BIOETHICS: HEALTH CARE, HUMAN RIGHTS AND THE LAW

Second Edition

Arthur Birmingham LaFrance
Professor of Law
Lewis & Clark Law School

Library of Congress Cataloging-in-Publication Data

LaFrance, Arthur B.
Bioethics : health care, human rights, and the law / by Arthur B. LaFrance. --2nd ed.
p. cm.
Includes bibliographical references and index.
ISBN 1-4224-0587-7 (hard cover : alk. paper)
1. Medical laws and legislation--United States. 2. Medical ethics --United States. I. Title.
[DNLM: 1. Bioethical Issues--legislation & jurisprudence--United States. 2. Human Rights--legislation & jurisprudence--United States. 3. Ethics, Clinical--United States. 4. Ethics, Medical--United States.
WB 33 AA1 L169b 2006]
KF3821.A7L34 2006
174'.2--dc22 2006030610

Editorial Offices
744 Broad Street, Newark, NJ 07102 (973) 820-2000
201 Mission St., San Francisco, CA 94105-1831 (415) 908-3200
701 East Water Street, Charlottesville, VA 22902-7587 (434) 972-7600
www.lexis.com

(Pub.1136)

This book is dedicated to
Sierra, Devon, Pele and Trotman LaFrance,
grandchildren all,
citizens of a brave new world.

PREFACE

This text is designed for professionals and students interested in bioethics, healthcare and the law, as viewed through the lens of court decisions, many resting on constitutional grounds. Judicial opinions concerning bioethical principles and issues are extremely important. They reflect disciplined, tough minded decision-making and translate abstraction into action. In this effort, judges must seek and be guided by the ethical values a community holds dear. Judicial commentary increasingly interprets legislation, such as the Americans with Disabilities Act, through which the community declares its ethical position and priorities. Thus, judicial decisions may be viewed as a rich and important source of literature on bioethics.

This book employs a definition of "bioethics" considerably broader than the definition usually reflected in treatments of this subject. All too often, "bioethics" is viewed as being limited to issues arising from the impact of new technology on the human body, as with reproductive technology or organ transplants, often viewed from the limited perspective of medical doctors. That is certainly included in the present volume, in such subjects as defining death, test tube babies, genetic screening, surrogacy, organ transplants and physician-assisted death. But a moment's reflection is sufficient to establish that a proper focus on bioethics, with its concern for personhood, privacy and autonomy, would include other subjects such as maternal-fetal conflict, experimentation, repressed memory, gender alteration, same sex marriage, compulsory testing, managed care and medical necessity. Bioethics should also include matters of conscience, as they affect human biology, as with religious beliefs or transfusions or abortion or creationism.

The cases in the Table of Contents reflect the extent to which bioethical decision making by courts has come to rest upon fundamental constitutional precepts. To a surprising extent, the Supreme Court itself has been involved in the exposition of bioethics as a constitutional concern. Cases concerning life, death, abortion, sterilization and institutionalization are commonplace, as are cases dealing with privacy, autonomy and conscience. Frequently, as in the *Cruzan* and *Quinlan* cases, courts are concerned not only with the ethics of outcome but also of process — the "who" of ethics. An important contribution of this volume is to reorganize and analyze constitutional case law in terms of traditional ethical and bioethical analysis.

The "who decides" question in bioethics is fundamental and of pervasive significance. One of the essential principles of bioethics posits autonomy as a starting point for bioethical decision making. Most writers agree that ethical relations require a respect for the autonomy of others. These two concerns — autonomy and respect for autonomy — are not only involved in the relations of patients and care givers, but also in the relation between the community — represented by the courts — and individual citizens. Courts must frequently decide when to defer to the autonomy, however misguided or dubious, of competent individuals. They must also seek and respect their own limits in dealing with institutions or individuals, competent or otherwise. With these concerns, for the individuals and for the limits of judicial processes, courts must also contend with the competing claims of others, including friends, family and health care providers. Thus, in every judicial decision, there is implicit both a consideration of what principles apply and who shall decide what those principles mean. Who will determine these questions is every bit as important as how they should be answered.

Of equal significance is the treatment in this work of the subject denominated "community," not the "who" but the "us" of ethics. Bioethics is properly concerned with those *included* and those *excluded* in ethical entitlements and obligations. For want of a better word, those to whom we owe duties, in varying forms, may be considered to be "citizens" of our community. The community must respect the citizen, but it must also protect him or her. And the reverse is true — individuals must respect each other and the community. Any consideration of ethics must therefore begin, as this book does, with the question of who is in, and who is outside, the community and what duty — if any — is owed outsiders. This text therefore considers cases which have treated people as property or aliens or, in some fashion, less than human, as with sexual predators, the unborn or the undead. Equally important are subclasses of community members — the incompetent or mentally ill or prisoners, people who are historically subject to abuse, neglect and exploitation.

Once it is determined who is in the "community", ethics requires describing those elements of individual personhood which must be respected. A person is not a self defining concept. Chapter II deals with the characteristics of a person — identity (memory, gender), integrity (testing), psychological control, association (marriage, privacy) and conscience (religion, belief). The cases deal with dimensions of biology and technology in these concepts, such as repressed memory and hypnosis, gender alteration, plethysmographs, ECT and psychosurgery, same sex marriage, predator identification, and ritual animal slaughter. Throughout are the recurring questions of what may the individual do? When may the community intervene? When must it hold back? When, for example, may the state amputate an incompetent woman's leg or transfer a kidney from an incompetent brother to his brother?

The ethical relationship between community and individual is most often confronted in the physician-patient relationship, the subject of Chapter III. Here are cases on sale of body parts, warning of third parties, sexual relations with patients, therapeutic privilege, experimentation, standard of care and measuring of injury. These are problems on the edge of developing concept and caselaw. But they fit well within traditional fiduciary strictures of fidelity (conflicts of interest, confidentiality), candor (informed consent, therapeutic privilege), and competence (best efforts). This "fiduciary" framework for analysis is preferable to the customary, yet awkward, four-point analysis of beneficence/nonmaleficence/autonomy and justice for several reasons. It is a traditional description of power relations in many legal contexts. It has the potential for growth which managed care mandates. And it realistically recognizes the needs of the healthcare provider.

Finally, the fourth chapter examines a number of bioethical contexts for patients' choices: maternal-fetal conflict, self abuse, AIDS treatments, refusal of treatment and assisted suicide. The fourth chapter serves up a number of recurring, current contexts involving the concepts of the first three chapters. The emphasis is on *choice* because ethics is preeminently a philosophy of *action.* And so maternal-fetal conflict, self-abuse, AIDS disclosure, and femal genital mutilation all appear in the fourth chapter. Managed care does as well, since seeking and denying healthcare coverage powerfully impacts the conduct of patients and providers. As might be expected, the last chapter closes with death, DNR orders and physician assisted suicide — the last opportunities for choice in life.

The author contemplated a fifth chapter, on issues of public health, such as rationing healthcare, funding research and quarantining disease. While these are "ethical" issues, they are of a different order. This text is mainly concerned with individual choice and the community. Moving to a level of generality, as with rationing, loses that focus and the uniquely ethical dilemmas posed for individuals as they choose among their various interests and those of the community. Still, some community level issues are included, particularly those arising from managed care. In the most elemental of terms, managed care restricts choices by patients and physicians, intruding on a fiduciary relationship. This casebook examines that process in a number of contexts, for example the denial of HMO/MCO coverage for bone marrow transplant or peripheral stem cell rescue in the treatment of cancer on the grounds that it is "experimental," or the denial of physical therapy to MS patients on the ground that it is not "medically necessary."

These materials are organized for teaching purposes. Generally, there are two or three cases, each followed by notes and questions designed to highlight important issues raised, resolved or remaining for future resolution. Each unit has at least one problem presented. These are based on current factual situations from practice or the literature, involving difficult bioethical issues for discussion and resolution. Some of the problems are based on court cases; others are drawn from articles and reports in the New England Journal of Medicine and the Journal of the American Medical Association; others are from the current news media. The problems are particularly important in bringing the primary court cases to bear upon medical or biotechnical contexts and practices.

One or two comments on editing may be in order. Whenever and wherever possible, technical citations, references and language have been omitted. Also, large portions of text have been omitted from some cases. Much of the omitted text was related to procedural or technical matters which would only detract from the ethical and substantive concerns, which are the focus of this text. At all times, the text as presented is accurate and, the author hopes, remains faithful to the intent and sense of the authors. The objective at all times is to enhance ease of reading and comprehension.

The author wishes to acknowledge a considerable debt to a number of people. Chief among these are his students, past and present, at Lewis and

Clark Law School and at Murdoch University in Perth, Australia. I have found myself badly in need of instruction about the principles and practices of the health care professions. Fortunately, I have had readily at hand a number of students who themselves were nurses, physicians, emergency medical technicians, hospital administrators, nursing home administrators and other health care professionals. It has been a pleasure and a delight over the years to be taught with kindness and consideration by such gifted people.

Several people warrant individual recognition. First, my thanks go to Linda Anderson, Becky Johnson, R.N., and Robin Craig, Ph.D., my student assistants, who made invaluable contributions to this text. Secondly, as always, my thanks particularly go to Lenair Mulford and Shannon Floyd, whose word processing talents and immense patience made this manuscript possible. Appreciation goes as well to Dean James Huffman, who in perilous financial times, nevertheless found the funds to make two summer grants possible, to bring this work to fruition. A special note of thanks goes as well to Professor John Grant of the University of Glasgow, Scotland, for his many helpful comments on the human rights and international dimensions of this subject matter.

Finally, it seems appropriate (if foolhardy) to define the subject of this book. For this author, at least, bioethics is the set of values by which people make choices that affect themselves and others as biologically-grounded beings. It defines the content and boundaries of individuals; the communities to which they belong; and the relations between them. It uses the body as a lens into, and a home for, the human spirit. Bioethics assumes a person of free choice and moral conscience, with an obligation not only to others, but also to ourselves, as physical, temporal beings in an infinite universe.

Arthur B. LaFrance
Professor of Law
Lewis and Clark Law School
Portland, Oregon

TABLE OF CONTENTS

Page

Chapter 1

MEMBERSHIP IN THE COMMUNITY

§ 1.01 Introduction

Every system of ethics defines not only rights and obligations but the community which will protect those rights and obligations. Some communities include only human beings; some include all living entities, human or otherwise. Most also include the spirits of those now dead and others — perhaps most — are concerned for those unborn.

Nevertheless, however broadly, people have tended to limit their communities to "us," excluding "them." Only the former are entitled to full respect and it is only to them that ethical recognition is fully extended. Those "outside" the community may be entitled to limited protections, since even in war time it has been traditionally recognized that noncombatants and prisoners must be treated according to certain codes of behavior. Still, every society throughout time defines those who are members of its community, however bounded, by race, religion, nationality, belief, consanguinity or locale.

There have been persons who belonged to no community or were shunned or banished from the communities to which they belonged. This might be said of Gypsies. It might be said of Jews in Nazi Germany. It might be said of the lepers throughout millenia or "untouchables" of India. A few nations occupy unique positions: they have welcomed peoples from different nations and therefore defined themselves through the threshold proposition that new groups *must* be included, drawing upon the tired, the poor and the teeming masses yearning to be free. While doing this, paradoxically, Americans and Australians conquered native races, imported — as slaves — others, and are still today working out the place and entitlement of subgroups, of race, nationality, gender, disability, and status.

The way the United States has gone about including and excluding people, favoring or discriminating against them, *illustrates* how a system of ethics defines its community. We have treated some people as property, as with African slaves or Chinese laborers or, more recently, surrogate mothers. We have set immigration quotas, favoring some nations and peoples over others; perhaps more significant, we have treated some peoples (*e.g.*, Native Americans, Japanese Americans) as "internal" aliens. And still others, we have disfavored, such as prisoners or the mentally retarded or sexual predators.

As a nation, we have had to develop guiding principles even as we implemented — or violated — them, and so our reach often exceeds our grasp. The community draws its legitimacy from this, as reflected in the United States Constitution and the United Nations Charter. More recently, civil rights legislation in the 1960s and the Americans with Disabilities Act in the 1990s have broadened our definition of an ethical community.

The cases in this chapter begin with the issue of when — if ever — people may treat others as "property," that is, nonpersons. The two examples are slavery or surrogacy. We then go on to deal with the special status of aliens, prisoners, the mentally ill and sexual predators. The subjects of these cases are concededly "human" but may be — and often are — accorded lesser liberty and respect than full "persons." We must ask, ethically, why and to what end? Nowhere are such questions more urgent than in dealing with issues of abortion or death, so this chapter deals with how a community may ethically treat the unborn, the undead, and the partially dead.

To begin, we need an overview of ethics, a concise statement of a comprehensive system, analyzing the interrelationship of society and individual, working out rights and responsibilities. There are many such systems, from Aristotle to Aquinas to Rousseau, Locke and Bentham and Foucault. An excellent survey of different systems may be found in Beauchamp and Childress, Principles of Biomedical Ethics (4th ed. Oxford Univ. Press, 1994). The most useful single statement, however, for our purposes appears in an early article by John Rawls, perhaps the most influential writer on ethics of our time.

That article appears next, and provides a framework for reference throughout this book.

John Rawls, *Justice as Fairness**

I

It might seem at first sight that the concepts of justice and fairness are the same, and that there is no reason to distinguish them, or to say that one is more fundamental than the other. I think that this impression is mistaken. In this paper I wish to show that the fundamental idea in the concept of justice is fairness — and I offer an analysis of the concept of justice from this point of view. To bring out the force of this claim, and the analysis based upon it, I shall then argue that it is this aspect of justice for which utilitarianism, in its classical form, is unable to account, but which is expressed, even if misleadingly, by the idea of the social contract.

To start with I shall develop a particular conception of justice by stating and commenting upon two principles which specify it, and by considering the circumstances and conditions under which they may be thought to arise. The principles defining this conception, and the conception itself, are, of course, familiar. It may be possible, however, by using the notion of fairness as a framework, to assemble and to look at them in a new way. Before stating this conception, however, the following preliminary matters should be kept in mind.

Throughout I consider justice only as a virtue of social institutions or what I shall call practices.[2] The principles of justice are regarded as formulating

* Reprinted from *The Philosophical Review*, Vol. 67. The first footnote making reference to an earlier version of this article has been omitted.

[2] I use the word "practice" throughout as a sort of technical term meaning any form of activity specified by a system of rules which defines offices, roles, moves, penalties, defense and so on, and which gives the activity its structure. As examples one may think of games and rituals, trials and parliaments, markets and systems of property.

restrictions as to how practices may define positions and offices, and assign thereto powers and liabilities, rights and duties. Justice as a virtue of particular actions or of persons I do not take up at all. It is important to distinguish these various subjects of justice, since the meaning of the concept varies according to whether it is applied to practices, particular actions, or persons. These meanings are, indeed, connected, but they are not identical. I shall confine my discussion to the sense of justice as applied to practices, since this sense is the basic one. Once it is understood, the other senses should go quite easily.

Justice is to be understood in its customary sense as representing but *one* of the many virtues of social institutions, for these may be antiquated, inefficient, degrading, or any number of other things, without being unjust. Justice is not to be confused with an all-inclusive vision of a good society; it is only one part of any such conception. It is important, for example, to distinguish that sense of equality which is an aspect of the concept of justice from that sense of equality which belongs to a more comprehensive social ideal. There may well be inequalities which one concedes are just, or at least not unjust, but which, nevertheless, one wishes, on other grounds, to do away with. I shall focus attention, then, on the usual sense of justice in which it is essentially the elimination of arbitrary distinctions and the establishment, within the structure of a practice, of a proper balance between competing claims.

Finally, there is no need to consider the principles discussed below as *the* principles of justice. For the moment it is sufficient that they are typical of a family of principles normally associated with the concept of justice. The way in which the principles of this family resemble one another, as shown by the background against which they may be thought to arise, will be made clear by the whole of the subsequent argument.

II

The conception of justice which I want to develop may be stated in the form of two principles as follows: first, each person participating in a practice, or affected by it, has an equal right to the most extensive liberty compatible with a like liberty for all; and second, inequalities are arbitrary unless it is reasonable to expect that they will work out for everyone's advantage, and provided the positions and offices to which they attach, or from which they may be gained, are open to all. These principles express justice as a complex of three ideas: liberty, equality, and reward for services contributing to the common good.[3]

[3] These principles are, of course, well known in one form or another and appear in many analyses of justice even where the writers differ widely on other matters. Thus if the principle of equal liberty is commonly associated with Kant (see *The Philosophy of Law*, tr. by W. Hastie, Edinburgh, 1887, pp. 56f.), it may be claimed that it can also be found in J.S. Mill's *On Liberty* and elsewhere, and in many other liberal writers. Recently H.L.A. Hart has argued for something like it in his paper "Are There Any Natural Rights?", *Philosophical Review*, LXIV (1955), 175-91. The injustice of inequalities which are not won in return for a contribution to the common advantage is, of course, widespread in political writings of all sorts. The conception of justice here discussed is distinctive, if at all, only in selecting these two principles in this form; but for another similar analysis, see the discussion by W.D. Lamont, *The Principles of Moral Judgment* (Oxford, 1946), ch. v.

The term "person" is to be construed variously depending on the circumstances. On some occasions it will mean human individuals, but in others it may refer to nations, provinces, business firms, churches, teams, and so on. The principles of justice apply in all these instances, although there is a certain logical priority to the case of human individuals. As I shall use the term "person," it will be ambiguous in the manner indicated.

The first principle holds, of course, only if other things are equal: that is, while there must always be a justification for departing from the initial position of equal liberty (which is defined by the pattern of rights and duties, powers and liabilities, established by a practice), and the burden of proof is placed on him who would depart from it, nevertheless, there can be, and often there is, a justification for doing so. Now, that similar particular cases, as defined by a practice, should be treated similarly as they arise, is part of the very concept of a practice; it is involved in the notion of an activity in accordance with rules. The first principle expresses an analogous conception, but as applied to the structure of practices themselves. It holds, for example, that there is a presumption against the distinctions and classifications made by legal systems and other practices to the extent that they infringe on the original and equal liberty of the persons participating in them. The second principle defines how this presumption may be rebutted.

It might be argued at this point that justice requires only an equal liberty. If, however, a greater liberty were possible for all without loss or conflict, then it would be irrational to settle on a lesser liberty. There is no reason for circumscribing rights unless their exercise would be incompatible, or would render the practice defining them less effective. Therefore no serious distortion of the concept of justice is likely to follow from including within it the concept of the greatest equal liberty.

The second principle defines what sorts of inequalities are permissible; it specifies how the presumption laid down by the first principle may be put aside. Now by inequalities it is best to understand not *any* differences between offices and positions, but differences in the benefits and burdens attached to them either directly or indirectly, such as prestige and wealth, or liability to taxation and compulsory services. Players in a game do not protest against there being different positions, such as batter, pitcher, catcher, and the like, nor to there being various privileges and powers as specified by the rules; nor do the citizens of a country object to there being the different offices of government such as president, senator, governor, judge, and so on, each with their special rights and duties. It is not differences of this kind that are normally thought of as inequalities, but differences in the resulting distribution established by a practice, or made possible by it, of the things men strive to attain or avoid. Thus they may complain about the pattern of honors and rewards set up by a practice (e.g., the privileges and salaries of government officials) or they may object to the distribution of power and wealth which results from the various ways in which men avail themselves of the opportunities allowed by it (e.g., the concentration of wealth which may develop in a free price system allowing large entrepreneurial or speculative gains).

It should be noted that the second principle holds that an inequality is allowed only if there is reason to believe that the practice with the inequality, or resulting in it, will work for the advantage of *every* party engaging in it. Here it is important to stress that *every* party must gain from the inequality. Since the principle applies to practices, it implies that the representative man in every office or position defined by a practice, when he views it as a going concern, must find it reasonable to prefer his condition and prospects with the inequality to what they would be under the practice without it. The principle excludes, therefore, the justification of inequalities on the grounds that the disadvantages of those in one position are outweighed by the greater advantages of those in another position. This rather simple restriction is the main modification I wish to make in the utilitarian principle as usually understood. When coupled with the notion of a practice, it is a restriction of consequence, and one which some utilitarians, e.g., Hume and Mill, have used in their discussions of justice without realizing apparently its significance, or at least without calling attention to it. Why it is a significant modification of principle, changing one's conception of justice entirely, the whole of my argument will show.

Further, it is also necessary that the various offices to which special benefits or burdens attach are open to all. It may be, for example, to the common advantage, as just defined, to attach special benefits to certain offices. Perhaps by doing so the requisite talent can be attracted to them and encouraged to give its best efforts. But any offices having special benefits must be won in a fair competition in which contestants are judged on their merits. If some offices were not open, those excluded would normally be justified in feeling unjustly treated, even if they benefited from the greater efforts of those who were allowed to compete for them. Now if one can assume that offices are open, it is necessary only to consider the design of practices themselves and how they jointly, as a system, work together. It will be a mistake to focus attention on the varying relative positions of particular persons, who may be known to us by their proper names, and to require that each such change, as a once for all transaction viewed in isolation, must be in itself just. It is the system of practices which is to be judged, and judged from a general point of view: unless one is prepared to criticize it from the standpoint of a putative man holding some particular office, one has no complaint against it.

III

Given these principles one might try to derive them from *a priori* principles of reason, or claim that they were known by intuition. These are familiar enough steps and, at least in the case of the first principle, might be made with some success. Usually, however, such arguments, made at this point, are unconvincing. They are not likely to lead to an understanding of the basis of the principles of justice, not at least as principles of justice. I wish, therefore, to look at the principles in a different way.

Imagine a society of persons amongst whom a certain system of practices is *already* well established. Now suppose that by and large they are mutually self-interested; their allegiance to their established practices is normally founded on the prospect of self-advantage. One need not assume that, in all senses of the term "person," the persons in this society are mutually self-interested. If the characterization as mutually self-interested applies when the line of division is the family, it may still be true that members of families are bound by ties of sentiment and affection and willingly acknowledge duties in contradiction to self-interest. Mutual self-interestedness in the relations between families, nations, churches, and the like, is commonly associated with intense loyalty and devotion on the part of individual members. Therefore, one can form a more realistic conception of this society if one thinks of it as consisting of mutually self-interested families, or some other association. Further, it is not necessary to suppose that these persons are mutually self-interested under all circumstances, but only in the usual situations in which they participate in their common practices.

Now suppose also that these persons are rational: they know their own interests more or less accurately; they are capable of tracing out the likely consequences of adopting one practice rather than another; they are capable of adhering to a course of action once they have decided upon it; they can resist present temptations and the enticements of immediate gain; and the bare knowledge or perception of the difference between their condition and that of others is not, within certain limits and in itself, a source of great dissatisfaction. Only the last point adds anything to the usual definition of rationality. This definition should allow, I think, for the idea that a rational man would not be greatly downcast from knowing, or seeing, that others are in a better position than himself, unless he thought their being so was the result of injustice, or the consequence of letting chance work itself out for no useful common purpose, and so on. So if these persons strike us as unpleasantly egoistic, they are at least free in some degree from the fault of envy.[4]

Finally, assume that these persons have roughly similar needs and interests, or needs and interests in various ways complementary, so that fruitful cooperation amongst them is possible; and suppose that they are sufficiently equal in power and ability to guarantee that in normal circumstances none is able to dominate the others. This condition (as well as the others) may seem excessively vague; but in view of the conception of justice to which the argument leads, there seems no reason for making it more exact here.

Since these persons are conceived as engaging in their common practices, which are already established, there is no question of our supposing them to come together to deliberate as to how they will set these practices up for the first time. Yet we can imagine that from time to time they discuss with one another whether any of them has a legitimate complaint against their established institutions. Such discussions are perfectly natural in any normal society. Now suppose that they have settled on doing this in the following way. They first try to arrive at the principles by which complaints, and so practices themselves, are to be judged. Their procedure for this is to let each person propose the principles upon which he wishes his complaints to be tried with the understanding that, if acknowledged, the complaints of others will be similarly tried, and that no complaints will be heard at all until everyone is

[4] It is not possible to discuss here this addition to the usual conception of rationality. If it seems peculiar, it may be worth remarking that it is analogous to the modification of the utilitarian principle which the argument as a whole is designed to explain and justify. In the same way that the satisfaction of interests, the representative claims of which violate the principles of justice, is not a reason for having a practice (see sec. 7), unfounded envy, within limits, need not to be taken into account.

roughly of one mind as to how complaints are to be judged. They each understand further that the principles proposed and acknowledged on this occasion are binding on future occasions. Thus each will be wary of proposing a principle which would give him a peculiar advantage, in his present circumstances, supposing it to be accepted. Each person knows that he will be bound by it in future circumstances the peculiarities of which cannot be known, and which might well be such that the principle is then to his disadvantage. The idea is that everyone should be required to make *in advance* a firm commitment, which others also may reasonably be expected to make, and that no one be given the opportunity to tailor the canons of a legitimate complaint to fit his own special condition, and then to discard them when they no longer suit his purpose. Hence each person will propose principles of a general kind which will, to a large degree, gain their sense from the various applications to be made of them, the particular circumstances of which being as yet unknown. These principles will express the conditions in accordance with which each is the least unwilling to have his interests limited in the design of practices, given the competing interests of the others, on the supposition that the interests of others will be limited likewise. The restrictions which would so arise might be thought of as those a person would keep in mind if he were designing a practice in which his enemy were to assign him his place.

The two main parts of this conjectural account have a definite significance. The character and respective situations of the parties reflect the typical circumstances in which questions of justice arise. The procedure whereby principles are proposed and acknowledged represents constraints, analogous to those of having a morality, whereby rational and mutually self-interested persons are brought to act reasonably. Thus the first part reflects the fact that questions of justice arise when conflicting claims are made upon the design of a practice and where it is taken for granted that each person will insist, as far as possible, on what he considers his rights. It is typical of cases of justice to involve persons who are pressing on one another their claims, between which a fair balance or equilibrium must be found. On the other hand, as expressed by the second part, having a morality must at least imply the acknowledgment of principles as impartially applying to one's own conduct as well as to another's, and moreover principles which may constitute a constraint, or limitation, upon the pursuit of one's own interests. There are, of course, other aspects of having a morality: the acknowledgment of moral principles must show itself in accepting a reference to them as reasons for limiting one's claims, in acknowledging the burden of providing a special explanation, or excuse, when one acts contrary to them, or else in showing shame and remorse and a desire to make amends, and so on. It is sufficient to remark here that having a morality is analogous to having made a firm commitment in advance; for one must acknowledge the principles of morality even when to one's disadvantage. A man whose moral judgments always coincided with his interests could be suspected of having no morality at all.

Thus the two parts of the foregoing account are intended to mirror the kinds of circumstances in which questions of justice arise and the constraints which having a morality would impose upon persons so situated. In this way one can see how the acceptance of the principles of justice might come about, for given all these conditions as described, it would be natural if the two principles of justice were to be acknowledged. Since there is no way for anyone to win special advantages for himself, each might consider it reasonable to acknowledge equality as an initial principle. There is, however, no reason why they should regard this position as final; for if there are inequalities which satisfy the second principle, the immediate gain which equality would allow can be considered as intelligently invested in view of its future return. If, as is quite likely, these inequalities work as incentives to draw out better efforts, the members of this society may look upon them as concessions to human nature: they, like us, may think that people ideally should want to serve one another. But as they are mutually self-interested, their acceptance of these inequalities is merely the acceptance of the relations in which they actually stand, and a recognition of the motives which lead them to engage in their common practices. *They* have no title to complain of one another. And so provided that the conditions of the principle are met, there is no reason why they should not allow such inequalities. Indeed, it would be short-sighted of them to do so, and could result, in most cases, only from their being dejected by the bare knowledge, or perception, that others are better situated. Each person will, however, insist on an advantage to himself, and so on a common advantage, for none is willing to sacrifice anything for the others.

These remarks are not offered as a rigorous proof that persons conceived and situated as the conjectural account supposes, and required to adopt the procedure described, would settle on the two principles of justice. For such a proof a more elaborate and formal argument would have to be given: there remain certain details to be filled in, and various alternatives to be ruled out. The argument should, however, be taken as a proof, or a sketch of a proof; for the proposition I seek to establish is a necessary one, that is, it is intended as a theorem: namely, that when mutually self-interested and rational persons confront one another in typical circumstances of justice; and when they are required by a procedure expressing the constraints of having a morality to jointly acknowledge principles by which their claims on the design of their common practices are to be judged, they will settle on these two principles as restrictions governing the assignment of rights and duties, and thereby accept them as limiting their rights against one another. It is this theorem which accounts for these principles as principles of justice, and explains how they come to be associated with this moral concept. Moreover, this theorem is analogous to those about human conduct in other branches of social thought. That is, a simplified situation is described in which rational persons pursuing certain ends and related to one another in a definite way, are required to act subject to certain limitations; then, given this situation, it is shown that they will act in a certain manner. Failure so to act would imply that one or more of the assumptions does not obtain. The foregoing account aims to establish, or to sketch, a theorem in this sense; the aim of the argument is to show the basis for saying that the principles of justice may be regarded as those principles which arise when the constraints of having a morality are imposed upon rational persons in typical circumstances of justice.

IV

These ideas are, of course, connected with a familiar way of thinking about justice which goes back at least to the Greek Sophists, and which regards the acceptance of the principles of justice as a compromise between persons of roughly equal power who would enforce their will on each other if they could, but who, in view of the equality of forces amongst them and for the sake of their own peace and security acknowledge certain forms of conduct in so far as prudence seems to require. Justice is thought of as a pact between rational egoists the stability of which is dependent on a balance of power and a similarity of circumstances. While the previous account is connected with this tradition, and with its most recent variant, the theory of games, it differs from it in several important respects which, to forestall misinterpretations, I will set out here.

First, I wish to use the previous conjectural account of the background of justice as a way of analyzing the concept. I do not want, therefore, to be interpreted as assuming a general theory of human motivation: when I suppose that the parties are mutually self-interested, and are not willing to have their (substantial) interests sacrificed to others, I am referring to their conduct and motives as they are taken for granted in cases where questions of justice ordinarily arise. Justice is the virtue of practices where there are assumed to be competing interests and conflicting claims, and where it is supposed that persons will press their rights on each other. That persons are mutually self-interested in certain situations and for certain purposes is what gives rise to the question of justice in practices covering those circumstances. Amongst an association of saints, if such a community could really exist, the disputes about justice could hardly occur; for they would all work selflessly together for one end, the glory of God as defined by their common religion, and reference to this end would settle every question of right. The justice of practices does not come up until there are several different parties (whether we think of these as individuals, associations, or nations and so on, is irrelevant) who do press their claims on one another, and who do regard themselves as representatives of interests which deserve to be considered. Thus the previous account involves no general theory of human motivation. Its intent is simply to incorporate into the conception of justice the relations of men to one another which set the stage for questions of justice. It makes no difference how wide or general these relations are, as this matter does not bear on the analysis of the concept.

Again, in contrast to the various conceptions of the social contract, the several parties do not establish any particular society or practice; they do not covenant to obey a particular sovereign body or to accept a given constitution. Nor do they, as in the theory of games (in certain respects a marvelously sophisticated development of this tradition), decide on individual strategies adjusted to their respective circumstances in the game. What the parties do is to *jointly* acknowledge certain *principles* of appraisal relating to their common *practices* either as already established or merely proposed. They accede to standards of judgment, not to a given practice; they do not make any specific agreement, or bargain, or adopt a particular strategy. The subject of their acknowledgment is, therefore, very general indeed; it is simply the acknowledgment of certain principles of judgment, fulfilling certain general conditions, to be used in criticizing the arrangement of their common affairs. The relations of mutual self-interest between the parties who are similarly circumstanced mirror the conditions under which questions of justice arise, and the procedure by which the principles of judgment are proposed and acknowledged reflects the constraints of having a morality. Each aspect, then, of the preceding hypothetical account serves the purpose of bringing out a feature of the notion of justice. One could, if one liked, view the principles of justice as the "solution" of this highest order "game" of adopting, subject to the procedure described, principles of argument for all coming particular "games" whose peculiarities one can in no way foresee. But this comparison, while no doubt helpful, must not obscure the fact that this highest order "game" is of a special sort.[5] Its significance is that its various pieces represent aspects of the concept of justice.

Finally, I do not, of course, conceive the several parties as necessarily coming together to establish their common practices for the first time. Some institutions may, indeed, be set up *de novo*; but I have framed the preceding account so that it will apply when the full complement of social institutions already exists and represents the result of a long period of development. Nor is the account in any way fictitious. In any society where people reflect on their institutions they will have an idea of what principles of justice would be acknowledged under the conditions described, and there will be occasions when questions of justice are actually discussed in this way. Therefore if their practices do not accord with these principles, this will affect the quality of their social relations. For in this case there will be some recognized situations wherein the parties are mutually aware that one of them is being forced to accept what the other would concede is unjust. The foregoing analysis may then be thought of as representing the actual quality of relations between persons as defined by practices accepted as just. In such practices the parties will acknowledge the principles on which it is constructed, and the general recognition of this fact shows itself in the absence of resentment and in the sense of being justly treated. Thus one common objection to the theory of the social contract, its apparently historical and fictitious character, is avoided.

V

That the principles of justice may be regarded as arising in the manner described illustrates an important fact about them. Not only does it bring out the idea that justice is a primitive moral notion in that it arises once the concept of morality is imposed on mutually self-interested agents similarly circumstanced, but it emphasizes that, fundamental to justice, is the concept of fairness which relates to right dealing between persons who are cooperating with or competing against one another, as when one speaks of fair games, fair competition, and fair bargains. The question of fairness arises when free persons, who have no authority over one another, are engaging in a joint activity and amongst themselves settling or acknowledging the rules which

5 The difficulty one gets into by a mechanical application of the theory of games to moral philosophy can be brought out by considering among several possible examples, R.B. Braithwaite's study, *Theory of Games as a Tool for the Moral Philosopher* (Cambridge, 1955). What is lacking is the concept of morality, and it must be brought into the conjectural account in some way or other. In the text this is done by the form of the procedure whereby principles are proposed and acknowledged (Section III). If one starts directly with the particular case as known, and if one accepts as given and definitive the preferences and relative positions of the parties, whatever they are, it is impossible to give an analysis of the moral concept of fairness.

define it and which determine the respective shares in its benefits and burdens. A practice will strike the parties as fair if none feels that, by participating in it, they or any of the others are taken advantage of, or forced to give in to claims which they do not regard as legitimate. This implies that each has a conception of legitimate claims which he thinks it reasonable for others as well as himself to acknowledge. If one thinks of the principles of justice as arising in the manner described, then they do define this sort of conception. A practice is just or fair, then, when it satisfies the principles which those who participate in it could propose to one another for mutual acceptance under the aforementioned circumstances. Persons engaged in a just, or fair, practice can face one another openly and support their respective positions, should they appear questionable, by reference to principles which it is reasonable to expect each to accept.

It is this notion of the possibility of mutual acknowledgment of principles by free persons who have no authority over one another which makes the concept of fairness fundamental to justice. Only if such acknowledgment is possible can there be true community between persons in their common practices; otherwise their relations will appear to them as founded to some extent on force. If, in ordinary speech, fairness applies more particularly to practices in which there is a choice whether to engage or not (e.g., in games, business competition), and justice to practices in which there is no choice (e.g., in slavery), the element of necessity does not render the conception of mutual acknowledgment inapplicable, although it may make it much more urgent to change unjust than unfair institutions. For one activity in which one can always engage is that of proposing and acknowledging principles to one another supposing each to be similarly circumstanced; and to judge practices by the principles so arrived at is to apply the standard of fairness to them.

Now if the participants in a practice accept its rules as fair, and so have no complaint to lodge against it, there arises a prima facie duty (and a corresponding prima facie right) of the parties to each other to act in accordance with the practice when it falls upon them to comply. When any number of persons engage in a practice, or conduct a joint undertaking according to rules, and thus restrict their liberty, those who have submitted to these restrictions when required have the right to a similar acquiescence on the part of those who have benefitted by their submission. These conditions will obtain if a practice is correctly acknowledged to be fair, for in this case all who participate in it will benefit from it. The rights and duties so arising are special rights and duties in that they depend on previous actions voluntarily undertaken, in this case on the parties having engaged in a common practice and knowingly accepted its benefits.[6] It is not, however, an obligation which presupposes a deliberate performative act in the sense of a promise, or contract, and the like. An unfortunate mistake of proponents of the idea of the social contract was to suppose that political obligation does require some such act, or at least to use language which suggests it. It is sufficient that one has knowingly participated in and accepted the benefits of a practice

[6] For the definition of this prima facie duty, and the idea that it is a special duty, I am indebted to H.L.A. Hart. See his paper "Are There Any Natural Rights?", *Philosophical Review*, LXIV (1955), 185 f.

acknowledged to be fair. This prima facie obligation may, of course, be overridden: it may happen, when it comes one's turn to follow a rule, that other considerations will justify not doing so. But one cannot, in general, be released from this obligation by denying the justice of the practice only when it falls on one to obey. If a person rejects a practice, he should, so far as possible, declare his intention in advance, and avoid participating in it or enjoying its benefits.

This duty I have called that of fair play, but it should be admitted that to refer to it in this way is, perhaps, to extend the ordinary notion of fairness. Usually acting unfairly is not so much the breaking of any particular rule, even if the infraction is difficult to detect (cheating), but taking advantage of loop-holes or ambiguities in rules, availing oneself of unexpected or special circumstances which make it impossible to enforce them, insisting that rules be enforced to one's advantage when they should be suspended, and more generally, acting contrary to the intention of a practice. It is for this reason that one speaks of the sense of fair play: acting fairly requires more than simply being able to follow rules; what is fair must often be felt, or perceived, one wants to say. It is not, however, an unnatural extension of the duty of fair play to have it include the obligation which participants who have knowingly accepted the benefits of their common practice owe to each other to act in accordance with it when their performance falls due; for it is usually considered unfair if someone accepts the benefits of a practice but refuses to do his part in maintaining it. Thus one might say of the tax-dodger that he violates the duty of fair play: he accepts the benefits of government but will not do his part in releasing resources to it; and members of labor unions often say that fellow workers who refuse to join are being unfair: they refer to them as "free riders," as persons who enjoy what are the supposed benefits of unionism, higher wages, shorter hours, job security, and the like, but who refuse to share in its burdens in the form of paying dues, and so on.

The duty of fair play stands beside other prima facie duties such as fidelity and gratitude as a basic moral notion; yet it is not to be confused with them. These duties are all clearly distinct, as would be obvious from their definitions. As with any moral duty, that of fair play implies a constraint on self-interest in particular cases; on occasion it enjoins conduct which a rational egoist strictly defined would not decide upon. So while justice does not require of anyone that he sacrifice his interests in that *general position* and procedure whereby the principles of justice are proposed and acknowledged, it may happen that in particular situations, arising in the context of engaging in a practice, the duty of fair play will often cross his interests in the sense that he will be required to forgo particular advantages which the peculiarities of his circumstances might permit him to take. There is, of course, nothing surprising in this. It is simply the consequence of the firm commitment which the parties may be supposed to have made, or which they would make, in the general position, together with the fact that they have participated in and accepted the benefits of a practice which they regard as fair.

Now the acknowledgment of this constraint in particular cases, which is manifested in acting fairly or wishing to make amends, feeling ashamed, and the like, when one has evaded it, is one of the forms of conduct by which participants in a common practice exhibit their recognition of each other as persons with similar interests and capacities. In the same way that, failing a special explanation, the criterion for the recognition of suffering is helping one who suffers, acknowledging the duty of fair play is a necessary part of the criterion for recognizing another as a person with similar interests and feelings as oneself.[7] A person who never under any circumstances showed a wish to help others in pain would show, at the same time, that he did not recognize that they were in pain; nor could he have any feelings of affection or friendship for anyone; for having these feelings implies, failing special circumstances, that he comes to their aid when they are suffering. Recognition that another is a person in pain shows itself in sympathetic action; this primitive natural response of compassion is one of those responses upon which the various forms of moral conduct are built.

Similarly, the acceptance of the duty of fair play by participants in a common practice is a reflection in each person of the recognition of the aspirations and interests of the others to be realized by their joint activity. Failing a special explanation, their acceptance of it is a necessary part of the criterion for their recognizing one another as persons with similar interests and capacities, as the conception of their relations in the general position supposes them to be. Otherwise they would show no recognition of one another as persons with similar capacities and interests, and indeed, in some cases perhaps hypothetical, they would not recognize one another as persons at all, but as complicated objects involved in a complicated activity. To recognize another as a person one must respond to him and act towards him in certain ways; and these ways are intimately connected with the various prima facie duties. Acknowledging these duties in *some* degree, and so having the elements of morality, is not a matter of choice, or of intuiting moral qualities, or a matter of the expression of feelings or attitudes (the three interpretations between which philosophical opinion frequently oscillates); it is simply the possession of one of the forms of conduct in which the recognition of others as persons is manifested.

These remarks are unhappily obscure. Their main purpose here, however, is to forestall, together with the remarks in Section IV, the misinterpretation that, on the view presented, the acceptance of justice and the acknowledgment of the duty of fair play depends in every day life solely on there being a *de facto* balance of forces between the parties. It would indeed be foolish to underestimate the importance of such a balance in securing justice; but it is not the only basis thereof. The recognition of one another as persons with similar interests and capacities engaged in a common practice must, failing a special explanation, show itself in the acceptance of the principles of justice and the acknowledgment of the duty of fair play.

The conception at which we have arrived, then, is that the principles of justice may be thought of as arising once the constraints of having a morality are imposed upon rational and mutually self-interested parties who are related and situated in a special way. A practice is just if it is in accordance

[7] I am using the concept of criterion here in what I take to be Wittgenstein's sense. That the response of compassion, under appropriate circumstances, is part of the criterion for whether or not a person understand what "pain" means, is, I think, in the *Philosophical Investigations.* The view in the text is simply an extension of this idea. I cannot, however, attempt to justify it here.

with the principles which all who participate in it might reasonably be expected to propose or to acknowledge before one another when they are similarly circumstanced and required to make a firm commitment in advance without knowledge of what will be their peculiar condition, and thus when it meets standards which the parties could accept as fair should occasion arise for them to debate its merits. Regarding the participants themselves, once persons knowingly engage in a practice which they acknowledge to be fair and accept the benefits of doing so, they are bound by the duty of fair play to follow the rules when it comes their turn to do so, and this implies a limitation on their pursuit of self-interest in particular cases.

Now one consequence of this conception is that, where it applies, there is no moral value in the satisfaction of a claim incompatible with it. Such a claim violates the conditions of reciprocity and community amongst persons, and he who presses it, not being willing to acknowledge it when pressed by another, has no grounds for complaint when it is denied; whereas he against whom it is pressed can complain. As it cannot be mutually acknowledged it is a resort to coercion; granting the claim is possible only if one party can compel acceptance of what the other will not admit. But it makes no sense to concede claims the denial of which cannot be complained of in preference to claims the denial of which can be objected to. Thus in deciding on the justice of a practice it is not enough to ascertain that it answers to wants and interests in the fullest and most effective manner. For if any of these conflict with justice, they should not be counted, as their satisfaction is no reason at all for having a practice. It would be irrelevant to say, even if true, that it resulted in the greatest satisfaction of desire. In tallying up the merits of a practice one must toss out the satisfaction of interests the claims of which are incompatible with the principles of justice.

VI

The discussion so far has been excessively abstract. While this is perhaps unavoidable, I should now like to bring out some of the features of the conception of justice as fairness by comparing it with the conception of justice in classical utilitarianism as represented by Bentham and Sidgwick, and its counterpart in welfare economics. This conception assimilates justice to benevolence and the latter in turn to the most efficient design of institutions to promote the general welfare. Justice is a kind of efficiency.

Now it is said occasionally that this form of utilitarianism puts no restrictions on what might be a just assignment of rights and duties in that there might be circumstances which, on utilitarian grounds, would justify institutions highly offensive to our ordinary sense of justice. But the classical utilitarian conception is not totally unprepared for this objection. Beginning with the notion that the general happiness can be represented by a social utility function consisting of a sum of individual utility functions with identical weights (this being the meaning of the maxim that each counts for one and no more than one), it is commonly assumed that the utility functions of individuals are similar in all essential respects. Differences between individuals are ascribed to accidents of education and upbringing, and they should not be taken into account. This assumption, coupled with that of diminishing marginal utility, results in a prima facie case for equality, e.g., of equality in the distribution of income during any given period of time, laying aside indirect effects on the future. But even if utilitarianism is interpreted as having such restrictions built into the utility function, and even if it is supposed that these restrictions have in practice much the same result as the application of the principles of justice (and appear, perhaps, to be ways of expressing these principles in the language of mathematics and psychology), the fundamental idea is very different from the conception of justice as fairness. For one thing, that the principles of justice should be accepted is interpreted as the contingent result of a higher order administrative decision. The form of this decision is regarded as being similar to that of an entrepreneur deciding how much to produce of this or that commodity in view of its marginal revenue, or to that of someone distributing goods to needy persons according to the relative urgency of their wants. The choice between practices is thought of as being made on the basis of the allocation of benefits and burdens to individuals (these being measured by the present capitalized value of their utility over the full period of the practice's existence), which results from the distribution of rights and duties established by a practice.

Moreover, the individuals receiving these benefits are not conceived as being related in any way: they represent so many different directions in which limited resources may be allocated. The value of assigning resources to one direction rather than another depends solely on the preferences and interests of individuals as individuals. The satisfaction of desire has its value irrespective of the moral relations between persons, say as members of a joint undertaking, and of the claims which, in the name of these interests, they are prepared to make on one another:[8] and it is this value which is to be taken into account by the (ideal) legislator who is conceived as adjusting the rules of the system from the center so as to maximize the value of the social utility function.

It is thought that the principles of justice will not be violated by a legal system so conceived provided these executive decisions are correctly made. In this fact the principles of justice are said to have their derivation and explanation; they simply express the most important general features of social institutions in which the administrative problem is solved in the best way. These principles have, indeed, a special urgency because, given the facts of

[8] An idea essential to the classical utilitarian conception of justice. Bentham is firm in his statement of it. (*The Principles of Morals and Legislation*, ch. II, sec. iv. See also ch. X, sec. x, footnote 1.) The same point is made in *The Limits of Jurisprudence Define D*, pp.115 f. Although much recent welfare economics, as found in such important works as I.M.D. Little, *A Critique of Welfare Economics*, 2d ed. (Oxford, 1957) and K.J. Arrow, *Social Choice and Individual Values* (New York, 1951), dispenses with the idea of cardinal utility, and use instead the theory of ordinal utility as stated by J.R. Hicks, *Value and Capital*, 2d ed. (Oxford, 1946), Pt. I, it assumes with utilitarianism that individual preferences have value as such, and so accepts the idea being criticized here. I hasten to add, however, that this is no objection to it as a means of analyzing economic policy, and for that purpose it may, indeed, be a necessary simplifying assumption. Nevertheless it is an assumption which cannot be made in so far as one is trying to analyze moral concepts, especially the concept of justice, as economists would, I think, agree. Justice is usually regarded as a separate and distinct part of any comprehensive criterion of economic policy. See, for example, Tibor Scitovsky, *Welfare and Competition* (London, 1952), pp. 59-69, and Little, op. cit., ch. VII.

human nature, so much depends on them; and this explains the peculiar quality of the moral feelings associated with justice. This assimilation of justice to a higher order executive decision, certainly a striking conception, is central to classical utilitarianism; and it also brings out its profound individualism, in one sense of this ambiguous word. It regards persons as so many *separate* directions in which benefits and burdens may be assigned; and the value of the satisfaction or dissatisfaction of desire is not thought to depend in any way on the moral relations in which individuals stand, or on the kinds of claims which they are willing, in the pursuit of their interests, to press on each other.

VII

Many social decisions are, of course, of an administrative nature. Certainly this is so when it is a matter of social utility in what one may call its ordinary sense: that is, when it is a question of the efficient design of social institutions for the use of common means to achieve common ends. In this case either the benefits and burdens may be assumed to be impartially distributed, or the question of distribution is misplaced, as in the instance of maintaining public order and security or national defense. But as an interpretation of the basis of the principles of justice, classical utilitarianism is mistaken. It *permits* one to argue, for example, that slavery is unjust on the grounds that the advantages to the slaveholder as slaveholder do not counterbalance the disadvantages to the slave and to society at large burdened by a comparatively inefficient system of labor. Now the conception of justice as fairness, when applied to the practice of slavery with its offices of slaveholder and slave, would not allow one to consider the advantages of the slaveholder in the first place. As that office is not in accordance with principles which could be mutually acknowledged, the gains accruing to the slaveholder, assuming them to exist, cannot be counted as in *any* way mitigating the injustice of the practice. The question whether these gains outweigh the disadvantages to the slave and to society cannot arise, since in considering the justice of slavery these gains have no weight at all which requires that they be overridden. Where the conception of justice as fairness applies, slavery is *always* unjust.

I am not, of course, suggesting the absurdity that the classical utilitarians approved of slavery. I am only rejecting a type of argument which their view allows them to use in support of their disapproval of it. The conception of justice as derivative from efficiency implies that judging the justice of a practice is always, in principle at least, a matter of weighing up advantages and disadvantages, each having an intrinsic value or disvalue as the satisfaction of interests, irrespective of whether or not these interests necessarily involve acquiescence in principles which could not be mutually acknowledged. Utilitarianism cannot account for the fact that slavery is always unjust, nor for the fact that it would be recognized as irrelevant in defeating the accusation of injustice for one person to say to another, engaged with him in a common practice and debating its merits, that nevertheless it allowed of the greatest satisfaction of desire. The charge of injustice cannot be rebutted in this way. If justice were derivative from a higher order executive efficiency, this would not be so.

But now, even if it is taken as established that, so far as the ordinary conception of justice goes, slavery is always unjust (that is, slavery by definition violates commonly recognized principles of justice), the classical utilitarian would surely reply that these principles, as other moral principles subordinate to that of utility, are only generally correct. It is simply for the most part true that slavery is less efficient than other institutions; and while common sense may define the concept of justice so that slavery is unjust, nevertheless, where slavery would lead to the greatest satisfaction of desire, it is not wrong. Indeed, it is then right, and for the very same reason that justice, as ordinarily understood, is usually right. If, as ordinarily understood, slavery is always unjust, to this extent the utilitarian conception of justice might be admitted to differ from that of common moral opinion. Still the utilitarian would want to hold that, as a matter of moral principle, his view is correct in giving no special weight to considerations of justice beyond that allowed for by the general presumption of effectiveness. And this, he claims, is as it should be. The everyday opinion is morally in error, although, indeed, it is a useful error, since it protects rules of generally high utility.

The question, then, relates not simply to the analysis of the concept of justice as common sense defines it, but the analysis of it in the wider sense as to how much weight considerations of justice, as defined, are to have when laid against other kinds of moral considerations. Here again I wish to argue that reasons of justice have a *special* weight for which only the conception of justice as fairness can account. Moreover, it belongs to the concept of justice that they do have this special weight. While Mill recognized that this was so, he thought that it could be accounted for by the special urgency of the moral feelings which naturally support principles of such high utility. But it is a mistake to resort to the urgency of feeling; as with the appeal to intuition, it manifests a failure to pursue the question far enough. The special weight of considerations of justice can be explained from the conception of justice as fairness. It is only necessary to elaborate a bit what has already been said as follows.

If one examines the circumstances in which a certain tolerance of slavery is justified, or perhaps better, excused, it turns out that these are of a rather special sort. Perhaps slavery exists as an inheritance from the past and it proves necessary to dismantle it piece by piece; at times slavery may conceivably be an advance on previous institutions. Now while there may be some excuse for slavery in special conditions, it is never an excuse for it that it is sufficiently advantageous to the slaveholder to outweigh the disadvantages to the slave and to society. A person who argues in this way is not perhaps making a wildly irrelevant remark; but he is guilty of a moral fallacy. There is disorder in his conception of the ranking of moral principles. For the slaveholder, by his own admission, has no moral title to the advantages which he receives as a slaveholder. He is no more prepared than the slave to acknowledge the principle upon which is founded the respective positions in which they both stand. Since slavery does not accord with principles which they could mutually acknowledge, they each may be supposed to agree that it is unjust: it grants claims which it ought not to grant and in doing so denies claims which it ought not to deny. Amongst persons in a general position who are debating the form of their common practices, it cannot, therefore, be offered as a reason for a practice that, in conceding these very claims that ought to be denied, it nevertheless meets existing interests more effectively. By their very nature the satisfaction of these claims is without weight and cannot enter into any tabulation of advantages and disadvantages.

Furthermore, it follows from the concept of morality that, to the extent that the slaveholder recognizes his position *vis-a-vis* the slave to be unjust, he would not choose to press his claims. His not wanting to receive his special advantages is one of the ways in which he shows that he thinks slavery is unjust. It would be fallacious for the legislator to suppose, then, that it is a ground for having a practice that it brings advantages greater than disadvantages, if those for whom the practice is designed, and to whom the advantages flow, acknowledge that they have no moral title to them and do not wish to receive them.

For these reasons the principles of justice have a special weight; and with respect to the principle of the greatest satisfaction of desire, as cited in the general position amongst those discussing the merits of their common practices, the principles of justice have an absolute weight. In this sense they are not contingent; and this is why their force is greater than can be accounted for by the general presumption (assuming that there is one) of the effectiveness, in the utilitarian sense, of practices which in fact satisfy them.

If one wants to continue using the concepts of classical utilitarianism, one will have to say, to meet this criticism, that at least the individual or social utility functions must be so defined that no value is given to the satisfaction of interests the representative claims of which violate the principles of justice. In this way it is no doubt possible to include these principles within the form of the utilitarian conception; but to do so is, of course, to change its inspiration altogether as a moral conception. For it is to incorporate within it principles which cannot be understood on the basis of a higher order executive decision aiming at the greatest satisfaction of desire.

It is worth remarking, perhaps, that this criticism of utilitarianism does not depend on whether or not the two assumptions, that of individuals having similar utility functions and that of diminishing marginal utility, are interpreted as psychological propositions to be supported or refuted by experience, or as moral and political principles expressed in a somewhat technical language. There are, certainly, several advantages in taking them in the latter fashion. For one thing, one might say that this is what Bentham and others really meant by them, at least as shown by how they were used in arguments for social reform. More importantly, one could hold that the best way to defend the classical utilitarian view is to interpret these assumptions as moral and political principles. It is doubtful whether, taken as psychological propositions, they are true of men in general as we know them under normal conditions. On the other hand, utilitarians would not have wanted to propose them merely as practical working principles of legislation, or as expedient maxims to guide reform, given the egalitarian sentiments of modern society. When pressed they might well have invoked the idea of a more or less equal capacity of men in relevant respects if given an equal chance in a just society. But if the argument above regarding slavery is correct, then granting these assumptions as moral and political principles makes no difference. To view individuals as equally fruitful lines for the allocation of benefits, even as a matter of moral principle, still leaves the mistaken notion that the satisfaction of desire has value in itself irrespective of the relations between persons as members of a common practice, and irrespective of the claims upon one another which the satisfaction of interests represents. To see the error of this idea one must give up the conception of justice as an executive decision altogether and refer to the notion of justice as fairness: that participants in a common practice be regarded as having an original and equal liberty and that their common practices be considered unjust unless they accord with principles which persons so circumstanced and related could freely acknowledge before one another, and so could accept as fair. Once the emphasis is put upon the concept of the mutual recognition of principles by participants in a common practice the rules of which are to define their several relations and give form to their claims on one another, then it is clear that the granting of a claim the principle of which could not be acknowledged by each in the general position (that is, in the position in which the parties propose and acknowledge principles before one another) is not a reason for adopting a practice. Viewed in this way, the background of the claim is seen to exclude it from consideration; that it can represent a value in itself arises from the conception of individuals as separate lines for the assignment of benefits, as isolated persons who stand as claimants on an administrative or benevolent largesse. Occasionally persons do so stand to one another; but this is not the general case, nor, more importantly, is it the case when it is a matter of the justice of practices themselves in which participants stand in various relations to be appraised in accordance with standards which they may be expected to acknowledge before one another. Thus however mistaken the notion of the social contract may be as history, and however far it may overreach itself as a general theory of social and political obligation, it does express, suitably interpreted, an essential part of the concept of justice.

VIII

By way of conclusion I should like to make two remarks: first, the original modification of the utilitarian principle (that it require of practices that the offices and positions defined by them be equal unless it is reasonable to suppose that the representative man in *every* office would find the inequality to his advantage), slight as it may appear at first sight, actually has a different conception of justice standing behind it. I have tried to show how this is so by developing the concept of justice as fairness and by indicating how this notion involves the mutual acceptance, from a general position, of the principles on which a practice is founded, and how this in turn requires the exclusion from consideration of claims violating the principles of justice. Thus the slight alteration of principle reveals another family of notions, another way of looking at the concept of justice.

Second, I should like to remark also that I have been dealing with the [illegible] set out the kinds of principles upon which judgments concerning the justice of practices may be said to stand. The analysis will be successful to the degree that it expresses the principles involved in these judgments when made by competent persons upon deliberation and reflection.[9] Now every people may be supposed to have the concept of justice, since in the life of every society there must be at least some relations in which the parties consider themselves to be circumstanced and related as the concept of justice as fairness requires. Societies will differ from one another not in having or in failing to have this notion but in the range of cases to which they apply it and in the emphasis which they give to it as compared with other moral concepts.

A firm grasp of the concept of justice itself is necessary if these variations, and the reasons for them, are to be understood. No study of the development of moral ideas and of the differences between them is more sound than the analysis of the fundamental moral concepts upon which it must depend. I have tried, therefore, to give an analysis of the concept of justice which should apply generally, however large a part the concept may have in a given morality, and which can be used in explaining the course of men's thoughts about justice and its relations to other moral concepts. How it is to be used for this purpose is a large topic which I cannot, of course, take up here. I mention it only to emphasize that I have been dealing with the concept of justice itself and to indicate what use I consider such an analysis to have.

NOTES AND QUESTIONS

1. Professor Rawls has written extensively on the subject of ethics and is generally regarded as the single most influential thinker on the subject in the latter half of the 20th century. The article presented here distills his thinking in a concise and useful way. *See also,* Rawls, A Theory of Justice (1972). Although not an article on "bioethics," the attempt to articulate justice as fairness is so fundamental that it pertains to most human relationships, including those usually encompassed by concerns about bioethics.
2. An excellent treatment more narrowly focused on bioethics may be found in Beauchamp & Childress, Principles of Biomedical Ethics, 4th ed. (Oxford Univ. Press 1994). The authors would characterize Rawls as articulating a "rights-based theory," in contrast to utilitarianism (consequence-based), Kantianism (obligation-based), character ethics (virtue-based) and communitarianism (community-based). Beauchamp and Childress themselves, in an excellent discussion of these various theories, acknowledge that the various approaches tend to overlap and merge. They then discuss the usual principles invoked by writers on

[9] For a further discussion of the idea expressed here, see my paper, "Outline of a Decision Procedure for Ethics," in the *Philosophical Review*, LX (1951), 177-97. For an analysis, similar in many respects but using the notion of the ideal observer instead of that of the considered judgment of a competent person, see Roderick Firth, "Ethical Absolutism and the Ideal Observer," *Philosophy and Phenomenological Research*, XII (1952), 317-45. While the similarities between these two discussions are more important than the differences, an analysis based on the notion of a considered judgment of a competent person, as it is based on a kind of judgment, may prove more helpful in understanding the features of moral judgment than an analysis based on the notion of an ideal observer, although this remains to be shown. A man who rejects the conditions imposed on a considered judgment of a competent person could no longer profess to *judge* at all. This seems more fundamental than his rejecting the conditions of observation, for these do not seem to apply, in an ordinary sense, to making a moral judgment.

bioethics: respect for autonomy, nonmaleficence, beneficence and justice. Placing these within the context of the professional-patient relationship, Beauchamp and Childress find essential requirements to be veracity, privacy, confidentiality and fidelity. In the end, an ethical system must recognize and reward "virtue," which includes compassion, discernment, trustworthiness and integrity. Society should respect and award conscientiousness and ideals. They conclude that any system of ethics should recognize moral excellence as its ultimate goal.

3. The difficulty with the analysis in Beauchamp and Childress, as excellent as it is, is that it proceeds from a particular context — usually physician/patient based — to work backwards toward a system of ethics. This tends to treat physician/patient relationships as different from, and apart from, other relationships in society and general ethical theory. The present text instead starts with Rawls' theory and proceeds from the general foundation thus provided toward more specific concerns in the realm of bioethics.

4. Rawls' two fundamental rules, providing for maximum liberty and for equality of opportunity, both govern ethical perspectives on societal obligations as well as individual entitlements. They would inform not only such "macro" issues as rationing health care, but also such "micro" issues as informed consent. They would also govern such traditional bioethical concerns as autonomy, beneficence and nonmaleficence. They find grounding in the United States Constitution, particularly the First Amendment protection of speech and belief and the Fourteenth Amendment guarantees of due process and equal protection. Freedom of contract — a concept out of favor in the social welfare state — is also both a constitutional and a Rawlsian concern.

5. What is perhaps most distinctive about Rawls' analysis is that he argues against compromising an individual's interests or "rights" as a means of assuring the interests of others. That idea that there is an irreducible minimum to human dignity underlies the American Bill of Rights and the United Nations Declaration of Human Rights. Rawls' essential touchstone is the emphasis on the agreement of parties to an arrangement. This is the essence of such central legal concepts as informed consent and the Nuremberg judgments concerning human experimentation. In Rawls' analysis, rationing of health care would be problematic, and concepts such as substituted judgment or community need in organ donations would be difficult to defend. That analysis would reject equally the utilitarian and communitarian approaches to organizing human relations and decision-making in bioethical settings.

6. It would be unfair to Rawls, however, to say that he advances a purely "rights-based" approach to ethics. His analysis finds limits to the autonomy of individuals who live in a community. They must act fairly and morally and respect ethical obligations to others and to the [illegible] which follow, this is a recurring theme and should particularly be considered in the opinions of the courts in dealing with maternal/fetal conflict, status of embryos, professional abuse and problems of privacy or confidentiality.

7. Ethical analysis, whether that of Rawls or of other writers, is chiefly deficient in defining the community by which ethical obligations are enforced or defined. Most writers *assume* the existence of a community or its creation from a "state of nature" by people who then form a community. But the process of creation, inclusion and exclusion is itself an ethical process and one of an ongoing nature. Thus, these materials begin with the fundamental issue of community membership, examining cases which confront the treatment of people as property, as aliens or prisoners, or as somehow of lesser dignity, as with the mentally retarded, the unborn and the undead.

   In looking to a community to determine membership of "personhood," it may be useful to reverse the process: to define "person" and infer a community from the essential, irreducible nature of persons. Writers such as Rousseau and Hobbes did this, portraying society as rising from the essential qualities of the human person, as found in a primitive state of nature. This is useful in a bioethical sense, because it starts with a fundamental biological unit — a human being. Any system of ethics would then have a firm, biological footing. Such an effort appears in the following essay by Fletcher. Consider whether it is accurate and useful.

Joseph Fletcher, *Humanness* *

We are constantly seeing lists, which grow longer all the time, of ethical questions in biomedical research and clinical practice. What ought we to do, or not do, about such things as truthtelling in medical diagnosis, sterilization, transplants and implants, intensive care and "crash" treatments, defective newborns and high-risk pregnancies, *in vitro* fertilizations in embryology, triage decisions about things like complicated hepatic coma, abortions, and genetic therapy and design proposals. We should include, also, behavior control by psychosurgery or chemotherapy, positive and negative euthanasia, cyborg amplifications, transsexual surgery, selection procedures for hemodialysis and other scarcity allocations, artificial insemination and inovulation, refusals of consent to indicated treatment, "ghost" surgery and medical care, the nonmedicinal use of drugs, clinical experiments, fetologic interventions. The list is long and, as I say, growing.

Physicians and biologists are notoriously conservative people, but by their "intranaut" research into the chemical depths of men they have precipitated an ethical and social revolution far more portentous than the astronauts' moon-walks and rock collecting. Now, with man's new control over man himself, by the new genetics, birth technologies, and life-support systems — now, what ought we to be doing and not doing, and how do we understand this "man" who makes and remakes men?

Abortion provides a clinical context in which we can see the need of a consensual answer to the question, What is a human being? and our serious

* From *Humanhood: Essays in Biomedical Ethics*, by Joseph Fletcher (1979), pp. 7-19. (Amherst, NY: Prometheus Books).

lack of one. There are other medical situations in which it is equally critical, however. I recall the decision making of a California prison's medical staff when confronted by a nonpsychotic prisoner's request for a prefrontal lobotomy. He had been imprisoned for committing murder in a rage, then murdered a fellow inmate — and finally almost killed a prison guard. What would he be like after the operation? What was risked? Could it be justified? Quality-of-life analyses obviously depend on some presuppositions about human biology and social welfare, but those who make their moral judgments by a quality-of-life ethics will, especially, need a list of criteria for humanness to supply the parameters of quality judgments and selections.

We all know the dangers of reductionism, i.e., the tendency to explain personality in terms of physiology, physiology in terms of metabolism, metabolism in terms of biochemistry, biochemistry in terms of chemistry, chemistry in terms of molecules, and molecules in terms of atoms, so that since the behavior of atoms is notoriously random, you end up with a question mark! Nevertheless, I would want to defend old Thomas Huxley's point made a hundred years ago, defending Darwin from the charge of godlessness; using a physical model to understand nature, including man, does not make us materialists or atheists any more than eating food or wearing clothes do.

By the phrase *nature of man* I would hope we do not mean *human nature*. The phrase *nature of man* is acceptable because it calls for a description, which is our task in meta-ethics. *Human nature* however, connotes a substantive and even fixed nature, as something "given in the nature of things," *de rerum natura*, an idea which may be seen classically in the old natural law tradition of prescientific reasoning. As recently as 1924, we find T.E. Hulme saying, "Man is an extraordinarily fixed and limited animal whose nature is absolutely constant." Less radical versions assign a kind of residual and unchanging core of human being. Contrasted to this is the opinion of Ren Dubos that man "has the privilege and responsibility of shaping his self and his future." In our investigation I would range myself with Ortega y Gasset's argument that man has no nature, only a history, and with Ashley Montagu's observation that babies are not born with human nature, but only with more or less capacity to become human. To some people in medical education this will seem a very abstruse issue, but such thinking is superficial.

Another point of prolegomena is that our analysis of the question, "What is a man?" needs to be converted in its form to, "What is a person?" A glance at arguments about the ethics of abortion and euthanasia is enough to make my reasons clear. Sometimes discussants say that whether it is right or not to terminate a pregnancy depends on whether an embryo or fetus is a human life. But that is not the critical question any more. Of course it is alive. Cell division goes forward from fertilization. And of course it is human, since any biologist could quickly identify even a blastula as of the species *Homo sapiens* — not as a monkey's or a rabbit's. No: the question is not whether it is a life or even whether it is a human life. The question is whether we may assign [illegible] people speak of "a truly human being."

Defective fetuses, defective newborns, moribund patients — all of these are human lives. Some physicians would "sacrifice" such human lives sometimes, others would not. But do they understand the import of their policy? If there is any ground at all, ethically, as I would contend there is, for allowing or hastening the end of such lives, it must be on a qualitative ground, that such human lives are subpersonal. What is critical is personal status, not merely human status. This is why the law does not allow that a fetus is a person.

Mark Twain complained that people are always talking about the weather but they never do anything about it. The same is true of humanhood criteria. In biomedical ethics writers constantly say that we need to explicate humanness or humaneness, what it means to be a truly human being, but they never follow their admission of the need with an actual inventory or profile, no matter how tentatively offered. Yet this is what must be done, or at least attempted.

Synthetic concepts such as human and man and person require operational terms, spelling out the which and what and when. Only in that way can we get down to cases — to normative decisions. There are always some people who prefer to be visceral and affective in their moral choices, with no desire to have any rationale for what they do. But ethics is precisely the business of rational, critical reflection (encephalic and not merely visceral) about the problems of the moral agent — in biology and medicine as much as in law, government, education, or anything else.

To that end, then, for the purposes of biomedical ethics, I now turn to a *profile of man* in concrete and discrete terms.

1. Minimum intelligence

Any individual of the species *Homo sapiens* who falls below an I.Q. grade of 40 in a standard Stanford-Binet test, amplified if you like by other tests, is questionably a person; below the mark of 20, not a person. *Homo* is indeed *sapiens*, in order to be *Homo*. The *ratio*, in another turn of speech, is what makes a person of the *vita*. Mere biological life, before minimal intelligence is achieved or after it is lost irretrievably, is without personal status. This has bearing, obviously, on decision making in gynecology, obstetrics, and pediatrics, as well as in general surgery and medicine.

2. Self-awareness

Self-consciousness, as we know, is the quality we watch developing in a baby; we watch it with fascination and glee. Its essential role in personality development is a basic datum of psychology. Its existence or function in animals at or below the primate level is debatable. It is clearly absent in the lower vertebrates, as well as in the nonvertebrates. In psychotherapy non-self-awareness is pathological; in medicine, unconsciousness when it is incorrigible at once poses quality-of-life judgments — for example, in neurosurgical cases of irreversible damage to the brain cortex.

3. Self-control

If an individual is not only not controllable by others (unless by force) but not controllable by the individual himself or herself, a low level of life is reached about on a par with that of a paramecium. If the condition cannot be rectified medically, so that means-ends behavior is out of the question, the individual is not a person — not ethically, and certainly not in the eyes of the law — just as a fetus is not legally a person.

4. A sense of time

Time consciousness. By this is meant clock time or *chronos*, not timeliness or *kairos*, i.e., not the "fullness of time" or the pregnant moment (remember Paul Tillich?). A sense, that is, of the passage of time. Dr. Thomas Hunter, a colleague of mine and Professor of Medicine at the University of Virginia, remarked recently, "Life is the allocation of time." We can disagree legitimately about how relatively important this indicator is, but it is hard to understand why anybody would minimize it or eliminate it as a trait of humanness.

5. A sense of futurity

How "truly human" is any man who cannot realize there is a time yet to come as well as the present? Subhuman animals do not look forward in time; they live only on what we might call visceral strivings, appetites. Philosophical anthropologies (one recalls that of William Temple, the Archbishop of Canterbury, for instance) commonly emphasize purposiveness as a key to humanness. Chesterton once remarked that we would never ask a puppy what manner of dog it wanted to be when it grows up. The assertion here is that men are typically teleological, although certainly not eschatological. For the latter sense of futurity, the eschatological outlook, and its ethical input, see Ramsey, who reasons that we ought not to aim teleologically at what is good (a consequentialist ethics) but act according to whatever we may believe about the "eschaton," or man's eternal and supernatural destiny.

6. A sense of the past

Memory. Unlike other animals, men as a species have reached a unique level of neurologic development, particularly in the cerebrum and especially its neocortex. They are linked to the past by conscious recall — not only, as with subhuman animals, by conditioning and the reactivation of emotions (reactivated, that is, externally rather than autonomously). It is this trait, in particular, that makes man, alone among all species, a cultural instead of an instinctive creature. An existentialist focus on "nowness" truncates the nature of man.

7. The capability to relate to others

Interpersonal relationships, of the sexual-romantic and friendship kind, are of the greatest importance for the fullness of what we idealize as being truly personal. Medical piety in the past has always held its professional ethics to be only a one-to-one, physician-patient obligation. However, there are also the more diffuse and comprehensive social relations of our vocational, economic, and political life. Aristotle's characterization of man as a social animal, *zoon politikon*, must surely figure prominently in the inventory. It is true that even insects live in social systems, but the cohesion of all subhuman societies is based on instinct. Man's society is based on culture — that is, on a conscious knowledge of the system and on the exercise in some real measure of either consent or opposition.

8. Concern for others

Some people may be skeptical about our capacity to care about others (what in Christian ethics is often distinguished from romance and friendship as "neighbor love" or "neighbor concern"). The extent to which this capacity is actually in play is debatable. But whether concern for others is disinterested or inspired by enlightened self-interest, it seems plain that a conscious extra-ego orientation is a trait of the species; the absence of this ambience is a clinical indication of psychopathology.

9. Communication

Utter alienation or disconnection from others, if it is irreparable, is dehumanization. This is not so much a matter of not being disposed to receive and send "messages" as of the inability to do so. This criterion comes into question in patients who cannot hear, speak, feel, or see others. It may come about as a result of mental or physical trauma, infection, genetic or congenital disorder, or from psychological causes. Completely and finally isolated individuals are subpersonal. The problem is perhaps most familiar in terminal illnesses and the clinical decision making required.

10. Control of existence

It is of the nature of man that he is not helplessly subject to the blind workings of physical or physiological nature. He has only finite knowledge, freedom, and initiative, but what he has of it is real and effective. Invincible ignorance and total helplessness are the antithesis of humanness, and to the degree that a man lacks control he is not responsible, and to be irresponsible is to be subpersonal. This item in the agenda applies directly, for example, in psychiatric medicine, especially to severe cases of toxic and degenerative psychosis.

11. Curiosity

without affect, sunk in *anomie*, is to be not a person. Indifference is inhuman. Man is a learner and a knower as well as a tool maker and user. This raises a question, therefore, about demands to stop some kinds of biomedical inquiry. For example, an AMA committee recently imposed a ban on *in vitro* fertilization and embryo transplants on the ground that they are dangerous. But dangerous ignorance is more dangerous than dangerous knowledge. It is dehumanizing to impose a moratorium on research. No doubt this issue arises, or will arise, in many other phases of medical education and practice.

12. Change and changeability

To the extent that an individual is unchangeable or opposed to change, he denies the creativity of personal beings. It means not only the fact of biological and physiological change, which goes on as a condition of life, but the capacity and disposition for changing one's mind and conduct as well. Biologically, human beings are developmental: birth, life, health, and death are processes, not events, and are to be understood progressively, not episodically. All human existence is on a continuum, a matter of becoming. In this perspective, are we to regard potentials *als ob*, as if they were actual? I think not. The question arises prominently in abortion ethics.

13. Balance of rationality and feeling

To be "truly human," to be a wholesome person, one cannot be either Apollonian or Dionysian. As human beings we are not coldly rational or cerebral, nor are we merely creatures of feeling and intuition. It is a matter of being both, in different combinations from one individual to another. To be one rather than the other is to distort the *humanum.*

14. Idiosyncrasy

The human being is idiomorphous, a distinctive individual. As Helmut Schoeck has shown, even the function of envy in human behavior is entirely consistent with idiosyncrasy. To be a person is to have an identity, to be recognizable and callable by name. It is this criterion which lies behind the fear that to replicate individuals by so-called cloning would be to make carbon copies of the parent source and thus dehumanize the clone by denying it its individuality. One or two writers have even spoken of a "right" to a "unique genotype," and while such talk is ethically and scientifically questionable, it nonetheless reflects a legitimate notion of something essential to an authentic person.

15. Neocortical function

In a way, this is the cardinal indicator, the one all the others are hinged upon. Before cerebration is in play, or with its end, in the absence of the synthesizing function of the cerebral cortex, the person is nonexistent. Such individuals are objects but not subjects. This is so no matter how many other spontaneous or artificially supported functions persist in the heart, lungs, neurologic and vascular systems. Such noncerebral processes are not personal. Like the Harvard Medical School's *ad hoc* committee report on "brain death," some state statutes require the absence of brain function. So do the guidelines for the legal determination of death recently adopted by the Italian Council of Ministers. But what is definitive in determining death is the loss of cerebration, not just of any or all brain function. Personal reality depends on cerebration and to be dead "humanly" speaking is to be excerebral, no matter how long the body remains alive.

The five negative points I have can be put even more briefly than the fifteen positive ones, although I am inclined to believe that they merit just as much critical scrutiny and elaboration.

1. Man is not non or anti-artificial

Men are characterized by technique, and for a human being to oppose technology is self-hatred. We are often confused on this score, attitudinally. A "test tube baby," for example, although conceived and gestated *ex corpo*, would nonetheless be humanly reproduced and of human value. A baby made artificially, by deliberate and careful contrivance, would be more human than one resulting from sexual roulette — the reproductive mode of the subhuman species.

2. Man is not essentially parental

People can be fully personal without reproducing, as the religious vows of nuns, monks, and celibate priests of the past have asserted, as the law has implied by refusing to annul [illegible], and as we see in the ethos reversal of contemporary family and population control — and, more militantly, in the nonparental rhetoric of women's liberation and a growing rejection of the "baby trap."

3. Man is not essentially sexual

Sexuality, a broader and deeper phenomenon than sex, is of the fullness but not of the essence of man. It is not even necessary to human species survival. I will not try here to indicate the psychological entailments of this negative proposition, but it is biologically apparent when we look at such nonsexual reproduction as cloning from somatic cells and parthenogenetic reproduction by both androgenesis and gynogenesis. What light does this biology throw on the nature of man? What does a personistic view of man say about the ethics of such biology? (N.B. I do not refer here to personalism, which has more metaphysical freight than many of us want to carry.)

4. Man is not a bundle of rights

The notion of a human nature has served as a conceptual bucket to contain "human rights" and certain other given things, like "original sin" and "the sense of oughtness" and "conscience." The idea behind this is that such things are objective, pre-existent phenomena, not contingent on biological or social relativities. People sometimes speak of rights to live, to die, to be healthy, to reproduce, and so on, as if they were absolute, eternal, intrinsic. But as the law makes plain, all rights are imperfect and may be set aside if human need requires it. We shall have to think through the relation of rights and needs, as it bears on clinical medicine's decision-making problems, as well as society's problems of health care delivery. One example: What is the "humane" policy if we should reach the point (I think we will) of deciding for or against compulsory birth control? Or, how are we to relate rights and needs if, to take only one example, an ethnic group protests against mass screening for sickle cell anemia? Or if after genetic counseling, a couple elects to proceed with a predictably degenerate pregnancy?

5. Man is not a worshipper

Faith in supernatural realities and attempts to be in direct association with them are choices some human beings make and others do not. Mystique is not essential to being truly a person. Like sexuality, it may arguably be of the fullness of humanness but it is not of the essence. This negative proposition is required by our basic guideline, the premise that a workable biomedical ethics is humanistic, whatever reasons we may have for putting human well-being at the center of concern.

These are the criteria, but how are we to go about testing them? And how are we to compare and combine the results of our criticism? How are we to rank-order or give priority to the items in our man-hood profile? Which are only optimal, what are essential? What are the applications of these or other indicators to the normative decisions of biologists and physicians? In my own list, here, which factors can be eliminated, in whole or in part, without lowering individuals and patients below the personal line? I trust that by this time it is plain that I do not claim to have produced the pure gospel of humanness. I remain open to correction.

I rather suspect that we are more apt to find good answers inductively and empirically, from medical science and the clinicians, than by the necessarily syllogistic reasoning of the humanities, which proceeds deductively from abstract premises. Syllogisms always contain their conclusions in their major or first premises. Divorced from the laboratory and the hospital, talk about what it means to be human could easily become inhumane.

NOTES AND QUESTIONS

1. Consider carefully Fletcher's last point: the laboratory is a better starting place than the humanities for a system of ethics. Do you agree? Otherwise, Fletcher says, the study of humanities may "become inhumane." Does he include Rawls?

2. Fletcher says the inquiry, "what is a man?" must be converted to "what is a person?" Isn't there a difference, and isn't the former more fundamental and important? To be precise, in that shift Fletcher moves from biology to philosophy. Does he succeed?

3. Someone, perhaps Mark Twain, wrote that man is the only animal that understands shame or needs to. Shame is not on Fletcher's list; nor are spirit, humor, conscience, choice, compassion, self-sacrifice, ambition, avarice and psychosis. Should these be there? What else is missing? On the other hand, there are some dubious elements on Fletcher's list: IQ, self-control, communication, idiosyncrasy. Do these distinguish us from animals? From nonliving things? Are they present in all humans? All persons?

4. Doesn't Fletcher deny the three most powerful forces in humans: a lust for sexuality and a thirst for justice (hence a concern for the "bundle of rights") and a quest for divinity? Are these not true of all people, and not true of animals? Why does Fletcher deny them?

5. In his list of "negative points," Fletcher includes as number 4 that "Man is not a bundle of rights." Perhaps he means that that is not all that man is. Or perhaps he means there are no inherent rights of man. If the latter, it is an important declaration, conflicting with Rawls and much of Western thought, rejecting Locke and Rousseau and many of the sentiments expressed in the Bill of Rights to the United States Constitution and the 1948 Declaration on Human Rights of the United Nations.

6. Finally, what does one do with such a list? Can it be reconciled with Rawls' approach? Can it be used for (or against) slavery, human experimentation, abortion, or euthanasia? Can it be a basis for rationing health care and preferring certain people ahead of others? Are these applications so intrinsically problematic as to make the question too dangerous, leading — perhaps — to the Nazi experiments with concentration camps and the American experience with the Tuskegee prisoners.

7. We turn now from the philosophy of Rawls and biology of Fletcher to the law of nations, specifically that community known as the United Nations. After the Second [illegible] consensus that there are universal human rights, rights which could be identified, declared and protected. What follows is the 1948 Universal Declaration. As to its present day significance, see a recent excellent essay by Annas,

Human Rights and Health — The Universal Declaration of Human Rights at 50, 339 New Eng. J. Med. 1778 (1998).

Two questions: What is the nature of the community and its membership? And what is the nature of the person contemplated?

UNIVERSAL DECLARATION OF HUMAN RIGHTS*

Preamble

Whereas recognition of the inherent dignity and of the equal and inalienable rights of all members of the human family is the foundation of freedom, justice and peace in the world,

Whereas disregard and contempt for human rights have resulted in barbarous acts which have outraged the conscience of mankind, and the advent of a world in which human beings shall enjoy freedom of speech and belief and freedom from fear and want has been proclaimed as the highest aspiration of the common people,

Whereas the peoples of the United Nations have in the Charter reaffirmed their faith in fundamental human rights, in the dignity and worth of the human person and in the equal rights of men and women and have determined to promote social progress and better standards of life in larger freedom,

Now, therefore, The General Assembly, Proclaims this Universal Declaration of Human Rights as a common standard of achievement for all peoples and all nations, to the end that every individual and every organ of society, keeping this Declaration constantly in mind, shall strive by teaching and education to promote respect for these rights and freedoms and by progressive measures, national and international, to secure their universal and effective recognition and observance, both among the peoples of Member States themselves and among the peoples of territories under their jurisdiction.

Article 1

All human beings are born free and equal in dignity and rights. They are endowed with reason and conscience and should act towards one another in a spirit of brotherhood.

Article 2

Everyone is entitled to all the rights and freedoms set forth in this Declaration, without distinction of any kind, such as race, colour, sex, language, religion, political or other opinion, national or social origin, property, birth or other status.

Furthermore, no distinction shall be made on the basis of the political, jurisdictional or international status of the country or territory to which a person belongs, whether it be independent, trust, non-self-governing or under any other limitation of sovereignty.

---

* From H.J. Steiner & P. Alston, *International Human Rights in Context*, at 1156 (Oxford Univ. Press, 1996).

Article 3

Everyone has the right to life, liberty and security of person.

Article 6

Everyone has the right to recognition everywhere as a person before the law.

Article 7

All are equal before the law and are entitled without any discrimination to equal protection of the law. All are entitled to equal protection against any discrimination in violation of this Declaration and against any incitement to such discrimination.

Article 8

Everyone has the right to an effective remedy by the competent national tribunals for acts violating the fundamental rights granted him by the constitution or by the law.

Article 9

No one shall be subjected to arbitrary arrest, detention or exile.

Article 10

Everyone is entitled in full equality to a fair and public hearing by an independent and impartial tribunal, in the determination of his rights and obligations and of any criminal charges against him.

Article 13

1. Everyone has the right to freedom of movement and residence within the borders of each State.

2. Everyone has the right to leave any country, including his own, and to return to his country.

Article 15

1. Everyone has the right to a nationality.

2. No one shall be arbitrarily deprived of his nationality nor denied the right to change his nationality.

Article 16

1. Men and women of full age, without any limitation due to race, nationality or religion, have the right to marry and to found a family. They are entitled to equal rights as to marriage, during marriage and at its dissolution.

2. Marriage shall be entered into only with the free and full consent of the intending spouses.

3. The family is the natural and fundamental group unit of society and is entitled to protection by society and the State.

Article 17

1. Everyone has the right to own property alone as well as in association with others.

2. No one shall be arbitrarily deprived of his property.

Article 18

Everyone has the right to freedom of thought, conscience and religion; this right includes freedom to change his religion or belief, and freedom, either alone or in community with others and in public or private, to manifest his religion or belief in teaching, practice, worship and observance.

Article 19

Everyone has the right to freedom of opinion and expression; this right includes freedom to hold opinions without interference and to seek, receive and impart information and ideas through media and regardless of frontiers.

Article 20

1. Everyone has the right to freedom of peaceful assembly and association.

2. No one may be compelled to belong to an association.

Article 21

1. Everyone has the right to take part in the government of his country, directly or through freely chosen representatives.

2. Everyone has the right to equal access to public service in his country.

3. The will of the people shall be the basis of the authority of government; this will shall be expressed in periodic and genuine elections which shall be universal and equal suffrage and shall be held by secret vote or by equivalent free voting procedures.

Article 22

Everyone, as a member of society, has the right to social security and is entitled to realization, through national effort and international co-operation and in accordance with the organization and resources of each State, of the economic, social and cultural rights indispensable for his dignity and the free development of his personality.

Article 23

1. Everyone has the right to work, to free choice of employment, to just and favourable conditions of work and to protection against unemployment.

2. Everyone, without any discrimination, has the right to equal pay for equal work.

3. Everyone who works has the right to just and favourable remuneration ensuring for himself and his family an existence worthy of human dignity, and supplemented, if necessary, by other means of social protection.

4. Everyone has the right to form and to join trade unions for the protection of his interests.

Article 28

Everyone is entitled to a social and international order in which the rights and freedoms set forth in this Declaration can be fully realized.

Article 29

1. Everyone has duties to the community in which alone the free and full development of his personality is possible.

2. In the exercise of his rights and freedoms, everyone shall be subject only to such limitations as are determined by law solely for the purpose of securing due recognition and respect for the rights and freedoms of others and of meeting the just requirements of morality, public order and the general welfare in a democratic society.

3. These rights and freedoms may in no case be exercised contrary to the purposes and principles of the United Nations.

Article 30

Nothing in this Declaration may be interpreted as implying for any State, group or person any right to engage in any activity or to perform any act aimed at destruction of any of the rights and freedoms set forth herein

NOTES AND QUESTIONS

1. Are the United Nations principles consistent or inconsistent with the views of Rawls and Fletcher? Is it fair to say the Declaration melds the two views of Rawls and Fletcher finding political and human rights inherent in the biology of human beings? Or is it a third view entirely of ethics and rights?

2. Was the United Nations Declaration a statement of what is or what ought to be? Was it based on nature, history or conscience? And to whom was the Declaration directed — a community of peoples, of nations, or individuals? Or was it directed to itself, a community called the United Nations, and if so, when and how did that community come into being? Who is included; excluded; how may they leave?

3. What would you delete from or add to the United Nations Declaration? It was the product of World War II and the chaos and optimism which followed. At the start of a new millenium, how would we draft the Declaration differently?
4. Given the scope of the 1948 Declaration of Human Rights, should a separate Convention on Discrimination Against Women have been necessary in 1981? A separate Declaration on the Rights of Minorities (National, Ethnic, Religious or Linguistic) in 1993? Why? What did/might/should these conventions have added?
5. The history and experience of the United Nations and the Universal Declaration are the subjects of extensive literature in the fields of history and international law. A single, useful accounting is Jerome J. Shestak, *The World Had a Dream: Forty Years Ago, the Universal Declaration of Human Rights was Issued. A Look at What Has Happened Since*, Human Rights, Summer, 1988.
6. In the next section, we look at two cases — *Dred Scott* and *Baby M* — which deal with people as property. What would Rawls, Fletcher and the United Nations Declaration say about the issues in those two cases — slavery and surrogacy?
7. However, before proceeding, we should pause to consider one further document, the 1997 Convention of the Council of Europe which focused its attention on human rights in a bioethical context. What does it add to the United Nations Declaration? How does it differ?

CONVENTION ON HUMAN RIGHTS AND BIOMEDICINE *

Preamble

The Member States of the Council of Europe, the other States and the European Community signatories hereto,

Bearing in mind the *Universal Declaration of Human Rights* proclaimed by the General assembly of the United Nations on 10 December 1948;

Considering that the aim of the council of Europe is the achievement of a greater unity between its members and that one of the methods by which that aim is to be pursued is the maintenance and further realisation of human rights and fundamental freedoms;

Conscious of the accelerating developments in biology and medicine;

Convinced of the need to respect the human being both as an individual and as a member of the human species and recognising the importance of ensuring the dignity of the human being;

Resolving to take such measures as are necessary to safeguard human dignity and the fundamental rights and freedoms of the individual with regard to the application of biology and medicine;

---

* From H.J. Steiner & P. Alston, *International Human Rights in Context* (Oxford Univ. Press, 1996). Copyright © 1996. Reprinted with permission.

Have agreed as follows:

Chapter I — General provisions

Article 1 Purpose and object

Parties to this Convention shall protect the dignity and identity of all human beings and guarantee everyone, without discrimination, respect for their integrity and other rights and fundamental freedoms with regard to the application of biology and medicine.

Each Party shall take in its internal law the necessary measures to give effect to the provisions of this convention.

Article 2 Primacy of the human being

The interests and welfare of the human being shall prevail over the sole interest of society or science.

Article 5 General rule

An intervention in the health field may only be carried out after the person concerned has given free and informed consent to it.

This person shall beforehand be given appropriate information as to the purpose and nature of the intervention as well as on its consequences and risks.

The person concerned may freely withdraw consent at any time.

Article 6 Protection of persons not able to consent

1. Subject to Articles 17 and 20 below, an intervention may only be carried out on a person who does not have the capacity to consent, for his or her direct benefit.

2. Where, according to law, a minor does not have the capacity to consent to an intervention, the intervention may only be carried out with the authorisation of his or her representative or an authority or a person or body provided for by law.

3. The opinion of the minor shall be taken into consideration as an increasingly determining factor in proportion to his or her age and degree of maturity.

4. Where, according to law, an adult does not have the capacity to consent to an intervention because of a mental disability, a disease or for some similar reasons, the intervention may only be carried out with the authorisation of his or her representative or an authority or a person or body provided for by law.

The individual concerned shall as far as possible take part in the authorisation procedure.

Article 9 Previously expressed wishes

The previously expressed wishes relating to a medical intervention by a patient who is not, at the time of the intervention, in a state to express his or her wishes shall be taken into account.

Chapter III — Private life and right to information

Article 10 Private life and right to information

1. Everyone has the right to respect for private life in relation to information about his or her health.

2. Everyone is entitled to know any information collected about his or her health. However, the wishes of individuals not to be so informed shall be observed.

3. In exceptional cases, restrictions may be placed by law on the exercise of the rights contained in paragraph 2 in the interests of the patient.

Chapter IV — Human genome

Article 11 Nondiscrimination

Any form of discrimination against a person on grounds of his or her genetic heritage is prohibited.

Article 12 Predictive genetic tests

Tests which are predictive of genetic diseases or which serve either to identify the subject as a carrier of a gene responsible for a disease or to detect a genetic predisposition or susceptibility to a disease may be performed only for health purposes or for scientific research linked to health purposes, and subject to appropriate genetic counseling.

Article 13 Interventions on the human genome

An intervention seeking to modify the human genome may only be undertaken for preventive, diagnostic or therapeutic purposes and only if its aim is not to introduce any modification in the genome of any descendants.

Article 14 Nonselection of sex

The use of techniques of medically assisted procreation shall not be allowed for the purpose of choosing a future child's sex, except where serious hereditary sex-related disease is to be avoided.

Chapter V — Scientific research

Article 15 General rule

Scientific research in the field of biology and medicine shall be carried out freely, subject to the provisions of this Convention and the other legal provisions ensuring the protection of the human being.

Article 16 Protection of persons undergoing research

Research on a person may only be undertaken if all the following conditions are met:

(i) there is no alternative of comparable effectiveness to research on humans

(ii) the risks which may be incurred by that person are not disproportionate to the potential benefits of the research,

(iii) the research project has been approved by the competent body after independent examination of its scientific merit, including assessment of the importance of the aim of the research, and multidisciplinary review of its ethical acceptability,

(iv) the persons undergoing research have been informed of their rights and the safeguards prescribed by law for their protection,

(v) the necessary consent as provided for under Article 5 has been given expressly, specifically and is documented. Such consent may be freely withdrawn at any time.

Article 17 Protection of persons not able to consent to research

1. Research on a person without the capacity to consent as stipulated in Article 5 may be undertaken only if all the following conditions are met:

(i) the conditions laid down in Article 16, sub-paragraphs i to iv, are fulfilled;

(ii) the results of the research have the potential to produce real and direct benefit to his or her health;

(iii) research of comparable effectiveness cannot be carried out on individuals capable of giving consent;

(iv) the necessary authorisation provided for under Article 6 has been given specifically and in writing, and

(v) the person concerned does not object.

2. Exceptionally and under the protective conditions prescribed by law, where the research has not the potential to produce results of direct benefit to the health of the person concerned, such research may be authorised subject to the conditions laid down in paragraph 1, sub-paragraphs i, iii, iv, and v above, and to the following additional conditions:

(i) the research has the aim of contributing, through significant improvement in the scientific understanding of the individual's condition, disease or disorder, to the ultimate attainment of results capable of conferring benefit to the person concerned or to other persons in the same age category or afflicted with the same disease or disorder or having the same condition.

(ii) the research entails only minimal risk and minimal burden for the individual concerned.

Article 18 Research on embryos in vitro

1. Where the law allows research on embryos in vitro, it shall ensure adequate protection of the embryo.

2. The creation of human embryos for research purposes is prohibited.

Chapter VI — Organ and tissue removal from living donors for transplantation purposes

Article 19 General rule

1. Removal of organs or tissue from a living person for transplantation purposes may be carried out solely for the therapeutic benefit of the recipient and where there is no suitable organ or tissue available from a deceased person and no other alternative therapeutic method of comparable effectiveness.

2. The necessary consent is provided for under Article 5 must have been given expressly and specifically either in written form or before an official body.

Article 20 Protection of persons not able to consent to organ removal

1. No organ or tissue removal may be carried out on a person who does not have the capacity to consent under Article 5.

2. Exceptionally and under the protective conditions prescribed by law, the removal of regenerative tissue from a person who does nto have the capacity to consent may be authorised provided the following conditions are met:

(i) there is no compatible donor available who has the capacity to consent,

(ii) the recipient is a brother or sister of the donor,

(iii) the donation must have the potential to be life-saving for the recipient,

(iv) the authorisation provided for under paragraphs 2 and 3 of Article 6 has been given specifically and in writing, in accordance with the law and with the approval of the competent body,

(v) the potential donor concerned does not object.

Chapter VII — Prohibition of financial gain and disposal of a part of the human body

Article 21 Prohibition of financial gain

The human body and its parts shall not, as such, give rise to financial gain.

Article 22 Disposal of a removed part of the human body

When in the course of an intervention any part of a human body is removed, it may be stored and used for a purpose other than that for which it was removed, only if this is done in conformity with appropriate information and consent procedures.

NOTES AND QUESTIONS

1. The Convention was, of course, preceded by a number of documents bearing on human experimentation. These include the Nuremberg Convention and the Helsinki Convention, explored *infra* § 3.03[1]. This Convention is different, however, in attempting to provide for human rights across a broad array of biomedical and bioethical contexts. Does it succeed? What would you add, omit, change?
2. Specifically, is Article 5 adequate; Article 10 clear; Article 11 overbroad; Article 14 intrusive; Article 17 abusive; Articles 18 and 19 overprotective; and Article 21 unfair?
3. The Convention was originally silent as to cloning. In 1998, the Council amended the preceding Convention, adding another article which prohibits cloning a human being. *See infra* § 2.03[3]. Is this consistent with the Convention? A wise addition?
4. Broad frameworks such as the United Nations Declaration and the Council of Europe's Convention are designed to impose a superstructure of values upon a multiplicity of communities and custom. Some of these communities still practice slavery or female genital mutilation. To what extent must a larger community tolerate such diverse customs as a matter of respect for those communities and the people who live there?

In the United States, for example, in the Dred Scott case, one of the questions was could the national Congress abolish slavery in the newly admitted states? And along what lines might it legitimately distinguish between Indian tribes/nations and African tribes/peoples? *See infra* § 1.02[1].

PROBLEM 1-1 — Rumors of War

Two news reports in the United States in 1998 concerned the following:

(a) The Associated Press reported that the prestigious Soldier's Medal had been awarded to three veterans of the Vietnamese War. The three were operating a helicopter gun ship in the early morning of March 16, 1968 at the village of My Lai, where American troops were massacring 500 Vietnamese civilian villagers. They landed their gunship in the line of fire and pointed their guns at U.S. soldiers to prevent more murders. They reported the incident upon their return to base.

(b) Time magazine and CNN reported (both later withdrew the report as false), that during the Vietnam War a special U.S. armed forces team entered Laos seeking American deserters, whom they found and killed in a village which they then destroyed. This clandestine undertaking was called "Operation Tailwind." On departure, they encountered fierce opposition and called in air strikes using sarin, a nerve gas banned by international law, which killed a number of opposing soldiers.

What bearing do these introductory materials have on the conduct and the persons involved in My Lai and Operation Tailwind? What "communities" did the various actors belong to, and to which communities did they owe obligations? What were their obligations to nonmembers?

§ 1.02 Noncitizens

Every community has a system of rights and obligations, governing those within and those without its boundaries. Respect may be paid both groups, but those outside usually are accorded lesser dignity. Often they are killed, as in war, or enslaved, as in Imperial Rome or Colonial America. Outsiders brought into the community may be accorded protected status, as resident aliens, or they may be treated as nonpersons, even property, on the order of domestic animals. Questions arise — how are such persons so categorized? What are their ethical entitlements? Today, can we — do we — treat people as property?

DRED SCOTT v. SANDFORD*
60 U.S. 393 (1856)

Mr. Chief Justice **Taney** delivered the opinion of the court.

. . . .

The question is simply this: Can a negro, whose ancestors were imported into this country, and sold as slaves become a member of the political community formed and brought into existence by the Constitution of the United States, and as such become entitled to all the rights, and privileges, and immunities guarantied by that instrument of the citizen? One of which rights insure the privilege of suing in a court of the United States in the cases specified in the Constitution.

. . . .

This situation of this population was altogether unlike that of the Indian Race. The latter, it is true, formed no part of the colonial communities, and never amalgamated with them in social connections or in government. But although they were uncivilized, they were yet a free and independent people, associated together in nations or tribes, and governed by their own laws . . . . Treaties have been negotiated with them, and their alliance sought for in war;

* For purposes of brevity, significant portions of the following case were omitted, including one of the concurring opinions and one of the dissenting opinions.

and the people who compose these Indians political communities have always been treated as foreigners not living under our Government. It is true that the course of events has brought the Indian tribes within the limits of the United States under subjection to the white race; and it has been found necessary, for their sake as well as our own, to regard them as in a state of pupilage, and to legislate to a certain extent over them and the territory they occupy. [A]nd if an individual should leave his nation or tribe, and take up his abode among the white population, he would be entitled to all the rights and privileges which would belong to an emigrant from any other foreign people.

. . . .

The words "people of the United States" and "citizens" are synonymous terms, and they mean the same thing. They both describe the political body who, according to our republican institutions form the sovereignty, and who hold the power and conduct the government through their representatives. They are what we familiarly call the "sovereign people," and every citizen is of this people, and a constituent member of this sovereignty. The question before us is, whether the class of persons described [above] compose a portion of this people, and are constituent members of this sovereignty? We think they are not, and that they are not included, and were not intended to be included, under the word "citizens" in the Constitution, and can therefore claim none of the rights and privileges which that instrument provides for and secures to citizens of the United States. On the contrary, they were at that time considered as a subordinate and inferior class of beings, who had been subjugated by the dominant race, and whether emancipated or not, yet remained subject to their authority, and had no rights or privileges but such as those who held the power and the Government might choose to grant them.

It is not the province of the court to decide upon the justice or injustice, the policy or impolicy, of these laws. The decision of that question belonged to the political or law making power; to those who formed the sovereignty and framed the Constitution. The duty of the court is, to interpret the instrument they have framed, with the best lights we can obtain on the subject, and to administer it as we find it, according to its true intent and meaning when it was adopted.

. . . .

In the opinion of the court the legislation and histories of the times, and the language used in the Declaration of Independence, show, that neither the class of persons who had been imported as slaves, nor their descendants, whether they had become free or not, were then acknowledged as a part of the people, nor intended to be included in the general words used in that memorable instrument.

. . . .

They had for more than a century before been regarded as beings of an inferior order, and altogether unfit to associate with the white race, either in social or political relations; and so far inferior, that they had no rights which the white man was bound to respect; and that the negro might justly and lawfully be reduced to slavery for his benefit. He was bought and sold, and treated as an ordinary article of merchandise and traffic, whenever a profit could be made by it. This opinion was at that time fixed and universal in the civilized portion of the white race. It was regarded as an axiom in morals as well as in politics, which no one thought of disputing, or supposed to be open to dispute; and men in every grade and position in society daily and habitually acted upon it in their private pursuits, as well as in matters of public concern, without doubting for a moment the correctness of this opinion.

And in no nation was this opinion more firmly fixed or more uniformly acted upon than by the English Government and English people. They not only seized them on the coast of Africa, and sold them or held them in slavery for their own use; but they took them as ordinary articles of merchandise to every country where they could make profit on them, and were far more extensively engaged in this commerce than any other nation in the world.

. . . .

The legislation of the different colonies furnishes positive and indisputable proof of this fact.

. . . .

The language of the Declaration of Independence is equally conclusive:

It begins by declaring that, "when in the course of human events it becomes necessary for one people to dissolve the political bands which have connected them with another, and to assume among the powers of the earth the separate and equal station to which the laws of nature and nature's God entitle them, a decent respect for the opinions of mankind requires that they should declare the causes which impel them to the separation."

It then proceeds to say: "We hold these truths to be self-evident: that all men are created equal; that they are endowed by their Creator with certain inalienable rights; that among them is life, liberty, and the pursuit of happiness; that to secure these rights, Governments are instituted, deriving their just powers from the consent of the governed."

The general words above quoted would seem to embrace the whole human family, and if they were used in a similar instrument at this day would be so understood. But it is too clear for dispute, that the enslaved African race were not intended to be included, and formed no part of the people who framed and adopted this declaration; for if the language, as understood in that day, would embrace them, the conduct of the distinguished men who framed the Declaration of Independence would have been utterly and flagrantly inconsistent with the principles they asserted; and instead of the sympathy of mankind, to which they so confidently appealed, they would have deserved and received universal rebuke and reprobation.

Yet the men who framed this declaration were great men — high in literary acquirements — high in their sense of honor, and incapable of asserting principles inconsistent with those on which they were acting. They perfectly understood the meaning of the language they used, and how it would be understood by others; and they knew that it would not in any part of the civilized world be supposed to embrace the negro race, which, by common consent, had been excluded from civilized Governments and the family of nations, and doomed to slavery. They spoke and acted according to the then established doctrines and principles, and in the ordinary language of the day, and no one misunderstood them. The unhappy black race were separated from the white by indelible marks, and laws long before established, and were never thought of or spoken of except as property, and when the claims of the owner or the profit of the trader were supposed to need protection.

This state of public opinion had undergone no change when the Constitution was adopted, as is equally evident from its provisions and language.

. . . .

[T]here are two clauses in the Constitution which point directly and specifically to the negro race as a separate class of persons, and show clearly that they were not regarded as a portion of the people or citizens of the Government then formed.

One of these clauses reserves to each of the thirteen States the right to import slaves until the year 1808, if it thinks proper. And the importation which it thus sanctions was unquestionably of persons of the race of which we are speaking, as the traffic in slaves in the United States had always been confined to them. And by the other provision the States pledge themselves to each other to maintain the right of property of the master, by delivering up to him any slave who may have escaped from his service, and be found within their respective territories. . . .

. . . .

The plaintiff was a negro slave, belonging to Dr. Emerson, who was a surgeon in the army of the United States. In the year 1834, he took the plaintiff from the State of Missouri to the military post at Rock Island, in the State of Illinois, and held him there as a slave until the month of April or May, 1836. At the time last mentioned, Dr. Emerson removed the plaintiff from said military post at Rock Island to the military post at Fort Snelling, situate [sic] on the west bank of the Mississippi River, in the Territory known as Upper Louisiana, acquired by the United States of France, and situate north of the latitude of thirty-six degrees thirty minutes north, and north of the State of Missouri. Dr. Emerson held the plaintiff in slavery at Fort Snelling, from said last-mentioned date until the year 1838.

In the year 1835, Harriet was the negro slave of Major Taliaferro, who belonged to the army of the United States. In that year, 1835, Major Taliaferro took Harriet to Fort Snelling and kept her there as a slave until the year 1836, and then sold and delivered her as a slave unto Dr. Emerson. Dr. Emerson held Harriet in slavery at Fort Snelling until the year 1838.

In the year 1836, the plaintiff and Harriet intermarried, at Fort Snelling with the consent of Dr. Emerson, who then claimed to be their master and owner. Eliza and Lizzie are the fruit of that marriage. Eliza is about fourteen years old, and was born on board the steamboat Gipsey, north of the north line of the State of Missouri, and upon the river Mississippi. Lizzie is about seven years old, and was born in the State of Missouri, at the military post called Jefferson Barracks.

In the year 1838, said Dr. Emerson removed the plaintiff and Harriet, and their said daughter Eliza, from Fort Snelling to the State of Missouri, where they have ever since resided.

Before the commencement of this suit, Dr. Emerson sold and conveyed the plaintiff, and Harriet, Eliza, and Lizzie, to the defendant, as slaves, and the defendant has ever since claimed to hold them, and each of them, as slaves.

In considering this part of the controversy, two questions rise: 1. Was he, together with his family, free in Missouri by reason of the stay in the territory of the United States hereinbefore mentioned? And 2. If they were not, is Scott himself free by reason of his removal to Rock Island, in the State of Illinois?

We proceed to examine the first question.

The act of Congress, upon which the plaintiff relies, declares that slavery and involuntary servitude, except as a punishment for crime, shall be forever prohibited in all that part of the territory ceded by France, under the name of Louisiana, which lies north of thirty-six degrees thirty minutes north latitude, and not included within the limits of Missouri. And the difficulty which meets us at the threshold of this part of the inquiry is, whether Congress was authorized to pass this law under any of the powers granted to it by the Constitution. . . .

. . . .

For example, no one, we presume, will contend that Congress can make any law in a Territory respecting the establishment of religion, or the free exercise thereof, or abridging the freedom of speech or of the press, or the right of the people of the Territory peaceably to assemble, and to petition the Government for the redress of grievances.

Nor can Congress deny to the people the right to keep and bear arms, nor the right to trial by jury, nor compel any one to be a witness against himself in a criminal proceeding.

These powers, and others, in relation to rights of person, which it is not necessary here to enumerate, are, in express and positive terms, denied to the General Government; and the rights of private property have been guarded with equal care. Thus the rights of property are united with the rights of person, and placed on the same ground by the fifth amendment to the Constitution, which provides that no person shall be deprived of life, liberty, and property, without due process of law. And an act of Congress which deprives a citizen of the United States of his liberty or property, merely because he came himself or brought his property into a particular Territory of the United States, and who had committed no offense against the laws, could hardly be dignified with the name of due process of law.

. . . .

. . . The people of the United States have delegated to it certain enumerated powers, and forbidden it to exercise others. It has no power over the person or property of a citizen but what the citizens of the United States have granted. And no laws or usages of other nations, or reasoning of statesmen or jurists upon the relations of master and slave, can enlarge the powers of the Government, or take from the citizens the rights they have reserved. And if the Constitution recognizes the right of property of the master in a slave, and makes no distinction between that description of property and other property owned by a citizen, no tribunal, acting under the authority of the United

States, whether it be legislative, executive, or judicial, has a right to draw such a distinction, or deny to it the benefit of the provisions and guarantees which have been provided for the protection of private property against the encroachments of the Government.

. . . .

Upon these considerations, it is the opinion of the court that the act of Congress which prohibited a citizen from holding and owning property of this kind in the territory of the United States north of the line therein mentioned, is not warranted by the Constitution, and is therefore void; and that neither Dred Scott himself, nor any of his family, were made free by being carried into this territory; even if they had been carried there by the owner, with the intention of becoming a permanent resident.

We have so far examined the case, as it stands under the Constitution of the United States, and the powers thereby delegated to the Federal Government.

But there is another point in the case which depends on State power and State law. And it is contended, on the part of the plaintiff, that he is made free by being taken to Rock Island, in the State of Illinois, independently of his residence in the territory of the United States; and being so made free, he was not again reduced to a state of slavery by being brought back to Missouri.

Our notice of this part of the case will be very brief; for the principle on which it depends was decided in this court; upon much consideration, in the case of *Strader et al. v. Graham.* In that case, the slaves had been taken from Kentucky to Ohio, with the consent of the owner, and afterwards brought back to Kentucky. And this court held that their *status* or condition, as free or slave, depended upon the laws of Kentucky, when they were brought back into that State, and not of Ohio; and that this court had no jurisdiction to revise the judgment of State court upon its own laws. This was the point directly before the court, and the decision that this court had not jurisdiction turned upon it, as will be seen by the report of the case.

So in this case. As Scott was a slave when taken into the State of Illinois by his owner, and was there held as such, and brought back in that character, his *status*, as free or slave, depended on the laws of Missouri, and not of Illinois.

. . . .

Mr. Justice **Daniel.**

. . . .

Now, the following are truths which a knowledge of the history of the world, and particularly of that of our own country, compels us to know — that the African negro race never have been acknowledged as belonging to the family of nations; that as amongst them there never has been known or recognized by the inhabitants of other countries anything partaking of the character of nationality, or civil or political polity; that this race has been by all the nations of Europe regarded as subjects of capture or purchase; as subjects of commerce or traffic; and that the introduction of that race into every section of this country was not as members of civil or political society, but as slaves, as *property* in the strictest sense of the term.

. . . .

It may be assumed as a postulate, that to a slave, as such, there appertains and can appertain no relation, civil or political, with the State or the Government. He is himself strictly *property*, to be used in subserviency to the interests, the convenience, or the will, of his owner; and to suppose, with respect to the former, the existence of any privilege or discretion, or of any obligation to others incompatible with the magisterial rights just defined, would be by implication, if not directly, to deny the relation of master and slave, since none can possess and enjoy, as his own, that which another has a paramount right and power to withhold. Hence it follows, necessarily, that a slave, the *peculium* or property of a master, and possessing within himself no civil nor political rights or capacities, cannot be a citizen. For who, it may be asked, is a citizen? What do the character and *status* of citizen import? Without fear of contradiction, it does not import the condition of being private property, the subject of individual power and ownership. Upon a principle of etymology alone, the term *citizen*, as derived from *civitas*, conveys the ideas of connection or identification with the State or Government, and a participation of its functions. . . .

. . . .

But it has been insisted, in argument, that the emancipation of a slave, effected either by the direct act and assent of the master, or by causes operating in contravention of his will, produces a change in the *status* or capacities of the slave, such as will transform him from a mere subject of property, into a being possessing a social, civil, and political equality with a citizen. In other words, will make him a citizen of the State within which he was, previously to his emancipation, a slave.

It is difficult to conceive by what magic the mere *surcease* or renunciation of an interest in a subject of *property*, by an individual possessing that interest, can alter the essential character of that property with respect to persons or communities unconnected with such renunciation.

The institution of slavery, as it exists and has existed from the period of its introduction into the United States, though more humane and mitigated in character than was the same institution, either under the republic or the empire of Rome, bears, both in its tenure and in the simplicity incident to the mode of its exercise, a closer resemblance to Roman slavery than it does to the condition of *villanage*, as it formerly existed in England. Connected with the latter, there were peculiarities, from custom or positive regulation, which varied it materially from the slavery of the Romans, or from slavery at any period within the United States.

But with regard to slavery amongst the Romans, it is by no means true that emancipation, either during the republic or the empire, conferred, by the act itself, or implied, the *status* or the rights of citizenship.

. . . .

[The plaintiff] rests mainly if not solely upon the provision of the act of Congress of March 6, 1820, prohibiting slavery in Upper Louisiana, popularly called the *Missouri Compromise*, that assumption renews the question, formerly so zealously debated, as to the validity of the provision in the act of Congress, and upon the constitutional competency of Congress to establish it.

. . . .

. . . In this attempt, there is asserted a power in Congress, whether from incentives of interest, ignorance, faction, partiality, or prejudice, to bestow upon a portion of the citizens of this nation that which is the common property and privilege of all — the power, in fine, of confiscation, in retribution of no offence, or, if for an offence, for that of accidental locality only.

It may be that, with respect to future cases, like the one now before the court, there is felt an assurance of the impotence of such a pretension; still, the fullest conviction of that result can impart to it no claim to forbearance, nor dispense with the duty of antipathy and disgust at its sinister aspect, whenever it may be seen to scowl upon the justice, the order, the tranquility, and fraternal feeling, which are the surest, nay, the only means, of promoting or preserving the happiness and prosperity of the nation, and which were the great and efficient incentives to the formation of this Government.

The power of Congress to impose the prohibition in the eighth section of the Act of 1820 has been advocated upon an attempted construction of the second clause of the third section of the fourth article of the Constitution, which declares that "Congress shall have power to dispose of and to make all needful rules and regulations respecting the *territory* and *other property belonging* to the United States."

In the discussions in both houses of Congress, at the time of adopting this eighth section of the act of 1820, great weight was given to the peculiar language of this clause, viz: *territory* and *other property belonging* to the United States, as going to show that the power of disposing of and regulating, thereby vested in Congress, was restricted to a *proprietary interest in the territory or land* comprised therein, and did not extend to the personal or political rights of citizens or settlers . . . . Scarcely anything more illogical or extravagant can be imagined than the attempt to deduce from this provision in the Constitution a power to destroy or in any wise to impair the civil and political rights of the citizens of the United States, and much more so the power to establish inequalities amongst those citizens by creating privileges in one class of those citizens, and by the disfranchisement of other portions or classes, by degrading them from the position they previously occupied.

. . . .

. . . James Madison, in the year 1819, speaking with reference to the prohibitory power claimed by Congress, then threatening the very existence of the Union, remarks of the language "that it cannot be well extended beyond a power over the territory *as property*, and the power to make provisions really needful or necessary for the government of settlers, until ripe for admission into the Union."

Again he says,

> "with respect to what has taken place in the Northwest territory, it may be observed that the ordinance giving it its distinctive character

on the subject of slaveholding proceeded from the old Congress, acting with the best intentions, but under a charter which contains no shadow of the authority exercised; and it remains to be decided how far the States formed within that territory, and admitted into the Union, are on a different footing from its other members as to their legislative sovereignty. As to the power of admitting new States into the Federal compact, the questions offering themselves are, whether Congress can attach conditions, or the new States concur in conditions, which after admission would *abridge* or *enlarge* the constitutional rights of legislation common to other States; whether Congress can, by a compact with a new State, take power either to or from itself, or place the new member above or below the equal rank and rights possessed by the others; whether all such stipulations expressed or implied would not be nullities, and be so pronounced when brought to a practical test. It falls within the scope of your inquiry to state the fact, that there was a proposition in the convention to discriminate between the old and the new States by an article in the Constitution. The proposition, happily, was rejected. The effect of such a discrimination is sufficiently evident."*

. . . .

Mr. Justice **McLean** dissenting.

. . . .

In the argument, it was said that a colored citizen would not be an agreeable member of society. This is more a matter of taste than of law. Several of the States have admitted persons of color to the right of suffrage, and in this view have recognized them as citizens; and this has been done in the slave as well as the free States. On the question of citizenship, it must be admitted that we have not been very fastidious. Under the late treaty with Mexico, we have made citizens of all grades, combinations and colors. The same was done in the admission of Louisiana and Florida. No one ever doubted, and no court ever held, that the people of these Territories did not become citizens under the treaty. They have exercised all the rights of citizens, without being naturalized under the acts of Congress.

. . . .

There is no nation in Europe which considers itself bound to return to his master a fugitive slave, under the civil law or the law of nations. On the contrary, the slave is held to be free where there is no treaty obligation, or compact in some other form, to return him to his master. The Roman law did not allow freedom to be sold. An ambassador or any other public functionary could not take a slave to France, Spain, or any other country of Europe, without emancipating him. . . .

. . . .

Slavery is emphatically a State institution. In the ninth section of the first article of the Constitution, it is provided "that the migration or importation

* Letter from James Madison to Robert Walsh, November 27th, 1819, on the subject of the Missouri Compromise.

of such persons as any of the States now existing shall think proper to admit, shall not be prohibited by the Congress prior to the year 1808, but a tax or duty may be imposed on such importation, not exceeding ten dollars for each person."

. . . .

The only connection which the Federal Government holds with slaves in a State, arises from that provision of the Constitution which declares that "No person held to service or labor in one State, under the laws thereof, escaping into another, shall, in consequence of any law or regulation therein, be discharged from such service or labor, but shall be delivered up, on claim of the party to whom such service or labor may be due."

This being a fundamental law of the Federal Government, it rests mainly for its execution, as has been held, on the judicial power of the Union; and so far as the rendition of fugitives from labor has become a subject of judicial action, the Federal obligation has been faithfully discharged.

. . . .

We need not refer to the mercenary spirit which introduced the infamous traffic in slaves, to show the degradation of negro slavery in our country. This system was imposed upon our colonial settlements by the mother country, and it is due to truth to say that the commercial colonies and States were chiefly engaged in the traffic. But we know as a historical fact, that James Madison, that great and good man, a leading member in the Federal Convention, was solicitous to guard the language of that instrument so as not to convey the idea that there could be property in man.

I prefer the lights of Madison, Hamilton, and Jay, as a means of construing the Constitution in all its bearings, rather than to look behind that period, into a traffic which is now declared to be piracy, and punished with death by Christian nations. I do not like to draw the sources of our domestic relations from so dark a ground. Our independence was a great epoch in the history of freedom; and while I admit the Government was not made especially for the colored race, yet many of them were citizens of the New England States, and exercised the rights of suffrage when the Constitution was adopted, and it was not doubted by any intelligent person that its tendencies would greatly ameliorate their condition.

Many of the States, on the adoption of the Constitution, or shortly afterward, took measures to abolish slavery within their respective jurisdictions; and it is a well-known fact that a belief was cherished by the leading men, South as well as North, that the institution of slavery would gradually decline, until it would become extinct. The increased value of slave labor, in the culture of cotton and sugar, prevented the realization of this expectation. Like all other communities and States, the South *were* influenced by what they considered to be their own interests.

But if we are to turn our attention to the dark ages of the world, why confine our view to colored slavery? On the same principles, white men were made slaves. All slavery has its origin in power, and is against right.

The power of Congress to establish Territorial Governments, and to prohibit the introduction of slavery therein, is the next point to be considered.

. . . .

If Congress should deem slaves or free colored persons injurious to the population of a free Territory, as conducing to lessen the value of the public lands, or on any other ground connected with the public interest, they have the power to prohibit them from becoming settlers in it. This can be sustained on the ground of a sound national policy, which is so clearly shown in our history by practical results, that it would seem no considerate individual can question it. And, as regards any unfairness of such a policy to our Southern brethren, as urged in the argument, it is only necessary to say that, with one-fourth of the Federal population of the Union, they have in the slave States a larger extent of fertile territory than is included in the free States; and it is submitted, if masters of slaves be restricted from bringing them into free territory, that the restriction on the free citizens of nonslaveholding States, by bringing slaves into free territory, is four times greater than that complained of by the South. But, not only so; some three or four hundred thousand holders of slaves, by bringing them into free territory, impose a restriction on twenty millions of the free States. The repugnancy to slavery would probably prevent fifty or a hundred freemen from settling in a slave Territory, where one slaveholder would be prevented from settling in a free Territory.

This remark is made in answer to the argument urged, that a prohibition of slavery in the free Territories is inconsistent with the continuance of the Union. . . .

I would here simply remark, that the Constitution was formed for our whole country. An expansion or contraction of our territory required no change in the fundamental law. When we consider the men who laid the foundation of our Government and carried it into operation, the men who occupied the bench, who filled the halls of legislation and the Chief Magistracy, it would seem, if any question could be settled clear of all doubt, it was the power of Congress to establish Territorial Governments. Slavery was prohibited in the entire Northwestern Territory, with the approbation of leading men, South and North; but this prohibition was not retained when this ordinance was adopted for the government of Southern Territories, where slavery existed. In a late republication of a letter of Mr. Madison, dated November 27, 1819, speaking of this power of Congress to prohibit slavery in a Territory, he infers there is no such power, from the fact that it has not been exercised. This is not a very satisfactory argument against any power, as there are but few, if any, subjects on which the constitutional powers of Congress are exhausted. It is true, as Mr. Madison states, that Congress, in the act to establish a Government in the Mississippi Territory; prohibited the importation of slaves into it from foreign parts; but it is equally true, that in the act erecting Louisiana into two Territories, Congress declared, "it shall not be lawful for any person to bring into Orleans Territory, from any port or place within the limits of the United States, any slave which shall have been imported since 1798, or which may hereafter be imported, except by a citizen of the United States who settles in the Territory, under the penalty of the freedom of such slave." The inference of Mr. Madison, therefore, against the power of Congress, is of no force, as it was founded on a fact supposed, which did not exist.

. . . .

If Congress may establish a Territorial Government in the exercise of its discretion, it is a clear principle that a court cannot control that discretion. This being the case, I do not see on what ground the act is held to be void. It did not purport to forfeit property, or take it for public purposes. It only prohibited slavery; in doing which, it followed the ordinance of 1787.

I will now consider the fourth head, which is: "The effect of taking slaves into a State or Territory, and so holding them, where slavery is prohibited."

. . . .

By virtue of what law is it, that a master may take his slave into free territory, and exact from him the duties of a slave? The law of the Territory does not sanction it. No authority can be claimed under the Constitution of the United States, or any law of Congress. Will it be said that the slave is taken as property, the same as other property which the master may own? To this I answer, that colored persons are made property by the law of the State, and no such power has been given to Congress. Does the master carry with him the law of the State from which he removes into the Territory? and does that enable him to coerce his slave in the Territory? Let us test this theory. If this may be done by a master from one slave State, it may be done by a master from every other slave State. This right is supposed to be connected with the person of the master, by virtue of the local law. Is it transferable? May it be negotiated, as a promissory note or bill of exchange? If it be assigned to a man from a free State, may he coerce the slave by virtue of it? What shall this thing be denominated? Is it personal or real property? Or is it an indefinable fragment of sovereignty, which every person carries with him from his late domicile? One thing is certain, that its origin has been very recent, and it is unknown to the laws of any civilized country.

. . . .

. . . A slave is not a mere chattel. He bears the impress of his Maker, and is amenable to the laws of God and man; and he is destined to an endless existence.

. . . .

The States of Missouri and Illinois are bounded by a common line. The one prohibits slavery, the other admits it. This has been done by the exercise of that sovereign power which appertains to each. We are bound to respect the institutions of each, as emanating from the voluntary action of the people. Have the people of either any right to disturb the relations of the other? Each State rests upon the basis of its own sovereignty, protected by the Constitution. Our Union has been the foundation of our prosperity and national glory. Shall we not cherish and maintain it? This can only be done by respecting the legal rights of each state.

. . . .

. . . Having the same rights of sovereignty as the State of Missouri in adopting a Constitution, I can perceive no reason why the institutions of Illinois should not receive the same consideration as those of Missouri. Allowing to my brethren the same right of judgment that I exercise myself, I must be permitted to say that it seems to me the principle laid down will enable the people of a slave State to introduce slavery into a free State, for a longer or shorter time, as may suit their convenience; and by returning the slave to the State whence he was brought, by force or otherwise, the status of slavery attaches, and protects the rights of the master, and defies the sovereignty of the free State. There is no evidence before us that Dred Scott and his family returned to Missouri voluntarily. The contrary is inferable from the agreed case: "In the year 1838, Dr. Emerson removed the plaintiff and said Harriet, and their daughter Eliza, from Fort Snelling to the State of Missouri, where they have ever since resided." This is the agreed case; and can it be inferred from this that Scott and family returned to Missouri voluntarily? He was removed; which shows that he was passive, as a slave, having exercised no volition on the subject. He did not resist the master by absconding or force. But that was not sufficient to bring him within Lord Stowell's decision; he must have acted voluntarily. It would be a mockery of law and an outrage on his rights to coerce his return, and then claim that it was voluntary, and on that ground that his former status of slavery attached.

. . . .

I think the judgment of the court below should be reversed.

NOTES AND QUESTIONS

1. *Dred Scott* was the very first opinion in which the Supreme Court exercised its power of judicial review to invalidate an act of Congress — here, the Missouri Compromise — as contrary to the Constitution. What were the grounds? Could such a confrontation have been avoided?

   The Missouri Compromise had not been lightly reached, and so the issue is posed: who speaks for the community on matters of profound ethical import?

2. Also, the Court in *Dred Scott* dismisses "African negroes" as never having formed nations, and so not deserving respect. So the case is as much about what *communities* deserve respect as what *persons* do. How do such questions get resolved? What respect was due Nazi Germany? Imperial Japan? What about the competing claims of the nations of Spain and Chile in the Pinochet extradition proceedings before the British courts in 1999?

3. Note that Taney claims his view of African-Americans was universally shared. But clearly that was not true in 1787 or 1857. There were "slave" states and "free" states. Thus *Dred Scott* poses two problems (not just one) for an ethical community: what obligation is owed a subjugated internal group of slaves and what obligation is owed a coordinate community (say, Massachusetts or Illinois) which holds a contrary view?

4. The Court in *Dred Scott* proceeds as though it were simply interpreting the Constitution, which by 1856 was already over 70 years old. How much latitude did the Court have in its task and how much was it bound by precise wording in the Constitution? If the court had latitude, what

values other than original intent should have guided its decision-making? Respect for differing views? Avoidance of war? Preservation of property? Implementation of its decrees, e.g., politically and financially? Are such factors even relevant? If so, why not in *Dred Scott*?

5. The decision in *Dred Scott* cannot be dismissed as simply a product of corrupt bigots. Chief Justice Taney was viewed in his time as a statesman and is still viewed today (except for his *Dred Scott* decision opinion) as one of the great Chief Justices. And the holding in *Dred Scott* and the opinions therein reflect a history and a mode of thinking based upon centuries of philosophy and practice. Millions of Americans were held in slavery into the mid-1800s, providing the basis for a caste and property system whose linchpin was legal recognition that one person might "own" another and whose legitimacy was supported by millions of other Americans. In finding them ethically deficient, can you say (and with what degree of certainty) what your own views would have been, had you lived then?

6. Independently, if a member of the Court as a matter of individual conscience was opposed to slavery, what is the ethical obligation of that person? Suppose you were on the Court, opposed to slavery, but wanting to preserve the Union — as did Taney — how would you have voted? Suppose you believed it was a matter for state, not national resolution, how would you vote?

7. After the Civil War, Congress adopted a series of civil rights acts as a part of the Reconstruction. These are found at 42 U.S.C. §§ 1981-1988. They became the vehicle for the school integration case of *Brown v. Board of Education*. It was not until the 1960s, however, that these statutes finally became fully accepted. They have since become the basis for wide-ranging federal court enforcement of civil rights. *See Monroe v. Pape*, 365 U.S. 167 (1961). In the 1960s, a civil rights movement was at first met by massive resistance and then advanced by legislation and programs which began the process of equalizing opportunity and material status — a process which is still occurring today.

   Yet, at the same time, the United States in its urban areas became even more segregated than one hundred years before. Is it possible to grade America on an ethical "report card"? Were we more "ethical" in 1850 than in the year 2000?

8. And note that in 1800 one in five Americans were of African American descent; by 2000, the proportion was one in ten. American immigration policy has consistently favored European, Asian and Hispanic peoples, ignoring Africans and their political and economic calamities of the 1970s, 1980s and 1990s. The community thus redefined itself to the detriment of one of its earliest constituencies.

   Was there an ethical obligation to strengthen the position of African Americans?

9. In the system of slavery discussed in the *Dred Scott* case, were African Americans viewed as citizens, noncitizens, persons, nonpersons, a race apart, animals or simply property? Does it matter which? Is Justice Daniels correct, a slave has absolutely *no* rights?

10. How would Rawls analyze the Court's performance in *Dred Scott*? What of Fletcher? The United Nations Charter? The European Convention on Biomedicine?

11. The issue of people as "property" is not behind us as a nation. It recurs in the abortion context, the employment context, the contexts of organ transplantation, assisted death, maternal-fetal conflict. We turn now to the surrogacy context, in which one woman bears another's child. In *Baby M*, who had rights in the womb of Mary Beth Whitehead and the fetus she was carrying? And were they "property" rights?

12. For an excellent article, see Joey Asher, *How The United States Is Violating Its International Agreements To Combat Slavery*, 8 Emory Int'l L. Rev. 215 (1994); and see Tania Tetlow, *The Founders and Slavery: A Crisis of Conscience*, 2 Loy. J. Pub. Int. L. 1 (2001); see also Jessica Berg, *Owning Persons: the Application of Property Theory to Embryos and Fetuses*, 40 Wake Forest L. Rev. 159 (Spring, 2005), for an excellent discussion of whether to treat embryos as property or persons.

13. Currently, 31 states have laws regarding surrogacy. Of those, 16 states ban surrogacy or surrogacy contracts. However, New Jersey allows surrogacy volunteers (generally family members), even though surrogacy contracts are illegal. *J.F. v. D.B.*, 66 Pa. D. & C.4th 1 (2004).

IN THE MATTER OF BABY M

537 A.2d 1227 (N.J. 1988)

The opinion of the Court was delivered by **Wilentz**, C.J.

In this matter the Court is asked to determine the validity of a contract that purports to provide a new way of bringing children into a family. For a fee of $10,000, a woman agrees to be artificially inseminated with the semen of another woman's husband; she is to conceive a child, carry it to term, and after its birth surrender it to the natural father and his wife. The intent of the contract is that the child's natural mother will thereafter be forever separated from her child. The wife is to adopt the child, and she and the natural father are to be regarded as its parents for all purposes. The contract providing for this is called a "surrogacy contract," the natural mother inappropriately called the "surrogate mother."

We invalidate the surrogacy contract because it conflicts with the law and public policy of this State. While we recognize the depth of the yearning of infertile couples to have their own children, we find the payment of money to a "surrogate" mother illegal, perhaps criminal, and potentially degrading to women. Although in this case we grant custody to the natural father, the evidence having clearly proved such custody to be in the best interests of the infant, we void both the termination of the surrogate mother's parental rights and the adoption of the child by the wife/stepparent. We thus restore the "surrogate" as the mother of the child. We remand the issue of the natural mother's visitation rights to the trial court, since that issue was not reached below and the record before us it not sufficient to permit us to decide it de novo.

We find no offense to our present laws where a woman voluntarily and without payment agrees to act as a "surrogate" mother, provided that she is not subject to a binding agreement to surrender her child. Moreover, our holding today does not preclude the Legislature from altering the current statutory scheme, within constitutional limits, so as to permit surrogacy contracts. Under current law, however, the surrogacy agreement before us is illegal and invalid.

I. Facts

In February 1985, William Stern and Mary Beth Whitehead entered into a surrogacy contract. It recited that Stern's wife, Elizabeth, was infertile, that they wanted a child, and that Mrs. Whitehead was willing to provide that child as the mother with Mr. Stern as the father.

The contract provided that through artificial insemination using Mr. Stern's sperm, Mrs. Whitehead would become pregnant, carry the child to term, bear it, deliver it to the Sterns, and thereafter do whatever was necessary to terminate her maternal rights so that Mrs. Stern could thereafter adopt the child. Mrs. Whitehead's husband, Richard, was also a party to the contract; Mrs. Stern was not. Mr. Whitehead promised to do all acts necessary to rebut the presumption of paternity under the Parentage Act. Although Mrs. Stern was not a party to the surrogacy agreement, the contract gave her sole custody of the child in the event of Mr. Stern's death. Mrs. Stern's status as a nonparty to the surrogate parenting agreement presumably was to avoid the application of the baby-selling statute to this arrangement.

Mr. Stern, on his part, agreed to attempt the artificial insemination and to pay Mrs. Whitehead $10,000 after the child's birth, on its delivery to him. In a separate contract, Mr. Stern agreed to pay $7,500 to the Infertility Center of New York ("ICNY"). The Center's advertising campaigns solicit surrogate mothers and encourage infertile couples to consider surrogacy. ICNY arranged for the surrogacy contract by bringing the parties together, explaining the process to them, furnishing the contractual form, and providing legal counsel.

The history of the parties' involvement in this arrangement suggests their good faith. William and Elizabeth Stern were married in July 1974, having met at the University of Michigan, where both were Ph.D. candidates. Due to financial considerations and Mrs. Stern's pursuit of a medical degree and residency, they decided to defer starting a family until 1981. Before then, however, Mrs. Stern learned that she might have multiple sclerosis and that the disease in some cases renders pregnancy a serious health risk. Her anxiety appears to have exceeded the actual risk, which current medical authorities assess as minimal. Nonetheless that anxiety was evidently quite real, Mrs. Stern fearing that pregnancy might precipitate blindness, paraplegia, or other forms of debilitation. Based on the perceived risk, the Sterns decided to forego having their own children. The decision had special significant for Mr. Stern. Most of his family had been destroyed in the Holocaust. As the family's only survivor, he very much wanted to continue his bloodline.

. . . .

The paths of Mrs. Whitehead and the Sterns to surrogacy were similar. Both responded to advertising by ICNY. The Sterns' response, following their inquiries into adoption, was the result of their long-standing decision to have a child. Mrs. Whitehead's response apparently resulted from her sympathy with family members and others who could have no children (she stated that she wanted to give another couple the "gift of life"); she also wanted the $10,000 to help her family.

. . . .

. . . After several artificial inseminations over a period of months, Mrs. Whitehead became pregnant. The pregnancy was uneventful and on March 27, 1986, Baby M was born.

Mrs. Whitehead realized, almost from the moment of birth, that she could not part with this child. She had felt a bond with it even during pregnancy. Some indication of the attachment was conveyed to the Sterns at the hospital when they told Mrs. Whitehead what they were going to name the baby. She apparently broke into tears and indicated that she did not know if she could give up the child. She talked about how the baby looked like her other daughter, and made it clear that she was experiencing great difficulty with the decision.

Nonetheless, Mrs. Whitehead was, for the moment, true to her word. Despite powerful inclinations to the contrary, she turned her child over to the Sterns on March 30 at the Whiteheads' home.

. . . .

Later in the evening of March 30, Mrs. Whitehead became deeply disturbed, disconsolate, stricken with unbearable sadness. She had to have her child. She could not eat, sleep, or concentrate on anything other than her need for her baby. The next day she went to the Sterns' home and told them how much she was suffering.

The depth of Mrs. Whitehead's despair surprised and frightened the Sterns. She told them that she could not live without her baby, that she must have her, even if only for one week, that thereafter she would surrender her child. The Sterns, concerned that Mrs Whitehead might indeed commit suicide, not wanting under any circumstances to risk that, and in any event believing that Mrs. Whitehead would keep her word, turned the child over to her. It was not until four months later, after a series of attempts to regain possession of the child, that Melissa was returned to the Sterns, having been forcibly removed from the home where she was then living with Mr. and Mrs. Whitehead, the home in Florida owned by Mary Beth Whitehead's parents.

The struggle over Baby M began when it became apparent that Mrs. Whitehead could not return the child to Mr. Stern. Due to Mrs. Whitehead's refusal to relinquish the baby, Mr. Stern filed a complaint seeking enforcement of the surrogacy contract. . . . After the order was entered, ex parte, the process server, aided by the police, in the presence of the Sterns, entered Mrs. Whitehead's home to execute the order. Mr. Whitehead fled with the child, who had been handed to him through a window while those who came to enforce the order were thrown off balance by a dispute over the child's current name.

The Whiteheads immediately fled to Florida with Baby M. They stayed initially with Mrs. Whitehead's parents, where one of Mrs. Whitehead's children had been living. For the next three months, the Whiteheads and Melissa lived at roughly twenty different hotels, motels, and homes in order to avoid apprehension. From time to time Mrs. Whitehead would call Mr. Stern to discuss the matter; the conversations, recorded by Mr. Stern on advice of counsel, show an escalating dispute about rights, morality, and power, accompanied by threats of Mrs. Whitehead to kill herself, to kill the child, and falsely to accuse Mr. Stern of sexually molesting Mrs. Whitehead's other daughter.

Eventually the Sterns discovered where the Whiteheads were staying, commenced supplementary proceedings in Florida, and obtained an order requiring the Whiteheads to turn over the child. Police in Florida enforced the order, forcibly removing the child from her grandparents' home. She was soon thereafter brought to New Jersey and turned over to the Sterns. . . .

The Sterns' complaint, in addition to seeking possession and ultimately custody of the child, sought enforcement of the surrogacy contract. Pursuant to the contract, it asked that the child be permanently placed in their custody, that Mrs. Whitehead's parental rights be terminated, and that Mrs. Stern be allowed to adopt the child, i.e., that, for all purposes, Melissa become the Sterns' child.

The trial took thirty-two days over a period of more than two months. It included numerous interlocutory appeals and attempted interlocutory appeals. There were twenty-three witnesses to the facts recited above and fifteen expert witnesses, eleven testifying on the issue of custody and four on the subject of Mrs. Stern's multiple sclerosis; the bulk of the testimony was devoted to determining the parenting arrangement most compatible with the child's best interests. Soon after the conclusion of the trial, the trial court announced its opinion from the bench. It held that the surrogacy contract was valid; ordered that Mrs. Whitehead's parental rights be terminated and that sole custody of the child be granted to Mr. Stern; and, after hearing brief testimony from Mrs. Stern, immediately entered an order allowing the adoption of Melissa by Mrs. Stern, all in accordance with the surrogacy contract. Pending the outcome of the appeal, we granted a continuation of visitation to Mrs. Whitehead, although slightly more limited than the visitation allowed during the trial.

Although clearly expressing its view that the surrogacy contract was valid, the trial court devoted the major portion of its opinion to the question of the baby's best interests. The inconsistency is apparent. The surrogacy contract calls for the surrender of the child to the Sterns, permanent and sole custody in the Sterns, and termination of Mrs. Whitehead's parental rights, all without qualification, all regardless of any evaluation of the best interests of the child. . . .

On the question of best interests — and we agree, but for different reasons, that custody was the critical issue — the court's analysis of the testimony was perceptive, demonstrating both its understanding of the case and its considerable experience in these matters. We agree substantially with both its analysis and conclusions on the matter of custody.

The court's review and analysis of the surrogacy contract, however, is not at all in accord with ours. . . .

. . . .

Of considerable interest in this clash of views is the position of the child's guardian *ad litem,* wisely appointed by the court at the outset of the litigation. As the child's representative, her role in the litigation, as she viewed it, was solely to protect the child's best interests. She therefore took no position on the validity of the surrogacy contract, and instead devoted her energies to obtaining expert testimony uninfluenced by any interest other than the child's. We agree with the guardian's perception of her role in this litigation. She appropriately refrained from taking any position that might have appeared to compromise her role as the child's advocate. She first took the position, based on her experts' testimony, that the Sterns should have primary custody, and that while Mrs. Whitehead's parental rights should not be terminated, no visitation should be allowed for five years. As a result of subsequent developments, mentioned *infra*, her view has changed. She now recommends that no visitation be allowed at least until Baby M reaches maturity.

. . . This Court, therefore, is without guidance from the trial court on the visitation issue, an issue of considerable importance in any event, and especially important in view of our determination that the surrogacy contract is invalid.

II. Invalidity and Unenforceability of Surrogacy Contract

We have concluded that this surrogacy contract is invalid. Our conclusion has two bases: direct conflict with existing statutes and conflict with the public policies of this State, as expressed in its statutory and decisional law.

. . . .

A. Conflict With Statutory Provisions

The surrogacy contract conflicts with: (1) laws prohibiting the use of money in connection with adoptions; (2) laws requiring proof of parental unfitness or abandonment before termination of parental rights is ordered or an adoption is granted; and (3) laws that make surrender of custody and consent to adoption revocable in private placement adoptions.

Our law prohibits paying or accepting money in connection with any placement of a child for adoption. Violation is a high misdemeanor. Excepted are fees of an approved agency and certain expenses in connection with childbirth.

Considerable care was taken in this case to structure the surrogacy arrangement so as not to violate this prohibition. The arrangement was structured as follows: the adopting parent, Mrs. Stern, was not a party to the surrogacy contract; the money paid to Mrs. Whitehead was stated to be for her services — not for the adoption; the sole purpose of the contract was stated as being that "of giving a child to William Stern, its natural and biological father;" the money was purported to be "compensation for services and expenses and in no way . . . a fee for termination of parental rights or a payment in exchange for consent to surrender a child for adoption;" the fee to the Infertility Center ($7,500) was stated to be for legal representation, advice, administrative work, and other "services." Nevertheless, it seems clear that the money was paid and accepted in connection with an adoption.

The Infertility Center's major role was first as a "finder" of the surrogate mother whose child was to be adopted, and second as the arranger of all proceedings that led to the adoption. Its role as adoption finder is demonstrated by the provision requiring Mr. Stern to pay another $7,500 if he uses Mary Beth Whitehead again as a surrogate, and by ICNY's agreement to "coordinate arrangements for the adoption of the child by the wife." The surrogacy agreement requires Mrs. Whitehead to surrender Baby M for the purposes of adoption. The agreement notes that Mr. and Mrs. Stern wanted to have a child, and provides that the child be "placed" with Mrs. Stern in the event Mr. Stern dies before the child is born. The payment of the $10,000 occurs only on surrender of custody of the child and "completion of the duties and obligations" of Mrs. Whitehead, including termination of her parental rights to facilitate adoption by Mrs. Stern. As for the contention that the Sterns are paying only for services and not for an adoption, we need note only that they would pay nothing in the event the child died before the fourth month of pregnancy, and only $1,000 if the child were stillborn, even though the "services" had been fully rendered. Additionally, one of Mrs. Whitehead's estimated costs, to be assumed by Mr. Stern, was an "Adoption Fee," presumably for Mrs. Whitehead's incidental costs in connection with the adoption.

Mr. Stern knew he was paying for the adoption of a child; Mrs. Whitehead knew she was accepting money so that a child might be adopted; the Infertility Center knew that it was being paid for assisting in the adoption of a child. The actions of all three worked to frustrate the goals of the statute. It strains credulity to claim that these arrangements, touted by those in the surrogacy business as an attractive alternative to the usual route leading to an adoption, really amount to something other than a private placement adoption for money.

. . . .

Baby-selling potentially results in the exploitation of all parties involved. Conversely, adoption statutes seek to further humanitarian goals, foremost among them the best interests of the child. The negative consequences of baby-buying are potentially present in the surrogacy context, especially the potential for placing and adopting a child without regard to the interest of the child or the natural mother.

The termination of Mrs. Whitehead's parental rights, called for by the surrogacy contract and actually ordered by the court, fails to comply with the stringent requirements of New Jersey law. Our law, recognizing the finality of any termination of parental rights, provides for such termination only where there has been a voluntary surrender of a child to an approved agency or to the Division of Youth and Family Services ("DYFS"), accompanied by a formal document acknowledging termination of parental rights, or where there has been a showing of parental abandonment or unfitness. . . .

. . . .

As the trial court recognized, without a valid termination there can be no adoption. This requirement applies to all adoptions, whether they be private placements, or agency adoptions.

Our statutes, and the cases interpreting them, leave no doubt that where there has been no written surrender to an approved agency or to DYFS, termination of parental rights will not be granted in this state absent a very strong showing of abandonment or neglect. That showing is required in every context in which termination of parental rights is sought, be it an action by an approved agency, an action by DYFS, or a private placement adoption proceeding, even where the petitioning adoptive parent is, as here, a stepparent. While the statutes make certain procedural allowances when stepparents are involved, the substantive requirement for terminating the natural parents' rights is not relaxed one iota. It is clear that a "best interests" determination is never sufficient to terminate parental rights; the statutory criteria must be proved.

In this case a termination of parental rights was obtained not by proving the statutory prerequisites but by claiming the benefit of contractual provisions. From all that has been stated above, it is clear that a contractual agreement to abandon one's parental rights, or not to contest a termination action, will not be enforced in our courts. The Legislature would not have so carefully, so consistently, and so substantially restricted termination of parental rights if it had intended to allow termination to be achieved by one short sentence in a contract.

Since the termination was invalid, it follows, as noted above, that adoption of Melissa by Mrs. Stern could not properly be granted.

The provision in the surrogacy contract stating that Mary Beth Whitehead agrees to "surrender custody . . . and terminate all parental rights" contains no clause giving her a right to rescind. It is intended to be an irrevocable consent to surrender the child for adoption — in other words, an irrevocable commitment by Mrs. Whitehead to turn Baby M over to the Sterns and thereafter to allow termination of her parental rights. The trial court required a "best interests" showing as a condition to granting specific performance of the surrogacy contract. Having decided the "best interests" issue in favor of the Sterns, that court's order included, among other things, specific performance of this agreement to surrender custody and terminate all parental rights.

Mrs. Whitehead, shortly after the child's birth, had attempted to revoke her consent and surrender by refusing, after the Sterns had allowed her to have the child "just for one week," to return Baby M to them. The trial court's award of specific performance therefore reflects its view that the consent to surrender the child was irrevocable. We accept the trial court's construction of the contract; indeed it appears quite clear that this was the parties' intent. Such a provision, however, making irrevocable the natural mother's consent to surrender custody of her child in a private placement adoption, clearly conflicts with New Jersey law.

. . . .

Contractual surrender of parental rights is not provided for in our statutes as now written. . . . There is no doubt that a contractual provision purporting to constitute an irrevocable agreement to surrender custody of a child for adoption is invalid.

. . . .

. . . The provision in the surrogacy contract, agreed to before conception, requiring the natural mother to surrender custody of the child without any right of revocation is one more indication of the essential nature of this transaction: the creation of a contractual system of termination and adoption designed to circumvent our statutes.

B. Public Policy Considerations

. . . .

The surrogacy contract guarantees permanent separation of the child from one of its natural parents. Our policy, however, has long been that to the extent possible, children should remain with and be brought up by both of their natural parents. The impact of failure to follow that policy is nowhere better shown than in the results of this surrogacy contract. A child, instead of starting off its life with as much peace and security as possible, finds itself immediately in a tug-of-war between contending mother and father.[1]

The surrogacy contract violates the policy of this State that the rights of natural parents are equal concerning their child, the father's right no greater than the mother's. . . . The whole purpose and effect of the surrogacy contract was to give the father the exclusive right to the child by destroying the rights of the mother.

. . . Here there is no counseling, independent or otherwise, of the natural mother, no evaluation, no warning.

The only legal advice Mary Beth Whitehead received regarding the surrogacy contract was provided in connection with the contract that she previously entered into with another couple. Mrs. Whitehead's lawyer was referred to her by the Infertility Center, with which he had an agreement to act as counsel for surrogate candidates. His services consisted of spending one hour going through the contract with the Whiteheads, section by section, and answering their questions. Mrs. Whitehead received no further legal advice prior to signing the contract with the Sterns.

Mrs. Whitehead was examined and psychologically evaluated, but if it was for her benefit, the record does not disclose that fact. The Sterns regarded the evaluation as important, particularly in connection with the question of whether she would change her mind. Yet they never asked to see it, and were content with the assumption that the Infertility Center had made an evaluation and had concluded that there was no danger that the surrogate mother would change her mind. From Mrs. Whitehead's point of view, all that she

[1] And the impact on the natural parents, Mr. Stern and Mrs. Whitehead, is severe and dramatic. The depth of their conflict about Baby M, about custody, visitation, about the goodness or badness of each of them, comes through in their telephone conversations, in which each tried to persuade the other to give up the child. The potential adverse consequences of surrogacy are poignantly captured here — Mrs. Whitehead threatening to kill herself and the baby, Mr. Stern begging her not to, each blaming the other. The dashed hopes of the Sterns, the agony of Mrs. Whitehead, their suffering, their hatred — all were caused by the unraveling of this arrangement.

learned from the evaluation was that "she had passed." It is apparent that the profit motive got the better of the Infertility Center. Although the evaluation was made, it was not put to any use, and understandably so, for the psychologist warned that Mrs. Whitehead demonstrated certain traits that might make surrender of the child difficult and that there should be further inquiry into this issue in connection with her surrogacy. To inquire further, however, might have jeopardized the Infertility Center's fee. The record indicates that neither Mrs. Whitehead nor the Sterns were ever told of this fact, a fact that might have ended their surrogacy arrangement.

Under the contract, the natural mother is irrevocably committed before she knows the strength of her bond with her child. She never makes a totally voluntary, informed decision, for quite clearly any decision prior to the baby's birth is, in the most important sense, uninformed, and any decision after that, compelled by a preexisting contractual commitment, the threat of a lawsuit, and the inducement of a $10,000 payment, is less than totally voluntary. Her interests are of little concern to those who controlled this transaction.

. . . .

Worst of all, however, is the contract's total disregard of the best interests of the child. There is not the slightest suggestion that any inquiry will be made at any time to determine the fitness of the Sterns as custodial parents, of Mrs. Stern as an adoptive parent, their superiority to Mrs. Whitehead, or the effect on the child of not living with her natural mother.

This is the sale of a child, or, at the very least, the sale of a mother's right to her child, the only mitigating factor being that one of the purchasers is the father. Almost every evil that prompted the prohibition on the payment of money in connection with adoptions exists here.

. . . .

The point is made that Mrs. Whitehead *agreed* to the surrogacy arrangement, supposedly fully understanding the consequences. Putting aside the issue of how compelling her need for money may have been, and how significant her understanding of the consequences, we suggest that her consent is irrelevant. There are, in a civilized society, some things that money cannot buy. In America, we decided long ago that merely because conduct purchased by money was "voluntary" did not mean that it was good or beyond regulation and prohibition. *West Coast Hotel Co. v. Parrish*. Employers can no longer buy labor at the lowest price they can bargain for, even though that labor is "voluntary," or buy women's labor for less money than paid to men for the same job, or purchase the agreement of children to perform oppressive labor, or purchase the agreement of workers to subject themselves to unsafe or unhealthful working conditions. There are, in short, values that society deems more important than granting to wealth whatever it can buy, be it labor, love, or life. . . .

. . . .

Beyond that is the potential degradation of some women that may result from this arrangement. In many cases, of course, surrogacy may bring satisfaction, not only to the infertile couple, but to the surrogate mother herself. The fact, however, that many women may not perceive surrogacy negatively but rather see it as an opportunity does not diminish its potential for devastation to other women.

In sum, the harmful consequences of this surrogacy arrangement appear to us all too palpable. In New Jersey the surrogate mother's agreement to sell her child is void. Its irrevocability infects the entire contract, as does the money that purports to buy it.

III. Termination

. . . .

Nothing in this record justifies a finding that would allow a court to terminate Mary Beth Whitehead's parental rights under the statutory standard. It is not simply that obviously there was no "intentional abandonment or very substantial neglect of parental duties without a reasonable expectation of reversal of that conduct in the future," quite the contrary, but furthermore that the trial court never found Mrs. Whitehead an unfit mother and indeed affirmatively stated that Mary Beth Whitehead had been a good mother to her other children.

Although the question of best interests of the child is dispositive of the custody issue in a dispute between natural parents, it does not govern the question of termination. It has long been decided that the mere fact that a child would be better off with one set of parents than with another is an insufficient basis for terminating the natural parent's rights. Furthermore, it is equally well settled that surrender of a child and a consent to adoption through private placement do not alone warrant termination. It must be noted, despite some language to the contrary, that the interests of the child are not the only interests involved when termination issues are raised. The parent's rights, both constitutional and statutory, have their own independent vitality.

. . . .

. . . Mary Beth Whitehead had custody of Baby M for four months before the child was taken away. Her initial surrender of Baby M was pursuant to a contract that we have declared illegal and unenforceable. The Sterns knew almost from the very day that they took Baby M that their rights were being challenged by the natural mother. . . .

There is simply no basis to warrant termination of Mrs. Whitehead's parental rights. We therefore conclude that the natural mother is entitled to retain her rights as a mother.

IV. Constitutional Issues

Both parties argue that the Constitutions — state and federal — mandate approval of their basic claims. The source of their constitutional arguments is essentially the same: the right of privacy, the right to procreate, the right to the companionship of one's child, those rights flowing either directly from the fourteenth amendment or by its incorporation of the Bill of Rights, or from the ninth amendment, or through the penumbra surrounding all of the Bill of Rights. They are the rights of personal intimacy, of marriage, of sex, of family, of procreation. Whatever their source, it is clear that they are fundamental rights protected by both the federal and state Constitutions. The right asserted by the Sterns is the right of procreation; that asserted by Mary Beth Whitehead is the right to the companionship of her child. We find that the right of procreation does not extend as far as claimed by the Sterns. As for the right asserted by Mrs. Whitehead,[2] since we uphold it on other grounds (i.e., we have restored her as mother and recognized her right, limited by the child's best interests, to her companionship), we need not decide that constitutional issue, and for reasons set forth below, we should not.

The right to procreate, as protected by the Constitution, has been ruled on directly only once by the United States Supreme Court. *See Skinner v. Oklahoma*. Although *Griswold v. Connecticut* is obviously of a similar class, strictly speaking it involves the right not to procreate. The right to procreate very simply is the right to have natural children, whether through sexual intercourse or artificial insemination. It is no more than that. Mr. Stern has not been deprived of that right. Through artificial insemination of Mrs. Whitehead, Baby M is his child. The custody, care, companionship, and nurturing that follow birth are not parts of the right to procreation; they are rights that may also be constitutionally protected, but that involve many considerations other than the right of procreation. To assert that Mr. Stern's right of procreation gives him the right to the custody of Baby M would be to assert that Mrs. Whitehead's right of procreation does not give her the right to the custody of Baby M; it would be to assert that the constitutional right of procreation includes within it a constitutionally protected contractual right to destroy someone else's right of procreation.

We conclude that the right of procreation is best understood and protected if confined to its essentials, and that when dealing with rights concerning the resulting child, different interests come into play. There is nothing in our culture or society that even begins to suggest a fundamental right on the part of the father to the custody of the child as part of his right to procreate when opposed by the claim of the mother to the same child. . . .

. . . .

Mrs. Whitehead, on the other hand, asserts a claim that falls within the scope of a recognized fundamental interest protected by the Constitution. As a mother, she claims the right to the companionship of her child. This is a fundamental interest, constitutionally protected. . . . By virtue of our decision Mrs. Whitehead's constitutional complaint — that her parental rights have been unconstitutionally terminated — is moot. . . .

Having held the contract invalid and having found no other grounds for the termination of Mrs. Whitehead's parental rights, we find that nothing remains of her constitutional claim. It seems obvious to us that since custody and visitation encompass practically all of what we call "parental rights," a total denial of both would be the equivalent of termination of parental rights. We express no opinion on whether a prolonged suspension of visitation would constitute a termination of parental rights, or whether, assuming it would, a showing of unfitness would be required.

---

[2] Opponents of surrogacy have also put forth arguments based on the thirteenth amendment, as well as the Peonage Act, 42 U.S.C. § 1994 (1982). We need not address these arguments because we have already held the contract unenforceable on the basis of state law.

V. Custody

. . . With the surrogacy contract disposed of, the legal framework becomes a dispute between two couples over the custody of a child produced by the artificial insemination of one couple's wife by the other's husband. Under the Parentage Act the claims of the natural father and the natural mother are entitled to equal weight, i.e., one is not preferred over the other solely because he or she is the father or the mother. The applicable rule given these circumstances is clear: the child's best interests determine custody.

. . . .

. . . Some of Mrs. Whitehead's alleged character failings, as testified to by experts and concurred in by the trial court, were demonstrated by her actions brought on by the custody crisis. For instance, in order to demonstrate her impulsiveness, those experts stressed the Whiteheads' flight to Florida with Baby M; to show her willingness to use her children for her own aims, they noted the telephone threats to kill Baby M and to accuse Mr. Stern of sexual abuse of her daughter; in order to show Mrs. Whitehead's manipulativeness, they pointed to her threat to kill herself; and in order to show her unsettled family life, they noted the innumerable moves from one hotel or motel to another in Florida. Furthermore, the argument continues, one of the most important factors, whether mentioned or not, in favor of custody in the Sterns is their continuing custody during the litigation, now having lasted for one-and-a-half years. . . .

. . . .

There were eleven experts who testified concerning the child's best interests, either directly or in connection with matters related to that issue. Our reading of the record persuades us that the trial court's decision awarding custody to the Sterns (technically to Mr. Stern) should be affirmed. . . .

Our custody conclusion is based on strongly persuasive testimony contrasting both the family life of the Whiteheads and the Sterns and the personalities and characters of the individuals. The stability of the Whitehead family life was doubtful at the time of trial. Their finances were in serious trouble (foreclosure by Mrs. Whitehead's sister on a second mortgage was in process). Mr. Whitehead's employment, though relatively steady, was always at risk because of his alcoholism, a condition that he seems not to have been able to confront effectively. Mrs. Whitehead had not worked for quite some time, her last two employments having been part-time. One of the Whiteheads' positive attributes was their ability to bring up two children, and apparently well, even in so vulnerable a household. Yet substantial question was raised even about that aspect of their home life. The expert testimony contained criticism of Mrs. Whitehead's handling of her son's educational difficulties. Certain of the experts noted that Mrs. Whitehead perceived herself as omnipotent and omniscient concerning her children. She knew what they were thinking, what they wanted, and she spoke for them. As to Melissa, Mrs. Whitehead expressed the view that she alone knew what that child's cries and sounds meant. Her inconsistent stories about various things engendered grave doubts about her ability to explain honestly and sensitively to Baby M — and at the right time — the nature of her origin. Although faith in professional counseling is not a sine qua non of parenting, several experts believed that Mrs. Whitehead's contempt for professional help, especially professional psychological help, coincided with her feelings of omnipotence in a way that could be devastating to a child who most likely will need such help. In short, while love and affection there would be, Baby M's life with the Whiteheads promised to be too closely controlled by Mrs. Whitehead. The prospects for wholesome, independent psychological growth and development would be at serious risk.

The Sterns have no other children, but all indications are that their household and their personalities promise a much more likely foundation for Melissa to grow and thrive. There is a track record of sorts — during the one-and-a-half years of custody Baby M has done very well, and the relationship between both Mr. and Mrs. Stern and the baby has become very strong. The household is stable, and likely to remain so. Their finances are more than adequate, their circle of friends supportive, and their marriage happy. Most important, they are loving, giving, nurturing, and open-minded people. They have demonstrated the wish and ability to nurture and protect Melissa, yet at the same time to encourage her independence. Their lack of experience is more than made up for by a willingness to learn and to listen, a willingness that is enhanced by their professional training, especially Mrs. Stern's experience as a pediatrician. They are honest; they can recognize error, deal with it, and learn from it. They will try to determine rationally the best way to cope with problems in their relationship with Melissa. When the time comes to tell her about her origins, they will probably have found a means of doing so that accords with the best interests of Baby M. All in all, Melissa's future appears solid, happy, and promising with them.

. . . .

It seems to us that given her predicament, Mrs. Whitehead was rather harshly judged — both by the trial court and by some of the experts. She was guilty of a breach of contract, and indeed, she did break a very important promise, but we think it is expecting something well beyond normal human capabilities to suggest that this mother should have parted with her newly born infant without a struggle. Other than survival, what stronger force is there? . . . The Sterns suffered, but so did she. And if we go beyond suffering to an evaluation of the human stakes involved in the struggle, how much weight should be given to her nine months of pregnancy, the labor of childbirth, the risk to her life, compared to the payment of money, the anticipation of a child and the donation of sperm?

. . . .

VI. Visitation

The trial court's decision to terminate Mrs. Whitehead's parental rights precluded it from making any determination on visitation. . . .

. . . .

We also note the following for the trial court's consideration: First, this is not a divorce case where visitation is almost invariably granted to the noncustodial spouse. To some extent the facts here resemble cases where the noncustodial spouse has had practically no relationship with the child, but it only "resembles" those cases. In the instant case, Mrs. Whitehead spent the first four months of this child's life as her mother and has regularly visited the child since then. Second, she is not only the natural mother, but also the legal mother, and is not to be penalized one iota because of the surrogacy contract. Mrs. Whitehead, as the mother (indeed, as a mother who nurtured her child for its first four months — unquestionably a relevant consideration), is entitled to have her own interest in visitation considered. Visitation cannot be determined without considering the parents' interests along with those of the child.

. . . .

We have decided that Mrs. Whitehead is entitled to visitation at some point, and that question is not open to the trial court on this remand. The trial court will determine what kind of visitation shall be granted to her, with or without conditions, and when and under what circumstances it should commence. It also should be noted that the guardian's recommendation of a five-year delay is most unusual — one might argue that it begins to border on termination. Nevertheless, if the circumstances as further developed by appropriate proofs or as reconsidered on remand clearly call for that suspension under applicable legal principles of visitation, it should be so ordered.

. . . .

While probably unlikely, we do not deem it unthinkable that, the major issues having been resolved, the parties' undoubted love for this child might result in a good faith attempt to work out the visitation themselves, in the best interests of the child.

Conclusion

. . . .

We have found that our present laws do not permit the surrogacy contract used in this case. Nowhere, however, do we find any legal prohibition against surrogacy when the surrogate mother volunteers, without any payment, to act as a surrogate and is given the right to change her mind and to assert her parental rights. Moreover, the Legislature remains free to deal with this most sensitive issue as it sees fit, subject only to constitutional constraints.

. . . .

The judgment is affirmed in part, reversed in part, and remanded for further proceedings consistent with this opinion.

NOTES AND QUESTIONS

1. The question of surrogacy arrangements has been addressed by a number of state supreme courts. In general, such arrangements are legal and permissible. They are largely unregulated. They vary in considerable detail, including on such important matters as whether there is compensation; whether the egg and sperm are from the couple,

the surrogate or a total stranger; and whether the surrogate mother retains any rights as to visitation or, indeed, retention after the birth. Increasingly, the contracts are being standardized.

2. *Baby M* is, of course, quite different from *Dred Scott*. However, both involve the central concept of dominion and control over another person. At first blush, this may not readily appear in the *Baby M* context. On reconsideration, are not both Mary Beth Whitehead *and* the fetus being treated as property? As to Mrs. Whitehead, may we simply conclude that a freely consenting adult may agree, for a period of time, to serve as a "warehouse" for others? Are there societal concerns in such an arrangement?

3. In the Court's view, what is *wrong* with the arrangement the Sterns made with Mary Beth Whitehead? The Court implies that economic disparity in bargaining is present — but what is the evidence? And what is wrong with the disparity? Would the Court feel differently if the amount of money given to the surrogate mother were greater? How much would you charge to be a surrogate mother, to be at risk for nine months and then lose the child you carried and delivered? Would it matter if the genetic composition of the child was partly yours?

4. The Court returns to the question of compensation at the end of its opinion, suggesting that a woman may "volunteer" to be a surrogate mother and that such an arrangement would be binding. Is this gender discrimination? Of all of the services which women may provide and employ for earning a living, the only one which is unique is the conception and bearing of a child. Why should this be denied a woman as a source of support and compensation? Is similar denial extended to men when they contribute sperm to a sperm bank?

5. The Court implies that discrimination is at work against Mary Beth Whitehead. But is there not, as well, discrimination against Mrs. Stern? And does not the Court's ultimate disposition, favoring only Mr. Stern, simply continue the pattern of discrimination which it found initially disfavored Mrs. Whitehead?

6. Does *Baby M* address the question of the status of a fetus? Is it property, a person or simply a potentiality? If Mary Beth Whitehead could choose to carry the Sterns' child, can she choose to terminate that pregnancy at any time? May she choose to sell the fetus to someone else? Might they even conceive the fetus with the *intent* of disposing of it in a commercial fashion rather than raising it as a human being?

7. In *Baby M*, does it matter whether the egg came from Mrs. Stern, from Mary Beth Whitehead or from a third party donor? Does it matter whether, if it came from Whitehead or a donor, it was transplanted into Mrs. Stern? And what if, in any or all of these alternatives, the sperm was not Doctor Stern's, but a third person's, perhaps that of Mr. Whitehead?

8. Such questions raise the issue of how and whether courts can deal with such issues. What do you think of the *ex parte* process of the trial court and the trauma it engendered? How could it — and the later month-long trial — be avoided?

9. Is it possible that a child may be delivered through IVF who has *no* parents? *See In Re Marriage of Buzzanca*, 72 Cal. Rptr. 280 (Ct. App. 4th Dist. 1998) (H and W agree with S to carry egg of D, fertilized by sperm of X, to delivery; parentage later denied by H and S. Trial court found *no* parentage.) If so, should such arrangements be permitted?
10. The Supreme Court of California explored the complicated issues surrounding surrogacy in *Johnson v. Calvert*, 851 P.2d 776 (Cal. 1993), where Anna was to bear the child of Mark and Crispina, whose sperm and egg would produce the child. The Court resolved the litigation in favor of the biological parents under the Uniform Parentage Act, but only with great difficulty, enforcing the contract and rejecting the best interests of the child analysis used by the dissent and by the *Baby M* court. Note that the outcome may turn on the form of IVF; *Johnson* was different from *Baby M* in that regard.
11. For an excellent article, see *Choices for a Child: An Ethical and Legal Analysis of a Failed Surrogate Birth Contract*, 30 U. Rich. L. Rev. 275 (1996); and see *Report of the New York State Task Force on Life and the Law* (1998).

PROBLEM 1-2 — Eggs for Sale

The New York Times carried an article* on the sale of human eggs which is excerpted below:

> The American Society for Assisted Reproductions' voluntary guidelines say egg donors "should be compensated for the direct and indirect expenses associated with their participation, their inconvenience and time, and to some degree, for the risk and discomfort undertaken." It also says "financial payments should not be so excessive as to constitute undue inducement."
>
> Dr. J. Benjamin Younger, executive director of the assisted reproduction society, explained that the goal was to avoid "the enticement or exploitation of young women."
>
> It is a tradition in this country, Dr. Younger said, to forbid payments for body parts, like kidneys, and to allow compensation for body products, like blood. Some, who say human eggs are body parts, would prefer that women not be paid at all. The fertility society's ethics committee, however, takes the view that eggs are body products, permitting limited payments, which is consistent with the Federal Government's policies.
>
> In other countries, like England and Japan, governments forbid payments to egg donors and there are essentially no such donors available.
>
> It would have to be a very generous woman who would provide eggs to a stranger at no cost. To donate eggs, a woman has to inject herself with hormones for about two weeks, making her ovaries swell until

* Gina Kolata, *Price of Donor Eggs Soars, Setting Off a Debate on Ethics*, A1, A14 (Feb. 25, 1998). Copyright © 1998 The New York Times Co. Reprinted with permission.

they grow, in some cases, to the size of grapefruits. During that time, she must have frequent blood tests and ultrasound examinations to assess the ripening clusters of eggs in her ovaries. Then she must visit a medical center so her eggs can be "harvested," meaning that a thin needle is inserted through her vagina to her ovaries and eggs are suctioned out.

. . . .

Ever since egg donation began, in 1984, the price paid to the donors was passed on to the infertile couples seeking eggs. But that price started out very low. In 1984, donors got just $250, said Dr. Mark Sauer, a fertility specialist at Columbia-Presbyterian Medical Center in New York. By 1987, the price had risen to $500, and it reached $1,500 in 1993. A few years ago, it jumped to $2,500 in many cities, including New York. The price in other cities is similar.

Some donors may get even more. Dr. Arthur Caplan, director of the Center for Bioethics at the University of Pennsylvania, said he had seen advertisements in American newspapers placed by Japanese couples seeking donors of Japanese descent and offering them $10,000. Dr. Caplan said infertile couples from countries, like Japan, that forbid payments to egg donors simply find their donors in the United States.

Dr. Rawlins said there were no formal guidelines on how often a woman could provide eggs.

Dr. Scott of St. Barnabas said he had raised his rate to $5,000 to draw in more donors, but he added that he still considered it compensation for a woman's "time and trouble." And, he said, considering what is involved, "I'm not sure $5,000 is enough."

Dr. Sauer, whose center competes with Dr. Scott's for donors, maintained that $5,000 was much too much.

"Where does it stop?" Dr. Sauer asked. "Egg donation is becoming like an auction."

. . . .

But some ethicists and fertility doctors say it is time to call human eggs what they are: a commodity whose price is set by whatever the market will bear.

Dr. Rawlins said women now finally realized just how valuable their eggs were.

And there is nothing inherently wrong with bidding for human eggs, said Dr. Norman Fost, an ethicist at the University of Wisconsin. After all, he asked, who is harmed?

"The point is to make sure that children come into the world in a loving way, that they are nurtured and that they grow up happy," Dr. Fost said.

Dr. Joseph Schulman, director of the Genetics and IVF Institute in Fairfax, Va., said the right price for human eggs was "ultimately determined by the balance between supply and demand."

And, Dr. Schulman said, since the patients are the ones paying for eggs, "the price is determined by the patient."

PROBLEM 1–3 — Market Forces and Federalism

On July 9, 2006, the *Portland Oregonian* reported that surrogate mothers are receiving between $20,000 and $30,000 for their services in Oregon. Because such arrangements are legal, people travel to Oregon from as far away as Washington State and Australia (and presumably, New Jersey) to arrange a surrogate pregnancy and birth. According to the article, surrogacy may cost $70,000, with the surrogate's insurance covering medical expenses. The mothers interviewed said they needed the money (for a house addition); were motivated by the gift they were giving; bristled at efforts to control them during pregnancy (such as requiring classical music); felt great responsibility; and were happy to get back to their lives — although missing the child.

Does this experience change your view of the opinion in *Baby M*?

Note (as the article did) the economic exclusivity and imbalance of these arrangements — what are the implications of this?

Suppose a successful Oregon surrogacy becomes embroiled in the New Jersey courts — say, the surrogate sues for nonpayment or the parents sue for nondisclosure of HIV+ status — what result?

Questions

1. Is there *any* harm in the sale of human eggs pursuant to "market" forces, as with chicken eggs?
2. If you would regulate sale, what *exactly* would you regulate — price? uses? purchasers? sellers? venders?
3. At what point, exactly, would (if at all) you change your position in the development process towards fetal evolution?
4. Go to Google or another search engine on the web; are eggs for sale, on what terms, with what safeguards? Does what you find change your answers to questions 2 and 3?

[1] Aliens Among Us

The community of America is built on immigration and naturalization of those who come from other nations and cultures. But *how* they shall be treated after arrival is an endlessly evolving inquiry. Discrimination endures, on race, nationality, language, wealth and locale. Korematsu, Schmidt and Edwards, the three cases in this section, examine the law and ethics governing the treatment of aliens among us. This is, of course, a far more enduring and catastrophic concern for those elsewhere, including Jews in Germany or Russia, Albanians in Kosovo, Tutsis in Africa, Catholics in Northern Ireland, and the residents of Darfur.

TOYOSABURO KOREMATSU v. UNITED STATES

323 U.S. 214 (1944)

Mr. Justice **Black** delivered the opinion of the Court.

The petitioner, an American citizen of Japanese descent, was convicted in a federal district court for remaining in San Leandro, California, a "Military Area," contrary to Civilian Exclusion Order No. 34 of the Commanding General of the Western Command, U.S. Army, which directed that after May 9, 1942, all persons of Japanese ancestry should be excluded from that area. No question was raised as to petitioner's loyalty to the United States. The Circuit Court of Appeals affirmed, and the importance of the constitutional question involved caused us to grant certiorari.

It should be noted, to begin with, that all legal restrictions which curtail the civil rights of a single racial group are immediately suspect. That is not to say that all such restrictions are unconstitutional. It is to say that courts must subject them to the most rigid scrutiny. Pressing public necessity may sometimes justify the existence of such restrictions; racial antagonism never can.

. . . .

Exclusion Order No. 34, which the petitioner knowingly and admittedly violated, was one of a number of military orders and proclamations, all of which were substantially based upon Executive Order No. 9066. That order, issued after we were at war with Japan, declared that "the successful prosecution of the war requires every possible protection against espionage and against sabotage to national-defense material, national-defense premises, and national-defense utilities . . . .

One of the series of orders and proclamations, a curfew order, which like the exclusion order here was promulgated pursuant to Executive Order 9066, subjected all persons of Japanese ancestry in prescribed West Coast military areas to remain in their residences from 8 p.m. to 6 a.m. As is the case with the exclusion order here, that prior curfew order was designed as a "protection against espionage and against sabotage." In *Kiyoshi Hirabayashi v. United States*, we sustained a conviction obtained for violation of the curfew order. The *Hirabayashi* conviction and this one thus rest on the same 1942 Congressional Act and the same basic executive and military orders, all of which orders were aimed at the twin dangers of espionage and sabotage.

. . . .

In the light of the principles we announced in the *Hirabayashi* case, we are unable to conclude that it was beyond the war power of Congress and the Executive to exclude those of Japanese ancestry from the West Coast war area at the time they did. True, exclusion from the area in which one's home is located is a far greater deprivation than constant confinement to the home from 8 p.m. to 6 a.m. Nothing short of apprehension by the proper military authorities of the gravest imminent danger to the public safety can constitutionally justify either. But exclusion from a threatened area, no less than curfew, has a definite and close relationship to the prevention of espionage and sabotage. The military authorities, charged with the primary responsibility of defending our shores, concluded that curfew provided inadequate protection and ordered exclusion. They did so, as pointed out in our *Hirabayashi* opinion, in accordance with congressional authority to the military to say who should, and who should not, remain in the threatened areas.

In this case the petitioner challenges the assumptions upon which we rested our conclusions in the *Hirabayashi* case. He also urges that by May 1942, when Order No. 34 was promulgated, all danger of Japanese invasion of the West Coast had disappeared. After careful consideration of these contentions we are compelled to reject them.

Here, as in the *Hirabayashi* case, ". . . we cannot reject as unfounded the judgment of the military authorities and of Congress that there were disloyal members of that population, whose number and strength could not be precisely and quickly ascertained. We cannot say that the war-making branches of the Government did not have ground for believing that in a critical hour such persons could not readily be isolated and separately dealt with, and constituted a menace to the national defense and safety, which demanded that prompt and adequate measures be taken to guard against it."

Like curfew, exclusion of those of Japanese origin was deemed necessary because of the presence of an unascertained number of disloyal members of the group, most of whom we have no doubt were loyal to this country. It was because we could not reject the finding of the military authorities that it was impossible to bring about an immediate segregation of the disloyal from the loyal that we sustained the validity of the curfew order as applying to the whole group. In the instant case, temporary exclusion of the entire group was rested by the military on the same ground. The judgment that exclusion of the whole group was for the same reason a military imperative answers the contention that the exclusion was in the nature of group punishment based on antagonism to those of Japanese origin. That there were members of the group who retained loyalties to Japan has been confirmed by investigations made subsequent to the exclusion. Approximately five thousand American citizens of Japanese ancestry refused to swear unqualified allegiance to the United States and to renounce allegiance to the Japanese Emperor, and several thousand evacuees requested repatriation to Japan.

We uphold the exclusion order as of the time it was made and when the petitioner violated it. In doing so, we are not unmindful of the hardships imposed by it upon a large group of American citizens. But hardships are part of war, and war is an aggregation of hardships. All citizens alike, both in and out of uniform, feel the impact of war in greater or lesser measure. Citizenship has its responsibilities as well as its privileges, and in time of war the burden is always heavier. Compulsory exclusion of large groups of citizens from their homes, except under circumstances of direst emergency and peril, is inconsistent with our basic governmental institutions. But when under conditions of modern warfare our shores are threatened by hostile forces, the power to protect must be commensurate with the threatened danger.

. . . .

We are thus being asked to pass at this time upon the whole subsequent detention program in both assembly and relocation centers, although the only issues framed at the trial related to petitioner's remaining in the prohibited area in violation of the exclusion order. Had petitioner here left the prohibited area and gone to an assembly center we cannot say either as a matter of fact or law, that his presence in that center would have resulted in his detention in a relocation center. . . .

. . . .

Since the petitioner has not been convicted of failing to report or to remain in an assembly or relocation center, we cannot in this case determine the validity of those separate provisions of the order. It is sufficient here for us to pass upon the order which petitioner violated. To do more would be to go beyond the issues raised, and to decide momentous questions not contained within the framework of the pleadings or the evidence in this case. It will be time enough to decide the serious constitutional issues which petitioner seeks to raise when an assembly or relocation order is applied or is certain to be applied to him, and we have its terms before us.

Some of the members of the Court are of the view that evacuation and detention in an Assembly Center were inseparable. After May 3, 1942, the date of Exclusion Order No. 34, Korematsu was under compulsion to leave the area not as he would choose but via an Assembly Center. The Assembly Center was conceived as a part of the machinery for group evacuation. The power to exclude includes the power to do it by force if necessary. And any forcible measure must necessarily entail some degree of detention or restraint whatever method of removal is selected. But whichever view is taken, it results in holding that the order under which petitioner was convicted was valid.

It is said that we are dealing here with the case of imprisonment of a citizen in a concentration camp solely because of his ancestry, without evidence or inquiry concerning his loyalty and good disposition towards the United States. Our task would be simple, our duty clear, were this a case involving the imprisonment of a loyal citizen in a concentration camp because of racial prejudice. Regardless of the true nature of the assembly and relocation centers — and we deem it unjustifiable to call them concentration camps with all the ugly connotations that term implies — we are dealing specifically with nothing but an exclusion order. To cast this case into outlines of racial prejudice, without reference to the real military dangers which were presented, merely confuses the issue. Korematsu was not excluded from the Military Area because of hostility to him or his race. He was excluded because we are at war with the Japanese Empire, because the properly constituted military authorities feared an invasion of our West Coast and felt constrained to take proper security measures, because they decided that the military urgency of the situation demanded that all citizens of Japanese ancestry be segregated from the West Coast temporarily, and finally, because Congress, reposing its confidence in this time of war in our military leaders — as inevitably it must — determined that they should have the power to do just this. There was evidence of disloyalty on the part of some, the military authorities considered that the need for action was great, and time was short. We cannot — by availing ourselves of the calm perspective of hindsight — now say that at that time these actions were unjustified.

Affirmed.

. . . .

Mr. Justice **Roberts**.

I dissent, because I think the indisputable facts exhibit a clear violation of Constitutional rights.

This is not a case of keeping people off the streets at night as was *Kiyoshi Hirabayashi v. United States*, nor a case of temporary exclusion of a citizen from an area for his own safety or that of the community, nor a case of offering him an opportunity to go temporarily out of an area where his presence might cause danger to himself or to his fellows. On the contrary, it is the case of convicting a citizen as a punishment for not submitting to imprisonment in a concentration camp, based on his ancestry, and solely because of his ancestry, without evidence or inquiry concerning his loyalty and good disposition towards the United States. If this be a correct statement of the facts disclosed by this record, and facts of which we take judicial notice, I need hardly labor the conclusion that Constitutional rights have been violated.

. . . .

The predicament in which the petitioner thus found himself was this: He was forbidden, by Military Order, to leave the zone in which he lived; he was forbidden, by Military Order, after a date fixed, to be found within that zone unless he were in an Assembly Center located in that zone. General DeWitt's report to the Secretary of War concerning the program of evacuation and relocation of Japanese makes it entirely clear, if it were necessary to refer to that document, — and, in the light of the above recitation, I think it is not, — that an Assembly Center was a euphemism for a prison. No person within such a center was permitted to leave except by Military Order.

In the dilemma that he dare not remain in his home, or voluntarily leave the area, without incurring criminal penalties, and that the only way he could avoid punishment was to go to an Assembly Center and submit himself to military imprisonment, the petitioner did nothing.

. . . .

As I have said above, the petitioner, prior to his arrest, was faced with two diametrically contradictory orders given sanction by the Act of Congress of March 21, 1942. The earlier of those orders made him a criminal if he left the zone in which he resided; the latter made him a criminal if he did not leave.

. . . .

These stark realities are met by the suggestion that it is lawful to compel an American citizen to submit to illegal imprisonment on the assumption that he might, after going to the Assembly Center, apply for his discharge by suing out a writ of habeas corpus, as was done in the *Endo* case, *supra*. The answer, of course, is that where he was subject to two conflicting laws he was not bound, in order to escape violation of one of the other, to surrender his liberty for any period. Nor will it do to say that the detention was a necessary part of the process of evacuation, and so we are here concerned only with the validity of the latter.

Again it is a new doctrine of constitutional law that one indicted for disobedience to an unconstitutional statute may not defend on the ground of the invalidity of the statute but must obey it though he knows it is no law and, after he has suffered the disgrace of conviction and lost his liberty by sentence, then, and not before, seek, from within prison walls, to test the validity of the law.

Moreover, it is beside the point to rest decision in part on the fact that the petitioner, for his own reasons, wished to remain in his home. If, as is the fact he was constrained so to do, it is indeed a narrow application of constitutional rights to ignore the order which constrained him, in order to sustain his conviction for violation of another contradictory order.

I would reverse the judgment of conviction.

Mr. Justice **Murphy**, dissenting.

This exclusion of "all persons of Japanese ancestry, both alien and nonalien," from the Pacific Coast area on a plea of military necessity in the absence of martial law ought not to be approved. Such exclusion goes over "the very brink of constitutional power" and falls into the ugly abyss of racism.

. . . .

The judicial test of whether the Government, on a plea of military necessity, can validly deprive an individual of any of his constitutional rights is whether the deprivation is reasonably related to a public danger that is so "immediate, imminent, and impending" as not to admit of delay and not to permit the intervention of ordinary constitutional processes to alleviate the danger. *United States v. Russell*, *Mitchell v. Harmony*, *Raymond v. Thomas*. Civilian Exclusion Order No. 34, banishing from a prescribed area of the Pacific Coast "all persons of Japanese ancestry, both alien and nonalien," clearly does not meet that test. Being an obvious racial discrimination, the order deprives all those within its scope of the equal protection of the laws as guaranteed by the Fifth Amendment. It further deprives these individuals of their constitutional rights to live and work where they will, to establish a home where they choose and to move about freely. In excommunicating them without benefit of hearings, this order also deprives them of all their constitutional rights to procedural due process. Yet no reasonable relation to an "immediate, imminent, and impending" public danger is evident to support this racial restriction which is one of the most sweeping and complete deprivations of constitutional rights in the history of this nation in the absence of martial law.

It must be conceded that the military and naval situation in the spring of 1942 was such as to generate a very real fear of invasion of the Pacific Coast, accompanied by fears of sabotage and espionage in that area. The military command was therefore justified in adopting all reasonable means necessary to combat these dangers. In adjudging the military action taken in light of the then apparent dangers, we must not erect too high or too meticulous standards; it is necessary only that the action have some reasonable relation to the removal of the dangers of invasion, sabotage and espionage. But the exclusion, either temporarily or permanently, of all persons with Japanese blood in their veins has no such reasonable relation. And that relation is lacking because the exclusion order necessarily must rely for its reasonableness upon the assumption that all persons of Japanese ancestry may have a dangerous tendency to commit sabotage and espionage and to aid our

Japanese enemy in other ways. It is difficult to believe that reason, logic or experience could be marshalled in support of such an assumption.

. . . .

Justification for the exclusion is sought, instead, mainly upon questionable racial and sociological grounds not ordinarily within the realm of expert military judgment, supplemented by certain semi-military conclusions drawn from an unwarranted use of circumstantial evidence. Individuals of Japanese ancestry are condemned because they are said to be "a large, unassimilated, tightly knit racial group, bound to an enemy nation by strong ties of race, culture, custom and religion." They are claimed to be given to "emperor worshipping ceremonies" and to "dual citizenship." Japanese language schools and allegedly pro-Japanese organizations are cited as evidence of possible group disloyalty, together with facts as to certain persons being educated and residing at length in Japan. It is intimated that many of these individuals deliberately resided "adjacent to strategic points," thus enabling them "to carry into execution a tremendous program of sabotage on a mass scale should any considerable number of them have been inclined to do so." The need for protective custody is also asserted. The report refers without identity to "numerous incidents of violence" as well as to other admittedly unverified or cumulative incidents . . . .

. . . .

The military necessity which is essential to the validity of the evacuation order thus resolves itself into a few intimations that certain individuals actively aided the enemy, from which it is inferred that the entire group of Japanese Americans could not be trusted to be or remain loyal to the United States. No one denies, of course, that there were some disloyal persons of Japanese descent on the Pacific Coast who did all in their power to aid their ancestral land. Similar disloyal activities have been engaged in by many persons of German, Italian and even more pioneer stock in our country. But to infer that examples of individual disloyalty prove group disloyalty and justify discriminatory action against the entire group is to deny that under our system of law individual guilt is the sole basis for deprivation of rights. Moreover, this inference, which is at the very heart of the evacuation orders, has been used in support of the abhorrent and despicable treatment of minority groups by the dictatorial tyrannies which this nation is now pledged to destroy. To give constitutional sanction to that inference in this case, however well-intentioned may have been the military command on the Pacific Coast, is to adopt one of the cruelest of the rationales used by our enemies to destroy the dignity of the individual and to encourage and open the door to discriminatory actions against other minority groups in the passions of tomorrow.

. . . .

I dissent, therefore, from this legalization of racism. Racial discrimination in any form and in any degree has no justifiable part whatever in our democratic way of life. It is unattractive in any setting but it is utterly revolting among a free people who have embraced the principles set forth in the Constitution of the United States. All residents of this nation are kin in some way by blood or culture to a foreign land. Yet they are primarily and necessarily a part of the new and distinct civilization of the United States. They must accordingly be treated at all times as the heirs of the American experiment and as entitled to all the rights and freedoms guaranteed by the Constitution.

Mr. Justice **Jackson**, dissenting.

Korematsu was born on our soil, of parents born in Japan. The Constitution makes him a citizen of the United States by nativity and a citizen of California by residence. No claim is made that he is not loyal to this country. There is no suggestion that apart from the matter involved here he is not law-abiding and well disposed. Korematsu, however, has been convicted of an act not commonly a crime. It consists merely of being present in the state whereof he is a citizen, near the place where he was born, and where all his life he has lived.

. . . .

Now, if any fundamental assumption underlies our system, it is that guilt is personal and not inheritable. Even if all of one's antecedents had been convicted of treason, the Constitution forbids its penalties to be visited upon him, for it provides that "no Attainder of Treason shall work Corruption of Blood, or Forfeiture except during the Life of the Person attained." Article 3, § 3, cl. 2. But here is an attempt to make an otherwise innocent act a crime merely because this prisoner is the son of parents as to whom he had no choice, and belongs to a race from which there is no way to resign. If Congress in peace-time legislation should enact such a criminal law, I should suppose this Court would refuse to enforce it.

. . . .

Much is said of the danger to liberty from the Army program for deporting and detaining these citizens of Japanese extraction. But a judicial construction of the due process clause that will sustain this order is a far more subtle blow to liberty than the promulgation of the order itself. A military order, however unconstitutional, is not apt to last longer than the military emergency. Even during that period a succeeding commander may revoke it all. But once a judicial opinion rationalizes such an order to show that it conforms to the Constitution, or rather rationalizes the Constitution to show that the Constitution sanctions such an order, the Court for all time has validated the principle of racial discrimination in criminal procedure and of transplanting American citizens. The principle then lies about like a loaded weapon ready for the hand of any authority that can bring forward a plausible claim of an urgent need. Every repetition imbeds that principle more deeply in our law and thinking and expands it to new purposes. All who observe the work of courts are familiar with what Judge Cardozo described as "the tendency of a principle to expand itself to the limit of its logic." A military commander may overstep the bounds of constitutionality, and it is an incident. But if we review and approve, that passing incident becomes the doctrine of the Constitution. There it has a generative power of its own, and all that it creates will be in its own image. Nothing better illustrates this danger than does the Court's opinion in this case.

. . . .

NOTES AND QUESTIONS

1. Scholars in the last two decades have been highly critical of *Korematsu* and of *Hirabayashi*. Both cases raised the question of whether people whose citizenship had been established and whose loyalty had been unquestioned might nevertheless be denied basic rights of citizenship (*e.g.*, home ownership, freedom of movement, choice of employment) because of race and national origin without individualized findings of wrongdoing or fault. The Supreme Court simply affirmed the decisions of the military to suspend citizenship status to American citizens. Congress — the Court said — had authorized this. Thus, all three branches of government combined in a way which subsequently seems (at least) to have been unwarranted and excessive.
2. Suppose that, as the Court suggests, the military accurately found that Americans of Japanese descent were members of cultural and religious organizations which were tight knit and exclusivist in nature. Would that not be sufficient to justify moving them to a locaton which would disable them for military purposes and subject them to careful and continuing surveillance? Was it realistic to think that individualized determinations could be made? To put the matter somewhat differently, is the issue in *Korematsu* whether to treat Japanese-Americans as citizens or whether, as citizens, they could be expected to submit to discriminatory treatment?
3. In the 1980s Korematsu brought a petition for a writ of *coram nobis* to vacate his conviction on the grounds of governmental misconduct. *Korematsu v. United States*, 584 F. Supp. 1406 (N.D. Cal. 1984). Although the court denied Korematsu the relief he desired, they made clear that his original case no longer had any precedential effect and the case was useful only as an example of our legal and political history. In 1988, Congress undertook a program of reparations and compensation for those whose homes, businesses and employment had been lost during the time of internment. *The Civil Liberties Act of 1988*, Pub. L. No. 100-383, § 102, 102 Stat. 904 (1988). This, of course, came almost 50 years after the event.
4. California's Proposition 187 mandates denial of public education, health services and social services to illegal aliens. For an examination of the constitutional issues implicated by Proposition 187, see Robert S. Ryan, *Proposition 187: California's Stance Against Illegal Immigration*, 25 Cap. U.L. Rev. 613 (1996). Also, for United States Supreme Court cases concerning limitations on public benefits to aliens, see *Graham v. Richardson*, 403 U.S. 365 (1971); *Mathews v. Diaz*, 426 U.S. 67 (1976); *Plyler v. Doe*, 457 U.S. 202 (1982).
5. In addition to Japan, of course, the United States confronted Germany during the Second World War. There was hostility toward Americans of German descent. However, they were not rounded up and detained in concentration camps. Was this due to the color of their skin, or can the discriminatory treatment be justified on other grounds? The next case, *United States v. Schmidt*, deals with a naturalized citizen from Germany.

UNITED STATES v. SCHMIDT
923 F.2d 1253 (D.C. Cir. 1991)

Bauer, Chief Judge.

The Constitution empowers Congress "[t]o establish an uniform Rule of Naturalization." Article I, sec. 8, cl. 4. Any alien who seeks to acquire the "precious right" of American citizenship must meet all the requirements fixed by Congress. One of the requirements Congress established for citizenship is entry into the United states by means of a legally procured immigration visa. [A]ny individual who advocated or assisted in the persecution of persons because of race, religion or national origin is ineligible to obtain a visa. In the judgment appealed from here, the district court revoked Michael Schmidt's citizenship and canceled his certificate of naturalization . . . The district court found that because Schmidt served as an armed guard with the Nazi "Death's Head Battalion" at the Sachsenhausen concentration camp during World War II, he was ineligible to receive a visa. The court concluded that, because Schmidt's visa was invalid, he did not have lawful permission to enter the United States, and thus his subsequent naturalization was procured unlawfully under section 316(a)(1) of the Immigration and Nationality Act. For the following reasons, we affirm.

I

Michael Schmidt was born in Scharosch, Romania, of German parentage. In June, 1943, he was inducted into the German Army as a private and assigned to serve at the Sachsenhausen concentration camp near Oraneinburg, Germany. In the district court, the government presented extensive evidence concerning the history of the Nazi regime and its plan to exterminate systematically individuals who disagreed with its policies, as well as groups it considered to be racially and socially inferior. The Nazis used concentration camps to carry out the Third Reich's plan to exterminate enemies or to exploit them through forced labor. The Gestapo, the Nazi secret police force, arrested and detained all persons thought to be enemies of the state. Those held in this manner could be incarcerated without trial for indefinite periods of time.

During Schmidt's service at Sachsenhausen, the camp was the second largest Nazi concentration camp after Auschwitz. Among those incarcerated there were Jews, Gypsies, Jehovah's Witnesses, certain Eastern European ethnics, political dissidents, homosexuals, and various individuals considered social "misfits," including beggars, vagrants, and the mentally ill. Each category of prisoner was forced to wear a colored triangle on the outside of its uniform: Jews, yellow; political prisoners, red; social misfits, black/brown; Jehovah's Witnesses, violet; homosexuals, pink. At the height of its operation, Sachsenhausen contained approximately 50,000 prisoners.

The "Death Head's Battalion" — the SS-Totenkopf Sturmbann — was organized as part of the armed SS for the purpose of guarding Nazi concentration camps. The military command assigned Schmidt to guard prisoners on forced labor crews outside Sachsenhausen. His duties included escorting prisoners to and from work sites, counting prisoners before returning them to the concentration camp, and keeping prisoners in formation. Schmidt wore on his SS uniform the skull and crossbones insignia of the Death Head's Battalion. He carried a rifle and ammunition and had orders to shoot at prisoners who attempted to escape. Because concentration camp guards were not permitted to enter the camps themselves, Schmidt was confined to patrol outside the camp wall. Although there is no evidence that Schmidt personally killed prisoners, it has been documented that during the period he served at Sachsenhausen, two Jews were intentionally murdered and at least thirteen prisoners were executed by being shot through the nape of the neck.

In addition, tens of thousands died in Sachsenhausen as a result of starvation, exhaustion, beatings, exposure, disease, and medical experimentation. The grim history of Sachsenhausen has been well-documented by historians and tribunals that have tried Nazi war criminals. . . .

Schmidt continued to serve as an armed guard at Sachsenhausen until at least September, 1944. He then served in the Third Battalion of the 38th SS Armored Infantry Division, "Goetz von Berlichingen," and was wounded in combat in Lorraine, France on November 28, 1944. He remained in military hospitals until he became a British prisoner of war. He was released on July 8, 1946.

Schmidt made his way to the United States under the authority of the Displaced Persons Act of 1948 ("DPA"). Congress enacted the DPA to accommodate the large number of European refugees wishing to emigrate to the United States after World War II. A person seeking to obtain an immigration visa under the DPA was required to obtain a designation of "displaced person" status as defined by the Constitution of the International Refugee Organization of the United Nations ("IRO"). Annex I, Part II of the IRO Constitution provided that war criminals and others who "assisted the enemy in persecuting civil populations of countries" were not "the concern" of the IRO. These individuals thus were excluded from the definition of "displaced persons" under the DPA.

. . . .

After living in Germany and Austria for several years following the war, Schmidt applied for a determination from the DPC that he was conscripted into the "German Army, Waffen-SS 'Goetz von Berlichingen,' " but he did not indicate his service as a guard at Sachsenhausen. Based on Schmidt's representations in his questionnaire, on February 28, 1952, DPC case analyst John F. Zipf, Jr. certified Schmidt as a displaced person eligible for a visa. Paul B. Lanius, Jr., the American Vice-Consul in Salzburg, Austria, issued Schmidt a visa in April, 1952. Schmidt entered the United States pursuant to this visa on May 24, 1952.

On March 1, 1968, Schmidt filed an application to become a United States citizen. Question 7 of the application form required him to list "present and past membership in every organization, association, fund, foundation, party, club, society, or similar group in the United States and in any other place, and your foreign military service." Schmidt entered his military service in the German army from 1943 to 1945, but did not indicate that he had served as an armed guard at Sachsenhausen from June, 1943 to September, 1944. On April 2, 1968, the United States District Court for the Northern District of

Illinois issued a certificate of naturalization granting Schmidt United States citizenship.

Schmidt lived a quiet life in the Chicago area, where he worked as a janitor until his retirement. Following a determination by the Criminal Division of the Office of Special Investigations of the United States Department of Justice that there was good cause to revoke Schmidt's citizenship, the Government filed a complaint in federal district court on November 2, 1988. The court ordered Schmidt's citizenship revoked and, in February, 1990, Schmidt surrendered his certificate of naturalization to the Attorney General of the United States. This appeal followed.

II

At issue is whether, under section 13 of the Displaced Persons Act, Schmidt's service in the SS as a guard at Sachsenhausen concentration camp rendered him ineligible to obtain a visa, in that his activities constituted assistance in the persecution of persons because of race, religion or national origin. . . .

Citizenship is procured illegally any time the applicant has failed to comply with "all the congressionally imposed prerequisites to the acquisition of citizenship." Section 316(a)(1) of the Immigration and Nationality Act of 1952 requires that the person seeking naturalization has been "lawfully admitted for permanent residence," that is, possess a valid visa. In denaturalization proceedings for illegal acquisition of citizenship, an individual's failure to enter the United States lawfully by means of a valid immigration visa, a condition precedent to naturalization, commands denaturalization. Further, section 13 of the DPA mandates that an individual is ineligible for a visa if a member of a specifically excluded category of persons: those who assisted in persecution.

. . . .

Schmidt first maintains that the court failed to consider that he involuntarily joined the SS. In *Fedorenko*, the Supreme Court stated that "[u]nder traditional principles of statutory construction, the deliberate omission of the word 'voluntary' from the DPA compels the conclusion that the statute made all who assisted in the persecution of civilians ineligible for visas." The Court rejected the distinction between voluntary and involuntary service for DPA purposes, and held that service as an armed guard in a concentration camp constitutes assistance to the enemy under the DPA as a matter of law. Therefore, Schmidt's involuntary service argument is meritless.

Schmidt also argues that he personally did not commit atrocities against the Sachsenhausen prisoners. He contends that because armed guards were not permitted to enter the camp, he had no knowledge of the persecution occurring within Sachsenhausen's walls. Whether or not Schmidt personally engaged in acts of violence, however, does not affect our conclusion that he assisted in persecution. Concerned that concentration camp survivors might become ineligible for visas because of "assistance" they had provided to their Nazi captors in the death camps, the *Fedorenko* Court drew a continuum of conduct ranging from passive acceptance to active, personal participation. The

Court distinguished between a person who only cut the hair of fellow inmates before they were killed and an armed guard who shot a fleeing inmate, finding that the former should not be found to have assisted in the persecution of civilians, but that the latter should. It is more difficult to determine whether conduct falling elsewhere on the continuum may be considered persecution. The difficulty of the problem is magnified by the task of determining the contribution of a single individual to the collective wrongdoing of a nation or group.

Whatever close questions may be presented by the application of the *Fedorenko* continuum to other factual situations, it is clear that service as an armed concentration camp guard constitutes assisting in persecution under the DPA. In *Schellong v. INS*, we observed that "Nazi concentration camps were places of persecution; individuals who, armed with guns, held the prisoners captive and prodded them into forced labor with threats of death or capital punishment cannot deny that they aided the Nazis in their program of racial, political, and religious oppression." When examined in context, the activities of an armed concentration guard must be viewed as contributing to the collective effort of the Nazis to persecute innocent civilians.

. . . .

Thus, even if Schmidt personally did not participate in the brutal acts committed at Sachsenhausen, the fact of his armed, uniformed service is sufficient to establish that he assisted in persecution. . . .

. . . [W]e conclude that Schmidt assisted in persecution of persons because of race, religion or national origin as contemplated by section 13 of the DPA. He carried a gun and wore the uniform of the dreaded "Death Head's Battalion." He guarded Jews, Gypsies, Jehovah's Witnesses, Eastern European nationals, and other persecuted peoples and forced them to do the bidding of the Third Reich. Schmidt prevented these prisoners from fleeing, and subjected them to forced labor under unspeakably brutal conditions. Such employment removed Schmidt from the intended scope of those to be aided by the DPA.

III

In affirming the district court's revocation of Schmidt's citizenship, we are mindful of the fact that Schmidt has lived in the United States for many years, and that he has raised a family and established roots in this country. At the same time, we are mindful of the fact that Schmidt entered the United States on an invalid visa and acquired that "precious right" of citizenship unlawfully. When Congress enacted the DPA, it sought to help those who had been persecuted by the enemy because of their religious, nationalistic, and ethnic identities. By excluding those who "assisted in persecution" in section 13 of the DPA, Congress intended to prevent those who contributed to the Nazi persecution of innocent civilians from obtaining visas to enter the United States as refugees. It would defeat the paramount purpose of the DPA — to assist those whose lives had been disrupted by persecution — to extend the statute's benefits to the persecutors themselves.

As we held in *Kulle* and the Supreme Court held in *Fedorenko*, an armed guard at a Nazi concentration camp is not eligible for a visa under the Displaced Persons Act. Schmidt, therefore, was not eligible for the visa he obtained pursuant to the DPA. Because he did not fulfill all of the statutory requirements for naturalization, his citizenship was illegally procured. Accordingly, the district court's entry of summary judgment revoking his citizenship and canceling his certificate of naturalization was correct as a matter of law and is, therefore,

Affirmed.

Pell, Senior Circuit Judge, dissenting.

. . . .

There is substantial reference in the record of this case to the depths of depravity to which the Third Reich descended. No one disputes that now. The question before this court, however, in a sense, is the extent, if any, that Schmidt was smeared by the evil brush of the governmental activities inside Sachsenhausen.

The record is, of course, sparse because this case is here without a trial. But there is no evidence that this defendant participated in any wrongful act toward any prisoner; there is affirmative evidence that he was never inside Sachsenhausen prison camp; there is affirmative evidence that he was a work-party guard and that he obeyed the regulation which forbade mistreatment of prisoners on work parties; and there is affirmative evidence that his service to the Third Reich of Germany, not his native country, in World War II was hardly "voluntary." It was, accepting all of this, the district court's judgment that a violation was shown solely on the basis of participation as a guard outside the walls of the camp.

. . . .

In the case before us, the only straw that would appear to seem to suggest Schmidt had some idea that some of the work prisoners were persecuted because of beliefs would be found in that he knew from their triangles that they were homosexuals. But, as his counsel pointed out, homosexuals were jailed in some of the states of this country at that very period of time.

The district court in its ruling found it did not make any difference whether Schmidt had knowledge or not. I disagree. As a matter of what was involved in the Displaced Persons Act, I cannot conceive how a person can be rendering assistance in persecution without some showable knowledge, or at the very least evidence of facts known to him which could lead only to a conclusion that the work prisoners were being persecuted. Schmidt, in my opinion, as a citizen was entitled to a trial on the issue of knowledge.

Cases interpreting *Fedorenko* hold (while finding) that "in order to establish 'participation' or 'assistance' the act of participation must involve some personal activity involving persecution." . . .

. . . .

It is true that this concept of "assistance" is not "capable of a precise definition," but it is also true that the "facts and the law should be construed as far as is reasonably possible in favor of the citizen . . . ."

The Government relied on *Kulle v. INS* as holding that there is no requirement of "knowledge" for "assisting."

Sergeant Kulle was deported on a record that included this question and answer:

> Q: Okay, was it your understanding at the time you made these lies, that if you had told the truth about your SS service you would have been denied admission to the United States?
>
> A: That's correct.

Kulle had denied SS service. Schmidt put it on his application. Kulle was decorated with the Iron Cross; Schmidt's service record shows nothing except that he came and went as a private, with no decorations. Kulle was a training leader, Schmidt was not. Kulle participated in a forced evacuation from a camp in the East to Mauthausen. Schmidt did not. The Court distinguished a "deportation" case from a denaturalization case (such as Schmidt's), and, with Kulle's admitted lies, ordered him deported.

As in *Schellong v. INS*, this court held that Kulle (on a trial record) had enough knowledge to be found to have assisted in persecution. In the present case, the facts in the record developed thus far did not reach the point of establishing knowledge on the part of Schmidt. In *Kulle*, a judgment was made on the basis of an INS record after a hearing at which Kulle's attorney was granted cross examination. Schmidt is to lose his citizenship without a fact hearing.

It may be at a trial, the trier of fact, evaluating the credibility of witnesses, might conclude that it is incredible that Schmidt during the relatively short period he was an outside guard could not help being aware that he was assisting in persecution. But that is a matter of credibility. Schmidt did not have such a chance. One might now think it is incredible that a presumably intelligent airline pilot could believe in good faith that the Internal Revenue Act is unconstitutional. He, however, was entitled to a fair trial and so should Schmidt be. Our system of justice that guilt should not be predicated on anything less than a fair trial is too important to tolerate any deviation or diminution.

NOTES AND QUESTIONS

1. Following World War II, a number of groups undertook to pursue and prosecute Nazis who had fled Germany. One of the more famous cases involved Adolph Eichmann, captured in South America and kidnapped there, ultimately to be tried in Israel. Less notorious cases were pursued in the United States, where Nazis had gained citizenship or entry by misrepresenting the role they had played. With the passage of time, the margin for error in identifying such people increased, in proportion to their contribution to the American community.

   The question thus posed was whether excluding such people from the American community made sense. And on what grounds? And with what procedures?

2. Why should the United States be concerned about what Schmidt (or others) may have done during the war? As American citizens, or as applicants for citizenship, should not the American community be concerned with Schmidt's performance as a member of *that* (our) community? Has the American community any obligation, ethical or otherwise, to members of another community (specifically, Jewish citizens, Gypsies, homosexuals, the mentally ill) some 40 to 60 years ago?

3. Should we, in quite conventional criminal law terms, consider the purposes of punishing Mr. Schmidt? Isn't culpability — knowledge or action or failure to act — necessary? Or is a showing of deterrence appropriate? Or possible? Should not Mr. Schmidt at least be able to show that, with the passage of time, his service to the American community outweighed his disservice years or decades earlier? When does a person become a member of our community?

4. In terms of ethical considerations, is it not enough to know that Schmidt helped to maintain the second largest Nazi concentration camp? Is it necessary to show that he actually *knew* the nature of the camp? What were Schmidt's ethical obligations as a guard toward the prisoners at Sachsenhausen? With actual knowledge, what were his options? As a member of then German society, or as a member of a larger community in geography, time or values? What would *you* have done, if *you* had been Herr Schmidt, standing guard outside Sachsenhausen?

5. Suppose the government — to avoid the denial of due process so apparent in *Korematsu* — undertook an individualized inquiry into Mr. Schmidt's culpability and he refused to answer questions. Should *that* be grounds for exclusions? *See United States v. Balsys*, U.S. 666 (1998). Or suppose citizenship was determined by gender. *See Miller v. Albright*, 523 U.S. 420 (1998).

6. A deportation context provides an occasion not only for defining who is in or out of a community, but also what conduct is acceptable. In §4.03[4], we return to this issue in dealing with female genital mutilation, where citizens of other countries resist deportation from the United States, on the ground that the common cultural practices of their nations are cruel and barbaric.

EDWARDS v. CALIFORNIA
314 U.S. 160 (1941)

Mr. Justice **Byrnes** delivered the opinion of the Court.

The facts of this case are simple and are not disputed. Appellant is a citizen of the United States and a resident of California. In December, 1939, he left his home in Marysville, California, for Spur, Texas, with the intention of bringing back to Marysville, his wife's brother, Frank Duncan, a citizen of the United States and a resident of Texas. When he arrived in Texas, appellant learned that Duncan had last been employed by the Works Progress Administration. Appellant thus became aware of the fact that Duncan was an indigent person and he continued to be aware of it throughout the period involved in this case. The two men agreed that appellant should transport Duncan from Texas to Marysville in appellant's automobile. Accordingly, they left Spur on January 1, 1940, entered California by way of Arizona on January 3, and reached Marysville on January 5. When he left Texas, Duncan had about $20. It had all been spent by the time he reached Marysville. He lived with appellant for about ten days until he obtained financial assistance from the Farm Security Administration. During the ten day interval, he had no employment.

In Justice Court a complaint was filed against appellant under the Welfare and Institutions Code of California, which provides: 'Every person, firm or corporation, or officer or agent thereof that brings or assists in bringing into the State any indigent person who is not a resident of the State, knowing him to be an indigent person, is guilty of a misdemeanor.' [T]he cause was tried, appellant was convicted and sentenced to six months imprisonment in the county jail, and sentence was suspended.

. . . .

The grave and perplexing social and economic dislocation which this statute reflects is a matter of common knowledge and concern. We are not unmindful of it. We appreciate that the spectacle of large segments of our population constantly on the move has given rise to urgent demands upon the ingenuity of government. Both the brief of the Attorney General of California and that of the Chairman of the Select Committee of the House of Representatives of the United States as amicus curiae have sharpened this appreciation. The State asserts that the huge influx of migrants into California in recent years has resulted in problems of health, morals, and especially finance, the proportions of which are staggering. It is not for us to say that this is not true. . . .

But this does not mean that there are no boundaries to the permissible area of State legislative activity. There are. And none is more certain than the prohibition against attempts on the part of any single State to isolate itself from difficulties common to all of them by restraining the transportation of persons and property across its borders. It is frequently the case that a State might gain a momentary respite from the pressure of events by the simple expedient of shutting its gates to the outside world. But, in the words of Mr. Justice Cardozo: "The Constitution was framed under the dominion of a political philosophy less parochial in range. It was framed upon the theory that the peoples of the several states must sink or swim together, and that in the long run prosperity and salvation are in union and not division."

It is difficult to conceive of a statute more squarely in conflict with this theory than the Section challenged here. Its express purpose and inevitable effect is to prohibit the transportation of indigent persons across the California border. The burden upon interstate commerce is intended and immediate; it is the plain and sole function of the statute. Moreover, the indigent nonresidents who are the real victims of the statute are deprived of the opportunity to exert political pressure upon the California legislature in order to obtain a change in policy. We think this statute must fail under any known test of the validity of State interference with interstate commerce.

It is urged, however, that the concept which underlies Section 2615 enjoys a firm basis in English and American history. This is the notion that each community should care for its own indigent, that relief is solely the responsibility of local government. Of this it must first be said that we are not now called upon to determine anything other than the propriety of an attempt by a State to prohibit the transportation of indigent nonresidents into its territory. The nature and extent of its obligation to afford relief to newcomers is not here involved. We do, however, suggest that the theory of the Elizabethan poor laws no longer fits the facts. Recent years, and particularly the past decade, have been marked by a growing recognition that in an industrial society the task of providing assistance to the needy has ceased to be local in character. The duty to share the burden, if not wholly to assume it, has been recognized not only by State governments, but by the Federal government as well. The changed attitude is reflected in the Social Security laws under which the Federal and State governments cooperate for the care of the aged, the blind and dependent children. It is reflected in the works programs under which work is furnished the unemployed, with the States supplying approximately 25% and the Federal government approximately 75% of the cost. It is further reflected in the Farm Security laws, under which the entire cost of the relief provisions is borne by the Federal government.

. . . .

What has been said with respect to financing relief is not without its bearing upon the regulation of the transportation of indigent persons. For the social phenomenon of large-scale interstate migration is as certainly a matter of national concern as the provision of assistance to those who have found a permanent or temporary abode. Moreover, and unlike the relief problem, this phenomenon does not admit of diverse treatment by the several States. The prohibition against transporting indigent nonresidents into one State is an open invitation to retaliatory measures, and the burdens upon the transportation of such persons become cumulative. Moreover, it would be a virtual impossibility for migrants and those who transport them to acquaint themselves with the peculiar rules of admission of many states. . . . There remains to be noticed only the contention that the limitation upon State power to interfere with the interstate transportation of persons is subject to an exception in the case of "paupers." It is true that support for this contention may be found in early decisions of this Court. In *City of New York v. Miln*, it was said that it is "as competent and as necessary for a state to provide precautionary measures against the moral pestilence of paupers, vagabonds, and possibly convicts; as it is to guard against the physical pestilence, which may arise from unsound and infectious articles imported . . . ." This language has been casually repeated in numerous later cases up to the turn of the century. In none of these cases, however, was the power of a State to exclude "paupers" actually involved.

Whether an able-bodied but unemployed person like Duncan is a 'pauper' within the historical meaning of the term is open to considerable doubt. But assuming that the term is applicable to him and to persons similarly situated, we do not consider ourselves bound by the language referred to. *City of New York v. Miln* was decided in 1836. Whatever may have been the notion then prevailing, we do not think that it will now be seriously contended that because a person is without employment and without funds he constitutes a 'moral pestilence'. Poverty and immorality are not synonymous.

We are of the opinion that Section 2615 is not a valid exercise of the police power of California, that it imposes an unconstitutional burden upon interstate commerce, and that the conviction under it cannot be sustained. In the view we have taken it is unnecessary to decide whether the Section is repugnant to other provisions of the Constitution.

Reversed.

Mr. Justice **Douglas**, concurring.

I express no view on whether or not the statute here in question runs afoul of Art. I, Sec. 8 of the Constitution granting to Congress the power 'to regulate Commerce with foreign Nations, and among the several States.' But I am of the opinion that the right of persons to move freely from State to State occupies a more protected position in our constitutional system than does the movement of cattle, fruit, steel and coal across state lines. While the opinion of the Court expresses no view on that issue, the right involved is so fundamental that I deem it appropriate to indicate the reach of the constitutional question which is present.

The right to move freely from State to State is an incident of *national* citizenship protected by the privileges and immunities clause of the Fourteenth Amendment against state interference. . . . Now it is apparent that this right is not specifically granted by the Constitution. Yet before the Fourteenth Amendment it was recognized as a right fundamental to the national character of our Federal government. . . .

So, when the Fourteenth Amendment was adopted in 1868 it had been squarely and authoritatively settled that the right to move freely from State to State was a right of national citizenship. As such it was protected by the privileges and immunities clause of the Fourteenth Amendment against state interference. And Chief Justice Fuller in *Williams v. Fears* stated: "Undoubtedly the right of locomotion, the right to remove from one place to another according to inclination, is an attribute of personal liberty, and the right, ordinarily, of free transit from or through the territory of any state is a right secured by the 14th Amendment and by other provisions of the Constitution."

. . . .

. . . That result necessarily follows unless perchance a State can curtail the right of free movement of those who are poor or destitute. But to allow such an exception to be engrafted on the rights of *national* citizenship would be to contravene every conception of national unity. It would also introduce a caste system utterly incompatible with the spirit of our system of government. It would permit those who were stigmatized by a State as indigents, paupers, or vagabonds to be relegated to an inferior class of citizenship. It would prevent a citizen because he was poor from seeking new horizons in other States. It might thus withhold from large segments of our people that mobility which is basic to any guarantee of freedom of opportunity. The result would be a substantial dilution of the rights of *national* citizenship, a serious impairment of the principles of equality. Since the state statute here challenged involves such consequences, it runs afoul of the privileges and immunities clause of the Fourteenth Amendment.

Mr. Justice **Black** and Mr. Justice **Murphy** join in this opinion. Mr. Justice **Jackson**, concurring.

I concur in the result reached by the Court, and I agree that the grounds of its decision are permissible ones under applicable authorities. But the migrations of a human being, of whom it is charged that he possesses nothing that can be sold and has no wherewithal to buy, do not fit easily into my notions as to what is commerce. To hold that the measure of his rights is the commerce clause is likely to result eventually either in distorting the commercial law or in denaturing human rights. I turn, therefore, away from principles by which commerce is regulated to that clause of the Constitution by virtue of which Duncan is a citizen of the United States and which forbids any state to abridge his privileges or immunities as such.

This clause was adopted to make United States citizenship the dominant and paramount allegiance among us. The return which the law had long associated with allegiance was protection. The power of citizenship as a shield against oppression was widely known from the example of Paul's Roman citizenship, which sent the centurion scurrying to his higher-ups with the message: "Take heed what thou doest: for this man is a Roman." I suppose none of us doubts that the hope of imparting to American citizenship some of this vitality was the purpose of declaring in the Fourteenth Amendment: "All persons born or naturalized in the United States, and subject to the jurisdiction thereof, are citizens of the United States and of the State wherein they reside. No State shall make or enforce any law which shall abridge the privileges or immunities of citizens of the United States . . . ."

. . . .

Even as to an alien who had "been admitted to the United States under the Federal law," this Court, through Mr. Justice Hughes, declared that "He was thus admitted with the privilege of entering and abiding in the United States, and hence of entering and abiding in any state in the Union." *Truax v. Raich*, 239 U.S. 33, 39. Why we should hesitate to hold that federal citizenship implies rights to enter and abide in any state of the Union at least equal to those possessed by aliens passes my understanding. The world is even more upside down than I had supposed it to be, if California must accept aliens in deference to their federal privileges but is free to turn back citizens of the United States unless we treat them as subjects of commerce.

. . . .

It is here that we meet the real crux of this case. Does "indigence" as defined by the application of the California statute constitute a basis for restricting the freedom of a citizen, as crime or contagion warrants its restriction? We should say now, and in no uncertain terms, that a man's mere property status, without more, cannot be used by a state to test, qualify, or limit his rights as a citizen of the United States. "Indigence" in itself is neither a source of rights nor a basis for denying them. The mere state of being without funds is a neutral fact — constitutionally an irrelevance, like race, creed, or color.

I agree with what I understand to be the holding of the Court that cases which may indicate the contrary are overruled.

. . . .

If I doubted whether his federal citizenship alone were enough to open the gates of California to Duncan, my doubt would disappear on consideration of the obligations of such citizenship. Duncan owes a duty to render military service, and this Court has said that this duty is the result of his citizenship. A contention that a citizen's duty to render military service is suspended by "indigence" would meet with little favor. Rich or penniless, Duncan's citizenship under the Constitution pledges his strength to the defense of California as a part of the United States, and his right to migrate to any part of the land he must defend is something she must respect under the same instrument. Unless this Court is willing to say that citizenship of the United States means at least this much to the citizen, then our heritage of constitutional privileges and immunities is only a promise to the ear to be broken to the hope, a teasing illusion like a munificent bequest in a pauper's will.

NOTES AND QUESTIONS

1. Frank Duncan, in Edwards, is different from the defendants in Korematsu and Schmidt, in the sense that he does not appear to be subjected to a denial of citizenship in quite the same, categorical terms. However, freedom of movement is an essential quality of personhood and citizenship. As John Steinbeck wrote in the Grapes of Wrath, the plight of the dust bowl farmers during the 1930s was of such critical proportions that, to maintain their lives, it was essential for them to be able to move elsewhere to seek a living and home for themselves and their families. In *Edwards*, the very issue was whether the poor could be confined to a limited, inferior citizenship in the American community.
2. Earlier, in *City of New York v. Miln*, the Supreme Court had held that the City of New York could exclude immigrants, even American citizens, coming in on ships unless they could demonstrate the ability to support themselves. The Court had said that the State of New York could deal with poverty just as with any other plague or pestilence. *Edwards* declines to follow *Miln*. Subsequent to *Edwards*, in *Shapiro v. Thompson*, the Supreme Court invalidated the statutes of a number of states which provided that a new migrant could be denied welfare until he or she had lived within the state for at least a year. The Court cited the same considerations as in *Edwards*, saying that a person might move to a state to improve his or her living conditions and those of the family, whether the move was for better parks, schooling or welfare. Thus, *Edwards* stands at a critical juncture between *Miln* and *Shapiro*.
3. Does it matter whether the Court's rationale is based on the interstate commerce clause, as with Justice Byrnes' opinion; or on national citizenship and the privileges and immunities of the Fourteenth Amendment, as in Justice Jackson's opinion; or on the privileges and immunities clause reflected in Article IV, Section 2, discussed by Justice Douglas?

4. Is the California legislation in *Edwards*, making it a crime to bring in a poor person from elsewhere, an unethical treatment of citizens from elsewhere or, instead, an ethical protection of citizens within California? In other words, is it not fair for California as a community to define its obligations and benefits as extending only as far as its state borders?
5. As the vote for Proposition 187 in the California 1994 elections indicated, immigrants from elsewhere may pose a significant burden on the state resources, a burden which the citizens and taxpayers of that state may choose not to assume. Is such a choice, aimed in Proposition 187 against Hispanic immigrants illegally entering from Mexico, an ethical option for denying such essential public services as schooling, housing and food? Similar burdens have been imposed on the Miami area, as the Cuban immigration has radically changed the entire identity of the community. Might a community fight to preserve, not its services, but its identity? Did we not do that by ending importation of slaves in 1808 and directing future immigration towards whites?

PROBLEM 1-4 — Health Among the Homeless

The New England Journal of Medicine carried a special article,* the abstract of which read as follows:

Abstract

Background: Homelessness is believed to be a cause of health problems and high medical costs, but data supporting this association have been difficult to obtain. We compared lengths of stay and reasons for hospital admission among homeless and other low-income persons in New York City to estimate the hospitalization costs associated with homelessness.

Methods: We obtained hospital-discharge data on 18,864 admissions of homeless adults to New York City's public general hospitals (excluding admissions for childbirth) and 383,986 nonmaternity admissions of other low-income adults to all general hospitals in New York City during 1992 and 1993. The differences in length of stay were adjusted for diagnosis-related group, principal diagnosis, selected co-existing illnesses, and demographic characteristics.

Results: Of the admissions of homeless people, 51.5 percent were for treatment of substance abuse or mental illness, as compared with 22.8 percent for the other low-income patients, and another 19.7 percent of the admissions of homeless people were for trauma, respiratory diseases (excluding the acquired immunodeficiency syndrome [AIDS]), many of which are potentially preventable medical conditions. For the homeless, 80.6 percent of the admissions involved either a principal or secondary diagnosis of substance abuse or mental illness — roughly twice the rates for the other patients. The homeless patients stayed 4.1 days, or 36 percent, longer per admission on

* Salit et al., *Hospitalization Costs Associated with Homelessness in New York City*, 338 New Eng. J. Med. 1734-40 (1998).

average than the other patients, even after adjustments were made for differences in the rates of substance abuse and mental illness and other clinical and demographic characteristics. The costs of the additional days per discharge averaged $4,094 for psychiatric patients, $3,370 for patients with AIDS, and $2,414 for all types of patients.

Conclusions: Homelessness is associated with substantial excess costs per hospital stay in New York City. Decisions to fund housing and supportive services for the homeless should take into account the potential of these services to reduce the high costs of hospitalization in this population.

Two tables provided the following data on the illnesses of the homeless.

TABLE 2. DISCHARGES ACCORDING TO PRINCIPAL DIAGNOSIS.*

PRINCIPAL-DIAGNOSIS CATEGORY	HOMELESS PATIENTS (N=18,864)	PUBLIC-HOSPITAL PATIENTS (N=244,345)	PRIVATE-HOSPITAL PATIENTS (N=139,641)
	Percentage of discharges		
Substance Abuse	28.5	9.2	22.2
Mental Illness	23.0	9.2	5.0
Subtotal	51.5	18.4	27.2
	(N=9149)	**(N=199,427)**	**(N=101,646)**
Other†			
Respiratory system	17.2	12.4	13.3
AIDS	16.6	6.3	11.2
Trauma	12.9	12.9	5.4
Skin	8.4	4.0	3.7
Circulatory system	8.4	16.7	16.6
Digestive system	5.8	7.5	8.1
Nervous system	5.4	5.6	6.3
Endocrine or metabolic system	3.6	3.6	4.4
Kidney or urinary tract	3.2	4.7	5.3
Liver or pancreas	2.9	3.6	4.9
Musculoskeletal system	2.8	2.5	3.4
Female reproductive system	2.3	8.6	6.6
Infections or parasites	2.2	1.3	1.5
Ears, nose, and throat	2.2	2.1	1.6
Blood or immunologic system	1.3	1.4	2.5
Neoplasms	0.5	1.1	2.5
Other	4.3	5.7	2.7

Table 3. Discharges with Selected Coexisting Illnesses.

Variable	Homeless Patients (N = 18,864)	Public-Hospital Patients (N = 244,345)	Private-Hospital Patients (N = 139,641)
	Percentage of discharges		
Coexisting illness‡			
Substance abuse	42.9	18.7	16.1
Mental illness	7.4	3.2	2.3
AIDS	6.4	2.8	4.8
Principal or coexisting diagnosis			
Substance abuse	71.4	27.9	38.3
Mental illness	30.3	12.4	7.3
Substance abuse or mental illness	80.6	33.4	41.3
AIDS	14.5	8.0	12.9

*P<0.001 for the differences between the homeless patients and each of the other two groups.

†Discharges of patients with a principal diagnosis of any of these conditions have been excluded.

‡Discharges of patients with the condition present as a principal or co-existing diagnosis have been included.

What strategies should the greater community devise to cope with the additional costs imposed by the homeless upon the community's healthcare system? What obligations does the community have toward the homeless? Should the response be punitive? Preventive? Curative? Abandonment?

§ 1.03 Nonequals

The preceding section dealt with the question of *what* ethical obligations — if any — are owed by a community to those "outside" the "community," both concepts requiring definition. And so in the problem concerning "Operation Tailwind," one must ask what obligation America owed to combatant Vietnam and neutral Laos. But that case also raises the question of diminished obligations owed to those admittedly *within* the community including American deserters (killed on sight without a finding of guilt) and servicemen (ordered into a neutral country, to use poison gas, a double violation of international law). This duality often exists when a community acts towards a subject community.

Within the community, similarly, there have historically been unequal or subject groups. They may be defined by hostile conduct or tendencies, as with the poor, the homeless, prisoners or sexual predators. Or they may simply be less able to cope, as with those who are mentally ill or mentally incompetent. With the latter, we often assume an ethical obligation to act *for* them in a manner which may be patronizing or destructive; a recurring case in point historically has been the status of women. With hostile or criminal groups, we may impose the death penalty or life in prison (under newly fashionable "three strikes" legislation or "Megan's Laws"), and — having such power — neglect or abuse prisoners or even use them for experimental purposes.

In all of this, there are important bioethical issues: With the mentally ill or incompetent, who speaks for them? What can we do to or for them that we could not with a fully equal person? With hostile groups, may we banish them? Deny all — or most — rights in prison? Identify biologically grounded causes of their criminality and respond by castration or psychosurgery?

We begin with prisoners, proceed toward sexual predators, then consider the ethical obligations towards — and entitlements of — those deemed incompetent or mentally ill.

[1] Prisoners

[a] Privacy and Protection

The treatment of prisoners is a litmus test for the ethical sense of a community. The next several cases explore this area, leaving for separate treatment the problem of medical experimentation on those confined in prisons or institutions. As to that, see § 3.03[3]. The first issue — perhaps the most critical — is whether there is an obligation to protect prisoners — either their rights or their persons — while in prison. A different range of concerns is how far prisons may go in controlling prisoners, indeed invading their bodies or minds. We close with a consideration of the ethical right of society to "alter" prisoners by surgery.

BELL v. WOLFISH

441 U.S. 520 (1979)

Mr. Justice **Rehnquist** delivered the opinion of the Court.

Over the past five Terms, this Court has in several decisions considered constitutional challenges to prison conditions or practices by convicted prisoners. This case requires us to examine the constitutional rights of pretrial detainees — those persons who have been charged with a crime but who have not yet been tried on the charge. The parties concede that to ensure their presence at trial, these persons legitimately may be incarcerated by the Government prior to a determination of their guilt or innocence . . . and it is the scope of their rights during this period of confinement prior to trial that is the primary focus of this case.

. . . .

I

The MCC [Metropolitan Correctional Center] was constructed in 1975 to replace the converted waterfront garage on West Street that had served as New York City's federal jail since 1928. It is located adjacent to the Foley Square federal courthouse and has as its primary objective the housing of persons who are being detained in custody prior to trial for federal criminal offenses in the United States District Courts for the Southern and Eastern Districts of New York and for the District of New Jersey. . . .

The MCC differs markedly from the familiar image of a jail: there are no barred cells, dank, colorless corridors, or clanging steel gates. It was intended to include the most advanced and innovative features of modern design of detention facilities. . . .

. . . While the MCC was under construction the number of persons committed to pretrial detention began to rise at an "unprecedented" rate. The Bureau of Prisons took several steps to accommodate this unexpected flow of persons assigned to the facility, but despite these efforts, the inmate population at the MCC rose above its planned capacity within a short time after its opening. To provide sleeping space for this increased population, the MCC replaced the single bunks in many of the individual rooms and dormitories with double bunks. Also, each week some newly arrived inmates had to sleep on cots in the common areas until they could be transferred to residential rooms as space became available.

. . . .

II

As a first step in our decision, we shall address "double-bunking" as it is referred to by the parties, since it is a condition of confinement that is alleged only to deprive pretrial detainees of their liberty without due process of law in contravention of the Fifth Amendment. . . .

. . . .

B

In evaluating the constitutionality of conditions or restrictions of pretrial detention that implicate only the protection against deprivation of liberty without due process of law, we think that the proper inquiry is whether those conditions amount to punishment of the detainee. For under the Due Process Clause, a detainee may not be punished prior to an adjudication or guilt in accordance with due process of law. . . .

Not every disability imposed during pretrial detention amounts to "punishment" in the constitutional sense, however. Once the Government has exercised its conceded authority to detain a person pending trial, it obviously is entitled to employ devices that are calculated to effectuate this detention. . . . And the fact that such detention interferes with the detainee's understandable desire to live as comfortably as possible and with as little restraint as possible during confinement does not convert the conditions or restrictions of detention into "punishment."

. . . .

One further point requires discussion. The petitioners assert, and respondents concede, that the "essential objective of pretrial confinement is to insure the detainees' presence at trial." The Government also has legitimate interests that stem from its need to manage the facility in which the individual is detained. These legitimate operational concerns may require administrative measures that go beyond those that are, strictly speaking, necessary to ensure that the detainee shows up at trial. For example, the Government must be able to take steps to maintain security and order at the institution and make certain no weapons or illicit drugs reach detainees. Restraints that are reasonably related to the institution's interest in maintaining jail security do not, without more, constitute unconstitutional punishment, even if they are discomforting and are restrictions that the detainee would not have experienced had he been released while awaiting trial. . . .

C

Judged by this analysis, respondents' claim that "double-bunking" violated their due process rights fails. Neither the District Court nor the Court of Appeals intimated that it considered "double-bunking" to constitute punishment; instead, they found that it contravened the compelling-necessity test, which today we reject. On this record, we are convinced as a matter of law that "double-bunking" as practiced at the MCC did not amount to punishment and did not, therefore, violate respondents' rights under the Due Process Clause of the Fifth Amendment.

Each of the rooms at the MCC that house pretrial detainees has a total floor space of approximately 75 square feet. Each of them designated for "double-bunking," contains a double bunkbed, certain other items of furniture, a wash basin, and an uncovered toilet. Inmates generally are locked into their rooms from 11 p.m. to 6:30 a.m. and for brief periods during the afternoon and evening head counts. During the rest of the day, they may move about freely between their rooms and the common areas.

Based on affidavits and a personal visit to the facility, the District Court concluded that the practice of "double-bunking" was unconstitutional. The court relied on two factors for its conclusion: (1) the fact that the rooms were designed to house only one inmate and (2) its judgment that confining two persons in one room or cell of this size constituted a "fundamental denia[l] of decency, privacy, personal security, and, simply, civilized humanity . . . ."

We disagree with both the District Court and the Court of Appeals that there is some sort of "one man, one cell" principle lurking in the Due Process Clause of the Fifth Amendment. While confining a given number of people in a given amount of space in such a manner as to cause them to endure genuine privations and hardship over an extended period of time might raise serious questions under the Due Process Clause as to whether those conditions amounted to punishment, nothing even approaching such hardship is shown by this record.

. . . .

III

Respondents also challenged certain MCC restrictions and practices that were designed to promote security and order at the facility on the ground that these restrictions violated the Due Process Clause of the Fifth Amendment, and certain other constitutional guarantees, such as the First and Fourth Amendments. . . .

Our cases have established several general principles that inform our evaluation of the constitutionality of the restrictions at issue. First, we have held that convicted prisoners do not forfeit all constitutional protections by reason of their conviction and confinement in prison. . . . *A fortiori,* pretrial detainees, who have not been convicted of any crimes, retain at least those constitutional rights that we have held are enjoyed by convicted prisoners.

But our cases also have insisted on a second proposition: simply because prison inmates retain certain constitutional rights does not mean that these rights are not subject to restrictions and limitations. . . . This principle applies equally to pretrial detainees and convicted prisoners. A detainee simply does not possess the full range of freedoms of an unincarcerated individual.

Third, maintaining institutional security and preserving internal order and discipline are essential goals that may require limitation or retraction of the retained constitutional rights of both convicted prisoners and pretrial detainees. . . .

A

At the time of the lower courts' decisions, the Bureau of Prisons' "publisher-only" rule, which applies to all Bureau facilities, permitted inmates to receive books and magazines from outside the institution only if the materials were mailed directly from the publisher or a book club. The warden of the MCC stated in an affidavit that "serious" security and administrative problems were caused when bound items were received by inmates from unidentified sources outside the facility. He noted that in order to make a "proper and thorough" inspection of such items, prison officials would have to remove the covers of hardback books and to leaf through every page of all books and magazines to ensure that drugs, money, weapons, or other contraband were not secreted in the material. . . .

. . . .

Our conclusion that this limited restriction on receipt of hardback books does not infringe the First Amendment rights of MCC inmates is influenced by several other factors. The rule operates in a neutral fashion, without regard to the content of the expression. . . . To the limited extent the rule might possibly increase the cost of obtaining published materials, this Court has held that where "other avenues" remain available for the receipt of materials by inmates, the loss of "cost advantages does not fundamentally implicate free speech values." We are also influenced in our decision by the fact that the rule's impact on pretrial detainees is limited to a maximum period of approximately 60 days. . . .

B

Inmates at the MCC were not permitted to receive packages from outside the facility containing items of food or personal property, except for one package of food at Christmas. This rule was justified by MCC officials on three grounds. First, officials testified to "serious" security problems that arise from the introduction of such packages into the institution, the "traditional file in the cake kind of situation" as well as the concealment of drugs "in heels of shoes [and] seams of clothing." As in the case of the "publisher-only" rule, the warden testified that if such packages were allowed, the inspection process necessary to ensure the security of the institution would require a "substantial and inordinate amount of available staff time." Second, officials were concerned that the introduction of personal property into the facility would increase the risk of thefts, gambling, and inmate conflicts, the "age-old problem of you have it and I don't." Finally, they noted storage and sanitary problems that would result from inmates' receipt of food packages. . . .

We think that the District Court and the Court of Appeals have trenched too cavalierly into areas that are properly the concern of MCC officials. It is plain from their opinions that the lower courts simply disagreed with the judgment of MCC officials about the extent of the security interests affected and the means required to further those interests. But our decisions have time and again emphasized that this sort of unguided substitution of judicial judgment for that of the expert prison administrators on matters such as this is inappropriate. . . .

C

The MCC staff conducts unannounced searches of inmate living areas at irregular intervals. These searches generally are formal unit "shakedowns" during which all inmates are cleared of the residential units, and a team of guards searches each room. Prior to the District Court's order, inmates were not permitted to watch the searches. Officials testified that permitting inmates to observe room inspections would lead to friction between the inmates and security guards and would allow the inmates to attempt to frustrate the search by distracting personnel and moving contraband from one room to another ahead of the search team.

. . . .

It is difficult to see how the detainee's interest in privacy is infringed by the room-search rule. No one can rationally doubt that room searches represent an appropriate security measure and neither the District Court nor the Court of Appeals prohibited such searches. And even the most zealous advocate of prisoners' rights would not suggest that a warrant is required to conduct such a search. Detainees' drawers, beds, and personal items may be searched, even after the lower courts' rulings. Permitting detainees to observe the searches does not lessen the invasion of their privacy; its only conceivable beneficial effect would be to prevent theft or misuse by those conducting the search. The room-search rule simply facilitates the safe and effective performance of the search which all concede may be conducted. The rule itself, then, does not render the searches "unreasonable" within the meaning of the Fourth Amendment.

D

Inmates at all Bureau of Prison facilities, including the MCC, are required to expose their body cavities for visual inspection as a part of a strip search conducted after every contact visit with a person from outside the institution. Corrections officials testified that visual cavity searches were necessary not only to discover but also to deter the smuggling of weapons, drugs, and other contraband into the institution. . . .

Admittedly, this practice instinctively gives us the most pause. However, assuming for present purposes that inmates, both convicted prisoners and pretrial detainees, retain some Fourth Amendment rights upon commitment to a corrections facility we nonetheless conclude that these searches do not violate that Amendment. . . .

. . . A detention facility is a unique place fraught with serious security dangers. Smuggling of money, drugs, weapons, and other contraband is all too common an occurrence. And inmate attempts to secrete these items into the facility by concealing them in body cavities are documented in this record . . . That there has been only one instance where an MCC inmate was discovered attempting to smuggle contraband into the institution on his person may be more a testament to the effectiveness of this search technique as a deterrent than to any lack of interest on the part of the inmates to secrete and import such items when the opportunity arises.

We do not underestimate the degree to which these searches may invade the personal privacy of inmates. Nor do we doubt, as the District Court noted, that on occasion a security guard may conduct the search in an abusive fashion . . . . Such an abuse cannot be condoned. The searches must be conducted in a reasonable manner . . . . But we deal here with the question whether visual body-cavity inspections as contemplated by the MCC rules can ever be conducted on less than probable cause. Balancing the significant and legitimate security interests of the institution against the privacy interests of the inmates, we conclude that they can.

. . . .

V

There was a time not too long ago when the federal judiciary took a completely "hands-off" approach to the problem of prison administration. In recent years, however, these courts largely have discarded this "hands-off" attitude and have waded into this complex arena. The deplorable conditions and Draconian restrictions of some of our Nation's prisons are too well known to require recounting here, and the federal courts rightly have condemned these sordid aspects of our prison systems. But many of these same courts have, in the name of the Constitution, become increasingly enmeshed in the minutiae of prison operations. Judges, after all, are human. They, no less than others in our society, have a natural tendency to believe that their individual solutions to often intractable problems are better and more workable than those of the persons who are actually charged with and trained in the running of the particular institution under examination. But under the Constitution, the first question to be answered is not whose plan is best, but in what branch of the Government is lodged the authority to initially devise the plan. This does not mean that constitutional rights are not to be scrupulously observed. It does mean, however, that the inquiry of federal courts into prison management must be limited to the issue of whether a particular system violates any prohibition of the Constitution or, in the case of a federal prison, a statute. The wide range of "judgment calls" that meet constitutional and statutory requirements are confided to officials outside of the Judicial Branch of Government.

The judgment of the Court of Appeals is, accordingly, reversed, and the case is remanded for proceedings consistent with this opinion.

It is so ordered.

. . . .

NOTES AND QUESTIONS

1. At common law, conviction of a felony meant loss of many of the rights of citizenship, such as the right to vote. Indeed, in the 1600s, conviction of a felony was usually accompanied by the death penalty. It could also lead to loss of property or the imposition of penalties on the children of the felon. The United States Constitution prohibits cruel and unusual punishments and imposing penalties on anyone other than the felon, and also prohibits excessive fines or forfeitures.
2. Still, the American history of treatment of prisoners is a sorry one. In terms of bioethical concerns, human experimentation has been directed at prisoners in a number of notorious instances. Perhaps the most notorious and appalling was begun in the 1930s concerning syphilis with African-American prisoners in Tuskegee, Alabama, and continued into the early 1970s, long after a cure for syphilis had been developed and long after the Public Health Service had any legitimate reason for continuing the experimentation or denying treatment to prisoners long since released to the community. *See The Final Report of the Tuskegee Syphilis Study Ad Hoc Panel*, in Jonsen et al., Source Book in Bioethics, A Documentary History, (Georgetown Univ. Press 1998). In the 1930s and 1940s, similarly, human experimentation with prisoners in Indiana was of such gross proportions that it provided a defense for the Nazi doctors tried at Nuremburg for their "experiments" on concentration camp prisoners.
3. In *Bell v. Wolfish*, are the conditions at the Metropolitan Correctional Center consistent with the community's obligation toward those whom it has incarcerated and who hope, someday at least, to return to the community? The practice of double bunking and overcrowding, the practice of pre-trial detention, the practices of opening mail, conducting shakedowns and undertaking body cavity searches, are all serious intrusions upon physical and personal liberty and dignity. Is there a difference between personal liberty and personal dignity, at least in terms of what may be done to a prisoner? What showing must or should

be made before liberties are restricted? With a sufficiently compelling showing, is there no limit to what may be done to a prisoner?

4. What of the corollary, of the obligation *toward* prisoners? When the community restricts a person and undertakes custody of a person, what is the community's obligation to provide for that person's safety and welfare? Can it be said that a prisoner may forfeit the right to care and consideration, in the form of food, housing, education and marital or family association, or religious expression, if the person's conduct is sufficiently heinous, as with rape and murder?

5. The Supreme Court has addressed such questions in a range of cases, finding that certain minimum guarantees must be afforded prisoners. Among these are the right to practice one's religion, the right to present one's case in court and the right, consistent with prison discipline, to marry. By and large, however, prisoners' liberty and personal dignity may be regulated as needed by prison discipline. The limits of that regulation are the subject of *Peckham v. Wisconsin*, the next case.

PECKHAM v. WISCONSIN DEPARTMENT OF CORRECTIONS

141 F.3d 694 (7th Cir. 1998)

Before **Cudahy**, **Easterbrook**, and **Evans**, Circuit Judges.

Evans, Circuit Judge.

Here we have yet another case about prison strip searches. This one began when Jane Peckham filed a pro se complaint alleging that Wisconsin prison and jail officials subjected her to around 35 strip searches (we use the term "strip search" to refer to a visual inspection of a naked inmate without intrusion into the person's body cavities). . . .

Our case concerns events at the Taycheedah Correctional Institution and the Outagamie (Wisconsin) County Jail, which contracted with the State of Wisconsin to hold prisoners in order to alleviate overcrowding at state prisons. Peckham, who is serving time for a variety of offenses and has been in both facilities, sued the Wisconsin Department of Corrections and its chief administrative officers, along with the sheriff who oversees the county jail.

Guards at the Outagamie jail regularly conduct strip searches of prisoners in four situations: whenever a prisoner first arrives at the jail from another facility, whenever a prisoner returns to the jail from a visit with a doctor or from court, whenever a prisoner finishes a contact visit with a nonprisoner, and whenever prison officials undertake a general search of a cell block. Officers of the Wisconsin Department of Corrections, under the Wisconsin Administrative Code, conduct strip searches under similar circumstances and also whenever a prisoner moves into segregation or when time is tacked onto a prisoner's term in segregation (this additional time is known, in Corrections' lingo, as "adjustment time"). None of the searches about which Peckham complains occurred outside these general policy guidelines.

Peckham points out that many of the strip searches she endured occurred even though she never left the sight of her guard escorts and even though she often continuously wore handcuffs and leg irons. She explains that guards often searched her even though she did not have physical contact with other inmates or outsiders. Peckham notes that her "adjustment time" searches at Taycheedah took place even though she never left the segregation unit. In her only allegation regarding a specific search, Peckham says she was strip-searched (by a female guard) on one occasion when a male guard "was in the area."

According to Peckham, the strip searches caused psychological injury, increased tensions, and deterred her and other inmates from pursuing things like medical attention. When describing the damage caused by the searches, Peckham argues on behalf of all inmates, not just herself. She produced "expert" affidavits attesting to the deleterious effects of strip searches and to their ineffectiveness at detecting the presence of contraband, which is their main objective. In her complaint she made no claim that specific searches violated particular rights; instead, she broadly alleged that the "strip searches constituted a general infringement of the constitutional rights of plaintiff."

The defendants advanced several reasons why they were entitled to summary judgment: (1) the court must accord deference to prison officials in matters of prison security, (2) prison officials do not need probable cause to conduct strip searches, and (3) the strip search policies at Taycheedah and the jail are needed to prevent the entry of contraband into the facilities.

Judge Goodstein viewed Peckham's suit as an attack on the security and orderly operation of prisons. He characterized the complaint as "challenging the practices and policies relating to the use of strip searches." Examining the case under *Bell v. Wolfish*, the leading Supreme Court case on strip searches, the judge concluded:

> In each type of instance cited by plaintiff, considering the deferential treatment which prison officials are entitled to in matters affecting the security of the institutions they run, the legitimate interests of plaintiff in avoiding a strip search are outweighed by the needs of prison authorities to such an extent that no reasonable fact-finder could find in plaintiff's favor.

. . . .

Peckham's appeal presents an unspecified generalized claim that the strip searches in this case were unconstitutional. The magistrate judge's approach to the case, as urged by the parties, focused on the question of reasonableness — an indication that the case was considered under the Fourth Amendment. But if it is a Fourth Amendment case we are surprised the parties failed to cite, here or in the district court, the Supreme Court's decision in *Hudson v. Palmer*, 468 U.S. 517 (1984). . . .

In *Hudson* an inmate's cell was searched during a general "shakedown" at a Virginia correctional institution. The Court of Appeals for the Fourth Circuit had held that a prisoner had a "limited privacy right" in his cell, but the Supreme Court reversed, holding:

Notwithstanding our caution in approaching claims that the Fourth Amendment is inapplicable in a given context, we hold that society is not prepared to recognize as legitimate any subjective expectation of privacy that a prisoner might have in his prison cell and that, accordingly, the Fourth Amendment proscription against unreasonable searches does not apply within the confines of the prison cell. The recognition of privacy rights for prisoners in their individual cells simply cannot be reconciled with the concept of incarceration and the needs and objectives of penal institutions.

. . . .

So, does a prison inmate enjoy any protection at all under the Fourth Amendment against unreasonable searches and seizures? . . . [W]e think the answer is "yes," but we hasten to add that given the considerable deference prison officials enjoy to run their institutions it is difficult to conjure up too many real-life scenarios where prison strip searches of inmates could be said to be unreasonable under the Fourth Amendment. In that regard, we agree with Judge Goodstein that the searches, including those for medical visits about which Peckham complains, were not unreasonable. More importantly, regardless of how one views the Fourth Amendment in this context, it is the Eighth Amendment that is more properly posed to protect inmates from unconstitutional strip searches, notably when their aim is punishment, not legitimate institutional concerns. So how does Peckham's case stack up under the Eighth Amendment? Unfortunately for her, not too well. There is nothing alleged here which could lead a fact finder to conclude that any of the searches were for harassment purposes or any purposes that could reasonably be said to be punishment. The searches were for legitimate, identifiable purposes, and given the deference we accord to prison authorities to run their institutions, there is no way the Eighth Amendment, on these facts, could come to Peckham's defense.

. . . .

Affirmed.

Easterbrook, Circuit Judge, concurring in the judgment.

. . . .

". . . Guards take control of where and how prisoners live; they do not retain any right of seclusion or secrecy against their captors, who are entitled to watch and regulate every detail of daily life. After Wolfish and Hudson monitoring of naked prisoners is not only permissible — wardens are entitled to take precautions against drugs and weapons (which can be passed through the alimentary canal or hidden in the rectal cavity and collected from a toilet bowl) — but also sometimes mandatory. Interprisoner violence is endemic, so constant vigilance without regard to the state of the prisoners' dress is essential. Vigilance over showers, vigilance over cells — vigilance everywhere, which means that guards gaze upon naked inmates."

. . . .

A right of privacy in traditional Fourth Amendment terms is fundamentally incompatible with the close and continual surveillance of inmates and their cells required to ensure institutional security and internal order. We are satisfied that society would insist that the prisoner's expectation of privacy always yield to what must be considered the paramount interest in institutional society. We believe that it is accepted by our society that "loss of freedom of choice and privacy are inherent incidents of confinement."

. . . .

A principal reason why both *Hudson* and [*Johnson v. Phelan*, 69 F.3d 144 (7th Cir.)] held that claims of this kind must be analyzed under the eighth amendment is that the cruel and unusual punishments clause builds in deference to prison administrators through a combination of objective and subjective elements. If the only way to use the fourth amendment in strip-search cases is to make it functionally identical to the cruel and unusual punishments clause, then what's the point? Far better to leave the fourth amendment out of the analysis and avoid watering down the role of courts in specifying objective standards.

. . . .

NOTES AND QUESTIONS

1. What are the personal interests, essential to personhood, which are offended when a person is "strip-searched"? Aren't they all already lost by reason of confinement? If not, can it not be said that they were forfeited by conviction?
2. Is there a difference between *Hudson* (involving a cell "shakedown") and *Canedy v. Boardman*, 16 F.3d 183 (7th Cir. 1994) (men being strip-searched by female guards) on the one hand, and Peckham's case (involving visual observation of a nude body) on the other? And what of the difference between a "strip" search and a "body cavity" search?
3. Why does the Court view strip searches as better analyzed under the Eighth Amendment's cruel and unusual punishment clause, rather than the Fourth Amendment's ban on unreasonable searches?
4. Note that Judge Easterbrook disagrees with the majority, reading *Bell v. Wolfish* and the Constitution as simply barring protection of privacy for prisoners under the Fourth Amendment. Is he correct? And what of his point that the Fourth and Eighth should *not* be used as synonymous in this context?
5. This leads us to ultimate invasion and imposition upon a prisoner, through forcible rape by other prisoners. In the next case, *Farmer v. Brennan*, is it possible to distinguish between society's obligation to respect a prisoner's choice of gender and its obligation to protect him or her from abuse by others? And does it matter that the prisoner could avoid (or minimize) abuse by simply conforming?

FARMER v. BRENNAN
511 U.S. 825 (1994)

Justice **Souter** delivered the opinion of the Court.

. . . .

I

The dispute before us stems from a civil suit brought by petitioner, Dee Farmer, alleging that respondents, federal prison officials, violated the Eighth Amendment by their deliberate indifference to petitioner's safety. Petitioner, who is serving a federal sentence for credit card fraud, has been diagnosed by medical personnel of the Bureau of Prisons as a transsexual, one who has "[a] rare psychiatric disorder in which a person feels persistently uncomfortable about his or her anatomical sex," and who typically seeks medical treatment, including hormonal therapy and surgery, to bring about a permanent sex change. American Medical Association, Encyclopedia of Medicine 1006 (1989); see also American Psychiatric Association, Diagnostic and Statistical Manual of Mental Disorders 74-75 (3d rev. ed. 1987). For several years before being convicted and sentenced in 1986 at the age of 18, petitioner, who is biologically male, wore women's clothing (as petitioner did at the 1986 trial), underwent estrogen therapy, received silicone breast implants, and submitted to unsuccessful "black market" testicle-removal surgery. Petitioner's precise appearance in prison is unclear from the record before us, but petitioner claims to have continued hormonal treatment while incarcerated by using drugs smuggled into prison, and apparently wears clothing in a feminine manner, as by displaying a shirt "off one shoulder." The parties agree that petitioner "projects feminine characteristics."

. . . .

On March 9, 1989, petitioner was transferred for disciplinary reasons from the Federal Correctional Institute in Oxford, Wisconsin (FCI-Oxford), to the United States Penitentiary in Terre Haute, Indiana (USP-Terre Haute). Though the record before us is unclear about the security designations of the two prisons in 1989, penitentiaries are typically higher security facilities that house more troublesome prisoners than federal correctional institutes. After an initial stay in administrative segregation, petitioner was placed in the USP-Terre Haute general population. Petitioner voiced no objection to any prison official about the transfer to the penitentiary or to placement in its general population. Within two weeks, according to petitioner's allegations, petitioner was beaten and raped by another inmate in petitioner's cell. Several days later, after petitioner claims to have reported the incident, officials returned petitioner to segregation to await, according to respondents, a hearing about petitioner's HIV-positive status.

. . . As later amended, the complaint alleged that respondents either transferred petitioner to USP-Terre Haute or placed petitioner in its general population despite knowledge that the penitentiary had a violent environment and a history of inmate assaults, and despite knowledge that petitioner, as a transsexual who "projects feminine characteristics," would be particularly vulnerable to sexual attack by some USP-Terre Haute inmates. This allegedly amounted to a deliberately indifferent failure to protect petitioner's safety, and thus to a violation of petitioner's Eighth Amendment rights. Petitioner sought compensatory and punitive damages, and an injunction barring future confinement in any penitentiary, including USP-Terre Haute.

. . . .

II

A

The Constitution "does not mandate comfortable prisons," but neither does it permit inhumane ones, and it is now settled that "the treatment a prisoner receives in prison and the conditions under which he is confined are subject to scrutiny under the Eighth Amendment." In its prohibition of "cruel and unusual punishments," the Eighth Amendment places restraints on prison officials, who may not, for example, use excessive physical force against prisoners. The Amendment also imposes duties on these officials, who must provide humane conditions of confinement. Prison officials must ensure that inmates receive adequate food, clothing, shelter and medical care, and must "take reasonable measures to guarantee the safety of the inmates."

In particular, as the lower courts have uniformly held, and as we have assumed, "prison officials have a duty . . . to protect prisoners from violence at the hands of other prisoners." Having incarcerated "persons [with] demonstrated proclivities for antisocial criminal, and often violent, conduct." Having stripped them of virtually every means of self-protection and foreclosed their access to outside aid, the government and its officials are not free to let the state of nature take its course. Prison conditions may be "restrictive and even harsh," but gratuitously allowing the beating or rape of one prisoner by another serves no "legitimate penological objective," any more than it squares with " 'evolving standards of decency.' " Being violently assaulted in prison is simply not "part of the penalty that criminal offenders pay for their offenses against society."

It is not, however, every injury suffered by one prisoner at the hands of another that translates into constitutional liability for prison officials responsible for the victim's safety. Our cases have held that a prison official violates the Eighth Amendment only when two requirements are met. First, the deprivation alleged must be, objectively, "sufficiently serious;" a prison official's act or omission must result in the denial of "the minimal civilized measure of life's necessities." For a claim (like the one here) based on a failure to prevent harm, the inmate must show that he is incarcerated under conditions posing a substantial risk of serious harm.

The second requirement follows from the principle that "only the unnecessary and wanton infliction of pain implicates the Eighth Amendment." To violate the Cruel and Unusual Punishments Clause, a prison official must have a "sufficiently culpable state of mind." In prison-conditions cases that state of mind is one of "deliberate indifference" to inmate health or safety, a standard the parties agree governs the claim in this case. The parties disagree, however, on the proper test for deliberate indifference, which we must therefore undertake to define.

B

1.

Although we have never paused to explain the meaning of the term "deliberate indifference," the case law is instructive. The term first appeared in the United States Reports in *Estelle v. Gamble* and its use there shows that deliberate indifference describes a state of mind more blameworthy than negligence. In considering the inmate's claim in Estelle that inadequate prison medical care violated the Cruel and Unusual Punishments Clause, we distinguished "deliberate indifference to serious medical needs of prisoners," from "negligence in diagnosing or treating a medical condition," holding that only the former violates the Clause. We have since read Estelle for the proposition that Eighth Amendment liability requires "more than ordinary lack of due care for the prisoner's interests or safety." *Whitley v. Albers*, 475 U.S. 312, 319 (1986).

While *Estelle* establishes that deliberate indifference entails something more than mere negligence, the cases are also clear that it is satisfied by something less than acts or omissions for the very purpose of causing harm or with knowledge that harm will result. . . .

. . . .

That does not, however, fully answer the pending question about the level of culpability deliberate indifference entails, for the term recklessness is not self-defining. The civil law generally calls a person reckless who acts or (if the person has a duty to act) fails to act in the face of an unjustifiably high risk of harm that is either known or so obvious that it should be known. The criminal law, however, generally permits a finding of recklessness only when a person disregards a risk of harm of which he is aware. The standards proposed by the parties in this case track the two approaches (though the parties do not put it that way): petitioner asks us to define deliberate indifference as what we have called civil-law recklessness, and respondents urge us to adopt an approach consistent with recklessness in the criminal law.

We reject petitioner's invitation to adopt an objective test for deliberate indifference. We hold instead that a prison official cannot be found liable under the Eighth Amendment for denying an inmate humane conditions of confinement unless the official knows of and disregards an excessive risk to inmate health or safety; the official must both be aware of facts from which the inference could be drawn that a substantial risk of serious harm exists, and he must also draw the inference. This approach comports best with the text of the Amendment as our cases have interpreted it. The Eighth Amendment does not outlaw cruel and unusual "conditions;" it outlaws cruel and unusual "punishments." . . .

. . . .

We are no[t] persuaded by petitioner's argument that, without an objective test for deliberate indifference, prison officials will be free to ignore obvious dangers to inmates. Under the test we adopt today, an Eighth Amendment claimant need not show that a prison official acted or failed to act believing that harm actually would befall an inmate; it is enough that the official acted or failed to act despite his knowledge of a substantial risk of serious harm. . . .

Nor may a prison official escape liability for deliberate indifference by showing that, while he was aware of an obvious, substantial risk to inmate safety, he did not know that the complainant was especially likely to be assaulted by the specific prisoner who eventually committed the assault. The question under the Eighth Amendment is whether prison officials, acting with deliberate indifference, exposed a prisoner to a sufficiently substantial "risk of serious damage to his future health," and it does not matter whether the risk comes from a single source or multiple sources, any more than it matters whether a prisoner faces an excessive risk of attack for reasons personal to him or because all prisoners in his situation face such a risk. If, for example, prison officials were aware that inmate "rape was so common and uncontrolled that some potential victims dared not sleep [but] instead . . . would leave their beds and spend the night clinging to the bars nearest the guards' station," *Hutto v. Finney*, 437 U.S., 678, 681-682 n. 3, (1978), it would obviously be irrelevant to liability that the officials could not guess beforehand precisely who would attack whom. . . .

. . . .

IV

The judgment of the Court of Appeals is vacated, and the case is remanded for further proceedings consistent with this opinion.

Justice **Blackmun**, concurring.

I agree with Justice Stevens that inhumane prison conditions violate the Eighth Amendment even if no prison official has an improper, subjective state of mind. This Court's holding in *Wilson v. Seiter*, 501 U.S. 294 (1991), to the effect that barbaric prison conditions may be beyond the reach of the Eighth Amendment if no prison official can be deemed individually culpable, in my view is insupportable in principle and is inconsistent with our precedents interpreting the Cruel and Unusual Punishments Clause. Whether the Constitution has been violated "should turn on the character of the punishment rather than the motivation of the individual who inflicted it." *Wilson v. Seiter* should be overruled.

I

Petitioner is a transsexual who is currently serving a 20-year sentence in an all-male federal prison for credit-card fraud. Although a biological male, petitioner has undergone treatment for silicone breast implants and unsuccessful surgery to have his testicles removed. Despite his overtly feminine characteristics, and his previous segregation at a different federal prison because of safety concerns, prison officials at the United States Penitentiary in Terre Haute, Indiana, housed him in the general population of that maximum-security prison. Less than two weeks later, petitioner was brutally beaten and raped by another inmate in petitioner's cell.

. . . The horrors experienced by many young inmates, particularly those who, like petitioner, are convicted of nonviolent offenses, border on the unimaginable. Prison rape not only threatens the lives of those who fall prey to their aggressors, but is potentially devastating to the human spirit. Shame, depression, and a shattering loss of self-esteem, accompany the perpetual terror the victim thereafter must endure. See *Note, Rape in Prison and AIDS: A Challenge for the Eighth Amendment Framework of* Wilson v. Seiter, 44 Stan. L. Rev. 1541, 1545 (1992). Unable to fend for himself without the protection of prison officials, the victim finds himself at the mercy of larger, stronger, and ruthless inmates. Although formally sentenced to a term of incarceration, many inmates discover that their punishment, even for nonviolent offenses like credit-card fraud or tax evasion, degenerates into a reign of terror unmitigated by the protection supposedly afforded by prison officials.

The fact that our prisons are badly overcrowded and understaffed may well explain many of the shortcomings of our penal systems. But our Constitution sets minimal standards governing the administration of punishment in this country, and thus it is no answer to the complaints of the brutalized inmate that the resources are unavailable to protect him from what, in reality, is nothing less than torture. . . .

. . . .

. . . Where a legislature refuses to fund a prison adequately, the resulting barbaric conditions should not be immune from constitutional scrutiny simply because no prison official acted culpably. The responsibility for subminimal conditions in any prison inevitably is diffuse, and often borne, at least in part, by the legislature. Yet, regardless of what state actor or institution caused the harm and with what intent, the experience of the inmate is the same. A punishment is simply no less cruel or unusual because its harm is unintended. . . .

. . . The Cruel and Unusual Punishments Clause was not adopted to protect prison officials with arguably benign intentions from lawsuits. The Eighth Amendment guarantees each prisoner that reasonable measures will be taken to ensure his safety. Where a prisoner can prove that no such reasonable steps were taken and, as a result, he experienced severe pain or suffering without any penological justification, the Eighth Amendment is violated regardless of whether there is an easily identifiable wrongdoer with poor intentions.

. . . .

NOTES AND QUESTIONS

1. Prisoners are held in conditions and facilities which deny most of the normal rights and much of the conventional dignity we all take for granted. Mobility, association, expression, privacy, all are lost. The present case, *Farmer v. Brennan*, deals with the incidental brutalizing of

prisoners, specifically by male/male rape, thereby posing the question of whether society has an obligation to guard against such brutalization. If so, how much?

2. The case here is about liability, with the majority and Justice Blackmun disagreeing about the standard. Justice Souter says it should be "deliberate indifference," meaning something more than the standard civil law definition when the issue concerns prison conditions, as opposed to an act or omission. Justice Blackmun disagrees, saying the Eighth Amendment guarantees that reasonable steps will be taken to assure safety. Which view is more persuasive?
3. Are there limits to the extent to which Mr. Farmer may create/impose obligations on prison officials? What rights can prison officals deny? Religious observances? Reading? Marital relations? Extramarital relations? Could a prison, for example, flatly prohibit the marriage of Carla Faye Tucker — executed in 1998 by Texas, the first woman to receive that penalty in 100 years — to the prison Chaplain, Dana Brown?
4. Mr. Farmer dresses, even in prison, "in a feminine manner." Does he have a right to do so? If he knows it will provoke assaultive responses, why does he do it? Does he have a right to protection against the very attacks he "invites"?
5. For an excellent article, see Sharon I. Fiedler, *Past Wrongs, Present Futility, and the Future of Prisoner Relief: A Reasonable Interpretation of "Available" in ihe Context of the PLRA*, 33 U.C. Davis L. Rev. 713 U.C (2000); and see Nicholas P. Miller, *Prisoner Claims for Religious Freedom and State RFRAS*, 32 U.C. Davis L. Rev. 573 (1999).

PROBLEM 1-5 — Hormone Therapy in Prison

In January of 1988, the Portland *Oregonian* reported the arrest of Anny May Stevens for the stabbing death of Robert I. Dove. Stevens, the article reported, "is a man but has said she takes female hormones and wants to be known as a woman." A spokeswoman for the state Department of Corrections said Anny would go to the state penitentiary and be kept in a single cell. "We consider them male if there is any male genitalia," she said. The state will not pay for hormone treatment or surgery. Comment, in light of *Bell v. Wolfish*, *Farmer v. Brennan*, the succeeding cases, and the cases on *Gender and Choice, infra*, § 2.02[2], on whether Anny May is entitled to hormone therapy.

[b] Health and Well-being

The preceding cases dealt with privacy of prisoners and the protection they must be accorded. This next section goes farther, considering the extent to which a prisoner's mind or body may be invaded or neglected as a matter of control, or simple neglect.

WASHINGTON v. HARPER

494 U.S. 210 (1990)

Justice **Kennedy** delivered the opinion of the Court.

The central question before us is whether a judicial hearing is required before the State may treat a mentally ill prisoner with antipsychotic drugs against his will. Resolution of the case requires us to discuss the protections afforded the prisoner under the Due Process Clause of the Fourteenth Amendment.

I

Respondent Walter Harper was sentenced to prison in 1976 for robbery. From 1976 to 1980, he was incarcerated at the Washington State Penitentiary. Most of that time, respondent was housed in the prison's mental health unit, where he consented to the administration of antipsychotic drugs. Antipsychotic drugs, sometimes called "neuroleptics" or "psychotropic drugs," are medications commonly used in treating mental disorders such as schizophrenia. As found by the trial court, the effect of these and similar drugs is to alter the chemical balance in the brain, the desired result being that the medication will assist the patient in organizing his or her thought processes and regaining a rational state of mind.[1]

Respondent was paroled in 1980 on the condition that he participate in psychiatric treatment. While on parole, he continued to receive treatment at the psychiatric ward at Harborview Medical Center in Seattle, Washington, and was later sent to Western State Hospital pursuant to a civil commitment order. In December 1981, the State revoked respondent's parole after he assaulted two nurses at a hospital in Seattle.

Upon his return to prison, respondent was sent to the Special Offender Center (SOC or Center), a 144-bed correctional institute established by the Washington Department of Corrections to diagnose and treat convicted felons with serious mental disorders. At the Center, psychiatrists first diagnosed respondent as suffering from a manic-depressive disorder. At first, respondent gave voluntary consent to treatment, including the administration of antipsychotic medications. In November 1982, he refused to continue taking the prescribed medications. The treating physician then sought to medicate respondent over his objections, pursuant to SOC Policy 600.30.

Policy 600.30 was developed in partial response to this Court's decision in Vitek v. Jones. The Policy has several substantive and procedural components. First, if a psychiatrist determines that an inmate should be treated with antipsychotic drugs but the inmate does not consent, the inmate may be subjected to involuntary treatment with the drugs only if he (1) suffers from a "mental disorder" and (2) is "gravely disabled" or poses a "likelihood of serious harm" to himself, others, or their property.[2] Only a psychiatrist may

---

[1] The drugs administrated to respondent included Trialafon, Haldol, Prolixin, Taractan, Loxitane, Mellaril, and Navane. Like the Washington Supreme Court, we limit our holding to the category of antipsychotic drugs.

[2] The Policy's definitions of the terms "mental disorder," "gravely disabled," and "likelihood of

order or approve the medication. Second, an inmate who refuses to take the medication voluntarily is entitled to a hearing before a special committee consisting of a psychiatrist, a psychologist, and the Associate Superintendent of the Center, none of whom may be, at the time of the hearing, involved in the inmate's treatment or diagnosis. If the committee determines by a majority vote that the inmate suffers from a mental disorder and is gravely disabled or dangerous, the inmate may be medicated against his will, provided the psychiatrist is in the majority.

Third, the inmate has certain procedural rights before, during, and after the hearing. He must be given at least 24 hours' notice of the Center's intent to convene an involuntary medication hearing, during which time he may not be medicated. In addition, he must receive notice of the tentative diagnosis, the factual basis for the diagnosis, and why the staff believes medication is necessary. At the hearing, the inmate has the right to attend; to present evidence, including witnesses; to cross-examine staff witnesses; and to the assistance of a lay adviser who has not been involved in his case and who understands the psychiatric issues involved. Minutes of the hearing must be kept, and a copy provided to the inmate. The inmate has the right to appeal the committee's decision to the Superintendent of the Center within 24 hours, and the Superintendent must decide the appeal within 24 hours after its receipt. The inmate may seek judicial review of a committee decision in state court by means of a personal restraint petition or extraordinary writ.

Fourth, after the initial hearing, involuntary medication can continue only with periodic review. When respondent first refused medication, a committee, again composed of a nontreating psychiatrist, a psychologist, and the Center's Associate Superintendent, was required to review an inmate's case after the first seven days of treatment. If the committee reapproved the treatment, the treating psychiatrist was required to review the case and prepare a report for the Department of Corrections medical director every 14 days while treatment continued.

In this case, respondent was absent when members of the Center staff met with the committee before the hearing. The committee then conducted the hearing in accordance with the Policy, with respondent being present and assisted by a nurse practitioner from another institution. The committee found that respondent was a danger to others as a result of a mental disease or

---

serious harm" are identical to the definitions of the terms as they are used in the state involuntary commitment statute. "Mental disorder" means "any organic, mental, or emotional impairment which has substantial adverse effects on an individual's cognitive or volitional functions." "Gravely disabled" means "a condition in which a person, as a result of a mental disorder: (a) [i]s in danger of serious physical harm resulting from a failure to provide for his essential human needs of health or safety, or (b) manifests severe deterioration in routine functioning evidenced by repeated and escalating loss of cognitive or volitional control over his or her actions and is not receiving such care as is essential for his or her health or safety." "Likelihood of serious harm" means "either (a) [a] substantial risk that physical harm will be inflicted by an individual upon his own person, as evidenced by threats or attempts to commit suicide or inflict physical harm on one's self, (b) a substantial risk that physical harm will be inflicted by an individual upon another, as evidenced by behavior which has caused such harm or which places another person or persons in reasonable fear of sustaining such harm, or (c) a substantial risk that physical harm will be inflicted by an individual upon the property of others, as evidenced by behavior which has caused substantial loss or damage to the property of others."

disorder, and approved the involuntary administration of antipsychotic drugs. On appeal, the Superintendent upheld the committee's findings. Beginning on November 23, 1982, respondent was involuntarily medicated for about one year. Periodic review occurred in accordance with the Policy.

In November 1983, respondent was transferred from the Center to the Washington State Reformatory. While there, he took no medication, and as a result, his condition deteriorated. He was retransferred to the Center after only one month. Respondent was the subject of another committee hearing in accordance with Policy 600.30, and the committee again approved medication against his will. Respondent continued to receive antipsychotic drugs, subject to the required periodic reviews, until he was transferred to the Washington State Penitentiary in June 1986.

. . . .

III

The Washington Supreme Court gave its primary attention to the procedural component of the Due Process Clause. It phrased the issue before it as whether "a prisoner [is] entitled to a judicial hearing before antipsychotic drugs can be administered against his will." The court, however, did more than establish judicial procedures for making the factual determinations called for by Policy 600.30. It required that a different set of determinations than those set forth in the Policy be made as a precondition to medication without the inmate's consent. Instead of having to prove, pursuant to the Policy, only that the mentally ill inmate is "gravely disabled" or that he presents a "serious likelihood of harm" to himself or others, the court required the State to prove that it has a compelling interest in administering the medication and that the administration of the drugs is necessary and effective to further that interest. The decision maker was required further to consider and make written findings regarding either the inmate's desires or a "substituted judgment" for the inmate analogous to the medical treatment decision for an incompetent person.

. . . .

Restated in the terms of this case, the substantive issue is what factual circumstances must exist before the State may administer antipsychotic drugs to the prisoner against his will; the procedural issue is whether the State's nonjudicial mechanisms used to determine the facts in a particular case are sufficient. The Washington Supreme Court in effect ruled upon the substance of the inmate's right, as well as the procedural guarantees, and both are encompassed by our grant of certiorari. We address these questions beginning with the substantive one.

. . . .

We have no doubt that, in addition to the liberty interest created by the State's Policy, respondent possesses a significant liberty interest in avoiding the unwanted administration of antipsychotic drugs under the Due Process Clause of the Fourteenth Amendment. Upon full consideration of the state administrative scheme, however, we find that the Due Process Clause confers upon respondent no greater right than that recognized under state law.

Respondent contends that the State, under the mandate of the Due Process Clause, may not override his choice to refuse antipsychotic drugs unless he has been found to be incompetent, and then only if the factfinder makes a substituted judgment that he, if competent, would consent to drug treatment. We disagree. The extent of a prisoner's right under the Clause to avoid the unwanted administration of antipsychotic drugs must be defined in the context of the inmate's confinement. The Policy under review requires the State to establish, by a medical finding, that a mental disorder exists which is likely to cause harm if not treated. Moreover, the fact that the medication must first be prescribed by a psychiatrist, and then approved by a reviewing psychiatrist, ensures that the treatment in question will be ordered only if it is in the prisoner's medical interests, given the legitimate needs of his institutional confinement. These standards, which recognize both the prisoner's medical interests and the State's interests, meet the demands of the Due Process Clause.

The legitimacy, and the necessity, of considering the State's interests in prison safety and security are well established by our cases. In *Turner v. Safley*, we held that the proper standard for determining the validity of a prison regulation claimed to infringe on an inmate's constitutional rights is to ask whether the regulation is "reasonably related to legitimate penological interests." This is true even when the constitutional right claimed to have been infringed is fundamental, and the State under other circumstances would have been required to satisfy a more rigorous standard of review. . . .

. . . .

Applying these factors to the regulation before us, we conclude that the Policy comports with constitutional requirements. There can be little doubt as to both the legitimacy and the importance of the governmental interest presented here . . . . Where an inmate's mental disability is the root cause of the threat he poses to the inmate population, the State's interest in decreasing the danger to others necessarily encompasses an interest in providing him with medical treatment for his illness.

Special Offender Center Policy 600.30 is a rational means of furthering the State's legitimate objectives. Its exclusive application is to inmates who are mentally ill and who, as result of their illness, are gravely disabled or represent a significant danger to themselves or others. The drugs may be administered for no purpose other than treatment, and only under the direction of a licensed psychiatrist. There is considerable debate over the potential side effects of antipsychotic medications, but there is little dispute in the psychiatric profession that proper use of the drugs is one of the most effective means of treating and controlling a mental illness likely to cause violent behavior.

The alternative means proffered by respondent for accommodating his interest in rejecting the forced administration of antipsychotic drugs do not demonstrate the invalidity of the State's policy . . . . The suggested rule takes no account of the legitimate governmental interest in treating him where medically appropriate for the purpose of reducing the danger he poses . . . . Nor are physical restraints or seclusion "alternative[s] that fully accommodat[e] the prisoner's rights at de minimis cost to valid penological interests."

Physical restraints are effective only in the short term, and can have serious physical side effects when used on a resisting inmate, as well as leaving the staff at risk of injury while putting the restraints on or tending to the inmate who is in them. Furthermore, respondent has failed to demonstrate that physical restraints or seclusion are acceptable substitutes for antipsychotic drugs, in terms of either their medical effectiveness or their toll on limited prison resources.

. . . .

IV

. . . The Washington Supreme Court held that a full judicial hearing, with the inmate being represented by counsel, was required by the Due Process Clause before the State could administer antipsychotic drugs to him against his will. In addition, the court held that the State must justify the authorization of involuntary administration of antipsychotic drugs by "clear, cogent, and convincing" evidence. We hold that the administrative hearing procedures set by the SOC Policy do comport with procedural due process, and conclude that the Washington Supreme Court erred in requiring a judicial hearing as a prerequisite for the involuntary treatment of prison inmates.

A

The primary point of disagreement between the parties is whether due process requires a judicial decision maker. As written, the Policy requires that the decision whether to medicate an inmate against his will be made by a hearing committee composed of a psychiatrist, a psychologist, and the Center's Associate Superintendent. None of the committee members may be involved, at the time of the hearing, in the inmate's treatment or diagnosis; members are not disqualified from sitting on the committee, however, if they have treated or diagnosed the inmate in the past. The committee's decision is subject to review by the Superintendent; if the inmate so desires, he may seek judicial review of the decision in a state court. Respondent contends that only a court should make the decision to medicate an inmate against his will.

. . . .

Notwithstanding the risks that are involved, we conclude that an inmate's interests are adequately protected, and perhaps better served, by allowing the decision to medicate to be made by medical professionals rather than a judge. The Due Process Clause "has never been thought to require that the neutral and detached trier of fact be law trained or a judicial or administrative officer." Though it cannot be doubted that the decision to medicate has societal and legal implications, the Constitution does not prohibit the State from permitting medical personnel to make the decision under fair procedural mechanisms. Particularly where the patient is mentally disturbed, his own intentions will be difficult to assess and will be changeable in any event. Respondent's own history of accepting and then refusing drug treatment illustrates the point. We cannot make the facile assumption that the patient's intentions, or a substituted judgment approximating those intentions, can be determined in a single judicial hearing apart from the realities of frequent and ongoing clinical observation by medical professionals. . . . Nor can we ignore the fact that requiring judicial hearings will divert scarce prison resources, both money and the staff's time, from the care and treatment of mentally ill inmates.

. . . .

. . . Adequate procedures exist here. In particular, independence of the decision maker is addressed to our satisfaction by these procedures. None of the hearing committee members may be involved in the inmate's current treatment or diagnosis. The record before us, moreover, is limited to the hearings given to respondent. There is no indication that any institutional biases affected or altered the decision to medicate respondent against his will. The trial court made specific findings that respondent has a history of assaultive behavior which his doctors attribute to his mental disease, and that all of the Policy's requirements were met. The court found also that the medical treatment provided to respondent, including the administration of antipsychotic drugs, was at all times consistent "with the degree of care, skill, and learning expected of a reasonably prudent psychiatrist in the State of Washington, acting in the same or similar circumstances." In the absence of record evidence to the contrary, we are not willing to presume that members of the staff lack the necessary independence to provide an inmate with a full and fair hearing in accordance with the Policy. . . .

. . . .

Justice **Stevens**, with whom Justice **Brennan** and Justice **Marshall** join, concurring in part and dissenting in part.

I

. . . .

The record of one of Walter Harper's involuntary medication hearings at the Special Offense Center (SOC) notes: "Inmate Harper stated he would rather die th[a]n take medication." That Harper would be so opposed to taking psychotropic drugs is not surprising: as the Court acknowledges, these drugs both "alter the chemical balance in a patient's brain" and can cause irreversible and fatal side effects. The prolixin injections that Harper was receiving at the time of his statement exemplify the intrusiveness of psychotropic drugs on a person's body and mind. Prolixin acts "at all levels of the central nervous system as well as on multiple organ systems."[3] It can induce catatonic-like states, alter electroencephalographic tracings, and cause swelling of the brain. Adverse reactions include drowsiness, excitement, restlessness, bizarre dreams, hypertension, nausea, vomiting, loss of appetite, salivation, dry mouth, perspiration, headache, constipation, blurred vision, impotency, eczema, jaundice, tremors, and muscle spasms. As with all psychotropic drugs, prolixin may cause tardive dyskinesia, an often irreversible syndrome of uncontrollable movements that can prevent a person from exercising basic functions such

[3] Physician's Desk Reference 1639 (43d ed. 1989).

as driving an automobile, and neuroleptic malignant syndrome, which is 30% fatal for those who suffer from it. The risk of side effects increases over time.[4]

The Washington Supreme Court properly equated the intrusiveness of this mind altering drug treatment with electroconvulsive therapy or psychosurgery. It agreed with the Supreme Judicial Court of Massachusetts' determination that the drugs have a "profound effect" on a person's "thought processes" and "well-established likelihood of severe and irreversible adverse side effects," and that they therefore should be treated "in the same manner we would treat psychosurgery or electroconvulsive therapy." There is no doubt, as the State Supreme Court and other courts that have analyzed the issue have concluded, that a competent individual's right to refuse such medication is a fundamental liberty interest deserving the highest order of protection.

II

Arguably, any of three quite different state interests might be advanced to justify a deprivation of this liberty interest. The State might seek to compel Harper to submit to a mind altering drug treatment program as punishment for the crime he committed in 1976, as a "cure" for his mental illness, or as a mechanism to maintain order in the prison. The Court today recognizes Harper's liberty interest only as against the first justification.

Forced administration of antipsychotic medication may not be used as a form of punishment. . . .

Policy 600.30 permits forced administration of psychotropic drugs on a mentally ill inmate based purely on the impact that his disorder has on the security of the prison environment. The provisions of the Policy make no reference to any expected benefit to the inmate's medical condition . . . . Thus, the Policy authorizes long-term involuntary medication not only of any mentally ill inmate who, as a result of a mental disorder, appears to present a future risk to himself, but also of an inmate who presents a future risk to other people or mere property.

Although any application of Policy 600.30 requires a medical judgment as to a prisoner's mental condition and the cause of his behavior, the Policy does not require a determination that forced medication would advance his medical interest. Use of psychotropic drugs, the State readily admits, serves to ease the institutional and administrative burdens of maintaining prison security and provides a means of managing an unruly prison population and preventing property damage. By focusing on the risk that the inmate's mental condition poses to other people and property, the Policy allows the State to exercise either parens patriae authority or police authority to override a prisoner's liberty interest in refusing psychotropic drugs. Thus, most unfortunately, there is simply no basis for the Court's assertion that medication under the Policy must be to advance the prisoner's medical interest.

---

[4] Physician's Desk Reference, *supra*, at 1639. Harper voluntarily took psychotropic drugs for six years before involuntary medication began in 1982, by which time he had already exhibited dystonia (acute muscle spasms) and akathesia (physical-emotional agitation). Although avoidance of akathesia and the risk of tardive dyskinesia require reduction or discontinuance of psychotropics, Harper's involuntary medication was continuous from November 1982 to June 1986, except for one month spent at Washington State Reformatory.

. . . .

III

The procedures of Policy 600.30 are also constitutionally deficient. Whether or not the State ever may order involuntary administration of psychotropic drugs to a mentally ill person who has been committed to its custody but has not been declared incompetent, it is at least clear that any decision approving such drugs must be made by an impartial professional concerned not with institutional interests, but only with the individual's best interests. The critical defect in Policy 600.30 is the failure to have the treatment decision made or reviewed by an impartial person or tribunal.[5]

. . . .

These decision makers have two disqualifying conflicts of interest. First, the panel members must review the work of treating physicians who are their colleagues and who, in turn, regularly review their decisions. Such an in-house system pits the interests of an inmate who objects to forced medication against the judgment not only of his doctor, but often his doctor's colleagues. Furthermore, the Court's conclusion that "[n]one of the hearing committee members may be involved in the inmate's current treatment or diagnosis," overlooks the fact that Policy 600.30 allows a treating psychiatrist to participate in all but the initial *7-day* medication approval. This revolving door operated in Harper's case. Dr. Petrich treated Harper through 1982 and recommended involuntary medication on October 27, 1982. Dr. Loeken, staff psychologist Giles, and Assistant Superintendent Stark authorized medication for seven days after a 600.30 hearing on November 23, 1982. Dr. Petrich then replaced Dr. Loeken on the committee, and with Giles and Stark approved long-term involuntary medication on December 8, 1982. Solely under this authority, Dr. Petrich prescribed more psychotropic medication for Harper on December 8, 1982, and throughout the following year.

Second, the panel members, as regular staff of the Center, must be concerned not only with the inmate's best medical interests, but also with the most convenient means of controlling the mentally disturbed inmate. The mere fact that a decision is made by a doctor does not make it "certain that professional judgment in fact was exercised." The structure of the SOC committee virtually insures that it will not be. While the initial inquiry into the mental bases for an inmate's behavior is medical, the ultimate medication decision under Policy 600.30 turns on an assessment of the risk that an inmate's condition imposes on the institution. . . .

. . . For example, Dr. Petrich added Taractan, a psychotropic drug, to Harper's medication around October 27, 1982, noting: "The goal of the increased medication to sedate him at night and relieve the residents and

[5] It is not necessary to reach the question whether the decision to force psychotropic drugs on a competent person against his will must be approved by a judge, or by an administrative tribunal of professionals who are not members of the prison staff, in order to conclude that the mechanism of Policy 600.30 violates procedural due process. The choice is not between medical experts on the one hand and judges on the other; the choice is between decision makers who are biased and those who are not.

evening [sic] alike of the burden of supervising him as intensely." A 1983 examination by non-SOC physicians also indicated that Harper was prophylactically medicated absent symptoms that would qualify him for involuntary medication.

The institutional bias that is inherent in the identity of the decision makers is unchecked by other aspects of Policy 600.30. The committee need not consider whether less intrusive procedures would be effective, or even if the prescribed medication would be beneficial to the prisoner, before approving involuntary medication. Findings regarding the severity or the probability of potential side effects of drugs and dosages are not required. And, although the Policy does not prescribe a standard of proof necessary for any factual determination upon which a medication decision rests, the Court gratuitously advises that the "clear, cogent, and convincing" standard adopted by the State Supreme Court would be unnecessary.

. . . .

In sum, it is difficult to imagine how a committee convened under Policy 660.30 could conceivably discover, much less be persuaded to overrule, an erroneous or arbitrary decision to medicate or to maintain a specific dosage or type of drug. *See Mathews v. Eldridge*, 424 U.S. 319 (1976). Institutional control infects the decision makers and the entire procedure. The state courts that have reviewed comparable procedures have uniformly concluded that they do not adequately protect the significant liberty interest implicated by the forced administration of psychotropic drugs. I agree with that conclusion. . . .

. . . .

NOTES AND QUESTIONS

1. For a comprehensive discussion of the constitutional rights impaired by incarceration, see Katya Lezin, *Life at Lorton: An Examination of Prisoner's Rights at the District of Columbia Correctional Facilities*, 5 B.U. Pub. Int. L.J. 165 (Winter, 1996).
2. *Washington v. Harper* is concerned with the personal dignity of a prisoner, in contrast to the liberty issues in *Bell v. Wolfish*. In ethical terms, is the invasion in *Harper* more powerful and direct, as an assault upon the "person" of the prisoner, than the searches in *Bell* and *Peckham*? All three cases together present the essential dimensions of personhood: relation to others and integrity of the self. Which is at stake in *Harper*?
3. The majority holds that the state of Washington's policy adequately protects the individual prisoner, subjecting him to involuntary treatment only if he suffers from a "mental disorder" and is "greatly disabled" or poses "a likelihood of serious harm." Even then, a hearing must be afforded. Why is that not a sufficient protection of the inmate's interest? These procedures would be sufficient to commit a citizen civilly. Why are they not sufficient to medicate a prisoner in a correctional institution?

4. Note that the state supreme court not only disagreed with the procedural components of the policy, insisting that a court hearing (rather than an administrative hearing) would be required prior to medication, but also went on to insist that the criteria for medication be changed. The *state* supreme court said that the state of Washington must prove it had a compelling interest in medicating the prisoner and that the drugs would further that interest. Moreover, weight must be given to the prisoner's wishes. The United States Supreme Court therefore notes that the Washington State Supreme Court ruled upon the "substance of the inmate's right"; the United States Supreme Court then goes on to reject that ruling. Constitutionally, does it have that power? Ethically, which court — the state supreme court or the United States Supreme Court — should decide the issue? Who takes the better approach?
5. It is true, of course, that the state had the option of simply restraining Mr. Harper, rather than medicating him. How do the majority and dissent treat this consideration differently? Is the state simply free to choose whichever means it desires? Which is more consistent with Mr. Harper's dignity?
6. The dissent argues that there will be conflicts of interest among the various professionals within the prison as they sit to hear cases for medication in which they themselves may previously have been involved or in which associates are involved. As a matter of professional ethics, to whom do the panel members owe their loyalty: to each other, to the prisoner as patient or to the institution? Is it fair to say that they must inevitably experience a *conflict* of interest? Consider these questions later in connection with Chapter Three and the physician's fiduciary obligation.
7. In *Enis v. Wisconsin*, 962 F.Supp 1192 (W.D. Wis. 1996), the Court invalidated Wisconsin's statute authorizing involuntary administration of psychotropic drugs upon persons found not guilty by reason of insanity, upon a finding they were not competent to consent. There was no requirement that the prisoner, who was in a mental health institute, be dangerous. Nor did the statute require a finding that there were no less intrusive alternatives. The Court relied on *Harper*; was it correct in doing so? Aren't *Harper*, *Farmer* and *Bell v. Wolfish* authority to the contrary?

SELL v. UNITED STATES
539 U.S. 166 (2003)

Justice **Breyer** delivered the opinion of the Court.

The question presented is whether the Constitution permits the Government to administer antipsychotic drugs involuntarily to a mentally ill criminal defendant — in order to render that defendant competent to stand trial for serious, but nonviolent, crimes. We conclude that the Constitution allows the Government to administer those drugs, even against the defendant's will, in limited circumstances, *i.e.*, upon satisfaction of conditions that we shall describe. Because the Court of Appeals did not find that the requisite circumstances existed in this case, we vacate its judgment.

I

A

Petitioner Charles Sell, once a practicing dentist, has a long and unfortunate history of mental illness. In September 1982, after telling doctors that the gold he used for fillings had been contaminated by communists, Sell was hospitalized, treated with antipsychotic medication, and subsequently discharged. In June 1984, Sell called the police to say that a leopard was outside his office boarding a bus, and he then asked the police to shoot him. Sell was again hospitalized and subsequently released. On various occasions, he complained that public officials, for example, a State Governor and a police chief, were trying to kill him. In April 1997, he told law enforcement personnel that he "spoke to God last night," and that "God told me every [Federal Bureau of Investigation] person I kill, a soul will be saved."

In May 1997, the Government charged Sell with submitting fictitious insurance claims for payment. See 18 U.S.C. § 1035(a)(2) [18 USCS § 1035(a)(2)]. A Federal Magistrate Judge (Magistrate), after ordering a psychiatric examination, found Sell "currently competent," but noted that Sell might experience "a psychotic episode" in the future. App. 321. The judge released Sell on bail. A grand jury later produced a superseding indictment charging Sell and his wife with 56 counts of mail fraud, 6 counts of Medicaid fraud, and 1 count of money laundering.

In early 1998, the Government claimed that Sell had sought to intimidate a witness. The Magistrate held a bail revocation hearing. Sell's behavior at his initial appearance was, in the judge's words, " 'totally out of control,' " involving "screaming and shouting," the use of "personal insults" and "racial epithets," and spitting "in the judge's face." A psychiatrist reported that Sell could not sleep because he expected the FBI to " 'come busting through the door,' " and concluded that Sell's condition had worsened. After considering that report and other testimony, the Magistrate revoked Sell's bail.

In April 1998, the grand jury issued a new indictment charging Sell with attempting to murder the FBI agent who had arrested him and a former employee who planned to testify against him in the fraud case. The attempted murder and fraud cases were joined for trial.

In early 1999, Sell asked the Magistrate to reconsider his competence to stand trial. The Magistrate sent Sell to the United States Medical Center for Federal Prisoners at Springfield, Missouri, for examination. Subsequently the Magistrate found that Sell was "mentally incompetent to stand trial." He ordered Sell to "be hospitalized for treatment" at the Medical Center for up to four months, "to determine whether there was a substantial probability that [Sell] would attain the capacity to allow his trial to proceed."

Two months later, Medical Center staff recommended that Sell take antipsychotic medication. Sell refused to do so. The staff sought permission to administer the medication against Sell's will. That effort is the subject of the present proceedings.

B

We here review the last of five hierarchically ordered lower court and Medical Center determinations. First, in June 1999, Medical Center staff sought permission from institutional authorities to administer antipsychotic drugs to Sell involuntarily. A reviewing psychiatrist held a hearing and considered Sell's prior history; Sell's current persecutional beliefs (for example, that Government officials were trying to suppress his knowledge about events in Waco, Texas, and had sent him to Alaska to silence him); staff medical opinions (for example, that "Sell's symptoms point to a diagnosis of Delusional Disorder but . . . there well may be an underlying Schizophrenic Process"); staff medical concerns (for example, about "the persistence of Dr. Sell's belief that the Courts, FBI, and federal government in general are against him"); an outside medical expert's opinion (that Sell suffered only from delusional disorder, which, in that expert's view, "medication rarely helps"); and Sell's own views, as well as those of other laypersons who know him (to the effect that he did not suffer from a serious mental illness).

The reviewing psychiatrist then authorized involuntary administration of the drugs, both (1) because Sell was "mentally ill and dangerous, and medication is necessary to treat the mental illness," and (2) so that Sell would "become competent for trial." The reviewing psychiatrist added that he considered Sell "dangerous based on threats and delusions if outside, but not necessarily inside prison" and that Sell was "able to function" in prison in the "open population."

The reviewing official "upheld" the "hearing officer's decision that [Sell] would benefit from the utilization of anti-psychotic medication."

In August 2000, the Magistrate found that "the government has made a substantial and very strong showing that Dr. Sell is a danger to himself and others at the institution in which he is currently incarcerated"; that "the government has shown that anti-psychotic medication is the only way to render him less dangerous"; that newer drugs and/or changing drugs will "ameliorate" any "serious side effects"; that "the benefits to Dr. Sell . . . far outweigh any risks"; and that "there is a substantial probability that" the drugs will "return" Sell "to competency." The Magistrate concluded that "the government has shown in as strong a manner as possible, that antipsychotic medications are the only way to render the defendant not dangerous and competent to stand trial."

The District Court *affirmed* the Magistrate's order permitting Sell's involuntary medication. The court wrote that "anti-psychotic drugs are medically appropriate," that "they represent the only viable hope of rendering defendant competent to stand trial," and that "administration of such drugs appears necessary to serve the government's compelling interest in obtaining an adjudication of defendant's guilt or innocence of numerous and serious charges" (including fraud and attempted murder). The court added that it was "premature" to consider whether "the effects of medication might prejudice [Sell's] defense at trial."

II

We conclude that the District Court order from which Sell appealed was an appealable "collateral order." The Eighth Circuit had jurisdiction to hear the appeal. And we consequently have jurisdiction to decide the question presented, whether involuntary medication violates Sell's constitutional rights.

III

We turn now to the basic question presented: Does forced administration of antipsychotic drugs to render Sell competent to stand trial unconstitutionally deprive him of his "liberty" to reject medical treatment? U.S. Const., Amdt. 5 (Federal Government may not "deprive" any person of "liberty . . . without due process of law"). Two prior precedents, [*Washington v.*] *Harper,* . . . 494 U.S. 210 [(1990)], and *Riggins* [*v. Nevada*], . . . 504 U.S. 127 [(1992)], set forth the framework for determining the legal answer. These two cases, *Harper* and *Riggins*, indicate that the Constitution permits the Government involuntarily to administer antipsychotic drugs to a mentally ill defendant facing serious criminal charges in order to render that defendant competent to stand trial, but only if the treatment is medically appropriate, is substantially unlikely to have side effects that may undermine the fairness of the trial, and, taking account of less intrusive alternatives, is necessary significantly to further important governmental trial-related interests.

This standard will permit involuntary administration of drugs solely for trial competence purposes in certain instances. But those instances may be rare. That is because the standard says or fairly implies the following:

> First, a court must find that *important* governmental interests are at stake. The Government's interest in bringing to trial an individual accused of a serious crime is important. That is so whether the offense is a serious crime against the person or a serious crime against property. In both instances the Government seeks to protect through application of the criminal law the basic human need for security. Courts, however, must consider the facts of the individual case in evaluating the Government's interest in prosecution. Special circumstances may lessen the importance of that interest. The defendant's failure to take drugs voluntarily, for example, may mean lengthy confinement in an institution for the mentally ill — and that would diminish the risks that ordinarily attach to freeing without punishment one who has committed a serious crime. We do not mean to suggest that civil commitment is a substitute for a criminal trial. The Government has a substantial interest in timely prosecution. And it may be difficult or impossible to try a defendant who regains competence after years of commitment during which memories may fade and evidence may be lost. The potential for future confinement affects, but does not totally undermine, the strength of the need for prosecution. The same is true of the possibility that the defendant has already been confined for a significant amount of time (for which he would receive credit toward any sentence ultimately imposed, see 18 U.S.C.

> § 3585(b) [18 USCS § 3585(b)]). Moreover, the Government has a concomitant, constitutionally essential interest in assuring that the defendant's trial is a fair one.
>
> Second, the court must conclude that involuntary medication will *significantly further* those concomitant state interests. It must find that administration of the drugs is substantially likely to render the defendant competent to stand trial. At the same time, it must find that administration of the drugs is substantially unlikely to have side effects that will interfere significantly with the defendant's ability to assist counsel in conducting a trial defense, thereby rendering the trial unfair.
>
> Third, the court must conclude that involuntary medication is *necessary* to further those interests. The court must find that any alternative, less intrusive treatments are unlikely to achieve substantially the same results. *Cf.* Brief for American Psychological Association as *Amicus Curiae* (nondrug therapies may be effective in restoring psychotic defendants to competence); *but cf.* Brief for American Psychiatric Association *et al.* as *Amici Curiae* (alternative treatments for psychosis commonly not as effective as medication). And the court must consider less intrusive means for administering the drugs, *e.g.*, a court order to the defendant backed by the contempt power, before considering more intrusive methods.
>
> Fourth, as we have said, the court must conclude that administration of the drugs is *medically appropriate, i.e.*, in the patient's best medical interest in light of his medical condition. The specific kinds of drugs at issue may matter here as elsewhere. Different kinds of antipsychotic drugs may produce different side effects and enjoy different levels of success.

We emphasize that the court applying these standards is seeking to determine whether involuntary administration of drugs is necessary significantly to further a particular governmental interest, namely, the interest in rendering the defendant *competent to stand trial.* A court need not consider whether to allow forced medication for that kind of purpose, if forced medication is warranted for a *different* purpose, such as the purposes set out in *Harper* related to the individual's dangerousness, or purposes related to the individual's own interests where refusal to take drugs puts his health gravely at risk. There are often strong reasons for a court to determine whether forced administration of drugs can be justified on these alternative grounds *before* turning to the trial competence question.

If a court authorizes medication on these alternative grounds, the need to consider authorization on trial competence grounds will likely disappear. Even if a court decides medication cannot be authorized on the alternative grounds, the findings underlying such a decision will help to inform expert opinion and judicial decision-making in respect to a request to administer drugs for trial competence purposes. At the least, they will facilitate direct medical and legal focus upon such questions as: Why is it medically appropriate forcibly to administer antipsychotic drugs to an individual who (1) is *not* dangerous *and*

(2) *is* competent to make up his own mind about treatment? Can bringing such an individual to trial *alone* justify in whole (or at least in significant part) administration of a drug that may have adverse side effects, including side effects that may to some extent impair a defense at trial? We consequently believe that a court, asked to approve forced administration of drugs for purposes of rendering a defendant competent to stand trial, should ordinarily determine whether the Government seeks, or has first sought, permission for forced administration of drugs on these other *Harper*-type grounds; and, if not, why not.

IV

The Medical Center and the Magistrate in this case, applying standards roughly comparable to those set forth here and in *Harper*, approved forced medication substantially, if not primarily, upon grounds of Sell's dangerousness to others. But the District Court and the Eighth Circuit took a different approach. The District Court found "clearly erroneous" the Magistrate's conclusion regarding dangerousness, and the Court of Appeals agreed. Both courts approved forced medication solely in order to render Sell competent to stand trial.

The District Court's opinion, while more thorough, places weight upon the Medical Center's decision, taken after the Magistrate's hearing, to return Sell to the general prison population. It does not explain whether that return reflected an improvement in Sell's condition or whether the Medical Center saw it as permanent rather than temporary.

Regardless, as we have said, we must assume that Sell was not dangerous. And on that hypothetical assumption, we find that the Court of Appeals was wrong to approve forced medication solely to render Sell competent to stand trial. For one thing, the Magistrate's opinion makes clear that he did *not* find forced medication legally justified on trial competence grounds alone. Rather, the Magistrate concluded that Sell *was* dangerous, and he wrote that forced medication was "the only way to render the defendant *not dangerous and* competent to stand trial."

Moreover, the record of the hearing before the Magistrate shows that the experts themselves focused mainly upon the dangerousness issue. Consequently the experts did not pose important questions — questions, for example, about trial-related side effects and risks — the answers to which could have helped determine whether forced medication was warranted on trial competence grounds alone. Rather, the Medical Center's experts conceded that their proposed medications had "significant" side effects and that "there has to be a cost benefit analysis. And in making their "cost-benefit" judgments, they primarily took into account Sell's dangerousness, not the need to bring him to trial.

The failure to focus upon trial competence could well have mattered. Whether a particular drug will tend to sedate a defendant, interfere with communication with counsel, prevent rapid reaction to trial developments, or diminish the ability to express emotions are matters important in determining the permissibility of medication to restore competence, but not necessarily relevant when dangerousness is primarily at issue. We cannot tell whether the side effects of antipsychotic medication were likely to undermine the fairness of a trial in Sell's case.

Finally, the lower courts did not consider that Sell has already been confined at the Medical Center for a long period of time, and that his refusal to take antipsychotic drugs might result in further lengthy confinement. Those factors, the first because a defendant ordinarily receives credit toward a sentence for time served, 18 U.S.C. § 3585(b) [18 USCS § 3585(b)], and the second because it reduces the likelihood of the defendant's committing future crimes, moderate — though they do not eliminate — the importance of the governmental interest in prosecution.

V

For these reasons, we believe that the present orders authorizing forced administration of anti-psychotic drugs cannot stand. The Government may pursue its request for forced medication on the grounds discussed in this opinion, including grounds related to the danger Sell poses to himself or others. Since Sell's medical condition may have changed over time, the Government should do so on the basis of current circumstances.

The judgment of the Eighth Circuit is vacated, and the case is remanded for further proceedings consistent with this opinion.

It is so ordered.

Justice **Scalia**, with whom Justice **O'Connor** and Justice **Thomas** join, dissenting.

. . .

II

B

Today's narrow holding will allow criminal defendants in petitioner's position to engage in opportunistic behavior. They can, for example, voluntarily take their medication until halfway through trial, then abruptly refuse and demand an interlocutory appeal from the order that medication continue on a compulsory basis. This sort of concern for the disruption of criminal proceedings — strangely missing from the Court's discussion today — is what has led us to state many times that we interpret the collateral-order exception narrowly in criminal cases.

But the adverse effects of today's narrow holding are as nothing compared to the adverse effects of the new rule of law that underlies the holding. The Court's opinion announces that appellate jurisdiction is proper because review after conviction and sentence will come only after "Sell will have undergone forced medication — the very harm that he seeks to avoid." This analysis effects a breathtaking expansion of appellate jurisdiction over interlocutory orders. If it is applied faithfully (and some appellate panels will be eager to apply it faithfully), any criminal defendant who asserts that a trial court order will, if implemented, cause an immediate violation of his constitutional (or perhaps even statutory?) rights may immediately appeal. He is empowered to hold up the trial for months by claiming that review after final judgment "would come too late" to prevent the violation. A trial-court order requiring the defendant to wear an electronic bracelet could be attacked as an immediate infringement of the constitutional right to "bodily integrity"; an order refusing to allow the defendant to wear a Tshirt that says "Black Power" in front of the jury could be attacked as an immediate violation of First Amendment rights; and an order compelling testimony could be attacked as an immediate denial [of] Fifth Amendment rights. All these orders would be immediately appealable. *Flanagan* [*v. United States,* 465 U.S. 259 (1984)] and *Carroll* [*v. United States,* 354 U.S. 394 (1957)], which held that appellate review of orders that might infringe a defendant's constitutionally protected rights *still* had to wait until final judgment, are seemingly overruled. The narrow gate of entry to the collateral-order doctrine — hitherto traversable by only (1) orders unreviewable on appeal from judgment and (2) orders denying an asserted right not to be tried — has been generously widened.

. . . .

NOTES AND QUESTIONS

1. What of the standard in *Sell*? Can it — will it — ever be met?
2. Shouldn't the Court have thrown into the calculus the seriousness of the crime? Of the possibility of taking and preserving testimony? Of the appointment of a guardian ad litem?
3. How would you advise an incompetent defendant, especially in light of Justice Scalia's dissent?
4. Is medication seen as a type of rehabilitation in *Washington v. Harper*? Why or why not? What is the role of rehabilitation in the prison system? Is it fair to medicate a prisoner during trial if the medication is not continued, or if treatment is not pursued? *See* Kyrsten Sinema, *Overton v. Bazzetta: How the Supreme Court used Turner to Sound the Death Knell for Prisoner Rehabilitation*, 36 Ariz. St. L.J. 471 (Spring, 2004).

HELLING v. McKINNEY

509 U.S. 25 (1993)

Justice **White** delivered the opinion of the Court.

This case requires us to decide whether the health risk posed by involuntary exposure of a prison inmate to environmental tobacco smoke (ETS) can form the basis of a claim for relief under the Eighth Amendment.

I

Respondent is serving a sentence of imprisonment in the Nevada prison system. At the time that this case arose, respondent was an inmate in the Nevada State Prison in Carson City, Nevada. The complaint, dated December 18, 1986, alleged that respondent was assigned to a cell with another inmate who smoked five packs of cigarettes a day. The complaint also stated that cigarettes were sold to inmates without properly informing of the health hazards a nonsmoking inmate would encounter by sharing a room with an inmate who smoked, and that certain cigarettes burned continuously releasing some type of chemical. Respondent complained of certain health problems allegedly caused by exposure to cigarette smoke. Respondent sought injunctive relief and damages for, inter alia, subjecting him to cruel and unusual punishment by jeopardizing his health.

. . . The Magistrate, after citing applicable authority, concluded that respondent had no constitutional right to be free from cigarette smoke: While "society may be moving toward an opinion as to the propriety of nonsmoking and a smoke-free environment," society cannot yet completely agree on the resolution of these issues. The Magistrate found that respondent nonetheless could state a claim for deliberate indifference to serious medical needs if he could prove the underlying facts, but held that respondent had failed to present evidence showing either medical problems that were traceable to cigarette smoke or deliberate indifference to them.

. . . .

III

It is undisputed that the treatment a prisoner receives in prison and the conditions under which he is confined are subject to scrutiny under the Eighth Amendment. As we said in *Deshaney v. Winnebago County Dept. of Social Services*, 489 U.S. 189, 199-200 (1989):

> "[W]hen the State takes a person into its custody and holds him there against his will, the Constitution imposes upon it a corresponding duty to assume some responsibility for his safety and general well being . . . . The rationale for this principle is simple enough: when the State by the affirmative exercise of its power so restrains an individual's liberty that it renders him unable to care for himself, and at the same time fails to provide for his basic human needs — e.g., food, clothing, shelter, medical care, and reasonable safety — it transgresses the substantive limits on state action set by the Eighth Amendment . . . ."

Contemporary standards of decency require no less. . . .

. . . .

That the Eighth Amendment protects against future harm to inmates is not a novel proposition. The Amendment, as we have said, requires that inmates be furnished with the basic human needs, one of which is "reasonable safety." . . . We thus reject petitioners' central thesis that only deliberate indifference to current serious health problems of inmates is actionable under the Eighth Amendment.

The United States as *amicus curiae* supporting petitioners does not contend that the Amendment permits "even those conditions of confinement that truly pose a significant risk of proximate and substantial harm to an inmate, so long as the injury has not yet occurred and the inmate does not yet suffer from its effects." . . . But the United States submits that the harm to any particular individual from exposure to ETS is speculative, that the risk is not sufficiently grave to implicate a " 'serious medical need[d],' " and that exposure to ETS is not contrary to current standards of decency. It would be premature for us, however, as a matter of law to reverse the Court of Appeals on the basis suggested by the United States. The Court of Appeals has ruled that McKinney's claim is that the level of ETS to which he has been involuntarily exposed is such that his future health is unreasonably endangered and has remanded to permit McKinney to attempt to prove his case. In the course of such proof, he must also establish that it is contrary to current standards of decency for anyone to be so exposed against his will and that prison officials are deliberately indifferent to his plight. We cannot rule at this juncture that it will be impossible for McKinney, on remand, to prove an Eighth Amendment violation based on exposure to ETS.

IV

. . . .

With respect to the objective factor, McKinney must show that he himself is being exposed to unreasonably high levels of ETS. Plainly relevant to this determination is the fact that McKinney has been moved from Carson City to Ely State Prison and is no longer the cellmate of a five-pack-a-day smoker. While he is subject to being moved back to Carson City and to being placed again in a cell with a heavy smoker, the fact is that at present he is not so exposed. Moreover, the director of the Nevada State Prisons adopted a formal smoking policy on January 10, 1992. This policy restricts smoking in "program, food preparation/serving, recreational and medical areas" to specifically designated areas. . . .

Also with respect to the objective factor, determining whether McKinney's conditions of confinement violate the Eighth Amendment requires more than a scientific and statistical inquiry into the seriousness of the potential harm and the likelihood that such injury to health will actually be caused by exposure to ETS. It also requires a court to assess whether society considers the risk that the prisoner complains of to be so grave that it violates contemporary standards of decency to expose anyone unwillingly to such a risk. In other words, the prisoner must show that the risk of which he complains is not one that today's society chooses to tolerate.

. . . .

Justice **Thomas**, with whom Justice **Scalia** joins, dissenting.

. . . .

I

The Eighth Amendment provides that "[e]xcessive bail shall not be required, nor excessive fines imposed, nor cruel and unusual punishments inflicted." . . .

A

At the time the Eighth Amendment was ratified, the word "punishment" referred to the penalty imposed for the commission of a crime. . . . And this understanding of the word, of course, does not encompass a prisoner's injuries that bear no relation to his sentence.

Nor, as far as I know, is there any historical evidence indicating that the framers and ratifiers of the Eighth Amendment had anything other than this common understanding of "punishment" in mind. . . .

. . . .

Judicial interpretations of the Cruel and Unusual Punishments Clause were, until quite recently, consistent with its text and history. . . .

Thus, although the evidence is not overwhelming, I believe that the text and history of the Eighth Amendment, together with the decisions interpreting it, support the view that judges or juries — but not jailers — impose "punishment." At a minimum, I believe that the original meaning of "punishment," the silence in the historical record, and the 185 years of uniform precedent shift the burden of persuasion to those who would apply the Eighth Amendment to prison conditions. In my view, that burden has not yet been discharged.

. . . .

Accordingly, I would reverse the judgment of the Court of Appeals.

NOTES AND QUESTIONS

1. This text returns to the subject of tobacco abuse in Chapter 4. The focus there is on self-abuse, not imposition on others, as in *Helling v. McKinney*.
2. Note the burden of proof imposed by the majority. How feasible or realistic is it?
3. Why must the prisoner prove the warden's state of mind? Or society's view of smoking? Or the probability of harm? Shouldn't the duty be to provide the maximum possible protection to prisoners? The exacting standards imposed by *Helling* seem to offer little protection. *See Scott v. District of Columbia*, 139 F.3d 940 (D. Col. Cir. 1998).
4. Justice Thomas' dissent may have force in narrowly defining the cruel and unusual "punishment" clause of the Constitution, but doesn't his view sweep too far? Would he *allow* any and all prison abuse to escape review? What of analyses under the equal protection and due process clauses?
5. Should the prison properly consider that other prisoners *need* to smoke cigarettes? Without that emotional release, prison administration might be cruel or impossible. Would Rawls countenance such thinking?
6. Might an equally tenable view be that the prisoner by his misconduct and conviction forfeited, or waived, any right to be free of normal habits or proclivities of other prisoners? He may have a right to be free from

rape, as in *Farmer v. Brennan*, but not from the normal impositions of society, such as the smoking of cigarettes by others.

7. This is not a text on prisoners' rights and so a number of issues and concerns must be omitted here, for example, freedom of religion. *See, e.g., O'Lone v. Estate of Shabazz*, 482 U.S. 342 (1987); *Chatin v. State of New York*, 1998 U.S. Dist. LEXIS 8351 (S.D. NY). The concern at this point is the extent to which society must protect those whom it imprisons, with special deference to their unique, individual characteristics, such as sexual orientation or sensitivity to second-hand smoke. One more case will develop this focus further, by looking at the position of handicapped or disabled prisoners under the Americans with Disabilities Act. This is a complex inquiry, for while prisoners may be a disfavored group in society, citizens suffering with a disability are the beneficiaries of corrective legislation. How then should they be treated behind bars?

YESKEY v. COMMONWEALTH OF PENNSYLVANIA DEPARTMENT OF CORRECTIONS

118 F.3d 168 (3d Cir. 1997)

Becker, Circuit Judge

Ronald R. Yeskey is a Pennsylvania prison inmate who was denied admission to the Pennsylvania Department of Correction's Motivational Boot Camp program because of a history of hypertension, despite the recommendation of the sentencing judge that he be placed therein.[6] Yeskey brought suit in the district court under the Americans With Disabilities Act (ADA), 42 U.S.C. § 12101 et seq., alleging that his exclusion from the program violated that enactment.

. . . The question of the applicability of the ADA to prisons is an important one, especially in view of the increased number of inmates, including many older, hearing-impaired, and HIV-positive inmates, in the nation's jails. See generally Ira P. Robbins, George Bush's America Meets Dante's Inferno: The Americans with Disabilities Act in Prison, 15 Yale L. & Pol'y Rev. 49, 56-63 (1996). . . .

I

. . . .

Title II of the ADA provides in pertinent part:

"no qualified individual with a disability shall, by reason of such disability, be excluded from participation in or be denied the benefits of the Services,

[6] The Motivational Boot Camp Act established a "motivational boot camp" to which certain inmates may be assigned by the Department of Corrections to serve their sentences for a period of six months.

The boot camp provides rigorous physical activity, intensive regimentation and discipline, work on public projects, and other treatment. Pursuant to statute, placement of inmates in the boot camp is discretionary, and, as such, no inmate has a right to such placement. Upon successful completion of the six months incarceration, the inmate is released on parole for intensive supervision as determined by the Pennsylvania Board of Probation and Parole.

programs, or activities of a public entity, or be subjected to discrimination by any such entity." 42 U.S.C. § 12132.

The statutory definition of "[p]rogram or activity" in Section 504 indicates that the terms were intended to be all-encompassing. . . .

. . . Certainly, operating a prison facility falls within the "duties or functions" of local government authorities. Moreover, Title II's definition of a "public entity" clearly encompasses a state or local correctional facility or authority: "any department, agency, . . . or other instrumentality of a State or States or local government[.]"

This conclusion is bolstered by the Department of Justice (DOJ) regulations implementing both Section 504 and Title II of the ADA. . . .

The regulations promulgated by DOJ to enforce Section 504 define the kinds of programs and benefits that should be afforded to individuals with disabilities on a nondiscriminatory basis. The regulations define "program" to mean "the operations of the agency or organizational unit of government receiving or substantially benefiting from the Federal assistance awarded, e.g., a police department or department of corrections." The term "[b]enefit" includes "provision of services, financial aid or disposition (i.e., treatment, handling, decision, sentencing, confinement, or other prescription of conduct.)" This coverage is broad, and includes "jails, prisons, reformatories and training schools, work camps, reception and diagnostic centers, prerelease and work release facilities, and community-based facilities."

. . . .

The regulations promulgated under Title II of the ADA afford similar protections to persons with disabilities who are incarcerated in prisons, or otherwise institutionalized by the state or its instrumentalities, regardless of the public institution's receipt of federal financial assistance. The regulations state that the statute's coverage extends to "all services, programs, and activities provided or made available by public entities." The preamble to the ADA regulations also refers explicitly to prisons, stating that, where an individual with disabilities "is an inmate of a custodial or correctional institution," the entity is required to provide "assistance in toileting, eating, or dressing to [that] individual[]."

In sum, Section 504 of the Rehabilitation Act, Title II of the ADA, and the specific provisions in the DOJ's regulations listing correctional facilities or departments as covered entities confirm that the Rehabilitation Act and the ADA apply to state and locally-operated correctional facilities.

II

The weight of judicial authority also supports our conclusion that the ADA applies to prison programs. . . .

. . . .

III

Despite the Commonwealth's contention to the contrary, moreover, prisoners (in contrast to prisons) are not excluded from coverage because Section

504 and Title II protect only "qualified individual[s] with a disability." That term is defined in Title II to mean:

> an individual with a disability who, with or without reasonable modifications . . . meets the essential eligibility requirements for the receipt of services or the participation in programs or activities provided by a public entity. . . .

Judge Posner addressed a related aspect of the case quite incisively:

> It might seem absurd to apply the Americans with Disabilities Act to prisoners. Prisoners are not a favored group in society; the propensity of some of them to sue at the drop of a hat is well known; prison systems are strapped for funds; the practical effect of granting disabled prisoners rights of access that might require costly modifications of prison facilities might be the curtailment of educational, recreational, and rehabilitative programs for prisoners, in which event everyone might be worse off. But . . . there is another side to the issue. The Americans with Disabilities Act was cast in terms not of subsidizing an interest group but of eliminating a form of discrimination that Congress considered unfair and even odious. The Act assimilates the disabled to groups that by reason of sex, age, race, religion, nationality, or ethnic origin are believed to be victims of discrimination. Rights against discrimination are among the few rights that prisoners do not park at the prison gates. Although the special conditions of the prison setting license a degree of discrimination that would not be tolerated in a free environment, there is no general right of prison officials to discriminate against prisoners on grounds of race, sex, religion, and so forth. If a prison may not exclude blacks from the prison dining hall and force them to eat in their cells, and if Congress thinks that discriminating against a blind person is like discriminating against a black person, it is not obvious that the prison may exclude the blind person from the dining hall, unless allowing him to use the dining hall would place an undue burden on prison management. . . .

. . . .

IV

The foregoing discussion establishes that the ADA applies to Yeskey's claim. His claim for injunctive relief is, apparently, moot in view of the impending (or actual) completion of his prison term. His claim for damages will turn, presumably, on whether he should (or would) have been admitted to the boot camp. Even with the ADA applicable, Yeskey might not have been admitted for a number of reasons, which will have to be explored on remand.

. . . .

NOTES AND QUESTIONS

1. The *Yeskey* case is the first in this text dealing with the ADA. That statute will reappear later in a number of cases. It is particularly important since the definition of "disability" not only includes conditions which *in fact* impair performance, but also those *perceived* to do so.

Consequently, the ADA is a powerful tool in dealing with prejudice. See, *infra*, § 3.02 and § 4.03[3], dealing with AIDS.

2. Note that, despite the *Yeskey* Court's assertion, there is substantial authority that the ADA does not apply to prisons. *See Amos v. Maryland Dept. of Public Safety*, 126 F.3d 589 (4th Cir. 1997) (denying coverage to prisoners who alleged such disabilities as paralysis, wheelchair confinement and cerebral palsy. But see there the powerful dissent of Judge Murnaghan.).
3. The United States Supreme Court affirmed the *Yeskey* decision in *Pennsylvania Department of Corrections v. Yeskey*, 524 U.S. 206, 118 S.Ct. 1952 (1998). It also affirmed another ADA case involving the obligation of a dentist to serve an HIV positive patient in *Bragdon v. Abbott*, 524 U.S. 624, 118 S.Ct. 2196 (1998) *infra,* § 3.02[3]. The Americans with Disabilities Act is thus a powerful engine for dealing with a range of cases where citizens are disadvantaged by *perceived* disabilities. See also, *infra,* cases collected at § 4.02.
4. Note that the *Yeskey* case must return to the District Court and the prisoner must show that he could/would have been eligible for boot camp. As in *Helling*, the "win" may yet be lost. How?
5. More broadly, *should* the ADA and § 504 apply to prisons? Disabled persons *are* subject to discrimination. But isn't that lost in the greater reclassification as a prisoner? And shouldn't prison administrators be accorded the latitude and deference extended them in *Bell* and *Harper*?

OLMSTEAD v. ZIMRING
527 U.S. 581 (2000)

Justice **Ginsburg** announced the judgment of the Court and delivered the opinion of the Court with respect to Parts I, II, and III-A, and an opinion with respect to Part III-B, in which **O'Connor, Souter,** and **Breyer**, JJ., joined.

I

This case concerns the proper construction of the anti-discrimination provision contained in the public services portion (Title II) of the Americans with Disabilities Act of 1990, 104 Stat. 337, 42 U.S.C. § 12132. Specifically, we confront the question whether the proscription of discrimination may require placement of persons with mental disabilities in community settings rather than in institutions. The answer, we hold, is a qualified yes. Such action is in order when the State's treatment professionals have determined that community placement is appropriate, the transfer from institutional care to a less restrictive setting is not opposed by the affected individual, and the placement can be reasonably accommodated, taking into account the resources available to the State and the needs of others with mental disabilities. In so ruling, we affirm the decision of the Eleventh Circuit in substantial part. We remand the case, however, for further consideration of the appropriate relief, given the range of facilities the State maintains for the care and treatment of persons with diverse mental disabilities, and its obligation to administer services with an even hand.

In the opening provisions of the ADA, Congress stated findings applicable to the statute in all its parts. Most relevant to this case, Congress determined that

> "(2) historically, society has tended to isolate and segregate individuals with disabilities, and, despite some improvements, such forms of discrimination against individuals with disabilities continue to be a serious and pervasive social problem;
>
> "(3) discrimination against individuals with disabilities persists in such critical areas as . . . institutionalization . . . ;
>
> "(5) individuals with disabilities continually encounter various forms of discrimination, including outright intentional exclusion, . . . failure to make modifications to existing facilities and practices, . . . [and] segregation"

. . . .

42 U.S.C. §§ 12101(a)(2), (3), (5).

II

With the key legislative provisions in full view, we summarize the facts underlying this dispute. Respondents L.C. and E.W. are mentally retarded women; L.C. has also been diagnosed with schizophrenia, and E.W., with a personality disorder. Both women have a history of treatment in institutional settings. In May 1992, L.C. was voluntarily admitted to Georgia Regional Hospital at Atlanta (GRH), where she was confined for treatment in a psychiatric unit. By May 1993, her psychiatric condition had stabilized, and L.C.'s treatment team at GRH agreed that her needs could be met appropriately in one of the community-based programs the State supported. Despite this evaluation, L.C. remained institutionalized until February 1996, when the State placed her in a community-based treatment program.

E.W. was voluntarily admitted to GRH in February 1995; like L.C., E.W. was confined for treatment in a psychiatric unit. In March 1995, GRH sought to discharge E.W. to a homeless shelter, but abandoned that plan after her attorney filed an administrative complaint. By 1996, E.W.'s treating psychiatrist concluded that she could be treated appropriately in a community-based setting. She nonetheless remained institutionalized until a few months after the District Court issued its judgment in this case in 1997.

III

Endeavoring to carry out Congress' instruction to issue regulations implementing Title II, the Attorney General, in the integration and reasonable-modifications regulations. . ., made two key determinations. The first concerned the scope of the ADA's discrimination proscription, 42 U.S.C. § 12132; the second concerned the obligation of the States to counter discrimination. As to the first, the Attorney General concluded that unjustified placement or retention of persons in institutions, severely limiting their exposure to the outside community, constitutes a form of discrimination based on disability prohibited by Title II. Regarding the States' obligation to avoid unjustified isolation of individuals with disabilities, the Attorney General provided that States could resist modifications that "would fundamentally alter the nature of the service, program, or activity."

The Court of Appeals essentially upheld the Attorney General's construction of the ADA. We affirm the Court of Appeals' decision in substantial part. Unjustified isolation, we hold, is properly regarded as discrimination based on disability. But we recognize, as well, the States' need to maintain a range of facilities for the care and treatment of persons with diverse mental disabilities, and the States' obligation to administer services with an even hand. Accordingly, we further hold that the Court of Appeals' remand instruction was unduly restrictive. In evaluating a State's fundamental-alteration defense, the District Court must consider, in view of the resources available to the State, not only the cost of providing community-based care to the litigants, but also the range of services the State provides others with mental disabilities, and the State's obligation to mete out those services equitably.

A

The State argues that L.C. and E.W. encountered no discrimination "by reason of" their disabilities because they were not denied community placement on account of those disabilities. Nor were they subjected to "discrimination," the State contends, because " 'discrimination' necessarily requires uneven treatment of similarly situated individuals," and L.C. and E.W. had identified no comparison class, *i.e.*, no similarly situated individuals given preferential treatment. We are satisfied that Congress had a more comprehensive view of the concept of discrimination advanced in the ADA.

The ADA stepped up earlier measures to secure opportunities for people with developmental disabilities to enjoy the benefits of community living. The Developmentally Disabled Assistance and Bill of Rights Act (DDABRA), a 1975 measure, stated in aspirational terms that "the treatment, services, and habilitation for a person with developmental disabilities . . . *should be* provided in the setting that is least restrictive of the person's personal liberty." Ultimately, in the ADA, enacted in 1990, Congress not only required all public entities to refrain from discrimination, additionally, in findings applicable to the entire statute, Congress explicitly identified unjustified "segregation" of persons with disabilities as a "form of discrimination."

Recognition that unjustified institutional isolation of persons with disabilities is a form of discrimination reflects two evident judgments. First, institutional placement of persons who can handle and benefit from community settings perpetuates unwarranted assumptions that persons so isolated are incapable or unworthy of participating in community life. Second, confinement in an institution severely diminishes the everyday life activities of individuals, including family relations, social contacts, work options, economic independence, educational advancement, and cultural enrichment. Dissimilar treatment correspondingly exists in this key respect: In order to receive needed medical services, persons with mental disabilities must, because of those disabilities, relinquish participation in community life they could enjoy given reasonable accommodations, while persons without mental disabilities can receive the medical services they need without similar sacrifice.

The State urges that, whatever Congress may have stated as its findings in the ADA, the Medicaid statute "reflected a congressional policy preference for treatment in the institution over treatment in the community." The State correctly used the past tense. Since 1981, Medicaid has provided funding for state-run home and community-based care through a waiver program.

B

The State's responsibility, once it provides community-based treatment to qualified persons with disabilities, is not boundless. The reasonable-modifications regulation speaks of "reasonable modifications" to avoid discrimination, and allows States to resist modifications that entail a "fundamental alteration" of the States' services and programs. 28 CFR § 35.130(b)(7) (1998). The Court of Appeals construed this regulation to permit a cost-based defense "only in the most limited of circumstances," 138 F.3d at 902, and remanded to the District Court to consider, among other things, "whether the additional expenditures necessary to treat L.C. and E.W. in community-based care would be unreasonable given the demands of the State's mental health budget," 138 F.3d at 905.

The Court of Appeals' construction of the reasonable-modifications regulation is unacceptable for it would leave the State virtually defenseless once it is shown that the plaintiff is qualified for the service or program she seeks. Sensibly construed, the fundamental-alteration component of the reasonable-modifications regulation would allow the State to show that, in the allocation of available resources, immediate relief for the plaintiffs would be inequitable, given the responsibility the State has undertaken for the care and treatment of a large and diverse population of persons with mental disabilities.

As already observed, the ADA is not reasonably read to impel States to phase out institutions, placing patients in need of close care at risk. Nor is it the ADA's mission to drive States to move institutionalized patients into an inappropriate setting, such as a homeless shelter, a placement the State proposed, then retracted, for E.W. Some individuals, like L.C. and E.W. in prior years, may need institutional care from time to time "to stabilize acute psychiatric symptoms." For other individuals, no placement outside the institution may ever be appropriate.

To maintain a range of facilities and to administer services with an even hand, the State must have more leeway than the courts below understood the fundamental-alteration defense to allow. If, for example, the State were to demonstrate that it had a comprehensive, effectively working plan for placing qualified persons with mental disabilities in less restrictive settings, and a waiting list that moved at a reasonable pace not controlled by the State's endeavors to keep its institutions fully populated, the reasonable-modifications standard would be met. In such circumstances, a court would have no warrant effectively to order displacement of persons at the top of the community-based treatment waiting list by individuals lower down who commenced civil actions.

For the reasons stated, we conclude that, under Title II of the ADA, States are required to provide community-based treatment for persons with mental disabilities when the State's treatment professionals determine that such placement is appropriate, the affected persons do not oppose such treatment, and the placement can be reasonably accommodated, taking into account the resources available to the State and the needs of others with mental disabilities. The judgment of the Eleventh Circuit is therefore affirmed in part and vacated in part, and the case is remanded for further proceedings consistent with this opinion.

It is so ordered.

Justice **Stevens**, concurring in part and concurring in the judgment. . . . Justice **Kennedy**, with whom Justice **Breyer** joins as to Part I, concurring in the judgment.

I

Despite remarkable advances and achievements by medical science, and agreement among many professionals that even severe mental illness is often treatable, the extent of public resources to devote to this cause remains controversial. Knowledgeable professionals tell us that our society, and the governments which reflect its attitudes and preferences, have yet to grasp the potential for treating mental disorders, especially severe mental illness. As a result, necessary resources for the endeavor often are not forthcoming. During the course of a year, about 5.6 million Americans will suffer from severe mental illness. E. Torrey, Out of the Shadows 4 (1997). Some 2.2 million of these persons receive no treatment. Millions of other Americans suffer from mental disabilities of less serious degree, such as mild depression. These facts are part of the background against which this case arises. In addition, of course, persons with mental disabilities have been subject to historic mistreatment, indifference, and hostility. *See, e.g., Cleburne v. Cleburne Living Center, Inc.*, 473 U.S. 432, 461–464 (1985) (Marshall, J., concurring in judgment in part and dissenting in part) (discussing treatment of the mentally retarded).

Despite these obstacles, the States have acknowledged that the care of the mentally disabled is their special obligation. They operate and support facilities and programs, sometimes elaborate ones, to provide care. It is a continuing challenge, though, to provide the care in an effective and humane way, particularly because societal attitudes and the responses of public authorities have changed from time to time.

Beginning in the 1950's, many victims of severe mental illness were moved out of state-run hospitals, often with benign objectives. According to one estimate, when adjusted for population growth, "the actual decrease in the numbers of people with severe mental illnesses in public psychiatric hospitals between 1955 and 1995 was 92 percent." This was not without benefit or justification. The so-called "deinstitutionalization" has permitted a substantial number of mentally disabled persons to receive needed treatment with greater freedom and dignity. It may be, moreover, that those who remain institutionalized are indeed the most severe cases. With reference to this case, as the Court points out, it is undisputed that the State's own treating professionals determined that community-based care was medically appropriate for respondents. Nevertheless, the depopulation of state mental hospitals has its dark side. According to one expert:

> "For a substantial minority. . . deinstitutionalization has been a psychiatric *Titanic*. Their lives are virtually devoid of 'dignity' or 'integrity of body, mind, and spirit.' 'Self-determination' often means merely that the person has a choice of soup kitchens. The 'least restrictive setting' frequently turns out to be a cardboard box, a jail cell, or a terror-filled existence plagued by both real and imaginary enemies."

It must be remembered that for the person with severe mental illness who has no treatment the most dreaded of confinements can be the imprisonment inflicted by his own mind, which shuts reality out and subjects him to the torment of voices and images beyond our own powers to describe.

It would be unreasonable, it would be a tragic event, then, were the Americans with Disabilities Act of 1990 (ADA) to be interpreted so that States had some incentive, for fear of litigation, to drive those in need of medical care and treatment out of appropriate care and into settings with too little assistance and supervision. The opinion of a responsible treating physician in determining the appropriate conditions for treatment ought to be given the greatest of deference. It is a common phenomenon that a patient functions well with medication, yet, because of the mental illness itself, lacks the discipline or capacity to follow the regime the medication requires. This is illustrative of the factors a responsible physician will consider in recommending the appropriate setting or facility for treatment. Justice Ginsburg's opinion takes account of this background. It is careful, and quite correct, to say that it is not "the ADA's mission to drive States to move institutionalized patients into an inappropriate setting, such as a homeless shelter. . . ."

In light of these concerns, if the principle of liability announced by the Court is not applied with caution and circumspection, States may be pressured into attempting compliance on the cheap, placing marginal patients into integrated settings devoid of the services and attention necessary for their condition. This danger is in addition to the federalism costs inherent in referring state decisions regarding the administration of treatment programs and the allocation of resources to the reviewing authority of the federal courts. It is of central importance, then, that courts apply today's decision with great deference to the medical decisions of the responsible, treating physicians and, as the Court makes clear, with appropriate deference to the program funding decisions of state policymakers.

II

Putting aside issues of animus or unfair stereotype, I agree with Justice Thomas that on the ordinary interpretation and meaning of the term, one who alleges discrimination must show that she "received differential treatment vis-a-vis members of a different group on the basis of a statutorily described characteristic." In my view, however, discrimination so defined might be shown here.

If they could show that persons needing psychiatric or other medical services to treat a mental disability are subject to a more onerous condition than are persons eligible for other existing state medical services, and if removal of the condition would not be a fundamental alteration of a program or require the creation of a new one, then the beginnings of a discrimination case would be established. In terms more specific to this case, if respondents could show that Georgia (i) provides treatment to individuals suffering from medical problems of comparable seriousness, (ii) as a general matter, does so in the most integrated setting appropriate for the treatment of those problems (taking medical and other practical considerations into account), but (iii) without adequate justification, fails to do so for a group of mentally disabled persons (treating them instead in separate, locked institutional facilities), I believe it would demonstrate discrimination on the basis of mental disability.

Of course, it is a quite different matter to say that a State without a program in place is required to create one. No State has unlimited resources and each must make hard decisions on how much to allocate to treatment of diseases and disabilities. If, for example, funds for care and treatment of the mentally ill, including the severely mentally ill, are reduced in order to support programs directed to the treatment and care of other disabilities, the decision may be unfortunate. The judgment, however, is a political one and not within the reach of the statute. Grave constitutional concerns are raised when a federal court is given the authority to review the State's choices in basic matters such as establishing or declining to establish new programs. It is not reasonable to read the ADA to permit court intervention in these decisions.

Unlike Justice Thomas, I deem it relevant and instructive that Congress in express terms identified the "isolation and segregation" of disabled persons by society as a "form of discrimination," §§ 12101(a)(2), (5), and noted that discrimination against the disabled "persists in such critical areas as . . . institutionalization," § 12101(a)(3). These findings do not show that segregation and institutionalization are always discriminatory or that segregation or institutionalization are, by their nature, forms of prohibited discrimination. Nor do they necessitate a regime in which individual treatment plans are required, as distinguished from broad and reasonable classifications for the provision of health care services. Instead, they underscore Congress' concern that discrimination has been a frequent and pervasive problem in institutional settings and policies and its concern that segregating disabled persons from others can be discriminatory. Both of those concerns are consistent with the normal definition of discrimination — differential treatment of similarly situated groups.

The possibility therefore remains that, on the facts of this case, respondents would be able to support a claim under § 12132 by showing that they have been subject to discrimination by Georgia officials on the basis of their disability. This inquiry would not be simple. Comparisons of different medical conditions and the corresponding treatment regimens might be difficult, as would be assessments of the degree of integration of various settings in which medical treatment is offered. For example, the evidence might show that, apart from services for the mentally disabled, medical treatment is rarely offered in a community setting but also is rarely offered in facilities comparable to state mental hospitals. Determining the relevance of that type of evidence would require considerable judgment and analysis. However, as petitioners observe, "in this case, no class of similarly situated individuals was even identified, let alone shown to be given preferential treatment."

I would remand the case to the Court of Appeals or the District Court for it to determine in the first instance whether a statutory violation is sufficiently alleged and supported in respondents' summary judgment materials and, if not, whether they should be given leave to replead and to introduce evidence and argument along the lines suggested above.

For these reasons, I concur in the judgment of the Court.

Justice **Thomas**, with whom **The Chief Justice** and Justice **Scalia** join, dissenting.

Until today, this Court has never endorsed an interpretation of the term "discrimination" that encompassed disparate treatment among members of the *same* protected class. Discrimination, as typically understood, requires a showing that a claimant received differential treatment vis-a-vis members of a different group on the basis of a statutorily described characteristic. This interpretation comports with dictionary definitions of the term discrimination, which means to "distinguish," to "differentiate," or to make a "distinction in favor of or against, a person or thing based on the group, class, or category to which that person or thing belongs rather than on individual merit." Our decisions construing various statutory prohibitions against "discrimination" have not wavered from this path.

At bottom, the type of claim approved of by the majority does not concern a prohibition against certain conduct (the traditional understanding of discrimination), but rather imposition of a standard of care. As such, the majority can offer no principle limiting this new species of "discrimination" claim apart from an affirmative defense because it looks merely to an individual in isolation, without comparing him to otherwise similarly situated persons, and determines that discrimination occurs merely because that individual does not receive the treatment he wishes to receive. By adopting such a broad view of discrimination, the majority drains the term of any meaning other than as a proxy for decisions disapproved of by this Court.

Further, I fear that the majority's approach imposes significant federalism costs, directing States how to make decisions about their delivery of public services. We previously have recognized that constitutional principles of federalism erect limits on the Federal Government's ability to direct state officers or to interfere with the functions of state governments. The majority's affirmative defense will likely come as cold comfort to the States that will now be forced to defend themselves in federal court every time resources prevent the immediate placement of a qualified individual. In keeping with our traditional deference in this area, see *Alexander* [*v. Choate,* 469 U.S. 287 (1985)], the appropriate course would be to respect the States' historical role as the dominant authority responsible for providing services to individuals with disabilities.

Finally, it is also clear petitioners did not "discriminate" against respondents "by reason of [their] disabilities," as § 12132 requires. We have previously interpreted the phrase "by reason of" as requiring proximate causation. Such an interpretation is in keeping with the vernacular understanding of the phrase. This statute should be read as requiring proximate causation as well. Respondents do not contend that their disabilities constituted the proximate cause for their exclusion. Nor could they — community placement simply is not available to those without disabilities. Continued institutional treatment of persons who, though now deemed treatable in a community placement, must wait their turn for placement, does not establish that the denial of community placement occurred "by reason of" their disability. Rather, it establishes no more than the fact that petitioners have limited resources.

For the foregoing reasons, I respectfully dissent.

NOTES AND QUESTIONS

1. *Olmstead* is based on a statute, the Americans with Disabilities Act, which recurs a number of times elsewhere in this text, in dealing, for example, with AIDS or alcoholism in employment settings. There, a defense may be offered that the person poses an unacceptable risk, or that alternative placement has been offered, and so discrimination is permissible. Here, what is the defense? Put somewhat differently, what may the State of Georgia argue on remand?
2. What was the State's argument, that there had been no discrimination "by reason" of disabilities because there was no "comparison class"? How does Justice Ginsburg respond?
3. Isn't Justice Ginsburg's rationale really that it is simply *unreasonable* to institutionalize someone who *could* be placed in the community? If so, why not say so?
4. Where does Justice Stevens find the discrimination required by the ADA? As a trial attorney, would you prefer his burden or Justice Ginsburg's?
5. And what of Justice Stevens' fear of "compliance on the cheap," under Justice Ginsburg's standard? Is he right? How would he avoid that danger? Is his concern one of resources? Enforcement? Or is it for the "psychiatric Titanic" experienced by those subjected to deinstitutionalization over the past decades?
6. If a state without a program escapes liability, couldn't a state *with* one simply end it?
7. And doesn't Justice Thomas have it right — isn't this case really about a standard of care, not discrimination? If so, what *is* the standard (least restrictive alternative? right to treatment?)? And, anyway, what is *wrong* with that?

8. Finally, what is a community's obligation to protect or support or compensate those members who are disabled? Does it matter what the disability is — congenital, developmental, self-inflicted (what *is* a disability, anyway?) — and whether the citizen has done all possible to cope? Are the answers different when we ask the same questions of *other* community members, such as employers or landlords?

PROBLEM 1–6 — Lobotomies of Murderers

Consider the following research summary* on the biological factor in crime:

> Previous research has suggested that links between autonomic nervous system functioning and violence are strongest in those who come from benign home backgrounds, but there appears to be no similar research using brain-imaging measures of central nervous system functioning. It was hypothesized that murderers who had no early psychosocial deprivation (*e.g.,* no childhood abuse, family neglect) would demonstrate lower prefrontal glucose metabolism than murderers with early psychosocial deprivation and a group of normal controls. Murderers from a previous study, which showed prefrontal deficits in murderers, were assessed for psychosocial deprivation and divided into those with and without deprivation. Murderers without any clear psychosocial deficits were significantly lower on prefrontal glucose metabolism than murderers with psychosocial deficits and controls. These results suggest that murderers lacking psychosocial deficits are characterized by prefrontal deficits. It is argued that among violent offenders without deprived home backgrounds, the "social push" to violence is minimized, and consequently, brain abnormalities provide a relatively stronger predisposition to violence in this group.

In the light of this research and the preceding cases, can murderers be subjected to psychosurgery? Consensually, as a condition of release or an alternative to the death penalty?

PROBLEM 1–7 — Prisoners, Experimentation and AIDS

Northern States Penitentiary has a death row, on which 27 inmates reside, awaiting execution pursuant to sentences of capital punishment. The warden has been approached by the Dean of State University Medical School, seeking permission to enroll the prisoners on death row in a controlled experiment, testing a new vaccine for AIDS. All of the patients will be exposed to the HIV virus and will become infected by it. Half of them would receive the new vaccine, in a double blind process. The other half would receive a placebo. The experiment would take three years, at the end of which time — if the vaccine is effective — it would be too late to administer the vaccine to the untreated control group. The proposal is that all of the participating prisoners at the end of the three-year period of time would have avoided the death penalty

* Reprinted with permission from Raine et al., *Prefrontal Glucose Deficits in Murderers,* 11 Neuropsychiatry, Neuropsychology and Behavorial Neurology 1-7 (1998).

for that length of time, and the suspension might be extended if scientifically necessary. As an ethical matter, is the "consent" of the prisoners necessary? Is their knowledge necessary? Should they, even with their consent and knowledge, be enrolled in such an experiment? Would it matter if the *quid pro quo* was commutation of the death penalty sentences to life imprisonment? Consider here the case law on informed consent and experimentation, *infra* § 3.03.

PROBLEM 1–8 — Torture and Terrorism (and Doctors)

In February, 2006, the Forum section of *USA Today* (2/20/2006, p. 11A) carried a column that stated two-thirds of Americans believe torturing suspected terrorists is permissible under certain circumstances. The column reported that a Jesuit priest, John Perry, discusses practices in Torture: Religious Ethics and National Security, which would justify, for example, killing a terrorist in order to gain information to prevent an attack like the one that killed 3000 people in New York City on September 11, 2001. (Or presumably, a similar number at Pearl Harbor on December 7, 1941.) The author of the column, Rabbi Gerald Zalizer, then reports that Israel's Supreme Court has banned torture, except under "ticking bomb" circumstances, and concludes that "torture degrades the victim, but it also degrades the society condoning it."

Is Rabbi Zalizer right? If so, is torture never permitted? If it may be allowed, how should the Israeli Supreme Court define the circumstances and techniques, and with what safeguards and oversight?

And what role should doctors play in torture? See Lifton, *Doctors and Torture,* New Eng. J. Med. 351:415 (7/29/2004) and Annas, *Unspeakably Cruel — Torture, Medical Ethics, and the Law,* New Eng. J. Med. 352:20 (5/19/2005), discussing the obligation of physicians to avoid participating in torture, even when in the military, in the light of events at the Abu Graihb and Guantanamo prisons during the Iraq war. *See also* Bloche, *When Doctors Go to War*, New Eng. J. Med. 352:1 (1/6/2005).

[2] Incompetents

Of the groups in society most subject to physical control and abuse, prisoners are followed closely by those deemed mentally unfit — "incompetent" — to handle their own affairs. Of the ranges of imposition historically inflicted by society, two — sterilization and surgery — are most troublesome. They are the subjects of the following cases.

[a] Sterilization

BUCK v. BELL
274 U.S. 200 (1927)

Mr. Justice **Holmes** delivered the opinion of the Court.

. . . .

Carrie Buck is a feeble-minded white woman who was committed to the State Colony. She is the daughter of a feeble-minded mother in the same institution, and the mother of an illegitimate feeble-minded child. She was eighteen years old at the time of the trial of her case in the Circuit Court in the latter part of 1924. An Act of Virginia approved March 20, 1924 recites that the health of the patient and the welfare of society may be promoted in certain cases by the sterilization of mental defectives, under careful safeguard, etc.; that the sterilization may be effected in males by vasectomy and in females by salpingectomy, without serious pain or substantial danger to life; that the Commonwealth is supporting in various institutions many defective persons who if now discharged would become a menace but if incapable of procreating might be discharged with safety and become self-supporting with benefit to themselves and to society; and that experience has shown that heredity plays an important part in the transmission of insanity, imbecility, etc. The statute then enacts that whenever the superintendent of certain institutions including the above-named State Colony shall be of opinion that it is for the best interest of the patients and of society that an inmate under his care should be sexually sterilized, he may have the operation performed upon any patient afflicted with hereditary forms of insanity, imbecility, etc., on complying with the very careful provisions by which the act protects the patients from possible abuse.

. . . .

The attack is not upon the procedure but upon the substantive law. It seems to be contended that in no circumstances could such an order be justified. It certainly is contended that the order cannot be justified upon the existing grounds. The judgment finds the facts that have been recited and that Carrie Buck "is the probable potential parent of socially inadequate offspring, likewise afflicted, that she may be sexually sterilized without detriment to her general health and that her welfare and that of society will be promoted by her sterilization," and thereupon makes the order. In view of the general declarations of the Legislature and the specific findings of the Court obviously we cannot say as matter of law that the grounds do not exist, and if they exist they justify the result. We have seen more than once that the public welfare may call upon the best citizens for their lives. It would be strange if it could not call upon those who already sap the strength of the State for these lesser sacrifices, often not felt to be such by those concerned, in order to prevent our being swamped with incompetence. It is better for all the world, if instead of waiting to execute degenerate offspring for crime, or to let them starve for their imbecility, society can prevent those who are manifestly unfit from continuing their kind. The principle that sustains compulsory vaccination is broad enough to cover cutting the Fallopian tubes. Three generations of imbeciles are enough.

But, it is said, however it might be if this reasoning were applied generally, it fails when it is confined to the small number who are in the institutions named and is not applied to the multitudes outside. It is the usual last resort of constitutional arguments to point out shortcomings of this sort. But the answer is that the law does all that is needed when it does all that it can, indicates a policy, applies it to all within the lines, and seeks to bring within the lines all similarly situated so far and so fast as its means allow. Of course so far as the operations enable those who otherwise must be kept confined to be returned to the world, and thus open the asylum to others, the equality aimed at will be more nearly reached.

Judgment affirmed.

Mr. Justice **Butler** dissents.

NOTES AND QUESTIONS

1. Justice Holmes was capable of reasoning by aphorism, as in "three generations of imbeciles are enough." These, however, can too easily dismiss legitimate argumentation, which for Carrie Buck included the following: (a) there was no need to sterilize her while she was institutionalized; (b) there was no showing that she proposed to have other children or that they would necessarily also be "feeble minded;" (c) sterilization against only the institutionalized denies equal protection of the laws; (d) sterilization under any circumstances denies due process, since it affects a fundamental human interest.

   How well does Justice Holmes do in dealing with these arguments?

2. Mr. Justice Butler dissented, but without stating his reasons. What might they have been in 1927?

3. The concern for society "being swamped with incompetents," having its strength "sapped" and having "to execute degenerate offspring for crime" bespeaks a concern for eugenics. During the early 20th century, the rise of social Darwinism, along with developments in the science of genetics, became woven into the preexisting law of public health. It spread broadly throughout the Western world and held open the promise of improving the human race by eliminating "those who are manifestly unfit from continuing their kind."

   Ethically, may a community set about defining (and "improving") itself in this manner? For an account of how one community went astray using eugenics as part of its public health program see Lifton, The Nazi Doctors (Basic Books, 1986).

4. Eugenics became discredited as a "science" by the Nazi obsession with preserving the Aryan "super race." But with the mapping of the human genome in the 1990s and the advent of genetic engineering and cloning, the possibility of eliminating undesirable characteristics (or people) from the human race again lies before us. What are the ethical dimensions of such a quest? *See* Chapter 4.

SKINNER v. OKLAHOMA
316 U.S. 535 (1942)

Mr. Justice **Douglas** delivered the opinion of the Court.

This case touches a sensitive and important area of human rights. Oklahoma deprives certain individuals of a right which is basic to the perpetuation of a race — the right to have offspring. Oklahoma has decreed the enforcement of its law against petitioner, overruling his claim that it violated the Fourteenth Amendment. . . .

. . . .

If the court or jury finds that the defendant is an "habitual criminal" and that he "may be rendered sexually sterile without detriment to his or her general health," then the court "shall render judgment to the effect that said defendant be rendered sexually sterile" by the operation of vasectomy in case of a male and of salpingectomy in case of a female. Only one other provision of the Act is material here and that is section 195 which provides that "offenses arising out of the violation of the prohibitory laws, revenue acts, embezzlement, or political offenses, shall not come or be considered within the terms of this Act."

Petitioner was convicted in 1926 of the crime of stealing chickens and was sentenced to the Oklahoma State Reformatory. In 1929 he was convicted of the crime of robbery with fire arms and was sentenced to the reformatory. In 1934 he was convicted again of robbery with firearms and was sentenced to the penitentiary. He was confined there in 1935 when the Act was passed. In 1936 the Attorney General instituted proceedings against him. . . .

Several objections to the constitutionality of the Act have been pressed upon us. It is urged that the Act cannot be sustained as an exercise of the police power in view of the state of scientific authorities respecting inheritability of criminal traits. It is argued that due process is lacking because under this Act, unlike the act upheld in *Buck v. Bell*, the defendant is given no opportunity to be heard on the issue as to whether he is the probable potential parent of socially undesirable offspring. It is also suggested that the Act is penal in character and that the sterilization provided for is cruel and unusual punishment and violative of the Fourteenth Amendment. We pass those points without intimating an opinion on them, for there is a feature of the Act which clearly condemns it. That is its failure to meet the requirements of the equal protection clause of the Fourteenth Amendment.

We do not stop to point out all of the inequalities of this Act. A few examples will suffice. In Oklahoma grand larceny is a felony. Larceny is grand larceny when the property taken exceeds $20 in value. Embezzlement is punishable "in the manner prescribed for feloniously stealing property of the value of that embezzled." Hence he who embezzles property worth more than $20 is guilty of a felony. A clerk who appropriates over $20 from his employer's till and a stranger who steals the same amount are thus both guilty of felonies. If the latter repeats his act and is convicted three times, he may be sterilized. But the clerk is not subject to the pains and penalties of the Act no matter how large his embezzlements nor how frequent his convictions. A person who enters a chicken coop and steals chickens commits a felony; and he may be sterilized if he is thrice convicted. If, however, he is a bailee of the property and fraudulently appropriates it, he is an embezzler. Hence no matter how habitual his proclivities for embezzlement are and no matter how often his conviction, he may not be sterilized. Thus the nature of the two crimes is intrinsically the same and they are punishable in the same manner. Furthermore, the line between them follows close distinctions — distinctions comparable to those highly technical ones which shaped the common law as to "trespass" or "taking." . . .

It was stated in *Buck v. Bell* that the claim that state legislation violates the equal protection clause of the Fourteenth Amendment is "the usual last resort of constitutional arguments." Under our constitutional system the States in determining the reach and scope of particular legislation need not provide "abstract symmetry." . . . Thus, if we had here only a question as to a State's classification of crimes, such as embezzlement or larceny, no substantial federal question would be raised. For a State is not constrained in the exercise of its police power to ignore experience which marks a class of offenders or a family of offenses for special treatment. Nor is it prevented by the equal protection clause from confining "its restrictions to those classes of cases where the need is deemed to be clearest." As stated in *Buck v. Bell*, "the law does all that is needed when it does all that it can, indicates a policy, applies it to all within the lines, and seeks to bring within the lines all similarly situated so far and so fast as its means allow."

But the instant legislation runs afoul of the equal protection clause, though we give Oklahoma that large deference which the rule of the foregoing cases requires. . . . Marriage and procreation are fundamental to the very existence and survival of the race. The power to sterilize, if exercised, may have subtle, far-reaching and devastating effects. In evil or reckless hands it can cause races or types which are inimical to the dominant group to wither and disappear. There is no redemption for the individual whom the law touches. Any experiment which the State conducts is to his irreparable injury. He is forever deprived of a basic liberty. We mention these matters not to reexamine the scope of the police power of the States. We advert to them merely in emphasis of our view that strict scrutiny of the classification which a State makes in a sterilization law is essential, lest unwittingly or otherwise invidious discriminations are made against groups or types of individuals in violation of the constitutional guaranty of just and equal laws. . . . In terms of fines and imprisonment the crimes of larceny and embezzlement rate the same under the Oklahoma code. Only when it comes to sterilization are the pains and penalties of the law different. The equal protection clause would indeed be a formula of empty words if such conspicuously artificial lines could be drawn. In *Buck v. Bell*, the Virginia statute was upheld though it applied only to feebleminded persons in institutions of the State. But it was pointed out that "so far as the operations enable those who otherwise must be kept confined to be returned to the world, and thus open the asylum to others, the equality aimed at will be more nearly reached." Here there is no such saving feature. Embezzlers are forever free. Those who steal or take in other ways are not. If such a classification were permitted, the technical common law concept of a "trespass" based on distinctions which are "very largely dependent upon history for explanation" could readily become a rule of human genetics.

. . . .

Reversed.

Mr. Chief Justice **Stone** concurring.

I concur in the result, but I am not persuaded that we are aided in reaching it by recourse to the equal protection clause.

If Oklahoma may resort generally to the sterilization of criminals on the assumption that their propensities are transmissible to future generations by inheritance, I seriously doubt that the equal protection clause requires it to apply the measure to all criminals in the first instance, or to none.

Moreover, if we must presume that the legislature knows — what science has been unable to ascertain — that the criminal tendencies of any class of habitual offenders are transmissible regardless of the varying mental characteristics of its individuals, I should suppose that we must likewise presume that the legislature, in its wisdom, knows that the criminal tendencies of some classes of offenders are more likely to be transmitted than those of others. And so I think the real question we have to consider is not one of equal protection, but whether the wholesale condemnation of a class to such an invasion of personal liberty, without opportunity to any individual to show that his is not the type of case which would justify resort to it, satisfies the demands of due process.

. . . .

Science has found and the law has recognized that there are certain types of mental deficiency associated with delinquency which are inheritable. But the State does not contend — nor can there be any pretense — that either common knowledge or experience, or scientific investigation, has given assurance that the criminal tendencies of any class of habitual offenders are universally or even generally inheritable. In such circumstances, inquiry whether such is the fact in the case of any particular individual cannot rightly be dispensed with. Whether the procedure by which a statute carries its mandate into execution satisfies due process is a matter of judicial cognizance. A law which condemns, without hearing, all the individuals of a class to so harsh a measure as the present because some or even many merit condemnation, is lacking in the first principles of due process. And so, while the state may protect itself from the demonstrably inheritable tendencies of the individual which are injurious to society, the most elementary notions of due process would seem to require it to take appropriate steps to safeguard the liberty of the individual by affording him, before he is condemned to an irreparable injury in his person, some opportunity to show that he is without such inheritable tendencies. The state is called on to sacrifice no permissible end when it is required to reach its objective by a reasonable and just procedure adequate to safeguard rights of the individual which concededly the Constitution protects.

Mr. Justice **Jackson** concurring.

I join the Chief Justice in holding that the hearings provided are too limited in the context of the present Act to afford due process of law. I also agree with the opinion of Mr. Justice Douglas that the scheme of classification set forth in the Act denies equal protection of the law. I disagree with the opinion of each in so far as it rejects or minimizes the grounds taken by the other.

. . . .

I also think the present plan to sterilize the individual in pursuit of a eugenic plan to eliminate from the race characteristics that are only vaguely identified and which in our present state of knowledge are uncertain as to transmissibility presents other constitutional questions of gravity. This Court has sustained such an experiment with respect to an imbecile, a person with definite and observable characteristics where the condition had persisted through three generations and afforded grounds for the belief that it was transmissible and would continue to manifest itself in generations to come.

There are limits to the extent to which a legislatively represented majority may conduct biological experiments at the expense of the dignity and personality and natural powers of a minority — even those who have been guilty of what the majority define as crimes. But this Act falls down before reaching this problem, which I mention only to avoid the implication that such a question may not exist because not discussed. On it I would also reserve judgment.

NOTES AND QUESTIONS

1. How is *Skinner* different from *Buck v. Bell*? Both involve sterilization of people in custody of the state and both are presumably grounded on public health concerns. How does Justice Douglas distinguish *Buck* from *Skinner*?
2. Is Justice Douglas' concern *truly* that "marriage and procreation are fundamental," or is it that the "power to sterilize, if exercised, may have . . . devastating effects?" In other words, is he concerned about the right involved or about the potential abuse of the power asserted? And why is it important to him that the power of procreation is important to the *race*? If so, does that mean it can be regulated?
3. Justice Douglas is unpersuaded that embezzlers are different from those who steal or take "in other ways." There is no basis, he says, for distinguishing between these classes of criminals in terms of inheritability of "criminal traits." But is he missing the point? Could not the state simply justify sterilization as a punishment for certain crimes, without regard to the traits of the criminals themselves? And if the line between embezzlement and larceny is too close, what about sterilization of those who commit rape, robbery or homicide?
4. Suppose there were — as there is coming to be — evidence that certain behavioral patterns *are* inherited, and persons having those traits can be reliably identified. Would Justice Douglas then support sterilization?
5. Should there be a requirement that the subject not appreciate or understand the nature of the sterilization procedure and the resulting loss in reproductive capability? Is sterilization more or less objectionable when the subject does not *understand*?
6. Statutes authorizing sterilization of "mental defectives" remain on the books of many states and have been held constitutional. *See North Carolina Association for Retarded Children v. State of North Carolina*, 420 F. Supp. 451 (D.N.C. 1976). Generally, such statutes must provide elaborate procedures and safeguards and must authorize sterilization only where the evidence is that the cause of mental retardation was inherited, capable of transmission, and that the subject would be

incapable of caring for any child. Consider whether these satisfy the questions and objections in *Skinner* as you read the next case.

IN THE MATTER OF EDITH M.M. HAYES

608 P.2d 635 (Wa. 1980)

Horowitz, Justice

This appeal raises the question whether the Superior Court for Grant County has authority to grant a petition for sterilization of a severely mentally retarded person.

. . . .

Edith Hayes is severely mentally retarded as a result of a birth defect. Now 16 years old, she functions at the level of a four to five year old. Her physical development, though, has been commensurate with her age. She is thus capable of conceiving and bearing children, while being unable at present to understand her own reproductive functions or exercise independent judgment in her relationship with males. Her mother and doctors believe she is sexually active and quite likely to become pregnant. Her parents are understandably concerned that Edith is engaging in these sexual activities. Furthermore, her parents and doctors feel the long term effects of conventional birth control methods are potentially harmful, and that sterilization is the most desirable method to ensure that Edith does not conceive an unwanted child.

Edith's parents are sensitive to her special needs and concerned about her physical and emotional health, both now and in the future. They have sought appropriate medical care and education for her, and provided her with responsible and adequate supervision. During the year or so that Edith has been capable of becoming pregnant, though, they have become frustrated, depressed and emotionally drained by the stress of seeking an effective and safe method of contraception. They believe it is impossible to supervise her activities closely enough to prevent her from becoming involved in sexual relations. Thus, with the consent of Edith's father, Sharon Hayes petitioned for an order appointing her guardian and authorizing a sterilization procedure for Edith.

I. Jurisdiction

. . . .

Persuasive authority for the principle that courts of general jurisdiction do have jurisdiction over a petition by a parent or guardian for an order authorizing sterilization is found in the United States Supreme Court in *Stump v. Sparkman*, 435 U.S. 349 (1978). In that case a woman sterilized pursuant to court order when she was a child later brought a civil rights action against the judge who issued the order. The question was whether the judge lacked judicial immunity for the act. The Court determined the judge's conduct in entertaining and approving the petition for sterilization constituted a judicial act, and that he had not acted in the clear absence of all jurisdiction. With regard to the jurisdiction issue, the Court noted the judge was a member of a court which had broad jurisdiction at law and in equity, and which was not prohibited from considering a petition for sterilization by either statute or controlling case law. It concluded the judge had "the power to entertain and act upon the petition for sterilization" and was entitled to judicial immunity in the suit.

The courts of this state have long recognized the inherent power of the superior court "to hear and determine all matters legal and equitable in all proceedings known to the common law." . . .

Nor is a statute required to empower a superior court to exercise its jurisdiction by granting a petition for sterilization. We recognize the power of the legislature, subject to the state and federal Constitutions, to enact statutes regulating sterilization of mentally incompetent persons in the custody of a parent or guardian. It has not done so, however. The relevant guardianship statute defines the duties of a guardian to care for, maintain, and provide education for an incompetent person. The statute neither provides nor prohibits sterilization procedures at a guardian's request. It does not in any event derogate from the judicial power of the court which includes the power to authorize such a procedure where it is necessary. In the absence of any limiting legislative enactment, the Superior Court has full power to take action to provide for the needs of a mentally incompetent person, just as it has authority to do so to protect the interests of a child. We hold the Superior Court of the State of Washington has authority under the state constitution to entertain and act upon a petition for an order authorizing sterilization of a mentally incompetent person, and in the absence of legislation restricting the exercise of that power, the court has authority to grant such a petition.

. . . .

II. Standards for Sterilization

Our conclusion that superior courts have the power to grant a petition for sterilization does not mean that power must be exercised. Sterilization touches upon the individual's right of privacy and the fundamental right to procreate. It is an unalterable procedure with serious effects on the lives of the mentally retarded person and those upon whom he or she may depend. Therefore, it should be undertaken only after careful consideration of all relevant factors. We conclude this opinion with a set of guidelines setting out of the questions which must be asked and answered before an order authorizing sterilization of a mentally incompetent person could be issued. First, however, the considerations which are important to this determination can be best illuminated by discussing briefly the historical context from which they arise.

Sterilization of the mentally ill, mentally retarded, criminals, and sufferers from certain debilitating diseases became popular in this country in the early 20th century. The theory of "eugenic sterilization" was that the above-named traits and diseases, widely believed at that time to be hereditary, could be eliminated to the benefit of all society by simply preventing procreation.

. . . .

More recently scientific evidence has demonstrated little or no relationship between genetic inheritance and such conditions as mental retardation, criminal behavior, and diseases such as epilepsy. Geneticists have discovered, for example, that some forms of mental retardation appear to have no hereditary component at all, while in some others the element of heredity is only one of a number of factors which may contribute to the condition. In short, the theoretical foundation for eugenic sterilization as a method of improving society has been disproved.

At the same time other previously unchallenged assumptions about mentally retarded persons have been shown to be unreliable. It has been found, for example, that far from being an insignificant event for the retarded person, sterilization can have longlasting detrimental emotional effects. Furthermore, while retarded persons, especially children, are often highly suggestible, there is evidence they are also capable of learning and adhering to strict rules of social behavior. Many retarded persons are capable of having normal children and being good parents.

Of great significance for the problem faced here is the fact that, unlike the situation of a normal and necessary medical procedure, in the question of sterilization the interests of the parents of a retarded person cannot be presumed to be identical to those of the child. The problem of parental consent to sterilization is of great concern to professionals in the field of mental health, and the overwhelming weight of opinion of those who have studied the problem appears to be that consent of a parent or guardian is a questionable or inadequate basis for sterilization. It is thus clear that in any proceedings to determine whether an order for sterilization should issue, the retarded person must be represented, as here, by a disinterested guardian ad litem.

. . . .

Among the factors to be considered are the age and educability of the individual. For example, a child in her early teens may be incapable at present of understanding the consequences of sexual activity, or exercising judgment in relations with the opposite sex, but may also have the potential to develop the required understanding and judgment through continued education and developmental programs.

A related consideration is the potential of the individual as a parent. As noted above, many retarded persons are capable of becoming good parents, and in only a fraction of cases is it likely that offspring would inherit a genetic form of mental retardation that would make parenting more difficult.

Another group of relevant factors involve the degree to which sterilization is medically indicated as the last and best resort for the individual. Can it be shown by clear, cogent and convincing evidence, for example, that other methods of birth control are inapplicable or unworkable?

. . . .

The decision can only be made in a superior court proceeding in which (1) the incompetent individual is represented by a disinterested guardian ad litem, (2) the court has received independent advice based upon a comprehensive medical, psychological, and social evaluation of the individual, and (3) to the greatest extent possible, the court has elicited and taken into account the view of the incompetent individual.

Within this framework, the judge must first find by clear, cogent and convincing evidence that the individual is (1) incapable of making his or her own decision about sterilization, and (2) unlikely to develop sufficiently to make an informed judgment about sterilization in the foreseeable future.

Next, it must be proved by clear, cogent and convincing evidence that there is a need for contraception. The judge must find that the individual is (1) physically capable of procreation, and (2) likely to engage in sexual activity at the present or in the near future under circumstances likely to result in pregnancy, and must find in addition that (3) the nature and extent of the individual's disability, as determined by empirical evidence and not solely on the basis of standardized tests, renders him or her permanently incapable of caring for a child, even with reasonable assistance.

Finally, there must be no alternatives to sterilization. The judge must find that by clear, cogent and convincing evidence (1) all less drastic contraceptive methods, including supervision, education and training, have been proved unworkable or inapplicable, and (2) the proposed method of sterilization entails the least invasion of the body of the individual. In addition, it must be shown by clear, cogent and convincing evidence that (3) the current state of scientific and medical knowledge does not suggest either (a) that a reversible sterilization procedure or other less drastic contraceptive method will shortly be available, or (b) that science is on the threshold of an advance in the treatment of the individual's disability.

There is a heavy presumption against sterilization of an individual incapable of informed consent that must be overcome by the person or entity requesting sterilization. This burden will be even harder to overcome in the case of a minor incompetent, whose youth may make it difficult or impossible to prove by clear, cogent and convincing evidence that he or she will never be capable of making an informed judgment about sterilization or of caring for a child.

Review of the facts in this case in light of these standards make it clear that the burden has not yet been met. It cannot be said that Edith Hayes will be unable to understand sexual activity or control her behavior in the future. The medical testimony and report of the mental health board are not detailed enough to provide clear, cogent and convincing evidence in this regard. Edith's youth is of particular concern, since she has many years of education before her. Furthermore, although there is evidence that some methods of birth control have already been tried, there is insufficient proof that no conventional form of contraception is a reasonable and medically acceptable alternative to sterilization. Nor is there any evidence such a procedure would not have detrimental effects on Edith's future emotional or physical health. Finally, there is no evidence that a pregnancy would be physically or emotionally hazardous to Edith, and insufficient evidence that she would never be capable of being a good parent.

Additional factfinding at the trial level will help the superior court judge answer the questions set out in this opinion. Therefore, the case is reversed and remanded for further proceedings consistent with this opinion.

Utter, C.J., and **Dolliver** and **Williams**, J.J., concur.

Stafford, Justice (concurring specially in part in the majority and dissenting in part).

. . . .

. . . [D]espite the cautious approach employed, I am compelled to depart from the majority. I acknowledge existence of the judicial power to act. Possession of such power, however, neither requires that it be exercised nor necessarily supports the wisdom of its exercise under all circumstances.

. . . .

It seems to me that having clearly declared the judiciary's power to act, wisdom dictates we should defer articulation of this complex public policy to the legislature. Such deferral, done with a clear declaration of judicial power, is not an abdication of that power. Rather, it is a recognition that the declared power can be rationally coupled with a conscious choice not to exercise it.

. . . .

Since, contrary to my views, the judiciary plans to exercise its power to act in cases of this nature, it should do so only under strict protective standards. Most of the standards enunciated by the majority fulfill this objective.

Without question those who seek intervention of the judiciary on "behalf" of an alleged mentally incompetent person usually will do so with the best of intentions. If the judiciary is willing to furnish the means of resolving such a critical issue, it should not on the one hand make the forum available and on the other hand make the burden of proof so impossible of accomplishment that the forum cannot be used. Unfortunately, the final standard proposed by the majority does just that.

The moving party is required to prove by clear, cogent and convincing evidence that "(3) the current state of scientific and medical knowledge does not suggest (a) that a reversible sterilization procedure or other less drastic contraceptive method will shortly be available, or (b) that science is on the threshold of an advance in the treatment of the individual's disability." First, the standard requires the moving party to prove a negative. Second, it involves the judiciary in a questionable contest at three levels: (a) whether the movant has done sufficient research to establish that no medical breakthrough is possible in the foreseeable future; (b) whether a medical procedure possible in the next few years will become an actuality; and (c) whether the alleged mentally incompetent person will be able to take advantage of the nebulous scientific advance for physical or emotional reasons.

It is too much to ask the moving party, the alleged mentally ill person or the judiciary to litigate such nebulous eventualities of science.

Hicks, J., concurs.

Rosellini, Justice (dissenting).

In the exercise of the police power, the legislature has provided for sterilization of certain criminals, evidently upon the mistaken belief that the tendencies exhibited by such criminals are inheritable. Today, the court has enacted its own statute, providing for the sterilization of children upon the petition of parents.

The majority recognizes that it has no real statutory authority to act in this area. It cites no authority supporting the proposition that the ordering of sterilization of human beings is among the inherent powers reserved to the courts. [T]he inherent powers of a court do not increase its jurisdiction; they are limited to such powers as are essential to the existence of the court and the orderly and efficient exercise of its jurisdiction. [T]he powers pertain to matters procedural rather than substantive. They do not include the power to determine what laws will best serve the public welfare.

. . . .

The majority of courts in the United States which have considered the question have held that, in the absence of specific statutory authorization, courts are not empowered to order sterilization of incompetents. . . .

. . . .

The United States Supreme Court has not held that a state court has inherent power to order sterilization. In *Stump v. Sparkman*, cited by the majority, the issue was whether a judge who had ordered a minor girl sterilized was immune from liability to that girl when she reached majority, married, and discovered the author of her inability to have children. The court held that judges of the courts of superior or general jurisdiction are not liable in a civil action for their judicial acts, even when such acts are in excess of their jurisdiction and are alleged to have been done maliciously or corruptly and even though grave procedural errors occur.

The Supreme Court majority was obviously intent upon protecting the judge's immunity. The opinion certainly does not stand as an endorsement of judicially ordered sterilizations but rather as an uncompromising assertion of such immunity. I would say that it also stands as an ominous warning of how easily the asserted power to order sterilization can be mistakenly exercised.

. . . .

The majority assumes that it is established that sterilization may be beneficial to society. And yet scientific studies cast grave doubts upon the correctness of this assumption. In a Note, *Eugenic Sterilization A Scientific Analysis*, 46 Denver L.J. 631, 633-34 (1969), the author says:

> [T]he fact that *some* sterilizations continue to be performed and that, in any event, the threat remains of possible sterilization being imposed, even though there is questionable scientific value in such procedures, makes this a topic of continuing timeliness and interest. Numerous legal, medical, and sociological reviews have been published on the subject, most of them unfavorable in their appraisal. The basic criticisms have been that eugenic sterilization does not accomplish its stated objective of "human betterment," and, at the same time, it interferes with important freedoms either expressly guaranteed by the *United States Constitution* or brought within its ambit by judicial construction.

My great concern is that the courts do not become "an imperial judiciary," a phrase coined, I believe, by Nathan Glaser. In his book, Power, written late in his career, Adolph Berle spoke of the United States Supreme Court as a benevolent dictatorship. And Phillip Kurland has often traced the Supreme Court's wandering in the political thicket with no compass for a guide, save its own subjective fancies.

The rule of law is not well served by handing unrestricted policymaking power to a shifting majority of as few as five whose judgment, as Justice Jackson would say, is not final because it is infallible, but infallible because it is final.

I would affirm the judgment of dismissal.

Wright and **Brachtenbach**, J.J., concur.

NOTES AND QUESTIONS

1. In deciding whether to sterilize a young woman, how important is it that her parents "have become frustrated, depressed and emotionally drained by the stress of seeking an effective and safe method of contraception?" Is the significant portion of this consideration the fact that the parents are drained or that no alternative exists? If one did exist, for example, the Norplant implant, would sterilization then become impermissible?

2. Are you satisfied that a "court of general jurisdiction" does have, or should have, authority to authorize sterilization without specific statutory permission from the Legislature? Is not sterilization of such personal importance to the individual and of community importance to society, that it should be discussed and reviewed by a democratic agency? What source does the court refer to in asserting its claim of implicit authority? *See Wirsing v. Michigan Protection and Advocacy Service*, 542 N.W.2d 594, *rev'd*, 573 NW2d 51 (Mich. 1998).

3. The court lists a group of "relevant factors," including the age and educationability of the individual, the potential as a parent, and the availability of other methods of birth control. It does not, however, establish any priority among these factors, develop a gradient scale as to each, or determine whether other factors might exist. What is your view as to these factors or others?

4. Assume for the moment that the mentally deficient individual can be shown *not* to suffer from a condition which may be transmitted, but would be incapable of caring for a child. Since society is capable of providing for such care, should sterilization be prohibited? Ethically, must society respect the right of the individual, even if retarded, to procreate?

5. The dissents emphasized the importance of the right of procreation to the individual, both ethically and constitutionally. If it could be shown that the subject had no awareness of the importance of procreation or of his or her capacity to so conform, does the "right" diminish in importance?

6. Norplant is an available alternative and perhaps a "least intrusive means" to solving problems of mentally disabled women reproducing. Norplant is a small (4 to 6 inch), thin device inserted under the skin

of the upper arm, slowly releasing over several years a substance which suppresses ovulation and, hence, conception. For a discussion of this alternative, see Roberta Cepko, *Involuntary Sterilization of Mentally Disabled Women,* 8 Berkeley Women's L.J. 122 (1993).

7. Sterilization of the mentally disabled is a controversial and perplexing issue. For a comprehensive review of this matter, see Joe Zumpano-Canto, J.D., M.P.H., *Nonconsensual Sterilization of the Mentally Disabled in North Carolina: An Ethics Critique of the Statutory Standard and its Judicial Interpretation*, 13 J. Contemp. Health L. & Pol'y 79 (Fall, 1996).

8. For an excellent article, see John Handy Culver, III, *Wentzel v. Montgomery General Hospital — Maryland's Equitable Jurisdiction Over Sterilization Petitions: A Constitutional Analysis*, 42 Md. L. Rev. 549 (1983); and see Steven J. Cleveland, *Sterilization Of The Mentally Disabled: Applying Error Cost Analysis To The "Best Interest" Inquiry*, 86 Geo. L.J. 137 (1997).

9. For an excellent discussion of balancing autonomy and need, see Nancy J. Knauer, *"Lawyering for the Mentally Ill: Defining Capacity: Balancing the Competing Interests of Autonomy and Need,"* 12 Temp. Pol. & Civ. Rts. L. Rev. 321 (Spring 2003).

PROBLEM 1-9 — Don't Get Pregnant

In *People v. Zaring*, 10 Cal. Rptr. 2d 263 (Ct. App. 5th Dist. 1992), the defendant was sentenced for heroin possession to five years probation on condition she not get pregnant. The reasons the judge gave were as follows:

> I want make [sic] to make clear that one of the reasons I am making this order is you've got five children. You're thirty years old. None of your children are in your custody or control. Two of them on AFDC. And I'm afraid that if you get pregnant we're going to get a cocaine or heroin addicted baby.
>
> So come in and report to the Court on the first day of November. Make sure that you comply with the terms and conditions. If you get pregnant, I'm going to send you to prison in large part because I want to protect the un-born child. But more importantly — that's the most important reason, but second of all, because you have violated a term and condition of your probation. Do you understand that?
>
> [APPELLANT]: Yes.

On appeal, what result?

[b] Compelled Surgery

Surgery upon a person may be for that person's benefit or for the benefit of others, as with an organ transplant. If someone is not competent to make those decisions, then the "benefit" question must be defined and resolved by some one else. Who that person shall be — and by what standard — are difficult issues at best, as the following cases illustrate.

DEPARTMENT OF HUMAN SERVICES v. NORTHERN

563 S.W.2d 197 (Ct. App. Tenn. 1978)

. . . .

On January 24, 1978, the Tennessee Department of Human Services filed this suit alleging that Mary C. Northern was 72 years old, with no available help from relatives; that Miss Northern resided alone under unsatisfactory conditions as a result of which she had been admitted to and was a patient in Nashville General Hospital; that the patient suffered from gangrene of both feet which required the removal of her feet to save her life; that the patient lacked the capacity to appreciate her condition or to consent to necessary surgery.

Attached to the complaint are identical letters from Drs. Amos D. Tackett and R. Benton Adkins which read as follows:

> Mrs. Mary Northern is a patient under our care at Nashville General Hospital. She has gangrene of both feet probably secondary to frost bite and then thermal burning of the feet. She has developed infection along with the gangrene of her feet. This is placing her life in danger. Mrs. Northern does not understand the severity or consequences of her disease process and does not appear to understand that failure to amputate the feet at this time would probably result in her death. It is our recommendation as the physicians in charge of her case, that she undergo amputation of both feet as soon as possible.

On January 24, 1978, the Chancellor appointed a guardian ad litem to defend the cause and to receive service of process pursuant to Rule 4.04(2) T.R.C.P.

On January 25, 1978, the guardian ad litem answered as follows:

> The Respondent, by and through her guardian ad litem, states as follows:
>
> 1. She is 72 years of age and a resident of Davidson County, Tennessee.
> 2. She is presently in the intensive care unit of General Hospital, Nashville, Tennessee, because of gangrenous condition in her two feet.
> 3. She feels very strongly that her present physical condition is improving, and that she will recover without the necessity of surgery.
> 4. She is in possession of a good memory and recall, responds accurately to questions asked her, is coherent and intelligent in her conversation and is of sound mind.
> 5. She is aware that the Tennessee Department of Human Services has filed this complaint, knows the nature of the complaint, and does not wish for her feet to be amputated.
> 6. There is no psychiatric report of her mental capacity, and there is nothing in the hospital or court record to support

the statement that she lacks the capacity to realize the need for protective services.

. . . .

On January 26, 1978, there was filed in this cause a letter from Dr. John J. Griffin, reporting that he found the patient to be generally lucid and sane, but concluding:

> Nonetheless, I believe that she is functioning on a psychotic level with respect to ideas concerning her gangrenous feet. She tends to believe that her feet are black because of soot or dirt. She does not believe her physicians about the serious infection. There is an adamant belief that her feet will heal without surgery, and she refused to even consider the possibility that amputation is necessary to save her life. There is no desire to die, yet her judgment concerning recovery is markedly impaired. If she appreciated the seriousness of her condition, and her physicians' opinions, and concluded against an operation, then I would believe she understood and could decide for herself. But my impression is that she does not appreciate the dangers to her life. I conclude that she is incompetent to decide this issue. A corollary to this denial is seen in her unwillingness to consider any future plans. Here again I believe she was utilizing a psychotic mechanism of denial.
>
> This is a schizoid woman who has been urged by everyone to have surgery. Having been self-sufficient previously (albeit a marginal adjustment), she is continuing to decide alone. The risks with surgery are great and her lifestyle has been permanently disrupted. If she has surgery there is a tremendous danger for physical and psychological complications. The chances for a post-operative psychosis are immense, yet the surgeons believe an operation is necessary to save her life. I would advise delaying surgery (if feasible) for a few days in order to attempt some work for strengthening her psychologically. Even if she does not consent to the operation after that time, however, I believe she is incompetent to make the decision.

. . . .

On January 28, 1978, a certified transcript was filed, and two members of this Court heard argument on behalf of the parties and on behalf of a proposed amicus curiae, after which it was announced that this Court would act to investigate the facts.

On the same date two members of this Court heard testimony of the three doctors previously mentioned and visited the patient in the intensive care unit of the hospital. Said testimony and the conversation with the patient were preserved by bill of exceptions filed with the Clerk of this Court.

On the same date, January 28, 1978, this Court entered an order reciting the following:

> From all of the above Court Finds:

1. That the respondent is not now in 'imminent danger of death' in the extreme sense of the words, but that her present condition is such that 'imminent danger of death' may reasonably be expected during her continued hospitalization.
2. That both feet of respondent are severely necrotic and affected by wet gangrene, an infection which probably will result in death unless properly treated by amputation of the feet.
3. That the probability of respondent's survival without amputation is from 5% to 10%; and the probability of survival after amputation is about 50%, with possible severe psychotic results.
4. That, with or without amputation, the prognosis of respondent's condition is poor.
5. That respondent is an intelligent, lucid, communicative and articulate individual who does not accept the fact of the serious condition of her feet and is unwilling to discuss the seriousness of such condition or its fatal potentiality.
6. That, because of her inability or unwillingness to recognize the actual condition of her feet which is clearly observable by her, she is incompetent to make a rational decision as to the amputation of her feet.
7. That respondent has no wish to die, but is unable or unwilling to recognize an obvious condition which will probably result in her death if untreated.

This Court is therefore of the opinion that a responsible individual should be named with authority to consent to amputation of respondent's feet when urgently recommended in writing by respondent's physicians because of the development of (symptoms) indicating an emergency and severe imminence of death. . . .

. . . .

This controversy arises from the fact that Miss Northern's attending physicians have determined that all of the soft tissue of her feet has been killed by frostbite, that said dead tissue has become infected with gangrene and that the feet must be removed to prevent loss of life from spreading of gangrene and its effects to the entire body. Miss Northern has refused to consent to the surgery.

The physicians have determined, and the Chancellor and this Court have found, that Miss Northern's life is critically endangered; that she is mentally incapable of comprehending the facts which constitute that danger; and that she is, to that extent, incompetent, thereby justifying State action to preserve her life.

As will be observed from the bill of exceptions, a member of this Court asked Miss Northern if she would prefer to die rather than lose her feet, and her answer was "possibly." This is the most definitive expression of her desires in this record.

The patient has not expressed a desire to die. She evidences a strong desire to live and an equally strong desire to keep her dead feet. She refuses to make a choice.

If the patient would assume and exercise her rightful control over her own destiny by stating that she prefers death to the loss of her feet, her wish would be respected. The doctors so testified; this Court so informed her; and this Court here and now reiterates its commitment to this principle.

For the reasons just stated, this is *not* a "right to die" case.

. . . .

Capacity is not necessarily synonymous with sanity. A blind person may be perfectly capable of observing the shape of small articles by handing them, but not capable of observing the shape of a cloud in the sky.

A person may have "capacity" as to some matters and may lack "capacity" as to others.

. . . .

In the present case, this Court has found the patient to be lucid and apparently of sound mind generally. However, on the subjects of death and amputation of her feet, her comprehension is blocked, blinded or dimmed to the extent that she is incapable of recognizing facts which would be obvious to a person of normal perception.

For example, in the presence of this Court, the patient looked at her feet and refused to recognize the obvious fact that the flesh was dead, black, shriveled, rotting and stinking.

The record also discloses that the patient refuses to consider the eventuality of death which is or ought to be obvious in the face of such dire bodily deterioration.

As described by the doctors and observed by this Court, the patient wants to live and keep her dead feet, too, and refuses to consider the impossibility of such a desire. In order to avoid the unpleasant experience of facing death and/or loss of feet, her mind or emotions have resorted to the device of denying the unpleasant reality so that, to the patient, the unpleasant reality does not exist. This is the "delusion" which renders the patient incapable of making a rational decision as to whether to undergo surgery to save her life or to forego surgery and forfeit her life.

The physicians speak of probabilities of death without amputation as 90 to 95%. And the probability of death with surgery as 50-50 (1 in 2). Such probabilities are not facts, but the existence and expression of such opinions are facts which the patient is unwilling or unable to recognize or discuss.

If, as repeatedly stated, this patient could and would give evidence of a comprehension of the facts of her condition and could and would express her unequivocal desire in the face of such comprehended facts, then her decision, however unreasonable to others, would be accepted and honored by the Courts and by her doctors. The difficulty is that she cannot or will not comprehend the facts.

. . . .

This Court is painfully and acutely aware of the possible tragic results of amputation. According to the doctors, the patient has only a 50% chance of surviving the surgery; and, if she survives, she will never be able to walk and may suffer severe mental and emotional problems.

On the other hand, the doctors testified, and this Court finds, that the patient's chances of survival without amputation are from 5% to 10%. A rather remote and fragile chance. Moreover, as testified by the doctors and found by this Court, even if the patient should survive without amputation, she will never walk because the dead flesh will fall off the bones of her feet leaving only bare bones.

. . . .

This is not a case of wrongful custody or detention, but a case limited to the issue of competency to consent to surgery and the furnishing of competent consent.

. . . .

Modified, Affirmed and Remanded. [1]

Drowota, Judge, concurring.

While I am in complete agreement with the opinion of the Court, I believe it worthwhile to try to elucidate and emphasize the central issue around which this entire litigation revolves: Is Miss Mary Northern at this time mentally and emotionally competent to decide whether or not to permit amputation of her gangrenous feet? . . . .

. . . .

In the instant case, the Court found that Miss Northern does not have the capacity to decide whether her feet should or should not be amputated . . . . These facts include the appearance of her feet, which are disfigured, coal black, crusty, cracking, oozing, and rancid. Yet, Miss Northern looks at them and insists that nothing is wrong . . . . But from our honest evaluation of the facts and evidence of this case, we have been forced to conclude that Miss Northern does not comprehend such basic facts and hence is currently incompetent to decide this particular question. While this finding was made more difficult by Miss Northern's apparent ability to grasp facts not related to the condition of her feet, it is nonetheless correct.

Since Miss Northern was not competent to decide the question of amputation, it fell to the Chancellor and then to this Court to do so. Again, the question for me is what would Miss Northern decide if she understood the facts. The presumption with any person must be that he would want surgery that would increase the chance of life from 5-10% to 50%, unless some statement made or attitude held while the patient was competent contradicts the presumption . . . . In these circumstances, this Court simply could not find that Miss Northern, if she had a basic understanding of the situation, would

[1] On May 1, 1978, Mary Northern died in a Nashville hospital as the result of a clot from the gangrenous tissue migrating through the bloodstream to a vital organ. Because of complications rendering surgery more dangerous, the proposed surgery was never performed.

not choose the substantially greater chance of life that surgery offers. Our decision has been made accordingly, but we have modified and narrowed the Chancellor's order so that consent may only be given by one responsible individual and only when Miss Northern's doctors certify that surgery is necessary immediately to save her life. This is our best approximation of what a competent Mary Northern would want under these circumstances.

. . . .

. . . I have also tried to emphasize that this Court bases its negative answer to that question not on Miss Northern's failure to "conform" or to do what we or the community might think is "sensible," but on her inability to comprehend basic concrete facts relating to her condition. No one lacking such comprehension of facts essential to an informed decision would be competent to make that decision . . . .

NOTES AND QUESTIONS

1. The decision by the Court of Appeals was affirmed by the Tennessee Supreme Court one month later, on March 14, 1978. As the footnote indicates, two months later, on May 1, 1978, Mary Northern died of complications from the gangrene, the amputation having been deferred indefinitely. In the transcript of testimony, to which the Court of Appeals refers, Mary Northern is quoted as saying that her feet looked normal to her, that she thought they would get better by themselves, that she did not believe she would die of gangrene, that she did not want the surgery, and that she did not want to die. She also stated that she did not want to discuss the matter, she did not like doctors, and she wanted to be left alone. After she died, the Department of Human Services tried to collect the cost of the legal proceeding from her estate.
2. The procedure followed by the Court in the case of Mary Northern was quite unusual. Appellate judges going directly to someone's hospital room is, indeed, a rare occasion. We shall see that again, however. Judge Skelly Wright did it in the *Georgetown College* case, which appears in § 4.02, as did the Court in the next case, *In Re A.C.* In that instance, as in this, judges who might otherwise have to make decisions based on a cold record, with all the deficiencies in such an artifact, instead are able to fill in the missing pieces by being in the presence of the person herself. In each instance, the judges ruled against the woman. Does it seem, then, that what is at first an act of compassion may actually be a compounding and confusing of roles, to the disadvantage of autonomy and privacy, both perhaps better protected by a respect for conventional procedure?
3. Writers on the subject of competence, in the narrowest sense, refer to it as a standard testing whether a person can perform a task. Competence, then, can range from whether a person can remove the cap from a bottle of soda, try a criminal case or manage life's decisions. In this last context, the broadest, an inquiry into competence may ask whether a person simply *knows* his or her past and present whereabouts and relations to important people, such as family members. At the next

level, the inquiry would be whether the person has the *capacity* to understand the nature of the decision or task presented. If so, has the person *learned* and *appreciated* the relevant facts and imponderables for making the decision (for example, whether to have open-heart surgery)? Then the next level of inquiry would be has the person in fact *done so* (that is, *made* a decision)? Often times, there are two additional levels of inquiry: was the decision, if made, a *rational* one? If it was not rational, must it be *respected*?

4. In what ways, or at what level of inquiry, was the decision by Mary Northern deemed not "competent"? Or, quite without regard to the decision, was she herself deemed not a competent *person*? Are these different questions? If Mary Northern made it through the various levels of competence inquiry, all the way to the last two levels, was the decision rational? If not, need it be respected? Does the outcome of the case suggest that the last two levels should be discarded?

5. An important element of bioethics is the concept of autonomy. The point of autonomy, and respect for it, is that an individual may make a "wrong" decision and yet that decision must stand. Are there "wrong" decisions by autonomous persons which are so *badly* wrong that the person's autonomy may be overridden? Whose values determine what decision to override?

6. Is the point of *Mary Northern* simply that she was not competent to make a decision? Is it unfair to suggest that the judges and the doctors acted because they disliked the decision, rather than because they concluded — fairly — that Mary Northern was not competent? Or did they attempt (and succeed) to decide as she *would* have?

7. Can you, as a healthy, 35-year-old woman (or man) place yourself in the position of a relatively frail yet feisty woman in her 70s, who had learned to dislike doctors and to trust in the regenerative processes of the body, even to the point of losing her fear of death? At that point, different as she (and you) would be, is it fair to say that Mary Northern is not "competent"? If so, are you concerned that there might be a point when you (and I) would be declared "incompetent" so that other people can do to us what we (now) would do to Mary Northern?

8. The Court of Appeals says it would treat the case differently if Mary Northern had said she wanted to die. Do you credit this view? Is it reasonable? Ethical? Consider these questions in connection with the next case, *In Re A.C.*

IN RE A.C.

573 A.2d 1235 (D.C. Ct. App. 1990)

Terry, Associate Judge.

. . . .

We are confronted here with two profoundly difficult and complex issues. First, we must determine who has the right to decide the course of medical treatment for a patient who, although near death, is pregnant with a viable fetus. Second, we must establish how that decision should be made if the patient cannot make it for herself — more specifically, how a court should proceed when faced with a pregnant patient, in extremis, who is apparently incapable of making an informed decision regarding medical care for herself and her fetus. We hold that in virtually all cases the question of what is to be done is to be decided by the patient — the pregnant woman — on behalf of herself and the fetus. If the patient is incompetent or otherwise unable to give an informed consent to a proposed course of medical treatment, then her decision must be ascertained through the procedure known as substituted judgment. Because the trial court did not follow that procedure, we vacate its order and remand the case for further proceedings.

This case came before the trial court when George Washington University Hospital petitioned the emergency judge in chambers for declaratory relief as to how it should treat its patient, A.C., who was close to death from cancer and was twenty-six and one-half weeks pregnant with a viable fetus. After a hearing lasting approximately three hours, which was held at the hospital (though not in A.C.'s room), the court ordered that a caesarean section be performed on A.C. to deliver the fetus. Counsel for A.C. immediately sought a stay in this court, which was unanimously denied by a hastily assembled division of three judges. The caesarean was performed, and a baby girl, L.M.C., was delivered. Tragically, the child died within two and one-half hours, and the mother died two days later.

. . . .

II

A.C. was first diagnosed as suffering from cancer at the age of thirteen. In the ensuing years she underwent major surgery several times, together with multiple radiation treatments and chemotherapy. A.C. married when she was twenty-seven, during a period of remission, and soon thereafter she became pregnant. She was excited about her pregnancy and very much wanted the child. Because of her medical history, she was referred in her fifteenth week of pregnancy to the high-risk pregnancy clinic at George Washington University Hospital.

On Tuesday, June 9, 1987, when A.C. was approximately twenty-five weeks pregnant, she went to the hospital for a scheduled checkup. Because she was experiencing pain in her back and shortness of breath, an x-ray was taken, revealing an apparently inoperable tumor which nearly filled her right lung. On Thursday, June 11, A.C. was admitted to the hospital as a patient. By Friday her condition had temporarily improved, and when asked if she really wanted to have her baby, she replied that she did.

Over the weekend A.C.'s condition worsened considerably. Accordingly, on Monday, June 15, members of the medical staff treating A.C. assembled, along with her family, in A.C.'s room. The doctors then informed her that her illness was terminal, and A.C. agreed to palliative treatment designed to extend her life until at least her twenty-eighth week of pregnancy. The "potential outcome [for] the fetus," according to the doctors, would be much better at twenty-eight weeks than at twenty-six weeks if it were necessary to "intervene." A.C. knew that the palliative treatment she had chosen presented some increased risk to the fetus, but she opted for this course both to prolong her life for at least another two weeks and to maintain her own comfort. When asked if she still wanted to have the baby, A.C. was somewhat equivocal, saying "something to the effect of 'I don't know, I think so.' " As the day moved toward evening, A.C.'s condition grew still worse, and at about 7:00 or 8:00 p.m. she consented to intubation to facilitate her breathing.

The next morning, June 16, the trial court convened a hearing at the hospital in response to the hospital's request for a declaratory judgment. The court appointed counsel for both A.C. and the fetus, and the District of Columbia was permitted to intervene for the fetus as parens patriae. The court heard testimony on the facts as we have summarized them, and further testimony that at twenty-six and a half weeks the fetus was viable, i.e., capable of sustained life outside of the mother, given artificial aid. A neonatologist, Dr. Maureen Edwards, testified that the chances of survival for a twenty-six-week fetus delivered at the hospital might be as high as eighty percent, but that this particular fetus, because of the mother's medical history, had only a fifty to sixty percent chance of survival. Dr. Edwards estimated that the risk of substantial impairment for the fetus, if it were delivered promptly, would be less than twenty percent. However, she noted that the fetus' condition was worsening appreciably at a rapid rate, and another doctor — Dr. Alan Weingold, an obstetrician who was one of A.C.'s treating physicians — stated that any delay in delivering the child by caesarean section lessened its chances of survival.

Regarding A.C.'s ability to respond to questioning and her prognosis, Dr. Louis Hamner, another treating obstetrician, testified that A.C. would probably die within twenty-four hours "if absolutely nothing else is done. . . . As far as her ability to interact, she has been heavily sedated in order to maintain her ventilatory function. She will open her eyes sometimes when you are in the room, but as far as her being able to . . . carry on a meaningful-type conversation . . . at this point, I don't think that is reasonable." When asked whether reducing her medication to "permit recovery of enough cognitive function on her part that we could get any sense from her as to what her preference would be as to therapy," Dr. Hamner replied, "I don't think so. I think her respiratory status has deteriorated to the point where she is [expending] an enormous amount of energy just to keep the heart going." Dr. Weingold, asked the same question, gave a similar answer: that A.C.'s few remaining hours of life "will be shortened by attempting to raise her level of consciousness because that is what is keeping her, in a sense, physiologically compliant with the respirator. If you remove that, then I think that will shorten her survival."

There was no evidence before the court showing that A.C. consented to, or even contemplated, a caesarean section before her twenty-eighth week of pregnancy. There was, in fact, considerable dispute as to whether she would have consented to an immediate caesarean delivery at the time the hearing was held. A.C.'s mother opposed surgical intervention, testifying that A.C. wanted "to live long enough to hold that baby" and that she expected to do so, "even though she knew she was terminal." Dr. Hamner testified that, given A.C.'s medical problems, he did not think she would have chosen to deliver a child with a substantial degree of impairment. Asked whether A.C. had been "confronted with the question of what to do if there were a choice that ultimately had to be made between her own life expectancy and that of her fetus," he replied that the question "was addressed [but] at a later gestational age. We had talked about the possibility at twenty-eight weeks, if she had to be intubated, if this was a terminal event, would we intervene, and the expression was yes, that we would, because we felt at twenty-eight weeks we had much more to offer as far as taking care of the child." Finally, Dr. Hamner stated that "the department as a whole" concluded that "we should abide by the wishes of the family." Dr. Lawrence Lessin, an oncologist and another of A.C.'s treating physicians, testified that in meetings with A.C. he had heard nothing to indicate that, if faced with the decision, she would have refused permission for a caesarean section. Dr. Weingold opposed the operation because he believed A.C. had not seriously considered that she might not survive the birth of her baby. Dr. Weingold made explicit what was implicit in Dr. Hamner's testimony: that "in dealing with her, a message that was sent to her was that the earliest we would feel comfortable in intervening, should there be indication as to either maternal or fetal grounds, would be twenty-eight weeks." . . .

. . . [T]he court ordered that a caesarean section be performed to deliver A.C.'s child.

The court's decision was then relayed to A.C., who had regained consciousness. When the hearing reconvened later in the day, R. Hamner told the court:

> I explained to her essentially what was going on . . . . I said it's been deemed we should intervene on behalf of the baby by caesarean section and it would give it the only possible chance of it living. Would you agree to this procedure? She said yes. I said, do you realize that you may not survive the surgical procedure? She said yes. And I repeated the two questions to her again [and] asked her did she understand. She said yes.

When the court suggested moving the hearing to A.C.'s bedside, Dr. Hamner discouraged the court from doing so, but he and Dr. Weingold, together with A.C.'s mother and husband, went to A.C.'s room to confirm her consent to the procedure. What happened then was recounted to the court a few minutes later:

> THE COURT: Will you bring us up to date? Did you have a conversation with [A.C.]?
>
> DR. WEINGOLD: I did not. I observed the conversation between Dr. Hamner and [A.C.]. Dr. Hamner went into the room to attempt to verify his previous discussion with the patient, with the patient's husband at her right hand and her mother at her left hand. He, to my satisfaction, clearly communicated with [A.C.]. She understood.
>
> THE COURT: You could hear what the parties were saying to one another?
>
> DR. WEINGOLD: She does not make sound because of the tube in her windpipe. She nods and she mouths words. One can see what she's

> saying rather readily. She asked whether she would survive the operation. She asked [Dr.] Hamner if he would perform the operation. He told her he would only perform it if she authorized it but it would be done in any case. She understood that. She then seemed to pause for a few moments and then very clearly mouthed words several times, I don't want it done. I don't want it done. Quite clear to me.
>
> I would obviously state the obvious and that is this is an environment in which, from my perspective as a physician, this would not be an informed consent one way or the other. She's under tremendous stress with the family on both sides, but I'm satisfied that I heard clearly what she said.
>
> THE COURT: Dr. Hamner, did you wish to elaborate?
>
> DR. HAMNER: That's accurate. I noticed she was much more alert than she had been earlier in the day and was responding to the nurses in the room as well as to all the physicians and went through the same sequence Dr. Weingold noted.

Dr. Weingold later qualified his opinion as to A.C.'s ability to give an informed consent, stating that he thought the environment for an informed consent was nonexistent because A.C. was in intensive care, flanked by a weeping husband and mother. He added:

> I think she's in contact with reality, clearly understood who Dr. Hamner was. Because of her attachment to him [she] wanted him to perform the surgery. Understood he would not unless she consented and did not consent.
>
> That is, in my mind, very clear evidence that she is responding, understanding, and is capable of making such decisions.

Dr. Hamner stated that the sedation had "worn off enough for her to wake up to this state" and that "the level of drugs in her body is much different from several hours ago." Consequently, despite A.C.'s continued sedation, Dr. Weingold said that she was "quite reactive," and Dr. Hamner concurred.

After hearing this new evidence, the court found that it was "still not clear what her intent is" and again ordered that a caesarean section be performed. . . . The operation took place, but the baby lived for only a few hours, and A.C. succumbed to cancer two days later.

A. Informed Consent and Bodily Integrity

[T]here is only one published decision from an appellate court that deals with the question of when, or even whether, a court may order a caesarean section: *Jefferson v. Griffin Spalding County Hospital Authority*, 247 Ga. 86, 274 S.E.2d 457 (1981).

. . . .

Jefferson is of limited relevance, if any at all, to the present case. In *Jefferson* there was a competent refusal by the mother to undergo the proposed surgery, but the evidence showed that performance of the caesarean was in the medical interests of both the mother and the fetus. In the instant case, by contrast, the evidence is unclear as to whether A.C. was competent when she mouthed her apparent refusal of the caesarean ("I don't want it done"), and it was generally assumed that while the surgery would most likely be highly beneficial to the fetus, it would be dangerous for the mother. Thus there was no clear maternal-fetal conflict in this case arising from a competent decision by the mother to forego a procedure for the benefit of the fetus. The procedure may well have been against A.C.'s medical interest, but if she was competent and given the choice, she may well have consented to an operation of significant risk to herself in order to maximize her fetus' chance for survival. From the evidence, however, we simply cannot tell whether she would have consented or not.

Thus our analysis of this case begins with the tenet common to all medical treatment cases: that any person has the right to make an informed choice, if competent to do so, to accept or forego medical treatment. The doctrine of informed consent, based on this principle and rooted in the concept of bodily integrity, is ingrained in our common law. Under the doctrine of informed consent, a physician must inform the patient, "at a minimum," of "the nature of the proposed treatment, any alternative treatment procedures, and the nature and degree of risks and benefits inherent in undergoing and in abstaining from the proposed treatment." To protect the right of every person to bodily integrity, courts uniformly hold that a surgeon who performs an operation without the patient's consent may be guilty of a battery, or that if the surgeon obtains an insufficiently informed consent, he or she may be liable for negligence. Furthermore, the right to informed consent "also encompasses a right to informed refusal."

In the same vein, courts do not compel one person to permit a significant intrusion upon his or her bodily integrity for the benefit of another person's health. *See, e.g.*, *Bonner v. Moran* (parental consent required for skin graft from fifteen-year-old for benefit of cousin who had been severely burned); *McFall v. Shimp*. In *McFall* the court refused to order Shimp to donate bone marrow which was necessary to save the life of his cousin, McFall. . . . Even though Shimp's refusal would mean death for McFall, the court would not order Shimp to allow his body to be invaded. It has been suggested that fetal cases are different because a woman who "has chosen to lend her body to bring [a] child into the world" has an enhanced duty to assure the welfare of the fetus, sufficient even to require her to undergo caesarean surgery. Surely, however, a fetus cannot have rights in this respect superior to those of a person who has already been born.

Courts have generally held that a patient is competent to make his or her own medical choices when that patient is capable of "the informed exercise of a choice, and that entails an opportunity to evaluate knowledgeably the options available and the risks attendant upon each." *Canterbury v. Spence*. Thus competency in a case such as this turns on the patient's ability to function as a decision maker, acting in accordance with her preferences and values. . . .

. . . .

This court has recognized as well that, above and beyond common law protections, the right to accept or forego medical treatment is of constitutional magnitude. Other courts also have found a basis in the Constitution for refusing medical treatment.

This court and others, while recognizing the right to accept or reject medical treatment, have consistently held that the right is not absolute. In some cases, especially those involving life-or-death situations or incompetent patients, the courts have recognized four countervailing interests that may involve the state as parens patriae: preserving life, preventing suicide, maintaining the ethical integrity of the medical profession, and protecting third parties. Neither the prevention of suicide nor the integrity of the medical profession has any bearing on this case. Further, the state's interest in preserving life must be truly compelling to justify overriding a competent person's right to refuse medical treatment. This is equally true for incompetent patients, who have just as much right as competent patients to have their decisions made while competent respected, even in a substituted judgment framework.

. . . .

From the record before us, we simply cannot tell whether A.C. was ever competent, after being sedated, to make an informed decision one way or the other regarding the proposed caesarean section. The trial court never made any finding about A.C.'s competency to decide. Undoubtedly, during most of the proceedings below, A.C. was incompetent to make a treatment decision; that is, she was unable to give an informed consent based on her assessment of the risks and benefits of the contemplated surgery. The court knew from the evidence that A.C. was sedated and unconscious, and thus it could reasonably have found her incompetent to render an informed consent; however, it made no such finding. On the other hand, there was no clear evidence that A.C. was competent to render an informed consent after the trial court's initial order was communicated to her.

We think it is incumbent on any trial judge in a case like this, unless it is impossible to do so, to ascertain whether a patient is competent to make her own medical decisions. Whenever possible, the judge should personally attempt to speak with the patient and ascertain her wishes directly, rather than relying exclusively on hearsay evidence, even from doctors. It is improper to presume that a patient is incompetent. We have no reason to believe that, if competent, A.C. would or would not have refused consent to a caesarean. We hold, however, that without a competent refusal from A.C. to go forward with the surgery, and without a finding through substituted judgment that A.C. would not have consented to the surgery, it was error for the trial court to proceed to a balancing analysis, weighing the rights of A.C. against the interests of the state.

. . . .

B. Substituted Judgment

In the previous section we discussed the right of an individual to accept or reject medical treatment. We concluded that if a patient is competent and has made an informed decision regarding the course of her medical treatment, that decision will control in virtually all cases. Sometimes, however, as our analysis presupposes here, a once competent patient will be unable to render an informed decision. In such a case, we hold that the court must make a substituted judgment on behalf of the patient, based on all the evidence. This means that the duty of the court, "as surrogate for the incompetent, is to determine as best it can what choice that individual, if competent, would make with respect to medical procedures." *In re Boyd.*

Under the substituted judgment procedure, the court as decision maker must "substitute itself as nearly as may be for the incompetent, and . . . act upon the same motives and considerations as would have moved her . . . ." In recent times the procedure has been used to authorize organ "donations" by incompetents, and to prohibit the forced administration of medical treatment to incompetents, over religious objections, where life itself was not at stake. Most cases involving substituted judgment, however, have arisen in the "right to die" context, and the courts have generally concluded that giving effect to the perceived decision of the incompetent is the proper course, even though doing so will result in the incompetent's death.

. . . .

Because it is the patient's decisional rights which the substituted judgment inquiry seeks to protect, courts are in accord that the greatest weight should be given to the previously expressed wishes of the patient. This includes prior statements, either written or oral, even though the treatment alternatives at hand may not have been addressed. The court should also consider previous decisions of the patient concerning medical treatment, especially when there may be a discernibly consistent pattern of conduct or of thought. Thus in a case such as this it would be highly relevant that A.C. had consented to intrusive and dangerous surgeries in the past, and that she chose to become pregnant and to protect her pregnancy by seeking treatment at the hospital's high-risk pregnancy clinic. It would also be relevant that she accepted a plan of treatment which contemplated caesarean intervention at the twenty-eighth week of pregnancy, even though the possibility of a caesarean during the twenty-sixth week was apparently unforeseen. On the other hand, A.C. agreed to a plan of palliative treatment which posed a greater danger to the fetus than would have been necessary if she were unconcerned about her own continuing care. Further, when A.C. was informed of the fatal nature of her illness, she was equivocal about her desire to have the baby.

. . . .

Although treating physicians may be an invaluable source of such information about a patient, the family will often be the best source. Family members or other loved ones will usually be in the best position to say what the patient would do if competent. The court should be mindful, however, that while in the majority of cases family members will have the best interests of the patient in mind, sometimes family members will rely on their own judgments or predilections rather than serving as conduits for expressing the patient's wishes. This is why the court should endeavor, whenever possible, to make an in-person appraisal "of the patient's personal desires and ability for rational choice. In this way the court can always know, to the extent possible, that the judgment is that of the individual concerned and not that of those who believe, however well-intentioned, that they speak for the person whose life is in the balance." *In re Osborne.*

. . . .

After considering the patient's prior statements, if any, the previous medical decisions of the patient, and the values held by the patient, the court may still be unsure what course the patient would choose. In such circumstances the court may supplement its knowledge about the patient by determining what most persons would likely do in a similar situation. When the patient is pregnant, however, she may not be concerned exclusively with her own welfare. Thus it is proper for the court, in a case such as this, to weigh (along with all the other factors) the mother's prognosis, the viability of the fetus, the probable result of treatment or nontreatment for both mother and fetus, and the mother's likely interest in avoiding impairment for her child together with her own instincts for survival.

. . . .

C. The Trial Court's Ruling

. . . [I]t is clear to us that the trial court did not follow the substituted judgment procedure. On the contrary, the court's specific finding before its decision was communicated to A.C. was as follows:

The court is of the view that it does not clearly know what [A.C.'s] present views are with respect to the issue of whether or not the child should live or die. She's presently unconscious. As late as Friday of last week, she wanted the baby to live. As late as yesterday, she did not know for sure.

The court did not go on, as it should have done, to make a finding as to what A.C. would have chosen to do if she were competent. Instead, the court undertook to balance the state's and L.M.C.'s interests in surgical intervention against A.C.'s perceived interest in not having the caesarean performed.

After A.C. was informed of the court's decision, she consented to the caesarean; moments later, however, she withdrew her consent. The trial court did not then make a finding as to whether A.C. was competent to make the medical decision or whether she had made an informed decision one way or the other. Nor did the court then make a substituted judgment for A.C. Instead, the court said that it was "still not clear what her intent is" and again ordered the caesarean.

It is that order which we must now set aside. What a trial court must do in a case such as this is to determine, if possible, whether the patient is capable of making an informed decision about the course of her medical treatment. If she is, and if she makes such a decision, her wishes will control in virtually all cases. If the court finds that the patient is incapable of making an informed consent (and thus incompetent), then the court must make a substituted judgment. This means that the court must ascertain as best it can what the patient would do if faced with the particular treatment question. Again, in virtually all cases the decision of the patient, albeit discerned through the mechanism of substituted judgment, will control. We do not quite foreclose the possibility that a conflicting state interest may be so compelling that the patient's wishes must yield, but we anticipate that such cases will be extremely rare and truly exceptional. This is not such a case.

. . . .

Vacated and remanded.

Belson, Associate Judge, concurring in part and dissenting in part:

. . . .

. . . Given the testimony that A.C. was unable to communicate her attitude toward the proposed surgery, if she had one, I submit that the most reasonable reading of the record is that the judge found her incompetent. . . .

. . . .

I think it appropriate, nevertheless, to state my disagreement with the very limited view the majority opinion takes of the circumstances in which the interests of a viable unborn child can afford such compelling reasons. The state's interest in preserving human life and the viable unborn child's interest in survival are entitled, I think, to more weight than I find them assigned by the majority when it states that "in virtually all cases the decision of the patient . . . will control." I would hold that in those instances, fortunately rare, in which the viable unborn child's interest in living and the state's parallel interest in protecting human life come into conflict with the mother's decision to forgo a procedure such as a caesarean section, a balancing should be struck in which the unborn child's and the state's interests are entitled to substantial weight.

It was acknowledged in *Roe v. Wade* that the state's interest in potential human life becomes compelling at the point of viability. Even before viability, the state has an "important and legitimate interest in protecting the potentiality of human life." . . . When the unborn child reaches the state of viability, the child becomes a party whose interests must be considered.

Without going into the difficult question of the extent to which an unborn viable child may be entitled to protection under the Fifth, the Fourteenth, or other Amendments to the Constitution, the already recognized rights and interests mentioned above are sufficient to indicate the need for a balancing process in which the rights of the viable unborn child are assigned substantial weight. . . .

. . . .

. . . In a case, however, where the court in an exercise of a substituted judgment has concluded that the patient would probably opt against a caesarean section, the court should vary the weight to be given this factor in proportion to the confidence the court has in the accuracy of its conclusion. Thus, in a case where the indicia of the incompetent patient's judgment are equivocal, the court should accord this factor correspondingly less weight. The appropriate weight to be given other factors will have to be worked out by the development of law in this area, and cannot be prescribed in a single court opinion. Some considerations obviously merit special attention in the balancing process. One such consideration is any danger to the mother's life or health, physical or mental, including the relatively small but still significant danger that necessarily inheres in any caesarean delivery, and including especially any danger that exceeds that level. The mother's religious beliefs as they relate to the operation would appear to deserve inclusion in the balancing process.

On the other side of the analysis, it is appropriate to look to the relative likelihood of the unborn child's survival. This could range from the situation where the full-term child's chances for survival were apparently excellent, through a case like the one before us where the unborn child's chances for survival were from fifty to sixty percent, and on to cases where the child's chances for survival are less than even. The child's interest in being born with as little impairment as possible should also be considered. . . .

. . . .

Weighed in the balance against ordering the procedure were two considerations that were central to the entire proceeding: the invasive and serious nature of the proposed surgery and the fact that such surgery cannot ordinarily be performed without the consent of the patient. Under the peculiar circumstances of this case, the influence of these factors was diminished by the fact that it was not clear whether A.C. would have consented to the surgery or not. Before events began to close in on her, A.C. had agreed to a caesarean at twenty-eight weeks. Thus, she was not averse, in principle, to having that particular type of surgery. What was unresolved was whether she would consent to that surgery at twenty-six and one-half weeks, when the unborn child's chances of survival were somewhat reduced and the chances of impairment to the child somewhat enhanced. It was clear that she had intended all along to carry her unborn child until the point the child could be successfully delivered, and she persevered in that intention even when she knew she would not live long, if at all, after her child was born. Even in the tragically difficult circumstances in which A.C. found herself at the very time of the court's proceedings, she first appeared in her sedated state to agree to the procedure and then apparently to disagree. Under the circumstances, the court could deem these matters, usually most pertinent to a determination of substituted judgment, to lessen the net weight of the factors that weighed against the performance of the surgery. Also to be considered in the balance was the rather minimal, but nevertheless undisputable, additional risk that caesarean delivery presented for the mother.

Turning to the interest of the unborn child in living and the parallel interest of the state in protecting that life, the evidence indicated that the child had a fifty to sixty percent chance of survival and a less than twenty percent chance of entering life with a serious handicap such as cerebral palsy or mental retardation. The evidence also showed that a delay in delivering the child would have increased the likelihood of a handicap. In view of the record before Judge Sullivan, and on the basis that there had been no plain error in not applying the sort of substituted judgment analysis that we for the first time mandate in today's ruling, I think it cannot be said that he abused his discretion in the way he struck the balance between the considerations that favored the procedure and those that went against it.

For the reasons stated above, I would affirm.

NOTES AND QUESTIONS

1. The court becomes concerned with whether or not A.C. was ever competent after being sedated. Recall now the case law, particularly the case of Mary Northern. *When* is the important time for determining competency? What is the relevant standard? And how, exactly, was the trial court to introduce the "substituted judgment" standard in this case? If it had done so correctly, what should have been the trial court's conclusion?
2. It seems clear initially that the mother chose to put her life at risk to assure the birth of her child, and then later chose not to expand the risk further, thereby increasing the likelihood that the unborn child would be stillborn or "dead." Which decision was ethical?
3. Are such issues of maternal-fetal conflict properly left to mothers? Ordinarily, in our society, choices implicating another's death or even our own must be made by legislatures and courts. Suicide, after all, is illegal. On the other hand, abortion is not. How *should* society handle a case like that of *A.C.*?
4. There is a narrow, but powerful, conflict between the majority view — emphasizing substituted judgment — and the dissent, emphasizing a balancing standard. Which do you favor? Which would Rawls favor?
5. What is your reaction to *McFall v. Shimp*, where Shimp refused a bone marrow transplant, even though it would mean the death of his cousin, and the court honored the refusal? Would *you* have refused? Recall these issues when reading the next case, *Strunk v. Strunk*.

STRUNK v. STRUNK
445 S.W.2d 145 (Ky. 1969)

Osborne, Judge.

The specific question involved upon this appeal is: Does a court of equity have the power to permit a kidney to be removed from an incompetent ward of the state upon petition of his committee, who is also his mother, for the purpose of being transplanted into the body of his brother, who is dying of a fatal kidney disease? We are of the opinion it does.

The facts of the case are as follows: Arthur L. Strunk, 54 years of age, and Ava Strunk, 52 years of age, of Williamstown, Kentucky, are the parents of two sons. Tommy Strunk is 28 years of age, married, an employee of the Penn State Railroad and a part-time student at the University of Cincinnati. Tommy is now suffering from chronic glomerulus nephritis, a fatal kidney disease. He is now being kept alive by frequent treatment on an artificial kidney, a procedure which cannot be continued much longer.

Jerry Strunk is 27 years of age, incompetent, and through proper legal proceedings has been committed to the Frankfort State Hospital and School, which is a state institution maintained for the feebleminded. He has an I.Q. of approximately 35, which corresponds with the mental age of approximately six years. He is further handicapped by a speech defect, which makes it difficult for him to communicate with persons who are not well acquainted with him. When it was determined that Tommy, in order to survive, would have to have a kidney the doctors considered the possibility of using a kidney from a cadaver if and when one became available or one from a live donor if this could be made available. The entire family, his mother, father and a number of collateral relatives were tested. Because of incompatibility of blood type or tissue none were medically acceptable as live donors. As a last resort, Jerry was tested and found to be highly acceptable. This immediately presented the legal problem as to what, if anything, could be done by the family, especially the mother and the father to procure a transplant from Jerry to Tommy. The mother as a committee petitioned the county court for authority to proceed with the operation. The court found that the operation was necessary, that under the peculiar circumstances of this case it would not only be beneficial to Tommy but also beneficial to Jerry because Jerry was greatly dependent upon Tommy, emotionally and psychologically, and that his well-being would be jeopardized more severely by the loss of his brother than by the removal of a kidney.

. . . .

A psychiatrist, in attendance to Jerry, who testified in the case, stated in his opinion the death of Tommy under these circumstances would have "an extremely traumatic effect upon him [Jerry]."

The Department of Mental Health of this Commonwealth has entered the case as amicus curiae and on the basis of its evaluation of the seriousness of the operation as opposed to the traumatic effect upon Jerry as a result of the loss of Tommy, recommended to the court that Jerry be permitted to undergo the surgery. Its recommendations are as follows:

> It is difficult for the mental defective to establish a firm sense of identity with another person and the acquisition of this necessary identity is dependent upon a person whom one can conveniently accept as a model and who at the same time is sufficiently flexible to allow the defective to detach himself with reassurances of continuity. His need to be social is not so much the necessity of a formal and mechanical contact with other human beings as it is the necessity of a close intimacy with other men, the desirability of a real community of feeling, an urgent need for a unity of understanding. Purely mechanical and formal contact with other men does not offer any treatment for the behavior of a mental defective; only those who are able to communicate intimately are of value of hospital treatment in these cases. And this generally is a member of the family.
>
> In view of this knowledge, we now have particular interest in this case. Jerry Strunk, a mental defective, has emotions and reactions on a scale comparable to that of a normal person. He identifies with his brother Tom; Tom is his model, his tie with his family. Tom's life is vital to the continuity of Jerry's improvement at Frankfort State Hospital and School.
>
> The necessity of Tom's life to Jerry's treatment and eventual rehabilitation is clearer in view of the fact that Tom is his only living sibling and at the death of their parents, now in their fifties, Jerry

> will have no concerned, intimate communication so necessary to his stability and optimal functioning.
>
> The evidence shows that at the present level of medical knowledge, it is quite remote that Tom would be able to survive several cadaver transplants. Tom has a much better chance of survival if the kidney transplant from Jerry takes place.

Upon this appeal we are faced with the fact that all members of the immediate family have recommended the transplant. The Department of Mental Health has likewise made its recommendation. The county court has given its approval. The circuit court has found that it would be to the best interest of the ward of the state that the procedure be carried out. Throughout the legal proceedings, Jerry has been represented by a guardian ad litem, who has continually questioned the power of the state to authorize the removal of an organ from the body of an incompetent who is a ward of the state. . . .

. . . .

In this state we have delegated substantial powers to committees of persons of unsound minds, and to county courts in their supervision. However, . . . these statutes were not intended to divest the equity courts of their inherent common law powers. These powers we have continued to exercise in spite of the jurisdiction granted to the county courts.

The medical practice of transferring tissue from one part of the human body to another (autografting) and from one human being to another (homografting) is rapidly becoming a common clinical practice. In many cases the transplants take as well where the tissue is dead as when it is alive. This has made practicable the establishment of tissue banks where such material can be stored for future use. Vascularized grafts of lungs, kidneys and hearts are becoming increasingly common. These grafts must be of functioning, living cells with blood vessels remaining anatomically intact. The chance of success in the transfer of these organs is greatly increased when the donor and the donee are genetically related. . . .

The renal transplant is becoming the most common of the organ transplants. This is because the normal body has two functioning kidneys, one of which it can reasonably do without, thereby making it possible for one person to donate a kidney to another. Testimony in this record shows that there have been over 2500 kidney transplants performed in the United States up to this date. The process can be effected under present techniques with minimal danger to both the donor and the donee. . . .

Review of our cases leads us to believe that the power given to a committee would not extend so far as to allow a committee to subject his ward to the serious surgical techniques here under consideration unless the life of his ward be in jeopardy. Nor do we believe the powers delegated to the county court by virtue of the above statutes would reach so far as to permit the procedure which we are dealing with here.

We are of the opinion that a chancery court does have sufficient inherent power to authorize the operation. The circuit court having found that the operative procedures in this instance are to the best interest of Jerry Strunk and this finding having been based upon substantial evidence, we are of the opinion the judgment should be affirmed.

Affirmed.

Steinfeld, Judge (dissenting).

Apparently because of my indelible recollection of a government which, to the everlasting shame of its citizens, embarked on a program of genocide and experimentation with human bodies I have been more troubled in reaching a decision in this case than in any other. My sympathies and emotions are torn between a compassion to aid an ailing young man and a duty to fully protect unfortunate members of society.

The opinion of the majority is predicated upon the authority of an equity court to speak for one who cannot speak for himself. However, it is my opinion that in considering such right in this instance we must first look to the power and authority vested in the committee, the appellee herein. Courts have restricted the activities of the committee to that which is for the best interest of the incompetent. The authority and duty have been to protect and maintain the ward, to secure that to which he is entitled and preserve that which he has. "A curator or guardian cannot dispose of his ward's property by donation, even though authorized to do so by the court on advice of a family meeting, unless a gift by the guardian is authorized by statute."

. . . [In] *Baker v. Thomas*, a man and woman had lived together out of wedlock. Two children were born to them. After the man was adjudged incompetent, his committee, acting for him, together with his paramour, instituted proceedings to adopt the two children. In rejecting the application and refusing to speak for the incompetent the opinion stated:

> The statute does not contemplate that the committee of a lunatic may exercise any other power than to have the possession, care, and management of the lunatic's or incompetent's estate. No authority is given by any statute to which our attention has been called, or that we have been by careful research able to locate, giving the committee of a lunatic or an incompetent authority to petition any court for the adoption of a person or persons as heirs capable of the inheritance of his or her estate.

. . . .

The majority opinion is predicated upon the finding of the circuit court that there will be psychological benefits to the ward but points out that the incompetent has the mentality of a six-year-old child. It is common knowledge beyond dispute that the loss of a close relative or a friend to a six-year-old child is not of major impact. Opinions concerning psychological trauma are at best most nebulous. Furthermore, there are no guarantees that the transplant will become a surgical success, it being well known that body rejection of transplanted organs is frequent. The life of the incompetent is not in danger, but the surgical procedure advocated creates some peril.

It is written in *Prince v. Massachusetts*, 321 U.S. 158 (1944), that "Parents may be free to become martyrs themselves. But it does not follow they are free, in identical circumstances, to make martyrs of their children before they have reached the age of full and legal discretion when they can make that choice for themselves." The ability to fully understand and consent is a prerequisite to the donation of a part of the human body.

. . . .

I am unwilling to hold that the gates should be open to permit the removal of an organ from an incompetent for transplant, at least until such time as it is conclusively demonstrated that it will be of significant benefit to the incompetent. The evidence here does not rise to that pinnacle. To hold that committees, guardians or courts have such awesome power even in the persuasive case before us, could establish legal precedent, the dire result of which we cannot fathom. Regretfully I must say no.

. . . .

NOTES AND QUESTIONS

1. Does the Court in *Strunk* use the same substituted judgment standard as in *A.C.*? Or does it use the balancing test of the dissent in that case?
2. Are you troubled, as was Judge Steinfeld, by a best interest approach to sacrifice one person, or putting that person at risk, for the life of another? Is his reference to Nazi Germany fair? Consider here the earlier materials from Rawls and the European Convention.
3. Suppose other members of the Strunk family *had* tested as being appropriate donors, but had declined. Could they be compelled to act as donors? Would their refusal exclude Jerry as a donor?
4. For a different perspective on compelled surgery, see *infra*, § 4.03[4], for materials on female genital mutilation in foreign countries as a ground for granting political asylum in the United States.
5. For an excellent article, see Adrieene E. Quinn, *Who Should Make Medical Decisions For Incompetent Adults? A Critique of RCW 7.70.065*, 20 Seattle U. L. Rev. 573 (1997); and see Krista L. Newkirk, *State-Compelled Fetal Surgery: The Viability Test Is Not Viable*, 4 Wm. & Mary J. Women & L. 467 (1998).

PROBLEM 1–10 — Organ Donation

The Smith family has been in an automobile accident, a head-on collision with the Jones family. Mr. Smith is in a coma, tests with a flat brain wave and is maintained by artificial respiration. His children are badly crushed, and will die unless his heart and liver are transplanted to each. Mr. Smith had previously executed a living will, a durable power of attorney and organ donation form, while saying he did not want to be "kept alive like Quinlan." He appointed his wife as attorney. Mrs. Smith refuses permission, since this would cause Mr. Smith's death.

Mr. Jones is fully conscious, having recovered from a coma following the accident. His youngest daughter, however, is badly crushed, and both of her kidneys have been destroyed. Because of years of alcohol abuse, Mr. Jones has only one functioning kidney, which he intends to donate to his daughter, although — even with dialysis — this means he will die within the year. He expresses the view that God spoke to him "through the accident," telling him during the coma that he must do this. Mrs. Jones reports that, until the accident, Mr. Jones had been unchurched, professing atheism.

Should the transplants be allowed to the children? Does it matter that there are (could be) other donors? What would your position be as guardian for the fathers? For the children?

You may consider here — although it is not necessary — the materials in Chapter 4 on death and dying.

PROBLEM 1-11 — Have Faith In Your Doctors

Faith Myers has been committed (again) to a psychiatric hospital, and found not competent to care for herself or to medicate herself. The staff intends to administer psychotropic drugs to which Faith strenuously objects. Two staff physicians testify they will help; two opposing experts say they will not, they are potentially harmful, and there are alternatives.

What is the relevant standard?

Besides incompetence, should the court find:

(a) if competent, Faith would have consented, or

(b) medical judgment is reasonable and entitled to deference, or

(c) medication will/may help Faith, or

(d) will calm her and ease administrative care, or

(e) there are no (reasonable) alternatives, or

(f) won't harm her, or

(g) an emergency exists, or

(h) some or all of the above, or

(i) none — the court just stays out of it once commitment is ordered

See Myers v. Alaska Psychiatric Institute, 138 P.3d 238 (Alaska 2006); *Rogers v. Commissioner*, 458 N.E.2d 308 (Mass. 1983); *Rivers v. Katz*, 495 N.E.2d 337 (N.Y. 1986); *Steele v. Hamilton County*, 736 N.E. 2d 10 (Ohio 2000).

[3] Sexual Predators

The final subgroup for consideration as citizens within a community subject to reduced status and viewed as significantly disfavored is the group loosely denominated as "sexual predators." They share some of the characteristics of the earlier groups: they may have been convicted and placed in prison, they may be incompetent (in some sense), they may pose a danger to society. But they have certain special qualities — their conduct, while pathological, seems a matter of choice and yet not amenable to deterrence or treatment.

Traditionally, people who engaged in offending conduct were — after the fact — imprisoned, or institutionalized, and then released. Sexual predators depart from the usual model in two ways — they seem to warrant *prospective* intervention and their condition seems to justify indeterminate custody. Moreover, sexual predators do not "fit" well in prisons, in institutions, or in the community. As citizens, society seems to [illegible] predators are pariahs and [illegible] in the community or in institutions — in ways protecting all other groups in society from such predators. Prevailing attitudes towards such people are reminiscent of the attitudes and barriers imposed for millenia upon lepers.

We begin with *Kansas v. Crane*.

KANSAS v. CRANE
534 U.S. 407 (2002)

Justice **Breyer** delivered the opinion of the Court.

This case concerns the constitutional requirements substantively limiting the civil commitment of a dangerous sexual offender — a matter that this Court considered in *Kansas v. Hendricks*, 521 U.S. 346 (1997). The State of Kansas argues that the Kansas Supreme Court has interpreted our decision in *Hendricks* in an overly restrictive manner. We agree and vacate the Kansas court's judgment.

. . .

II

In the present case the State of Kansas asks us to review the Kansas Supreme Court's application of *Hendricks*. The State here seeks the civil commitment of Michael Crane, a previously convicted sexual offender who, according to at least one of the State's psychiatric witnesses, suffers from both exhibitionism and antisocial personality disorder. After a jury trial, the Kansas District Court ordered Crane's civil commitment. But the Kansas Supreme Court reversed. In that court's view, the Federal Constitution as interpreted in *Hendricks* insists upon "a finding that the defendant cannot control his dangerous behavior" — even if (as provided by Kansas law) problems of "emotional capacity" and not "volitional capacity" prove the "source of bad behavior" warranting commitment.

Kansas now argues that the Kansas Supreme Court wrongly read *Hendricks* as requiring the State *always* to prove that a dangerous individual is *completely* unable to control his behavior. That reading, says Kansas, is far too rigid.

III

We agree with Kansas insofar as it argues that *Hendricks* set forth no requirement of *total* or *complete* lack of control. *Hendricks* referred to the Kansas Act as requiring a "mental abnormality" or "personality disorder" that makes it "*difficult*, if not impossible, for the [dangerous] person to control his dangerous behavior." The word "difficult" indicates that the lack of control to which this Court referred was not absolute. Indeed, as different *amici* on opposite sides of this case agree, an absolutist approach is unworkable. Insistence upon absolute lack of control would risk barring the civil commitment of highly dangerous persons suffering severe mental abnormalities.

We do not agree with the State, however, insofar as it seeks to claim that the Constitution permits commitment of the type of dangerous sexual offender considered in *Hendricks* without *any* lack-of-control determination. *Hendricks* underscored the constitutional importance of distinguishing a dangerous sexual offender subject to civil commitment "from other dangerous persons who are perhaps more properly dealt with exclusively through criminal proceedings." That distinction is necessary lest "civil commitment" become a "mechanism for retribution or general deterrence" — functions properly those of criminal law, not civil commitment.

In recognizing that fact, we did not give to the phrase "lack of control" a particularly narrow or technical meaning. And we recognize that in cases where lack of control is at issue, "inability to control behavior" will not be demonstrable with mathematical precision. It is enough to say that there must be proof of serious difficulty in controlling behavior. And this, when viewed in light of such features of the case as the nature of the psychiatric diagnosis, and the severity of the mental abnormality itself, must be sufficient to distinguish the dangerous sexual offender whose serious mental illness, abnormality, or disorder subjects him to civil commitment from the dangerous but typical recidivist convicted in an ordinary criminal case.

IV

The State also questions how often a volitional problem lies at the heart of a dangerous sexual offender's serious mental abnormality or disorder. It points out that the Kansas Supreme Court characterized its state statute as permitting commitment of dangerous sexual offenders who (1) suffered from a mental abnormality properly characterized by an "emotional" impairment and (2) suffered no "volitional" impairment. It adds that, in the Kansas court's view, *Hendricks* absolutely forbids the commitment of any such person. And the State argues that it was wrong to read *Hendricks* in this way.

We agree that *Hendricks* limited its discussion to volitional disabilities. And that fact is not surprising. The case involved an individual suffering from pedophilia — a mental abnormality that critically involves what a lay person might describe as a lack of control. DSM-IV 571–572 (listing as a diagnostic criterion for pedophilia that an individual have acted on, or been affected by, "sexual urges" toward children). Hendricks himself stated that he could not " 'control the urge' " to molest children. In addition, our cases suggest that civil commitment of dangerous sexual offenders will normally involve individuals who find it particularly difficult to control their behavior — in the general sense described above. And it is often appropriate to say of such individuals, in ordinary English, that they are "unable to control their dangerousness."

Regardless, *Hendricks* must be read in context. The Court did not draw a clear distinction between the purely "emotional" sexually related mental abnormality and the "volitional." Here, as in other areas of psychiatry, there may be "considerable overlap between a . . . defective understanding or appreciation and . . . [an] ability to control . . . behavior." American Psychiatric Association Statement on the Insanity Defense, 140 Am. J. Psychiatry 681, 685 (1983) (discussing "psychotic" individuals). Nor, when considering civil commitment, have we ordinarily [illegible] purposes [illegible], and cognitive impairments. The Court in *Hendricks* had no occasion to consider whether confinement based solely on "emotional" abnormality would be constitutional, and we likewise have no occasion to do so in the present case.

For these reasons, the judgment of the Kansas Supreme Court is vacated, and the case is remanded for further proceedings not inconsistent with this opinion.

It is so ordered.

Justice **Scalia**, with whom Justice **Thomas** joins, dissenting.

I

Respondent was convicted of lewd and lascivious behavior and pleaded guilty to aggravated sexual battery for two incidents that took place on the same day in 1993. In the first, respondent exposed himself to a tanning salon attendant. In the second, 30 minutes later, respondent entered a video store, waited until he was the only customer present, and then exposed himself to the clerk. Not stopping there, he grabbed the clerk by the neck, demanded she perform oral sex on him, and threatened to rape her, before running out of the store. Following respondent's plea to aggravated sexual battery, the State filed a petition in State District Court to have respondent evaluated and adjudicated a sexual predator under the SVPA. That Act permits the civil detention of a person convicted of any of several enumerated sexual offenses, if it is proven beyond a reasonable doubt that he suffers from a "mental abnormality" — a disorder affecting his "emotional or volitional capacity which predisposes the person to commit sexually violent offenses" — or a "personality disorder," either of "which makes the person likely to engage in repeat acts of sexual violence."

II

The first words of our opinion dealing with the merits of the case were as follows: "Kansas argues that the Act's definition of 'mental abnormality' satisfies 'substantive' due process requirements. We agree." *Hendricks*, 521 U.S. at 356.

And the *reason* it found substantive due process satisfied was clearly stated:

> The Kansas Act is plainly of a kind with these other civil commitment statutes [that we have approved]: It requires a finding of future dangerousness [viz., that the person committed is "likely to engage in repeat acts of sexual violence"], and then links that finding to the existence of a 'mental abnormality' or 'personality disorder' *that makes it difficult, if not impossible, for the person to control his dangerous behavior.*

Kan. Stat. Ann. § 59-29a02(b) (1994)." 521 U.S. at 358 (emphasis added).

It is the italicized language in the foregoing excerpt that today's majority relies upon as establishing the requirement of a separate *finding* of inability to control behavior.

That is simply not a permissible reading of the passage, for several reasons. First, because the authority cited for the statement — in the immediately following reference to the Kansas Statutes Annotated — is the section of the SVPA that defines "mental abnormality," *which contains no requirement of inability to control*. What the opinion was obviously saying was that the SVPA's required finding of a *causal connection* between the likelihood of repeat acts of sexual violence and the existence of a "mental abnormality" or "personality disorder" *necessarily* establishes "difficulty if not impossibility" in controlling behavior. This is clearly confirmed by the very next sentence of the opinion, which reads as follows:

> The precommitment requirement of a "mental abnormality" or "personality disorder" is consistent with the requirements of . . . other statutes that we have upheld in that it narrows the class of persons eligible for confinement to those who are unable to control their dangerousness.

It could not be clearer that, in the Court's estimation, the very existence of a mental abnormality or personality disorder *that causes* a likelihood of repeat sexual violence in itself *establishes* the requisite "difficulty if not impossibility" of control.

III

Not content with holding that the SVPA cannot be applied as written because it does not require a separate "lack-of-control determination," the Court also reopens a question closed by *Hendricks:* whether the SVPA also cannot be applied as written because it allows for the commitment of people who have mental illnesses other than volitional impairments. "*Hendricks*," the Court says, "had no occasion to consider" this question.

But how could the Court possibly have avoided it? The jury whose commitment we affirmed in *Hendricks* had not been asked to find a volitional impairment, but had been charged in the language of the statute, which quite clearly covers nonvolitional impairments. And the fact that it did so had not escaped our attention. To the contrary, our *Hendricks* opinion explicitly and repeatedly recognized that the SVPA reaches individuals with personality disorders, 521 U.S. at 352, 353, 357, 358, and quoted the Act's definition of mental abnormality (§ 59-29a02(b)), which makes plain that it embraces both emotional and volitional impairments.

I cannot resist observing that the distinctive status of volitional impairment which the Court mangles *Hendricks* to preserve would not even be worth preserving by more legitimate means. There is good reason why, as the Court accurately says, "when considering civil commitment . . . we [have not] ordinarily distinguished for constitutional purposes between volitional, emotional, and cognitive impairments," . . . We have not done so because it makes no sense. It is obvious that a person may be able to exercise volition and yet be unfit to turn loose upon society. The man who has a will of steel, but who delusionally believes that every woman he meets is inviting [illegible] sexual advances, is surely a dangerous [illegible] predator.

IV

I not only disagree with the Court's gutting of our holding in *Hendricks;* I also doubt the desirability, and indeed even the coherence, of the new constitutional test which (on the basis of no analysis except a misreading of *Hendricks*) it substitutes. Under our holding in *Hendricks*, a jury in an SVPA commitment case would be required to find, beyond a reasonable doubt, (1) that the person previously convicted of one of the enumerated sexual offenses is suffering from a mental abnormality or personality disorder, and (2) that this condition renders him likely to commit future acts of sexual violence. Both of these findings are coherent, and (with the assistance of expert testimony) well within the capacity of a normal jury.

Today's opinion says that the Constitution requires the addition of a third finding: (3) that the subject suffers from an inability to control behavior — not utter inability, . . . and not even inability in a particular constant degree, but rather inability in a degree that will vary "in light of such features of the case as the nature of the psychiatric diagnosis, and the severity of the mental abnormality itself."

This formulation of the new requirement certainly displays an elegant subtlety of mind. Unfortunately, it gives trial courts, in future cases under the many commitment statutes similar to Kansas's SVPA, *not a clue* as to how they are supposed to charge the jury! Indeed, it does not even provide a clue to the trial court, on remand, *in this very case*. What is the judge to ask the jury to find? It is fine and good to talk about the desirability of our "proceeding deliberately and contextually, elaborating generally stated constitutional standards and objectives as specific circumstances require," . . . but one would think that this plan would at least produce the "elaboration" of what the jury charge should be in the "specific circumstances" of the present case. "Proceeding deliberately" is not synonymous with not proceeding at all.

I suspect that the reason the Court avoids any elaboration is that elaboration which passes the laugh test is impossible. How *is* one to frame for a jury the degree of "inability to control" which, in the particular case, "the nature of the psychiatric diagnosis, and the severity of the mental abnormality" require? Will it be a percentage ("Ladies and gentlemen of the jury, you may commit Mr. Crane under the SVPA only if you find, beyond a reasonable doubt, that he is 42% unable to control his penchant for sexual violence")? Or a frequency ratio ("Ladies and gentlemen of the jury, you may commit Mr. Crane under the SVPA only if you find, beyond a reasonable doubt, that he is unable to control his penchant for sexual violence 3 times out of 10")? Or merely an adverb ("Ladies and gentlemen of the jury, you may commit Mr. Crane under the SVPA only if you find, beyond a reasonable doubt, that he is appreciably — or moderately, or substantially, or almost totally — unable to control his penchant for sexual violence")? None of these seems to me satisfactory.

But if it is indeed possible to "elaborate" upon the Court's novel test, surely the Court has an obligation to do so in the "specific circumstances" of the present case, so that the trial court will know what is expected of it on remand. It is irresponsible to leave the law in such a state of utter indeterminacy.

NOTES AND QUESTIONS

1. In *Kansas v. Crane*, the Supreme Court revisits the same statute that it interpreted in *Hendricks*. Note that the Court did so, as well, in yet another case, holding that a prisoner may be isolated under the Kansas Act for refusing to admit guilt as a precondition to treatment as a sexual predator. *See McKune v. Lile*, 536 U.S. 24 (2002).
2. In *Crane*, the Court is drawing distinctions between "volitional disabilities" (in *Hendricks*) and "emotional abnormalities" (not involved in *Hendricks*). It then adds a third, "cognitive impairments." Do these terms have grounding in psychology? Moral philosophy? And why are they relevant — under the Constitution, the statute, logic, criminal law tradition?
3. Which covers pedophilia? Which category does the Court *say* it fits into?
4. Separately, are these concepts useful? Do they overlap? Or describe readily apparent conditions? Persons? Conduct? Is commitment appropriate for all three? One? Which?
5. Of course, the Court doesn't reach or resolve such questions. It simply says that, with respect to volitional disabilities, there need not be a complete or total lack of control. But how much is enough? The Court says, "serious difficulty" controlling behavior, enough to separate the dangerous sex offender from "the typical recidivist convicted in an ordinary criminal case."
6. And isn't Justice Scalia right: the standard is impossible to apply? Shall the judge charge that 42% suffices? A penchant for violence 3 times out of 10?
7. Finally, do these considerations suggest that the legislation in *Hendricks* and *Crane* provides no guidelines because it reaches and punishes people solely because of a (fairly reliable) prediction of future conduct, on evidence insufficient to satisfy usual requirements of inchoate crimes?
8. Note that the Kansas Act deals only with presently confined people, once convicted of a sexually violent crime. Nonprisoners are not subject to indefinite commitment. Nor are others with equally violent propensities or habitiual patterns, such as addicts. Should they be? What about wife-beaters and alcoholics?

   Can you tell from the Kansas legislation how "serious" the conviction must have been? How "high" the likelihood of repeated behavior must be to justify commitment? How imminent? How frequent? What proof, after commitment, will suffice to get the prisoner out?

   The model for Kansas legislation is commitment of the mentally ill suffering from a mental disease which may cause a crime or may keep the defendant from being able to care for himself. But here, the risk is to the public, from violence (predatory conduct) caused by a mental abnormality predisposing a person to violence. Are th[illegible] Does it matter?

9. I[illegible] SVP completes "treatment" but must still [illegible] under Megan's Laws? According to the Supreme Court of Pennsylvania, sexually violent behavior may not be "cured" as other criminal behavior may be. (*See Commonwealth v. Williams*, 832 A.2d 962 (2003)).

   Does this then render treatment programs worthless in the eyes of the court?

10. For an excellent article, see Jennifer L. Poller, *Provisions of Megan's Law Held Unconstitutional: State Should Bear Burden of Proof in Sexually Violent Predator Proceeding*, 1 No. 12 Lawyers J. 2 (1999); and see Rebecca Kesler, *Running in Circles: Defining Mental Illness and Dangerousness in the Wake of* Kansas v. Hendricks, 44 Wayne L. Rev. 1871 (1999).

11. The Kansas Act reaches sexual predators by *imprisoning* them. Other states deal with them by identifying them in the community, to isolate and impeded them. Such an approach is of dubious effectiveness and poses special ethical and constitutional issues, as the next case involving "Megan's Law" illustrates.

DOE v. PORITZ
662 A.2d 367 (N.J. 1995)

Wilentz, C.J.

On October 31, 1994, a group of bills concerning sex offenders became law. They are generally referred to as "Megan's Law," named after the second female child abducted, raped, and murdered during the prior year. The question before us is whether two of those bills, the Registration and Community Notification Laws, are constitutional. We hold that they are, but that the prosecutor's decision to provide community notification, including the manner of notification, is subject to judicial review before such notification is given, and that such review is constitutionally required.

. . . .

I. The Legislative Purpose: Addressing the Problem of Repetitive Sex Offenders

The challenged laws before us in this case have two basic provisions. First, they require registration with law enforcement authorities of certain convicted sex offenders and spell out the offenses that trigger the registration requirement, registration of those convicted prior to their passage limited to offenders found to have repetitive and compulsive characteristics. Second, they provide for notice of the presence of such offenders in the community, the scope of that notice measured by the likelihood that such offenders will commit another sex offense: where the risk of such reoffense is low, only law enforcement authorities are notified; where it is moderate, institutions and organizations having the responsibility to care for and supervise children and women are notified; and where the risk is high, those members of the public likely to encounter the offender are notified.

. . . .

Based on statistical and other studies the Legislature could have found, and presumably did find, the following facts, essentially reflected in its statement of purpose, and its enactment of the laws:

[S]tudies describing recidivism by sex offenders indicate the severity of the problem the Legislature addressed in Megan's Law. Studies report that rapists recidivate at a rate of 7 to 35%; offenders who molest young girls, at a rate of 10 to 29%, and offenders who molest young boys, at a rate of 13 to 40%. Further, of those who recidivate, many commit their second crime after a long interval without offense. In cases of sex offenders, as compared to other criminals, the propensity to commit crimes does not decrease over time . . . . [I]n one study, 48% of the recidivist sex offenders repeated during the first five years and 52% during the next 17 years . . . .

As Doe acknowledges, successful treatment of sex offenders appears to be rare. He correctly notes that very few offenders sentenced to ADTC [Adult Diagnostic and Treatment Center] ever meet the dual standards required for parole from ADTC. Indeed, according to Department of Correction's statistics between 1980 and 1994 only 182 inmates were paroled from ADTC. While plaintiff was among the few who were released as "capable of making an acceptable social adjustment in the community," the large majority of ADTC inmates leave only after having served their maximum sentences. During the same time frame, 1980-1994, 712 inmates were released from ADTC at expiration of term.

Further information gleaned from similar studies strongly reinforces the foregoing: Sexual crimes are notoriously underreported. Such data as are available, however, demonstrate that their impact is substantial and widespread. A nationwide sampling of households by the Justice Department for the years 1987 to 1991 indicates that every year nearly 133,000 women in the United States age 12 or older were victims of rape or attempted rape, 44% committed by strangers. Twenty-one percent of the total involved weapons (29% of stranger rapes), and 47% of all victims (60% of victims of strangers) sustained injuries in addition to the rape itself. The Justice Department also estimates from police reports that nationwide about 17,000 girls under age 12 were raped in 1992, 54% by nonfamily members (acquaintances and strangers). And based solely on incidents reported to the police, a Justice Department study shows that in 1988 as many as 4,600 children of both sexes were abducted or detained by nonfamily members, nearly always by force (85-87%) and usually with a weapon (75-85%), and more than two-thirds of these children were sexually assaulted.

Sexual assault takes a heavy toll on its victims, particularly on children. Recent research indicates that a number of psychosocial problems — including chronic depression and anxiety, isolation and poor social adjustment, substance abuse, suicidal behavior, and involvement in physically or sexually abusive relationships as either aggressor or victim — are more common among adults molested as children than among those with no such childhood experiences. Victims of sexual abuse can suffer an impaired abilit[illegible] evaluate the motives and behavior of [illegible] vulnerable to revictimization [illegible] finding about child sexual abuse [illegible] generational pattern; in particular, due to the psychological impact of their own abuse, sexually abused boys have been found to be more likely than nonabused boys to turn into offenders against the next generation of children, and sexually abused girls are more likely to become mothers of children who are abused. And studies show that adult male aggressive behavior, particularly sexual aggression, is associated with the trauma of childhood sexual abuse. Thus, apart from the substantial personal trauma caused to the victims of such crimes, sexual crimes against children exact heavy social costs as well.

. . . Sex offender recidivism compounds the problem. As a group, sex offenders are significantly more likely than other repeat offenders to reoffend with sex crimes or other violent crimes, and that tendency persists over time. A 15-year follow-up study by the California Department of Justice of 1,362 sex offenders arrested in 1973 found that 19.7% were rearrested for a subsequent sexual offense. Those first arrested for rape by force or threat had the highest recidivism rate, 63.8% for any offense, and 25.2% for a subsequent sex offense. Sex offenders were five times as likely as other violent offenders, and more than six times as likely as all types of offenders, to reoffend with a sex offense. Similarly, a Washington State study of 1,373 adult male sex offenders convicted between 1985 and 1991 and released by the end of 1991 showed that after seven years of follow-up, 12% were rearrested for sex offenses and an additional 3% were rearrested for violent offenses. Of the 110 offenders reconvicted of a sex offense, 43% were reconvicted of a more serious sex offense.

These figures comport with other data on sex offender recidivism. A major Justice Department study of state prisoners released in one year showed that 7.7% of released rapists were rearrested for rape within three years. Moreover, 27.5% of released rapists were rearrested during that period for some kind of violent offense (murder, rape, robbery, or assault). Released rapists were 10.5 times more likely to be rearrested for rape than were other released prisoners; likewise, prisoners who had served time for other sexual assaults were 7.5 times more likely than other released prisoners to be rearrested for sexual assault. A recent review of the most frequently cited studies of sex offender recidivism indicates that rapists repeat their offenses at [] rates up to 35%; offenders who molest young girls, at [] rates up to 29%; and offenders who molest young boys, at [] rates up to 40%. Moreover, the recidivism rates do not appreciably decline over time, and thus, in contrast with other types of offenders, the tendency to reoffend does not appear to decline with an offender's increasing age. It has been estimated that extrafamilial child molesters have an average of as many as 19.8 victims (for those molesting a girl) and 150 victims (for those molesting a boy).

. . . .

. . . The spectacle of offenses committed by neighbors, known in the public records as significantly potential reoffenders, but not known to anyone else, and especially not known to those most likely to be affected, their neighbors, suggested the most obvious and practical degree of protection: a law that would tell neighbors and others who might be affected, of the presence of such offenders, no more and no less.

The concern for the potential unfairness of identification has some justification, but it is wrong to assume the people of this State and the media will not understand that potential. The Attorney General points to information, far from complete because of the injunction against the implementation of these laws, that suggests that harassment and vigilantism have been minimal. This Court has no right to assume that the public will be punitive when the Legislature was not, that the public, instead of protecting itself as the laws intended, will attempt to destroy the lives of those subject to the laws, and this Court has no right to assume that community leaders, public officials, law enforcement authorities, will not seek to educate the public concerning the Legislature's intent, including appropriate responses to notification information, responses that are not at all punitive, but seek merely to protect their children, their families, and others from reoffense. And this Court has no right to assume the media will not act responsibly.

. . . .

II. The Laws and the Attorney General's Guidelines

Despite complexities of detail, the Registration Law is basically simple. It requires registration of sex offenders convicted after its effective date and all prior-convicted offenders whose conduct was found to be repetitive and compulsive. The sex offenses that trigger the laws for those previously convicted are aggravated sexual assault, sexual assault, aggravated criminal sexual contact, kidnapping, and for those convicted after their effective date, added to the foregoing are various laws concerning endangering the welfare of a child, luring or enticing, criminal sexual contact if the victim is a minor, and kidnapping, criminal restraint, or false imprisonment if the victim is a minor and the offender not the parent; and in all cases an attempt to commit any of the foregoing.

Registration requires, in the case of those no longer in custody — generally those who committed the offense before adoption of the laws — appearance at a local police station for fingerprinting, photographing, and providing information for a registration form that will include a physical description, the offense involved, home address, employment or school address, vehicle used, and license plate number. For those in custody, the procedure is effected at that location. . . .

All of these are lifetime requirements unless the registrant has been offense-free for fifteen years following conviction or release from a correctional facility (whichever is later) and, on application to terminate these obligations, can persuade the court that he or she is not likely to pose a threat to the safety of others. . . .

The Community Notification Law requires the local chief of police to give notification of the registrant's presence in the community, such notification is also required if the registrant changes address (presumably whether within or outside of the community although the statutory language refers only to the latter). The law provides for three levels of notification (referred to as Tiers One, Two and Three in the Guidelines) depending on the [illegible]

(1) If risk of reoffense is low [illegible] likely to encounter the [illegible] notified;

(2) [illegible] risk of reoffense is moderate, organizations in the community including schools, religious and youth organizations shall be notified in accordance with the Attorney General's Guidelines, in addition to the notice required by paragraph (1) of this subsection;

(3) If risk of reoffense is high, the public shall be notified through means in accordance with the Attorney General's Guidelines designed to reach members of the public likely to encounter the person registered, in addition to the notice required by paragraphs (1) and (2) of this subsection.

. . . .

IV

. . . The basic attack on these laws is the alleged excessiveness of community notification. Our interpretation and revisions strictly confine that notification in accordance with legislative intent. The judicial review required by our opinion assures implementation of that intent. It is therefore also described in this section.

We have interpreted the statute to require for Tier Two notification that the institution or organization to be notified is one that is "likely to encounter" the offender. Later in this section we have defined, both for Tiers Two and Three, what "likely to encounter the offender" means and have also set forth standards intended to clarify the difference between low, moderate, and high risk. As for the Guidelines, we have clarified or revised them in order to assure that they conform to the statute. We have required that the statutory factor "behavior in the community following service of sentence" be considered in all Tier classifications; that the statutory factor "whether psychological or psychiatric profiles indicate a risk of recidivism" be available not only to increase the risk assessment, but to decrease it.

Having interpreted the statute to require Tier Two notification to be based on "likely to encounter," we have modified the automatic nature of Tier Two notification so as to require an individual determination concerning such institutions and organizations. We have underlined the Attorney General's interpretation, and accepted it, limiting Tier Two notification to those organizations that actually are in charge of the care or supervision of children or women. We have limited Tier Three notification to conform to the "likely to encounter" requirement of the statute, thereby revising those provisions of the Guidelines that suggest the possibility that notification would be extended to the entire community regardless of whether those notified are likely to encounter the offender.

The most significant change, of course, is the requirement, on application, of judicial review of the Tier classification and the manner of notification prior to actual notification. Because we have concluded that despite its constitutionality, the statute sufficiently impinges on liberty interests to trigger both procedural due process and the fairness doctrine in our state, see *infra* Section IX, those subject to the statute are entitled to the protection of procedures designed to assure that the risk of reoffense and the extent of notification are fairly evaluated before Tier Two or Tier Three notification is implemented. . . .

. . . .

The only issue for the court on the Tier level of notification is the risk of reoffense. In that sense the factors of the Guidelines noting the characteristics of prior offenses or of the offender are relevant only to the risk of reoffense, i.e., the likelihood of its occurrence. That is the clear intent of the statute. All offenders required to register are, by statute, subject to at least Tier One notification, meaning that no matter how low the risk of reoffense, the Legislature has concluded Tier One notification is required.

We conclude that the legislative intent was to use the word "moderate" in comparison to the "low" risk that the Legislature found was minimally characteristic of all those sex offenders required to register. Where Tier Two notification is sought, the State's prima facie case shall include a description of the class of sex offenders required to register who constitute low-risk offenders, including a description of that risk, which need not necessarily be statistical; a further description of that class of sex offenders required to register who constitute moderate-risk offenders, including a description of that risk, not necessarily statistical; some proof, in the form of expert opinion or otherwise, that the moderate-risk offender class poses a risk of reoffense substantially higher than the low-risk class, and that the offender before the court is a moderate-risk offender who poses such a substantially higher risk.

Where Tier Three notification is sought, the State's prima facie case shall include, in addition to the description of low-risk and moderate-risk offenders and of the risks associated with each class, a description of the class of sex offenders required to register who constitute high-risk offenders, including a description of that risk, not necessarily statistical; some proof, in the form of expert opinion or otherwise, that the high-risk offender class poses a risk of reoffense substantially higher than the moderate-risk offender class, and that the offender before the court is a high-risk offender who poses that substantially higher risk.

. . . .

In these proceedings the prosecutor, or someone designated by the prosecutor, shall, if offered as such, be presumptively accepted by the court as an expert on the risk of reoffense. We do not mean to diminish the court's power to reject that person as an expert, but simply note that a fair degree of experience with sex offenders and their characteristics, along with adequate knowledge of the research in this area — much of which is conflicting in its conclusions — should ordinarily be regarded as sufficient. . . .

As for the manner of notification, the limitations set forth in our opinion are mandatory. For Tier Two notification, only those community organizations that own or operate an establishment where children gather under their care, or where women are cared for, shall qualify, and only those that are "likely to encounter" the offender as discussed in connection with Tier Three. The notice that goes out to such [illegible] intent of the statute as interpreted by the Attorney General, an interpretation with which we agree. Organizations concerned with the welfare of children and women, but not having them under their custody or care, do not qualify. . . .

As for the manner and extent of notification under Tier Three, "likely to encounter" clearly includes the immediate neighborhood of the offender's residence and not just the people next door. It presumably would include (since Tier Three includes Tier Two notification) all schools within the municipality, depending on its size, and we see no reason why it should not include schools and other institutions in adjacent municipalities depending upon their distance from the offender's residence, place of work, or school. We find the Attorney General's Guidelines, however, more extensive in the Tier Three proposed notification than authorized by statute. The statute confines public notification under Tier Three to "means . . . designed to reach members of the public likely to encounter the person registered," and it is that standard with which the Attorney General's Guidelines must comply. We do not understand how "community meetings, speeches in schools and religious congregations" conform to the statutory mandate. Those are means apparently designed to inform the entire community of the offender's presence, rather than means designed, as the statute requires, "to reach members of the public likely to encounter the person registered." They are means that exceed the statutory standard and are therefore not permitted.

. . . .

We assume that the media will exercise responsibility in this matter in recognition of the critical societal interest involved. In particular, we assume that the media will not knowingly frustrate the explicit legislative goal of confining notification to those likely to encounter the offender. In other settings, all sectors of the media have voluntarily and on their own initiative, where they thought the public interest was served, consistently restrained their articles, coverage and reporting, e.g., withholding the name of rape victims. We do not believe that the response of the media to this law, whatever it may be, can determine or affect its constitutionality, but clearly there is no occasion to pass on that issue for to do so assumes conduct on the part of the media that should not be attributed to it hypothetically in this litigation, and, we believe, unfairly. . . .

. . . .

V. Challenges Based on the Claim That the Laws Constitute Punishment

. . . .

A

The parties and all amici are in general agreement that the laws' validity, measured against the various constitutional attacks, depends on whether they inflict punishment. The determination of punishment has ordinarily consisted of several components. An initial inquiry is whether the legislative intent was regulatory or punitive: if the latter, that generally is the end of the inquiry, for punishment results; if the former, the inquiry changes to whether the impact, despite the legislative intent to regulate, is in fact punitive, usually analyzed in terms of the accepted goals of punishment, retribution and deterrence. Despite some ambivalent language, a punitive impact — one that effects retribution or accomplishes deterrence — renders the law or the specific provision of the law that is attacked, punishment, but only if the sole explanation for that impact is a punitive intent.

. . . .

In *De Veau v. Braisted*, 363 U.S. 144 (1960), a New York law that prohibited unions from collecting dues if any officer or agent of the union was a convicted felon was attacked on *ex post facto* grounds. The claim was that the felon, convicted before the passage of the law, was subjected to additional punishment because of the law's impact in causing the union to suspend him from his position as an officer in order to enable it to continue to collect dues, the response being that the law was regulatory, its only goal being to cleanse the unions that controlled the waterfront of criminal control. In ruling that there was no punishment the Court said:

> The mark of an ex post facto law is the imposition of what can fairly be designated punishment for past acts. The question in each case where unpleasant consequences are brought to bear upon an individual for prior conduct, is whether the legislative aim was to punish that individual for past activity, or whether the restriction of the individual comes about as a relevant incident to a regulation of a present situation, such as the property qualifications for a profession. . . .

. . . .

The federal law permitting pretrial detention of those accused of certain crimes on the basis of future dangerousness was sustained in the face of a substantive due process claim in *Salerno, supra*, 481 U.S. at 739. Although none of the constitutional clauses aimed at restraining government's power to punish was involved, the question whether such detention constituted punishment was critical, for the government "never argued that pretrial detention could be upheld if it were 'punishment.'" . . .

. . . .

The contention, therefore, . . . that even the slightest deterrent consequence, whether intended or not, whether the inevitable consequence of remedial provisions or not, renders the statute or the sanction involved "punishment" is not borne out either by a careful reading of the language relied on or by the judicial analysis of the issue. Furthermore, the contention is not supported by the outcome in various cases where the claim of punishment is rejected despite some obvious deterrent impact. . . .

. . . .

D

The laws, as we have described them above, when measur[illegible] the standards of the cases that determine wheth[illegible], statute or sanction constitutes punishment [illegible] doubt that they are remedial. . . .

W[illegible] it difficult to accept the notion that the Registration and Notification Laws are designed or are likely to deter repetitive and compulsive offenders who were not previously deterred by the threat of long-term incarceration. Even assuming that removing the shield of anonymity constitutes deterrence, and therefore is arguably punitive, that is the inevitable consequence of these remedial provisions, uniformly sustained in other cases. It is not intended as punishment. . . .

. . . .

Plaintiff's additional claims that the challenged provisions of Megan's Law violate the Bill of Attainder and Cruel and Unusual Punishment Clauses of the State and Federal Constitutions rest upon the premise that the provisions impose punishment. . . .

. . . In determining whether a statute imposes punishment under the Bill of Attainder Clause, the Court has applied this test: (1) whether the challenged statute falls within the historical meaning of legislative punishment; (2) whether the statute, "viewed in terms of the type and severity of burdens imposed, reasonably can be said to further nonpunitive legislative purposes;" and (3) whether the legislative record "evinces a [legislative] intent to punish." . . .

Because that historical factor is not dispositive, even if we were to find, and we do not, that the "public stigma" and "ostracism" that petitioner claims is inextricably linked to the registration and notification provisions of Megan's Law is historically associated with punishment, those provisions would not violate the ban against bills of attainder. The relation between any burdens imposed and the nonpunitive purpose and legislative intent must be accorded greater weight, and we have already concluded that the challenged provisions do not constitute punishment under those inquiries.

VI. Privacy

. . . .

We first address plaintiff's expectation of privacy in the information disclosed under the Registration Law. Information that is readily available to the public, which an individual cannot expect to remain private, is not within the ambit of constitutional protection. "[A]n individual cannot expect to have a constitutionally protected privacy interest in matters of public record." Requiring disclosure of plaintiff's prior arrest and conviction, therefore, does not implicate the right to privacy, as those records are publicly available.

New Jersey specifically guarantees public access to all court records, including criminal records. In most New Jersey counties, it is possible to go to the courthouse and request an individual's criminal record within that vicinage, providing only the individual's name and address. . . .

Since 1979, moreover, the Parole Board has been required to give public notice prior to considering any adult inmate for release. The inmate's name, crimes, and place of conviction are released to the local prosecutor's offices of each county, police departments, and the press. It should be noted, furthermore, that pursuant to an amendment — which was enacted along with the Registration and Notification Laws but is not a subject of this appeal — crime victims are notified by prosecutors of a defendant's release from custody.

Likewise, requiring the disclosure of other information, such as plaintiff's age and legal residence or a description of his vehicle, does not infringe on any expectation of privacy. As the trial court noted, that information is readily available through public records. The records of the Division of Motor Vehicles, which are public records, include applications for driver's licenses and vehicle registrations, and indicate an applicant's name, street address of residence or business, and a vehicle description. Plaintiff therefore cannot have a reasonable expectation of privacy in the information contained therein.

. . . .

Having found no expectation of privacy in the information disclosed under the Registration Law, we now address plaintiff's expectation of privacy in the information disclosed under the Notification Law. With respect to that information, the analysis is substantially the same as that under the Registration Law. Plaintiff has no expectation of privacy in many of the individual pieces of information disclosed, such as his name, convictions, appearance, place of employment or school attended, and the fact of public disclosure of these pieces of information, rather than mere disclosure to the State, does not alter the analysis.

. . . .

Our analysis is altered, however, by the disclosure of plaintiff's home address, and more importantly, by the totality of the information disclosed to the public. We believe that public disclosure of plaintiff's home address does implicate privacy interests. "We are reluctant to disparage the privacy of the home, which is accorded special consideration in our Constitution, laws, and traditions." *United States Dep't of Defense v. Federal Labor Relations Authority*, 510 U.S. 487, ___, 114 S.Ct. 1006, 1015, 127 L.Ed.2d 325, 338 (1994).

. . . .

. . . In this case, where as a result of the information disclosed under the Notification Law, plaintiff may be exposed to uninvited harassment, we conclude that disclosure of plaintiff's home address, particularly when coupled with the other information disclosed, implicates a privacy interest.

We underscore that while we recognize the possibility of such action on the part of the public in determining plaintiff's privacy interests, we expect that the information disclosed will be used as intended: as a means of protection, not as a means of harassment. It should be unmistakably clear that the Registration and Notification Laws are not a license for public lawlessness against registered sex offenders. . . .

We find, moreover, that considering the totality of the information disclosed to the public, the Notification Law implicates a privacy interest. . . .

. . . .

The distinction between merely providing access to information and compiling and disclosing that information is evident in this [illegible] government dissemination of information to which the [illegible] merely has access through various sources eliminates [illegible] costs, in time, effort, and expense, that members of the public would incur in assembling the information themselves. Those costs, however, may severely limit the extent to which the information becomes a matter of public knowledge. The Notification Law therefore exposes various bits of information that, although accessible to the public, may remain obscure. Indeed, if the information disclosed under the Notification Law were, in fact, freely available, there would be no need for the law.

. . . .

Having found privacy interests implicated only by the Notification Law, however diminished those interests may be by the public nature of the individual pieces of information disclosed, we must determine whether the state interest justifies disclosure. . . .

We find, based on those factors, that the state interest in public disclosure substantially outweighs plaintiff's interest in privacy. First, the information requested is not deserving of a particularly high degree of protection. . . .

Counterbalanced against plaintiff's diminished privacy interest is a strong state interest in public disclosure. There is an express public policy militating toward disclosure: the danger of recidivism posed by sex offenders. The state interest in protecting the safety of members of the public from sex offenders is clear and compelling. . . .

We note that the degree and scope of disclosure is carefully calibrated to the need for public disclosure: the risk of reoffense. The greater the risk of reoffense, the greater is the scope of disclosure. The extent or degree of the information disclosed is similarly limited by the need for disclosure. . . .

. . . .

Thus, we conclude, under both the State and Federal Constitutions, that neither the Registration, nor the Notification Law, violates the right to privacy.

VII. Equal Protection

Plaintiff Doe asserts that the notification and registration requirements of the statute violate his right to equal protection under the Federal and State Constitutions. Plaintiff argues that he is entitled to be treated as an individual and not classified with other sex offenders who, unlike plaintiff, have not successfully completed treatment at Avenel. He emphasizes that he is one of few offenders who have been determined to be repetitive compulsive offenders but have earned release from Avenel because they have been determined to be no longer dangerous. He asserts that his right to equal protection requires that he be viewed by the law individually rather than as part of a class. This argument mischaracterizes the Equal Protection Clause.

Equal protection does not preclude the use of classifications, but requires only that those classifications not be arbitrary. . . .

A classification that does not impact a suspect class or impinge upon a fundamental constitutional right will be upheld if it is rationally related to a legitimate government interest. . . .

It is well settled that classifying offenders according to the offense committed is subject to rational basis analysis. This Court, moreover, has specifically held that creating a separate classification for repetitive-compulsive sex offenders is not arbitrary and "has a rational basis." . . .

Plaintiff argues nonetheless that he should not be classified with other repetitive compulsive sex offenders because, unlike most offenders in this category, he was determined to have successfully completed treatment and released on parole. However, the requirements of equal protection, when measured under rational basis standards, are not offended merely because the classification is not narrowly tailored. . . .

. . . .

Plaintiff asserts that he has the right to individual treatment but, as we have already concluded, there is no such right under either Constitution. More than that, plaintiff's significant individual characteristics are assured recognition under these laws. He is a repetitive and compulsive offender, and his inclusion in the initial class of those required to register is not only rational, but closely related to a strong state interest. These are the sex offenders most likely to reoffend. Thereafter, he will be placed in a class that is carefully defined to reflect his specific characteristics that reasonably predict his specific risk of reoffense. He will not be lumped together with all sex offenders but will be placed either in Tier One, Two or Three, depending upon his characteristics alone, the notification that results again directly related to a strong state interest.

. . . .

IX. Procedural Due Process and Fairness and Rightness

The United States Constitution provides that no State shall "deprive any person of life, liberty, or property, without due process of law." U.S. Const. amend. XIV, § 1. . . .

We deal here not with the question of substantive constitutional deprivation, for we have held that there is none. The question treated in this section is whether in the implementation of notification, procedural protections are required beyond those found in these laws in order to assure fairness and accuracy in carrying them out. . . .

. . . .

"The question of whether one's good name and standing, and the interest in protecting that reputation, constitutes a protectible liberty interest" has been addressed in a number of cases. In *Wisconsin v. Constantineau*, 400 U.S. 433, 434 (1971), a statute authorized the posting of a notice prohibiting the sale or gift of liquor to any person who " 'by excessive drinking' produces described conditions or exhibits specified traits, such as exposing himself or family 'to want' or becoming 'dangerous to the peace' of the community." Stating that "[i]t would be naive not to recognize that such 'posting' or characterization of an individual will expose him to public embarrassment and ridicule," the Court held that a protectible liberty interest is implicated "[w]here a person's good name, reputation, honor [illegible] at stake because of what the government [illegible] him."

In *Paul*, *supra*, 424 U.S. at 701, however, the Court concluded that "reputation alone, apart from some more tangible interests such as employment, is [not] either 'liberty' or 'property' by itself sufficient to invoke the procedural protection of the Due Process Clause." According to the Court, harm to reputation must be accompanied by the alteration of "a right or status previously recognized by state law," for it is that "alteration, officially removing the interest from the recognition and protection previously afforded by the State, which [the Court has] found sufficient to invoke the procedural guarantees contained in the Due Process Clause of the Fourteenth Amendment." The Court held, therefore, that because the circulation of flyers publicizing the plaintiff's arrest for shoplifting and labelling him an "active shoplifter" only harmed his reputation, and did not alter his status as a matter of state law, there was no deprivation of a protectible liberty interest.

Paul has been interpreted to require "stigma plus" to establish a constitutional deprivation.

We therefore must assess whether plaintiff has established damage to reputation and impairment of some additional interest.

Plaintiff has plainly established that classification in Tiers Two or Three will result in damage to his reputation. In *Constantineau*, *supra*, the Court recognized that public embarrassment and ridicule would result from the posting, and that a person's good name or reputation would therefore be at stake. . . . Thus, we conclude that classification in Tiers Two or Three, with the requisite public notification, would expose plaintiff to public opprobrium, not only identifying him as a sex offender but also labelling him as potentially currently dangerous, and thereby undermining his reputation and standing in the community.

The harm to plaintiff's reputation, when coupled with the incursion on his right of privacy, although justified by the compelling state interest, constitutes a protectible interest. . . . Thus, we conclude that because the stigma resulting from notification is tied to the protectible interest in privacy, which has been grounded in the Fourteenth Amendment, plaintiff has a protectible interest in his reputation.

. . . .

. . . If not for the Registration and Notification Laws, or if classified in Tier One, plaintiff would be stigmatized only to the extent that the fact of his incarceration and the crime for which he was convicted might be publicly known. Because only the prosecutor and local law enforcement would receive notification under Tier One, he would be free, to the degree possible, to rehabilitate his name and standing in the community. However, if classified in Tier Two or Three, plaintiff's name and standing in the community would be threatened to the extent that his prior undisclosed criminal history and his new classification become known. We conclude that the consequences to plaintiff's reputation from classification in Tier Two or Three implicate a liberty interest.

. . . .

Although we have applied the doctrine of fundamental fairness in a variety of contexts, there is one common denominator in all of those cases: a determination that someone was being subjected to potentially unfair treatment and there was no explicit statutory or constitutional protection to be invoked. Fundamental fairness is a doctrine that is an integral part of due process, and is often extrapolated from or implied in other constitutional guarantees. The doctrine effectuates imperatives that government minimize arbitrary action, and is often employed when narrowed constitutional standards fall short of protecting individual defendants against unjustified harassment, anxiety, or expense.

In plaintiff's case, there is no question that he may be subject to serious consequences if he is classified as either Two or Three. Fundamental fairness is appropriately applied to require procedural protections that will ensure that his classification, and its related consequences, are tailored to his particular characteristics and are not the product of arbitrary action.

X. Conclusion

We sail on truly uncharted waters, for no other state has adopted such a far-reaching statute. All other notification statutes apparently make public notification discretionary on the part of officials; the statute before us, however, mandates it. Despite the unavoidable uncertainty of our conclusion, we remain convinced that the statute is constitutional. To rule otherwise is to find that society is unable to protect itself from sexual predators by adopting the simple remedy of informing the public of their presence. That the remedy has a potentially severe effect arises from no fault of government, or of society, but rather from the nature of the remedy and the problem; it is an unavoidable consequence of the compelling necessity to design a remedy.

. . . .

Stein, J., dissenting.

. . . .

The Legislature's rationale for enacting these statutes obviates any inquiry about the purpose for their retroactive application to those sex offenders whose offenses had been committed before the statutes were enacted, as well as to those prior offenders who had fully served sentences imposed on them for their offenses and had returned to their communities. If the Registration and Notification Laws did not apply to those offenders their effectiveness would be severely limited, and as a practical matter, delayed for many years. Nevertheless, despite its obvious importance to the statutory scheme, the retroactive application of the notification statute to prior offenders poses, in my view, a fundamental constitutional impediment to its validity.

The Constitution's prohibition of bills of attainder and Ex Post Facto laws is not to be taken lightly. As the Court acknowledges, "These are towering constitutional provisions of great importance to individual dignity, freedom, and liberty." . . .

Because the Community Notifica[illegible] makes more burdensome the punish[illegible] crime, after its commission," I conclude that that law, despite its understandable objectives, violates the constitutional prohibition against *ex post facto* laws. . . .

. . . .

B

The federal statute, 42 U.S.C.A. § 14071, was passed as part of the Violent Crime Control and Law Enforcement Act of 1994, and codified under Subchapter VI — Crimes Against Children. To be entitled to funds under 42 U.S.C.A. § 3756 (providing funds for drug control), states must comply with 42 U.S.C.A. § 14071, which mandates that states implement programs requiring "a person who is convicted of a criminal offense against a victim who is a minor or who is convicted of a sexually violent offense to register" with the state in which he or she resides. The federal statute does not require that states apply their sex-offender registration statutes retroactively to offenses committed before the state law was enacted, reflecting a congressional determination that, despite the enhanced effectiveness of retroactive registration statutes, states would be in full compliance with federal law by adopting statutes that apply only prospectively. Moreover, the federal law is more restrictive regarding the personal information about the offender that may be released. . . .

In respect of the state sex-offender registration statutes, ten states have not adopted sex-offender registration laws. . . . Of the forty states that have adopted sex-offender registration laws (which includes New Jersey), five states do not apply their laws retroactively. . . . In addition, of those states that have adopted sex-offender registration laws, twenty states, excluding New Jersey, provide for some type of community notification.

Excluding New Jersey, eighteen states have notification provisions that apply retroactively. . . . Most important, none of the states with retroactive notice provisions provides for notification as extensive as that mandated by New Jersey's statute. . . .

Furthermore, the remaining ten states that have retroactive notification provisions either do not require law enforcement to notify the public, or authorize far more limited public notification than that mandated by New Jersey's statute. . . .

C

At this time, the future effects of "Megan's Law" on those subject to community and individual notification are not possible to discern. The only relevant information before the Court consists of newspaper accounts of actions taken against two sex offenders who were subject to the registration and notification provisions. Although I do not suggest that those accounts are typical of the character and nature of the response of the public to the discovery that a sex offender lives among them, I include them to reflect fully the record before the Court.

On December 27, 1994, residents of Phillipsburg were informed of the whereabouts of a recently released sex offender. This individual was "the first Warren County resident subject to community notification under 'Megan's Law.' " (Donna M. Weston, *Vigilantes Beat Wrong Man After Rapist's Release*, The Trentonian, Jan. 11, 1995, at 5.) Law-enforcement authorities provided neighbors with the address at which the offender was to reside and distributed photographs of him. On January 8, 1995, "[a] father and his son broke into [that] Phillipsburg row house . . . looking for [the] released child molester who had been identified by the police." (Iver Peterson, *Mix-Ups and Worse Arising from Sex-Offender Notification*, N.Y. Times, Jan. 12, 1995, at B1, B6.) Once inside, the two "attacked a man they thought was a rapist." (Sandy McClure, Christie: *Vigilantism Intolerable*, The Trentonian, Jan. 12, 1995, at 4.) "But the two ended up attacking the wrong man," (John Connolly & Phyllis Plitch, *"Megan's Law" Brings Snafus, Vigilantism*, The Trentonian, Jan. 12, 1995, at 4) allegedly assaulting a forty-one-year-old truck driver who was also staying in the house. The severity of the beating required the man to be hospitalized. (Weston, *supra*, The Trentonian, at 5.)

Another example also involves "one of the first people to fall under the law's strictures." (Peterson, *supra*, N.Y. Times, at B6.) On January 1, 1995, Carlos Diaz was released from prison after serving a sentence for rape. Diaz informed authorities that upon his release he intended to reside in Passaic with his mother. (Fredrick Kunkle, *Rapist's Plan to Live in Passaic Sparks Demonstration*, The Record, Jan. 6, 1995, at A-11.) Diaz sought a preliminary injunction in federal district court, seeking to enjoin the dissemination to schools and community groups of Tier Two level information by law-enforcement officials until he had been afforded the opportunity to enforce his constitutional rights. The district court granted the preliminary injunction on January 3, 1995, determining that Diaz demonstrated a reasonable likelihood of success on the merits and faced the danger of irreparable injury.

Although the preliminary injunction delayed law-enforcement officials from implementing the provisions of Megan's Law, the Guardian Angels, a New York-based civilian group, organized a community protest outside the residence of Diaz's mother. "And up and down the streets, Guardian Angel founder Curtis Sliwa and his men walked yesterday, handing out fliers with a large photo of Diaz, the warning 'BEWARE' in big black block letters and a phone number to call if Diaz [was] spotted." (Rosemarie Ross, *Rapist, Beware: Residents' Fear Turns to Anger, Revenge*, The North Jersey Herald & News, Jan. 6, 1995, at A1, A4.) "Hundreds of . . . students streamed down [the street] . . . clutching pictures of convicted rapist Carlos Diaz, handed to them by Guardian Angels who descended on the city to rally in support of Megan's Law." (Ron Day, *Rapist, Beware: Angels Hand Out His Photo in Passaic*, The North Jersey Herald & News, Jan. 6, 1995, at A1.) "Some . . . residents sounded like would-be vigilantes . . . hinting they might take the law into their own hands if Diaz appeared." (*Id.* at A4.) Two young men, residents of Passaic, stated: "We're waiting for him to come down[.] . . . We're going to beat him up. He can go back upstairs, come down, we'll beat him up again."

(Ross, *supra*, The North Jersey Herald & News, at A1, A4.) "Sliwa suggested that convicted criminals deserve to be treated as outcasts, and that their ostracism would [illegible] there should be a stigma,' Sliwa said." (Kunkle, *supra*, The Record, at A-11.) Sliwa stated, "Let the criminal have a taste of being the victim." (Day, *supra*, The North Jersey Herald & News, at A1.)

II

. . . .

Undoubtedly, the Registration and Community Notification Laws apply retroactively to sex offenses committed before their enactment. Their retroactive application potentially affects every living person who has ever been convicted of a sex offense in this State "if the court found that the offender's conduct was characterized by a pattern of repetitive, compulsive behavior." The critical issue is whether the actual effect of the notification statute's retroactive application constitutes punishment within the meaning of the *Ex Post Facto* Clause.

. . . .

The Court's exclusive reliance on legislative intent as the test of punishment is misplaced, the decisions advocating that narrow and formalistic approach having been long since superseded. The appropriate standard extends significantly beyond legislative intent. "[I]n determining whether a particular civil sanction constitutes criminal punishment, it is the purposes actually served by the sanction in question, not the underlying nature of the proceeding giving rise to the sanction, that must be evaluated," *United States v. Halper*, 490 U.S. 435, 447 n. 7, (1989). That standard requires that a court "assess [] the character of the actual sanctions imposed on the individual by the machinery of the state."

. . . .

The Court's gradual abandonment of its previously exclusive reliance on legislative intent to determine punishment culminated with its decision in Halper, *supra*, in 1989. Halper had previously been convicted on multiple counts of submitting false claims for Medicare reimbursement and causing governmental overpayments of $585, the convictions resulting in a prison sentence and $5,000 fine. Subsequently, the government instituted a civil action under the False Claims Act to recover $130,000 ($2,000 for each of the sixty-five counts), and Halper challenged the proceeding as imposing multiple punishments in violation of the Double Jeopardy Clause. The government contended that the question whether the civil proceeding constituted "punishment" was solely a matter of statutory intent. The Court firmly rejected that approach. . . .

In rejecting exclusive reliance on legislative intent as "not well suited to the context of the 'humane interests' safeguarded by the Double Jeopardy Clause's proscription of multiple punishments," the Court indicated that for purposes of double jeopardy, and the analogous protections afforded by the Ex Post Facto and Bill of Attainder Clauses, the determination of punishment would largely depend on a functional test that focused on the purposes actually served by the sanction:

It is commonly understood that civil proceedings may advance punitive as well as remedial goals, and, conversely, that both punitive and remedial goals may be served by criminal penalties. The notion of punishment, as we commonly understand it, cuts across the division between the civil and the criminal law, and for the purposes of assessing whether a given sanction constitutes multiple punishment barred by the Double Jeopardy Clause, we must follow the notion where it leads. . . .

. . . .

III

The Supreme Court's punishment jurisprudence confirms that the Court's opinion misses the mark when it holds that "a statute that can fairly be characterized as remedial, both in its purpose and implementing provisions, does not constitute punishment even though its remedial provisions have some inevitable deterrent impact, and even though it may indirectly and adversely affect, potentially severely, some of those subject to its provisions." The legislature's ostensible purpose, which rarely can be definitively determined, is relevant but hardly decisive on the issue of punishment. A comprehensive and balanced inquiry into whether the Notification Law imposes punishment would include consideration of whether its impact, the widespread publicizing of information concerning sex offenders within their community, is consistent with practices historically employed as punishment in the past. In addition, a functional inquiry is essential to consider, even on this sparse record, the probable effects of the Notification Law on those sex offenders to whom it is applied.

A

. . . .

In colonial times, "[t]he colonial frame of mind and the structure of colonial society influenced not only what was punished but also how crimes were punished." Lawrence M. Friedman, Crime and Punishment in American History 36 (1993). Because "[t]he aim was not just to punish, but to teach a lesson, so that sinful sheep would want to get back to the flock," public stigmatization, marking, disgrace, and humiliation of the offender served as a means by which collective society expressed its disapproval.

. . . .

"Shaming punishments were colorful [and] they were certainly used with great frequency." Friedman, *supra*, at 38. Floggings at the whipping-post, hangings, and ritualistic mutilations "were carried out publicly in a ceremonial fashion," which served to "focus[] the community's attention on the humiliation component of punishment." The branding of offenders was a common feature in colonial American jurisprudence, having been in wide use in England as well. The practice consisted of burning a letter roughly corresponding to the nature of the crime committed upon the face of the criminal. Murderers were branded with the letter M; thieves with a T; fighters and brawlers with an F; vagrants with a V. "In the laws of colonial New Jersey it [illegible] that for burglary the first offense was to be punished by branding with a T on his hand, while the second offense was to be punished by branding an R on his forehead." "The message was that this offender was not likely to mend his ways; disgrace would and should last until death." Friedman, *supra*, at 40. "This cruel method of marking would preclude those who were branded from finding employment and thus 'render[ing] them desperate.' " Brilliant, *supra*, 1989 Duke L.J. at 1361 (quoting G. Ives, A History of Penal Methods 53 (1914)).

. . . Often, "shaming punishments" were offered as alternatives to fines or other forms of punishment. In Maine, in 1671, "Sarah Morgan, who had the effrontery to strike her husband, was ordered" 'to stand with a gagg in her Mouth halfe an houre at Kittery at a Publique Town meeting & the cause of her offence writt upon her forhead, or pay 50 s[hillings] to the County.' "Friedman, *supra*, at 38 (quoting 2 Province & Court Records of Maine (Charles T. Libby ed. 1931)).

"Esteem has always meant much in intimate communities. . . ." Hirsch, *supra*, 80 Mich.L.Rev. at 1226. Humiliation and stigma were the essential, and at times sole, elements of colonial punishment.

B

. . . .

The Court holds that for Tier Two notification, schools and other organizations that operate establishments that care for women or children qualify for notification if they are likely to encounter the offender. The Court's opinion suggests that all schools and qualifying organizations within the municipality, depending on its size, shall be notified as well as schools and qualifying organizations in adjacent municipalities "depending upon their distance from the offender's residence, place of work, or school." The notice to schools and organizations must direct the recipient not to notify anyone else, but the Court does not specifically limit the personnel in the schools and organizations to whom the notice may be distributed. Presumably, all administrators, teachers, and other employees directly engaged in providing instruction and care for children, and comparable personnel in organizations providing care for women, will receive copies of the notice. In addition, day-care centers, nursery schools, day camps, little-league organizations, and similar community athletic programs for children all would appear to qualify for Tier Two notice. In a small municipality with a population of under 10,000 residents, hundreds of persons presumably will be entitled to receive the Tier Two notice and, although instructed to inform no one else about its contents, no enforcement mechanism conceivably can prevent word-of-mouth dissemination of the information contained in the notice required to be distributed.

Tier Three notification includes all entitled to Tier Two notice and members of the public likely to encounter the offender, which the Court construes to include "the immediate neighborhood of the offender's residence and not just the people next door." The Court expressly authorizes, if appropriate, notification of parents and school children in a neighborhood school if they are deemed likely to encounter the offender. In addition, because the Court instructs that geography as well as an offender's likely whereabouts and proclivity for certain locations are significant factors in determining the scope of notice, the law might require notice to members of the public who live or work in the vicinity of the offender's place of employment, or in the vicinity of establishments (such as bars or bowling alleys) that the offender regularly frequents, without regard to municipal boundaries. Although the Court has limited Tier Three notification from that authorized by the Attorney General's Guidelines, no creative imagination is necessary for one fairly to conclude that the public notice mandated by the law is expansive. If Tier Two notice typically would reach hundreds of persons employed in a municipality, Tier Three notification could involve double or triple that number, and the numbers of people notified would be even greater in communities of larger size and population.

To receive the notice mandated by law and not to disclose information contained in the notice to family members or neighbors would be contrary to human nature. The Court assumes that the media will act responsibly and not frustrate the legislative goal of targeted notification. Even if the media heeds the Court's admonition, which cannot be assured, the virtual certainty is that the notification mandated by the law, especially Tier Three but probably Tier Two as well, will result as a practical matter in broad and pervasive notice, community-wide in many smaller municipalities, of the presence within the community of someone convicted of a sex offense.

The community's reaction to such notice is impossible to predict, but given the normal range of human emotion one reasonably could anticipate that notice of the presence of a sex offender will trigger fear, suspicion, hostility, anger, evasive behavior, ostracism, and in some cases derision, epithets and violence. To be sure, the sex offender's quality of life will be adversely affected. Depending on circumstances, the sex offender might lose employment, friends, standing in the community, and might very well be subjected to community hostility so pervasive as to induce the offender to relocate. A likely, although unintended, result of New Jersey's notification statute might be to induce the sex offenders subject to the Community Notification Law to leave the State.

. . . .

IV

. . . .

The question whether the Registration and Community Notification Laws are "reasonably designed" to protect society from convicted sex offenders is exclusively a legislative determination, but the availability of alternative means of protection may be pertinent to the overriding constitutional issue. . . . Moreover, continued treatment of convicted sex offenders through State-supported voluntary counseling and rehabilitation programs arguably might be more effective than notification over the long term. In addition, the Legislature undoubtedly recognizes that the limited protection afforded by the Community Notification Law does not address the concern that a sex offender could commit an offense a substantial distance from that offender's community. Finally, the tier classification procedure lacks criteria and reliability, the statute distinguishing only among low, moderate, and high risk of re-offense without specific standards, and the classification decision being left [illegible] the county prosecutor. The likelihood is strong that prosecutors, in making tier-classification decisions, will err on the side of caution and in favor of broader notification, and that courts reviewing those determinations will disturb them infrequently. Thus, the process by which prior sex offenders are classified and subjected to broad community notification, although a subject remitted initially to legislative discretion, is hardly flawless.

. . . .

The Constitution's prohibition against ex post facto laws reflects an enduring value that transcends the most pressing concerns of this or any day and age. Today, our concern is with prior sex offenders; in the 1950's the legislative concern focused on Communists; and in the 1860's Congress was determined to punish legislatively those who had supported the Confederacy. Future legislatures will doubtlessly find reasons to deal harshly with other groups that pose an apparent threat to the public safety.

. . . .

Despite the Legislature's understandable concern about the danger presented by prior sex offenders, the judicial role, mindful of the compelling pressures that led to the statute's enactment, is to test the statute on the basis of the Constitution's fundamental protection against punitive retroactive legislation. I would hold that the devastating impact on prior sex offenders that will occur from implementation of the Community Notification Law constitutes retroactively imposed punishment prohibited by the *Ex Post Facto* Clause of the Constitution.

NOTES AND QUESTIONS

1. It is unclear, but seems likely, that virtually all of the states have adopted "Megan's Laws" or their equivalents. Independently, a number of state court judges have — as a condition of probation — imposed requirements that sex offenders put signs on houses, fences or automobiles giving notice to neighbors. Is judicial discretion a desirable alternative or complement to legislation such as Megan's Law?
2. Note that Megan's Law has two components — lifetime registration and community notification. Are *both* necessary? And should it be, as the Court in *Doe v. Poritz* observes, that even the least "risky" offender *must* provide not only registration but also, in every instance, at least Tier One notification? Only New Jersey's statute has mandatory notification. How should "Tiers" be determined?
3. Are the Court's efforts to limit dissemination of information to those receiving notices persuasive? What of the recipient's freedom of speech and association? And at Tier 3, does the Court's exclusion of meetings, speeches in schools and religious congregations make sense? Particularly, if — as the Court says — geography and proximity are the critical factors?

4. Are you persuaded by the Court's conclusion that Megan's Law is not "criminal," not "punishment," because it does not serve deterrence? Isn't that its very purpose — to deter and prevent re-offending? And quite apart from deterrence, what of the stigma and shame and shunning to which offenders will be subject? Does the Court persuade you in its reading of legislative intent and its emphasis on that intent, despite the *effects* of the statute?

5. More particularly, what of the danger of vindictiveness and vigilante action by neighbors or townspeople? If there is no control against such misconduct, doesn't that heighten the importance of the citizen's privacy as the last, best protection against public oppression? What of the conduct of the Guardian Angels picketing Mr. Diaz's mother's home? Was it ethical? Protected by the First Amendment? If not, should their misconduct invalidate a statute otherwise badly needed by the public? Is that what Justice Stein argues?

6. In ruling against the privacy claim, isn't the New Jersey Court being disingenuous? It isn't the *information*, but the *delivery* of it that intrudes upon the citizen's privacy in the community. The Court seems to agree, for example, that *compiling* information *is* significant, but finds the citizen's interest is reasonably outweighed by the public's interest, although there is no assurance of how the public will *use* the information. Are you persuaded?

7. Doesn't the Court miss the point of Doe's equal protection argument? It is not that he is grouped inappropriately for administrative purposes, but that doing so stigmatizes him. He is grouped with people viewed by the public *and* him as dangerous and repugnant. This stigma carries an insult, and would be offensive to you or me. Do we care less about a sexual predator?

8. Should Megan's Law apply only to sex offenders? What of addicts? Spousal or child abusers? Those with several convictions while driving under the influence? And who should be added to the list of those receiving notification — employers? spouses? club or church associates?

9. The Court does find "stigma plus" in the notification process, requiring a prior judicial hearing. But what good is such a hearing without standards for classification, treatment or protection?

   The Court ultimately upholds Megan's Law because, it says, there is no alternative and because there is no point in predicting the extent of ostracism. Do you agree? Equally important, do the 40 other states summarized in Justice Stein's dissent agree? Was it clear to *them* that there are alternatives and less intrusive means? And that the punitive reactions described by Justice Stein were predictable and to be avoided?

10. It should be noted that the Halper decision relied on heavily by the dissent and discussed by the majority was reversed by the United States Supreme Court in *Hudson v. United States*, 522 U.S. 93 (1997), but on grounds which — arguably — leave both majority and dissenting positions intact. *But see United States v. Bajakajian*, 524 U.S. 321 (1998).

11. Justice Stein makes a strong case that stigma is punishment, believing this will invalidate Megan's Law as imposing *ex post facto* punishment on th[illegible]. But does that mean he must concede that the colonial methods of punishment — branding, signing, shaming — are *legitimate*? Would you agree? What of banishment?

    And what is Stein's point about the breadth of notification — hundreds, perhaps thousands, of residents even in a small town of 5,000? Doesn't this actually heighten the prospect of rational response and broad security, improving the rationality of Megan's Law?

12. Justice Stein dissents only on the ground that Megan's Law violates the Constitution's ban on *ex post facto* laws. What of plaintiff's Due Process and Equal Protection arguments? What of the right to privacy?

13. A number of other courts have dealt with the Megan's Laws of other states, generally upholding them, since New Jersey's is by far the most draconian. One decision worth noting is *Doe v. Pataki*, 3 F. Supp. 2d 456 (S.D. N.Y. 1998), where a preliminary injunction was granted because state judicial hearings on classifying offenders for notification purposes often denied basic protections of evidence, counsel and due process, leading to numerous erroneous determinations. Does this surprise you? Should it lead to reconsideration by the New Jersey Supreme Court? The Court in *Pataki* summarized the following two proceedings under New York's Megan's Law:

    > The case of proposed plaintiff Charles Coe illustrates vividly the deficiencies in the process of assigning risk levels under the Act. Coe pled guilty in 1990 to attempted sexual abuse for kissing a neighbor and touching her breasts while riding in an elevator. At his sentencing in December 1990, the court noted that Coe suffered from borderline mental retardation. In December 1996, Coe received a notice advising him that the court was required to make a "final determination" of his risk level under the Act. The notice did not advise Coe of his proposed classification or the ramifications thereof. Although he had been found indigent and was represented by Legal Aid in the earlier criminal proceedings, no lawyer was notified to appear at the classification hearing on his behalf.
    >
    > At the classification hearing, the court read from a document, provided by the Board of Examiners of Sex Offenders (the "Board"), that incorrectly described the case as one that involved, not kissing and grabbing someone on an elevator, but sexual contact with a 15-year-old girl, including pulling her pants down and lying on top of her. The report stated, incorrectly, that Coe had been charged with rape. The court noted that the Board had recommended that Coe be classified at risk level two, and ruled that it was going to "adhere" to the Board's recommendation.
    >
    > Coe, who appeared without a lawyer, attempted to tell the court that "[t]he description of the crime . . . [was] totally different from what originally happened." The court responded as follows:

The Board has given me a summary of what happened, and the Board — based upon what they have recommended that you receive, risk level two, I don't agree with it wholly, but the law is there and I must carry it out as long as I sit on the bench . . . .

The court refused to change its classification of Coe as a risk level two. The court did not inform Coe that he had a right to a lawyer. The court did advise Coe to contact a lawyer and apparently gave him the name and telephone number of Legal Aid, but the court did not do so until after it had classified Coe as a risk level two.

Hence, Coe was assigned risk level two, a classification that subjects him to community notification, on the basis of an incorrect report that recited facts from the wrong case. Moreover, the "hearing" could not have lasted much more than five minutes, and Coe, who apparently was indigent and borderline mentally retarded, was not provided with counsel or prior notice of the Board's recommendation or disclosure of the evidence relied on by the Board. Although the court noted that it did not "wholly" agree with the Board, it concluded that it was required to adhere to the Board's recommendation. Despite these serious problems in the proceedings, Coe was not permitted to appeal.

The case of Samuel Poe provides another example. Poe was convicted of attempted sodomy in 1989. On March 26, 1997, he was produced from prison for a classification hearing. The transcript of the hearing — which is reproduced here in its entirety — speaks for itself:

THE CLERK: Bring out [Mr. Samuel Poe].

THE COURT: Let's see what they say about him.

(Whereupon, the defendant was escorted into the courtroom.)

THE CLERK: People versus [Samuel Poe].

[THE ASSISTANT DISTRICT ATTORNEY]: This is [Poe]?

THE COURT: Mr. [Poe], you're basically here for me to make a risk offender assessment in the case. They've assessed you a total of a hundred and twenty points. Is there anything about that that you contest?

THE DEFENDANT: Yes. I don't even know what a hundred and twenty points means.

THE COURT: Okay. That means you're a risk level three.

THE DEFENDANT: First of all, I didn't do the crime.

THE COURT: That's a separate matter.

THE DEFENDANT: Okay. Second of all, for twenty-five years I went from house to house. I'm a plumber. I went from house to house, to house to house. Never had a complaint of any kind. I can't see how I can be a risk of any kind.

THE COURT: Okay. Is that what you wanted to tell me about it?

> THE DEFENDANT: I don't know what else to tell you. I haven't talked to anyone. I haven't been able to hear anyone.
>
> THE COURT: I'll just confirm this risk level three that they said after a hearing, after hearing from you. I appreciate it.
>
> THE CLERK: Hold on a second. This is for him. Bring out Mr. Rahman.
>
> THE COURT: Have a good day.
>
> (Hendricks Reply Decl. Ex. A at 2-3). The entire proceeding could not have lasted more than two minutes. Although the assignment of risk level three subjected Poe to the highest level of community notification, he was not represented by counsel; he was not advised that he had a right to counsel; he apparently did not understand what the 120 points meant; he was not advised how the 120 points were calculated; and he was given no meaningful opportunity to challenge his classification. The court undertook no independent review of the Board's risk level recommendation, nor was Poe even provided with a copy of the risk assessment instrument or the case summary.

In view of *Doe v. Pataki*, should the New Jersey Supreme Court reconsider its conclusions with respect to public vigilantism and judicial assurance of citizen rights? If so, should it reverse its conclusion that Megan's Law is consistent with due process?

14. Suppose a Tier Three Offender moved onto your block. Would you want to know? What would you do with that knowledge? Does your answer vary depending upon whether sexual abuse has been directed toward your child? You? Recently? By this offender?

15. Suppose you are a psychiatrist and you learn by Tier Three notification that a predator has moved onto the same block as one of your patients. However, the notice forbids communication with your patient. Do you have an ethical obligation to communicate with him or her? Before answering, consider the *Tarasoff* case, *infra*, § 3.02[2].

PROBLEM 1–12 — Sexual Predators

Your state presently lacks a Megan's Law. You are clerk to the Chair of your State Senate's Judiciary Committee. She has followed closely the legislative experience reflected in Hendricks, Doe, and Pataki, the three preceding cases. In the light of those and earlier cases, particularly *Bell v. Wolfish*, *Washington v. Harper*, and *Skinner v. Oklahoma*, she asks you to draft a memorandum and proposed legislation:

(a) providing incarcerated sexual predators the option of immediate parole on condition they undergo an orchotomy or psychosurgery. She understands Texas has legislation on the former and that California has legislation on the latter, referring you to *Aden v. Younger*, *infra* § 3.03[1]. She also inquires whether delayed release medication like

Norplant, electronic control devices as in *Terminal Man*, or aversion therapy as in *A Clockwork Orange* might be imposed;

(b) adopting Megan's Law for your state but extending to categories other than sexual offenders. She suggests drunk drivers, wife and child abusers and narcotics "pushers." She also asks whether arm bands and signs on automobiles could be added to mandated notices.

Your memoranda should be no longer than five pages each. Your bills should be no more than three pages.

PROBLEM 1–13 — Sexual Predators and You

You have just learned that a third tier sexual offender has moved onto Main Street, Yourtown. What do you do, if:

(a) the notice came to you as a minister of the Main Street Four Square Bible Church. Do you have an obligation to your parish? What if you know that one of the children in your parish was a victim of sexual abuse? What if the offender is a parishioner?

(b) you are a psychiatrist; the offender is a patient; you learn he has moved to Main Street; *and* you know Nancy Smith's daughter was abused sexually; by your patient (consider these alternatively and cumulatively).

The notice received by the minister and the psychiatrist both warn them to say nothing to anyone.

In considering your rights and obligations, consider not only the preceding cases but also *Tarasoff v. Regents of the University of California*, *infra* § 3.02[2].

§ 1.04 Nonpersons

Defining a community includes a number of factors determining whether the being in question is enough like us to be considered *one* of us: race, religion, language, ancestry, gender, age and education, to name a few. The preceding section dealt with certain *groups* of persons having characteristics causing the community to treat them as nonequals: prisoners, incompetent individuals, sexual predators. The question arises of whether — and to what extent — there may be others so "different" that, although part of the community in some fashion, they are simply — explicitly or functionally — nonpersons.

Such questions arise with great controversy in the abortion context. But they arise as well in the increasingly complex and troubling field of assisted reproduction. This section therefore includes the unborn. It includes as well the "undead," those born into this world, but who show none of Fletcher's qualities of "life," for example anencephalic babies or adults in a persistent vegetative state.

The questions are: Are these individuals "persons"? And, if they are "nonpersons," are they still entitled to ethical respect? If so, to what extent?

[1] The Unborn

[a] Unwanted Fetuses: Abortion

The Roe and Casey opinions deal with one of the great bioethical issues of our time — abortion. Both cases are so familiar that the obvious needs re-emphasis: the two cases hold only that fetuses are not "persons" under the Constitution's political definitions. They do *not* say a community may *not* consider the interests of a fetus for ethical or public health purposes. Indeed, *Roe* and *Casey* are clear that the community has a very substantial interest in the care and well-being of a third trimester fetus.

ROE v. WADE
410 U.S. 113 (1973)

Mr. Justice **Blackmun** delivered the opinion of the Court.

This Texas federal appeal and its Georgia companion, *Doe v. Bolton*, present constitutional challenges to state criminal abortion legislation. The Texas statutes under attack here are typical of those that have been in effect in many States for approximately a century. The Georgia statutes, in contrast, have a modern cast and are a legislative product that, to an extent at least, obviously reflects the influences of recent attitudinal change, of advancing medical knowledge and techniques, and of new thinking about an old issue.

We forthwith acknowledge our awareness of the sensitive and emotional nature of the abortion controversy, of the vigorous opposing views, even among physicians, and of the deep and seemingly absolute convictions that the subject inspires. One's philosophy, one's experiences, one's exposure to the raw edges of human existence, one's religious training, one's attitudes toward life and family and their values, and the moral standards one establishes and seeks to observe, are all likely to influence and to color one's thinking and conclusions about abortion.

In addition, population growth, pollution, poverty, and racial overtones tend to complicate and not to simplify the problem.

. . . .

I

The Texas statutes that concern us here are Arts. 1191-1194 and 1196 of the State's Penal Code. These make it a crime to "procure an abortion," as therein defined, or to attempt one, except with respect to "an abortion procured or attempted by medical advice for the purpose of saving the life of the mother." Similar statutes are in existence in a majority of the States.

. . . .

V

The principal thrust of appellant's attack on the Texas statutes is that they improperly invade a right, said to be possessed by the pregnant woman, to choose to terminate her pregnancy. Appellant would discover this right in the concept of personal "liberty" embodied in the Fourteenth Amendment's Due Process Clause; or in personal, marital, familial, and sexual privacy said to be protected by the Bill of Rights or its penumbras; or among those rights reserved to the people by the Ninth Amendment. . . .

VI

It perhaps is not generally appreciated that the restrictive criminal abortion laws in effect in a majority of States today are of relatively recent vintage. Those laws, generally proscribing abortion or its attempt at any time during pregnancy except when necessary to preserve the pregnant woman's life, are not of ancient or even of common-law origin. Instead, they derive from statutory changes effected, for the most part, in the latter half of the 19th century.

. . . .

2. *The Hippocratic Oath*. . . . The Oath varies somewhat according to the particular translation, but in any translation the content is clear: "I will give no deadly medicine to anyone if asked, nor suggest any such counsel; and in like manner I will not give to a woman a pessary to produce abortion," or "I will neither give a deadly drug to anybody if asked for it, nor will I make a suggestion to this effect. Similarly, I will not give to a woman an abortive remedy."

Although the Oath is not mentioned in any of the principal briefs in this case, it represents the apex of the development of strict ethical concepts in medicine, and its influence endures to this day. Why did not the authority of Hippocrates dissuade abortion practice in his time and that of Rome? The late Dr. Edelstein provides us with a theory: The Oath was not uncontested even in Hippocrates' day; only the Pythagorean school of philosophers frowned upon the related act of suicide. Most Greek thinkers, on the other hand, commended abortion, at least prior to viability. . . .

. . . .

3. *The Common Law*. It is undisputed that at common law, abortion performed *before* "quickening" — he first recognizable movement of the fetus in utero, appearing usually from the 16th to the 18th week of pregnancy — was not an indictable offense. Although Christian theology and the canon law came to fix the point of animation at 40 days for a male and 80 days for a female, a view that persisted until the 19th century, there was otherwise little agreement about the precise time of formation or animation. There was agreement, however, that prior to this point the fetus was to be regarded as part of the mother, and its destruction, therefore, was not homicide. . . .

Whether abortion of a *quick* fetus was a felony at common law, or even a lesser crime, is still disputed. Bracton, writing early in the 13th century, thought it homicide. But the later and predominant view, following the great common-law scholars, has been that it was, at most, a lesser offense. In a frequently cited passage, Coke took the position that abortion of a woman "quick with childe" is "a great misprision, and no murder." Blackstone followed, saying that while abortion after quickening had once been considered manslaughter (though not murder), "modern law" took a less severe [illegible]

6. *The Position of the American Medical Association.* The anti-abortion mood prevalent in this country in the late 19th century was shared by the medical profession. Indeed, the attitude of the profession may have played a significant role in the enactment of stringent criminal abortion legislation during that period.

An AMA Committee on Criminal Abortion was appointed in May 1857. It presented its report to the Twelfth Annual Meeting. That report observed that the Committee had been appointed to investigate criminal abortion "with a view to its general suppression." It deplored abortion and its frequency . . . .

Except for periodic condemnation of the criminal abortionist, no further formal AMA action took place until 1967. In that year, the Committee on Human Reproduction urged the adoption of a stated policy of opposition to induced abortion, except when there is "documented medical evidence" of a threat to the health or life of the mother, or that the child "may be born with incapacitating physical deformity or mental deficiency," or that a pregnancy "resulting from legally established statutory or forcible rape or incest may constitute a threat to the mental or physical health of the patient," and two other physicians "chosen because of their recognized professional competence have examined the patient and have concurred in writing," and the procedure "is performed in a hospital accredited by the Joint Commission on Accreditation of Hospitals." The providing of medical information by physicians to state legislatures in their consideration of legislation regarding therapeutic abortion was "to be considered consistent with the principles of ethics of the American Medical Association." This recommendation was adopted by the House of Delegates.

. . . .

7. *The position of the American Public Health Association.* In October 1970, the Executive Board of the APHA adopted Standards for Abortion Services. These were five in number:

a. Rapid and simple abortion referral must be readily available through state and local public health departments, medical societies, or other nonprofit organizations.

b. An important function of counseling should be to simplify and expedite the provision of abortion services; it should not delay the obtaining of these services.

c. Psychiatric consultation should not be mandatory. As in the case of other specialized medical services, psychiatric consultation should be sought for definite indications and not on a routine basis.

d. A wide range of individuals from appropriately trained, sympathetic volunteers to highly skilled physicians may qualify as abortion counselors.

e. Contraception and/or sterilization should be discussed with each abortion patient." Recommended Standards for Abortion Services, 61 Am. J. Pub. Health 396 (1971).

. . . .

VII

Three reasons have been advanced to explain historically the enactment of criminal abortion laws in the 19th century and to justify their continued existence.

It has been argued occasionally that these laws were the product of a Victorian social concern to discourage illicit sexual conduct. Texas, however, does not advance this justification in the present case, and it appears that no court or commentator has taken the argument seriously. The appellants and amici contend, moreover, that this is not a proper state purpose at all and suggest that, if it were, the Texas statutes are overbroad in protecting it since the law fails to distinguish between married and unwed mothers.

A second reason is concerned with abortion as a medical procedure. When most criminal abortion laws were first enacted, the procedure was a hazardous one for the woman. . . .

Modern medical techniques have altered this situation. Appellants and various amici refer to medical data indicating that abortion in early pregnancy, this is, prior to the end of the first trimester, although not without its risk, is now relatively safe. Mortality rates for women undergoing early abortions, where the procedure is legal, appear to be as low as or lower than the rates for normal childbirth. Consequently, any interest of the State in protecting the woman from an inherently hazardous procedure, except when it would be equally dangerous for her to forgo it, has largely disappeared. Of course, important state interests in the area of health and medical standards do remain. . . .

The third reason is the State's interest — some phrase it in terms of duty — in protecting prenatal life. Some of the argument for this justification rests on the theory that a new human life is present from the moment of conception. The State's interest and general obligation to protect life then extends, it is argued, to prenatal life. Only when the life of the pregnant mother herself is at stake, balanced against the life she carries within her, should the interest of the embryo or fetus not prevail. Logically, of course, a legitimate state interest in this area need not stand or fall on acceptance of the belief that life begins at conception or at some other point prior to live birth. In assessing the State's interest, recognition may be given to the less rigid claim that as long as at least *potential* life is involved, the State may assert interests beyond the protection of the pregnant woman alone.

. . . .

It is with these interests, and the weight to be attached to them, that this case is concerned.

VIII

The Constitution does not explicitly mention any right of privacy. In a line of decisions, the Court has recognized that a right of personal privacy, or a guarantee of certain areas or zones of privacy, does exist under the Constitution . . . . These decisions make it clear that only personal rights th[illegible] be deemed "fundamental" [illegible] the concept of ordered liberty," *Palko v. Connecticut*, are included in this guarantee of personal privacy. They also make it clear that the right has some extension to activities relating to marriage, *Loving v. Virginia*; family relationships, *Prince v. Massachusetts*; and child rearing and education, *Pierce v. Society of Sisters*.

This right of privacy, whether it be founded in the Fourteenth Amendment's concept of personal liberty and restrictions upon state action, as we feel it is, or, as the District Court determined, in the Ninth Amendment's reservation of rights to the people, is broad enough to encompass a woman's decision whether or not to terminate her pregnancy. The detriment that the State would impose upon the pregnant woman by denying this choice altogether is apparent. Specific and direct harm medically diagnosable even in early pregnancy may be involved. Maternity, or additional offspring, may force upon the woman a distressful life and future. Psychological harm may be imminent. Mental and physical health may be taxed by child care. There is also the distress, for all concerned, associated with the unwanted child, and there is the problem of bringing a child into a family already unable, psychologically and otherwise, to care for it. . . .

. . . .

We, therefore, conclude that the right of personal privacy includes the abortion decision, but that this right is not unqualified and must be considered against important state interests in regulation.

. . . .

Where certain "fundamental rights" are involved, the Court has held that regulation limiting these rights may be justified only by a "compelling state interest," *Kramer v. Union Free School District*, *Shapiro v. Thompson*, *Sherbert V. Verner*, and that legislative enactments must be narrowly drawn to express only the legitimate state interests at stake. *Griswold v. Connecticut*.

. . . .

IX

. . . Appellant, as has been indicated, claims an absolute right that bars any state imposition of criminal penalties in the area. Appellee argues that the State's determination to recognize and protect prenatal life from and after conception constitutes a compelling state interest. As noted above, we do not agree fully with either formulation.

A

The appellee and certain *amici* argue that the fetus is a "person" within the language and meaning of the Fourteenth Amendment. In support of this, they outline at length and in detail the well-known facts of fetal development. If this suggestion of personhood is established, the appellant's case, of course, collapses, for the fetus' right to life is then guaranteed specifically by the Amendment. . . .

The Constitution does not define "person" in so many words. Section 1 of the Fourteenth Amendment contains three references to "person." The first, in defining "citizens," speaks of "persons born or naturalized in the United States." The word also appears both in the Due Process Clause and in the Equal Protection Clause. "Person" is used in other places in the Constitution . . . . But in nearly all these instances, the use of the word is such that it has application only postnatally. None indicates, with any assurance, that it has any possible prenatal application.[1]

All this, together with our observation, *supra*, that throughout the major portion of the 19th century prevailing legal abortion practices were far freer than they are today, persuades us that the word "person," as used in the Fourteenth Amendment, does not include the unborn. . . .

This conclusion, however, does not of itself fully answer the contentions raised by Texas, and we pass on to other considerations.

B

The pregnant woman cannot be isolated in her privacy. She carries an embryo and, later, a fetus, if one accepts the medical definitions of the developing young in the human uterus. The situation therefore is inherently different from marital intimacy, or bedroom possession of obscene material, or marriage, or procreation, or education, with which *Eisenstadt, Griswold, Stanley, Loving, Skinner, Pierce,* and *Meyer* were respectively concerned. As we have intimated above, it is reasonable and appropriate for a State to decide that at some point in time another interest, that of health of the mother or that of potential human life, becomes significantly involved. The woman's privacy is no longer sole and any right of privacy she possesses must be measured accordingly.

Texas urges that, apart from the Fourteenth Amendment, life begins at conception and is present throughout pregnancy, and that, therefore, the State has a compelling interest in protecting that life from and after conception. We need not resolve the difficult question of when life begins. When those trained in the respective disciplines of medicine, philosophy, and theology are unable to arrive at any consensus, the judiciary, at this point in the development of man's knowledge, is not in a position to speculate as to the answer.

It should be sufficient to note briefly the wide divergence of thinking on this most sensitive and difficult question. There has always been strong support for the view that life does not begin until live birth. This was the belief of the Stoics. It appears to be the predominant, though not the unanimous, attitude of the Jewish faith. It may be taken to represent also the position of a large segment of the Protestant community, insofar as that can be

[1] When Texas urges that a fetus is entitled to Fourteenth Amendment protection as a person, it faces a dilemma. Neither in Texas nor in any other State are all abortions prohibited. Despite broad proscription, an exception always exists. The exception contained in Art. 1196, for an abortion procured or attempted by medical advice for the purpose of saving the life of the mother, is typical. But if the fetus is a person who is not to be deprived of life without due process of law, and if the mother's condition is the sole determinant, does not the Texas exception appear to be out of line with the Amendment's command?

ascertained; organized groups that have taken a formal position on the abortion issue have generally regarded abortion as a matter for the conscience of the individual and her famil[illegible] noted, the common law found greater significance in quickening. Physicians and their scientific colleagues have regarded that event with less interest and have tended to focus either upon conception, upon live birth, or upon the interim point at which the fetus becomes "viable," that is, potentially able to live outside the mother's womb, albeit with artificial aid. Viability is usually placed at about seven months but may occur earlier, even at 24 weeks. The Aristotelian theory of "mediate animation," that held sway throughout the Middle Ages and the Renaissance in Europe, continued to be official Roman Catholic dogma until the 19th century, despite opposition to this "ensoulment" theory from those in the Church who would recognize the existence of life from the moment of conception. The latter is now, of course, the official belief of the Catholic Church. As one of the briefs amicus discloses, this is a view strongly held by many non-Catholics as well, and by many physicians. Substantial problems for precise definition of this view are posed, however, by new embryological data that purport to indicate that conception is a "process" over time, rather than an event, and by new medical techniques such as menstrual extraction, the "morning-after" pill, implantation of embryos, artificial insemination, and even artificial wombs.

In areas other than criminal abortion, the law has been reluctant to endorse any theory that life, as we recognize it, begins before live birth or to accord legal rights to the unborn except in narrowly defined situations and except when the rights are contingent upon live birth . . . . Perfection of the interests involved, again, has generally been contingent upon live birth. In short, the unborn have never been recognized in the law as persons in the whole sense.

X

In view of all this, we do not agree that, by adopting one theory of life, Texas may override the rights of the pregnant woman that are at stake. We repeat, however, that the State does have an important and legitimate interest in preserving and protecting the health of the pregnant woman, whether she be a resident of the State or a nonresident who seeks medical consultation and treatment there, and that it has still *another* important and legitimate interest in protecting the potentiality of human life. These interests are separate and distinct. Each grows in substantiality as the woman approaches term and, at a point during pregnancy, each becomes "compelling."

With respect to the State's important and legitimate interest in the health of the mother, the "compelling" point, in the light of present medical knowledge, is at approximately the end of the first trimester. This is so because of the now-established medical fact, that until the end of the first trimester mortality in abortion may be less than mortality in normal childbirth. It follows that, from and after this point, a State may regulate the abortion procedure to the extent that the regulation reasonably relates to the preservation and protection of maternal health. Examples of permissible state regulation in this area are requirements as to the qualifications of the person who is to perform the abortion; as to the licensure of that person; as to the facility in which the procedure is to be performed, that is, whether it must be a hospital or may be a clinic or some other place of less-than-hospital status; as to the licensing of the facility; and the like.

This means, on the other hand, that, for the period of pregnancy prior to this "compelling" point, the attending physician, in consultation with his patient, is free to determine, without regulation by the State, that, in his medical judgment, the patient's pregnancy should be terminated. If that decision is reached, the judgment may be effectuated by an abortion free of interference by the State.

With respect to the State's important and legitimate interest in potential life, the "compelling" point is at viability. This is so because the fetus then presumably has the capability of meaningful life outside the mother's womb. State regulation protective of fetal life after viability thus has both logical and biological justifications. If the State is interested in protecting fetal life after viability, it may go so far as to proscribe abortion during that period, except when it is necessary to preserve the life or health of the mother.

Measured against these standards, Art. 1196 of the Texas Penal Code, in restricting legal abortions to those "procured or attempted by medical advice for the purpose of saving the life of the mother," sweeps too broadly. The statute makes no distinction between abortions performed early in pregnancy and those performed later, and it limits to a single reason, "saving" the mother's life, the legal justification for the procedure. The statute, therefore, cannot survive the constitutional attack made upon it here.

. . . .

The judgment of the District Court as to intervenor Hallford is reversed, and Dr. Hallford's complaint in intervention is dismissed. In all other respects, the judgment of the District Court is affirmed. Costs are allowed to the appellee.

It is so ordered.

Mr. Chief Justice **Douglas**, concurring.

I agree that, under the Fourteenth Amendment to the Constitution, the abortion statutes of Georgia and Texas impermissibly limit the performance of abortions necessary to protect the health of pregnant women, using the term health in its broadest medical context. I am somewhat troubled that the Court has taken notice of various scientific and medical data in reaching its conclusion; however, I do not believe that the Court has exceeded the scope of judicial notice accepted in other contexts.

The Ninth Amendment obviously does not create federally enforceable rights. It merely says, "The enumeration in the Constitution, of certain rights, shall not be construed to deny or disparage others retained by the people." But a catalogue of these rights includes customary, traditional, and time-honored rights, amenities, privileges, and immunities that come within the sweep of "the Blessings of Liberty" mentioned in the preamble to the Constitution. Many of them, in my view, come within the meaning of the term "liberty" as used in the Fourteenth Amendment.

First is the autonomous control over the development and expression of one's intellect, interests, tastes, and personality.

These are rights protected by the First Amendment and, in my view, they are absolute, permitting of no exceptions. The Free Exercise Clause of the First Amendment is one facet of this constitutional right. The right to remain silent as respects one's own beliefs is protected by the First and the Fifth. The First Amendment grants the privacy of first-class mail. All of these aspects of the right of privacy are rights "retained by the people" in the meaning of the Ninth Amendment.

Second is the freedom of choice in the basic decisions of one's life respecting marriage, divorce, procreation, contraception, and the education and upbringing of children.

These rights, unlike those protected by the First Amendment, are subject to some control by the police power. Thus, the Fourth Amendment speaks only of "unreasonable searches and seizures" and of "probable cause." These rights are "fundamental," and we have held that in order to support legislative action the statute must be narrowly and precisely drawn and that a "compelling state interest" must be shown in support of the limitation.

The liberty to marry a person of one's own choosing, *Loving v. Virginia*; the right of procreation, *Skinner v. Oklahoma*; the liberty to direct the education of one's children; and the privacy of the marital relation, *Griswold v. Connecticut, supra*, are in this category.

This right of privacy was called by Mr. Justice Brandeis the right "to be let alone." *Olmstead v. United States*. That right includes the privilege of an individual to plan his own affairs, for, " 'outside areas of plainly harmful conduct, every American is left to shape his own life as he thinks best, do what he pleases, go where he pleases.' " *Kent v. Dulles*.

Third is the freedom to care for one's health and person, freedom from bodily restraint or compulsion, freedom to walk, stroll, or loaf.

These rights, though fundamental, are likewise subject to regulation on a showing of "compelling state interest." We stated in *Papachristou v. City of Jacksonville*, that walking, strolling, and wandering "are historically part of the amenities of life as we have known them." As stated in *Jacobson v. Massachusetts*:

> There is, of course, a sphere within which the individual may assert the supremacy of his own will and rightfully dispute the authority of any human government, especially of any free government existing under a written constitution, to interfere with the exercise of that will.

In *Meyer v. Nebraska*, the Court said:

> Without doubt, [liberty] denotes not merely freedom from bodily restraint but also the right of the individual to contract, to engage in any of the common occupations of life, to acquire useful knowledge, to marry, establish a home and bring up children, to worship God according to the dictates of his own conscience, and generally to enjoy those privileges long recognized at common law as essential to the orderly pursuit of happiness by free men.

Elaborate argument is hardly necessary to demonstrate that childbirth may deprive a woman of her preferred lifestyle and force upon her a radically different and undesired future. For example, rejected applicants under the Georgia statute are required to endure the discomforts of pregnancy; to incur the pain, higher mortality rate, and after effects of childbirth; to abandon educational plans, to sustain loss of income; to forgo the satisfactions of careers; to tax further mental and physical health in providing child care; and, in some cases, to bear the lifelong stigma of unwed motherhood, a badge which may haunt, if not deter, later legitimate family relationships.

II

In summary, the enactment is overbroad. It is not closely correlated to the aim of preserving prenatal life. In fact, it permits its destruction in several cases, including pregnancies resulting from sex acts in which unmarried females are below the statutory age of consent. At the same time, however, the measure broadly proscribes aborting other pregnancies which may cause severe mental disorders. Additionally, the statute is overbroad because it equates the value of embryonic life immediately after conception with the worth of life immediately before birth.

Mr. Justice **Stewart** concurring.

In 1963, this Court, in *Ferguson v. Skrupa*, purported to sound the death knell for the doctrine of substantive due process, a doctrine under which many state laws had in the past been held to violate the Fourteenth Amendment. . . .

Barely two years later, in *Griswold v. Connecticut*, the Court held a Connecticut birth control law unconstitutional. In view of what had been so recently said in *Skrupa*, the Court's opinion in *Griswold* understandably did its best to avoid reliance on the Due Process Clause of the Fourteenth Amendment as the ground for decision. Yet, the Connecticut law did not violate any provision of the Bill of Rights, nor any other specific provision of the Constitution. So it was clear to me then, and it is equally clear to me now, that the *Griswold* decision can be rationally understood only as a holding that the Connecticut statute substantively invaded the "liberty" that is protected by the Due Process Clause of the Fourteenth Amendment. . . .

As Mr. Justice Harlan once wrote: "[T]he full scope of the liberty guaranteed by the Due Process Clause cannot be found in or limited by the precise terms of the specific guarantees elsewhere provided in the Constitution. This 'liberty' is not a series of isolated points pricked out in terms of the taking of property; the freedom of speech, press, and religion; the right to keep and bear arms; the freedom from unreasonable searches and seizures; and so on. It is a rational continuum which, broadly speaking, includes a freedom from all substantial arbitrary impositions and purposeless restraints . . . and which also recognizes, what a reasonable and sensitive judgment must, that certain interests require particularly careful scrutiny of the state needs asserted to justify their abridgment." *Poe v. Ullman*. . . .

. . . .

Clearly, therefore, the Court today is correct in holding that the right asserted by Jane Roe is embraced within the personal liberty protected by the Due Process Clause of the Fourteenth Amendment.

. . . .

Mr. Justice **White**, with whom Mr. Justice **Rehnquist** joins, dissenting.

At the heart of the controversy in these cases are those recurring pregnancies that pose no danger whatsoever to the life or health of the mother but are, nevertheless, unwanted for any one or more of a variety of reasons — convenience, family planning, economics, dislike of children, the embarrassment of illegitimacy, etc. The common claim before us is that for any one of such reasons, or for no reason at all, and without asserting or claiming any threat to life or health, any woman is entitled to an abortion at her request if she is able to find a medical advisor willing to undertake the procedure.

With all due respect, I dissent. I find nothing in the language or history of the Constitution to support the Court's judgment. The Court simply fashions and announces a new constitutional right for pregnant mothers and, with scarcely any reason or authority for its action, invests that right with sufficient substance to override most existing state abortion statutes. The upshot is that the people and the legislatures of the 50 States are constitutionally disentitled to weigh the relative importance of the continued existence and development of the fetus, on the one hand, against a spectrum of possible impacts on the mother, on the other hand. As an exercise of raw judicial power, the Court perhaps has authority to do what it does today; but in my view its judgment is an improvident and extravagant exercise of the power of judicial review that the Constitution extends to this Court.

Mr. Justice **Rehnquist**, dissenting.

The Court's opinion brings to the decision of this troubling question both extensive historical fact and a wealth of legal scholarship. While the opinion thus commands my respect, I find myself nonetheless in fundamental disagreement with those parts of it that invalidate the Texas statute in question, and therefore dissent.

I

. . . .

. . . I have difficulty in concluding, as the Court does, that the right of "privacy" is involved in this case. Texas, by the statute here challenged, bars the performance of a medical abortion by a licensed physician on a plaintiff such as Roe. A transaction resulting in an operation such as this is not "private" in the ordinary usage of that word. Nor is the "privacy" that the Court finds here even a distant relative of the freedom from searches and seizures protected by the Fourth Amendment to the Constitution, which the Court has referred to as embodying a right to privacy.

If the Court means by the term "privacy" no more than that the claim of a person to be free from unwanted state regulation of consensual transactions may be a form of "liberty" protected by the Fourteenth Amendment, there is no doubt that similar claims have been upheld in our earlier decisions on the basis of that liberty. I agree with the statement of Mr. Justice Stewart in his concurring opinion that the "liberty," against deprivation of which without due process the Fourteenth Amendment protects, embraces more than the rights found in the Bill of Rights. But that liberty is not guaranteed absolutely against deprivation, only against deprivation without due process of law. The test traditionally applied in the area of social and economic legislation is whether or not a law such as that challenged has a rational relation to a valid state objective. *Williamson v. Lee Optical Co.* The Due Process Clause of the Fourteenth Amendment undoubtedly does place a limit, albeit a broad one, on legislative power to enact laws such as this. If the Texas statute were to prohibit an abortion even where the mother's life is in jeopardy, I have little doubt that such a statute would lack a rational relation to a valid state objective under the test stated in *Williamson, supra.* But the Court's sweeping invalidation of any restrictions on abortion during the first trimester is impossible to justify under that standard, and the conscious weighing of competing factors that the Court's opinion apparently substitutes for the established test is far more appropriate to a legislative judgment than to a judicial one.

. . . .

While the Court's opinion quotes from the dissent of Mr. Justice Holmes in *Lochner v. New York*, the result it reaches is more closely attuned to the majority opinion of Mr. Justice Peckham in that case. As in *Lochner* and similar cases applying substantive due process standards to economic and social welfare legislation, the adoption of the compelling state interest standard will inevitably require this Court to examine the legislative policies and pass on the wisdom of these policies in the very process of deciding whether a particular state interest put forward may or may not be "compelling." The decision here to break pregnancy into three distinct terms and to outline the permissible restrictions the State may impose in each one, for example, partakes more of judicial legislation than it does of a determination of the intent of the drafters of the Fourteenth Amendment.

The fact that a majority of the States reflecting, after all, the majority sentiment in those States, have had restrictions on abortions for at least a century is a strong indication, it seems to me, that the asserted right to an abortion is not "so rooted in the traditions and conscience of our people as to be ranked as fundamental," *Snyder v. Massachusetts*. Even today, when society's views on abortion are changing, the very existence of the debate is evidence that the "right" to an abortion is not so universally accepted as the appellants would have us believe.

. . . .

NOTES AND QUESTIONS

1. *Roe v. Wade* is perhaps, along with *Brown v. Board of Education* (school integration) and *Miranda v. Arizona* (criminal confessions), one of the most controversial opinions by the United States Supreme Court in the latter half of the 20th century. All three opinions provoked ongoing storms of controversy, massive efforts at amendment and resistance,

and continuing criticism and attacks on the authors of the majority opinions. Mr. Justice Blackmun often expressed regret that his opinion in *Roe* received such overwhelming attention [illegible] important opinions [illegible] in the tumult created by *Roe v. Wade*.

3. These questions, of course, go well beyond the scope of the opinion in *Roe*. By comparison, that scope is quite narrow. The majority simply held that during the first trimester of pregnancy, the state has virtually no interest in whether a pregnancy is terminated. In the second trimester, the state's interest is in the health and safety of the mother. In the third trimester, the state has an interest in protecting the potentiality for life. This mechanical approach has been criticized as inadequate, in the light of scientific advances which move earlier in time the point of "viability;" that is, the time when a fetus may be delivered from the mother and be expected to survive. Science also has moved *back* the time when an abortion may be safely and routinely performed, so that it is no longer limited to the first or second trimesters. Is a better approach available than Mr. Justice Blackmun's "arithmetic" approach?

4. *Roe* has also been criticized in its constitutional grounding. It rests upon a right of "privacy," nowhere explicitly created in the Constitution. In a very literal sense, an abortion is rarely "private," since it almost always involves a medical provider, frequently in a clinical or hospital setting. The closest guarantee is that found in the Fourth Amendment, which protects the rights of citizens to be "secure" in their persons from unreasonable searches and seizures. Other "fundamental rights" involve association, as in marriage. But none of these comes close to creating a "right of privacy." Why would not the Court have agreed upon the Ninth Amendment, invoked by Chief Justice Burger, or the liberty clause of the Fourteenth Amendment, invoked by Mr. Justice Stewart?

5. Of the various opinions in *Roe*, it is the opinion of Chief Justice Douglas which comes closest to invoking ethical principles. He invokes concepts of "autonomous control," "freedom of choice," and "freedom to care for one's health and person," "freedom from bodily restraint or compulsion." A central concept of ethics, including bioethics, is the respect which must be given to the choices of autonomous individuals. Which opinion in *Roe* would Rawls write?

6. The fetus involved in *Roe v. Wade* is the same entity as involved in the earlier cases of *Baby M* and *In Re A.C.*, discussed in the preceding sections of this text and the *Davis* case, discussed later in this section. In *Baby M*, the fetus was of such great significance that the surrogate mother bonded with it *in utero* and the New Jersey Supreme Court held that it could not be transferred like so much property, but instead was protected by, and subject to, fundamental principles of family law. There, as in *A.C.* and *Davis,* the state is protecting the "best interests" of the child. Is this mode of analysis consistent with the approach taken in *Roe v. Wade*?

7. Similarly, is a fetus entitled to sufficient protection so that a class action might prevent either the state or pregnant women from conceiving and

developing fetuses, the issue in *Davis* — but for sale, for human experimentation or for organ transplantation? Clearly, a state may have an interest in the third trimester of pregnancy in the potentiality for life, after the decision in *Roe v. Wade*. But may it have an interest prior to that time, in preventing unethical conception or the unethical termination of a pregnancy? When *might* abortion be considered unethical?

PLANNED PARENTHOOD v. CASEY

505 U.S. 833 (1992)

Justice **O'Connor**, Justice **Kennedy**, and Justice **Souter** announced the judgment of the Court and delivered the opinion of the Court with respect to Parts I, II, III, V-A, V-C, and VI, an opinion with respect to Part V-E, in which Justice **Stevens** joins, and an opinion with respect to Parts IV, V-B, and V-D.

I

Liberty finds no refuge in a jurisprudence of doubt. Yet 19 years after our holding that the Constitution protects a woman's right to terminate her pregnancy in its early stages, *Roe v. Wade*, that definition of liberty is still questioned. Joining the respondents as amicus curiae, the United States, as it has done in five other cases in the last decade, again asks us to overrule *Roe*.

At issue in these cases are five provisions of the Pennsylvania Abortion Control Act of 1982 as amended in 1988 and 1989. The Act requires that a woman seeking an abortion give her informed consent prior to the abortion procedure, and specifies that she be provided with certain information at least 24 hours before the abortion is performed. For a minor to obtain an abortion, the Act requires the informed consent of one of her parents, but provides for a judicial bypass option if the minor does not wish to or cannot obtain a parent's consent. Another provision of the Act requires that, unless certain exceptions apply, a married woman seeking an abortion must sign a statement indicating that she has notified her husband of her intended abortion. The Act exempts compliance with these three requirements in the event of a "medical emergency." In addition to the above provisions regulating the performance of abortions, the Act imposes certain reporting requirements on facilities that provide abortion services.

. . . .

After considering the fundamental constitutional questions resolved by *Roe*, principles of institutional integrity, and the rule of *stare decisis*, we are led to conclude this: the essential holding of *Roe v. Wade* should be retained and once again reaffirmed.

It must be stated at the outset and with clarity that *Roe*'s essential holding, the holding we reaffirm, has three parts. First is a recognition of the right of the woman to choose to have an abortion before viability and to obtain it without undue interference from the State. Before viability, the State's interests are not strong enough to support a prohibition of abortion or the imposition of a substantial obstacle to the woman's effective right to elect the procedure. Second is a confirmation of the State's power to restrict abortions after fetal viability, if the law contains exceptions for pregnancies which endanger a woman's life or health. And third is the principle that the State has legitimate interests from the outset of the pregnancy in protecting the health of the woman and the life of the fetus that may become a child. These principles do not contradict one another; and we adhere to each.

II

. . . .

Men and women of good conscience can disagree, and we suppose some always shall disagree, about the profound moral and spiritual implications of terminating a pregnancy, even in its earliest stage. Some of us as individuals find abortion offensive to our most basic principles of morality, but that cannot control our decision. Our obligation is to define the liberty of all, not to mandate our own moral code. The underlying constitutional issue is whether the State can resolve these philosophic questions in such a definitive way that a woman lacks all choice in the matter, except perhaps in those rare circumstances in which the pregnancy is itself a danger to her own life or health, or is the result of rape or incest.

. . . .

Our law affords constitutional protection to personal decisions relating to marriage, procreation, contraception, family relationships, child rearing, and education. *Carey v. Population Services International*. Our cases recognize "the right of the *individual*, married or single, to be free from unwarranted governmental intrusion into matters so fundamentally affecting a person as the decision whether to bear or beget a child." *Eisenstadt v. Baird*. Our precedents "have respected the private realm of family life which the state cannot enter." *Prince v. Massachusetts*. These matters, involving the most intimate and personal choices a person may make in a lifetime, choices central to personal dignity and autonomy, are central to the liberty protected by the Fourteenth Amendment. At the heart of liberty is the right to define one's own concept of existence, of meaning, of the universe, and of the mystery of human life. Beliefs about these matters could not define the attributes of personhood were they formed under compulsion of the State.

These considerations begin our analysis of the woman's interest in terminating her pregnancy but cannot end it, for this reason: though the abortion decision may originate within the zone of conscience and belief, it is more than a philosophic exercise. Abortion is a unique act. It is an act fraught with consequences for others: for the woman who must live with the implications of her decision; for the persons who perform and assist in the procedure; for the spouse, family, and society which must confront the knowledge that these procedures exist, procedures some deem nothing short of an act of violence against innocent human life; and, depending on one's beliefs, for the life or potential life that is aborted. Though abortion is conduct, it does not follow that the State is entitled to proscribe it in all instances. That is because the liberty of the woman is at stake in a sense unique to the human condition and so unique to the law. The mother who carries a child to full term is subject to anxieties, to physical constraints, to pain that only she must bear. That these sacrifices have from the beginning of the human race been endured by woman with a pride that ennobles her in the eyes of others and gives to the infant a bond of love cannot alone be grounds for the State to insist she make the sacrifice. Her suffering is too intimate and personal for the State to insist, without more, upon its own vision of the woman's role, however dominant that vision has been in the course of our history and our culture. The destiny of the woman must be shaped to a large extent on her own conception of her spiritual imperatives and her place in society.

. . . .

IV

From what we have said so far it follows that it is a constitutional liberty of the woman to have some freedom to terminate her pregnancy. We conclude that the basic decision in *Roe* was based on a constitutional analysis which we cannot now repudiate. The woman's liberty is not so unlimited, however, that from the outset the State cannot show its concern for the life of the unborn, and at a later point in fetal development the State's interest in life has sufficient force so that the right of the woman to terminate the pregnancy can be restricted.

That brings us, of course, to the point where much criticism has been directed at *Roe*, a criticism that always inheres when the Court draws a specific rule from what in the Constitution is but a general standard. We conclude, however, that the urgent claims of the woman to retain the ultimate control over her destiny and her body, claims implicit in the meaning of liberty, require us to perform that function. Liberty must not be extinguished for want of a line that is clear. And it falls to us to give some real substance to the woman's liberty to determine whether to carry her pregnancy to full term.

We conclude the line should be drawn at viability, so that before that time the woman has a right to choose to terminate her pregnancy. We adhere to this principle for two reasons. First, as we have said, is the doctrine of *stare decisis*. . . .

The second reason is that the concept of viability, as we noted in *Roe*, is the time at which there is a realistic possibility of maintaining and nourishing a life outside the womb, so that the independent existence of the second life can in reason and all fairness be the object of state protection that now overrides the rights of the woman. Consistent with other constitutional norms, legislatures may draw lines which appear arbitrary without the necessity of offering a justification. But courts may not. We must justify the lines we draw. And there is no line other than viability which is more workable. To be sure, as we have said, there may be some medical developments that affect the precise point of viability, but this is an imprecision within tolerable limits given that the medical community and all those who must apply its discoveries will continue to explore the matter. The viability line also has, as a practical matter, an element of fairness. In some broad sense it might be said that a woman who fails to act before viability has consented to the State's intervention on behalf of the developing child.

Though the woman has a right to choose to terminate or continue her pregnancy before viability, it does not at all follow that the State is prohibited from taking steps to ensure that this choice is thoughtful and informed. Even in the earliest stages of pregnancy, the State may enact rules and regulations designed to encourage her to know that there are philosophic and social arguments of great weight that can be brought to bear in favor of continuing the pregnancy to full term and that there are procedures and institutions to allow adoption of unwanted children as well as a certain degree of state assistance if the mother chooses to raise the child herself. It follows that States are free to enact laws to provide a reasonable framework for a woman to make a decision that has such profound and lasting meaning. This, too, we find consistent with *Roe's* central premises, and indeed the inevitable consequence of our holding that the State has an interest in protecting the life of the unborn.

We reject the trimester framework, which we do not consider to be part of the essential holding of *Roe*. Measures aimed at ensuring that a woman's choice contemplates the consequences for the fetus do not necessarily interfere with the right recognized in *Roe*, although those measures have been found to be inconsistent with the rigid trimester framework announced in that case. A logical reading of the central holding in *Roe* itself, and a necessary reconciliation of the liberty of the woman and the interest of the State in promoting prenatal life, require, in our view, that we abandon the trimester framework as a rigid prohibition on all previability regulation aimed at the protection of fetal life. The trimester framework suffers from these basic flaws: in its formulation it misconceives the nature of the pregnant woman's interest; and in practice it undervalues the State's interest in potential life, as recognized in *Roe*.

. . . .

The very notion that the State has a substantial interest in potential life leads to the conclusion that not all regulations must be deemed unwarranted. Not all burdens on the right to decide whether to terminate a pregnancy will be undue. In our view, the undue burden standard is the appropriate means of reconciling the State's interest with the woman's constitutionally protected liberty.

. . . .

A finding of an undue burden is a shorthand for the conclusion that a state regulation has the purpose or effect of placing a substantial obstacle in the path of a woman seeking an abortion of a nonviable fetus. A statute with this purpose is invalid because the means chosen by the State to further the interest in potential life must be calculated to inform the woman's free choice, not hinder it. And a statute which, while furthering the interest in potential life or some other valid state interest, has the effect of placing a substantial obstacle in the path of a woman's choice cannot be considered a permissible means of serving its legitimate ends. . . .

. . . .

V

The Court of Appeals applied what it believed to be the undue burden standard and upheld each of the provisions except for the husband notification requirement. We agree generally with this conclusion, but refine the undue burden analysis in accordance with the principles articulated above. We now consider the separate statutory sections at issue.

. . . .

C

Section 3209 of Pennsylvania's abortion law provides, except in cases of medical emergency, that no physician shall perform an abortion on a married woman without receiving a signed statement from the woman that she has notified her spouse that she is about to undergo an abortion. The woman has the option of providing an alternative signed statement certifying that her husband is not the man who impregnated her; that her husband could not be located; that the pregnancy is the result of spousal sexual assault which she has reported; or that the woman believes that notifying her husband will cause him or someone else to inflict bodily injury upon her. A physician who performs an abortion on a married woman without receiving the appropriate signed statement will have his or her license revoked, and is liable to the husband for damages.

The District Court heard the testimony of numerous expert witnesses, and made detailed findings of fact regarding the effect of this statute. These included:

> 273. The vast majority of women consult their husbands prior to deciding to terminate their pregnancy . . . .
>
> . . . .
>
> 281. Studies reveal that family violence occurs in two million families in the United States. This figure, however, is a conservative one that substantially understates (because battering is usually not reported until it reaches life-threatening proportions) the actual number of families affected by domestic violence. In fact, researchers estimate that one of every two women will be battered at some time in their life . . . .
>
> 282. A wife may not elect to notify her husband of her intention to have an abortion for a variety of reasons, including the husband's illness, concern about her own health, the imminent failure of the marriage, or the husband's absolute opposition to the abortion . . . .
>
> 283. The required filing of the spousal consent form would require plaintiff-clinics to change their counseling procedures and force women to reveal their most intimate decision-making on pain of criminal sanctions. The confidentiality of these revelations could not be guaranteed, since the woman's records are not immune from subpoena . . . .

> . . . .
>
> 289. Mere notification of pregnancy is frequently a flashpoint for battering and violence within the family. The number of battering incidents is high during the pregnancy and often the worst abuse can be associated with pregnancy . . . . The battering husband may deny parentage and use the pregnancy as excuse for abuse . . . .
>
> . . . .
>
> 296. It is common for battered women to have sexual intercourse with their husbands to avoid being battered. While this type of coercive sexual activity would be spousal sexual assault as defined by the Act, many women may not consider it to be so and others would fear disbelief . . . .

These findings are supported by studies of domestic violence. The American Medical Association (AMA) has published a summary of the recent research in this field, which indicates that in an average 12-month period in this country, approximately two million women are the victims of severe assaults by their male partners. . . .

Other studies fill in the rest of this troubling picture. Physical violence is only the most visible form of abuse. Psychological abuse, particularly forced social and economic isolation of women, is also common. L. Walker, The Battered Woman Syndrome 27-28 (1984). Many victims of domestic violence remain with their abusers, perhaps because they perceive no superior alternative. . . .

The limited research that has been conducted with respect to notifying one's husband about an abortion, although involving samples too small to be representative, also supports the District Court's findings of fact. The vast majority of women notify their male partners of their decision to obtain an abortion. In many cases in which married women do not notify their husbands, the pregnancy is the result of an extramarital affair. Where the husband is the father, the primary reason women do not notify their husbands is that the husband and wife are experiencing marital difficulties, often accompanied by incidents of violence.

This information and the District Court's findings reinforce what common sense would suggest. In well-functioning marriages, spouses discuss important intimate decisions such as whether to bear a child. But there are millions of women in this country who are the victims of regular physical and psychological abuse at the hands of their husbands. Should these women become pregnant, they may have very good reasons for not wishing to inform their husbands of their decision to obtain an abortion. . . .

The spousal notification requirement is thus likely to prevent a significant number of women from obtaining an abortion. It does not merely make abortions a little more difficult or expensive to obtain; for many women, it will impose a substantial obstacle. We must not blind ourselves to the fact that the significant number of women who fear for their safety and the safety of their children are likely to be deterred from procuring an abortion as surely as if the Commonwealth had outlawed abortion in all cases.

Respondents attempt to avoid the conclusion that § 3209 is invalid by pointing out that it imposes almost no burden at all for the vast majority of women seeking abortions. They begin by noting that only about 20 percent of the women who obtain abortions are married. They then note that of these women about 95 percent notify their husbands of their own volition. Thus, respondents argue, the effects of § 3209 are felt by only one percent of the women who obtain abortions. . . .

The analysis does not end with the one percent of women upon whom the statute operates; it begins there. Legislation is measured for consistency with the Constitution by its impact on those whose conduct it affects. . . .

. . . Of course, as we have said, § 3209's real target is narrower even than the class of women seeking abortions identified by the State: it is married women seeking abortions who do not wish to notify their husbands of their intentions and who do not qualify for one of the statutory exceptions to the notice requirement. The unfortunate yet persisting conditions we document above will mean that in a large fraction of the cases in which § 3209 is relevant, it will operate as a substantial obstacle to a woman's choice to undergo an abortion. It is an undue burden, and therefore invalid.

. . . .

We recognize that a husband has a "deep and proper concern and interest . . . in his wife's pregnancy and in the growth and development of the fetus she is carrying." With regard to the children he has fathered and raised, the Court has recognized his "cognizable and substantial" interest in their custody. *Stanley v. Illinois*. If this case concerned a State's ability to require the mother to notify the father before taking some action with respect to a living child raised by both, therefore, it would be reasonable to conclude as a general matter that the father's interest in the welfare of the child and the mother's interest are equal.

Before birth, however, the issue takes on a very different cast. It is an inescapable biological fact that state regulation with respect to the child a woman is carrying will have a far greater impact on the mother's liberty than on the father's. The effect of state regulation on a woman's protected liberty is doubly deserving of scrutiny in such a case, as the State has touched not only upon the private sphere of the family but upon the very bodily integrity of the pregnant woman. This conclusion rests upon the basic nature of marriage and the nature of our Constitution: "[T]he marital couple is not an independent entity with a mind and heart of its own, but an association of two individuals each with a separate intellectual and emotional makeup. If the right of privacy means anything, it is the right of the *individual*, married or single, to be free from unwarranted governmental intrusion into matters so fundamentally affecting a person as the decision whether to bear or beget a child." *Eisenstadt v. Baird*. The Constitution protects individuals, men and women alike, from unjustified state interference, even when that interference is enacted into law for the benefit of their spouses.

. . . .

. . . For the great many women who are victims of abuse inflicted by their husbands, or whose children are the victims of such abuse, a spousal notice requirement enables the husband to wield an effective veto over his wife's decision. Whether the prospect of notification itself deters such women from seeking abortions, or whether the husband, through physical force or psychological pressure or economic coercion, prevents his wife from obtaining an abortion until it is too late, the notice requirement will often be tantamount to the veto found unconstitutional in *Danforth.* The women most affected by this law — those who most reasonably fear the consequences of notifying their husbands that they are pregnant — are in the gravest danger.

The husband's interest in the life of the child his wife is carrying does not permit the State to empower him with this troubling degree of authority over his wife. The contrary view leads to consequences reminiscent of the common law. A husband has no enforceable right to require a wife to advise him before she exercises her personal choices. If a husband's interest in the potential life of the child outweighs a wife's liberty, the State could require a married woman to notify her husband before she uses a postfertilization contraceptive. Perhaps next in line would be a statute requiring pregnant married women to notify their husbands before engaging in conduct causing risks to the fetus. After all, if the husband's interest in the fetus' safety is a sufficient predicate for state regulation, the State could reasonably conclude that pregnant wives should notify their husbands before drinking alcohol or smoking. Perhaps married women should notify their husbands before using contraceptives or before undergoing any type of surgery that may have complications affecting the husband's interest in his wife's reproductive organs. And if a husband's interest justifies notice in any of these cases, one might reasonably argue that it justifies exactly what the *Danforth* Court held it did not justify — a requirement of the husband's consent as well. A State may not give to a man the kind of dominion over his wife that parents exercise over their children.

Section 3209 embodies a view of marriage consonant with the common-law status of married women but repugnant to our present understanding of marriage and of the nature of the rights secured by the Constitution. Women do not lose their constitutionally protected liberty when they marry. The Constitution protects all individuals, male or female, married or unmarried, from the abuse of governmental power, even where that power is employed for the supposed benefit of a member of the individual's family. These considerations confirm our conclusion that § 3209 is invalid.

D

. . . .

The judgment in No. 91-902 is affirmed. The judgment in No. 91-744 is affirmed in part and reversed in part, and the case is remanded for proceedings consistent with this opinion including consideration of the question of severability.

It is so ordered.

. . . .

Chief Justice **Rehnquist**, with whom Justice **White**, Justice **Scalia**, and Justice **Thomas** join, concurring in the judgment in part and dissenting in part.

The joint opinion, following its newly-minted variation on *stare decisis*, retains the outer shell of *Roe v. Wade*, but beats a wholesale retreat from the substance of that case. We believe that *Roe* was wrongly decided, and that it can and should be overruled consistently with our traditional approach to *stare decisis* in constitutional cases.

. . . .

III

C

Section 3209 of the Act contains the spousal notification provision. It requires that, before a physician may perform an abortion on a married woman, the woman must sign a statement indicating that she has notified her husband of her planned abortion. A woman is not required to notify her husband if (1) her husband is not the father, (2) her husband, after diligent effort, cannot be located, (3) the pregnancy is the result of a spousal sexual assault that has been reported to the authorities, or (4) the woman has reason to believe that notifying her husband is likely to result in the infliction of bodily injury upon her by him or by another individual. In addition, a woman is exempted from the notification requirement in the case of a medical emergency.

. . . .

The question before us is therefore whether the spousal notification requirement rationally furthers any legitimate state interests. We conclude that it does. First, a husband's interests in procreation within marriage and in the potential life of his unborn child are certainly substantial ones. *See Planned Parenthood of Central Mo. v. Danforth.* ("We are not unaware of the deep and proper concern and interest that a devoted and protective husband has in his wife's pregnancy and in the growth and development of the fetus she is carrying"); *Skinner v. Oklahoma ex rel. Williamson.* The State itself has legitimate interests both in protecting these interests of the father and in protecting the potential life of the fetus, and the spousal notification requirement is reasonably related to advancing those state interests. By providing that a husband will usually know of his spouse's intent to have an abortion, the provision makes it more likely that the husband will participate in deciding the fate of his unborn child, a possibility that might otherwise have been denied him. This participation might in some cases result in a decision to proceed with the pregnancy. . . .

The State also has a legitimate interest in promoting "the integrity of the marital relationship." This Court has previously recognized "the importance of the marital relationship in our society." *Planned Parenthood of Central Mo. v. Danforth, supra.* In our view, the spousal notice requirement is a rational attempt by the State to improve truthful communication between spouses and encourage collaborative decision making, and thereby fosters marital integrity. . . . In our view, it is unrealistic to assume that every husband-wife relationship is either (1) so perfect that this type of truthful and important communication will take place as a matter of course, or (2) so imperfect that, upon notice, the husband will react selfishly, violently, or contrary to the best interests of his wife. . . .

. . . .

Justice **Scalia**, with whom **The Chief Justice**, Justice **White**, and Justice **Thomas** join, concurring in the judgment in part and dissenting in part.

. . . The States may, if they wish, permit abortion on demand, but the Constitution does not *require* them to do so. The permissibility of abortion, and the limitations upon it, are to be resolved like most important questions in our democracy: by citizens trying to persuade one another and then voting. As the Court acknowledges, "where reasonable people disagree the government can adopt one position or the other." . . .

That is, quite simply, the issue in these cases: not whether the power of a woman to abort her unborn child is a "liberty" in the absolute sense; or even whether it is a liberty of great importance to many women. Of course it is both. The issue is whether it is a liberty protected by the Constitution of the United States. I am sure it is not. I reach that conclusion not because of anything so exalted as my views concerning the "concept of existence, of meaning, of the universe, and of the mystery of human life." Rather, I reach it for the same reason I reach the conclusion that bigamy is not constitutionally protected — because of two simple facts: (1) the Constitution says absolutely nothing about it, and (2) the longstanding traditions of American society have permitted it to be legally proscribed.

. . . .

. . . The whole argument of abortion opponents is that what the Court calls the fetus and what others call the unborn child *is a human life*. Thus, whatever answer *Roe* came up with after conducting its "balancing" is bound to be wrong, unless it is correct that the human fetus is in some critical sense merely potentially human. There is of course no way to determine that as a legal matter; it is in fact a value judgment. Some societies have considered newborn children not yet human, or the incompetent elderly no longer so.

. . . .

The emptiness of the "reasoned judgment" that produced *Roe* is displayed in plain view by the fact that, after more than 19 years of effort by some of the brightest (and most determined) legal minds in the country, after more than 10 cases upholding abortion rights in this Court, and after dozens upon dozens of *amicus* briefs submitted in this and other cases, the best the Court can do to explain how it is that the word "liberty" must be thought to include the right to destroy human fetuses is to rattle off a collection of adjectives that simply decorate a value judgment and conceal a political choice. . . . Those adjectives might be applied, for example, to homosexual sodomy, polygamy, adult incest, and suicide, all of which are equally "intimate" and "deep[ly] personal" decisions involving "personal autonomy and bodily integrity," and all of which can constitutionally be proscribed because it is our unquestionable constitutional tradition that they are proscribable. It is not reasoned judgment that supports the Court's decision; only personal predilection. . . .

. . . .

The joint opinion explains that a state regulation imposes an "undue burden" if it "has the purpose or effect of placing a substantial obstacle in the path of a woman seeking an abortion of a nonviable fetus." An obstacle is "substantial," we are told, if it is "calculated[,] [not] to inform the woman's free choice, [but to] hinder it." This latter statement cannot possibly mean what it says. *Any* regulation of abortion that is intended to advance what the joint opinion concedes is the State's "substantial" interest in protecting unborn life will be "calculated [to] hinder" a decision to have an abortion. It thus seems more accurate to say that the joint opinion would uphold abortion regulations only if they do not unduly hinder the woman's decision. That, of course, brings us right back to square one: Defining an "undue burden" as an "undue hindrance" hardly "clarifies" the test. Consciously or not, the joint opinion's verbal shell game will conceal raw judicial policy choices concerning what is "appropriate" abortion legislation.

. . . .

. . . Reason finds no refuge in this jurisprudence of confusion.

. . . .

. . . All manner of "liberties," the Court tells us, inhere in the Constitution and are enforceable by this Court — not just those mentioned in the text or established in the traditions of our society. Why even the Ninth Amendment — which says only that "[t]he enumeration in the Constitution of certain rights shall not be construed to deny or disparage others retained by the people" — is, despite our contrary understanding for almost 200 years, a literally boundless source of additional, unnamed, unhinted — at "rights," definable and enforceable by us, through "reasoned judgment."

What makes all this relevant to the bothersome application of "political pressure" against the Court are the twin facts that the American people love democracy and the American people are not fools. As long as this Court thought (and the people thought) that we Justices were doing essentially lawyers' work up here — reading text and discerning our society's understanding of that text — the public pretty much left us alone. Texts and traditions are facts to study, not convictions to demonstrate about. But if in reality our process of constitutional adjudication consists primarily of making *value judgments*; if we can ignore a long and clear tradition clarifying an ambiguous text, as we did, for example, five days ago in declaring unconstitutional invocations and benedictions at public high school graduation ceremonies, *Lee v. Weisman*; if as I say, our pronouncement of constitutional law rests primarily on value judgments, then a free and intelligent people's attitude towards us can be expected to be (ought to be) quite different. The people know that their value judgments are quite as good as those taught in any law school — maybe better. If, indeed, the "liberties" protected by the Constitution are, as the Court says, undefined and unbounded, then the people *should* demonstrate, to protest that we do not implement *their* values instead of *ours*. . . .

. . . .

. . . [B]y foreclosing all democratic outlet for the deep passions this issue arouses, by banishing the issue from the political forum that gives all participants, even the losers, the satisfaction of a fair hearing and an honest fight, by continuing the imposition of a rigid national rule instead of allowing for regional differences, the Court merely prolongs and intensifies the anguish.

We should get out of this area, where we have no right to be, and where we do neither ourselves nor the country any good by remaining.

NOTES AND QUESTIONS

1. Following *Roe v. Wade*, the Supreme Court undertook a course of decision-making which involved some dozen major cases concerning abortion. Critics suggested that these involved a "retreat" from *Roe* and that ultimately *Roe v. Wade* itself would be overturned. The opinion in *Casey* is proof to the contrary, although it may — in significant respects — be seen as a very lukewarm affirmation of *Roe.*

2. The state legislation in *Casey* was attacked on five points: it was sustained as to four of the five. Would those first four have been invalidated under the reasoning of *Roe v. Wade*? If so, is *Casey* indeed a "retreat"?

3. The Court in *Casey* does invalidate one portion of the Pennsylvania legislation, that which required notice to a husband prior to an abortion. Not only is this consistent with *Roe*, but it may be an expansion. Unlike the criminal legislation in *Roe*, the Pennsylvania statute did not bar or inhibit the obtaining of an abortion, at least by the express statutory terms. A woman who felt she could not give notice safely was, by the statute, exempted from doing so. Nevertheless, Justice O'Connor wrote for the Court that the spousal notification requirement might deter 1% of women from seeking an abortion for fear of abuse or punitive retaliation by their husbands. It was, therefore, unconstitutional as a "burden" on the exercise of a right. Was this an expansion of *Roe*?

4. On a different level of analysis, does a proper ethical appreciation of the interests of both parents in a pregnancy require that each must at least be *informed* of the other's intentions prior to terminating the pregnancy? Respect for the autonomy of the mother may give her desires priority. But respect for the marital commitments of both parties should, one would assume, require candor and fidelity, in the form of notice at least, prior to an abortion. In a small number of cases, such notice might lead to abuse or retaliation; but is it fair to assume that this will be the case in a larger number of cases? Is it fair to deny notice to those husbands for whom abuse would *not* be a risk?

5. Assuming that the analysis of *Casey* is correct, did the Court make the wrong choices? The informed consent requirement and the 24-hour waiting period apply in *all* cases and are a substantial intrusion on the autonomy and liberty of women, particularly in their relationships with their physicians. On the other hand, the spousal notification requirement only required that the woman provide a signed statement that she had given notice to her husband, or had a reason for not doing so, arguably imposing only a minimal burden. Is it fair to say, then, that the reason for invalidating the notification statement requirement is

not that it constituted a significant burden but that, instead, it recognized spousal interest in the fetus?

6. This, in turn, raises the question of the status of the fetus after *Casey.* Since the trimester mode of analysis is rejected, it is now possible for the state to assert an "interest" in the pregnancy at an earlier point than was true in *Roe.* To the extent that such an interest is asserted, the fetus acquires enhanced stature legally. Why was it necessary to reject *Roe's* trimester analysis? Was it a good choice?

7. Note that the Pennsylvania legislation required a physician to warn a woman *against* abortion, under the guise of "informed consent." We previously met this concept in *Zinermon v. Burch* and will return to it in Chapter 3. Is not the Pennsylvania legislation an *intrusion* on informed consent, in the sense of dictating a script for it, when the woman is seeking a personalized dialogue with her physician as advisor, not as agent for the state?

8. *Planned Parenthood v. Casey* has had profound effects on not only abortion, but also on other issues such as women's procreative rights, birth control methods and *in vitro* fertilization. For a discussion of Casey's far-ranging implications, see Paul D. Simmons, *Casey, Bray and Beyond: Religious Liberty and the Abortion Debate*, 13 St. Louis U. Pub. L. Rev. 46 (1993). We will return to *Casey* throughout this book — particularly when we turn to physician-assisted death — for its emphasis on the bioethical; concept of autonomy in interpreting the Constitution. Autonomy is the subject of the next chapter and its relation to dignity is analyzed in Shepherd, *Dignity and Autonomy*, 7 Cornell J. Law & Pub. Pol'y. 431 (1998).

9. For an excellent article, see Judith A.M. Scully, *Book Review*, 8 UCLA Women's L.J. 125 (1997) (reviewing *Breaking The Abortion Deadlock: From Choice to Consent&EIT;, by Eileen L. Mcdonagh); and see Lynne Marie Kohm, Sex Selection Abortion and the Boomerang Effect of a Woman's Right to Choose: A Paradox of the Skeptics, 4 Wm. & Mary J. Women & L. 91 (1997).*

10. For an excellent article on the emerging topic of fetal protection, see Dena M. Marks, *Person v. Potential: Judicial Struggles to Decide Claims Arising from the Death of an Embryo or Fetus and Michigan's Struggle to Settle the Question*, 37 Akron L. Rev. 41 (2004).

11. The problem in *Roe* and *Casey* was the availability of abortion. A separate issue is the methodology of abortion; the next case, *Stenberg v. Carhart* addresses the constitutionality of bans on "late term" or "partial birth" abortion.

PROBLEM 1-14 — 500,000 Missing Girls

In March of 2006, *The Associated Press* reported, based on an article in *Lancet*, the British medical journal, that pre-natal testing allowed parents in India to choose to abort female embryos. Some 500,000 fewer girls, as a result, are born each year.

Criticisms were strong: Dipankar Gupta, a sociologist, blamed the failure on the government's inability to implement laws against fetal sex determination and medical termination of pregnancy on the [illegible]. "Everybody knows [illegible] where these tests are carried out. It's tantamount to murder. The guilty should be tried for that. The government has to be proactive to change people's attitude," he said. Zoya Hasan, a professor of political science at Jawaharlal Nehru University in New Delhi, said the matter could not be dealt with by the government alone. "Civil society and various organizations have to intervene. However, the government has to ensure that tests for determining the sex of the child are now not allowed," she said. "Ultimately, it boils down to building public opinion and social consciousness that there is no difference between a man and a woman and protecting women's rights."

Do you agree? What of a woman's right to choose, under *Roe*? What of a woman's right to be born? What of gender discrimination by physicians?

PROBLEM 1-15 — Abortion: Notifying Parents

The Supreme Court has upheld the right of states to require pregnant girls or their doctors to notify parents prior to an abortion. Opponents argue this infringes a (young) woman's autonomy. They also argue that it will reduce the number of abortions and delay the remainder.

A study in *The New England Journal of Medicine* supports both conclusions. Joyce et al., *Changes In Abortions and Births and the Texas Parental Notification Law*, 354 New Eng. J. Med. 1031 (3/9/06). They found abortions declined about 20% among 15- to 17-year-olds, Table 2. The change was greatest with white minors, and virtually non-existent with blacks (p. 1036), a difference the authors attribute to greater communication with black parents. Other studies have shown a decline of 42% after passage of a parental notification law.

What are the implications of this data for abortion rights? Parental notification statutes? Constitutional analysis? Would you expect similar results with spousal notification statutes?

STENBERG v. CARHART
530 U.S. 914 (2000)

Justice **Breyer** delivered the opinion of the Court.

We again consider the right to an abortion. We understand the controversial nature of the problem. Millions of Americans believe that life begins at conception and consequently that an abortion is akin to causing the death of an innocent child; they recoil at the thought of a law that would permit it. Other millions fear that a law that forbids abortion would condemn many American women to lives that lack dignity, depriving them of equal liberty and leading those with least resources to undergo illegal abortions with the attendant risks of death and suffering. Taking account of these virtually irreconcilable points of view, aware that constitutional law must govern a society whose different members sincerely hold directly opposing views, and considering the matter in light of the Constitution's guarantees of fundamental individual liberty, this Court, in the course of a generation, has determined and then redetermined that the Constitution offers basic protection to the woman's right to choose. We shall not revisit those legal principles. Rather, we apply them to the circumstances of this case. We apply these principles to a Nebraska law banning "partial birth abortion." The statute reads as follows:

> "No partial birth abortion shall be performed in this state, unless such procedure is necessary to save the life of the mother whose life is endangered by a physical disorder, physical illness, or physical injury, including a life-endangering physical condition caused by or arising from the pregnancy itself."

Neb. Rev. Stat. Ann. § 28-328(1) (Supp. 1999).

The statute defines "partial birth abortion" as:

> "an abortion procedure in which the person performing the abortion partially delivers vaginally a living unborn child before killing the unborn child and completing the delivery."

§ 28-326(9).

It further defines "partially delivers vaginally a living unborn child before killing the unborn child" to mean

> "deliberately and intentionally delivering into the vagina a living unborn child, or a substantial portion thereof, for the purpose of performing a procedure that the person performing such procedure knows will kill the unborn child and does kill the unborn child."

Ibid.

The law classifies violation of the statute as a "Class III felony" carrying a prison term of up to 20 years, and a fine of up to $ 25,000. §§ 28-328(2), 28-105. It also provides for the automatic revocation of a doctor's license to practice medicine in Nebraska. § 28-328(4). We hold that this statute violates the Constitution.

I

B

The evidence before the trial court, as supported or supplemented in the literature, indicates the following:

1. About 90% of all abortions performed in the United States take place during the first trimester of pregnancy, before 12 weeks of gestational age. Centers for Disease Control and Prevention, Abortion Surveillance — United States, 1996, p. 41 (July 30, 1999) (hereinafter Abortion Surveillance). During the first trimester, the predominant abortion method is "vacuum aspiration,"

which involves insertion of a vacuum tube (cannula) into the uterus to evacuate the contents. Such an abortion is typically performed on an outpatient basis under local anesthesia.

2. Approximately 10% of all abortions are performed during the second trimester of pregnancy (12 to 24 weeks). In the early 1970's, inducing labor through the injection of saline into the uterus was the predominant method of second trimester abortion. Today, however, the medical profession has switched from medical induction of labor to surgical procedures for most second trimester abortions. The most commonly used procedure is called "dilation and evacuation" (D&E). That procedure (together with a modified form of vacuum aspiration used in the early second trimester) accounts for about 95% of all abortions performed from 12 to 20 weeks of gestational age.

3. D&E "refers generically to transcervical procedures performed at 13 weeks gestation or later." The AMA Report, adopted by the District Court, describes the process as follows.

Between 13 and 15 weeks of gestation:

> "D&E is similar to vacuum aspiration except that the cervix must be dilated more widely because surgical instruments are used to remove larger pieces of tissue. Osmotic dilators are usually used. Intravenous fluids and an analgesic or sedative may be administered. A local anesthetic such as a paracervical block may be administered, dilating agents, if used, are removed and instruments are inserted through the cervix into the uterus to removal fetal and placental tissue. Because fetal tissue is friable and easily broken, the fetus may not be removed intact. The walls of the uterus are scraped with a curette to ensure that no tissue remains."

After 15 weeks:

> "Because the fetus is larger at this stage of gestation (particularly the head), and because bones are more rigid, dismemberment or other destructive procedures are more likely to be required than at earlier gestational ages to remove fetal and placental tissue."

After 20 weeks:

> "Some physicians use intrafetal potassium chloride or digoxin to induce fetal demise prior to a late D&E (after 20 weeks), to facilitate evacuation."

There are variations in D&E operative strategy; compare *ibid.* with W. Hern, Abortion Practice 146–156 (1984), and Medical and Surgical Abortion 133–135. However, the common points are that D&E involves (1) dilation of the cervix; (2) removal of at least some fetal tissue using nonvacuum instruments; and (3) (after the 15th week) the potential need for instrumental disarticulation or dismemberment of the fetus or the collapse of fetal parts to facilitate evacuation from the uterus.

4. When instrumental disarticulation incident to D&E is necessary, it typically occurs as the doctor pulls a portion of the fetus through the cervix into the birth canal. Dr. Carhart testified at trial as follows:

> "Dr. Carhart: . . . 'The dismemberment occurs between the traction of . . . my instrument and the counter-traction of the internal os of the cervix . . . .
>
> "Counsel: 'So the dismemberment occurs after you pulled a part of the fetus through the cervix, is that correct?
>
> "Dr. Carhart: 'Exactly. Because you're using — The cervix has two strictures or two rings, the internal os and the external os . . . that's what's actually doing the dismembering . . . .
>
> "Counsel: 'When we talked before or talked before about a D&E, that is not — where there is not intention to do it intact, do you, in that situation, dismember the fetus in utero first, then remove portions?
>
> "Dr. Carhart: 'I don't think so. . . . I don't know of any way that one could go in and intentionally dismember the fetus in the uterus. . . . It takes something that restricts the motion of the fetus against what you're doing before you're going to get dismemberment.' "

5. The D&E procedure carries certain risks. The use of instruments within the uterus creates a danger of accidental perforation and damage to neighboring organs. Sharp fetal bone fragments create similar dangers. And fetal tissue accidentally left behind can cause infection and various other complications. Nonetheless studies show that the risks of mortality and complication that accompany the D&E procedure between the 12th and 20th weeks of gestation are significantly lower than those accompanying induced labor procedures (the next safest midsecond trimester procedures).

6. At trial, Dr. Carhart and Dr. Stubblefield described a variation of the D&E procedure, which they referred to as an "intact D&E." Like other versions of the D&E technique, it begins with induced dilation of the cervix. The procedure then involves removing the fetus from the uterus through the cervix "intact," *i.e.*, in one pass, rather than in several passes. It is used after 16 weeks at the earliest, as vacuum aspiration becomes ineffective and the fetal skull becomes too large to pass through the cervix. The intact D&E proceeds in one of two ways, depending on the presentation of the fetus. If the fetus presents head first (a vertex presentation), the doctor collapses the skull; and the doctor then extracts the entire fetus through the cervix. If the fetus presents feet first (a breech presentation), the doctor pulls the fetal body through the cervix, collapses the skull, and extracts the fetus through the cervix. The breech extraction version of the intact D&E is also known commonly as "dilation and extraction," or D&X. In the late second trimester, vertex, breech, and traverse/compound (sideways) presentations occur in roughly similar proportions.

7. The intact D&E procedure can also be found described in certain obstetric and abortion clinical textbooks, where two variations are recognized. The first, as just described, calls for the physician to adapt his method for extracting the intact fetus depending on fetal presentation.

8. The American College of Obstetricians and Gynecologists describes the D&X procedure in a manner corresponding to a breech-conversion intact D&E including the following steps:

> "1. deliberate dilatation of the cervix, usually over a sequence of days;
>
> "2. instrumental conversion of the fetus to a footling breech;
>
> "3. breech extraction of the body excepting the head; and
>
> "4. partial evacuation of the intracranial contents of a living fetus to effect vaginal delivery of a dead but otherwise intact fetus."

American College of Obstetricians and Gynecologists Executive Board, Statement on Intact Dilation and Extraction (Jan. 12, 1997) (hereinafter ACOG Statement), App. 599–560.

Despite the technical differences we have just described, intact D&E and D&X are sufficiently similar for us to use the terms interchangeably.

9. Dr. Carhart testified he attempts to use the intact D&E procedure during weeks 16 to 20 because (1) it reduces the dangers from sharp bone fragments passing through the cervix, (2) minimizes the number of instrument passes needed for extraction and lessens the likelihood of uterine perforations caused by those instruments, (3) reduces the likelihood of leaving infection-causing fetal and placental tissue in the uterus, and (4) could help to prevent potentially fatal absorption of fetal tissue into the maternal circulation. The District Court made no findings about the D&X procedure's overall safety. The District Court concluded, however, that "the evidence is both clear and convincing that Carhart's D&X procedure is superior to, and safer than, the . . . other abortion procedures used during the relevant gestational period in the 10 to 20 cases a year that present to Dr. Carhart."

II

The question before us is whether Nebraska's statute, making criminal the performance of a "partial birth abortion," violates the Federal Constitution. We conclude that it does for at least two independent reasons. First, the law lacks any exception " 'for the preservation of the . . . health of the mother.' " Second, it "imposes an undue burden on a woman's ability" to choose a D&E abortion, thereby unduly burdening the right to choose abortion itself. We shall discuss each of these reasons in turn.

A

The fact that Nebraska's law applies both pre-and postviability aggravates the constitutional problem presented. The State's interest in regulating abortion previability is considerably weaker than postviability. Since the law requires a health exception in order to validate even a postviability abortion regulation, it at a minimum requires the same in respect to previability regulation.

The quoted standard also depends on the state regulations "promoting [the State's] interest in the potentiality of human life." The Nebraska law, of course, does not directly further an interest "in the potentiality of human life" by saving the fetus in question from destruction, as it regulates only a *method* of performing abortion. Nebraska describes its interests differently. It says the law "shows concern for the life of the unborn," "prevents cruelty to partially born children," and "preserves the integrity of the medical profession." But we cannot see how the interest-related differences could make any difference to the question at hand, namely, the application of the "health" requirement.

Consequently, the governing standard requires an exception "where it is necessary, in appropriate medical judgment for the preservation of the life or health of the mother," for this Court has made clear that a State may promote but not endanger a woman's health when it regulates the methods of abortion.

. . .

2

Nebraska, along with supporting *amici*, replies that these findings are irrelevant, wrong, or applicable only in a tiny number of instances. It says (1) that the D&X procedure is "little-used," (2) by only "a handful of doctors." It argues (3) that D&E and labor induction are at all times "safe alternative procedures." It refers to the testimony of petitioners' medical expert, who testified (4) that the ban would not increase a woman's risk of several rare abortion complications (disseminated intravascular coagulopathy and amniotic fluid embolus).

The Association of American Physicians and Surgeons *et al.*, *amici* supporting Nebraska, argue (5) that elements of the D&X procedure may create special risks, including cervical incompetence caused by overdilitation, injury caused by conversion of the fetal presentation, and dangers arising from the "blind" use of instrumentation to pierce the fetal skull while lodged in the birth canal. Nebraska further emphasizes (6) that there are no medical studies "establishing the safety of the partial-birth abortion/ D&X procedure." It points to (7) an American Medical Association policy statement that " 'there does not appear to be any identified situation in which intact D&X is the only appropriate procedure to induce abortion.' " And it points out (8) that the American College of Obstetricians and Gynecologists qualified its statement that D&X "may be the best or most appropriate procedure," by adding that the panel "could identify no circumstances under which [the D&X] procedure . . . would be the only option to save the life or preserve the health of the woman."

3

We find these eight arguments insufficient to demonstrate that Nebraska's law needs no health exception. For one thing, certain of the arguments are beside the point. The D&X procedure's relative rarity (argument (1)) is not highly relevant. The D&X is an infrequently used abortion procedure; but the health exception question is whether protecting women's health requires an exception for those infrequent occasions. A rarely used treatment might be necessary to treat a rarely occurring disease that could strike anyone — the

State cannot prohibit a person from obtaining treatment simply by pointing out that most people do not need it. Nor can we know whether the fact that only a "handful" of doct[illegible] (argument (2)) reflects the comparative rarity of late second term abortions, the procedure's recent development.

For another thing, the record responds to Nebraska's (and *amici*'s) medically based arguments. In respect to argument (3), for example, the District Court agreed that alternatives, such as D&E and induced labor, are "safe" but found that the D&X method was significantly *safer* in certain circumstances. In respect to argument (4), the District Court simply relied on different expert testimony — testimony stating that "another advantage of the Intact D&E is that it eliminates the risk of embolism of cerebral tissue into the woman's blood stream."

In response to *amici*'s argument (5), the American College of Obstetricians and Gynecologists, in its own *amici* brief, denies that D&X generally poses risks greater than the alternatives. It says that the suggested alternative procedures involve similar or greater risks of cervical and uterine injury, for "D&E procedures, involve similar amounts of dilitation" and "of course childbirth involves even greater cervical dilitation."

In sum, Nebraska has not convinced us that a health exception is "never necessary to preserve the health of women." Rather, a statute that altogether forbids D&E creates a significant health risk. The statute consequently must contain a health exception.

. . .

B

The Eighth Circuit found the Nebraska statute unconstitutional because, in *Casey*'s words, it has the "effect of placing a substantial obstacle in the path of a woman seeking an abortion of a nonviable fetus." It thereby places an "undue burden" upon a woman's right to terminate her pregnancy before viability. Nebraska does not deny that the statute imposes an "undue burden" *if* it applies to the more commonly used D&E procedure as well as to D&X. And we agree with the Eighth Circuit that it does so apply.

The judgment of the Court of Appeals is *affirmed.*

Justice **Stevens**, with whom Justice **Ginsburg** joins, concurring.

Although much ink is spilled today describing the gruesome nature of late-term abortion procedures, that rhetoric does not provide me a *reason* to believe that the procedure Nebraska here claims it seeks to ban is more brutal, more gruesome, or less respectful of "potential life" than the equally gruesome procedure Nebraska claims it still allows. Justice Ginsburg and Judge Posner have, I believe, correctly diagnosed the underlying reason for the enactment of this legislation — a reason that also explains much of the Court's rhetoric directed at an objective that extends well beyond the narrow issue that this case presents. The rhetoric is almost, but not quite, loud enough to obscure the quiet fact that during the past 27 years, the central holding of *Roe v. Wade*, 410 U.S. 113 (1973), has been endorsed by all but 4 of the 17 Justices who have addressed the issue. That holding — that the word "liberty" in the Fourteenth Amendment includes a woman's right to make this difficult and extremely personal decision — makes it impossible for me to understand how a State has any legitimate interest in requiring a doctor to follow any procedure other than the one that he or she reasonably believes will best protect the woman in her exercise of this constitutional liberty. But one need not even approach this view today to conclude that Nebraska's law must fall. For the notion that either of these two equally gruesome procedures performed at this late stage of gestation is more akin to infanticide than the other, or that the State furthers any legitimate interest by banning one but not the other, is simply irrational. *See* U.S. Const., Amdt. 14.

Justice **O'Connor**, concurring.

It is important to note that, unlike Nebraska, some other States have enacted statutes more narrowly tailored to proscribing the D&X procedure alone. Some of those statutes have done so by specifically excluding from their coverage the most common methods of abortion, such as the D&E and vacuum aspiration procedures. For example, the Kansas statute states that its ban does not apply to the "(A) suction curettage abortion procedure; (B) suction aspiration abortion procedure; or (C) dilation and evacuation abortion procedure involving dismemberment of the fetus prior to removal from the body of the pregnant woman." Kan Stat. Ann. § 65-6721(b)(2) (Supp. 1998). The Utah statute similarly provides that its prohibition "does not include the dilation and evacuation procedure involving dismemberment prior to removal, the suction curettage procedure, or the suction aspiration procedure for abortion." Utah Code Ann. § 76-7-310.5(1)(a) (1999). Likewise, the Montana statute defines the banned procedure as one in which "(A) the living fetus is removed intact from the uterus until only the head remains in the uterus; (B) all or a part of the intracranial contents of the fetus are evacuated; (C) the head of the fetus is compressed; and (D) following fetal demise, the fetus is removed from the birth canal." Mont. Code Ann. § 50-20-401(3)(c)(ii) (Supp. 1999). By restricting their prohibitions to the D&X procedure exclusively, the Kansas, Utah, and Montana statutes avoid a principal defect of the Nebraska law.

Justice **Ginsburg**, with whom Justice **Stevens** joins, concurring.

I write separately only to stress that amidst all the emotional uproar caused by an abortion case, we should not lose sight of the character of Nebraska's "partial birth abortion" law. As the Court observes, this law does not save any fetus from destruction, for it targets only "a *method* of performing abortion." Nor does the statute seek to protect the lives or health of pregnant women.

Chief Justice **Rehnquist**, dissenting.

I did not join the joint opinion in *Planned Parenthood of Southeastern Pa. v. Casey*, 505 U.S. 833 (1992), and continue to believe that case is wrongly decided. Despite my disagreement with the opinion, under the rule laid down in *Marks v. United States*, 430 U.S. 188 (1977), the *Casey* joint opinion represents the holding of the Court in that case. I believe Justice **Kennedy** and Justice **Thomas** have correctly applied *Casey*'s principles and join their dissenting opinions.

Justice **Scalia**, dissenting.

be assigned its rightful place in the history of this Court's jurisprudence beside *Korematsu* and *Dred Scott*. The method of killing a human child — one cannot even accurately say an entirely unborn human child — proscribed by this statute is so horrible that the most clinical description of it evokes a shudder of revulsion. And the Court must know (as most state legislatures banning this procedure have concluded) that demanding a "health exception" — which requires the abortionist to assure himself that, in his expert medical judgment, this method is, in the case at hand, marginally safer than others (how can one prove the contrary beyond a reasonable doubt?) — is to give live-birth abortion free rein. The notion that the Constitution of the United States, designed, among other things, "to establish Justice, insure domestic Tranquility, . . . and secure the Blessings of Liberty to ourselves and our Posterity," prohibits the States from simply banning this visibly brutal means of eliminating our half-born posterity is quite simply absurd.

Even so, I had not intended to write separately here until the focus of the other separate writings (including the one I have joined) gave me cause to fear that this case might be taken to stand for an error different from the one that it actually exemplifies. Because of the Court's practice of publishing dissents in the order of the seniority of their authors, this writing will appear in the reports before those others, but the reader will not comprehend what follows unless he reads them first.

The two lengthy dissents in this case have, appropriately enough, set out to establish that today's result does not follow from this Court's most recent pronouncement on the matter of abortion, *Planned Parenthood of Southeastern Pa. v. Casey*, 505 U.S. 833 (1992). It would be unfortunate, however, if those who disagree with the result were induced to regard it as merely a regrettable misapplication of *Casey*. It is not that, but is *Casey*'s logical and entirely predictable consequence.

But the Court gives a second and independent reason for invalidating this humane (not to say anti-barbarian) law: That it fails to allow an exception for the situation in which the abortionist believes that this livebirth method of destroying the child might be safer for the woman. (As pointed out by Justice Thomas, and elaborated upon by Justice Kennedy, there is no good reason to believe this is ever the case, but — who knows? — it sometime *might* be.)

I have joined Justice Thomas's dissent because I agree that today's decision is an "unprecedented expansion" of our prior cases, "is not mandated" by *Casey*'s "undue burden" test, and can even be called (though this pushes me to the limit of my belief) "obviously irreconcilable with *Casey*'s explication of what its undue-burden standard requires." But I never put much stock in *Casey*'s explication of the inexplicable. In the last analysis, my judgment that *Casey* does not support today's tragic result can be traced to the fact that what I consider to be an "undue burden" is different from what the majority considers to be an "undue burden" — a conclusion that can not be demonstrated true or false by factual inquiry or legal reasoning. It is a value judgment, dependent upon how much one respects (or believes society ought to respect) the life of a partially delivered fetus, and how much one respects (or believes society ought to respect) the freedom of the woman who gave it life to kill it. Evidently, the five Justices in today's majority value the former less, or the latter more, (or both), than the four of us in dissent. Case closed. There is no cause for anyone who believes in *Casey* to feel betrayed by this outcome. It has been arrived at by precisely the process *Casey* promised — a democratic vote by nine lawyers, not on the question whether the text of the Constitution has anything to say about this subject (it obviously does not); nor even on the question (also appropriate for lawyers) whether the legal traditions of the American people would have sustained such a limitation upon abortion (they obviously would); but upon the pure policy question whether this limitation upon abortion is "undue" — *i.e.*, goes too far.

In my dissent in *Casey*, I wrote that the "undue burden" test made law by the joint opinion created a standard that was "as doubtful in application as it is unprincipled in origin." Today's decision is the proof. As long as we are debating this issue of necessity for a health-of-the-mother exception on the basis of *Casey*, it is really quite impossible for us dissenters to contend that the majority is *wrong* on the law — any more than it could be said that one is *wrong in law* to support or oppose the death penalty, or to support or oppose mandatory minimum sentences. The most that we can honestly say is that we disagree with the majority on their policy-judgment-couchedas-law. And those who believe that a 5 to 4 vote on a policy matter by unelected lawyers should not overcome the judgment of 30 state legislatures have a problem, not with the *application* of *Casey*, but with its *existence*. *Casey* must be overruled.

Justice **Kennedy**, with whom **The Chief Justice** joins, dissenting.

I

The Court's failure to accord any weight to Nebraska's interest in prohibiting partial-birth abortion is erroneous and undermines its discussion and holding. The Court's approach in this regard is revealed by its description of the abortion methods at issue, which the Court is correct to describe as "clinically cold or callous." The majority views the procedures from the perspective of the abortionist, rather than from the perspective of a society shocked when confronted with a new method of ending human life. Words invoked by the majority, such as "transcervical procedures," "osmotic dilators," "instrumental disarticulation," and "paracervical block," may be accurate and are to some extent necessary; but for citizens who seek to know why laws on this subject have been enacted across the Nation, the words are insufficient. Repeated references to sources understandable only to a trained physician may obscure matters for persons not trained in medical terminology. Thus it seems necessary at the outset to set forth what may happen during an abortion.

As described by Dr. Carhart, the D&E procedure requires the abortionist to use instruments to grasp a portion (such as a foot or hand) of a developed and living fetus and drag the grasped portion out of the uterus into the vagina. Dr. Carhart uses the traction created by the opening between the uterus and vagina to dismember the fetus, tearing the grasped portion away from the remainder of the body. The traction between the uterus and vagina is essential to the procedure because attempting to abort a fetus without [illegible] by Dr. Carhart as “pulling the cat's tail” or “dragging a string across the floor, you'll just keep dragging it. It's not until something grabs the other end that you are going to develop traction.” The fetus, in many cases, dies just as a human adult or child would: It bleeds to death as it is torn from limb from limb. The fetus can be alive at the beginning of the dismemberment process and can survive for a time while its limbs are being torn off. Dr. Carhart agreed that “when you pull out a piece of the fetus, let's say, an arm or a leg and remove that, at the time just prior to removal of the portion of the fetus, . . . the fetus [is] alive.” Dr. Carhart has observed fetal heartbeat via ultrasound with “extensive parts of the fetus removed,” and testified that mere dismemberment of a limb does not always cause death because he knows of a physician who removed the arm of a fetus only to have the fetus go on to be born “as a living child with one arm.” At the conclusion of a D&E abortion no intact fetus remains. In Dr. Carhart's words, the abortionist is left with “a tray full of pieces.”

The other procedure implicated today is called “partial-birth abortion” or the D&X. The D&X can be used, as a general matter, after 19 weeks gestation because the fetus has become so developed that it may survive intact partial delivery from the uterus into the vagina. In the D&X, the abortionist initiates the woman's natural delivery process by causing the cervix of the woman to be dilated, sometimes over a sequence of days. The fetus' arms and legs are delivered outside the uterus while the fetus is alive; witnesses to the procedure report seeing the body of the fetus moving outside the woman's body. At this point, the abortion procedure has the appearance of a live birth. As stated by one group of physicians, “as the physician manually performs breech extraction of the body of a live fetus, excepting the head, she continues in the apparent role of an obstetrician delivering a child.” With only the head of the fetus remaining in utero, the abortionist tears open the skull. According to Dr. Martin Haskell, a leading proponent of the procedure, the appropriate instrument to be used at this stage of the abortion is a pair of scissors. Witnesses report observing the portion of the fetus outside the woman react to the skull penetration. The abortionist then inserts a suction tube and vacuums out the developing brain and other matter found within the skull. The process of making the size of the fetus' head smaller is given the clinically neutral term “reduction procedure.” Brain death does not occur until after the skull invasion, and, according to Dr. Carhart, the heart of the fetus may continue to beat for minutes after the contents of the skull are vacuumed out. The abortionist next completes the delivery of a dead fetus, intact except for the damage to the head and the missing contents of the skull.

Of the two described procedures, Nebraska seeks only to ban the D&X. In light of the description of the D&X procedure, it should go without saying that Nebraska's ban on partial-birth abortion furthers purposes States are entitled to pursue.

States may take sides in the abortion debate and come down on the side of life, even life in the unborn:

> "Even in the earliest stages of pregnancy, the State may enact rules and regulations designed to encourage [a woman] to know that there are philosophic and social arguments of great weight that can be brought to bear in favor of continuing the pregnancy to full term and that there are procedures and institutions to allow adoption of unwanted children as well as a certain degree of state assistance if the mother chooses to raise the child herself."

States also have an interest in forbidding medical procedures which, in the State's reasonable determination, might cause the medical profession or society as a whole to become insensitive, even disdainful, to life, including life in the human fetus. Abortion, *Casey* held, has consequences beyond the woman and her fetus. The States' interests in regulating are of concomitant extension. *Casey* recognized that abortion is, "fraught with consequences for . . . the persons who perform and assist in the procedure [and for] society which must confront the knowledge that these procedures exist, procedures some deem nothing short of an act of violence against innocent human life."

A State may take measures to ensure the medical profession and its members are viewed as healers, sustained by a compassionate and rigorous ethic and cognizant of the dignity and value of human life, even life which cannot survive without the assistance of others.

Nebraska was entitled to find the existence of a consequential moral difference between the procedures. We are referred to substantial medical authority that D&X perverts the natural birth process to a greater degree than D&E, commandeering the live birth process until the skull is pierced. Witnesses to the procedure relate that the fingers and feet of the fetus are moving prior to the piercing of the skull; when the scissors are inserted in the back of the head, the fetus' body, wholly outside the woman's body and alive, reacts as though startled and goes limp. D&X's stronger resemblance to infanticide means Nebraska could conclude the procedure presents a greater risk of disrespect for life and a consequent greater risk to the profession and society, which depend for their sustenance upon reciprocal recognition of dignity and respect. The Court is without authority to second-guess this conclusion.

II

No studies support the contention that the D&X abortion method is safer than other abortion methods. Leading proponents of the procedure acknowledge that the D&X has "disadvantages" versus other methods because it requires a high degree of surgical skill to pierce the skull with a sharp instrument in a blind procedure. Other doctors point to complications that may arise from the D&X.

Substantial evidence supports Nebraska's conclusion that its law denies no woman a safe abortion. The most to be said for the D&X is it may present an unquantified lower risk of complication for a particular patient but that other proven safe procedures remain available even for this patient. Under these circumstances, the Court is wrong to limit its inquiry to the relative physical safety of the two procedures, with the slightest potential difference requiring the invalidation of the law.

Courts are ill-equipped to evaluate the relative worth of particular surgical procedures. The legislatures of the several States have superior factfinding capabilities in th[illegible] to acknowledge substantial authority allowing the State to take sides in a medical debate, even when fundamental liberty interests are at stake and even when leading members of the profession disagree with the conclusions drawn by the legislature.

Instructive is *Jacobson v. Massachusetts*, 197 U.S. 11 (1905), where the defendant was convicted because he refused to undergo a smallpox vaccination. The defendant claimed the mandatory vaccination violated his liberty to "care for his own body and health in such way as to him seems best." He offered to prove that members of the medical profession took the position that the vaccination was of no value and, in fact, was harmful. The Court rejected the claim, establishing beyond doubt the right of the legislature to resolve matters upon which physicians disagreed:

> "Those offers [of proof by the defendant] in the main seem to have had no purpose except to state the general theory of those of the medical profession who attach little or no value to vaccination as a means of preventing the spread of smallpox, or who think that vaccination causes other diseases of the body. What everybody knows the court must know, and therefore the state court judicially knew, as this court knows, that an opposite theory accords with the common belief, and is maintained by high medical authority. We must assume that, when the statute in question was passed, the legislature of Massachusetts was not unaware of these opposing theories, and was compelled, of necessity, to choose between them. It was not compelled to commit a matter involving the public health and safety to the final decision of a court or jury. It is no part of the function of a court or a jury to determine which one of two modes was likely to be the most effective for the protection of the public against disease. That was for the legislative department to determine in the light of all the information it had or could obtain. It could not properly abdicate its function to guard the public health and safety."

From the decision, the reasoning, and the judgment, I dissent.

Justice **Thomas**, with whom **The Chief Justice** and Justice **Scalia** join, dissenting.

In 1973, this Court struck down an Act of the Texas Legislature that had been in effect since 1857, thereby rendering unconstitutional abortion statutes in dozens of States. *Roe v. Wade*. As some of my colleagues on the Court, past and present, demonstrated that decision was grievously wrong.

In the years following *Roe*, this Court applied, and, worse, extended, that decision to strike down numerous state statutes that purportedly threatened a woman's ability to obtain an abortion.

I

In the almost 30 years since *Roe*, this Court has never described the various methods of aborting a second-or third-trimester fetus. From reading the majority's sanitized description, one would think that this case involves state regulation of a widely accepted routine medical procedure. Nothing could be further from the truth. The most widely used method of abortion during this stage of pregnancy is so gruesome that its use can be traumatic even for the physicians and medical staff who perform it. And the particular procedure at issue in this case, "partial birth abortion," so closely borders on infanticide that 30 States have attempted to ban it.

Use of the partial birth abortion procedure achieved prominence as a national issue after it was publicly described by Dr. Martin Haskell, in a paper entitled "Dilation and Extraction for Late Second Trimester Abortion" at the National Abortion Federation's September 1992 Risk Management Seminar. In that paper, Dr. Haskell described his version of the procedure as follows:

> "With a lower [fetal] extremity in the vagina, the surgeon uses his fingers to deliver the opposite lower extremity, then the torso, the shoulders and the upper extremities.
>
> "The skull lodges at the internal cervical os. Usually there is not enough dilation for it to pass through. The fetus is oriented dorsum or spine up.
>
> "At this point, the right-handed surgeon slides the fingers of the left hand along the back of the fetus and 'hooks' the shoulders of the fetus with the index and ring fingers (palm down).
>
> "The surgeon takes a pair of blunt curved Metzenbaum scissors in the right hand. He carefully advances the tip, curved down, along the spine and under his middle finger until he feels it contact the base of the skull under the tip of his middle finger.
>
> "The surgeon then forces the scissors into the base of the skull or into the foramen magnum. Having safely entered the skull, he spreads the scissors to enlarge the opening.
>
> "The surgeon removes the scissors and introduces a suction catheter into this hole and evacuates the skull contents. With the catheter still in place, he applies traction to the fetus, removing it completely from the patient."

In cases in which the physician inadvertently dilates the woman to too great a degree, the physician will have to hold the fetus inside the woman so that he can perform the procedure. (statement of Pamela Smith, M. D.) ("In these procedures, one basically relies on cervical entrapment of the head, along with a firm grip, to help keep the baby in place while the practitioner plunges a pair of scissors into the base of the baby's skull"). *See also* S.6 and H.R. 929 Joint Hearing 45 ("I could put dilapan in for four or five days and say I'm doing a D&E procedure and the fetus could just fall out. But that's not really the point. The point here is you're attempting to do an abortion . . . . Not to see how do I manipulate the situation so that I get a live birth instead") (quoting Dr. Haskell).

IV

Having resolved that Nebraska's partial birth abortion statute permits doctors to perform D&E abortions, the question remains whether a State can constitutionally prohibit the partial birth abortion procedure without a health exception. Although the majority and Justice **O'Connor** purport to rely on the standard articulated in the *Casey* joint opinion in concluding that a State may not, they in fact disregard it entirely.

B

There is no question that the State of Nebraska has a valid interest — one not designed to strike at the right itself — in prohibiting partial birth abortion. *Casey* itself noted that States may "express profound respect for the life of the unborn." States may, without a doubt, express this profound respect by prohibiting a procedure that approaches infanticide, and thereby dehumanizes the fetus and trivializes human life. The AMA has recognized that this procedure is "ethically different from other destructive abortion techniques because the fetus, normally twenty weeks or longer in gestation, is killed *outside* the womb. The 'partial birth' gives the fetus an autonomy which separates it from the right of the woman to choose treatments for her own body." Thirty States have concurred with this view.

Although the description of this procedure set forth above should be sufficient to demonstrate the resemblance between the partial birth abortion procedure and infanticide, the testimony of one nurse who observed a partial birth abortion procedure makes the point even more vividly:

> "The baby's little fingers were clasping and unclasping, and his little feet were kicking. Then the doctor stuck the scissors in the back of his head, and the baby's arms jerked out, like a startle reaction, like a flinch, like a baby does when he thinks he is going to fall.
>
> "The doctor opened up the scissors, stuck a high-powered suction tube into the opening, and sucked the baby's brains out. Now the baby went completely limp."

The question whether States have a legitimate interest in banning the procedure does not require additional authority. In a civilized society, the answer is too obvious, and the contrary arguments too offensive to merit further discussion.

C

The next question, therefore, is whether the Nebraska statute is unconstitutional because it does not contain an exception that would allow use of the procedure whenever "necessary in appropriate medical judgment, for the preservation of the . . . health of the mother."

It is clear that the Court's understanding of when a health exception is required is not mandated by our prior cases. In fact, we have, post-*Casey*, approved regulations of methods of conducting abortion despite the lack of a health exception.

The majority effectively concedes that *Casey* provides no support for its broad health exception rule by relying on pre-*Casey* authority, including a case that was specifically disapproved of in *Casey* for giving too little weight to the State's interest in fetal life. *See Casey, supra*, at 869, 882 (overruling the parts of *Thornburgh v. American College of Obstetricians and Gynecologists*, 476 U.S. 747, that were "inconsistent with *Roe*'s statement that the State has a legitimate interest in promoting the life or potential life of the unborn," 505 U.S. at 870.

And even if I were to assume that the pre-*Casey* standards govern, the cases cited by the majority provide no support for the proposition that the partial birth abortion ban must include a health exception because some doctors believe that partial birth abortion is safer.

As if this state of affairs were not bad enough, the majority expands the health exception rule articulated in *Casey* in one additional and equally pernicious way. Although *Roe* and *Casey* mandated a health exception for cases in which abortion is "necessary" for a woman's health, the majority concludes that a procedure is "necessary" if it has any comparative health benefits. In other words, according to the majority, so long as a doctor can point to support in the profession for his (or the woman's) preferred procedure, it is "necessary" and the physician is entitled to perform it. But such a health exception requirement eviscerates *Casey*'s undue burden standard and imposes unfettered abortion-on-demand. The exception entirely swallows the rule. In effect, no regulation of abortion procedures is permitted because there will always be *some* support for a procedure and there will always be some doctors who conclude that the procedure is preferable. If Nebraska reenacts its partial birth abortion ban with a health exception, the State will not be able to prevent physicians like Dr. Carhart from using partial birth abortion as a routine abortion procedure.

D

The majority assiduously avoids addressing the *actual* standard articulated in *Casey* — whether prohibiting partial birth abortion without a health exception poses a substantial obstacle to obtaining an abortion. And for good reason: Such an obstacle does not exist. There are two essential reasons why the Court cannot identify a substantial obstacle. First, the Court cannot identify any real, much less substantial, barrier to any woman's ability to obtain an abortion. And second, the Court cannot demonstrate that any such obstacle would affect a sufficient number of women to justify invalidating the statute on its face.

. . . .

2

Even if I were willing to assume that the partial birth method of abortion is safer for some small set of women, such a conclusion would not require invalidating the Act, because this case comes to us on a facial challenge. The only question before us is whether respondent has shown that "no set of circumstances exists under which the Act would be valid." Courts may not invalidate on its face a state statute regulating abortion "based upon a worst-case analysis that may never occur."

Invalidation of the statute would be improper even assuming that *Casey* rejected this standard *sub silentio* (at least so far as abortion cases are concerned) in favor of a so-called " 'large fraction' " test. See also *Janklow v. Planned Parenthood, Sioux Falls Clinic*, 517 U.S. 1174, 1177–1179 (1996) (Scalia, J., dissenting from denial of certiorari). In *Casey*, the Court was presented with a facial challenge to, among other provisions, a spousal notice requirement. The question, according to the majority was whether the spousal notice provision operated as a "substantial obstacle" to the women "whose conduct it affects," namely, "married women seeking abortions who do not wish to notify their husbands of their intentions and who do not qualify for one of the statutory exceptions to the notice requirement." The Court determined that a "large fraction" of the women in this category were victims of psychological or physical abuse. For this subset of women, according to the Court, the provision would pose a substantial obstacle to the ability to obtain an abortion because their husbands could exercise an effective veto over their decision.

None of the opinions supporting the majority so much as mentions the large fraction standard, undoubtedly because the Nebraska statute easily survives it. I will assume, for the sake of discussion, that the category of women whose conduct Nebraska's partial birth abortion statute might affect includes any woman who wishes to obtain a safe abortion after 16 weeks' gestation. I will also assume (although I doubt it is true) that, of these women, every one would be willing to use the partial birth abortion procedure if so advised by her doctor. Indisputably, there is no "large fraction" of these women who would face a substantial obstacle to obtaining a safe abortion because of their inability to use this particular procedure. In fact, it is not clear that *any* woman would be deprived of a safe abortion by her inability to obtain a partial birth abortion. More medically sophisticated minds than ours have searched and failed to identify a single circumstance (let alone a large fraction) in which partial birth abortion is required. But no matter. The "ad hoc nullification" machine is back at full throttle.

We were reassured repeatedly in *Casey* that not all regulations of abortion are unwarranted and that the States may express profound respect for fetal life. Under *Casey*, the regulation before us today should easily pass constitutional muster. But the Court's abortion jurisprudence is a particularly virulent strain of constitutional exegesis. And so today we are told that 30 States are prohibited from banning one rarely used form of abortion that they believe to border on infanticide. It is clear that the Constitution does not compel this result.

I respectfully dissent.

NOTES AND QUESTIONS

1. Many of the opinions below and in the Supreme Court (and in other Courts of Appeal) dwell on the gory, grotesque and ghastly details of D&E and D&X (mercifully abbreviated in the editing here). Why? Do

these shocking, graphic depictions have significance other than as a broad based attack on abortion?

2. Note that this is the first "abortion" case in which the Supreme Court has dealt with the *method* of abortion, rather than its availability, a point made by Justices Ginsburg and Stevens. This seems significant, but why?

3. Note also that the Nebraska statute had no "health exception," permitting an abortion to save, not the life, but the health of the mother. Justice Breyer places considerable emphasis on this omission. Why? What has this to do with the central issue of the case — partial birth abortion?

4. In this connection, is Justice O'Connor saying that a more narrowly crafted statute (as in Kansas, Utah, and Montana) would survive challenge?

5. And how, in Breyer's view, does the ban on partial birth abortion "burden" the right to choose abortion itself? D&E or D&X is so rarely used, and so late in the process, how can it be said that unavailability "burdens" the choices routinely available earlier?

6. And what of the State's asserted interests? Truly, isn't the method at issue in *Carhart* in fact a killing? And what impact could this have on medical practitioners — if ever the morale and mission of the medical community are relevant, indeed controlling, isn't this such a case? Even if not, isn't D&X it so grotesque and shocking that a state may ban it in the public interest?

7. On another level, is the *Carhart* decision about methodology or choice? Or is it instead about the meaning of, or the defining of, a "person"? *Roe* and *Casey* turn centrally on the proposition that a fetus is not a "person" for constitutional purposes. Yet moments and millimeters after passage from the birth canal, it becomes a "person." It is exactly that passage and transition which is at issue in *Carhart*. So, does D&X destroy a person?

8. More basically, do these methods destroy life, or "a" life? The state has a powerful interest in preserving life. Isn't life being destroyed in *Carhart* by use of these methods?

9. When does the fetus in *Carhart* die? Did it ever live?

10. A ban on Partial Birth Abortion was passed by Congress in 2003, and subsequently invalidated under the Fifth Amendment in *Planned Parenthood v. Ashcroft*, 320 F. Supp. 2d 957 (Cal. Dist. Ct. App. 2004). There was no exception for the health of the mother, Congress specifically finding none was necessary. Why? What result before the Supreme Court?

    On appeal to the Eighth Circuit, the lower court was unanimously affirmed in *Carhart v. Gonzales*, 413 F. 3d 791 (8th Cir. 2005), a decision which will be reviewed by the Supreme Court in the 2006-07 term. The Court of Appeals dismissed Congress' fact-finding that late term abortions are never needed for medical necessity as "adjudicatory" facts, and beyond Congress' purview. 413 F. 3d at 799.

Do you agree? Will the Supreme Court?

11. The importance of having an exception for the life of th[illegible] abortion, as *Roe* and *Carhart* make clear. What of medications? Ohio has banned mifepristone (RU-486). The Sixth circuit reversed the trial court which had held that *every* law must contain an exception for life-saving treatment, but found such an exception was necessary with RU 486, since surgery might be more risky. *See Planned Parenthood v. Taft*, ___ F.3d ___ (6th Cir. 2006), 74 U.S.L.W. 1633 (4/25/06).

 Is this an accurate reading of *Carhart*? Of *Roe*? How is a court to determine such risks and facts?

 In the July 6, 2006 issue of *The New England Journal of Medicine*, New Eng. J. Med. 1 (7/6/06), in an article entitled *Roe versus Reality*, the authors detail the scarcity of resources for those seeking abortions in rural areas. In 2000, only 3% of rural areas had an abortion provider; 87% of counties had none; 18 states had fewer than 10 willing doctors. Doctor Carhart's clinic in Nebraska draws patients from multiple states; they performed 1250 abortions last year. In 1991, his house, barns and stables were burned to the ground — 17 horses died. Today, his clinic has a shabby exterior, with a welcoming interior, surrounded by community signs of disapprobation. (*See* photo, 355 New Eng. J. Med. at p.7.)

[b] Wanted Fetuses: Assisted Reproduction

Modern technology now can assist infertile couples by fertilizing and returning eggs to a woman, often leading to multiple births. Fertilized eggs may also be placed in a "surrogate mother," as in *Baby M*, *supra*. Disputes may arise *in transitu*, while the fertilized eggs are *outside* the womb. Courts must decide not only *what* to do, but *who* to respect, and — more fundamentally — whether the case is decided as a matter of contract, property, equity, family or constitutional law. Implicit is deciding whether a fetus *is* a person . . . .

DAVIS v. DAVIS

842 S.W.2d 588 (Tenn. 1992)

Daughtrey, Justice.

This appeal presents a question of first impression, involving the disposition of the cryogenically-preserved product of *in vitro* fertilization (IVF), commonly referred to in the popular press and the legal journals as "frozen embryos." The case began as a divorce action, filed by the appellee, Junior Lewis Davis, against his then wife, appellant Mary Sue Davis. The parties were able to agree upon all terms of dissolution, except one: who was to have "custody" of the seven "frozen embryos" stored in a Knoxville fertility clinic that had attempted to assist the Davises in achieving a much-wanted pregnancy during a happier period in their relationship.

I. Introduction

Mary Sue Davis originally asked for control of the "frozen embryos" with the intent to have them transferred to her own uterus, in a post-divorce effort to become pregnant. Junior Davis objected, saying that he preferred to leave the embryos in their frozen state until he decided whether or not he wanted to become a parent outside the bounds of marriage.

Based on its determination that the embryos were "human beings" from the moment of fertilization, the trial court awarded "custody" to Mary Sue Davis and directed that she "be permitted the opportunity to bring these children to term through implantation." The Court of Appeals reversed, finding that Junior Davis has a "constitutionally protected rights not to beget a child where no pregnancy has taken place" and holding that "there is no compelling state interest to justify [] ordering implantation against the will of either party." The Court of Appeals further held that "the parties share an interest in the seven fertilized ova" and remanded the case to the trial court for entry of an order vesting them with "joint control . . . and equal voice over their disposition."

. . . .

We note, in this latter regard, that their positions have already shifted: both have remarried and Mary Sue Davis (now Mary Sue Stowe) has moved out of state. She no longer wishes to utilize the "frozen embryos" herself, but wants authority to donate them to a childless couple. Junior Davis is adamantly opposed to such donation and would prefer to see the "frozen embryos" discarded. The result is, once again, an impasse, but the parties' current legal position does have an effect on the probable outcome of the case, as discussed below.

At the outset, it is important to note the absence of two critical factors that might otherwise influence or control the result of this litigation: When the Davises signed up for the IVF program at the Knoxville clinic, they did not execute a written agreement specifying what disposition should be made of any unused embryos that might result from the cryopreservation process. Moreover, there was at that time no Tennessee statute governing such disposition, nor has one been enacted in the meantime.

In addition, because of the uniqueness of the question before us, we have no case law to guide us to a decision in this case. Despite the fact that over 5,000 IVF babies have been born in this country and the fact that some 20,000 or more "frozen embryos" remain in storage, there are apparently very few other litigated cases involving the disputed disposition of untransferred "frozen embryos," and none is on point with the facts in this case.

. . . .

. . . We conclude that given the relevant principles of constitutional law, the existing public policy of Tennessee with regard to unborn life, the current state of scientific knowledge giving rise to the emerging reproductive technologies, and the ethical considerations that have developed in response to that scientific knowledge, there can be no easy answer to the question we now face. We conclude, instead, that we must weight the interests of each party to the dispute, in terms of the facts and analysis set out below, in order to resolve that dispute in a fair and responsible manner.

II. The Facts

. . . .

Beginning in 1985, the Davises went through six attempts at IVF, at a total cost of $35,000, but the hoped-for pregnancy never occurred. Despite her fear of needles, at each IVF attempt Mary Sue underwent the month of subcutaneous injections necessary to shut down her pituitary gland and the eight days of intermuscular injections necessary to stimulate her ovaries to produce ova. She was anesthetized five times for the aspiration procedure to be performed. Forty-eight to 72 hours after each aspiration, she returned for transfer back to her uterus, only to receive a negative pregnancy test result each time.

The Davises then opted to postpone another round of IVF until after the clinic with which they were working was prepared to offer them cryogenic preservation, scheduled for November 1988. Using this process, if more ova are aspirated and fertilized than needed, the conceptive product may be cryogenically preserved (frozen in nitrogen and stored at sub-zero temperatures) for later transfer if the transfer performed immediately does not result in a pregnancy. The unavailability of this procedure had not been a hindrance to previous IVF attempts by the Davises because Mary Sue had produced at most only three or four ova, despite hormonal stimulation. However, on their last attempt, on December 8, 1988, the gynecologist who performed the procedure was able to retrieve nine ova for fertilization. The resulting one-celled entities, referred to before division as zygotes, were then allowed to develop in petri dishes in the laboratory until they reached the four-to eight-cell state.

. . . .

After fertilization was completed, a transfer was performed as usual on December 10, 1988; the rest of the four-to eight-cell entities were cryogenically preserved. Unfortunately, a pregnancy did not result from the December 1988 transfer, and before another transfer could be attempted, Junior Davis filed for divorce — in February 1989. He testified that he had known that their marriage "was not very stable" for a year or more, but had hoped that the birth of a child would improve their relationship. Mary Sue Davis testified that she had no idea that there was a problem with their marriage. As noted earlier, the divorce proceedings were complicated only by the issue of the disposition of the "frozen embryos."

III. The Scientific Testimony

In the record, and especially in the trial court's opinion, there is a great deal of discussion about the proper descriptive terminology to be used in this case. Although this discussion appears at first glance to be a matter simply of semantics, semantical distinctions are significant in this context, because language defines legal status and can limit legal rights. Obviously, an "adult" has a different legal status than does a "child." Likewise, "child" means something other than "fetus." A "fetus differs from an "embryo." There was much dispute at trial about whether the four-to eight-cell entities in this case should properly be referred to as "embryos" or as "preembryos," with resulting differences in legal analysis.

One expert, a French geneticist named Dr. Jerome Lejeune, insisted that there was no recognized scientific distinction between the two terms. He referred to the four-to eight-cell entities at issue here as "early human beings," as "tiny persons," and as his "kin." Although he is an internationally recognized geneticist, Dr. Lejeune's background fails to reflect any degree of expertise in obstetrics or gynecology (specifically in the field of infertility) or in medical ethics. His testimony revealed a profound confusion between science and religion. For example, he was deeply moved that "Madame [Mary Sue], the mother, wants to rescue babies from this concentration can," and he concluded that Junior Davis has a moral duty to try to bring these "tiny human beings" to term.

Dr. LeJeune's opinion was disputed by Dr. Irving Ray King, the gynecologist who performed the IVF procedures in this case. Dr. King is a medical doctor who had practiced as a sub-specialty in the areas of infertility and reproductive endocrinology for 12 years. He established the Fertility Center of East Tennessee in Knoxville in 1984 and had worked extensively with IVF and cryopreservation. He testified that the currently accepted term for the zygote immediately after division is "preembryo" and that this term applies up until 14 days after fertilization. He testified that this 14-day period defines the accepted period for preembryo research. At about 14 days, he testified, the group of cells begins to differentiate in a process that permits the eventual development of the different body parts which will become an individual.

Dr. King's testimony was corroborated by the other experts who testified at trial, with the exception of Dr. Lejeune. It is further supported by the American Fertility Society, an organization of 10,000 physicians and scientists who specialize in problems of human infertility. The Society's June 1990 report on Ethical Considerations of the New Reproductive Technologies indicates that from the point of fertilization, the resulting one-cell zygote contains "a new hereditary constitution (genome) contributed to by both parents through the union of sperm and egg." Continuing, the report notes:

> The stage subsequent to the zygote is cleavage, during which the single initial cell undergoes successive equal divisions with little or no intervening growth. As a result, the product cells (blastomeres) become successively smaller, while the size of the total aggregate of cells remains the same. After three such divisions, the aggregate contains eight cells in relatively loose association . . . [E]ach blastomere, if separated from the others, has the potential to develop into a complete adult . . . . Stated another way, at the 8-cell stage, the developmental singleness of one person has not been established.
>
> Beyond the 8-cell stage, individual blastomeres begin to lose their zygote-like properties. Two divisions after the 8-cell stage, the 32 blastomeres are increasingly adherent, closely packed, and no longer of equal developmental potential. The impression now conveyed is of a multicellular entity, rather than of a loose packet of identical cells.

> As the number of cells continues to increase, some are formed into a surface layer, surrounding [illegible] changed in properties toward trophoblast . . ., which is destined [to become part of the placenta]. The less-altered inner cells will be the source of the later embryo. The developing entity is now referred to as a blastocyst, characterized by a continuous peripheral layer of cells and a small cellular population within a central cavity . . . . It is at about this stage that the [normally] developing entity usually completes its transit through the oviduct to enter the uterus.
>
> Cell division continues and the blastocyst enlarges through increase of both cell number and [volume]. The populations of inner and outer cells become increasingly different, not only in position and shape but in synthetic activities as well. The change is primarily in the outer population, which is altering rapidly as the blastocyst interacts with and implants into the uterine wall . . . . Thus, the first cellular differentiation of the new generation relates to physiologic interaction with the mother, rather than to the establishment of the embryo itself. *It is for this reason that it is appropriate to refer to the developing entity up to this point as a preembryo, rather than an embryo.*

Admittedly, this distinction is not dispositive in the case before us. It deserves emphasis only because inaccuracy can lead to misanalysis such as occurred at the trial level in this case. The trial court reasoned that if there is no distinction between embryos and preembryos, as Dr. Lejeune theorized, then Dr. Lejeune must also have been correct when he asserted that "human life begins at the moment of conception." . . .

. . . .

IV. The "Person" vs. "Property" Dichotomy

One of the fundamental issues the inquiry poses is whether the preembryos in this case should be considered "persons" or "property" in the contemplation of the law. The Court of Appeals held, correctly, that they cannot be considered "persons" under Tennessee law. . . .

. . . .

To our way of thinking, the most helpful discussion on this point is found not in the minuscule number of legal opinions that have involved "frozen embryos," but in the ethical standards set by The American Fertility Society, as follows:

> Three major ethical positions have been articulated in the debate over preembryo status. At one extreme is the view of the preembryo as a human subject after fertilization, which requires that it be accorded the rights of a person. This position entails an obligation to provide an opportunity for implantation to occur and tends to ban any action before transfer that might harm the preembryo or that is not immediately therapeutic, such as freezing and some preembryo research.

> At the opposite extreme is the view that the preembryo has a status no different from any other human tissue. With the consent of those who have decision-making authority over the preembryo, no limits should be imposed on actions taken with preembryos.
>
> A third view — one that is most widely held — takes an intermediate position between the other two. It holds that the preembryo deserves respect greater than that accorded to human tissue but not the respect accorded to actual persons. The preembryo is due greater respect than other human tissue because of its potential to become a person and because of its symbolic meaning for many people. Yet, it should not be treated as a person, because it has not yet developed the features of personhood, is not yet established as developmentally individual, and may never realize its biologic potential.

Report of the Ethics Committee of The American Fertility Society, *supra*, at 34S-35S.

. . . .

We conclude that preembryos are not, strictly speaking, either "persons" or "property," but occupy an interim category that entitles them to special respect because of their potential for human life. It follows that any interest that Mary Sue Davis and Junior Davis have in the preembryos in this case is not a true property interest. However, they do have an interest in the nature of ownership, to the extent that they have decision-making authority concerning disposition of the preembryos, within the scope of policy set by law.

V. The Enforceability of Contract

. . . .

We believe, as a starting point, that an agreement regarding disposition of any untransferred preembryos in the event of contingencies (such as the death of one or more of the parties, divorce, financial reversals, or abandonment of the program) should be presumed valid and should be enforced as between the progenitors. This conclusion is in keeping with the proposition that the progenitors, having provided the gametic material giving rise to the preembryos, retain decision-making authority as to their disposition.

At the same time, we recognize that life is not static, and that human emotions run particularly high when a married couple is attempting to overcome infertility problems. It follows that the parties' initial "informed consent" to IVF procedures will often not be truly informed because of the near impossibility of anticipating, emotionally and psychologically, all the turns that events may take as the IVF process unfolds. Providing that the initial agreements may later be modified by agreement will, we think, protect the parties against some of the risks they face in this regard. But, in the absence of such agreed modification, we conclude that their prior agreements should be considered binding.

. . . .

We are therefore left with this situation: there was initially no agreement between the parties concerning disposition of the preembryos [illegible] circumstances [illegible] has been no agreement since; and there is no formula in the Court of Appeals opinion for determining the outcome if the parties cannot reach an agreement in the future.

In granting joint custody to the parties, the Court of Appeals must have anticipated that, in the absence of agreement, the preembryos would continue to be stored, as they now are, in the Knoxville fertility clinic. One problem with maintaining the status quo is that the viability of the preembryos cannot be guaranteed indefinitely. Experts in cryopreservation who testified in this case estimated the maximum length of preembryonic viability at two years. Thus, the true effect of the intermediate court's opinion is to confer on Junior Davis the inherent power to veto any transfer of the preembryos in this case and thus to ensure their eventual discard or self-destruction.

. . . Nevertheless, for the reasons set out in Section VI of this opinion, we conclude that it is not the best route to take, under all the circumstances.

VI. The Right of Procreational Autonomy

Although an understanding of the legal status of preembryos is necessary in order to determine the enforceability of agreements about their disposition, asking whether or not they constitute "property" is not an altogether helpful question. As the appellee points out in his brief, "[as] two or eight cell tiny lumps of complex protein, the embryos have no [intrinsic] value to either party." Their value lies in the "potential to become, after implantation, growth and birth, children." Thus, the essential dispute here is not where or how or how long to store the preembryos, but whether the parties will become parents. The Court of Appeals held in effect that they will become parents if they both agree to become parents. The Court did not say what will happen if they fail to agree. We conclude that the answer to this dilemma turns on the parties' exercise of their constitutional right to privacy.

. . . .

. . . None of the concerns about a woman's bodily integrity that have previously precluded men from controlling abortion decisions is applicable here. We are not unmindful of the fact that the trauma (including both emotional stress and physical discomfort) to which women are subjected in the IVF process is more severe than is the impact of the procedure on men. In this sense, it is fair to say that women contribute more to the IVF process than men. Their experience, however, must be viewed in light of the joys of parenthood that is desired or the relative anguish of a lifetime of unwanted parenthood. As they stand on the brink of potential parenthood, Mary Sue Davis and Junior Lewis Davis must be seen as entirely equivalent gamete-providers.

. . . .

Certainly, if the state's interests do not become sufficiently compelling in the abortion context until the end of the first trimester, after very significant developmental stages have passed, then surely there is no state interest in these preembryos which could suffice to overcome the interests of the gamete-providers. . . . When weighed against the interests of the individuals and the burdens inherent in parenthood, the state's interest in the potential life of these preembryos is not sufficient to justify any infringement upon the freedom of these individuals to make their own decisions as to whether to allow a process to continue that may result in such a dramatic change in their lives as becoming parents.

The unique nature of this case requires us to note that the interests of these parties in parenthood are different in scope than the parental interest considered in other cases. Previously, courts have dealt with the child-bearing and child-rearing aspects of parenthood. Abortion cases have dealt with gestational parenthood. In this case, the Court must deal with the question of genetic parenthood. We conclude, moreover, that an interest in avoiding genetic parenthood can be significant enough to trigger the protections afforded to all other aspects of parenthood. The technological fact that someone unknown to these parties could gestate these preembryos does not alter the fact that these parties, the gamete-providers, would become parents in that event, at least in the genetic sense. The profound impact this would have on them supports their right to sole decisional authority as to whether the process of attempting to gestate these preembryos should continue. This brings us directly to the question of how to resolve the dispute that arises when one party wishes to continue the IVF process and the other does not.

VII. Balancing the Parties' Interest

. . . .

Beginning with the burden imposed on Junior Davis, we note that the consequences are obvious. Any disposition which results in the gestation of the preembryos would impose unwanted parenthood on him, with all of its possible financial and psychological consequences. The impact that this unwanted parenthood would have on Junior Davis can only be understood by considering his particular circumstances, as revealed in the record.

Junior Davis testified that he was the fifth youngest of six children. When he was five years old, his parents divorced, his mother had a nervous breakdown, and he and three of his brothers went to live at a home for boys run by the Lutheran Church. Another brother was taken in by an aunt, and his sister stayed with their mother. From that day forward, he had monthly visits with his mother but saw his father only three more times before he died in 1976. Junior Davis testified that, as a boy, he had severe problems caused by separation from his parents. He said that it was especially hard to leave his mother after each monthly visit. He clearly feels that he has suffered because of his lack of opportunity to establish a relationship with his parents and particularly because of the absence of his father.

In light of his boyhood experiences, Junior Davis is vehemently opposed to fathering a child that would not live with both parents. Regardless of whether he or Mary Sue had custody, he feels that the child's bond with the noncustodial parent would not be satisfactory. He testified very clearly that his concern was for the psychological obstacles a child in such a situation would face, as well as the burdens it would impose on him. Likewise, he is opposed to donation because the recipient couple might divorce, leaving the child (which he definitely would consider his own) in a single-parent setting.

Balanced against Junior Davis' interest in avoiding parenthood is Mary Sue Davis' interest in donating the preembryos to another couple for implantation. Refusal to permit donation of the preembryos would impose on her the burden of knowing that the lengthy IVF procedures she underwent were futile, and that the preembryos to which she contributed genetic material would never become children. While this is not an insubstantial emotional burden, we can only conclude that Mary Sue Davis' interest in donation is not as significant as the interest Junior Davis has in avoiding parenthood. If she were allowed to donate these preembryos, he would face a lifetime of either wondering about his parental status or knowing about his parental status but having no control over it. He testified quite clearly that if these preembryos were brought to term he would fight for custody of his child or children. Donation, if a child came of it, would rob him twice — his procreational autonomy would be defeated and his relationship with his offspring would be prohibited.

The case would be closer if Mary Sue Davis were seeking to use the preembryos herself, but only if she could not achieve parenthood by any other reasonable means. We recognize the trauma that Mary Sue has already experienced and the additional discomfort to which she would be subjected if she opts to attempt IVF again. Still, she would have a reasonable opportunity, through IVF, to try once again to achieve parenthood in all its aspects — genetic, gestational, bearing, and rearing.

Further, we note that if Mary Sue Davis were unable to undergo another round of IVF, or opted not to try, she could still achieve the child-rearing aspects of parenthood through adoption. The fact that she and Junior Davis pursued adoption indicates that, at least at one time, she was willing to forego genetic parenthood and would have been satisfied by the child-rearing aspects of parenthood alone.

VIII. Conclusion

In summary, we hold that disputes involving the disposition of preembryos produced by *in vitro* fertilization should be resolved, first, by looking to the preferences of the progenitors. If their wishes cannot be ascertained, or if there is dispute, then their prior agreement concerning disposition should be carried out. If no prior agreement exists, then the relative interests of the parties in using or not using the preembryos must be weighed. Ordinarily, the party wishing to avoid procreation should prevail, assuming that the other party has a reasonable possibility of achieving parenthood by means other than use of the preembryos in question. If no other reasonable alternatives exist, then the argument in favor of using the preembryos to achieve pregnancy should be considered. However, if the party seeking control of the preembryos intends merely to donate them to another couple, the objecting party obviously has the greater interest and should prevail.

. . . .

Reid, C.J., and **Drowota, O'Brien** and **Anderson,** J.J., concur.

NOTES AND QUESTIONS

1. Note that *Davis* is unmistakably a decision about ethics, strongly informed by professional associations and their ethical pronouncements. Is this surprising?

2. In all four cases, *Baby M*, *Roe v. Wade*, *Casey*, and *Davis v. Davis*, it would be possible to resolve the issues as a matter of simple contract law. That is, courts could acknowledge the autonomy of individuals to make agreements and then their obligation to be bound by such agreements. As an ethical matter, would this be sufficient? What if the contract was inconsistent with the "special respect" the Tennessee Supreme Court says is due these embryos? Why do courts go on to invoke communitarian values limiting the rights of consenting adults to surrogacy, abortion and *in vitro* fertilization?

3. What should the contract in *Davis* provide? The Court notes that resolution of the issues cannot, at least under the circumstances of *Davis*, be done simply as a matter of contract law. The parents as "gamete-providers" have an interest in "genetic parenthood," or avoiding that status, which in the Court's view "can be significant enough to trigger the protections afforded to all other aspects of parenthood." Is this consistent with the Court's concern in *Casey*, protecting the autonomy of the mother against the husband's interest in an ongoing pregnancy? And is it useful, since it reduces the concept of "parenthood" to the mechanical transmission of personal characteristics by biological means, without any of the attending involvements or associations which make parenting a true relationship.

4. *Davis v. Davis* is the sixth case in these materials dealing with procreation, the first being *Baby M* and the second being *In Re A.C.*, followed by *Roe v. Wade*, *Casey*, and *Carhart*. Each case involved varying the "norm" of conception and delivery of children within a marital union of two partners. In *Baby M*, the concern was that a third party (the surrogate mother) was being brought into the picture. In *A.C.*, a mother sought delivery, then became (perhaps) incompetent to abort. In *Roe* and *Casey*, the concern was that a pregnancy would be terminated; in *Davis* the concern is that fertilized eggs, the subject of a pregnancy, might be transferred to, or terminated by, a third party.

   Each case involves the "unborn" and each court is reluctant to apply the term "person" to such entities. And yet, ethically, is not such a conclusion unavoidable? Indeed, is it not fair to say that the reason these cases express so much societal interest and concern is *precisely* because the unborn encapsulate the fullest range of personhood, from maximum vulnerability to maximum potential? If so, is the *Davis* court correct in finding the State's interest to be minimal, at best?

5. Is it significant that the Ethical Considerations Report of the American Fertility Society picks the point of implantation by the pre-embryo into the uterus wall as the point at which the developing blastomere/blastocyst moves from being a pre-embryo to an embryo? Attachment to the uterus is a physiologically significant event, coinciding with

cellular differentiation which lends identity to the emerging entity itself. But should this be of either ethical or legal [illegible] [illegible], if the cellular development is arrested at the attachment stage, precisely because attachment is withheld where the pre-embryo is *outside* the human body, what is the legal status of the entity, what are societal concerns about it and ethically what may or should be done with it?

6. Is the disposition achieved by the Tennessee Supreme Court preferable to the result in the Court of Appeals, which had simply remanded the case to the trial court for entry of an order vesting Junior and Mary Sue "with joint control . . . " and an equal voice over "the disposition of the fertilized eggs?"
7. For a thoughtful depiction of the status of embryos procured for *in vitro* fertilization, see Dan Fabricant, *International Law Revisisted: Davis v. Davis and the Need for Coherent Policy on the Status of the Embryo,* 6 Conn. J. Int'l L. 173 (Fall, 1990). Also, after three physicians in California were accused of stealing eggs and embryos of women and giving them to other patients or using them in research, many concerns arose in relation to *in vitro* fertilization. For a thorough exploration of the actual process of *in vitro* fertilization, potential problems inherent in the procedure and possible solutions to these problems, see Shirley J. Paine, Patrick K. Moore & David L. Hill, *Ethical Dilemmas in Reproductive Medicine*, 18 Whittier L. Rev. 51 (1996).
8. To see how a similar case might be decided as a matter of contract law, we now turn to the decision of the New York Court of Appeals in *Kass v. Kass*.

KASS v. KASS
696 N.E.2d 554 (N.Y. Ct. App. 1998)

Kaye, Chief Judge:

Although *in vitro* fertilization (IVF) procedures are now more than two decades old and in wide use, this is the first such dispute to reach our Court. Specifically in issue is the disposition of five frozen, stored pre-embryos, or "pre-zygotes," created five years ago, during the parties' marriage, to assist them in having a child. Now divorced, appellant (Maureen Kass) wants the pre-zygotes implanted, claiming this is her only chance for genetic motherhood; respondent (Steven Kass) objects to the burdens of unwanted fatherhood, claiming that the parties agreed at the time they embarked on the effort that in the present circumstances the pre-zygotes would be donated to the IVF program for approved research purposes. Like the two-Justice plurality at the Appellate Division, we conclude that the parties' agreement providing for donation to the IVF program controls. The Appellate Division order should therefore be affirmed.

Facts

Appellant and respondent were married on July 4, 1988, and almost immediately began trying to conceive a child. While appellant believed that, owing to prenatal exposure to diethylstilbestrol (DES) she might have difficulty carrying a pregnancy to term, her condition in fact was more serious — she failed to become pregnant. In August 1989, the couple turned to John T. Mather Memorial Hospital in Port Jefferson, Long Island and, after unsuccessful efforts to conceive through artificial insemination, enrolled in the hospital's IVF program.

. . . .

Beginning in March 1990, appellant underwent the egg retrieval process five times and fertilized eggs were transferred to her nine times. She became pregnant twice — once in October 1991, ending in a miscarriage and again a few months later, when an ectopic pregnancy had to be surgically terminated.

Before the final procedure, for the first time involving cryopreservation, the couple on May 12, 1993 signed four consent forms provided by the hospital. Each form begins on a new page, with its own caption and "Patient Name." The first two forms, "GENERAL INFORMED CONSENT FORM NO. 1: IN VITRO FERTILIZATION AND EMBRYO TRANSFER" and "ADDENDUM NO. 1-1," consist of 12 single-spaced typewritten pages explaining the procedure, its risks and benefits, at several points indicating that, before egg retrieval could begin, it was necessary for the parties to make informed decisions regarding disposition of the fertilized eggs. ADDENDUM NO. 1-1 concludes as follows:

> "We understand that it is general IVF Program Policy, as medically determined by our IVF physician, to retrieve as many eggs as possible and to inseminate and transfer 4 of those mature eggs in this IVF cycle, unless our IVF physician determines otherwise. It is necessary that we decide . . . [now] how excess eggs are to be handled by the IVF Program and how many embryos to transfer. *We are to indicate our choices by signing our initials where noted below.*
>
> . . . .
>
> "III. Disposition of Pre-Zygotes. We understand that our frozen pre-zygotes will be stored for a maximum of 5 years. We have the principal responsibility to decide the disposition of our frozen pre-zygotes. Our frozen pre-zygotes will not be released from storage for any purpose without the written consent of both of us, consistent with the policies of the IVF Program and applicable law. In the event of divorce, we understand that legal ownership of any stored pre-zygotes must be determined in a property settlement and will be released as directed by order of a court of competent jurisdiction. Should we for any reason no longer wish to attempt to initiate a pregnancy, we understand that we may determine the disposition of our frozen pre-zygotes remaining in storage. . . .
>
> . . . .
>
> "2. In the event that we no longer wish to initiate a pregnancy or are unable to make a decision regarding the disposition of our stored, frozen pre-zygotes, we now indicate our desire for the disposition of our pre-zygotes and direct the IVF program to (choose one):

. . . .

> "(b) Our frozen [illegible] IVF Program for biological studies and be disposed of by the IVF Program for approved research investigation as determined by the IVF Program" (emphasis in original).

On May 20, 1993, doctors retrieved 16 eggs from appellant, resulting in nine pre-zygotes. Two days later, four were transferred to appellant's sister, who had volunteered to be a surrogate mother, and the remaining five were cryopreserved. The couple learned shortly thereafter that the results were negative and that appellant's sister was no longer willing to participate in the program. They then decided to dissolve their marriage. The total cost of their IVF efforts exceeded $75,000.

With divorce imminent, the parties themselves on June 7, 1993 — barely three weeks after signing the consents — drew up and signed an "uncontested divorce" agreement, typed by appellant, including the following:

> "The disposition of the frozen 5 pre-zygotes at Mather Hospital is that they should be disposed of [in] the manner outlined in our consent form and that neither Maureen Kass[,] Steve Kass or anyone else will lay claim to custody of these pre-zygotes."

On June 28, 1993, appellant by letter informed the hospital and her IVF physician of her marital problems and expressed her opposition to destruction or release of the pre-zygotes.

One month later, appellant commenced the present matrimonial action, requesting sole custody of the pre-zygotes so that she could undergo another implantation procedure. . . .

. . . .

Supreme Court granted appellant custody of the pre-zygotes and directed her to exercise her right to implant them within a medically reasonable time. The court reasoned that a female participant in the IVF procedure has exclusive decisional authority over the fertilized eggs created through that process, just as a pregnant woman has exclusive decisional authority over a nonviable fetus, and that appellant had not waived her right either in the May 12, 1993 consents or in the June 7, 1993 "uncontested divorce" agreement.

. . . .

We now [reverse, on the ground] that the parties clearly expressed their intent that in the circumstances presented the pre-zygotes would be donated to the IVF program for research purposes.

Analysis

A

The Legal Landscape Generally. We begin analysis with a brief description of the broader legal context of this dispute. In the past two decades, thousands of children have been born through IVF, the best known of several methods of assisted reproduction. Additionally, tens of thousands of frozen embryos annually are routinely stored in liquid nitrogen canisters, some having been in that state for more than ten years with no instructions for their use or disposal (see, New York State Task Force on Life and the Law, Assisted Reproductive Technologies: Analysis and Recommendations for Public Policy [April 1998], at 289 ["Assisted Reproductive Technologies"]; Caplan, Due Consideration: Controversy in the Age of Medical Miracles 63 [1998]). As science races ahead, it leaves in its trail mind-numbing ethical and legal questions (*see generally*, Robertson, Children of Choice: Freedom and the New Reproductive Technologies [1994] ["Children of Choice"]).

The law, whether statutory or decisional, has been evolving more slowly and cautiously. A handful of states — New York not among them — have adopted statutes touching on the disposition of stored embryos.

In the case law, only *Davis v. Davis* attempts to lay out an analytical framework for disputes between a divorcing couple regarding the disposition of frozen embryos. . . . In the absence of any prior written agreement between the parties — which should be presumed valid, and implemented — according to *Davis*, courts must in every case balance these competing interests, each deserving of judicial respect. . . .

. . . Some commentators would vest control in one of the two gamete providers (*see, e.g., Poole, Allocation of Decision-Making Rights to Frozen Embryos*, 4 Am. J. Fam. L. 67 [1990] [pre-zygotes to party wishing to avoid procreation]; Andrews, *The Legal Status of the Embryo*, 32 Loy. L. Rev. 357 [1986] [woman retains authority when she desires to implant]). Others would imply a contract to procreate from participation in an IVF program (*see, e.g.*, Note, Davis v. Davis: *What About Future Disputes?* 26 Conn. L. Rev. 305 [1993]; Comment, *Frozen Embryos: Towards An Equitable Solution*, 46 U. Miami L. Rev. 803 [1992]).

Yet a third approach is to regard the progenitors as holding a "bundle of rights" in relation to the pre-zygote that can be exercised through joint disposition agreements (*see*, Robertson, *Prior Agreements for Disposition of Frozen Embryos*, 51 Ohio St. L. Rev. 407 [1990] ["Prior Agreements"]; Robertson, *In the Beginning: The Legal Status of Early Embryos*, 76 Va. L. Rev. 437 [1990] ["Early Embryos"]). The most recent view — a "default rule" — articulated in the report of the New York State Task Force on Life and the Law, is that, while gamete bank regulations should require specific instructions regarding disposition, no embryo should be implanted, destroyed or used in research over the objection of an individual with decision-making authority (*see*, Assisted Reproductive Technologies, at 317-320, *supra*).

Proliferating cases regarding the disposition of embryos, as well as other assisted reproduction issues, will unquestionably spark further progression of the law. What is plain, however, is the need for clear, consistent principles to guide parties in protecting their interests and resolving their disputes, and the need for particular care in fashioning such principles as issues are better defined and appreciated. Against that backdrop we turn to the present appeal.

B. The Appeal Before Us

Like the Appellate Division, we conclude that disposition of these pre-zygotes does not implicate a woman's right of privacy or bodily integrity in the area of reproductive choice; nor are the pre-zygotes recognized as "persons" for constitutional purposes. The relevant inquiry thus becomes who has dispositional authority over them. Because that question is answered in this case by the parties' agreement, for purposes of resolving the present appeal we have no cause to decide whether the pre-zygotes are entitled to "special respect" (*cf., Davis v. Davis*).

Agreements between progenitors, or gamete donors, regarding disposition of their pre-zygotes should generally be presumed valid and binding, and enforced in any dispute between them. Indeed, parties should be encouraged in advance, before embarking on IVF and cryopreservation, to think through possible contingencies and carefully specify their wishes in writing. Explicit agreements avoid costly litigation in business transactions; they are all the more necessary and desirable in personal matters of reproductive choice, where the intangible costs of any litigation are simply incalculable. . . .

. . . .

Applying those principles, we agree that the informed consents signed by the parties unequivocally manifest their mutual intention that in the present circumstances the pre-zygotes be donated for research to the IVF program.

The conclusion that emerges most strikingly from reviewing these consents as a whole is that appellant and respondent intended that disposition of the pre-zygotes was to be their joint decision. The consents manifest that what they above all did not want was a stranger taking that decision out of their hands. Even in unforeseen circumstances, even if they were unavailable, even if they were dead, the consents jointly specified the disposition that would be made.

That sentiment explicitly appears again and again throughout the lengthy documents. Words of shared understanding — "we," "us" and "our" — permeate the pages. The overriding choice of these parties could not be plainer: "We have the principal responsibility to decide the disposition of our frozen pre-zygotes. Our frozen pre-zygotes will not be released from storage for any purpose without the written consent of both of us, consistent with the policies of the IVF Program and applicable law" . . . .

. . . .

As they embarked on the IVF program, appellant and respondent — "husband" and "wife," signing as such — clearly contemplated the fulfillment of a life dream of having a child during their marriage. The consents they signed provided for other contingencies, most especially that in the present circumstances the pre-zygotes would be donated to the IVF program for approved research purposes. These parties having clearly manifested their intention, the law will honor it.

. . . .

NOTES AND QUESTIONS

1. Note that the IVF efforts by the Kasses cost $75,000. An adoption costs $2,000–$5,000; a foreign adoption (Russia, China and Korea are the most common sources) may cost $10–15,000. Why would the Kasses choose against adoption? Is it a responsible choice, particularly in light of the cost, physical and emotional burdens and the high risk of failure?
2. The New York Court of Appeals sketches five (counting *Davis*) different approaches to the abandoned pre-embryo problem. Which does it use? Which makes sense to you — Administratively? Constitutionally? Ethically?
3. The Court says it need not consider whether the "pre-zygotes" are entitled to "special respect," because the parties' contract governs. Would the *Davis* Court agree? Do you?
4. The Court finds the contract unambiguous in seeking to have the parties — not the Court — decide disposition. So much may be conceded. But *did* they, in fact, unambiguously *decide*? Did they preclude later changes? And — if they *did* decide — shouldn't the Court, as in any commercial contract, consider whether the contract was unconscionable? (Was it?)
5. In a footnote 4 (omitted), the Court of Appeals indicated that despite its determination to honor contracts, a contract might be void, as contrary to public policy. Why might that be? For reasons expressed in *Davis v. Davis*? In The Council of Europe Convention? How then would a court be guided to decision?

PROBLEM 1–16 — Conception for Sacrifice

During 1990, it was reported that Abe and Mary Ayala of Walnut, California decided to conceive a child. They were both in their 40s and had intended to have no more children. However, their teenage daughter contracted leukemia and a bone marrow transplant donor could not be found. If they conceived a child, there was a one in four chance that the child might qualify as a perfect match. The Ayalas set about conceiving a donor.

A storm of controversy followed. There was particular objection to one method of donation which would have involved aspirating the tissue from the fetus by a needle injected into the fetus while still in the uterus and transferring it to the teenage daughter *before the fetus was born.* More broadly, critics argued that it was unethical to conceive a child for the purpose of "harvesting" organs or materials for the living. Issues of autonomy, privacy, competence, dignity and integrity seemed implicated.

In response, the Ayalas replied that they were conceiving this child in love; that they would love the child and raise the child as well as they had the teenage daughter even if the child could not serve as a donor; that the child would grow up knowing, quite possibly, that she had saved her sister's life. And, in point of fact, that is precisely what happened. Marissa-Eve celebrated her 8th birthday in June of 1998; her sister Anissa, now 26, is the beneficiary of the successful transplant.

1. Was it ethical to create life for such a purpose?
2. [illegible] of the necessary material might have been possible in the third trimester. Was this use of fetal material ethical? Should an abortion then have been allowed? Deemed ethically mandatory?
3. Reconsider here the *A.C.*, *Strunk* and *Davis* cases. Is the fetus a noncompetent donor? Is it entitled to "special respect" as in *Davis*? Consider also *In Re T.A.C.P.*, below in this section, where parents were not allowed to use their anencephalic baby as a donor. Should a similar prohibition have been imposed on the Ayalas?
4. Would you feel differently if the Ayalas had conceived the child and aborted the fetus in order to sell the bone marrow commercially to a perfect stranger?

[2] The Undead

In bioethical terms, the very meaning of death has become a matter of concern and ambiguity as science has expanded both our ability to keep people "alive" on machines and our need to declare them "dead" in order to transplant body parts for organ donation purposes. The resulting tension has both pragmatic and philosophical implications of a profound nature — whether to keep someone "alive" is by itself often a difficult question; when to declare such a person — breathing, warm, on life support machines — "dead" to save another compounds that difficulty. This section deals with defining the point in time when people may be deemed dead, and explores the question of what may be done with those who remain in the twilight zone between life and death.

[a] Defining Death

Death is both an event and a process, intermixed with elements of condition, causation, culture and culpability. It is equally a medical, an ethical, and a legal concept. In its most elemental terms, we say that death "occurs" when the heart and lungs stop. But this may be a matter of choice; and if they are kept going by machines, a person may still be "dead" in the sense that he or she cannot exist otherwise — the brain is gone. And then there are those — anencephalics, those in a persistent, vegetative state — who may breathe independently with no higher brain — are they "dead" too?

Defining death is important for many reasons, including determining when organs become available for transplantation. That decision has traditionally been left to those who "own" the body — either the deceased person or his or her family. The reason, partly, is the meaning of life and death to the dead and the living. This is a profound part of our culture and community, now being challenged by the technology which seeks body parts.

NEWMAN v. SATHYAVAGLSWARAN

287 F.3d 786 (9th Cir. 2002)

Fisher, Circuit Judge.

Parents, whose deceased children's corneas were removed by the Los Angeles County Coroner's office without notice or consent, brought this 42 U.S.C. § 1983 action alleging a taking of their property without due process of law. The complaint was dismissed by the district court for a failure to state a claim upon which relief could be granted. We must decide whether the longstanding recognition in the law of California, paralleled by our national common law, that next of kin have the exclusive right to possess the bodies of their deceased family members creates a property interest, the deprivation of which must be accorded due process of law under the Fourteenth Amendment of the United States Constitution. We hold that it does. The parents were not required to exhaust post deprivation procedures prior to bringing this suit. Thus, we hold that they properly stated a claim under § 1983.

I. FACTUAL AND PROCEDURAL BACKGROUND

Robert Newman and Barbara Obarski (the parents) each had children, Richard Newman and Kenneth Obarski respectively, who died in Los Angeles County in October 1997. Following their deaths, the Office of the Coroner for the County of Los Angeles (the coroner) obtained possession of the bodies of the children and, under procedures adopted pursuant to California Government Code § 27491.47 as it then existed, removed the corneas from those bodies without the knowledge of the parents and without an attempt to notify them and request consent. The parents became aware of the coroner's actions in September 1999 and subsequently filed this § 1983 action alleging a deprivation of their property without due process of law in violation of the Fourteenth Amendment.

II. PROPERTY INTERESTS IN DEAD BODIES

A. History of Common Law Interests in Dead Bodies

Duties to protect the dignity of the human body after its death are deeply rooted in our nation's history. In a valuable history of the subject, the Supreme Court of Rhode Island recounted:

> By the civil law of ancient Rome, the charge of burial was first upon the person to whom it was delegated by the deceased; second, upon the *scripti haeredes* (to whom the property was given), and if none, then upon the *haeredes legitimi* or *cognati* in order. . . . The heirs might be compelled to comply with the provisions of the will in regard to burial. And the Pontifical College had the power of providing for the burial of those who had no place of burial in their own right.

Pierce v. Proprietors of Swan Point Cemetery, 10 R.I. 227, 235–36, 1872 WL 3575 (1872) (citations omitted).

In 17th century England, and in much of Europe, duties to bury the dead and protect the dignified disposition of the body, described as flowing from a "*right of burial, . . .* a person's *right* to be buried," *id.* at 238–39; *accord*

In re Johnson's Estate, 169 Misc. 215, 7 N.Y.S.2d 81, 84 (N.Y. Surr. Ct. 1938) (explaining that in 17th century England, "[a] man had a right to the decent interment of his own body in expectation of the day of resurrection"), were borne primarily by churches, which had a duty to bury the bodies of those residing in their parishes. *Pierce*, 10 R.I. at 236. These duties, and the explanation of their genesis in the rights of the dead, carried over into New England colonial practice where "[i]n many parts . . . the parish system prevailed, and every family was considered to have a right of burial in the churchyard of the parish in which they lived."

The Roman practice of including duties to protect the body of the dead in civil law had no parallel in the early English common law because burials were matters of ecclesiastical cognizance. Thus, Blackstone explained that "though the heir has a property [interest] in the monuments and escutcheons of his ancestors, yet he has none in their bodies or ashes; nor can he bring any suit or action against such as indecently, at least, if not injuriously, violate and disturb their remains, when dead and buried."

A change in the common law in England can be traced to the 1840 case of *Rex v. Stewart,* 12 AD. & E. 773 (1840). In that case, the socially recognized right of the dead to a dignified disposition, previously enforced only through ecclesiastical courts, was interpreted as creating enforceable common law duties. The question before the court was whether the hospital in which "a pauper" died or the parish in which she was to be buried was under a duty to carry the body to the grave. *Id.* at 774. The court expressed "extreme difficulty in placing . . . any legal foundation" for either rule, but stated it was unwilling to discharge the case "considering how long the practice had prevailed, and been sanctioned, of burying such persons at the expense of the parish, and the general consequences of holding that such practice ha[d] no warrant in law." It stated the premises that, under long-standing tradition, "[e]very person . . . has a right to Christian burial . . . that implies the right to be carried from the place where his body lies to the parish cemetery" and "bodies . . . carried in a state of naked exposure to the grave [ ] would be a real offence to the living, as well as an apparent indignity to the dead." From these traditional understandings, the court concluded that "[t]he feelings and interests of the living require" that "the common law cast [ ] on some one the duty of carrying to the grave, decently covered, the dead body of any person dying in such a state of indigence as to leave no funds for that purpose."

Many early American courts adopted Blackstone's description of the common law, holding that "a dead body is not the subject of property right." *Bessemer Land*, 18 So. at 567. The duty to protect the body by providing a burial was often described as flowing from the "universal . . . right of sepulture," rather than from a concept of property law. *Wynkoop v. Wynkoop*, 42 Pa. 293, 300–01, 1861 WL 5846 (1862). As cases involving unauthorized mutilation and disposition of bodies increased toward the end of the 19th century, paralleling the rise in demand for human cadavers in medical science and use of cremation as an alternative to burial, *see In re Johnson's Estate*, 7 N.Y.S.2d at 85–86 (describing "an outpouring" of such cases), courts began to recognize an exclusive right of the next of kin to possess and control the disposition of the bodies of their dead relatives, the violation of which was actionable at law. Thus, in holding that a city council could not "seize upon existing private burial grounds, make them public, and exclude the proprietors from their management," the Supreme Court of Indiana commented that "the burial of the dead can [not] . . . be taken out of the hands of the relatives thereof" because "we lay down the proposition, that the bodies of the dead belong to the surviving relations, in the order of inheritance, as property, and that they have the right to dispose of them as such, within restrictions analogous to those by which the disposition of other property may be regulated." *Bogert v. City of Indianapolis*, 13 Ind. 134, 136, 138 (1859).

. . . .

C. The Right to Transfer Body Parts

The first successful transplantation of a kidney in 1954 led to an expansion of the rights of next of kin to the bodies of the dead. In 1968, the National Conference of Commissioners on Uniform State Laws approved the Uniform Anatomical Gift Act (UAGA), adopted by California the same year, which grants next of kin the right to transfer the parts of bodies in their possession to others for medical or research purposes. Cal. Health & Safety Code § 7150 *et seq.* The right to transfer is limited. The California UAGA prohibits any person from "knowingly, for valuable consideration, purchas[ing] or sell[ing] a part for transplantation, therapy, or reconditioning, if removal of the part is intended to occur after the death of the decedent," Cal. Health & Safety Code § 7155, as does federal law, 42 U.S.C. § 274e (prohibiting the "transfer [of] any human organ for valuable consideration").

In the 1970s and 1980s, medical science improvements and the related demand for transplant organs prompted governments to search for new ways to increase the supply of organs for donation. *See* National Organ Transplant Act, Pub.L. No. 98-507, 98 Stat 2339 (1984) (establishing Task Force on Organ Transplantation and the Organ Procurement and Transplantation Network); S.Rep. No. 98-382, at 2–4 (1984), *reprinted in* 1984 U.S.C.C.A.N. 3975, 3976–78 (discussing "major advances . . . in the science of human organ transplantation," and the "need[ ] . . . to encourage organ donation" to meet a supply "far short" of demand). Many perceived as a hindrance to the supply of needed organs the rule implicit in the UAGA that donations could be effected only if consent was received from the decedent or next of kin.

III. DUE PROCESS ANALYSIS

"[T]o provide California non-profit eye banks with an adequate supply of corneal tissue," S. Com. Rep. SB 21 (Cal.1983), § 27491.47(a) authorized the coroner to "remove and release or authorize the removal and release of corneal eye tissue from a body within the coroner's custody" without any effort to notify and obtain the consent of next of kin "if . . . [t]he coroner has no knowledge of objection to the removal." The law also provided that the coroner or any person acting upon his or her request "shall [not] incur civil liability for such removal in an action brought by any person who did not object prior to the removal . . . nor be subject to criminal prosecution." § 27491.47(b).

In two decisions the Sixth Circuit, the only federal circuit to address the issue until now, held that the interests of next of kin in dead bodies recognized in Michigan and Ohio allowed next of kin to bring § 1983 actions challenging implementation of cornea removal statutes similar to California's. *Whaley v. County of Tuscola*, 58 F.3d 1111 (6th Cir 1995) (Michigan); *Brotherton v. Cleveland*, 923 F.2d 477 (6th Cir.1991) (Ohio). The Sixth Circuit noted that courts in each state had recognized a right of next of kin to possess the body for burial and a claim by next of kin against others who disturb the body. Those common law rights, combined with the statutory right to control the disposition of the body recognized in each state's adoption of the UAGA, was held to be sufficient to create in next of kin a property interest in the corneas of their deceased relatives that could not be taken without due process of law.

We agree with the reasoning of the Sixth Circuit and believe that reasoning is applicable here. Under traditional common law principles, serving a duty to protect the dignity of the human body in its final disposition that is deeply rooted in our legal history and social traditions, the parents had exclusive and legitimate claims of entitlement to possess, control, dispose and prevent the violation of the corneas and other parts of the bodies of their deceased children. With California's adoption of the UAGA, Cal. Health and Safety Code § 7151.5, it statutorily recognized other important rights of the parents in relation to the bodies of their deceased children — the right to transfer body parts and refuse to allow their transfer. These are all important components of the group of rights by which property is defined, each of which carried with it the power to exclude others from its exercise, "traditionally . . . one of the most treasured strands in an owner's bundle of property rights." *Loretto v. Teleprompter Manhattan CATV Corp*. Thus, we hold that the parents had property interests in the corneas of their deceased children protected by the Due Process Clause of the Fourteenth Amendment.

Our holding is not affected by California's labeling of the interests of the next of kin as "quasi property," a term with little meaningful legal significance.

Nor does the fact that California forbids the trade of body parts for profit mean that next of kin lack a property interest in them. The Supreme Court has "never held that a physical item is not 'property' simply because it lacks a positive economic or market value."

Because the property interests of next of kin to dead bodies are firmly entrenched in the "background principles of property law," based on values and understandings contained in our legal history dating from the Roman Empire, California may not be free to alter them with exceptions that lack "a firm basis in traditional property principles." We need not, however, decide whether California has transgressed basic property principles with enactment of § 27491.47 because that statute did not extinguish California's legal recognition of the property interests of the parents to the corneas of their deceased children. It allowed the removal of corneas only if "the coroner has no knowledge of objection," a provision that implicitly acknowledges the ongoing property interests of next of kin.

The effect of § 27491.47 was to remove a procedure — notice and request for consent prior to the deprivation — and a remedy — the opportunity to seek redress for the deprivation in California's courts. A state may not evade due process analysis by defining " '[p]roperty' . . . by the procedures provided for its deprivation." *Cleveland Bd. of Educ. v. Loudermill*, 470 U.S. 532, 541 (1985). "While the legislature may elect not to confer a property interest . . .

it may not constitutionally authorize the deprivation of such an interest, once conferred, without appropriate procedural safeguards."

When the coroner removed the corneas from the bodies of the parents' deceased children and transferred them to others, the parents could no longer possess, control, dispose or prevent the violation of those parts of their children's bodies. To borrow a metaphor used when the government physically occupies property, the coroner did not merely "take a single 'strand' from the 'bundle' of property rights: it chop[ped] through the bundle, taking a slice of every strand." *Loretto*, 458 U.S. at 435. This was a deprivation of the most certain variety.

IV. POSTDEPRIVATION PROCESS

The scope of the process of law that was due the parents is not a question that we can answer based on the pleadings alone. This question must be addressed in future proceedings.

The coroner's argument that, as a matter of law, post-deprivation process is sufficient and the parents should therefore be required to exhaust postdeprivation procedures must fail. "[T]he State may not finally destroy a property interest without first giving the putative owner an opportunity to present his claim of entitlement." *Logan v. Zimmerman Brush Co.*, 455 U.S. 422, 434 (1982). The timing of a hearing depends upon the accommodation of competing interests including the importance of the private interests, the length or finality of the deprivation and the magnitude of governmental interest. *Mathews v. Eldridge*, 424 U.S. 319, 335 (1976). But, absent "extraordinary situations," *Boddie v. Connecticut*, 401 U.S. 371, 379 (1971), such as " 'the necessity of quick action by the State or the impracticality of providing any predeprivation process,' " the deprivation of property resulting from an established state procedure does not meet due process requirements without a predeprivation hearing. The coroner's removal of corneas was in accordance with the state procedures. Whether extraordinary situations justify the failure of the coroner to afford a predeprivation hearing turns on issues of fact that cannot be properly examined at this stage of the litigation.

We do not hold that California lacks significant interests in obtaining corneas or other organs of the deceased in order to contribute to the lives of the living. Courts are required to evaluate carefully the state's interests in deciding what process must be due the holders of property interests for their deprivation. An interest so central to the state's core police powers as improving the health of its citizens is certainly one that must be considered seriously in determining what process the parents were due. But our Constitution requires the government to assert its interests and subject them to scrutiny when it invades the rights of its subjects. Accordingly, we reverse the district court's dismissal of the parents' complaint and remand for proceedings in which the government's justification for its deprivation of parents' interests may be fully aired and appropriately scrutinized.

The dismissal of the parents' § 1983 claim is reversed and remanded for further proceedings.

Fernandez, Circuit Judge, Dissenting:

I dissent because I do not believe that the asthenic legal interest in a decedent's body, which California confers upon relatives and others, should be treated as a puissant giant for federal constitutional purposes.

To begin with, it has always been true in California that absent a statute "there is no property in a dead body." For that reason, no action for conversion will lie against someone who is said to have damaged or taken a part of the body. To the extent that any right exists, it is, in general, merely a right to possession. That right exists solely "for the limited purpose of determining who shall have its custody for burial."

Of course, any civilized state desires that the bodies of its deceased members be disposed of in an appropriate way, on grounds of decency, consideration for others, and pragmatism. And it should be done with reasonable haste and without undue acrimony.

California's statutory scheme reflects all of that. It decidedly does not confer a property right upon anyone. Assuming that a decedent has not made his own arrangements for disposal of his own earthly remains, the state makes sure that somebody else will both do so and pay for it. To that end, California has provided that "[t]he right to control the disposition of the remains of a deceased person . . . vests in, and the duty of disposition and the liability for the reasonable cost of disposition of the remains devolves upon," a list of individuals. Cal. Health & Safety Code § 7100(a). Thus, this so-called right is actually in the nature of a duty and expense designed to assure that the remains will not simply be left about, but will be quickly interred.

This leads, I think, to a fairly simple proposition: when the state sees to it that the duty, with its necessarily associated right, devolves upon a person, it can constitutionally limit that duty and the right that goes with it. And that is precisely what California did when it declared that the coroner can, in the course of an autopsy, release corneal eye tissue if he "has no knowledge of objection to the removal and release of corneal tissue having been made by the decedent or any other person specified in Section 7151.5 of the Health and Safety Code." Cal. Gov't Code § 27491.47(a) (1983). In that respect, it should be noted that the people referred to in § 7151.5 are not precisely the same as the people referred to in § 7100(a). The so-called right to consent, therefore, does not follow the so-called duty, and right, to see to interment. This, again, demonstrates just how asthenic the right conferred by § 7100(a) really is.

Nobody who has had the misfortune of having his loved ones die can fail to be moved by the prospect that somebody else will treat the loved one's former earthly vessel with disrespect. That feeling does not, however, demonstrate that California has conferred a constitutionally protected property right upon family members. In fact, it has not; it has merely given them enough of a right to allow them to fulfill their duty, and it has limited that in a number of ways. One of those ways has to do with corneal tissue. As to that, the duty may not devolve, and concomitantly the right will be neither necessary nor constitutionally protected.

Thus, I respectfully dissent.

NOTES AND QUESTIONS

1. In *Newman v. Sathyavaglswaran*, the suit is brought under 42 U.S.C. § 1983, a Civil War/Reconstruction Era statute conferring damages on anyone denied — under color of state law — any rights guaranteed by the "Constitution and laws" of the United States. Usually it is invoked for such civil rights as speech, religion, or privacy, or to protect against denial of due process or equal protection of the laws. What is the comparable civil right involved in *Newman*?
2. As Judge Fisher recounts, over the centuries, cadavers became the "property" of surviving relatives. But less than a century later, the advent of organ transplantation created a public interest in body parts. Shouldn't a state be allowed to effectuate such policy? Isn't the problem in *Newman* simply that California left the property interest of the parents intact, but provided it could be deprived without notice?
3. Or is there more here? Is it that "every person has a right to a Christian burial," and so the parents are not enforcing *their* rights, but rather their children's rights? But what are those rights? If death is the end of life, what "rights" do the dead have? Are they "persons" anymore than the aborted fetus in *Roe v. Wade*? Is the *Newman* case about life or death?
4. Most societies provide, by law or religion or otherwise, for respect for the dead. Desecrating a corpse or a graveyard is a serious crime. And administering estates, even intestate succession, honors the wishes of the dead. But is there *dishonor* here? Should we inquire into what the children would have wanted?
5. Anyway, whether it is the children's loss or the parents, what is it worth? The corneas are valuable only to those with sight. The loss to the dead has no cash consequences. And if the jury is to make an award for pain and suffering, how is that to be measured? Would it matter that, if they had been asked, the parents would readily (or *should* readily) have agreed to donate the corneas?
6. Could California provide that all bodies, upon death, become the property of the State? Could it provide instead that removable organs become the property of the State? Should it do so?
7. In the 1960s, a committee of the Harvard Medical School grappled with defining death, as we learn in the next case, *People v. Eulo*, and those following as to anencephaly.

PEOPLE v. EULO

482 N.Y.S.2d 436 (Ct. App. 1984)

Cooke, Chief Judge.

These appeals involve a question of criminal responsibility in which defendants, charged with homicide, contend that their conduct did not cause death.

The term "death," as used in this State's statutes, may be construed to embrace a determination, made according to accepted medical standards, that a person has suffered an irreversible cessation of breathing and heartbeat or, when these functions are artificially maintained, an irreversible cessation of the functioning of the entire brain, including the brain stem. Therefore, a defendant will not necessarily be relieved of criminal liability for homicide by the removal of the victim's vital organs after the victim has been declared dead according to brain-based criteria, notwithstanding that, at that time, the victim's heartbeat and breathing were being continued by artificial means.

I

On the evening of July 19, 1981, defendant and his girlfriend attended a volunteer firemen's fair in Kings Park, Suffolk County. Not long after they arrived, the two began to argue, reportedly because defendant was jealous over one of her former suitors, whom they had seen at the fair. The argument continued through the evening; it became particularly heated as the two sat in defendant's pick-up truck, parked in front of the home of the girlfriend's parents. Around midnight, defendant shot her in the head with his unregistered handgun.

The victim was rushed by ambulance to the emergency room of St. John's Hospital. A gunshot wound to the left temple causing extreme hemorrhaging was apparent. A tube was placed in her windpipe to enable artificial respiration and intravenous medication was applied to stabilize her blood pressure.

Shortly before 2:00 a.m., the victim was examined by a neurosurgeon, who undertook various tests to evaluate damage done to the brain. Painful stimuli were applied and yielded no reaction. Various reflexes were tested and, again, there was no response. A further test determined that the victim was incapable of spontaneously maintaining respiration. An electroencephalogram (EEG) resulted in "flat," or "isoelectric," readings indicating no activity in the part of the brain tested.

Over the next two days, the victim's breathing was maintained solely by a mechanical respirator. Her heartbeat was sustained and regulated through medication. Faced with what was believed to be an imminent cessation of these two bodily functions notwithstanding the artificial maintenance, the victim's parents consented to the use of certain of her organs for transplantation.

On the afternoon of July 23, a second neurosurgeon was called in to evaluate whether the victim's brain continued to function in any manner. A repetition of all of the previously conduct tests led to the same diagnosis: the victim's entire brain had irreversibly ceased to function. This diagnosis was reviewed and confirmed by the Deputy Medical Examiner for Suffolk County and another physician.

The victim was pronounced dead at 2:20 p.m. on July 23, although at that time she was still attached to a respirator and her heart was still beating. Her body was taken to a surgical room where her kidneys, spleen, and lymph nodes were removed. The mechanical respirator was then disconnected, and her breathing immediately stopped, followed shortly by a cessation of the heartbeat.

Defendant was indicted for second degree murder. After a jury trial, he was convicted of manslaughter. The Appellate Division unanimously affirmed the conviction, without opinion.

. . . .

II

Defendants' principal point in each of these appeals is that the respective Trial Judges failed to adequately instruct the juries as to what constitutes a person's death, the time at which criminal liability for a homicide would attach. It is claimed that in New York, the time of death has always been set by reference to the functioning of the heart and the lungs; that death does not occur until there has been an irreversible cessation of breathing and heartbeat.

. . . .

(a)

A person's passing from life has long been an event marked with a variety of legal consequences. A determination of death starts in motion the legal machinery governing the disposition of the deceased's property. It serves to terminate certain legal relationships, including marriage, and business partnerships. The period for initiation of legal actions brought against, by, or on behalf of the deceased is extended. And, in recent times, death marks the point at which certain of the deceased's organs, intended to be donated upon death, may be transferred. In the immediate context, pertinent here, determination of a person's "death" is relevant because our Penal Law defines homicide in terms of "conduct which causes the *death* of a person."

Death has been conceptualized by the law as, simply, the absence of life: "Death is the opposite of life; it is the termination of life." But, while erecting death as a critical milepost in a person's legal life, the law has had little occasion to consider the precise point at which a person ceases to live.

. . . .

(b)

Within the past two decades, machines that artificially maintain cardiorespiratory functions have come into widespread use. This technical accomplishment has called into question the universal applicability of the traditional legal and medical criteria for determining when a person has died.[1]

---

[1] *See generally Report of President's Comm. for Study of Ethical Problems in Medicine and Biomedical and Behavioral Research on Defining Death: Medical, Legal and Ethical Issues in Determination of Death* (1981) [hereinafter Comm. Report], U.S. Supt. Docs. No. Pr. 40.8; ET 3/ D34, pp.13-42; Walton, *On Defining Death*, pp.1-17; Abram, *Need for Uniform Law on the Determination of Death*, 27 NYLS L. Rev. 1187, 1187-1193; Compton, *Telling The Time of Human Death by Statute: An Essential and Progressive Trend*, 31 Wash. & Lee L. Rev. 521, 521-532; Capron & Kass, *A Statutory Definition of the Standards for Determining Human Death: An Appraisal and a Proposal*, 121 U. of Pa. L. Rev. 87, 87-92.

These criteria were cast into flux as the medical community gained a better understanding of human physiology. It is widely understood that the human brain may be anatomically divided, generally, into three parts: the cerebrum, the cerebellum, and the brain stem. The cerebrum, known also as the "higher brain," is deemed largely to control cognitive functions such as thought, memory, and consciousness. The cerebellum primarily controls motor coordination. The brain stem, or "lower brain," which itself has three parts known as the midbrain, pons, and medulla, controls reflexive or spontaneous functions such as breathing, swallowing, and "sleep-wake" cycles.

. . . .

Notwithstanding a total irreversible loss of the entire brain's functioning, contemporary medical techniques can maintain, for a limited period, the operation of the heart and the lungs. Respirators or ventilators can substitute for the lower brain's failure to maintain breathing. This artificial respiration, when combined with a chemical regimen, can support the continued operation of the heart. This is so because, unlike respiration, the physical contracting or "beating" of the heart occurs independently of impulses from the brain: so long as blood containing oxygen circulates to the heart, it may continue to beat and medication can take over the lower brain's limited role in regulating the rate and force of the heartbeat.

It became clear in medical practice that the traditional "vital signs" — breathing and heartbeat — are not independent indicia of life, but are, instead, part of an integration of functions in which the brain is dominant. As a result, the medical community began to consider the cessation of brain activity as a measure of death.[2]

The movement in law towards recognizing cessation of brain functions as criteria for death followed this medical trend. The immediate motive for adopting this position was to ease and make more efficient the transfer of donated organs. Organ transfers, to be successful, require a "viable, intact organ." Once all of a person's vital functions have ceased, transferable organs swiftly deteriorate and lose their transplant value. The technical ability to artificially maintain respiration and heartbeat after the entire brain has ceased to function was sought to be applied in cases of organ transplant to preserve the viability of donated organs.

Thus, the first legal recognition of cessation of brain functions as a criterion for determining death came in the form of a Kansas statute enacted in 1970. Denominated "[a]n Act relating to and defining death," the statute states, in

---

[2] *See Comm. Report* n.3, at pp.21-29; *but see* Biorck, *When is Death?*, 1968 Wis. L. Rev. 484. The initial problem for doctors was to devise a technical means of verifying when the entire brain ceases to function. Unlike tests for determining the cessation of breathing and heartbeat, more sophisticated means were necessary to measure the less obvious functioning of the brain. A seminal study was issued in 1968, under the auspices of Harvard Medical School (*see* Harvard Report, n.7), setting forth a multistep test designed to identify the existence of physical indicia of brain activity. Under it, responsiveness to painful stimuli is to be tested. The subject is also to be observed for any spontaneous movement or respiration and any operation of various bodily reflexes. The absence of brain activity, when demonstrated under these tests, is then sought to be confirmed by reapplication of the tests at least 24 hours later and through the reading of an EEG, which when "flat" has confirmatory value. This test has served as the foundation for currently applied tests for determining when the brain has ceased to function.

part, that death will be deemed to have occurred when a physician applying ordinary medical standards determines that there is an "absence of spontaneous respiratory and cardiac functions and . . . attempts to resuscitation are considered hopeless . . . or . . . there is the absence of spontaneous brain function."[3]

In the years following enactment of this statute, a growing number of sister States enacted statutes of their own. Some opted for the Kansas approach. Others defined death solely in terms of brain-based criteria as determined by accepted methods of medical practice. And still others retain the cardiorespiratory yardstick, but provide that when artificial means of sustaining respiration and heartbeat preclude application of the traditional criteria, death may be determined according to brain-based criteria, namely the irreversible cessation of brain functions. In the absence of any statute defining death, some jurisdictions have judicially adopted brain-based criteria for determining death. Professional and quasi-governmental groups (including the American Bar Association, the American Medical Association, the President's Commission for the Study of Ethical Problems in Medicine and Biomedical and Behavioral Research, and the National Conference of Commissioners on Uniform State Laws) have jointly endorsed a single standard that includes both cardiorespiratory and brain-based criteria.[4]

(c)

In New York, the term "death," although used in many statutes, has not been expressly defined by the Legislature. This raises the question of how this court may construe these expressions of the term "death" in the absence of clarification by the Legislature. When the Legislature has failed to assign definition to a statutory term, the courts will generally construe that term according to "its ordinary and accepted meaning as it was understood at the time." . . .

Bearing these principles in mind, it must be added that statutory construction is not "a ritual to be observed by unimaginative adherence to well-worn professional phrases." . . .

---

[3] Following the second part of the disjunctive definition, as originally enacted, is the statement: "Death is to be pronounced before artificial means of supporting respiratory and circulatory function are terminated and before any vital organ is removed for purposes of transplantation." This final sentence, which intimates that the brain-based criteria are to be utilized only in transplant cases, precipitated some criticism of the statute. Two commentators noted that "[t]he primary fault with this legislation is that it appears to be based on, or at least gives voice to, the misconception that there are two separate phenomena of death. This dichotomy is particularly unfortunate because it seems to have been inspired by a desire to establish a special definition for organ transplantation" (Capron & Kass at p.109). They added that the two-part definition set forth in the Kansas statute leaves "open the prospect 'that X at a certain stage in the process of dying can be pronounced dead, whereas Y, having arrived at the same point, is not said to be dead' " (at p.110, quoting Kennedy, *Kansas Statute on Death: An Appraisal*, 285 New Neg. J. Med. 946, 948). This provision was subsequently deleted from the statute. (*See* Kan. Stats. Ann. § 77-202, L. 1979, ch. 199, § 11.)

[4] The recommended standard provides: "An individual who has sustained either (1) irreversible cessation of circulatory and respiratory functions, or (2) irreversible cessation of all functions of the entire brain, including the brain stem, is dead. A determination of death must be made in accordance with accepted medical standards" (see Comm. Report, n.3, at p.2).

It has been called to this court's attention that the Legislature has, on a number of occasions, had bills before it that would expressly recognize brain-based criteria for determining death and has taken no affirmative action. This legislative void in no way impedes this court from fulfilling its obligation to construe laws of the State. Indeed, advances made in medical science have caused a focus on the issues of when a jury may find criminal responsibility for homicide, of when physicians may transfer donated organs, and of when a person's body may be accorded the dignity of final repose. It is incumbent upon this court to instill certainty and uniformity in these important areas.

We hold that a recognition of brain-based criteria for determining death is not unfaithful to prior judicial definitions of "death," as presumptively adopted in the many statutes using that term. Close examination of the common-law conception of death and the traditional criteria used to determine when death has occurred leads inexorably to this conclusion.

. . . .

Death remains the single phenomenon identified at common law; the supplemental criteria are merely adapted to account for the "changed conditions" that a dead body may be attached to a machine so as to exhibit demonstrably false indicia of life. It reflects an improved understanding that in the complete and irreversible absence of a functioning brain, the traditional foci of life — the heart and the lungs — function only as a result of stimuli originating from outside of the body and will never again function as part of an integrated organism.[5]

. . . .

(d)

One must be careful to distinguish the effect of this decision — determining when a person has died — from issues raised in related but qualitatively distinct cases — determining when a person may be allowed to die. In Matter of Storar, 52 N.Y.2d 363, this court reviewed two separate applications brought on behalf of two terminally ill patients. One sought permission to terminate extraordinary medical care. The other sought permission, over the patient's mother's objection to administer medically necessary blood transfusions that would have prolonged the patient's short-lived life. A personal right to decline medical care, founded at common law, was applied in the first case

[5] In reaching this conclusion, this court is aware of the criticism from some quarters that the perceived motivation for the development and recognition of brain-based criteria for death renders these criteria "theoretically impure." This is asserted on the ground that the prospect of more easily accessible transplants serves to "adulterate the purity of [the] scientific case by baiting it with the prospect of this extraneous — though extremely appealing — gain" (Jonas, n.16, at p.52). Although, practically speaking, adoption of these supplemental criteria will indeed facilitate organ transplants, it has been found that "the need for viable organs to transplant does not account fully for the interest in diagnosing irreversible loss of brain functions" (Comm. Report, n.3, at p.23). The Presidential Commission, charged with evaluating how death should be determined, cited studies reporting "that organs are procured in only a small percentage of cases in which brain-based criteria might be applied." The Commission itself found that the "medical concern over the determination of death rests much less with any wish to facilitate organ transplantation than with the need both to render appropriate care to patients and to replace artificial support with more fitting and respectful behavior when a patient has become a dead body" (at pp.23-24).

as there existed clear and convincing evidence that this was the patient's personal desire. But, in the second case, the court held that, in the absence of such evidence of personal intent (there, due to the patient's incompetence), a third party has no recognized right to decide that the patient's quality of life has declined to a point where treatment should be withheld and the patient should be allowed to die.

Today's decision is no retreat from that holding. Under existing law, third parties are without authority to determine on behalf of the terminally ill that they should be permitted to die. This court will make no judgment as to what is for another an unacceptable quality of life. But, when a determination has been made according to accepted medical standards[6] that a person has suffered an irreversible cessation of heartbeat and respiration, or, when these functions are maintained solely by extraordinary mechanical means, an irreversible cessation of all functions of the entire brain, including the brain stem, no life traditionally recognized by the law is present in that body.

III

. . . .

The courts here adequately conveyed to the juries their obligation to determine the fact and causation of death. The courts defined the criteria of death in relation to the chain of causation. By specifically charging the juries that they might consider the surgical procedures as superseding causes of death, the courts made clear by ready implication that death should be deemed to have occurred after all medical procedures had ended.

. . . .

Even though each of these cases was presented to a jury which had been charged that death should be deemed to have occurred after the medical intervention had ended, testimony concerning the attending physicians' diagnoses of the victims as dead, according to brain-based criteria, was nonetheless highly relevant. It was these medical pronouncements that caused the victims to be removed from the medical systems that maintained their breathing and heartbeat. If the victims were properly diagnosed as dead, of course, no subsequent medical procedure such as the organ removals would be deemed a cause of death. If victims' deaths were prematurely pronounced due to a doctor's negligence, the subsequent procedures may have been a cause of death, but that negligence would not constitute a superseding cause of death relieving defendants of liability. If, however, the pronouncements of death were premature due to the gross negligence or the intentional wrongdoing of doctors, as determined by a grave deviation from accepted medical practices or disregard for legally cognizable criteria for determining death, the intervening medical procedure would interrupt the chain of causation and become the

[6] This court has rejected judicial attempts to formulate detailed legal standards governing procedures leading to medical diagnoses. Today we decline to set forth what particular medical diagnostic tests should be performed before a person's brain functions may be found to have irreversibly ceased. Any attempt to establish a specific procedure might inhibit the development and application of more sophisticated diagnostic methods. Therefore, it is sufficient that a particular determination be made according to accepted medical standards.

legal cause of death. Thus, the propriety of the medical procedures is integral to the question of causation

. . . .

Accordingly, in each case, the order of the Appellate Division should be affirmed.

NOTES AND QUESTIONS

1. As the court notes, until the mid-1960s, the definition of "death" was cessation of cardiac or pulmonary activity. As it became increasingly possible to maintain people on machines, helping their hearts and their lungs to function, this definition became inadequate. In addition, by the mid-1960s, the technology and transportation available to national transplant networks made it imperative that organ donations be facilitated for transplantation purposes by adopting a more manageable definition of death. Specifically, transplantation would be facilitated if a person could be declared "dead" while his or her heart and lungs were still functioning, keeping a body part "fresh" for transplanting.

   Therefore, the Harvard *Ad Hoc* Committee in 1968 provided an alternative to the cardio/pulmonary definition of death, concluding that death might be found to have occurred where the brain has wholly ceased to function. This would be confirmed by electroencephalogram examination, as well as clinical examination. It must be found that the patient is unresponsive to painful stimuli, that there is an absence of spontaneous movements or breathing and that, third, there is an absence of reflexes. With this, a person could be declared dead.

2. The Harvard definition required "whole" brain death. However, the brain is made up of three large components, and multiple subdivisions, and cognitive function may be lost although the brain stem remains intact. With such a person, the semblance of "life" remains, although any hope of autonomy or identity is lost. Thus, in the latter part of the 20th century, the debate became whether or not to expand the definition of "brain death" to include a person who might function independently off a ventilator, respirator or heart assistance machine, but who would never recover from a coma or persistent vegetative state. In the main, the answer has been negative. Should it be?

3. The requirement of "whole brain death" is presently universal. A person whose brain is partially functioning is not deemed to be "dead." Yet such a person may be irretrievably lost, as was Nancy Beth Cruzan in the case which appears, *infra*, § 1.04[2][c]. Prevailing wisdom is that so long as such a person breathes independently, he or she is not dead and, for example, organs could not be removed. There may be good reason to reach an opposite conclusion — for the dignity of the person and the resources of society and the needs of those whose organs are failing. As to this, see Robert M. Veatch, *The Impending Collapse of the Whole Brain Definition of Death*, 23 Hastings. Cent. Rep. 18, 24 (1993), preferring a principled definition based upon "integrated

functioning of mind and body," requiring "some version of a higher-brain-oriented formulation."

4. Quite clearly, in the above case the removal of the victim's kidneys would have caused her death. Equally clear, removing her from the mechanical respirator was itself a sufficient cause of death. Should Mr. Eulo, then, be convicted of killing the victim? Can it be said that he effectively "caused" in a proximate and culpable sense her death?

   Wasn't there an obligation to keep his girlfriend "alive" as long as possible? And suppose she were conscious and made the choice *herself*, to avoid a life of dependency on machines and paralysis. Who "caused" the death for homicide purposes? *See People v. Caldwell*, 692 N.E.2d 448 (Ill. App. Ct. 1998).

5. Note that the victim was pronounced dead at 2:20 p.m. on July 23 only four days after the shooting and at a time when her heart was still beating and she was still attached to a respirator. Her body was taken to an operating room where her kidneys, spleen and lymph nodes were removed. Without a court's "brain death" definition of death, she would have been deemed "alive." Is there something ghoulish here? Is society diminished by the spectre of warm, functioning bodies being "parted out" like old automobiles, or "harvested" like crops?

6. Numerous articles over the past decade have detailed the shortage of organ donors and the inadequacy of the organ supply to meet the need for transplants, particularly heart, liver, lungs, and kidneys. The presumption is that people do not wish to be donors unless they have expressed a willingness. Should the presumption be reversed? Should it be presumed that people who die in a hospital wish to be organ donors, and are available for organ donation, unless they have expressed an *unwillingness*? Should one be concerned about the propriety of the hospital, its staff, or the surgeons and physicians attending the victim, approaching the family or surviving relatives and seeking their permission for a donation or transplant?

7. Recently, articles have discussed differing cultural beliefs about death and dying. Navajos, for instance, believe that language and thought "have the power to shape reality and control events." Therefore, it is seen as both disrespectful and unhealthy for doctors to discuss the possibility of death or advance planning. (*See* Carerese and Rhodes, *Western Bioethics on the Navajo Reservation: Benefit or Harm?* JAMA Sept 13, 1995.) This poses an interesting dilemma for doctors and those advising them: violate cultural values in order to obtain informed consent or facilitate the planning of death?

PROBLEM 1–17 — Feticide

On Halloween night William killed his former wife with a machete, knowing her to be eight months pregnant. The fetus, with multiple wounds, was expelled from the womb; there was no air in its lungs when found later, dead. California treats as murder the killing of a human being or a fetus, but manslaughter is only the killing of a human being, that is, a live "person."

Is this statute, with that distinction, valid? If William was provoked, what crime did he commit? *See People v. Dennis*, 450 P.2d 1035 (Cal. S. Ct. 1998) and *State v. Horne*, 319 S.E.2d 703 (S.C. 1984).

A number of states now punish an assault which kills a fetus, some requiring that it have been "viable," others treating a fetus as a "human being" from conception. Which is the better approach? *See Kentucky v. Morris*, 142 S.W.3d 654 (Ky. 2004); *People v. Taylor*, 86 P.3d 881 (Cal. 2004); *People v. Davis*, 872 P.2d 591 (Cal. 1994). How can you square the latter with *Roe v. Wade* and *Casey*? *See Minnesota v. Merrill*, 450 N.W.2d 318 (Minn. 1990). Must the defendant have known the woman was pregnant? Intended to harm the fetus?

In 2004, Congress adopted the Unborn Victims of Violence Act, 18 U.S.C.A. 1841, which provides as follows:

> 1841 Protection of unborn children
>
> (a)(1) Whoever engages in conduct that violates any of the provisions of law listed in subsection (b) and thereby causes the death of, or bodily injury (as defined in section 1365 [18 USCS 1365]) to, a child, who is in utero at the time the conduct takes place, is guilty of a separate offense under this section.
>
> (2)(A) Except as otherwise provided in this paragraph, the punishment for that separate offense is the same as the punishment provided under Federal law for that conduct had that injury or death occurred to the unborn child's mother.
>
> (B) An offense under this section does not require proof that —
>
> (i) the person engaging in the conduct had knowledge or should have had knowledge that the victim of the underlying offense was pregnant; or
>
> (ii) the defendant intended to cause the death of, or bodily injury to, the unborn child.
>
> (C) If the person engaging in the conduct thereby intentionally kills or attempts to kill the unborn child, that person shall instead of being punished under subparagraph (A), be punished as provided under sections 1111, 1112, 1113, of this title [18 USCS 1111, 1112, and 1113] for intentionally killing or attempting to kill a human being.
>
> (D) Notwithstanding any other provision of law, the death penalty shall not be imposed for an offense under this section.
>
> * * * * * *
>
> (1) of any person for conduct relating to an abortion for which the consent of the pregnant woman, or a person authorized by law to act on her behalf, has been obtained or for which such consent is implied by law;
>
> (2) of any person for any medical treatment of the pregnant woman or her unborn child; or
>
> (3) of any woman with respect to her unborn child.

(d) As used in this section, the term "unborn child" means a child in utero, and the term "child in utero" or "child, who is in utero" means a member of the species homo sapiens, at any stage of development, who is carried in the womb.

Does this statute answer the questions above? Is it constitutional?

For recent, excellent discussions of fetal prosecutions, see Note, *Recognizing Unborn Victims*, 31 N.E.J. on Crim & Civ. Conf. 461 (2005); Note, *The Unborn Victims of Violence Act*, 1 Tenn. J. L. & Pol'y 277 (2005); *Recent Development, The Unborn Victims of Violence Act*, 39 Harv. J. on Legis. 215 (2002).

[b] Brain Death: Anencephalic and Conjoint Babies

Some children are born without brains or with only a partial brain. Most die within days. Such children, anencephalics, could never develop personalities or even motor skills. Must they be kept "alive;" can they be put to "death"? Do these terms have any meaning with such beings which — although "human" — can hardly be called "persons"?

IN THE MATTER OF BABY "K"
832 F. Supp. 1022 (E.D. Va. 1993)

Hilton, Justice.

Findings of Fact

1. Plaintiff Hospital is a general acute care hospital located in Virginia that is licensed to provide diagnosis, treatment, and medical and nursing services to the public as provided by Virginia law. Among other facilities, the Hospital has a Pediatric Intensive Care Department and an Emergency Department.
2. The Hospital is a recipient of federal and state funds including those from Medicare and Medicaid and is a "participating hospital" pursuant to 42 U.S.C. § 1395cc.
3. The Hospital and its staff (including emergency doctors, pediatricians, neonatologists and pediatric intensivists) treat sick children on a daily basis.
4. Defendant Ms. H, a citizen of the Commonwealth of Virginia, is the biological mother of Baby K, an infant girl born by Caesarean section at the Hospital on October 13, 1992. Baby K was born with anencephaly.
5. Anencephaly is a congenital defect in which the brain stem is present but the cerebral cortex is rudimentary or absent. There is no treatment that will cure, correct, or ameliorate anencephaly. Baby K is permanently unconscious and cannot hear or see. Lacking a cerebral function, Baby K does not feel pain. Baby K has brain stem functions primarily limited to reflexive actions such as feeding reflexes (rooting, sucking, swallowing), respiratory reflexes (breathing, coughing), and reflexive responses to sound or touch. Baby K has a normal heart rate, blood

pressure, liver function, digestion, kidney function, and bladder function and has gained weight since her birth. Most anencephalic infants die within days of birth.

6. Baby K was diagnosed prenatally as being anencephalic. Despite the counseling of her obstetrician and neonatologist that she terminate her pregnancy, Ms. H refused to have her unborn child aborted.

7. A Virginia court of competent jurisdiction has found defendant Mr. K, a citizen of the Commonwealth of Virginia, to be Baby K's biological father.

8. Ms. H and Mr. K have never been married.

9. Since Baby K's birth, Mr. K has, at most, been only distantly involved in matters relating to the infant. Neither the Hospital nor Ms. H ever sought Mr. K's opinion or consent in providing medical treatment to Baby K.

10. Because Baby K had difficulty breathing immediately upon birth, Hospital physicians provided her with mechanical ventilator treatment to allow her to breathe.

11. Within days of Baby K's birth, Hospital medical personnel urged Ms. H to permit a "Do Not Resuscitate Order" for Baby K that would discontinue ventilator treatment. Her physicians told her that no treatment existed for Baby K's anencephalic condition, no therapeutic or palliative purpose was served by the treatment, and that ventilator care was medically unnecessary and inappropriate. Despite this pressure, Ms. H continued to request ventilator treatment for her child.

12. Because of Ms. H's continued insistence that Baby K receive ventilator treatment, her treating physicians requested the assistance of the Hospital's "Ethics Committee" in overriding the mother's wishes.

13. A three person Ethics Committee subcommittee, composed of a family practitioner, a psychiatrist, and a minister, met with physicians providing care to Baby K. On October 22, 1992, the group concluded that Baby K's ventilator treatment should [illegible] decided to "wait a reasonable time for the family to help the caregiver terminate aggressive therapy." If the family refused to follow this advice, the committee recommended that the Hospital should "attempt to resolve this through our legal system."

14. Ms. H subsequently rejected the committee's recommendation. Before pursuing legal action to override Ms. H's position, the Hospital decided to transfer the infant to another health care facility.

15. Baby K was transferred to a nursing home ("Nursing Home") in Virginia on November 30, 1992 during a period when she was not experiencing respiratory distress and thus did not need ventilator treatment. A condition of the transfer was that the Hospital agreed to take the infant back if Baby K again developed respiratory distress to receive ventilator treatment which was unavailable at the Nursing Home. Ms. H agreed to this transfer.

16. Baby K returned to the Hospital on January 15, 1993 after experiencing respiratory distress to receive ventilator treatment. Hospital officials again attempted to persuade Ms. H to discontinue ventilator treatment for her child. Ms. H again refused. After Baby K could breathe on her own, she was transferred back to the Nursing Home on February 12, 1993.
17. Baby K again experienced breathing difficulties on March 3, 1993 and returned to the Hospital to receive ventilator treatment.
18. On March 15, 1993, Baby K received a tracheotomy, a procedure in which a breathing tube is surgically implanted in her windpipe, to facilitate ventilator treatment. Ms. H agreed to this operation.
19. After no longer requiring ventilator treatment, Baby K was transferred back to the Nursing Home on April 13, 1993 where she continues to live.
20. Baby K will almost certainly continue to have episodes of respiratory distress in the future. In the absence of the ventilator treatment during these episodes, she would suffer serious impairment of her bodily functions and soon die.
21. Ms. H visits Baby K daily. The mother opposes the discontinuation of ventilator treatment when Baby K experiences respiratory distress because she believes that all human life has value, including her anencephalic daughter's life. Ms. H has a firm Christian faith that all life should be protected. She believes that God will work a miracle if that is his will. Otherwise, Ms. H believes, God, and not other humans, should decide the moment of her daughter's death. As Baby K's mother and as the only parent who has participated in the infant's care, Ms. H believes that she has the right to decide what is in her child's best interests.
22. On the Hospital's motion, a guardian *ad litem* to represent Baby K was appointed.
23. Both the guardian *ad litem* and Mr. K share the Hospital's position that ventilator treatment should be withheld from Baby K when she experiences respiratory distress.
24. The Hospital has stipulated that it is not proposing to deny ventilator treatment to Baby K because of any lack of adequate resources or any inability of Ms. H to pay for the treatment.

Conclusions of Law

. . . [T]he Hospital has sought declaratory and injunctive relief under four federal statutes and one Virginia statute: the Emergency Medical Treatment and Active Labor Act, the Rehabilitation Act of 1973, the Americans with Disabilities Act of 1990, the Child Abuse Amendments of 1984, and the Virginia Medical Malpractice Act. . . .

I. Emergency Medical Treatment and Active Labor Act

Plaintiff seeks a declaration that its refusal to provide Baby K with life-supporting medical care would not transgress the Emergency Medical

Treatment and Active Labor Act. EMTALA requires that participating hospitals provide stabilizing medical treatment to any person who comes to an emergency department in an "emergency medical condition" when treatment is requested on that person's behalf. An "emergency medical condition" is defined in the statute as "acute symptoms of sufficient severity . . . such that the absence of immediate medical attention could reasonably be expected to result in . . . serious impairment to bodily functions, or serious dysfunction of any bodily organ or part." "Stabilizing" medical treatment is defined as "such medical treatment of the condition as may be necessary to assure, within reasonable medical probability, that no material deterioration of the condition" will result. The statute's legislative history includes a position paper by the American College of Emergency Physicians stating that "stabilization" should include "[e]stablishing and assuring an adequate airway and adequate ventilation."

The Hospital admits that Baby K would meet these criteria if she is brought to the Hospital while experiencing breathing difficulty. As stated in the Hospital's complaint, when Baby K is in respiratory distress, that condition is "such that the absence of immediate medical attention could reasonably be expected to cause serious impairment to her bodily functions" — i.e., her breathing difficulties constitute an "emergency medical condition." The Hospital also concedes in its complaint that ventilator treatment is required in such circumstances to assure "that no material deterioration of Baby K's condition is likely to occur" — i.e., a ventilator is necessary to "stabilize" the baby's condition. These admissions establish that the Hospital would be liable under EMTALA if Baby K arrived there in respiratory distress (or some other emergency medical condition) and the Hospital failed to provide mechanical ventilation (or some other medical treatment) necessary to stabilize her acute condition.

The Hospital would also have an obligation to continue to provide stabilizing medical treatment to Baby K even is she were admitted to the pediatric intensive care unit or other unit of the Hospital and to provide the treatment until she could be transferred back to the Nursing Home or to another facility willing to accept her. . . .

Despite EMTALA's clear requirements and in the face of the Hospital's admissions, the Hospital seeks an exemption from the statute for instances in which the treatment at issue is deemed "futile" or "inhumane" by the hospital physicians. The plain language of the statute requires stabilization of an emergency medical condition. The statute does not admit of any "futility" or "inhumanity" exceptions. Any argument to the contrary should be directed to the U.S. Congress, not to the Federal Judiciary. . . .

Even if EMTALA contained the exceptions advanced by the Hospital, these exceptions would not apply here. The use of a mechanical ventilator to assist breathing is not "futile" or "inhumane" in relieving the acute symptoms of respiratory difficulty which is the emergency medical condition that must be treated under EMTALA. To hold otherwise would allow hospitals to deny emergency treatment to numerous classes of patients, such as accident victims who have terminal cancer or AIDS, on the grounds that they eventually will die anyway from those diseases and that emergency care for them would therefore be "futile."

II. Rehabilitation Act

. . . [T]he Rehabilitation Act prohibits discrimination against an "otherwise qualified" handicapped individual, solely by reason of his or her handicap, under any program or activity receiving federal financial assistance. Hospitals such as plaintiff that accept Medicare and Medicaid funding are subject to the Act. Baby K is a "handicapped" and "disabled" person within the meaning of the Rehabilitation Act. A "handicapped individual" under the Rehabilitation Act "includes an infant who is born with a congenital defect." *Bowen v. American Hospital Ass'n*.

Section 504's plain text spells out the necessary scope of inquiry: is Baby K otherwise qualified to receive ventilator treatment and is ventilator treatment being threatened with being denied because of an unjustified consideration of her anencephalic handicap? The Hospital has admitted that the sole reason it wishes to withhold ventilator treatment for Baby K over her mother's objections, is because of Baby K's anencephaly — her handicap and disability.

To evade this textual mandate, the Hospital relies on two cases which held that a hospital's decision not to override the desire of the parents of babies with congenital defects to withhold treatment did not violate section 504. Because the parents in *Johnson* and *University Hospital* consented to the withholding of treatment, the two cases are factually distinguishable from this case.[1]

When the Rehabilitation Act was passed in 1973, Congress intended that discrimination on the basis of a handicap be treated in the same manner that Title VI of the Civil Rights Act treats racial discrimination. This analogy to race dispels any ambiguity about the extent to which Baby K has statutory rights not to be discriminated against on the basis of her handicap. It also shatters the Hospital's contention that ventilator treatment should be withheld because Baby K's recurring breathing troubles are intrinsically related to her handicap. No such distinction would be permissible within the context of racial discrimination. . . .

III. Americans with Disabilities Act

[T]he Americans with Disabilities Act ("ADA") prohibits discrimination against disabled individuals by "public accommodations." A "disability" is "a physical or mental impairment that substantially limits one or more of the major life activities" of an individual. This includes any physiological disorder or condition affecting the neurological system, musculoskeletal system, or sense organs, among others. Anencephaly is a disability, because it affects the baby's neurological functioning, ability to walk, and ability to see or talk. "Public accommodation" is defined to include a "professional office of a health care provider, hospital, or other service establishment." The Hospital is a public accommodation under the ADA.

[1] Department of Health and Human Services guidelines addressing hospital reporting obligations under the Act if parents seek to withhold treatment from anencephalic infants are similarly inapplicable because of their silence regarding whether hospitals are allowed to terminate care in spite of a parent's wishes to the contrary. *See* 45 C.F.R. Pt. 84, App. C., para. (a)(5)(iii) (1992).

. . . In contrast to the Rehabilitation Act, the ADA does not require that a handicapped individual be "otherwise qualified" to receive the benefits of participation. Further, the ADA states that "[i]t shall be discriminatory to subject an individual or class of individuals on the basis of a disability . . . to denial of the opportunity of the individual or class to participate in or benefit from the goods, services, facilities, privileges, advantages, or accommodations of an entity."

The Hospital asks this court for authorization to deny the benefits of ventilator services to Baby K by reason of her anencephaly. The Hospital's claim is that it is "futile" to keep alive an anencephalic baby, even though the mother has requested such treatment. But the plain language of the ADA does not permit the denial of ventilator services that would keep alive an anencephalic baby when those life-saving services would otherwise be provided to a baby without disabilities at the parent's request. The Hospital's reasoning would lead to the denial of medical services to anencephalic babies as a class of disabled individuals. Such discrimination against a vulnerable population class is exactly what the American with Disabilities Act was enacted to prohibit. The Hospital would therefore violate the ADA if it were to withhold ventilator treatment from Baby K.

. . . .

VI. Constitutional and Common Law Issues

Baby K's parents disagree over whether or not to continue medical treatment for her. Mr. K and Baby K's guardian ad litem join the Hospital in seeking the right to override the wishes of Ms. H, Baby K's mother. Regardless of the questions of statutory interpretation presented in this case, Ms. H retains significant legal rights regarding her insistence that her daughter be kept alive with ventilator treatment. A parent has a constitutionally protected right to "bring up children" grounded in the Fourteenth Amendment's due process clause. *Meyer v. Nebraska*; *Pierce v. Society of Sisters*. Parents have the "primary role" in the "nurture and upbringing of their children." *Wisconsin v. Yoder*; *Prince v. Massachusetts*. Decisions for children can be based in the parent's free exercise of religion, protected by the First Amendment.

These constitutional principles extend to the right of parents to make medical treatment decisions for their minor children. Absent a finding of neglect or abuse, parents retain plenary authority to seek medical care for their children, even when the decision might impinge on a liberty interest of the child. Indeed, there is a "presumption that the parents act in the best interests of their child" because the "natural bonds of affection lead parents to act in the best interests of their children."

State law rights to make medical and surgical treatment decisions for a minor child are grounded in the common law and can also be inferred from state statutes. . . .

Based on Ms. H's "natural bonds of affection," *Parham*, and the relative noninvolvement of Baby K's biological father, the constitutional and common law presumption must be that Ms. H. is the appropriate decision maker. This presumption arises from the explicit guarantees of a right to life in the United States Constitution, Amendments V and XIV, and the Virginia Constitution.

. . . .

At the very least, the Hospital must establish by clear and convincing evidence that Ms. H's treatment decision should not be respected because it would constitute abuse or neglect of Baby K. This clear and convincing evidence standard has been adopted by numerous courts and was upheld by the Supreme Court in *Cruzan* in authorizing the withdrawal of life-supporting treatment from an incompetent patient. In this case, where the choice essentially devolves to a subjective determination as to the quality of Baby K's life, it cannot be said that the continuation of Baby K's life is so unreasonably harmful as to constitute child abuse or neglect.

NOTES AND QUESTIONS

1. The trial court decision in *Baby K* was affirmed by the Fourth Circuit Court of Appeals in 1994, 16 F.3d 590, on the ground that the EMTALA gives rise to a duty on the part of the hospital to provide respiratory treatment to Baby K. Judge Sprouse dissented, on the ground that the EMTALA was directed at hospital "dumping" of indigent or uninsured emergency patients. Such a suggestion, he said, was not involved. Moreover, the EMTALA was aimed at "emergency" conditions; Baby K's condition was anencephalic, not the subsidiary respiratory failure, and so was a *continuing* condition, not an emergency one. Do you agree?

2. Note that *Baby K* continued to live for a number of months after birth. Indeed, she was able to survive outside the hospital. And yet, the customary view, as discussed in *In re T.A.C.P.*, is that an anencephalic baby lasts only a brief period of time, perhaps only a few days. Since the customary wisdom seems flawed, should one reconsider one's willingness to define anencephalic babies as "dead"?

3. In addition to the Emergency Medical Treatment and Act of Labor Act, the plaintiffs relied on the Rehabilitation Act. Baby K was a "handicapped" and "disabled" person; as such, she had a protected interest under the Rehabilitation Act. The same, the trial court said, was true under the Americans With Disabilities Act. Neither of these rulings was upheld by the Court of Appeals. Should they have been? We will revisit the ADA in a number of later contexts, chiefly involving AIDS — which has been held to be a "disability" by the Supreme Court. *See Bragdon v. Abbott*, Ch. 3 *infra*.

4. Baby K's parents disagreed over whether or not to continue medical treatment for her. The court ruled in favor of the mother, based on "natural bonds of affection" and the relative noninvolvement of the biological father. It also relied upon the mother's religious conviction that all life is sacred. *Should* it have favored the mother? In the *Baby M* case and *Davis v. Davis*, the courts there found an interest to be protected in *both parents*. The same may be true in the *Casey* opinion, although it clearly favored women. Should that be true here as well?

5. Was the mother acting ethically in seeking to continue the existence of Baby K? How would [illegible] What sources would *you* look to?

IN RE T.A.C.P.
609 So. 2d 588 (Fla. 1992)

Kogan, Justice.

We have for review an order of the trial court certified by the Fourth District Court of Appeal as touching on a matter of great public importance requiring immediate resolution by this Court. We frame the issue as follows:

Is an anencephalic newborn considered "dead" for purposes of organ donation solely by reason of its congenital deformity? . . .

I. Facts

At or about the eighth month of pregnancy, the parents of the child T.A.C.P. were informed that she would be born with anencephaly. This is a birth defect invariably fatal,[1] in which the child typically is born with only a "brain stem" but otherwise lacks a human brain. In T.A.C.P.'s case, the back of the skull was entirely missing and the brain stem was exposed to the air, except for medical bandaging. The risk of infection to the brain stem was considered very high. Anencephalic infants sometimes can survive several days after birth because the brain stem has a limited capacity to maintain autonomic bodily functions such as breathing and heartbeat. This ability soon ceases, however, in the absence of regulation from the missing brain.

In this case, T.A.C.P. actually survived only a few days after birth. The medical evidence in the record shows that the child T.A.C.P. was incapable of developing any sort of cognitive process, may have been unable to feel pain or experience sensation due to the absence of the upper brain,[2] and at least for part of the time was placed on a mechanical ventilator to assist her breathing. At the time of the hearing below, however, the child was breathing unaided, although she died soon thereafter.

On the advice of physicians, the parents continued the pregnancy to term and agreed that the mother would undergo caesarean section during birth. The parents agreed to the caesarean procedure with the express hope that the infant's organs would be less damaged and could be used for transplant in other sick children. Although T.A.C.P. had no hope of life herself, the parents both testified in court that they wanted to use this opportunity to give life to others. However, when the parents requested that T.A.C.P. be declared legally dead for this purpose, her health care providers refused out of concern that they thereby might incur civil or criminal liability.

---

[1] We are mindful that some parties argue that anencephaly is not invariably fatal and that some anencephalics actually live for many years. We find that this argument arises from a misperception about the nature of anencephaly as it is defined by a consensus in the medical community. The living children described by the parties actually are not anencephalic, because they do not meet the definitive medical criteria. These medical criteria are discussed below.

[2] There was some dispute about this point. Our resolution of the case, however, renders the dispute moot.

. . . .

II. The Medical Nature of Anencephaly

Although appellate courts appear never to have confronted the issue, there already is an impressive body of published medical scholarship on anencephaly. From our review of this material, we find that anencephaly is a variable but fairly well defined medical condition. Experts in the field have written that anencephaly is the most common severe birth defect of the central nervous system seen in the United States, although it apparently has existed throughout human history.

A statement by the Medical Task Force on Anencephaly ("Task Force") printed in the New England Journal of Medicine[3] generally described "anencephaly" as "a congenital absence of major portions of the brain, skull, and scalp, with its genesis in the first month of gestation." The large opening in the skull accompanied by the absence or severe congenital disruption of the cerebral hemispheres is the characteristic feature of the condition.

. . . .

After the advent of new transplant methods in the past few decades, anencephalic infants have successfully been used as a source of organs for donation. However, the Task Force was able to identify only twelve successful transplants using anencephalic organs by 1990. Transplants were most successful when the anencephalic immediately was placed on life support and its organs used as soon as possible, without regard to the existence of brain-stem activity. However, this only accounted for a total of four reported transplants.

There appears to be general agreement that anencephalics usually have ceased to be suitable organ donors by the time they meet all the criteria for "whole brain death," i.e., the complete absence of brain-stem function. . . .

III. Legal Definitions of "Death" & "Life"

As the parties and *amici* have argued, the common law in some American jurisdictions recognized a cardiopulmonary definition of "death": A human being was not considered dead until breathing and heartbeat had stopped entirely, without possibility of resuscitation.

. . . .

In light of the inadequacies of a cardiopulmonary definition of "death," a number of jurisdictions began altering their laws in an attempt to address the medical community's changing conceptions of the point in time at which life ceases. An effort was made to synthesize many of the new concerns into a Uniform Determination of Death Act issued by the National Conference of Commissioners on Uniform State Laws. The uniform statute states:

> An individual who has sustained either (1) irreversible cessation of circulatory and respiratory functions, or (2) irreversible cessation of

[3] The statement also was approved by the American Academy of Pediatrics, the American Academy of Neurology, the American College of Obstetricians and Gynecologists, the American Neurological Association, and the Child Neurology Society.

> all functions of the entire brain, including the brain stem, is dead. A [illegible] medical standards.

Unif. Determination of Death Act § 1, 12 U.L.A. 340 (Supp. 1991). Thus, the uniform act both codified the earlier common law standard and extended it to deal with the specific problem of "whole brain death." While some American jurisdictions appear to have adopted substantially the same language, Florida is not among these.

Indeed, Florida appears to have struck out on its own. The statute cited as controlling by the trial court does not actually address itself to the problem of anencephalic infants, nor indeed to any situation other than patients actually being sustained by artificial life support. The statute provides:

> For legal and medical purposes, where respiratory and circulatory functions are maintained by artificial means of support so as to preclude a determination that these functions have ceased, the occurrence of death may be determined where there is the irreversible cessation of the functioning of the entire brain, including the brain stem, determined in accordance with this section.

A later subsection goes on to declare:

> Except for a diagnosis of brain death, the standard set forth in this section is not the exclusive standard for determining death or for the withdrawal of life-support systems.

This language is highly significant for two reasons.

First, the statute does not purport to codify the common law standard applied in some other jurisdictions, as does the uniform act. The use of the permissive word "may" in the statute in tandem with the savings clause of section 382.009(4) buttresses the conclusion that the legislature envisioned other ways of defining "death." Second, the statutory framers clearly did not intend to apply the statute's language to the anencephalic infant not being kept alive by life support. To the contrary, the framers expressly limited the statute to that situation in which "respiratory and circulatory functions are maintained by artificial means of support."

There are a few Florida authorities that have addressed the definitions of "life" and "death" in somewhat analogous though factually distinguishable contexts. Florida's Vital Statistics Act, for example, defines "live birth" as the complete expulsion or extraction of a product of human conception from its mother, irrespective of the duration of pregnancy, which, after such expulsion, breathes or shows any other evidence of life such as beating of the heart, pulsation of the umbilical cord, and definite movement of the voluntary muscles, whether or not the umbilical cord has been cut or the placenta is attached.

Conversely, "fetal death" is defined as death prior to the complete expulsion or extraction of a product of human conception from its mother if the 20th week of gestation has been reached and the death is indicated by the fact that after such expulsion or extraction the fetus does not breathe or show any other evidence of life such as beating of the heart, pulsation of the umbilical cord, or definite movement of voluntary muscles.

From these definitions, it is clear that T.A.C.P. was a "live birth" and not a "fetal death," at least for purposes of the collection of vital statistics in Florida. These definitions obviously are inapplicable to the issues at hand today, but they do shed some light on the Florida legislature's thoughts regarding a definition of "life" and "death."

Similarly, an analogous (if distinguishable) problem has arisen in Florida tort law. In cases alleging wrongful death, our courts have held that fetuses are not "persons" and are not "born alive" until they acquire an existence separate and independent from the mother. We believe the weight of the evidence supports the conclusion that T.A.C.P. was "alive" in this sense because she was separated from the womb, and was capable of breathing and maintaining a heartbeat independently of her mother's body for some duration of time thereafter. Once again, however, this conclusion arises from law that is only analogous and is not dispositive of the issue at hand.

We also note that the 1988 Florida Legislature considered a bill that would have defined "death" to include anencephaly. The bill died in committee. While the failure of legislation in committee does not establish legislative intent, it nevertheless supports the conclusion that as recently as 1988 no consensus existed among Florida's lawmakers regarding the issue we confront today.

The parties have cited to no authorities directly dealing with the question of whether anencephalics are "alive" or "dead." Our own research has disclosed no other federal or Florida law or precedent arguably on point or applicable by analogy. We thus are led to the conclusion that no legal authority binding upon this Court has decided whether an anencephalic child is alive for purposes of organ donation. In the absence of applicable legal authority, this Court must weigh and consider the public policy considerations at stake here.

IV. Common Law & Policy

Initially, we must start by recognizing that section 382.009, Florida Statutes (1991), provides a method for determining death in those cases in which a person's respiratory and circulatory functions are maintained artificially. Likewise, we agree that a cardiopulmonary definition of death must be accepted in Florida as a matter of our common law, applicable whenever section 382.009 does not govern. Thus, if cardiopulmonary function is not being maintained artificially as stated in section 382.009, a person is dead who has sustained irreversible cessation of circulatory and respiratory functions as determined in accordance with accepted medical standards. We have found no credible authority arguing that this definition is inconsistent with the existence of death, and we therefore need not labor the point further.

The question remaining is whether there is good reason in public policy for this Court to create an additional common law standard applicable to anencephalics. Alterations of the common law, while rarely entertained or allowed, are within this Court's prerogative. However, the rule we follow is that the common law will not be altered or expanded unless demanded by public [illegible] example, that our adoption of the cardiopulmonary definition of death today is required by public necessity and, in any event, merely formalizes what has been the common practice in this state for well over a century.

Such is not the case with petitioners' request. Our review of the medical, ethical, and legal literature on anencephaly discloses absolutely no consensus that public necessity or fundamental rights will be better served by granting this request.

We are not persuaded that a public necessity exists to justify this action, in light of the other factors in this case — although we acknowledge much ambivalence about this particular question. We have been deeply touched by the altruism and unquestioned motives of the parents of T.A.C.P. The parents have shown great humanity, compassion, and concern for others. The problem we as a Court must face, however, is that the medical literature shows unresolved controversy over the extent to which anencephalic organs can or should be used in transplants.

There is an unquestioned need for transplantable infant organs. Yet some medical commentators suggest that the organs of anencephalics are seldom usable, for a variety of reasons, and that so few organ transplants will be possible from anencephalics as to render the enterprise questionable in light of the ethical problems at stake — even if legal restrictions were lifted.

Others note that prenatal screening now is substantially reducing the number of anencephalics born each year in the United States and that, consequently, anencephalics are unlikely to be a significant source of organs as time passes. And still others have frankly acknowledged that there is no consensus and that redefinition of death in this context should await the emergence of a consensus.

A presidential commission in 1981 urged strict adherence to the Uniform Determination of Death Act's definition, which would preclude equating anencephaly with death. . . .

Some legal commentators have argued that treating anencephalics as dead [illegible] regard to all other persons who lack cognition for whatever reason. Others have quoted physicians involved in infant-organ transplants as stating, "[T]he slippery slope is real," because some physicians have proposed transplants from infants with defects less severe than anencephaly.

We express no opinion today about who is right and who is wrong on these issues — if any "right" or "wrong" can be found here. The salient point is that no consensus exists as to: (a) the utility of organ transplants of the type at issue here; (b) the ethical issues involved; or (c) the legal and constitutional problems implicated.

. . . .

NOTES AND QUESTIONS

1. For an extensive discussion of *In Re T.A.C.P.* and the issues surrounding this case, see J. Steven Justice, *Personhood and Death — The Proper*

Treatment of Anencephalic Organ Donors Under the Law: In Re T.A.C.P., 62 U. Cin. L. Rev. 1227 (Winter, 1994).

2. It seems clear that the parents of the little girl could have aborted the pregnancy rather than have her born alive. Thus, the only reason for bringing this life into being was for it to serve as an organ donor. Was this an ethical choice? Would Rawls view this as sacrificing one "person's" life for another? What would be the view of the Council of Europe?

3. What of the role of the doctors in opposing the parents? On whose behalf were they acting? Was the conduct ethical? Suppose it breached an understanding reached *prior* to birth?

4. Could the Court have reached an opposite result? *Should* it have? Should the Florida definition of death be amended to permit what the parents here desired?

5. Is what the parents proposed here similar to the sacrificing of one being for another, opposed by the dissent in *Strunk v. Strunk* and by Rawls in the opening essay?

6. For an excellent article, see David Randolph Smith, *Legal Recognition Of Neocortical Death*, 71 Cornell L. Rev. 850 (1986); and see S. Bard, *The Diagnosis Is Anencephaly and the Parents Ask About Organ Donation: Now What? A Guide for Hospital Counsel and Ethics Committees*, 21 W. New Eng. L. Rev. 49 (1999).

BRITELL v. UNITED STATES

372 F.3d 1370 (1st Cir. 2004)

Michel, Circuit Judge.

Defendant-Appellant United States ("the government") appeals from the May 29, 2002 Order of the United States District Court for the District of Massachusetts granting summary judgment to Plaintiff-Appellee Maureen M. Britell ("Britell") in this Little Tucker Act case seeking reimbursement for the cost of an abortion. The district court ruled that 10 U.S.C. § 1093(a) violated the Equal Protection Clause of the Fifth Amendment to the United States Constitution under a rational-basis review because its ban on funding abortions could not be justified on the basis of the state's interest in "potential human life" because such an interest was not relevant as to anencephalic fetuses. *Britell v. United States*, 204 F. Supp. 2d 182, 192–93 (D. Mass. 2002) (*"Britell II"*). Because we hold that under Supreme Court precedent section 1093(a)'s funding ban is rationally related to the state's legitimate interest in potential human life, even in cases of anencephaly, section 1093(a) does not violate the *Equal Protection Clause* under a rational-basis review, and so we must reverse.

BACKGROUND

In January 1994, Britell and her husband, a Captain in the Air National Guard, were expecting their second child. A routine checkup about twenty weeks into her pregnancy revealed that Britell's fetus suffered from a rare condition called anencephaly;[1] the diagnosis of [illegible] by a second ultrasound. Faced with this horrific diagnosis, and the certain death of the fetus or newborn, the Britells consulted their family, doctors, grief counselors, psychiatrists, and their parish priest, all of whom agreed that the Britells should abort the fetus. On February 18, 1994, Britell had an abortion at the New England Medical Center — after thirteen hours of physically and emotionally painful labor, the fetus died during delivery. The diagnosis of anencephaly was confirmed.

Anencephaly also poses health risks to the mother. Towards the end of the pregnancy, women carrying anencephalic fetuses produce excessive amniotic fluid, increasing the risk of placental abruption (premature separation of the placenta from the uterine wall), which can, in turn, cause abnormally accelerated blood clotting and simultaneous uncontrolled bleeding (disseminated intravascular coagulopathy), placing the mother at grave risk. Moreover, because anencephalic fetuses have abnormally small adrenal glands (which play a critical role in triggering labor), the mothers of anencephalic fetuses must often have delivery induced or face the many health risks associated with late-term pregnancy.

Beyond these physical risks, the emotional toll of anencephaly is undeniable. These mothers are faced with the horrifying knowledge that the fetus they are carrying will die, never having achieved consciousness.

After the abortion, the New England Medical Center sought payment for its services from Britell's insurer, the Civilian Health and Medical Program ("CHAMPUS"). In fulfilling its statutory mandate to "provide an improved and uniform program of medical and dental care for members . . . of [the uniformed] services, and their dependents," 10 U.S.C. § 1071 (2000), CHAMPUS funds all "medically necessary services and supplies associated with maternity care." 32 C.F.R. § 199.4(e)(16)(i) (2003). In the present case, however, CHAMPUS denied the claim based on 10 U.S.C. § 1093(a) and corresponding regulations. *Britell II,* 204 F. Supp. 2d at 186. Section 1093(a) provides in relevant part that "funds available to the Department of Defense may not be used to perform abortions except where the life of the mother would be endangered if the fetus is carried to term." 10 U.S.C. § 1093(a) (2000). The CHAMPUS regulations specifically provide that abortions performed in the case of "fetal abnormalities" including anencephaly are not covered by CHAMPUS. 32 C.F.R. § 199.4(e)(2)(2003).

Because the Supreme Court had previously held, in *Harris v. McRae,* 448 U.S. 297 (1980), that the language of the *Hyde Amendment* (language in the Medicaid statute prohibiting the use of federal funds to reimburse the cost of abortions "except where the life of the mother would be endangered if the

[1] Anencephaly is a neural tube defect in which the fetus develops without forebrain, cerebellum, or cranium. *Britell II*, 204 F. Supp. 2d at 185. In place of a brain, the fetus develops with a gelatinous tissue covering the crown of the head. The condition is fatal: most anencephalic fetuses die during pregnancy or birth, and the few (thirty-two percent) of anencephalic fetuses that are carried to term can survive for up to two months with continuous life support and intensive care. Without life support and intensive care, fewer than two percent of anencephalic fetuses carried to term will survive longer than seven days. Even those that survive, with or without intensive care and life support, will never gain consciousness because they possess no cerebrum.

fetus were carried to term") was facially constitutional under the *Equal Protection Clause*, Britell's challenge was narrow in scope. Britell argued that section 1093(a) was only unconstitutional "as applied" to her and similarly-situated pregnant women because the ban on CHAMPUS funding for abortions in cases of anencephaly does not further any of the legitimate state interests identified in *McRae* as supporting the facial constitutionality of congressional abortion funding restrictions. The government responded by arguing that there is no such thing as an "as applied" equal protection challenge to a statute whose facial constitutionality has been sustained, and that, in any event, the denial of funding in Britell's case passes muster under rational basis review because it encourages childbirth and is thus rationally related to the legitimate state interest in potential human life.

DISCUSSION

On appeal, the parties' arguments are essentially identical to those made before the district court. The government argues that Britell does not have a valid as-applied challenge and that *McRae* thus controls. Further, to the extent Britell's as-applied challenge is valid, the government argues that section 1093(a) is constitutional because the statute is rationally related to legitimate state interests, including the protection and promotion of potential human life. Britell, on the other hand, argues that the district court correctly held that her challenge is a valid as-applied challenge, and that as applied to her, section 1093(a) is unconstitutional because the distinction between medically necessary services and what she argues are medically necessary abortions in cases of anencephaly is not rationally related to any legitimate state interest.

. . . .

II.

With regard to the merits of Britell's appeal, the parties argue two core issues on appeal: (1) does the decision in *McRae*, upholding the facial validity of an abortion funding restriction identical to the one here, preclude Britell's as-applied challenge; and (2) if *McRae* does not preclude Britell's as-applied challenge, is the challenged statutory provision rationally related to a legitimate governmental interest? We address these issues in turn.

A.

As to the first issue — whether Britell has a valid as-applied challenge to section 1093(a) despite the ruling of *McRae* — we find that this court need not reach the issue because, even if Britell has a valid as-applied challenge, Britell's equal protection challenge fails because section 1093(a) passes a rational basis review. Accordingly, we move directly to the second, outcome-determinative issue.

B.

"The guarantee of equal protection under the *Fifth Amendment* is not a source of substantive rights or liberties, but rather a right to be free from invidious discrimination in statutory classifications and other governmental activity. It is well settled that where a statutory classification does not itself impinge on a right or liberty protected by the Constitution, the validity of classification must be sustained unless 'the classification rests on grounds wholly irrelevant to the achievement of [any legitimate governmental] objective.' " *McRae,* 448 U.S. at 322 (*quoting McGowan v. Maryland*, 366 U.S. 420, 425 (1961)). The presumption of constitutional validity does not exist, however, where the statutory classification is predicated on "suspect" criteria, *e.g.*, race.

In *McRae*, the Supreme Court determined that the Hyde Amendment, restricting Medicaid funding to abortions where the life of the mother is at risk, "places no governmental obstacle in the path of a woman who chooses to terminate her pregnancy," and does not "impinge[] on the constitutional protected freedom of choice recognized in Wade" because every woman has the same range of choice in deciding whether to obtain an abortion. The Supreme Court also noted that the language of the Hyde Amendment "is not predicated on a constitutionally suspect classification" because the Supreme Court had "held repeatedly that poverty, standing alone is not a suspect classification." In light of the uniformity between the language of the Hyde Amendment and that in section 1093(a), there can be no doubt that the classification drawn in section 1093(a) neither impinges on a fundamental right guaranteed by the Constitution nor is predicated on a suspect classification.

Accordingly, the remaining question is whether section 1093(a) is "rationally related to a legitimate governmental objective." The government suggests several possible legitimate governmental objectives in justification of section 1093(a): (1) the protection and promotion of potential human life; (2) the creation of a bright-line rule that no birth defect justifies the use of federal funds for abortion; and (3) the accommodation of taxpayers who are strongly and sincerely opposed to abortion by not expending taxpayer funds on abortion. Because we find that section 1093(a) is rationally related to the first of these proffered interests, we need not address the other two suggested governmental interests.[7]

In *McRae*, the Supreme Court found a rational relationship between the Hyde Amendment and the state's interest in protecting potential human life. The Supreme Court's analysis of the rational relationship bears repeating.

The remaining question then is whether the Hyde Amendment is rationally related to a legitimate governmental objective. It is the Government's position that the Hyde Amendment bears a rational relationship to its legitimate interest in protecting the potential life of the fetus. We agree.

In [*Roe v.*] *Wade*, the Court recognized that the State has an "important and legitimate interest in protecting the potentiality of human life." That interest was found to exist throughout a pregnancy, "growing in substantiality as the woman approaches term." Moreover, in *Maher* [*v. Roe*], the Court held

[7] Nor need we address the government's argument that congressional funding determinations should be given even greater deference than non-funding determinations reviewed under a rational basis review.

that Connecticut's decision to fund the costs associated with childbirth but not those associated with nontherapeutic abortions was a rational means of advancing the legitimate state interest in protecting potential life by encouraging childbirth.

It follows that the Hyde Amendment, by encouraging childbirth except in the most urgent circumstances, is rationally related to the legitimate governmental objective of protecting potential life. By subsidizing the medical expenses of indigent women who carry their pregnancies to term while not subsidizing the comparable expenses of women who undergo abortions (except those whose lives are threatened), Congress has established incentives that make childbirth a more attractive alternative than abortion for persons eligible for Medicaid. These incentives bear a direct relationship to the legitimate congressional interest in protecting potential life. Nor is it irrational that Congress has authorized federal reimbursement for medically necessary services generally, but not for certain medically necessary abortions. Abortion is inherently different from other medical procedures, because no other procedure involves the purposeful termination of a potential life.

Recognizing, as she must, the long line of precedent supporting the government's argument that the state has a legitimate governmental interest in protecting potential human life, Britell argues that there is no legitimate governmental interest in protecting an anencephalic fetus because the fetus will never gain consciousness. Accordingly, Britell seeks a reading of the statute to require an additional exception to the abortion-funding ban in cases of anencephaly. *Britell I*, 150 F. Supp. 2d at 223 ("Judgment in Britell's favor would simply require that this Court (1) excise the parenthetical '(e.g., anencephalic)' from 32 C.F.R. § 199.4(e)(2), and (2) declare that 10 U.S.C. § 1093(a) may not be interpreted to proscribe funding for abortions in cases of fetal anencephaly."). And indeed, the district court so held, relying on *Karlin v. Foust, 188* F.3d 446 (7th Cir. 1999), which it characterized as recognizing that "where a fetus suffers from a condition that guarantees both imminent death and no hope of ever functioning or attaining consciousness, it makes little sense to maintain that measures aimed at encouraging women to carry to term serve the interest of protecting 'potential life.' " *Britell II,* 204 F. Supp. 2d at 193.

It is here that we must disagree with both the district court and *Britell.* As an initial matter, it is worth noting that *Karlin* is neither binding upon this court nor factually analogous to the present case. *Karlin* involved a challenge to an informed consent law under an "undue burden" analysis. In a single footnote, the Seventh Circuit noted that the defendants did not contest that the informational requirements of the informed consent law (requiring that women seeking an abortion be informed of the father's obligations concerning child assistance) would not apply in cases of lethal fetal anomalies, but nevertheless went on to reject such informational requirements on the ground that they did not further a legitimate state interest. The *Karlin* court explained that it viewed the term "lethal anomaly" to signal that "the child will die at birth," *Karlin,* 188 F.3d at 489 n.16; nowhere did the *Karlin* court address anencephaly specifically. The distinction is important because, despite both the district court's and Britell's intimations to the contrary, an anencephalic fetus does not necessarily die at birth. Thus, even if the *Karlin* court is correct that the [illegible] have a legitimate interest in potential human life in cases of "lethal anomaly," it does not follow that anencephaly [illegible] a condition. More importantly, however, we reject both the district court's and Britell's reliance upon *Karlin* because we find it inconsistent with Supreme Court precedent as discussed below.

Supreme Court precedent makes clear that, from the very start of the pregnancy, there is a legitimate state interest in the potential human life. [*Planned Parenthood v.*] *Casey*, 505 U.S. at 846 ("The State has legitimate interests from the outset of the pregnancy in protecting the health of the woman and the life of the fetus that may become a child. . . . Even in the earliest stages of pregnancy, the State may enact rules and regulations designed to encourage her to know that there are philosophic and social arguments of great weight that can be brought to bear in favor of continuing the pregnancy to full term . . . ."); *Webster* [*v. Reproductive Health Services*], 492 U.S. at 519 ("We do not see why the State's interest in protecting potential human life should come into existence only at the point of viability, and that there should therefore be a rigid line allowing state regulation after viability, but prohibiting it before viability."); *Beal* [*v. Doe*], 432 U.S. at 446 (noting in the context of an abortion funding case that "it [potential human life] is a significant state interest existing throughout the course of the woman's pregnancy"). The state has a legitimate interest in potential human life before anyone knows whether the fetus will be carried to term, or even reach viability, and this legitimate state interest exists even where the fetus is diagnosed with an abnormality or birth defect. Indeed, the Supreme Court has expressly noted that states have an "'unqualified interest in the preservation of human life' . . . regardless of physical or mental condition." *Washington v. Glucksberg,* 521 U.S. 702, 728–29 (1997) (*quoting Cruzan v. Director, Mo. Dep't of Health*, 497 U.S. 261, 282 (1990)).

For us to hold, as Britell urges, that in some circumstances a birth defect or fetal abnormality is so severe as to remove the state's interest in potential human life would require this court to engage in line-drawing of the most non-judicial and daunting nature. This we will not do. We agree with the government's argument that the type of line-drawing urged by Britell can create a slippery slope. It is not the role of the courts to draw lines as to which fetal abnormalities or birth defects are so severe as to negate the state's otherwise legitimate interest in the fetus' potential life. The district court opined that there was no slippery slope with regard to anencephaly because "anencephaly is a very distinctive physical condition with not just life-threatening, but fundamentally life-incompatible consequences for the fetus." *Britell II*, 204 F. Supp. 2d at 198 (emphasis in original). We cannot agree. No reason has been presented, nor do we see one, to explain why consciousness (or extended life span) is the lynchpin of potential human life. Indeed, it could reasonably be argued that other birth defects or abnormalities, while different in their effects on the fetus, are also so severe as to negate the state's interest in potential human life. If that is the case, courts will be forced to determine on a condition-by-condition or abnormality-by-abnormality basis whether a fetus' condition is so severe as to eliminate the state's interest. Such line-drawing is something for which courts are ill-equipped, and is inconsistent with existing Supreme Court jurisprudence on what constitutes a "potential human life."

Without question, Congress could have drafted the abortion-funding ban of section 1093(a) differently, perhaps allowing exceptions in cases of severe birth defects or fetal abnormalities or even in cases where the health of the mother is at risk. Congress chose not to draw those lines, and we must respect that decision. Under rational basis review, "the constitutionality of state classifications . . . cannot be determined on a person-by-person basis." *Kimel v. Fla. Bd. of Regents*, 528 U.S. 62, 85–86, 145 L. Ed. 2d 522, 120 S. Ct. 631 (2000). Indeed, congressional line-drawing "inevitably requires that some persons who have an almost equally strong claim to favored treatment be placed on different sides of the line," such that there will almost certainly be "some harsh and apparently arbitrary consequences." *Mathews v. Diaz*, 426 U.S. 67, 83–84, 85–86 (1976). Put simply, "perfection in making the necessary classifications is neither possible nor necessary." *Mass. Bd. of Retirement v. Murgia*, 427 U.S. 307, 314 (1976). And so it is that, even if Britell and the district court are correct that the funding ban of section 1093(a) is not perfect in that it does not allow for an exception in cases of anencephaly, Britell and the district court are incorrect that the statute fails under rational basis review. Supreme Court precedent makes clear that the state has a legitimate interest in any potential human life, even that of an anencephalic fetus. As much as in *McRae*, the language of *section 1093(a)* is rationally related to this state interest, and therefore section 1093(a) passes equal protection muster.

CONCLUSION

Although this court, and surely all humankind, feels great sympathy for any parent faced with the truly horrifying diagnosis of anencephaly, we find that the law is clear: the state has a legitimate interest in potential human life from the outset of a woman's pregnancy, regardless of a diagnosis of a severe birth defect or fetal abnormality. Because, by analogy to *McRae,* the language of section 1093(a) is rationally related to this legitimate state interest, section 1093(a), just as the Hyde Amendment to Medicaid, passes rational basis review. The language of the two bans on funding is virtually identical, and the differences, for constitutional rational basis review, between Medicaid and CHAMPUS are insignificant. Accordingly, the district court's entry of judgment for Britell, must be

Reversed.

NOTES AND QUESTIONS

1. The *Britell* case is yet another instance of anencephaly, perplexing the ethical community as to its obligation with respect to living (or as yet unborn) entities which cannot develop into "persons" or have a future or life we would recognize as worth living. Much the same conundrum is posed by the next case, *In Re A*, involving conjoined or "Siamese" twins.
2. Here, government has explicitly chosen to fund some abortions, where there is danger to the mother's life, but not others, including abortions of anencephalic children. It might have chosen altogether not to fund *any* abortions, as noted in *Harris v. McRae*. Why then does the Court

even need to inquire as to line drawing at all? And how is its analysis advanced by the principle of "as applied" versus "facial invalidity"?

3. Does it matter, *should* it matter, that the government program here, CHAMPUS, is in a sense *earned* by service people, unlike Medicaid, the welfare program in *Harris v. McRae*?

4. In more fundamental terms, how *should* one characterize an anencephalic fetus? If, as the Britells argue, it is difficult to characterize it as "potential life," why accord the full protections of "life" upon birth? Or is it not treated as such? Isn't the whole core of the Court's opinion the "slippery slope" argument — that saying an anencephalic has no life will require addressing other conditions? But so what? Isn't line drawing what courts are paid to do, when lines are possible?

5. Does refusal of plaintiff's insurance to pay for a (medically necessary) abortion impinge on the constitutionally protected freedom of choice recognized in *Roe v. Wade*? Suppose the Britells had been so poor, yet in the armed services, that they couldn't get an abortion?

6. And are you persuaded by the Court's effort to distinguish or reject *Karlin*?

PROBLEM 1-18 — Siamese Twins

In 1993, in Florida, Florence Williams gave birth to Siamese twins. They were both baptized in Mrs. Williams' church, and given the names Frederick Stephen and Winona Anne. They are joined at the thorax and abdomen. They share a single heart and set of lungs; there is one liver. It is a medical certainty that they cannot both survive. If one is separated and sacrificed to save the other, there is still less than a 50% chance of survival. If one survives, the surgery alone will cost $100,000 and, as the child grows, he or she will be limited by massive disabilities and attendant expense.

Mrs. Williams insists that they must both live or die together; separating one from the vital organs would be murder. Who makes the decision, and if it is to separate the children, which shall be chosen to survive? Does Mr. Williams have a say — although not currently married to the mother — and what of siblings and grandparents? Does the gender of the children matter? Does it matter which has the liver? Does it matter that one is blind and the other deaf? Does it matter whether Mrs. Williams is a welfare, Medicaid patient? Or that the Williams' insurance carrier considers separation surgery to be "experimental" and therefore not a "covered" (i.e., insurance-reimbursable) service? (*See infra,* § 4.04[2].)

Babies joined at birth may often be severed successfully. Sometimes not. And if left together, one may die, or both be condemned to marginal lives.

Who decides who lives and who dies? And how? For a lengthy discussion leading to the severing of conjoined twins, one of whom died as a result, see *In Re A (Children) (Conjoined Twins: Medical Treatment)* No. 1, [2000] H.R.L.R. 721, 2000 WL 1274054.

[c] Brain Death: Persistent Vegetative State

Unlike anencephalics, many fully functioning adults lapse into a condition of near-death, through strokes, or seizures, or trauma. If in a persistent vegetative state, they may breathe independently, but they must be maintained through artificial nutrition and hydration. Can they — should they — be allowed to die? When? Are they already dead? Who decides?

IN THE MATTER OF KAREN QUINLAN, AN ALLEGED INCOMPETENT

355 A.2d 647 (N.J. 1976)

Opinion by: **Hughes**

The central figure in this tragic case is Karen Ann Quinlan, a New Jersey resident. At the age of 22, she lies in a debilitated and allegedly moribund state at Saint Clare's Hospital in Denville, New Jersey. The litigation has to do, in final analysis, with her life, — its continuance or cessation, — and the responsibilities, rights and duties, with regard to any fateful decision concerning it, of her family, her guardian, her doctors, the hospital, the State through its law enforcement authorities, and finally the courts of justice.

. . . .

The matter is of transcendent importance, involving questions related to the definition and existence of death; the prolongation of life through artificial means developed by medical technology undreamed of in past generations of the practice of the healing arts; the impact of such durationally indeterminate and artificial life prolongation on the rights of the incompetent, her family and society in general; the bearing of constitutional right and the scope of judicial responsibility, as to the appropriate response of an equity court of justice to the extraordinary prayer for relief of the plaintiff. Involved as well is the right of the plaintiff, Joseph Quinlan, to guardianship of the person of his daughter.

. . . .

The Factual Base

. . . .

On the night of April 15, 1975, for reasons still unclear, Karen Quinlan ceased breathing for at least two 15 minute periods. She received some ineffectual mouth-to-mouth resuscitation from friends. She was taken by ambulance to Newton Memorial Hospital. There she had a temperature of 100 degrees, her pupils were unreactive and she was unresponsive even to deep pain. The history at the time of her admission to that hospital was essentially incomplete and uninformative.

Three days later, Dr. Morse examined Karen at the request of the Newton admitting physician, Dr. McGee. He found her comatose with evidence of decortication, a condition relating to derangement of the cortex of the brain causing a physical posture in which the upper extremities are flexed and the lower extremities are extended. She required a respirator to assist her breathing. When she was later transferred to Saint Clare's Hospital she was still unconscious, still on a respirator and a tracheotomy had been performed. On her arrival Dr. Morse conducted extensive and detailed examinations. An electroencephalogram (EEG) measuring electrical rhythm of the brain was performed and Dr. Morse characterized the result as "abnormal but it showed some activity and was consistent with her clinical state." Other significant neurological tests, including a brain scan, an angiogram, and a lumbar puncture were normal in result. Dr. Morse testified that Karen has been in a state of coma, lack of consciousness, since he began treating her. He explained that there are basically two types of coma, sleep-like unresponsiveness and awake unresponsiveness. Karen was originally in a sleep-like unresponsive condition but soon developed "sleep-wake" cycles, apparently a normal improvement for comatose patients occurring within three to four weeks. In the awake cycle she blinks, cries out and does things of that sort but is still totally unaware of anyone or anything around her.

Dr. Morse and other expert physicians who examined her characterized Karen as being in a "chronic persistent vegetative state." Dr. Fred Plum, one of such expert witnesses, defined this as a "subject who remains with the capacity to maintain the vegetative parts of neurological function but who . . . no longer has any cognitive function."

Dr. Morse, as well as the several other medical and neurological experts who testified in this case, believed with certainty that Karen Quinlan is not "brain dead." They identified the Ad Hoc Committee of Harvard Medical School report (*infra*) as the ordinary medical standard for determining brain death, and all of them were satisfied that Karen met none of the criteria specified in that report and was therefore not "brain dead" within its contemplation.

. . . .

Because Karen's neurological condition affects her respiratory ability (the respiratory system being a brain stem function) she requires a respirator to assist her breathing. From the time of her admission to Saint Clare's Hospital, Karen has been assisted by an MA-1 respirator, a sophisticated machine which delivers a given volume of air at a certain rate and periodically provides a "sigh" volume, a relatively large measured volume of air designed to purge the lungs of secretions. Attempts to "wean" her from the respirator were unsuccessful and have been abandoned.

. . . .

The further medical consensus was that Karen in addition to being comatose is in a chronic and persistent "vegetative" state, having no awareness of anything or anyone around her and existing at a primitive reflex level. Although she does have some brain stem function (ineffective for respiration) and has other reactions one normally associates with being alive, such as moving, reacting to light, sound and noxious stimuli, blinking her eyes, and the like, the quality of her feeling impulses is unknown. She grimaces, makes stereotyped cries and sounds and has chewing motions. Her blood pressure is normal.

. . . .

Karen is described as emaciated, having suffered a weight loss of at least 40 pounds, and undergoing a continuing deteriorative process. Her posture is described as fetal-like and grotesque; there is extreme flexion-rigidity of the arms, legs and related muscles and her joints are severely rigid and deformed.

. . . .

Developments in medical technology have obfuscated the use of the traditional definition of death. Efforts have been made to define irreversible coma as a new criterion for death, such as by the 1968 report of the Ad Hoc Committee of the Harvard Medical School (the Committee comprising ten physicians, an historian, a lawyer and a theologian). . . .

The Ad Hoc standards, carefully delineated, included absence of response to pain or other stimuli, pupillary reflexes, corneal, pharyngeal and other reflexes, blood pressure, spontaneous respiration, as well as "flat" or isoelectric electro-encephalograms and the like, with all tests repeated "at least 24 hours later with no change." . . .

But, as indicated, it was the consensus of medical testimony in the instant case that Karen, for all her disability, met none of these criteria, nor indeed any comparable criteria in the medical world and representing, as does the Ad Hoc Committee report, according to the testimony in this case, prevailing and accepted medical standards.

We have adverted to the "brain death" concept and Karen's disassociation with any of its criteria, to emphasize the basis of the medical decision made by Dr. Morse. When plaintiff and his family, finally reconciled to the certainty of Karen's impending death, requested the withdrawal of life support mechanisms, he demurred. . . .

. . . The character and general suitability of Joseph Quinlan as guardian for his daughter, in ordinary circumstances, could not be doubted. The record bespeaks the high degree of familial love which pervaded the home of Joseph Quinlan and reached out fully to embrace Karen, although she was living elsewhere at the time of her collapse. The proofs showed him to be deeply religious, imbued with a morality so sensitive that months of tortured indecision preceded his belated conclusion (despite earlier moral judgments reached by the other family members, but unexpressed to him in order not to influence him) to seek the termination of life-supportive measures sustaining Karen. . . .

To confirm the moral rightness of the decision he was about to make he consulted with his parish priest and later with the Catholic chaplain of Saint Clare's Hospital. He would not, he testified, have sought termination if that act were to be morally wrong or in conflict with the tenets of the religion he so profoundly respects. He was disabused of doubt, however, when the position of the Roman Catholic Church was made known to him as it is reflected in the record in this case. The position statement of Bishop Lawrence B. Casey, reproduced in the amicus brief, projects these views:

(a) The verification of the fact of death in a particular case cannot be deduced from any religious or moral principle and, under this aspect, does not fall within the competence of the church; — that dependence must be had upon traditional and medical standards, and by these standards Karen Ann Quinlan is assumed to be alive.

[illegible] The request of plaintiff for authority to terminate a medical procedure characterized as "an extraordinary means of treatment" would not involve euthanasia. This upon the reasoning expressed by Pope Pius XII in his "allocutio" (address) to anesthesiologists on November 24, 1957, when he dealt with the question:

> Does the anesthesiologist have the right, or is he bound, in all cases of deep unconsciousness, even in those that are completely hopeless in the opinion of the competent doctor, to use modern artificial respiration apparatus, even against the will of the family?

His answer made the following points:

1. In ordinary cases the doctor has the right to act in this manner, but is not bound to do so unless this is the only way of fulfilling another certain moral duty.
2. The doctor, however, has no right independent of the patient. He can act only if the patient explicitly or implicitly, directly or indirectly gives him the permission.
3. The treatment as described in the question constitutes extraordinary means of preserving life and so there is no obligation to use them nor to give the doctor permission to use them.
4. The rights and the duties of the family depend on the presumed will of the unconscious patient if he or she is of legal age, and the family, too, is bound to use only ordinary means.
5. This case is not to be considered euthanasia in any way; that would never be elicit. The interruption of attempts at resuscitation, even when it causes the arrest of circulation, is not more than an indirect cause of the cessation of life, and we must apply in this case the principle of double effect.

So it was that the Bishop Casey statement validated the decision of Joseph Quinlan

. . . The right to a natural death is one outstanding area in which the disciplines of theology, medicine and law overlap; or, to put it another way, it is an area in which these three disciplines convene.

. . . .

. . . Medical science is not authorized to directly cause natural death; nor, however, is it expected to prevent it when it is inevitable and all hope of a return to an even partial exercise of human life is irreparably lost. Religion is not expected to define biological death; nor, on its part, is it expected to relinquish its responsibility to assist man in the formation and pursuit of a correct conscience as to the acceptance of natural death when science has confirmed its inevitability beyond any hope other than that of preserving biological life in a merely vegetative state.

. . . .

Before turning to the legal and constitutional issues involved, we feel it essential to reiterate that the "Catholic view" of religious neutrality in the circumstances of this case is considered by the Court only in the aspect of its impact upon the conscience, motivation and purpose of the intending guardian, Joseph Quinlan, and not as a precedent in terms of the civil law.

. . . .

Constitutional and Legal Issues

. . . .

III. The Right of Privacy

. . . [N]o external compelling interest of the State could compel Karen to endure the unendurable, only to vegetate a few measurable months with no realistic possibility of returning to any semblance of cognitive or sapient life. We perceive no thread of logic distinguishing between such a choice on Karen's part and a similar choice which, under the evidence in this case, could be made by a competent patient terminally ill, riddled by cancer and suffering great pain; such a patient would not be resuscitated or put on a respirator in the example described by Dr. Korein, and *a fortiori* would not be kept *against his will* on a respirator.

Although the Constitution does not explicitly mention a right of privacy, Supreme Court decisions have recognized that a right of personal privacy exists and that certain areas of privacy are guaranteed under the Constitution. *Eisenstadt v. Baird*, 405 U.S. 438 (1972); *Stanley v. Georgia*, 394 U.S. 557 (1969). The Court has interdicted judicial intrusion into many aspects of personal decision, sometimes basing this restraint upon the conception of a limitation of judicial interest and responsibility, such as with regard to contraception and its relationship to family life and decision. *Griswold v. Connecticut*, 381 U.S. 479 (1965).

. . . .

The claimed interests of the State in this case are essentially the preservation and sanctity of human life and defense of the right of the physician to administer medical treatment according to his best judgment. In this case the doctors say that removing Karen from the respirator will conflict with their professional judgment. The plaintiff answers that Karen's present treatment serves only a maintenance function; that the respirator cannot cure or improve her condition but at best can only prolong her inevitable slow deterioration and death; and that the interests of the patient, as seen by her surrogate, the guardian, must be evaluated by the court as predominant, even in the face of an opinion contra by the present attending physicians. Plaintiff's distinction is significant. The nature of Karen's care and the realistic chances of her recovery are quite unlike those of the patients discussed in many of the cases where treatments were ordered. . . .

IV. The Medical Factor

Having declared the substantive legal basis upon which plaintiff's rights as representative of Karen must be deemed predicated, we face and respond to the assertion on behalf of defendants that our premise unwarrantably offends prevailing medical standards. We thus turn to [illegible] supporting the determination made below, conscious of the paucity of pre-existing legislative and judicial guidance as to the rights and liabilities therein involved. . . .

. . . When does the institution of life-sustaining procedures, ordinarily mandatory, become the subject of medical discretion in the context of administration to persons in extremis? And when does the withdrawal of such procedures, from such persons already supported by them, come within the orbit of medical discretion? When does a determination as to either of the foregoing contingencies court the hazard of civil or criminal liability on the part of the physician or institution involved?

. . . .

Courts in the exercise of their parens patriae responsibility to protect those under disability have sometimes implemented medical decisions and authorized their carrying out under the doctrine of "substituted judgment." . . .

. . . .

We glean from the record here that physicians distinguish between curing the ill and comforting and easing the dying; that they refuse to treat the curable as if they were dying or ought to die, and that they have sometimes refused to treat the hopeless and dying as if they were curable. In this sense, as we were reminded by the testimony of Drs. Korein and Diamond, many of them have refused to inflict an undesired prolongation of the process of dying on a patient in irreversible condition when it is clear that such "therapy" offers neither human nor humane benefit. We think these attitudes represent a balanced implementation of a profoundly realistic perspective on the meaning of life and death and that they respect the whole Judeo-Christian tradition of regard for human life. No less would they seem consistent with the moral matrix of medicine, "to heal," very much in the sense of the endless mission of the law, "to do justice."

Yet this balance, we feel, is particularly difficult to perceive and apply in the context of the development by advanced technology of sophisticated and artificial life-sustaining [illegible] possibly curable, such devices are of great value, and, as ordinary medical procedures, are essential. Consequently, as pointed out by Dr. Diamond, they are necessary because of the ethic of medical practice. But in light of the situation in the present case (while the record here is somewhat hazy in distinguishing between "ordinary" and "extraordinary" measures), one would have to think that the use of the same respirator or like support could be considered "ordinary" in the context of the possibly curable patient but "extraordinary" in the context of the forced sustaining by cardio-respiratory processes of an irreversibly doomed patient. And this dilemma is sharpened in the face of the malpractice and criminal action threat which we have mentioned.

. . . .

A technique aimed at the underlying difficulty (though in a somewhat broader context) is described by Dr. Karen Teel, a pediatrician and a director of Pediatric Education, who writes in the Baylor Law Review under the title

"The Physician's Dilemma: A Doctor's View: What The Law Should Be." Dr. Teel recalls:

. . . .

> I suggest that it would be more appropriate to provide a regular forum for more input and dialogue in individual situations and to allow the responsibility of these judgments to be shared. Many hospitals have established an Ethics Committee composed of physicians, social workers, attorneys, and theologians, . . . which serves to review the individual circumstances of ethical dilemma and which has provided much in the way of assistance and safeguards for patients and their medical caretakers. Generally, the authority of these committees is primarily restricted to the hospital setting and their official status is more that of an advisory body than of an enforcing body.

. . . .

[This would allow] some much needed dialogue regarding these issues and [force] the point of exploring all of the options for a particular patient. It diffuses the responsibility for making these judgments. Many physicians, in many circumstances, would welcome this sharing of responsibility. I believe that such an entity could lend itself well to an assumption of a legal status which would allow courses of action not now undertaken because of the concern for liability. [27 Baylor L. Rev. 6, 8-9 (1975)].

. . . .

We consider that a practice of applying to a court to confirm such decisions would generally be inappropriate, not only because that would be a gratuitous encroachment upon the medical profession's field of competence, but because it would be impossibly cumbersome. Such a requirement is distinguishable from the judicial overview traditionally required in other matters such as the adjudication and commitment of mental incompetents. This is not to say that in the case of an otherwise justiciable controversy access to the courts would be foreclosed; we speak rather of a general practice and procedure.

And although the deliberations and decisions which we describe would be professional in nature they should obviously include at some stage the feelings of the family of an incompetent relative. Decision-making within health care if it is considered as an expression of a primary obligation of the physician, primum non nocere, should be controlled primarily within the patient-doctor-family relationship, as indeed was recognized by Judge Muir in his supplemental opinion of November 12, 1975.

If there could be created not necessarily this particular system but some reasonable counterpart, we would have no doubt that such decisions, thus determined to be in accordance with medical practice and prevailing standards, would be accepted by society and by the courts, at least in cases comparable to that of Karen Quinlan.

. . . .

Declaratory Relief

. . . .

We thus arrive at the formulation of the declaratory relief which we have concluded is appropriate to this case. Some time has passed since Karen's physical and mental condition was described to the Court. At that time her continuing deterioration was plainly projected. Since the record has not been expanded we assume that she is now even more fragile and nearer to death than she was then. Since her present treating physicians may give reconsideration to her present posture in the light of this opinion, and since we are transferring to the plaintiff as guardian the choice of the attending physician and therefore other physicians may be in charge of the case who may take a different view from that of the present attending physicians, we herewith declare the following affirmative relief on behalf of the plaintiff. Upon the concurrence of the guardian and family of Karen, should the responsible attending physicians conclude that there is no reasonable possibility of Karen's ever emerging from her present comatose condition to a cognitive, sapient state and that the life-support apparatus now being administered to Karen should be discontinued, they shall consult with the hospital "Ethics Committee" or like body of the institution in which Karen is then hospitalized. If that consultative body agrees that there is no reasonable possibility of Karen's ever emerging from her present comatose condition to a cognitive, sapient state, the present life-support system may be withdrawn and said action shall be without any civil or criminal liability therefor on the part of any participant, whether guardian, physician, hospital or others. We herewith specifically so hold.

. . . .

NOTES AND QUESTIONS

1. Now, thirty years later, the *Quinlan* case remains a landmark decision and the source of continuing commentary and significance. It is frequently paired with the next case, involving Nancy Beth Cruzan, but that case turns on a narrower issue of whether Missouri [illegible] convincing proof of the patient's desire to discontinue life support. *Quinlan,* in contrast, deals with the full range of issues — the interests of the patient, parents, physicians and courts in that decision.
2. What of the parents' interest? Clearly if Karen Quinlan had been ten instead of twenty-one, their interests would have been separate and significant. Why not now, when she is — again — a "child"?
3. And do the physicians not have the right to their own, separate ethical imperatives? If their professional standards preclude withdrawing support, shouldn't that fact be significant? Can they be forced to act contrary to their beliefs?
4. What of the emphasis placed on the Catholic Church and its views? Should the Church have been allowed to participate as an intervener, or would you say its views should be treated as irrelevant? Were you, incidentally, surprised by the court's treatment?

5. Where, then, does the Court find the overarching interest in the patient? The right of "privacy" is nowhere mentioned in the Constitution. (As to that, see *Griswold v. Connecticut*, *infra* § 2.02[2]). And, anyway, how is "privacy" affected in keeping alive a young woman in a hospital, where there is no privacy?
6. Why and how does the *Quinlan* case get out of the hospitals and into the Court? *Should* it? Isn't the Court really acting like a family court, exercising *parens patriae* authority, like the *Davis* Court or, more properly, the *Baby M* Court? Is there anything wrong with that?
7. Does everything turn, as the court says, on the prognosis? And the diagnosis — isn't Karen Ann Quinlan really "dead"? As to that, see the *Eulo* and *T.A.C.P.* cases, *supra*.
8. Note the relief. The Court is careful to say there is to be no criminal or civil liability, if Karen is removed after hearing on remand. But isn't it impossible, before hand, to make such a declaration?
9. On remand, the life support was removed. Karen Ann Quinlan continued to live in a persistent vegetative state for nine years afterward.

CRUZAN v. DIRECTOR, MO. HEALTH DEPT.
497 U.S. 261 (1990)

Chief Justice **Rehnquist** delivered the opinion of the Court.

. . . .

On the night of January 11, 1983, Nancy Cruzan lost control of her car as she traveled down Elm Road in Jasper County, Missouri. The vehicle overturned, and Cruzan was discovered lying face down in a ditch without detectable respiratory or cardiac function. Paramedics were able to restore her breathing and heartbeat at the accident site, and she was transported to a hospital in an unconscious state. An attending neurosurgeon diagnosed her as having sustained probable cerebral contusions compounded by significant anoxia (lack of oxygen). The Missouri trial court in this case found that permanent brain damage generally results after six minutes in an anoxic state; it was estimated that Cruzan was deprived of oxygen from 12 to 14 minutes. She remained in a coma for approximately three weeks and then progressed to an unconscious state in which she was able to orally ingest some nutrition. In order to ease feeding and further the recovery, surgeons implanted a gastrostomy feeding and hydration tube in Cruzan with the consent of her then husband. Subsequent rehabilitative efforts proved unavailing. She now lies in a Missouri state hospital in what is commonly referred to as a persistent vegetative state: generally, a condition in which a person exhibits motor reflexes but evinces no indications of significant cognitive function.[1] The State of Missouri is bearing the cost of her care.

---

[1] The State Supreme Court, adopting much of the trial court's findings, described Nancy Cruzan's medical condition as follows:

> ". . . (1) [H]er respiration and circulation are not artificially maintained and are within the normal limits of a thirty-year-old female; (2) she is oblivious to her environment except for reflexive responses to sound and perhaps painful stimuli; (3)

After it had become apparent that Nancy Cruzan had virtually no chance of regaining her mental faculties, her parents asked hospital employees to terminate the artificial [illegible] and hydration procedures. All agree that such a removal would cause her death. The employees refused to honor the request without court approval. The parents then sought and received authorization from the state trial court for termination. The court found that a person in Nancy's condition had a fundamental right under the State and Federal Constitutions to refuse or direct the withdrawal of "death prolonging procedures." The court also found that Nancy's "expressed thoughts at age twenty-five in somewhat serious conversation with a housemate friend that if sick or injured she would not wish to continue her life unless she could live at least halfway normally suggests that given her present condition she would not wish to continue on with her nutrition and hydration."

The Supreme Court of Missouri reversed by a divided vote. . . .

We granted certiorari to consider the question whether Cruzan has a right under the United States Constitution which would require the hospital to withdraw life-sustaining treatment from her under these circumstances.

At common law, even the touching of one person by another without consent and without legal justification was a battery. Before the turn of the century, this Court observed that "[n]o right is held more sacred, or is more carefully guarded, by the common law, than the right of every individual to the possession and control of his own person, free from all restraint or interference of others, unless by clear and unquestionable authority of law." *Union Pacific R. Co. v. Botsford*. This notion of bodily integrity has been embodied in the requirement that informed consent is generally required for medical treatment. Justice Cardozo, while on the Court of Appeals of New York, aptly described this doctrine: "Every human being of adult years and sound mind has a right to determine what shall be done with his own body; and a surgeon who performs an operation without his patient's consent commits an assault, for which he is liable in damages." *Schloendorff v. Society of New York Hospital*. The informed consent doctrine has become firmly entrenched in American tort law.

---

she suffered anoxia of the brain resulting in a massive enlargement of the ventricles filling with cerebrospinal fluid in the [illegible] the brain has degenerated and [her] cerebral cortical atrophy is irreversible, permanent, progressive and ongoing; (4) her highest cognitive brain function is exhibited by her grimacing perhaps in recognition of ordinarily painful stimuli, indicating the experience of pain and apparent response to sound; (5) she is a spastic quadriplegic; (6) her four extremities are contracted with irreversible muscular and tendon damage to all extremities; (7) she has no cognitive or reflexive ability to swallow food or water to maintain her daily essential needs and . . . she will never recover her ability to swallow sufficient [sic] to satisfy her needs. In sum, Nancy is diagnosed as in a persistent vegetative state. She is not dead. She is not terminally ill. Medical experts testified that she could live another thirty years." . . .

Dr. Fred Plum, the creator of the term "persistent vegetative state" and a renowned expert on the subject, has described the "vegetative state" in the following terms:

> " 'Vegetative state describes a body which is functioning entirely in terms of its internal controls. It maintains temperature. It maintains heart beat and pulmonary ventilation. It maintains digestive activity. It maintains reflex activity of muscles and nerves for low level conditioned responses. But there is no behavioral evidence of either self-awareness or awareness of the surroundings in a learned manner.' "

. . . .

The Fourteenth Amendment provides that no State shall "deprive any person of life, liberty, or property, without due process of law." The principle that a competent person has a constitutionally protected liberty interest in refusing unwanted medical treatment may be inferred from our prior decisions. . . .

. . . .

But determining that a person has a "liberty interest" under the Due Process Clause does not end the inquiry, "whether respondent's constitutional rights have been violated must be determined by balancing his liberty interests against the relevant state interests."

Petitioners insist that under the general holdings of our cases, the forced administration of life-sustaining medical treatment, and even of artificially delivered food and water essential to life, would implicate a competent person's liberty interest. Although we think the logic of the cases discussed above would embrace such a liberty interest, the dramatic consequences involved in refusal of such treatment would inform the inquiry as to whether the deprivation of that interest is constitutionally permissible. But for purposes of this case, we assume that the United States Constitution would grant a competent person a constitutionally protected right to refuse lifesaving hydration and nutrition.

. . . .

. . . The more stringent the burden of proof a party must bear, the more that party bears the risk of an erroneous decision. We believe that Missouri may permissibly place an increased risk of an erroneous decision on those seeking to terminate an incompetent individual's life-sustaining treatment. An erroneous decision not to terminate results in a maintenance of the status quo; the possibility of subsequent developments such as advancements in medical science, the discovery of new evidence regarding the patient's intent, changes in the law, or simply the unexpected death of the patient despite the administration of life-sustaining treatment at least create the potential that a wrong decision will eventually be corrected or its impact mitigated. An erroneous decision to withdraw life-sustaining treatment, however, is not susceptible of correction. . . .

. . . .

Petitioners alternatively contend that Missouri must accept the "substituted judgment" of close family members even in the absence of substantial proof that their views reflect the views of the patient. They rely primarily upon our decisions in *Michael H. v. Gerald D.* But we do not think these cases support their claim. In *Michael H*, we *upheld* the constitutionality of California's favored treatment of traditional family relationships; such a holding may not be turned around into a constitutional requirement that a State *must* recognize the primacy of those relationships in a situation like this. And in *Parham*, where the patient was a minor, we also *upheld* the constitutionality of a state scheme in which parents made certain decisions for mentally ill minors. Here again petitioners would seek to turn a decision which allowed a State to rely on family decision making into a constitutional requirement that the State recognize such decision making. But constitutional law does not work that way.

No [illegible] is engendered by anything in this record but that Nancy Cruzan's mother and father are loving and caring parents. If the State were required by the United States Constitution to repose a right of "substituted judgment" with anyone, the Cruzans would surely qualify. But we do not think the Due Process Clause requires the State to repose judgment on these matters with anyone but the patient herself. Close family members may have a strong feeling — a feeling not at all ignoble or unworthy, but not entirely disinterested, either — that they do not wish to witness the continuation of the life of a loved one which they regard as hopeless, meaningless, and even degrading. But there is no automatic assurance that the view of close family members will necessarily be the same as the patient's would have been had she been confronted with the prospect of her situation while competent. All of the reasons previously discussed for allowing Missouri to require clear and convincing evidence of the patient's wishes lead us to conclude that the State may choose to defer only to those wishes, rather than confide the decision to close family members.

The judgment of the Supreme Court of Missouri is affirmed.

Justice **O'Connor**, concurring.

I agree that a protected liberty interest in refusing unwanted medical treatment may be inferred from our prior decisions, and that the refusal of artificially delivered food and water is encompassed within that liberty interest. I write separately to clarify why I believe this to be so.

As the Court notes, the liberty interest in refusing medical treatment flows from decisions involving the State's invasions into the body. Because our notions of liberty are inextricably entwined with our idea of physical freedom and self-determination, the Court has often deemed state incursions into the body repugnant to the interests protected by the Due Process Clause. *See, e.g., Rochin v. California*; *Union Pacific R. Co. v. Botsford*. Our Fourth Amendment jurisprudence has echoed this same concern. *See Schmerber v. California*.The State's imposition of medical treatment on an unwilling competent adult necessarily involves some form of restraint [illegible] intrusion. A seriously ill or dying patient whose wishes are not honored may feel a captive of the machinery required for life-sustaining measures or other medical interventions. Such forced treatment may burden that individual's liberty interests as much as any state coercion. . . .

. . . Accordingly, the liberty guaranteed by the Due Process Clause must protect, if it protects anything, an individual's deeply personal decision to reject medical treatment, including the artificial delivery of food and water.

I also write separately to emphasize that the Court does not today decide the issue whether a State must also give effect to the decisions of a surrogate decision maker. In my view, such a duty may well be constitutionally required to protect the patient's liberty interest in refusing medical treatment. Few individuals provide explicit oral or written instructions regarding their intent to refuse medical treatment should they become incompetent. States which decline to consider any evidence other than such instructions may frequently fail to honor a patient's intent. Such failures might be avoided if the State considered an equally probative source of evidence: the patient's appointment of a proxy to make health care decisions on her behalf. Delegating the authority to make medical decisions to a family member of friend is becoming a common method of planning for the future. Several States have recognized the practical wisdom of such a procedure by enacting durable power of attorney statutes that specifically authorize an individual to appoint a surrogate to make medical treatment decisions.[1] Some state courts have suggested that an agent appointed pursuant to a general durable power of attorney statute would also be empowered to make health care decisions on behalf of the patient.[2] Other States allow an individual to designate a proxy to carry out the intent of a living will.[3] These procedures for surrogate decision making, which appear to be rapidly gaining in acceptance, may be a valuable additional safeguard of the patient's interest in directing his medical care. Moreover, as patients are likely to select a family member as a surrogate, giving effect to a proxy's decisions may also protect the "freedom of personal choice in matters of . . . family life." *Cleveland Board of Education v. LaFleur.*

Today's decision, holding only that the Constitution permits a State to require clear and convincing evidence of Nancy Cruzan's desire to have artificial hydration and nutrition withdrawn, does not preclude a future determination that the Constitution requires the States to implement the decisions of a patient's duly appointed surrogate. Nor does it prevent States from developing other approaches for protecting an incompetent individual's liberty interest in refusing medical treatment. . . .

Justice **Scalia**, concurring.

The various opinions in this case portray quite clearly the difficult, indeed agonizing, questions that are presented by the constantly increasing power of science to keep the human body alive for longer than any reasonable person would want to inhabit it. The States have begun to grapple with these problems through legislation. I am concerned, from the tenor of today's opinions, that we are poised to confuse that enterprise as successfully as we have confused the enterprise of legislating concerning abortion — requiring it to be conducted against a background of federal constitutional imperatives that are unknown because they are being newly crafted from Term to Term. That would be a great misfortune.

While I agree with the Court's analysis today, and therefore join in its opinion, I would have preferred that we announce, clearly and promptly, that the federal courts have no business in this field; that American law has always

[1] At least 13 States and the District of Columbia have durable power of attorney statutes expressly authorizing the appointment of proxies for making health care decisions. *See* Alaska Stat. Ann. §§ 13.26.335, 13.26.344(l) (Supp. 1989); Cal. Civ. Code Ann. § 2500 (West Supp. 1990); DC Code § 21-2205 (1989); Idaho Code § 39-4505 (Supp. 1989); Ill. Rev. Stat., ch. 110 ¶¶ 804-1 to 804-12 (Supp. 1988); Kan. Stat. Ann. § 58-625 (Supp. 1989); Me. Rev. Stat. Ann. Tit. 18-A, § 5-501 (Supp. 1989); Nev. Rev. Stat. § 449.800 (Supp. 1989); Ohio Rev. Code Ann. §§ 1337.11 *et seq.* (Supp. 1989); Or. Rev. Stat. § 127.510 (1989); Pa. Stat. Ann., Tit. 20, § 5603(h) (Purdon Supp. 1989); R.I. Gen. Laws §§ 23-4.10-1 *et seq.* (1989); Tex. Rev. Civ. Stat. Ann., Art. 4590h-1 (Vernon Supp. 1990); Vt. Stat. Ann., Tit. 14, §§ 3451 *et seq.* (1989).

[2] All 50 States and the District of Columbia have general durable power of attorney statutes.

[3] Thirteen States have living will statutes authorizing the appointment of health care proxies.

accorded the State the power to prevent, by force if necessary, suicide — including suicide by refusing to take appropriate measures necessary to preserve one's life; that the point at which life becomes "worthless," and the point at which the means necessary to preserve it become "extraordinary" or "inappropriate," are neither set forth in the Constitution nor known to the nine Justices of this Court any better than they are known to nine people picked at random from the Kansas City telephone directory. . . .

. . . .

Petitioners rely on three distinctions to separate Nancy Cruzan's case from ordinary suicide: (1) that she is permanently incapacitated and in pain; (2) that she would bring on her death not by any affirmative act but by merely declining treatment that provides nourishment; and (3) that preventing her from effectuating her presumed wish to die requires violation of her bodily integrity. None of these suffices. Suicide was not excused even when committed "to avoid those ills which [persons] had not the fortitude to endure." . . .

The second asserted distinction — suggested by the recent cases canvassed by the Court concerning the right to refuse treatment — relies on the dichotomy between action and inaction. Suicide, it is said, consists of an affirmative act to end one's life; refusing treatment is not an affirmative act "causing" death, but merely a passive acceptance of the natural process of dying. I readily acknowledge that the distinction between action and inaction has some bearing upon the legislative judgment of what ought to be prevented as suicide — though even there it would seem to me unreasonable to draw the line precisely between action and inaction, rather than between various forms of inaction. . . .

Starving oneself to death is no different from putting a gun to one's temple as far as the common-law definition of suicide is concerned; the cause of death in both cases is the suicide's conscious decision to "pu[t] an end to his own existence." . . .

. . . .

The third asserted basis of distinction — that frustrating Nancy Cruzan's wish to die in the present case requires interference with her bodily integrity — is likewise inadequate, because such interference is impermissible only if one begs the question whether her refusal to undergo the treatment on her own is suicide. It has always been lawful not only for the State, but even for private citizens, to interfere with bodily integrity to prevent a felony. It is not even reasonable, much less required by the Constitution, to maintain that although the State has the right to prevent a person from slashing his wrists, it does not have the power to apply physical force to prevent him from doing so, nor the power, should he succeed, to apply, coercively if necessary, medical measures to stop the flow of blood. . . .

. . . .

. . . Are there, then, no reasonable and humane limits that ought not to be exceeded in requiring an individual to preserve his own life? There obviously are, but they are not set forth in the Due Process Clause. What assures us that those limits will not be exceeded is the same constitutional guarantee that is the source of most of our protection — what protects us, for example, from being assessed a tax of 100% of our income above the subsistence level, from being forbidden to drive cars, or from being required to send our children to school for 10 hours a day, none of which horribles are categorically prohibited by the Constitution. Our salvation is the Equal Protection Clause, which requires the democratic majority to accept for themselves and their loved ones what they impose on you and me. This Court need not, and has no authority to, inject itself into every field of human activity where irrationality and oppression may theoretically occur, and if it tries to do so it will destroy itself.

Justice **Brennan**, with whom Justice **Marshall** and Justice **Blackmun** join, dissenting.

> "Medical technology has effectively created a twilight zone of suspended animation where death commences while life, in some form, continues. Some patients, however, want no part of a life sustained only by medical technology. Instead, they prefer a plan of medical treatment that allows nature to take its course and permits them to die with dignity."[1]

Nancy Cruzan has dwelt in that twilight zone for six years. She is oblivious to her surroundings and will remain so. . . . Because she cannot swallow, her nutrition and hydration are delivered through a tube surgically implanted in her stomach.

A grown woman at the time of the accident, Nancy had previously expressed her wish to forgo continuing medical care under circumstances such as these. Her family and her friends are convinced that this is what she would want. A guardian *ad litem* appointed by the trial court is also convinced that this is what Nancy would want. Yet the Missouri Supreme Court, alone among state courts deciding such a question, has determined that an irreversibly vegetative patient will remain a passive prisoner of medical technology — for Nancy, perhaps for the next 30 years.

. . . .

I

A

. . . .

The question before this Court is a relatively narrow one: whether the Due Process Clause allows Missouri to require a now-incompetent patient in an irreversible persistent vegetative state to remain on life support absent rigorously clear and convincing evidence that avoiding the treatment represents the patient's prior, express choice. If a fundamental right is at issue, Missouri's rule of decision must be scrutinized under the standards this Court has always applied in such circumstances. . . .

[1] Rasmussen v. Fleming, 154 Ariz. 207, 211, 741 P.2d 674, 678 (1987) (*en banc*).

B

The right to be free from medical attention without consent, to determine what shall be done with one's own body, *is* deeply rooted in this Nation's traditions, as the majority acknowledges. This right has long been "firmly entrenched in American tort law" and is securely grounded in the earliest common law. . . . Thus, freedom from unwanted medical attention is unquestionably among those principles "so rooted in the traditions and conscience of our people as to be ranked as fundamental." *Snyder v. Massachusetts.*[2]

No material distinction can be drawn between the treatment to which Nancy Cruzan continues to be subject — artificial nutrition and hydration — and any other medical treatment. The artificial delivery of nutrition and hydration is undoubtedly medical treatment. The technique to which Nancy Cruzan is subject — artificial feeding through a gastrostomy tube — involves a tube implanted surgically into her stomach through incisions in her abdominal wall. It may obstruct the intestinal tract, erode and pierce the stomach wall, or cause leakage of the stomach's contents into the abdominal cavity. The tube can cause pneumonia from reflux of the stomach's contents into the lung, and in this case, commercially prepared formulas are used, rather than fresh food. . . .

. . . .

Nor does the fact that Nancy Cruzan is now incompetent deprive her of her fundamental rights. . . . [T]he question is not whether an incompetent has constitutional rights, but how such rights may be exercised. As we explained in *Thompson v. Oklahoma*, "[t]he law must often adjust the manner in which it affords rights to those whose status renders them unable to exercise choice freely and rationally. Children, the insane, and *those who are irreversibly ill with loss of brain function, for instance, all retain 'rights,'* to be sure, but often such rights are only meaningful as they are exercised by agents acting with the best interests of their principals in mind."

II

A

The right to be free from unwanted medical attention is a right to evaluate the potential benefit of treatment and its possible consequences according to one's own values and to make a personal decision whether to subject oneself to the intrusion. For a patient like Nancy Cruzan, the sole benefit of medical treatment is being kept metabolically alive. Neither artificial nutrition nor

---

2 . . . .

See, e.g., Canterbury v. Spence, 150 U.S. App. D.C. 263, 271, 464 F.2d 772, 780, *cert denied*, 409 U.S. 1064, 34 L. Ed. 2d 518, 93 S. Ct. 560 (1972) ("The root premise" of informed consent "is the concept, fundamental in American jurisprudence, that '[e]very human being of adult years and sound mind has a right to determine what shall be done with his own body' ") (quoting Schloendorff v. Society of New York Hospital, 211 N.Y. 125, 129-130, 105 N.E. 92, 93 (1914) (Cardozo, J.)). *See generally* Washington v. Harper, 494 U.S. 210, 241, 108 L. Ed. 2d 178, 110 S. Ct. 1028 (1990).

any other form of medical treatment available today can cure or in any way ameliorate her condition. Irreversibly vegetative patients are devoid of thought, emotion, and sensation; they are permanently and completely unconscious. . . .

There are also affirmative reasons why someone like Nancy might choose to forgo artificial nutrition and hydration under these circumstances. Dying is personal. And it is profound. For many, the thought of an ignoble end, steeped in decay, is abhorrent. A quiet, proud death, bodily integrity intact, is a matter of extreme consequence. . . .

Such conditions are, for many, humiliating to contemplate,[10] as is visiting a prolonged and anguished vigil on one's parents, spouse, and children. A long, drawn-out death can have a debilitating effect on family members. For some, the idea of being remembered in their persistent vegetative states rather than as they were before their illness or accident may be very disturbing.

B

Although the right to be free of unwanted medical intervention, like other constitutionally protected interests, may not be absolute, no state interest could outweigh the rights of an individual in Nancy Cruzan's position. Whatever a State's possible interests in mandating life-support treatment under other circumstances, there is no good to be obtained here by Missouri's insistence that Nancy Cruzan remain on life-support systems if it is indeed her wish not to do so. Missouri does not claim, nor could it, that society as a whole will be benefitted by Nancy's receiving medical treatment. No third party's situation will be improved and no harm to others will be averted.[13]

The only state interest asserted here is a general interest in the preservation of life. But the State has no legitimate general interest in someone's life, completely abstracted from the interest of the person living that life, that could outweigh the person's choice to avoid medical treatment. Thus, the State's general interest in life must accede to Nancy Cruzan's particularized and intense interest in self-determination in her choice of medical treatment.

---

[10] Nancy Cruzan, for instance, is totally and permanently disabled. All four of her limbs are severely contracted; her fingernails cut into her wrists. She is incontinent of bowel and bladder. The most intimate aspects of her existence are exposed to and controlled by strangers. Her family is convinced that Nancy would find this state degrading.

[13] Were such interests at stake, however, I would find that the Due Process Clause places limits on what invasive medical procedures could be forced on an unwilling comatose patient in pursuit of the interests of a third party. If Missouri were correct that its interests outweigh Nancy's interest in avoiding medical procedures as long as she is free of pain and physical discomfort, it is not apparent why a State could not choose to remove one of her kidneys without consent on the ground that society would be better off if the recipient of that kidney were saved from renal poisoning. Nancy cannot feel surgical pain. Nor would removal of one kidney be expected to shorten her life expectancy. Patches of her skin could also be removed to provide grafts for burn victims and scrapings of bone marrow to provide grafts for someone with leukemia. Perhaps the State could lawfully remove more vital organs for transplanting into others who would then be cured of their ailments, provided the State placed Nancy on some other life-support equipment to replace the lost function. Indeed, why could the State not perform medical experiments on her body, experiments that might save countless lives, and would cause her no greater burden than she already bears by being fed through the gastrostomy tube? This would be too brave a new world for me and, I submit, for our Constitution.

There is simply nothing legitimately within the State's purview to be gained by superseding her decision.

. . . .

III

This is not to say that the State has no legitimate interests to assert here. Missouri has a *parens patriae* interest in providing Nancy Cruzan, now incompetent, with as accurate as possible a determination of how she would exercise her rights under these circumstances. Second, if and when it is determined that Nancy Cruzan would want to continue treatment, the State may legitimately assert an interest in providing that treatment. But *until* Nancy's wishes have been determined, the only state interest that may be asserted is an interest in safeguarding the accuracy of that determination.

Accuracy, therefore, must be our touchstone. . . .

A

The majority offers several justifications for Missouri's heightened evidentiary standard. . . . To be sure, courts have long erected clear and convincing evidence standards to place the greater risk of erroneous decisions on those bringing disfavored claims. In such cases, however, the choice to discourage certain claims was a legitimate, constitutional policy choice. In contrast, Missouri has no such power to disfavor a choice by Nancy Cruzan to avoid medical treatment, because Missouri has no legitimate interest in providing Nancy with treatment until it is established that this represents her choice. . . .

Second, the majority offers two explanations for why Missouri's clear and convincing evidence standard is a means of enhancing accuracy, but neither is persuasive. The majority initially argues that a clear and convincing evidence standard is necessary to compensate for the possibility that such proceedings will lack the "guarantee of accurate fact-finding that the adversary process brings with it." . . .

. . . .

. . . Missouri's heightened evidentiary standard attempts to achieve balance by discounting evidence; the guardian ad litem technique achieves balance by probing for additional evidence. Where, as here, the family members, friends, doctors, and guardian ad litem agree, it is not because the process has failed, as the majority suggests. It is because there is no genuine dispute as to Nancy's preference.

. . . .

The majority claims that the allocation of the risk of error is justified because it is more important not to terminate life support for someone who would wish it continued than to honor the wishes of someone who would not. An erroneous decision to terminate life support is irrevocable, says the majority, while an erroneous decision not to terminate "results in a maintenance of the status quo." But, from the point of view of the patient, an erroneous decision in either direction is irrevocable. An erroneous decision to terminate artificial nutrition and hydration, to be sure, will lead to failure of that last remnant of physiological life, the brain stem, and result in complete brain death. An erroneous decision not to terminate life support, however, robs a patient of the very qualities protected by the right to avoid unwanted medical treatment. His own degraded existence is perpetuated; his family's suffering is protracted; the memory he leaves behind becomes more and more distorted.

. . . .

B

Even more than its heightened evidentiary standard, the Missouri court's categorical exclusion of relevant evidence dispenses with any semblance of accurate factfinding. The court adverted to no evidence supporting its decision, but held that no clear and convincing, inherently reliable evidence had been presented to show that Nancy would want to avoid further treatment. In doing so, the court failed to consider statements Nancy had made to family members and a close friend.[19] The court also failed to consider testimony from Nancy's mother and sister that they were certain that Nancy would want to discontinue artificial nutrition and hydration,[20] even after the court found that

[19] The trial court had relied on the testimony of Athena Comer, a longtime friend, co-worker, and housemate for several months, as sufficient to show that Nancy Cruzan would wish to be free of medical treatment under her present circumstances. Comer described a conversation she and Nancy had while living together, concerning Ms. Comer's sister who had become ill suddenly and died during the night. The Comer family had been told that if she had lived through the night, she would have been in a vegetative state. Nancy had lost a grandmother a few months before. Ms. Comer testified that: "Nancy said she would never want to live [in a vegetative state] because if she couldn't be normal or even, you know, like half way, and do things for yourself, because Nancy always did, that she didn't want to live . . . and we talked about it a lot." She said "several times" that "she wouldn't want to live that way because if she was going to live, she wanted to be able to live, not to just lay in a bed and not be able to move because you can't do anything for yourself." "[S]he said that she hoped that [all the] people in her family knew that she wouldn't want to live [in a vegetative state] because she knew it was usually up to the family whether you lived that way or not."

The conversation took place approximately a year before Nancy's accident and was described by Ms. Comer as a "very serious" conversation that continued for approximately half an hour without interruption. The Missouri Supreme Court dismissed Nancy's statement as "unreliable" on the ground that it was an informally expressed reaction to other people's medical conditions.

The Missouri Supreme Court did not refer to other evidence of Nancy's wishes or explain why it was rejected. Nancy's sister Christy, to whom she was very close, testified that she and Nancy had had two very serious conversations about a year and a half before the accident. A day or two after their niece was stillborn (but would have been badly damaged if she had lived), Nancy had said that maybe it was part of a "greater plan" that the baby had been stillborn and did not have to face "the possible life of mere existence." A month later, after their grandmother had died after a long battle with heart problems, Nancy said that "it was better for my grandmother not to be kind of brought back and forth [by] medical [treatment], brought back from a critical near point of death . . . ."

[20] Nancy's sister Christy, Nancy's mother, and another of Nancy's friends testified that Nancy would want to discontinue the hydration and nutrition. Christy said that "Nancy would be horrified at the state she is in." She would also "want to take that burden away from [her family]." Based on "a lifetime of experience [I know Nancy's wishes] are to discontinue the hydration and the nutrition." Nancy's mother testified: "Nancy would not want to be like she is now. [I]f it were me up there or Christy or any of us, she would be doing for us what we are trying to do for her. I know she would, . . . as her mother."

Nancy's family was loving and without malignant motive. The court also failed to consider the conclusions of the guardian ad litem, appointed by the trial court, that th[illegible] evidence that Nancy would want to discontinue medical treatment and that this was in her best interests. . . .

. . . .

IV

. . . .

. . . The new medical technology can reclaim those who would have been irretrievably lost a few decades ago and restore them to active lives. For Nancy Cruzan, it failed, and for others with wasting incurable disease, it may be doomed to failure. In these unfortunate situations, the bodies and preferences and memories of the victims do not escheat to the State; nor does our Constitution permit the State or any other government to commandeer them. . . . Yet Missouri and this Court have displaced Nancy's own assessment of the processes associated with dying. They have discarded evidence of her will, ignored her values, and deprived her of the right to a decision as closely approximating her own choice as humanly possible. They have done so disingenuously in her name and openly in Missouri's own. That Missouri and this Court may truly be motivated only by concern for incompetent patients makes no matter. As one of our most prominent jurists warned us decades ago: "Experience should teach us to be most on our guard to protect liberty when the government's purposes are beneficent. . . . The greatest dangers to liberty lurk in insidious encroachment by men of zeal, well meaning but without understanding." *Olmstead v. United States* (Brandeis, J., dissenting).

. . . .

NOTES AND QUESTIONS

1. *Should* "clear and convincing" evidence be the standard for withdrawing life support in vegetative states? *Must* it be? For a thorough discussion of standards applied in vegetative state [illegible] Dale E. Moore, *Afterword: The Case of Daniel Joseph Fiori*, 57 Alb. L. Rev. 811 (1994).
2. On remand to the Missouri court, there was a further hearing at the trial level. At that time, new evidence was offered to establish that Nancy's desire would have been not to be maintained in a persistent vegetative state. The tube-feedings were ended and Nancy Beth Cruzan died on December 26, 1990. For an excellent, moving account of the human and legal saga of the *Cruzan* case, see *Long Goodbye, The Deaths of Nancy Cruzan*, by William Colby, her attorney.
3. Chief Justice Rehnquist states that the *Cruzan* case variously involves the right to refuse treatment, the right to die, and the right to insist upon informed consent prior to medical treatment. Are these all rephrasings of the same thing? If they are different, how so? And where is the constitutional basis for them? What would the European Convention say?

4. Why should Missouri presume that a person, such as Nancy Cruzan, would want to continue her existence in a persistent vegetative state? Should not the reverse presumption be true: that a person's existence should not be so continued unless he or she has expressly declared a desire to that effect? How does maintenance of a persistent vegetative state advance the state of Missouri's declared interest in "life"?

5. As a practical matter, most people will not have anticipated the plight confronting Nancy Cruzan; nor are we likely in our everyday conversations to discuss such matters. Thus, insisting upon evidence of such discussions, and insisting that the proof be clear and convincing, is likely to lead to erroneous decision-making. That is, although it may be assumed that most of us would *not* want to be maintained in a persistent vegetative state, the Missouri approach is likely to enforce such maintenance on us. A procedure which maximizes the margin for error ordinarily is thought to violate due process of laws. Why does the court conclude otherwise in *Cruzan*?

6. Why did the court reject the "substituted judgment" approach offered by Nancy Cruzan's parents? Was it out of fear that the inconvenience or emotional distress of the parents might influence their testimony? Or, put somewhat differently, was it a conclusion that there should be no balancing between Nancy's "right to life" and her parents' right to peace of mind? What would Rawls say?

7. Justice Stevens' view was quite different. He did not argue for Nancy Cruzan's right to refuse treatment or to choose to die. Instead, he argued for a judicial determination of her "best interests," especially when "buttressed by the interest of all related third parties." These best interests, he said, "must prevail over any general state policy." But, such an approach would be enforced by the state itself. And, thus, the state which cannot be trusted to enforce Nancy Cruzan's wishes would, paradoxically, be entrusted to protect her best interests. Is such an approach safe? Ethical? What would Rawls say?

8. Would it make sense to declare a person who is in a persistent vegetative state to be "dead"? Would the 1968 Harvard Committee agree? Would the more recent legislation, reflected in the preceding cases, support such a conclusion? If not, should they be amended?

9. For an excellent article, see Adam J. Hildebrand, *Masked Intentions: The Masquerade of Killing Thoughts Used to Justify Dehydrating and Starving People in a "Persistent Vegetative State" and People with Other Profound Neurological Impairments*, 16 Issues L. & Med. 143 (2000); and see Ronald E. Cranford, *Michael Martin and Robert Wendland: Beyond the Vegetative State*, 15 J. Contemp. Health L. & Pol'y 427 (1999).

10. Does a State's Attorney General have the authority to override the decisions of the patient's family, the hospital's medical staff and ethics committee, and clergy, to make a decision which refuses artificial hydration for a patient who is not, and has never been, mentally competent? (*See Blouin v. Spitzer*, 213 F. Supp. 2d 184 (2d Cir. N.Y., 2004)).

11. For what seemed a painful eternity of months during 2004 and 2005, much of the nation was consumed by the saga of Theresa (Terry) Schiavo), a young woman in a persistent vegetative state in Florida. After more than ten years of keeping Terry on artificial life support, her husband, Michael, and her parents, Robert and Mary, were pitted against each other in an exceptional number of cases that drew the attention and intervention of Governor Jeb Bush and the Florida legislature, and the state and federal Courts, as well as the United States Congress. The Speaker of the House, Congressman Thomas DeLay, himself under ethics investigation, called for impeachment of those federal judges who refused Congress' call to intervene. Below are three of the decisions, spanning four years of the rancorous family and political debate.

SCHINDLER v. SCHIAVO (In re Schiavo)

780 So. 2d 176 (Fla. Dist. Ct. App. 2001)

(*Schiavo I*)

Altenbernd, Judge.

Robert and Mary Schindler, the parents of Theresa Marie Schiavo, appeal the trial court's order authorizing the discontinuance of artificial life support to their adult daughter. Michael Schiavo, Theresa's husband and guardian, petitioned the trial court in May 1998 for entry of this order. We have carefully reviewed the record. The trial court made a difficult decision after considering all of the evidence and the applicable law. We conclude that the trial court's decision is supported by competent, substantial evidence and that it correctly applies the law. Accordingly, we affirm the decision.

Theresa Marie Schindler was born on December 3, 1963, and lived with or near her parents in Pennsylvania until she married Michael Schiavo on November 10, 1984. Michael and Theresa moved to Florida in 1986. They were happily married and both were employed. They had no children.

On February 25, 1990, their lives changed. Theresa, age 27, suffered a cardiac arrest as a result of a potassium imbalance. Michael called 911, and Theresa was rushed to the hospital. She never regained consciousness.

Since 1990, Theresa has lived in nursing homes with constant care. She is fed and hydrated by tubes. The staff changes her diapers regularly. She has had numerous health problems, but none have been life threatening.

The evidence is overwhelming that Theresa is in a permanent or persistent vegetative state. It is important to understand that a persistent vegetative state is not simply a coma.[1] She is not asleep. She has cycles of apparent wakefulness and apparent sleep without any cognition or awareness. As she breathes, she often makes moaning sounds. Theresa has severe contractures of her hands, elbows, knees, and feet.

---

[1] For more extensive discussions of persistent vegetative state, see Dorothy J. McNoble, The Cruzan Decision-A Surgeon's Perspective, 20 Mem. St. U. L. Rev. 569, 610 n.3 (1990); John B. Oldershaw, M.D., J.D., et al., Persistent Vegetative State: Medical, Religious, Economic and Legal Perspectives, 1 DePaul J. Health Care L. 495–536 (1997).

Over the span of this last decade, Theresa's brain has deteriorated because of the lack of oxygen it suffered at the time of the heart attack. By mid-1996, the CAT scans of her brain showed a severely abnormal structure. At this point, much of her cerebral cortex is simply gone and has been replaced by cerebral spinal fluid. Medicine cannot cure this condition. Unless an act of God, a true miracle, were to recreate her brain, Theresa will always remain in an unconscious, reflexive state, totally dependent upon others to feed her and care for her most private needs. She could remain in this state for many years.

Theresa has been blessed with loving parents and a loving husband. Many patients in this condition would have been abandoned by friends and family within the first year. Michael has continued to care for her and to visit her all these years. He has never divorced her. He has become a professional respiratory therapist and works in a nearby hospital. As a guardian, he has always attempted to provide optimum treatment for his wife. He has been a diligent watch guard of Theresa's care, never hesitating to annoy the nursing staff in order to assure that she receives the proper treatment.

Theresa's parents have continued to love her and visit her often. No one questions the sincerity of their prayers for the divine miracle that now is Theresa's only hope to regain any level of normal existence. No one questions that they have filed this appeal out of love for their daughter.

This lawsuit is affected by an earlier lawsuit. In the early 1990's, Michael Schiavo, as Theresa's guardian, filed a medical malpractice lawsuit. That case resulted in a sizable award of money for Theresa. This fund remains sufficient to care for Theresa for many years. If she were to die today, her husband would inherit the money under the laws of intestacy. If Michael eventually divorced Theresa in order to have a more normal family life, the fund remaining at the end of Theresa's life would presumably go to her parents.

Since the resolution of the malpractice lawsuit, both Michael and the Schindlers have become suspicious that the other party is assessing Theresa's wishes based upon their own monetary self-interest. The trial court discounted this concern, and we see no evidence in this record that either Michael or the Schindlers seek monetary gain from their actions. Michael and the Schindlers simply cannot agree on what decision Theresa would make today if she were able to assess her own condition and make her own decision.

There has been discussion among the parties that the money remaining when Theresa dies should be given to a suitable charity as a lasting memorial. If anything is undeniable in this case, it is that Theresa would never wish for this money to drive a wedge between the people she loves. We have no jurisdiction over the disposition of this money, but hopefully these parties will consider Theresa's desires and her memory when a decision about the money is ultimately required.

This is a case to authorize the termination of life-prolonging procedures under chapter 765, Florida Statutes (1997), and under the constitutional guidelines enunciated in *In re Guardianship of Browning*, 568 So. 2d 4 (Fla.

1990).[2] The Schindlers have raised three legal issues that warrant brief discussion.

First, the Schindlers maintain that the trial court was required to appoint a guardian ad litem for this proceeding because Michael stands to inherit under the laws of intestacy. When a living will or other advance directive does not exist, it stands to reason that the surrogate decision-maker will be a person who is close to the patient and thereby likely to inherit from the patient. *See* § 765.401, Fla. Stat. (2000). Thus, the fact that a surrogate decision-maker may ultimately inherit from the patient should not automatically compel the appointment of a guardian. On the other hand, there may be occasions when an inheritance could be a reason to question a surrogate's ability to make an objective decision.

In this case, however, Michael Schiavo has not been allowed to make a decision to disconnect life-support. The Schindlers have not been allowed to make a decision to maintain life-support. Each party in this case, absent their disagreement, might have been a suitable surrogate decision-maker for Theresa. Because Michael Schiavo and the Schindlers could not agree on the proper decision and the inheritance issue created the appearance of conflict, Michael Schiavo, as the guardian of Theresa, invoked the trial court's jurisdiction to allow the trial court to serve as the surrogate decision-maker.

In this case, Michael Schiavo used the first approach. Under these circumstances, the two parties, as adversaries, present their evidence to the trial court. The trial court determines whether the evidence is sufficient to allow it to make the decision for the ward to discontinue life support. In this context, the trial court essentially serves as the ward's guardian. Although we do not rule out the occasional need for a guardian in this type of proceeding, a guardian ad litem would tend to duplicate the function of the judge, would add little of value to this process, and might cause the process to be influenced by hearsay or matters outside the record. Accordingly, we affirm the trial court's discretionary decision in this case to proceed without a guardian ad litem.

Second, the Schindlers argue that the trial court should not have heard evidence from Beverly Tyler, [illegible] director of Georgia Health Decisions. Al though it is doubtful that this issue is preserved for appeal, we have reviewed the issue as if it were. Ms. Tyler has studied American values, opinions, and attitudes about the decision to discontinue life support systems. As a result, she has some special expertise concerning the words and expressions that Americans often use in discussing these difficult issues. She also has knowledge about trends within American attitudes on this subject.

We have considerable doubt that Ms. Tyler's testimony provided much in the way of relevant evidence. She testified about some social science surveys. Apparently most people, even those who favor initial life-supporting medical treatment, indicate that they would not wish this treatment to continue indefinitely once their medical condition presented no reasonable basis for a

[2] This case does not involve section 765.404, Florida Statutes (2000). This new legislative enactment permits use of a "best interests" standard for discontinuing life-prolonging procedures when a patient in a persistent vegetative state has no friend or family member to serve as a proxy.

cure. There is some risk that a trial judge could rely upon this type of survey evidence to make a "best interests" decision for the ward. In this case, however, we are convinced that the trial judge did not give undue weight to this evidence and that the court made a proper surrogate decision rather than a best interests decision.

Finally, the Schindlers argue that the testimony, which was conflicting, was insufficient to support the trial court's decision by clear and convincing evidence. We have reviewed that testimony and conclude that the trial court had sufficient evidence to make this decision. The clear and convincing standard of proof, while very high, permits a decision in the face of inconsistent or conflicting evidence. *See In re Guardianship of Browning*, 543 So. 2d at 273.

The testimony in this case establishes that Theresa was very young and very healthy when this tragedy struck. Like many young people without children, she had not prepared a will, much less a living will. She had been raised in the Catholic faith, but did not regularly attend mass or have a religious advisor who could assist the court in weighing her religious attitudes about life-support methods. Her statements to her friends and family about the dying process were few and they were oral. Nevertheless, those statements, along with other evidence about Theresa, gave the trial court a sufficient basis to make this decision for her.

In the final analysis, the difficult question that faced the trial court was whether Theresa Marie Schindler Schiavo, not after a few weeks in a coma, but after ten years in a persistent vegetative state that has robbed her of most of her cerebrum and all but the most instinctive of neurological functions, with no hope of a medical cure but with sufficient money and strength of body to live indefinitely, would choose to continue the constant nursing care and the supporting tubes in hopes that a miracle would somehow recreate her missing brain tissue, or whether she would wish to permit a natural death process to take its course and for her family members and loved ones to be free to continue their lives. After due consideration, we conclude that the trial judge had clear and convincing evidence to answer this question as he did.

Affirmed.

Parker, A.C.J., and **Blue**, J., Concur.

NOTES AND QUESTIONS

1. The Florida Court in *Schiavo I* notes the self-interest of the husband and parents. In light of this, shouldn't they have been displaced by guardians? Or the fund transferred to a state trustee? How should the Court best protect against underlying motives?
2. What of the Florida procedure in which a judge "essentially serves as the ward's guardian"? Can a judge do so and — at the same time — perform the usual functions of a judge? Is a judge's training appropriate? The court is at pains to draw a distinction: the trial court made a proper "surrogate" decision, not a "best interests" decision. What does this mean? How do they know?

3. In *Schiavo I*, the Court notes a new statute, 765.404, Florida Statutes (2000), permits a "best interest" analysis when there is no friend or family available. Could that have been applied here? And why not apply it if friends or family are acting contrary to best interests? What do you think of such a standard?

4. The next opinion follows on *Schiavo I*, and the extraordinary maneuvering of the parents, challenging past witnesses and offering new evidence. Next is *Schiavo III*.

SCHINDLER v. SCHIAVO (In re Schiavo)
800 So. 2d 640 (Fla. Dist. Ct. App. 2001)
(*Schiavo III*)

Altenbernd, Judge.

This is the third opinion issued by this court addressing a bitter dispute among the members of Mrs. Theresa Schiavo's family over her medical condition and her right to forego life-prolonging medical procedures.

We conclude that the Schindlers' motion for relief from judgment and the supporting affidavits state a "colorable entitlement" to relief concerning the issue of whether Mrs. Schiavo might elect to pursue a new medical treatment before withdrawing life-prolonging procedures.

. . . .

II. THE AMENDED MOTION FOR RELIEF FROM JUDGMENT

The Schindlers contend in their amended motion for relief from judgment that it is no longer equitable for the judgment permitting the withdrawal of life-prolonging measures to have prospective application for two reasons. First, in May 2001, the Schindlers discovered three new witnesses whose proffered testimony is primarily impeachment evidence of the testimony of Mr. Schiavo at the original trial before the guardianship court. Two of these witnesses were women who were friends of Mr. Schiavo during a period ending in approximately 1993. The third witness was the husband of one of these women. The Schindlers filed lengthy depositions from the husband and wife, and a lengthy affidavit from the second woman. The Schindlers maintained that this new evidence was sufficient to change the trial court's determination that, in February 2000, Mrs. Schiavo would have chosen to withdraw life-prolonging procedures.

We have also reviewed this evidence and conclude that the trial court committed no reversible error in determining that this new evidence failed to present a colorable claim for entitlement to relief from the judgment.

As a second reason for relief from judgment, the Schindlers argued that Mrs. Schiavo's medical condition in February 2000 was misrepresented to the trial court and to this court throughout these proceedings. They claim that she is not in a persistent vegetative state. What is more important, they maintain that current accepted medical treatment exists to restore her ability to eat and speak. The initial trial focused on what Mrs. Schiavo would have decided given her current medical condition and not on whether any available medical treatment could improve her condition. The Schindlers argue that in light of this new evidence of additional medical procedures intended to improve her condition, Mrs. Schiavo would now elect to undergo new treatment and would reverse the prior decision to withdraw life-prolonging procedures.

In support of these arguments, the Schindlers filed numerous affidavits from licensed physicians who have reviewed Mrs. Schiavo's medical records, who have considered affidavits providing anecdotal evidence from lay people about her condition, and who have watched a brief videotape of her interaction with her mother at a time close to the original trial. Mr. Schiavo, as the ward's guardian, has not permitted these doctors to physically examine Mrs. Schiavo or conduct any diagnostic tests.

The affidavits of the several doctors vary in content and rhetoric. Among the affidavits filed by the Schindlers, however, the most significant evidence comes from Dr. Fred Webber. Dr. Webber is an osteopathic physician practicing in Clearwater, Florida, who claims that Mrs. Schiavo is not in a persistent vegetative state and that she exhibits "purposeful reaction to her environment." He swore under oath as follows:

> Within the past year, I have treated patients with brain defects similar to Mrs. Schiavo's. In most cases, using cardiovascular medication style of therapy, my patients have shown some improvement, although the degree of that improvement is variable. By "improvement" I mean cognitive and physical items such as speech recovery, enhanced speech clarity and complexity, release of contractures, and better awareness of the patient's surroundings. In my opinion and judgment, based on my 26 years of practice, Mrs. Schiavo has a good opportunity to show some degree of improvement if treated with this type of therapy, although I cannot anticipate how much improvement.

Purely from a lay perspective, this court must express skepticism concerning Dr. Webber's affidavit. Nevertheless, when a doctor claims under oath that he may be able to restore Mrs. Schiavo's ability to speak and otherwise restore her cognitive function, and when numerous doctors dispute the diagnosis of persistent vegetative state based on the records available to them, it is difficult for judges untrained in any medical specialty to summarily reject their opinions without additional evidence.

In our last opinion, we suggested that a medical improvement might need to rise to the level of a "complete cure" before the trial court would be required to conduct an additional evidentiary hearing. *Schiavo II*, 2001 Fla. App. LEXIS 9578, 26 Fla. L. Weekly at D1702. We described extreme hypothetical examples in our opinion to demonstrate that circumstances could exist where all would agree that the trial court should grant relief under rule 1.540(b)(5). We conclude that our examples misled the trial court into believing that only those types of allegations would suffice, and we apologize for the confusion we created.

This court has repeatedly stated that, in cases of termination of life support, the courts must assume that a patient would choose to defend life in exercising the right of privacy. *See Schiavo I*, 780 So. 2d at 179; *In re Guardianship of Browning*, 543 So. 2d 258, 273 (Fla. 2d DCA 1989). This default position requires this court to conclude that the medical affidavits are sufficient to create a colorable entitlement to relief sufficient to warrant an evidentiary hearing on the motion for relief from judgment. We therefore reverse the summary denial of this portion of the motion and remand to the trial court to conduct an evidentiary hearing on these specific claims.

As we view the unusual and difficult posture of this case, the question before the trial court in the evidentiary hearing on remand is whether this new evidence concerning additional medical treatment is sufficient to establish that the current final judgment is no longer equitable. Under these circumstances, we conclude that the Schindlers, as the proponents of the motion, must prove only by a preponderance of the evidence that the initial judgment is no longer equitable. To meet this burden, they must establish that new treatment offers sufficient promise of increased cognitive function in Mrs. Schiavo's cerebral cortex — significantly improving the quality of Mrs. Schiavo's life — so that she herself would elect to undergo this treatment and would reverse the prior decision to withdraw life-prolonging procedures.

In order to obtain the best available medical evaluation and because at least one of the Schindlers' experts in his affidavit has accused the treating physicians of malpractice, we further conclude that the trial court should appoint a new independent physician to examine and evaluate Mrs. Schiavo's current condition. This physician should not be one of the doctors who has already provided testimony or an affidavit in this case and should be independent of those physicians and without any prior involvement with this family. If possible, this new physician should be very experienced in the treatment of brain damage and in the diagnosis and treatment of persistent vegetative state. This new physician should be board-certified in neurology or neurosurgery. We instruct lead counsel in the trial court for both parties to locate and agree upon the selection of this new physician. In the event that counsel are unable to stipulate to the selection of a new physician for the purposes of this independent examination, the trial court shall make the selection.

Once the Schindlers and Mr. Schiavo have each designated their two physicians and the independent physician has been selected, the physicians shall have the opportunity to examine Mrs. Schiavo. The court shall authorize the expenditure and payment of the reasonable fees of the independent physician appointed by the court and all reasonable diagnostic tests. We anticipate that the physicians will want to obtain current EEG readings as well as brain scans performed using current technology. They may need to obtain diagnostic results from the tests typically given at a general physical. In the event that the doctors disagree upon the necessary tests or the guardian objects to a test on grounds that it may be too invasive or harmful to Mrs. Schiavo, the trial court will need to resolve the dispute.8 We recommend to the trial court that all five designated physicians file written reports with the trial court, and that the court then schedule an evidentiary hearing to resolve this matter.

Affirmed in part, reversed in part, and remanded.

Blue, C.J., and **Parker**, J., concur.

NOTES AND QUESTIONS

1. In *Schiavo III*, the parents offer new depositions of three witnesses as to what Terry would want. Should that be the standard? If she is in a persistent vegetative state, why should her wishes control? Would the answer be different if the state was paying hospital bills?
2. Should there be finality in these proceedings to bar after-acquired evidence? Should the standard be different from that in other cases?
3. The Schindlers argued new treatment and health evidence, breaking into three parts:
   a. Terry was not really in a PVS;
   b. Even if she were, new treatment could help her eat and speak;
   c. She would now, knowing this, choose such treatment.

   Are these arguments consistent with the "surrogacy" approach?
4. Also, Dr. Webber's affidavit spoke of "some" improvement. By not requiring a "complete cure," isn't the Court forced to weigh gradations of quality of life, determining at what level life is not worth living — the very task courts seek to avoid?

BUSH v. SCHIAVO

885 So. 2d 321 (Fla. Dist. Ct. App. 2004)

CORRECTED OPINION

Pariente, C.J.

The narrow issue in this case requires this Court to decide the constitutionality of a law passed by the Legislature that directly affected Theresa Schiavo, who has been in a persistent vegetative state since 1990. This Court, after careful consideration of the arguments of the parties and amici, the constitutional issues raised, the precise wording of the challenged law, and the underlying procedural history of this case, concludes that the law violates the fundamental constitutional tenet of separation of powers and 8 We emphasize again that we are authorizing diagnostic tests, not treatment. is therefore unconstitutional both on its face and as applied to Theresa Schiavo. Accordingly, we affirm the trial court's order declaring the law unconstitutional.

On October 21, 2003, the Legislature enacted chapter 2003-418, the Governor signed the Act into law, and the Governor issued executive order No. 03-201 to stay the continued withholding of nutrition and hydration from Theresa. The nutrition and hydration tube was reinserted pursuant to the Governor's executive order.

On the same day, Michael Schiavo brought the action for declaratory judgment in the circuit court. Relying on undisputed facts and legal argument, the circuit court entered a final summary judgment on May 6, 2004, in favor of Michael Schiavo, finding the Act unconstitutional both on its face and as applied to Theresa. Specifically, the circuit court found that chapter 2003-418 was unconstitutional on its face as an unlawful delegation of legislative authority and as a violation of the right to privacy, and unconstitutional as applied because it allowed the Governor to encroach upon the judicial [illegible] abolish Theresa's vested right to privacy.

ANALYSIS

We begin our discussion by emphasizing that our task in this case is to review the constitutionality of chapter 2003-418, not to reexamine the guardianship court's orders directing the removal of Theresa's nutrition and hydration tube, or to review the Second District's numerous decisions in the guardianship case. Although we recognize that the parties continue to dispute the findings made in the prior proceedings, these proceedings are relevant to our decision only to the extent that they occurred and resulted in a final judgment directing the withdrawal of life-prolonging procedures.

The language of chapter 2003-418 is clear. It states in full:

> Section 1. (1) The Governor shall have the authority to issue a one-time stay to prevent the withholding of nutrition and hydration from a patient if, as of October 15, 2003:
>
> (a) That patient has no written advance directive;
>
> (b) The court has found that patient to be in a persistent vegetative state;
>
> (c) That patient has had nutrition and hydration withheld; and
>
> (d) A member of that patient's family has challenged the withholding of nutrition and hydration.
>
> (2) The Governor's authority to issue the stay expires 15 days after the effective date of this act, and the expiration of the authority does not impact the validity or the effect of any stay issued pursuant to this act. The Governor may lift the stay authorized under this act at any time. A person may not be held civilly liable and is not subject to regulatory or disciplinary sanctions for taking any action to comply with a stay issued by the Governor pursuant to this act.
>
> (3) Upon issuance of a stay, the chief judge of the circuit court shall [illegible] guardian ad litem for the patient to make recommendations to the Governor and the court.
>
> Section 2. This act shall take effect upon becoming a law.

Ch. 2003-418, Laws of Fla. Thus, chapter 2003-418 allowed the Governor to issue a stay to prevent the withholding of nutrition and hydration from a patient under the circumstances provided for in subsections (1)(a)-(d). Under the fifteen-day sunset provision, the Governor's authority to issue the stay expired on November 5, 2003. The Governor's authority to lift the stay continues indefinitely.

SEPARATION OF POWERS

The cornerstone of American democracy known as separation of powers recognizes three separate branches of government — the executive, the legislative, and the judicial — each with its own powers and responsibilities. In Florida, the constitutional doctrine has been expressly codified in article II, section 3 of the Florida Constitution, which not only divides state government into three branches but also expressly prohibits one branch from exercising the powers of the other two branches: Branches of Government. — The powers of the state government shall be divided into legislative, executive and judicial branches. No person belonging to one branch shall exercise any powers appertaining to either of the other branches unless expressly provided herein.

"This Court . . . has traditionally applied a strict separation of powers doctrine," *State v. Cotton*, 769 So. 2d 345, 353 (Fla. 2000), and has explained that this doctrine "encompasses two fundamental prohibitions. The first is that no branch may encroach upon the powers of another. The second is that no branch may delegate to another branch its constitutionally assigned power." *Chiles v. Children A, B, C, D, E, & F*, 589 So. 2d 260, 264 (Fla. 1991) (citation omitted).

Encroachment on the Judicial Branch

We begin by addressing the argument that, as applied to Theresa Schiavo, the Act encroaches on the power and authority of the judicial branch. More than 140 years ago this Court explained the foundation of Florida's express separation of powers provision:

> The framers of the Constitution of Florida, doubtless, had in mind the omnipotent power often exercised by the British Parliament, the exercise of judicial power by the Legislature in those States where there are no written Constitutions restraining them, when they wisely prohibited the exercise of such powers in our State.
>
> That Convention was composed of men of the best legal minds in the country — men of experience and skilled in the law — who had witnessed the breaking down by unrestrained legislation all the security of property derived from contract, the divesting of vested rights by doing away the force of the law as decided, the overturning of solemn decisions of the Courts of the last resort, by, under the pretence of remedial acts, enacting for one or the other party litigants such provisions as would dictate to the judiciary their decision, and leaving everything which should be expounded by the judiciary to the variable and ever-changing mind of the popular branch of the Government.

Trustees Internal Improvement Fund v. Bailey, 10 Fla. 238, 250 (1863). Similarly, the framers of the United States Constitution recognized the need to establish a judiciary independent of the legislative branch. Indeed, the desire to prevent Congress from using its power to interfere with the judgments of the courts was one of the primary motivations for the separation of powers established at this nation's founding:

> This sense of a sharp necessity to separate the legislative from the judicial power, prompted by the crescendo of legislative interference

> with private judgments of the courts, triumphed among the Framers of the new Federal Constitution. The Convention made the critical decision to establish a judicial department independent of the Legislative Branch . . . . Before and during the debates on ratification, Madison, Jefferson, and Hamilton each wrote of the factional disorders and disarray that the system of legislative equity had produced in the years before the framing; and each thought that the separation of the legislative from the judicial power in the new Constitution would cure them. Madison's Federalist No. 48, the famous description of the process by which "the legislative department is every where extending the sphere of its activity, and drawing all power into its impetuous vortex," referred to the report of the Pennsylvania Council of Censors to show that in that State "cases belonging to the judiciary department [had been] frequently drawn within legislative cognizance and determination." Madison relied as well on Jefferson's Notes on the State of Virginia, which mentioned, as one example of the dangerous concentration of governmental powers into the hands of the legislature, that "the Legislature . . . in many instances decided rights which should have been left to judiciary controversy."

Plaut v. Spendthrift Farm, Inc., 514 U.S. 211, 221-22 (1995) (citations omitted).

The Act, as applied in this case, resulted in an executive order that effectively reversed a properly rendered final judgment and thereby constituted an unconstitutional encroachment on the power that has been reserved for the independent judiciary. *Cf. Bailey*, 10 Fla. at 249-50 (noting that had the statute under review "directed a rehearing, the hearing of the case would necessarily carry with it the right to set aside the judgment of the Court, and there would be unquestionably an exercise of judicial power").

The Governor and amici assert that the Act does not reverse a final court order because an order to discontinue life-prolonging procedures may be challenged at any time prior to the death of the ward. In advancing this argument, the Governor and amici rely on the Second District's conclusion that as long as the ward is alive, an order discontinuing life-prolonging procedures "is subject to recall and is executory in nature." *Schiavo II*, 792 So. 2d at 559. However, the Second District did not hold that the guardianship court's order was not a final judgment but, rather, that the Schindlers, as interested parties, could file a motion for relief from judgment under Florida Rule of Civil Procedure 1.540(b)(5) if they sufficiently alleged that it is no longer equitable that the judgment have prospective application. Rule 1.540(b) expressly states that a motion filed pursuant to its terms "does not affect the finality of a judgment." Further, the fact that a final judgment may be subject to recall under a rule of procedure, if certain circumstances can be proved, does not negate its finality. Unless and until the judgment is vacated by judicial order, it is "the last word of the judicial department with regard to a particular case or controversy." *Plaut*, 514 U.S. at 227.

Delegation of Legislative Authority

In addition to concluding that the Act is unconstitutional as applied in this case because it encroaches on the power of the judicial branch, we further conclude that the Act is unconstitutional on its face because it delegates legislative power to the Governor. The Legislature is permitted to transfer subordinate functions "to permit administration of legislative policy by an agency with the expertise and flexibility to deal with complex and fluid conditions." However, under article II, section 3 of the constitution the Legislature "may not delegate the power to enact a law or the right to exercise unrestricted discretion in applying the law. This prohibition, known as the nondelegation doctrine, requires that "fundamental and primary policy decisions . . . be made by members of the legislature who are elected to perform those tasks, and [that the] administration of legislative programs must be pursuant to some minimal standards and guidelines ascertainable by reference to the enactment establishing the program."

In the final analysis it is the courts, upon a challenge to the exercise or nonexercise of administrative action, which must determine whether the administrative agency has performed consistently with the mandate of the legislature. When legislation is so lacking in guidelines that neither the agency nor the courts can determine whether the agency is carrying out the intent of the legislature in its conduct, then, in fact, the agency becomes the lawgiver rather than the administrator of the law.

In this case, the circuit court found that chapter 2003-418 contains no guidelines or standards that "would serve to limit the Governor from exercising completely unrestricted discretion in applying the law to" those who fall within its terms. The circuit court explained:

> The terms of the Act affirmatively confirm the discretionary power conferred upon the Governor. He is given the "authority to issue a one-time stay to prevent the withholding of nutrition and hydration from a patient" under certain circumstances but, he is not required to do so. Likewise, the act provides that the Governor "may lift the stay authorized under this act at any time. The Governor may revoke the stay upon a finding that a change in the condition of the patient warrants revocation." (Emphasis added). In both instances there is nothing to provide the Governor with any direction or guidelines for the exercise of this delegated authority. The Act does not suggest what constitutes "a change in condition of the patient" that could "warrant revocation." Even when such an undefined "change" occurs, the Governor is not compelled to act. The Act confers upon the Governor the unfettered discretion to determine what the terms of the Act mean and when, or if, he may act under it.

We agree with this analysis. In enacting chapter 2003-418, the Legislature failed to provide any standards by which the Governor should determine whether, in any given case, a stay should be issued and how long a stay should remain in effect. Further, the Legislature has failed to provide any criteria for lifting the stay. This absolute, unfettered discretion to decide whether to issue and then when to lift a stay makes the Governor's decision virtually unreviewable.

The Governor asserts that by enacting chapter 2003-418 the Legislature determined that he should be permitted to act as proxy for an incompetent patient in very narrow circumstances and, therefore, that his discretion is limited by the provisions of chapter 765. However, the Act does not refer to the provisions of chapter 765. Specifically, the Act does not amend section 765.401(1), Florida Statutes (2003), which sets forth an order of priority for determining who should act as proxy for an incapacitated patient who has no advance directive. Nor does the Act require that the Governor's decision be made in conformity with the requirement of section 765.401 that the proxy's decision be based on "the decision the proxy reasonably believes that patient would have made under the circumstances" or, if there is no indication of what the patient would have chosen, in the patient's best interests. § 765.401(2)-(3), Fla. Stat. (2003).

We also reject the Governor's argument that this legislation provides an additional layer of due process protection to those who are unable to communicate their wishes regarding end-of-life decisions. Parts I, II, III, and IV of chapter 765, enacted by the Legislature in 1992 and amended several times, n4 provide detailed protections for those who are adjudicated incompetent, including that the proxy's decision be based on what the patient would have chosen under the circumstances or is in the patient's best interest, and be supported by competent, substantial evidence.

In contrast to the protections set forth in chapter 765, chapter 2003-418's standardless, open-ended delegation of authority by the Legislature to the Governor provides no guarantee that the incompetent patient's right to withdraw life-prolonging procedures will in fact be honored. *See In re Guardianship of Browning*, 568 So. 2d 4, 12 (Fla. 1990) (reaffirming that an incompetent person has the same right to refuse medical treatment as a competent person). As noted above, the Act does not even require that the Governor consider the patient's wishes in deciding whether to issue a stay, and instead allows a unilateral decision by the Governor to stay the withholding of life-prolonging procedures without affording any procedural process to the patient.

Moreover, the argument that the Act broadly protects those who cannot protect themselves is belied by the case-specific criteria under which the Governor can exercise his discretion. The Act applies only if a court has found the individual to be in a persistent vegetative state and food and hydration have been ordered withdrawn. It does not authorize the Governor to intervene if a person in a persistent vegetative state is dependent upon another form of life support. Nor does the Act apply to a person who is not in a persistent vegetative state but a court finds, contrary to the wishes of another family member, that life support should be withdrawn. In theory, the Act could have applied during its fifteen-day window to more than one person, but it is undeniable that in fact the criteria fit only Theresa Schiavo.

In sum, although chapter 2003-418 applies to a limited class of people, it provides no criteria to guide the Governor's decision about whether to act. In addition, once the Governor has issued a stay as provided for in the Act, there are no criteria for the Governor to evaluate in deciding whether to lift the stay. Thus, chapter 2003-418 allows the Governor to act "through whim, show[] favoritism, or exercise unbridled discretion," *Lewis*, 346 So. 2d at 56, and is therefore an unconstitutional delegation of legislative authority.

CONCLUSION

The continuing vitality of our system of separation of powers precludes the other two branches from nullifying the judicial branch's final orders. If the Legislature with the assent of the Governor can do what was attempted here, the judicial branch would be subordinated to the final directive of the other branches. Also subordinated would be the rights of individuals, including the well established privacy right to self determination. *See Browning*, 568 So. 2d at 11-13. No court judgment could ever be considered truly final and no constitutional right truly secure, because the precedent of this case would hold to the contrary. Vested rights could be stripped away based on popular clamor. The essential core of what the Founding Fathers sought to change from their experience with English rule would be lost, especially their belief that our courts exist precisely to preserve the rights of individuals, even when doing so is contrary to popular will.

It is so ordered.

Wells, **Anstead, Lewis, Quince, Cantero** and **Bell**, JJ., concur.

NOTES AND QUESTIONS

1. The Florida legislature's efforts to repose unfettered authority in Governor Bush's hands were paralleled by Congress' efforts to confer jurisdiction on the federal courts to interfere. That hasty amendment to the United States Judicial Code provided as follows:

   > The United States District Court for the Middle District of Florida shall have jurisdiction to hear, determine, and render judgment on a suit or claim by or on behalf of Theresa Marie Schiavo for the alleged violation of any right of Theresa Marie Schiavo under the Constitution or laws of the United States relating to the withholding or withdrawal of food, fluids, or medical treatment necessary to sustain life.

   Pub. L. No. 109-3 (March 21, 2005).

   The Federal Courts rejected this legislation.

2. Why? Why were the legislative bodies of Florida and the United States so driven to act precipitiously and recklessly in the Schiavo case? Why were the courts not similarly motivated? Is it possible the legislatures could act as they did only because they knew the courts would defeat their efforts?

3. Is there a better way for these controversies to be resolved? What is it?

PROBLEM 1-19 — Unconscious Conception

A young lady, Cruzan Quinlan, recently married, was in an automobile accident with her new husband on the way back from their honeymoon. Both experienced terrible injuries but survived. Young Cruzan, however, is in a persistent vegetative state and, to a medical certainty, will never recover cognition. She was a recent law school graduate, and had discussed both the *Quinlan* and *Cruzan* cases with her parents and her new spouse, stating clearly two propositions: (a) she would not want to be continued in a persistent vegetative state and (b) should she be found in such a state before she and her new husband had children, she would want to conceive and bear a child and then be allowed to die.

The technology is available to arrange for Cruzan to conceive a child by her new husband and to carry the child to term. She and her husband had sought assistance of fertility experts and their fertilized eggs (pre-embryos) are available for return to her uterus. The physicians assure her family that this may be done and there is a normal likelihood that the child will be normal. The husband seeks such a pregnancy; her parents oppose it.

What should be done?

PROBLEM 1-20 — Futility and Baby Sun

In February and March of 2005, in Houston, Texas, a major controversy developed over the care and future of Baby Sun. He had been born without the capacity to develop lungs which would support him as he grew. Yet his mother, who believed she had conceived her son through a relationship with the Sun god (hence, the name), insisted on maximum care.

The attending physician entered a conclusion that care was futile: it would not cure Baby Sun's condition; he would die of the condition; and he could never develop naturally. The mother insisted care was not "futile," since it would prolong his life.

Who was right?

The case was referred to the hospital's Institutional Ethics Committee, which supported the physician's conclusion. Under Texas law, the hospital could then terminate after giving the mother ten days to transfer to another facility. Is this a good statute? Policy? Consistent with EMTALA?

As to futility of care, see generally, Report of the Council on Ethical and Judicial Affairs, *Medical Futility in End of Life Care*, JAMA 281: 937 (1999).

Withholding or withdrawing life support, nutrition and hydration may lead to death of a patient. If he or she is comatose or in a persistent vegetative state effecting death may be tolerable, but the calculus shifts when the patient is conscious and sentient.

WENDLAND v. WENDLAND

28 P.3d 151 (Cal. 2001)

Werdegar, J.

In this case we consider whether a conservator of the person may withhold artificial nutrition and hydration from a conscious conservatee who is not terminally ill, comatose, or in a persistent vegetative state, and who has not left formal instructions for health care or appointed an agent or surrogate for health care decisions. Interpreting Probate Code § 2355 in light of the relevant provisions of the California Constitution, we conclude a conservator may not withhold artificial nutrition and hydration from such a person absent clear and convincing evidence the conservator's decision is in accordance with either the conservatee's own wishes or best interest.

I. FACTS AND PROCEDURAL HISTORY

On September 29, 1993, Robert Wendland rolled his truck at high speed in a solo accident while driving under the influence of alcohol. The accident injured Robert's brain, leaving him conscious yet severely disabled, both mentally and physically, and dependent on artificial nutrition and hydration. Two years later, Rose Wendland, Robert's wife and conservator, proposed to direct his physician to remove his feeding tube and allow him to die. Florence Wendland and Rebekah Vinson (respectively Robert's mother and sister) objected to the conservator's decision. This proceeding arose under the provisions of the Probate Code authorizing courts to settle such disputes. (Prob. Code, §§ 2355, 2359.)

Following the accident, Robert remained in a coma, totally unresponsive, for several months. During this period Rose visited him daily, often with their children, and authorized treatment as necessary to maintain his health.

Robert eventually regained consciousness. His subsequent medical history is described in a comprehensive medical evaluation later submitted to the court. According to the report, Rose "first noticed signs of responsiveness sometime in late 1994 or early 1995 and alerted [Robert's] physicians and nursing staff." Intensive therapy followed. Robert's "cognitive responsiveness was observed to improve over a period of several months such that by late spring of 1995 the family and most of his health care providers agreed that he was inconsistently interacting with his environment. A video recording of [Robert] in July 1995 demonstrated clear, though inconsistent, interaction with his environment in response to simple commands. At his highest level of function between February and July, 1995, Robert was able to do such things as throw and catch a ball, operate an electric wheelchair with assistance, turn pages, draw circles, draw an 'R' and perform two-step commands." For example, "he was able to respond appropriately to the command 'close your eyes and open them when I say the number 3.' . . . He could choose a requested color block out of four color blocks. He could set the right peg in a pegboard. Augmented communication was met with inconsistent success. He remained unable to vocalize. Eye blinking was successfully used as a communication mode for a while, however no consistent method of communication was developed."

After Robert regained consciousness and while he was undergoing therapy, Rose authorized surgery three times to replace [illegible] physicians sought her permission a fourth time, she declined. She discussed the decision with her daughters and with Robert's brother Michael, all of whom believed that Robert would not have approved the procedure even if necessary to sustain his life. Rose also discussed the decision with Robert's treating physician, Dr. Kass, other physicians, and the hospital's ombudsman, all of whom apparently supported her decision. Dr. Kass, however, inserted a nasogastric feeding tube to keep Robert alive pending input from the hospital's ethics committee.

Eventually, the 20-member ethics committee unanimously approved Rose's decision. In the course of their deliberations, however, the committee did not speak with Robert's mother or sister. Florence learned, apparently through an anonymous telephone call, that Dr. Kass planned to remove Robert's feeding tube. Florence and Rebekah applied for a temporary restraining order to bar him from so doing, and the court granted the motion ex parte.

The trial generated the evidence set out above. The testifying physicians agreed that Robert would not likely experience further cognitive recovery. Dr. Kass, Robert's treating physician, testified that, to the highest degree of medical certainty, Robert would never be able to make medical treatment decisions, walk, talk, feed himself, eat, drink, or control his bowel and bladder functions. Robert was able, however, according to Dr. Kass, to express "certain desires . . . . Like if he's getting tired in therapy of if he wants to quit therapy, he's usually very adamant about that. He'll either strike out or he'll refuse to perform the task." Dr. Kobrin, Robert's neurologist, testified that Robert recognized certain caregivers and would allow only specific caregivers to bathe and help him. Both Dr. Kass and Dr. Kobrin had prescribed medication for Robert's behavioral problems. Dr. Sundance, who was retained by appointed counsel to evaluate Robert, described him as being in a "minimally conscious state in that he does have some cognitive function" and the ability to "respond to his environment," but not to "interact" with it "in a more proactive way."

On April 29, 1997, Dr. Kass asked Robert a series of questions using an augmented [illegible] tions about Robert's physical state, such as "Are you sitting up?" and "Are you lying down?" that Robert appeared to answer correctly "most times," Dr. Kass asked the following questions and received the following answers:

"Do you have pain? Yes.

"Do your legs hurt? No.

"Does your buttocks hurt? No.

"Do you want us to leave you alone? Yes.

"Do you want more therapy? No.

"Do you want to get into the chair? Yes.

"Do you want to go back to bed? No.

"Do you want to die? No answer.

"Are you angry? Yes.

"At somebody? No."

So far as Dr. Kass knew, no one had previously asked Robert the same questions. Dr. Kass acknowledged there was no way to verify whether Robert "really understood the questions or not," but "the reason I asked those questions," Dr. Kass continued, "is because [Robert] was able to answer the previous questions mostly correctly. So I thought perhaps he could understand more questions." Dr. Kass believed Robert probably understood some but not all of the questions. Robert's speech pathologist, Lowana Brauer, testified generally that Robert used the augmented communications device primarily as therapy and not with enough consistency to justify leaving the device in his room for communication with other people. She did not, however, testify specifically about the interaction between Robert and Dr. Kass.

Robert's wife, brother and daughter recounted pre-accident statements Robert had made about his attitude towards life-sustaining health care. Robert's wife recounted specific statements on two occasions. The first occasion was Rose's decision whether to turn off a respirator sustaining the life of her father, who was near death from gangrene. Rose recalls Robert saying: "I would never want to live like that, and I wouldn't want my children to see me like that and look at the hurt you're going through as an adult seeing your father like that." On cross-examination, Rose acknowledged Robert said on this occasion that Rose's father "wouldn't want to live like a vegetable" and "wouldn't want to live in a comatose state."

II. DISCUSSION

A. The Relevant Legal Principles

1. Constitutional and common law principles

One relatively certain principle is that a competent adult has the right to refuse medical treatment, even treatment necessary to sustain life. That a competent person has the right to refuse treatment is a statement both of common law and of state constitutional law. In its common law form, the principle is often traced to *Union Pacific Railway Co. v. Botsford* (1891) 141 U.S. 250, 251, in which the United States Supreme Court wrote that "no right is held more sacred, or is more carefully guarded, by the common law, than the right of every individual to the possession and control of his own person, free from all restraint or interference of others, unless by clear and unquestionable authority of law." Applying this principle, the high court held that the plaintiff in a personal injury case was not required to submit to a surgical examination intended to reveal the extent of her injuries. Courts in subsequent cases relied on the same principle to award damages for operations performed without the patient's consent. The landmark case is *Schloendorff v. Society of New York Hospital* (N.Y. 1914) 211 N.Y. 125, 105 N.E. 92, 93, in which Judge Cardozo wrote that "every human being of adult years and sound mind has a right to determine what shall be done with his own body; and a surgeon who performs an operation without his patient's consent commits an assault, for which he is liable in damages." We adopted this principle in *Cobbs v. Grant* (1972) 8 Cal. 3d 229, 242, 104 Cal. Rptr. 505, 502 P.2d 1 [illegible]

The Courts of Appeal have found another source for the same right in the California Constitution's privacy clause. (Cal. Const., art. I, § 1.) The court in *Bartling v. Superior Court* (1984) 163 Cal. App. 3d 186, 209 Cal. Rptr. 220 held that a competent adult with serious, probably incurable illnesses was entitled to have life-support equipment disconnected over his physicians' objection even though that would hasten his death. To the same effect is the decision in *Bouvia v. Superior Court* (1986) 179 Cal. App. 3d 1127, 225 Cal. Rptr. 297, in which the court directed injunctive relief requiring a public hospital to comply with a competent, terminally ill patient's direction to remove a nasogastric feeding tube. "The right to refuse medical treatment," the court wrote, "is basic and fundamental. . . . Its exercise requires no one's approval. It is not merely one vote subject to being overridden by medical opinion." (*Id.* at p. 1137; see also *Rains v. Belshe* (1995) 32 Cal. App. 4th 157, 169.

Federal law has little to say about the competent person's right to refuse treatment, but what it does say is not to the contrary. The United States Supreme Court spoke provisionally to the point in *Cruzan v. Director, Missouri Dept. of Health* (1990) 497 U.S. 261, 111 L. Ed. 2d 224, 110 S. Ct. 2841 (*Cruzan*).

In view of these authorities, the competent adult's right to refuse medical treatment may be safely considered established, at least in California.

The same right survives incapacity, in a practical sense, if exercised while competent pursuant to a law giving that act lasting validity. For some time, California law has given competent adults the power to leave formal directions for health care in the event they later become incompetent; over time, the Legislature has afforded ever greater scope to that power. Briefly, and as relevant here, the new law permits a competent person to execute an advance directive about "any aspect" of health care. (§ 4701.) Among other things, a [illegible] under conditions specified by the person and not limited to terminal illness, permanent coma, or persistent vegetative state. A competent person may still use a power of attorney for health care to give an agent the power to make health care decisions, but a patient may also orally designate a surrogate to make such decisions by personally informing the patient's supervising health care provider. Under the new law, agents and surrogates are required to make health care decisions "in accordance with the principal's individual health care instructions, if any, and other wishes to the extent known to the agent."

In contrast, decisions made by conservators typically derive their authority from a different basis — the *parens patriae* power of the state to protect incompetent persons. Unlike an agent or a surrogate for health care, who is voluntarily appointed by a competent person, a conservator is appointed by the court because the conservatee "has been adjudicated to lack the capacity to make health care decisions."

2. Section 2355

The ultimate focus of our analysis, as mentioned at the outset, must be section 2355, the statute under which the conservator claims the authority to end the conservatee's life. The statute's history indicates that the Law Revision Commission, which drafted the current version, was aware of and intended to incorporate some, but not all, of the *Drabick* court's construction of the former statute.

As originally enacted in 1979, and at the time the lower courts ruled in this case, section 2355 provided: "If the conservatee has been adjudicated to lack the capacity to give informed consent for medical treatment, the conservator has the exclusive authority to give consent for such medical treatment to be performed on the conservatee as the conservator in good faith based on medical advice determines to be necessary and the conservator may require the conservatee to receive such medical treatment, whether or not the conservatee objects."

In other respects, the current version of section 2355 departs from the decision in [*In Re Conservatorship of*] *Drabick*, '200 Cal. App. 3d 185. The *Drabick* court viewed the informally expressed wishes of the incompetent conservatee simply as a factor for the conservator to consider in determining the conservatee's best interest. In contrast to *Drabick*, section 2355 assigns dispositive weight to the conservatee's informally expressed wishes, when known. Under the statute, "the conservator shall make health care decisions for the conservatee in accordance with the conservatee's individual health care instructions, if any, and other wishes to the extent known to the conservator." (§ 2355, subd. (a).) The best interest standard applies only when the conservatee's wishes are not known, as a fall-back standard embodied in the statute's next sentence: "Otherwise, the conservator shall make the decision in accordance with the conservator's determination of the conservatee's best interest. In determining the conservatee's best interest, the conservator shall consider the conservatee's personal values to the extent known to the conservator."

B. The Present Case

This background illuminates the parties' arguments, which reduce in essence to this: The conservator has claimed the power under section 2355, as she interprets it, to direct the conservatee's health care providers to cease providing artificial nutrition and hydration. In opposition, the objectors have contended the statute violates the conservatee's rights to privacy and life under the facts of this case if the conservator's interpretation of the statute is correct.

1. The primary standard: a decision in accordance with the conservatee's wishes

The conservator argues the Legislature understood and intended that the low preponderance of the evidence standard would apply. Certainly this was the Law Revision Commission's understanding.

The objectors, in opposition, argue that section 2355 would be unconstitu- [illegible] vatee based on a finding by the low preponderance of the evidence standard that the latter would not want to live. We see no basis for holding the statute unconstitutional on its face. We do, however, find merit in the objectors' argument. We therefore construe the statute to minimize the possibility of its unconstitutional application by requiring clear and convincing evidence of a conscious conservatee's wish to refuse life-sustaining treatment when the conservator relies on that asserted wish to justify withholding life-sustaining treatment.

The only apparent purpose of requiring conservators to make decisions in accordance with the conservatee's wishes, when those wishes are known, is to enforce the fundamental principle of personal autonomy. The same requirement, as applied to agents and surrogates freely designated by competent persons, enforces the principles of agency. A reasonable person presumably will designate for such purposes only a person in whom the former reposes the highest degree of confidence. A conservator, in contrast, is *not* an agent of the conservatee, and unlike a freely designated agent cannot be presumed to have special knowledge of the conservatee's health care wishes. A person with "sufficient capacity . . . to form an intelligent preference" may nominate his or her own conservator (§ 1810), but the nomination is not binding because the appointment remains "solely in the discretion of the court" (§ 1812, subd. (a)). Furthermore, while statutory law gives preference to spouses and other persons related to the conservatee (*id.*, subd. (b)), who might know something of the conservatee's health care preferences, the law also permits the court in its sole discretion to appoint unrelated persons and even public conservators (*ibid.*). While it may be constitutionally permissible to assume that an agent freely designated by a formerly competent person to make all health care decisions, including life-ending ones, will resolve such questions "in accordance with the principal's . . . wishes" (§ 4684), one cannot apply the same assumption to conservators and conservatees (cf. § 2355, subd, (a)). For this reason, when the legal premise of a conservator's decision to end a conservatee's life by withholding medical care is that the conservatee would refuse such care, to apply a high standard of proof will help to ensure the reliability of the decision.

In this case, the importance of the ultimate decision and the risk of error are manifest. So too should be the degree of confidence required in the necessary findings of fact. The ultimate decision is whether a conservatee lives or dies, and the risk is that a conservator, claiming statutory authority to end a conscious conservatee's life "in accordance with the conservatee's . . . wishes" by withdrawing artificial nutrition and hydration, will make a decision with which the conservatee subjectively disagrees and which subjects the conservatee to starvation, dehydration and death. This would represent the gravest possible affront to a conservatee's state constitutional right to privacy, in the sense of freedom from unwanted bodily intrusions, and to life.

2. *The best interest standard*

Having rejected the conservator's argument that withdrawing artificial hydration and nutrition would have been "in accordance with the conservatee's

. . . wishes," we must next consider her contention that the same action would have been proper under the fall-back best interest standard. Under that standard, "the conservator shall make the decision in accordance with the conservator's determination of the conservatee's best interest. In determining the conservatee's best interest, the conservator shall consider the conservatee's personal values to the extent known to the conservator." The trial court, as noted, ruled the conservator had the burden of establishing that the withdrawal of artificially delivered nutrition and hydration was in the conservatee's best interest, and had not met that burden.

Here, as before, the conservator argues that the trial court applied too high a standard of proof. This follows, she contends, from section 2355, which gives her as conservator "the *exclusive* authority" to give consent for such medical treatment as she "in good faith based on medical advice determines to be necessary."

The conservator's understanding of section 2355 is not correct. To be sure, the statute provides that "the conservator shall make the decision in accordance with *the conservator's determination* of the conservatee's best interest." But the conservator herself concedes the court must be able to review her decision for abuse of discretion. This much, at least, follows from the conservator's status as an officer of the court subject to judicial supervision. While the assessment of a conservatee's best interest belongs in the first instance to the conservator, this does not mean the court must invariably defer to the conservator regardless of the evidence.

In the exceptional case where a conservator proposes to end the life of a conscious but incompetent conservatee, we believe the same factor that principally justifies applying the clear and convincing evidence standard to a determination of the conservatee's wishes also justifies applying that standard to a determination of the conservatee's best interest: The decision threatens the conservatee's fundamental rights to privacy and life. While section 2355 is written with sufficient breadth to cover all health care decisions, the Legislature cannot have intended to authorize every conceivable application without meaningful judicial review. Taken to its literal extremes, the statute would permit a conservator to withdraw health care necessary to life from any conservatee who had been adjudicated incompetent to make health care decisions, regardless of the degree of mental and physical impairment, and on no greater showing than that the conservator in good faith considered treatment not to be in the conservatee's best interest. The result would be to permit a conservator freely to end a conservatee's life based on the conservator's subjective assessment, albeit "in good faith [and] based on medical advice," that the conservatee enjoys an unacceptable quality of life. We find no reason to believe the Legislature intended section 2355 to confer power so unlimited and no authority for such a result in any judicial decision. Under these circumstances, we may properly construe the statute to require proof by clear and convincing evidence to avoid grave injury to the fundamental rights of conscious but incompetent conservatees. . . .

III. CONCLUSION

For the reasons set out above, we conclude the superior court correctly required the conservator to prove, by clear and convincing evidence, either that the conservatee wished to refuse life-sustaining treatment or that to [illegible] evidence, the superior court correctly denied the conservator's request for permission to withdraw artificial hydration and nutrition. We emphasize, however, that the clear and convincing evidence standard does not apply to the vast majority of health care decisions made by conservators under section 2355. Only the decision to withdraw life-sustaining treatment, because of its effect on a conscious conservatee's fundamental rights, justifies imposing that high standard of proof. Therefore, our decision today affects only a narrow class of persons: conscious conservatees who have not left formal directions for health care and whose conservators propose to withhold life-sustaining treatment for the purpose of causing their conservatees' deaths. Our conclusion does not affect permanently unconscious patients, including those who are comatose or in a persistent vegetative state, persons who have left legally cognizable instructions for health care, persons who have designated agents or other surrogates for health care, or conservatees for whom conservators have made medical decisions other than those intended to bring about the death of a conscious conservatee.

The decision of the Court of Appeal is reversed.

NOTES AND QUESTIONS

1. The *Wendland* case goes beyond existing case law, such as *Cruzan* and *Quinlan*. In those cases, the patient was comatose, or in a persistent vegetative state, unlikely ever to recover or resume a functioning life. Moreover, and more importantly, there was no evidence of a capacity to experience sensations, communicate, or perceive surroundings. All of those capabilities seemed possessed by Robert Wendland. Do they matter? If he is to die, we must differentiate him from those of us who will live. How shall we do that?

2. As is often the case, one may ask how this case gets into court. Who brought it, and how does that person have a cognizable interest — a right or obligation to sue? Might a court best resolve these issues by simply denying such a right?

3. Is the issue whether to withdraw nutrition and hydration, or to authorize surgery to restore a tube for those purposes? Does it matter? And is it correct to characterize this as involving "treatment"? Isn't it just custodial care?

4. Also, if the standard is different for an "attorney" than for a "conservator" (is it?), which is Mrs. Wendland? Does it matter? How does the Court and § 2355 treat the *Drabick* opinion in this regard?

5. Should the conservator be required to respect the conservatee's wishes? What of the *public's* interests? Why does the Court treat the wishes of hospitals, doctors, funding agencies as irrelevant? Shouldn't these be considered at least in the "fall-back" situation, where the patient's wishes are unknown?

PROBLEM 1-21 — Anthrax

Following the terrorist attacks of September 11, 2001, in New York City and Washington DC, a number of citizens were vaccinated against Anthrax, a deadly bacteria used as a biological weapon. The fatality rate is over 86% in American studies, but is estimated over 97% in the UK. (From CDC website/ ACIP guidelines: *www.cdc.gov.*)

Many of the reported severe reactions to the vaccine have not been proven by the CDC or military; nevertheless the anthrax vaccine is not recommended for most citizens, and is considered an "investigational new drug."

In 1999, an active serviceman, Schwartz, refused the vaccine, and was subsequently discharged for bad conduct.

Is refusal of this vaccine by a service member covered under the scope of *Cruzan* and *Quinlan* and the right of refusal of medical treatments? Why or why not? Should military personnel have a lesser right of refusal than others? How about emergency care providers? Would you give more credence to the wishes of a doctor against vaccination as opposed to a military serviceman?

How are your views influenced by your own knowledge (or fear?) of recent terror activities? Should it matter that Mr. Schwartz' refusal came *before* the September 11th attacks and the July 2005 bombings in London and Egypt?

PROBLEM 1-22 — Tennis, Anyone?

The September 2006 issue of *Science* magazine carries a piece by neurologist Adrian M. Owen in which a woman in a persistent vegetative state was told that in a few minutes they would say the word "tennis" to her and they wanted her to visualize that she was serving and volleying. They then measured brain wave activity identical to that of a fully-functioning individual. There was a similar result when they asked her to visualize moving from room to room in her home...When words were spoken to her, the language processing part of the brain was activitated, as with normal people, but not when nonsense words were spoken.

What are the implications of these findings for cases like those of *Quinlan*, *Cruzan*, and *Schiavo*? At a minimum, do these findings mean that these tests, or similar ones, must be performed before withdrawal of life support or nutrition may be authorized? Or, furthermore, do they mean that life support and nutrition simply must be maintained on the assumption that there may be activity or sentience which simply cannot be measured?

Chapter 2

AUTONOMY AND RIGHTS

§ 2.01 Introduction

The preceding chapter was concerned with defining the community. Exclusion may affect people by deeming them to be "property" or "aliens." Even if included in the community, some humans are accorded lesser dignity and respect, as with "prisoners" or the "insane." And those who are unborn or who are deemed "dead" may not even be considered to be members of the community. The community deals inconsistently with such beings and has ambiguous and confused criteria in categorizing them.

The present chapter is concerned with those whom we agree are persons: what we must respect about them, how we impose upon them, how they may insist on integrity or privacy, and how, when confronted by community demands, they may resist and assert the dictates of their own consciences or protect the integrity of their identities. These are important matters of human rights, addressed by philosophers over millennia, from Aristotle to Aquinas, from Locke to Rawls, from Thoreau to Ghandi to King. Our lens is contemporary, limited to judicial opinions, and focused on bioethics considerations, but the view is of ancient lankmarks.

The United States Constitution protects "liberty," which means that it is concerned with defining the elements of "liberty" and the circumstances under which they may make a difference. The Constitution and the United Nations Declaration of Human Rights specifically protect matters of belief, speech and conscience. These are particularly important areas of liberty. The Declaration and the Constitution also protect the "security" of people from unreasonable searches and seizures, and invasions, ensuring that their privacy and personal dignity can be compromised only for good cause. Perhaps most important, and yet curiously overlooked in most bioethics discussions, the Constitution protects the right of people to sexual intimacy, to associate in families, and to marry. In this constitutional jurisprudence, liberty rests on a biologically-grounded core of values, and it includes the right — recognized by the Council of Europe — to control one's own biological destiny. *Cruzan* and *Casey* are both authority to that end.

The first part of this chapter draws upon the preceding chapter in determining not who *qualifies* as a person within the community, but how that person's *identity* is established and protected. Issues of memory, gender and language are important here. These are a function not only of biology but also *choice*. This chapter then deals with bodily integrity and society's need for bodily invasion, testing or control, as with polygraphs or psychosurgery or ECT (electro-convulsive therapy). Because integrity implicates identity, this chapter also deals with cloning humans, the ultimate expression (or compromise) of identity. This chapter also addresses privacy, the zone of interests around a person — usually called a "home" or "family," into which the state may simply not go. And it closes with matters of conscience and dissent, as they relate to bioethical issues, such as homosexuality and the origin of the species.

§ 2.02 Identity

Identity is a complex of factors distinguishing one person from another. No two people are alike, being separated by parentage, race, gender, size, age, culture, language and life experience. This individuality is both a treasure and a burden for persons and society; it marks the boundary between rights and responsibility.

In ethical and legal terms, identity at least includes the concepts of memory and gender. These are both organic and mutable; each involves choice and judgment. Yet we commonly believe there are fixed groundings to memory and gender — that things exist objectively, in the body or in "reality." The proposition that identity — memory, gender and other elements such as language or even age and height — can be influenced by *choice* is highly controversial. Language — dealt with in the third part of this section — is the ultimate expression of choice in identity. Language is an amalgam of our memory, history and ethnicity, our place and our association, and our own self-image — how we choose to present ourselves to the world. It raises the truly important question — if choice is present even with fundamentals such as gender or memory, then what are the ethics of such choices? And how shall they be made?

[1] Repressed Memory

By "memory" we mean at least two things: the accumulated *contents* of a person's experience and the *process* of accumulation and recall. That *process* is essential to autonomy. The question posed is, to what extent may others facilitate or displace the process, reshaping memory and identity? And since we usually expect memory to accord with "reality," what do we *mean* by "reality" and *how* do we establish or find it?

ROCK v. ARKANSAS
483 U.S. 44 (1987)

Justice **Blackmun** delivered the opinion of the Court.

The issue presented in this case is whether Arkansas' evidentiary rule prohibiting the admission of hypnotically refreshed testimony violated petitioner's constitutional right to testify on her own behalf as a defendant in a criminal case.

I

Petitioner Vickie Lorene Rock was charged with manslaughter in the death of her husband, Frank Rock, on July 2, 1983. A dispute had been simmering about Frank's wish to move from the couple's small apartment adjacent to Vickie's beauty parlor to a trailer she owned outside town. That night a fight erupted when Frank refused to let petitioner eat some pizza and prevented her from leaving the apartment to get something else to eat. When police [illegible] they found Frank on the floor with a bullet wound in his chest. Petitioner urged the officers to help her husband, and cried to a sergeant who took her in charge, "please save him" and "don't let him die." . . .

Because petitioner could not remember the precise details of the shooting, her attorney suggested that she submit to hypnosis in order to refresh her memory. Petitioner was hypnotized twice by Doctor Betty Back, a licensed neuropsychologist with training in the field of hypnosis. Doctor Back interviewed petitioner for an hour prior to the first hypnosis session, taking notes on petitioner's general history and her recollections of the shooting. Both hypnosis sessions were recorded on tape. Petitioner did not relate any new information during either of the sessions, but, after the hypnosis, she was able to remember that at the time of the incident she had her thumb on the hammer of the gun, but had not held her finger on the trigger. She also recalled that the gun had discharged when her husband grabbed her arm during the scuffle. As a result of the details that petitioner was able to remember about the shooting, her counsel arranged for a gun expert to examine the handgun, a single-action Hawes .22 Deputy Marshal. That inspection revealed that the gun was defective and prone to fire, when hit or dropped, without the trigger's being pulled.

When the prosecutor learned of the hypnosis sessions, he filed a motion to exclude petitioner's testimony. The trial judge held a pretrial hearing on the motion and concluded that no hypnotically refreshed testimony would be admitted. The court issued an order limiting petitioner's testimony to "matters remembered and stated to the examiner prior to being placed under hypnosis." At trial, petitioner introduced testimony by the gun expert, but the court limited petitioner's own description of the events on the day of the shooting to a reiteration of the sketchy information in Doctor Back's notes. The jury convicted petitioner on the manslaughter charge and she was sentenced to 10 years' imprisonment and a $10,000 fine.

. . . .

III

The question now before the Court is whether a criminal defendant's right to testify may be restricted by a state rule that excludes her posthypnosis testimony. This is not the first time this Court has faced a constitutional challenge to a state rule, designed to ensure trustworthy evidence, that interfered with the ability of a defendant to offer testimony. In *Washington v. Texas*, 388 U.S. 14 (1967), the Court was confronted with a state statute that prevented persons charged as principals, accomplices, or accessories in the same crime from being introduced as witnesses for one another.

. . . .

[T]he Court reasoned that the Sixth Amendment was designed in part "to make the testimony of a defendant's witnesses admissible on his behalf in court."

. . . .

Just as a State may not apply an arbitrary rule of competence to exclude a material defense witness from taking the stand, it also may not apply a rule of evidence that permits a witness to take the stand, but arbitrarily excludes material portions of his testimony. . . .

Of course, the right to present relevant testimony is not without limitation. The right "may, in appropriate cases, bow to accommodate other legitimate interests in the criminal trial process." But restrictions of a defendant's right to testify may not be arbitrary or disproportionate to the purposes they are designed to serve. In applying its evidentiary rules a State must evaluate whether the interests served by a rule justify the limitation imposed on the defendant's constitutional right to testify.

IV

The Arkansas rule enunciated by the state courts does not allow a trial court to consider whether post-hypnosis testimony may be admissible in a particular case; it is a *per se* rule prohibiting the admission at trial of any defendant's hypnotically refreshed testimony on the ground that such testimony is always unreliable. Thus, in Arkansas, an accused's testimony is limited to matters that he or she can prove were remembered *before* hypnosis. This rule operates to the detriment of any defendant who undergoes hypnosis, without regard to the reasons for it, the circumstances under which it took place, or any independent verification of the information it produced.

In this case, the application of that rule had a significant adverse effect on petitioner's ability to testify. It virtually prevented her from describing any of the events that occurred on the day of the shooting, despite corroboration of many of those events by other witnesses. Even more importantly, under the court's rule petitioner was not permitted to describe the actual shooting except in the words contained in Doctor Back's notes. The expert's description of the gun's tendency to misfire would have taken on greater significance if the jury had heard petitioner testify that she did not have her finger on the trigger and that the gun went off when her husband hit her arm.

In establishing its *per se* rule, the Arkansas Supreme Court simply followed the approach taken by a number of States that have decided that hypnotically enhanced testimony should be excluded at trial on the ground that it tends to be unreliable. Other States that have adopted an exclusionary rule, however, have done so for the testimony of *witnesses*, not for the testimony of a *defendant*. The Arkansas Supreme Court failed to perform the constitutional analysis that is necessary when a defendant's right to testify is at stake.

. . . .

Responses of individuals to hypnosis vary greatly. The popular belief that hypnosis guarantees the accuracy of recall is as yet without established foundation and, in fact, hypnosis often has no effect at all on memory. The most common response to hypnosis, however, appears to be an increase in both correct and incorrect recollections.[1] Three general characteristics of hypnosis may lead to the introduction of inaccurate memories: the subject becomes "suggestible" and may try to please the hypnotist with answers the subject thinks will be met with approval; the subject is likely to "confabulate," that is, to fill in details from the imagination in order to make an answer more coherent and complete; and, the subject experiences "memory hardening," which gives him great confidence in both true and false memories, making effective cross-examination more difficult. Despite the unreliability that hypnosis concededly may introduce, however, the procedure has been credited as instrumental in obtaining investigative leads or identifications that were later confirmed by independent evidence. . . .

The inaccuracies the process introduces can be reduced, although perhaps not eliminated, by the use of procedural safeguards. One set of suggested guidelines calls for hypnosis to be performed only by a psychologist or psychiatrist with special training in its use and who is independent of the investigation. These procedures reduce the possibility that biases will be communicated to the hypersuggestive subject by the hypnotist. Suggestion will be less likely also if the hypnosis is conducted in a neutral setting with no one present but the hypnotist and the subject. Tape or video recording of all interrogations, before, during, and after hypnosis, can help reveal if leading questions were asked. Such guidelines do not guarantee the accuracy of the testimony, because they cannot control the subject's own motivations or any tendency to confabulate, but they do provide a means of controlling overt suggestions.

. . . .

We are not now prepared to endorse without qualifications the use of hypnosis as an investigative tool; scientific understanding of the phenomenon and of the means to control the effects of hypnosis is still in its infancy. Arkansas, however, has not justified the exclusion of *all* of a defendant's testimony that the defendant is unable to prove to be the product of prehypnosis memory. A State's legitimate interest in barring unreliable evidence does not extend to *per se* exclusions that may be reliable in an individual case. Wholesale inadmissibility of a defendant's testimony is an arbitrary restriction on the right to testify in the absence of clear evidence by the State repudiating the validity of all posthypnosis recollections. . . .

. . . .

The judgment of the Supreme Court of Arkansas is vacated, and the case is remanded to that court for further proceedings not inconsistent with this opinion.

. . . .

[1] "[W]hen hypnosis is used to refresh recollection, one of the following outcomes occurs: (1) hypnosis produces recollections that are not substantially different from nonhypnotic recollections; (2) it yields recollections that are more inaccurate than nonhypnotic memory; or, most frequently, (3) it results in more information being reported, but these recollections contain both accurate and inaccurate details. There are no data to support a fourth alternative, namely, that hypnosis increases remembering of only accurate information."

NOTES AND QUESTIONS

1. The most elementary and fundamental aspect of identity and of competence is memory. Whether as a plumber, attorney or student, whether as a mother, astronaut, or homemaker shopping at a supermarket, if a person cannot observe, recall and communicate from his or her memory, then the person's identity and competence as an individual are severely compromised. Without memory, a "person" simply vanishes. This is the tragedy of Alzheimer's Disease.
2. Who "is" Vickie Rock? Which — before or after hypnosis — is the "real" person?
3. Ultimately, is there any way, realistically, that hypnosis can avoid affecting all aspects of a person's recall? How would the impact of newly introduced or created memories, whether refreshed or fabricated, ever be traced adequately subsequent to the event of refreshment through hypnosis?
4. How would you as counsel for either side in *Rock,* on remand, prepare to explain or demonstrate to the jury the significance of hypnosis? What *is* its significance?
5. In *Rock*, if you were the prosecutor on remand, what would you seek by way of protective procedures? Protective orders? What lines of cross-examination would you develop?
6. In *Rock,* it is possible that the defendant might have told the hypnotherapist information that would tend to incriminate her. If so, what obligation to disclose would the hypnotist have had?

S.V. v. R.V.

933 S.W.2d 1 (Tex. 1996)

Opinion by: Nathan L. **Hecht.**

. . . .

II

. . . .

S. was born in 1942. He received a B.A. degree and an M.B.A. degree, entered the U.S. Army as a commissioned officer, and served eighteen months in the medical corps in Vietnam. In March 1970, a few months after his discharge from the Army, S., then 27, married B., then 22, who had received her B.A. degree in elementary education and had just begun teaching when she met S. Neither had previously been married. Shortly after the birth of their first child, R., on October 15, 1970, S. was fired from his job, and the family moved to Texas. S. and B.'s only other child, H., was born in August 1975.

. . . .

From all outward appearances, however, they seemed a model family. R. and H. were bright, well-behaved children. They attended a private girls' school. R. was at least an average student and her teachers liked her. . . .

R. expressed interest in the subject of incest. She participated in an improvisational theater group for teenagers, taking part in a sketch dealing with incest. In 1988, her junior year in high school, she wrote a term paper on father-daughter incest. Citing several books on the subject, the paper described the impact of incest on the victim daughter, the abusing father, and innocent family members. R. worked on another paper on incest her freshman year of college.

. . . .

At the end of her first year she returned to Dallas. On May 18, 1990, B. told R. that she, B., had been sexually abused as a child. B.'s first recollection of her own experiences had come to her a year earlier during an annual physical examination administered by her physician. She remembers that he asked her without warning, "Who sexually abused you as a child?" Instantly she recalled two instances, both involving her mother's father, that she had never before remembered. . . .

. . . .

Just before Thanksgiving, R. had her first image of incest. She testified that she had been napping in her room

> and was kind of half asleep and half awake, and was dreaming. And I had this dream of this authority — this man, but it was an authority figure — and he didn't have a face, it was just this, it was just that authority figure over this young girl. And he was forcing himself upon her. And it wasn't all real clear, it was a dream. The girl just had kind of brownish, blondish hair, kind of long, and as I said, the man didn't have a face. At first R. assumed the little girl was her mother, but then she began to feel what the little girl must have felt. She did not recognize the faceless man at the time, and never has.

R. called Frazier [a counselor] and told her about the dream. Frazier suggested that they meet at Thanksgiving while R. was home. During that meeting R. told Frazier that she believed the dream had something to do with her father. Frazier had her lie on the floor, breathe deeply, and say whatever [illegible] "[illegible] work" or free association. R. testified: "I had this, just this picture of myself and my dad and we were sitting on the edge of the bed in his room and he just had his hand on my chest, like inside my blouse. That was all."

Later the same day R. was trying to do homework when she started writing about the little girl she had seen in her first dream. The little girl was three or four years old, and her father was forcing her to touch his genitals, telling her that she was loving him and making him feel good. As she wrote, R. realized that she was the little girl and S. was the father.

A week or so later R. met with her mother and sister in Frazier's office and told them what she had recalled. B. and H. knew nothing to indicate that S. had abused R., and they found it hard to imagine, but they nevertheless believed R. Knowing the family as she did, Frazier was surprised by R.'s account of abuse, but as their discussions continued, Frazier also became convinced R. was telling the truth.

. . . .

As her memories flooded back, R. became increasingly dysfunctional. She did not return to college until January 1992 but remained at home with her mother and sister. She continued to meet with Frazier and began seeing a psychiatrist. Eventually R. recalled numerous instances when S. forced her to engage in a variety of sexual contacts. She also recalls that S.'s father fondled her.

The memories R. took longest in recalling were of the two occasions S. had intercourse with her. The first time she was at home with her family on her seventeenth birthday, in October 1987. The second time was in a motel room in August 1990, when S. had driven R. back to college for the start of her sophomore year. Although R. was nearly twenty years old at the time, and began to recall instances of abuse three months later, she had no memory of the occurrence until shortly before trial, which took place in June 1992. (R. does not include the August 1990 event in her allegations in this case. In her pleadings she specifically limited the period for which she is claiming damages to 1973-1988, and she does not seek recovery for any abuse that occurred within two years of her filing suit.)

At trial, R.'s experts explained how she could have been abused so often for so long without remembering anything until November 1990. They attributed the phenomenon to two psychological defense mechanisms — dissociation and repression — which we discuss more fully in Part IV. As explained by the experts at trial, dissociation is the segregation of part of a person's mental process from the rest of it, so that certain ideas or experiences are removed from the main stream of consciousness. Repression blocks all memory of a traumatic event until the mind is prepared to cope with it. The experts testified that because S.'s abuse was so traumatic, she insulated herself first by being mentally "absent" while it was happening, and then by blocking all memory of it. . . . The experts agreed that R. was not consciously aware of S.'s abuse until November 1990.

Frazier, the counselor who helped R. recover her memories, based her therapy on the treatment for post-traumatic stress disorder. In more than seventy sessions with R., Frazier encouraged her to recognize that her symptoms were based on a trauma, then re-experience the trauma, and then "own" the experience. Frazier considered that it was her responsibility, not to attempt to verify R.'s recollections, but to provide R. a safe place in which to remember them. Although Frazier never hypnotized R., she had her relax and recount whatever came into her head, a technique Frazier described as similar to hypnosis. Frazier also used a technique she called "guided imagery": she would read aloud memory fragments R. had written down earlier, and R. would fill in other recollections. Frazier had R. write down her dreams and then helped her interpret them. Frazier also instructed R. to write questions about her experiences with one hand and answers with the other. Switching hands, Frazier testified, helps a patient access her subconscious.

. . . .

Frazier testified that she had never known a patient to have a false memory of childhood abuse and did not believe that it happened. Two other experts who testified for R., Dr. Madigan, a psychiatrist, and Dr. Powitsky, a forensic clinical psychologist, acknowledged that patients sometimes have false memories, but they were both convinced, for several reasons, that R.'s recollections were valid. First, her symptomatology was consistent with that of other survivors of childhood sexual abuse: headaches, gastrointestinal problems, fatigue, nightmares, low self-esteem, depression, anxiety, body memories, gagging, distraction, fear of sexual intercourse, and lack of emotion in recounting memories. . . .

Second, the Minnesota Multiphasic Personality Inventory test administered to R. showed a classic "V" profile, shared by many survivors of sexual abuse. The experts admitted, however, that the test was not conclusive of abuse. Dr. Powitsky also noted that R. has traits of a borderline personality disorder, although she does not have that disorder. People with this disorder, he testified, are prone to distort the truth.

. . . .

Finally, all three experts noted the consistent, vivid details of R.'s memories. They were each convinced that R. could not have made up the events she claimed to recall. Dr. Madigan testified that R. did not appear to be the sort of person who was highly suggestible or who could be brainwashed. As Dr. Powitsky confirmed at trial, R. would "have to get an Oscar to give those details if they weren't true."

. . . .

III

R. sued S. for negligence "during the years 1973 through 1988, inclusively," in engaging or attempting to engage in sexual acts or contacts with her, and exposing himself to her while he was nude and aroused. She alleged that S.'s negligence was a breach of her right to privacy and caused her damages not in excess of $10 million. . . .

. . . .

The only physical evidence to support R.'s allegations consists of her symptoms and to a lesser extent her behavioral traits, as described by her and the experts who testified on her behalf. In every instance this evidence was inconclusive. The experts testified that R.'s symptoms could have been caused by other things than sexual abuse by her father. While R. fit a behavioral profile for someone who has been sexually abused, the experts acknowledged that did not mean she had actually been abused. Tests on S. were also inconclusive. While he had many of the characteristics of a sex abuser, he did not match a characteristic profile, and even if he had, it would not prove that he abused R. . . .

. . . .

IV

Dr. Madigan, a psychiatrist who examined R. and testified at trial on her behalf, stated that psychiatry is not an exact science. Recognizing the reality of false claims of sexual abuse and the danger they pose to innocent people,

Dr. Madigan told the jury: "I think it's a tremendous burden for everybody in this room to figure it out."

Dr. Madigan accurately characterized the problems of trying to determine whether childhood sexual abuse has occurred when the victim has repressed all memory of it for a long period of time. The scientific literature on memory in general and recovered memory in particular establishes the wealth of uncertainty about these subjects. There is some agreement among psychiatrists concerning psychiatric treatment in this area. See American Psychiatric Ass'n, Statement on Memories of Sexual Abuse (1993), *reprinted in* 42 Int'L J. Clinical & Experimental Hypnosis 261 (1994) [hereinafter Memories of Sexual Abuse]. But there is little agreement on the validity of recovered memories or on the techniques used to retrieve them.

. . . .

There is basic agreement about the workings of the memory process. The senses register an event; these sense images are organized into meaningful units; the organized images are stored or "encoded" in the brain's neural structure; and finally, memories are retrieved and recounted. Elizabeth Loftus & Katherine Ketcham, The Myth of Repressed Memory: False Memories And Allegations of Sexual Abuse 75 (1994). See also Roberta L. Klatzky, Human Memory: Structure and Processes 2-9 (2d ed. 1980). People commonly recall little from the first five to seven years of life, and very infrequently anything before the age of two or three, principally because the brain has not matured sufficiently to assimilate and carry forward meaningful memories.

Explicit, or declarative, memory refers to the ability to consciously recall events or facts. Implicit, or procedural, memory is behavioral knowledge of an experience without conscious recall. Examples of the latter are knowing how to ride a bicycle and a combat veteran's feeling of panic upon hearing helicopters without remembering specifically the helicopter crash that killed a friend. These two types of memory appear to be supported by different brain systems. Some have posited that procedural memory may remain after declarative memory of the event that generated it has vanished. Procedural memory could therefore play a role in tending to confirm or belie an accusation of abuse. The problem, of course, is that a certain type of procedural memory, like gagging, may indicate child abuse, but the fact that a person gags does not indicate why; it does not eliminate all other possible causes except abuse. Thus, procedural memories may be misinterpreted by a patient or therapist, and that misinterpretation may solidify into "truth."

Memory is a multifarious, complex, usually reconstructive process. It does not retrieve information the way a video recorder or computer does. Everything sensed is not stored; recall of picture-perfect images is not automatic. A variety of social, psychological, and developmental factors commonly cause distortions at each stage of the process. The real possibility of such distortions cannot be overlooked or minimized in determining what relation recalled memories bear to what really happened.

. . . .

Some therapists believe that repressed material can be restored to consciousness if the anxiety associated with the memory is removed. This belief, of course, assumes that the material has not been "simply forgotten" or confabulated. In addition, since recalling is a constructive process, a host of defense mechanisms may distort images or feelings at that phase as well. . . .

. . . .

Recovered memories come to be regarded as true for a variety of reasons. Therapists who expect to find abuse often do. And because the therapist occupies a position of authority and trust with the patient, this "confirmatory bias" can lead to leading questions and other forms of suggestion. Therapists also may interpret certain symptoms as indicating childhood sexual abuse, but those symptoms may be so general that they do not eliminate other possible ills.

In short, the preconceptions of the therapist, the suggestibility of the patient, the aleatory nature of memory recall, and the need to find a clear culprit for a diffuse set of symptoms may lead to false memories. Or they may not. Even assuming the reliability of all the studies and reports on the theory and techniques underlying recovered memory, the possibility of confabulation still exists. But it does not always occur. The point is this: the scientific community has not reached consensus on how to gauge the truth or falsity of "recovered" memories. . . .

. . . .

The expert testimony in this case, from qualified, competent therapists, shows the pitfalls of recalled memory therapy and the difficulties in using the results of such therapy as objective verification of abuse. Before she entered therapy, R. had no memories of abuse. She recovered her memories with Frazier, a licensed therapist who was not a specialist in memory. Some of Frazier's views may have influenced R.: Frazier had never had a patient make an untrue allegation of childhood sexual abuse, did not know of an instance when anyone had made such an untrue allegation, and did not think it could happen; she felt it was not her role to question the veracity of R.'s memories; she accepted the idea that R. could recover memories from around age three; and she had already found that R.'s mother had been the victim of childhood sexual abuse. The American Psychiatric Association has recognized clinicians' need to guard against their own possible preconceptions:

> Psychiatrists should maintain an empathic, non-judgmental, neutral stance towards reported memories of sexual abuse. . . . Care must be taken to avoid prejudging the cause of the patient's difficulties, or the veracity of the patient's reports. A strong prior belief by the psychiatrist that sexual abuse, or other factors, are or are not the cause of the patient's problems is likely to interfere with appropriate assessment and treatment.

Memories of Sexual Abuse, *supra,* at 263.

In addition to Frazier's possible confirmatory bias, her technique to recover memories may have increased R.'s suggestibility. Frazier had R. relax and recount whatever came into her head, a technique she described as similar to hypnosis. She also used what she called "guided imagery," reading aloud fragments R. had written down earlier and having R. fill in other recollections. Both hypnosis and guided, leading questioning have been criticized as over suggestive. Frazier's interpretation of various events may have also stemmed from a "confirmation bias." R.'s first dream involved a faceless man; this man never got a face. R.'s procedural memory, gagging, did not of itself point to having been forced to perform oral sex. The record does not show that other possible causes were sufficiently explored. Other possible influences on or sources of R.'s recovered memories include: B.'s detailing of her own abuse, R.'s research on incest, her anger with her father, and Frazier's comment that R.'s relationship with a boyfriend "sounded like incest" to her.

. . . .

In addition, post-traumatic stress disorder, from which R. suffered, presupposes "an event outside the range of usual human experience that would be markedly distressing to almost anyone." Obviously, a PTSD diagnosis cannot establish the occurrence of a trauma that it presupposes. . . .

In sum, the literature on repression and recovered memory syndrome establishes that fundamental theoretical and practical issues remain to be resolved. These issues include the extent to which experimental psychological theories of amnesia apply to psychotherapy, the effect of repression on memory, the effect of screening devices in recall, the effect of suggestibility, the difference between forensic and therapeutic truth, and the extent to which memory restoration techniques lead to credible memories or confabulations. . . .

V

. . . .

Legislatures have been far more active than courts in addressing the problem. Though fewer than fifteen state supreme courts have addressed the problem of limitations and childhood sexual abuse, since the mid-1980s, over half of the state legislatures have enacted or amended statutes of limitations to specifically address the problem of childhood sexual abuse claims.

. . . Essentially, there are two generations of statutes addressing the problem of delayed accrual for childhood sexual abuse cases. The first generation simply adopted the discovery rule or extended the statute of limitations for some fixed, extended period after the minor reached majority. The second generation of statutes, including amendments to existing statutes, is more complex and gives greater weight to avoiding the danger of possibly fraudulent claims. For example, in 1986 the California Legislature adopted the discovery rule for childhood sexual abuse. Later amendments to the statute require "certificates of merit" for plaintiffs 26 years or older. These certificates of merit must be executed by the plaintiff's attorney and a licensed mental health practitioner. The attorney must state that he has reviewed the facts of the case with at least one licensed mental heath practitioner, who is not a party to the litigation, and that on the basis of this review and consultation, there is reasonable and meritorious cause to file the action. The mental health practitioner must state that he is licensed in California, is not treating or has not treated the plaintiff, has interviewed the plaintiff, and on the basis of that interview has concluded the plaintiff was subject to childhood sexual abuse. Later amendments to California's Section 340.1 require greater protection of the defendant's identity. . . .

. . . .

The Texas Legislature entered this area just last year, enacting a special statute of limitations for civil actions for sexual abuse which extends the period for filing suit from two years to five years. However, the new limitations period, like the old one, begins on the day the cause of action accrues. We must assume that the Legislature did not intend for sexual abuse cases to be treated differently from any other case in applying the discovery rule. The Legislature is in the best position to determine and accommodate the complex and conflicting policies involved in determining an appropriate limitations period, and it has done so.

(The Court reinstated the trial court's dismissal of plaintiff's case.)

Owen, Justice, dissenting.

. . . .

. . . The number of children sexually abused in the United States each year has been estimated to be between 60,000 and 100,000.

We know that the psychological scars from that abuse can continue into adulthood and in many cases, can impact the victims throughout their lives. Some victims develop sexual disorders; others may suffer from multiple personality disorders or borderline psychosis. . . . We also know that an allegation of sexual abuse can be devastating to the one accused and that there can be faulty memories, or worse, false accusations.

. . . .

II

. . . .

The Court also argues that there would be . . . "[n]o basis, ever" for putting a time limit on when suit could be brought. Limitations would serve no purpose at all. Cutting off even some valid claims is the price of repose, the Court recites. The danger of stale evidence and stale claims is too great. . . .

[illegible] would not create a "special limitations jurisprudence unique to sexual abuse cases." We would be following the principles we have articulated in other of our decisions. The Court has aptly identified the "common thread" in prior decisions where we have deferred the running of limitations:

> The common thread in these cases is that when the wrong and injury were unknown to the plaintiff because of their very nature and not because of any fault of the plaintiff, accrual of the cause of action was delayed.

The wrong and the injury inflicted on R.V. was by its very nature unknown to her through no fault of her own. The Court declines to apply its own rationale in this case.

A

The linchpin of the Court's decision today is its conclusion that repressed memory does not warrant the application of the discovery rule unless the sexual abuse is "objectively verifiable." In so holding, the Court ignores the fact that physical evidence may have been available at the time of the molestation but repression of memory and thus the unavailability of such evidence is often the direct consequence of the abuser's reprehensible acts. Allowing the statute of limitations to preclude R.V.'s cause of action would violate the principle "deeply rooted in our jurisprudence" that "no man may take advantage of his own wrong." Because of the age of the victims and their psychological vulnerability, many years may pass before they are able to recall the event. In many cases, recollections do not occur until the victims are able to distance themselves from the physical presence and the emotional influence of the abuser.

. . . .

This is reminiscent of the days when the crime of rape went unpunished unless corroborating evidence, above and beyond the victim's testimony, was available. The Court's opinion perpetuates the attitudes reflected in that era. Today in Texas, no corroboration is required to convict a criminal defendant of the rape of a minor. Similarly, no corroboration should be required of a victim of childhood sexual abuse who seeks to invoke the discovery rule in a civil suit.

. . . .

A

As the Court recognizes, there is little dispute that the repression of traumatic memories does occur. . . . These memories may surface after the statute of limitations has expired. As one of the experts who treated R.V. testified, "Repression is really the only defense mechanism that a very small child has."

. . . .

The Court skillfully explains the "reconstructive process" of memory retrieval and the possibility that memories may be a distortion of historical truth. But the Court's description of the unreliability of memory applies to some extent to all memories, not just recovered ones. For example, studies have shown that eyewitness testimony is often surprisingly unreliable. S.V. did not challenge the admissibility of the testimony of R.V.'s experts on the basis that it was not scientifically reliable.

. . . .

B

The testimony of qualified, reputable mental health experts should suffice as "corroboration."

Under California's statutory discovery rule, a plaintiff in a childhood sexual abuse case who is age twenty-six or older at the time suit is filed must submit certificates of merit, including a certificate from a non-treating mental health practitioner, setting forth facts showing: . . .

> that the practitioner is not treating and has not treated the plaintiff, and that the practitioner has interviewed the plaintiff and is knowledgeable of

> the relevant facts and issues involved in the particular action, and has concluded, on the basis of his or her knowledge of the facts and issues, that in his or her professional opinion there is a reasonable basis to believe that the plaintiff had been subject to childhood sexual abuse.

New Mexico's statute similarly provides that the plaintiff's claim must be corroborated, but that the corroboration requirement is satisfied by "competent medical or psychological testimony." Such a course is preferable to the approach adopted by the Court today.

The testimony of three mental health experts corroborated R.V.'s testimony: Dr. Robert Powitsky, a forensic clinical psychologist, Dr. Michael Madigan, a medical doctor practicing in psychiatry with a Ph.D. in experimental psychology, and Alice Frazier, a licensed counselor with a master's degree in psychology. All three testified that in their expert opinions R.V. had been sexually abused. . . .

Dr. Madigan, who diagnosed R.V. with post-traumatic stress disorder, testified that he did not believe that R.V. had fabricated her memories of sexual abuse because in such cases, the person usually suffers other forms of pathology, such as anti-social behaviors, manipulativeness, stealing, lying, and being dishonest in other parts of her life. Dr. Powitsky testified that the way in which R.V.'s memories surfaced, with the most traumatic memories surfacing last, was a typical sequence for the recovery of memories of sexual abuse.

All three experts testified that R.V. experienced "body memories" or procedural memories, including a gagging reaction, which are common to survivors of sexual abuse. . . .

Dr. Powitsky testified that R.V.'s Minnesota Multiphasic Personality Inventory test showed that she fit the classic "V profile" of someone who has been abused. The results of psychological tests performed on her father, according to Dr. Powitsky, also fit the profile of one kind of sexual abuser. . . .

. . . Dr. Powitsky reviewed Frazier's deposition detailing her treatment of R.V. and testified that her method of treatment seemed appropriate. Further, R.V. was not in a therapy session when her first images of sexual abuse surfaced; she was away at college. Frazier testified that she never hypnotized R.V., but she did use a relaxation technique similar to hypnosis. Frazier also testified that she had never suggested to R.V. that she had been the victim of incest before she recovered her first memory, although she did tell R.V. that her relationship with her boyfriend "sounded like incest" to her. I agree that the corroborative testimony provided by R.V.'s experts is "inconclusive," but it does lend some objective support to her allegations. . . .

Other circumstantial evidence also corroborates R.V.'s memories. She testified that her father tied her up with bandannas during several incidents of sexual abuse. Her mother B.V. similarly testified that S.V. had tied her up with headscarves during sexual relations. Other events recounted by R.V. paralleled experiences between her mother and father, and there was no indication that R. and B.V. had shared those recollections with one another. Although this evidence does not in and of itself *prove* that S.V. sexually abused his daughter, it does provide some circumstantial corroboration of R.V.'s claims. Again, nothing in the record suggests that R.V. knew the details of her parents' sexual relations.

. . . .

I am concerned that statutes of limitations, including section 16.003, have been steadily eroded by doctrines such as fraudulent concealment, the discovery rule, and by an expansive reading of the open courts provision of our Texas Constitution. However, our Court embarked down this path some time ago. While I may well not have reached the same conclusions as our Court in its past decisions, they remain part of our precedent.

Our prior decisions and equitable considerations weigh in favor of extending the discovery rule in the case before us.

. . . .

NOTES AND QUESTIONS

1. This case differs from *Rock*, where the State was excluding refreshed recollection. Here, the State of Texas is considering whether to admit testimony of memories which arise years after the event. Suit would normally be barred by the statute of limitations, although the discovery rule allows the statute of limitations to begin running from the date of "discovery."
2. Should repressed memories, recaptured from years or decades earlier, be the basis of testimony in court? The Court in *S.V. v. R.V.* says they may not be the basis for suspending the statute of limitations in a tort action. But isn't the court's real point that expert testimony about recapturing repressed memories is simply "junk science"? Do you agree?
3. The Texas Court's extensive citations have been omitted in the interest of readability, but should be consulted for a good source of authority. See also, to the same effect, *State v. Hungerford*, 697 A.2d 916 (N.H. 1997), affirming dismissal of sexual assault charges by the trial court after extensive testimony by experts (including the ubiquitous Dr. Elizabeth Loftus), on the grounds that the offered testimony could not be understood by the average juror without expert assistance; that literature and expertise on the subject of repressed memory is dubious; and that the memories themselves were suspect. Given all of that, shouldn't the issue have been left to the jury?
4. For articles criticizing repressed memory theory and the litigation it has generated, see Loftus, *Patient-Psychotherapist Privilege, Repressed Memory Litigation,* 30 U. Rich. L. Rev. 109 (1996); Murray, *Repression, Memory and Suggestibility,* 66 U. Colo. L. Rev. 477 (1995); Richmond, *Bad Science: Repressed and Recovered Memories,* 44 U. of Kan. L. Rev. 517 (1996); and *State v. Ereth, 964 P.2d 26 (Mont. 1998)*
5. Note that the daughter sued as a part of the parents' divorce proceeding. Does this seem odd? Wise? Do you think such a suit should be disallowed, as a matter of public policy, where the parents' marriage remains intact?

6. And what of the Court's treatment of the counselor, Frazier? Was she unfairly treated? Would you say [illegible] ethical tradition, or that she abused her young client? Was there a conflict of interest, since she ultimately treated both mother and daughter? And ultimately, did she hurt the daughter?
7. Why would the mother believe the daughter under these circumstances? Do you?
8. Hypnosis is only one way of recovering or perhaps "creating" memories. Another — even more problematic — is used in interviewing young children, using devices such as anatomically correct dolls. Here, there are two "witnesses": the child who reacts to the doll and the interviewer who administers the examination and later testifies. All the usual problems of memory are present (observation, absorption, recall, relating) plus two others: the bias of the interviewer and the dubious "science" underlying the utility of such mnemonic devices. Courts are divided on the utility of such testimony, as is reflected in the next case, *United States v. Dorian.*

UNITED STATES v. DORIAN
803 F.2d 1439 (8th Cir. 1986)

Magill, Circuit Judge.

. . . The defendant ordered his wife to leave him alone with their five-year-old daughter; instead she went to the police station. . . . Three days later, the daughter was interviewed by a caseworker, using anatomically correct dolls. Ms. Virchow asked Roxanne if her mother touched her anywhere on her body to hurt or scare her, and Roxanne nodded no. When asked the same question about her father, Roxanne nodded yes. Ms. Virchow then repeated the question as she pointed to various parts of the girl doll's body. Roxanne gave negative responses except when Ms. Virchow pointed to the doll's chest. She then indicated that she felt scared when her father touched her there, and that although she was fully clothed when he did so, her father was not wearing a shirt.

Then, later, with two witnesses present, Ms. Virchow pointed with the hand of the male doll to parts of the girl doll's body, and asked Roxanne if it scared her when her father touched her on the chest. She became very uneasy and uncommunicative during the course of the interview, and indicated that she wanted Penny Virchow to leave. Thereafter, Monica Whiting and Priscilla Hornby continued the interview, and at some point, asked Roxanne if her father ever put anything between her legs. Roxanne shook her head no.

On June 24 Hornby and Whiting interviewed Roxanne a third time. Roxanne found it easier to speak only with Monica Whiting, so Virchow and Hornby waited in the living room. Roxanne told Monica about a time when her father carried her from the kitchen of the Dorian home into the bedroom, where he took off his pants and undershorts. Roxanne said her mother then came into the room and told her father to get out, and he left. Later, Ms. Hornby asked Roxanne again if her father had ever put anything between her legs, and this time Roxanne responded that he had put his finger there.

Two weeks later, at the child's home, the caseworker, Monica, suggested the child use dolls to show what had happened with her father.

Monica testified that Roxanne then showed the Roxanne doll hitting the daddy doll on the chest. According to Monica, Roxanne became very frightened when she showed this, as though she thought she had done something very bad. However, when Monica reassured her that hitting her father was okay, Roxanne relaxed and continued her story. She then showed the daddy doll hitting the Roxanne doll in the stomach, and the Roxanne doll falling to the floor. Roxanne then had the daddy doll pick up the Roxanne doll, carry her back into the bedroom, and lay her on the bed. She showed the daddy doll pulling the Roxanne doll's dress up to her shoulders, and taking the panties off the Roxanne doll. Roxanne had the daddy doll kneel on the bed next to the Roxanne doll, and then moved the daddy doll between the Roxanne doll's legs. Monica testified that when she asked what happened next, Roxanne said, "he put his boy thing in the hole between my legs." Roxanne then showed the daddy doll lying down beside the Roxanne doll on the bed, with his arm over the Roxanne doll's body.

Monica asked Roxanne if she saw her father's "boy thing," and Roxanne said "yes." Monica asked Roxanne if her father's boy thing looked like the doll they were using, and Roxanne said "yes," but then grabbed the daddy doll's penis, put it in an erect position, and said, "This was up here." . . .

. . . .

At trial, Roxanne was unable to testify meaningfully, because of age and fright. Monica was then called and testified to the statements above.

. . . .

Dorian contends that the challenged evidence (1) did not have the necessary guarantees of trustworthiness; (2) was not more probative than any other evidence the government could have procured through reasonable efforts; and (3) did not serve the purposes of the Federal Rules or the interests of justice. We reject these claims.

1. Trustworthiness

Dorian first argues that Roxanne's July 10, 1985 statement did not possess sufficient circumstantial guarantees of trustworthiness to be admissible under Rule 803(24). In particular, he emphasizes the length of time between Roxanne's description of the sexual abuse, and the date when any such abuse could have occurred (at least twenty-five days); the contradictions in the statements Roxanne gave during the various interviews (e.g., indicating on June 19 that her father never put anything between her legs, on June 24 that he put his finger between her legs, and on July 10 that he put his "boy thing" between her legs); and the possibility that Roxanne's statement to Monica Whiting was the result of suggestiveness and pressure by the social workers. In addition, Dorian submits that the mere use of anatomically correct dolls is suggestible to a young child.

. . . .

To begin with, the women who interviewed Roxanne — including her foster mother, Monica Whiting — [illegible] in interviewing children and in the use of anatomical dolls.[1] All three testified that they were careful not to use leading or suggestive questions during any of the interviews. They also indicated that, because of Roxanne's withdrawn behavior and her obvious discomfort with sharing the things that frightened her, the initial interviews were stopped before they were complete. Indeed, it appears that the reason Roxanne did not make the challenged statement until July 10 was because she was able fully to reveal what happened only after she had developed a relationship of trust with Monica Whiting.

Nor do the conflicts in Roxanne's statements necessarily render her July 10 statement untrustworthy. As a clinical psychologist testifying as an expert witness explained, the contradictions may well have been a function of Roxanne's concern about how the information would be received, and whether she would be punished for what she said. According to the psychologist, it frequently takes a long time for children to share what is really going on and they may then do so in stages, telling a little more each time. Furthermore, because defense counsel cross-examined Penny Virchow, Priscilla Hornby, and Monica Whiting extensively about the contradictions in Roxanne's statements and the circumstances in which her statements were made, the jury was certainly in a position to consider those factors in deciding what weight to give her July 10 statement.

However, the reliability of Roxanne's statement is perhaps best supported by the nature of her graphic but child-like description of the incident. In particular, we note Roxanne's statement that her father "put his boy thing in the hole between my legs," and her ability to describe an erect penis. As the clinical psychologist observed, an erect penis is not normally a matter within the knowledge of a five-year-old girl. . . .

Finally, we note that Roxanne's statement was corroborated by other evidence: the descriptions of her fearful behavior around men; her terror when the physician's assistant prepared to conduct a vaginal examination; her disturbed behavior when told she was going home, which stopped when she learned her father would not be there; Dorian's unprecedented act of washing Roxanne's underwear; and Norma [Roxanne's mother]'s statements that Ferlin [Dorian] was trying to rape her daughter. Furthermore, the medical evidence, although inconclusive, was certainly consistent with sexual abuse. We therefore conclude that the requirement of trustworthiness was satisfied in this case.

. . . .

Bright, J., dissenting.

---

[1] Although Monica was not a social worker, her background included experience in both teaching and child development. During college she worked with children in a mental hospital, teaching reading and other skills. She received training in child development as a high school home economics teacher. During the three years she had been licensed as an emergency foster parent, she had taken care of approximately 60 children. In addition, to maintain her certification as a foster parent, Monica attended a number of classes offered by the State Department of Social Services. Those classes included some training on interviewing children and the use of anatomical dolls.

. . . .

II

. . . .

First, Monica Whiting cannot be considered an objective observer. Between Roxanne and Monica existed a strong foster mother-daughter relationship although Roxanne had been living as a member of the Whiting household for less than a month at the time of Roxanne's interviews. Despite this bond, it was Monica who conducted the interviews of Roxanne which sought, as their purpose, to learn whether Ferlin Dorian had sexually abused his daughter. The relationship between Monica and Roxanne may have influenced Roxanne to relate statements to please, or which she thought might please, Monica, regardless of Monica's sincere desire to obtain truthful information.

Second, because Monica, to whom Roxanne first gave her version of the assault, was not at the time a qualified social worker and possessed minimal experience interviewing children, her efforts to elicit the facts of the incident from Roxanne cannot be considered a reliable interrogation. At trial, Monica testified that subsequent to her first interview with Roxanne, but before the July 10, 1985 interview, she attended one lecture on the interviewing of children given by a State Social Services agent. Monica conceded that her instruction with regard to the use of anatomical dolls, which she used to facilitate her interviews with Roxanne, was "limited." She also stated that she had never before been involved in this type of interviewing. Monica's lack of qualifications and experience in child interviewing detracts from the reliability of the story she obtained from Roxanne.

Third, Roxanne was interviewed amidst what appears to have been considerable suggestiveness by Monica, Priscilla Hornby, the Supervisor for the South Dakota Department of Social Services and Penny Virchow, an on-call child protection worker in the same state agency. In her initial interview, Roxanne was asked whether her father touched her while her mother was gone. In a later interview, she was asked whether her father touches her any place on her body and whether that touch hurts or scares her. At still another interview, Roxanne was asked by a social worker, "Is this a scary place that your dad touched you?" She was also asked if her father ever put anything between her legs. Moreover, many of the questions put to Roxanne were asked through the manipulation of anatomically correct dolls. While I would not go so far as to hold, as the appellant urges, that the mere use of anatomically correct dolls is per se suggestive, the record of Roxanne's interviews indicates that the use of these dolls to question a very young child adduces a relatively high degree of suggestiveness.

Fourth, Roxanne's own statements, as related by Monica, are too inconsistent to be afforded any significant amount of reliability. During the interview of June 17, 1985, Roxanne indicated that her father did not touch her any place on her body to scare her except her chest. During the interview conducted on June 19, 1985, Roxanne indicated that her father had never put anything between her legs. During her June 24, 1985 interview, Roxanne indicated that her father had placed his finger in the opening between her legs. Finally, during the course of an interview conducted on July 10, 1985, Roxanne told Monica Wilding that her father had put his [illegible] “hole” between her legs.

In an effort to explain these inconsistencies at trial, the Government called an expert witness to testify that contradictions in a child’s statements do not necessarily indicate a lack of trustworthiness. Children, testified this expert, will often contradict themselves in their desire to tell an adult about something scary that has happened to them without being punished for what they believe is their wrongful involvement in the incident. As a child receives assurances that he will not be punished and will instead be believed, the expert testified that he will gradually tell an adult the real truth of what occurred. The Government’s expert spoke only of children in general, however, and not of Roxanne in particular. Thus we have no idea whether these behavioral assumptions even apply to Roxanne. The expert did not and could not testify whether Roxanne’s statements were true or false. Moreover, the very need for an expert witness to testify to the credibility of children’s stories told in an inconsistent manner demonstrates the unreliability of the declaration here offered in evidence.

. . . .

NOTES AND QUESTIONS

1. Abuse, as with any trauma, impacts the mind in subtle ways. Survivors of concentration camps, wars, fires, auto accidents and bank robberies, all suppress memories — they may even suppress *impressions* — of events. How can a present-time psychologist *avoid* creating *new* “impressions,” or filling in the missing ones with fabrications? Will not the child-witness (perhaps decades later) respond to suggestion, the need to please, the logic of context, by *creating* “facts”? If so, should not the witness be left alone? This was the problem in the preceding case, with an adult woman recalling abuse as a child.

2. With young children as witnesses, as in *Dorian*, the problem is not only one of memory and recall, but absorption and communication. The use of “anatomically correct” dolls may provide the “language” for the child to understand and describe events. But what are the risks of fabrication and — for that matter — psychological upset? If a child refuses to speak, or cannot, is there good reason to leave the child alone? In this sense, are *Dorian* and the preceding case similar?

3. As science, does the reliability of the method used in *Dorian* seem more or less reliable than the repressed memory methodology of Counselor Frazier in the preceding case or than the polygraphs and plethysmographs discussed in § 2.03[2] below? Would you allow expert testimony as to any?

4. And now consider a related but significantly different situation — imposition upon a defendant by psychotropic drugs.

RIGGINS v. NEVADA

504 U.S. 127 (1992)

Justice **O'Connor** delivered the opinion of the Court.

Petitioner David Riggins challenges his murder and robbery convictions on the ground that the State of Nevada unconstitutionally forced an Anti-psychotic drug upon him during trial. Because the Nevada courts failed to make findings sufficient to support forced administration of the drug, we reverse.

I

During the early hours of November 20, 1987, Paul Wade was found dead in his Las Vegas apartment. An autopsy revealed that Wade died from multiple stab wounds, including wounds to the head, chest, and back. David Riggins was arrested for the killing 45 hours later.

A few days after being taken into custody, Riggins told Dr. R. Edward Quass, a private psychiatrist who treated patients at the Clark County Jail, about hearing voices in his head and having trouble sleeping. Riggins informed Dr. Quass that he had been successfully treated with Mellaril in the past. Mellaril is the trade name for thioridazine, an anti-psychotic drug. After this consultation, Dr. Quass prescribed Mellaril at a level of 100 milligrams per day. Because Riggins continued to complain of voices and sleep problems in the following months, Dr. Quass gradually increased the Mellaril prescription to 800 milligrams per day. Riggins also received a prescription for Dilantin, an antiepileptic drug.

In January 1988, Riggins successfully moved for a determination of his competence to stand trial. Three court-appointed psychiatrists performed examinations during February and March, while Riggins was taking 450 milligrams of Mellaril daily. Dr. William O'Gorman, a psychiatrist who had treated Riggins for anxiety in 1982, and Dr. Franklin Master concluded that Riggins was competent to stand trial. The third psychiatrist, Dr. Jack Jurasky, found that Riggins was incompetent. The Clark County District Court determined that Riggins was legally sane and competent to stand trial, so preparations for trial went forward.

In early June, the defense moved the District Court for an order suspending administration of Mellaril and Dilantin until the end of Riggins' trial. . . .

. . . .

II

The record in this case narrowly defines the issues before us. The parties have indicated that once the District Court denied Riggins' motion to terminate use of Mellaril, subsequent administration of the drug was involuntary. . . .

We also presume that administration of Mellaril was medically appropriate. Although defense counsel stressed that Riggins received a very high dose of the drug, at no point did he suggest to the Nevada courts that administration [illegible]

. . . .

With these considerations in mind, we turn to Riggins' core contention that involuntary administration of Mellaril denied him " 'a full and fair' trial." Our discussion in *Washington v. Harper* provides useful background for evaluating this claim. In *Harper,* a prison inmate alleged that the State of Washington and various individuals violated his right to due process by giving him Mellaril and other anti-psychotic drugs against his will. Although the inmate did not prevail, we agreed that his interest in avoiding involuntary administration of anti-psychotic drugs was protected under the Fourteenth Amendment's Due Process Clause. "The forcible injection of medication into a non-consenting person's body," we said, "represents a substantial interference with that person's liberty." . . .

. . . .

Although we have not had occasion to develop substantive standards for judging forced administration of such drugs in the trial or pretrial settings, Nevada certainly would have satisfied due process if the prosecution had demonstrated and the District Court had found that treatment with Anti-psychotic medication was medically appropriate and, considering less intrusive alternatives, essential for the sake of Riggins' own safety or the safety of others. Similarly, the State might have been able to justify medically appropriate, involuntary treatment with the drug by establishing that it could not obtain an adjudication of Riggins' guilt or innocence by using less intrusive means. We note that during the July 14 hearing Riggins did not contend that he had the right to be tried without Mellaril if its discontinuation rendered him incompetent. The question whether a competent criminal defendant may refuse anti-psychotic medication if cessation of medication would render him incompetent at trial is not before us.

. . . .

Were we to divine the District Court's logic from the hearing transcript, we would have to conclude that the court simply weighed the risk that the defense would be prejudiced by changes in Riggins' outward appearance against the chance that Riggins would become incompetent if taken off Mellaril, and struck the balance in favor of involuntary medication. The court did not acknowledge the defendant's liberty interest in freedom from unwanted anti-psychotic drugs.

This error may well have impaired the constitutionally protected trial rights Riggins invokes. At the hearing to consider terminating medication, Dr. O'Gorman suggested that the dosage administered to Riggins was within the toxic range and could make him "uptight." Dr. Master testified that a patient taking 800 milligrams of Mellaril each day might suffer from drowsiness or confusion. It is clearly possible that such side effects impacted not just Riggins' outward appearance, but also the content of his testimony on direct or cross-examination, his ability to follow the proceedings, or the substance of his communication with counsel.

Efforts to prove or disprove actual prejudice from the record before us would be futile, and guesses whether the outcome of the trial might have been different if Riggins' motion had been granted would be purely speculative. We accordingly reject the dissent's suggestion that Riggins should be required to demonstrate how the trial would have proceeded differently if he had not been given Mellaril. . . .

. . . .

The judgment of the Nevada Supreme Court is reversed, and the case is remanded for further proceedings not inconsistent with this opinion.

It is so ordered.

Justice **Kennedy**, concurring in the judgment.

. . . .

The question is whether the State's interest in conducting the trial allows it to ensure the defendant's competence by involuntary medication, assuming of course there is a sound medical basis for the treatment. . . .

. . . .

. . . The drugs can prejudice the accused in two principal ways: (1) by altering his demeanor in a manner that will prejudice his reactions and presentation in the courtroom, and (2) by rendering him unable or unwilling to assist counsel.

It is a fundamental assumption of the adversary system that the trier of fact observes the accused throughout the trial, either while the accused is on the stand or sitting at the defense table. This assumption derives from the right to be present at trial, which in turn derives from the right to testify and rights under the Confrontation Clause. At all stages of the proceedings, the defendant's behavior, manner, facial expressions, and emotional responses, or their absence, combine to make an overall impression on the trier of fact, an impression that can have a powerful influence on the outcome of the trial. . . .

The side effects of anti-psychotic drugs may alter demeanor in a way that will prejudice all facets of the defense. Serious due process concerns are implicated when the State manipulates the evidence in this way. The defendant may be restless and unable to sit still. The drugs can induce a condition called Parkinsonism, which, like Parkinson's disease, is characterized by tremor of the limbs, diminished range of facial expression, or slowed movements and speech. Some of the side effects are more subtle. Anti-psychotic drugs such as Mellaril can have a "sedation-like effect" that in severe cases may affect thought processes. At trial, Dr. Jurasky testified that Mellaril has "a tranquilizer effect." ("If you are dealing with someone very sick then you may prescribe up to 800 milligrams which is the dose he had been taking which is very, very high. I mean you can tranquilize an elephant with 800 milligrams.") Dr. Jurasky listed the following side effects of large doses of Mellaril: "Drowsiness, constipation, perhaps lack of alertness, changes in blood pressure. . . . Depression of the psychomotor functions. If you take a lot of it you become stoned for all practical purposes and can barely function."

. . . .

Concerns about medication extend also to the issue of cooperation with [illegible] counsel is impaired when he cannot cooperate in an active manner with his lawyer. . . . The State interferes with this relation when it administers a drug to dull cognition.

It is well established that the defendant has the right to testify on his own behalf, a right we have found essential to our adversary system. . . . In my view medication of the type here prescribed may be for the very purpose of imposing constraints on the defendant's own will, and for that reason its legitimacy is put in grave doubt.

If the State cannot render the defendant competent without involuntary medication, then it must resort to civil commitment, if appropriate, unless the defendant becomes competent through other means. If the defendant cannot be tried without his behavior and demeanor being affected in this substantial way by involuntary treatment, in my view the Constitution requires that society bear this cost in order to preserve the integrity of the trial process. The state of our knowledge of Anti-psychotic drugs and their side effects is evolving and may one day produce effective drugs that have only minimal side effects. Until that day comes, we can permit their use only when the State can show that involuntary treatment does not cause alterations raising the concerns enumerated in this separate opinion.

With these observations, I concur in the judgment reversing the conviction.

Justice **Thomas**, with whom Justice **Scalia** joins except as to Part II-A, dissenting.

. . . .

The Court's opinion, in my view, conflates two distinct questions: whether Riggins had a full and fair criminal trial and whether Nevada improperly forced Riggins to take medication. In this criminal case, Riggins is asking, and may ask, only for the reversal of his conviction and sentence. He is not seeking, and may not seek, an injunction to terminate his medical treatment or damages for an infringement of his personal rights. I agree with the [illegible] Court: Even if the State truly forced Riggins to take medication, and even if this medication deprived Riggins of a protected liberty interest in a manner actionable in a different legal proceeding, Riggins nonetheless had the fundamentally fair criminal trial required by the Constitution. I therefore would affirm his conviction.

. . . .

B

Riggins also argued in the Nevada Supreme Court, although not in his briefs to this Court, that he did not have a "'full and fair' trial" because Mellaril had side effects that interfered with his ability to participate in his defense. He alleged, in particular, that the drug tended to limit his powers of perception. The Court accepts this contention, stating: "It is clearly possible that such side effects impacted . . . the content of his testimony on direct examination or cross-examination, his ability to follow the proceedings, or the substance of his communication with counsel." I disagree. We cannot conclude that Riggins had less than a full and fair trial merely because of the possibility that Mellaril had side effects.

. . . .

Riggins has no claim of legal incompetence in this case. The trial court specifically found him competent while he was taking Mellaril under a statute requiring him to have "sufficient mentality to be able to understand the nature of the criminal charges against him, and . . . to aid and assist his counsel in the defense interposed upon the trial." Riggins does not assert that due process imposes a higher standard.

The record does not reveal any other form of unfairness relating to the purported side affects of Mellaril. Riggins has failed to allege specific facts to support his claim that he could not participate effectively in his defense. He has not stated how he would have directed his counsel to examine or cross-examine witnesses differently. He has not identified any testimony or instructions that he did not understand. The record, moreover, does not even support his assertion that Mellaril made him worse off. As Justice Rose noted in his concurring opinion below: "Two psychiatrists who had prescribed Mellaril for Riggins, Dr. Quass and Dr. O'Gorman, testified that they believed it was helpful to him. Additional psychiatric testimony established that Mellaril may have increased Riggins' cognitive ability. . . ." I thus see no basis for reversing the Nevada Supreme Court.

. . . .

A

Riggins may not complain about a deprivation of the liberty interest that we recognized in *Harper* because the record does not support his version of the facts. Shortly after his arrest, as the Court notes, Riggins told a psychiatrist at his jail that he was hearing voices and could not sleep. The psychiatrist prescribed Mellaril. When the prescription did not eliminate the problem, Riggins sought further treatment and the psychiatrist increased the dosage. Riggins thus began taking the drug voluntarily.

. . . .

B

The *Harper* issue, in any event, does not warrant reversal of Riggins' conviction. The Court correctly states that Riggins, as a detainee awaiting trial, had at least the same liberty interest in avoiding unwanted medication that the inmate had in *Harper*. This case, however, differs from *Harper* in a very significant respect. When the inmate in *Harper* complained that physicians were drugging him against his will, he sought damages and an injunction against future medication in a civil action. Although Riggins also complains of forced medication, he is seeking a reversal of his criminal conviction. I would not expand *Harper* to include this remedy.

. . . .

NOTES AND QUESTIONS

1. The simple demeanor of a person during a trial may, at least in the eyes of some jurors, reveal a good deal about a person. Obviously, heavy sedation or tranquilization would severely affect all of this, and a jury would never come to "know" the witness or the accused in a normal state if overcome by required medications. Also, of course, the defendant in a case functions as a decision maker. While the defendant may be represented by counsel, it is the defendant who instructs counsel as to how counsel shall proceed. If the defendant is under medication, there will be an inevitable effect on his or her ability to make decisions, to understand advice and information and to remember and relate important data.

2. May a defendant be subjected to medication (or hypnosis, for that matter) to render him or her competent to stand trial? Does the court in *Riggins* answer that question? What *should* the answer be?

3. It is not clear, but assume that absent medication, Riggins could not be tried. Assume, further, as appears to be the case, that with medication he could stand trial as meeting the standard test of competence: he could "aid and assist" in his own defense, by recalling events and by participating in decision-making. If so, then which course shows greater respect for Riggins' autonomy as an individual: leaving him as he is and hospitalizing him or changing him so that he is more like the rest of us and jailing or imprisoning him? Does your answer vary, depending upon whether you are a physician, a judge or defense counsel?

4. In a setting like *Riggins,* or in the earlier case, *Rock*, what are the ethical obligations of the physicians? Ordinarily, it is said that their ethical obligations are to do good; to do no harm; and, essentially, to advance the interests of their "patient." But in *Riggins,* the physicians were hired by the prosecution, to medicate the "patient," potentially at least, pushing toward a conviction. Indeed, treatment with Antipsychotic drugs was the only way to ensure that Riggins would stand trial and be convicted. What should a physician do?

5. In *Khiem v. United States,* 612 A.2d 160 (D.C. 1992), the court ordered a defendant medicated so he could be tried. Defendant relied upon *In Re A.C.*, *Cruzan*, *Riggins*, and *Harper*. Should he have prevailed — on a right to refuse treatment? As to this right, see also *Guardianship of Boyle*, 674 A.2d 912 (Me. 1996).

6. For an excellent article, see Joseph A. Spadaro, *An Elusive Search For The Truth: The Admissibility Of Repressed And Recovered Memories In Light Of Daubert v. Merrell Dow Pharmaceuticals, Inc.*, 30 Conn. L. Rev. 1147 (1998); and see Douglas R. Richmond, *Bad Science: Repressed and Recovered Memories of Childhood Sexual Abuse*, 44 U. Kan. L. Rev. 517 (1996).

7. See also Bower and Michaels, *Dying to Have a Family*, Time, p. 78 (March 11, 2002) on the ethical considerations involved in the assisted reproduction of a woman, 33, with early onset Alzheimer's disease.

PROBLEM 2-1 — Child Abuse

Marsha Smith is now 35. For years, she has had troubling dreams and suffered from a panic disorder related to a deep-seated anxiety which psychoanalysts had concluded stemmed from traumatic events in her childhood. Of these, Marsha has no present memory. Marsha lives with her father, of whom she is uncommonly fond and upon whom she is inordinately dependent; her mother died 15 years ago.

You are Marsha's counselor and you now believe Marsha suffers from a post-traumatic stress disorder, leading her to bury memories deeply within her personality in order to assure her psychological survival. These memories typically relate to abuse as a child, at a very young age. Through hypnosis and medication, as in *S.V. v. R.V.*, it may be possible to reach the level of the subconscious where these memories may (or may not) be buried. Even if this journey is successful, there is no guarantee that the memories may be there still, or that they can be retrieved. Indeed, the very psychological processes which buried the memories may continue to conflate reality, perceived now some 30 years later, and it may create present beliefs of a prior series of events which are false.

Moreover, if the past memories or newly created beliefs are to the effect that her father molested her as a child, those beliefs will destroy Marsha's present time reality and relationship with her father. There is the risk that without her present relationship with her father, Marsha is sufficiently fragile so that she cannot function or survive. It is clear that her present relationship with her father is excellent, presenting no risk of harm.

As Marsha's counselor or a consulting hypnotherapist or psychiatrist, what would you do? If you were Marsha, what would you do? Should the father participate in these decisions? How? Are these questions of psychology, criminal law or professional ethics? Recall this problem when we come to problems of professional ethics, candor and competence, in the next chapter and consider related problems of professionalism on the facts in *State v. Ereth*, 964 P.2d 26 (Mont. 1998).

[2] Gender and Sexuality

Every person has a gender component in their identity. It is, for most, a central, core element, anchoring the individual in manifold biological, psychological and social relationships. Gender therefore is entitled to community respect as central to such choices as marriage and procreation. But such respect becomes problematic when the choices are as to identity itself, and the choices run counter to powerful community norms and taboos. May a person choose *not* to procreate, or *not* to be heterosexual, or *not* to retain genitalia?

Are these choices which society must permit a person to make? Must it support such changes? Are they — *can* they be — ethical? May it instead insist on the binary order of sexual order, in which all people (as on Noah's ark) are either male or female, and change or permutation is not allowed? At this point, the reader should recall and reconsider *Farmer v. Brennan*, *supra*

§ 1.03[1], where Mr. Farmer's "feminine" mode of dress while in prison generated hostile responses [illegible] prison administrators. A thoughtful discussion of these issues may be found in the May-June 1998 issue of the Hastings Center Report in two articles, Driger, "*Ambiguous Sex*" — *or Ambivalent Medicine,* 28 Hast. Cent. Rep. 24 (1998) and Elliott, *Why Can't We Go On As Three?* 28 Hast. Cent. Rep. 36 (1998).

This section examines contraception, homosexuality and sex change.

GRISWOLD v. CONNECTICUT
381 U.S. 479 (1965)

Mr. Justice **Douglas** delivered the opinion of the Court.

Appellant Griswold is Executive Director of the Planned Parenthood League of Connecticut. Appellant Buxton is a licensed physician and a professor at the Yale Medical School who served as Medical Director for the League at its Center in New Haven — a center open and operating from November 1 to November 10, 1961, when appellants were arrested.

They gave information, instruction, and medical advice to *married persons* as to the means of preventing conception. They examined the wife and prescribed the best contraceptive device or material for her use. Fees were usually charged, although some couples were served free.

The statutes whose constitutionality is involved in this appeal are §§ 53-32 and 54-196 of the General Statutes of Connecticut (1958 rev.). The former provides:

> "Any person who uses any drug, medicinal article or instrument for the purpose of preventing conception shall be fined not less than fifty dollars or imprisoned not less than sixty days nor more than one year or be both fined and imprisoned. . . ."

The appellants were found guilty as accessories and fined $100 each, against the claim that the accessory statute as so applied violated the Fourteenth Amendment. . . .

. . . .

Coming to the merits, we are met with a wide range of questions that implicate the Due Process Clause of the Fourteenth Amendment. Overtones of some arguments suggest that *Lochner v. New York* should be our guide. But we decline that invitation. We do not sit as a super-legislature to determine the wisdom, need, and propriety of laws that touch economic problems, business affairs, or social conditions. This law, however, operates directly on an intimate relation of husband and wife and their physician's role in one aspect of that relation.

The association of people is not mentioned in the Constitution nor in the Bill of Rights. The right to educate a child in a school of the parents' choice — whether public or private or parochial — is also not mentioned. Nor is the right to study any particular subject or any foreign language. Yet the First Amendment has been construed to include certain of those rights.

. . . .

. . . The right of "association," like the right of belief, is more than the right to attend a meeting; it includes the right to express one's attitudes or philosophies by membership in a group or by affiliation with it or by other lawful means. Association in that context is a form of expression of opinion; and while it is not expressly included in the First Amendment its existence is necessary in making the express guarantees fully meaningful.

[S]pecific guarantees in the Bill of Rights have penumbras, formed by emanations from those guarantees that help give them life and substance. Various guarantees create zones of privacy. The right of association contained in the penumbra of the First Amendment is one, as we have seen. The Third Amendment in its prohibition against the quartering of soldiers "in any house" in time of peace without the consent of the owner is another facet of that privacy. The Fourth Amendment explicitly affirms the "right of the people to be secure in their persons, houses, papers, and effects, against unreasonable searches and seizures." The Fifth Amendment in its Self-Incrimination Clause enables the citizen to create a zone of privacy which government may not force him to surrender to his detriment. The Ninth Amendment provides: "The enumeration in the Constitution, of certain rights, shall not be construed to deny or disparage others retained by the people."

. . . .

The present case, then, concerns a relationship lying within the zone of privacy created by several fundamental constitutional guarantees. And it concerns a law which, in forbidding the *use* of contraceptives rather than regulating their manufacture or sale, seeks to achieve its goals by means having a maximum destructive impact upon that relationship. Such a law cannot stand in light of the familiar principle, so often applied by this Court, that a "governmental purpose to control or prevent activities constitutionally subject to state regulation may not be achieved by means which sweep unnecessarily broadly and thereby invade the area of protected freedoms." Would we allow the police to search the sacred precincts of marital bedrooms for telltale signs of the use of contraceptives? The very idea is repulsive to the notions of privacy surrounding the marriage relationship.

We deal with a right of privacy older than the Bill of Rights — older than our political parties, older than our school system. Marriage is a coming together for better or for worse, hopefully enduring, and intimate to the degree of being sacred. It is an association that promotes a way of life, not causes; a harmony in living, not political faiths; a bilateral loyalty, not commercial or social projects. Yet it is an association for as noble a purpose as any involved in our prior decisions.

Reversed.

Mr. Justice **Goldberg**, whom the **Chief Justice** and Mr. Justice **Brennan** join, concurring.

I agree with the Court that Connecticut's birth-control law unconstitutionally intrudes upon the right of marital privacy, and I join in its opinion and judgment. Although I have not accepted the view that "due process" as used in the Fourteenth Amendment incorporates all of the first eight Amendments,

I do agree that the concept of liberty protects those personal rights that are fundamental, and is not [illegible] My conclusion that the concept of liberty is not so restricted and that it embraces the right of marital privacy though that right is not mentioned explicitly in the Constitution is supported both by numerous decisions of this Court, referred to in the Court's opinion, and by the language and history of the Ninth Amendment. . . .

. . . .

The Ninth Amendment reads, "The enumeration in the Constitution, of certain rights, shall not be construed to deny or disparage others retained by the people." The Amendment is almost entirely the work of James Madison. It was introduced in Congress by him and passed the House and Senate with little or no debate and virtually no change in language. It was proffered to quiet express fears that a bill of specifically enumerated rights could not be sufficiently broad to cover all essential rights and that the specific mention of certain rights would be interpreted as a denial that others were protected.

. . . .

. . . The Ninth Amendment to the Constitution may be regarded by some as a recent discovery and may be forgotten by others, but since 1791 it has been a basic part of the Constitution which we are sworn to uphold. To hold that a right so basic and fundamental and so deep-rooted in our society as the right of privacy in marriage may be infringed because that right is not guaranteed in so many words by the first eight amendments to the Constitution is to ignore the Ninth Amendment and to give it no effect whatsoever. Moreover, a judicial construction that this fundamental right is not protected by the Constitution because it is not mentioned in explicit terms by one of the first eight amendments or elsewhere in the Constitution would violate the Ninth Amendment, which specifically states that "[t]he enumeration in the Constitution, of certain rights, shall not be *construed* to deny or disparage others retained by the people." (Emphasis added.)

. . . .

In determining which rights are fundamental, judges are not left at large to decide cases in light of their personal and private notions. Rather, they must look to the "traditions and [collective] conscience of our people" to determine whether a principle is "so rooted [there] . . . as to be ranked as fundamental." The inquiry is whether a right involved "is of such a character that it cannot be denied without violating those 'fundamental principles of liberty and justice which lie at the base of all our civil and political institutions. . . .' "

. . . .

I agree with Mr. Justice Harlan's statement in his dissenting opinion in *Poe v. Ullman*: "Certainly the safeguarding of the home does not follow merely from the sanctity of property rights. The home derives its preeminence as the seat of family life. And the integrity of that life is something so fundamental that it has been found to draw to its protection the principles of more than one explicitly granted Constitutional right. . . . Of this whole' private realm of family life' it is difficult to imagine what is more private or more intimate than a husband and wife's marital relations."

The entire fabric of the Constitution and the purposes that clearly underlie its specific guarantees demonstrate that the rights to marital privacy and to marry and raise a family are of similar order and magnitude as the fundamental rights specifically protected.

Although the Constitution does not speak in so many words of the right of privacy in marriage, I cannot believe that it offers these fundamental rights no protection. The fact that no particular provision of the Constitution explicitly forbids the State from disrupting the traditional relation of the family — a relation as old and as fundamental as our entire civilization — surely does not show that the Government was meant to have the power to do so. Rather, as the Ninth Amendment expressly recognizes, there are fundamental personal rights such as this one, which are protected from abridgment by the Government though not specifically mentioned in the Constitution.

. . . .

In a long series of cases this Court has held that where fundamental personal liberties are involved, they may not be abridged by the States simply on a showing that a regulatory statute has some rational relationship to the effectuation of a proper state purpose. "Where there is a significant encroachment upon personal liberty, the State may prevail only upon showing a subordinating interest which is compelling." The law must be shown "necessary, and not merely rationally related, to the accomplishment of a permissible state policy." . . .

. . . .

Mr. Justice **Harlan**, concurring in the judgment.

I fully agree with the judgment of reversal, but find myself unable to join the Court's opinion. . . .

. . . .

In my view, the proper constitutional inquiry in this case is whether this Connecticut statute infringes the Due Process Clause of the Fourteenth Amendment because the enactment violates basic values "implicit in the concept of ordered liberty." For reasons stated at length in my dissenting opinion in *Poe v. Ullman* believe that it does. While the relevant inquiry may be aided by resort to one or more of the provisions of the Bill of Rights, it is not dependent on them or any of their radiations. The Due Process Clause of the Fourteenth Amendment stands, in my opinion, on its own bottom.

. . . .

Mr. Justice **White**, concurring in the judgment.

In my view this Connecticut law as applied to married couples deprives them of "liberty" without due process of law, as that concept is used in the Fourteenth Amendment. I therefore concur in the judgment of the Court reversing these convictions under Connecticut's aiding and abetting statute.

It would be unduly repetitious, and belaboring the obvious, to expound on the impact of this statute on the liberty guaranteed by the Fourteenth Amendment against arbitrary or capricious denials or on the nature of this liberty. Suffice it to say that this is not the first time this Court has had [illegible] teenth Amendment includes the right "to marry, establish a home and bring up children," and "the liberty . . . to direct the upbringing and education of children," and that these are among "the basic civil rights of man." These decisions affirm that there is a "realm of family life which the state cannot enter" without substantial justification. Surely the right invoked in this case, to be free of regulation of the intimacies of the marriage relationship, "come[s] to this Court with a momentum for respect lacking when appeal is made to liberties which derive merely from shifting economic arrangements."

. . . .

In these circumstances one is rather hard pressed to explain how the ban on use by married persons in any way prevents use of such devices by persons engaging in illicit sexual relations and thereby contributes to the State's policy against such relationships. Perhaps the theory is that the flat ban on use prevents married people from possessing contraceptives and without the ready availability of such devices for use in the marital relationship, there will be no or less temptation to use them in extramarital ones. This reasoning rests on the premise that married people will comply with the ban in regard to their marital relationship, notwithstanding total nonenforcement in this context and apparent nonenforcibility, but will not comply with criminal statutes prohibiting extramarital affairs and the anti-use statute in respect to illicit sexual relationships, a premise whose validity has not been demonstrated and whose intrinsic validity is not very evident. At most the broad ban is of marginal utility to the declared objective. . . .

Mr. Justice **Black**, with whom Mr. Justice **Stewart** joins, dissenting.

. . . .

The Court talks about a constitutional "right of privacy" as though there is some constitutional provision or provisions forbidding any law ever to be passed which might abridge the "privacy" of individuals. But there is not. There are, of course, guarantees in certain specific constitutional provisions which are designed in part to protect privacy at certain times and places with [illegible] guarantee against "unreasonable searches and seizures." But I think it belittles that Amendment to talk about it as though it protects nothing but "privacy." . . .

One of the most effective ways of diluting or expanding a constitutionally guaranteed right is to substitute for the crucial word or words of a constitutional guarantee another word or words more or less flexible and more or less restricted in meaning. . . . I like my privacy as well as the next one, but I am nevertheless compelled to admit that government has a right to invade it unless prohibited by some specific constitutional provision. For these reasons I cannot agree with the Court's judgment and the reasons it gives for holding this Connecticut law unconstitutional.

. . . My disagreement with the Court's opinion holding that there is such a violation here is a narrow one, relating to the application of the First Amendment to the facts and circumstances of this particular case. But my disagreement with Brothers Harlan, White and Goldberg is more basic. I think that if properly construed neither the Due Process Clause nor the Ninth Amendment, nor both together, could under any circumstances be a proper basis for invalidating the Connecticut law. I discuss the due process and Ninth Amendment arguments together because on analysis they turn out to be the same thing — merely using different words to claim for this Court and the federal judiciary power to invalidate any legislative act which the judges find irrational, unreasonable or offensive.

. . . .

NOTES AND QUESTIONS

1. *Griswold v. Connecticut* is a centrally important decision in the development of constitutional law as it pertains to personal identity and autonomy, dealing as it does with the sexual component of personhood. Each person in various ways engages in practices involved with that person's sexual orientation, either as a cause of the orientation, as a result, or as an inevitable, central expression of it. The heterosexual relations in *Griswold* accompanied by contraception are not for the purposes of procreation, but for the purposes of intimacy and association. Thus, *Griswold,* properly viewed, bears directly on the sexual identity of individuals and their right of privacy in affirming or acting upon that identity.

2. The Court in *Griswold* seems to believe that it is important that the contraception ban could apply to married couples. Suppose it did not? Would the ban on contraception stand if it exempted the use of contraceptive devices by married couples? Could not the state of Connecticut *then* say that this placed a premium on being married and supported the integrity of the family in a way which was consistent with the Supreme Court's own emphasis on family association as a constitutionally protected zone of interests?

3. It may be, as Justice Douglas says, that various provisions of the Constitution create "penumbras" and that there are certain liberties which are enumerated in the Constitution itself; but is it possible to tell where and how the particular activity of heterosexual intercourse without contraception *is* protected? Justice Goldberg, at least, relies upon the Ninth Amendment as preserving rights "retained by the people." Justices Harlan and White would rely upon the concept of "liberty" in the Fifth and Fourteenth Amendments. Which makes the most sense? Which later prevails in *Casey*?

4. *Griswold* may be seen as a precursor to *Roe v. Wade* and *Pennsylvania Planned Parenthood v. Casey*, discussed in Ch. 1, *supra.* Constitutionally, how does it differ in its grounding or mode of analysis from these later cases?

5. Given the holding in *Griswold,* how is it possible for the federal government over the last decade to ban the importation and use of the French drug RU 486? That drug operates safely for contraceptive purposes as a "morning after" pill. Politically, it has been controversial as a form of early abortion. But given the opinions in *Griswold, Roe* and

Casey, can there be any doubt as to the unconstitutionality of barring its development and sale in the United States.

6. What would Rawls, The United Nations Declaration and the Council of Europe Convention say about the issues in *Griswold*? Would the privacy interests in *Griswold* protect homosexual relations? That is the subject of the next case, *Lawrence v. Texas*, in which the Supreme Court reversed an almost identical case, *Bowers v. Hardwick*, decided less than twenty years earlier.

LAWRENCE v. TEXAS
539 U.S. 558 (2003)

Justice **Kennedy** delivered the opinion of the Court.

Liberty protects the person from unwarranted government intrusions into a dwelling or other private places. In our tradition the State is not omnipresent in the home. And there are other spheres of our lives and existence, outside the home, where the State should not be a dominant presence. Freedom extends beyond spatial bounds. Liberty presumes an autonomy of self that includes freedom of thought, belief, expression, and certain intimate conduct. The instant case involves liberty of the person both in its spatial and more transcendent dimensions.

The question before the Court is the validity of a Texas statute making it a crime for two persons of the same sex to engage in certain intimate sexual conduct.

In Houston, Texas, officers of the Harris County Police Department were dispatched to a private residence in response to a reported weapons disturbance. They entered an apartment where one of the petitioners, John Geddes Lawrence, resided. The right of the police to enter does not seem to have been questioned. The officers observed Lawrence and another man, Tyron Garner, engaging in a sexual act. The two petitioners were arrested, held in custody over night, and charged and convicted before a Justice of the Peace.

The complaints described their crime as "deviate sexual intercourse, namely anal sex, with a member of the same sex (man)." The applicable state law is Tex. Penal Code provides: "A person commits an offense if he engages in deviate sexual intercourse with another individual of the same sex." The statute defines "[d]eviate sexual intercourse" as follows:

> "(A) any contact between any part of the genitals of one person and the mouth or anus of another person; or
>
> "(B) the penetration of the genitals or the anus of another person with an object."

We conclude the case should be resolved by determining whether the petitioners were free as adults to engage in the private conduct in the exercise of their liberty under the Due Process Clause of the Fourteenth Amendment to the Constitution. For this inquiry we deem it necessary to reconsider the Court's holding in *Bowers* [*v. Hardwick*].

After Griswold it was established that the right to make certain decisions regarding sexual conduct extends beyond the marital relationship. In *Eisenstadt v. Baird*, 405 U.S. 438 (1972), the Court invalidated a law prohibiting the distribution of contraceptives to unmarried persons. The case was decided under the Equal Protection Clause, but with respect to unmarried persons, the Court went on to state the fundamental proposition that the law impaired the exercise of their personal rights.

The *Bowers* Court began its substantive discussion as follows: "The issue presented is whether the Federal Constitution confers a fundamental right upon homosexuals to engage in sodomy and hence invalidates the laws of the many States that still make such conduct illegal and have done so for a very long time." That statement, we now conclude, discloses the Court's own failure to appreciate the extent of the liberty at stake. To say that the issue in *Bowers* was simply the right to engage in certain sexual conduct demeans the claim the individual put forward, just as it would demean a married couple were it to be said marriage is simply about the right to have sexual intercourse. The laws involved in *Bowers* and here are, to be sure, statutes that purport to do no more than prohibit a particular sexual act. Their penalties and purposes, though, have more far-reaching consequences, touching upon the most private human conduct, sexual behavior, and in the most private of places, the home. The statutes do seek to control a personal relationship that, whether or not entitled to formal recognition in the law, is within the liberty of persons to choose without being punished as criminals.

This, as a general rule, should counsel against attempts by the State, or a court, to define the meaning of the relationship or to set its boundaries absent injury to a person or abuse of an institution the law protects. It suffices for us to acknowledge that adults may choose to enter upon this relationship in the confines of their homes and their own private lives and still retain their dignity as free persons. When sexuality finds overt expression in intimate conduct with another person, the conduct can be but one element in a personal bond that is more enduring. The liberty protected by the Constitution allows homosexual persons the right to make this choice.

At the outset it should be noted that there is no longstanding history in this country of laws directed at homosexual conduct as a distinct matter. Beginning in colonial times there were prohibitions of sodomy derived from the English criminal laws passed in the first instance by the Reformation Parliament of 1533. The English prohibition was understood to include relations between men and women as well as relations between men and men. See, *e.g.*, *King v. Wiseman*, 92 Eng. Rep. 774, 775 (K.B.1718) (interpreting "mankind" in Act of 1533 as including women and girls). Nineteenth-century commentators similarly read American sodomy, buggery, and crime-against-nature statutes as criminalizing certain relations between men and women and between men and men. The absence of legal prohibitions focusing on homosexual conduct may be explained in part by noting that according to some scholars the concept of the homosexual as a distinct category of person did not emerge until the late 19th century. Thus early American sodomy laws were not directed at homosexuals as such but instead sought to prohibit non-procreative sexual activity more generally. This does not suggest approval of homosexual conduct. It does tend to show that this particular form of conduct was not thought of as a separate category from like conduct between heterosexual persons.

Laws prohibiting sodomy do not seem to have been enforced against consenting adults acting in private. A substantial number of sodomy prosecutions and convictions for which there are surviving records were for predatory acts against those who could not or did not consent, as in the case of a minor or the victim of an assault. As to these, one purpose for the prohibitions was to ensure there would be no lack of coverage if a predator committed a sexual assault that did not constitute rape as defined by the criminal law. Thus the model sodomy indictments presented in a 19th-century treatise. Instead of targeting relations between consenting adults in private, 19th-century sodomy prosecutions typically involved relations between men and minor girls or minor boys, relations between adults involving force, relations between adults implicating disparity in status, or relations between men and animals.

To the extent that there were any prosecutions for the acts in question, 19th-century evidence rules imposed a burden that would make a conviction more difficult to obtain even taking into account the problems always inherent in prosecuting consensual acts committed in private. Under then-prevailing standards, a man could not be convicted of sodomy based upon testimony of a consenting partner, because the partner was considered an accomplice. A partner's testimony, however, was admissible if he or she had not consented to the act or was a minor, and therefore incapable of consent.

The policy of punishing consenting adults for private acts was not much discussed in the early legal literature. We can infer that one reason for this was the very private nature of the conduct. Despite the absence of prosecutions, there may have been periods in which there was public criticism of homosexuals as such and an insistence that the criminal laws be enforced to discourage their practices. But far from possessing "ancient roots," American laws targeting same-sex couples did not develop until the last third of the 20th century. The reported decisions concerning the prosecution of consensual, homosexual conduct between adults for the years 1880-1995 are not always clear in the details, but a significant number involved conduct in a public place.

It was not until the 1970's that any State singled out same-sex relations for criminal prosecution, and only nine States have done so. Post-*Bowers* even some of these States did not adhere to the policy of suppressing homosexual conduct. Over the course of the last decades, States with same-sex prohibitions have moved toward abolishing them.

In summary, the historical grounds relied upon in *Bowers* are more complex than the majority opinion and the concurring opinion by Chief Justice Burger indicate. Their historical premises are not without doubt and, at the very least, are overstated.

It must be acknowledged, of course, that the Court in *Bowers* was making the broader point that for centuries there have been powerful voices to condemn homosexual conduct as immoral. The condemnation has been shaped by religious beliefs, conceptions of right and acceptable behavior, and respect for the traditional family. For many persons these are not trivial concerns but profound and deep convictions accepted as ethical and moral principles to which they aspire and which thus determine the course of their lives. These considerations do not answer the question before us, however. The issue is whether the majority may use the power of the State to enforce these views on the whole society through operation of the criminal law. "Our obligation is to define the liberty of all, not to mandate our own moral code." *Planned Parenthood of Southeastern Pa. v. Casey.*

In *Bowers* the Court referred to the fact that before 1961 all 50 States had outlawed sodomy, and that at the time of the Court's decision 24 States and the District of Columbia had sodomy laws. Justice Powell pointed out that these prohibitions often were being ignored, however. Georgia, for instance, had not sought to enforce its law for decades. ("The history of nonenforcement suggests the moribund character today of laws criminalizing this type of private, consensual conduct.")

The sweeping references by Chief Justice Burger to the history of Western civilization and to Judeo-Christian moral and ethical standards did not take account of other authorities pointing in an opposite direction. A committee advising the British Parliament recommended in 1957 repeal of laws punishing homosexual conduct. Parliament enacted the substance of those recommendations 10 years later.

In our own constitutional system the deficiencies in *Bowers* became even more apparent in the years following its announcement. The 25 States with laws prohibiting the relevant conduct referenced in the *Bowers* decision are reduced now to 13, of which 4 enforce their laws only against homosexual conduct. In those States where sodomy is still proscribed, whether for same-sex or heterosexual conduct, there is a pattern of nonenforcement with respect to consenting adults acting in private. The State of Texas admitted in 1994 that as of that date it had not prosecuted anyone under those circumstances.

Two principal cases decided after *Bowers* cast its holding into even more doubt. In *Planned Parenthood of Southeastern Pa. v. Casey*, the Court reaffirmed the substantive force of the liberty protected by the Due Process Clause. The *Casey* decision again confirmed that our laws and tradition afford constitutional protection to personal decisions relating to marriage, procreation, contraception, family relationships, child rearing, and education. In explaining the respect the Constitution demands for the autonomy of the person in making these choices, we stated as follows:

> "These matters, involving the most intimate and personal choices a person may make in a lifetime, choices central to personal dignity and autonomy, are central to the liberty protected by the Fourteenth Amendment. At the heart of liberty is the right to define one's own concept of existence, of meaning, of the universe, and of the mystery of human life. Beliefs about these matters could not define the attributes of personhood were they formed under compulsion of the State."

Persons in a homosexual relationship may seek autonomy for these purposes, just as heterosexual persons do. The decision in *Bowers* would deny them this right.

The second post-*Bowers* case of principal relevance is *Romer v. Evans*. There the Court struck down class-based legislation directed at homosexuals as a violation of the Equal Protection Clause. Romer invalidated an amendment to Colorado's constitution which named as a solitary class persons who were homosexuals, lesbians, or bisexual either by "orientation, conduct, practices or relationships," and deprived them of protection under state antidiscrimination laws. We concluded that the provision was "born of animosity toward the class of persons affected" and further that it had no rational relation to a legitimate governmental purpose.

Equality of treatment and the due process right to demand respect for conduct protected by the substantive guarantee of liberty are linked in important respects, and a decision on the latter point advances both interests. If protected conduct is made criminal and the law which does so remains unexamined for its substantive validity, its stigma might remain even if it were not enforceable as drawn for equal protection reasons. When homosexual conduct is made criminal by the law of the State, that declaration in and of itself is an invitation to subject homosexual persons to discrimination both in the public and in the private spheres. The central holding of *Bowers* has been brought in question by this case, and it should be addressed. Its continuance as precedent demeans the lives of homosexual persons.

The rationale of *Bowers* does not withstand careful analysis. In his dissenting opinion in *Bowers* Justice Stevens came to these conclusions:

> "Our prior cases make two propositions abundantly clear. First, the fact that the governing majority in a State has traditionally viewed a particular practice as immoral is not a sufficient reason for upholding a law prohibiting the practice; neither history nor tradition could save a law prohibiting miscegenation from constitutional attack. Second, individual decisions by married persons, concerning the intimacies of their physical relationship, even when not intended to produce offspring, are a form of 'liberty' protected by the Due Process Clause of the Fourteenth Amendment. Moreover, this protection extends to intimate choices by unmarried as well as married persons."

Justice Stevens' analysis, in our view, should have been controlling in *Bowers* and should control here.

The petitioners are entitled to respect for their private lives. The State cannot demean their existence or control their destiny by making their private sexual conduct a crime. Their right to liberty under the Due Process Clause gives them the full right to engage in their conduct without intervention of the government. "It is a promise of the Constitution that there is a realm of personal liberty which the government may not enter." The Texas statute furthers no legitimate state interest which can justify its intrusion into the personal and private life of the individual.

Had those who drew and ratified the Due Process Clauses of the Fifth Amendment or the Fourteenth Amendment known the components of liberty in its manifold possibilities, they might have been more specific. They did not presume to have this insight. They knew times can blind us to certain truths and later generations can see that laws once thought necessary and proper in fact serve only to oppress. As the Constitution endures, persons in every generation can invoke its principles in their own search for greater freedom.

The judgment of the Court of Appeals for the Texas Fourteenth District is reversed, and the case is remanded for further proceedings not inconsistent with this opinion.

It is so ordered.

Justice **O'Connor**, concurring in the judgment.

The Court today overrules *Bowers v. Hardwick*, 478 U.S. 186 (1986). I joined *Bowers*, and do not join the Court in overruling it. Nevertheless, I agree with the Court that Texas' statute banning same-sex sodomy is unconstitutional. Rather than relying on the substantive component of the Fourteenth Amendment's Due Process Clause, as the Court does, I base my conclusion on the Fourteenth Amendment's Equal Protection Clause.

The Equal Protection Clause of the Fourteenth Amendment "is essentially a direction that all persons similarly situated should be treated alike." Under our rational basis standard of review, "legislation is presumed to be valid and will be sustained if the classification drawn by the statute is rationally related to a legitimate state interest."

Laws such as economic or tax legislation that are scrutinized under rational basis review normally pass constitutional muster, since "the Constitution presumes that even improvident decisions will eventually be rectified by the democratic processes." We have consistently held, however, that some objectives, such as "a bare . . . desire to harm a politically unpopular group," are not legitimate state interests. When a law exhibits such a desire to harm a politically unpopular group, we have applied a more searching form of rational basis review to strike down such laws under the Equal Protection Clause.

The statute at issue here makes sodomy a crime only if a person "engages in deviate sexual intercourse with another individual of the same sex." Sodomy between opposite-sex partners, however, is not a crime in Texas. That is, Texas treats the same conduct differently based solely on the participants. Those harmed by this law are people who have a same-sex sexual orientation and thus are more likely to engage in behavior prohibited by § 21.06.

The Texas statute makes homosexuals unequal in the eyes of the law by making particular conduct — and only that conduct — subject to criminal sanction.

And the effect of Texas' sodomy law is not just limited to the threat of prosecution or consequence of conviction. Texas' sodomy law brands all homosexuals as criminals, thereby making it more difficult for homosexuals to be treated in the same manner as everyone else. Indeed, Texas itself has previously acknowledged the collateral effects of the law, stipulating in a prior challenge to this action that the law "legally sanctions discrimination against [homosexuals] in a variety of ways unrelated to the criminal law," including in the areas of "employment, family issues, and housing." *State v. Morales*, 826 S.W.2d 201, 203 (Tex.App.1992).

Texas attempts to justify its law, and the effects of the law, by arguing that the statute satisfies rational basis review because it furthers the legitimate governmental interest of the promotion of morality. In *Bowers*, we held that a state law criminalizing sodomy as applied to homosexual couples did not [illegible] We rejected the argument that no rational basis existed to justify the law, pointing to the government's interest in promoting morality. The only question in front of the Court in *Bowers* was whether the substantive component of the Due Process Clause protected a right to engage in homosexual sodomy. *Bowers* did not hold that moral disapproval of a group is a rational basis under the Equal Protection Clause to criminalize homosexual sodomy when heterosexual sodomy is not punished.

This case raises a different issue than *Bowers*: whether, under the Equal Protection Clause, moral disapproval is a legitimate state interest to justify by itself a statute that bans homosexual sodomy, but not heterosexual sodomy. It is not. Moral disapproval of this group, like a bare desire to harm the group, is an interest that is insufficient to satisfy rational basis review under the Equal Protection Clause. *See, e.g., Department of Agriculture v. Moreno*, [413 U.S. 528] at 534; *Romer v. Evans*, 517 U.S. [610], at 634–635. Indeed, we have never held that moral disapproval, without any other asserted state interest, is a sufficient rationale under the Equal Protection Clause to justify a law that discriminates among groups of persons.

Texas argues, however, that the sodomy law does not discriminate against homosexual persons. Instead, the State maintains that the law discriminates only against homosexual conduct. While it is true that the law applies only to conduct, the conduct targeted by this law is conduct that is closely correlated with being homosexual. Under such circumstances, Texas' sodomy law is targeted at more than conduct. It is instead directed toward gay persons as a class.

A State can of course assign certain consequences to a violation of its criminal law. But the State cannot single out one identifiable class of citizens for punishment that does not apply to everyone else, with moral disapproval as the only asserted state interest for the law. The Texas sodomy statute subjects homosexuals to "a lifelong penalty and stigma. A legislative classification that threatens the creation of an underclass . . . cannot be reconciled with" the Equal Protection Clause.

Whether a sodomy law that is neutral both in effect and application would violate the substantive component of the Due Process Clause is an issue that need not be decided today. I am confident, however, that so long as the Equal Protection Clause requires a sodomy law to apply equally to the private consensual conduct of homosexuals and heterosexuals alike, such a law would not long stand in our democratic society.

That this law as applied to private, consensual conduct is unconstitutional under the Equal Protection Clause does not mean that other laws distinguishing between heterosexuals and homosexuals would similarly fail under rational basis review. Texas cannot assert any legitimate state interest here, such as national security or preserving the traditional institution of marriage. Unlike the moral disapproval of same-sex relations — the asserted state interest in this case — other reasons exist to promote the institution of marriage beyond mere moral disapproval of an excluded group.

A law branding one class of persons as criminal based solely on the State's moral disapproval of that class and the conduct associated with that class runs contrary to the values of the Constitution and the Equal Protection Clause, under any standard of review. I therefore concur in the Court's judgment that Texas' sodomy law banning "deviate sexual intercourse" between consenting adults of the same sex, but not between consenting adults of different sexes, is unconstitutional.

Justice **Scalia**, with whom **The Chief Justice** and Justice **Thomas** join, dissenting.

Having decided that it need not adhere to stare decisis, the Court still must establish that *Bowers* was wrongly decided and that the Texas statute, as applied to petitioners, is unconstitutional.

Texas Penal Code Ann. § 21.06(a) (2003) undoubtedly imposes constraints on liberty. So do laws prohibiting prostitution, recreational use of heroin, and, for that matter, working more than 60 hours per week in a bakery. But there is no right to "liberty" under the Due Process Clause, though today's opinion repeatedly makes that claim. ("The liberty protected by the Constitution allows homosexual persons the right to make this choice"); (" 'These matters . . . are central to the liberty protected by the Fourteenth Amendment' "); ("Their right to liberty under the Due Process Clause gives them the full right to engage in their conduct without intervention of the government"). The Fourteenth Amendment expressly allows States to deprive their citizens of "liberty," so long as "due process of law" is provided:

"No state shall . . . deprive any person of life, liberty, or property, without due process of law." Amdt. 14 (emphasis added).

Our opinions applying the doctrine known as "substantive due process" hold that the Due Process Clause prohibits States from infringing fundamental liberty interests, unless the infringement is narrowly tailored to serve a compelling state interest. *Washington v. Glucksberg*, We have held repeatedly, in cases the Court today does not overrule, that only fundamental rights qualify for this so-called "heightened scrutiny" protection — that is, rights which are " 'deeply rooted in this Nation's history and tradition.' " *Ibid.*

Bowers held, first, that criminal prohibitions of homosexual sodomy are not subject to heightened scrutiny because they do not implicate a "fundamental right" under the Due Process Clause. Noting that "[p]roscriptions against that conduct have ancient roots," that "[s]odomy was a criminal offense at common law and was forbidden by the laws of the original 13 States when they ratified the Bill of Rights," *ibid.*, and that many States had retained their bans on sodomy, *id.*, at 193, *Bowers* concluded that a right to engage in homosexual sodomy was not " 'deeply rooted in this Nation's history and tradition.' "

The Court today does not overrule this holding. Not once does it describe homosexual sodomy as a "fundamental right" or a "fundamental liberty interest," nor does it subject the Texas statute to strict scrutiny. Instead, having failed to establish that the right to homosexual sodomy is " 'deeply rooted in this Nation's history and tradition,' " the Court concludes that the application of Texas's statute to petitioners' conduct fails the rational-basis test, and overrules *Bowers*' holding to the contrary. "The Texas statute furthers no legitimate state interest which can justify its intrusion into the personal and private life of the individual."

I shall address that rational-basis holding presently. First, however, I address some aspersions that the Court casts upon *Bowers'* conclusion that homosexual sodomy is not a "fundamental right" — even though, as I have said, the Court does not have the boldness to reverse that conclusion.

. . . .

III

It is (as *Bowers* recognized) entirely irrelevant whether the laws in our long national tradition criminalizing homosexual sodomy were "directed at homosexual conduct as a distinct matter." Whether homosexual sodomy was prohibited by a law targeted at same-sex sexual relations or by a more general law prohibiting both homosexual and heterosexual sodomy, the only relevant point is that it was criminalized — which suffices to establish that homosexual sodomy is not a right "deeply rooted in our Nation's history and tradition." The Court today agrees that homosexual sodomy was criminalized and thus does not dispute the facts on which *Bowers* actually relied.

Next the Court makes the claim, again unsupported by any citations, that "[l]aws prohibiting sodomy do not seem to have been enforced against consenting adults acting in private." There are 203 prosecutions for consensual, adult homosexual sodomy reported in the West Reporting system and official state reporters from the years 1880-1995. *See* W. Eskridge, *Gaylaw: Challenging the Apartheid of the Closet*, 375 (1999) (hereinafter Gaylaw). There are also records of 20 sodomy prosecutions and 4 executions during the colonial period. J. Katz, Gay/Lesbian Almanac 29, 58, 663 (1983). *Bowers'* conclusion that homosexual sodomy is not a fundamental right "deeply rooted in this Nation's history and tradition" is utterly unassailable.

Realizing that fact, the Court instead says: "[W]e think that our laws and traditions in the past half century are of most relevance here. These references show an emerging awareness that liberty gives substantial protection to adult persons in deciding how to conduct their private lives in matters pertaining to sex." Apart from the fact that such an "emerging awareness" does not establish a "fundamental right," the statement is factually false. States continue to prosecute all sorts of crimes by adults "in matters pertaining to sex": prostitution, adult incest, adultery, obscenity, and child pornography. Sodomy laws, too, have been enforced "in the past half century," in which there have been 134 reported cases involving prosecutions for consensual, adult, homosexual sodomy. In relying, for evidence of an "emerging recognition," upon the American Law Institute's 1955 recommendation not to criminalize " 'consensual sexual relations conducted in private,' " the Court ignores the fact that this recommendation was "a point of resistance in most of the states that considered adopting the Model Penal Code."

In any event, an "emerging awareness" is by definition not "deeply rooted in this Nation's history and tradition[s]," as we have said "fundamental right" status requires. Constitutional entitlements do not spring into existence because some States choose to lessen or eliminate criminal sanctions on certain behavior.

IV

I turn now to the ground on which the Court squarely rests its holding: the contention that there is no rational basis for the law here under attack. This proposition is so out of accord with our jurisprudence — indeed, with the jurisprudence of any society we know — that it requires little discussion.

The Texas statute undeniably seeks to further the belief of its citizens that certain forms of sexual behavior are "immoral and unacceptable," — the same interest furthered by criminal laws against fornication, bigamy, adultery, adult incest, bestiality, and obscenity. *Bowers* held that this was a legitimate state interest. The Court today reaches the opposite conclusion. This effectively decrees the end of all morals legislation. If, as the Court asserts, the promotion of majoritarian sexual morality is not even a legitimate state interest, none of the above-mentioned laws can survive rational-basis review.

V

Finally, I turn to petitioners' equal-protection challenge, which no Member of the Court save Justice O'Connor, embraces: On its face § 21.06(a) applies equally to all persons. Men and women, heterosexuals and homosexuals, are all subject to its prohibition of deviate sexual intercourse with someone of the same sex. To be sure, § 21.06 does distinguish between the sexes insofar as concerns the partner with whom the sexual acts are performed: men can violate the law only with other men, and women only with other women. But this cannot itself be a denial of equal protection, since it is precisely the same distinction regarding partner that is drawn in state laws prohibiting marriage with someone of the same sex while permitting marriage with someone of the opposite sex.

Justice O'Connor argues that the discrimination in this law which must be justified is not its discrimination with regard to the sex of the partner but its discrimination with regard to the sexual proclivity of the principal actor.

> "While it is true that the law applies only to conduct, the conduct targeted by this law is conduct that is closely correlated with being homosexual. Under such circumstances, Texas' sodomy law is targeted at more than conduct. It is instead directed toward gay persons as a class."

Of course the same could be said of any law. A law against public nudity targets "the conduct that is closely correlated with being a nudist," and hence "is targeted at more than conduct"; it is "directed toward nudists as a class." But be that as it may. Even if the Texas law does deny equal protection to "homosexuals as a class," that denial still does not need to be justified by anything more than a rational basis, which our cases show is satisfied by the enforcement of traditional notions of sexual morality.

Justice O'Connor simply decrees application of "a more searching form of rational basis review" to the Texas statute.

This reasoning leaves on pretty shaky grounds state laws limiting marriage to opposite-sex couples. Justice O'Connor seeks to preserve them by the conclusory statement that "preserving the traditional institution of marriage" is a legitimate state interest. But "preserving the traditional institution of marriage" is just a kinder way of describing the State's moral disapproval of same-sex couples. Texas's interest in § 21.06 could be recast in similarly euphemistic terms: "preserving the traditional sexual mores of our society." In the jurisprudence Justice O'Connor has seemingly created, judges can validate laws by characterizing them as "preserving the traditions of society" (good); or invalidate them by characterizing them as "expressing moral disapproval" (bad).

. . . .

Today's opinion is the product of a Court, which is the product of a law profession culture, that has largely signed on to the so-called homosexual agenda, by which I mean the agenda promoted by some homosexual activists directed at eliminating the moral opprobrium that has traditionally attached to homosexual conduct.

Many Americans do not want persons who openly engage in homosexual conduct as partners in their business, as scoutmasters for their children, as teachers in their children's schools, or as boarders in their home. They view this as protecting themselves and their families from a lifestyle that they believe to be immoral and destructive. The Court views it as "discrimination" which it is the function of our judgments to deter. So imbued is the Court with the law profession's anti-anti-homosexual culture, that it is seemingly unaware that the attitudes of that culture are not obviously "mainstream"; that in most States what the Court calls "discrimination" against those who engage in homosexual acts is perfectly legal; that proposals to ban such "discrimination" under Title VII have repeatedly been rejected by Congress, that in some cases such "discrimination" is mandated by federal statute, see 10 U.S.C. § 654(b)(1) (mandating discharge from the armed forces of any service member who engages in or intends to engage in homosexual acts); and that in some cases such "discrimination" is a constitutional right, see *Boy Scouts of America v. Dale*.

Let me be clear that I have nothing against homosexuals, or any other group, promoting their agenda through normal democratic means. Social perceptions of sexual and other morality change over time, and every group has the right to persuade its fellow citizens that its view of such matters is the best.

One of the benefits of leaving regulation of this matter to the people rather than to the courts is that the people, unlike judges, need not carry things to their logical conclusion. The people may feel that their disapprobation of homosexual conduct is strong enough to disallow homosexual marriage, but not strong enough to criminalize private homosexual acts — and may legislate accordingly. The Court today pretends that it possesses a similar freedom of action. Do not believe it. Today's opinion dismantles the structure of constitutional law that has permitted a distinction to be made between heterosexual and homosexual unions, insofar as formal recognition in marriage is concerned. This case "does not involve" the issue of homosexual marriage only if one entertains the belief that principle and logic have nothing to do with the decisions of this Court. Many will hope that, as the Court comfortingly assures us, this is so.

Justice **Thomas**, dissenting.

I join Justice **Scalia**'s dissenting opinion.

NOTES AND QUESTIONS

1. Should *Lawrence* be decided on equal protection grounds? Overbreadth? Under the First Amendment? If "privacy" or "liberty," where shall these be grounded in the Constitution?
2. Justice Kennedy relies on *Casey* and *Romer*, but isn't he missing the point? Those cases related to established rights — in *Lawrence*, the issue was whether there *was* a right.
3. And what is the right protected in *Lawrence* — to have a homosexual relationship? To engage in same-sex sexual activity? If the latter, must it be within the former? And within the home?
4. Justice Kennedy's reading of history is in dramatic contrast to that in *Bowers v. Hardwick*, where Chief Justice Burger traced the ban on homosexual activity and sodomy to truly "ancient roots." Who has it right? And what does it matter?
5. Justice O'Connor finds a law restricted to homosexuals discriminatory and irrational. But does this mean Texas could ban sodomy by homosexuals and heterosexuals? And is it irrational — or is it directed at nonprocreative sexual activity (or is that irrational?)?
6. Does Justice O'Connor succeed in distinguishing *Bowers*? Does she preserve a constitutional role for morality? What is it?
7. And what of Justice Scalia's dissent? Does he persuade you that stare decisis has been mindlessly abandoned? That statistics of prosecution favor his point of view?
8. Justice Scalia argues that the decision in *Lawrence* means an end to morality as a basis for state legislation. Is that a bad thing? And is he right, since states may still ban forcible and "statutory" rape, child abuse, pornography as crimes? They may legislate favorably to marriage and child welfare. Or does he have something else in mind?
9. As to Justice Scalia's comments about same sex marriage, see *infra*, *Goodridge v. Dept. of Health*, (798 N.E.2d 941, Mass. 2003), where the Massachusetts high court held *for* same sex marriage.
10. *Lofton v. Secretary of the Dept of Children and Family Services* (358 F.3d 804 (11th Cir. 2004)) reaches the conclusion that homosexual adoption is also not protected under *Lawrence*. The court distinguishes adoption as a public act, not a private one, and discusses the reasoning behind the state's "legitimate interest" in placing children in nuclear-type families. The court discusses how this is in the best interests of the children, even if in certain cases, a homosexual family may provide better care than a nuclear one. How can this be rationalized? If the state must look at the best interests of each child when deciding adoption, should it be able to rule out certain types of families, without looking further at the individuals involved?

IN RE: BRIAN HARRIS, a/k/a LISA HARRIS*

707 A.2d 225 (Pa. Super. Ct. 1997)

Olszewski, Judge.

As Tammy Wynette so aptly observed, sometimes it's hard to be a woman. This is especially true in the instant matter, which calls this Court to decide the case of Brian Harris, a thirty-nine-year-old man who, for the past twenty-two years, has lived as a woman. During this time, petitioner has consistently dressed and appeared in public as a female and has assumed the name "Lisa." In addition to his years of intensive psychological counseling, petitioner has undergone a number of medical procedures designed to make himself appear more feminine. Specifically, petitioner receives routine estrogen hormone therapy and has had permanent reconstructive facial surgeries as well as breast implants. Although petitioner desires to have the sex reassignment surgery which involves the removal of the male genitalia and the construction of female genitalia, financial constraints have thus far made reassignment unavailable.

On April 30, 1996, petitioner filed an unopposed petition for name change. . . . The first witness to testify was Dr. Constance Saunders, petitioner's counselor of twenty years. Dr. Saunders testified that, in her expert medical opinion, petitioner's desire to live as a woman was permanent and unassailable. In support of this opinion, Dr. Saunders relied upon petitioner's long history of living as a woman and the extensive surgical measures he had undergone in order to present himself more convincingly as a female. Additionally, Dr. Saunders testified that petitioner's hormonal makeup was naturally more female than male.

When asked whether the name change would benefit petitioner, Dr. Saunders testified that, both professionally and personally, the name change would be beneficial. Because of petitioner's outwardly feminine appearance, Dr. Saunders testified, he oftentimes encounters problems when required to present official identification. That is, the disparity between petitioner's female appearance and the male name on his license leads to confrontations and allegations of deceit. In fact, Dr. Saunders [illegible] accompanies petitioner to appointments in order to vouch that petitioner is, in fact, a man. Personally, Dr. Saunders testified that allowance of the name change would provide petitioner with a degree of dignity that is presently lacking in his life and, additionally, would afford an affirmance of petitioner's belief that he is genetically and hormonally more female than male.

Following Dr. Saunders testimony, petitioner briefly testified. In essence, petitioner stated that his desire to have his name legally changed was twofold. First, petitioner stated that he has used the name "Lisa" socially for over twenty years and that his gender identification is completely female. Additionally, petitioner swore that he desired additional surgeries, including reassignment, but that at present the costs of such procedures were prohibitive. Secondly, petitioner stated that the change of name would result in less confusion for those people requesting official identification from him in

* The citation references has been omitted from this case.

addition to eliminating the personal embarrassment that petitioner feels when he is forced to adamantly and repeatedly aver that he is a man.

At the close of testimony, the court reserved its decision. By order dated September 19, 1996, the court denied the petition for change of name. . . .

. . . .

. . . [T]he court in the instant matter held that "absent reassignment surgery it would not comport with common sense, common decency and fairness to all concerned, especially the public, to allow a change of name at this juncture." In essence, the court interpreted the caselaw from its sister courts as creating a bright-line test for determining when a transsexual may successfully petition for a name change.

The trial court's own interpretation is fundamentally flawed, however, for this petitioner has undergone permanent reconstructive surgeries whose only possible benefit is to advance his stated desire to become a woman in all respects. Accordingly, we believe the trial court's reading to be unnecessarily narrow and decline to adopt it.

Instead, we believe that the better-reasoned approach is to require such a petitioner to demonstrate that he or she is permanently committed to living as a member of the opposite sex. While proof of reassignment surgery would undoubtedly fulfill this criteria, the absence of such surgery does not automatically doom a petition to failure. . . .

. . . .

Moreover, we must disagree with the trial court's determination that permitting a name change at this juncture would be unfair to the general public. The uncontroverted evidence adduced at the hearing proved that a legal name change would actually prevent the daily confusion and public confrontations which presently plague petitioner's dealings with the public.

While saddled with a male name and a female visage, petitioner must constantly convince the public that his name is "Brian." Should petitioner be allowed to change his name to "Lisa," however, the general public's outward perception of petitioner would be reaffirmed by petitioner's legal name. Thus, rather then perpetrating a fraud upon the public, the name change would eliminate what many presently believe to be a fraud; that is, that petitioner is a man.

. . . .

Reversed. Court to grant the petition seeking a legal name change from "Brian Harris" to "Lisa Harris"; jurisdiction relinquished.

Concurring statement by **Popovich**, J.:

This court must determine whether a petitioner has complied with the statutory requirements and to ensure that the person has no fraudulent intentions in changing his name. This is where the inquiry ends. Herein, appellant filed an unopposed petition for change of name in accordance with the statutory requirements of 54 Pa.C.S.A. § 701 et seq. There is no evidence to suggest that appellant was attempting to change his name to avoid any financial obligation. In light of the statutory language and the legislature's intent, I believe that appellant's petition should be granted without probing into appellant's sex or his [illegible] manner of his choosing.

Moreover, if parents have an absolute right to choose to name their male child an obvious "female" name at birth, it is illogical that an adult does not have the same right to change his name in the future if he so desires, whatever the name shall be, provided that the person does not seek the change for fraudulent purposes.

Dissenting statement by **Saylor**, J.:

Because such petitions for a formal change of name implicate the judicial process in sanctioning the petitioner's choice of name, I believe that the trial court properly considered not only the literal requirements of the name change statute but also public policy interests.

Here, petitioner is a pre-operative transsexual. Although petitioner receives routine hormone therapy, has undergone permanent facial reconstructive surgery, and has had breast implants, the fact remains that he has not yet had gender reassignment surgery, which involves the removal of the male genitalia and the construction of female genitalia. Therefore, although he possesses some of the outward physical characteristics of a female, his physical transformation to the opposite gender is not yet complete. To permit him to adopt an obviously female name would be to perpetuate a fiction, since the fact remains that petitioner is anatomically a male until he undergoes reassignment surgery. Only after such procedure would petitioner be a female, physically as well as psychologically. See, Matter of Anonymous, (court granted name change from male name to female name where petitioner was a male-to-female transsexual who had already undergone sex reassignment surgery and was both anatomically and psychologically female "in fact"). To judicially sanction a pre-operative male transsexual's adoption of an obviously female name would grant legal recognition to a physiological fiction.

Accordingly, I would affirm the trial court's denial of the petition for legal change of name.

NOTES AND QUESTIONS

1. A name is essential to a person's identity, frequently establishing gender, race, ethnicity and religion, in a succinct, public way. It also is frequently a matter of family tradition and heritage. And political significance may attach to a name or a name change. All of these dimensions in a name may prove burdensome to a person, especially if he or she wishes to change the identity or position society assigns to that name. Many immigrants to America shortened or Anglicized their names. And many women in businesses use initials or middle names (which are often gender-neutral, based on the mother's family name) to avoid gender discrimination. That is what Brian Harris, in a reverse way, was seeking to do.
2. Why, then, resist name changes? Does it matter whether we are known as Prince, The Artist Formerly Known As Prince, or — latterly —

simply, the Artist? In a world where we are all known by Social Security numbers, why not allow name changes at will? What should be the criteria in the Pennsylvania statute for denying a name change? Allowing one?

3. Dissenting Judge Saylor writes that public policy should not endorse a "physiological fiction." Is it clear that Brian as Lisa *would* be a fiction? Isn't Brian *as Brian* a greater fiction? Or is it, as the court in *In re Richardson*, 23 Pa. D & C.3d 199 (1982), wrote, that sex change operations are a "freakish rechristening," "combin[ing] incompatibles," in a way which would "prevent the judicial process"?

4. Should Brian, after he becomes Lisa, be allowed to marry a man? *See Baehr v. Lewin, infra,* § 2.04. Would your answer be different if Brian/ Lisa completed the gender-change process by undergoing complete sex change surgery? *See In Re Ladrach*, 513 N.E.2d 828 (Ohio Prob. Ct. 1987).

5. Could the prisoner in *Farmer v. Brennan, supra* § 1.03[1], qualify for a name change under the reasoning of the *Brian* court?

6. In the next case, the issue of gender choice is raised in a different context: may a trans-sexual insist on Medicaid funding for sex re-assignment surgery?

RUSH v. JOHNSON

565 F. Supp. 856 (N.D. Ga. 1983)

Richard C. **Freeman**, District Judge.

This is an action for declaratory, injunctive and mandamus relief and damages instituted by plaintiff Carolyn Rush, an individual eligible for Medicaid coverage against the Director of the Georgia Department of Medical Assistance [hereinafter "State"], who denied the plaintiff's application for Medicaid reimbursement of proposed transsexual surgery expenses for inpatient hospital and physician's services. . . .

. . . .

I. Findings of Fact

A. Whether the State had a Policy

In early 1974, plaintiff Rush applied to the Medicaid program of the Georgia Department of Medical Assistance for payment of the cost of transsexual surgery. At that time, the Georgia Medicaid program contained: (1) a written policy prohibiting payment for "[s]ervices which are not reasonable and necessary for the diagnosis or the treatment of an illness or injury"; (2) a written policy prohibiting payment for "[c]osmetic surgery, except when furnished in connection with prompt repair of accidental injury or for the improvement of function in a malformed body member"; (3) a written policy providing that "[t]he diagnostic justification of the claimed services, as well as the customary methods of handling similar cases by the individual practitioner, are also reviewed"; (4) a written policy providing that "[p]rior authorization is used to determine medical necessity, to consider alternate methods of care, and to curb over-utilization"; and (5) a written policy requiring prior authorization for certain out-of-state services. Prior to May 1975, the program contained no express prohibition concerning the funding of experimental surgery. In May 1975, the Department adopted an express written policy prohibiting payment for "[e]xperimental surgery, e.g., transsexual operations." . . .

Rush's application for payment of the cost of transsexual surgery was reviewed by Ms. Cathy Harbin, who processed Medicaid claims for out-of-state services. At the time it was filed, Rush's application contained the opinion of her physician, Dr. Lee Shelton, who stated firmly that the plaintiff "is female functionally and physically and is handicapped severely by having no suitable arifice [sic] for sexual intercourse with a male." Dr. Shelton recommended surgery for the creation of a vagina and modification of existing genitalia.

. . . .

In November 1974, Dr. Dewitt C. Alfred, Jr., Associate Professor of Psychiatry, Emory University School of Medicine, Atlanta, Georgia, evaluated the plaintiff. While he found no evidence of organic brain syndrome or mental deficiency, he noted evidence of a psychiatric condition known as "Male Sex Role Inversion," which is "characterized by desire for Transsexualism and Psychoneurotic Traits (tendency toward depression dominating) and Character Neurotic Traits (manipulative patterns dominating)." Defendant's Exh. J. Dr. Alfred related that he had no knowledge of a particular surgeon or surgical group that was performing transsexual surgery in Georgia. He then stated:

> Because of the presence of significant evidence of unconscious Ambivalence in the patient toward Transsexual Surgery, I cannot state an unqualified approval of such surgery for this patient, in spite of the overt and consciously expressed wish to have the surgery. It is necessary however to take the following authoritative quote into consideration: "So far as is known, there is not a single case of clearly established adult inversion that has been cured by psychotherapy or any other form of treatment. . . . The fact that the transsexualist-invert belongs biologically to one sex but psychologically to the other sex commonly creates a deep rooted, underlying pattern of maladjustment among such individuals. A healthy integration of the personality is hardly possible in such cases. Some authorities are of the opinion, however, that these individuals do improve in their adjustment to life after they have undergone the 'change-over' operative procedure." (From: The Encyclopedia of Sexual Behavior: Ellis and Abarbanel (Ed.), Hawthorn Books, Inc., New York, 1964, Volume II, "Sex Role Inversion," pages 1020 and 1021.) On the basis of this authoritative opinion, Dr. Alfred recommended that Rush be referred to an out-of-state surgical group who would make the final decision as to whether surgery should be performed on Rush.

On March 11, 1975, Mr. Moore [Chief of the Medicaid Section] sent a memorandum relating to the plaintiff's file to Mr. Thurmond [Director of the Department]. He stated:

> . . . .
>
> My recommendation is to deny Medicaid coverage for this type of operation as it remains experimental in nature and the Medical Schools in Georgia do not perform this type procedure and Dean Richardson at Emory Medical School also stated that they do not contemplate in the immediate future of having anyone with the expertise to carry out this procedure. . . .
>
> I feel we will get repercussions regardless of the decision but expending money for this type procedure I feel could really be the worst move we could make at this point in time. . . .

On March 26, 1975, upon considering Dr. Alfred's letter, the Foundation's letter, Mr. Moore's memorandum, and the plaintiff's Medicaid file, Mr. Thurmond denied the plaintiff's application for payment of the cost of transsexual surgery. . . .

After Mr. Thurmond denied Rush's application, she requested that the Department reconsider its decision. Rush supplemented her application with several articles and medical reports. In August 1976, Mr. Thurmond again denied Rush's application, stating:

> This denial is based on a careful review of the request and previous correspondence to determine the necessity of treatment based on any present pathological condition. Such determination indicated that no apparent pathological condition exists and since the Georgia Medicaid Program specifically eliminates payment for such procedures, in accordance with the physician policy manual, authorization is denied.

. . . .

B. Whether the State's Determination that Transsexual Surgery Is Experimental Is Reasonable

Transsexualism is a recognized psychosexual disorder whose essential feature is an incongruence between anatomic and gender identity. A transsexual experiences a persistent sense of discomfort and inappropriateness about his anatomic sex and a persistent wish to be rid of his genitals and to live as a member of the other sex. Plaintiff's Exh. F, American Psychological Association, Diagnostic and Statistical Manual of Mental Disorders (hereinafter "DSM"), 261 (3d ed. 1980). A diagnosis of transsexualism is made only if the disturbance has been continuous for at least two years, is not due to another mental disorder, and is not associated with physical intersex or genetic abnormality. Generally a transsexual suffers from moderate to severe co-existing personality disturbances and frequently from considerable anxiety and depression, which the individual may attribute to his inability to live in the role of the desired sex. Without treatment, the curse of transsexualism "is 'chronic and unremitting.' " With respect to the efficacy of transsexual surgery, the DSM provides: "Since surgical sex reassignment is a recent development, the long-term course of the disorder with this treatment is unknown."

R. called Frazier [a counselor] and told her about the dream. Frazier suggested that they meet at Thanksgiving while R. was home. During that meeting R. told Frazier that she believed the dream had something to do with her father. Frazier had her lie on the floor, breathe deeply, and say whatever crossed her mind. Frazier refers to this as "imagery work" or free association. R. testified: "I had this, just this [illegible] and my dad and we were sitting on the edge of the bed in his room and he just had his hand on my chest, like inside my blouse. That was all."

Contrary to the Court's assertions, applying the discovery rule in this case would not create a "[illegible] jurisprudence unique to sexual abuse cases." We would be following the principles we have articulated in other of our decisions. The Court has aptly identified the "common thread" in prior decisions where we have deferred the running of limitations:

Concerns about medication extend also to the issue of cooperation with counsel. We have held that a defendant's right to the effective assistance of counsel is impaired when he cannot cooperate in an active manner with his lawyer. . . . The State interferes with this relation when it administers a drug to dull cognition.

liberty. Suffice it to say that this is not the first time this Court has had occasion to articulate that the liberty entitled to protection under the Fourteenth Amendment includes the right "to marry, establish a home and bring up children," and "the liberty . . . to direct the upbringing and education of children," and that these are among "the basic civil rights of man." These decisions affirm that there is a "realm of family life which the state cannot enter" without substantial justification. Surely the right invoked in this case, to be free of regulation of the intimacies of the marriage relationship, "come[s] to this Court with a momentum for respect lacking when appeal is made to liberties which derive merely from shifting economic arrangements."

The Court talks about a constitutional "right of privacy" as though there is some constitutional provision or provisions forbidding any law ever to be passed which might abridge the "privacy" of individuals. But there is not. There are, of course, guarantees in certain specific constitutional provisions which are designed in part to protect privacy at certain times and places with respect to certain activities. Such, for example, is the Fourth Amendment's guarantee against "unreasonable searches and seizures." But I think it belittles that Amendment to talk about it as though it protects nothing but "privacy." . . .

. . . .

If trans[illegible]gnosed, sex reassignment surgery is available as a method of treatment. Male-to-female surgery consists of castration and vaginal construction. A variety of methods have been used, involving single-stage and multi-stage procedures. Post-operative results of surgery vary with the skill of the treating physicians and the healing ability of the transsexual. Post-surgical patients live their lives in their new gender role.

. . . .

. . . Dr. Walker testified that the etiology of transsexualism is not yet known. He noted that while there is general agreement among researchers that biology and the environment play a part in causing transsexualism no consensus exists as to which component plays a greater role. Dr. Walker testified that various methods are used to treat transsexuals. He stated that over the years psychotherapists have attempted to use psychotherapy both to cure and to palliate a transsexual's condition. According to Dr. Walker, a psychotherapeutic cure would consist of a change in the patient's gender identity to conform to his anatomic sex. Successful palliative psychotherapy relieves or lessens the psychological symptoms of the disorder, e.g., depression and anxiety, and would assist the patient in adjusting to his condition. Dr. Walker believes that psychotherapy is not an effective form of treatment for transsexualism and that the professional medical community concurs in his belief.

According to Dr. Walker, approximately six thousand individuals have had sex-reassignment surgery in this country. Sex-reassignment surgery was first performed in the United States in 1965. Dr. Walker stated that the surgery has generally been accepted by the informed medical community as the treatment of choice in carefully selected patients and as a safe and effective treatment for properly screened and diagnosed transsexuals. His experience has led him to conclude that surgery has several positive results: it provides a feeling of psychological relief, improves social functioning, decreases anxiety, and lessens the pervasive unhappiness and depression that is attributable to transsexualism. . . .

Dr. S[illegible] experience in the field of transsexualism has also been extensive. She has treated over two hundred fifty transsexuals and has conducted empirical research on transsexualism. In 1980, Dr. Satterfield conducted a study of twenty-five transsexuals who had had surgery. Her research revealed a strong positive correlation between the degree of preoperative gender dysphoria present and the overall post-operative improvement, and a positive correlation between intelligence quotient and vocational adjustment. She found no evidence of negative results from the surgery.

. . . .

Dr. Satterfield noted that psychotherapy has been used to treat transsexualism. She routinely attempts this form of treatment before she refers patients

2 Transsexualism is generally viewed as distinguishable from transvestism. Transsexuals and transvestites engage in cross-dressing (dressing in clothes of the other sex). However, the individual with transvestism considers himself to be basically male, whereas the anatomically male transsexual has a female sexual identity.

for surgery. In her opinion it has not been uniformly curative and has sometimes been palliative. She stated that she believed surgery to be safe and effective. She stated that given the high risk of suicide without surgery, it is the treatment of choice. She also testified that transsexual surgery is accepted by a majority of the informed medical community.

. . . .

Dr. Meyer, a leading expert in the field of transsexualism, testified that there is a difference of opinion in the medical community as to the etiology of transsexualism and as to the appropriate form of treatment for transsexualism. He noted that there are three main hypotheses of etiology: biological, conflictual identity, and conflict of defense psychosis. A professional who adopts the biological point of view considers "the transsexual a kind of psychological intersex on biological grounds," and therefore, transsexual surgery, which makes the body fit with the mind, is an acceptable mode of treatment. On the other hand, a professional who adopts the psychogenic point of view that the disorder is borne out of psychic conflict believes the treatment of choice is psychotherapy. And a professional who holds the view that the disorder is a product of "more than conflictual identity formation," is inclined to support the use of surgery.

According to Dr. Meyer, there is a great diversity of opinion in the professional community as to whether transsexual surgery is an effective and proven treatment for the condition of transsexualism. Dr. Meyer testified that in his earlier writings he had stated: "It may be that the only alternative open to the adult patient is a surgical reversal of the external genitalia, in which case reassignment surgery is indicated." He further testified that he had since changed his view with respect to the effectiveness and appropriateness of sex-reassignment surgery and that the general medical community does not accept the surgery. Dr. Meyer now believes that the question whether the surgery is safe[3] in terms of psychological status of the patient remains unanswerable. He believes firmly that surgery is not any more effective than the passage of time. This view is based on his clinical experience with transsexuals and on his empirical research on transsexuals.

. . . .

Dr. Volkan's experience in the field of transsexualism includes familiarity with approximately one hundred transsexuals. For several years, he served as a psychiatrist on the staff of the Gender Identity Clinic of the University of Virginia. Dr. Volkan testified that there is a difference of opinion in the medical community as to the etiology of transsexualism. Dr. Volkan personally holds a psychogenic view, and believes that surgery cannot cure the disorder. In his opinion, the professional medical community remains undecided as to whether transsexual surgery is effective treatment for transsexualism.

Dr. Sheldon expressed an opinion similar to that of Dr. Volkan. . . .

---

[3] Dr. Meyer stated that the surgery is essentially major surgery with various attendant risks and complications.

II. Conclusions of Law

A. Plaintiff's Statutory Claim

The Medicaid program created by Title XIX is a cooperative endeavor in which the federal government provides financial assistance to participating states to aid them in furnishing health care. Title XIX states that "[a] State plan for medical assistance must . . . include reasonable standards . . . for determining eligibility for and the extent of medical assistance under the plan which . . . are consistent with the objectives of this [Title]." . . . The considerations that go into determining whether a particular service is experimental are:

> "Whether the service has come to be generally accepted by the professional medical community as an effective and proven treatment for the condition for which it is being used. . . . On the other hand, if the service or treatment is not yet generally accepted, is rarely used, novel or relatively unknown, then authoritative evidence must be obtained that it is safe and effective before Medicaid may make payment."

. . . .

The expert testimony presented by the parties is irreconcilably conflicting. The testimony demonstrates that the etiology of transsexualism is still debated by the medical community. Although Dr. Walker stated that etiology is not necessarily relevant to the question whether surgery is effective treatment for transsexualism, substantial evidence demonstrated a link between the various theories as to etiology and the recommended treatment. Moreover, while Drs. Walker and Satterfield testified that sex reassignment surgery is generally recognized by the informed medical community as an effective and proven treatment for the condition of transsexualism, Drs. Meyer, Volkan, and Cohen testified that it was not so recognized. Substantial evidence presents a picture of growing concern in the medical literature over the long-term effectiveness of sex-reassignment surgery as a generally accepted form of treatment. Furthermore, although Drs. Walker and Satterfield testified that the surgery is safe and effective, the evidence taken as a whole shows that it constitutes major surgery with various attendant risks and complications and that there is no consensus in the professional medical community that the surgery is effective treatment for transsexualism. Finally, the DSM, an authoritative text which is an expression of the consensus of the professional psychiatric community as of 1980, states that the long-term course of the treatment of transsexualism with surgical reassignment is unknown. This statement supports the conclusion that the long-term effects of the procedure have yet to be determined.

In light of this evidence, the court finds that the State could reasonably determine that transsexual surgery is experimental. The evidence demonstrates that it is neither generally accepted as a proven and effective treatment nor is there authoritative evidence that the surgery is safe and effective.

B. Plaintiff's Constitutional Claim

The Constitution imposes no obligation on the states to pay any of the medical expenses of indigents. When a state decides to alleviate some of the hardships of poverty by providing medical care, the manner in which it dispenses benefits is subject to constitutional limitations. Plaintiff's claim is that the State's policy prohibiting reimbursement for transsexual surgery violates the equal protection clause of the fourteenth amendment "by invidiously discriminating between transsexuals who require inpatient hospital services and physicians' services for such condition, and others who require such services for other conditions."

"The guarantee of equal protection under the fourteenth amendment is not a source of substantive rights or liberties, but rather a right to be free from invidious discrimination in statutory classifications and other governmental activity." . . . Applying this analysis to the present case, the court finds that the State's policy did not violate the equal protection clause of the fourteenth amendment.

This case involves no discrimination against a suspect classification. "Examining the traditional indicia of suspect classification, [the court] finds that transsexuals are not necessarily a 'discrete and insular minority,' nor has it been established that transsexuality is an "immutable characteristic determined solely by accident of birth' like race or national origin."

Under the rational basis standard, the State's prohibition against reimbursement for experimental surgery, including transsexual surgery, is rationally related to a legitimate governmental interest. The State has a legitimate governmental interest in protecting the public health. The court has found reasonable the State's determination that transsexual surgery is not generally accepted by the professional medical community as a proven and effective treatment for the condition for which it is being used and that there is no authoritative evidence that the surgery is safe and effective. Thus, the State's determination that medically necessary services do not include experimental surgery "with all its attendant risks to the recipient population," withstands judicial scrutiny.

Accordingly, the Clerk of Court is hereby ordered to enter judgment for the defendant against the claims of plaintiff.

It is so ordered.

NOTES AND QUESTIONS

1. Are you surprised to learn that by 1983, 6,000 individuals had received sex-reassignment surgery? That meant, since 1965, an average of over 300 per year. Although information is incomplete, since 1985, the average has been approximately 1,000 per year.
2. Is the plaintiff a male or female? Footnote 24 of the court's opinion includes an excerpt from the American Psychiatric Association, Diagnostic and Statistical Manual of Mental Disorders (3d ed. 1980), to the effect that gender identity is "the sense of knowing to which sex one belongs," that is, the awareness that "I am a male" or "I am a female." This would imply, then, that a person's own sense of self, or choice as

to self, determines gender, rather than physiological appurtenances or genetic inheritance. In this [illegible]

3. It appears, as well, that transsexualism involves changing gender, possibly out of choice, possibly out of need. It is characterized as a "psychosexual disorder," frequently accompanied by personality disturbances, anxiety and depression. As such, is transsexualism a "disease"? What is the significance of this label?

4. A sex change operation involves removing organs and/or creating the organs of the opposite gender, in a process of extensive major surgery, and in a manner which most people would view as mutilation. In Chapter 3, we review the obligations of physicians to "do no harm" and to render only "effective" care. There is also a significant inhibition on the performance of "experimentation." For all of these reasons, should the surgery in *Rush v. Johnson* have been refused, not by the state, but by the participating physicians because of their individual, ethical obligations?

5. The issue posed in the case, of course, is not whether physicians may or should refuse, but whether the state may refuse to provide *funding* for physician services. The reason given is that transsexual surgery is "experimental." Presumably, removal of male organs and the creation of female organs is well within the compass of medical science. What, then, is the meaning of the term "experimental"? Infrequency of performance? Unclarity of need? Unlikelihood of success of the surgery? Unlikelihood of success as a "treatment" for the condition? HMOs will also, like Medicaid, refuse to cover "experimental" surgery (*see infra*, § 4.04).

6. Suppose that transsexual surgery was *not* "experimental." Could the state nevertheless refuse to provide funding? Would it matter whether the reason was (a) shortage of money, (b) a belief that the surgery was mutilation, (c) a belief that surgery was unethical, immoral and contrary to God's law? Reconsider here *Bowers v. Hardwick*, *supra*.

7. If the state took such a position, then the plaintiff's due [illegible] equal protection arguments would begin to operate. *Are* transsexuals a "discrete and insular minority"; is transsexuality an "immutable characteristic determined by accident of birth," like race or national origin? Even if not, would not the refusal to fund the surgery condemn transsexuals to a continuing medical condition profoundly affecting their identity and autonomy as human beings? How justify such discrimination, when Medicaid is regularly provided to women who wish to have children, men who wish to have vasectomies and women who need hysterectomies?

8. For material on female genital mutilation in foreign countries as a basis for granting asylum in the United States, see § 4.03[3] *infra*.

9. For an excellent article, see Elvia R. Arriola, *The Penalties for Puppy Love: Institutionalized Violence Against Lesbian, Gay, Bisexual and Transgendered Youth*, 1 J. Gender Race & Just. 429 (1998); also see Hasan Shafiqullah, *Shape-Shifters, Masqueraders, & Subversives: An*

Argument for the Liberation of Transgendered Individuals, 8 Hastings Women's L.J. 195 (1997).

IN THE MATTER OF THE ESTATE OF GARDINER

22 P.3d 1086 (Kan. App. 2001)

Gernon, J.: This is an appeal from an order issued by the district court granting summary judgment to Joseph M. Gardiner, III, (Joe) finding the marriage between Joe's father, Marshall G. Gardiner, and J'Noel Gardiner to be void under Kansas law and denying partial summary judgment to J'Noel. We reverse and remand with instructions.

. . . .

I

Marriage Issue

I-A Court Procedural Background

Marshall died intestate on August 12, 1999. He was a resident of Leavenworth County, Kansas.

Joe filed a petition for letters of administration with the District Court of Leavenworth County, Kansas. Joe named himself and J'Noel, Marshall's surviving spouse, as Marshall's heirs. In his petition, Joe argued that J'Noel had waived any rights to Marshall's estate, and, thus, he was the sole heir-at-law to Marshall.

J'Noel filed an objection to Joe's petition. J'Noel also applied for letters of administration. The court then appointed a special administrator to handle the estate. Joe filed an objection to J'Noel's application.

Joe then petitioned the district court to amend his pleadings. In his amended petition, Joe named himself as Marshall's sole heir. Joe denied that Marshall and J'Noel were validly married. He contended that J'Noel was previously known as Jay N. Ball and was born a man. He argued that despite surgery, a name change, and other steps taken by J'Noel to change sex, she remains a man for the purposes of Kansas law relating to the issuance of a marriage license. Joe argued that the marriage between Marshall and J'Noel is void since, pursuant to K.S.A. 2000 Supp. 23-101, marriages between persons of the same sex are prohibited. Therefore, Joe claimed, J'Noel had no right to a share of Marshall's estate as the surviving spouse.

J'Noel filed a response to Joe's objection to her petition for issuance of letters. In the response, J'Noel asserted that her marriage to Marshall was valid. J'Noel argued that she is a biological female, and, as such, under K.S.A. 2000 Supp. 23-101,she is not prohibited from marrying Marshall, a biological male. J'Noel also stated that there is no evidence that she, through a memo written to Marshall, intended to waive any interest in Marshall's property and that no premarital agreement was ever entered into by her and Marshall. J'Noel further asserted that she told Marshall about the sex reassignment surgery she had undergone before the marriage.

J'Noel met Marshall while on the faculty at Park College in May 1998. Marshall was a donor to the [illegible] fourth date, J'Noel testified that Marshall brought up marriage. J'Noel wanted to get to know Marshall better, so they went to Utah for a trip. When asked about when they became sexually intimate, J'Noel testified that on this trip, Marshall had an orgasm. J'Noel stated that sometime in July 1998, Marshall was told about J'Noel's prior history as a male. The two were married in Kansas on September 25, 1998.

There is no evidence in the record to support Joe's suggestion that Marshall did not know about J'Noel's sex reassignment. It had been completed years before Marshall and J'Noel met. Nor is there any evidence that Marshall and J'Noel were not compatible.

Both parties agree that J'Noel has gender dysphoria or is a transsexual. J'Noel agrees that she was born with male genitalia. In a deposition, J'Noel testified that she was born with a "birth defect" — a penis and testicles. J'Noel stated that she thought something was "wrong" even prepuberty and that she viewed herself as a girl but had a penis and testicles.

J'Noel's journey from perceiving herself as one sex to the sex her brain suggests she was, deserves to be detailed. In 1991 and 1992, J'Noel began electrolysis and then thermolysis to remove body hair on the face, neck, and chest. J'Noel was married at the time and was married for 5 years. Also, beginning in 1992, J'Noel began taking hormones, and, in 1993, she had a tracheal shave. A tracheal shave is surgery to the throat to change the voice. All the while, J'Noel was receiving therapy and counseling.

In February 1994, J'Noel had a bilateral orchiectomy to remove the testicles. J'Noel also had a forehead/eyebrow lift at this time and rhinoplasty. Rhinoplasty refers to plastic surgery to alter one's nose. In July 1994, J'Noel consulted with a psychiatrist, who opined that there were no signs of thought disorder or major affective disorder, that J'Noel fully understood the nature of the process of transsexual change, and that her life history was consistent with a diagnosis of transsexualism. The psychiatrist recommended to J'Noel that total sex reassignment was the next appropriate step in her treatment.

In August 1994, J'Noel underwent further sex reassignment surgery. In this surgery, Eugene Schrang, M.D., J'Noel's doctor, essentially cut and inverted the penis, using part of the skin to form a female vagina, labia, and clitoris. Dr. Schrang, in a letter dated October 1994, stated that J'Noel has a "fully functional vagina" and should be considered "a functioning, anatomical female." In 1995, J'Noel also had cheek implants. J'Noel continues to take hormone replacements.

Regardless of whether one agrees with the concept of sex reassignment, one must be impressed with the resolve of, and have compassion for, any human being who undergoes such a demanding set of procedures.

After the surgery in 1994, J'Noel petitioned the Circuit Court of Outagamie County, Wisconsin, for a new birth certificate which would reflect her new name as J'Noel Ball and sex as female. The court issued a report ordering the state registrar to make these changes and issue a new birth certificate. A new birth certificate was issued on September 26, 1994. The birth certificate indicated the child's name as J'Noel Ball and sex as female. J'Noel also has had her driver's license, passport, and health documents changed to reflect her new status. Her records at two universities have also been changed to reflect her new sex designation.

. . . .

I-C The Kansas Statute: K.S.A. 2000 Supp. 23-101

J'Noel argues that the district court erred when it held that her marriage to Marshall violated K.S.A. 2000 Supp. 23-101. J'Noel argues that the legislature, through the language in K.S.A. 2000 Supp. 23-101, intended to prohibit only homosexual marriages and that her marriage to Marshall was not such a marriage.

K.S.A. 2000 Supp. 23-101 states:

> "The marriage contract is to be considered in law as a civil contract *between two parties who are of opposite sex. All other marriages are declared to be contrary to the public policy of this state and are void.* The consent of the parties is essential. The marriage ceremony may be regarded either as a civil ceremony or as a religious sacrament, but the marriage relation shall only be entered into, maintained or abrogated as provided by law." (Emphasis added.)

There is no dispute that the legislature meant to void any marriage between members of the same sex.

The question here is whether J'Noel should have been considered a female under Kansas law at the time the marriage license was issued. Subparts to that question are the criteria used to determine sex and the timing of the determination. Stated another way: Is this marriage, between a post-operative male-to-female transsexual and a male, prohibited under Kansas law?

The interpretation of a statute is a question of law for which appellate review is unlimited. *Rose & Nelson v. Frank*, 25 Kan. App. 2d 22, 24, 956 P.2d 729, rev. denied 265 Kan. 886, 1998 Kan. LEXIS 482 (1998).

The amendment to 23-101 limiting marriage to two parties of the opposite sex began its legislative history in 1975. The minutes of the Senate Committee on Judiciary for January 21, 1976, state that the amendment would "affirm the traditional view of marriage." The proposed amendment was finally enacted in 1980.

K.S.A. 23-101 was again amended in 1996, when language was added, stating: "All other marriages are declared to be contrary to the public policy of this state and are void." This sentence was inserted immediately after the sentence limiting marriage to two parties of the opposite sex.

In 1996, K.S.A. 23-115 was amended, with language added stating: "It is the strong public policy of this state only to recognize as valid marriages from other states that are between a man and a woman."

The legislative history contains discussions about gays and lesbians, but nowhere is there any testimony that specifically states that marriage should be prohibited by two parties if one is a post-operative male-to-female or female-to-male [illegible] Was J'Noel a female at the time the license was issued for the purpose of the statute?

I-D The Science

It is perhaps well to pause and attempt to define what a transsexual is by stating what a transsexual is not. A transsexual is not a homosexual. A homosexual is one who prefers the same sex for sexual contact. Nor is a transsexual a transvestite. A transvestite is one who remains one sex but gains pleasure from dressing like the other sex. A transsexual is one who experiences himself or herself as being of the opposite sex, despite having some biological characteristics of one sex, or one whose sex has been changed externally by surgery and hormones. A transsexual might be a homosexual or a transvestite also, but one does not define the other.

A recent study that autopsied the brains of transsexuals and others supports a conclusion that there is a scientific basis for J'Noel's assertion that she was born with a condition — specifically that she had a penis and testicles, which was evidence that she was male, but in most other senses of the word, she was female. The same science which allows us to map the genome and explore our DNA requires us to recognize these discoveries in all aspects of our lives, including the legal ramifications. We can no longer be permitted to conclude who is male or who is female by the amount of facial hair one has or the size of one's feet.

A study in the respected medical journal, *The Journal of Clinical Endocrinology & Metabolism*, analyzed the brains of homosexual males, heterosexual males, heterosexual females, and male-to-female transsexuals. It concluded:

> "Regardless of sexual orientation, men had almost twice as many somatostatin neurons as women. The number of neurons in . . . male-to-female transsexuals was similar to that of the females. . . . In contrast, the neuron number of female-to-male transsexual was found to be in the male range. . . . The present findings of somatostatin neuronal sex differences in the BSTc (a part of the brain) and its sex reversal in the transsexual brain clearly support the paradigm that in transsexuals sexual differentiation of the brain and genitals may go into opposite directions and point to a neurobiological basis of gender identity disorder."
>
> "According to medical professionals, the typical criteria of sex include:
>
> 1. Genetic or chromosomal sex — XY or XX;
>
> 2. Gonadal sex (reproductive sex glands) — testes or ovaries;
>
> 3. Internal morphologic sex (determined after three months gestation) — seminal vesicles/prostrate [sic] or vagina/uterus/ fallopian tubes;
>
> 4. External morphologic sex (genitalia) — penis/scrotum or clitoris/labia;

5. Hormonal sex — androgens or estrogens;

6. Phenotypic sex (secondary sexual features) — facial and chest hair or breasts;

7. Assigned sex and gender of rearing; and

8. Sexual identity.

"For most people, these factors are all congruent, and one's status as a man or woman is uncontroversial. For intersexuals, some of these factors may be incongruent, or an ambiguity within a factor may exist.

" 'The assumption is that there are two separate roads, one leading from XY chromosomes at conception to manhood, the other from XX chromosomes at conception to womanhood. The fact is that there are not two roads, but one road with a number of forks that turn in the male or female direction. Most of us turn in the same direction at each fork.'

"The bodies of the millions of intersexed people have taken a combination of male and female forks and have followed the road less traveled. These individuals have noncongruent sexual attributes. For these individuals, the law must determine which of the eight sexual factors will determine their sex and whether any one factor should be dispositive for all legal purposes.

"Because the law has typically looked to biology and the medical community for guidance in determining how an individual's sex should be legally established, the complex nature of sexual differentiation must be understood. . . .

"A. Sexual Differentiation — The Typical Path

"During the first seven weeks after conception, all human embryos are sexually undifferentiated. At seven weeks, the embryonic reproductive system consists of a pair of gonads that can grow into either ovaries (female) or testes (male). The genital ridge that exists at this point can develop either into a clitoris and labia (female) or a penis and a scrotum (male). Two primordial duct systems also exist at this stage. The female ducts are called Mullerian ducts and develop into the uterus, fallopian tubes and the upper part of the vagina if the fetus follows a female path. The male ducts are called Wolffian ducts and are the precursors of the seminal vesicles, vas deferens and epididymis.

"Because the typical female fetus is 46XX and does not have a Y chromosome, the master switch that leads to the development of male organs is not turned on. The fetus continues on what is considered the default path and in the thirteenth week the gonads start to transform into ovaries. Because no testes exist to produce male hormones, the remainder of the sexual system develops along a female path. During this time, the Wolffian (male) ducts shrivel up. In other words, unless the body is triggered by hormonal production to follow the male path, the fetus will normally develop as a female. Therefore, although chromosomes generally control the hormones that are produced, it is actually the hormones that directly affect sexual development.

. . . .

"B. Sexual Differentiation — Intersexuals: The Paths Less Followed

"Two circumstances may lead to an intersexual condition: (1) failure to meet the typical criteria within any one factor; or (2) one or more factors may be incongruent with the other factors.

"1. Ambiguity Within a Factor

"a. Chromosomal Ambiguity — Certain individuals have chromosomes that differ from the typical pattern of either XY or XX. Doctors have discovered people with a variety of combinations including: XXX, XXY, XXXY, XYY, XYYY, XYYYY, and XO.

"b. Gonadal Ambiguity — Some intersexuals do not have typical ovaries or testes. Instead, they have 'streak' gonads that do not appear to function as either ovaries or testes. Others have ovotestes, a combination of both male and female gonads. Still others have one ovary and one testis.

"c. External Morphologic Sex — Some individuals' external genitalia are neither clearly male nor clearly female. In addition, some women have clitoral hypertrophy, a clitoris that is larger than the typical clitoris, may more closely resemble a penis, and is sometimes accompanied by an internal vagina.

"d. Internal Morphologic Sex — Some individuals have incomplete internal sex organs or a complete absence of an internal sex organ. In addition, some individuals are born with a combination of male and female internal organs.

"e. Hormonal Sex — The male hormones are referred to as androgens. The female hormones are estrogen and progesterone. Although they are referred to as male and female hormones, all human sex hormones are shared by men and women. Typically, men and women have hormones of each type, but the levels of production and reception of each hormone are highly variable among all individuals. Different medical disorders further influence levels of hormone production and/or reception.

"f. Phenotypic Sex — Individuals may have a variety of combinations of incongruent phenotypic characteristics. In other words, an individual may have characteristics that are typically associated with a male (heavy facial hair) and characteristics that are typically associated with a female (developed breasts).

"g. Assigned Sex/Gender of Rearing — Although it occurs rarely, some parents have raised their child as a gender other than the sex that was assigned by the medical attendant at birth. In addition, in some circumstances, doctors have recommended that a child be raised as the sex different from the one assigned at birth.

"h. Sexual Identity — Sexual identity refers to how individuals would identify themselves; gender identity refers to how society would identify an individual. Some individuals do not consider themselves to be either male or female; they identify themselves as a third sex.

"2. Ambiguity Among Factors

"Some individuals have an incongruence among the eight factors due to a sexual differentiation disorder. In other words, some factors may be clearly male, some may be clearly female, and others may be a mixture of male and female. Incongruity among factors can result from a number of disorders and circumstances including:

a. Chromosomal sex disorders;

b. Gonadal sex disorders;

c. Internal organ anomalies;

d. External organ anomalies;

e. Hormonal disorders;

f. Gender identity disorders; and

g. Surgical creation of an intersexed condition.

"These conditions are described in detail below. . . .

"Klinefelter Syndrome

"Approximately one in 500 to 1000 'males' is affected by Klinefelter Syndrome, a condition in which a mostly phenotypic male does not fall neatly into the XY chromosome complement. Individuals with Klinefelter Syndrome will typically have two or more X chromosomes. The testes, and often the penis, are smaller than in unaffected XY males.

"Turner Syndrome

"Disorders of chromosomal sex also appear in phenotypic females. Turner Syndrome is a condition that affects approximately one in 5000 newborn females. Individuals with Turner Syndrome will typically have an XO chromosomal pattern, not falling neatly into the XX, XY binary system. Individuals with Turner Syndrome typically have bilateral 'streak' gonads (unformed and non-functioning gonads) instead of clearly defined ovaries or testes. The absence of complete ovaries or testes in-utero means that the fetus has little exposure to either female or male hormones. In the absence of male hormones, the fetus will follow the female path.

"Individuals with Turner Syndrome are typically shorter than XX females. They have female appearing genitalia, but little breast development in the absence of exogenous estrogen administration.

"d. External Organ Anomalies: Hermaphroditism

"Individuals who have ambiguous external genitalia (neither clearly male nor female) are commonly referred to as hermaphrodites. Hermaphrodites are often classified into three categories: true hermaphrodites, male pseudo-hermaphrodites, and female pseudo-hermaphrodites. A 'true hermaphrodite' has some ovarian and some testicular tissue. So-called 'true hermaphrodites' have either one ovary and one testis, two ovotestes (a combination of an ovary and testis in a single gonad) or some combination thereof (e.g. one ovotestes and one ovary). True hermaphroditic condi[illegible] as the other intersex conditions described in this section. A male pseudohermaphrodite has testes and no ovaries but some aspect of female genitalia. A female pseudohermaphrodite has ovaries and no testes and some aspect of male genitalia.

"A variety of disorders can lead to hermaphroditic conditions. Hermaphroditic conditions are named according to their etiology (e.g. Partial Androgen Insensitivity Syndrome ['PAIS'] or Congenital Adrenal Hyperplasia ['CAH']) unless the etiology of the condition remains unknown.

"True hermaphroditism is rare and the exact incidence is unknown. The chromosome count may vary but is predominantly 46XX.

"e. Hormonal Disorders

"Androgen Insensitivity Syndrome

"Androgen Insensitivity Syndrome ('AIS') affects approximately 1 out of every 20,000 genetic males. AIS can be either complete ("CAIS") or partial (PAIS). Individuals with AIS are born with XY chromosomes and normally-functioning testes, which would otherwise suggest a normal male fetus. Individuals with CAIS, however, have a receptor defect and are unable to process the androgens produced by the testes.

"Because the body cannot process the androgens, the fetus will follow the default path of female development. External female genitalia will form. No internal reproductive organs will form because the Mullerian inhibiting factor produced by the testes will inhibit the growth of the uterus and fallopian tubes. The vagina will be shorter than in the typical woman (or may only be a dimple) and will end blindly because there are no female internal reproductive organs with which to connect.

"5-Alpha-Reductase Deficiency

"This condition is similar to the androgen [illegible] individuals with 5-Alpha-Reductase Deficiency have XY chromosomes and testes but appear phenotypically female at birth. This condition results from the body's failure to convert testosterone to dihydrotestosterone, the more powerful form of androgen responsible for the development of male external genitalia. Despite a female appearance during childhood, by the onset of puberty, the body will masculinize. The testes descend, the voice deepens, muscle mass substantially increases, and a 'functional' penis that is capable of ejaculating develops from what was thought to be the clitoris. The prostate, however, remains small and beard growth is scanty. Although the individual is typically raised as a girl, at puberty, psychosexual orientation typically becomes male. In other words, virilization will occur at puberty in the absence of medical intervention.

"5-Alpha-Reductase Deficiency is an inheritable condition, and has resulted in a large group of affected individuals in some communities in the Dominican Republic. In some cases, a diagnosis is made in early puberty, male external development is arrested, and the individual will take exogenous female hormones to simulate a female puberty. In these cases, the individual will often have a female sexual identity. Other individuals with 5-Alpha-Reductase Deficiency will develop a masculine appearance in conformity with their genotype and will also develop a male psychosexual identification.

"Congenital Adrenal Hyperplasia

"Some individuals with XX chromosomes, ovaries, and other female internal structures have a more masculinized external appearance and/or demeanor due to an abundance of androgen production in-utero. Typical of this category is 21-Hydroxylase Deficiency Congenital Adrenal Hyperplasia ('CAH'). It occurs in approximately one out of 5000 to 15,000 births.

"Progestin-Induced Virilization

"Similar to CAH is Progestin-Induced Virilization ('PIV'), which results from an abundance of male hormones in an otherwise normal XX female. PIV is caused by exposure inutero to progestin that has been taken by the mother during pregnancy. Like individuals with CAH, PIV women will frequently have clitoral hypertrophy. In all other respects, however, they have completely female gonads.

"f. Gender Identity Disorder

"Some individuals may be seemingly harmonious in all of the first six factors, but do not identify themselves with the sex associated with these factors. These individuals may be said to have gender dysphoria or gender identity disorder ('GID'). Often these individuals are called transsexuals. Science has yet to definitely isolate a biological common denominator that causes these individuals to feel transgendered. A recent study, however, has determined that a section of the brain area that is essential for sexual behavior is larger in men than in women and that the brain structure of genetically male transsexuals is more similar to female brains than to male brains. Some transgendered individuals choose to undergo hormonal treatment and/or surgery so that their bodies comport with their sexual identity while other transsexuals do not choose to undergo such treatment.

"Transsexualism is not necessarily related to sexual orientation. Some transsexuals identify themselves as gays or lesbians while others identify themselves as heterosexuals. In other words, a male-to-female transsexual who has undergone surgery to acquire female genitalia may still prefer to have sex with another female, and a female-to-male transsexual may still prefer to have sex with another male.

"g. Surgical Creation of an Intersexed Condition

"In addition to cases in which intersexed individuals may be assigned a sex that does not comport with their own sexual identity, some persons have had their sexual features altered either accidentally or purposefully. For instance, some individuals have had their penises removed at a young age because they were mistakenly identified as females and the penis was considered an oversized clitoris that required reduction. Although these cases are rare, they are illustrative of the complex nature of sexual identity.

"The significance of these two reports is that they exemplify the difficulty law and medicine must confront in defining sex. At birth, these infants' sex factors were congruent and were male. After the original intervention, they were turned into intersexuals but were treated by society as if they were females. They had male chromosomes, ambiguous genitalia, and female gender assignment. As adults, one person selfidentifies as a heterosexual male while the other selfidentifies as a bi-sexual female.

"These studies and other reports about intersexuals have forced the medical and psychiatric communities to question their long-held beliefs about sex and sexual identity. Just as current scientific studies have caused the scientific communities to question their beliefs about sex and sexual identity, the legal community must question its long-held assumptions about the legal definitions of sex, gender, male, and female."

Greenberg, *Defining Male and Female: Intersexuality and the Collision Between Law and Biology*, 41 Ariz. L. Rev. 265, 278–92 (1992).

I-E Case Law

This is a case of first impression in Kansas. A discussion of case law on transsexualism from other jurisdictions, including another nation, may prove helpful.

The cases generally fall into three categories: cases dealing with the amendment of identification records, usually birth certificate name and/or sex changes; cases dealing with discrimination, most pointedly in the workplace; and cases dealing with marriage between a transsexual and a nontranssexual. An additional case which will be discussed deals with transsexuals and competition in sporting events. The analysis will follow the cases chronologically.

The first case in the United States to deal with transsexualism involved a petition for a change of sex on a birth certificate. *In Mtr. of Anonymous v. Weiner*, 50 Misc. 2d 380, 270 N.Y.S.2d 319 (1966), a post-operative transsexual who had assumed the name and role of a female applied to the Bureau of Vital Statistics in the New York City Health Department for a new birth certificate.

The transsexual's application in *Weiner* was denied. In a resolution passed by the Board of Health, it was stated that " 'an individual born one sex cannot be changed for the reasons proposed by the request which was made to us. Sex can be changed where there is an error, of course, but not when there is a later attempt to change psychological orientation of the patient and including such surgery as goes with it.' " 50 Misc. 2d at 383.

However, a civil court in New York, in 1968 and then again in 1970, granted an application for a change of name to a post-operative transsexual. *Matter of Anonymous*, 57 Misc. 2d 813, 293 N.Y.S.2d 834 (1968); Matter of Anonymous, 64 Misc. 2d 309, 314 N.Y.S.2d 668 (1970).In the 1968 case of *Anonymous*, a male-to-female transsexual petitioned the court to order the Bureau of Vital Statistics of the Department of Health of the City of New York to change his birth certificate to reflect a name and sex change.

The next case, often cited, but perhaps colored by the fact that the parties lived together only 14 days of their 3-month marriage, is *Corbett v. Corbett*, 2 All E.R. 33 (1970), an English opinion dealing with transsexualism. One of the parties was a male-to-female transsexual and former female impersonator named April Ashley, who married Arthur Corbett. Arthur was a homosexual and transvestite "prone to all kinds of sexual fantasies and practices." 2 All E.R. at 38. An English court in the probate, divorce, and admiralty division ruled that a marriage between a post-operative male-tofemale transsexual and a male was void. 2 All E.R. at 50.

In dealing with the argument that it is illogical for the court to treat the respondent as a male while other paperwork may have been changed to say differently, the court declared: "Marriage is a relationship which depends on sex and not on gender." 2 All E.R. at 49. The court distinguished marriage from other social situations. 2 All E.R. at 49. Sex is clearly an essential determinant of the relationship in marriage, the court stated, as it is recognized as the union between a man and woman. The court established a three-part test in determining what is a person's sex for purposes of the law, stating:

> "Having regard to the essentially heterosexual character of the relationship which is called marriage, the criteria must . . . be biological, for even the most extreme degree of transsexualism in a male or the most severe hormonal imbalance which can exist in a person with male chromosomes, male gonads and male genitalia cannot reproduce a person who is naturally capable of performing the essential role of a woman in marriage. In other words, the law should adopt in the first place . . . the chromosomal, gonadal, and genital tests, and if all three are congruent, determine the sex for the purpose of marriage accordingly, and ignore any operative intervention." 2 All E.R. at 48.

The case of *M.T. v. J.T.*, 140 N.J. Super. 77, 355 A.2d 204, cert. denied, 71 N.J. 345, 364 A.2d 1076 (1976), deserves greater attention, in our view, than *Corbett*, [*Mtr. of*] *Hartin* [*v. Dir. of Bur. of Recs.*, 75 Misc. 2d 229, 232, 347 N.Y.S.2d 515 (1973)], or *Darnell* [*v. Lloyd*, 395 F. Supp. 1210 (D. Conn. 1975)].

In *M.T.*, a husband and wife were divorcing, and the issue was support and maintenance. The husband argued that he should not have to pay support to his wife because she was a male, making the marriage void. The issue before the court, similar to that before this court, was whether the marriage of a post-operative male-to-female transsexual and a male was a lawful marriage between a man and a woman. The court found that it was a valid marriage.

The importance of the holding in *M.T.* is that it replaces the biological sex test with dual tests of anatomy and gender, where "for marital purposes if the anatomical or genital features of a genuine transsexual are made to conform to the person's gender, psyche or psychological sex, then identity by sex must be governed by the congruence of these standards."

The *M.T.* court further stated:

> In this case the transsexual's gender and genitalia are no longer discordant; they have been harmonized through medical treatment. Plaintiff has become physically and psychologically unified and fully capable of sexual activity consistent with her reconciled sexual attributes of gender and anatomy. Consequently, plaintiff should be considered a member of the female sex for marital purposes. It follows that such an individual would have the capacity to enter into a valid marriage relationship *with* a person of the opposite sex and did so here. In so ruling we do no more than give legal effect to a *fait accompli*, based upon medical judgment and action which are irreversible. Such recognition will promote the individual's quest for inner peace and personal happiness, while in no way disserving any societal interest, principle of public order or precept of morality."

In 1984, the United States Court of Appeals, Seventh Circuit, analyzed an issue concerning transsexualism and workplace discrimination. In *Ulane v. Eastern Airlines, Inc.*, 742 F.2d 1081 (7th Cir. 1984), cert. denied 471 U.S. 1017 (1985), a post-operative male-to-female transsexual who was a pilot for Eastern Airlines was fired in 1981, shortly after sex reassignment surgery. The transsexual sued the airline, alleging that the employer violated Title VII by discharging her from her position as a pilot.

After noting that nothing was said in the legislative history about transsexuals, the court stated that it appears clear that Congress did not intend the legislation to apply to anything other than "the traditional concept of sex." Had Congress intended it to apply, surely it would have said so, the court explained. Thus, the court declined to expand the definition of "sex" as used in Title VII beyond its "common and traditional interpretation," stating: "We agree with the Eighth and Ninth Circuits that if the term 'sex' as it is used in Title VII is to mean more than biological male or biological female, the new definition must come from Congress."

The most recent decision in the United States [illegible] decided by the Texas Court of Appeals in *Littleton v. Prange*, 9 S.W.3d 223 (Tex. Civ. App. 1999), cert. denied 531 U.S. 872 (2000). In J'Noel's case, the district court appears to rely heavily on this case in rendering its decision that J'Noel is a male, quoting some of its language verbatim. In *Littleton*, a transsexual, now called Christie, who was born a man but had undergone sex reassignment surgery, brought a medical malpractice suit under Texas' wrongful death statute as a surviving spouse of a male patient. The doctor who was sued filed a motion for summary judgment, asserting that Christie was a male and, therefore, could not be the surviving spouse of another man. The trial court granted summary judgment to the doctor, and Christie appealed.

Christie had a name and sex change made on her birth certificate during pendency of the suit. During the surgical procedures, Christie's penis, scrotum, and testicles were removed, and a vagina and labia were constructed. Christie also had breast construction surgery. One of Christie's doctors testified that Christie "has the capacity to function sexually as a female" after the surgery. Doctors testified that medically Christie was a woman.

After a review of the case law, the court concluded that Christie was a male as a matter of law. The court noted that this was an issue of first impression in Texas. In line with previous cases, the court stated: "It is for the legislature, should it choose to do so, to determine what guidelines should govern the recognition of marriages involving transsexuals. . . . It would be intellectually impossible for this court to write a protocol for when transsexuals would be recognized as having successfully changed their sex."

Thus, the court found that even though surgery and hormones can make a transsexual male look like a woman, including female genitalia, and in Christie's case, even breasts, transsexual medicine does not create the internal sex organs of a woman (except for a man-made vaginal canal). There is no womb, cervix, or ovaries in the post-operative transsexual female. The chromosomes do not change. Biologically, the post-operative female is still a male. Even though some doctors would consider Christie a female and some a male, the court concluded: "Her female anatomy, however, is all man-made. The body that Christie inhabits is a male body in all aspects other than what the physicians have supplied."

I-F Other Laws, Cases, Regulations, and Considerations

Kansas law allows individuals to change the sex designation on their birth certificates "with a medical certificate substantiating that a physiological or anatomical change occurred." K.A.R. 28-17-20(b)(1)(A)(i).

K.S.A. 2000 Supp. 65-2416(a) states that a birth certificate is "prima facie evidence of the facts therein stated."

Kansas does not require proof of one's sex to obtain a marriage license.

The Kansas Supreme Court has stated that the " 'public policy relating to marriage is to foster and protect it, to make it a permanent and public institution, to encourage the parties to live together and to prevent separation.' " *Ranney v. Ranney*, 219 Kan. 428, 431, 548 P.2d 734 (1976).

Transsexual issues have or will arise in situations involving penal institutions, schools, sports, employment, and every other situation in which perceived gender is important.

. . . .

III-EQUAL PROTECTION

J'Noel argues that the district court's decision violates the Equal Protection Clause of the 14th Amendment of the United States Constitution by not recognizing J'Noel's legal status as female and denying J'Noel the right to marry.

A new legal theory may not be asserted for the first time on appeal or raised in a reply brief. *Jarboe v. Board of Sedgwick County Comm'rs*, 262 Kan. 615, 622, 938 P.2d 1293 (1997). J'Noel did not note this in her response to Joe's objection to her petition for issuance of letters, her suggestions in opposition to Joe's motion for summary judgment, her motion for partial summary judgment, or at oral argument on the motions.

J'Noel argues that she could not have raised this issue at the district court level because the district court had not yet ruled on the issue of the validity of J'Noel and Marshall's marriage. J'Noel argues that she is not arguing that K.S.A. 2000 Supp. 23-101 is unconstitutional on its face but as applied to her marriage.

J'Noel's argument concerning equal protection fails. The Fourteenth Amendment to the United States Constitution provides that no state shall "deny to any person within its jurisdiction the equal protection of the laws." When J'Noel was found by the district court to be a male for purposes of Kansas law, she was denied the right to marry a male. It logically follows, therefore, that the court did not forbid J'Noel from marrying a female. Federal law allows a state to not give effect to another state's recognition of a same-sex marriage. 28 U.S.C. § 1738C (1996). Kansas law forbids same-sex marriages.

. . . .

CONCLUSION

This court rejects the reasoning of the majority in the *Littleton* case as a rigid and simplistic approach to issues that are far more complex than addressed in that opinion.

We conclude that a trial court must consider and decide whether an individual was male or female at the time the individual's marriage license was issued and the individual was married, not simply what the individual's chromosomes were or were not at the moment of birth.

The court may use chromosome makeup as one factor, but not the exclusive factor, in arriving at a decision.

Aside from chromosomes, we adopt the criteria set forth by Professor Greenberg. On remand, the trial court is directed to consider factors in addition to chromosome makeup, including: gonadal sex, internal morphologic sex, external morphologic sex, hormonal sex, phenotypic sex, assigned sex and gender of rearing, and sexual identity. The listed criteria we adopt as significant in resolving the case before us should not preclude the consideration of other criteria as science advances.

If fraud be shown, a marriage can always be annulled, under any circumstances. While we find no badges of fraud in the record before us, it remains a potential alternative basis to void the marriage. Here, the evidence in the appellate record to date points to a conclusion that Marshall knew of the transsexual nature of J'Noel, approved, married, and enjoyed a consummated marriage relationship with her.

This court looks with favor on the reasoning and the language of *M.T. v. J.T.*, 140 N.J. Super. 77, 355 A.2d 204, *cert. denied*, 71 N.J. 345, 364 A.2d 1076 (1976).

Last, we note the conclusion of William Reiner, M.D., a researcher at The Johns Hopkins Hospital:

"In the end it is only the children themselves who can and must identify who and what they are. It is for us as clinicians and researchers to listen and to learn. Clinical decisions must ultimately be based not on anatomical predictions, nor on the 'correctness' of sexual function, for this is neither a question of morality nor of social consequence, but on that path most appropriate to the likeliest psychosexual developmental pattern of the child. In other words, the organ that appears to be critical to psychosexual development and adaptation is not the external genitalia, but the brain."

NOTES AND QUESTIONS

1. *In The Matter of the Estate of Gardiner* is perhaps the most extensive discussion in a court opinion of the nature, treatment and legal status of transsexualism. It directly addresses the tension in gender concepts between genetic destiny and conscious choice. It also raises questions as to society's assignment of significance to gender in a number of contexts.
2. Why did J'Noel, the former Jay N. Ball, go to such great lengths to change her physiologic sex? Did she succeed? Is the decision in *Casey* relevant to these considerations?
3. The court summarizes cases dealing with transsexualism in a number of contexts — records, discrimination, marriage and sports. Are the results consistent? Should they be? And what of the Supreme Court's decision in *Lawrence*, which was rendered two years after *Gardiner*?
4. What was J'Noel's equal protection argument? How does the court resolve it? Are there other lines of constitutional analysis that should be considered?
5. Is the distinction between a homosexual and a transsexual meaningful? For what purposes? Within the Kansas statutory scheme, would it make sense to honor marriages of transsexuals, but not homosexuals? Realistically, wouldn't an average Kansas legislator fail to see the difference; indeed, be equally appalled by both?
6. On remand, what evidence and criteria must the trial court consider? How should it decide the case?
7. Finally, are you surprised that the court did not devote more time to discussing the nature of marriage? Isn't that really what the case is all about?

PROBLEM 2-2 — Sex Change and Disability

In *Conway v. City of Hartford*, 1997 Conn. Super. LEXIS 282, Trevor Conway brought an action against the city for firing him after he underwent surgery which changed his gender to male. In eight counts, Trevor alleged discrimination based on: (a) mental disorder; (b) physical disability; (c) sex; and (d) sexual orientation. How should the court have ruled on the central questions of whether transsexualism or gender dysphoria is either a mental disorder or a physical disability?

Does it help to know that transsexualism is explicitly excluded from coverage under the Federal Rehabilitation Act, 29 USC § [illegible] et seq., and the Americans with Disabilities Act, 42 USC § 12101 et seq., but that it is a listed diagnosis in the American Psychiatric Associations Diagnostic and Statistical Manual of Mental Disorders (3d ed. 1987 (DSM-IVR)). *Should* it be so excluded?

PROBLEM 2–3 — David or Diane

A job applicant was turned away from The Library of Congress for a position as a terrorism research analyst, having interviewed as a male and gotten the offer, whereupon he disclosed that he/she was undergoing sex reassignment and would come to work as a female, the beginning phase of reassignment therapy, to be followed by hormone therapy and, possibly, surgery.

Some courts have held Title VII does not protect transsexualism. *See Vlane v. Eastern Airlines*, 742 F2d 1081 (7th Cir. 1984). In *Price Waterhouse v. Hopkins*, 490 U.S. 228 (1989), the Supreme Court seemed to support this view, and so the trial court held Diane lost on her claim of sex stereotyping. The Library did not turn her down as an effeminate male or masculine female — she presented as a feminine female. But it upheld her claim on simpler grounds — discrimination on the basis of sex. *Schroer v. Billington*, ___ F. Supp. 2d ___ (D.D.C. Mar. 31, 2006), 74 U.S.L.W. 1647 (May 2, 2006).

Does this make sense? If so, might an employer find good cause (if true) in the probability that Diane will lose time from work and run up medical bills because of her future therapy and surgery? Because she will likely be a disruptive factor?

Why did Diane not first present as female? Why not wait until after accepting the offer to disclose the transition?

§ 2.03 Physical Integrity: Testing and Cloning

Every person has a physical embodiment, through which we experience the sensations of life. Our bodies are essential to our active functioning in society — holding jobs, learning, associating with others, procreating. Our bodies are also essential in passive ways — for containing and protecting our inner selves, our emotional, reflective, spiritual processes and principles. Who we are, what we do, what we may become, our secrets, all of this is protected and held within. The extent to which our bodies are respected and left to our own control is a measure of our integrity and dignity.

Ethical values are compromised whenever our bodies may be invaded against our wills. The earlier cases dealt with these concerns in such areas as slavery, surrogacy, amputation, sterilization, abortion and memory. The present section deals specifically with two related, but different, areas: forcible entry of the body or mind, and replication of the body through cloning.

It is important to highlight an assumption so basic to society and personhood that it is often ignored — each person is a unique individual. Conventional procreation assures this genetically. Society affirms it as a fundamental value.

The science of cloning poses a profound challenge to this centerpiece of the order of things. Or does it?

[1] Bodily Invasions

ROCHIN v. PEOPLE OF CALIFORNIA
342 U.S. 165 (1952)

Mr. Justice **Frankfurter** delivered the opinion of the Court.

Having "some information that (the petitioner here) was selling narcotics," three deputy sheriffs of the County of Los Angeles, on the morning of July 1, 1949, made for the two-story dwelling house in which Rochin lived with his mother, common-law wife, brothers and sisters. Finding the outside door open, they entered and then forced open the door to Rochin's room on the second floor. Inside they found petitioner sitting partly dressed on the side of the bed, upon which his wife was lying. On a "night stand" beside the bed the deputies spied two capsules. When asked "Whose stuff is this?" Rochin seized the capsules and put them in his mouth. A struggle ensued, in the course of which the three officers "jumped upon him" and attempted to extract the capsules. The force they applied proved unavailing against Rochin's resistance. He was handcuffed and taken to a hospital. At the direction of one of the officers a doctor forced an emetic solution through a tube into Rochin's stomach against his will. This "stomach pumping" produced vomiting. In the vomited matter were found two capsules which proved to contain morphine.

Rochin was brought to trial before a California Superior Court, sitting without a jury, on the charge of possessing "a preparation of morphine" in violation of the California Health and Safety Code. Rochin was convicted and sentenced to sixty days' imprisonment. The chief evidence against him was the two capsules. They were admitted over petitioner's objection, although the means of obtaining them was frankly set forth in the testimony by one of the deputies, substantially as here narrated.

. . . .

. . . Regard for the requirements of the Due Process Clause "inescapably imposes upon this Court an exercise of judgment upon the whole course of the proceedings (resulting in a conviction) in order to ascertain whether they offend those canons of decency and fairness which express the notions of justice of English-speaking peoples even toward those charged with the most heinous offenses." These standards of justice are not authoritatively formulated anywhere as though they were specifics. Due process of law is a summarized constitutional guarantee of respect for those personal immunities which, as Mr. Justice Cardozo twice wrote for the Court, are "so rooted in the traditions and conscience of our people as to be ranked as fundamental." . . .

. . . In dealing not with the machinery of government but with human rights, the absence of formal exactitude, or want of fixity of meaning, is not an unusual or even regrettable attribute of constitutional provisions. Words being symbols do not speak without a gloss. On the one hand the gloss may be the deposit of history, whereby a term gains technical content. . . .

When the gloss has thus not been fixed but is a function of the process of [illegible] at different times and differently at the same time through different judges. Even more specific provisions, such as the guaranty of freedom of speech and the detailed protection against unreasonable searches and seizures, have inevitably evoked as sharp divisions in this Court as the least specific and most comprehensive protection of liberties, the Due Process Clause.

. . . .

Applying these general considerations to the circumstances of the present case, we are compelled to conclude that the proceedings by which this conviction was obtained do more than offend some fastidious squeamishness or private sentimentalism about combating crime too energetically. This is conduct that shocks the conscience. Illegally breaking into the privacy of the petitioner, the struggle to open his mouth and remove what was there, the forcible extraction of his stomach's contents — this course of proceeding by agents of government to obtain evidence is bound to offend even hardened sensibilities. They are methods too close to the rack and the screw to permit of constitutional differentiation.

. . . It would be a stultification of the responsibility which the course of constitutional history has cast upon this Court to hold that in order to convict a man the police cannot extract by force what is in his mind but can extract what is in his stomach.

. . . Coerced confessions offend the community's sense of fair play and decency. So here, to sanction the brutal conduct which naturally enough was condemned by the court whose judgment is before us, would be to afford brutality the cloak of law. Nothing would be more calculated to discredit law and thereby to brutalize the temper of a society.

. . . .

Mr. Justice **Black,** concurring.

Adamson v. People of State of California sets out reasons for my belief that state as well as federal courts and law enforcement officers must obey the Fifth Amendment's command that "No person . . . shall be compelled in any criminal case to be a witness against himself." I think a person is compelled to be a witness against himself not only when he is compelled to testify, but also when as here, incriminating evidence is forcibly taken from him by a contrivance of modern science. California convicted this petitioner by using against him evidence obtained in this manner, and I agree with Mr. Justice **Douglas** that the case should be reversed on this ground.

. . . .

. . . There is, however, no express constitutional language granting judicial power to invalidate *every* state law of *every* kind deemed "unreasonable" or contrary to the Court's notion of civilized decencies; yet the constitutional philosophy used by the majority has, in the past, been used to deny a state the right to fix the price of gasoline; and even the right to prevent bakers from palming off smaller for larger loaves of bread. These cases, and others, show the extent to which the evanescent standards of the majority's philosophy have been used to nullify state legislative programs passed to suppress evil economic practices. What paralyzing role this same philosophy will play in the future economic affairs of this country is impossible to predict. Of even graver concern, however, is the use of the philosophy to nullify the Bill of Rights. I long ago concluded that the accordion-like qualities of this philosophy must inevitably imperil all the individual liberty safeguards specifically enumerated in the Bill of Rights. Reflection and recent decisions of this Court sanctioning abridgment of the freedom of speech and press have strengthened this conclusion.

Mr. Justice **Douglas,** concurring.

The evidence obtained from this accused's stomach would be admissible in the majority of states where the question has been raised. So far as the reported cases reveal, the only states which would probably exclude the evidence would be Arkansas, Iowa, Michigan, and Missouri. Yet the Court now says that the rule which the majority of the states have fashioned violates the "decencies of civilized conduct." To that I cannot agree. It is a rule formulated by responsible courts with judges as sensitive as we are to the proper standards for law administration.

As an original matter it might be debatable whether the provision in the Fifth Amendment that no person "shall be compelled in any criminal case to be a witness against himself" serves the ends of justice. Not all civilized legal procedures recognize it. But the Choice was made by the Framers, a choice which sets a standard for legal trials in this country. The Framers made it a standard of due process for prosecutions by the Federal Government. If it is a requirement of due process for a trial in the federal courthouse, it is impossible for me to say it is not a requirement of due process for a trial in the state courthouse. I think that words taken from his lips, capsules taken from his stomach, blood taken from his veins are all inadmissible provided they are taken from him without his consent. They are inadmissible because of the command of the Fifth Amendment.

. . . .

NOTES AND QUESTIONS

1. *Rochin* was decided in 1952, some twenty-five years before the international traffic in narcotics posed a health and criminal problem of pandemic proportions. Would the case be decided the same way today?
2. Even assuming that the force and means used against Mr. Rochin were shocking, still, should his conviction be reversed? The evidence was essential to the case; possession was illegal; it was not (unlike a confession) influenced by illegal force. Why not *use* the evidence and let Mr. Rochin, after conviction, sue for damages? Isn't *that* better justice? Are the stomach pump in *Rochin,* and the accompanying force, used thereby to produce drug capsules, as shocking as if the product had been a confession? Wouldn't the latter be more shocking?
3. What of Justice Frankfurter's panegyric in favor of vagueness, uncertainty and unequal treatment, due to shifting interpretations of human

rights? Are you persuaded that lack of clarity is unavoidable? Acceptable, in the field of human rights? Do you agree with Justice Black?

4. And why — may one ask? — does Frankfurter think there would be derision if his views were denominated "natural law"? What is *wrong* with natural law? Isn't it the set of rules by which one's "conscience" may be informed, a breach of which may "shock the conscience"?

5. *How* does Justice Frankfurter (a former Harvard Law Professor, New Deal "brain truster," and then Supreme Court Justice) inform himself, with requisite conformity, about the "community's sense of fair play and decency"? And if the community, upon being polled, favored *convicting* Mr. Rochin, what *then* would Justice Frankfurter say? Justice Black? Doesn't Justice Douglas have the better part of the argument when he notes that all states but four would admit this evidence?

6. Is *Rochin* a part of the same tradition as *Meyer*, *Griswold*, *Roe* and *Casey*? If so, how can a system of law avoid the aberration of personal predeliction reflected — and later disavowed — in *Lochner v. New York*, *infra* § 4.03[2]? How would the United Nations Declaration treat Mr. Rochin? Rawls?

7. In *Schmerber v. California*, 384 U.S. 757 (1966), the Supreme Court upheld taking a blood sample from an unconscious automobile driver by medically administered means. Was this consistent with *Rochin*?

WINSTON v. LEE
470 U.S. 753 (1985)

Justice **Brennan** delivered the opinion of the Court.

. . . .

I

A

At approximately 1 a.m. on July 18, 1982, Ralph E. Watkinson was closing his shop for the night. As he was locking the door, he observed someone armed with a gun coming toward him from across the street. Watkinson was also armed and when he drew his gun, the other person told him to freeze. Watkinson then fired at the other person, who returned his fire. Watkinson was hit in the legs, while the other individual, who appeared to be wounded in his left side, ran from the scene. The police arrived on the scene shortly thereafter, and Watkinson was taken by ambulance to the emergency room of the Medical College of Virginia (MCV) Hospital.

Approximately 20 minutes later, police officers responding to another call found respondent eight blocks from where the earlier shooting occurred. Respondent was suffering from a gunshot wound to his left chest area and told the police that he had been shot when two individuals attempted to rob him. An ambulance took respondent to the MCV Hospital. Watkinson was still in the MCV emergency room and, when respondent entered that room, said "[t]hat's the man that shot me." After an investigation, the police decided that respondent's story of having been himself the victim of a robbery was untrue and charged respondent with attempted robbery, malicious wounding, and two counts of using a firearm in the commission of a felony.

B

The Commonwealth shortly thereafter moved in state court for an order directing respondent to undergo surgery to remove an object thought to be a bullet lodged under his left collarbone. The court conducted several evidentiary hearings on the motion. At the first hearing, the Commonwealth's expert testified that the surgical procedure would take 45 minutes and would involve a three to four percent chance of temporary nerve damage, a one percent chance of permanent nerve damage, and a one-tenth of one percent chance of death. At the second hearing, the expert testified that on reexamination of respondent, he discovered that the bullet was not "back inside close to the nerves and arteries," as he originally had thought. Instead, he now believed the bullet to be located "just beneath the skin." He testified that the surgery would require an incision of only one and one-half centimeters (slightly more than one-half inch), could be performed under local anesthesia, and would result in "no danger on the basis that there's no general anesthesia employed."

. . . .

On October 18, 1982, just before the surgery was scheduled, the surgeon ordered that X rays be taken of respondent's chest. The X rays revealed that the bullet was in fact lodged two and one-half to three centimeters (approximately one inch) deep in muscular tissue in respondent's chest, substantially deeper than had been thought when the state court granted the motion to compel surgery. The surgeon now believed that a general anesthetic would be desirable for medical reasons.

Respondent moved the state trial court for a rehearing based on the new evidence. After holding an evidentiary hearing, the state trial court denied the rehearing, and the Virginia Supreme Court affirmed. Respondent then returned to federal court, where he moved to alter or amend the judgment previously entered against him. After an evidentiary hearing, the District Court enjoined the threatened surgery. . . .

II

. . . Putting to one side the procedural protections of the warrant requirement, the Fourth Amendment generally protects the "security" of "persons, houses, papers, and effects" against official intrusions up to the point where the community's need for evidence surmounts a specified standard, ordinarily "probable cause." Beyond this point, it is ordinarily justifiable for the community to demand that the individual give up some part of his interest in privacy and security to advance the community's vital interests in law enforcement; such a search is generally "reasonable" in the Amendment's terms.

A compelled surgical intrusion into an individual's body for evidence, however, implicates expectations of privacy and security of such magnitude that the intrusion may be "unreasonable" even if likely to produce evidence [illegible]. . . .

. . . .

The reasonableness of surgical intrusions beneath the skin depends on a case-by-case approach, in which the individual's interests in privacy and security are weighed against society's interests in conducting the procedure. In a given case, the question whether the community's need for evidence outweighs the substantial privacy interests at stake is a delicate one admitting of few categorical answers. . . .

. . . .

Another factor is the extent of intrusion upon the individual's dignitary interests in personal privacy and bodily integrity. . . .

. . . .

III

. . . .

The threats to the health or safety of respondent posed by the surgery are the subject of sharp dispute between the parties. Before the new revelations of October 18, the District Court found that the procedure could be carried out "with virtually no risk to [respondent]." On rehearing, however, with new evidence before it, the District Court held that "the risks previously involved have increased in magnitude even as new risks are being added."

The Court of Appeals examined the medical evidence in the record and found that respondent would suffer some risks associated with the surgical procedure. One surgeon had testified that the difficulty of discovering the exact location of the bullet "could require extensive probing and retracting of the muscle tissue," carrying with it "the concomitant risks of injury to the muscle as well as injury to the nerves, blood vessels and other tissue in the chest and pleural cavity." the court further noted that "the greater intrusion and the larger incisions increase the risks of infection." Moreover, there was conflict in the testimony concerning the nature and the scope of the operation. One surgeon stated that it would take 15-20 minutes, while another predicted the procedure could take up to two and one-half hours. The court properly took the resulting uncertainty about the medical risks into account.

Both lower courts in this case believed that the proposed surgery, which for purely medical reasons required the use of a general anesthetic, would be an "extensive" intrusion on respondent's personal privacy and bodily integrity. When conducted with the consent of the patient, surgery requiring general anesthesia is not necessarily demeaning or intrusive. In such a case, the surgeon is carrying out the patient's own will concerning the patient's body and the patient's right to privacy is therefore preserved. In this case, however, the Court of Appeals noted that the Commonwealth proposes to take control of respondent's body, to "drug this citizen — not yet convicted of a criminal offense — with narcotics and barbiturates into a state of unconsciousness," and then to search beneath his skin for evidence of a crime. This kind of surgery involves a virtually total divestment of respondent's ordinary control over surgical probing beneath his skin.

The other part of the balance concerns the Commonwealth's need to intrude into respondent's body to retrieve the bullet. . . . The Commonwealth has available substantial additional evidence that respondent was the individual who accosted Watkinson on the night of the robbery. No party in this case suggests that Watkinson's entirely spontaneous identification of respondent at the hospital would be inadmissible. In addition, petitioners can no doubt prove that respondent was found a few blocks from Watkinson's store shortly after the incident took place. And petitioners can certainly show that the location of the bullet (under respondent's left collarbone) seems to correlate with Watkinson's report that the robber "jerked" to the left. . . .

In weighing the various factors in this case, we therefore reach the same conclusion as the courts below. The operation sought will intrude substantially on respondent's protected interests. The medical risks of the operation, although apparently not extremely severe, are a subject of considerable dispute; the very uncertainty militates against finding the operation to be "reasonable." In addition, the intrusion on respondent's privacy interests entailed by the operation can only be characterized as severe. On the other hand, although the bullet may turn out to be useful to the Commonwealth in prosecuting respondent, the Commonwealth has failed to demonstrate a compelling need for it. We believe that in these circumstances the Commonwealth has failed to demonstrate that it would be "reasonable" under the terms of the Fourth Amendment to search for evidence of this crime by means of the contemplated surgery.

. . . .

Affirmed.

. . . .

NOTES AND QUESTIONS

1. The court analyzes the proposed surgery under the "reasonableness" standard of the Fourth Amendment. This permits a balancing of interests, as suggested in the note immediately above. But is this wrong or not? Should there not be an absolute provision for bodily integrity, perhaps found in the Ninth Amendment, as discussed in *Griswold v. Connecticut*?
2. What are the ethical constraints bearing on the facts and circumstances in *Winston v. Lee*? Rather than invading the defendant's body, should not the court simply give him a choice? If so, and the defendant declines the surgery, what would be an appropriate sanction?
3. Should it matter that magnetic resonance imaging would now be available as an alternative to surgery for the scanning and ballistics analysis of a bullet while in the body? Furthermore, should it also matter that laporoscopic surgery would now make surgery minimally invasive?

4. Is *Winston v. Lee* consistent with *Washington v. Harper* and the *Mary Northern* case, *supra* § 1.06 and *Riggins v. Nevada*, *supra* § 2.02[1].

PROBLEM 2–4 — Do Rite, Mr. Hanna

Consider the following factual scenario taken from *People v. Hanna*, 567 N.W.2d 12 (Mich. Ct. of App. 1997).

> After the police stopped the defendant for speeding, he stumbled out of his vehicle, stood unsteadily, and with slurred speech admitted that he had been drinking. Thereafter, defendant failed a field sobriety test, refused to take a Breathalyzer examination, and vomited in his jail cell. While arresting officers Bradley LaCross and Michael Troyer drove [the] defendant to a hospital to execute a warrant to draw a sample of defendant's blood, defendant proclaimed repeatedly in a loud, angry voice that he would not permit anyone to draw his blood.
>
> Defendant became "very uncooperative" at the hospital and refused to lie on the examination table. Defendant jerked his arm away from the laboratory technician who attempted to draw his blood. Concerned about the safety threat posed by defendant's evasive conduct, the two officers restrained defendant by laying him on the examination table and applying for "a few seconds" "Do-Rite sticks" to pressure points on defendant's wrists. The pressure subdued defendant, who then relaxed and permitted the laboratory technician to draw his blood.
>
> Officer LaCross described Do-Rite sticks as being two plastic rods connected with a one-inch cord. The device is used by wrapping the cord around certain pressure points and exerting pressure by briefly pulling or twisting the handles. LaCross testified that the device inflicts a "quick and simple" discomfort that causes no injury or lasting pain. According to LaCross, all Sault Sainte Marie police officers receive training before receiving certification to carry and use Do-Rite sticks. Officer LaCross described the nature of Do-Rite sticks, and the use of the devices on defendant to obtain his compliance with the taking of a blood sample, as follows:
>
> Q: What steps occurred then to get a hold of the situation?
>
> A: He was asked to lay [sic] down on the bed, which he refused to do. Finally, he was informed to lay [sic] down or we would lay him down on the bed, at which time Officer Troyer and myself laid Eric Hanna down on the bed and the do right [sic] sticks were applied to his wrists.
>
> Q: What effect do they have upon the person they are applied to?
>
> A: They are designed to gain compliance. Once compliance is gained the pressure is supposed to be relieved in order to not cause injury or long-term pain.
>
> Q: You say there was control on the amount of pressure?
>
> A: I applied it at the wrist with soft hands. I applied pressure when the lab technician was coming up to draw the blood because Mr.

Hanna started to pull away. Pressure was applied. He was told repeatedly. At which time he complied after the pain was applied to him.

Q: Pain, it sounds pretty bad. Was it pinching? How does it all work?

A: It's just through pressure points that are learned through our training. It's not a permanent pain. It's just real quick and simple. It is used for compliance for subjects that aren't cooperative.

Q: You indicated. I thought, soft hands, if I am quoting you correctly. What does that denote and relate it to other types of procedures that you might have used.

A: It wasn't used as a training instrument or any type of a weapon for use of force that way.

Q: Okay. Are they able to be used in that manner?

A: Yes, they are.

. . . .

Q: If you had not had the right [sic] devices at this time, Officer, would you have been able to get the blood?

A: No.

. . . .

Q: In the case here with Mr. Hanna how long did you have them applied to him?

A: A few seconds.

Q: And was the same degree of pressure constant as far as the pair of restraints you were controlling?

A: There was a short, very short period of pressure, maybe two seconds, at which time he laid [sic] still. At that time the pressure was released and Mr. Hanna was informed if he didn't comply further pressure was going to be reapplied.

Q: Now, what was his response to that statement?

A: At that time he laid [sic] still.

Does it seem that a blood sample of Mr. Hanna was necessary? Excessive? Justified by the preceding case law or the needs of prosecution? Mr. Hanna was a third offender, receiving a two–to–five year imprisonment sentence.

PROBLEM 2–5 — Insulin Injections

August T. Vogel was convicted of murder, receiving a 90-year sentence, to be released in the year 2016. He is 64, has diabetes, is taking insulin regularly, attends State College, works at the Radisson Inn and is eligible for parole. The Parole Board has recently denied parole eligibility for the next two years. August has stopped eating and stopped taking his insulin. A psychiatrist says Vogel is competent, "stubborn and angry" and has "asserted his control" by those refusals in "an attempt to manipulate the system and blackmail the officials," to be returned to minimum security and his job at the Radisson Inn.

Vogel replies that he has a right to refuse medical treatment, a right to humane care, and a right to protest. The prison physician says Vogel will soon die.

Should a court order forcible injections of insulin? Feeding of food through a nasogastric tube? Consider here not only the *Rochin* and *Winston* cases but also *Bell*, *Harper*, *Riggins*, and *Cruzan supra* Ch. 1. *See also State of North Dakota v. Vogel*, 537 N.W.2d 358 (N.D. 1995).

[2] Testing: Urine, Plethysmograph, Polygraph, and Genes

Society exercises controls over people in different ways, in different settings. Testing is one such control. It may be a precondition of employment, marriage, education, insurance or other associations and benefits. As a public health measure, testing for communicable diseases, such as tuberculosis or AIDS, has long been an acceptable technique to assure the safety of society.

Serious questions arise when disclosure compromises privacy, leads to prosecution, or is unrelated to legitimate public concerns. Some questions relate to the manner and circumstances of testing, which often is physically and psychologically intrusive. Other concerns relate to *who* is tested and why. And always there is the issue of proper disclosure and use of the results of testing.

These concerns are particularly compelling when the tests, as with the polygraph and plethysmograph, are psychologically invasive and of dubious validity. Then, the imposition on dignity may outweigh the benefit to society.

Less invasive — it may seem, perhaps — are the requirement and testing of urine samples. We begin with those. Consider who is selected, how and why, as well as the uses (legitimate or otherwise) of the tests and the method of administration. In this connection consider not only the following cases, but also *Long v. Great West Life*, *infra* § [illegible], [illegible] of the application of the Americans with Disabilities Act to testing (there urine samples).

NATIONAL TREASURY EMPLOYEES UNION v. VON RAAB
489 U.S. 656 (1989)

Justice **Kennedy** delivered the opinion of the Court.

We granted certiorari to decide whether it violates the Fourth Amendment for the United States Customs Service to require a urinalysis test from employees who seek transfer or promotion to certain positions.

I

A

. . . .

In December 1985, respondent, the Commissioner of Customs, established a Drug Screening Task Force to explore the possibility of implementing a drug-screening program within the Service. After extensive research and consultation with experts in the field, the task force concluded that "drug screening through urinalysis is technologically reliable, valid and accurate." Citing this conclusion, the Commissioner announced his intention to require drug tests of employees who applied for, or occupied, certain positions within the Service. The Commissioner stated his belief that "Customs is largely drug-free," but noted also that "unfortunately no segment of society is immune from the threat of illegal drug use." Drug interdiction has become the agency's primary enforcement mission, and the Commissioner stressed that "there is no room in the Customs Service for those who break the laws prohibiting the possession and use of illegal drugs."

In May 1986, the Commissioner announced implementation of the drug-testing program. Drug tests were made a condition of placement or employment for positions that meet one or more of three criteria. The first is direct involvement in drug interdiction or enforcement of related laws, an activity the Commissioner deemed fraught with obvious dangers to the mission of the agency and the lives of Customs agents. The second criterion is a requirement that the incumbent carry firearms, as the Commissioner concluded that "[p]ublic safety demands that employees who carry deadly arms and are prepared to make instant life or death decisions be drug free." The third criterion is a requirement for the incumbent to handle "classified" material, which the Commissioner determined might fall into the hands of smugglers if accessible to employees who, by reason of their own illegal drug use, are susceptible to bribery or blackmail.

After an employee qualifies for a position covered by the Customs testing program, the Service advises him by letter that his final selection is contingent upon successful completion of drug screening. An independent contractor contacts the employee to fix the time and place for collecting the sample. On reporting for the test, the employee must produce photographic identification and remove any outer garments, such as a coat or a jacket, and personal belongings. The employee may produce the sample behind a partition, or in the privacy of a bathroom stall if he so chooses. To ensure against adulteration of the specimen, or substitution of a sample from another person, a monitor of the same sex as the employee remains close at hand to listen for the normal sounds of urination. Dye is added to the toilet water to prevent the employee from using the water to adulterate the sample.

. . . .

Customs employees who test positive for drugs and who can offer no satisfactory explanation are subject to dismissal from the Service. Test results may not, however, be turned over to any other agency, including criminal prosecutors, without the employee's written consent.

II

In *Skinner v. Railway Labor Executives' Assn.*, 489 U.S. 602, we held that federal regulations requiring employees of private railroads to produce urine samples for chemical testing implicate the Fourth Amendment, as those tests invade reasonable expectations of privacy. Our earlier cases have settled that the Fourth Amendment protects individuals from unreasonable searches conducted by the Government, even when the Government acts as an employer, and, in view of our holding in *Railway Labor Executives* that urine tests are searches, it follows that the Customs Service's drug-testing program must meet the reasonableness requirement of the Fourth Amendment.

. . . .

It is clear that the Customs Service's drug-testing program is not designed to serve the ordinary needs of law enforcement. Test results may not be used in a criminal prosecution of the employee without the employee's consent. The purposes of the program are to deter drug use among those eligible for promotion to sensitive positions within the Service and to prevent the promotion of drug users to those positions. These substantial interests, no less than the Government's concern for safe rail transportation at issue in *Railway Labor Executives,* present a special need that may justify departure from the ordinary warrant and probable-cause requirements.

. . . .

B

. . . We think the Government's need to conduct the suspicionless searches required by the Customs program outweighs the privacy interests of employees engaged directly in drug interdiction, and of those who otherwise are required to carry firearms.

The Customs Service is our Nation's first line of defense against one of the greatest problems affecting the health and welfare of our population. We have adverted before to "the veritable national crisis in law enforcement caused by smuggling of illicit narcotics." Our cases also reflect the traffickers' seemingly inexhaustible repertoire of deceptive practices and elaborate schemes for importing narcotics. The record in this case confirms that, through the adroit selection of source locations, smuggling routes, and increasingly elaborate methods of concealment, drug traffickers have managed to bring into this country increasingly large quantities of illegal drugs. The record also indicates, and it is well known, that drug smugglers do not hesitate to use violence to protect their lucrative trade and avoid apprehension.

. . . .

It is readily apparent that the Government has a compelling interest in ensuring that front-line interdiction personnel are physically fit, and have unimpeachable integrity and judgment. Indeed, the Government's interest here is at least as important as its interest in searching travelers entering the country. We have long held that travelers seeking to enter the country may be stopped and required to submit to a routine search without probable cause, or even founded suspicion, "because of national self protection reasonably requiring one entering the country to identify himself as entitled to come in, and his belongings as effects which may be lawfully brought in." . . .

. . . .

We think Customs employees who are directly involved in the interdiction of illegal drugs or who are required to carry firearms in the line of duty likewise have a diminished expectation of privacy in respect to the intrusions occasioned by a urine test. Unlike most private citizens or government employees in general, employees involved in drug interdiction reasonably should expect effective inquiry into their fitness and probity. Much the same is true of employees who are required to carry firearms. Because successful performance of their duties depends uniquely on their judgment and dexterity, these employees cannot reasonably expect to keep from the Service personal information that bears directly on their fitness. . . .

Without disparaging the importance of the governmental interests that support the suspicionless searches of these employees, petitioners nevertheless contend that the Service's drug-testing program is unreasonable in two particulars. First, petitioners argue that the program is unjustified because it is not based on a belief that testing will reveal any drug use by covered employees. In pressing this argument, petitioners point out that the Service's testing scheme was not implemented in response to any perceived drug problem among Customs employees, and that the program actually has not led to the discovery of a significant number of drug users. Counsel for petitioners informed us at oral argument that no more than 5 employees out of 3,600 have tested positive for drugs. Second, petitioners contend that the Service's scheme is not a "sufficiently productive mechanism[] to justify [its] intrusion upon Fourth Amendment interests," because illegal drug users can avoid detection with ease by temporary abstinence or by surreptitious adulteration of their urine specimens. These contentions are unpersuasive.

. . . .

The mere circumstance that all but a few of the employees tested are entirely innocent of wrongdoing does not impugn the program's validity. The same is likely to be true of householders who are required to submit to suspicionless housing code inspections, and of motorists who are stopped at the checkpoints we approved in *United States v. Martinez-Fuerte*. The Service's program is designed to prevent the promotion of drug users to sensitive positions as much as it is designed to detect those employees who use drugs. Where, as here, the possible harm against which the Government seeks to guard is substantial, the need to prevent its occurrence furnishes an ample justification for reasonable searches calculated to advance the Government's goal.[1]

We think petitioners' second argument — that the Service's testing program is ineffective because employees may attempt to deceive the test by a brief

[1] The point is well illustrated also by the Federal Government's practice of requiring the search of all passengers seeking to board commercial airliners, as well as the search of their carry-on luggage, without any basis for suspecting any particular passenger of an untoward motive.

abstention before the test date, or by adulterating their urine specimens — overstates the case. As the Court of Appeals noted, addicts may be unable to abstain even for a limited period of time, or may be unaware of the "fade-away effect" of certain drugs. More importantly, the avoidance techniques suggested by petitioners are fraught with uncertainty and risks for those employees who venture to attempt them. A particular employee's pattern of elimination for a given drug cannot be predicted with perfect accuracy, and, in any event, this information is not likely to be known or available to the employee. . . . Nor can he expect attempts at adulteration to succeed, in view of the precautions taken by the sample collector to ensure the integrity of the sample. In all the circumstances, we are persuaded that the program bears a close and substantial relation to the Service's goal of deterring drug users from seeking promotion to sensitive positions.

. . . .

C

We are unable, on the present record, to assess the reasonableness of the Government's testing program insofar as it covers employees who are required "to handle classified material." We readily agree that the Government has a compelling interest in protecting truly sensitive information from those who, "under compulsion of circumstances or for other reasons, . . . might compromise [such] information." . . .

It is not clear, however, whether the category defined by the service's testing directive encompasses only those Customs employees likely to gain access to sensitive information. Employees who are tested under the Service's scheme include those holding such diverse positions as "Accountant," "Accounting Technician," "Animal Caretaker," "Attorney (All)," "Baggage Clerk," "Co-op Student (All)," "Electric Equipment Repairer," "Mail Clerk/Assistant," and "Messenger." . . .

We cannot resolve this ambiguity on the basis of the record before us, and we think it is appropriate to remand the case to the Court of Appeals for such proceedings as may be necessary to clarify the scope of this category of employees subject to testing. Upon remand the Court of Appeals should examine the criteria used by the Service in determining what materials are classified and in deciding whom to test under this rubric. In assessing the reasonableness of requiring tests of these employees, the court should also consider pertinent information bearing upon the employees' privacy expectations, as well as the supervision to which these employees are already subject.

III

. . . .

The judgment of the Court of Appeals for the Fifth Circuit is affirmed in part and vacated in part, and the case is remanded for further proceedings consistent with this opinion.

It is so ordered.

. . . .

Justice **Scalia**, with whom Justice **Stevens** joins, dissenting.

. . . .

Until today this Court had upheld a bodily search separate from arrest and without individualized suspicion of wrongdoing only with respect to prison inmates, relying upon the uniquely dangerous nature of that environment. Today, in *Skinner,* we allow a less intrusive bodily search of railroad employees involved in train accidents. I joined the Court's opinion there because the demonstrated frequency of drug and alcohol use by the targeted class of employees, and the demonstrated connection between such use and grave harm, rendered the search a reasonable means of protecting society. I decline to join the Court's opinion in the present case because neither frequency of use nor connection to harm is demonstrated or even likely. In my view the Customs Service rules are a kind of immolation of privacy and human dignity in symbolic opposition to drug use.

. . . .

The Court's opinion in the present case, however, will be searched in vain for real evidence of a real problem that will be solved by urine testing of Customs Service employees. . . . The only pertinent points, it seems to me, are supported by nothing but speculation, and not very plausible speculation at that. It is not apparent to me that a Customs Service employee who uses drugs is significantly more likely to be bribed by a drug smuggler, any more than a Customs Service employee who wears diamonds is significantly more likely to be bribed by a diamond smuggler — unless, perhaps, the addiction to drugs is so severe, and requires so much money to maintain, that it would be detectable even without benefit of a urine test. . . .

What is absent in the Government's justifications — notably absent, revealingly absent, and as far as I am concerned dispositively absent — is the recitation of even a single instance in which any of the speculated horribles actually occurred: an instance, that is, in which the cause of bribe-taking, or of poor aim, or of unsympathetic law enforcement, or of compromise of classified information, was drug use. Although the Court points out that several employees have in the past been removed from the Service for accepting bribes and other integrity violations, and that at least nine officers have died in the line of duty since 1974, there is no indication whatever that these incidents were related to drug use by Service employees. . . . According to the Service's counsel, out of 3,600 employees tested, no more than 5 tested positive for drugs.

. . . .

Today's decision would be wrong, but at least of more limited effect, if its approval of drug testing were confined to that category of employees assigned specifically to drug interdiction duties. Relatively few public employees fit that description. But in extending approval of drug testing to that category consisting of employees who carry firearms, the Court exposes vast numbers of public employees to this needless indignity. Logically, of course, if those who carry guns can be treated in this fashion, so can all others whose work, if performed under the influence of drugs, may endanger others — automobile drivers, operators of other potentially dangerous equipment, construction workers, school crossing guards. A similarly broad scope attaches to the Court's approval of drug testing for those with access to 'sensitive information." . . .

. . . I do not believe for a minute that the driving force behind these drug-testing rules was any of the feeble justifications put forward by counsel here and accepted by the Court. The only plausible explanation, in my view, is that the Commissioner himself offered in the concluding sentence of his memorandum to Customs Service employees announcing the program: "Implementation of the drug screening program would set an important example in our country's struggle with this most serious threat to our national health and security." What better way to show that the Government is serious about its "war on drugs" than to subject its employees on the front line of that war to this invasion of their privacy and affront to their dignity? To be sure, there is only a slight chance that it will prevent some serious public harm resulting from Service employee drug use, but it will show to the world that the Service is "clean," and — most important of all — will demonstrate the determination of the Government to eliminate this scourge of our society! I think it obvious that this justification is unacceptable; that the impairment of individual liberties cannot be the means of making a point; that symbolism, even symbolism for so worthy a cause as the abolition of unlawful drugs, cannot validate an otherwise unreasonable search.

There is irony in the Government's citation, in support of its position, Justice Brandeis' statement in *Olmstead v. United States*, 277 U.S. 438 (1928) that "[f]or good or for ill, [our Government] teaches the whole people by its example." Brandeis was there dissenting from the Court's admission of evidence obtained through an unlawful Government wiretap. He was not praising the Government's example of vigor and enthusiasm in combating crime, but condemning its example that "the end justifies the means." An even more apt quotation from that famous Brandeis dissent would have been the following:

> "[I]t is . . . immaterial that the intrusion was in aid of law enforcement. Experience should teach us to be most on our guard to protect liberty when the Government's purposes are beneficent. Men born to freedom are naturally alert to repel invasion of their liberty by evil-minded rulers. The greatest dangers to liberty lurk in insidious encroachment by men of zeal, well-meaning but without understanding." . . .

NOTES AND QUESTIONS

1. In a companion case, *Skinner v. Railway Labor Executives' Ass'n.*, the Supreme Court upheld the Federal Railroad Safety Act of 1970, and regulations pursuant to it, mandating blood and urine tests of employees involved in certain train accidents. Justices Marshall and Brennan dissented, but Justices Scalia and Stevens (who dissented in *Von Raab*) did not. Why?
2. Contrast the searches in *Von Raab* with those in *Rochin*, *Schmerber* and *Winston v. Lee*, where — in all of those cases — crimes had been

committed, the defendants had been identified, and the probable cause to believe evidence existed was clear. Are there similarly "compelling circumstances" in *Von Raab* ? If not, how can the Fourth Amendment be satisfied?

3. The preceding cases, *Rochin, Schmerbert* and *Winston v. Lee*, all involved physical *entry* into the body; that is not involved in *Von Raab.* In addition, those cases involved criminal prosecutions; the issue in *Von Raab* is simply employment. Which cases involve more important issues, in terms of integrity and dignity?

4. How does giving a urine sample in private implicate fundamental, personal values? It does, after all, simply involve bodily waste material — discarded daily by all of us. How, exactly, are sensitive issues of privacy implicated in urinalysis?

5. *Should* classified employees be subject to the urinalysis testing programs? What of police, school teachers, bus drivers and law students? Lawyers? Doctors?

6. Ethically, should not employees, as members of the community, be willing to take the burden of proof in establishing that they are law abiding? Put somewhat differently, should not society be able to impose *any* conditions which it chooses on public employment?

7. In *Vernonia School District v. Acton*, 515 U.S. 646 (1995), the Supreme Court upheld a school's policy of random urinalysis of athletes for drugs. Justice Scalia wrote for the majority — are you surprised? Should it matter that the subjects were children? That drug use impacts athletic performance? That this was a school? Should a less intrusive means — if available — be required? Should suspicion (if not probable cause) be required?

8. The Supreme Court held in 2002 that no "special need" had to exist within the public schools — they were the "special need" themselves. (*Board of Education v. Earls*, 536 U.S. 822 (2002)). This allowed public schools to administer drug tests to student athletes, even without "particularized suspicion."

9. Is it reasonable that the court held that public schools provided the "special needs" previously required in drug testing cases involving children? Does this mean that private schools may not meet the special need?

10. Is a generalized belief that a drug problem has existed since 1970 enough to assert probable cause? Why does the court allow it now, when it wasn't allowed before? What are the limits of this decision: could the court find that "special needs" exist in other locales or professions, such as public housing or practicing law? How about in neighborhoods known to have drug problems?

11. However, random search of students' belongings is a violation of the Fourth Amendment: *Jane Doe v. Little Rock School District*, 380 F.3d 349 (8th Cir. 2004). What might distinguish this case from *Board of Ed v. Earls*? Would you agree that your possessions are more private

than your body fluids (urine)? Is participation in school clubs or sports enough of a distinction?

NORMAN-BLOODSAW v. LAWRENCE BERKELEY LABORATORY*

135 F.3d 1260 (9th Cir. 1998)

Reinhardt, Circuit Judge:

. . . .

Plaintiffs Marya S. Norman-Bloodsaw, Eulalio R. Fuentes, Vertis B. Ellis, Mark E. Covington, John D. Randolph, Adrienne L. Garcia, and Brendolyn B. Smith are current and former administrative and clerical employees of defendant Lawrence Berkeley Laboratory ("Lawrence"), a research facility operated by the appellee Regents of the University of California pursuant to a contract with the United States Department of Energy (the Department). . . .

. . . .

With the exception of Ellis, who was hired in 1968 and underwent an examination after beginning employment, each of the plaintiffs received written offers of employment expressly conditioned upon a "medical examination," "medical approval," or "health evaluation." All accepted these offers and underwent preplacement examinations, and Randolph and Smith underwent subsequent examinations as well. . . .

The blood and urine samples given by all employees during their preplacement examinations were tested for syphilis; in addition, certain samples were tested for sickle cell trait; and certain samples were tested for pregnancy. . . . Defendants further contend that "for many years" signs posted in the health examination rooms and "more recently" in the reception area stated that the tests at issue would be administered.

. . . Plaintiffs allege that the testing of their blood and urine samples for syphilis, sickle cell trait, and pregnancy occurred without their knowledge or consent, and without any subsequent notification that the tests had been conducted. They also allege that only black employees were tested for sickle cell trait and assert the obvious fact that only female employees were tested for pregnancy. Finally, they allege that Lawrence failed to provide safeguards to prevent the dissemination of the test results. . . .

. . . .

The record, indeed, contains considerable evidence that the manner in which the tests were performed was inconsistent with sound medical practice. Plaintiffs introduced before the district court numerous expert declarations by medical scholars roundly condemning Lawrence's alleged practices and explaining, inter alia, that testing for syphilis, sickle cell trait, and pregnancy is not an appropriate part of an occupational medical examination and is rarely if ever done by employers as a matter of routine; that Lawrence lacked any reasonable medical or public health basis for performing these tests on clerical and

* Citation material has been omitted from this case.

administrative employees such as plaintiffs; and that the performance of such tests without explicit notice and informed consent violates prevailing medical standards. . . .

. . . .

Furthermore, if plaintiffs' evidence concerning reasonable medical practice is to be credited, they had no reason to think that tests would be performed without their consent simply because they had answered some questions on a form and had then, in addition, provided bodily fluid samples: Plaintiffs could reasonably have expected Lawrence to seek their consent before running any tests not usually performed in an occupational health exam — particularly tests for intimate medical conditions bearing no relationship to their responsibilities or working conditions as clerical employees. . . .

In sum, the district court erred in holding as a matter of law that the plaintiffs knew or had reason to know of the nature of the tests as a result of their submission to the preemployment medical examinations. . . .

The district court also ruled, in the alternative, on the merits of all of plaintiffs' claims except the ADA claims. We first examine its ruling with respect to the claim for violation of the federal constitutional right to privacy. While acknowledging that the government had failed to identify any "undisputed legitimate governmental purpose" for the three tests, the district court concluded that no violation of plaintiffs' right to privacy could have occurred because any intrusions arising from the testing were de minimis in light of (1) the "large overlap" between the subjects covered by the medical questionnaire and the three tests and (2) the "overall intrusiveness" of "a full-scale physical examination." We hold that the district court erred.

The constitutionally protected privacy interest in avoiding disclosure of personal matters clearly encompasses medical information and its confidentiality. Although cases defining the privacy interest in medical information have typically involved its disclosure to "third" parties, rather than the collection of information by illicit means, it goes without saying that the most basic violation possible involves the performance of unauthorized tests — that is, the non-consensual retrieval of previously unrevealed medical information that may be unknown even to plaintiffs. These tests may also be viewed as searches in violation of Fourth Amendment rights that require Fourth Amendment scrutiny. The tests at issue in this case thus implicate rights protected under both the Fourth Amendment and the Due Process Clause of the Fifth or Fourteenth Amendments.

. . . .

One can think of few subject areas more personal and more likely to implicate privacy interests than that of one's health or genetic make-up. . . . Furthermore, the facts revealed by the tests are highly sensitive, even relative to other medical information. With respect to the testing of plaintiffs for syphilis and pregnancy, it is well established in this circuit "that the Constitution prohibits unregulated, unrestrained employer inquiries into personal sexual matters that have no bearing on job performance." The fact that one has syphilis is an intimate matter that pertains to one's sexual history and may invite tremendous amounts of social stigma. Pregnancy is likewise, for many, an intensely private matter, which also may pertain to one's sexual history and often carries far-reaching societal implications. . . . Finally, the carrying of sickle cell trait can pertain to sensitive information about family history and reproductive decisionmaking. Thus, the conditions tested for were aspects of one's health in which one enjoys the highest expectations of privacy.

As discussed above, with respect to the question of the statute of limitations, there was little, if any, "overlap" between what plaintiffs consented to and the testing at issue here. Nor was the additional invasion only incremental. In some instances, the tests related to entirely different conditions. In all, the information obtained as the result of the testing was qualitatively different from the information that plaintiffs provided in their answers to the questions, and was highly invasive. . . .

Lawrence further contends that the tests in question, even if their intrusiveness is not de minimis, would be justified by an employer's interest in performing a general physical examination. This argument fails because issues of fact exist with respect to whether the testing at issue is normally part of a general physical examination. There would of course be no violation if the testing were authorized, or if the plaintiffs reasonably should have known that the blood and urine samples they provided would be used for the disputed testing and failed to object. However, as we concluded in Section I, material issues of fact exist as to those questions. . . .

. . . .

The district court also dismissed the Title VII counts on the merits on the ground that plaintiffs had failed to state a claim because the "alleged classifications, standing alone, do not suffice to provide a cognizable basis for relief under Title VII" and because plaintiffs had neither alleged nor demonstrated how these classifications had adversely affected them.

Section 703(a) of Title VII of the Civil Rights Act of 1964 provides that it is unlawful for any employer:

> (1) to fail or refuse to hire or to discharge any individual, or otherwise to discriminate against any individual with respect to his compensation, terms, conditions, or privileges of employment, because of such individual's race, color, religion, sex, or national origin; or
>
> (2) to limit, segregate, or classify his employees or applicants for employment in any way which would deprive or tend to deprive any individual of employment opportunities or otherwise adversely affect his status as an employee, because of such individual's race, color, religion, sex, or national origin.

42 U.S.C. § 2000e-2(a). The Pregnancy Discrimination Act further provides that discrimination on the basis of "sex" includes discrimination "on the basis of pregnancy, childbirth, or related medical conditions." . . .

Despite defendants' assertions to the contrary, plaintiffs' Title VII claims fall neatly into a Title VII framework: Plaintiffs allege that black and female employees were singled out for additional nonconsensual testing and that defendants thus selectively invaded the privacy of certain employees on the basis of race, sex, and pregnancy. The district court held that (1) the tests did not constitute discrimination in the "terms" or "conditions" of plaintiffs' employment; and that (2) plaintiffs have failed to show any "adverse effect" as a result of the tests. It also granted the plaintiffs leave to amend their complaint to show adverse effect.

. . . .

In this case, the term or condition for black employees was undergoing a test for sickle cell trait; for women it was undergoing a test for pregnancy. It is not disputed that the preplacement exams were, literally, a condition of employment: the offers of employment stated this explicitly. Thus, the employment of women and blacks at Lawrence was conditioned in part on allegedly unconstitutional invasions of privacy to which white and/or male employees were not subjected. . . .

The district court also erred in finding as a matter of law that there was no "adverse effect" with respect to the tests as required under § 2000e-2(a)(2). The unauthorized obtaining of sensitive medical information on the basis of race or sex would in itself constitute an "adverse effect," or injury, under Title VII. Thus, it was error to rule that as a matter of law no "adverse effect" could arise from a classification that singled out particular groups for unconstitutionally invasive, nonconsensual medical testing, and the district court erred in dismissing the Title VII claims on this ground as well.

. . . .

Affirmed in Part, Reversed in Part, and Remanded.

NOTES AND QUESTIONS

1. *Norman-Bloodsaw* is *Von Raab* run amuck, isn't it? If you were the attorneys for the laboratories, what defenses would you offer?

2. Note the plaintiffs' theories — Americans with Disabilities Act, right of privacy, California Constitutional privacy, racial discrimination. Why these theories, and what are their relative merits? What of others? For example, isn't there a simple issue of informed consent, or lack thereof? *See infra* § 3.03[1].

3. In testing situations such as *Von Raab* and *Norman-Bloodsaw,* physicians are involved — directly or indirectly — in administering the tests, evaluating results and communicating the outcomes. To whom do their obligations run? To the employees? Employers only? And what do the obligations *include*: just results or advice on needed therapy? Reconsider these questions in §§ 3.02 and 3.03.

4. As attorney for the plaintiffs, how would you describe *what* they lost? How they were injured? How much should they recover in damages? For example, if the results were disclosed to no one, if nobody lost employment or compensation, what is the injury? The measure of damages?

5. Note the defendant, Lawrence Laboratory is a governmental agency, subject to the Fourth Amendment. Suppose it were private? Would that matter?

IN THE INTEREST OF A.V.

849 S.W.2d 393 (1993)

Hopkins, Justice (Retired).

In this post-divorce proceeding, Thomas V. appeals the termination of his parental rights with his daughter, A.V., born June 15, 1984.

. . . .

A.V.'s parents are both therapists; appellant has a master's degree in psychology, and appellee has a Ph.D. in psychology. They were married in 1973, and their daughter, A.V., was born on June 15, 1984. The parties were divorced on May 12, 1987, and appellee was appointed managing conservator of their daughter, A.V., who was then almost three years old. In June 1989, appellee filed a petition seeking to terminate appellant's parental rights, alleging appellant had sexually abused A.V., which conduct endangered the physical and emotional well-being of the child.

After a bench trial, the court found that appellant had engaged in conduct that endangers the physical and emotional well-being of the child, and that termination of the parent-child relationship between appellant and A.V. is in the child's best interest. . . .

Appellant's second and third points of error address the admission into evidence of testimony of a social worker, John Brogden, concerning his interpretation and conclusions based on the results of a penile plethysmography test which was administered to appellant in August 1989 by Robert Powitzky, Ph.D. Dr. Powitzky's two-page report was offered into evidence by appellee, and admitted without objection, as a part of the case file maintained by the Child Protective Services division of the Texas Department of Human Services. Dr. Powitzky did not testify at trial.

Appellee called as a witness John Brogden, a supervisor of a sexual abuse unit with Child Protective Services. Brogden is a certified social worker in the State of Texas, and holds a master's degree in Science and Social Work. He testified that since 1976 he has held many jobs in which he attempted to rehabilitate accused sex offenders. He never interviewed or tested appellant, but stated that he was familiar with the pending investigation concerning alleged abuse of A.V. by appellant. Brogden explained that when he works on a case, he routinely uses a psychologist's interpretative test results of various tests which the psychologist has performed upon the patient, including a penile plethysmography. Brogden testified that in his practice he uses the results of a penile plethysmography to evaluate the absence or presence of deviant arousal in a patient, and to measure whether someone is making progress in treatment.

The following is Brogden's description of how a penile plethysmography is performed:

> Basically it's a plastic tube generally. It feels very sensitive [with a] metallic substance such as mercury, perhaps with cable coming off that. It goes around the man's penis. It runs in the computer software and various designs and then different stimuli are shown to the individual visually and generally orally listen to audio tapes and

> watch slides and calibrations, et cetera are quite complicated actually, but the bottom line is to test arousal and see what someone is turned on to and what they're turned off to.

Over appellant's objections, appellee was permitted to question Brogden about his interpretation of the penile plethysmography which Dr. Powitzky had performed upon appellant. In his report, Dr. Powitzky stated that appellant had been referred to him by appellant's attorney, who requested an evaluation of appellant's personality, specifically regarding allegations of sexual abuse. Dr. Powitzky performed five evaluation techniques: clinical interview; Minnesota Multiphasic Personality Inventory (MMPI); Millon Clinical Multiaxial Inventory (MCMI); Multiphasic Sex Inventory (MSI); and Penile Plethysmography. Dr. Powitzky listed various facts concerning appellant's personal and professional background.

The following portions of Dr. Powitzky's report are relevant to appellant's contention that John Brogden should not have been permitted to testify about Brogden's interpretation of the test results of appellant's penile plethysmography:

> EVALUATION RESULTS:
>
> The results of the psychological inventories and clinical interview indicated that [Thomas V.] is experiencing agitated depression, probably situationally related. He stated that the most stressful part of his situation is that he has always been in positions of trust and helping, and now professional colleagues question his honesty and behavior. There were no indications of sexual pathology.
>
> The Multiphasic Sexual Inventory also revealed no indications of sexual problems. Tom scored in the normal range of social sexual desirability and of sexual knowledge. The plethysmography data revealed no significant arousal to any of the stimuli. His highest individual score was to adult females. Although his actual arousal was not significant, he self-reported moderate arousal only to adult females.
>
> SUMMARY:
>
> The results of [Thomas V.'s] evaluation revealed no sexual or psychological pathology. He was exhibiting acute agitated depression, as a result of the current situation. The plethysmography data revealed no deviant arousal pattern; moreover, there was no significant arousal to any age/sex group. There was a slight, though not significant, trend only for adult females.

In conclusion, no psychosexual evaluation can prove or disprove guilt of any act; however, there were none of the indicators of sexual abuse patterns that one would expect. This evaluation is offered as one component of the overall decision-making process.

Appellant did not object either at trial or on appeal to the introduction into evidence of Dr. Powitzky's report; therefore, we will not address the admissibility of the written report. However, appellant did object that Brogden's interpretation of the penile plethysmography administered by Dr. Powitzky was inadmissible hearsay, and that appellee had not established any predicate for Brogden to testify about a test that he had not conducted. Appellant further objected that the reliability of a penile plethysmography had not been shown. Although the trial judge stated "I do have some concerns about that exam. I really do," she found Brogden's testimony was admissible and overruled appellant's motion to strike the complained of testimony or alternatively to grant a mistrial.

. . . .

Brogden was asked about his opinion that he found an internal inconsistency between appellant's statement to Dr. Powitzky that appellant has a great sex life, and the results of the penile plethysmography which indicate a low flat arousal pattern by appellant. The following dialogue ensued:

> [Guardian Ad Litem:]
>
> Q: Okay. I need for you to explain to me again why there is an inconsistency in the report that Dr. Powitsky [sic] did?
>
> A: A person that's taking a test honestly you will find congruence between the verbal statements about their sexual lives and also the plethysmography results.
>
> In other words the person honestly taking the test will have very similar results. If an individual says I'm primarily interested in adult women, they will find that a significant interest in adult women on the test.
>
> What I find interesting in this one is: I'm having a great sex life. I'm really into [the] women sort of thing. Yet on the test we find basically no significant arousal to any stimuli and no significant difference amongst the stimuli. In other words a low flat pattern.
>
> Q: All right. And it's your testimony that those kinds of facts that are reported in this report are consistent with someone who is not telling the truth?
>
> A: It can be consistent with that, but there is another thing that's often seen in literature. There are two things that are seen in literature. One is the person try [sic] to dissimulate the results. In other words to not peak out. In other words look bad on the test, but the pattern is decreased. Generally so it's a low flat pattern. The person is messing with the test.
>
> Second possibility that is referred to in the literature is particularly targeted incest and that is a common pattern in incest. Very common. This is, in fact, the most common plethysmography pattern with incestuous offenders.
>
> In other words they're not primarily interested in children. One of the major problems is their sexual interest in adult women is too low. So there is very little discrimination when it comes to children and adults. So their preference is certainly not children, but when push comes to shove and things are going bad in life, a kid will do.

. . . .

When asked about Dr. Powitzky's conclusion that the plethysmography data revealed no deviant arousal pattern in appellant, Brogden stated he disagreed with this conclusion and the test does reveal such a pattern. He said:

> If these test results are correct. If there is no dissimulation here, if these are accurate readings on this individual, you have a man in my opinion that needs a lot of help. He must have number one a lower increase arousal to adults definitely. No doubt about that. If this is an honest test. All right. Then I would want to see some lowering of the arousal to children.

. . . .

Responding to questions from the attorney ad litem, Brogden testified regarding the reliability of the test results as follows:

> Q: What is your opinion, if you have one, about whether or not the arousal pattern that shows on a plethysmography is controllable at will by the patient?
>
> A: Plethysmography is perhaps the most manipulable test because someone who is of high intelligence and does some reading you can figure out real easily how to lower arousal. It's not difficult to do.
>
> Q: All right. So would it be fairly easy for someone who is quite educated and intelligent to have a flat pattern if they wanted to?
>
> A: Oh, yes. But there is a distinction there. What happens when people are dissimulating is they lower the arousal but not necessarily change the pattern. That's what's most informative.

In support of his contention that Brogden's testimony about the test results of the penile plethysmography was inadmissible, appellant directs us to several out-of-state criminal cases which comment upon the admissibility of such a test. . . .

. . . .

None of the cited cases directly supports the arguments of either party in the case at bar regarding the weight we should place upon the conflicting expert opinions interpreting the penile plethysmography which Dr. Powitzky administered to appellant. . . .

In the instant case, we have grave reservations whether appellee has established that the penile plethysmography is a reliable test of a person's alleged sexual deviancy, and whether such a test is generally accepted in the scientific community as a valid indicator of sexual preferences or disorders. There was no medical testimony presented on the issue of reliability, and Brogden himself admitted that a person of high intelligence who does some reading can easily manipulate the results of the penile plethysmography. Based upon the record before us, we are unable to conclude that appellee has established the reliability of the penile plethysmography. Therefore, in our review of the sufficiency of the evidence to support the judgment we will not [illegible] weight upon any evidence regarding the results of the penile plethysmography that was administered to appellant.[1]

NOTES AND QUESTIONS

1. The test involved in the case, *In the Interest of A.V.*, has a widespread currency in those areas of the law which are concerned with human motivation, and is oftentimes a condition of probation in cases where the defendant has been convicted of sexually deviant misconduct. As the testimony indicates, the technique of administering the plethysmograph is not well standardized or understood. Nor are the patterns of interpretation or reaction well understood. The basic approach of the law of evidence is to allow evidence to be admitted if it has *any* relevance, leaving the weight to be ascribed for the jury. Does this make sense in this case?

2. The plethysmograph has been challenged in other cases, for example, in *Berthiaume v. Caron*, 142 F.3d 12 (1st Cir. 1998) and *Harrington v. Almy*, 977 F.2d 37 (1st Cir. 1992), as demeaning and degrading to the subject. Is it more so than a stomach pump or the taking of a blood sample? Is it more so than a urine sample? Do *Winston v. Lee* and *Rochin* have relevance here? If you feel a certain squeamishness as we move from routine surgical procedures to procedures which affect reproductive organs, how can the increasing reservations about such testing be expressed? What are the values offended?

3. Or is it that the test is intended to bypass normal psychological defenses and probe directly a person's psyche and sexual predelictions, perhaps to a depth the person himself represses? Are the earlier cases on repressed memory, *supra* §2.02, relevant here?

4. The plethysmograph not only *measures* reactions, but *stimulates* them. Is that a significant difference? Suppose the defendant claims a moral revulsion toward the material shown him? Consider then the relevance of the cases *infra* § 2.04 and § 2.05.

5. Tests such as the plethysmograph, [illegible] must be performed by professionals, frequently physicians, whose ordinary role is that of *helping people.* Yet, in a testing context, they may be seeking evidence to incriminate or convict people or perhaps cause them to lose custody of their children. What are the ethical limitations on such responsibilities? As we shall see in Chapter 3, ordinarily professionals have a fiduciary relationship involving fidelity, candor and care. How is that involved in a case such as *In the Interest of A.V.* ? What relevance does the European Convention have here?

6. Note that here a social worker, John Brogden, testifies about a test administered by another person, Dr. Powitzky, who did not testify.

---

[1] Appellant also compares the unreliability of a penile plethysmography with a polygraph, the results of which are not admissible into evidence in civil suits in Texas. *See Bufkin v. Texas Farm Bureau Mut. Ins. Co.*, 658 S.W.2d 317, 322 (Tex. App. Tyler 1983, no writ); *Pierson v. McClanahan*, 531 S.W.2d 672, 676 (Tex. Civ. App. Austin 1975, writ ref'd n.r.e.). In view of our holding that we will not consider any testimony regarding the penile plethysmography, we need not discuss this aspect of appellant's argument.

Brogden disagreed with Powitzky. Should Brogden have been allowed to testify? If the appellant did not object to the evidence of Powitzky's report, should he then be allowed to object to Brogden? The problems here are not simply hearsay upon hearsay; they are also interpretation *contra* interpretation.

7. The plethysmograph seeks to bypass normal psychological controls by directly testing automatic physiologic responses. It is regarded as scientifically reliable (although barely) in court proceedings. The more conventional test, widely used in industry, is the polygraph, largely excluded by courts, and the subject of the next case.

UNITED STATES v. SCHEFFER

523 U.S. 303 (1998)

I

In March 1992, respondent Edward Scheffer, an airman stationed at March Air Force Base in California, volunteered to work as an informant on drug investigations for the Air Force Office of Special Investigations (OSI). His OSI supervisors advised him that, from time to time during the course of his undercover work, they would ask him to submit to drug testing and polygraph examinations. In early April, one of the OSI agents supervising respondent requested that he submit to a urine test. Shortly after providing the urine sample, but before the results of the test were known, respondent agreed to take a polygraph test administered by an OSI examiner. In the opinion of the examiner, the test "indicated no deception" when respondent denied using drugs since joining the Air Force.

On April 30, respondent unaccountably failed to appear for work and could not be found on the base. He was absent without leave until May 13, when an Iowa state patrolman arrested him following a routine traffic stop and held him for return to the base. OSI agents later learned that respondent's urinalysis revealed the presence of methamphetamine.

Respondent was tried by general court-martial on charges of using methamphetamine, failing to go to his appointed place of duty, wrongfully absenting himself from the base for 13 days, and, with respect to an unrelated matter, uttering 17 insufficient funds checks. He testified at trial on his own behalf, relying upon an "innocent ingestion" theory and denying that he had knowingly used drugs while working for OSI. On cross-examination, the prosecution attempted to impeach respondent with inconsistencies between his trial testimony and earlier statements he had made to OSI.

Respondent sought to introduce the polygraph evidence in support of his testimony that he did not knowingly use drugs. The military judge denied the motion, relying on Military Rule of Evidence 707, which provides, in relevant part:

> "(a) Notwithstanding any other provision of law, the results of a polygraph examination, the opinion of a polygraph examiner, or any reference to an offer to take, failure to take, or taking of a polygraph examination, shall not be admitted into evidence." . . .

Respondent was convicted on all counts and was sentenced to a bad-conduct discharge, confinement for 30 month[illegible] of all pay and allowances, and reduction to the lowest enlisted grade. The Air Force Court of Criminal Appeals affirmed in all material respects, explaining that Rule 707 "does not arbitrarily limit the accused's ability to present reliable evidence."

. . . .

II

A defendant's right to present relevant evidence is not unlimited, but rather is subject to reasonable restrictions. . . .

Rule 707 serves several legitimate interests in the criminal trial process. These interests include ensuring that only reliable evidence is introduced at trial, preserving the jury's role in determining credibility, and avoiding litigation that is collateral to the primary purpose of the trial. The rule is neither arbitrary nor disproportionate in promoting these ends. Nor does it implicate a sufficiently weighty interest of the defendant to raise a constitutional concern under our precedents.

A

. . . .

The contentions of respondent and the dissent notwithstanding, there is simply no consensus that polygraph evidence is reliable. To this day, the scientific community remains extremely polarized about the reliability of polygraph techniques. Some studies have concluded that polygraph tests overall are accurate and reliable. Others have found that polygraph tests assess truthfulness significantly less accurately — that scientific field studies suggest the accuracy rate of the "control question technique" polygraph is "little better than could be obtained by the toss of a coin," that is, 50 percent. . . .

. . . .

The approach taken by the President in adopting Rule 707 [illegible] [illegible] evidence in all military trials — is a rational and proportional means of advancing the legitimate interest in barring unreliable evidence. Although the degree of reliability of polygraph evidence may depend upon a variety of identifiable factors, there is simply no way to know in a particular case whether a polygraph examiner's conclusion is accurate, because certain doubts and uncertainties plague even the best polygraph exams. Individual jurisdictions therefore may reasonably reach differing conclusions as to whether polygraph evidence should be admitted. We cannot say, then, that presented with such widespread uncertainty, the President acted arbitrarily or disproportionately in promulgating a *per se* rule excluding all polygraph evidence.

B

It is equally clear that Rule 707 serves a second legitimate governmental interest: Preserving the jury's core function of making credibility determinations in criminal trials. A fundamental premise of our criminal trial system is that "the jury is the lie detector." . . .

By its very nature, polygraph evidence may diminish the jury's role in making credibility determinations. The common form of polygraph test measures a variety of physiological responses to a set of questions asked by the examiner, who then interprets these physiological correlates of anxiety and offers an opinion to the jury about whether the witness — often, as in this case, the accused — was deceptive in answering questions about the very matters at issue in the trial.[2] Unlike other expert witnesses who testify about factual matters outside the jurors' knowledge, such as the analysis of fingerprints, ballistics, or DNA found at a crime scene, a polygraph expert can supply the jury only with another opinion, in addition to its own, about whether the witness was telling the truth. . . .

C

A third legitimate interest served by Rule 707 is avoiding litigation over issues other than the guilt or innocence of the accused. Such collateral litigation prolongs criminal trials and threatens to distract the jury from its central function of determining guilt or innocence. Allowing proffers of polygraph evidence would inevitably entail assessments of such issues as whether the test and control questions were appropriate, whether a particular polygraph examiner was qualified and had properly interpreted the physiological responses, and whether other factors such as countermeasures employed by the examinee had distorted the exam results. Such assessments would be required in each and every case. . . .

. . . .

DISSENTING OPINION

Justice **Stevens**, dissenting.

. . . .

I

Rule 707 is a blanket rule of exclusion. No matter how reliable and how probative the results of a polygraph test may be, Rule 707 categorically denies the defendant any opportunity to persuade the court that the evidence should be received for any purpose. Indeed, even if the parties stipulate in advance that the results of a lie detector test may be admitted, the Rule requires exclusion.

. . . .

---

[2] The examiner interprets various physiological responses of the examinee, including blood pressure, perspiration, and respiration, while asking a series of questions, commonly in three categories: direct accusatory questions concerning the matter under investigation, irrelevant or neutral questions, and more general "control" questions concerning wrongdoing by the subject in general. The examiner forms an opinion of the subject's truthfulness by comparing the physiological reactions to each set of questions.

. . . Those opinions correctly observe that the rules of evidence generally recognized in the trial of civil and criminal [illegible] federal courts do not [illegible] any blanket prohibition against the admissibility of polygraph evidence.

. . . .

Rule 707 has no counterpart in either the Federal Rules of Evidence or the Federal Rules of Criminal Procedure. Moreover, to the extent that the use of the lie detector plays a special role in the military establishment, military practices are more favorable to a rule of admissibility than is the less structured use of lie detectors in the civilian sector of our society. That is so because the military carefully regulates the administration of polygraph tests to ensure reliable results. The military maintains "very stringent standards for polygraph examiners" and has established its own Polygraph Institute, which is "generally considered to be the best training facility for polygraph examiners in the United States." The military has administered hundreds of thousands of such tests and routinely uses their results for a wide variety of official decisions.

. . . .

The Court's opinion barely acknowledges that a person accused of a crime has a constitutional right to present a defense. . . .

II

. . . Over the years, with respect to category after category, strict rules of exclusion have been replaced by rules that broaden the discretion of trial judges to admit potentially unreliable evidence and to allow properly instructed juries to evaluate its weight. While that trend has included both rulemaking and non-constitutional judicial decisions, the direction of the trend has been consistent and it has been manifested in constitutional holdings as well.

. . . .

III

The constitutional requirement that a blanket exclusion of potentially unreliable evidence must be proportionate to the purposes served by the rule obviously makes it necessary to evaluate the interests on both sides of the balance. Today the Court all but ignores the strength of the defendant's interest in having polygraph evidence admitted in certain cases. As the facts of this case illustrate, the Court is quite wrong in assuming that the impact of Rule 707 on respondent's defense was not significant because it did not preclude the introduction of any "factual evidence" or prevent him from conveying "his version of the facts to the court-martial members." Under such reasoning, a rule that excluded the testimony of alibi witnesses would not be significant as long as the defendant is free to testify himself. But given the defendant's strong interest in the outcome — an interest that was sufficient to make his testimony presumptively untrustworthy and therefore inadmissible at common law — his uncorroborated testimony is certain to be less persuasive than that of a third-party witness. A rule that bars him "from introducing expert opinion testimony to bolster his own credibility," unquestionably impairs any "meaningful opportunity to present a complete defense"; indeed, it is sure to be outcome-determinative in many cases.

. . . .

The question, then, is whether the three interests on which the Government relies are powerful enough to support a categorical rule excluding the results of all polygraph tests no matter how unfair such a rule may be in particular cases.

Reliability

There are a host of studies that place the reliability of polygraph tests at 85% to 90%. While critics of the polygraph argue that accuracy is much lower, even the studies cited by the critics place polygraph accuracy at 70%. Moreover, to the extent that the polygraph errs, studies have repeatedly shown that the polygraph is more likely to find innocent people guilty than vice versa. Thus, exculpatory polygraphs — like the one in this case — are likely to be more reliable than inculpatory ones.

. . . .

. . . Studies indicate that handwriting analysis, and even fingerprint identifications, may be less trustworthy than polygraph evidence in certain cases.[3] . . .

The Role of the Jury

It is the function of the jury to make credibility determinations. In my judgment evidence that tends to establish either a consciousness of guilt or a consciousness of innocence may be of assistance to the jury in making such determinations. That also was the opinion of Dean Wigmore. . . .

---

[3] One study compared the accuracy of fingerprinting, handwriting analysis, polygraph tests, and eyewitness identification. The study consisted of 80 volunteers divided into 20 groups of 4. Fingerprints and handwriting samples were taken from all of the participants. In each group of four, one person was randomly assigned the role of "perpetrator." The perpetrator was instructed to take an envelope to a building doorkeeper (who knew that he would later need to identify the perpetrator), sign a receipt, and pick up a package. After the "crime," all participants were given a polygraph examination.

The fingerprinting expert (comparing the original fingerprints with those on the envelope), the handwriting expert (comparing the original samples with the signed receipt), and the polygrapher (analyzing the tests) sought to identify the perpetrator of each group. In addition, two days after the "crime," the doorkeeper was asked to pick the picture of the perpetrator out of a set of four pictures.

The results of the study demonstrate that polygraph evidence compares favorably with other types of evidence. Excluding "inconclusive" results from each test, the fingerprinting expert resolved 100% of the cases correctly, the polygrapher resolved 95% of the cases correctly, the handwriting expert resolved 94% of the cases correctly, and the eyewitness resolved only 64% of the cases correctly. Interestingly, when "inconclusive" results were included, the polygraph test was more accurate than any of the other methods: The polygrapher resolved 90% of the cases correctly, compared with 85% for the handwriting expert, 35% for the eyewitness, and 20% for the fingerprinting expert. Widacki & Horvath, An Experimental Investigation of the Relative Validity and Utility of the Polygraph Technique and Three Other Common Methods of Criminal Identification, 23 J. Forensic Sciences 596, 596-600 (1978); see also Honts & Perry 365.

. . . .

Collateral Litigation

The potential burden of collateral proceedings to determine the examiner's qualifications is a manifestly insufficient justification for a categorical exclusion of expert testimony. Such proceedings are a routine predicate for the admission of any expert testimony, and may always give rise to searching cross-examination. If testimony that is critical to a fair determination of guilt or innocence could be excluded for that reason, the right to a meaningful opportunity to present a defense would be an illusion.

It is incongruous for the party that selected the examiner, the equipment, the testing procedures, and the questions asked of the defendant to complain about the examinee's burden of proving that the test was properly conducted. While there may well be a need for substantial collateral proceedings when the party objecting to admissibility has a basis for questioning some aspect of the examination, it seems quite obvious that the Government is in no position to challenge the competence of the procedures that it has developed and relied upon in hundreds of thousands of cases.

. . . .

IV

. . . Accordingly, I respectfully dissent.

NOTES AND QUESTIONS

1. In the *Scheffer* case, the polygraph seeks to go directly to a person's automatic reactions, to belie what he seeks to keep secret. He becomes a witness against himself. Is this more or less offensive (if at all) than the plethysmograph?
2. Justice Thomas writes there is no consensus on the validity of polygraph testing, mustering authority for the proposition. So what? Shouldn't that be part of the proof for the fact-finder, to determine weight of evidence and credibility of witnesses?
3. What of the other "legitimate" interests in excluding polygraph testimony — leaving credibility to the jury and avoiding litigation over collateral issues? Are these more problematic with polygraphs than other forms of technical testimony?
4. What of Justice Stevens' point that the military trains polygraph examiners, and uses their service extensively, under the most rigorous of standards? And the concerns which compel exclusion — he argues — have less significance in the military than elsewhere. Are you persuaded that these observations are relevant (even if true)?
5. Suppose the rule in the military were the opposite — polygraphs are to be administered in all cases and the results admitted in all cases?
6. For an excellent article, see Michael J. Elbert, *The Use of Creatinine and Specific Gravity Measurement to Combat Urine Test Dilution*, 61-DEC Fed. Probation 3 (1997); and see Jonathan M. Ettman, *Vernonia*

Case Comment: High School Students Lose Their Rights When They Don Their Uniforms, 13 N.Y.L. Sch. J. Hum. Rts. 625 (1997).

PROBLEM 2-6 — Thermal Imaging

Kyllo and Luanne live in one unit of a triplex and are rumored to grow marijuana, there. Agent Jumbo Bill Elliott of the Federal Bureau of Land Management subpoenas their electric bills, which seem high. He asks Sergeant Danny Haas of the National Guard to use an Agema Thermovision 210 thermal imaging device to examine the house. This device reflects in great detail the differential heat patterns emanating from various objects.

The examination reveals high intensity lights used to grow marijuana. Warrants and a conviction are obtained. Is the use of the Agema Thermovision troublesome? Suppose it also reflected Kyllo and Luanne in their daily activities — regularly having coffee, arguments, and sex? *See United States v. Kyllo*, 140 F.3d 1249 (9th Cir. 1998); *United States v. Cusumano*, 67 F.3d 1497 (10th Cir. 1995); *United States v. Robinson*, 62 F.3d 1325 (11th Cir. 1995); *United States v. Meyers*, 46 F.3d 668 (7th Cir. 1995).

Testing is a part of standard medical treatment, including pregnancy.

It is assumed patient's consent to treatment includes all routine tests. But when the purpose is not treatment, but prosecution, consent may not be implied. Can it be dispensed with if the purpose is public health, or the health of the unborn? The answer has profound implications for individual autonomy, community health, and the doctrine of informed consent.

FERGUSON v. CITY OF CHARLESTON
532 U.S. 67 (2001)

Justice **Stevens** delivered the opinion of the Court.

In this case, we must decide whether a state hospital's performance of a diagnostic test to obtain evidence of a patient's criminal conduct for law enforcement purposes is an unreasonable search if the patient has not consented to the procedure. More narrowly, the question is whether the interest in using the threat of criminal sanctions to deter pregnant women from using cocaine can justify a departure from the general rule that an official nonconsensual search is unconstitutional if not authorized by a valid warrant.

I

In the fall of 1988, staff members at the public hospital operated in the city of Charleston by the Medical University of South Carolina (MUSC) became concerned about an apparent increase in the use of cocaine by patients who were receiving prenatal treatment.[1] In response to this perceived increase, as of April 1989, MUSC began to order drug screens to be performed on urine samples from maternity patients who were suspected of using cocaine. If a

[1] As several witnesses testified at trial, the problem of "crack babies" was widely perceived in the late 1980's as a national epidemic, prompting considerable concern both in the medical community and among the general populace.

patient tested positive, she was then referred by MUSC staff to the county substance abuse commission for counseling and treatment. However, despite the referrals, the incidence of cocaine use among the patients at MUSC did not appear to change.

Some four months later, Nurse Shirley Brown, the case manager for the MUSC obstetrics department, heard a news broadcast reporting that the police in Greenville, South Carolina, were arresting pregnant users of cocaine on the theory that such use harmed the fetus and was therefore child abuse.[2] Nurse Brown discussed the story with MUSC's general counsel, Joseph C. Good, Jr., who then contacted Charleston Solicitor Charles Condon in order to offer MUSC's cooperation in prosecuting mothers whose children tested positive for drugs at birth.[3]

The task force that Condon formed included representatives of MUSC, the police, the County Substance Abuse Commission and the Department of Social Services. Their deliberations led to MUSC's adoption of a 12-page document entitled "POLICY M-7," dealing with the subject of "Management of Drug Abuse During Pregnancy."

The first three pages of Policy M-7 set forth the procedure to be followed by the hospital staff to "identify/assist pregnant patients suspected of drug abuse." The first section, entitled the "Identification of Drug Abusers," provided that a patient should be tested for cocaine through a urine drug screen if she met one or more of nine criteria.[4] It also stated that a chain of custody should be followed when obtaining and testing urine samples, presumably to make sure that the results could be used in subsequent criminal proceedings. The policy also provided for education and referral to a substance abuse clinic for patients who tested positive. Most important, it added the threat of law enforcement intervention that "provided the necessary ' leverage' to make the policy effective." That threat was, as respondents candidly acknowledge, essential to the program's success in getting women into treatment and keeping them there.

The threat of law enforcement involvement was set forth in two protocols, the first dealing with the identification of drug use during pregnancy, and

---

[2] Under South Carolina law, a viable fetus has historically been regarded as a person, in 1995, the South Carolina Supreme Court held that the ingestion of cocaine during the third trimester of pregnancy constitutes criminal child neglect. *Whitner v. South Carolina*, 328 S.C. 1, 492 S.E.2d 777 (1995), cert. denied, 523 U.S. 1145 (1998).

[3] In his letter dated August 23, 1989, Good wrote: "Please advise us if your office is anticipating future criminal action and what if anything our Medical Center needs to do to assist you in this matter." App. to Pet. for Cert. A-67.

[4] Those criteria were as follows:

"1. No prenatal care

"2. Late prenatal care after 24 weeks gestation

"3. Incomplete prenatal care

"4. Abruptio placentae

"5. Intrauterine fetal death

"6. Preterm labor 'of no obvious cause'

"7. IUGR [intrauterine growth retardation] ' of no obvious cause'

"8. Previously known drug or alcohol abuse

"9. Unexplained congenital anomalies."

the second with identification of drug use after labor. Under the latter protocol, the police were to be notified without delay and the patient promptly arrested. Under the former, after the initial positive drug test, the police were to be notified (and the patient arrested) only if the patient tested positive for cocaine a second time or if she missed an appointment with a substance abuse counselor.[5] In 1990, however, the policy was modified at the behest of the solicitor's office to give the patient who tested positive during labor, like the patient who tested positive during a prenatal care visit, an opportunity to avoid arrest by consenting to substance abuse treatment.

The last six pages of the policy contained forms for the patients to sign, as well as procedures for the police to follow when a patient was arrested. The policy also prescribed in detail the precise offenses with which a woman could be charged, depending on the stage of her pregnancy. If the pregnancy was 27 weeks or less, the patient was to be charged with simple possession. If it was 28 weeks or more, she was to be charged with possession and distribution to a person under the age of 18 — in this case, the fetus. If she delivered "while testing positive for illegal drugs," she was also to be charged with unlawful neglect of a child. Under the policy, the police were instructed to interrogate the arrestee in order "to ascertain the identity of the subject who provided illegal drugs to the suspect." Other than the provisions describing the substance abuse treatment to be offered to women who tested positive, the policy made no mention of any change in the prenatal care of such patients, nor did it prescribe any special treatment for the newborns.

II

Petitioners are 10 women who received obstetrical care at MUSC and who were arrested after testing positive for cocaine. Four of them were arrested during the initial implementation of the policy; they were not offered the opportunity to receive drug treatment as an alternative to arrest. The others were arrested after the policy was modified in 1990; they either failed to comply with the terms of the drug treatment program or tested positive for a second time. Respondents include the city of Charleston, law enforcement officials who helped develop and enforce the policy, and representatives of MUSC.

III

Because MUSC is a state hospital, the members of its staff are government actors, subject to the strictures of the Fourth Amendment. *New Jersey v. T. L. O.*, 469 U.S. 325, 335–337 (1985). Moreover, the urine tests conducted by those staff members were indisputably searches within the meaning of the Fourth Amendment. *Skinner v. Railway Labor Executives' Assn.*, 489 U.S. 602, 617 (1989). Neither the District Court nor the Court of Appeals concluded that any of the nine criteria used to identify the women to be searched provided either probable cause to believe that they were using cocaine, or even the basis

[5] Despite the conditional description of the first category, when the policy was in its initial stages, a positive test was immediately reported to the police, who then promptly arrested the patient.

for a reasonable suspicion of such use. Rather, the District Court and the Court of Appeals viewed the case as one involving MUSC's right to conduct searches without warrants or probable cause. Furthermore, given the posture in which the case comes to us, we must assume for purposes of our decision that the tests were performed without the informed consent of the patients.

Because the hospital seeks to justify its authority to conduct drug tests and to turn the results over to law enforcement agents without the knowledge or consent of the patients, this case differs from the four previous cases in which we have considered whether comparable drug tests "fit within the closely guarded category of constitutionally permissible suspicionless searches." In three of those cases, we sustained drug tests for railway employees involved in train accidents, for United States Customs Service employees seeking promotion to certain sensitive positions, and for high school students participating in interscholastic sports, In the fourth case, we struck down such testing for candidates for designated state offices as unreasonable. *Chandler v. Miller*, 520 U.S. 305 (1997).

In each of those cases, we employed a balancing test that weighed the intrusion on the individual's interest in privacy against the "special needs" that supported the program. As an initial matter, we note that the invasion of privacy in this case is far more substantial than in those cases. In the previous four cases, there was no misunderstanding about the purpose of the test or the potential use of the test results, and there were protections against the dissemination of the results to third parties.

In this case, however, the central and indispensable feature of the policy from its inception was the use of law enforcement to coerce the patients into substance abuse treatment. This fact distinguishes this case from circumstances in which physicians or psychologists, in the course of ordinary medical procedures aimed at helping the patient herself, come across information that under rules of law or ethics is subject to reporting requirements, which no one has challenged here.

Respondents argue in essence that their ultimate purpose — namely, protecting the health of both mother and child — is a beneficent one. In *Chandler*, however, we did not simply accept the State's invocation of a "special need." Instead, we carried out a "close review" of the scheme at issue before concluding that the need in question was not "special," as that term has been defined in our cases.

Moreover, throughout the development and application of the policy, the Charleston prosecutors and police were extensively involved in the day-to-day administration of the policy. Police and prosecutors decided who would receive the reports of positive drug screens and what information would be included with those reports. Law enforcement officials also helped determine the procedures to be followed when performing the screens. In the course of the policy's administration, they had access to Nurse Brown's medical files on the women who tested positive, routinely attended the substance abuse team's meetings, and regularly received copies of team documents discussing the women's progress. Police took pains to coordinate the timing and circumstances of the arrests with MUSC staff, and, in particular, Nurse Brown.

While the ultimate goal of the program may well have been to get the women in question into substance abuse treatment and off of drugs, the immediate objective of the searches was to generate evidence *for law enforcement purposes* in order to reach that goal. The threat of law enforcement may ultimately have been intended as a means to an end, but the direct and primary purpose of MUSC's policy was to ensure the use of those means. In our opinion, this distinction is critical. Because law enforcement involvement always serves some broader social purpose or objective, under respondents' view, virtually any nonconsensual suspicionless search could be immunized under the special needs doctrine by defining the search solely in terms of its ultimate, rather than immediate, purpose. Such an approach is inconsistent with the Fourth Amendment. Given the primary purpose of the Charleston program, which was to use the threat of arrest and prosecution in order to force women into treatment, and given the extensive involvement of law enforcement officials at every stage of the policy, this case simply does not fit within the closely guarded category of "special needs."

As respondents have repeatedly insisted, their motive was benign rather than punitive. Such a motive, however, cannot justify a departure from Fourth Amendment protections, given the pervasive involvement of law enforcement with the development and application of the MUSC policy. The stark and unique fact that characterizes this case is that Policy M-7 was designed to obtain evidence of criminal conduct by the tested patients that would be turned over to the police and that could be admissible in subsequent criminal prosecutions.

Accordingly, the judgment of the Court of Appeals is reversed, and the case is remanded for further proceedings consistent with this opinion.

It is so ordered.

Justice **Kennedy**, concurring in the judgment.

. . . .

II

The beginning point ought to be to acknowledge the legitimacy of the State's interest in fetal life and of the grave risk to the life and health of the fetus, and later the child, caused by cocaine ingestion. Infants whose mothers abuse cocaine during pregnancy are born with a wide variety of physical and neurological abnormalities. See Chiriboga, Brust, Bateman, & Hauser, *Dose-Response Effect of Fetal Cocaine Exposure on Newborn Neurologic Function*, 103 Pediatrics 79 (1999) (finding that, compared with unexposed infants, cocaine-exposed infants experienced higher rates of intrauterine growth retardation, smaller head circumference, global hypertonia, coarse tremor, and extensor leg posture). Prenatal exposure to cocaine can also result in developmental problems which persist long after birth. See Arendt, Angelopoulos, Salvator, & Singer, *Motor Development of Cocaine-exposed Children at Age Two Years*, 103 Pediatrics 86 (1999) (concluding that, at two years of age, children who were exposed to cocaine in utero exhibited significantly less fine and gross motor development than those not so exposed); Chasnoff *et al.*, *Prenatal Exposure to Cocaine and Other Drugs: Outcome at Four to Six Years*,

846 Annals of the New York Academy of Sciences 314, 319–320 (J. Harvey and B. Kosofsky eds. 1998) (finding that four to six year olds who were exposed to cocaine in utero exhibit higher instances of depression, anxiety, social, thought, and attention problems, and delinquent and aggressive behaviors than their unexposed counterparts). There can be no doubt that a mother's ingesting this drug can cause tragic injury to a fetus and a child. There should be no doubt that South Carolina can impose punishment upon an expectant mother who has so little regard for her own unborn that she risks causing him or her lifelong damage and suffering. The State, by taking special measures to give rehabilitation and training to expectant mothers with this tragic addiction or weakness, acts well within its powers and its civic obligations.

The holding of the Court, furthermore, does not call into question the validity of mandatory reporting laws such as child abuse laws which require teachers to report evidence of child abuse to the proper authorities, even if arrest and prosecution is the likely result. That in turn highlights the real difficulty. As this case comes to us, and as reputable sources confirm, see K. Farkas, *Training Health Care and Human Services Personnel in Perinatal Substance Abuse, in Drug & Alcohol Abuse Reviews, Substance Abuse During Pregnancy and Childhood,* 13, 27–28 (R. Watson ed. 1995); U.S. Dept. of Health and Human Services, Substance Abuse and Mental Health Services Administration, Pregnant, Substance-Using Women 48 (1993), we must accept the premise that the medical profession can adopt acceptable criteria for testing expectant mothers for cocaine use in order to provide prompt and effective counseling to the mother and to take proper medical steps to protect the child. If prosecuting authorities then adopt legitimate procedures to discover this information and prosecution follows, that ought not to invalidate the testing. One of the ironies of the case, then, may be that the program now under review, which gives the cocaine user a second and third chance, might be replaced by some more rigorous system. We must, however, take the case as it comes to us; and the use of handcuffs, arrests, prosecutions, and police assistance in designing and implementing the testing and rehabilitation policy cannot be sustained under our previous cases concerning mandatory testing.

With these remarks, I concur in the judgment.

Justice **Scalia**, with whom **The Chief Justice** and Justice **Thomas** join as to Part II, dissenting.

There is always an unappealing aspect to the use of doctors and nurses, ministers of mercy, to obtain incriminating evidence against the supposed objects of their ministration — although here, it is correctly pointed out, the doctors and nurses were ministering not just to the mothers but also to the children whom their cooperation with the police was meant to protect. But whatever may be the correct social judgment concerning the desirability of what occurred here, that is not the issue in the present case.

I

It is rudimentary Fourth Amendment law that a search which has been consented to is not unreasonable. There is no contention in the present case that the urine samples were extracted forcibly. The only conceivable bases for saying that they were obtained without consent are the contentions (1) that the consent was coerced by the patients' need for medical treatment, (2) that the consent was uninformed because the patients were not told that the tests would include testing for drugs, and (3) that the consent was uninformed because the patients were not told that the results of the tests would be provided to the police.

Until today, we have *never* held — or even suggested — that material which a person voluntarily entrusts to someone else cannot be given by that person to the police, and used for whatever evidence it may contain. Without so much as discussing the point, the Court today opens a hole in our Fourth Amendment jurisprudence, the size and shape of which is entirely indeterminate. Today's holding would be remarkable enough if the confidential relationship violated by the police conduct were at least one protected by state law. It would be surprising to learn, for example, that in a State which recognizes a spousal evidentiary privilege the police cannot use evidence obtained from a cooperating husband or wife. But today's holding goes even beyond that, since there does not exist any physician-patient privilege in South Carolina. Since the Court declines even to discuss the issue, it leaves law enforcement officials entirely in the dark as to when they can use incriminating evidence obtained from "trusted" sources.

II

I think it clear, therefore, that there is no basis for saying that obtaining of the urine sample was unconstitutional. The special-needs doctrine is thus quite irrelevant, since it operates only to validate searches and seizures that are otherwise unlawful. In the ensuing discussion, however, I shall assume (contrary to legal precedent) that the taking of the urine sample was (either because of the patients' necessitous circumstances, or because of failure to disclose that the urine would be tested for drugs, or because of failure to disclose that the results of the test would be given to the police) coerced. Indeed, I shall even assume (contrary to common sense) that the testing of the urine constituted an unconsented search of the patients' effects. On those assumptions, the special-needs doctrine *would* become relevant; and, properly applied, would validate what was done here.

The conclusion of the Court that the special-needs doctrine is inapplicable rests upon its contention that respondents "undertook to obtain [drug] evidence from their patients" not for any medical purpose, but "*for the specific purpose of incriminating those patients*." In other words, the purported medical rationale was merely a pretext; there was no special need. This contention contradicts the District Court's finding of fact that the goal of the testing policy "was not to arrest patients but to facilitate their treatment and protect both the mother and unborn child." This finding is binding upon us unless clearly erroneous. Not only do I find it supportable; I think any other finding would have to be overturned.

In sum, there can be no basis for the Court's purported ability to "distinguish this case from circumstances in which physicians or psychologists, in the course of ordinary medical procedures aimed at helping the patient herself, come across information that . . . is subject to reporting [illegible] That the *addition* of a law-enforcement-related purpose *to* a legitimate medical purpose destroys applicability of the "special-needs" doctrine. But that is quite impossible, since the special-needs doctrine was developed, and is ordinarily employed, precisely to enable searches *by law enforcement officials* who, of course, ordinarily have a law enforcement objective.

As I indicated at the outset, it is not the function of this Court — at least not in Fourth Amendment cases — to weigh petitioners' privacy interest against the State's interest in meeting the crisis of "crack babies" that developed in the late 1980's. I cannot refrain from observing, however, that the outcome of a wise weighing of those interests is by no means clear. The initial goal of the doctors and nurses who conducted cocaine-testing in this case was to refer pregnant drug addicts to treatment centers, and to prepare for necessary treatment of their possibly affected children. When the doctors and nurses agreed to the program providing test results to the police, they did so because (in addition to the fact that child abuse was required by law to be reported) they wanted to use the sanction of arrest as a strong incentive for their addicted patients to undertake drug-addiction treatment. And the police themselves used it for that benign purpose, as is shown by the fact that only 30 of 253 women testing positive for cocaine were ever arrested, and only 2 of those prosecuted. It would not be unreasonable to conclude that today's judgment, authorizing the assessment of damages against the county solicitor and individual doctors and nurses who participated in the program, proves once again that no good deed goes unpunished.

But as far as the Fourth Amendment is concerned: There was no unconsented search in this case. And if there was, it would have been validated by the special-needs doctrine. For these reasons, I respectfully dissent.

NOTES AND QUESTIONS

1. *Ferguson* finds drug testing violates the Fourth [illegible] purpose was to involve law enforcement to get pregnant women to drug treatment. Would the result be different if results were not disclosed to the police? If the fact of the testing was made known to the patients as a condition of treatment?
2. Also, if the tests were being run on blood samples already drawn in the routine, how is there a "search" for Fourth Amendment purposes? There is no further intrusion on the person and any privacy interest is already foregone. Isn't Justice Scalia, then, correct?
3. In *Ferguson*, the concern was not to prosecute adult patients, but to protect unborn "patients." As to them, there was no criminal prosecutorial purpose. Is that distinction helpful? Tenable? Is this Justice Kennedy's point?
4. More broadly, what of the public health and ethical interests involved here? Drug addiction is a national epidemic. How should society

respond? Doesn't the "special needs" doctrine validate what was done here?

5. And were you surprised to learn that South Carolina does not have physician-patient privilege? If so, is informed consent still required? And, if not, what is the legal basis for Ferguson's complaint?

6. Finally, note that subsequent to *Ferguson* the Supreme Court upheld a school district's requirement of random drug testing of all students engaged in interscholastic competitions. *See Board of Education of Independent School District No. 92 of Pottawatomie County v. Earls*, 536 U.S. 822 (2002). Is that consistent with *Ferguson*?

[3] Genetics, Cloning and Chimeras

The preceding section dealt with bodily integrity and invasion by tests — blood, urine, and psychological, among others. The values at risk are essentially those of privacy and autonomy. Our bodies are the embodiment of our identity and our identities are essential to any system of ethics. What we choose to keep inside is *ours,* it is *private.*

The present section deals with similar concerns, but in a manner *external* to the body. If each of us has an identity worthy of protection, it is because that identity is *ours* — in its individuality, and its uniqueness. Modern bioscience threatens both of those qualities. Genetic engineering may change our composition, prior or subsequent to birth, by insertion of engineered DNA or RNA material into our cells. More radically, exact copies of an individual may be produced by cloning, so that no individual remains — in traditional terms — unique.

These techniques may be combined. Genetic engineering across species may produce "chimeras" — animals having genetic materials and physical or behavioral characteristics of more than one species. Such transgenic creatures already exist, and have already been employed in treating disease in humans. Thus, radically new innovations, in modest ways, have been put to good use. Such transgenic creatures may — potentially, at least — be cloned. A new race might then emerge.

The most dramatic genetic manipulation thus far is cloning of individuals. This was first envisioned in the late 1930s, undertaken with mice in 1981 (from embryo cells), achieved with sheep in 1984, and performed with sheep from adult cells in 1997. That sheep, Dolly, was the only survivor from among 277 eggs fused with adult cells. A variation of the technique was employed to clone two calves, George and Charlie, by adding a gene to cells extracted from a cow's fetus; a nucleus was then removed from an egg and replaced with the nucleus from the altered cell; the egg was incubated, then placed in a surrogate mother. The result is a cow with genes from only the original cell.

Ian Wilmut, the Scottish scientist who produced Dolly, has declared his opposition to cloning humans. In 1998, Congress expressed opposition, President Clinton banned federal funds for human cloning research, and the Food and Drug Administration declared it had authority to ban human cloning.

Beyond reproducing humans, and far more troublesome, is the potential creation of human/animal chimeras. In 1998, scientists at the University of

Wisconsin announced at a meeting in Boston that they had successfully cloned five different species, using the technique employed at the [illegible] Institute in Edinburgh, Scotland (to clone Dolly, a sheep, the first mammal from an adult cell). Other animals prior to Dolly were cloned from embryonic or fetal tissue. The Wisconsin scientists went one step further: they combined different species, producing a chimera. Other firms have cloned transgenic cows, by removing egg nuclei and transferring nuclei, some with the purpose of producing better milk, others to produce human serum albumin. This all suggests that eggs of one species could be used as a universal incubator for cloning any adult mammal cell, including cells of human beings.

Mice, goats, sheep, cows and pigs have already been altered genetically to carry certain human genes; transgenic mice and rats are used for research. The PTO has issued 79 patents on altered animals. The PTO's position on human chimeras is based on an 1817 Circuit Court decision, *Lowell v. Lewis infra* that the "utility" requirement in the 1793 Patent Act has a morality element. A patent could not issue to poison people, promote debauchery, or facilitate private assassination. Until 1977, patents were denied for gambling machines under *Lowell*. The PTO has consistently refused to patent humans, which would violate the Thirteenth Amendment ban on slavery. A "chimera" might have only one human cell — or 99% human cells.

The closest species to humans — monkeys — were cloned by scientists in Oregon in 1997 from embryo cells. Hence — unlike the Scottish sheep, Dolly — they were not identical. But it would be possible to clone eight or more from a single embryo, and these would be identical. Through genetic engineering, the scientists at the Oregon Primate Center say, colonies of identical animals with specific characteristics or diseases could be developed for experimentation.

Not surprisingly, the next step would be to clone an entire human being. A physicist, Richard Steed, in early 1998, claimed the capacity to do this, given the requisite funds — he put the number at ten to thirty million dollars. A storm of controversy followed, with legislation introduced in Congress and a number of state legislatures to ban cloning humans. Senate Bill 1601 introduced by Senators Bond, Frist, Lott and Gregg, would have banned not only cloning of humans, but also cloning technology to treat diseases such as leukemia, diabetes, and Alzheimer's, on the ground that even such techniques require creating an embryo and then using it to repair or generate tissues.

A National Advisory Commission on Bioethics — in a lengthy paper — recommended a moratorium on cloning, as did European bodies. Those materials are excerpted later in this section.

All of this raises profound questions with respect to cloning specifically but also genetic engineering generally:

1) May an altered species or a cloned individual be patented or otherwise "owned"? What may be done pursuant to such ownership?

2) Are cloned individuals or species entitled to respect from the rest of us? In the same manner and degree as noncloned individuals? And are we entitled to respect from them?

3) Consider the conundrum of the *Baby M* and *Davis v. Davis* courts in Chapter 1. Will family law govern cloned humans? What of negligence? Of the fiduciary obligations in the next chapter?

4) And may we "improve" a species? By increasing strength, intelligence, talent, longevity? By imparting consciousness? Fidelity to us? Or — may we do the exact reverse — dumb down a species (say, our own) so the new group is happy doing what the rest of us choose against or refuse to do?

5) In genetically altering a species, what is our obligation to the pre-existing species? Must it be preserved? May it be subordinated to (extinguished by) the new species? Finally — if we are able to do so — may we deliberately extinguish the species which will (in all probability) replace us on the evolutionary scale?

There presently is no single forum for resolving these questions. In other areas of the law, courts or administrative or legislative bodies are actively engaged, setting standards, enforcing duties and assessing liability. Such efforts presently remain in the future for genetic engineering and cloning. The present focus of attention has been in the area of patenting processes. And so these materials will present some of the judicial treatment of genetic engineering, pursuant to the patent provisions of the United States Code, 25 U.S.C. § 101, which provides simply:

§ 101. Inventions patentable

> Whoever invents or discovers any new and useful process, machine, manufacture, or composition of matter, or any new and useful improvement thereof, may obtain a patent therefor, subject to the conditions and requirements of this title.

An early interpretation of § 101 was rendered by Judge — later, Justice — Story, sitting as a federal trial judge in Massachusetts in 1817, in a patent infringement case, *Lowell v. Lewis*. The defendant was represented by Daniel Webster.

LOWELL v. LEWIS

15 F.Cas. 1018 (C.C.D. Mass. 1817)

This was an action on the case for the infringement of a patent-right. March 23, 1813, Mr. Jacob Perkins obtained a patent for a new and useful invention in the construction of pumps, and afterwards assigned his interest therein to the plaintiff [Francis C. Lowell]. The defendant [Winslow Lewis], became the assignee of a similar patent, taken out in 1817, by a Mr. James Baker; and it was for the constructing and vending pumps under this second patent, that the action was brought. The principal object of both the inventions, was, by dispensing with the box used in the common pumps, to obtain a larger water-way.

A great number of witnesses were produced on both sides to sustain these positions.

Story, Circuit Justice (charging jury).

The present action is brought by the plaintiff for a supposed infringement of a patent-right, granted, in 1813, to Mr. Jacob Perkins, (under whom the plaintiff claims by assignment) for a new and useful improvement in the construction of pumps. The defendant asserts, in the first place, that the invention is neither new nor useful; and, in the next place, that the pumps used by him are not of the same construction as those of Mr. Perkins, but are of a new invention of a Mr. Baker, under whom the defendant claims by assignment.

To entitle the plaintiff to a verdict, he must establish, that his machine is a new and useful invention; and of these facts his patent is to be considered merely prima facie evidence of a very slight nature. He must, in the first place, establish it to be a useful invention; for the law will not allow the plaintiff to recover, if the invention be of a mischievous or injurious tendency. The defendant, however, has asserted a much more broad and sweeping doctrine; and one, which I feel myself called upon to negate in the most explicit manner. He contends, that it is necessary for the plaintiff to prove, that his invention is of general utility; so that in fact, for the ordinary purposes of life, it must supersede the pumps in common use. In short, that it must be, for the public, a better pump than the common pump; and that unless the plaintiff can establish this position, the law will not give him the benefit of a patent, even though in some peculiar cases his invention might be applied with advantage. I do not so understand the law. In my judgment the argument is utterly without foundation. All that the law requires is, that the invention should not be frivolous or injurious to the well-being, good policy, or sound morals of society. The word 'useful,' therefore, is incorporated into the act in contradistinction to mischievous or immoral. For instance, a new invention to poison people, or to promote debauchery, or to facilitate private assassination, is not a patentable invention. But if the invention steers wide of these objections, whether it be more or less useful is a circumstance very material to the interests of the patentee, but of no importance to the public. If it be not extensively useful, it will silently sink into contempt and disregard. There is no pretence, that Mr. Perkins' pump is a mischievous invention; and if it has been used injuriously to the patentee by the defendant, it certainly does not lie in his mouth to contest its general utility. Indeed the defendant asserts, that Baker's pump is useful in a very eminent degree, and, if it be substantially the same as Perkins's, there is an end of the objection; if it be not substantially the same, then the plaintiff must fail in his action. So that, in either view, the abstract question seems hardly of any importance in this case.

The next question is, whether Mr. Perkins's pump be a new invention. In the present improved state of mechanics, this is often a point of intrinsic difficulty. It has been often decided, that a patent cannot be legally obtained for a mere philosophical or abstract theory; it can only be for such a theory reduced to practice in a particular structure or combination of parts. In short, the patent must be for a specific machine, substantially new in its structure and mode of operation, and not merely changed in form, or in the proportion of its parts. Mr. Perkins's pump is square, and it is agreed, that a piston exactly fitted, and used as in his pump, cannot be found described in any scientific treatise and has never been seen in operation.

An objection of a more general cast (and which might more properly have been considered at the outset of the cause, as it is levelled against the sufficiency of the patent itself) is, that the specification is expressed in such obscure and inaccurate terms, that it does not either definitely state, in what the invention consists, or describe the mode of constructing the machine so, as to enable skilful persons to make one. The reason of this principle of law will be manifest upon the slightest examination. A patent is grantable only for a new and useful invention; and, unless it be distinctly stated, in what that invention specifically consists, it is impossible to say, whether it ought to be patented or not; and it is equally difficult to know, whether the public infringe upon or violate the exclusive right secured by the patent.

A question nearly allied to the foregoing, is, whether (supposing the invention itself be truly and definitely described in the patent) the specification is in such full, clear, and exact terms, as not only to distinguish the same from all things before known; but 'to enable any person skilled in the art or science, of which it is a branch, or with which it is most nearly connected, to make, compound, and use the same.' Unless, therefore, such a specification was made, as would at all events enable other persons of competent skill to construct similar machines, the advantage to the public, which the act contemplates, would be entirely lost, and its principal object would be defeated.

The manner, in which Mr. Perkins's invention is, in his specification, proposed to be used, is in a square pump, with triangular valves, connected in the centre, and resting without any box on the sides of the pump, at such an angle as exactly to fit the four sides. The pump of Mr. Baker, on the other hand, is fitted only for a circular tube, with butterfly valves of an oval shape, connected in the centre, and resting, not on the sides of the pump, but on a metal rim, at a given angle, so that the rim may not be exactly in contact with the sides, but the valve may be. If from the whole evidence the jury is satisfied, that these differences are mere changes of form, without any material alteration in real structure, then the plaintiff is entitled to recover; if they are substantially different combinations of mechanical parts to effect the same purposes, then the defendant is entitled to a verdict. This is a question of fact, which I leave entirely to the sound judgment of the jury.

Verdict for the defendant.

NOTES AND QUESTIONS

1. Judge Story's comments about morality in the law of patents are unnecessary to the decision in *Lowell v. Lewis*. The pumps at issue did not pose a risk to the public welfare. But Story's comments in 1817 are useful for understanding the intent of the framers of the Constitution and the members of Congress in the late 1700s when they decided to encourage inventiveness by granting exclusive property rights — "patents" — to inventors.
2. The morality component of the patent law has been used, until recent times, to prevent patenting of gambling machines. Might it have been used to preclude patenting birth control devices, such as the Dalkon

Shield in the 1970s? Or RU 486 in the 1980s? Or machines/devices for assisting suicide in one's own home in the 1990s? Or hum[illegible] Or virtual reality computerized prostitution via the Internet in the year 2010?

3. What criteria shall determine when an invention is "moral"? The values of 1797? 1897? 1997? And is it the intended use, or potential for abuse? *How* shall judges *inform* themselves — the problem faced by Justice Frankfurter in *Rochin*? And what if the public is simply wrong-headed; shall a Supreme Court Justice rule the way morality *would* dictate if it were well-informed?

4. Judge Story goes on to consider two other criteria of later importance in patenting genetic inventions: that the invention be new and not already "obvious" from prior development and literature, and that it be described with sufficient clarity as to "enable" a skilled person to build the device from the patent. These requirements pose unique difficulty in the world of biological engineering for the paradoxical reasons that patents at once build upon extensive, pre-existing research from around the world but — at the same time — can be understood by relatively few people — indeed, this may be a hallmark of patentability in bio-science.

5. That raises the issue of whether genetic research is so fundamentally far-reaching, widely shared and coordinated through the Human Genome Project, that patenting and property applications are simply obsolete? *See Moore v. California, infra* § 3.02[1].

6. Genetic engineering is different from the mechanical engineering in *Lowell v. Lewis* in that DNA and RNA and the cellular material providing them are naturally occurring in nature. Unlike the box pump in *Lowell,* genetic proteins are "found," then may be altered and then may be inserted into animal or human cells. The question posed is whether such endeavors, within the language of the statute involve "inventing or discovering" any "new and useful . . . composition of matter"? The Patent and Trademark Office confronted this question in an application for patenting a genetically altered bacterium which could eat oil spills; the PTO [illegible] the application. The Supreme Court reversed, in *Diamond v. Chakrabarty.*

DIAMOND v. CHAKRABARTY*

447 U.S. 303 (1980)

Mr. Chief Justice **Burger** delivered the opinion of the Court.

We granted certiorari to determine whether a live, human-made micro-organism is patentable subject matter under 35 U.S.C. § 101.

I

In 1972, respondent Chakrabarty, a microbiologist, filed a patent application, assigned to the General Electric Co. The application asserted 36 claims

* Citation material has been omitted from this case.

related to Chakrabarty's invention of "a bacterium from the genus Pseudomonas containing therein at least two stable energy-generating plasmids, each of said plasmids providing a separate hydrocarbon degradative pathway." This human-made, genetically engineered bacterium is capable of breaking down multiple components of crude oil. Because of this property, which is possessed by no naturally occurring bacteria, Chakrabarty's invention is believed to have significant value for the treatment of oil spills.

Chakrabarty's patent claims were of three types: first, process claims for the method of producing the bacteria; second, claims for an inoculum comprised of a carrier material floating on water, such as straw, and the new bacteria; and third, claims to the bacteria themselves. The patent examiner allowed the claims falling into the first two categories, but rejected claims for the bacteria. His decision rested on two grounds: (1) that micro-organisms are "products of nature," and (2) that as living things they are not patentable subject matter under 35 U.S.C. § 101. Chakrabarty appealed the rejection of these claims to the Patent Office Board of Appeals, and the Board affirmed the Examiner on the second ground.[1] Relying on the legislative history of the 1930 Plant Patent Act, in which Congress extended patent protection to certain asexually reproduced plants, the Board concluded that § 101 was not intended to cover living things such as these laboratory created micro-organisms.

. . . .

II

The Constitution grants Congress broad power to legislate to "promote the Progress of Science and useful Arts, by securing for limited Times to Authors and Inventors the exclusive Right to their respective Writings and Discoveries." Art. I, § 8, cl. 8. The patent laws promote this progress by offering inventors exclusive rights for a limited period as an incentive for their inventiveness and research efforts.

. . . .

The question before us in this case is a narrow one of statutory interpretation requiring us to construe 35 U.S.C. § 101, which provides:

> "Whoever invents or discovers any new and useful process, machine, manufacture, or composition of matter, or any new and useful improvement thereof, may obtain a patent therefor, subject to the conditions and requirements of this title."

Specifically, we must determine whether respondent's micro-organism constitutes a "manufacture" or "composition of matter" within the meaning of the statute.[2]

[1] The Board concluded that the new bacteria were not "products of nature," because Pseudomonas bacteria containing two or more different energy-generating plasmids are not naturally occurring.

[2] This case does not involve the other "conditions and requirements" of the patent laws, such as novelty and nonobviousness. 35 U.S.C. §§ 102, 103.

III

In [illegible] construction we begin, of course, with the language of the statute. . . .

. . . [T]his Court has read the term "manufacture" in § 101 in accordance with its dictionary definition to mean "the production of articles for use from raw or prepared materials by giving to these materials new forms, qualities, properties, or combinations, whether by hand-labor or by machinery." Similarly, "composition of matter" has been construed consistent with its common usage to include "all compositions of two or more substances and . . . all composite articles, whether they be the results of chemical union, or of mechanical mixture, or whether they be gases, fluids, powders or solids." In choosing such expansive terms as "manufacture" and "composition of matter," modified by the comprehensive "any," Congress plainly contemplated that the patent laws would be given wide scope.

The relevant legislative history also supports a broad construction. The Patent Act of 1793, authored by Thomas Jefferson, defined statutory subject matter as "any new and useful art, machine, manufacture, or composition of matter, or any new or useful improvement . . . [thereof]." The Act embodied Jefferson's philosophy that "ingenuity should receive a liberal encouragement." In 1952, when the patent laws were recodified, Congress replaced the word "art" with "process," but otherwise left Jefferson's language intact. The Committee Reports accompanying the 1952 Act inform us that Congress intended statutory subject matter to "include anything under the sun that is made by man."

This is not to suggest that § 101 has no limits or that it embraces every discovery. The laws of nature, physical phenomena, and abstract ideas have been held not patentable. Thus, a new mineral discovered in the earth or a new plant found in the wild is not patentable subject matter. Likewise, Einstein could not patent his CELEBRATED law that E=mc2 nor could Newton have patented the law of gravity. Such discoveries are "manifestations of . . . nature, free to all men and reserved exclusively to none."

Judged in this light, respondent's micro-organism plainly qualifies [illegible] matter. His claim is not to a hitherto unknown natural phenomenon, but to a nonnaturally occurring manufacture or composition of matter — a product of human ingenuity "having a distinctive name, character . . . [and] use." The point is underscored dramatically by comparison of the invention here with that in Funk. [*Brothers Seed Co. v. Kalo.*] There, the patentee had discovered that there existed in nature certain species of root-nodule bacteria which did not exert a mutually inhibitive effect on each other. He used that discovery to produce a mixed culture capable of inoculating the seeds of leguminous plants. Concluding that the patentee had discovered "only some of the handiwork of nature," the Court ruled the product nonpatentable:

> "Each of the species of root-nodule bacteria contained in the package infects the same group of leguminous plants which it always infected. No species acquires a different use. The combination of species produces no new bacteria, no change in the six species of bacteria, and no enlargement of the range of their utility. Each species has the same

effect it always had. The bacteria perform in their natural way. Their use in combination does not improve in any way their natural functioning. They serve the ends nature originally provided and act quite independently of any effort of the patentee."

Here, by contrast, the patentee has produced a new bacterium with markedly different characteristics from any found in nature and one having the potential for significant utility. His discovery is not nature's handiwork, but his own; accordingly it is patentable subject matter under § 101.

IV

Two contrary arguments are advanced, neither of which we find persuasive.

(A)

The petitioner's first argument rests on the enactment of the 1930 Plant Patent Act, which afforded patent protection to certain asexually reproduced plants, and the 1970 Plant Variety Protection Act, which authorized protection for certain sexually reproduced plants but excluded bacteria from its protection.[3] In the petitioner's view, the passage of these Acts evidences congressional understanding that the terms "manufacture" or "composition of matter" do not include living things; if they did, the petitioner argues, neither Act would have been necessary.

We reject this argument. Prior to 1930, two factors were thought to remove plants from patent protection. The first was the belief that plants, even those artificially bred, were products of nature for purposes of the patent law. The second obstacle to patent protection for plants was the fact that plants were thought not amenable to the "written description" requirement of the patent law. See 35 U.S.C. § 112. Because new plants may differ from old only in color or perfume, differentiation by written description was often impossible.

In enacting the Plant Patent Act, Congress addressed both of these concerns. It explained at length its belief that the work of the plant breeder "in aid of nature" was patentable invention. And it relaxed the written description requirement in favor of "a description . . . as complete as is reasonably possible." 35 U.S.C. § 162. No Committee or Member of Congress, however, expressed the broader view, now urged by the petitioner, that the terms

---

[3] The Plant Patent Act of 1930, 35 U.S.C. § 161, provides in relevant part:

> "Whoever invents or discovers and asexually reproduces any distinct and new variety of plant, including cultivated sports, mutants, hybrids, and newly found seedlings, other than a tuber propagated plant or a plant found in an uncultivated state, may obtain a patent therefor . . . ."

The Plant Variety Protection Act of 1970, provides in relevant part:

> "The breeder of any novel variety of sexually reproduced plant (other than fungi, bacteria, or first generation hybrids) who has so reproduced the variety, or his successor in interest, shall be entitled to plant variety protection therefor . . . ."

84 Stat. 1547, 7 U.S.C. § 2402(a). See generally, 3 A. Deller, Walker on Patents, ch. IX (2d ed. 1964); R. Allyn, The First Plant Patents (1934).

"manufacture" or "composition of matter" exclude living things. . . . The Reports observe:

> "There is a clear and logical distinction between the discovery of a new variety of plant and of certain inanimate things, such, for example, as a new and useful natural mineral. The mineral is created wholly by nature unassisted by man. . . . On the other hand, a plant discovery resulting from cultivation is unique, isolated, and is not repeated by nature, nor can it be reproduced by nature unaided by man. . . ."

Congress thus recognized that the relevant distinction was not between living and inanimate things, but between products of nature, whether living or not, and human-made inventions. Here, respondent's micro-organism is the result of human ingenuity and research. Hence, the passage of the Plant Patent Act affords the Government no support. Nor does the passage of the 1970 Plant Variety Protection Act support the Government's position. As the Government acknowledges, sexually reproduced plants were not included under the 1930 Act because new varieties could not be reproduced true-to-type through seedlings. By 1970, however, it was generally recognized that true-to-type reproduction was possible and that plant patent protection was therefore appropriate. The 1970 Act extended that protection. There is nothing in its language or history to suggest that it was enacted because § 101 did not include living things.

In particular, we find nothing in the exclusion of bacteria from plant variety protection to support the petitioner's position. The legislative history gives no reason for this exclusion. . . . [I]t may reflect the fact that prior to 1970 the Patent Office had issued patents for bacteria under § 101.[4] . . .

(B)

The petitioner's second argument is that micro-organisms cannot qualify as patentable subject matter until Congress expressly authorizes such protection. His position rests on the fact that genetic technology was unforeseen when Congress enacted § 101. From this it is argued that resolution of the patentability of inventions such as respondent's should be left to Congress. The legislative process, the petitioner argues, is best equipped to weigh the competing economic, social, and scientific considerations involved, and to determine whether living organisms produced by genetic engineering should receive patent protection. . . .

. . . .

To buttress his argument, the petitioner, with the support of amicus, points to grave risks that may be generated by research endeavors such as respondent's. The briefs present a gruesome parade of horribles. Scientists, among them Nobel laureates, are quoted suggesting that genetic research may pose a serious threat to the human race, or, at the very least, that the dangers

[4] In 1873, the Patent Office granted Louis Pasteur a patent on "yeast, free from organic germs of disease, as an article of manufacture." And in 1967 and 1968, immediately prior to the passage of the Plant Variety Protection Act, that Office granted two patents which, as the petitioner concedes, state claims for living micro-organisms.

are far too substantial to permit such research to proceed apace at this time. We are told that genetic research and related technological developments may spread pollution and disease, that it may result in a loss of genetic diversity, and that its practice may tend to depreciate the value of human life. These arguments are forcefully, even passionately, presented; they remind us that, at times, human ingenuity seems unable to control fully the forces it creates — that with Hamlet, it is sometimes better "to bear those ills we have than fly to others that we know not of."

It is argued that this Court should weigh these potential hazards in considering whether respondent's invention is patentable subject matter under § 101. We disagree. The grant or denial of patents on micro-organisms is not likely to put an end to genetic research or to its attendant risks. The large amount of research that has already occurred when no researcher had sure knowledge that patent protection would be available suggests that legislative or judicial fiat as to patentability will not deter the scientific mind from probing into the unknown any more than Canute could command the tides. Whether respondent's claims are patentable may determine whether research efforts are accelerated by the hope of reward or slowed by want of incentives, but that is all.

What is more important is that we are without competence to entertain these arguments — either to brush them aside as fantasies generated by fear of the unknown, or to act on them. The choice we are urged to make is a matter of high policy for resolution within the legislative process after the kind of investigation, examination, and study that legislative bodies can provide and courts cannot. That process involves the balancing of competing values and interests, which in our democratic system is the business of elected representatives. Whatever their validity, the contentions now pressed on us should be addressed to the political branches of the Government, the Congress and the Executive, and not to the courts.

. . . .

Accordingly, the judgment of the Court of Customs and Patent Appeals is Affirmed.

Mr. Justice **Brennan**, with whom Mr. Justice **White**, Mr. Justice **Marshall**, and Mr. Justice **Powell** join, dissenting.

I agree with the Court that the question before us is a narrow one. Neither the future of scientific research, nor even, the ability of respondent Chakrabarty to reap some monopoly profits from his pioneering work, is at stake. Patents on the processes by which he has produced and employed the new living organism are not contested. The only question we need decide is whether Congress, exercising its authority under Art. I, § 8, of the Constitution, intended that he be able to secure a monopoly on the living organism itself, no matter how produced or how used. Because I believe the Court has misread the applicable legislation, I dissent.

. . . .

In this case, however, we do not confront a complete legislative vacuum. The sweeping language of the Patent Act of 1793, as re-enacted in 1952, is not the last pronouncement Congress has made in this area. In 1930 Congress enacted the Plant Patent Act affording patent protection to developers of certain asexually reproduced plants. In 1970 Congress enacted the Plant Variety Protection Act to extend protection to certain new plant varieties capable of sexual reproduction. Thus, we are not dealing — as the Court would have it — with the routine problem of "unanticipated inventions." In these two Acts Congress has addressed the general problem of patenting animate inventions and has chosen carefully limited language granting protection to some kinds of discoveries, but specifically excluding others. These Acts strongly evidence a congressional limitation that excludes bacteria from patentability.

First, the Acts evidence Congress' understanding, at least since 1930, that § 101 does not include living organisms. If newly developed living organisms not naturally occurring had been patentable under § 101, the plants included in the scope of the 1930 and 1970 Acts could have been patented without new legislation. Those plants, like the bacteria involved in this case, were new varieties not naturally occurring. Although the Court, rejects this line of argument, it does not explain why the Acts were necessary unless to correct a pre-existing situation. . . .

Second, the 1970 Act clearly indicates that Congress has included bacteria within the focus of its legislative concern, but not within the scope of patent protection. Congress specifically excluded bacteria from the coverage of the 1970 Act. 7 U.S.C. § 2402(a). The Court's attempts to supply explanations for this explicit exclusion ring hollow. It is true that there is no mention in the legislative HISTORY of the exclusion, but that does not give us license to invent reasons. The fact is that Congress, assuming that animate objects as to which it had not specifically legislated could not be patented, excluded bacteria from the set of patentable organisms.

The Court protests that its holding today is dictated by the broad language of § 101, which cannot "be confined to the 'particular application[s] . . . contemplated by the legislators.'" But as I have shown, the Court's decision does not follow the unavoidable implications of the statute. Rather, it extends the patent system to cover living material even though Congress plainly has legislated in the belief that § 101 does not encompass living organisms. It is the role of Congress, not this Court, to broaden or narrow the reach of the patent laws. This is especially true where, as here, the composition sought to be patented uniquely implicates matters of public concern.

NOTES AND QUESTIONS

1. In *Chakrabarty*, the Patent Board affirmed the examiner's rejection of the patent on only the *second* ground (living things are not patentable), not the first (the bacteria were "products of nature"). Apart from problems of statutory interpretation, what is *wrong* with the first ground? Wasn't it accurate? (*See* footnote 1.) *Should* products of nature be appropriated by patent law as the property of a single person?

2. Wasn't the oil-eating bacterium as much a "hitherto unknown natural phenomenon" (and hence unpatentable) as the root-nodule bacteria in *Funk Brothers*? Both are products of nature, previously unknown. Both

can exist independently, as living creatures. Or is the issue that in *Funk,* the bacterium was *already* existing? If so, are we then rewarding Chakrabarty (really, General Electric Corp.) for playing God? Is this what Thomas Jefferson and Congress intended?

3. More broadly the question is — through patent law or otherwise — do we want to encourage the creation of new and different creatures? The issue in *Chakrabarty* did not concern just a *process* of genetic engineering, but a product, claimed as not naturally occurring in nature. Historically, introducing exotic species, whether plants or animals, to vulnerable environments has meant ecological disasters. Should we — by patent law — encourage that risk? How can we, if we choose, discourage it?

4. Note that Congress actually addressed these issues twice, in 1930 and in 1970. Both times Congress granted patent protection to new varieties of plants, but not bacteria, such as those involved in *Chakrabarty.* The dissent by Justice Brennan makes this argument. Who has the more tenable view — the majority or the minority? How *should* Congress legislate with respect to wholly new organisms — plant or animal? Note the Court's passing reference to the concerns expressed to it by leading scientists; what might those concerns be?

5. Much of the litigation subsequent to *Chakrabarty* has not been about wholly new organisms (there are now, for example, patents on lines of mice for laboratory research), but about patent infringement claims concerning genetically altered or constructed material for treatment of diseases and conditions. In these, the policy issues are often obscured. They are somewhat better illuminated in the following case, *Foundation on Economic Trends v. Bowen*, where the plaintiffs insist that before the federal government may fund AIDS research and cancer research involving cloning HIV and cancer genes into bacteria or animals, it must file environmental impact statements.

FOUNDATION ON ECONOMIC TRENDS v. BOWEN

722 F. Supp. 787 (D.D.C. 1989)

Revercomb, District Judge.

The plaintiffs have sued the chiefs of various federal government entities to enjoin the National Institute of Health (NIH) from supporting any research involving various aspects of genetic, AIDS, and cancer research until NIH completes an Environmental Impact Statement (EIS) on the research, pursuant to the National Environmental Policy Act (NEPA), 42 U.S.C. § 4332. . . .

I. The Current Legal Standards

NEPA requires the federal government to create a "detailed" statement on all "major Federal actions significantly affecting the quality of the human environment." Such a statement must discuss:

(i) the environmental impact of the proposed action,

(ii) any adverse environmental effects which cannot be avoided should the proposal be implemented

. . . .

Such statements are to be made available to the public, id., and are designed to inform the governmental policy-makers and the public about the environmental effects of action undertaken with governmental support.

Once an agency has completed an EIS on a major federal action, the agency must supplement the EIS if (1) the agency makes substantial changes to the action that changes the environmental impact, or (2) there are "significant new circumstances or information relevant to environmental concerns and bearing on the proposed action or its impacts." . . .

There is no hard-and-fast rule regarding when there are significant enough new circumstances to require a new EIS. It is clear to the Court, however, that an agency should not have to generate an EIS every time a researcher develops a new project — such a requirement would be oppressively burdensome and would effectively prevent a tremendous amount of research from going forward. Rather, a supplementary EIS should be required when new developments have so increased the effects and risks to the environment that the old EIS does not properly address them. It is safe to say, then, that a supplementary EIS should not be required when there are new developments in a field of research that scientists believe either have less effect than preceding research or that reveal that the field of research is likely to have less effect on the environment than originally estimated.

The NIH in 1976 published detailed Guidelines on NIH-sponsored DNA research. The Guidelines set standards for safety and environmental protection in DNA research, including physical containment of particular experiments, and discouraged certain experiments. They also established groups to review research and determine whether the Guidelines were being followed properly.

In 1977, NIH published the final draft of an EIS on the 1976 Guidelines after accepting public comments. The statement evaluated the likely consequences of research under the Guidelines and concluded that although following the Guidelines would guard against many possible environmental harms, they would not and could not guarantee that rDNA research would be free from all risk. The EIS also stated that the Guidelines should remain flexible in order to take account of new biological developments and new evaluations of the environmental impact of certain research.

. . . .

In the years after the formulation of 1976 Guidelines, the experts at NIH determined that the initial level of concern over the dangers of DNA research was too high, and that some relaxation of the Guidelines was warranted. This conclusion was based on the fact that there had been little or no environmental harm caused by DNA research and that additional research showed that DNA did not pose the level of risk that was once feared. The Guidelines thus have been relaxed somewhat nearly each year since 1976, most recently in 1987. The defendants' position is that there is no need for a new EIS on the revised

Guidelines because both the new scientific evidence and the excellent environmental record of rDNA research so far prove that the environmental impact of rDNA research is likely to be less than expected in 1977.

II. The Standard of Review

The Court reviews the decision of an agency that an EIS is not necessary under the deferential "arbitrary or capricious" test, which essentially means that the Court cannot "second-guess" the agency unless it has acted unreasonably. The Court must give a hard and thorough look at the evidence presented to it on the record. Nonetheless, the Court thus must uphold scientific evaluations and conclusions by an agency if the decision was a reasonable one, even if there are good — or even, in the Court's opinion, slightly more convincing — arguments made on the other side.

III. The Plaintiff's Challenges

It is settled that NIH approval of experiments involving DNA constitute "major federal action" under NEPA and thus is subject to the EIS requirement when appropriate. The plaintiffs in this case allege that certain research and experimentation approved by NIH in the years after the 1977 EIS have triggered the requirement of an EIS supplement, but that NIH has failed to create such a supplement.

The plaintiffs disagree that the 1977 EIS is legally sufficient under NEPA to cover all current DNA research conducted under the auspices of NIH since 1977. Specifically, plaintiffs argue that there are three new areas of research and experimentation that were not evaluated by the 1977 EIS: (1) the ability to clone oncogenes into bacteria using shuttle vectors; (2) the cloning of the HIV (human immunodefiency virus); and (3) the engineering of genetic codes of AIDS (acquired immune deficiency syndrome) into animal species. On each of these three broad points, the Court concludes that it is reasonable to maintain that the new developments are not so significant in their likely impact on the environment that a new EIS is necessary.

A. Oncogenic Cloning

The first area of debate is over the purported new development of the ability to clone oncogenic — i.e., tumor-causing — viruses into bacteria by using shuttle vectors. Vectors are DNA molecules used to introduce foreign DNA into a cell. The plaintiffs fear that this ability could lead to a situation in which oncogenic viruses entered into E. coli could reproduce, causing danger to other organisms.

The defendants argue persuasively, however, that the ability to clone oncogenic viruses using shuttle vectors does not create any greater risk or harm than cloning using other methods. Indeed, in 1978 NIH published an Environmental Assessment (EA) on changes in oncogenic research. Noting that the new Guidelines removed the ban on research involving oncogenic viruses classified as moderated risk, the EA stated that the change would not have a significant environmental impact and that cloning oncogenic viruses posed a "conceivable" but "unlikely" biohazard. The principles of basic molecular biology provide that it is virtually impossible f[illegible] generate an oncogenic virus. This conclusion, and the decision to remove the ban on research involving oncogenic viruses, resulted from an in-depth analysis that included a series of workshops attended by experts from all over the world, various reviews of the workshop conclusions, examination of the guidelines of other countries, hours of public hearings, and various public and scientific comment.

The new technique of using shuttle vectors is still the use of gene or DNA segments and therefore does not increase the risk beyond that was evaluated carefully by the EA in 1978. The Court concludes that there was substantial evidence and that it was reasonable to conclude that the new oncogenic cloning research does not require a supplementary EIS.

B. Cloning the HIV Virus

The second area of new research and experimentation identified by plaintiffs is the ability to genetically engineer the HIV virus into HeLa cells and other types of cells not normally susceptible to HIV. Because these HeLa cells would for the first time be a host to the HIV virus, the plaintiffs argue, this new development would increase the risk of environmental harm.

The defendants note, however, that the new capabilities *do not* extend the host range of the HIV virus. Making HeLa cell lines — which are human cell lines — susceptible to the HIV virus does not put any new species at greater risk, the defendants point out, because humans are already susceptible to HIV and AIDS. Because the practical effect of the development does not appear to pose any serious additional threat, the Court concludes that it reasonable [sic] not to require a supplement to the EIS for this research.

C. Transgenic Experimentation

Finally, the third area of research and experimentation about which the plaintiffs allege that the government has failed to provide adequate environmental impact statement concerns the engineering of the genetic code for viruses causing human disease in other animals. This transgenic research, the plaintiffs claim, has the potential for serious harm should these animals enter man's environment. Particularly, the plaintiffs point to current experimentation at NIH in which the AIDS DNA has been placed in mice.

NIH approved the mice/AIDS experimentation pursuant to the NIH Guidelines. NIH concluded that if the experimentation was controlled using the highest safety level under the Guidelines, there would be no chance that any of the mice could escape the contained environment.

The plaintiffs argue that NIH is legally required to prepare a supplementary EIS to set forth and assess the possible environmental impact of the experiment and other similar experiments. NIH is in the process, however, of working on amendments to its Guidelines regarding the use of transgenic animals. As part of the Guideline amendments, NIH is preparing an environmental assessment (EA). The Court concludes that this EA should satisfy the legal requirements of NEPA.

The Court also concludes that NIH is acting reasonably in permitting the mice/AIDS experimentation to go forward while the EA is being prepared. First, the Court notes that although the AIDS virus was discovered after the original NIH EIS was published in 1977, the mere existence of a new disease that is being researched does not mean that the analyses, safeguards, and assessments of previous environmental evaluations are worthless.

Second, even if the mice/AIDS research does raise new environmental concerns and problems that have not been addressed satisfactorily to the requirements of NEPA, the Court concludes that the proper legal solution is to await the creation of the EA by NIH, instead of enjoining the mice/AIDS research.

NIH has presented persuasive evidence that mice/AIDS experimentation poses only the smallest possible risk to the environment. Under the highest-level containment pursuant to the NIH Guidelines, the mice are stored in "glove box" — a completely sealed unit with built-in gloves for handling the mice without having to open the box. The mice area is surrounded by a Clorox-filled dunk tank designed to stop the mice. Even if a mouse somehow did escape the unit, it would then have to work its way out of the high-level contained laboratory, which contains mouse traps, and a screen door to enable scientists to examine the area before entering. The defendant states that each of the safety features is inspected once every 10 days.

NIH also has guarded against the harm to humans should the mice somehow escape the laboratory building altogether. The mice have been blinded, to prevent their escape and to put them at a selective disadvantage in the wild. Mice injected with the viral DNA while still in embryo have all died before reaching sexual maturity. Finally, the AIDS virus has not been found in the saliva or the urine of the mice — making further remote the possibility that a mouse biting a human or an escaping mouse could spread the AIDS virus.

In sum, the Court does not subscribe completely to the argument that because the mice are not released to the general environment there is no environmental impact. The Court realizes that the environmental impact of an experiment or research should be judged while considering the possibility that the experiment could affect the environment, as well as the expected impact. In the NIH's mice/AIDS experimentation, the Court concludes that the EA currently being created appears to satisfy the requirements of NEPA, and that the proven very low possibility of any environmental impact before the EA is complete justifies not enjoining NIH from continuing to sponsor the research pending the publication of the EA.

The defendants' motion for summary judgment is granted.

NOTES AND QUESTIONS

1. Do you suppose that the authors of the National Environmental Policy Act *intended* it to cover research funded by NIH into genetic, AIDS and cancer concerns? Why or why not?
2. The issues involved in the *Bowen* case are important, concerning the cloning of oncogenic viruses into bacteria, genetically engineering the

HIV virus into HeLa cells and the engineering of genetic virus codes [illegible] experiment. The Court says that these matters are either covered or will be covered by environmental assessment reports or, in the instance of HIV, pose no *additional* threat. Are you persuaded? If not, is it because the Court has not done its job or is ill-equipped to do the job assigned to it?

3. If the Court had been persuaded that NIH had not submitted appropriate filings under NEPA, what would those filings look like? What *should* an agency such as NIH do in areas such as these? Would it, in your judgment, simply be better to ban such research?
4. Is NIH, as it supports research of a transgenic nature, undertaking the risk undertaken in the 1800s, when communities introduced new animals or species from elsewhere ("exotics"), to control native species, only to find the newly introduced animals (or plants) created a far greater danger than the preexisting problem?
5. And what are the limits of the experimentation funded by NIH? Funding for research on fetal material was banned in the 1970s and 1980s, only to be resumed in the 1990s. *See* § 4.02[3] *infra*. What of cloning of humans? Should such experimentation be banned? Funded? The subject of EIS? See below for some views on these subjects.
6. On a somewhat different note, should we be concerned for the mice into whom the AIDS virus is inserted? Most die as embryos; the rest are blinded and imprisoned. Are there ethical concerns in such acts?
7. The preceding cases raised the question of how government might control patent, research and appropriation of knowledge for product making purposes. Would tort law help? We will now turn to this question in the next case, *Miles v. Scripps Clinic*.
8. But before so doing, what might an EIS look like if NIH should ever fund research leading to development of a human chimera?

MILES, INC. v. SCRIPPS CLINIC AND RESEARCH FOUNDATION

810 F. Supp. 1091 (S.D. Cal. 1993)

Rhoades, District Judge.

I. Statement of Facts

A. The Parties

Scripps-Miles, Inc. ("Scripps-Miles") was a corporation jointly owned by Plaintiff Miles, Inc. ("Miles"), a pharmaceutical company, and Defendant Scripps Clinic and Research Foundation ("Scripps"), a non-profit research foundation. One purpose of forming the corporation was to prepare and sell immunochemical materials. . . .

. . . .

C. The Technology

This case concerns monoclonal antibodies. The antibodies at issue in this case were used by Dr. Zimmerman to create a purified Factor VIII:C. Factor VIII:C is a substance that permits a hemophiliac's blood to clot. Without Factor VIII:C, hemophiliacs run great risks of blood loss. Purified Factor VIII:C serves its vital function without risk of transmitting AIDS or hepatitis through treatment.

Dr. Zimmerman provided the Scripps-Miles Monoclonal Laboratory with the antigen that eventually led to the production of cell line 2.2.9 — the cell line at issue in this suit. A cell line is "a clone or a population of identical cells, derived from a single cell." "Created through genetic engineering, cell lines produce cells capable of continuous culture, immortalizing the rare and valuable qualities of a particular cell." Dr. Zimmerman later used cell line 2.2.9 to develop a patented process of purifying Factor VIII:C. Dr. Zimmerman assigned his patent rights to Scripps, which later licensed the rights to Armour and Revlon.

D. Other Facts and Allegations

In 1982, Scripps-Miles, Inc. adopted a plan of dissolution and Miles received ownership of the Monoclonal Lab. Dr. Zimmerman and Scripps continued to use cell line 2.2.9, published articles on the purification of Factor VIII:C through monoclonal antibodies, and obtained a patent for the process of producing Factor VIII:C. Dr. Zimmerman assigned the patent to Scripps, who licensed the patent exclusively to Armour and Revlon. Revlon later sold Armour to Rorer.

Plaintiff alleges that prior to the Scripps-Miles dissolution, Scripps conspired with Dr. Zimmerman and Nakamura to transfer the right to commercialize the cell line to Scripps. Plaintiff further contends that the transfers of the cell line itself from Dr. Zimmerman to Armour and Revlon, and later to Rorer, were inconsistent with Miles's ownership interest in the right to commercialization of the cell line. Plaintiffs further contend that Defendants Scripps, Dr. Zimmerman, and Nakamura breached a fiduciary duty, committed acts of deceit and fraudulent concealment, and committed actual fraud.

. . . .

II. Discussion

A. Conversion

All Defendants allege that California does not recognize an action for conversion of the "right to commercialize" a cell line. I agree. . . .

Under California law, the elements of a conversion claim are (1) plaintiff's ownership or right to possession of the property at the time of the conversion; (2) defendants' conversion by a wrongful act or dispossession of plaintiff's property rights; and (3) damages. The first of these elements is at issue in this case.

Plaintiff agrees that the conversion claim is not as to the cell line itself. [illegible] Defendants. . . . That Dr. Zimmerman physically was given cell line 2.2.9 is not relevant here; the "property" at issue is the intangible right to commercialize the cell line, not the cell line itself.

The claim of conversion here relates to an intangible right — a kind of property not traditionally considered capable of being converted. Generally, California law only recognizes "conversion of intangibles represented by documents, such as bonds, notes, bills of exchange, stock certificates, and warehouse receipts." Ordinarily, there can be no conversion of the goodwill of a business, trade secrets, a newspaper route, or a laundry list of customers.

. . . .

The commercialization of a cell line is an interest capable of precise definition. First, it is undisputed that a cell line is patentable subject matter under 35 U.S.C. § 101. Second, under 35 U.S.C. § 271, the holder of a patent may enforce the exclusive rights flowing from the sale or use of the patentable invention. Thus, using patents as an analogy, the interest at stake here — making money from the commercialization of a cell line — is capable of precise definition.

. . . .

Since cell lines may be patented, and since a patent provides the patent holder with exclusive possession or control of the right to exploit the patent for financial gain, the right to commercialize a cell line is, by analogy, also capable of exclusive possession or control. The contract analogy also demonstrates that the interest in commercialization is capable of exclusive possession or control, since contracts are often used to protect similar interests in reaping commercial rewards from biomedical technology.

. . . .

3. California Approach to Conversion of Cell Lines

The California Supreme Court recently analyzed the issue of conversion of cell lines in *Moore v. Regents of University of California*, (*infra*, § 3.02):

> Thousands of human cell lines already exist in tissue repositories, such as the American Type Culture Collection and those operated by the National Institutes of Health and the American Cancer Society. . . . Since the patent office requires the holders of patents on cell lines to make samples available to anyone, many patent holders place their cell lines in repositories to avoid the administrative burden of responding to requests. At present, human cell lines are routinely copied and distributed to other researchers for experimental purposes, usually free of charge.

The *Moore* court also noted that exchange of cell lines is "increasingly limited by contract" as "a result of concerns over patent and ownership rights." In refusing to extend California law of conversion to cell lines, the Moore court denied that Moore had a property interest in the cells from his removed spleen.

The instant case is distinguishable because Plaintiff does have a property interest in the right to commercialization of the cell line. However, it is not uncommon for a person to have an intangible property right without a cause of action in conversion to protect that right. . . .

California has not recognized a cause of action for conversion of the intangible right to commercialization of a cell line and this Court refuses to extend California conversion law. Instead, this Court follows California's trend of rejecting new theories of tort liability based on contracts, especially when such decisions are more appropriately the subject of legislative deliberation and resolution. Here, Plaintiff is essentially asserting a breach of contract claim. Had the contract claim been brought in a timely manner, the conversion claim would have been unnecessary. Now, Plaintiff seeks to attach a tort action to an expired contract claim. This Court refuses to create a new cause of action under California law.

. . . .

4. Policy Implications After Moore

In *Moore*, *supra*, the California Supreme Court addressed the issue of the rights of a human donor whose cells, through research and experimentation, were eventually engineered to create a profitable drug.

Moore involved the creation of a cell line using cells from plaintiff's diseased spleen, which was removed by defendant out of medical necessity. Although defendant knew of the possible commercial value of the cells before they were removed, plaintiff was never notified of defendant's use of the cells from his spleen. The Moore defendants developed a cell line from plaintiff's cells and received a patent covering the cell line and various methods for using the cell line for commercially valuable medical procedures.

. . . .

According to the *Moore* court, extending conversion law into this area would threaten the economic incentive to conduct important medical research. "If the use of cells in research is a conversion, then with every cell sample a researcher purchases a ticket in a litigation lottery."

. . . .

The *Moore* court's concerns that permitting conversion actions for cell line use are only partially related to the instant case. Whereas the Moore plaintiff supplied the raw cells that eventually led to the development of a cell line, here the cell line is the starting point. Thus, Justice Arabian's policy concern that courts may overstep the limits of their competency in fashioning a remedy is not implicated here. No human donor is involved in the analysis at this level of medical research. For this reason, the Moore court's discussion of California's Health and Safety Code is likewise inapplicable here. Furthermore, the chilling effect on medical research that the Moore court feared is not identical here since the parties developing the cell lines are sophisticated researchers capable of protecting themselves legally, not patients who may be unaware of the economic uses for discarded body parts.

The expansion of conversion law into this realm could, however, implicate [illegible] Currently, a regime exists under which readily available cell lines are protected by contract or patent law and parties are on notice of possible claims on ownership and control. If these "protections" were expanded to include the strict-liability tort of conversion, then the threat of conversion actions would take away a measure of reliability of source materials and could create a chilling effect on research. The threat of a conversion action would thereby impose a duty of investigation on all subsequent users of cells and cell lines. Researchers would need to determine the "consensual pedigree" of cell lines before beneficial research could be conducted. "Title insurance companies" for cell lines could become the norm. This costly result would add an entirely new procedural dimension to important medical research; time and money would necessarily be diverted to fund the search efforts for ownership rights. This result is unwarranted. Furthermore, it is beyond the competence of this Court to extend California's conversion law, to create a new cell-registry regime. Such a result is better left to the California Legislature.

Plaintiff raises a counter policy consideration, one that was raised in Rasmussen: Since the starting point in this action is with a human-engineered product (and not simply a naturally occurring cell), the opposite chilling effect could result. If entrepreneurs are not permitted the exclusive right to profit from their developments, then inventors will be less likely to invest the necessary time, money and energy into innovation. . . .

While this economic consideration of profit motive is a valid concern, even devotees of Ayn Rand could not dispute that the available protections provide adequate profit incentives for inventors. Patent and contract law already protect the financial incentives for development of new technologies. No disincentive to ingenuity is created by the absence of a conversion cause of action. . . .

. . . .

5. Conclusion

[illegible] a property right which is deserving of protection. The protections for that right, however, are not found in an action for conversion. Under existing California law, there is no cause of action for conversion for commercialization of a cell line and strong policy considerations weigh against expanding the conversion cause of action. This Court refuses to extend California law to impose liability — especially a strict-liability tort — for conversion of this type of property.

. . . .

NOTES AND QUESTIONS

1. The Court finds a property interest in *Miles* in the right to "commercialize" a cell line. Why, then, does it deny a remedy for breach or interference with that right? The contract remedy is barred by the statute of limitations, but wouldn't a tort remedy encourage care and consideration, of a fiduciary nature? Wouldn't that be desirable?

2. Is this case similar to *Moore*, *infra* § 3.02, where a patient's spleen was fraudulently appropriated by his physicians to develop a cancer-fighting cell line? Here, there is no doctor-patient relationship, but there *is* a clear *property* relationship. Why, then, does Mr. Moore win, but Miles, Inc. lose?

3. What of the policy analysis? *Would* granting a conversion claim discourage research? In *Moore*? Here? Is advancement of research better left — as the Court concludes — exclusively to patent and contract law — with shorter statutes of limitations than conversion?

4. Gene patenting, like patenting of life forms in *Chakrabarty*, raises profound questions. Eliminating disease is one thing; "improving" an existing species is quite another; and acquiring an exclusive property right either in the mechanism of improvement or the improvement itself raises concern to yet a higher level. Is trepidation at this level warranted? Truly, is there some point at which humanity comes close to playing at God?

   Consider the comments of Mark Hanson, *Religious Voices in Biotechnology: the Case of Gene Patenting*,*

   > In addition, assertions by critics of patenting that genes are the common heritage of humanity place genetic material in a further category of things that cannot be owned, namely, as Andre notes, when "the use of some things cannot be confined to any individual or group" (p.33). So even if patenting does not confer ownership, Andre's analysis helps illustrate the sense people may have that certain things, by their nature, may be inappropriate subjects of any sort of proprietary discourse, including patenting. Use of the term *ownership* by critics serves to make this point more sharply in public rhetoric.
   >
   > The second set of claims on which the ownership objection depends relates to the issue of sovereignty. Because of the special status of living things generally, and human beings especially, as created recipients of the gift of life, they are necessarily in relationship with the Creator. According to the critics, the creator's sovereignty over the creation is such that human beings may be thought of as "owned" by God, such that certain other forms of "ownership" are inappropriate.
   >
   > What would it mean to be owned by God? The view that God's ownership entails a right to use, dispose, or alter any thing, and also to prohibit such activity by others, would be consistent with a narrow conception of ownership as well as certain (but not all) doctrines of God. But clearly, to be owned by God could not be strictly analogous to the relationship that human beings have with things that they own. While one might believe that all things "belong" to God, most religious traditions understand God to have given life as a gift to living creatures, and the rest of creation as

gifts to be shared among creatures. Jewish and Christian traditions also believe that human beings have been given dominion over the rest of creation, within which they have established various systems of ownership.

So how might God's ownership be more accurately understood? Protestant theologian Ronald Cole-Turner argues that

> God's ownership of all things is best understood as God's reserving the right to define their purpose, value, and relationship to other creatures. God owns the land, not to exclude creatures from it, but to give it for their use and to set the limits of proper use and care.
>
> . . . Human beings may own individual animals and plants, and their components may be bought, sold, and used for food. That is, we may own these things as long as God's prior claim of ownership is acknowledged, as long as we own them in a way that is consistent with God's definition of their purpose. It is wrong to own any of these things in a way that denies God's prior ownership.

Cole-Turner does not believe that patenting itself could violate this sense of God's ownership — although certain forms of genetic engineering, such as the Harvard oncomouse, would.

I believe his conclusion to be correct.

. . . .

Similarly, the ownership objection may offer critics of biological parents a way to assert that patents, as claims or corporate control, symbolize a denial of the sovereignty of God over life and those processes involved in its creation and modification. This may be how patents link up with what defenders believe is the deeper motivation for critics, namely, objection to biotechnologies themselves. Biotechnology does involve the hand of humanity in the creation and modification of life forms in a way that is more direct and efficient than more so called natural processes, such as breeding. In short, it is one thing to be fruitful and multiply; it is another to be fruitful and modify. To claim this latter sort of power, the critics might assert, is to act *as if* one owned what is being manipulated.

Even though a patent does not legally entail usage rights, it claims for the patent holder a sovereignty over the information that enables the exercise of such power. In this sense, intellectual property rights may be more offensive to critics than full ownership rights. For example, the counter argument to the ownership objection has been that human beings own all sorts of living things, such as mules. Land and Mitchell invoke Leon Kass's argument in response that "It is one thing to own a mule; it is another to own *mule*." The sense of species ownership invoked here is not the same as would apply if a person legally owned every mule in existence. Rather, what is objectionable is the intellectual property claim to sovereignty over the ideas, that enable control over the creation of an entire and *uniquely created* species. The religious offense at the sovereignty implied by the "ownership" of these sorts of ideas — even for a limited time — is part of what the ownership objection is likely capturing. This argument, however, is obviously more powerful and relevant to the patenting of entire life forms than to genes or body parts.

5. There was a fiduciary claim in *Miles*, as there had been in *Moore*, where it prevailed. How should it have been resolved in *Miles*?
6. This section began with a brief note, summarizing recent developments in genetic manipulation, particularly human cloning. We now close with that subject. In 1997, President Clinton appointed a commission to look into the subject of human cloning. That commission was to report in 90 days. Recall here the five questions raised at the beginning of the section. How well does the Advisory Commission respond?

What follows is the executive summary of that Report and some of the critical commentary it provoked.

Cloning Symposium

*Report and Recommendations of the National Bioethics Advisory Commission: Cloning Human Beings**

The idea that humans might someday be cloned — created from a single somatic cell without sexual reproduction — moved further away from science fiction and closer to a genuine scientific possibility on February 23, 1997. On that date, *The Observer* broke the news that Ian Wilmut, a Scottish scientist, and his colleagues at the Roslin Institute were about to announce the successful cloning of a sheep by a new technique which had never before been fully successful in mammals. The technique involved transplanting the genetic material of an adult sheep, apparently obtained from a differentiated somatic cell, into an egg from which the nucleus had been removed. The resulting birth of the sheep, named Dolly, on July 5, 1996, was different from prior attempts to create identical offspring since Dolly contained the genetic material of only one parent, and was, therefore, a "delayed" genetic twin of a single adult sheep.

This cloning technique is an extension of research that had been ongoing for over 40 years using nuclei derived from non-human embryonic and fetal cells. The demonstration that nuclei from cells derived from an adult animal could be "reprogrammed," or that the full genetic complement of such a cell could be reactivated well into the chronological life of the cell, is what sets the results of this experiment apart from prior work. In this report we refer to the technique, first described by Wilmut, of nuclear transplantation using nuclei derived from somatic cells other than those of an embryo or fetus as "somatic cell nuclear transfer."

* "Cloning Human Beings: Report and Recommendations of the National Bioethics Advisory Commission," *Executive Summary*, published in *Jurimetrics*, Vol. 38, No. 1, Fall 1997. Copyright © 1997 by the American Bar Association. Reprinted with permission.

Within days of the published report of Dolly, President Clinton instituted a ban on federal funding related to attempts to clone human beings in this manner. In addition, the President asked the recently appointed National Bioethics Advisory Commission (NBAC) to address within ninety days the ethical and legal issues that surround the subject of cloning human beings. This provided a welcome opportunity for initiating a thoughtful analysis of the many dimensions of the issue, including a careful consideration of the potential risks and benefits. It also presented an occasion to review the current legal status of cloning and the potential constitutional challenges that might be raised if new legislation were enacted to restrict the creation of a child through somatic cell nuclear transfer cloning.

The Commission began its discussions fully recognizing that any effort in humans to transfer a somatic cell nucleus into an enucleated egg involves the creation of an embryo, with the apparent potential to be implanted in utero and developed to term. Ethical concerns surrounding issues of embryo research have recently received extensive analysis and deliberation in our country. Indeed, federal funding for human embryo research is severely restricted, although there are few restrictions on human embryo research carried out in the private sector. Thus, under current law, the use of somatic cell nuclear transfer to create an embryo solely for research purposes is already restricted in cases involving federal funds. There are, however, no current federal regulations on the use of private funds for this purpose.

The unique prospect, vividly raised by Dolly, is the creation of a new individual genetically identical to an existing (or previously existing) person — a "delayed" genetic twin. This prospect has been the source of the overwhelming public concern about such cloning. While the creation of embryos for research purposes alone always raises serious ethical questions, the use of somatic cell nuclear transfer to create embryos raises no new issues in this respect. The unique and distinctive ethical issues raised by the use of somatic cell nuclear transfer to create children relate to, for example, serious safety concerns, individuality, family integrity, and treating children as objects. Consequently, the Commission focused its attention on the use of such techniques for the purpose of creating an embryo which would then be implanted in a woman's uterus and brought to term. It also expanded its analysis of this particular issue to encompass activities in both the public and private sector.

. . . .

In addition to concerns about specific harms to children, people have frequently expressed fears that the widespread practice of somatic cell nuclear transfer cloning would undermine important social values by opening the door to a form of eugenics or by tempting some to manipulate others as if they were objects instead of persons. Arrayed against these concerns are other important social values, such as protecting the widest possible sphere of personal choice, particularly in matters pertaining to procreation and child rearing, maintaining privacy and the freedom of scientific inquiry, and encouraging the possible development of new biomedical breakthroughs.

To arrive at its recommendations concerning the use of somatic cell nuclear transfer techniques to create children, NBAC also examined long-standing religious traditions that guide many citizens' responses to new technologies and found that religious positions on human cloning are pluralistic in their premises, modes of argument, and conclusions. Some religious thinkers argue that the use of somatic cell nuclear transfer cloning to create a child would be intrinsically immoral and thus could never be morally justified. Other religious thinkers contend that human cloning to create a child could be morally justified under some circumstances, but hold that it should be strictly regulated in order to prevent abuses.

. . . .

Beyond the issue of the safety of the procedure, however, NBAC found that concerns relating to the potential psychological harms to children and effects on the moral, religious, and cultural values of society merited further reflection and deliberation. Whether upon such further deliberation our nation will conclude that the use of cloning techniques to create children should be allowed or permanently banned is, for the moment, an open question. Time is an ally in this regard, allowing for the accrual of further data from animal experimentation, enabling an assessment of the prospective safety and efficacy of the procedure in humans, as well as granting a period of fuller national debate on ethical and social concerns. The Commission therefore concluded that there should be imposed a period of time in which no attempt is made to create a child using somatic cell nuclear transfer.

Within this overall framework the Commission came to the following conclusions and recommendations:

I. The Commission concludes that at this time it is morally unacceptable for anyone in the public or private sector, whether in a research or clinical setting, to attempt to create a child using somatic cell nuclear transfer cloning. We have reached a consensus on this point because current scientific information indicates that this technique is not safe to use in humans at this point. Indeed, we believe it would violate important ethical obligations were clinicians or researchers to attempt to create a child using these particular technologies, which are likely to involve unacceptable risks to the fetus and/or potential child. Moreover, in addition to safety concerns, many other serious ethical concerns have been identified, which require much more widespread and careful public deliberation before this technology may be used.

The Commission, therefore, recommends the following for immediate action:

- A continuation of the current moratorium on the use of federal funding in support of any attempt to create a child by somatic cell nuclear transfer.
- An immediate request to all firms, clinicians, investigators, and professional societies in the private and non-federally funded sectors to comply voluntarily with the intent of the federal moratorium. Professional and scientific societies should make clear that any attempt to create a child by somatic cell nuclear transfer and implantation into a woman's body would at this time be an irresponsible, unethical, and unprofessional act. II. The Commission further recommends that:

- Federal legislation should be enacted to prohibit anyone from attempting, whether in a research or clinical setting, to create a child through somatic cell nuclear transfer cloning. It is critical, however, that such legislation include a sunset clause to ensure that Congress will review the issue after a specified time period (three to five years) in order to decide whether the prohibition continues to be needed. If state legislation is enacted, it should also contain such a sunset provision. Any such legislation or associated regulation also ought to require that at some point prior to the expiration of the sunset period, an appropriate oversight body will evaluate and report on the current status of somatic cell nuclear transfer technology and on the ethical and social issues that its potential use to create human beings would raise in light of public understandings at that time.

III. The Commission also concludes that:

- Any regulatory or legislative actions undertaken to effect the foregoing prohibition on creating a child by somatic cell nuclear transfer should be carefully written so as not to interfere with other important areas of scientific research. In particular, no new regulations are required regarding the cloning of human DNA sequences and cell lines, since neither activity raises the scientific and ethical issues that arise from the attempt to create children through somatic cell nuclear transfer, and these fields of research have already provided important scientific and biomedical advances. Likewise, research on cloning animals by somatic cell nuclear transfer does not raise the issues implicated in attempting to use this technique for human cloning, and its continuation should only be subject to existing regulations regarding the humane use of animals and review by institution-based animal protection committees.
- If a legislative ban is not enacted, or if a legislative ban is ever lifted, clinical use of somatic cell nuclear transfer techniques to create a child should be preceded by research trials that are governed by the twin protections of independent review and informed consent, consistent with existing norms of human subjects protection.

NOTES AND QUESTIONS

1. Note that the Commission's conclusions are limited to somatic cell nuclear transfer. Why? What of earlier techniques using fetal material?
2. What — exactly — are the differing concerns of the Commission? Autonomy? Eugenics? Children's safety? Identity of individuals? Morality? How does it propose addressing these issues?
3. The Commission proposes legislation, but does not describe its content. What should it be? It would include banning the cloning of a human; should it include prohibiting research? And what should the sanctions be?
4. As brief as it is, the Commission Report has provoked considerable criticism, among which are the following.

Susan M. Wolf, *Ban Cloning? Why NBAC Is Wrong**

In its report on cloning, NBAC recommended a ban of unprecedented scope. Based on commission consensus that human cloning would currently be unsafe, NBAC called for congressional prohibition throughout the public and private sectors of all somatic cell nuclear transfer with the intent of creating a child. President Clinton promptly responded by proposing legislation to enact such a ban for five years.

NBAC was wrong to urge a ban. Cloning undoubtedly warrants regulation. But the ban proposed will not yield the sort of regulation required. Instead, it will reduce cloning to a political football in Congress, raise serious constitutional problems, and chill important research. NBAC defends its ban as a limited one, prohibiting somatic cell nuclear transfer (not all forms of cloning), when used to create a child (not in research), and for three to five years (not indefinitely). A congressional ban, however, is likely to be far broader.

. . . .

A better approach would extend human subjects protection into the private sphere and regulate reproductive technologies effectively, with a central advisory body for novel issues such as cloning. By failing to tackle private research and reproductive technologies, NBAC avoided the real job and instead proposed an isolated and misguided response to cloning.

. . .[B]y responding to these worries with a congressional ban, NBAC missed the target. Protecting human subjects in private research and regulating reproductive technologies are both long overdue. A ban on cloning just suppresses one technology, while these two systemic problems guarantee the development of other technologies in need of regulation. Some would argue that somatic cell cloning deserves to be singled out as the most threatening possibility. But that assumes a conclusion we have not had time to reach, that Dolly-style cloning raises radically more difficult problems than, for example, cloning by embryo splitting (which can also lead to a delayed twin, with cryopreservation).

NBAC admits that protecting human subjects in private research offers advantages over a ban on cloning. Yet the commission balks. It first complains that extending human subjects protections requires legislation and thus delay. But Senator John Glenn (Dem., Ohio) has already proposed legislation, and enacting a congressional ban involves delay as well. The commission further complains that human subjects legislation would rely on decentralized institutional review boards (IRBs). But others have suggested creating a national IRB for novel questions, and NBAC ought to be considering this among other improvements in human subjects protection anyway. Moreover, IRBs are actually part of a larger mechanism providing centralized federal agency review when needed. The commission's final objection is that human subjects legislation would not reach beyond research activity to clinical use, as in infertility clinics. But this merely counsels supplemental regulation of those clinics.

No other bioethics controversy has been addressed by a ban as broad as the one NBAC advocates and the president now proposes. Its prohibition reaches all public and private institutions, whether or not federal money is involved or FDA approval is required. Limits on the use of federal money are common, but federal prohibitions on medical and scientific work in the private sector are not.

Moreover, the ban threatens substantial damage. The president's bill prohibits "somatic cell nuclear transfer with the intent of introducing the product of that transfer into a woman's womb or in any other way creating a human being," and would impose significant fines. Though NBAC insists it does not want to tamper with research in the private sphere, merely baby-making, this ban cannot avoid the former. The policing necessary to enforce the ban will require intruding into labs and monitoring the "intent" of scientists. Research will thus be chilled. It will be chilled further by the vagueness of a prohibition that is meant to ban baby-making, but seems to reach intent to "transfer," even if a researcher knows no child will result, plus the intent to create a human being in any unspecified "other way."

The ban proposed thus raises serious constitutional questions. The ban's prohibition of somatic cell nuclear transfer with the wrong intent and its unavoidable chilling effect on research may infringe freedom of scientific inquiry in violation of the First Amendment. And the ban as proposed by the president may well by unconstitutionally vague in its statement of the prohibited intent. The ban may also represent an unconstitutional infringement on the procreative liberty of infertile couples. In any case, it may exceed the limits of federal power, especially since the regulation of health and clinical practice has traditionally fallen to the states.

. . . .

Moreover, a ban may cause harm to infertile couples, especially if it hardens into an indefinite prohibition. After all, cloning offers potential benefit in infertility cases. NBAC points to a couple each carrying a recessive gene for a serious disorder. Cloning would allow them to avoid conceiving an embryo with the disorder and facing selective abortion. In another case, a woman might carry a dominant gene for a disorder. Cloning would permit her to avoid genetic contribution from an egg donor and thus would keep the genetic parenting between the woman and her partner, something of value to many couples. Other cases would include a couple entirely lacking gametes.

A federal ban on cloning thus misses the big picture. Cloning is only one of many reproductive technologies that should be safe before application, be it intracytoplasmic sperm injection, cytoplasm transfer, or beyond. The task is to devise a regulatory approach that addresses safety while permitting research and progress in a sphere of immense importance to couples. Cloning should spur us to that delicate balancing act. Simply lowering the boom on cloning does the opposite.

A Better Model

There is a better way. Certainly, we need improved regulation of assisted reproduction and human subjects experimentation in the private sphere. But we have to combine that regulation with an advisory body providing oversight for cloning and other novel reproductive and genetic technologies.

The commission, president, and Congress should consider a model we have used before: agency regulation guided by an advisory body able to respond to improvements in the technology over time and more removed than Congress from partisan politics. Though NBAC's report compared policy options, strangely this was not among them.

Certainly the details of the model can be debated. Indeed, rather than create a new advisory body, using a reinvigorated RAC, another preexisting entity, or NBAC itself (if its mission were restructured) might be considered. And some may argue we need two bodies, one for human subjects and the other for reproductive technologies. But surrendering cloning to a congressional ban, as NBAC suggests, attempts a delicate operation with far too blunt an instrument. It is slim consolation that under the president's proposal, NBAC will be continuing discussion on the sidelines.

James F. Childress, *The Challenges of Public Ethics: Reflections on NBAC's Report**

These reflections build on my participation in the commission, but I do not profess to speak for the commission in my attempt to illuminate its discourse, deliberations, and conclusions about cloning humans. Others inside and outside the commission may have quite different interpretations.

Is human cloning intrinsically wrong or does it depend on the circumstances? There is disagreement in this society and possibly also in NBAC about whether any conceivable acts of human cloning could ever be justified if the technique were safe for the children so created. On the one hand, some thinkers, especially but not only in the Roman Catholic tradition, hold that cloning humans is wrong in and of itself (intrinsically wrong), and that it would thus be wrong under any conceivable circumstances. Any use would violate human dignity, the natural law, the natural order, or some other fundamental principle or value, perception of this violation often being expressed, as Leon Kass suggests, in the language of repugnance and revulsion.

On the other hand, many hold that human cloning would be wrong in some, perhaps most, circumstances but not in others that could be imagined.

Several scenarios are considered — cloning because of problems of infertility; cloning to provide a compatible source of biological material, such as bone marrow, for treatment; cloning a dying child; cloning to prevent genetic diseases. Many who hold that human cloning could be justified under some circumstances would not view all these scenarios as ethically acceptable. In any event, most religious and secular positions that accept some possible cases of human cloning presuppose that the procedure is sufficiently safe for the child created by cloning and that the child's rights and interests will be adequately protected. Otherwise human cloning even for legitimate purposes would be morally unjustifiable.

Practical reasoning: principled or casuistical or both? After NBAC's deliberations, one commissioner suggested to me that we had not appealed to principles at all in our reasoning and wondered whether I wanted to reconsider my defense of a principle-based approach. I responded that NBAC's concern for safety reflects the principle of nonmaleficence and that NBAC at this time could not identify benefits of human cloning that outweigh the risks to children (a consideration of beneficence) or claims of autonomy in reproduction or in scientific inquiry strong enough to outweigh the risks to children. In addition, concerns about respect for persons, including their dignity as well as their autonomy, surfaced in discussions about objectifying and commodifying children.

Much of our discourse also moved casuistically, as we looked for settled cases that could provide helpful analogies. For instance, we referred to what was more or less settled in the 1994 federal policy regarding embryo splitting, and to what is currently accepted in various reproductive and genetic technologies. These two approaches — principled and casuistical — are, in my judgment, quite compatible with and even essential to each other in deliberations about public policy.

Religious perspectives on human cloning. When President Clinton asked NBAC to consider the cloning of human beings, he commented that "any discovery that touches upon human creation is not simply a matter of scientific inquiry, it is a matter of morality and spirituality as well." Shortly thereafter, the commission set up two days of hearings, with particular attention to scientific, ethical, and religious perspectives.

NBAC believed that it was important to examine religious as well as philosophical perspectives on human cloning for several reasons.

First, religious communities, several with ancient roots and long traditions of moral reflection, significantly shape the moral positions taken by many U.S. citizens on new technological developments. Hence, it is important to understand how these communities view human cloning, including how they argue for their positions as well as the conclusions they reach. NBAC wanted to hear and weigh religious and philosophical arguments in their own integrity. Though some questions pressed for translation into a more secular idiom, NBAC was interested in the arguments that religious communities actually use to guide their own adherents as well as to guide public policy.

Second, religious traditions often present moral arguments that rest on premises that are not merely or exclusively religious in nature. For instance, they may invoke categories such as "nature" or "basic human values" or "family values" that are not reducible to particular faith commitments and that are accessible to citizens of different or no faith commitments.

Third, NBAC sought to determine the extent to which religious traditions — and secular traditions — overlap on moral positions on human cloning to create children. It wanted to learn whether these diverse traditions have reached a moral consensus on human cloning — and, if so, the nature of that consensus.

Fourth, NBAC sought to engender and sustain in its own meetings and in its report serious national moral discourse about human cloning and about public policies regarding human cloning. Hence, it listened to and attempted to understand as fully as possible various religious and philosophical positions.

Fifth, many different factors determine whether particular public policies are feasible and effective and whether their social benefits outweigh their social costs. One such factor is the nature, extent, and depth of opposition to those policies by various religious and secular communities. It was thus important to NBAC to identify the basic concerns both religious and secular communities have about human cloning.

On one point a strong consensus, perhaps even unanimity, exists among Jewish, Roman Catholic, and Protestant thinkers: A child created through somatic cell nuclear transfer cloning would still be created in the image of God. It is important to make this point because so many commentators on religious perspectives miss or neglect it. Even when religious thinkers maintain that cloning would always or at least sometimes violate the dignity of the child created this way, they also contend that it would not *diminish* that child's dignity (Pope John Center testimony to NBAC, 13 March 1997). In different language, Rabbi Elliot Dorff (also in testimony to NBAC, 14 March 1997) stressed that cloning would create "a new person, an integrated body and mind, with unique experiences," however difficult it may be for such persons to "establish their own identity and for their creators to acknowledge and respect it."

Religious and secular thinkers alike insist that it is morally obligatory not to inflict serious harm on children created through human cloning. One such harm is physical. Cloning would be wrong at least for now because cloners could not be sure that they would not be doing unacceptable harm to children. This is also the position NBAC took, based on broad societal moral norms, in holding that safety is a fundamental ethical issue, and that, at least for the time being, human cloning to create a child should not be undertaken and should even be prohibited through legislation. Such prohibitive legislation would provide a window of opportunity for society to determine whether *safe* human cloning would have unacceptable moral costs and should be severely restricted or even banned.

John A. Robertson, *Wrongful Life, Federalism, and Procreative Liberty: A Critique of the NBAC Cloning Report*[*]

. . . .

Far from settling the public policy issues, the NBAC Report is best viewed as a first stab at dealing with the complicated issues raised by human cloning and other genetic selection techniques. With the NBAC's limited staff and time in mind, this critique focuses on the ethical and policy arguments it made for a federal criminal ban on cloning "at this time."

II. PHYSICAL SAFETY AND THE ETHICS OF HUMAN CLONING

[*] "Cloning Human Beings: Report and Recommendations of the National Bioethics Advisory Commission," *Executive Summary*, published in *Jurimetrics*, Vol. 38, No. 1, Fall 1997. Copyright © 1997 by the American Bar Association. Reprinted with permission.

The NBAC justified its main recommendation in favor of a time-limited federal ban on all human cloning on grounds of physical safety. Its position deserves careful analysis not only because it underpins the Report's call for a present ban, but also because of the implications of its premises for other issues in cloning and genetic selection.

The Report's emphasis on physical safety is somewhat surprising. Issues about physical safety arise with any new medical procedure, but they were not at the top of anyone's list of fears about human cloning. There is always a danger that physicians, who have an interest in developing and using innovative procedures, will mislead patients about the prospect of success. In some cases, patients may demand procedures when the risks and likelihood of success are unknown. While both are possibilities with somatic cell nuclear transfer, in a more realistic scenario few couples and doctors would be willing to use this technique if there were a significant risk of physical damage to offspring. People might differ somewhat in their willingness to accept risks, but it is highly unlikely that therapeutic or clinical transfers of embryos created by cloning would occur without extensive animal and laboratory research that first established its safety and efficacy.

The concern about harm to children is more problematic than the Report recognizes because the underlying principle on which it rests would make it unethical knowingly or intentionally to give birth to children who are not fully healthy, physically or psychologically. Such a principle is difficult to defend. Since it is not followed in most other reproductive situations, it is unclear why human cloning should be treated differently.

For example, most courts and commentators have objected to the idea of holding women criminally responsible for prenatal behavior that causes postnatal harm to offspring, even when the child would otherwise have been born healthy if the woman or man had not engaged in the behavior at issue. Indeed, some persons object to any moral condemnation of pregnant women, even when they have knowingly or recklessly engaged in behavior that will cause a child who would otherwise have been born healthy to be born with mental or physical impairments.

Similarly, people are loath to sanction couples who knowingly bring genetically handicapped children into the world. Thus we do not normally think that couples who are carriers for Tay Sachs, sickle cell, or cystic fibrosis are acting wrongfully if they have not been screened for their carrier status, if they know they are carriers and yet intentionally conceive, or, if having conceived, they then refuse prenatal diagnosis and abortion. Yet their conduct will cause a child to be born with a severe, physically debilitating disease.

The NBAC Report assumes that being born less than healthy or whole is always a harm to the child who results from nuclear transfer cloning, even when it has no alternative way to be born. It rejects the claim that the cloned child is not harmed when this is the only way it has to be born:

But the argument that somatic cell nuclear transfer cloning experiments are "beneficial" to the resulting child rest on the notion that it is a "benefit" to be brought into the world as compared to being left unconceived and unborn. This metaphysical argument, in which one is forced to compare existence with nonexistence, is problematic. Not only does it require us to compare something unknowable — non-existence — with something else, it also can lead to absurd conclusions if taken to its logical extreme.

For example, it would support the argument that there is no degree of pain and suffering that cannot be inflicted on a child, provided that the alternative is never to have been conceived.

There are several mistakes here. First, the claim that there is no harm to a cloned child from the fact of cloning because it had no other way to come into existence is not a "metaphysical" one based on the interests of nonexisting, potential children. The claim is made instead from the standpoint of the cloned child who now exists, not from the standpoint of someone waiting to exist. It asks whether the child's present life is so full of suffering that it would now prefer nonexistence. This is comparing a present state of existence with nonexistence as it appears from the perspective of the now existing person. True, we do not know what nonexistence is, but we do know that it is the absence of life and experience. This is a judgment that we allow people in terminal or debilitating conditions to make in refusing necessary medical treatment. There is no reason that we cannot apply it to existing persons whose very lives are said to harm them because they are the product of cloning or other controversial procedures.

Second, the Report is incorrect about the logical extreme to which this reasoning would lead. If cloning or other possible reproduction techniques impose such a high degree of physical harm on the resulting offspring, few couples would be interested in using them, because would-be parents are interested in having a healthy child. If the technique at issue does in fact produce such enormous suffering that from the born child's own perspective nonexistence would have been preferable, then continuing the child's life would indeed be wrongful. But that extreme state is highly unlikely to occur. Its possibility hardly provides a basis for finding harm in situations that amount to much less than a wrongful life.

A third mistake is inconsistency. In calling for a ban on human cloning on grounds of the risk of physical safety to resulting offspring, the Report relies on the very assumptions that it criticizes. If bringing the child into being is to harm it, even if there is no alternative way to be born, then, according to NBAC, it is preferable that the child not exist at all. The NBAC is thus explicitly comparing existence and nonexistence, while at the same time asserting that they cannot be compared.

III. SHOULD FEDERAL LAW CRIMINALIZE CLONING?

Even if one accepted the Report's premise that children born after somatic cell nuclear transfer are harmed by their very existence, it would not follow that the alleged unethical behavior involved with bringing them into the world should be a crime under federal law. There are many forms of unethical, even harmful, conduct in medicine and other endeavors for which we do not pass a federal criminal law. Why is a federal law necessary to prevent human cloning but not these other actions?

. . . .

B. Problems and Critique

. . . .

The idea that federal criminal law is needed to prevent potential harmful or unethical uses of a reproductive or other medical innovation is unique in bioethics. Most federal bioethical regulation has occurred through the federal funding power, not through the use of direct criminal sanctions. For example, the extensive federal regulation of human subjects research has occurred in the guise of the conditional spending power. It is not a crime to conduct human subject research without IRB review or compliance with other federal regulations, though such practices might lead to withdrawal of federal funds or independently violate state law. The Patient Self-Determination Act of 1990, which requires hospitals to inform patients of their rights to refuse medical treatment and to issue advance directives, is based on the federal power to condition Medicare spending on compliance with certain conditions. Although failure to inform patients of their rights could lead to unnecessary suffering, criminal penalties were not deemed necessary to protect those interests. Nor are criminal sanctions attached to violations of the reporting requirements of the Fertility Clinic Success Rate and Laboratory Certification Act of 1992, even though false reports could cause great suffering to infertile couples who relied on them in choosing a fertility clinic.

. . . .

But the view that an unneeded federal law that is enacted for symbolic or political reasons is costless is itself highly dubious. If cloning quickly turns out to be a safe and effective way for some couples to rear biologically related children, a time-limited ban will exact a price from couples who have legitimate reasons for wishing to clone. In addition, there is the danger that once Congress is moved to outlaw cloning, it may attach no time limit at all, or place the burden on proponents of cloning to have the policy changed.

. . . .

Finally, the recommended ban sets an unwise precedent for invoking federal criminal law to settle a bioethics issue. If a federal law is justified here, then it is justified for many other reproductive and genetic situations. For example, the same principles could be invoked to make it a crime for couples not to undergo genetic screening prior to conception, or to refuse prenatal testing after conception. It could also lead to a federalization of rules for assisted reproduction, or for future developments in gene therapy and genetic alteration. If so, the NBAC's cloning report will truly have been historical. It will have started the process by which federal criminal law is used to regulate the use of all new reproductive and genetic selection technologies.

IV. CLONING POLICY IN THE FUTURE

Our ethical, legal, and social commitment to reproductive and family liberty should place the burden on opponents to show that family-centered uses of cloning are not truly procreative, or that they impose such a high risk of severe harm that they should be prohibited. Such an approach is necessary to give procreative liberty and family autonomy its due. Speculation, hypothetical harms, and moral objection alone are not a sufficient basis for limiting coital reproduction. They should not be sufficient to limit the use of noncoital and genetic selection techniques essential to a couple seeking healthy, biologically-related children to rear.

This means that future inquiries into the ethics and public policy issues raised by human cloning and other genetic selection techniques should begin with an examination of their role in helping families have healthy children to rear. As I argue elsewhere, a plausible case exists for viewing cloning in some circumstances as an essential way for a married couple intent on gestating and rearing children to accomplish that goal. Once the connection with procreative choice is established, proper respect for family and reproductive liberty requires that opponents of the practice show that legitimate family uses would produce such great harm to others that prohibition or regulation is justified.

Ira H. Carmen, *Should Human Cloning Be Criminalized?*[*]

The work of Ian Wilmut and his colleagues clearly demonstrates that "sheep cloning," that is to say, "somatic cell nuclear transfer" ("SCNT"), can now be considered a viable mammalian reproductive procedure.

The NBAC's essential conclusion was that Congress should pass a law making human cloning via SCNT a crime, and several bills addressing the issue have now been drafted, formally introduced, and referred to committee. The purpose of this paper is to assess that policy recommendation. Central to the inquiry is fleshing out the assumptions and the values that should guide us in determining whether such proposed legislation is consistent with the public interest and the Constitution of the United States.

I

The NBAC proceeded to delimit its task and its role in the narrowest fashion consistent with its responsibilities. It investigated and made recommendations relevant to SCNT and only SCNT. This strategy is in sharp contrast to lost opportunities. For example, Mr. Clinton's moratorium on federal funding seemingly covers all procedures leading to the "cloning of human beings." Such procedures include implanting embryonic (as opposed to adult) cells and implanting "twinned" preembryos. The NBAC explicitly found the latter to lie beyond its purview, and never discussed the former in its report at all. With respect to twinned preembryos, it is well documented that when Jerry Hall demonstrated the ability to cleave human blastomeres, with no thought whatever of implanting any of the resulting clones, many bioethicists were more than disturbed by the possible consequences. "[W]hat we are talking about," said one, "is the ability to mass-produce humans." Needless to say, no humans have been produced, much less mass-produced, via the twinning procedure, even though the liberty to indulge such procreative choices in privately funded laboratories remains unfettered by federal legal constraint. With respect to implanting embryonic cells, the notoriety accompanying Wilmut's announcement evidently prompted Don Wolf and his associates at the Oregon Regional Primate Research Center to disclose that they had several months earlier [illegible] rhesus monkeys, albeit from immature cells. Cloning sheep and cattle in this fashion was no novelty, but cloning primates using embryonic cell nuclear transfer (“ECNT”), one could reasonably submit, brought scientists much closer to the reality of “cloning human beings” than anything Wilmut had done, especially given the fact that in Homo sapiens, DNA “reprogramming” apparently would commence at the four-cell stage rather than at the eight-cell stage as with sheep. The point requiring emphasis is that while President Clinton’s executive memorandum itself had opened the door to a national policy paper treating the ethical, legal, and social implications of “implantational cloning” as a whole, the committee failed to take up this broader challenge. When one addresses only the most extreme of controversial cases, extreme solutions are most likely to suggest themselves.

A more pervasive limitation in the NBAC’s definition of the problem is that it says nothing about SCNT as a purely scientific enterprise. The committee apparently took the view that national policy on preembryo research was not properly on the table because of recent high-profile debates and consequent executive and legislative decisions governing the matter. This writer has elsewhere reported on the work of the NIH’s Human Embryo Research Panel (“HERP”): The fact that this blue-ribbon committee had recommended that the moratorium (ban!) on federal funding of human preembryonic research — the kind of research that Robert Winston and Alan Handyside have for years conducted in their UK laboratories — be lifted; and the fact that President Clinton, on his own authority, had rejected this recommendation virtually out of hand. Congress would eventually place into appropriations act legislation Mr. Clinton’s administrative order.

. . . .

The NBAC was quite candid in rejecting self-evident ethical truths as dispositive. “[T]here is no universally accepted ethical theory [in this country],” the panel found, and “the Commission itself is unable to agree at this time on all the ethical issues [involving such matters as ‘’self-identity’ and “human dignity’] that surround the issue of cloning human beings in this manner.” When Congress enacts legislation, it is textbook law that ordinarily the constitutionality of the statute be tested by the criterion of rationality. The straightforward way to proceed is for Congress to advance a valid national interest and then show how the statute rationally advances that interest. What the NBAC was saying was that the national interest relied upon in its recommendation was not some set of commonly-shared theological or philosophical values.

Instead, the rationale relied upon to sustain a claim of valid federal interest is that old technological assessment standby, safety. Cloning humans via SCNT is terra incognita, argued the NBAC, and “it seems clear to all of us . . . [that it is therefore] unacceptably dangerous to the fetus and [so] morally unacceptable.” There can be little argument that the Wilmut procedure applied to humans is risky business and that a rational, objective person might find it so risky that it should be proscribed. The tougher question is whether a criminal law punishing all those who utilize the procedure can clear some higher level of scrutiny. What higher level of scrutiny?

As indicated earlier, a good argument could be made that the Supreme Court's reproductive rights cases should not be read to include SCNT. The NBAC, while keeping an open mind on this issue, concluded that if reproductively-directed SCNT is considered a bona fide form of procreation lying within the ambit of *the Roe v. Wade* doctrine, then Congress (and the states) would have to demonstrate a compelling interest to regulate it. That assertion appears false and makes enemies among reasonable observers fearful of human cloning's excesses where none need be made. The latest word on the subject is *Planned Parenthood v. Casey* . There, Justice O'Connor's prevailing opinion makes it clear that the right to create or terminate a pregnancy is protected only against "undue burdens." If this be so, then the right to clone a human being by any procedure is substantial but certainly not comparable to regulations that must satisfy strict scrutiny.

Strongly supporting what would eventually be the proposed committee recommendation and attempting to finesse what they rightly perceived as a constitutional roadblock in the path of their policy preferences, bioethicists George Annas and Leon Kass argued in testimony before a congressional panel and the NBAC itself that creating a child through SCNT was not "reproduction" at all; it was "replication." Had the NBAC endorsed the Annas-Kass position, it certainly could have built a case for its proposal without having to belabor the true meaning of *Roe v. Wade* in 1997. This, however, the NBAC never did. Nor does an argument for criminalizing SCNT human creation based on the Annas-Kass theory suffice. Replication may not be reproduction, but in many contexts it is scientific inquiry, perhaps even pure research. Scientific inquiry, including genetic engineering, implicates First Amendment freedom of expression values. How can scientists understand the structure and function of genes without experimentation, without in some cases "engineering" DNA, without in some cases replicating DNA? Of course DNA replication is not an absolute right. The question, as always, is one of balancing competing interests. Annas and Kass see the SCNT version of human cloning (query: what do they think of other "versions"?) as so pernicious that there is nothing to balance, that is, there is no interest in scientific inquiry to include in the constitutional debate relevant to this particular species of human cloning. Without any empirical data to support this position, their moral outrage directed toward any and all work in this area is itself constitutionally suspect.

The NBAC neither accepted nor rejected Annas-Kass. So what, ultimately, was the committee's constitutional rationale? Essentially, it came to this: No matter how weighty one thinks is the researcher's freedom of inquiry interest in performing SCNT child creation, and no matter how weighty one thinks is the mother's procreative interest in conceiving a child through the medium of SCNT, both of these interests combined cannot overcome Congress' authority to protect the safety of human cloned fetuses through the device of legislation criminalizing the procedure. This theory is neither as clean and neat and parsimonious as the Annas-Kass theory, nor is it as constitutionally viable.

In its commentary, the NBAC noted how well the moratorium on human gene therapy had worked in the 1980s. The report did not mention that if the moratorium worked, it was in large measure because the RAC developed a

"Points to Consider" document informing researchers of what they needed to do if they wanted to receive a full and fair hearing for their human somatic cell gene transfer/therapy protocols. Incidentally, when the RAC finally conducted a full-dress review of a specimen project, the Anderson-Blaese-Rosenberg metastatic melanoma NEO gene marker investigation, the principle investigators failed to provide the committee with any animal model research data, exactly the sort of experimental data which the NBAC contended is so critical to developing ethical consensus on safety issues before SCNT human reproductive protocols ever pass scrutiny. The RAC's experience with the NEO project bears ample witness to the fact that empirical research on human subjects may sometimes be required before viable theory on human subjects research can be formulated. In any event, it is difficult to recall a single objective, knowledgeable voice arguing in the 1980s that Congress should pass a criminal statute — with or without the sunset feature — making illegal human somatic cell gene transfer/therapy.

. . . .

III

Anthropologists and historians of human community and culture tell us that for each civilization there is a body of knowledge that is taboo, whose content it is forbidden even for the great minds of past and present to probe. For Western Civilization, much of this forbidden knowledge has traditionally involved human genetics, particularly human genetic experimentation. What the NBAC has decided is that implantational human cloning via SCNT sits at the apex of the human genetic experimentation pyramid of taboos, and that scientists who indulge in the practice should be punished accordingly. Provided above is a sketch of the twenty-five-year history of genetic engineering knowledge — all of it at one time forbidden knowledge — in its complex political trappings. In its most enlightened moments it is a history of experts, scholars representing the diverse fields of the liberal arts and sciences, sitting around a table in full public view, debating and voting on research issues great and small. In this fashion, the political system provides an ordered, accountable process for demystifying taboos, for balancing competing interests so as to separate out in some rational, patterned way legitimate as opposed to illegitimate research practices. In the context of human cloning taken as a whole, the dialogue would include the sorts of questions that the RAC has put, in its more edifying moments and with varying degrees of success to be sure, to a variety of investigators challenging the boundaries of genetic understanding: What is the dominant purpose of the investigation? Is this a search for knowledge or a search in pursuit of utilitarian ends? How does one compare procreative with therapeutic interests? Are the means employed as appropriate to the ends in view as circumstances permit? What are the prospects for patentability? What is the influence of corporate money and direction? What manner of informed consent has the practitioner received from what kinds of human subjects? Incredibly, the NBAC finds nothing in such a process worth commending to the American people. All it would take is an amendment to the NIH guidelines giving the RAC authority over human cloning. We should consider it, and not the voice of Congress, the forum of first choice.

NOTES AND QUESTIONS

1. Susan Wolf argues for an advisory body with regulatory authority over human cloning. But, what would be its purpose, jurisdiction and criteria? Would it permit the couples described to engage in cloning? If not, do they have constitutional arguments?

2. Childress argues that the NABC did, in fact, undertake a principle-based approach. But *did* it? In dealing only with safety and autonomy, the Commission essentially simply deferred to parents and scientists. What of the principles Childress referred to, of "human dignity, the natural law, the natural order, or some other fundamental principle or value"?

3. Childress says there was "strong consensus" on one point: "A child created through somatic cell transfer cloning would still be created in the image of God." What does this mean? Suppose the child is deliberately made *less* than human? *More,* in some fashion? If religious leaders truly support this consensus, should they oppose human cloning?

4. Robertson opposes a criminal statute banning cloning, partly because we do not generally impose sanctions for maternal misconduct during pregnancy or for wrongfully conceiving defective children. But in fact, authority exists for doing so (see *infra,* § 4.02) and — even if this weren't true — doesn't it make particularly good sense in cloning? How persuasive is Robertson in arguing that even if cloned children are harmed by the very fact of their existence, criminal sanctions would still be inappropriate?

5. Carmen joins Robertson in critiquing the Commission's recommendation of a criminal ban on cloning, but does in part because the Commission would ban only SCNT. Does this make sense? *Should* the Commission have included implanting embryonic and "twinned" embryos?

6. Carmen also criticizes the Commission for using only safety as a rationale for its ban, and not "some sort of commonly-shared theological or philosophical values." What would he suggest? And is his following argument that the ban need not meet "strict scrutiny" under the *Casey* decision accurate? Isn't the "undue burdens" test itself a form of strict scrutiny? Other cases requiring strict scrutiny involve race, religion and procreation, as with *Griswold* and *Roe v. Wade, supra,* § 2.02[2] and § 1.04. Shouldn't Carmen argue — consistent with his position — *for* strict scrutiny?

7. And what *of* the Annas-Kass position that cloning is not reproduction but "replication"? Doesn't that make good, common sense, *biological* sense in simple, human terms? Why does Carmen reject that distinction? Where would it lead? And why does Carmen think there is no strict scrutiny involved in analyzing the Commission's criminal ban even while he argues cloning research is protected under the First Amendment?

8. Two more thoughtful, opposing views on whether cloning of humans should be banned appear in the July 9, 1998 issue of the *Journal of*

the American Medical Association, in essays by John Robertson and George Annas, at 330 JAMA 119-127 (1998).

9. At about the time the debate on human cloning was proceeding in the United States, the Council of Europe addressed the subject, and adopted the following protocol. Evaluate its terms in light of the preceding materials. In particular, what does the Council *mean* by the "instrumentalization" of human beings? And *why* is it "contrary to human dignity?"

10. For an excellent article, see Allison Lampert, *An Andy Warhol Society — First Coca-Cola, Now Humans: An Examination Of Whether A Ban On Human Cloning Violates Procreative Liberty*, 16 St. John's J. Legal Comment. 245 (2002); and see Shannon H. Smith, *Ignorance Is Not Bliss: Why a Ban on Human Cloning Is Unacceptable*, 9 Health Matrix 311 (1999).

    See also Dunn, *Cloning Trevor*, Atlantic Magazine, p. 31 *et seq.* (June 2002), for an excellent discussion of attempts to clone humans for treatment purposes.

11. A common criticism of genetic experimentation is the "slippery slope:" how far is too far, and how will we know? *See* National Science Foundation, *Ethics of Boosting Brainpower Debated by Researchers*, Health Law Weekly, May 29, 2004

    See also Cooper and Psaty, Genomics and Medicine: Distraction, Incremental Progress, or the Dawn of a New Age? Ann Intern Med 2003.

Additional Protocol to the Convention for the Protection of Human Rights with regard to the Application of Biology, on the Prohibition of Cloning Human Beings
Paris, 12.1.1998

The member States of the Council of Europe, the other States and the European Community Signatories to this Additional Protocol to the Convention for the Protection of Human Rights and Dignity of the Human Being with regard to the Application of Biology and Medicine,

Noting scientific developments in the field of mammal cloning, particularly through embryo splitting and nuclear transfer;

Mindful of the progress that some cloning techniques themselves may bring to scientific knowledge and its medical application;

Considering that the cloning of human beings may become a technical possibility;

Having noted that embryo splitting may occur naturally and sometimes result in the birth of genetically identical twins;

Considering however that the instrumentalization of human beings through the deliberate creation of genetically identical human beings is contrary to human dignity and thus constitutes a misuse of biology and medicine;

Considering also the serious difficulties of a medical, psychological and social nature that such a deliberate biomedical practice might imply for all the individuals involved;

Considering the purpose of the Convention on Human Rights and Biomedicine, in particular the principle mentioned in Article 1 aiming to protect the dignity and identity of all human beings,

Have agreed as follows:

Article 1

1. Any intervention seeking to create a human being genetically identical to another human being, whether living or dead, is prohibited.

2. For the purpose of this article, the term human being "genetically identical" to another human being means a human being sharing with another the same nuclear gene set.

Article 2

No derogation from the provisions of this Protocol shall be made under Article 26, paragraph 1, of the Convention.

PROBLEM 2–7 — The Human Chimera

In 1998, the magazine *Nature* reported that Doctor Stuart Newman, a professor at New York Medical College, had filed a patent for a process to make chimeras, part human and part nonhuman. He and his partner, Jeremy Rifkin, later accounts reported, believe there should be no such patents or such creatures, which would be a mixture of *both* contributing species. A chimera between a human and a chimpanzee might have a brain with *both* cells, but it could not breed "true" because its reproductive cells would be one or the other. There are already patents, Newman said, on organisms (e.g., a pig) which have some human cells. Newman accepts experimentation on transgenic species; he opposes genetically modifying human embryos or cloning humans or germ line modification — since "predetermined prototypes" are "really culturally a very negative thing."

On April 2, 1998, the United State Patent and Trademark Office declared that it would not issue a patent on a human chimera along the lines sought by Newman and Rifkin. Was this the correct decision?

PROBLEM 2–8 — Cloning, Chimeras and Other Things My Mother Never Thought Of

My mother believed she had pushed medical science to the limit by bearing twins, one weighing 6 pounds and the other weighing 6 pounds 6 ounces, since she was barely 60 inches tall and weighed 110 pounds at the time. But time marches on.

You are the United States Attorney for the Southern District of your state. The United States Congress has recently passed the following statute:

18 U.S.C. § 2010

Whoever shall engage, or aid, assi[illegible] another to engage, in the [illegible]ation of, or attempt to create, a human being by cloning shall be guilty of a class B felony. The term cloning shall be limited to somatic cell nuclear transfer and shall not include sexual reproduction. Any person who creates or attempts to create a human being with a composition not entirely human, or assists another in so doing, shall be guilty of a class A felony.

Dolly Steed has Huntington's Disease, an hereditary condition which manifests itself in a person's adult years, leading to a painful, wasting death. There is no cure. Dolly has therefore never married or had children, although she loves them and is actively involved with her nieces and nephews. She has read recently of a method of reproduction that would not pass Huntington's on to the next generation and has therefore decided to have a child by that method.

The method, developed in Scotland by a reproductive geneticist, J. Ishbel McCahon, involves removing the nucleus of one of her eggs, eliminating the offending markers or strands of DNA which cause the unwanted condition (here, Huntington's) and returning the altered nucleus to the egg. The egg is, by this process, stimulated as if fertilized through conventional sexual means, and begins cellular development for a period of six weeks in the laboratory. It is then implanted in the mother's uterus, where it develops into a full person. Its genetic makeup is identical to that of the donor (minus the offending gene), so the mother — in effect — has a "delayed twin."

The McCahon method requires implantation in the womb of a breed of laboratory sheep for the six week period of time. For reasons not understood, Ms. Steed's own body would reject her altered egg/pre-embryo during the six week period of development. The sheep are specially bred — themselves a product of genetic engineering which includes some human genetic material in the sheep uterus to assure compatibility, patented by McCahon's laboratory. Some of the child's cells will be derived from the sheep, in a method not fully understood, but — in McCahon's [illegible] these will be less than 10% of the genetic makeup of the child, which can be monitored during fetal development. If problematic, the fetus can be aborted. The transfer of the fetus at six weeks from the sheep to the mother is hazardous. There is an estimated 50% failure rate.

The local newspaper carries an article about Dolly Steed's planned trip to Scotland and the assistance she has received locally from her own physician and the director of the fertility laboratory at Your State University, where research on cloning has been conducted for a decade. Do you charge anyone with a crime? Who? For what? What defenses are available?

Would it matter if Dolly were first to conceive, then permit extraction of cells from the fetus, then abort, with the cells receiving nuclear material from her, after the offending Huntington's DNA had been eliminated? As to this, see *infra,* Ch. 4 on research concerning fetal material and maternal-fetal conflict generally. And consider whether the closed society protected in the next case, *Wisconsin v. Yoder*, doesn't achieve the same result as cloning of humans, with the same evils.

Consider the implications of a recent New York Times report (November 12, 1998 at A1, A24.) that for the first time human cells have been made to revert to the primordial, embryonic state by fusing them with cow eggs. The result is a hybrid fetus — part human, part cow.

PROBLEM 2-9 — Eggs and Employee Liability

The following article* appeared in *The New York Times*, November 25, 2005:

> TOKYO, Nov. 24 — The South Korean researcher who won world acclaim as the first scientist to clone a human embryo and extract stem cells from it apologized Thursday for lying over the sources of some human eggs used in his work and stepped down as director of a new research center.
>
> After months of denying rumors that swirled around his Seoul laboratory, the researcher, Dr. Hwang Woo Suk, confirmed that in 2002 and 2003, when his work had little public support, two of his junior researchers donated eggs and a hospital director paid about 20 other women for their eggs.
>
> On several earlier occasions, he had said that he did not use eggs harvested from subordinates and that no one was paid for egg donations.
>
> "Being too focused on scientific development, I may not have seen all the ethical issues related to my research," Dr. Hwang, a veterinarian by training, told a news conference in Seoul on Thursday. "I should be here reporting the successful results of our research, but I'm sorry instead to have to apologize." He said the staff donations had taken place without his knowledge.
>
> "We needed a lot of ova for the research, but there were not enough ova around," he said. "It was during this time when my researchers suggested making voluntary donations. I clearly turned it down."
>
> He said he later discovered they had donated eggs under false names in 2003.
>
> Although the egg donations by the junior researchers were not considered a legal or ethical violation, critics say that in the strict hierarchy of a scientific laboratory in a Confucian society like South Korea, junior members often feel great pressure to please their superiors. Under international medical ethics standards, researchers are warned against receiving eggs from members of their own research teams who are deemed to be in a dependent relationship.
>
> Payment for eggs was not illegal in 2003, but it was banned last January by South Korean law.

* James Brook, *Korean Leaves Cloning Center in Ethics Furor* (Nov. 25, 2005).

> Dr. Hwang and his team's production of stem cells from cloned human embryos in 2004 was considered [illegible] toward eventually treating conditions like Alzheimer's disease and spinal cord injuries. But the human eggs ethics controversy may give ammunition to his opponents, who warn that his work could lead to human cloning.
>
> His team also cloned a dog, an Afghan named Snuppy, who appeared on the cover of Time magazine, which declared his team's feat this year's most amazing invention.

What is the issue here? Informed consent? Breaching research protocols? Imposing on staff? Misrepresenting facts?

And do the answers vary from those in a Western culture, like the United States, to an Eastern, Confucian, or Hindu culture?

And are there issues to explore about Snuppy?

§ 2.04 Association and Privacy

[1] Family, Same-Sex Marriage and Parenting

Every person has a family of birth, from which we receive our physical inheritance and often our legacy of culture, language and social position. We also, most of us, have a family of choice, frequently through marriage. Because *that* family is the vehicle of nurture and transmission — and, hence, identity — for the next generation, family and marital associations are profoundly important relationships. Ethically, they command the highest respect and responsibility. Legally, and constitutionally, this is also true, as the *Casey* and *Griswold* (*supra*) opinions held.

And yet, in the 1990s between one-third and one-half of all children are born out of marriage; nearly one-half live with adults other than their biological parents. Many commentators consider the breakdown of the traditional family the gravest crisis facing this nation and other nations around the world. We therefore turn to the subject of the family of one's choice — its content and status, both within and beyond the bounds of traditional marriage.

We begin with a uniquely traditional, religiously-grounded old Amish family in the *Yoder* case and follow with an unconventional, same-sex family, in *Baehr v. Lewin.*

WISCONSIN v. YODER

406 U.S. 205 (1972)

Mr. Chief Justice **Burger** delivered the opinion of the Court.

. . . .

Respondents Jonas Yoder and Wallace Miller are members of the Old Order Amish religion, and respondent Adin Yutzy is a member of the Conservative Amish Mennonite Church. They and their families are residents of Green County, Wisconsin. Wisconsin's compulsory school-attendance law required them to cause their children to attend public or private school until reaching age 16 but the respondents declined to send their children, ages 14 and 15, to public school after they complete the eighth grade. The children were not enrolled in any private school, or within any recognized exception to the compulsory-attendance law, and they are conceded to be subject to the Wisconsin statute.

On complaint of the school district administrator for the public schools, respondents were charged, tried, and convicted of violating the compulsory-attendance law in Green County Court and were fined the sum of $5 each. Respondents defended on the ground that the application of the compulsory-attendance law violated their rights under the First and Fourteenth Amendments. The trial testimony showed that respondents believed, in accordance with the tenets of Old Order Amish communities generally, that their children's attendance at high school, public or private, was contrary to the Amish religion and way of life. They believed that by sending their children to high school, they would not only expose themselves to the danger of the censure of the church community, but, as found by the county court, also endanger their own salvation and that of their children. The State stipulated that respondents' religious beliefs were sincere.

In support of their position, respondents presented as expert witnesses scholars on religion and education whose testimony is uncontradicted. They expressed their opinions on the relationship of the Amish belief concerning school attendance to the more general tenets of their religion, and described the impact that compulsory high school attendance could have on the continued survival of Amish communities as they exist in the United States today. The history of the Amish sect was given in some detail, beginning with the Swiss baptists of the 16th century who rejected institutionalized churches and sought to return to the early, simple, Christian life deemphasizing material success, rejecting the competitive spirit, and seeking to insulate themselves from the modern world. As a result of their common heritage, Old Order Amish communities today are characterized by a fundamental belief that salvation requires life in a church community separate and apart from the world and worldly influence. This concept of life aloof from the world and its values is central to their faith.

A related feature of Old Order Amish communities is their devotion to a life in harmony with nature and the soil, as exemplified by the simply life of the early Christian era that continued in America during much of our early national life. Amish beliefs require members of the community to make their living by farming or closely related activities. Broadly speaking, the Old Order Amish religion pervades and determines the entire mode of life of its adherents. Their conduct is regulated in great detail by the Ordnung, or rules, of the church community. Adult baptism, which occurs in late adolescence, is the time at which Amish young people voluntarily undertake heavy obligations, not unlike the Bar Mitzvah of the Jews, to abide by the rules of the church community.

Amish objection to formal education beyond the eighth grade is firmly grounded in these central religious concepts. They object to the high school, and higher education generally, because the values they teach are in marked variance with Amish values and the Amish way of life; they view secondary school education as an impermissible exposure of their [illegible] worldly influence [illegible] their beliefs. The high school tends to emphasize intellectual and scientific accomplishments, self-distinction, competitiveness, worldly success, and social life with other students. Amish society emphasizes informal learning-through-doing; a life of "goodness," rather than a life of intellect; wisdom, rather than technical knowledge, community welfare, rather than competition; and separation from, rather than integration with [illegible] porary worldly society [illegible]

. . . .

The Amish do not object to elementary education through the first eight grades as a general proposition because they agree that their children must have basic skills in the "three R's" in order to read the Bible, to be good farmers and citizens, and to be able to deal with non-Amish people when necessary in the course of daily affairs. They view such a basic education as acceptable because it does not significantly expose their children to worldly values or interfere with their development in the Amish community during the crucial adolescent period. While Amish accept compulsory elementary education generally, wherever possible they have established their own elementary schools in many respects like the small local schools of the past. In the Amish belief higher learning tends to develop values they reject as influences that alienate man from God.

On the basis of such considerations, Dr. Hostetler testified that compulsory high school attendance could not only result in great psychological harm to Amish children, because of the conflicts it would produce, but would also, in his opinion, ultimately result in the destruction of the Old Order Amish church community as it exists in the United States today. . . .

. . . .

I

There is no doubt as to the power of a State, having a high responsibility for education of its citizens, to impose reasonable regulations [illegible] control and duration of [illegible] education. See, e.g., *Pierce v. Society of Sisters*, 268 U.S. 510, 534 (1925). Providing public schools ranks at the very apex of the function of a State. Yet even this paramount responsibility was, in *Pierce,* made to yield to the right of parents to provide an equivalent education in a privately operated system. There the Court held that Oregon's statute compelling attendance in a public school from age eight to age 16 unreasonably interfered with the interest of parents in directing the rearing of their offspring, including their education in church-operated schools. As that case suggests, the values of parental direction of the religious upbringing and education of their children in their early and formative years have a high place in our society. . . .

It follows that in order for Wisconsin to compel school attendance beyond the eighth grade against a claim that such attendance interferes with the practice of a legitimate religious belief, it must appear either that the State does not deny the free exercise of religious belief by its requirement, or that there is a state interest of sufficient magnitude to override the interest claiming protection under the Free Exercise Clause. Long before there was general acknowledgment of the need for universal formal education, the Religion Clauses had specifically and firmly fixed the right to free exercise of religious beliefs, and buttressing this fundamental right was an equally firm, even if less explicit, prohibition against the establishment of any religion by government. . . .

. . . .

II

We come then to the quality of the claims of the respondents concerning the alleged encroachment of Wisconsin's compulsory school-attendance statute on their rights and the rights of their children to the free exercise of the religious beliefs they and their forbears have adhered to for almost three centuries. In evaluating those claims we must be careful to determine whether the Amish religious faith and their mode of life are, as they claim, inseparable and interdependent. A way of life, however virtuous and admirable, may not be interposed as a barrier to reasonable state regulation of education if it is based on purely secular considerations. . . .

Giving no weight to such secular considerations, however, we see that the record in this case abundantly supports the claim that the traditional way of life of the Amish is not merely a matter of personal preference, but one of deep religious conviction, shared by an organized group, and intimately related to daily living. That the Old Order Amish daily life and religious practice stem from their faith is shown by the fact that it is in response to their literal interpretation of the Biblical injunction from the Epistle of Paul to the Romans, "be not conformed to this world. . . ." This command is fundamental to the Amish faith. . . .

The record shows that the respondents' religious beliefs and attitude toward life, family, and home have remained constant — perhaps some would say static — in a period of unparalleled progress in human knowledge generally and great changes in education. The respondents freely concede, and indeed assert as an article of faith, that their religious beliefs and what we would today call "life style" have not altered in fundamentals for centuries. . . .

. . . As the record so strongly shows, the values and programs of the modern secondary school are in sharp conflict with the fundamental mode of life mandated by the Amish religion; modern laws requiring compulsory secondary education have accordingly engendered great concern and conflict. . . .

. . . .

III

. . . .

The State attacks respondents' position as one fostering "ignorance" from which the child must be protected by the State. No one can question the State's duty to protect children from ignorance but this argument does not square with the facts disclosed in the record. Whatever their idiosyncrasies as seen by the majority, this record strongly shows that the Amish community has been a highly successful social unit within our society, even if apart from the conventional "mainstream." Its members are productive and very law-abiding members of society; they reject public welfare in any of its usual modern forms. The Congress itself recognized their self-sufficiency by authorizing exemption of such groups as the Amish from the obligation to pay social security taxes.

. . . .

The State, however, supports its interest in providing an additional one or two years of compulsory high school education to Amish children because of the possibility that some such children will choose to leave the Amish community, and that if this occurs they will be ill-equipped for life. The State argues that if Amish children leave their church they should not be in the position of making their way in the world without the education available in the one or two additional years the State requires. However, on this record, that argument is highly speculative. There is no specific evidence of the loss of Amish adherents by attrition, nor is there any showing that upon leaving the Amish community Amish children, with their practical agricultural training and habits of industry and self-reliance, would become burdens on society because of educational shortcomings. . . .

. . . .

Insofar as the State's claim rests on the view that a brief additional period of formal education is imperative to enable the Amish to participate effectively and intelligently in our democratic process, it must fall. The Amish alternative to formal secondary school education has enabled them to function effectively in their day-to-day life under self-imposed limitations on relations with the world, and to survive and prosper in contemporary society as a separate, sharply identifiable and highly self-sufficient community for more than 200 years in this country. In itself this is strong evidence that they are capable of fulfilling the social and political responsibilities of citizenship without compelled attendance beyond the eighth grade at the price of jeopardizing their free exercise of religious belief. . . .

. . . .

IV

Finally, the State, on authority of *Prince v. Massachusetts*, argues that a decision exempting Amish children from the State's requirement fails to recognize the substantive right of the Amish child to a secondary education, and fails to give due regard to the power of the State as parens patriae to extend the benefit of secondary education to children regardless of the wishes of their parents. Taken at its broadest sweep, the Court's language in *Prince,* might be read to give support to the State's position. However, the Court was not confronted in *Prince* with a situation comparable to that of the Amish as revealed in this record; this is shown by the Court's severe characterization of the evils that it thought the legislature could legitimately associate with child labor, even when performed in the company of an adult. The Court later took great care to confine *Prince* to a narrow scope in *Sherbert v. Verner*, when it stated:

> "On the other hand, the Court has rejected challenges under the Free Exercise Clause to governmental regulation of certain overt acts prompted by religious beliefs or principles, for 'even when the action is in accord with one's religious convictions, [it] is not totally free from legislative restrictions.' The conduct of actions so regulated have invariably posed some substantial threat to public safety, peace or order."

This case, of course, is not one in which any harm to the physical or mental health of the child or to the public safety, peace, order, or welfare has been demonstrated or may be properly inferred. The record is to the contrary, and any reliance on that theory would find no support in the evidence.

. . . .

Our holding in no way determines the proper resolution of possible competing interests of parents, children, and the State in an appropriate state court proceeding in which the power of the State is asserted on the theory that Amish parents are preventing their minor children from attending high school despite their expressed desires to the contrary. Recognition of the claim of the State in such a proceeding would, of course, call into question traditional concepts of parental control over the religious upbringing and education of their minor children recognized in this Court's past decisions. It is clear that such an intrusion by a State into family decisions in the area of religious training would give rise to grave questions of religious freedom comparable to those raised here and those presented in *Pierce v. Society of Sisters*. On this record we neither reach nor decide those issues.

. . . .

Indeed it seems clear that if the State is empowered, as *parens patriae,* to "save" a child from himself or his Amish parents by requiring an additional two years of compulsory formal high school education, the State will in large measure influence, if not determine, the religious future of the child. Even more markedly than in *Prince,* therefore, this case involves the fundamental interest of parents, as contrasted with that of the State, to guide the religious future and education of their children. The history and culture of Western civilization reflect a strong tradition of parental concern for the nurture and upbringing of their children. This primary role of the parents in the upbringing of their children is now established beyond debate as an enduring American tradition. . . .

. . . .

V

Aided by a history of three centuries as an identifiable religious sect and a long history as a successful and self-sufficient segment of American society, the Amish in this case have convincingly demonstrated the sincerity of their religious beliefs, the interrelationship of belief with their mode of life, the vital role that belief and daily conduct play in the continued survival of Old Order Amish communities and their religious organization, and the hazards presented by the State's enforcement of a statute generally valid as to others.

Beyond this, they have carried the even more difficult burden of demonstrating the adequacy of their alternative mode of continuing informal vocational education in terms of precisely those overall interests that the State advances in support of its program of compulsory high school education. In light of this convincing showing, one that probably few other religious groups or sects could make, and weighing the minimal difference between what the State would require and what the Amish already accept, it was incumbent on the State to show with more particularity how its admittedly strong interest in compulsory education would be adversely affected by granting an exemption to the Amish.

. . . .

Affirmed.

. . . .

Mr. Justice **Douglas**, dissenting in part.

I

. . . .

Religion is an individual experience. It is not necessary, nor even appropriate, for every Amish child to express his views on the subject in a prosecution of a single adult. Crucial, however, are the views of the child whose parent is the subject of the suit. Frieda Yoder has in fact testified that her own religious views are opposed to high-school education. I therefore join the judgment of the Court as to respondent Jonas Yoder. But Frieda Yoder's views may not be those of Vernon Yutzy or Barbara Miller. I must dissent, therefore, as to respondents Adin Yutzy and Wallace Miller as their motion to dismiss also raised the question of their children's religious liberty.

II

This issue has never been squarely presented before today. Our opinions are full of talk about the power of the parents over the child's education. And we have in the past analyzed similar conflicts between parent and State with little regard for the views of the child. *See Prince v. Massachusetts*. Recent cases, however, have clearly held that the children themselves have constitutionally protectible interests.

These children are "persons" within the meaning of the Bill of Rights. We have so held over and over again. . . .

. . . .

On this important and vital matter of education, I think the children should be entitled to be heard. While the parents, absent dissent, normally speak for the entire family, the education of the child is a matter on which the child will often have decided views. He may want to be a pianist or an astronaut or an oceanographer. To do so he will have to break from the Amish tradition.

It is the future of the student, not the future of the parents, that is imperiled by today's decision. If a parent keeps his child out of school beyond the grade school, then the child will be forever barred from entry into the new and amazing world of diversity that we have today. The child may decide that is the preferred course, or he may rebel. It is the student's judgment, not his parents', that is essential if we are to give full meaning to what we have said about the Bill of Rights and of the right of students to be masters of their own destiny. If he is harnessed to the Amish way of life by those in authority over him and if his education is truncated, his entire life may be stunted and deformed. The child, therefore, should be given an opportunity to be heard before the State gives the exemption which we honor today.

. . . .

III

The Court rightly rejects the notion that actions, even though religiously grounded, are always outside the protection of the Free Exercise Clause of the First Amendment. . . .

. . . .

NOTES AND QUESTIONS

1. *Wisconsin v. Yoder* is significant constitutionally in two very important ways: it affirms the importance of religion in a most important secular area, education, and, as well, it reaffirms the right of the family to make choices as to that same important secular field of education. The Court may treat the Old Order Amish as unique, in constituting a closed religious community which satisfies Wisconsin's need to provide education. But in so doing, the Court reaffirms two distinct preexisting bodies of law, concerning the exercise of religion and the association of family. Each of these is independently significant in determining the identity of individuals.
2. Ethically, the Amish seek to preserve their way of life and to preserve it for their children and future generations, in the belief that it is a *better* way of life. However, in so doing, they live within a greater society whose values are different from theirs, but whose resources are available to them and, in considerable measure, appropriated by them. To which community do they belong? Ethically, to which do they owe respect and responsibility?
3. There are within the greater community many distinct sub-communities: the Native Americans, the Mormons, Roman Catholic convents for nuns, gated enclaves for the wealthy, public housing, high-rise slums for the poor. In what ways, if at all, should the members of such groups be permitted to draw upon the identity thus conferred or created, rejecting majoritarian values? If it is the ethical commitment of America that all groups should have equal opportunity and all groups should make equal commitments, then is the result in *Wisconsin v. Yoder* an unethical result?
4. Does the Court in *Wisconsin v. Yoder* protect the free exercise of religion or does it instead favor the establishment of religion, which is prohibited by the First Amendment?

5. Justice Douglas argues in dissent that the Court is enabling the Amish families to frustrate the free exercise of religion by the [illegible] argues that their children should [illegible] be heard and that it is the [illegible] student, not the parents, that is imperiled by the majority's decision. What is your reaction to these arguments? If you objected — in the preceding section — to cloning humans because of the effect on the child created, shouldn't you have the same objections to what the Amish are doing to their children?

6. Suppose that the Old Order Amish [illegible] teach and speak in the German [illegible] spoken in The Netherlands in the early 1700s. And suppose that this was the language spoken in their homes and their churches. Could the state of Wisconsin declare that English is the official language of the state, or that only English may be taught in the public schools, or that any family failing to instruct in English could lose their children? As to these questions, see *Meyer v. Nebraska* and the cases in the previous sections of this chapter.

7. Suppose that a community of Hassidic Jews moved to a rural area of Your State, and incorporated as a municipality, with a separate school district? Could they exclude Christians from the schools? From property ownership? *Should* they be able to do so? See *Board of Education of Kiryas Joel Village v. Grumet*, 512 U.S. 687 (1994) and *Stark v. Independent School District*, 123 F.3d 1068 (8th Cir. 1997).

8. *Yoder* tests the *power* of the family when merged strongly with religion. We now turn to a different inquiry — the *meaning* of "family" when marriage — traditionally a heterosexual concept — is proposed for same-sex couples.

HERNANDEZ v. ROBLES

__ N.E.2d __, 2006 NY LEXIS 1836,
2006 N.Y. Slip Op. 05239 (July 6, 2006)

R.S. **Smith**, J.

We hold that the New York Constitution does not compel [illegible] marriages between members of the same [illegible] such marriages should be recognized [illegible] to be addressed by the Legislature.

Facts and Procedural History

Plaintiffs and petitioners (hereafter plaintiffs) are the members of 44 same-sex couples. Each couple tried unsuccessfully to obtain a marriage license.

Discussion

I

All the parties to these cases now acknowledge, implicitly or explicitly, that the Domestic Relations Law limits marriage to opposite-sex couples. Some *amici*, however, suggest that the statute can be read to permit same-sex marriage, thus mooting the constitutional issues. We find this suggestion untenable.

Articles 2 and 3 of the Domestic Relations Law, which govern marriage, nowhere say in so many words that only people of different sexes may marry each other, but that was the universal understanding when Articles 2 and 3 were adopted in 1909, an understanding reflected in several statutes. Domestic Relations Law § 12 provides that "the parties must solemnly declare . . . that they take each other as husband and wife." Domestic Relations Law § 15(a) requires town and city clerks to obtain specified information from "the groom" and "the bride." Domestic Relations Law § 5 prohibits certain marriages as incestuous, specifying opposite-sex combinations (brother and sister, uncle and niece, aunt and nephew), but not same-sex combinations. Domestic Relations Law § 50 says that the property of "a married woman . . . shall not be subject to her husband's control."

New York's statutory law clearly limits marriage to opposite-sex couples. The more serious question is whether that limitation is consistent with the New York Constitution.

III

It is undisputed that the benefits of marriage are many. The diligence of counsel has identified 316 such benefits in New York law, of which it is enough to summarize some of the most important: Married people receive significant tax advantages, rights in probate and intestacy proceedings, rights to support from their spouses both during the marriage and after it is dissolved, and rights to be treated as family members in obtaining insurance coverage and making health care decisions. Beyond this, they receive the symbolic benefit, or moral satisfaction, of seeing their relationships recognized by the State.

The critical question is whether a rational legislature could decide that these benefits should be given to members of opposite-sex couples, but not same-sex couples. The question is not, we emphasize, whether the Legislature must or should continue to limit marriage in this way; of course the Legislature may (subject to the effect of the Federal Defense of Marriage Act, Pub L 104-199, 110 Stat 2419) extend marriage or some or all of its benefits to same-sex couples. We conclude, however, that there are at least two grounds that rationally support the limitation on marriage that the Legislature has enacted. Others have been advanced, but we will discuss only these two, both of which are derived from the undisputed assumption that marriage is important to the welfare of children.

First, the Legislature could rationally decide that, for the welfare of children, it is more important to promote stability, and to avoid instability, in opposite-sex than in same-sex relationships. Heterosexual intercourse has a natural tendency to lead to the birth of children; homosexual intercourse does not. Despite the advances of science, it remains true that the vast majority of children are born as a result of a sexual relationship between a man and a woman, and the Legislature could find that this will continue to be true. The Legislature could also find that such relationships are all too often casual or temporary. It could find that an important function of marriage is to create more stability and permanence in the relationships that cause children to be born. It thus could choose to offer an inducement in th[illegible] of marriage and its attendant benefits to [illegible] sex couples who make a solemn, long-term [illegible]ment to each other.

The Legislature could find that this rationale for marriage does not apply with comparable force to same-sex couples. These couples can become parents by adoption, or by artificial insemination or other technological marvels, but they do not become parents as a result of accident or impulse. The [illegible] could find that unstable relationships [illegible] people of the opposite sex present a greater [illegible] that children will be born into or grow up in unstable homes than is the case with same-sex couples, and thus that promoting stability in opposite-sex relationships will help children more. This is one reason why the Legislature could rationally offer the benefits of marriage to opposite-sex couples only.

There is a second reason: The Legislature could rationally believe that it is better, other things being equal, for children to grow up with both a mother and a father. Intuition and experience suggest that a child benefits from having before his or her eyes, every day, living models of what both a man and a woman are like. It is obvious that there are exceptions to this general rule — some children who never know their fathers, or their mothers, do far better than some who grow up with parents of both sexes — but the Legislature could find that the general rule will usually hold.

In sum, there are rational grounds on which the Legislature could choose to restrict marriage to couples of opposite sex. Plaintiffs have not persuaded us that this long-accepted restriction is a wholly irrational one, based solely on ignorance and prejudice against homosexuals.

The traditional definition of marriage is not merely a by-product of historical injustice. Its history is of a different kind.

The idea that same-sex marriage is even possible is a relatively new one. Until a few decades ago, it was an accepted truth for almost everyone who ever lived, in any society in which marriage existed, that there could be marriages only between participants of different sex. A court should not lightly conclude that everyone who held this belief was irrational, ignorant or [illegible]. We do not so conclude.

A. Due Process

In deciding the validity of legislation under the Due Process Clause, courts first inquire whether the legislation restricts the exercise of a fundamental right, one that is "deeply rooted in this Nation's history and tradition." In this case, whether the right in question is "fundamental" depends on how it is defined. The right to marry is unquestionably a fundamental right. The right to marry someone of the same sex, however, is not "deeply rooted"; it has not even been asserted until relatively recent times. The issue then becomes whether the right to marry must be defined to include a right to same-sex marriage.

The difference between *Lawrence* and *Glucksberg* is that in *Glucksberg* the relatively narrow definition of the right at issue was based on rational line-drawing. In *Lawrence*, by contrast, the court found the distinction between homosexual sodomy and intimate relations generally to be essentially arbitrary. Here, there are, as we have explained, rational grounds for limiting the definition of marriage to opposite-sex couples. This case is therefore, in the relevant way, like *Glucksberg* and not at all like *Lawrence*. Plaintiffs here do not, as the petitioners in *Lawrence* did, seek protection against State intrusion on intimate, private activity. They seek from the courts access to a State-conferred benefit that the Legislature has rationally limited to opposite-sex couples. We conclude that, by defining marriage as it has, the New York Legislature has not restricted the exercise of a fundamental right (see also concurring op of Judge Graffeo at 5-13).

Where no fundamental right is at issue, legislation is valid under the Due Process Clause if it is rationally related to legitimate government interests.

B. Equal Protection

By limiting marriage to opposite-sex couples, New York is not engaging in sex discrimination. The limitation does not put men and women in different classes, and give one class a benefit not given to the other. Women and men are treated alike — they are permitted to marry people of the opposite sex, but not people of their own sex. Plaintiffs do not argue here that the legislation they challenge is designed to subordinate either men to women or women to men as a class.

However, the legislation does confer advantages on the basis of sexual preference. Those who prefer relationships with people of the opposite sex and those who prefer relationships with people of the same sex are not treated alike, since only opposite-sex relationships may gain the status and benefits associated with marriage. This case thus presents the question of what level of scrutiny is to be applied to legislation that classifies people on this basis.

We resolve this question in this case on the basis of the Supreme Court's observation that no more than rational basis scrutiny is generally appropriate "where individuals in the group affected by a law have distinguishing characteristics relevant to interests the State has the authority to implement" (*City of Cleburne v. Cleburne Living Ctr., Inc.*, 473 U.S. 432, 441 [1985]). Perhaps that principle would lead us to apply heightened scrutiny to sexual preference discrimination in some cases, but not where we review legislation governing marriage and family relationships. A person's preference for the sort of sexual activity that cannot lead to the birth of children is relevant to the State's interest in fostering relationships that will serve children best. In this area, therefore, we conclude that rational basis scrutiny is appropriate.

Plaintiffs argue that the category is underinclusive because, as we recognized above, same-sex couples, as well as opposite-sex couples, may have children. That is indeed a reason why the Legislature might rationally choose to extend marriage or its benefits to same-sex couples; but it could also, for the reasons we have explained, rationally make another choice, based on the different characteristics of opposite-sex and same-sex relationships. Our earlier discussion demonstrates that the definition of marriage to include only opposite-sex couples is not irrationally underinclusive.

In arguing that the definition is overinclusive, plaintiffs point out that many opposite-sex couples cannot have or do not want to have children. How can it be rational, they ask, to permit these couples, but not same-sex couples, to marry? The question is not a difficult one to answer. While same-sex couples and opposite-sex couples are easily distinguished, limiting marriage to opposite-sex couples likely to have children would require grossly intrusive inquiries, and arbitrary and unreliable line-drawing. A legislature that regarded marriage primarily or solely as an institution for the benefit of children could rationally find that an attempt to exclude childless opposite-sex couples from the institution would be a very bad idea.

V

We hold, in sum, that the Domestic Relations Law's limitation of marriage to opposite-sex couples is not unconstitutional. We emphasize once again that we are deciding only this constitutional question. It is not for us to say whether same-sex marriage is right or wrong. We have presented some (though not all) of the arguments against same-sex marriage because our duty to defer to the Legislature requires us to do so. We do not imply that there are no persuasive arguments on the other side — and we know, of course, that there are very powerful emotions on both sides of the question.

The dissenters assert confidently that "future generations" will agree with their view of this case (dissenting op at 28). We do not predict what people will think generations from now, but we believe the present generation should have a chance to decide the issue through its elected representatives. We therefore express our hope that the participants in the controversy over same-sex marriage will address their arguments to the Legislature; that the Legislature will listen and decide as wisely as it can; and that those unhappy with the result — as many undoubtedly will be — will respect it as people in a democratic state should respect choices democratically made.

Accordingly, the orders of the Appellate Division in each case should be affirmed without costs.

Kaye, Chief Judge (dissenting):

Plaintiffs (including petitioners) are 44 same-sex couples who wish to marry. They include a doctor, a police officer, a public school teacher, a nurse, an artist and a State legislator. Ranging in age from under 30 to 68, plaintiffs reflect a diversity of races, religions and ethnicities. They come from upstate and down, from rural, urban and suburban settings. Many have been together in committed relationships for decades, and many are raising children — from toddlers to teenagers. Many are active in their communities, serving on their local school board, for example, or their cooperative apartment building board. In short, plaintiffs represent a cross-section of New Yorkers who want only to live full lives, raise their children, better their communities and be good neighbors.

For most of us, leading a full life includes establishing a family. Indeed, most New Yorkers can look back on, or forward to, their wedding as among the most significant events of their lives. They, like plaintiffs, grew up hoping to find that one person with whom they would share their future, eager to express their mutual lifetime pledge through civil marriage. Solely because of their sexual orientation, however — that is, because of who they love — plaintiffs are denied the rights and responsibilities of civil marriage. This State has a proud tradition of affording equal rights to all New Yorkers. Sadly, the Court today retreats from that proud tradition.

I. *Due Process*

Simply put, fundamental rights are fundamental rights. They are not defined in terms of who is entitled to exercise them.

Instead, the Supreme Court has repeatedly held that the fundamental right to marry must be afforded even to those who have previously been excluded from its scope — that is, to those whose exclusion from the right was "deeply rooted." Well into the twentieth century, the sheer weight of precedent accepting the constitutionality of bans on interracial marriage was deemed sufficient justification in and of itself to perpetuate these discriminatory laws — much as defendants now contend that same-sex couples should be prohibited from marrying because historically they always have been.

Just 10 years before *Loving* declared unconstitutional state laws banning marriage between persons of different races, 96% of Americans were opposed to interracial marriage. Sadly, many of the arguments then raised in support of the anti-miscegenation laws were identical to those made today in opposition to same-sex marriage.

To those who appealed to history as a basis for prohibiting interracial marriage, it was simply inconceivable that the right of interracial couples to marry could be deemed "fundamental." Incredible as it may seem today, during the lifetime of every Judge on this Court, interracial marriage was forbidden in at least a third of American jurisdictions. In 1948, New York was one of only 18 states in the nation that did not have such a ban. By 1967, when *Loving* was decided, 17 states still outlawed marriages between persons of different races. Nevertheless, even though it was the ban on interracial marriage — not interracial marriage itself — that had a long and shameful national tradition, the Supreme Court determined that interracial couples could not be deprived of their fundamental right to marry.

The claim that marriage has always had a single and unalterable meaning is a plain distortion of history. In truth, the common understanding of "marriage" has changed dramatically over the centuries. Until well into the nineteenth century, for example, marriage was defined by the doctrine of coverture, according to which the wife's legal identity was merged into that of her husband, whose property she became. A married woman, by definition, could not own property and could not enter into contracts. Such was the very "meaning" of marriage. Only since the mid-twentieth century has the institution of marriage come to be understood as a relationship between two equal partners, founded upon shared intimacy and mutual financial and emotional support. Indeed, as amici professors note, "The historical record shows that, through adjudication and legislation, all of New York's sex-specific rules for marriage have been invalidated save for the one at issue here."

II. *Equal Protection*

By virtue of their being denied entry into civil marriage, plaintiff couples are deprived of a myriad of statutory benefits and protections extended to married couples under New York law. Unlike married spouses, same-sex partners may be denied hospital visitation of their critically ill life partners. They must spend more of their joint income to obtain equivalent levels of health care coverage. They may, upon the death of their partners, find themselves at risk of losing the family home. The record is replete with examples of the hundreds of ways in which committed same-sex couples and their children are deprived of equal benefits under New York law. Same-sex families are, among other things, denied equal treatment with respect to intestacy, inheritance, tenancy by the entirety, taxes, insurance, health benefits, medical decisionmaking, workers' compensation, the right to sue for wrongful death, and spousal privilege. Each of these statutory inequities, as well as the discriminatory exclusion of same-sex couples from the benefits and protections of civil marriage as a whole, violates their constitutional right to equal protection of the laws.

A. *Heightened Scrutiny*

1. *Sexual Orientation Discrimination*

Homosexuals meet the constitutional definition of a suspect class, that is, a group whose defining characteristic is "so seldom relevant to the achievement of any legitimate state interest that laws grounded in such considerations are deemed to reflect prejudice and antipathy — a view that those in the burdened class are not as worthy or deserving as others" (*Cleburne*, 473 U.S. at 440). Accordingly, any classification discriminating on the basis of sexual orientation must be narrowly tailored to meet a compelling state interest.

Although no single factor is dispositive, the Supreme Court has generally looked to three criteria in determining whether a group subject to legislative classification must be considered "suspect." First, the Court has considered whether the group has historically been subjected to purposeful discrimination. Homosexuals plainly have been, as the Legislature expressly found when it recently enacted the Sexual Orientation Non-Discrimination Act (SONDA), barring discrimination against homosexuals in employment, housing, public accommodations, education, credit and the exercise of civil rights. Specifically, the Legislature found "that many residents of this state have encountered prejudice on account of their sexual orientation, and that this prejudice has severely limited or actually prevented access to employment, housing and other basic necessities of life, leading to deprivation and suffering. The legislature further recognizes that this prejudice has fostered a general climate of hostility and distrust, leading in some instances to physical violence against those perceived to be homosexual or bisexual" (L 2002, ch 2, § 1; see also Br. of Parents, Families & Friends of Lesbians and Gays, Inc., et al. as Amici Curiae in Support of Plaintiffs, at 22-49 [detailing history of state-sanctioned discrimination against gays and lesbians]).

Second, the Court has considered whether the trait used to define the class is unrelated to the ability to perform and participate in society. When the State differentiates among its citizens "on the basis of stereotyped characteristics not truly indicative of their abilities" (*Mass. Bd. of Retirement v. Murgia*, 427 U.S. 307, 313 [1976]), the legislative classification must be closely scrutinized. Obviously, sexual orientation is irrelevant to one's ability to perform or contribute.

Third, the Court has taken into account the group's relative political powerlessness. Defendants contend that classifications based on sexual orientation should not be afforded heightened scrutiny because, they claim, homosexuals are sufficiently able to achieve protection from discrimination through the political process, as evidenced by the Legislature's passage of SONDA in 2002. SONDA, however, was first introduced in 1971. It failed repeatedly for 31 years, until it was finally enacted just four years ago. Further, during the Senate debate on the Hate Crimes Act of 2000, one Senator noted that "[i]t's no secret that for years we could have passed a hate-crimes bill if we were willing to take out gay people, if [we] were willing to take out sexual orientation." The simple fact is that New York has not enacted anything approaching comprehensive statewide domestic partnership protections for same-sex couples, much less marriage or even civil unions.

Nor is plaintiffs' claim legitimately answered by the argument that the licensing statute does not discriminate on the basis of sexual orientation since it permits homosexuals to marry persons of the opposite sex and forbids heterosexuals to marry persons of the same sex. The purported "right" of gays and lesbians to enter into marriages with different-sex partners to whom they have no innate attraction cannot possibly cure the constitutional violation actually at issue here. "The right to marry is the right of individuals, not of . . . groups." "Human beings are bereft of worth and dignity by a doctrine that would make them as interchangeable as trains." Limiting marriage to opposite-sex couples undeniably restricts gays and lesbians from marrying their chosen same-sex partners whom "to [them] may be irreplaceable" (*id.*) — and thus constitutes discrimination based on sexual orientation.[1]

2. *Sex Discrimination*

Under the Domestic Relations Law, a woman who seeks to marry another woman is prevented from doing so on account of her sex — that is, because she is not a man. If she were, she would be given a marriage license to marry that woman. That the statutory scheme applies equally to both sexes does not alter the conclusion that the classification here is based on sex. The "equal application" approach to equal protection analysis was expressly rejected by the Supreme Court in *Loving*: "[W]e reject the notion that the mere 'equal application' of a statute containing [discriminatory] classifications is enough

[1] Indeed, the true nature and extent of the discrimination suffered by gays and lesbians in this regard is perhaps best illustrated by the simple truth that each one of the plaintiffs here could lawfully enter into a marriage of convenience with a complete stranger of the opposite sex tomorrow, and thereby immediately obtain all of the myriad benefits and protections incident to marriage. Plaintiffs are, however, denied these rights because they each desire instead to marry the person they love and with whom they have created their family.

to remove the classifications from the [constitutional] proscription of all invidious . . . discriminations" (388 U.S. at 8). Instead, the *Loving* Court held that "[t]here can be no question but that Virginia's miscegenation statutes rest solely upon distinctions drawn according to race [where the] statutes proscribe generally accepted conduct if engaged in by members of different races."

B. *Rational-Basis Analysis*

Although the classification challenged here should be analyzed using heightened scrutiny, it does not satisfy even rational-basis review, which requires that the classification "rationally further a legitimate state interest." Rational-basis review requires both the existence of a legitimate interest and that the classification rationally advance that interest. Although a number of interests have been proffered in support of the challenged classification at issue, none is rationally furthered by the exclusion of same-sex couples from marriage. Some fail even to meet the threshold test of legitimacy.

1. *Children*

Defendants primarily assert an interest in encouraging procreation within marriage. But while encouraging opposite-sex couples to marry before they have children is certainly a legitimate interest of the State, the *exclusion* of gay men and lesbians from marriage in no way furthers this interest. There are enough marriage licenses to go around for everyone.

Nor does this exclusion rationally further the State's legitimate interest in encouraging heterosexual married couples to procreate. Plainly, the ability or desire to procreate is not a prerequisite for marriage. The elderly are permitted to marry, and many same-sex couples do indeed have children. Thus, the statutory classification here — which prohibits only same-sex couples, and no one else, from marrying — is so grossly underinclusive and overinclusive as to make the asserted rationale in promoting procreation "impossible to credit."[2] Indeed, even the *Lawrence* dissenters observed that "encouragement of procreation" could not "possibly" be a justification for denying marriage to gay and lesbian couples, "since the sterile and the elderly are allowed to marry."

Of course, there are many ways in which the government could rationally promote procreation — for example, by giving tax breaks to couples who have children, subsidizing child care for those couples, or mandating generous family leave for parents. Any of these benefits — and many more — might convince people who would not otherwise have children to do so. But no one rationally decides to have children because gays and lesbians are excluded from marriage.

---

[2] Although the plurality asserts that the Legislature could not possibly exclude from marriage opposite-sex couples unable to have children because to do so would require "grossly intrusive inquiries" (plurality op at 16), no explanation is given as to why the Legislature could not easily remedy the irrationality inherent in allowing all childless couples to marry — if, as the plurality believes, the sole purpose of marriage is procreation — by simply barring from civil marriage all couples in which both spouses are older than, say, 55. In that event, the State would have no need to undertake intrusive inquiries of any kind.

Marriage is about much more than producing children, yet same-sex couples are excluded from the entire spectrum of protections that come with civil marriage — purportedly to encourage other people to procreate. Indeed, the protections that the State gives to couples who do marry — such as the right to own property as a unit or to make medical decisions for each other — are focused largely on the adult relationship, rather than on the couple's possible role as parents. Nor does the plurality even attempt to explain how offering only heterosexuals the right to visit a sick loved one in the hospital, for example, conceivably furthers the State's interest in encouraging opposite-sex couples to have children, or indeed how excluding same-sex couples from each of the specific legal benefits of civil marriage — even apart from the totality of marriage itself — does not independently violate plaintiffs' rights to equal protection of the laws. The breadth of protections that the marriage laws make unavailable to gays and lesbians is "so far removed" from the State's asserted goal of promoting procreation that the justification is, again, "impossible to credit."

The State plainly has a legitimate interest in the welfare of children, but excluding same-sex couples from marriage in no way furthers this interest. In fact, it undermines it. Civil marriage provides tangible legal protections and economic benefits to married couples and their children, and tens of thousands of children are currently being raised by same-sex couples in New York. Depriving these children of the benefits and protections available to the children of opposite-sex couples is antithetical to their welfare, as defendants do not dispute

3. *Tradition*

That civil marriage has traditionally excluded same-sex couples — i.e., that the "historic and cultural understanding of marriage" has been between a man and a woman — cannot in itself provide a rational basis for the challenged exclusion. To say that discrimination is "traditional" is to say only that the discrimination has existed for a long time. A classification, however, cannot be maintained merely "for its own sake." Instead, the classification (here, the exclusion of gay men and lesbians from civil marriage) must advance a state interest that is separate from the classification itself. Because the "tradition" of excluding gay men and lesbians from civil marriage is no different from the classification itself, the exclusion cannot be justified on the basis of "history." Indeed, the justification of "tradition" does not explain the classification; it merely repeats it. Simply put, a history or tradition of discrimination — no matter how entrenched — does not make the discrimination constitutional.[3]

4. *Uniformity*

The State asserts an interest in maintaining uniformity with the marriage laws of other states. But our marriage laws currently are not uniform with

[3] Ultimately, as the Lawrence dissenters recognized, " preserving the traditional institution of marriage' is just a kinder way of describing the State's moral disapproval of same-sex couples" (539 U.S. at 601 [Scalia, J., dissenting] [emphasis in original]), an illegitimate basis for depriving gay and lesbian couples of the equal protection of the laws.

those of other states. For example, New York — unlike most other states in the nation — permits first cousins to marry (*see* Domestic Relations [illegible]). This disparity has caused [illegible], however, because well-settled principles of comity resolve any conflicts. The same well-settled principles of comity would resolve any conflicts arising from any disparity involving the recognition of same-sex marriages.

It is, additionally, already impossible to maintain uniformity among all the states, inasmuch as Massachusetts has now legalized same-sex marriage. Indeed, of the seven jurisdictions that border New York State, only Pennsylvania currently affords no legal status to same-sex relationships. Massachusetts, Ontario and Quebec all authorize same-sex marriage; Vermont and Connecticut provide for civil unions; and New Jersey has a statewide domestic partnership law. Moreover, insofar as a number of localities within New York offer domestic partnership registration, even the law within the State is not uniform. Finally, and most fundamentally, to justify the exclusion of gay men and lesbians from civil marriage because "others do it too" is no more a justification for the discriminatory classification than the contention that the discrimination is rational because it has existed for a long time. As history has well taught us, separate is inherently unequal.

It is uniquely the function of the Judicial Branch to safeguard individual liberties guaranteed by the New York State Constitution, and to order redress for their violation. The Court's duty to protect constitutional rights is an imperative of the separation of powers, not its enemy.

I am confident that future generations will look back on today's decision as an unfortunate misstep.

NOTES AND QUESTIONS

1. *Hernandez v. Robles* was decided as this Second Edition was going to press and replaces *Baehr v. Lewin*, 852 P. 2d 44 (Harv. 1993), a Hawaii case which held that Hawaii could not bar same-sex marriage. That case was followed by legislation protecting same-sex couples, and both the case and statute remain germane today. However, the *Robles* case accounts for Supreme Court decisions subsequent to *Baehr*, and so is included here. The next case, *Goodridge*, reaches the same conclusions as *Baehr*, and so provides an effective counterpoint to *Robles*.
2. Why do same-sex couples seek marriage? Is it for the 316 benefits? If so, what are they, and couldn't they be achieved by contract anyway? Is it to achieve social approbation and recognition of their union? Is it simply a declaration of support and fidelity? Or, perhaps, is it that asking the question is to engage in the very discrimination same-sex couples seek to avoid?
3. If the statutes, by their terms, do not *bar* same-sex marriages, why does Justice Smith find that is their effect? Does the dissent agree?
4. Justice Smith says the legislature *could* extend marriage to same-sex couples, "subject to the effect of the Federal Defense of Marriage Act, 110 Stat. 2419." What does he mean? What is that Act and how does

it limit state latitude? *See, e.g., Why the Defense of Marriage Act Is Not (Yet?) Unconstitutional*, 90 Minn. L. Rev. 915 (2006)

Suppose the DOMA overrides state legislation authorizing gay marriage; if so, would DOMA be unconstitutional?

5. What of Smith's purported due process rationale that heterosexual unions "are all too often casual or temporary," and thus children born into such homes face greater instability and such homes need to have greater support. Isn't this exactly the *opposite* of what you expected? Wouldn't you expect the legislature might — as the dissent in *Goodridge, infra*, argues — conclude same-sex unions are sufficiently lacking in reproductive "glue" that *they* do not merit marriage?

   And, if heterosexual unions have great need for the stability of marriage, how effective is it, really, when *half* end in divorce? Does any of this mean that mean same-sex marriages *would not* benefit from state validation?

6. The same questions arise as to the second due process rationale -that children need a mother and father "before their eyes daily," when half of such homes are divorced, and the remainder are a prolific source of domestic violence and child abuse. As for "models," shouldn't it be of loving relationships, which are not restricted to heterosexual pairing?

7. The *Lawrence* case, *supra*, § 2.02(2) and the *Glucksberg* case, *infra*, § 4.05(2), discussed in *Robles*, dealt respectively with banning homosexual relations (struck down) and assisted suicide (upheld), with Justice Smith saying that unlike the plaintiffs in *Lawrence*, the plaintiffs here do not seek protection from State intrusion, but access to a state-conferred benefit — rationally limited to heterosexuals — and so no fundamental right is at stake, for due process purposes.

   How persuasive is this reasoning? *Lawrence* involved societal privacy; so does *Robles*. At issue in both was the right to seek privacy and protection — in *Robles*, by marriage.

   And anyway — is marriage a state-created benefit, or a right antedating the Constitution, preserved by the Ninth Amendment? As to that, see *Griswold v. Connecticut*, discussed in *Roe* and *Casey,* supra § 1.04(1).

8. Partly, the due process issue in *Robles* is not whether a purported rationale has merit but how minimally meritorious it may be. Finding no fundamental right at issue means that only low-level scrutiny is needed — but how "low-level"?

   May the rationale be overinclusive, underinclusive, ineffective in fact, and never actually entertained by the legislature? The answers appear to be yes, yes, yes and yes.

9. The court in *Robles* finds, as with due process, that equal protection guarantees are not offended by denying marriage to same-sex couples. This means same-sex couples must differ from heterosexual couples — how? And this difference must be related to values served by withholding marriage — how?

Are the answers related to child-bearing potential? Same-sex children may conceive children or adopt them, and many do; ma[illegible] couples are [illegible] children or choose not to do so.

Again, as with due process, the answer(s) seem to turn partly on the level of scrutiny in equal protection cases. The Court concludes lesser scrutiny is required in family law cases. Shouldn't the conclusion be the opposite — where association, family and reproductive choice are all implicated?

10. The majority seeks to resolve the equal protection issue by sleight-of-hand: all are treated equally, because *neither* men *nor* women may enter same-sex relations. Dissenting Chief Judge Kaye equates this to the same argument rejected in *Loving v. Virginia*, when the Supreme Court found barring mixed-race marriage unconstitutional.

    Are they equivalent?

11. And what of *Loving*? Kaye argues it is controlling here. But are race and sexual preference equal, historically and societally, as foci of discrimination, such that each is a "suspect criterion" triggering heightened scrutiny of state rationales (unlike the majority's minimal scrutiny) and requiring a "compelling state interest"?

    What are Kaye's tests for whether a line of discrimination is so offensive as to qualify as suspect criteria, like race? Or gender?

12. Does *Robles* involve gender, or sexual preference? Does it matter?

13. Kaye argues that a rationale tying marriage to children is overinclusive (some heterosexual couples have none), underinclusive (some same-sex couples have children), and further, that marriage is about more than children — affecting a lot of "adult" interests, such as property and hospital visitation.

    What is this last argument? Is it a means/ends test, or a reality check on the purported rationale?

14. Kaye notes that Vermont and Connecticut have civil union laws (as does Hawaii, adopted after the *Baehr* decision). Shouldn't this support the majority view? And would such statute[illegible] needs of same-sex [illegible], permitting denial of marriage?

    What should a civil union or "domestic partner" statute provide? *See Symposium*, 54 Am J. Comp. Law, Fall 2006; *Symposium*, 8 U. Pa. J. Const. L., May 2006; *Mimicking Marriage*, 30 Univ. Dayton L. Rev. 119 (2004); *White Paper*, 38 Fam. L.Q. 339 (2004); *Civil Union Statutes*, 15 U. Fla. J. L. & Pub. Pol'y 229 (2004); *Symposium, Civil Unions*, 11 Widener J. Pub. L. 361 (2002).

15. Finally, is there a fundamental dishonesty and irresponsibility in the majority's position? As Kaye points out, the recent New York statute protecting gays had been held up for 30 years precisely because gays were included. Why not acknowledge that and proceed from there, nevertheless, to permit restricting marriage to heterosexual couples?

16. Would it be best simply to abolish marriage? *See Symposium On Abolishing Civil Marriage*, 27 Cardozo L. Rev. 1155 (2006).

GOODRIDGE v. DEPT. OF PUBLIC HEALTH

440 Mass. 309, 798 N.E.2d 941 (2003)

Marshall, C.J.

Marriage is a vital social institution. The exclusive commitment of two individuals to each other nurtures love and mutual support; it brings stability to our society. For those who choose to marry, and for their children, marriage provides an abundance of legal, financial, and social benefits. In return it imposes weighty legal, financial, and social obligations. The question before us is whether, consistent with the Massachusetts Constitution, the Commonwealth may deny the protections, benefits, and obligations conferred by civil marriage to two individuals of the same sex who wish to marry. We conclude that it may not. The Massachusetts Constitution affirms the dignity and equality of all individuals. It forbids the creation of second-class citizens. In reaching our conclusion we have given full deference to the arguments made by the Commonwealth. But it has failed to identify any constitutionally adequate reason for denying civil marriage to same-sex couples.

We are mindful that our decision marks a change in the history of our marriage law. Many people hold deep-seated religious, moral, and ethical convictions that marriage should be limited to the union of one man and one woman, and that homosexual conduct is immoral. Many hold equally strong religious, moral, and ethical convictions that same-sex couples are entitled to be married, and that homosexual persons should be treated no differently than their heterosexual neighbors. Neither view answers the question before us. Our concern is with the Massachusetts Constitution as a charter of governance for every person properly within its reach. "Our obligation is to define the liberty of all, not to mandate our own moral code." *Lawrence v. Texas,* 539 U.S. 558.

Barred access to the protections, benefits, and obligations of civil marriage, a person who enters into an intimate, exclusive union with another of the same sex is arbitrarily deprived of membership in one of our community's most rewarding and cherished institutions. That exclusion is incompatible with the constitutional principles of respect for individual autonomy and equality under law.

I

The plaintiffs are fourteen individuals from five Massachusetts counties. As of April 11, 2001, the date they filed their complaint, the plaintiffs Gloria Bailey, sixty years old, and Linda Davies, fifty-five years old, had been in a committed relationship for thirty years; the plaintiffs Maureen Brodoff, forty-nine years old, and Ellen Wade, fifty-two years old, had been in a committed relationship for twenty years and lived with their twelve year old daughter; the plaintiffs Hillary Goodridge, forty-four years old, and Julie Goodridge, forty-three years old, had been in a committed relationship for thirteen years and lived with their five year old daughter; the plaintiffs Gary Chalmers, thirty-five years old, and Richard Linnell, thirty-seven years old, had been in a committed relationship for thirteen years and lived with their eight year old daughter and Richard's mother; the plaintiffs Heidi Norton, thirty-six years old, and Gina Smith, thirty-six years old, had been in a committed relationship for eleven years and lived with their two [illegible] years and [illegible] plaintiffs Michael Horgan, forty-one years old, and Edward Balmelli, forty-one years old, had been in a committed relationship for seven years; and the plaintiffs David Wilson, fifty-seven years old, and Robert Compton, fifty-one years old, had been in a committed relationship for four years and had cared for David's mother in their home after a serious illness until she died.

The plaintiffs include business executives, lawyers, an investment banker, educators, therapists, and a computer engineer. Many are active in church, community, and school groups. They have employed such legal means as are available to them — for example, joint adoption, powers of attorney, and joint ownership of real property — to secure aspects of their relationships. Each plaintiff attests a desire to marry his or her partner in order to affirm publicly their commitment to each other and to secure the legal protections and benefits afforded to married couples and their children.

In March and April, 2001, each of the plaintiff couples attempted to obtain a marriage license from a city or town clerk's office. As required under G. L. c. 207, they completed notices of intention to marry on forms provided by the registry, and presented these forms to a Massachusetts town or city clerk, together with the required health forms and marriage license fees. In each case, the clerk either refused to accept the notice of intention to marry or denied a marriage license to the couple on the ground that Massachusetts does not recognize same-sex marriage. Because obtaining a marriage license is a necessary prerequisite to civil marriage in Massachusetts, denying marriage licenses to the plaintiffs was tantamount to denying them access to civil marriage itself, with its appurtenant social and legal protections, benefits, and obligations.

On April 11, 2001, the plaintiffs filed suit in the Superior Court against the department and the commissioner seeking a judgment that "the exclusion of the plaintiff couples and other qualified same-sex couples from access to marriage licenses, and the legal and social status of civil marriage, as well as the protections, benefits and obligations of [illegible] Massachusetts law." [illegible] G. L. c. 231A. The plaintiffs alleged violation of the laws of the Commonwealth, including but not limited to their rights under arts. 1, 6, 7, 10, 12, and 16, and Part II, c. 1, § 1, art. 4, of the Massachusetts Constitution.[7]

---

[7] Article 1, as amended by art. 106 of the Amendments to the Massachusetts Constitution, provides: "All people are born free and equal and have certain natural, essential and unalienable rights; among which may be reckoned the right of enjoying and defending their lives and liberties; that of acquiring, possessing and protecting property; in fine, that of seeking and obtaining their safety and happiness. Equality under the law shall not be denied or abridged because of sex, race, color, creed or national origin."

Article 6 provides: "No man, nor corporation, or association of men, have any other title to obtain advantages, or particular and exclusive privileges, distinct from those of the community, than what arises from the consideration of services rendered to the public . . . ."

Article 7 provides: "Government is instituted for the common good; for the protection, safety, prosperity, and happiness of the people; and not for the profit, honor, or private interest of any one man, family or class of men: Therefore the people alone have an incontestable, unalienable,

After the complaint was dismissed and summary judgment entered for the defendants, the plaintiffs appealed. Both parties requested direct appellate review, which we granted.

II

Although the plaintiffs refer in passing to "the marriage statutes," they focus, quite properly, on G. L. c. 207, the marriage licensing statute, which controls entry into civil marriage. As a preliminary matter, we summarize the provisions of that law.

General Laws c. 207 is both a gatekeeping and a public records statute. It sets minimum qualifications for obtaining a marriage license and directs city and town clerks, the registrar, and the department to keep and maintain certain "vital records" of civil marriages. The gatekeeping provisions of G. L. c. 207 are minimal. They forbid marriage of individuals within certain degrees of consanguinity, §§ 1 and 2, and polygamous marriages. (marriages solemnized in violation of §§ 1, 2, and 4, are void ab initio). They prohibit marriage if one of the parties has communicable syphilis, and restrict the circumstances in which a person under eighteen years of age may marry. See G. L. c. 207, §§ 7, 25, and 27. The statute requires that civil marriage be solemnized only by those so authorized. See G. L. c. 207, §§ 38-40.

The record-keeping provisions of G. L. c. 207 are more extensive. Marriage applicants file standard information forms and a medical certificate in any Massachusetts city or town clerk's office and tender a filing fee. The clerk issues the marriage license, and when the marriage is solemnized, the individual authorized to solemnize the marriage adds additional information to the form and returns it (or a copy) to the clerk's office. (This completed form is commonly known as the "marriage certificate"). The clerk sends a copy of the information to the registrar, and that information becomes a public record.

In short, for all the joy and solemnity that normally attend a marriage, G. L. c. 207, governing entrance to marriage, is a licensing law. The plaintiffs argue that because nothing in that licensing law specifically prohibits marriages between persons of the same sex, we may interpret the statute to permit "qualified same sex couples" to obtain marriage licenses, thereby avoiding the question whether the law is constitutional. We interpret statutes to carry out the Legislature's intent, determined by the words of a statute interpreted according to "the ordinary and approved usage of the language." The everyday meaning of "marriage" is "the legal union of a man and woman as husband and wife," Black's Law Dictionary 986 (7th ed. 1999), and the plaintiffs do not argue that the term "marriage" has ever had a different meaning under Massachusetts law.

The intended scope of G. L. c. 207 is also evident in its consanguinity provisions. Sections 1 and 2 of G. L. c. 207 prohibit marriages between a man and certain female relatives and a woman and certain male relatives, but are

---

and indefeasible right to institute government; and to reform, alter, or totally change the same, when their protection, safety, prosperity and happiness require it."

Article 10 provides, in relevant part: "Each individual of the society has a right to be protected by it in the enjoyment of his life, liberty and property, according to standing laws . . . ."

silent as to the consanguinity of male-male or female-female marriage applicants. See G. L. c. 207, §§ 1–2. The only reasonable explanation is that the Legislature did not intend that same-sex couples be licensed to marry. We conclude, as did the judge, that G. L. c. 207 may not be construed to permit same-sex couples to marry.

III

A

The larger question is whether, as the department claims, government action that bars same-sex couples from civil marriage constitutes a legitimate exercise of the State's authority to regulate conduct, or whether, as the plaintiffs claim, this categorical marriage exclusion violates the Massachusetts Constitution. We have recognized the long-standing statutory understanding, derived from the common law, that "marriage" means the lawful union of a woman and a man. But that history cannot and does not foreclose the constitutional question.

The plaintiffs' claim that the marriage restriction violates the Massachusetts Constitution can be analyzed in two ways. Does it offend the Constitution's guarantees of equality before the law? Or do the liberty and due process provisions of the Massachusetts Constitution secure the plaintiffs' right to marry their chosen partner? In matters implicating marriage, family life, and the upbringing of children, the two constitutional concepts frequently overlap, as they do here. Much of what we say concerning one standard applies to the other.

We begin by considering the nature of civil marriage itself. Simply put, the government creates civil marriage. In Massachusetts, civil marriage is, and since pre-Colonial days has been, precisely what its name implies: a wholly secular institution. No religious ceremony has ever been required to validate a Massachusetts marriage. While only the parties can mutually assent to marriage, the terms of the marriage — who may marry and what obligations, benefits, and liabilities attach to civil marriage — are set by the Commonwealth. Conversely, while only the parties can agree to end the marriage (absent the death of one of them or a marriage void *ab initio*), the Commonwealth defines the exit terms.

Civil marriage is created and regulated through exercise of the police power.

Without question, civil marriage enhances the "welfare of the community." It is a "social institution of the highest importance." Civil marriage anchors an ordered society by encouraging stable relationships over transient ones. It is central to the way the Commonwealth identifies individuals, provides for the orderly distribution of property, ensures that children and adults are cared for and supported whenever possible from private rather than public funds, and tracks important epidemiological and demographic data.

Marriage also bestows enormous private and social advantages on those who choose to marry. Civil marriage is at once a deeply personal commitment to another human being and a highly public celebration of the ideals of mutuality, companionship, intimacy, fidelity, and family. "It is an association that promotes a way of life, not causes; a harmony in living, not political faiths; a bilateral loyalty, not commercial or social projects." *Griswold v. Connecticut,* 381 U.S. 479, 486 (1965). Because it fulfils yearnings for security, safe haven, and connection that express our common humanity, civil marriage is an esteemed institution, and the decision whether and whom to marry is among life's momentous acts of self-definition.

Tangible as well as intangible benefits flow from marriage. The marriage license grants valuable property rights to those who meet the entry requirements, and who agree to what might otherwise be a burdensome degree of government regulation of their activities.

The benefits accessible only by way of a marriage license are enormous, touching nearly every aspect of life and death. The department states that "hundreds of statutes" are related to marriage and to marital benefits. With no attempt to be comprehensive, we note that some of the statutory benefits conferred by the Legislature on those who enter into civil marriage include, as to property: joint Massachusetts income tax filing; tenancy by the entirety (a form of ownership that provides certain protections against creditors and allows for the automatic descent of property to the surviving spouse without probate); extension of the benefit of the homestead protection (securing up to $ 300,000 in equity from creditors) to one's spouse and children; automatic rights to inherit the property of a deceased spouse who does not leave a will; the rights of elective share and of dower (which allow surviving spouses certain property rights where the decedent spouse has not made adequate provision for the survivor in a will); entitlement to wages owed to a deceased employee; eligibility to continue certain businesses of a deceased spouse; the right to share the medical policy of one's spouse, [domestic partners of city employees not included within the term "dependent" as used in G. L. c. 32B, § 2]); thirty-nine week continuation of health coverage for the spouse of a person who is laid off or dies; preferential options under the Commonwealth's pension system; preferential benefits in the Commonwealth's medical program, MassHealth (e.g., prohibiting placing a lien on long-term care patient's former home if spouse still lives there); access to veterans' spousal benefits and preferences; financial protections for spouses of certain Commonwealth employees (fire fighters, police officers, prosecutors, among others) killed in the performance of duty; the equitable division of marital property on divorce; temporary and permanent alimony rights; the right to separate support on separation of the parties that does not result in divorce; and the right to bring claims for wrongful death and loss of consortium, and for funeral and burial expenses and punitive damages resulting from tort actions.

Exclusive marital benefits that are not directly tied to property rights include the presumptions of legitimacy and parentage of children born to a married couple; and evidentiary rights, such as the prohibition against spouses testifying against one another about their private conversations, applicable in both civil and criminal cases. Other statutory benefits of a personal nature available only to married individuals include qualification for bereavement or medical leave to care for individuals related by blood or marriage; an automatic "family member" preference to make medical decisions for an incompetent or disabled spouse who does not have a contrary health care proxy; the application of predictable rules of child custody, visitation, support, and removal out-of-State when [illegible], priority [illegible] to administer the estate of a deceased spouse who dies without a will, and requirement that surviving spouse must consent to the appointment of any other person as administrator; and the right to interment in the lot or tomb owned by one's deceased spouse.

Where a married couple has children, their children are also directly or indirectly, but no less auspiciously, the recipients of the special legal and economic protections obtained by civil marriage. Notwithstanding the Commonwealth's strong public policy to abolish legal distinctions between marital and nonmarital children in providing for the support and care of minors, the fact remains that marital children reap a measure of family stability and economic security based on their parents' legally privileged status that is largely inaccessible, or not as readily accessible, to nonmarital children. Some of these benefits are social, such as the enhanced approval that still attends the status of being a marital child. Others are material, such as the greater ease of access to family-based State and Federal benefits that attend the presumptions of one's parentage.

It is undoubtedly for these concrete reasons, as well as for its intimately personal significance, that civil marriage has long been termed a "civil right."

Without the right to marry — or more properly, the right to choose to marry — one is excluded from the full range of human experience and denied full protection of the laws for one's "avowed commitment to an intimate and lasting human relationship." *Baker v. State, supra* at 229. Because civil marriage is central to the lives of individuals and the welfare of the community, our laws assiduously protect the individual's right to marry against undue government incursion. Laws may not "interfere directly and substantially with the right to marry."

B

For decades, indeed centuries, in much of this country (including Massachusetts) no lawful marriage was possible between white and black Americans. That long history [illegible] Supreme Court of California held in 1948 that a legislative prohibition against interracial marriage violated the due process and equality guarantees of the *Fourteenth Amendment*, *Perez v. Sharp,* 32 Cal.2d 711, 728, 198 P.2d 17 (1948), or when, nineteen years later, the United States Supreme Court also held that a statutory bar to interracial marriage violated the Fourteenth Amendment, *Loving v. Virginia,* 388 U.S. 1 (1967).

The Massachusetts Constitution protects matters of personal liberty against government incursion as zealously, and often more so, than does the Federal Constitution, even where both Constitutions employ essentially the same language.

The Massachusetts Constitution requires, at a minimum, that the exercise of the State's regulatory authority not be "arbitrary or capricious."

The plaintiffs challenge the marriage statute on both equal protection and due process grounds. With respect to each such claim, we must first determine the appropriate standard of review. Where a statute implicates a fundamental right or uses a suspect classification, we employ "strict judicial scrutiny." For all other statutes, we employ the " 'rational basis' test." For due process claims, rational basis analysis requires that statutes "bear[] a real and substantial relation to the public health, safety, morals, or some other phase of the general welfare." For equal protection challenges, the rational basis test requires that "an impartial lawmaker could logically believe that the classification would serve a legitimate public purpose that transcends the harm to the members of the disadvantaged class."

The department argues that no fundamental right or "suspect" class is at issue here, and rational basis is the appropriate standard of review. For the reasons we explain below, we conclude that the marriage ban does not meet the rational basis test for either due process or equal protection. Because the statute does not survive rational basis review, we do not consider the plaintiffs' arguments that this case merits strict judicial scrutiny.

The department posits three legislative rationales for prohibiting same-sex couples from marrying: (1) providing a "favorable setting for procreation"; (2) ensuring the optimal setting for child rearing, which the department defines as "a two-parent family with one parent of each sex"; and (3) preserving scarce State and private financial resources. We consider each in turn.

The judge in the Superior Court endorsed the first rationale, holding that "the state's interest in regulating marriage is based on the traditional concept that marriage's primary purpose is procreation." This is incorrect. Our laws of civil marriage do not privilege procreative heterosexual intercourse between married people above every other form of adult intimacy and every other means of creating a family. General Laws c. 207 contains no requirement that the applicants for a marriage license attest to their ability or intention to conceive children by coitus. Fertility is not a condition of marriage, nor is it grounds for divorce. People who have never consummated their marriage, and never plan to, may be and stay married.[22] People who cannot stir from their deathbed may marry. While it is certainly true that many, perhaps most, married couples have children together (assisted or unassisted), it is the exclusive and permanent commitment of the marriage partners to one another, not the begetting of children, that is the sine qua non of civil marriage.

The department's first stated rationale, equating marriage with unassisted heterosexual procreation, shades imperceptibly into its second: that confining

[22] Our marriage law does recognize that the inability to participate in intimate relations may have a bearing on one of the central expectations of marriage. Since the earliest days of the Commonwealth, the divorce statutes have permitted (but not required) a spouse to choose to divorce his or her impotent mate. While infertility is not a ground to void or terminate a marriage, impotency (the inability to engage in sexual intercourse) is, at the election of the disaffected spouse.

The "marriage is procreation" argument singles out the one unbridgeable difference between same-sex and opposite-sex couples, and transforms that difference into the essence of legal marriage. Like "*Amendment 2" to the Constitution of Colorado*, which effectively denied homosexual persons equality under the law and full access to the political process, the marriage restriction impermissibly "identifies persons by a single trait and then denies them protection across the board." *Romer v. Evans*, 517 U.S. 620, 633 (1996). In so doing, the State's action confers an official stamp of approval on the destructive stereotype that same-sex relationships are inherently unstable and inferior to opposite-sex relationships and are not worthy of respect.

marriage to opposite-sex couples ensures that children are raised in the "optimal" setting. Protecting the welfare of children is a paramount State policy. Restricting marriage to opposite-sex couples, however, cannot plausibly further this policy. Moreover, we have repudiated the commonlaw power of the State to provide varying levels of protection to children based on the circumstances of birth.

The department has offered no evidence that forbidding marriage to people of the same sex will increase the number of couples choosing to enter into opposite-sex marriages in order to have and raise children. There is thus no rational relationship between the marriage statute and the Commonwealth's proffered goal of protecting the "optimal" child rearing unit. Moreover, the department readily concedes that people in same-sex couples may be "excellent" parents. These couples (including four of the plaintiff couples) have children for the reasons others do — to love them, to care for them, to nurture them. But the task of child rearing for same-sex couples is made infinitely harder by their status as outliers to the marriage laws. While establishing the parentage of children as soon as possible is crucial to the safety and welfare of children, same-sex couples must undergo the sometimes lengthy and intrusive process of second-parent adoption to establish their joint parentage. While the enhanced income provided by marital benefits is an important source of security and stability for married couples and their children, those benefits are denied to families headed by same-sex couples. While the laws of divorce provide clear and reasonably predictable guidelines for child support, child custody, and property division on dissolution of a marriage, same-sex couples who dissolve their relationships find themselves and their children in the highly unpredictable terrain of equity jurisdiction. See *E.N.O. v. L.M.M., [429 Mass. 824 (1999)]*. Given the wide range of public benefits reserved only for married couples, we do not credit the department's contention that the absence of access to civil marriage amounts to little more than an inconvenience to same-sex couples and their children. Excluding same-sex couples from civil marriage will not make children of opposite-sex marriages more secure, but it does prevent children of same-sex couples from enjoying the immeasurable advantages that flow from the assurance of "a stable family structure in which children will be reared, educated, and socialized."

In this case, we are confronted with an entire, sizeable class of parents raising children who have absolutely no access to civil marriage and its protections because they are forbidden from procuring a marriage license. It cannot be rational under our laws, and indeed it is not permitted, to penalize children by depriving them of State benefits because the State disapproves of their parents' sexual orientation.

The third rationale advanced by the department is that limiting marriage to opposite-sex couples furthers the Legislature's interest in conserving scarce State and private financial resources. The marriage restriction is rational, it argues, because the General Court logically could assume that same-sex couples are more financially independent than married couples and thus less needy of public marital benefits, such as tax advantages, or private marital benefits, such as employer-financed health plans that include spouses in their coverage.

An absolute statutory ban on same-sex marriage bears no rational relationship to the goal of economy. First, the department's conclusory generalization — that same-sex couples are less financially dependent on each other than opposite-sex couples — ignores that many same-sex couples, such as many of the plaintiffs in this case, have children and other dependents (here, aged parents) in their care. The department does not contend, nor could it, that these dependents are less needy or deserving than the dependents of married couples. Second, Massachusetts marriage laws do not condition receipt of public and private financial benefits to married individuals on a demonstration of financial dependence on each other; the benefits are available to married couples regardless of whether they mingle their finances or actually depend on each other for support.

The department suggests additional rationales for prohibiting same-sex couples from marrying, which are developed by some amici. It argues that broadening civil marriage to include same-sex couples will trivialize or destroy the institution of marriage as it has historically been fashioned. Certainly our decision today marks a significant change in the definition of marriage as it has been inherited from the common law, and understood by many societies for centuries. But it does not disturb the fundamental value of marriage in our society.

Here, the plaintiffs seek only to be married, not to undermine the institution of civil marriage. They do not want marriage abolished. They do not attack the binary nature of marriage, the consanguinity provisions, or any of the other gate-keeping provisions of the marriage licensing law. Recognizing the right of an individual to marry a person of the same sex will not diminish the validity or dignity of opposite-sex marriage, any more than recognizing the right of an individual to marry a person of a different race devalues the marriage of a person who marries someone of her own race. If anything, extending civil marriage to same-sex couples reinforces the importance of marriage to individuals and communities. That same-sex couples are willing to embrace marriage's solemn obligations of exclusivity, mutual support, and commitment to one another is a testament to the enduring place of marriage in our laws and in the human spirit.

We also reject the argument suggested by the department, and elaborated by some amici, that expanding the institution of civil marriage in Massachusetts to include same-sex couples will lead to interstate conflict. We would not presume to dictate how another State should respond to today's decision. But neither should considerations of comity prevent us from according Massachusetts residents the full measure of protection available under the Massachusetts Constitution. The genius of our Federal system is that each State's Constitution has vitality specific to its own traditions, and that, subject to the minimum requirements of the Fourteenth Amendment, each State is free to address difficult issues of individual liberty in the manner its own Constitution demands.

The marriage ban works a deep and scarring hardship on a very real segment of the community for no rational reason. The absence of any reasonable relationship between, on the one hand, an absolute disqualification of same-sex couples who wish to enter into civil marriage and, on the other, protection of public health, safety, or general welfare, suggests that the marriage restriction is rooted in persistent prejudice against persons who are (or who are believed to be) homosexual. "The Constitution cannot control such prejudices but neither can it tolerate them. Private biases may be outside the reach of the law, but the law cannot, directly or indirectly, give them effect." *Palmore v. Sidoti,* 466 U.S. 429, 433, (1984) (construing Fourteenth Amendment). Limiting the protections, benefits, and obligations of civil marriage to opposite-sex couples violates the basic premises of individual liberty and equality under law protected by the Massachusetts Constitution.

IV

We consider next the plaintiffs' request for relief. We preserve as much of the statute as may be preserved in the face of the successful constitutional challenge.

Here, no one argues that striking down the marriage laws is an appropriate form of relief. Eliminating civil marriage would be wholly inconsistent with the Legislature's deep commitment to fostering stable families and would dismantle a vital organizing principle of our society.

We construe civil marriage to mean the voluntary union of two persons as spouses, to the exclusion of all others. This reformulation redresses the plaintiffs' constitutional injury and furthers the aim of marriage to promote stable, exclusive relationships. It advances the two legitimate State interests the department has identified: providing a stable setting for child rearing and conserving State resources. It leaves intact the Legislature's broad discretion to regulate marriage.

In their complaint the plaintiffs request only a declaration that their exclusion and the exclusion of other qualified same-sex couples from access to civil marriage violates Massachusetts law. We declare that barring an individual from the protections, benefits, and obligations of civil marriage solely because that person would marry a person of the same sex violates the Massachusetts Constitution. We vacate the summary judgment for the department. We remand this case to the Superior Court for entry of judgment consistent with this opinion. Entry of judgment shall be stayed for 180 days to permit the Legislature to take such action as it may deem appropriate in light of this opinion.

So ordered.

Greaney, J. (concurring). I agree with the result reached by the court, the remedy ordered, and much of the reasoning in the court's opinion. In my view, however, the case is more directly resolved using traditional equal protection analysis.

The equal protection infirmity at work here is strikingly similar to (although, perhaps, more subtle than) the invidious discrimination perpetuated by Virginia's antimiscegenation laws and unveiled in the decision of *Loving v. Virginia, supra.* In its landmark decision striking down Virginia's ban on marriages between Caucasians and members of any other race on both equal protection and substantive due process grounds, the United States Supreme

Court soundly rejected the proposition that the equal application of the ban (i.e., that it applied equally to whites and blacks) made unnecessary the strict scrutiny analysis traditionally required of statutes drawing classifications according to race, and concluded that "restricting the freedom to marry solely because of racial classifications violates the central meaning of the Equal Protection Clause." That our marriage laws, unlike antimiscegenation laws, were not enacted purposely to discriminate in no way neutralizes their present discriminatory character.

With these two propositions established (the infringement on a fundamental right and a sex-based classification), the enforcement of the marriage statutes as they are currently understood is forbidden by our Constitution unless the State can present a compelling purpose furthered by the statutes that can be accomplished in no other reasonable manner. (b) I am hopeful that our decision will be accepted by those thoughtful citizens who believe that same-sex unions should not be approved by the State. I am not referring here to acceptance in the sense of grudging acknowledgment of the court's authority to adjudicate the matter. My hope is more liberating. The plaintiffs are members of our community, our neighbors, our coworkers, our friends. As pointed out by the court, their professions include investment advisor, computer engineer, teacher, therapist, and lawyer. The plaintiffs volunteer in our schools, worship beside us in our religious houses, and have children who play with our children, to mention just a few ordinary daily contacts. We share a common humanity and participate together in the social contract that is the foundation of our Commonwealth. Simple principles of decency dictate that we extend to the plaintiffs, and to their new status, full acceptance, tolerance, and respect. We should do so because it is the right thing to do. The union of two people contemplated by G. L. c. 207 "is a coming together for better or for worse, hopefully enduring, and intimate to the degree of being sacred. It is an association that promotes a way of life, not causes; a harmony in living, not political faiths; a bilateral loyalty, not commercial or social projects. Yet it is an association for as noble a purpose as any involved in our prior decisions." *Griswold v. Connecticut,* 381 U.S. 479, 486 (1965). Because of the terms of art. 1, the plaintiffs will no longer be excluded from that association.

Spina, J. (dissenting, with whom **Sosman** and **Cordy, JJ.**, join).

What is at stake in this case is not the unequal treatment of individuals or whether individual rights have been impermissibly burdened, but the power of the Legislature to effectuate social change without interference from the courts, pursuant to art. 30 of the Massachusetts Declaration of Rights. The power to regulate marriage lies with the Legislature, not with the judiciary. See *Commonwealth v. Stowell,* 389 Mass. 171, 175, 449 N.E.2d 357 (1983). Today, the court has transformed its role as protector of individual rights into the role of creator of rights, and I respectfully dissent.

1. *Equal protection.* General Laws c. 207 enumerates certain qualifications for obtaining a marriage license. It creates no distinction between the sexes, but applies to men and women in precisely the same way. It does not create any disadvantage identified with gender, as both men and women are similarly limited to marrying a person of the opposite sex.

Similarly, the marriage statutes do not discriminate on the basis of sexual orientation. As the [illegible], constitutional protections are extended to individuals, not couples. .The marriage statutes do not disqualify individuals on the basis of sexual orientation from entering into marriage. All individuals, with certain exceptions not relevant here, are free to marry. Whether an individual chooses not to marry because of sexual orientation or any other reason should be of no concern to the court.

The court concludes, however, that G. L. c. 207 unconstitutionally discriminates against the individual plaintiffs because it denies them the "right to marry the person of one's choice" where that person is of the same sex. .To reach this result the court relies on *Loving v. Virginia*, and transforms "choice" into the essential element of the institution of marriage. The *Loving* case did not use the word "choice" in this manner, and it did not point to the result that the court reaches today.

Unlike the *Loving* and *Sharp* cases, the Massachusetts Legislature has erected no barrier to marriage that intentionally discriminates against anyone. Within the institution of marriage, anyone is free to marry, with certain exceptions that are not challenged. In the absence of any discriminatory purpose, the State's marriage statutes do not violate principles of equal protection.

2. *Due process.* The marriage statutes do not impermissibly burden a right protected by our constitutional guarantee of due process implicit in art. 10 of our Declaration of Rights. There is no restriction on the right of any plaintiff to enter into marriage. Each is free to marry a willing person of the opposite sex.

Substantive due process protects individual rights against unwarranted government intrusion. See *Aime v. Commonwealth*, 414 Mass. 667, 673, 611 N.E.2d 204 (1993). The court states, as we have said on many occasions, that the Massachusetts Declaration of Rights may protect a right in ways that exceed the protection afforded by the Federal Constitution. See *Arizona v. Evans*, 514 U.S. 1, 8, (1995) (State courts afforded broader protection of rights than granted by United States Constitution). However, today the court does not fashion a remedy that affords greater protection of a right. Instead, using the rubric of due process, it has redefined marriage.

Although this court did not state that same-sex marriage is a fundamental right worthy of strict scrutiny protection, it nonetheless deemed it a constitutionally protected right by applying rational basis review. Before applying any level of constitutional analysis there must be a recognized right at stake. Same-sex marriage, or the "right to marry the person of one's choice" as the court today defines that right, does not fall within the fundamental right to marry. Same-sex marriage is not "deeply rooted in this Nation's history," and the court does not suggest that it is.

The court has extruded a new right from principles of substantive due process, and in doing so it has distorted the meaning and purpose of due process. The purpose of substantive due process is to protect existing rights, not to create new rights. Its aim is to thwart government intrusion, not invite it. The court asserts that the Massachusetts Declaration of Rights serves to guard against government intrusion into each individual's sphere of privacy. Similarly, the Supreme Court has called for increased due process protection when individual privacy and intimacy are threatened by unnecessary government imposition. *See, e.g., Lawrence v. Texas, Eisenstadt v. Baird, Griswold v. Connecticut.* These cases, along with the *Moe* case, [*infra,*]focus on the threat to privacy when government seeks to regulate the most intimate activity behind bedroom doors. The statute in question does not seek to regulate intimate activity within an intimate relationship, but merely gives formal recognition to a particular marriage. The State has respected the private lives of the plaintiffs, and has done nothing to intrude in the relationships that each of the plaintiff couples enjoy. *Cf. Lawrence v. Texas,* (case "does not involve whether the government must give formal recognition to any relationship that homosexual persons seek to enter"). Ironically, by extending the marriage laws to same-sex couples the court has turned substantive due process on its head and used it to interject government into the plaintiffs' lives.

Sosman, J. (dissenting, with whom **Spina** and **Cordy, JJ.**, join).

In applying the rational basis test to any challenged statutory scheme, the issue is not whether the Legislature's rationale behind that scheme is persuasive to us, but only whether it satisfies a minimal threshold of rationality. Today, rather than apply that test, the court announces that, because it is persuaded that there are no differences between same-sex and opposite-sex couples, the Legislature has no rational basis for treating them differently with respect to the granting of marriage licenses.

Based on our own philosophy of child rearing, and on our observations of the children being raised by same-sex couples to whom we are personally close, we may be of the view that what matters to children is not the gender, or sexual orientation, or even the number of the adults who raise them, but rather whether those adults provide the children with a nurturing, stable, safe, consistent, and supportive environment in which to mature. Same-sex couples can provide their children with the requisite nurturing, stable, safe, consistent, and supportive environment in which to mature, just as opposite-sex couples do. It is therefore understandable that the court might view the traditional definition of marriage as an unnecessary anachronism, rooted in historical prejudices that modern society has in large measure rejected and biological limitations that modern science has overcome.

It is not, however, our assessment that matters. Conspicuously absent from the court's opinion today is any acknowledgment that the attempts at scientific study of the ramifications of raising children in same-sex couple households are themselves in their infancy and have so far produced inconclusive and conflicting results. Notwithstanding our belief that gender and sexual orientation of parents should not matter to the success of the child rearing venture, studies to date reveal that there are still some observable differences between children raised by opposite-sex couples and children raised by same-sex couples. Interpretation of the data gathered by those studies then becomes clouded by the personal and political beliefs of the investigators, both as to whether the differences identified are positive or negative, and as to the untested explanations of what might account for those differences. The Legislature can rationally view the state of the scientific evidence as unsettled on the critical question it now faces: Are families headed by same-sex parents [illegible] from infancy to adulthood as families headed by parents of opposite sexes? Our belief that children raised by same-sex couples should fare the same as children raised in traditional families is just that: a passionately held but utterly untested belief. The Legislature is not required to share that belief but may, as the creator of the institution of civil marriage, wish to see the proof before making a fundamental alteration to that institution.

Although ostensibly applying the rational basis test to the civil marriage statutes, it is abundantly apparent that the court is in fact applying some undefined stricter standard to assess the constitutionality of the marriage statutes' exclusion of same-sex couples. While avoiding any express conclusion as to any of the proffered routes by which that exclusion would be subjected to a test of strict scrutiny — infringement of a fundamental right, discrimination based on gender, or discrimination against gays and lesbians as a suspect classification — the opinion repeatedly alludes to those concepts in a prolonged and eloquent prelude before articulating its view that the exclusion lacks even a rational basis.

Shorn of these emotion-laden invocations, the opinion ultimately opines that the Legislature is acting irrationally when it grants benefits to a proven successful family structure while denying the same benefits to a recent, perhaps promising, but essentially untested alternate family structure. Placed in a more neutral context, the court would never find any irrationality in such an approach. For example, if the issue were government subsidies and tax benefits promoting use of an established technology for energy efficient heating, the court would find no equal protection or due process violation in the Legislature's decision not to grant the same benefits to an inventor or manufacturer of some new, alternative technology who did not yet have sufficient data to prove that that new technology was just as good as the established technology. That the early results from preliminary testing of the new technology might look very promising, or that the theoretical underpinnings of the new technology might appear flawless, would not make it irrational for the Legislature [illegible] tax breaks to the established technology and deny them to the still unproved newcomer in the field. While programs that affect families and children register higher on our emotional scale than programs affecting energy efficiency, our standards for what is or is not "rational" should not be bent by those emotional tugs. Where, as here, there is no ground for applying strict scrutiny, the emotionally compelling nature of the subject matter should not affect the manner in which we apply the rational basis test.

As a matter of social history, today's opinion may represent a great turning point that many will hail as a tremendous step toward a more just society. As a matter of constitutional jurisprudence, however, the case stands as an aberration. To reach the result it does, the court has tortured the rational basis test beyond recognition. I fully appreciate the strength of the temptation to find this particular law unconstitutional — there is much to be said for the argument that excluding gay and lesbian couples from the benefits of civil marriage is cruelly unfair and hopelessly outdated; the inability to marry has a profound impact on the personal lives of committed gay and lesbian couples (and their children) to whom we are personally close (our friends, neighbors, family members, classmates, and co-workers); and our resolution of this issue takes place under the intense glare of national and international publicity. Speaking metaphorically, these factors have combined to turn the case before us into a "perfect storm" of a constitutional question. In my view, however, such factors make it all the more imperative that we adhere precisely and scrupulously to the established guideposts of our constitutional jurisprudence, a jurisprudence that makes the rational basis test an extremely deferential one that focuses on the rationality, not the persuasiveness, of the potential justifications for the classifications in the legislative scheme. I trust that, once this particular "storm" clears, we will return to the rational basis test as it has always been understood and applied. Applying that deferential test in the manner it is customarily applied, the exclusion of gay and lesbian couples from the institution of civil marriage passes constitutional muster. I respectfully dissent.

Cordy, J. (dissenting, with whom **Spina** and **Sosman, JJ.**, join).

The Massachusetts marriage statute does not impair the exercise of a recognized fundamental right, or discriminate on the basis of sex in violation of the equal rights amendment to the Massachusetts Constitution. Consequently, it is subject to review only to determine whether it satisfies the rational basis test. Because a conceivable rational basis exists upon which the Legislature could conclude that the marriage statute furthers the legitimate State purpose of ensuring, promoting, and supporting an optimal social structure for the bearing and raising of children, it is a valid exercise of the State's police power.

A. *Limiting marriage to the union of one man and one woman does not impair the exercise of a fundamental right.* Civil marriage is an institution created by the State. In Massachusetts, the marriage statutes are derived from English common law, and were first enacted in colonial times. They were enacted to secure public interests and not for religious purposes or to promote personal interests or aspirations. As the court notes in its opinion, the institution of marriage is "the legal union of a man and woman as husband and wife," and it has always been so under Massachusetts law, colonial or otherwise.

The plaintiffs contend that because the right to choose to marry is a "fundamental" right, the right to marry the person of one's choice, including a member of the same sex, must also be a "fundamental" right. While the court stops short of deciding that the right to marry someone of the same sex is "fundamental" such that strict scrutiny must be applied to any statute that impairs it, it nevertheless agrees with the plaintiffs that the right to choose to marry is of fundamental importance ("among the most basic" of every person's "liberty and due process rights") and would be "hollow" if an individual was foreclosed from "freely choosing the person with whom to share . . . the . . . institution of civil marriage." Hence, it concludes that a marriage license cannot be denied to an individual who wishes to marry someone of the same sex. In reaching this result the court has transmuted the "right" to marry into a right to change the institution of marriage itself. This feat of reasoning succeeds only if one accepts the proposition that the definition of the institution of marriage as a union between a man and a woman is merely "conclusory" (as suggested, ante, rather than the basis on which the "right" to partake in it has been deemed to be of fundamental importance. In other words, only by assuming that "marriage" includes the union of two persons of the same sex does the court conclude that restricting marriage to opposite-sex couples infringes on the "right" of same-sex couples to "marry."[2]

The plaintiffs ground their contention that they have a fundamental right to marry a person of the same sex in a long line of Supreme Court decisions that discuss the importance of marriage. In context, all of these decisions and their discussions are about the "fundamental" nature of the institution of marriage as it has existed and been understood in this country, not as the court has redefined it today. Even in that context, its "fundamental" nature is derivative of the nature of the interests that underlie or are associated with it.[3] An examination of those interests reveals that they are either not shared by same-sex couples or not implicated by the marriage statutes.

Supreme Court cases that have described marriage or the right to marry as "fundamental" have focused primarily on the underlying interest of every individual in procreation, which, historically, could only legally occur within the construct of marriage because sexual intercourse outside of marriage was a criminal act. Because same-sex couples are unable to procreate on their own, any right to marriage they may possess cannot be based on their interest in procreation, which has been essential to the Supreme Court's denomination of the right to marry as fundamental.

Supreme Court cases recognizing a right to privacy in intimate decisionmaking, *e.g.*, *Griswold v. Connecticut, supra* (striking down statute prohibiting use of contraceptives); *Roe v. Wade,* 410 U.S. 113 (1973) (striking down statute criminalizing abortion), have also focused primarily on sexual relations and the decision whether or not to procreate, and have refused to recognize an "unlimited right" to privacy. Massachusetts courts have been no more willing than the Federal courts to adopt a "universal[]" "privacy doctrine," *Marcoux v. Attorney Gen.,* 375 Mass. 63, 67, 375 N.E.2d 688 (1978), or to derive "controversial 'new' rights from the Constitution." *Aime v. Commonwealth,* 414 Mass. 667, 674 n.10, 611 N.E.2d 204 (1993).

What the *Griswold* Court found "repulsive to the notions of privacy surrounding the marriage relationship" was the prospect of "allowing the police to search the sacred precincts of marital bedrooms for telltale signs of the use

2 The same semantic sleight of hand could transform every other restriction on marriage into an infringement of a right of fundamental importance. For example, if one assumes that a group of mature, consenting, committed adults can form a "marriage," the prohibition on polygamy (G. L. c. 207, § 4), infringes on their "right" to "marry." In legal analysis as in mathematics, it is fundamentally erroneous to assume the truth of the very thing that is to be proved.

3 Casting the right to civil marriage as a "fundamental right" in the constitutional sense is somewhat peculiar. It is not referred to as such in either the State or Federal Constitution, and unlike other recognized fundamental rights (such as the right to procreate, the right to be free of government restraint, or the right to refuse medical treatment), civil marriage is wholly a creature of State statute. If by enacting a civil marriage statutory scheme Massachusetts has created a fundamental right, then it could never repeal its own statute without violating the fundamental rights of its inhabitants.

of contraceptives." *Griswold v. Connecticut, supra at 485–486*. See *Moe v. Secretary of Admin. & Fin., 382 Mass. 629,* 658, 417 N.E.2d 387 (1981), quoting L. Tribe, American Constitutional Law 924 (1978) (finding it "difficult to imagine a clearer case of bodily intrusion" than being forced to bear a child). When Justice Goldberg spoke of "marital relations" in the context of finding it "difficult to imagine what is more private or more intimate than a husband and wife's marital relationship," *Griswold v. Connecticut, supra at 495* (Goldberg, J., concurring), he was obviously referring to sexual relations. Similarly, in *Lawrence v. Texas,* 539 U.S. 558 (2003), it was the criminalization of private sexual behavior that the Court found violative of the petitioners' liberty interest.

The marriage statute, which regulates only the act of obtaining a marriage license, does not implicate privacy in the sense that it has found constitutional protection under Massachusetts and Federal law. *Cf. Commonwealth v. King,* 374 Mass. 5, 14, 372 N.E.2d 196 (1977) (solicitation of prostitution "while in a place to which the public had access" implicated no "constitutionally protected rights of privacy"); *Marcoux v. Attorney Gen., supra at 68* (right to privacy, at most, protects conduct "limited more or less to the hearth"). It does not intrude on any right that the plaintiffs have to privacy in their choices regarding procreation, an intimate partner or sexual relations.[6] The plaintiffs' right to privacy in such matters does not require that the State officially endorse their choices in order for the right to be constitutionally vindicated.

Although some of the privacy cases also speak in terms of personal autonomy, no court has ever recognized such an open-ended right. "That many of the rights and liberties protected by the Due Process Clause sound in personal autonomy does not warrant the sweeping conclusion that any and all important, intimate, and personal decisions are so protected . . . ." *Washington v. Glucksberg.* While the institution of marriage is deeply rooted in the history and traditions of our country and our State, the right to marry someone of the same sex is not. No matter how personal or intimate a decision to marry someone of the same sex might be, the right to make it is not guaranteed by the right of personal autonomy.

The protected right to freedom of association, in the sense of freedom of choice "to enter into and maintain certain intimate human relationships," *Roberts v. United States Jaycees* (as an element of liberty or due process rather than free speech), is similarly limited and unimpaired by the marriage statute. As recognized by the Supreme Court, that right affords protection only to "certain kinds of highly personal relationships," such as those between husband and wife, parent and child, and among close relatives, that "have played a critical role in the culture and traditions of the Nation,"

Finally, the constitutionally protected interest in child rearing, recognized in *Meyer v. Nebraska, Pierce v. Society of Sisters,* and *Care & Protection of Robert*, is not implicated or infringed by the marriage statute here. The fact that the plaintiffs cannot marry has no bearing on their independently protected constitutional rights as parents which, as with opposite-sex parents,

[6] Contrast *Lawrence v. Texas*, 539 U.S. 558 (2003), in which the United States Supreme Court struck down the Texas criminal sodomy statute because it constituted State intrusion on some of these very choices.

are limited only by their continued fitness and the best interests of their children. *Bezio v. Patenaude*, 381 Mass. 563, 579, [illegible] (1980) (courts may not use parent's sexual orientation as reason to deny child custody).

Because the rights and interests discussed above do not afford the plaintiffs any fundamental right that would be impaired by a statute limiting marriage to members of the opposite sex, they have no fundamental right to be declared "married" by the State.

In the area of family-related rights in particular, the Supreme Court has emphasized that the "Constitution protects the sanctity of the family precisely because the institution of the family is deeply rooted." *Moore v. East Cleveland, supra.*

B. *The marriage statute, in limiting marriage to heterosexual couples, does not constitute discrimination on the basis of sex in violation of the Equal Rights Amendment to the Massachusetts Constitution.* In his concurrence, Justice Greaney contends that the marriage statute constitutes discrimination on the basis of sex in violation of art. 1 of the Declaration of Rights as amended by art. 106 of the Amendments to the Constitution of the Commonwealth, the Equal Rights Amendment (ERA).[12] Such a conclusion is analytically unsound and inconsistent with the legislative history of the ERA.

The central purpose of the ERA was to eradicate discrimination against women and in favor of men or vice versa. See *Attorney Gen. v. Massachusetts Interscholastic Athletic Ass'n,* 378 Mass. 342, 357, 393 N.E.2d 284 (1979). Consistent with this purpose, we have construed the ERA to prohibit laws that advantage one sex at the expense of the other, but not laws that treat men and women equally, (assuming that "separate but equal" treatment of males and females would be constitutionally permissible). The Massachusetts marriage statute does not subject men to different treatment from women; each is equally prohibited from precisely the same conduct.

Of course, a statute that on its face treats protected groups equally may still harm, stigmatize, or advantage one over the other. Such was the circumstance in *Loving v. Virginia.*

By contrast, h[illegible] evidence that limiting marriage to opposite-sex couples was motivated by sexism in general or a desire to disadvantage men or women in particular. Moreover, no one has identified any harm, burden, disadvantage, or advantage accruing to either gender as a consequence of the Massachusetts marriage statute. In the absence of such effect, the statute limiting marriage to couples of the opposite sex does not violate the ERA's prohibition of sex discrimination.

On October 19, 1976, just before the general election at which the amendment was to be considered, the commission filed its Interim Report, which focused on the effect of the Massachusetts ERA on the laws of the Commonwealth. 1976 Senate Doc. No. 1689. A section of the report, entitled "Areas Unaffected by the Equal Rights Amendment," addressed some of the legal regimes that would not be affected by the adoption of the ERA. One such area was "Homosexual Marriage," about which the commission stated:

[12] Article 106 is referred to as the Equal Rights Amendment.

> "An equal rights amendment will have no effect upon the allowance or denial of homosexual marriages. The equal rights amendment is not concerned with the relationship of two persons of the same sex; it only addresses those laws or public-related actions which treat persons of opposite sexes differently. The Washington Court of Appeals has already stated that the equal rights amendment to its state constitution did not afford a basis for validating homosexual marriages. In Colorado, the attorney general has likewise issued an opinion that the state equal rights amendment did not validate homosexual marriage. There are no cases which have used a state equal rights amendment to either validate or require the allowance of homosexual marriages." (Footnotes omitted.)

While the court, in interpreting a constitutional amendment, is not bound to accept either the views of a legislative commission studying and reporting on the amendment's likely effects, or of public commentary and debate contemporaneous with its passage, it ought to be wary of completely disregarding what appears to be the clear intent of the people recently recorded in our constitutional history. This is particularly so where the plain wording of the amendment does not require the result it would reach.

C. *The marriage statute satisfies the rational basis standard.* The burden of demonstrating that a statute does not satisfy the rational basis standard rests on the plaintiffs. It is a weighty one. "[A] reviewing court will presume a statute's validity, and make all rational inferences in favor of it. . . . The Legislature is not required to justify its classifications, nor provide a record or finding in support of them." (Citation omitted). The statute "only need[s to] be supported by a conceivable rational basis."

The "time tested wisdom of the separation of powers" requires courts to avoid "judicial legislation in the guise of new constructions to meet real or supposed new popular viewpoints, preserving always to the Legislature alone its proper prerogative of adjusting the statutes to changed conditions."

1. *Classification.* The nature of the classification at issue is readily apparent. Opposite-sex couples can obtain a license and same-sex couples cannot. The granting of this license, and the completion of the required solemnization of the marriage, opens the door to many statutory benefits and imposes numerous responsibilities. The fact that the statute does not permit such licenses to be issued to couples of the same sex thus bars them from civil marriage. The classification is not drawn between men and women or between heterosexuals and homosexuals, any of whom can obtain a license to marry a member of the opposite sex; rather, it is drawn between same-sex couples and opposite-sex couples.

2. *State purpose.* The court's opinion concedes that the civil marriage statute serves legitimate State purposes, but further investigation and elaboration of those purposes is both helpful and necessary.

Civil marriage is the institutional mechanism by which societies have sanctioned and recognized particular family structures, and the institution of marriage has existed as one of the fundamental organizing principles of human society. Marriage has not been merely a contractual arrangement for legally defining the private relationship between [illegible] (although [illegible] part of any marriage). Rather, on an institutional level, marriage is the "very basis of the whole fabric of civilized society," and it serves many important political, economic, social, educational, procreational, and personal functions.

Paramount among its many important functions, the institution of marriage has systematically provided for the regulation of heterosexual behavior, brought order to the resulting procreation, and ensured a stable family structure in which children will be reared, educated, and socialized. Admittedly, heterosexual intercourse, procreation, and child care are not necessarily conjoined (particularly in the modern age of widespread effective contraception and supportive social welfare programs), but an orderly society requires some mechanism for coping with the fact that sexual intercourse commonly results in pregnancy and childbirth. The institution of marriage is that mechanism.

The institution of marriage provides the important legal and normative link between heterosexual intercourse and procreation on the one hand and family responsibilities on the other. The partners in a marriage are expected to engage in exclusive sexual relations, with children the probable result and paternity presumed. Whereas the relationship between mother and child is demonstratively and predictably created and recognizable through the biological process of pregnancy and childbirth, there is no corresponding process for creating a relationship between father and child.[16] Similarly, aside from an act of heterosexual intercourse nine months prior to childbirth, there is no process for creating a relationship between a man and a woman as the parents of a particular child. The institution of marriage fills this void by formally binding the husband-father to his wife and child, and imposing on him the responsibilities of fatherhood.

The marital family is also the foremost setting for the education and socialization of children. Children learn about the world and their place in it primarily from those who raise them, and those children eventually grow up to exert some influence, great or small, positive or negative, on [illegible] The institution of [illegible] parents to remain committed to each other and to their children as they grow, thereby encouraging a stable venue for the education and socialization of children.

It is undeniably true that dramatic historical shifts in our cultural, political, and economic landscape have altered some of our traditional notions about marriage, including the interpersonal dynamics within it, the range of responsibilities required of it as an institution, and the legal environment in which it exists. Nevertheless, the institution of marriage remains the principal weave of our social fabric. A family defined by heterosexual marriage continues to be the most prevalent social structure into which the vast majority of children are born, nurtured, and prepared for productive participation in civil society, see Children's Living Arrangements and Characteristics: March, 2002, United States Census Bureau Current Population Reports at 3 (June, 2003)

[16] Modern DNA testing may reveal actual paternity, but it establishes only a genetic relationship between father and child.

(in 2002, 69% of children lived with two married parents, 23% lived with their mother, 5% lived with their father, and 4% lived in households with neither parent present).

It is difficult to imagine a State purpose more important and legitimate than ensuring, promoting, and supporting an optimal social structure within which to bear and raise children. At the very least, the marriage statute continues to serve this important State purpose.

3. *Rational relationship.* The question we must turn to next is whether the statute, construed as limiting marriage to couples of the opposite sex, remains a rational way to further that purpose. Stated differently, we ask whether a conceivable rational basis exists on which the Legislature could conclude that continuing to limit the institution of civil marriage to members of the opposite sex furthers the legitimate purpose of ensuring, promoting, and supporting an optimal social structure for the bearing and raising of children.[22]

We must assume that the Legislature (1) might conclude that the institution of civil marriage has successfully and continually provided this structure over several centuries; (2) might consider and credit studies that document negative consequences that too often follow children either born outside of marriage or raised in households lacking either a father or a mother figure, and scholarly commentary contending that children and families develop best when mothers and fathers are partners in their parenting; and (3) would be familiar with many recent studies that variously support the proposition that children raised in intact families headed by same-sex couples fare as well on many measures as children raised in similar families headed by opposite-sex couples; support the proposition that children of same-sex couples fare worse on some measures; or reveal notable differences between the two groups of children that warrant further study.[29]

We must also assume that the Legislature would be aware of the critiques of the methodologies used in virtually all of the comparative studies of children

[22] In support of its conclusion that the marriage statute does not satisfy the rational basis test, the court emphasizes that "the department has offered no evidence that forbidding marriage to people of the same sex will increase the number of couples choosing to enter into opposite-sex marriages in order to have and raise children." This surprising statement misallocates the burden of proof in a constitutional challenge to the rational basis of a statute (see *supra*). It is the plaintiffs who must prove that supporting and promoting one form of relationship by providing (as is pointed out) literally hundreds of benefits, could not conceivably affect the decision-making of anyone considering whether to bear and raise a child. The department is not required to present "evidence" of anything.

[29] This family structure raises the prospect of children lacking any parent of their own gender. For example, a boy raised by two lesbians as his parents has no male parent. Contrary to the suggestion that concerns about such a family arrangement is based on "stereotypical" views about the differences between sexes, concern about such an arrangement remains rational. It is, for example, rational to posit that the child himself might invoke gender as a justification for the view that neither of his parents "understands" him, or that they "don't know what he is going through," particularly if his disagreement or dissatisfaction involves some issue pertaining to sex. Given that same-sex couples raising children are a very recent phenomenon, the ramifications of an adolescent child's having two parents but not one of his or her own gender have yet to be fully realized and cannot yet even be tested in significant numbers. But see note 25, *supra*, regarding studies of children raised without parents of each gender.

raised in these different environments, cautioning that the sampling populations are not representative, that the [illegible] are too limited in [illegible] empirical data are unreliable, and that the hypotheses are too infused with political or agenda driven bias.

Taking all of this available information into account, the Legislature could rationally conclude that a family environment with married opposite-sex parents remains the optimal social structure in which to bear children, and that the raising of children by same-sex couples, who by definition cannot be the two sole biological parents of a child and cannot provide children with a parental authority figure of each gender, presents an alternative structure for child rearing that has not yet proved itself beyond reasonable scientific dispute to be as optimal as the biologically based marriage norm.

The eligibility of a child for adoption presupposes that at least one of the child's biological parents is unable or unwilling, for some reason, to participate in raising the child.

That the State does not preclude different types of families from raising children does not mean that it must view them all as equally optimal and equally deserving of State endorsement and support.

As long as marriage is limited to opposite-sex couples who can at least theoretically procreate, society is able to communicate a consistent message to its citizens that marriage is a (normatively) necessary part of their procreative endeavor; that if they are to procreate, then society has endorsed the institution of marriage as the environment for it and for the subsequent rearing of their children; and that benefits are available explicitly to create a supportive and conducive atmosphere for those purposes. If society proceeds similarly to recognize marriages between same-sex couples who cannot procreate, it could be perceived as an abandonment of this claim, and might result in the mistaken view that civil marriage has little to do with procreation: just as the potential of procreation would not be necessary for a marriage to be valid, marriage would not be necessary for optimal procreation and child rearing to occur.[34]

---

[34] The court contends that the exclusive and permanent commitment of the marriage partnership rather than the begetting of children is the *sine qua non of civil* [illegible] that the 'marriage is procreation' [illegible] out the one unbridgeable difference between same-sex and opposite-sex couples, and transforms that difference into the essence of legal marriage." The court has it backward. Civil marriage is the product of society's critical need to manage procreation as the inevitable consequence of intercourse between members of the opposite sex. Procreation has always been at the root of marriage and the reasons for its existence as a social institution. Its structure, one man and one woman committed for life, reflects society's judgment as how optimally to manage procreation and the resultant child rearing. The court, in attempting to divorce procreation from marriage, transforms the form of the structure into its purpose. In doing so, it turns history on its head. The court compounds its error by likening the marriage statute to *Colorado's "Amendment 2"* which was struck by the United States Supreme Court in *Romer v. Evans*, 517 U.S. 620, 633 (1996). That amendment repealed all Colorado laws and ordinances that barred discrimination against homosexuals, and prohibited any governmental entity from adopting similar statutes. The amendment withdrew from homosexuals, but no others, legal protection from a broad range of injuries caused by private and governmental discrimination, "imposing a broad and undifferentiated disability on a single named group." As the Court noted, its sheer breadth seems "inexplicable by anything but animus toward the class it affects." The comparison to the Massachusetts marriage statute, which limits the institution of marriage (created to manage procreation) to opposite-sex couples who can theoretically procreate, is completely inapposite.

The court recognizes this concern, but brushes it aside with the assumption that permitting same-sex couples to marry "will not diminish the validity or dignity of opposite-sex marriage," and that "we have no doubt that marriage will continue to be a vibrant and revered institution." Whether the court is correct in its assumption is irrelevant. What is relevant is that such predicting is not the business of the courts. A rational Legislature, given the evidence, could conceivably come to a different conclusion, or could at least harbor rational concerns about possible unintended consequences of a dramatic redefinition of marriage.

The advancement of the rights, privileges, and protections afforded to homosexual members of our community in the last three decades has been significant, and there is no reason to believe that that evolution will not continue. Changes of attitude in the civic, social, and professional communities have been even more profound. Thirty years ago, The Diagnostic and Statistical Manual, the seminal handbook of the American Psychiatric Association, still listed homosexuality as a mental disorder. Today, the Massachusetts Psychiatric Society, the American Psychoanalytic Association, and many other psychiatric, psychological, and social science organizations have joined in amicus brief on behalf of the plaintiffs' cause. A body of experience and evidence has provided the basis for change, and that body continues to mount. The Legislature is the appropriate branch, both constitutionally and practically, to consider and respond to it. It is not enough that we as Justices might be personally of the view that we have learned enough to decide what is best. So long as the question is at all debatable, it must be the Legislature that decides. The marriage statute thus meets the requirements of the rational basis test.

NOTES AND QUESTIONS

1. The *Goodridge* case concludes that Massachusetts may not deny marriage licenses to same sex couples. Contrast *Goodridge* with *Baehr* and compare their rationales. Which is better? And how would the *Goodridge* court view the Hawaii civil union statute?

2. *Goodridge* is decided under the state constitution, but all of the Justices discuss decisions by the United States Supreme Court under the federal Constitution. Who has the better reading of *Lawrence, Romer, Loving, Griswold*? Would *Goodridge* come out the same way under the United States Constitution?

3. What is it about marriage that makes it so important: child creation, child rearing, union of two individuals, transmission of property, sharing of support and care, or something else? Is it simply the status, marking someone as loved, reserved, committed, unavailable? Is it a place of refuge, a springboard for action, a resource?

   And if it is some, or all, or more of these, does it matter that all of the features or qualities may be found outside marriage, by persons solo or as couples or as groups?

4. What is the objection of same-sex couples to denial of marriage licenses? They have individually the same opportunity as other men and women

to *get* a license, or to enjoy the benefits noted in (3) above. And they are not the only ones excluded [illegible] more, people under age, people diseased — all of these may be denied licenses.

5. What is the Commonwealth's rationale for excluding same-sex couples: history? Stability? Procreation? State finances? Religion? Encouraging heterosexuals to marry? Research? Did the Commonwealth put forward the best possible rationale(s)? Are there others?

6. What of simply "saving" the institution of marriage as we know it?

7. Who has the burden, anyway? Those who challenge the existing order (to show it is irrational or harmful), or those who defend (to show it is effective, necessary, rational (minimally)? Is this what the case really turns on?

8. And what of the majority's analysis of the Commonwealth's rationales? Aren't they using "strict scrutiny" when they said they were just looking for (and not finding) "minimum rationality?" True, the fit and follow-through on the proffered rationales aren't perfect, but isn't there *some* minimum rationality? See dissenting opinions by Justices Cordy and Sosman.

9. Or is it simply that fundamental rights and suspect criteria, requiring "strict scrutiny" are involved? If so, why did the majority not use that mode of analysis? Justice Greany equates this with the racial discrimination in *Loving*. Is he right? Don't dissenting Justices Spina and Cordy have the better side of the argument?

10. And dissenting Justice Sosman is surely on good ground in arguing that the legislature is entitled to wait until there is solid scientific evidence before abandoning the restriction of marriage. Or should it be the other way around? And what, scientifically speaking, would be tested, exactly? For a comprehensive survey of the scientific studies concerning same sex marriage see Justice Cordy's dissent, notes 22–25, omitted in the text.

11. In this "perfect storm" of a case, what does Justice Cordy's dissent add? [illegible] his reference to polygamy in Note 2? By his argument that the cases holding marriage is a "fundamental" rest on interests not shared by same-sex couples, such as procreation? By his reliance on the Equal Rights Amendment? By his argument that the marriage statute passes the minimum rationality test? (What *are* the rationales, exactly?) — or is he just re-casting the historical and separation of powers arguments?

12. Note the difference between the majority opinion and Justice Cordy's dissent: he advances rationales for restricted marriage, arguing they do not need to have a perfect "fit" or apply in all instances. The majority argues they do. (See part 3 of Cordy's dissent.) Who is correct? Does it matter — *should* it — that some of the rationales are over-inclusive or under-inclusive, or could be achieved by less restrictive means?

13. What of Justice Cordy's closing argument: that if marriage is extended to those who cannot procreate, it may send a message that marriage

is no longer essential to procreation and the family, or society itself. *See* note 34. This "unintended consequence," he argues, might itself be the basis for staying within traditional definitions of marriage.

14. And, in the end, aren't the various opinions really about community: what are its building blocks, its traditions and values, its resources for continuing itself? So viewed, the same sex couples should be viewed as a threat and disruptive, shouldn't they?

    Or is the opposite true, in an era when 50% of (heterosexual) marriages end in divorce?

15. If a same-sex couple is legally wed in Canada or elsewhere, can they state on tax forms that they are married? How about file for bankruptcy jointly? *See In Re Kandu*, 315 B.R. 123 (W. Dist. Wa. 2004)

STANLEY v. ILLINOIS
405 U.S. 645 (1972)

Justice **White** delivered the opinion of the Court.

Joan Stanley lived with Peter Stanley intermittently for 18 years, during which time they had three children. When Joan Stanley died, Peter Stanley lost not only her but also his children. Under Illinois law, the children of unwed fathers become wards of the State upon the death of the mother. Accordingly, upon Joan Stanley's death, in a dependency proceeding instituted by the State of Illinois, Stanley's children were declared wards of the State and placed with court-appointed guardians. Stanley appealed, claiming that he had never been shown to be an unfit parent and that since married fathers and unwed mothers could not be deprived of their children without such a showing, he had been deprived of the equal protection of the laws guaranteed him by the Fourteenth Amendment. The Illinois Supreme Court accepted the fact that Stanley's own unfitness had not been established but rejected the equal protection claim, holding that Stanley could properly be separated from his children upon proof of the single fact that he and the dead mother had not been married. Stanley's actual fitness as a father was irrelevant.

. . . .

II

Illinois has two principal methods of removing nondelinquent children from the homes of their parents. In a dependency proceeding it may demonstrate that the children are wards of the State because they have no surviving parent or guardian. In a neglect proceeding it may show that children should be wards of the State because the present parent[s] or guardian does not provide suitable care.

The State's right — indeed, duty — to protect minor children through a judicial determination of their interests in a neglect proceeding is not challenged here. Rather, we are faced with a dependency statute that empowers state officials to circumvent neglect proceedings on the theory that an unwed father is not a "parent" whose existing relationship with his children must be considered. . . .

. . . .

The private interest here, that of a man in the children he has sired and raised, undeniably warrants deference and, absent a powerful countervailing interest, protection. It is plain that the interest of a parent in the companionship, care, custody, and management of his or her children "come[s] to this Court with a momentum for respect lacking when appeal is made to liberties which derive merely from shifting economic arrangements." *Kovacs v. Cooper.*

The Court has frequently emphasized the importance of the family. The rights to conceive and to raise one's children have been deemed "essential," *Meyer v. Nebraska*, "basic civil rights of man," and "[r]ight far more precious . . . than property rights," *May v. Anderson*. "It is cardinal with us that the custody, care and nurture of the child reside first in the parents, whose primary function and freedom include preparation for obligations the state can neither supply nor hinder." *Prince v. Massachusetts.* The integrity of the family unit has found protection in the Due Process Clause of the Fourteenth Amendment, the Equal Protection Clause of the Fourteenth Amendment, and the Ninth Amendment.

. . . .

These authorities make it clear that, at the least, Stanley's interest in retaining custody of his children is cognizable and substantial.

. . . .

But we are here not asked to evaluate the legitimacy of the state ends, rather, to determine whether the means used to achieve these ends are constitutionally defensible. What is the state interest in separating children from fathers without a hearing designed to determine whether the father is unfit in a particular disputed case? We observe that the State registers no gain towards its declared goals when it separates children from the custody of fit parents. Indeed, if Stanley is a fit father, the State spites its own articulated goals when it needlessly separates him from his family.

. . . .

It may be, as the State insists, that most unmarried fathers are unsuitable and neglectful parents. It may also be that Stanley is such a parent and that his children should be placed in other hands. But all unmarried fathers are not in this category; some are wholly suited to have custody of their children. This much the State readily concedes, and nothing in this record indicates that Stanley is or has been a neglectful father who has not cared for his children. Given the opportunity to make his case, Stanley may have been seen to be deserving of custody of his offspring. Had this been so, the State's statutory policy would have been furthered by leaving custody in him.

. . . .

Procedure by presumption is always cheaper and easier than individualized determination. But when, as here, the procedure forecloses the determinative issues of competence and care, when it explicitly disdains present realities in deference to past formalities, it needlessly risks running roughshod over the important interests of both parent and child. It therefore cannot stand.

. . . .

Reversed and remanded.

. . . .

Mr. Chief Justice **Burger**, with whom Mr. Justice **Blackmun** concurs, dissenting.

. . . .

Where there is a valid contract of marriage, the law of Illinois presumes that the husband is the father of any child born to the wife during the marriage; as the father, he has legally enforceable rights and duties with respect to that child. When a child is born to an unmarried woman, Illinois recognizes the readily identifiable mother, but makes no presumption as to the identity of the biological father. It does, however, provide two ways, one voluntary and one involuntary, in which that father may be identified. First, he may marry the mother and acknowledge the child as his own; this has the legal effect of legitimating the child and gaining for the father full recognition as a parent. Second, a man may be found to be the biological father of the child pursuant to a paternity suit initiated by the mother; in this case, the child remains illegitimate, but the adjudicated father is made liable for the support of the child until the latter attains age 18 or is legally adopted by another.

. . . .

Furthermore, I believe that a State is fully justified in concluding, on the basis of common human experience, that the biological role of the mother in carrying and nursing an infant creates stronger bonds between her and the child than the bonds resulting from the male's often casual encounter. This view is reinforced by the observable fact that most unwed mothers exhibit a concern for their offspring either permanently or at least until they are safely placed for adoption, while unwed fathers rarely burden either the mother or the child with their attentions or loyalties. Centuries of human experience buttress this view of the realities of human conditions and suggest that unwed mothers of illegitimate children are generally more dependable protectors of their children than are unwed fathers. While these, like most generalizations, are not without exceptions, they nevertheless provide a sufficient basis to sustain a statutory classification whose objective is not to penalize unwed parents but to further the welfare of illegitimate children in fulfillment of the State's obligations as *parens patriae*.

. . . .

NOTES AND QUESTIONS

1. Which position, the majority or the dissent, in *Stanley v. Illinois*, is most supportive of the family? Does the majority result work to the benefit of marriages, and their resulting families, or to their detriment?
2. What weight should be given, if any, to the fact that Mr. Stanley never married Joan Stanley? Are your answers different if posed under a legal standard rather than an ethical standard?
3. The majority discusses the importance of the family, but is that the linchpin of the decision? Or, is the most important element the failure

of the state to consider Mr. Stanley's fitness or unfitness as a parent? In other words, is the decision a *procedural du*[illegible] or a *substantive on*[illegible]?

4. As the Court notes, it has decided cases which found denial of benefits or imposition of discriminatory treatment on illegitimate children to be invalid. But it has also upheld discriminatory treatment in certain cases. How *should* society treat illegitimate children? If the Stanleys chose, for their own reasons, not to marry and "legitimate" their children, should society honor their choice?

5. Is Chief Justice Burger, in dissent, urging gender discrimination *against* women or in their *favor*? Or is he urging an associational — as opposed to a biological — grounding of the family? Which, ethically or legally, is preferable?

6. To put the matter simply, which is more important (indeed, a *sine qua non*), biology or association, in deciding issues of parenthood, marriage and family? Consider this question in connection with the next case.

LEHR v. ROBERTSON
463 U.S. 248 (1983)

Stevens, Justice delivered the opinion of the Court.

The question presented is whether New York has sufficiently protected an unmarried father's inchoate relationship with a child whom he has never supported and rarely seen in the two years since her birth. The appellant, Jonathan Lehr, claims that the Due Process and Equal Protection Clauses of the Fourteenth Amendment give him an absolute right to notice and an opportunity to be heard before the child is adopted. We disagree.

Jessica M. was born out of wedlock on November 9, 1976. Her mother, Orraine Robertson, married Richard Robertson eight months after Jessica's birth. On December 21, 1978, when Jessica was over two years old, the Robertsons filed an adoption petition in the Family Court of Ulster County, New York. The court heard their testimony and received a favorable report from the Ulster County Department of Social Services. On March 7, 1979, the [illegible] entered an order of adoption. In this proceeding, appellant contends that the adoption order is invalid because he, Jessica's putative father, was not given advance notice of the adoption proceeding.

. . . .

In addition to the persons whose names are listed on the putative father registry, New York law requires that notice of an adoption proceeding be given to several other classes of possible fathers of children born out of wedlock — those who have been adjudicated to be the father, those who have been identified as the father on the child's birth certificate, those who live openly with the child and the child's mother and who hold themselves out to be the father, those who have been identified as the father by the mother in a sworn written statement, and those who were married to the child's mother before the child was six months old. Appellant admittedly was not a member of any of those classes. . . .

On January 30, 1979, one month after the adoption proceeding was commenced in Ulster County, appellant filed a "visitation and paternity petition" in the Westchester County Family Court. . . . On March 3, 1979, appellant for the first time, learned that an adoption proceeding was pending in Ulster County.

On March 7, 1979, appellant's attorney telephoned the Ulster County judge to inform him that he planned to seek a stay of the adoption proceeding pending the determination of the paternity petition. In that telephone conversation, the judge advised the lawyer that he had already signed the adoption order earlier that day. According to appellant's attorney, the judge stated that he was aware of the pending paternity petition but did not believe he was required to give notice to appellant prior to the entry of the order of adoption.

. . . .

I

The intangible fibers that connect parent and child have infinite variety. They are woven throughout the fabric of our society, providing it with strength, beauty, and flexibility. It is self-evident that they are sufficiently vital to merit constitutional protection in appropriate cases. In deciding whether this is such a case, however, we must consider the broad framework that has traditionally been used to resolve the legal problems arising from the parent-child relationship.

. . . .

In some cases, however, this Court has held that the Federal Constitution supersedes state law and provides even greater protection for certain formal family relationships. In those cases, as in the state cases, the Court has emphasized the paramount interest in the welfare of children and has noted that the rights of the parents are a counterpart of the responsibilities they have assumed. Thus, the "liberty" of parents to control the education of their children that was vindicated in *Meyer v. Nebraska* was described as a "right, coupled with the high duty, to recognize and prepare [the child] for additional obligations." The linkage between parental duty and parental right was stressed again in *Prince v. Massachusetts* when the Court declared it a cardinal principal "that the custody, care and nurture of the child reside first in the parents, whose primary function and freedom include preparation for obligations the state can neither supply nor hinder." In these cases the Court has found that the relationship of love and duty in a recognized family unit is an interest in liberty entitled to constitutional protection. . . .

. . . .

The difference between the developed parent-child relationships that was implicated in *Stanley,* and the potential relationship involved in this case, is both clear and significant. When an unwed father demonstrates a full commitment to the responsibilities of parenthood by "com[ing] forward to participate in the rearing of his child," his interest in personal contact with his child acquires substantial protection under the due process clause. At that point it may be said that he "act[s] as a father toward his children." But the mere existence of a biological link does not merit equivalent constitutional protection. The actions of judges neither create nor sever genetic bonds. "[T]he importance of the familial relationship, to the individuals involved and to the society, stems from the emotional attachments that derive from the intimacy of daily association, and from the role it plays in 'promot[ing] a way of life' through the instruction of children as well as from the fact of blood relationship." *Smith v. Organization of Foster Families for Equality and Reform* (quoting *Wisconsin v. Yoder*).

The significance of the biological connection is that it offers the natural father an opportunity that no other male possesses to develop a relationship with his offspring. If he grasps that opportunity and accepts some measure of responsibility for the child's future, he may enjoy the blessings of the parent-child relationship and make uniquely valuable contributions to the child's development. If he fails to do so, the Federal Constitution will not automatically compel a state to listen to his opinion of where the child's best interests lie.

. . . .

II

The most effective protection of the putative father's opportunity to develop a relationship with his child is provided by the laws that authorize formal marriage and govern its consequences. But the availability of that protection is, of course, dependent on the will of both parents of the child. Thus, New York has adopted a special statutory scheme to protect the unmarried father's interest in assuming a responsible role in the future of his child.

After this Court's decision in *Stanley,* the New York Legislature appointed a special commission to recommend legislation that would accommodate both the interests of biological fathers in their children and the children's interest in prompt and certain adoption procedures. The commission recommended, and the legislature enacted, a statutory adoption scheme that automatically provides notice to seven categories of putative fathers who are likely to have assumed some responsibility for the care of their natural children. If this scheme were likely to omit many responsible fathers, and if qualification for notice were beyond the control of an interested putative father, it might be thought procedurally inadequate. Yet, as all of the New York courts that reviewed this matter observed, the right to receive notice was completely within appellant's control. By mailing a postcard to the putative father registry, he could have guaranteed that he would receive notice of any proceedings to adopt Jessica. . . .

Appellant argues, however, that even if the putative father's opportunity to establish a relationship with an illegitimate child is adequately protected by the New York statutory scheme in the normal case, he was nevertheless entitled to special notice because the court and the mother knew that he had filed an affiliation proceeding in another court. This argument amounts to nothing more than an indirect attack on the notice provisions of the New York statute. The legitimate state interests in facilitating the adoption of young children and having the adoption proceeding completed expeditiously that underlie the entire statutory scheme also justify a trial judge's determination to require all interested parties to adhere precisely to the procedural requirements of the statute. The Constitution does not require either a trial judge or a litigant to give special notice to nonparties who are presumptively capable of asserting and protecting their own rights. . . .

. . . .

The judgment of the New York Court of Appeals is *Affirmed.*

Justice **White**, with whom Justice **Marshall** and Justice **Blackmun** join, dissenting.

The question in this case is whether the State may, consistent with the Due Process Clause, deny notice and an opportunity to be heard in an adoption proceeding to a putative father when the State has actual notice of his existence, whereabouts, and interest in the child.

I

It is axiomatic that "[t]he fundamental requirement of due process is the opportunity to be heard 'at a meaningful time and in a meaningful manner.'" *Mathews v. Eldridge.* As Jessica's biological father, Lehr either had an interest protected by the Constitution or he did not. If the entry of the adoption order in this case deprived Lehr of a constitutionally protected interest, he is entitled to notice and an opportunity to be heard before the order can be accorded finality.

. . . .

Lehr's version of the "facts" paints a far different picture than that portrayed by the majority. Appellant has never been afforded an opportunity to present his case. The legitimation proceeding he instituted was first stayed, and then dismissed, on appellees' motions. Nor could appellant establish his interest during the adoption proceedings, for it is the failure to provide Lehr notice and an opportunity to be heard there that is at issue here. We cannot fairly make a judgment based on the quality or substance of a relationship without a complete and developed factual record. . . .

. . . .

"[T]he usual understanding of 'family' implies biological relationships, and most decisions treating the relation between parent and child have stressed this element." *Smith v. Organization of Foster Families.* The "biological connection" is itself a relationship that creates a protected interest. Thus the "nature" of the interest is the parent-child relationship; how well-developed that relationship has become goes to its "weight," not its "nature." Whether Lehr's interest is entitled to constitutional protection does not entail a searching inquiry into the quality of the relationship but a simple determination of the fact that the relationship exists — a fact that even the majority agrees must be assumed to be established.

. . . .

II

In this case, of course, there was no question about either the identity or the location of the putative father. The mother knew exactly who he was and both she and the court entering the order of adoption knew precisely where he was and how to give him actual notice that his parental rights were about to be terminated by an adoption order. Lehr was entitled to due process, and the right to be heard is one of the fundamentals of that right, which "has little reality or worth unless one is informed that the matter is pending and can choose for himself whether to appear or default, acquiesce or contest."

The State concedes this much but insists that Lehr has had all the process that is due to him. It relies on § 111-a, which designates seven categories of unwed fathers to whom notice of adoption proceedings must be given, including any unwed father who has filed with the State a notice of his intent to claim paternity. The State submits that it need not give notice to anyone who has not filed his name, as he is permitted to do, and who is not otherwise within the designated categories, even if his identity and interest are known or are reasonably ascertainable by the State.

I am unpersuaded by the State's position. In the first place, § 111-a defines six categories of unwed fathers to whom notice must be given even though they have not placed their names on file pursuant to the section. Those six categories, however, do not include fathers such as Lehr who have initiated filiation proceedings, even though their identity and interest are as clearly and easily ascertainable as those fathers in the six categories. . . . Indeed, there would appear to be more reason to give notice to those such as Lehr who acknowledge paternity than to those who have been adjudged to be a father in a contested paternity action.

. . . It makes little sense to me to deny notice and hearing to a father who has not placed his name in the register but who has unmistakably identified himself by filing suit to establish his paternity and has notified the adoption court of his action and his interest. I thus need not question the statutory scheme on its face. Even assuming that Lehr would have been foreclosed if his failure to utilize the register had somehow disadvantaged the State, he effectively made himself known by other means, and it is the sheerest formalism to deny him a hearing because he informed the State in the wrong manner.

. . . .

Respectfully, I dissent.

NOTES AND QUESTIONS

1. This case is the mirror image of *Stanley v. Illinois*, since there the unmarried father had participated fully in raising his children and providing a family for them, whereas in this case, Mr. Lehr never participated in the raising or support of young Jessica, who was adopted at age 2, cutting off Lehr's parental rights. Thus, this case asks the question, what is the minimum attachment necessary to constitute a "family," at least for constitutional protection purposes? What is the answer?

2. It is interesting that Justice Blackmun dissented in both *Stanley* and *Lehr v. Robertson*, arguing that Mr. Stanley was not entitled to a hearing, but that Mr. Lehr was. Are these positions inconsistent?

3. If the state had not had *actual* notice about Mr. Lehr, would the dissents have felt differently? Suppose that the mother had known who the father was, and deliberately failed to give notice to him because not required to do so by the statute. Should the father's interest be terminated, legally or ethically?

4. What do you make of the language quoting from the *Smith* case, in turn quoting from *Wisconsin v. Yoder*, to the effect that the importance of familial relationship stems from the emotional attachments that "derive from the intimacy of daily association"? Mr. Lehr was denied the opportunity to develop those relationships. Moreover, in the *Smith* case itself, the Court never fully addressed the rights or interests of foster parents, even those involved in the "intimacy of daily associations." Is the choice between nature and nurture, or are both required, and if so, how much?

5. For an excellent article, see Tami Dower, *Redefining Family: Should Lesbians Have Access To Assisted Reproduction?*, 25 Melb. U. L. Rev. 466 (2001); and see Allison B. Smith, *The Breakdown of the American Family: Why Welfare Reform Is Not the Answer*, 11 Notre Dame J.L. Ethics & Pub. Pol'y 761 (1997).

PROBLEM 2–10 — Lesbian Parenting

Janet Johnson and Linda Stowe are in a long-term, stable lesbian relationship. Both are professionally employed, well educated, the children of loving parents and were raised in conventional, intact homes. They have been denied consideration for adoption because of their lesbian home and life style. They are now considering artificial insemination of Janet, because Linda is infertile due to endometriosis. Linda suggests removing Janet's egg — fertilizing it outside her body and then implanting the egg in Linda. She further proposes the sperm be donated by her brother.

Linda's fear is that if Janet is simply inseminated, Linda would have no right to assert custody in the event of divorce or death, even if they jointly raise the child. Janet is concerned about the right of the brother in visitation and also about possible incest charges. Both inquire as to marriage.

How would you advise them under the law of your jurisdiction? If your jurisdiction had the Hawaii statute excerpted at Note 8 following *Baehr v. Lewin*? Consider particularly the materials in § 1.02 concerning surrogacy.

PROBLEM 2–11 — The Spirit Catches You and . . .

The Hmong people of Southeast Asia have moved in large numbers to the United States. In one California community, a Hmong baby girl had severe epileptic seizures, viewed by her Hmong parents as a matter of distinction, directed by spirits. Still, they took her to the local hospital for Western medical treatment. Continuing care generated increasing incursions on the Hmong views, home, and family by the Western physicians. Ultimately, the child —

who had been thriving with her parents, was taken from them, worsened and died. Given the complex interrelationship between family, health, and religion, as well as the importance of parental primacy, what is the proper course in such cases? *See* Anne Fadiman, *The Spirit Catches You and You Fall Down* (Farrar, Straus & Giroux, 1997). *See also* Carrese et al., *Western Bioethics on the Navajo Reservation*, JAMA 274:825 (1995), and Kagawa-Singer, et. al., *Negotiating Cross-Cultural Issues at the End of Life*, JAMA 286:2993 (Dec. 19, 2001; and Weissman, *Resident Physicians' Preparedness to Provide Cross Cultural Care*, JAMA 294:1058 (Sep. 17, 2005).

The concept of parenting has an essential, biologically-grounded core. We qualify this when we allow adoption by couples who might conceive children. The question is: Shall we stretch it further, indeed abandon it, to allow adoption by couples who could not jointly conceive a child because they are homosexual?

ADOPTIONS OF B.L.V.B. AND E.L.V.B.

628 A.2d 1271 (Vt. 1993)

Johnson, J.

Appellants are two women, Jane and Deborah, who have lived together in a committed, monogamous relationship since 1986. Together, they made the decision to have and raise children, and together, they consulted various sources to determine the best method for them to achieve their goal of starting a family. On November 2, 1988, Jane gave birth to a son, B.L.V.B., after being impregnated with the sperm of an anonymous donor. On August 27, 1992, after being impregnated with sperm from the same donor, she gave birth to a second son, E.L.V.B. Deborah assisted the midwife at both births, and she has been equally responsible for raising and parenting the children since their births.

Appellants sought legal recognition of their existing status as co-parents, and asked the probate court to allow Deborah to legally adopt the children, while leaving Jane's parental rights intact. The adoption petitions were uncontested. The Department of Social and Rehabilitation Services conducted a home study, determined the adoptions were in the best interests of the children, and recommended that they be allowed. A clinical and school psychologist who had evaluated the family testified that it was essential for the children to be assured of a continuing relationship with Deborah, and recommended that the adoptions be allowed for the psychological and emotional protection of the children.

Despite the lack of opposition, the probate court denied the adoptions, declining to reach whether the adoptions were in the best interests of the children because the proposed adoptive mother "does not satisfy the statutory prerequisite to adoption." The court relied on 15 V.S.A. §§ 431 and 448. Section 431, covering who may adopt, provides:

> A person or husband and wife together, of age and sound mind, may adopt any other person as his or their heir with or without change of name of the person adopted. A married man or a married woman shall not adopt a person or be adopted without the consent of the other

spouse. The petition for adoption and the final adoption decree shall be executed by the other spouse as provided in this chapter.

Section 448, which describes how the rights and obligations of both parents and children are altered by a final adoption decree, provides in pertinent part:

> The natural parents of a minor shall be deprived, by the adoption, of all legal right to control of such minor, and such minor shall be freed from all obligations of obedience and maintenance to them. . . . Notwithstanding the foregoing provisions of this section, when the adoption is made by a spouse of a natural parent, obligations of obedience to, and rights of inheritance by and through the natural parent who has intermarried with the adopting parent shall not be affected.

The court read the last sentence of § 448, the "step-parent exception," and § 431, as clearly requiring that "if a couple adopts together, they must be married. If one partner is the birth parent, and the other partner desires to adopt, then they must be married: otherwise, the birth parent will lose rights in the child under § 448."

Nothing in Vermont law, other than a restrictive interpretation of § 448, would exclude Deborah from adopting another person. Under15 V.S.A. § 431, which broadly grants the right to adopt to "a person or husband and wife together," an unmarried person is permitted to adopt, and the sole limitation — that the adoption of a married person requires the consent of the adoptee's spouse — does not apply here. Even reading § 431 in conjunction with § 448, we cannot conclude, as the probate court did, that the legislature meant to limit the categories of persons who were entitled to adopt.

When the statute is read as a whole, we see that its general purpose is to clarify and protect the legal rights of the adopted person at the time the adoption is complete, not to proscribe adoptions by certain combinations of individuals. Who may adopt is already covered by § 431. Section 448 is concerned with defining the lines of inheritance for adoptees, preserving their right to inherit from their natural parents and granting the right to inherit from the "person or persons" by whom they are adopted. The statute also terminates the natural parents' rights upon adoption, but this provision anticipates that the adoption of children will remove them from the home of the biological parents, where the biological parents elect or are compelled to terminate their legal obligations to the child. This legislative intent is evidenced by the step-parent exception, which saves the natural parent's rights in a step-parent adoption. The legislature recognized that it would be against common sense to terminate the biological parent's rights when that parent will continue to raise and be responsible for the child, albeit in a family unit with a partner who is biologically unrelated to the child.

Although the precise circumstances of these adoptions may not have been contemplated during the initial drafting of the statute, the general intent and spirit of § 448 is entirely consistent with them. The intent of the legislature was to protect the security of family units by defining the legal rights and responsibilities of children who find themselves in circumstances that do not include two biological parents. Despite the narrow wording of the step-parent exception, we cannot conclude that the legislature ever meant to terminate the parental rights of a biological parent who intended to continue raising a child with the help of a partner. Such a narrow construction would produce the unreasonable and irrational result of defeating adoptions that are otherwise indisputably in the best interests of children. (intent of statute is derived from consideration not only of language, but from entire enactment, its reason, purpose and consequence, and on presumption that no unjust or unreasonable result was intended).

When social mores change, governing statutes must be interpreted to allow for those changes in a manner that does not frustrate the purposes behind their enactment. To deny the children of same-sex partners, as a class, the security of a legally recognized relationship with their second parent serves no legitimate state interest. By allowing same-sex adoptions to come within the step-parent exception of § 448, we are furthering the purposes of the statute as was originally intended by allowing the children of such unions the benefits and security of a legal relationship with their de facto second parents.

As the case law from other jurisdictions illustrates, our paramount concern should be with the effect of our laws on the reality of children's lives. It is not the courts that have engendered the diverse composition of today's families. It is the advancement of reproductive technologies and society's recognition of alternative lifestyles that have produced families in which a biological, and therefore a legal, connection is no longer the sole organizing principle. But it is the courts that are required to define, declare and protect the rights of children raised in these families, usually upon their dissolution. At that point, courts are left to vindicate the public interest in the children's financial support and emotional well-being by developing theories of parenthood, so that "legal strangers" who are de facto parents may be awarded custody or visitation or reached for support.

We are not called upon to approve or disapprove of the relationship between the appellants. Whether we do or not, the fact remains that Deborah has acted as a parent of B.L.V.B. and E.L.V.B. from the moment they were born. To deny legal protection of their relationship, as a matter of law, is inconsistent with the children's best interests and therefore with the public policy of this state, as expressed in our statutes affecting children.

Reversed; judgment is entered granting the petitions for adoption in Docket Nos. 5813 and 5814 of the Washington Probate Court.

NOTES AND QUESTIONS

1. Suppose that the statute in *Adoptions of B.L.V.B. And E.L.V.B.* had, in fact, banned adoption by same-sex couples? Might a legislature conclude such "families" are never in the "best interests" of children?
2. Might a legislature, alternatively, impose such a ban as preserving the traditional nature of marriage and family?
3. Florida in fact has done so. *See Cox v. Florida Dept. of Rehabilitative Services*, 656 So. 2d 902 (Fla. 1995), *and* Florida Statute § 63.042 (2001).

4. The Florida statutes concerning adoption provide as follows:

Fla. Stat. § 63.042 (2001):

Who may be adopted; who may adopt.

(1) Any person, a minor or an adult, may be adopted.

(2) The following persons may adopt:

(a) A husband and wife jointly;

(b) An unmarried adult, including the birth parent of the person to be adopted;

(c) The unmarried minor birth parent of the person to be adopted; or

(d) A married person without the other spouse joining as a petitioner, if the person to be adopted is not his or her spouse, and if:

1. The other spouse is a parent of the person to be adopted and consents to the adoption; or

2. The failure of the other spouse to join in the petition or to consent to the adoption is excused by the court for reason of prolonged unexplained absence, unavailability, incapacity, or circumstances constituting an unreasonable withholding of consent.

(3) *No person eligible to adopt under this statute may adopt if that person is a homosexual.*

(4) No person eligible under this section shall be prohibited from adopting solely because such person possesses a physical disability or handicap, unless it is determined by the department or the license child-placing agency that such disability or handicap renders such person incapable of serving as an effective parent. (emphasis supplied).

5. Most states ban same-sex marriages. Can/should employers nevertheless extend health benefits to such unmarried partnerships? And what if they are extended only to same-sex domestic partners?

IRIZARRY v. BOARD OF EDUCATION OF THE CITY OF CHICAGO

251 F.3d 604 (7th Cir. 1993)

Posner, Circuit Judge.

Although Milagros Irizarry has lived with the same man for more than two decades and they have two (now adult) children, they have never married. As an employee of the Chicago public school system, she receives health benefits but he does not, even though he is her "domestic partner" (the term for persons who are cohabiting with each other in a relationship similar to marriage), though he would if he were her husband. In July 1999, the Chicago Board of Education extended spousal health benefits to domestic partners — but only if the domestic partner was of the same sex as the employee, which excluded Irizarry's domestic partner, an exclusion that she contends is unconstitutional.

Besides being of th[illegible], applicants for domestic-partner status must be unmarried, unrelated, at least 18 years old, and "each other's sole domestic partner, responsible for each other's common welfare." They must satisfy two of the following four additional conditions as well: that they have been living together for a year; that they jointly own their home; that they jointly own other property of specified kinds; that the domestic partner is the primary beneficiary named in the employee's will. Although the board's purpose in entitling domestic partners so defined to spousal benefits was to extend such benefits to homosexual employees, homosexual marriage not being recognized by Illinois, 750 ILCS 5/212, 5/213.1, entitlement to the benefits does not require proof of sexual orientation.

Irizarry's domestic partner satisfies all the conditions for domesticpartner benefits except being of the same sex. She argues that the board's policy denies equal protection and, secondarily, due process. The district court dismissed her suit for failure to state a claim.

The board of education makes two arguments for treating homosexual couples differently from unmarried heterosexual couples. First, since homosexual marriage is not possible in Illinois (or anywhere else in the United States, though it is now possible in the Netherlands), and heterosexual marriage of course is, the recognition of a domestic-partnership surrogate is more important for homosexual than for heterosexual couples, who can obtain the benefits simply by marrying. Second, the board wants to attract homosexual teachers in order to provide support for homosexual students. *Cf. Crawford v. City of Chicago*, 304 Ill.App.3d 818, 237 Ill.Dec. 668, 710 N.E.2d 91, 98–99 (1999). According to its brief, the board "believes that lesbian and gay male school personnel who have a healthy acceptance of their own sexuality can act as role models and provide emotional support for lesbian and gay students. . . . They can support students who are questioning their sexual identities or who are feeling alienated due to their minority sexual orientation. They can also encourage all students to be tolerant and accepting of lesbians and gay males, and discourage violence directed [illegible] groups.

Th[illegible] of argument will shock many people even today; it was not that long ago when homosexual teachers were almost universally considered a public menace likely to seduce or recruit their students into homosexuality, then regarded with unmitigated horror. The plaintiff does not argue, however, that the Chicago Board of Education is irrational in having turned the traditional attitude toward homosexual teachers upside down. It is not for a federal court to decide whether a local government agency's policy of tolerating or even endorsing homosexuality is sound. Even if the judges consider such a policy morally repugnant — even dangerous — they may not interfere with it unless convinced that it lacks even minimum rationality, which is a permissive standard. It is a fact that some school children are homosexual, and the responsibility for dealing with that fact is lodged in the school authorities, and (if they are public schools) ultimately in the taxpaying public, rather than in the federal courts.

The efficacy of the policy may be doubted. Although it had been in effect for a year and a half when the appeal was argued, only nine employees out of some 45,000 had signed up for domestic-partner benefits and none of the nine indicated whether he or she was homosexual; they may not all have been, as we shall see — perhaps none were. Nor is there any indication that any of the nine are new employees attracted to teach in the Chicago public schools by the availability of health benefits for same-sex domestic partners. Maybe it's too early, though, to assess the efficacy of the policy. No matter; limited efficacy does not make the policy irrational — not even if we think limited efficacy evidence that the policy is more in the nature of a political gesture than a serious effort to improve the lot of homosexual students — if only because with limited efficacy comes limited cost. Because homosexuals are a small fraction of the population, because the continuing stigma of homosexuality discourages many of them from revealing their sexual orientation, and because nowadays a significant number of heterosexuals substitute cohabitation for marriage in response to the diminishing stigma of cohabitation, extending domestic-partner benefits to mixed-sex couples would greatly increase the expense of the program.

Irizarry argues that the child of an unmarried couple ought equally to be entitled to the mentoring and role-model benefits of having teachers who live in the same way the student's parents do. Cost considerations to one side, the argument collides with a nationwide policy in favor of marriage. True, it is no longer widely popular to try to pressure homosexuals to marry persons of the opposite sex. But so far as heterosexuals are concerned, the evidence that on average married couples live longer, are healthier, earn more, have lower rates of substance abuse and mental illness, are less likely to commit suicide, and report higher levels of happiness — that marriage civilizes young males, confers economies of scale and of joint consumption, minimizes sexually transmitted disease, and provides a stable and nourishing framework for child rearing — see, *e.g.,* Linda J. Waite & Maggie Gallagher, *The Case for Marriage: Why Married People Are Happier, Healthier, and Better Off Financially* (2000); David Popenoe, *Life without Father: Compelling New Evidence That Fatherhood and Marriage Are Indispensable for the Good of Children and Society* (1996); George W. Dent, Jr., "*The Defense of Traditional Marriage,*" 15 J.L. & Pol. 581 (1999), refutes any claim that policies designed to promote marriage are irrational. The Chicago Board of Education cannot be faulted, therefore, for not wishing to encourage heterosexual cohabitation; and, though we need not decide the point, the refusal to extend domestic-partner benefits to heterosexual cohabitators could be justified on the basis of the policy favoring marriage for heterosexuals quite apart from the reasons for wanting to extend the spousal fringe benefits to homosexual couples.

Of course, self-selection is important; people are more likely to marry who believe they have characteristics favorable to a long-term relationship. Lee A. Lillard & Constantijn W.A. Panis, "*Marital Status and Mortality: The Role of Health,*" 33 Demography 313 (1996); Lee A. Lillard, Michael J. Brien & Linda J. Waite, "*Premarital Cohabitation and Subsequent Dissolution: A Matter of Self-Selection?*" 32 Demography 437 (1995). But the Chicago Board of Education would not be irrational (though it might be incorrect) in assigning some causal role to the relationship itself. Linda J. Waite, "*Does Marriage*

Matter?" 32 Demography 483, 498–99 (1995), finds that cohabitants are much less likely than married couples to pool financial resources, more likely to assume that each partner is responsible for supporting himself or herself financially, more likely to spend free time separately, and less likely to agree on the future of the relationship. This makes both investment in the relationship and specialization with this partner much riskier than in marriage, and so reduces them. Whereas marriage connects individuals to other important social institutions, such as organized religion, cohabitation seems to distance them from these institutions.

Irizarry and her domestic partner may, given the unusual duration of their relationship, be an exception to generalizations about the benefits of marriage. We are not aware of an extensive scholarly literature comparing marriage to long-term cohabitation. This may be due to the fact that longterm cohabitation is rare — only ten percent of such relationships last for five years or more, Pamela J. Smock, "*Cohabitation in the United States: An Appraisal of Research Themes, Findings, and Implications*," 26 Ann. Rev. Sociology 1 (2000). But there is evidence that the widespread substitution of cohabitation for marriage in Sweden has given that country the highest rate of family dissolution and single parenting in the developed world. David Popenoe, *Disturbing the Nest: Family Change and Decline in Modern Societies* 173–74 (1988). It is well known that divorce is harmful to children (see Jonathan Gruber, "*Is Making Divorce Easier Bad for Children? The Long Run Implications of Unilateral Divorce*," NBER Working Paper No. 7968 (Oct. 2000), for a survey of the evidence), and presumably the same is true for the dissolution of a cohabitation — and a cohabitation is more likely to dissolve than a marriage. True, Irizarry's cohabitation has not dissolved; but law and policy are based on the general rather than the idiosyncratic, as the Supreme Court noted with reference to other benefits tied to marital status in *Califano v. Jobst*, 434 U.S. 47, 53–54 (1977). Nor is it entirely clear that this couple ought to be considered an exception to the general concern with heterosexuals who choose to have a family outside of marriage. For when asked at argument why the couple had never married, Irizarry's counsel replied that he had asked his client that question and she had told him that "it just never came up." There may be good reasons why a particular couple would not marry even after producing children, but that the thought of marriage would not even occur to them is disquieting.

The Lambda Legal Defense and Education Fund has filed an amicus curiae brief surprisingly urging reversal — surprisingly because Lambda is an organization for the promotion of homosexual rights, and if it is the law that domestic-partnership benefits must be extended to heterosexual couples, the benefits are quite likely to be terminated for everyone lest the extension to heterosexual cohabiters impose excessive costs and invite criticism as encouraging heterosexual cohabitation and illegitimate births and discouraging marriage and legitimacy. But Lambda is concerned with the fact that state and national policy encourages (heterosexual) marriage in all sorts of ways that domestic-partner health benefits cannot begin to equalize. Lambda wants to knock marriage off its perch by requiring the board of education to treat unmarried heterosexual couples as well as it treats married ones, so that marriage will lose some of its luster.

This is further evidence of the essentially symbolic or political rather than practical significance of the board's policy. Lambda is not jeopardizing a substantial benefit for homosexuals because very few of them want or will seek the benefit. In any event, it would not be proper for judges to use the vague concept of "equal protection" to undermine marriage just because it is a heterosexual institution. The desire of the board of education to increase the employment of homosexual teachers is admittedly a striking manifestation of the sexual revolution that has characterized, some would say convulsed, the United States in the last forty years. The courts did not try to stop the revolution. On the contrary, they spurred it on, most pertinently to this case by their decisions removing legal disabilities of birth out of wedlock, *e.g.*, *Jimenez v. Weinberger*, 417 U.S. 628 (1974); *Gomez v. Perez*, 409 U.S. 535 (1973) (*per curiam*); *Weber v. Aetna Casualty & Surety Co.*, 406 U.S. 164 (1972); *Glona v. American Guarantee & Liability Insurance Co.*, 391 U.S. 73 (1968); *Levy v. Louisiana*, 391 U.S. 68 (1968), disabilities that if they still existed might have induced Ms. Irizarry and the father of her children to marry in order to remove those disabilities from their children. Likewise relevant are cases such as *Stanley v. Illinois*, 405 U.S. 645 (1972), that confer constitutional rights on unwed fathers. But no court has gone so far as to deem marriage a suspect classification because government provides benefits to married persons that it withholds from cohabiting couples. That would be a bizarre extension of case law already criticized as having carried the courts well beyond the point at which the Constitution might be thought to provide guidance to social policy.

To the board's argument that it has extended spousal benefits to the domestic partners of homosexual employees because homosexual marriage is not a status available to its employees, Irizarry replies that the argument depends on the board's groundless decision to provide benefits to spouses, rather than domestic partners, of its employees. She says that all the board has to do to purge the constitutional violation is to condition all nonemployee fringe benefits on satisfaction of its domestic-partnership conditions other than that the domestic partner be of the same sex as the employee; and then the "discrimination" in favor of heterosexuals that the extension of spousal benefits to homosexual domestic partners was intended to erase will be eliminated without discrimination against heterosexual domestic partners. She points to Chicago's Human Rights Ordinance, which forbids discrimination on the basis of marital status. But the purpose, at least the primary purpose, of such a prohibition is surely not to dethrone marriage; it is to prevent discrimination against married women, who employers might think have divided loyalties. Such laws are pro-marriage, not anti — as the plaintiff suggests.

All other considerations to one side, the board reaps cost savings by basing dependent benefits on marital status — savings distinct from those discussed earlier that depend simply on the much smaller number of homosexuals than heterosexuals likely to seek or qualify for domesticpartner benefits. It is easier to determine whether the claimant is married to an employee than to determine whether the claimant satisfies the multiple criteria for domestic partnership. Earlier we took for granted that cost is an admissible consideration in evaluating the rationality of a classification; here we add that the cases so hold. *Bankers Life & Casualty Co. v. Crenshaw*, 486 U.S. 71, 83–84

(1988); *LaGuerre v. Reno*, 164 F.3d 1035, 1041 (7th Cir.1998); *DeSousa v. Reno*, 190 F.3d 175, 185 (3d Cir.1999); *Silver v. Baggiano*, 804 F.2d [illegible] 1218–19 (11th Cir.198[illegible]). [illegible] understand the plaintiff to be arguing that the board of education must have anything more than a rational basis for its action in order to defeat the plaintiff's equal protection claim. Only when the plaintiff in an equal protection case is complaining of a form of discrimination that is suspect because historically it was irrational or invidious is there a heavier burden of justifying a difference in treatment than merely showing that it is rational. *E.g., Kimel v. Florida Bd. of Regents*, 528 U.S. 62, 83–84 (2000); *Milner v. Apfel*, 148 F.3d 812, 815–16 (7th Cir.1998); *Miller v. United States*, 73 F. 3d 878, 881–82 (9th Cir.1995); *Disabled American Veterans v. Dept. of Veterans Affairs*, 962 F. 2d 136, 141–42 (2d Cir.1992). Heterosexuals cohabiting outside of marriage are not such a class. There is a history of disapproval of (nonmarital) cohabitation, and some states still criminalize it. See, *e.g.*, Ariz.Rev.Stat.Ann. § 13-1409; Mich.Comp. Laws Ann. § 750.355; N.D. Cent.Code § 12.1-20-10 — as indeed Illinois did until 1990. *United States v. Nichols*, 937 F.2d 1257, 1263 (7th Cir.1991). But the disapproval is not necessarily irrational or invidious, *Doe v. Duling*, 782 F.2d 1202, 1207 (4th Cir.1986), given the benefits of marriage discussed earlier. It was rational for the board to refuse to extend domestic-partnership benefits to persons who can if they wish marry and by doing so spare the board from having to make a factual inquiry into the nature of their relationship.

The least rational feature of the board's policy, though not emphasized by the plaintiff, is that although domestic-partner benefits are confined to persons of the same sex, the partners need not be homosexual. They could be roommates who have lived together for a year and own some property jointly and for want of relatives are each other's "sole domestic-partner," and if so they would be entitled to domestic-partner benefits under the board of education's policy. To distinguish between roommates of the same and of different sexes, as the policy implicitly does, cannot be justified on the ground that the latter but not the former could marry each other!

So the policy does not make a very close fit between end and means. But it doesn't have to, provided there is a rational basis for the loose fit. See, *e.g.*, *Kimel v. Florida Bd. of Regents*, supra, 528 U.S. 62 at 83–84, [illegible] 145 L. Ed. 2d [illegible] *v. Bradley*, 440 U.S. 93, 108–109, 99 S. Ct. 939, 59 L. Ed. 2d 171 (1979); *Zehner v. Trigg*, 133 F.3d 459, 463 (7th Cir.1997); *Wedderburn v. INS*, 215 F.3d 795, 800 (7th Cir.2000). This follows from our earlier point that cost is a rational basis for treating people differently. Economy is one of the principal reasons for using rules rather than standards to govern conduct. Rules single out one or a few facts from the welter of possibly relevant considerations and make that one or those few facts legally determinative, thus dispensing with inquiry into the other considerations. A standard that takes account of all relevant considerations will produce fewer arbitrary differences in outcome, but at a cost in uncertainty, administrative burden, and sometimes even — as here — in invading people's privacy. It is easy to see why the board of education does not want to put applicants to the proof of their sexual preference. That would be resented. The price of avoiding an inquiry that would be costly because it would be obnoxious is that a few roommates may end up with windfall benefits. We cannot say that the board is being irrational in deciding to pay that price rather than snoop into people's sex lives. *Cf. Califano v. Jobst*, supra, 434 U.S. at 53–54.

If the result is, as it may be, that none of the nine employees who have opted for domestic-partner benefits is homosexual (or at least that none is willing to acknowledge his homosexuality publicly, for that is not required by the board's policy though it would seem implicit in the board's desire to attract homosexuals who have "a healthy acceptance of their own sexuality"), this would lend a note of irony to the board's policy and would reinforce our earlier conjecture that the purpose is to make a statement rather than to confer actual monetary benefits. But "making a statement" is a common purpose of legislation and does not condemn it as irrational.

The plaintiff has a second ground of appeal. Interpreting the city ordinance to which we referred earlier as forbidding discrimination on the basis of marital status, she argues that by depriving her of the right created by those laws the board has deprived her of "property" without due process of law. It is true that a legal claim can be "property" within the meaning of the due process clause *Logan v. Zimmerman Brush Co.*, 455 U.S. 422, 428–31 (1982); *Mullane v. Central Hanover Bank & Trust Co.*, 339 U.S. 306, 311–13 (1950); *Shvartsman v. Apfel*, 138 F.3d 1196, 1199 (7th Cir.1998), but it is not true that a violation of state or local law (or for that matter of federal law) as such is a deprivation of property. *Daniels v. Williams*, 474 U.S. 327, 331 (1986); *Paul v. Davis*, 424 U.S. 693, 700–01 (1976). How could it be? It is the violation that gives rise to the legal claim! Had the board not discriminated against the plaintiff on the basis of her (non)marital status, she would not have a claim that she could press (that she is pressing) before the Chicago Commission on Human Relations. We suspect that she has misinterpreted the ordinance as forbidding any preference for marital status. But that is an issue for the Commission to resolve in the first instance, and it is irrelevant to whether she has alleged a deprivation of constitutional property.

NOTES AND QUESTIONS

1. The *Irizarry* case stands convention on its head, doesn't it? Usually discrimination disfavors gays and lesbians; here it favors them. Why? What public interest is served?
2. And the policy denies benefits to unmarried heterosexual couples, presumably punishing them for not getting married. If the public value is to favor marriage, then why not deny benefits, as well, to gays and lesbians? Is it because gays and lesbians do not have the option of getting married?
3. Of course, as the Court notes, the benefits are accorded to same sex couples *even if they are not homosexuals*! And so a purpose to protect gays and lesbians would not be over-broad, and the statute is under-inclusive. Shouldn't the statute fail, then, under due process or equal protection analyses?
4. And if the value is chiefly symbolic or political, as the Court says, do you agree with the symbolism? What is the message being delivered? And how successfully?

5. The family is a basic, perhaps the basic, unit of society. It embodies many of the elements and strengths of the greater community while enabling family members to find refuge from society and to procreate and produce future family members. It is thus quintessentially a biological unit. Society may expand this. However, by allowing adoption or visitation by non-related individuals, the questions posed are who may qualify and what are the limits?

TROXEL v. GRANVILLE
530 U.S. 57 (2000)

Justice **O'Connor** announced the judgment of the Court and delivered an opinion, in which **The Chief Justice**, Justice **Ginsburg**, and Justice **Breyer** join.

Section 26.10.160(3) of the Revised Code of Washington permits "any person" to petition a superior court for visitation rights "at any time," and authorizes that court to grant such visitation rights whenever "visitation may serve the best interest of the child." Petitioners Jenifer and Gary Troxel petitioned a Washington Superior Court for the right to visit their grandchildren, Isabelle and Natalie Troxel. Respondent Tommie Granville, the mother of Isabelle and Natalie, opposed the petition. The case ultimately reached the Washington Supreme Court, which held that § 26.10.160(3) unconstitutionally interferes with the fundamental right of parents to rear their children.

I

Tommie Granville and Brad Troxel shared a relationship that ended in June 1991. The two never married, but they had two daughters, Isabelle and Natalie. Jenifer and Gary Troxel are Brad's parents, and thus the paternal grandparents of Isabelle and Natalie. After Tommie and Brad separated in 1991, Brad lived with his parents and regularly brought his daughters to his parents' home for weekend visitation. Brad committed suicide in May 1993. Although the Troxels at first continued to see Isabelle and Natalie on a regular basis after their son's death, Tommie Granville informed the Troxels in October 1993 that she wished to limit their visitation with her daughters to one short visit per month.

In December 1993, the Troxels commenced the present action by filing, in the Washington Superior Court for Skagit County, a petition to obtain visitation rights with Isabelle and Natalie. The Washington Supreme Court held that "parents have a right to limit visitation of their children with third persons," and that between parents and judges, "the parents should be the ones to choose whether to expose their children to certain people or ideas." Four justices dissented from the Washington Supreme Court's holding on the constitutionality of the statute.

II

The demographic changes of the past century make it difficult to speak of an average American family. The composition of families varies greatly from household to household. While many children may have two married parents and grandparents who visit regularly, many other children are raised in single-parent households. In 1996, children living with only one parent accounted for 28 percent of all children under age 18 in the United States. Understandably, in these single-parent households, persons outside the nuclear family are called upon with increasing frequency to assist in the everyday tasks of child rearing. In many cases, grandparents play an important role. For example, in 1998, approximately 4 million children — or 5.6 percent of all children under age 18 — lived in the household of their grandparents.

The nationwide enactment of nonparental visitation statutes is assuredly due, in some part, to the States' recognition of these changing realities of the American family. Because grandparents and other relatives undertake duties of a parental nature in many households, States have sought to ensure the welfare of the children therein by protecting the relationships those children form with such third parties. The States' nonparental visitation statutes are further supported by a recognition, which varies from State to State, that children should have the opportunity to benefit from relationships with statutorily specified persons — for example, their grandparents. The extension of statutory rights in this area to persons other than a child's parents, however, comes with an obvious cost. For example, the State's recognition of an independent third-party interest in a child can place a substantial burden on the traditional parent-child relationship.

The liberty interest at issue in this case — the interest of parents in the care, custody, and control of their children — is perhaps the oldest of the fundamental liberty interests recognized by this Court. More than 75 years ago, in *Meyer v. Nebraska*, 262 U.S. 390, 399, 401, 67 L. Ed. 1042, 43 S. Ct. 625 (1923), we held that the "liberty" protected by the Due Process Clause includes the right of parents to "establish a home and bring up children" and "to control the education of their own." Two years later, in *Pierce v. Society of Sisters*, 268 U.S. 510, 534–535, 69 L. Ed. 1070, 45 S. Ct. 571 (1925), we again held that the "liberty of parents and guardians" includes the right "to direct the upbringing and education of children under their control." We explained in Pierce that "the child is not the mere creature of the State; those who nurture him and direct his destiny have the right, coupled with the high duty, to recognize and prepare him for additional obligations."

Section 26.10.160(3), as applied to Granville and her family in this case, unconstitutionally infringes on that fundamental parental right. The Washington nonparental visitation statute is breathtakingly broad. According to the statute's text, "*any person* may petition the court for visitation rights *at any time*," and the court may grant such visitation rights whenever "visitation may serve *the best interest of the child*." § 26.10.160(3) (emphases added). That language effectively permits any third party seeking visitation to subject any decision by a parent concerning visitation of the parent's children to state-court review. Once the visitation petition has been filed in court and the matter is placed before a judge, a parent's decision that visitation would not be in the child's best interest is accorded no deference. Section 26.10.160(3) contains no requirement that a court accord the parent's decision any presumption of validity or any weight whatsoever. Instead, the Washington statute places the best-interest determination solely in the hands of the judge. Should the judge disagree with the parent's estimation of the child's best interests, the judge's view necessarily prevails. Thus, in practical effect, in the State of Washington a court can disregard and overturn any decision by a fit custodial parent concerning visitation whenever a third party affected by the decision files a visitation petition, based solely on the judge's determination of the child's best interests.

The Troxels did not allege, and no court has found, that Granville was an unfit parent. That aspect of the case is important, for there is a presumption that fit parents act in the best interests of their children. As this Court explained in *Parham [v. J.R., 442 U.S.584 (1979)]*:

> "Our constitutional system long ago rejected any notion that a child is the mere creature of the State and, on the contrary, asserted that parents generally have the right, coupled with the high duty, to recognize and prepare [their children] for additional obligations. . . . The law's concept of the family rests on a presumption that parents possess what a child lacks in maturity, experience, and capacity for judgment required for making life's difficult decisions. More important, historically it has recognized that natural bonds of affection lead parents to act in the best interests of their children." 442 U.S. at 602 (alteration in original) (internal quotation marks and citations omitted).

Accordingly, so long as a parent adequately cares for his or her children (*i.e.*, is fit), there will normally be no reason for the State to inject itself into the private realm of the family to further question the ability of that parent to make the best decisions concerning the rearing of that parent's children.

The problem here is not that the Washington Superior Court intervened, but that when it did so, it gave no special weight at all to Granville's determination of her daughters' best interests. More importantly, it appears that the Superior Court applied exactly the opposite presumption.

The decisional framework employed by the Superior Court directly contravened the traditional presumption that a fit parent will act in the best interest of his or her child. In that respect, the court's presumption failed to provide any protection for Granville's fundamental constitutional right to make decisions concerning the rearing of her own daughters.

Finally, we note that there is no allegation that Granville ever sought to cut off visitation entirely. Rather, the present dispute originated when Granville informed the Troxels that she would prefer to restrict their visitation with Isabelle and Natalie to one short visit per month and special holidays. In the Superior Court proceedings Granville did not oppose visitation but instead asked that the duration of any visitation order be shorter than that requested by the Troxels. While the Troxels requested two weekends per month and two full weeks in the summer, Granville asked the Superior Court to order only one day of visitation per month (with no overnight stay) and participation in the Granville family's holiday celebrations. The Superior Court gave no weight to Granville's having assented to visitation even before the filing of any visitation petition or subsequent court intervention. The court instead rejected Granville's proposal and settled on a middle ground, ordering one weekend of visitation per month, one week in the summer, and time on both of the petitioning grandparents' birthdays. Significantly, many other States expressly provide by statute that courts may not award visitation unless a parent has denied (or unreasonably denied) visitation to the concerned third party.

Considered together with the Superior Court's reasons for awarding visitation to the Troxels, the combination of these factors demonstrates that the visitation order in this case was an unconstitutional infringement on Granville's fundamental right to make decisions concerning the care, custody, and control of her two daughters. The Washington Superior Court failed to accord the determination of Granville, a fit custodial parent, any material weight. As we have explained, the Due Process Clause does not permit a State to infringe on the fundamental right of parents to make childrearing decisions simply because a state judge believes a "better" decision could be made. Neither the Washington nonparental visitation statute generally — which places no limits on either the persons who may petition for visitation or the circumstances in which such a petition may be granted — nor the Superior Court in this specific case required anything more. Accordingly, we hold that § 26.10.160(3), as applied in this case, is unconstitutional.

Because we rest our decision on the sweeping breadth of § 26.10.160(3) and the application of that broad, unlimited power in this case, we do not consider the primary constitutional question passed on by the Washington Supreme Court — whether the Due Process Clause requires all nonparental visitation statutes to include a showing of harm or potential harm to the child as a condition precedent to granting visitation. We do not, and need not, define today the precise scope of the parental due process right in the visitation context. In this respect, we agree with Justice Kennedy that the constitutionality of any standard for awarding visitation turns on the specific manner in which that standard is applied and that the constitutional protections in this area are best "elaborated with care." Because much state-court adjudication in this context occurs on a case-by-case basis, we would be hesitant to hold that specific nonparental visitation statutes violate the Due Process Clause as a *per se* matter.

Accordingly, the judgment of the Washington Supreme Court is affirmed.

It is so ordered.

Justice **Souter**, concurring in the judgment.

Justice **Thomas**, concurring in the judgment.

Justice **Stevens**, dissenting.

. . . .

II

In my view, the State Supreme Court erred in its federal constitutional analysis because neither the provision granting "any person" the right to petition the court for visitation, nor the absence of a provision requiring a "threshold . . . finding of harm to the child," provides a sufficient basis for holding that the statute is invalid in all its applications. [illegible] should fail whenever a statute has "a plainly legitimate sweep." Under the Washington statute, there are plainly any number of cases — indeed, one suspects, the most common to arise — in which the "person" among "any" seeking visitation is a once-custodial caregiver, an intimate relation, or even a genetic parent. Even the Court would seem to agree that in many circumstances, it would be constitutionally permissible for a court to award some visitation of a child to a parent or previous caregiver in cases of parental separation or divorce, cases of disputed custody, cases involving temporary foster care or guardianship, and so forth. As the statute plainly sweeps in a great deal of the permissible, the State Supreme Court majority incorrectly concluded that a statute authorizing "any person" to file a petition seeking visitation privileges would invariably run afoul of the Fourteenth Amendment.

The second key aspect of the Washington Supreme Court's holding — that the Federal Constitution requires a showing of actual or potential "harm" to the child before a court may order visitation continued over a parent's objections — finds no support in this Court's case law. While, as the Court recognizes, the Federal Constitution certainly protects the parent-child relationship from arbitrary impairment by the State, we have never held that the parent's liberty interest in this relationship is so inflexible as to establish a rigid constitutional shield, protecting every arbitrary parental decision from any challenge absent a threshold finding of harm. The presumption that parental decisions generally serve the best interests of their children is sound, and clearly in the normal case the parent's interest is paramount. But even a fit parent is capable of treating a child like a mere possession.

Cases like this do not present a bipolar struggle between the parents and the State over who has final authority to determine what is in a child's best interests. There is at a minimum a third individual, whose interests are implicated in every case to which the statute applies — the child.

While this Court has not yet had occasion to elucidate the nature of a child's liberty interests in preserving established familial [illegible] question), it seems to me extremely likely that, to the extent parents and families have fundamental liberty interests in preserving such intimate relationships, so, too, do children have these interests, and so, too, must their interests be balanced in the equation. At a minimum, our prior cases recognizing that children are, generally speaking, constitutionally protected actors require that this Court reject any suggestion that when it comes to parental rights, children are so much chattel.

But presumptions notwithstanding, we should recognize that there may be circumstances in which a child has a stronger interest at stake than mere protection from serious harm caused by the termination of visitation by a "person" other than a parent. The almost infinite variety of family relationships that pervade our ever-changing society strongly counsel against the creation by this Court of a constitutional rule that treats a biological parent's liberty interest in the care and supervision of her child as an isolated right that may be exercised arbitrarily. It is indisputably the business of the States, rather than a federal court employing a national standard, to assess in the first instance the relative importance of the conflicting interests that give rise to disputes such as this. Far from guaranteeing that parents' interests will be trammeled in the sweep of cases arising under the statute, the Washington law merely gives an individual — with whom a child may have an established relationship — the procedural right to ask the State to act as arbiter, through the entirely well-known best-interests standard, between the parent's protected interests and the child's. It seems clear to me that the Due Process Clause of the Fourteenth Amendment leaves room for States to consider the impact on a child of possibly arbitrary parental decisions that neither serve nor are motivated by the best interests of the child.

Accordingly, I respectfully dissent.

Justice **Scalia**, dissenting.

In my view, a right of parents to direct the upbringing of their children is among the "unalienable Rights" with which the Declaration of Independence proclaims "all Men . . . are endowed by their Creator." And in my view that right is also among the "other [rights] retained by the people" which the Ninth Amendment says the Constitution's enumeration of rights "shall not be construed to deny or disparage." The Declaration of Independence, however, is not a legal prescription conferring powers upon the courts; and the Constitution's refusal to "deny or disparage" other rights is far removed from affirming any one of them, and even farther removed from authorizing judges to identify what they might be, and to enforce the judges' list against laws duly enacted by the people. Consequently, while I would think it entirely compatible with the commitment to representative democracy set forth in the founding documents to argue, in legislative chambers or in electoral campaigns, that the state has *no power* to interfere with parents' authority over the rearing of their children, I do not believe that the power which the Constitution confers upon me *as a judge* entitles me to deny legal effect to laws that (in my view) infringe upon what is (in my view) that unenumerated right.

For these reasons, I would reverse the judgment below.

Justice **Kennedy,** dissenting.

Turning to the question whether harm to the child must be the controlling standard in every visitation proceeding, there is a beginning point that commands general, perhaps unanimous, agreement in our separate opinions: As our case law has developed, the custodial parent has a constitutional right to determine, without undue interference by the state, how best to raise, nurture, and educate the child. The parental right stems from the liberty protected by the Due Process Clause of the Fourteenth Amendment. *Pierce* and *Meyer*, had they been decided in recent times, may well have been grounded upon First Amendment principles protecting freedom of speech, belief, and religion. Their formulation and subsequent interpretation have been quite different, of course; and they long have been interpreted to have found in Fourteenth Amendment concepts of liberty an independent right of the parent in the "custody, care and nurture of the child," free from state intervention. The principle exists, then, in broad formulation; yet courts must use considerable restraint, including careful adherence to the incremental instruction given by the precise facts of particular cases, as they seek to give further and more precise definition to the right.

The State Supreme Court sought to give content to the parent's right by announcing a categorical rule that third parties who seek visitation must always prove the denial of visitation would harm the child. While it might be argued as an abstract matter that in some sense the child is always harmed if his or her best interests are not considered, the law of domestic relations, as it has evolved to this point, treats as distinct the two standards, one harm to the child and the other the best interests of the child. The judgment of the Supreme Court of Washington rests on that assumption, and I, too, shall assume that there are real and consequential differences between the two standards.

On the question whether one standard must always take precedence over the other in order to protect the right of the parent or parents, "our Nation's history, legal traditions, and practices" do not give us clear or definitive answers. The consensus among courts and commentators is that at least through the 19th century there was no legal right of visitation; court-ordered visitation appears to be a 20th-century phenomenon. A case often cited as one of the earliest visitation decisions, *Succession of Reiss*, 46 La. Ann. 347, 353, 15 So. 151, 152 (1894), explained that "the obligation ordinarily to visit grandparents is moral and not legal"

To say that third parties have had no historical right to petition for visitation does not necessarily imply, as the Supreme Court of Washington concluded, that a parent has a constitutional right to prevent visitation in all cases not involving harm. The State Supreme Court's conclusion that the Constitution forbids the application of the best interests of the child standard in any visitation proceeding, however, appears to rest upon assumptions the Constitution does not require.

My principal concern is that the holding seems to proceed from the assumption that the parent or parents who resist visitation have always been the child's primary caregivers and that the third parties who seek visitation have no legitimate and established relationship with the child. That idea, in turn, appears influenced by the concept that the conventional nuclear family ought to establish the visitation standard for every domestic relations case. As we all know, this is simply not the structure or prevailing condition in many households.

Indeed, contemporary practice should give us some pause before rejecting the best interests of the child standard in all third-party visitation cases, as the Washington court has done. The standard has been recognized for many years as a basic tool of domestic relations law in visitation proceedings. Since 1965 all 50 States have enacted a third-party visitation statute of some sort. Each of these statutes, save one, permits a court order to issue in certain cases if visitation is found to be in the best interests of the child.

The best interests of the child standard has at times been criticized as indeterminate, leading to unpredictable results. If a single parent who is struggling to raise a child is faced with visitation demands from a third party, the attorney's fees alone might destroy her hopes and plans for the child's future. Our system must confront more often the reality that litigation can itself be so disruptive that constitutional protection may be required; and I do not discount the possibility that in some instances the best interests of the child standard may provide insufficient protection to the parent-child relationship. We owe it to the Nation's domestic relations legal structure, however, to proceed with caution.

In my view the judgment under review should be vacated and the case remanded for further proceedings.

NOTES AND QUESTIONS

1. Is the problem in *Troxel* that "any person" may petition the court or that the court may award visitation rights to "any person"? Could the statute be saved by altering one — but not both — elements?
2. May the statute in *Troxel* be narrowed to grant visitation rights to grandparents? Brothers and sisters? Significant others of non-biological relation, such as stepparents or foster parents? What are the outer limits of the "family," and how is that to be defined? Compare the definition in *Moore v. City of East Cleveland, infra.*
3. And, in any event, must a showing be made not only that the proposed "visitor" is within the circle, but that visitation will be in the "best interests" of the child? Or should it be enough to show absence of harm? Or is the test the interest of the would-be visitor, and, if so, what *is* that interest. What does Justice Stevens say about this?
4. Why shouldn't the matter of visitation simply be left to the autonomous choice of the custodial parent, thus protecting her liberty interest?
5. Suppose Tommie Granville *had* sought to cut off the grandparent's visitation? Would/should the case come out differently? Might this be a basis for removing custody from her?
6. Why does Justice Kennedy dissent? Shouldn't he join the plurality?
7. May curfew laws which prevent parents from making decisions regarding their children be violative of equal protection laws? *See Hodgkins v. Peterson*, 2004 U.S. Dist. LEXIS 16359 (Southern Dist. Indiana, 2004). Under broad reading of Equal Protection, what activities pertaining to children *may* the government regulate?

PROBLEM 2–12 — Now Hear This

Your State's Department of Children's Services has filed a petition before you, seeking to take custody of young Adam Smith, born deaf to deaf parents, Sam and Sheila. Adam is three years of age. His older sister, Samantha, is thirteen, also deaf and fluent in ASL, American Sign Language, but with limited oral speech. Indeed, in testimony before you, you were largely unable to understand her or her parents and a sign language interpreter was necessary.

DCS seeks to compel the Smiths to agree to a cochlear implant for Adam. He has been tested by appropriate medical specialists who are unanimous that this device would enable Adam to have 90% of the hearing capability of children born with normal hearing. While this would [illegible] a "routine" procedure, not "experimental", with a high percentage of success. The prognosis is that Adam would then develop normal speech and attend public school without the need for special accommodation, training or financial support.

Sam, Sheila and Samantha are opposed. All three testify that they are a nonhearing family, members of the deaf culture and embrace deaf pride. The majoritarian obsession with hearing is a misguided imposition on their autonomy and identity, and would deny Adam the special benefits of nonhearing society and experience. Two clinical pyschologists and one sociologist support their position.

DCS calls its own experts as to the learning, speech, educational and employment limitations imposed by hearing disability. DCS also argues that the special accommodations required by the Americans with Disabilities Act for Sam and Sheila in their employment will not extend to Adam, because a disability which can be corrected cannot be said to affect a major life activity, much as a person who is legally blind may often correct his or her vision with eyeglasses. Moreover, DCS argues, the Smiths are not only hypocrites but have behaved irresponsibly in conceiving two children born deaf due to predictable genetic disorders.

How do you rule? In your deliberation, you may wish to consult Tucker, *Deaf Culture, Cochlear Implants and Elective Disability,* 28 Hast. Center Report 6 (1998); the *Casey*, *Griswold, Ruiz* and *Meyer* decisions, *supra*; the cases on family association, *infra* § 2.04; the *Bragdon* case, *infra* § 3.02[3]; § 4.03 on the ADA; and the cases at § 4.02[1] on maternal-fetal conflict.

[2] Privacy and Home

Earlier cases such as *Casey*, *Griswold*, and *Bowers v. Hardwick*, in addressing issues of autonomy and privacy, have assumed the presence and importance of a home. Indeed marriage and family — as *Yoder* suggests — would hardly be possible otherwise. The place and protection of the home deserve independent, separate [illegible] begin with *Moore v. City of East Cleveland.*

MOORE v. CITY OF EAST CLEVELAND, OHIO

431 U.S. 494 (1977)

Mr. Justice **Powell** announced the judgment of the Court, and delivered an opinion in which Mr. Justice **Brennan**, Mr. Justice **Marshall**, and Mr. Justice **Blackmun** joined.

East Cleveland's housing ordinance, like many throughout the country, limits occupancy of a dwelling unit to members of a single family. But the ordinance contains an unusual and complicated definitional section that recognizes as a "family" only a few categories of related individuals.[1] Because

[1] Section 1341.08 (1966) provides:

" 'Family' means a number of individuals related to the nominal head of the household or to the her family, living together in her home, fits none of those categories, appellant stands convicted of a criminal offense. The question in this case is whether the ordinance violates the Due Process Clause of the Fourteenth Amendment.

I

Appellant, Mrs. Inez Moore, lives in her East Cleveland home together with her son, Dale Moore Sr., and her two grandsons, Dale, Jr., and John Moore, Jr. The two boys are first cousins rather than brothers; we are told that John came to live with his grandmother and with the elder and younger Dale Moore after his mother's death.

In early 1973, Mrs. Moore received a notice of violation from the city, stating that John was an "illegal occupant" and directing her to comply with the ordinance. When she failed to remove him from her home, the city filed a criminal charge. Mrs. Moore moved to dismiss, claiming that the ordinance was constitutionally invalid on its face. Her motion was overruled, and upon conviction she was sentenced to five days in jail and a $25 fine. . . .

II

The city argues that our decision in *Village of Belle Terre v. Boraas*, 416 U.S. 1 (1974), requires us to sustain the ordinance attacked here. Belle Terre, like East Cleveland, imposed limits on the types of groups that could occupy a single dwelling unit. . . .

But one overriding factor sets this case apart from *Belle Terre*. The ordinance there affected only unrelated individuals. It expressly allowed all who were related by "blood, adoption, or marriage" to live together. East Cleveland, in contrast, has chosen to regulate the occupancy of its housing by slicing deeply into the family itself. This is no mere incidental result of the ordinance. On its face it selects certain categories of relatives who may live together and declares that others may not. In particular, it makes a crime of a grandmother's choice to live with her grandson in circumstances like those presented here.

When a city undertakes such intrusive regulation of the family . . . the usual judicial deference to the legislature is inappropriate. "This Court has long recognized that freedom of personal choice in matters of marriage and family life is one of the liberties protected by the Due Process Clause of the Fourteenth Amendment." A host of cases, tracing their lineage to *Meyer v.*

spouse of the nominal head of the household living as a single housekeeping unit in a single dwelling unit, but limited to the following: '(a) Husband or wife of the nominal head of the household.' '(b) Unmarried children of the nominal head of the household or of the spouse of the nominal head of the household, provided, however, that such unmarried children have no children residing with them.' '(c) Father or mother of the nominal head of the household or of the spouse of the nominal head of the household.' '(d) Notwithstanding the provisions of subsection (b) hereof, a family may include not more than one dependent married or unmarried child of the nominal head of the household or of the spouse of the nominal head of the household and the spouse and dependent children of such dependent child. For the purpose of this subsection, a dependent person is one who has more than fifty percent of his total support furnished for him by the nominal head of the household and the spouse of the nominal head of the household.' '(e) A family may consist of one individual.' "

Nebraska have consistently acknowledged a "private realm of family life which the state cannot enter." Of course, the family is not b[illegible] when the government intrudes on choices concerning family living arrangements, this Court must examine carefully the importance of the governmental interests advanced and the extent to which they are served by the challenged regulation.

When thus examined, this ordinance cannot survive. The city seeks to justify it as a means of preventing overcrowding, minimizing traffic and parking congestion, and avoiding an undue financial burden on East Cleveland's school system. Although these are legitimate goals, the ordinance before us serves them marginally, at best. For example, the ordinance permits any family consisting only of husband, wife, and unmarried children to live together, even if the family contains a half dozen licensed drivers, each with his or her own car. At the same time it forbids an adult brother and sister to share a household, even if both faithfully use public transportation. The ordinance would permit a grandmother to live with a single dependent son and children, even if his school-age children number a dozen, yet it forces Mrs. Moore to find another dwelling for her grandson John, simply because of the presence of his uncle and cousin in the same household. We need not labor the point. . . .

III

The city would distinguish the cases based on *Meyer* and *Pierce*. It points out that none of them "gives grandmothers any fundamental rights with respect to grandsons," and suggests that any constitutional right to live together as a family extends only to the nuclear family essentially a couple and their dependent children.

To be sure, these cases did not expressly consider the family relationship presented here. They were immediately concerned with freedom of choice with respect to childbearing, or with the rights of parents to the custody and companionship of their own children, or with traditional parental authority in matters of child rearing and education. But unless we close our eyes to the basic reasons why certain rights [illegible] the family have been accorded shelter under the Fourteenth Amendment's Due Process Clause, we cannot avoid applying the force and rationale of these precedents to the family choice involved in this case.

. . . .

. . . Our decisions establish that the Constitution protects the sanctity of the family precisely because the institution of the family is deeply rooted in this Nation's history and tradition. It is through the family that we inculcate and pass down many of our most cherished values, moral and cultural.

Ours is by no means a tradition limited to respect for the bonds uniting the members of the nuclear family. The tradition of uncles, aunts, cousins, and especially grandparents sharing a household along with parents and children has roots equally venerable and equally deserving of constitutional recognition. Over the years millions of our citizens have grown up in just such an environment, and most, surely, have profited from it. Even if conditions of modern society have brought about a decline in extended family households, they have not erased the accumulated wisdom of civilization, gained over the centuries and honored throughout our history, that supports a larger conception of the family. Out of choice, necessity, or a sense of family responsibility, it has been common for close relatives to draw together and participate in the duties and satisfactions of a common home. Decisions concerning child rearing, which *Yoder, Meyer, Pierce* and other cases have recognized as entitled to constitutional protection, long have been shared with grandparents or other relatives who occupy the same household indeed who may take on major responsibility for the rearing of the children. Especially in times of adversity, such as the death of a spouse or economic need, the broader family has tended to come together for mutual sustenance and to maintain or rebuild a secure home life. This is apparently what happened here.

Whether or not such a household is established because of personal tragedy, the choice of relatives in this degree of kinship to live together may not lightly be denied by the State. . . . [T]he Constitution prevents East Cleveland from standardizing its children and its adults by forcing all to live in certain narrowly defined family patterns.

Reversed.

Mr. Justice **Brennan**, with whom Mr. Justice **Marshall** joins, concurring.

. . . .

In today's America, the "nuclear family" is the pattern so often found in much of white suburbia. The Constitution cannot be interpreted, however, to tolerate the imposition by government upon the rest of us of white suburbia's preference in patterns of family living. The "extended family" that provided generations of early Americans with social services and economic and emotional support in times of hardship, and was the beachhead for successive waves of immigrants who populated our cities, remains not merely still a pervasive living pattern, but under the goad of brutal economic necessity, a prominent pattern virtually a means of survival for large numbers of the poor and deprived minorities of our society. For them compelled pooling of scant resources requires compelled sharing of a household.

The "extended" form is especially familiar among black families. We may suppose that this reflects the truism that black citizens, like generations of white immigrants before them, have been victims of economic and other disadvantages that would worsen if they were compelled to abandon extended, for nuclear, living patterns. Even in husband and wife households, 13% of black families compared with 3% of white families include relatives under 18 years old, in addition to the couple's own children. In black households whose head is an elderly woman, as in this case, the contrast is even more striking: 48% of such black households, compared with 10% of counterpart white households, include related minor children not offspring of the head of the household.

. . . .

Moreover, to sanction the drawing of the family line at the arbitrary boundary chosen by East Cleveland would surely conflict with prior decisions that protected "extended" family relationships. For the "private realm of family life which the state cannot enter," recognized as protected in *Prince v. Massachusetts*, was the relationship of aunt and niece. And in *Pierce v. Society of Sisters*, the protection held to have been unconstitutionally abridged was "the liberty of parents and guardians to direct the upbringing and education of children under their control." . . . The cited decisions recognized, as the plurality recognizes today, that the choice of the "extended family" pattern is within the "freedom of personal choice in matters of . . . family life [that] is one of the liberties protected by the Due Process Clause of the Fourteenth Amendment."

. . . .

Mr. Justice **Stevens**, concurring in the judgment.

In my judgment the critical question presented by this case is whether East Cleveland's housing ordinance is a permissible restriction on appellant's right to use her own property as she sees fit.

Long before the original States adopted the Constitution, the common law protected an owner's right to decide how best to use his own property. This basic right has always been limited by the law of nuisance which proscribes uses that impair the enjoyment of other property in the vicinity. But the question whether an individual owner's use could be further limited by a municipality's comprehensive zoning plan was not finally decided until this century.

. . . .

There appears to be no precedent for an ordinance which excludes any of an owner's relatives from the group of persons who may occupy his residence on a permanent basis. Nor does there appear to be any justification for such a restriction on an owner's use of his property. The city has failed totally to explain the need for a rule which would allow a homeowner to have two grandchildren live with her if they are brothers, but not if they are cousins. Since this ordinance has not been shown to have any "substantial relation to the public health, safety, morals, or general welfare" of the city of East Cleveland, and since it cuts so deeply into a fundamental right normally associated with the ownership of residential property that of an owner to decide who may reside on his or her property it must fall. . . . East Cleveland's unprecedented ordinance constitutes a taking of property without due process and without just compensation.

. . . .

Mr. Justice **Stewart**, with whom Mr. Justice **Rehnquist** joins, dissenting.

To suggest that the biological fact of common ancestry necessarily gives related persons constitutional rights of association superior to those of unrelated persons is to misunderstand the nature of the associational freedoms that the Constitution has been understood to protect. Freedom of association has been constitutionally recognized because it is often indispensable to effectuation of explicit First Amendment guarantees. But the scope of the associational right, until now, at least, has been limited to the constitutional need that created it; obviously not every "association" is for First Amendment purposes or serves to promote the ideological freedom that the First Amendment was designed to protect.

. . . .

The appellant is considerably closer to the constitutional mark in asserting that the East Cleveland ordinance intrudes upon "the private realm of family life which the state cannot enter." . . .

Although the appellant's desire to share a single-dwelling unit also involves "private family life" in a sense, that desire can hardly be equated with any of the interests protected in the cases just cited. The ordinance about which the appellant complains did not impede her choice to have or not to have children, and it did not dictate to her how her own children were to be nurtured and reared. The ordinance clearly does not prevent parents from living together or living with their unemancipated offspring.

But even though the Court's previous cases are not directly in point, the appellant contends that the importance of the "extended family" in American society requires us to hold that her decision to share her residence with her grandsons may not be interfered with by the State. This decision, like the decisions involved in bearing and raising children, is said to be an aspect of "family life" also entitled to substantive protection under the Constitution. Without pausing to inquire how far under this argument an "extended family" might extend, I cannot agree. When the Court has found that the Fourteenth Amendment placed a substantive limitation on a State's power to regulate, it has been in those rare cases in which the personal interests at issue have been deemed "implicit in the concept of ordered liberty." The interest that the appellant may have in permanently sharing a single kitchen and a suite of contiguous rooms with some of her relatives simply does not rise to that level. To equate this interest with the fundamental decisions to marry and to bear and raise children is to extend the limited substantive contours of the Due Process Clause beyond recognition.

. . . .

Obviously, East Cleveland might have as easily and perhaps as effectively hit upon a different definition of "family." But a line could hardly be drawn that would not sooner or later become the target of a challenge like the appellant's. If "family" included all of the householder's grandchildren there would doubtless be the hard case of an orphaned niece or nephew. If, as the appellant suggests, a "family" must include all blood relatives, what of longtime friends? The point is that any definition would produce hardships in some cases without materially advancing the legislative purpose. That this ordinance also does so is no reason to hold it unconstitutional, unless we are to use our power to interpret the United States Constitution as a sort of generalized authority to correct seeming inequity wherever it surfaces. It is not for us to rewrite the ordinance, or substitute our judgment for the discretion of the prosecutor who elected to initiate this litigation.

. . . .

NOTES AND QUESTIONS

1. What is this case about? Privacy or property? Poverty or race? Family or the individual? Biology or choice? All of these are rubrics, properly

invoked by the various Justices. But *what* is the *core* concern at stake here?

2. Why was Mrs. Moore prosecuted, do you suppose? There are serious ethical issues in an ordinance that breaks up a biologically-grounded family — as *Lehr* and *Stanley* illustrated. But there are *separate* ethical issues in choosing to prosecute any person under a law. Why was this case brought?

3. For our purposes, the significance of the case is that it defined "family" as being outside the marital union and outside the "normal" heterosexual, biological unit comprising the conventional "nuclear" family. How, then, *shall* a family be defined? Must there be a biological connection? If such a connection is necessary, is it sufficient? Do the previous cases, *Stanley v. Illinois* and *Lehr v. Robertson*, provide an answer to these questions?

4. An answer may lie in the notion of choice in personhood. A grandmother chooses, socially and biologically, to contribute to and incorporate the identities of her grandchildren. The reverse, in some degree, is also often true. This process of identity is both biological and genetic, on the one hand, and social and cultural, on the other. It is a matter, initially at least, of choice. Thus the paradox arises — choice is a matter of privacy; family is a matter of association. The dissents say such reasoning is too thin for constitutional line-drawing. Do you agree?

5. Suppose the grandmother was only a "foster grandmother"? In the latter part of the 20th century, with both parents working, day care providers to a considerable extent have replaced parents and families in America. If, as *Moore* suggests, the family is so important both to society and to the individual members of the family, what should be societal policy?

6. Does preserving the family, given existing parenting patterns, discriminate against women?

7. The issue of "home" in *Moore* turns out to be more about family than home. To focus on the latter [illegible] *California v. Carney*.

CALIFORNIA v. CARNEY

471 U.S. 386 (1985)

Chief Justice **Burger** delivered the opinion of the Court.

We granted certiorari to decide whether law enforcement agents violated the Fourth Amendment when they conducted a warrantless search, based on probable cause, of a fully mobile "motor home" located in a public place.

I

On May 31 1979, Drug Enforcement Agency Agent Robert Williams watched respondent, Charles Carney, approach a youth in downtown San Diego. The youth accompanied Carney to a Dodge Mini Motor Home parked in a nearby lot. Carney and the youth closed the window shades in the motor home, including one across the front window. Agent Williams had previously received uncorroborated information that the same motor home was used by another person who was exchanging marihuana for sex. Williams, with assistance from other agents, kept the motor home under surveillance for the entire one and one-quarter hours that Carney and the youth remained inside. When the youth left the motor home, the agents followed and stopped him. The youth told the agents that he had received marijuana in return for allowing Carney sexual contacts.

At the agents' request, the youth returned to the motor home and knocked on its door; Carney stepped out. The agents identified themselves as law enforcement officers. Without a warrant or consent, one agent entered the motor home and observed marihuana, plastic bags, and a scale of the kind used in weighing drugs on a table. Agent Williams took Carney into custody and took possession of the motor home. A subsequent search of the motor home at the police station revealed additional marihuana in the cupboards and refrigerator.

Respondent was charged with possession of marihuana for sale. At a preliminary hearing, he moved to suppress the evidence discovered in the motor home. The Magistrate denied the motion, upholding the initial search as a justifiable search for other persons, and the subsequent search as a routine inventory search.

. . . .

II

The Fourth Amendment protects the "right of the people to be secure in their persons, houses, papers, and effects, against unreasonable searches and seizures." This fundamental right is preserved by a requirement that searches be conducted pursuant to a warrant issued by an independent judicial officer. There are, of course, exceptions to the general rule that a warrant must be secured before a search is undertaken; one is the so-called "automobile exception" at issue in this case. This exception to the warrant requirement was first set forth by the Court 60 years ago in *Carroll v. United States*, 267 U.S. 132 (1925). There, the Court recognized that the privacy interests in an automobile are constitutionally protected; however, it held that the ready mobility of the automobile justifies a lesser degree of protection of those interests. . . .

. . . .

These reduced expectations of privacy derive not from the fact that the area to be searched is in plain view, but from the pervasive regulation of vehicles capable of traveling on the public highways. . . .

The public is fully aware that it is accorded less privacy in its automobiles because of this compelling governmental need for regulation. In short, the pervasive schemes of regulation, which necessarily lead to reduced expectations of privacy, and the exigencies attendant to ready mobility justify searches without prior recourse to the authority of a magistrate so long as the overriding standard of probable cause is met.

. . . .

Respondent urges us to distinguish his vehicle from other vehicles within the exception because it was capable of functioning as a home. In our increasingly mobile society, many vehicles used for transportation can be and are being used not only for transportation but for shelter, i.e., as a "home" or "residence." To distinguish between respondent's motor home and an ordinary sedan for purposes of the vehicle exception would require that we apply the exception depending upon the size of the vehicle and the quality of its appointments. Moreover, to fail to apply the exception to vehicles such as motor homes ignores the fact that a motor home lends itself easily to use as an instrument of illicit drug traffic and other illegal activity. . . .

Our application of the vehicle exception has never turned on the other uses to which a vehicle might be put. The exception has historically turned on the ready mobility of the vehicle, and on the presence of the vehicle in a setting that objectively indicates that the vehicle is being used for transportation.[1]

. . .

III

. . . .

The judgment of the California Supreme Court is reversed, and the case is remanded for further proceedings not inconsistent with this opinion.

It is so ordered.

Justice **Stevens**, with whom Justice **Brennan** and Justice **Marshall** join, dissenting.

. . . .

The hybrid character of the motor home places it at the crossroads between the privacy interests that generally forbid warrantless invasions of the home, and the law enforcement interests that support the exception for warrantless searches of automobiles based on probable cause. . . .

. . . .

III

. . . .

In this case, the motor home was parked in an off-the-street lot only a few blocks from the courthouse in downtown San Diego where dozens of magistrates were available to entertain a warrant application. The officers clearly had the element of surprise with them, and with curtains covering the windshield, the motor home offered no indication of any imminent departure. The officers plainly had probable cause to arrest the respondent and search the

[1] We need not pass on the application of the vehicle exception to a motor home that is situated in a way or place that objectively indicates that it is being used as a residence. Among the factors that might be relevant in determining whether a warrant would be required in such a circumstance is its location, whether the vehicle is readily mobile or instead, for instance, elevated on blocks, whether the vehicle is licensed, whether it is connected to utilities, and whether it has convenient access to a public road.

motor home, and on this record, it is inexplicable why they eschewed the safe harbor of a warrant.

. . . .

Unlike a brick bungalow or a frame Victorian, a motor home seldom serves as a permanent lifetime abode. The motor home in this case, however, was designed to accommodate a breadth of ordinary everyday living. Photographs in the record indicate that its height, length, and beam provided substantial living space inside: stuffed chairs surround a table; cupboards provide room for storage of personal effects; bunk beds provide sleeping space; and a refrigerator provides ample space for food and beverages. Moreover, curtains and large opaque walls inhibit viewing the activities inside from the exterior of the vehicle. The interior configuration of the motor home establishes that the vehicle's size, shape, and mode of construction should have indicated to the officers that it was a vehicle containing mobile living quarters.

. . . .

In my opinion, searches of places that regularly accommodate a wide range of private human activity are fundamentally different from searches of automobiles which primarily serve a public transportation function. Although it may not be a castle, a motor home is usually the functional equivalent of a hotel room, a vacation and retirement home, or a hunting and fishing cabin. These places may be as spartan as a humble cottage when compared to the most majestic mansion, but the highest and most legitimate expectations of privacy associated with these temporary abodes should command the respect of this Court. In my opinion, a warrantless search of living quarters in a motor home is "presumptively unreasonable absent exigent circumstances."

I respectfully dissent.

NOTES AND QUESTIONS

1. The question in *Carney* is, what qualifies as a home? What might be classified as an automobile, and hence accompanied by a lesser expectation of privacy, was asserted to be a "home," to be accorded the maximum zone of privacy. Paradoxically, the protection may turn upon such physical details as whether the trailer has been taken off its wheels, is in a leased space, is hooked up to utilities and even surrounded by potted plants. Does this trivialize central issues of privacy and dignity?
2. The issue should not turn upon the *physical* qualities of *place* and *space*. Rather, it is *people* who are being protected, and — as in *Moore* — we are concerned with physical space only to the extent it defines or expresses elements of personhood. *Carney* suggests we look to different reference points from *Moore* — to the "security" language of the Fourth Amendment, to the reasonable expectations of society. Should we instead look to the concepts invoked in *Moore*? *Roe/Casey*?
3. A citizen's interest in privacy and security travels with that person and attaches to normal activities. Yet these may often be subject to extensive regulation — say, making a telephone call from a glass booth, or renting a hotel room for a night — or oversight, as with fire and health

inspections of businesses. *See Katz v. United States*, 389 U.S. 347 (1967). The issue posed is the one recurring throughout this text. When do the interests of society outweigh the autonomy of the individual?

4. The question of privacy may arise in a hospital bed, a room in a nursing home or even an operating room. For example, must a nursing home treat its residents with the same respect, deference and formality as a resident in a boarding house or apartment house or someone in their own home? And how *far* must that treatment extend: to bureaus, suitcases, files, bedding, clothing and meals? Must similar deference be paid to staff nurses or physicians?

5. What of waiver? People in a hospital, a nursing home or a mental institution may be there as a matter of commitment, but more often are there as a matter of negotiated admission and presence. So also with employees. Ordinary contract law permits parties to negotiate any terms they want, including a waiver or abandonment of constitutional treatment. May abandonment of privacy be a condition of admission or tenancy in a nursing home or an apartment? Ethically and legally, is there an irreducible minimum of privacy which is essential to the dignity and integrity of the person such that forcing relinquishment would be unconscionable? What would Rawls say?

6. And what of the need for regulation, so heavily stressed in *Carney*? Doesn't it apply as well in public health settings, dealing — let's say — with AIDS? And doesn't it apply as well with housing, as in *Moore,* or the next case, *Stanley v. Georgia*?

STANLEY v. GEORGIA
394 U.S. 557 (1969)

Mr. Justice **Marshall** delivered the opinion of the Court.

An investigation of appellant's alleged bookmaking activities led to the issuance of a search warrant for appellant's home. Under authority of this warrant, federal and state agents secured entrance. They found very little evidence of bookmaking activity, but while looking through a desk drawer in an upstairs bedroom, one of the federal agents, accompanied by a state officer, found three reels of eight-millimeter film. Using a projector and screen found in an upstairs living room, they viewed the films. The state officer concluded that they were obscene and seized them. Since a further examination of the bedroom indicated that appellant occupied it, he was charged with possession of obscene matter and placed under arrest. . . .

Appellant raises several challenges to the validity of his conviction. We find it necessary to consider only one. Appellant argues here, and argued below, that the Georgia obscenity statute, insofar as it punishes mere private possession of obscene matter, violates the First Amendment, as made applicable to the States by the Fourteenth Amendment. For reasons set forth below, we agree that the mere private possession of obscene matter cannot constitutionally be made a crime.

. . . .

It is now well established that the Constitution protects the right to receive information and ideas. "This freedom [of speech and press] . . . necessarily protects the right to receive. . . ." This right to receive information and ideas, regardless of their social worth, is fundamental to our free society. Moreover, in the context of this case — a prosecution for mere possession of printed or filmed matter in the privacy of a person's own home — that right takes on an added dimension. For also fundamental is the right to be free, except in very limited circumstances, from unwanted governmental intrusions into one's privacy. "The makers of our Constitution undertook to secure conditions favorable to the pursuit of happiness. They recognized the significance of man's spiritual nature, of his feelings and of his intellect. They knew that only a part of the pain, pleasure and satisfactions of life are to be found in material things. They sought to protect Americans in their beliefs, their thoughts, their emotions and their sensations. They conferred, as against the government, the right to be let alone — the most comprehensive of rights and the right most valued by civilized man." *Olmstead v. United States*, 277 U.S. 438 (1928) (Brandeis, J., dissenting).

These are the rights that appellant is asserting in the case before us. He is asserting the right to read or observe what he pleases — the right to satisfy his intellectual and emotional needs in the privacy of his own home. He is asserting the right to be free from state inquiry into the contents of his library. Georgia contends that appellant does not have these rights, that there are certain types of materials that the individual may not read or even possess. Georgia justifies this assertion by arguing that the films in the present case are obscene. But we think that mere categorization of these films as "obscene" is insufficient justification for such a drastic invasion of personal liberties guaranteed by the First and Fourteenth Amendments. Whatever may be the justifications for other statutes regulating obscenity, we do not think they reach into the privacy of one's own home. If the First Amendment means anything, it means that a State has no business telling a man, sitting alone in his own house, what books he may read or what films he may watch. Our whole constitutional heritage rebels at the thought of giving government the power to control men's minds.

And yet, in the face of these traditional notions of individual liberty, Georgia asserts the right to protect the individual's mind from the effects of obscenity. We are not certain that this argument amounts to anything more than the assertion that the State has the right to control the moral content of a person's thoughts. To some, this may be a noble purpose, but it is wholly inconsistent with the philosophy of the First Amendment. . . .

Perhaps recognizing this, Georgia asserts that exposure to obscene materials may lead to deviant sexual behavior or crimes of sexual violence. There appears to be little empirical basis for that assertion. But more important, if the State is only concerned about printed or filmed materials inducing antisocial conduct, we believe that in the context of private consumption of ideas and information we should adhere to the view that "[a]mong free men, the deterrents ordinarily to be applied to prevent crime are education and punishment for violations of the law. . . ." Given the present state of knowledge, the State may no more prohibit mere possession of obscene matter on the ground that it may lead to antisocial conduct than it may prohibit possession of chemistry books on the ground that they may lead to the manufacture of homemade spirits.

. . . .

. . . As we have said, the States retain broad power to regulate obscenity; that power simply does not extend to mere possession by the individual in the privacy of his own home. Accordingly, the judgment of the court below is reversed and the case is remanded for proceedings not inconsistent with this opinion.

. . . .

NOTES AND QUESTIONS

1. In *Stanley*, the Court holds that a person may possess obscene materials, however "obscenity" may be defined, for personal consumption. Individuals have the right to satisfy their "intellectual and emotional needs in the privacy" of their own home. The question then is posed, what else may be enjoyed in the privacy of one's own home? A partial answer was provided by the earlier case of *Bowers v. Hardwick*, where the Supreme Court held that a citizen could be prosecuted for consensual homosexual relations in his own home. Are *Bowers* and *Stanley* consistent? And what of *Lawrence v. Texas*, *supra*, which reversed *Bowers*?

2. Between *Stanley* and *Bowers,* there is a spectrum of interests or activities which might fall under the umbrella of privacy: card playing, painting, consumption of narcotics, wallpapering or rewiring a kitchen, delivering a baby or performing an abortion. Sexual intercourse with one's own spouse would presumably fall within the protection of privacy; intercourse with a commercial prostitute might not. What are the values which set the limits and the content?

3. The issues in *Stanley v. Georgia* include what is privacy, what is a *home,* and what may a person *do* with privacy? Mr. Stanley is protected in his thoughts and impressions. But *possessing* pornography requires *acquiring* it. Possession also implies support of its production, and this involves others — often children. Thus privacy collides with the public interest.

4. Can it be argued that no one, anywhere, has a legitimate interest — intellectual or emotional — in pornography? That pornography "instrumentalizes" the people who appear in it or are portrayed by it? Would Rawls agree? If so, what are the difficulties in simply *banning* pornography? Definitional? Expressive? *See New York v. Ferber*, 458 U.S. 747 (1982); *American Booksellers v. Hudnut*, 771 F.2d 323 (7th Cir. 1985), *aff'd,* 475 U.S. 1001 (1986); *Osborne v. Ohio*, 495 U.S. 103 (1990); Brest & Vandenberg, *Politics, Feminism and the Constitution,* 39 Stan. L. Rev. 607 (1997); Baldwin, *Pornography and the Traffic in Women,* 1 Yale J.L. & Fem. III (1989); Dworkin, *Against the Male Flood,* 8 Harv. Women's L.J. 1 (1985); MacKinnon, *Pornography, Civil Rights and Speech,* 20 Harv. Civ. Rts. L. Rev. 1 (1985).

5. Since the decision in *Stanley,* the advent of computers and the Internet/ world wide web has linked homes to communication sources throughout the world. Pornography now is routinely available in the privacy of millions of home. This greater availability creates greater demand. What are the implications, on the one hand, for protecting autonomy and privacy and, on the other, protecting the privacy of those who do not want pornography in their homes?

6. Reconsider Problem 2-6 — Thermal Imaging, in light of *Moore, Carney* and *Stanley.*

7. For an excellent article, see Amy M. Intille, *Video Surveillance And Privacy: Implications for Wearable Computing*, 32 Suffolk U. L. Rev. 729 (1999); and see Michele L. Tyler, *Blowing Smoke: Do Smokers have a Right? Limiting the Privacy Rights of Cigarette Smokers*, 86 Geo. L.J. 783 (1998).

PROBLEM 2-13 — The Homeless

The 1990s saw the closing of many large institutions for the developmentally disabled, the mentally disadvantaged and others for whom society had no other place. People thus "mainstreamed" began appearing on streets, under bridges, on park benches, in doorways, and over the heating grates of the streets of American cities. Such people, denominated "street people" or "the homeless," often had no "home" other than a supermarket shopping cart, a cardboard carton, a sleeping bag or an abandoned automobile. In these, the "homeless" seek the protective values of privacy found in the hotel or motel rooms, the rooms of boarding houses, the apartments, condos, homes and mansions enjoyed by the more affluent.

In what ways can the privacy concepts extended to the more affluent be extended or assured to the homeless in the existing settings in which they may presently be found? Should society be ethically committed to such an effort or should it, instead, seek to change the situations of such people? If the latter, how can the task be performed in a way that preserves the privacy and dignity of people, contrary to the unacceptable treatment which prompted the closing of institutions and asylums?

Privacy: An essential aspect of privacy, the right to be left alone, is freedom to think and communicate. In deed, one's home, besides providing creature comforts, has the zone of privacy as one of its prime virtues. The question posed, as in *Stanley v. Georgia*, *Bowers v. Hardwick*, and *Griswold v. Connecticut,* is whether society may intrude on the home, or sequester it, in such a way as to exclude socially-offensive conduct or material, such as pornography on the internet. As to this, see *Ashcroft v. ACLU*, 535 U.S. 564 (2002).

Home: When the "home" is owned by the government or the state, a question is posed as to what conditions may be imposed, what limitations may be imposed on family, liberty and associational privacy. Similarly, when there is misconduct by one family member, to what extent may others be held responsible? Punished?

DEPT. OF HOUSING AND URBAN DEVELOPMENT v. RUCKER

535 U.S. 125 (2002)

Chief Justice **Rehnquist** delivered the opinion of the Court.

With drug dealers "increasingly imposing a reign of terror on public and other federally assisted low-income housing tenants," Congress passed the Anti-Drug Abuse Act of 1988. The Act, as later amended, provides that each "public housing agency shall utilize leases which . . . provide that any criminal activity that threatens the health, safety, or right to peaceful enjoyment of the premises by other tenants or any drug-related criminal activity on or off such premises, engaged in by a public housing tenant, any member of the tenant's household, or any guest or other person under the tenant's control, shall be cause for termination of tenancy." 42 U.S.C. § 1437d (*l*)(6) (1994 ed., Supp. V). Petitioners say that this statute requires lease terms that allow a local public housing authority to evict a tenant when a member of the tenant's household or a guest engages in drug-related criminal activity, regardless of whether the tenant knew, or had reason to know, of that activity. Respondents say it does not. We agree with petitioners.

In late 1997 and early 1998, OHA instituted eviction proceedings in state court against respondents, alleging violations of this lease provision. The complaint alleged: (1) that the respective grandsons of respondents William Lee and Barbara Hill, both of whom were listed as residents on the leases, were caught in the apartment complex parking lot smoking marijuana; (2) that the daughter of respondent Pearlie Rucker, who resides with her and is listed on the lease as a resident, was found with cocaine and a crack cocaine pipe three blocks from Rucker's apartment;[1] and (3) that on three instances within a 2-month period, respondent Herman Walker's caregiver and two others were found with cocaine in Walker's apartment. OHA had issued Walker notices of a lease violation on the first two occasions, before initiating the eviction action after the third violation.

United States Department of Housing and Urban Development (HUD) regulations administering § 1437d(l)(6) require lease terms authorizing evictions in these circumstances. The HUD regulations closely track the statutory language,[2] and provide that "in deciding to evict for criminal activity, the [public housing authority] shall have discretion to consider all of the circumstances of the case. . . ." 24 CFR § 966.4 (*l*)(5)(i) (2001). The agency made clear that local public housing authorities' discretion to evict for

[1] In February 1998, OHA dismissed the unlawful detainer action against Rucker, after her daughter was incarcerated, and thus no longer posed a threat to other tenants.

[2] The regulations require public housing authorities (PHAs) to impose a lease obligation on tenants:

> "To assure that the tenant, any member of the household, a guest, or another person under the tenant's control, shall not engage in:
>
> "(A) Any criminal activity that threatens the health, safety, or right to peaceful enjoyment of the PHA's public housing premises by other residents or employees of the PHA, or
>
> "(B) Any drug-related criminal activity on or near such premises. Any criminal activity in violation of the preceding sentence shall be cause for termination of tenancy, and for eviction from the unit." 24 CFR § 966.4(f)(12)(i) (2001).

drug-related activity includes those situations in which "[the] tenant did not know, could not foresee, or could not control behavior by other occupants of the unit." 56 Fed. Reg. 51560, 51567 (1991).

That this is so seems evident from the plain language of the statute. It provides that "each public housing authority shall utilize leases which . . . provide that . . . any drug-related criminal activity on or off such premises, engaged in by a public housing tenant, any member of the tenant's household, or any guest or other person under the tenant's control, shall be cause for termination of tenancy." The en banc Court of Appeals thought the statute did not address "the level of personal knowledge or fault that is required for eviction." [*Rucker v. Davis,*] 237 F.3d [1113,] 1120.Yet Congress' decision not to impose any qualification in the statute, combined with its use of the term "any" to modify "drug-related criminal activity," precludes any knowledge requirement. Thus, *any* drug-related activity engaged in by the specified persons is grounds for termination, not just drug-related activity that the tenant knew, or should have known, about.

Comparing § 1437d(*l*)(6) to a related statutory provision reinforces the unambiguous text. The civil forfeiture statute that makes all leasehold interests subject to forfeiture when used to commit drug-related criminal activities expressly exempts tenants who had no knowledge of the activity: "No property shall be forfeited under this paragraph . . . by reason of any act or omission established by that owner to have been committed or omitted without the knowledge or consent of the owner." Because this forfeiture provision was amended in the same Anti-Drug Abuse Act of 1988 that created 42 U.S.C. § 1437d (*l*)(6), the en banc Court of Appeals thought Congress "meant them to be read consistently" so that the knowledge requirement should be read into the eviction provision. But the two sections deal with distinctly different matters. The "innocent owner" defense for drug forfeiture cases was already in existence prior to 1988 as part of 21 U.S.C. § 881 (a)(7). All that Congress did in the 1988 Act was to add leasehold interests to the property interests that might be forfeited under the drug statute. And if such a forfeiture action were to be brought against a leasehold interest, it would be subject to the pre-existing "innocent owner" defense. But 42 U.S.C. § 1437 (d)(1)(6), with which we deal here, is a quite different measure. It is entirely reasonable to think that the Government, when seeking to transfer private property to itself in a forfeiture proceeding, should be subject to an "innocent owner defense," while it should not be when acting as a landlord in a public housing project. The forfeiture provision shows that Congress knew exactly how to provide an "innocent owner" defense. It did not provide one in § 1437d(*l*)(6).

Nor was the en banc Court of Appeals correct in concluding that this plain reading of the statute leads to absurd results. The statute does not *require* the eviction of any tenant who violated the lease provision. Instead, it entrusts that decision to the local public housing authorities, who are in the best position to take account of, among other things, the degree to which the housing project suffers from "rampant drug-related or violent crime," "the seriousness of the offending action," and "the extent to which the leaseholder has . . . taken all reasonable steps to prevent or mitigate the offending action." It is not "absurd" that a local housing authority may sometimes evict a tenant who had no knowledge of the drug-related activity. Such "no-fault" eviction is a common "incident of tenant responsibility under normal landlord-tenant law and practice." Strict liability maximizes deterrence and eases enforcement difficulties.

And, of course, there is an obvious reason why Congress would have permitted local public housing authorities to conduct no-fault evictions: Regardless of knowledge, a tenant who "cannot control drug crime, or other criminal activities by a household member which threaten health or safety of other residents, is a threat to other residents and the project." With drugs leading to "murders, muggings, and other forms of violence against tenants," and to the "deterioration of the physical environment that requires substantial governmental expenditures," it was reasonable for Congress to permit no-fault evictions in order to "provide public and other federally assisted low-income housing that is decent, safe, and free from illegal drugs."

In another effort to avoid the plain meaning of the statute, the en banc Court of Appeals invoked the canon of constitutional avoidance. But that canon "has no application in the absence of statutory ambiguity." There are, moreover, no "serious constitutional doubts" about Congress' affording local public housing authorities the discretion to conduct no-fault evictions for drug-related crime. *Reno v. Flores*, 507 U.S. 292, 314, n. 9 (1993) (emphasis deleted).

The en banc Court of Appeals held that HUD's interpretation "raises serious questions under the Due Process Clause of the Fourteenth Amendment," because it permits "tenants to be deprived of their property interest without any relationship to individual wrongdoing." 237 F.3d at 1124–1125 (*citing Scales v. United States*, 367 U.S. 203, 224–225 (1961); *Southwestern Telegraph & Telephone Co. v. Danaher*, 238 U.S. 482 (1915)). But both of these cases deal with the acts of government as sovereign. In *Scales*, the United States criminally charged the defendant with knowing membership in an organization that advocated the overthrow of the United States Government. In *Danaher*, an Arkansas statute forbade discrimination among customers of a telephone company. The situation in the present cases is entirely different. The government is not attempting to criminally punish or civilly regulate respondents as members of the general populace. It is instead acting as a landlord of property that it owns, invoking a clause in a lease to which respondents have agreed and which Congress has expressly required. *Scales* and *Danaher* cast no constitutional doubt on such actions.

The Court of Appeals sought to bolster its discussion of constitutional doubt by pointing to the fact that respondents have a property interest in their leasehold interest, citing *Greene v. Lindsey*, 456 U.S. 444, 72 L. Ed. 2d 249 (1982).This is undoubtedly true, and *Greene* held that an effort to deprive a tenant of such a right without proper notice violated the Due Process Clause of the Fourteenth Amendment. But, in the present cases, such deprivation will occur in the state court where OHA brought the unlawful detainer action against respondents. There is no indication that notice has not been given by OHA in the past, or that it will not be given in the future. Any individual factual disputes about whether the lease provision was actually violated can, of course, be resolved in these proceedings.[6]

We hold that "Congress has directly spoken to the precise question at issue." *Chevron U.S.A. Inc. v. Natural Resources Defense Council, Inc.*, 467 U.S. [837,] 842. Section 1437d(*l*)(6) requires lease terms that give local public housing authorities the discretion to terminate the lease of a tenant when a member of the household or a guest engages in drug-related activity, regardless of whether the tenant knew, or should have known, of the drug-related activity.

Accordingly, the judgment of the Court of Appeals is reversed, and the cases are remanded for further proceedings consistent with this opinion.

It is so ordered.

Justice **Breyer** took no part in the consideration or decision of these cases.

NOTES AND QUESTIONS

1. In *Rucker*, the Supreme Court upholds evicting a family from public housing where a member uses drugs. Can this be squared with our usual insistence, as a matter of ethics, on individual culpability prior to punishment? At a minimum, as a matter of due process, shouldn't a housing agency first be required to make inquiry as to individual responsibility?
2. It is true, of course, that drug trafficking and usage are of epidemic proportions in low income neighborhoods. But so is unhealthy housing. How realistic is it to believe one can have low income housing free of drugs?
3. Is the rationale that there is no "right" to public housing, and so it may be conditioned on any limitation government chooses? If so, can limits be imposed on religion or speech? Isn't there at least a "property interest" in tenancy and occupancy, such that a hearing on fault is required prior to eviction?
4. At a minimum, wouldn't fairness require proportionality? Note that the Parker children were allegedly using marijuana in a parking lot, and Rucker's daughter was found with cocaine *three blocks away*. How does this make the home or the project unsafe? And how *de minimis* may the relationship, the location, and the misconduct be and yet justify eviction?
5. More fundamentally, is there an obligation on the part of a just society to provide decent, safe housing for all? Is there a "right" to housing, education, healthcare, community safety? These same questions will

[6] The en banc Court of Appeals cited only the due process constitutional concern. Respondents raise two others: the First Amendment and the Excessive Fines Clause. We agree with Judge O'Scannlain, writing for the panel that reversed the injunction, that the statute does not raise substantial First Amendment or Excessive Fines Clause concerns. *Lyng v. Automobile Workers*, 485 U.S. 360 (1988), forecloses respondents claim that the eviction of unknowing tenants violates the First Amendment guarantee of freedom of association. See *Rucker v. Davis*, 203 F.3d 627, 647 (2000). And termination of tenancy "is neither a cash nor an in-kind payment imposed by and payable to the government" and therefore is "not subject to analysis as an excessive fine."

recur, *infra*, when we examine medical experimentation on children living in substandard housing ingesting lead [illegible] the *Grimes* case.

6. What are the implications of *Rucker* and the preceding cases for the tens of thousands of New Orleans residents still living in FEMA trailers years after the 2005 catastrophe of the Katrina hurricane?

§ 2.05 Conscience

Personhood is nowhere more clearly expressed than in matters of conscience, when a person acts on principles of ethics, often at great personal cost. It is that cost from personally accepting imposition of general rules which Rawls characterized as moral. Memorable figures of history — Socrates, Joan of Arc, William Penn, Gandhi, Martin Luther King, Nelson Mandela — were motivated by conscience, oftentimes challenging society and prevailing mores at great personal cost. In so doing, they were acting in "public," but for compelling "private" reasons. To the extent society tolerates deviance, it is respecting "privacy."

What is the obligation of society to respect conscientious objectors? What are their obligations towards society? The cause of conscience oftentimes comes garbed in the armor of arrogance, covered by the cloak of religious belief or fervor. Must society tolerate intolerance?

The place of religion in society is a vast subject. But the boundary between belief and conduct is often the line between tolerance and intolerance. And so the following cases track that line, in contexts where the use of peyote, the slaughtering of animals, and the obstruction of public facilities were all the product of profound beliefs, placing their adherents at risk of imprisonment.

In the age of managed care, the nonconforming doctor who challenges a "gag rule" or the dissident employee "whistleblower" who invokes legal process may equally suffer calamitous economic punishment. That subject we will defer to Chapter 3. Here we address the more basic place and role of conscience as an aspect of the deference due from and to individuals in an ethical society.

[1] Religion and the Price of Belief

SHERBERT v. VERNER
374 U.S. 398 (1963)

Mr. Justice **Brennan** delivered the opinion of the Court.

Appellant, a member of the Seventh-day adventists church was discharged by her South Carolina employer because she would not work on Saturday, the Sabbath Day of her faith. When she was unable to obtain other employment because from conscientious scruples she would not take Saturday work, she filed a claim for unemployment compensation benefits under the South Carolina Unemployment Compensation Act. That law provides that, to be eligible for benefits, a claimant must be "able to work and . . . is available for work"; and, further, that a claimant is ineligible for benefits "(i)f . . . he has failed, without good cause . . . to accept available suitable work when offered him by the employment office or the employer. . . ." The appellee Employment Security Commission, in administrative proceedings under the statute, found that appellant's restriction upon her availability for Saturday work brought her within the provision disqualifying for benefits insured workers who fail, without good cause, to accept "suitable work when offered . . . by the employment office or the employer. . . ." We reverse the judgment of the South Carolina Supreme Court and remand for further proceedings not inconsistent with this opinion.

I.

The door of the Free Exercise Clause stands tightly closed against any governmental regulation of religious beliefs as such. Government may neither compel affirmation of a repugnant belief, nor penalize or discriminate against individuals or groups because they hold religious views abhorrent to the authorities, nor employ the taxing power to inhibit the dissemination of particular religious views. On the other hand, the Court has rejected challenges under the Free Exercise Clause to governmental regulation of certain overt acts prompted by religious beliefs or principles, for "even when the action is in accord with one's religious convictions, (it) is not totally free from legislative restrictions." The conduct or actions so regulated have invariably posed some substantial threat to public safety, peace or order.

Plainly enough, appellant's conscientious objection to Saturday work constitutes no conduct prompted by religious principles of a kind within the reach of state legislation. If, therefore, the decision of the South Carolina Supreme Court is to withstand appellant's constitutional challenge, it must be either because her disqualification as a beneficiary represents no infringement by the State of her constitutional rights of free exercise, or because any incidental burden on the free exercise of appellant's religion may be justified by a "compelling state interest in the regulation of a subject within the State's constitutional power to regulate. . . ."

II.

We turn first to the question whether the disqualification for benefits imposes any burden on the free exercise of appellant's religion. We think it is clear that it does. In a sense the consequences of such a disqualification to religious principles and practices may be only an indirect result of welfare legislation within the State's general competence to enact; it is true that no criminal sanctions directly compel appellant to work a six-day week. But this is only the beginning, not the end, of our inquiry. For "(i)f the purpose or effect of a law is to impede the observance of one or all religions or is to discriminate invidiously between religions, that law is constitutionally invalid even though the burden may be characterized as being only indirect." *Braunfeld v. Brown*. Here not only is it apparent that appellant's declared ineligibility for benefits derives solely from the practice of her religion, but the pressure upon her to forego that practice is unmistakable. The ruling forces her to choose between following the precepts of her religion and forfeiting benefits, on the one hand,

and abandoning one of the precepts of her religion in order to accept work, on the other hand. Governmental imposition of such [illegible] same kind of burden [illegible] exercise of religion as would a fine imposed against appellant for her Saturday worship.

Nor may the South Carolina court's construction of the statute be saved from constitutional infirmity on the ground that unemployment compensation benefits are not appellant's 'right' but merely a'privilege.' It is too late in the day to doubt that the liberties of religion and expression may be infringed by the denial of or placing of conditions upon a benefit or privilege. . . .

. . . .

III.

We must next consider whether some compelling state interest enforced in the eligibility provisions of the South Carolina statute justifies the substantial infringement of appellant's First Amendment right. It is basic that no showing merely of a rational relationship to some colorable state interest would suffice; in this highly sensitive constitutional area, "(o)nly the gravest abuses, endangering paramount interest, give occasion for permissible limitation." No such abuse or danger has been advanced in the present case. The appellees suggest no more than a possibility that the filing of fraudulent claims by unscrupulous claimants feigning religious objections to Saturday work might not only dilute the unemployment compensation fund but also hinder the scheduling by employers of necessary Saturday work. But that possibility is not apposite here because no such objection appears to have been made before the South Carolina Supreme Court, and we are unwilling to assess the importance of an asserted state interest without the views of the state court. . . .

[T]he state interest asserted in the present case is wholly dissimilar to the interests which were found to justify the less direct burden upon religious practices in *Braunfeld v. Brown*, supra. The Court recognized that the Sunday closing law which that decision sustained undoubtedly served 'to make the practice of (the Orthodox Jewish merchants') religious [illegible]. But the statute [illegible] saved by a countervailing factor which finds no equivalent in the instant case — a strong state interest in providing one uniform day of rest for all workers. That secular objective could be achieved, the Court found, only by declaring Sunday to be that day of rest. Requiring exemptions for Sabbatarians, while theoretically possible, appeared to present an administrative problem of such magnitude, or to afford the exempted class so great a competitive advantage, that such a requirement would have rendered the entire statutory scheme unworkable. In the present case no such justifications underlie the determination of the state court that appellant's religion makes her ineligible to receive benefits.

. . . .

IV

Reversed and remanded.

. . . .

Mr. Justice **Stewart**, concurring in the result.

Although fully agreeing with the result which the Court reaches in this case, I cannot join the Court's opinion. This case presents a double-barreled dilemma, which in all candor I think the Court's opinion has not succeeded in papering over. The dilemma ought to be resolved.

I

. . . .

Because the appellant refuses to accept available jobs which would require her to work on Saturdays, South Carolina could not hold that she was not "available for work" within the meaning of its statute. . . . That being so, the Establishment Clause as construed by this Court not only permits but affirmatively requires South Carolina equally to deny the appellant's claim for unemployment compensation when her refusal to work on Saturdays is based upon her religious creed.

To require South Carolina to so administer its laws as to pay public money to the appellant under the circumstances of this case is thus clearly to require the State to violate the Establishment Clause as construed by this Court. . . .

. . . .

II.

My second difference with the Court's opinion is that I cannot agree that today's decision can stand consistently with *Braunfeld v. Brown*. The Court says that there was a 'less direct burden upon religious practices' in that case than in this. With all respect, I think the Court is mistaken, simply as a matter of fact. The Braunfeld case involved a state criminal statute. The undisputed effect of that statute, was that "Plaintiff, Abraham Braunfeld, will be unable to continue in his business if he may not stay open on Sunday and he will thereby lose his capital investment.' In other words, the issue in this case — and we do not understand either appellees or the Court to contend otherwise — is whether a State may put an individual to a choice between his business and his religion.

The impact upon the appellant's religious freedom in the present case is considerably less onerous. We deal here not with a criminal statute, but with the particularized administration of South Carolina's Unemployment Compensation Act. Even upon the unlikely assumption that the appellant could not find suitable non-Saturday employment, the appellant at the worst would be denied a maximum of 22 weeks of compensation payments. I agree with the Court that the possibility of that denial is enough to infringe upon the appellant's constitutional right to the free exercise of her religion. But it is clear to me that in order to reach this conclusion the court must explicitly reject the reasoning of *Braunfeld v. Brown*. I think the Braunfeld case was wrongly decided and should be overruled, and accordingly I concur in the result reached by the Court in the case before us.

Mr. Justice **Harlan**, whom Mr. Justice **White** joins, dissenting.

Today's decision is disturbing both in its rejection of existing precedent and in its implications for the future. . . .

. . . .

The South Carolina Supreme Court has uniformly applied this law in conformity with its clearly expressed purpose. It has consistently held that one is not 'available for work' if his unemployment has resulted not from the inability of industry to provide a job but rather from personal circumstances, no matter how compelling. The reference to 'involuntary unemployment' in the legislative statement of policy, whatever a sociologist, philosopher, or theologian might say, has been interpreted not to embrace such personal circumstances. . . .

In the present case all that the state court has done is to apply these accepted principles. Since virtually all of the mills in the Spartanburg area were operating on a six-day week, the appellant was 'unavailable for work,' and thus ineligible for benefits, when personal considerations prevented her from accepting employment on a full-time basis in the industry and locality in which she had worked. The fact that these personal considerations sprang from her religious convictions was wholly without relevance to the state court's application of the law. Thus in no proper sense can it be said that the State discriminated against the appellant on the basis of her religious beliefs or that she was denied benefits because she was a Seventh-day Adventist. She was denied benefits just as any other claimant would be denied benefits who was not "available for work" for personal reasons.

[D]espite the Court's protestations to the contrary, the decision necessarily overrules *Braunfeld v. Brown*, which held that it did not offend the 'Free Exercise' Clause of the Constitution for a State to forbid a Sabbatarian to do business on Sunday. The secular purpose of the statute before us today is even clearer than that involved in Braunfeld. . . .

Second, the implications of the present decision are far more troublesome than its apparently narrow dimensions would indicate at first glance. The meaning of today's holding, as already noted, is that the State must furnish unemployment benefits to one who is unavailable for work if the unavailability stems from the exercise of religious convictions. The State, in other words, must single out for financial assistance those whose behavior is religiously motivated, even though it denies such assistance to others whose identical behavior (in this case, inability to work on Saturdays) is not religiously motivated.

. . . .

[I] cannot subscribe to the conclusion that the State is constitutionally compelled to carve out an exception to its general rule of eligibility in the present case. Those situations in which the Constitution may require special treatment on account of religion are, in my view, few and far between, and this view is amply supported by the course of constitutional litigation in this area. Such compulsion in the present case is particularly inappropriate in light of the indirect, remote, and insubstantial effect of the decision below on the exercise of appellant's religion and in light of the direct financial assistance to religion that today's decision requires.

For these reasons I respectfully dissent from the opinion and judgment of the Court.

NOTES AND QUESTIONS

1. Justice Brennan's opinion in *Sherbert* for the Court remands for "further proceedings"; what would they be?
2. How can it be said that South Carolina is infringing Adell Sherbert's exercise of her religion when all it is doing is setting limits to a program (unemployment compensation) to which she has no right and which the State need not offer and for which she may qualify like any other citizen? Is it "clear" that her disqualification stems from the "practice of her religion"? Suppose her faith forbade *all* work? Required worship *at* work?
3. The Court finds a "burden" on Sherbert's religion, although there is no prohibition or punishment. What *exactly* is the "burden"? What is meant by the term? Is it different from the burden Justice O'Connor described in *Casey*, *supra* § 1.04[1]? Isn't Ms. Sherbert simply experiencing the consequence of exercising freedom — which society must abide, but needn't underwrite? Or must it?
4. The state interest in fraud is only one potential interest, isn't it? What others might there be? Is the interest equivalent to that of the state in Sunday closing laws, upheld in *Braunfeld v. Brown*?
5. Do Justices Stewart and Harlan have it right: the payment to Ms. Sherbert supports her religion in ways not extended to other faiths, violating the Establishment Clause of the First Amendment? There is further discrimination, in that assistance would be denied a mother (or father) declining work to stay home to care for children (or education or other legitimate reasons), is there not?
6. How far does *Sherbert* extend the free exercise of religion? Would it reach vaccination, transfusions, schooling, polygamy, military service, assisted death? Does it, in fact, mean that businesses can *not* be compelled to close on Sundays, reversing *Braunfeld v. Brown*, as the dissent argues? And how much is left after *Employment Div. v. Smith*, the next case to which we now turn?

EMPLOYMENT DIV., DEPT. OF H.R. OF OREGON v. SMITH
494 U.S. 872 (1990)

Justice **Scalia** delivered the opinion of the Court.

. . . .

I

Oregon law prohibits the knowing or intentional possession of a "controlled substance" unless the substance has been prescribed by a medical practitioner. . . . Persons who violate this provision by possessing a controlled substance listed on Schedule I are "guilty of a Class B felony." As compiled by the State Board of Pharmacy under its statutory authority, Schedule I contains the drug peyote, a hallucinogen derived from the plant *Lophophora Williamsii Lemaire*.

Respondents Alfred Smith and Galen Black were fired from their jobs with a private drug rehabilitation organization because they ingested peyote for sacramental purposes at a ceremony of the Native American Church, of which both are members. When respondents applied to petitioner Employment Division [hereinafter petitioner] for unemployment compensation, they were determined to be ineligible for benefits because they had been discharged for work-related "misconduct." . . .

. . . .

II

Respondents' claim for relief rests on our decisions in *Sherbert v. Verner, Thomas v. Review Bd. of Indiana Employment Security Div.* and *Hobbie v. Unemployment Appeals Comm'n of Florida*, in which we held that a State could not condition the availability of unemployment insurance on an individual's willingness to forgo conduct required by his religion. [H]owever, the conduct at issue in those cases was not prohibited by law. . . .

A

. . . The free exercise of religion means, first and foremost, the right to believe and profess whatever religious doctrine one desires. Thus, the First Amendment obviously excludes all "governmental regulation of religious beliefs as such." *Sherbert v. Verner.* The government may not compel affirmation of religious belief, punish the expression of religious doctrines it believes to be false, impose special disabilities on the basis of religious views or religious status, or lend its power to one or the other side in controversies over religious authority or dogma.

. . . .

Respondents in the present case, however, seek to carry the meaning of "prohibiting the free exercise [of religion]" one large step further. They contend that their religious motivation for using peyote places them beyond the reach of a criminal law that is not specifically directed at their religious practice, and that is concededly constitutional as applied to those who use the drug for other reasons. They assert, in other words, that "prohibiting the free exercise [of religion]" includes requiring any individual to observe a generally applicable law that requires (or forbids) the performance of an act that his religious belief forbids (or requires). As a textual matter, we do not think the words must be given that meaning. It is no more necessary to regard the collection of a general tax, for example, as "prohibiting the free exercise [of religion]" by those citizens who believe support of organized government to be sinful, than it is to regard the same tax as "abridging the freedom . . . of the press" of those publishing companies that must pay the tax as a condition of staying in business. It is a permissible reading of the text, in the one case as in the other, to say that if prohibiting the exercise of religion (or burdening the activity of printing) is not the object of the tax but merely the incidental effect of a generally applicable and otherwise valid provision, the First Amendment has not been offended.

. . . .

. . . In *Prince v. Massachusetts*, we held that a mother could be prosecuted under the child labor laws for using her children to dispense literature in the streets, her religious motivation notwithstanding. We found no constitutional infirmity in "excluding [these children] from doing there what no other children may do." . . .

. . . .

The only decisions in which we have held that the First Amendment bars application of a neutral, generally applicable law to religiously motivated action have involved not the Free Exercise Clause alone, but the Free Exercise Clause in conjunction with other constitutional protections, such as freedom of speech and of the press, or the right of parents, acknowledge in *Pierce v. Society of Sisters*, to direct the education of their children. *See Wisconsin v. Yoder*. . . .

The present case does not present such a hybrid situation, but a free exercise claim unconnected with any communicative activity or parental right. Respondents urge us to hold, quite simply, that when otherwise prohibitable conduct is accompanied by religious convictions, not only the convictions but the conduct itself must be free from governmental regulation. We have never held that, and decline to do so now. . . .

B

Respondents argue that even though exemption from generally applicable criminal laws need not automatically be extended to religiously motivated actors, at least the claim for a religious exemption must be evaluated under the balancing test set forth in *Sherbert v. Verner*. Under the *Sherbert* test, governmental actions that substantially burden a religious practice must be justified by a compelling governmental interest. Applying that test we have, on three occasions, invalidated state unemployment compensation rules that conditioned the availability of benefits upon an applicant's willingness to work under conditions forbidden by his religion. *See Sherbert v. Verner*, *Thomas v. Review Bd. of Indiana Employment Security Div.* and *Hobbie v. Unemployment Appeals Comm'n of Florida*. We have never invalidated any governmental action on the basis of the *Sherbert* test except the denial of unemployment compensation. . . .

Even if we were inclined to breathe into *Sherbert* some life beyond the unemployment compensation field, we would not apply it to require exemptions from a generally applicable criminal law. The *Sherbert* test, it must be recalled, was developed in a context that lent itself to individualized governmental assessment of the reasons for the relevant conduct. . . .

Whether or not the decisions are that limited, they at least have nothing to do with an across-the-board criminal prohibition on a particular form of conduct. Although, as noted earlier, we have sometimes used the *Sherbert* test to analyze free exercise challenges to such laws, we h[illegible] applied the [illegible]invalidate one. We conclude today that the sounder approach, and the approach in accord with the vast majority of our precedents, is to hold the test inapplicable to such challenges. The government's ability to enforce generally applicable prohibitions of socially harmful conduct, like its ability to carry out other aspects of public policy, "cannot depend on measuring the effects of a governmental action on a religious objector's spiritual development." . . .

. . . .

Because respondents' ingestion of peyote was prohibited under Oregon law, and because that prohibition is constitutional, Oregon may, consistent with the Free Exercise Clause, deny respondents unemployment compensation when their dismissal results from use of the drug. The decision of the Oregon Supreme Court is accordingly reversed.

It is so ordered.

Justice **O'Connor**, with whom Justice **Brennan**, Justice **Marshall**, and Justice **Blackmun** join as to Parts I and II, concurring in the judgment.

Although I agree with the result the Court reaches in this case, I cannot join its opinion. In my view, today's holding dramatically departs from well-settled First Amendment jurisprudence, appears unnecessary to resolve the question presented, and is incompatible with our Nation's fundamental commitment to individual religious liberty.

. . . .

II

The Court today extracts from our long history of free exercise precedents the single categorical rule that "if prohibiting the exercise of religion . . . is . . . merely the incidental effect of a generally applicable and otherwise valid provision, the First Amendment has not been offended." Indeed, the Court holds that where the law is a generally applicable criminal prohibition, our usual free exercise jurisprudence does not even apply. To reach this sweeping result, however, the Court must not only give a strained reading of the First Amendment but must also disregard our consistent application of free exercise doctrine to cases involving generally applicable regulations that burden religious conduct.

. . . .

The Court attempts to support its narrow reading of the Clause by claiming that "[w]e have never held that an individual's religious beliefs excuse him from compliance with an otherwise valid law prohibiting conduct that the State is free to regulate." But as the Court later notes, as it must, in cases such as *Cantwell* and *Yoder* we have in fact interpreted the Free Exercise Clause to forbid application of a generally applicable prohibition to religiously motivated conduct. *See Cantwell.* Indeed, in *Yoder* we expressly rejected the interpretation the Court now adopts. . . .

The Court endeavors to escape from our decisions in *Cantwell* and *Yoder* by labeling them "hybrid" decisions, but there is no denying that both cases expressly relied on the Free Exercise Clause, and that we have consistently regarded those cases as part of the mainstream of our free exercise jurisprudence. . . .

. . . .

III

The Court's holding today not only misreads settled First Amendment precedent; it appears to be unnecessary to this case. I would reach the same result applying our established free exercise jurisprudence.

A

There is no dispute that Oregon's criminal prohibition of peyote places a severe burden on the ability of respondents to freely exercise their religion. Peyote is a sacrament of the Native American Church and is regarded as vital to respondents' ability to practice their religion. [T]he Oregon Supreme Court concluded that "the Native American Church is a recognized religion, that peyote is a sacrament of that church, and that respondent's beliefs were sincerely held." Under Oregon law, as construed by that State's highest court, members of the Native American Church must choose between carrying out the ritual embodying their religious beliefs and avoidance of criminal prosecution. That choice is, in my view, more than sufficient to trigger First Amendment scrutiny.

. . . .

B

. . . Although the question is close, I would conclude that uniform application of Oregon's criminal prohibition is "essential to accomplish" its overriding interest in preventing the physical harm caused by the use of a Schedule I controlled substance. Oregon's criminal prohibition represents that State's judgment that the possession and use of controlled substances, even by one person, is inherently harmful and dangerous. Because the health effects caused by the use of controlled substances exist regardless of the motivation of the user, the use of such substances, even for religious purposes, violates the very purpose of the laws that prohibit them. Moreover, in view of the societal interest in preventing trafficking in controlled substances, uniform application of the criminal prohibition at issue is essential to the effectiveness of Oregon's stated interest in preventing any possession of peyote.

For these reasons, I believe that granting a selective exemption in this case would seriously impair Oregon's compelling interest in prohibiting possession of peyote by its citizens. Under such circumstances, the Free Exercise Clause does not require the State to accommodate respondents' religiously motivated conduct. . . .

. . . .

I would therefore adhere to our established free exercise jurisprudence and hold that the State in this case has a compelling interest in regulating peyote use by its citizens and that accommodating respondents' religiously motivated conduct "will unduly interfere with fulfillment of the governmental interest." *Lee,* 455 U.S. at 259. Accordingly, I concur in the judgment of the Court.

Justice **Blackmun**, with whom Justice **Brennan** and Justice **Marshall** join, dissenting.

This Court over the years painstakingly has developed a consistent and exacting standard to test the consistent and exacting standard to test the constitutionality of a state statute that burdens the free exercise of religion. Such a statute may stand only if the law in general, and the State's refusal to allow a religious exemption in particular, are justified by a compelling interest that cannot be served by less restrictive means.

. . . .

I

In weighing the clear interests of respondents Smith and Black [hereinafter respondents] in the free exercise of their religion against Oregon's asserted interest in enforcing its drug laws, it is important to articulate in precise terms of the state interest involved. It is not the State's broad interest in fighting the critical "war on drugs" that must be weighed against respondents' claim, but the State's narrow interest in refusing to make an exception for the religious, ceremonial use of peyote. . . .

. . . .

The carefully circumscribed ritual context in which respondents used peyote is far removed from the irresponsible and unrestricted recreational use of unlawful drugs. The Native American Church's internal restrictions on, and supervision of, its members' use of peyote substantially obviate the State's health and safety concerns. . . .

Moreover, just as in *Yoder,* the values and interests of those seeking a religious exemption in this case are congruent, to a great degree, with those the State seeks to promote through its drug laws. Not only does the church's doctrine forbid nonreligious use of peyote; it also generally advocates self-reliance, familial responsibility, and abstinence from alcohol. There is considerable evidence that the spiritual and social support provided by the church has been effective in combating the tragic effects of alcoholism on the Native American population. . . .

The State also seeks to support its refusal to make an exception for religious use of peyote by invoking its interest in abolishing drug trafficking. There is, however, practically no illegal traffic in peyote. . . .

. . . .

The State's apprehension of a flood of other religious claims is purely speculative. Almost half the States, and the Federal Government, have maintained an exemption for religious peyote use for many years, and apparently have not found themselves overwhelmed by claims to other religious exemptions. Allowing an exemption for religious peyote use would not necessarily oblige the State to grant a similar exemption to other religious groups. The unusual circumstances that make the religious use of peyote compatible with the State's interests in health and safety and in preventing drug trafficking would not apply to other religious claims. . . .

II

Finally, although I agree with Justice O'Connor that courts should refrain from delving into questions whether, as a matter of religious doctrine, a particular practice is "central" to the religion, I do not think this means that the courts must turn a blind eye to the severe impact of a State's restrictions on the adherents of a minority religion.

Respondents believe, and their sincerity has never been at issue, that the peyote plant embodies their deity, and eating it is an act of worship and communion. Without peyote, they could not enact the essential ritual of their religion. ("To the members, peyote is consecrated with powers to heal body, mind and spirit. It is a teacher; it teaches the way to spiritual life through living in harmony and balance with the forces of the Creation. The rituals are an integral part of the life process. They embody a form of worship in which the sacrament Peyote is the means for communicating with the Great Spirit.")

If Oregon can constitutionally prosecute them for this act of worship, they, like the Amish, may be "forced to migrate to some other and more tolerant region." This potentially devastating impact must be viewed in light of the federal policy — reached in reaction to many years of religious persecution and intolerance — of protecting the religious freedom of Native Americans. . . .

The American Indian Religious Freedom Act, in itself, may not create rights enforceable against government action restricting religious freedom, but this Court must scrupulously apply its free exercise analysis to the religious claims of Native Americans, however unorthodox they may be. Otherwise, both the First Amendment and the stated policy of Congress will offer to Native Americans merely an unfulfilled and hollow promise.

. . . .

NOTES AND QUESTIONS

1. Recall in *Smith* not only *Sherbert v. Verner* but also the *Yoder* case. Is *Smith* consistent with those cases? Of the separate opinions, who has the better argument, Justice O'Connor or Justice Brennan? Isn't the "burden" on religion here more compelling than in *Sherbert,* since here there is a complete ban?
2. Note that *Smith* involves the principle of "double effect." The point of the criminal law is not to deter religion. But it does have that incidental effect. Ethically, this is tolerable only if the good outweighs the bad and if there is no alternative. Does that seem true here? Is that the reasoning of the court?

3. Is the use of peyote like child labor or not paying social security? Are not those more detrimental to society than [illegible] not more important to religion? Can or should a court make such inquiries?

4. Note the majority's effort to limit *Sherbert v. Verner*, which held that a person unavailable for work on Saturdays could not be denied unemployment compensation as refusing work "without cause." Why does the majority do this? Are you persuaded by the dissent and the concurrence?

5. Following the decision in *Smith,* in 1993, Congress adopted the Religious Freedom Restoration Act ("RFRA"), 42 U.S.C. § 2000bb, a rare instance of Congress directly seeking to set aside an interpretation of the Constitution by the Court. *See* Berg, *What Hath Congress Wrought?,* 39 Vill. L. Rev. 1 (1994), and Ides, *The Text of the Free Exercise Clause,* 51 Wash. & Lee L. Rev. 135 (1994). Congress specifically found that "neutral" laws could burden religion and the "compelling interest" test was a workable approach, and expressed Congressional purpose to restore the test of *Yoder* and *Sherbert v. Verner.* It provided that government would have to show a compelling interest, furthered by the least restrictive means to justify a burden on religion, even by a neutral statute of general applicability, such as that in *Smith.*

   Litigation followed, capped by the Supreme Court's response in *City of Boerne v. Flores*, 521 U.S. 507 (1997), where local zoning authorities had denied a Catholic church the right to expand, under historic preservation laws. The church sued under; RFRA. The Court, per Justice Kennedy, held RFRA exceeded Congress' powers over the States under the Fourteenth Amendment, § 5, which authorizes legislation enforcing due process, equal protection and privileges and immunities guarantees. RFRA, it seemed, was not just "remedial," but substantive, and lacked "proportionality," not limited to religious bigotry, imposing a heavy burden on legitimate state legislation.

   Significantly, Justice O'Connor dissented in *City of Boerne.* She had concurred in *Smith* because the same result would have obtained under the *Sherbert* test, reinstated by RFRA. In her *Boerne* dissent, O'C[illegible] *Sherbert's* test in place, RFRA would be constitutional. The First Amendment is not simply a guarantee against discrimination, but an affirmative guarantee of religious practices. Justices Souter and Breyer dissented along related lines.

   After the decision in *City of Boerne,* a compelling state interest test still continues in two contexts. The first, as *Smith* itself notes, is where a law burdens religion *and* another right or is specifically *intended* to burden religion. The second is where RFRA rests not on the Fourteenth Amendment, but some other aspect of the Constitution, where Congress' power is not simply "remedial." *See, e.g., Young v. Crystal Evangelical Free Church*, 141 F.3d 854 (8th Cir. 1998) (upholding RFRA under federal bankruptcy law and Article I of the Constitution, against *federal* efforts to reach contributions to a church).

   What is left, then, are basic questions. Should a society affirmatively assist religious expression? When other values collide, how powerful must they be to override religious expression? And for an individual, in Rawls' terms, doesn't a proper sense of "morality" mean *accepting* society's burdens when accepting its benefits?

These questions are posed vividly in the next case, involving religious sacrifice of animals by a religious sect.

CHURCH OF THE LUKUMI BABALU AYE, INC. v. CITY OF HIALEAH
508 U.S. 520 (1993)

Justice **Kennedy** delivered the opinion of the Court, except as to Part II-A-2.*

The principle that government may not enact laws that suppress religious belief or practice is so well understood that few violations are recorded in our opinions. Concerned that this fundamental nonpersecution principle of the First Amendment was implicated here, however, we granted certiorari.

Our review confirms that the laws in question were enacted by officials who did not understand, failed to perceive, or chose to ignore the fact that their official actions violated the Nation's essential commitment to religious freedom. The challenged laws had an impermissible object; and in all events the principle of general applicability was violated because the secular ends asserted in defense of the laws were pursued only with respect to conduct motivated by religious beliefs. We invalidate the challenged enactments and reverse the judgment of the Court of Appeals.

I

A

This case involves practices of the Santeria religion, which originated in the nineteenth century. When hundreds of thousands of members of the Yoruba people were brought as slaves from eastern Africa to Cuba, their traditional African religion absorbed significant elements of Roman Catholicism. The resulting syncretion, or fusion, is Santeria, "the way of the saints." The Cuban Yoruba express their devotion to spirits, called *orishas*, through the iconography of Catholic saints, Catholic symbols are often present at Santeria rites, and Santeria devotees attend the Catholic sacraments. . . .

The Santeria faith teaches that every individual has a destiny from God, a destiny fulfilled with the aid and energy of the *orishas*. The basis of the Santeria religion is the nurture of a personal relation with the *orishas*, and one of the principal forms of devotion is an animal sacrifice. The sacrifice of animals as part of religious rituals has ancient roots. Animal sacrifice is mentioned throughout the Old Testament, and it played an important role in the practice of Judaism before destruction of the second Temple in

* The Chief Justice, Justice Scalia, and Justice Thomas join all but Part II-A-2 of this opinion. Justice White joins all but Part II-A of this opinion. Justice Souter joins only Parts I, III, and IV of this opinion.

Jerusalem. In modern Islam, there is an annual sacrifice commemorating Abraham's sacrifice of a ram in the stead of his son.

According to Santeria teaching, the *orishas* are powerful but not immortal. They depend for survival on the sacrifice. Sacrifices are performed at birth, marriage, and death rites, for the cure of the sick, for the initiation of new members and priests, and during an annual celebration. Animals sacrificed in Santeria rituals include chickens, pigeons, doves, ducks, guinea pigs, goats, sheep, and turtles. The animals are killed by the cutting of the carotid arteries in the neck. The sacrificed animal is cooked and eaten, except after healing and death rituals. . . .

. . . .

The prospect of a Santeria church in their midst was distressing to many members of the Hialeah community, and the announcement of the plans to open a Santeria church in Hialeah prompted the city council to hold an emergency public session on June 9, 1987. . . .

. . . First, the city council adopted Resolution 87-66, which noted the "concern" expressed by residents of the city "that certain religions may propose to engage in practices which are inconsistent with public morals, peace or safety," and declared that "[t]he City reiterates its commitment to a prohibition against any and all acts of any and all religious groups which are inconsistent with public morals, peace or safety." Next, the council approved an emergency ordinance that incorporated in full, except as to penalty, Florida's animal cruelty laws. Among other things, the incorporated state law subjected to criminal punishment "[w]however . . . unnecessarily or cruelly . . . kills any animal."

. . . .

In September 1987, the city council adopted three substantive ordinances addressing the issue of religious animal sacrifice. Ordinance 87-52 defined "sacrifice" as "to unnecessarily kill, torment, torture, or mutilate an animal in a public or private ritual or ceremony not for the primary purpose of food consumption," and prohibited owning or possessing an animal "intending to use such animal for food purposes." It restricted application of this prohibition, however, to any individual or group that "kills, slaughters or sacrifices animals for any type of ritual, regardless of whether or not the flesh or blood of the animal is to be consumed." The ordinance contained an exemption for slaughtering by "licensed establishment[s]" of animals "specifically raised for food purposes." Declaring, moreover, that the city council "has determined that the sacrificing of animals within the city limits is contrary to the public health, safety, welfare and morals of the community," the city council adopted Ordinance 87-71. That ordinance defined sacrifice as had Ordinance 87-52, and then provided that "[i]t shall be unlawful for any person, persons, corporations or associations to sacrifice any animal within the corporate limits of the City of Hialeah, Florida." . . .

. . . .

II

The Free Exercise Clause of the First Amendment, provides that "Congress shall make no law respecting an establishment of religion, or prohibiting the free exercise thereof. . . ." U.S. Const., Amdt. 1 (emphasis added). The city does not argue that Santeria is not a "religion" within the meaning of the First Amendment. Nor could it. Although the practice of animal sacrifice may seem abhorrent to some, "religious beliefs need not be acceptable, logical, consistent, or comprehensible to others in order to merit First Amendment protection." Given the historical association between animal sacrifice and religious worship, petitioners' assertion that animal sacrifice is an integral part of their religion "cannot be deemed bizarre or incredible." Neither the city nor the courts below, moreover, have questioned the sincerity of petitioners' professed desire to conduct animal sacrifices for religious reasons. We must consider petitioners' First Amendment claim.

In addressing the constitutional protection for free exercise of religion, our cases establish the general proposition that a law that is neutral and of general applicability need not be justified by a compelling governmental interest even if the law has the incidental effect of burdening a particular religious practice. *Employment Div., Dept. of Human Resources of Oregon v. Smith*, supra. Neutrality and general applicability are interrelated, and, as becomes apparent in this case, failure to satisfy one requirement is a likely indication that the other has not been satisfied. A law failing to satisfy these requirements must be justified by a compelling governmental interest and must be narrowly tailored to advance that interest. These ordinances fail to satisfy the Smith requirements. We begin by discussing neutrality.

A

. . . .

1

Although a law targeting religious beliefs as such is never permissible, if the object of a law is to infringe upon or restrict practices because of their religious motivation, the law is not neutral; and it is invalid unless it is justified by a compelling interest and is narrowly tailored to advance that interest. . . .

. . . .

The record in this case compels the conclusion that suppression of the central element of the Santeria worship service was the object of the ordinances. First, though use of the words "sacrifice" and "ritual" does not compel a finding of improper targeting of the Santeria religion, the choice of these words is support for our conclusion. . . .

It becomes evident that these ordinances target Santeria sacrifice when the ordinances' operation is considered. . . .

It is a necessary conclusion that almost the only conduct subject to Ordinances 87-40, 87-52, and 87-71 is the religious exercise of Santeria church members. The texts show that they were drafted in tandem to achieve this result. We begin with Ordinance 87-71. It prohibits the sacrifice of animals but defines sacrifice as "to unnecessarily kill . . . an animal in a public or private ritual or ceremony not for the primary purpose of food consumption."

The definition excludes almost all killings of animals except for religious sacrifice, and the primary purpose requirement narrows the [illegible], in particular by exempting Kosher slaughter. . . . Indeed, careful drafting ensured that, although Santeria sacrifice is prohibited, killings that are no more necessary or humane in almost all other circumstances are unpunished.

. . . .

Ordinance 87-40 incorporates the Florida animal cruelty statute. Its prohibition is broad on its face, punishing "[w]however . . . unnecessarily . . . kills any animal." The city claims that this ordinance is the epitome of a neutral prohibition. The problem, however, is the interpretation given to the ordinance by respondent and the Florida attorney general. Killings for religious reasons are deemed unnecessary, whereas most other killings fall outside the prohibition. The city, on what seems to be a per se basis, deems hunting, slaughter of animals for food, eradication of insects and pests, and euthanasia as necessary. There is no indication in the record that respondent has concluded that hunting or fishing for sport is unnecessary. Indeed, one of the few reported Florida cases concludes that the use of live rabbits to train greyhounds is not unnecessary. . . .

. . . .

The legitimate governmental interests in protecting the public health and preventing cruelty to animals could be addressed by restrictions stopping far short of a flat prohibition of all Santeria sacrificial practice. . . .

. . . With regard to the city's interest in ensuring the adequate care of animals, regulation of conditions and treatment, regardless of why an animal is kept, is the logical response to the city's concern, not a prohibition on possession for the purpose of sacrifice. The same is true for the city's interest in prohibiting cruel methods of killing. Under federal and Florida law and Ordinance 87-40, which incorporates Florida law in this regard, killing an animal by the "simultaneous and instantaneous severance of the carotid arteries with a sharp instrument" — the method used in Kosher slaughter — is approved as humane. The District Court found that, though Santeria sacrifice also results in [illegible] of the carotid arteries, the method used during sacrifice is less reliable and therefore not humane. If the city has a real concern that other methods are less humane, however, the subject of the regulation should be the method of slaughter itself, not a religious classification that is said to bear some general relation to it.

Ordinance 87-72 — unlike the three other ordinances — does appear to apply to substantial nonreligious conduct and not to be overbroad. For our purposes here, however, the four substantive ordinances may be treated as a group for neutrality purposes. . . .

. . . .

B

We turn next to a second requirement of the Free Exercise Clause, the rule that laws burdening religious practice must be of general applicability. . . .

. . . .

Respondent claims that Ordinances 87-40, 87-52, and 87-71 advance two interests: protecting the public health and preventing cruelty to animals. The ordinances are underinclusive for those ends. They fail to prohibit nonreligious conduct that endangers these interests in a similar or greater degree than Santeria sacrifice does. The underinclusion is substantial, not inconsequential. Despite the city's proffered interest in preventing cruelty to animals, the ordinances are drafted with care to forbid few killings but those occasioned by religious sacrifice. Many types of animal deaths or kills for nonreligious reasons are either not prohibited or approved by express provision. For example, fishing is legal. Extermination of mice and rats within a home is also permitted. Florida law sanctions euthanasia of "stray, neglected, abandoned, or unwanted animals," destruction of animals judicially removed from their owners "for humanitarian reasons" or when the animal "is of no commercial value," the infliction of pain or suffering "in the interest of medical science," the placing of poison in one's yard or enclosure, and the use of a live animal "to pursue or take wildlife or to participate in any hunting," and "to hunt wild hogs."

. . . .

The ordinances are also underinclusive with regard to the city's interest in public health, which is threatened by the disposal of animal carcasses in open public places and the consumption of uninspected meat. Neither interest is pursued by respondent with regard to conduct that is not motivated by religious conviction. The health risks posed by the improper disposal of animal carcasses are the same whether Santeria sacrifice or some nonreligious killing preceded it. The city does not, however, prohibit hunters from bringing their kill to their houses, nor does it regulate disposal after their activity. Despite substantial testimony at trial that the same public health hazards result from improper disposal of garbage by restaurants, restaurants are outside the scope of the ordinances. . . .

The ordinances are underinclusive as well with regard to the health risk posed by consumption of uninspected meat. Under the city's ordinances, hunters may eat their kill and fisherman may eat their catch without undergoing governmental inspection. . . .

Ordinance 87-72, which prohibits the slaughter of animals outside of areas zoned for slaughterhouses, is underinclusive on its face. The ordinance includes an exemption for "any person, group, or organization" that "slaughters or processes for sale, small numbers of hogs and/or cattle per week in accordance with an exemption provided by state law." Respondent has not explained why commercial operations that slaughter "small numbers" of hogs and cattle do not implicate its professed desire to prevent cruelty to animals and preserve the public health. Although the city has classified Santeria sacrifice as slaughter, subjecting it to this ordinance, it does not regulate other killings for food in like manner.

. . . .

IV

The Free Exercise Clause commits government itself to religious tolerance, and upon even slight suspicion that proposals for state intervention stem from animosity to religion or distrust of its practices, all officials must pause to remember their own high duty to the Constitution and to the rights it secures. Those in office must be resolute in resisting importunate demands and must ensure that the sole reasons for imposing the burdens of law and regulation are secular. Legislators may not devise mechanisms, overt or disguised, designed to persecute or oppress a religion or its practices. The laws here in question were enacted contrary to these constitutional principles, and they are void.

Reversed.

. . . .

Justice **Blackmun**, with whom Justice **O'Connor** joins, concurring in the judgment.

The Court holds today that the city of Hialeah violated the First and Fourteenth Amendments when it passed a set of restrictive ordinances explicitly directed at petitioners' religious practice. With this holding I agree. I write separately to emphasize that the First Amendment's protection of religion extends beyond those rare occasions on which the government explicitly targets religion (or a particular religion) for disfavored treatment, as is done in this case. In my view, a statute that burdens the free exercise of religion "may stand only if the law in general, and the State's refusal to allow a religious exemption in particular, are justified by a compelling interest that cannot be served by less restrictive means." . . .

. . . .

It is only in the rare case that a state or local legislature will enact a law directly burdening religious practice as such. Because the respondent here does single out religion in this way, the present case is an easy one to decide.

A harder case would be presented if petitioners were requesting an exemption from a generally applicable anticruelty law. The result in the case before the Court today, and the fact that every Member of the Court concurs in that result, does not necessarily reflect this Court's views of the strength of a State's interest in prohibiting cruelty to animals. This case does not present, and I therefore decline to reach, the question whether the Free Exercise Clause would require a religious exemption from a law that sincerely pursued the goal of protecting animals from cruel treatment. The number of organizations that have filed *amicus* briefs on behalf of this interest,* however, demonstrates that it is not a concern to be treated lightly.

* See Brief for Washington Humane Society in support of Respondent; Brief for People for the Ethical Treatment of Animals, New Jersey Animal Rights Alliance, and Foundation for Animal Rights Advocacy in support of Respondent; Brief for Humane Society of the United States, American Humane Association, American Society for the Prevention of Cruelty to Animals, Animal Legal Defense Fund, Inc., and Massachusetts Society for the Prevention of Cruelty to Animals in support of Respondent; Brief for International Society for Animal Rights, Citizens for Animals, Farm Animal Reform Movement, In Defense of Animals, Performing Animal Welfare Society, and Student Action Corps for Animals in support of Respondent; and Brief for Institute

NOTES AND QUESTIONS

1. Are the *Smith* and *Church of the Lukumi Babelu Aye* cases different? Is not each concerned with practices, rather than principles, of religious belief? And is not each equally directed at concerns of public health, whether consumption of peyote or the killing of wildlife? Why, then, the different results?
2. Would it matter if the killing of animals, except for consumption, was illegal, like the use of peyote? If this case involved a criminal prosecution? A public health prosecution?
3. We will return to issues of religion and conscience in Chapter 4 with cases addressing maternal-fetal conflict, vaccination and right to die. In such contexts, practitioners of certain religions, particularly Jehovah's Witnesses, object to certain medical treatments, such as blood transfusions. Should their convictions and choices be respected? Why might that be true and yet the Court might consistently reach the conclusion it reached in *Smith*?
4. In some ways, the *Church of the Lukumi Babula Aye* case was too easy was it not? The City specifically and openly targeted *this* religion and *this* practice. On remand, if you were the City Attorney, what would you advise? Is there a way to ban this practice? This Church?
5. For an excellent article, see Erin D. Coffman, *Pielech v. Massasoit Greyhound, Inc.: Can A "Sincerely Held Religious Belief" Have Meaning?* 32 New Eng. L. Rev. 117 (1997); and see James D. Gordon, III, *The New Free Exercise Clause*, 26 Cap. U. L. Rev. 65 (1997).

PROBLEM 2–14 — Daggers in the Heart

The Reverend Ali Ben Some teaches a medieval, Middle Eastern amalgam of mind over matter and invulnerability by faith. Those who believe cannot be harmed, and demonstrate their belief by undergoing various physical trials. These progress through levels of risk, from walking on hot coals, to sleeping on beds of nails, to levitating off high places, to plunging knives into themselves. They bring the Believer along The Way to The One.

The Reverend Ali's successor chose to enter the inner circle and requested passage by the Ritual of Knives. After ceremonies of purification, in the presence of the Elect, and repeated insistence on belief and desire, the successor stood before the Body, and the Reverend Ali plunged a dagger into the successor's heart.

He then died.

A jury has returned a verdict of murder. Should that be reduced to manslaughter? Criminal negligence? Not guilty?

See People v. Strong, 338 N.E.2d 602 (N.Y. 1975).

for Animal Rights Law, American Fund for Alternatives to Animal Research, Farm Sanctuary, Jews for Animal Rights, United Animal Nations, and United Poultry Concerns, in support of Respondent.

PROBLEM 2–15 — Denying the Holocaust

In February 2006, a historian, David Irving, was convicted in Austria of denying the Holocaust and arguing that 6,000,000 Jews, Gypsies, Poles, Russians and homosexuals were not killed by the Nazis prior to and during World War II, as well as denying the existence of the ovens used to kill them. He had done this 17 years earlier and claimed to have changed his mind. His sentence was three years in prison. *Should* this be a crime? Why should Austria care? What should the sentence be?

PROBLEM 2–16 — A Drugstore With A Conscience — Sort Of

Pharmacists in Illinois sued in federal court, challenging an Illinois regulation requiring them to dispense certain prescription contraceptives without delay. The rule also requires that they stock needed contraceptives. The pharmacists had refused to dispense certain contraceptive prescriptions and maintain a First Amendment right to refuse. Several maintain they have been fired by Walgreen's for this, contrary to Title VII of the 1964 Civil Rights Act. Walgreen's has been allowed to intervene.

Who is right ethically? Legally?

Are the interests of the pharmacy and the pharmacists identical? Divergent? Waived by employment? Licensure?

Suppose the rule applied to nurses or physicians in hospitals?

See 15 H.L. Rprtr. 163, 779, 782 (7/06)

[2] Dissent: War, Abortion, and Homosexuality

The preceding cases dealt with the extent to which society must accommodate groups within it, in search of a rationale for identifying which groups are entitled to respect and when societal interests — in public health, for example — may override the views and interests of such groups. These were religious groups. The present section takes a narrower focus, on the individual, who — often alone — asserts the right — indeed the necessity — to challenge the views and demands of a society.

Nonconformity is an aspect of liberty. It is also essential to individuality, almost as a matter of definition, whether physical, psychological, social or otherwise. It is this which is most troubling to those opposed to cloning, for example, or to the Amish position in the *Yoder* case. Individuals may dissent from society because of views they derive from groups, as in the *Summers* case, where the litigant is a Quaker. Or the individual may dissent because of his or her profoundly held, possibly biologically grounded, individual views. This was the context of *Archer*, where individuals obstructed an abortion clinic, and *Dale*, where a homosexual opposed the Boy Scouts' position on homosexuality.

In each instance, the common question is whether there is a right to dissent, and what is its price? And, perhaps all too rarely asked, what is the responsibility of the conscientious objector — to himself or herself, or to society?

IN RE SUMMERS

325 U.S. 561 (1945)

Mr. Justice **Reed** delivered the opinion of the Court.

Petitioner sought to review the action of the Supreme Court of Illinois in denying petitioner's prayer for admission to the practice of law in that state. It was alleged that the denial was 'on the sole ground that he is a conscientious objector to war' or to phrase petitioner's contention slightly differently 'because of his conscientious scruples against participation in war.' Petitioner challenges here the right of the Supreme Court to exclude him from the bar under the due process clause of the Fourteenth Amendment to the Constitution of the United States which secured to him protection against state action in violation of the principles of the First Amendment. . . .

. . . No report appears in the record from the Committee. An unofficial letter from the Secretary gives his personal views.[1] A petition was filed in the Supreme Court on August 2, 1943, which alleged that petitioner was informed in January, 1943, that the Committee declined to sign a favorable certificate. The petition set out that the sole reason for the Committee's refusal was that petitioner was a conscientious objector to war, and averred that such reason did not justify his exclusion because of the due process clause of the Fourteenth Amendment. . . .

. . . .

The Justices justify their refusal to admit petitioner to practice before the courts of Illinois on the ground of petitioner's inability to take in good faith the required oath to support the Constitution of Illinois. . . . A conscientious belief in non-violence to the extent that the believer will not use force to prevent wrong, no matter how aggravated, and so cannot swear in good faith to support the Illinois Constitution, the Justices contend, must disqualify such a believer for admission.

Petitioner appraises the denial of admission from the viewpoint of a religionist. He said in his petition:

'The so-called 'misconduct' for which petitioner could be reproached is his taking the New Testament too seriously. Instead of merely reading or preaching the Sermon on the Mount, he tries to practice it. The only fault of the petitioner consists in his attempt to act as a good Christian in accordance with his interpretation of the Bible, and according to the dictates of his conscience. We respectfully submit that the profession of law does not

---

[1] In part it read:

"I think the record establishes that you are a conscientious objector, — also that your philosophical beliefs go further. You eschew the use of force regardless of circumstances but the law which you profess to embrace and which you teach and would practice is not an abstraction observed through mutual respect. It is real. It is the result of experience of man in an imperfect world, necessary we believe to restrain the strong and protect the weak. It recognizes the right even of the individual to use force under certain circumstances and commands the use of force to obtain its observance."

. . . .

"I do not argue against your religious beliefs or your philosophy of nonviolence. My point is merely that your position seems inconsistent with the obligation of an attorney at law."

shut its gates to persons who have qualified in all other respects, even when they follow in the footsteps of that Great Teacher of [illegible] the Sermon on the Mount. We respectfully submit that under out Constitutional guarantees even good Christians who have met all the requirements for the admission to the bar may be admitted to practice law.

. . . Of course, under our Constitutional system, men could not be excluded from the practice of law, or indeed from following any other calling, simply because they belong to any of our religious groups, whether Protestant, Catholic, Quaker or Jewish, assuming it conceivable that any state of the Union would draw such a religious line. We cannot say that any such purpose to discriminate motivated the action of the Illinois Supreme Court.

. . . .

Illinois has constitutional provisions which require service in the militia in time of war of men of petitioner's age group. The return of the Justices alleges that petitioner has not made any showing that he would serve notwithstanding his conscientious objections. While under Section 5(g) of the Selective Training and Service Act, supra, conscientious objectors to participation in war in any form now are permitted to do non-war work of national importance, this is by grace of Congressional recognition of their beliefs. The Act may be repealed. No similar exemption during war exists under Illinois law. . . .

The United States does not admit to citizenship the alien who refuses to pledge military service. It is impossible for us to conclude that the insistence of Illinois that an officer who is charged with the administration of justice must take an oath to support the Constitution of Illinois and Illinois' interpretation of that oath to require a willingness to perform military service violates the principles of religious freedom which the Fourteenth Amendment secures against state action, when a like interpretation of a similar oath as to the Federal Constitution bars an alien from national citizenship.

Affirmed.

Mr. Justice **Black**, dissenting.

The State of Illinois has denied the petitioner the right to practice his profession and [illegible] a lawyer. . . .

The state does not deny that petitioner possesses the following qualifications:

> He is honest, moral, and intelligent, has had a college and a law school education. He has been a law professor and fully measures up to the high standards of legal knowledge Illinois has set as a prerequisite to admission to practice law in that State. He has never been convicted for, or charged with, a violation of law. That he would serve his clients faithfully and efficiently if admitted to practice is not denied. His ideals of what a lawyer should be indicate that his activities would not reflect discredit upon the bar, that he would strive to make the legal system a more effective instrument of justice. Because he thinks that 'Lawsuits do not bring love and brotherliness, they just create antagonisms,' he would, as a lawyer, exert himself to adjust controversies out of court, but would vigorously press his

client's cause in court if efforts to adjust failed. Explaining to his examiners some of the reasons why he wanted to be a lawyer, he told them: 'I think there is a lot of work to be done in the law. . . . I think the law has a place to see to it that every man has a chance to eat and a chance to live equally. I think the law has a place where people can go and get justice done for themselves without paying too much, for the bulk of people that are too poor.' No one contends that such a vision of the law in action is either illegal or reprehensible.

The petitioner's disqualifying religious beliefs stem chiefly from a study of the New Testament and a literal acceptance of the teachings of Christ as he understands them. Those beliefs are these:

> He is opposed to the use of force for either offensive or defensive purposes. The taking of human life under any circumstances he believes to be against the Law of God and contrary to the best interests of man. He would if he could, he told his examiners, obey to the letter these precepts of Christ: 'Love your Enemies; Do good to those that hate you; Even though your enemy strike you on your right cheek, turn to him your left cheek also.' . . .

. . . The conclusion seems to me inescapable that if Illinois can bar this petitioner from the practice of law it can bar every person from every public occupation solely because he believes in non-resistance rather than in force. For a lawyer is no more subject to call for military duty than a plumber, a highway worker, a Secretary of State, or a prison chaplain. It may be, as many people think, that Christ's Gospel of love and submission is not suited to a world in which men still fight and kill one another. But I am not ready to say that a mere profession of belief in that Gospel is a sufficient reason to keep otherwise well qualified men out of the legal profession, or to drive law-abiding lawyers of that belief out of the profession, which would be the next logical development.

Nor am I willing to say that such a belief can be penalized through the circuitous method of prescribing an oath, and then barring an applicant on the ground that his present belief might later prompt him to do or refrain from doing something that might violate that oath. Test oaths, designed to impose civil disabilities upon men for their beliefs rather than for unlawful conduct, were an abomination to the founders of this nation. This feeling was made manifest in Article VI of the Constitution which provides that 'no religious Test shall ever be required as a Qualification to any Office or public Trust under the United States.'

. . . .

The Illinois Constitution itself prohibits the draft of conscientious objectors except in time of war and also excepts from militia duty persons who are 'exempted by the laws of the United States.' It has not drafted men into the militia since 1864, and if it ever should again, no one can say that it will not, as has the Congress of the United States, exempt men who honestly entertain the views that this petitioner does. Thus the probability that Illinois would ever call the petitioner to serve in a war has little more reality than an imaginary quantity in mathematics.

I cannot agree that a state can lawfully bar from a semi-public position, a well-qualified man of good character solely because he entertains a religious belief which might prompt him at some time in the future to violate a law which has not yet been and may never be enacted. Under our Constitution men are punished for what they do or fail to do and not for what they think and believe. Freedom to think, to believe, and to worship, has too exalted a position in our country to be penalized on such an illusory basis.

I would reverse the decision of the State Supreme Court.

Mr. Justice **Douglas**, Mr. Justice **Murphy**, and Mr. Justice **Rutledge** concur in this opinion.

NOTES AND QUESTIONS

1. The decision *In Re Summers* precedes the decisions, in *Yoder*, *Sherbert v. Verner* and *Smith*. Would it — should it — be decided differently in the light of subsequent case law? In the light of the Vietnam Era experience with war? Is the decision a product of World War II mentality, in line with *Korematsu*? *See supra* § 1.02.
2. *May* a society legitimately insist that all of its members fight in its wars? *All* of its wars? (As to this, see *Clay v. United States*, 403 U.S. 698 (1971)). The Court holds there is no *right* to exemption, although Mr. Summers (later, Professor Summers of Yale Law School) qualified under federal law. Illinois granted no such dispensation. *Should* it have?
3. Separately, what should be the punishment for dissent? Imprisonment? Substituted service? Exclusion from the Bar? Is *this* the central issue in *Summers* — the *relevance* of his "misconduct" to practicing law, the proportionality of exclusion to the *harm* his "misconduct" inflicted on society. Is *this* the point of Justice Black's dissent?
4. Still, might one ask whether there is a kind of arrogance in Summers' position? M[illegible], only a few adopt the extreme position of the Quakers. Is it fair to question their sincerity? Their utility? Their respect for the rights of others and the society which makes their beliefs possible?
5. Where, then, shall a person of conscience find guidance, to avoid the sin of pride and the folly of arrogance? Respect is due the views and rights of others, according to the teaching of Rawls. A standard jury instruction in criminal cases across America tells jurors to form their own opinions and adhere to them, but to listen to the views of others and respect the weight of contrary views. While they are told a verdict must be unanimous, they are not told a single juror may dissent and "hang" a jury, producing a result, but not a decision. *Should* they be told this?
6. In a text on bioethics, it is perhaps surprising to find a case on conscientious objection and practicing law. But there is a view that

conscience is a biologically grounded aspect of consciousness, distinguishing humanity. And an enduring bioethical issue is posed by war. And a central issue of personhood is dissent, from war or other prevailing views of society. The *Archer* case — which is next — illustrates the point in a more contemporary setting, abortion.

PEOPLE v. ARCHER

537 N.Y.S.2d 726 (Monroe County, 1988)

John Manning **Regan**, Judge.

I. Facts

On Saturday morning, May 21, 1988, at 7:00 a.m., Timothy Archer, Gerald Crawford and 40 others entered Highland Hospital in Rochester, New York, and went at once to the fifth floor, east wing. Upon arrival at that location, all 42 persons sat down in the hallway which led to the examining, and clinical treatment, rooms where nine abortions were scheduled to be performed that day. The group sang hymns, greeted the women who came for abortions, and distributed pro-life literature to them. The Highland Obstetrical Group, a partnership of six physicians, had leased that floor of the east wing of the hospital, for the purpose of performing these abortions, and two members of the partnership, Doctors Wax and Eisenberg, were present that morning, and were anticipating attending to their patients. Around 7:30 a.m., the Director of Security for Highland Hospital notified police of this abortion "sit-in." When the police came, in response to his summons, they found that the 42 people had physically blocked access to the clinic and that no abortions were in progress. Over a period lasting about five hours, the police tried to evacuate these protestors with persuasion, admonition, threats and warnings. These measures having failed, the police resorted, finally, to arrests. They managed to clear the area, and to take all 42 people into custody, about 1:00 p.m. that afternoon.

This episode was free from overt violence to either person or property. The charges which the hospital and the police have filed against the 42 defendants are Criminal Trespass Third Degree, and Resisting Arrest.

II. Pre-Trial Proceedings

In August 1988, after the arraignment of all 42 defendants, and during the pre-trial discovery stage, the People moved, on written application, to preclude the defendants from asserting the "necessity defense" at the trial. At that point in the prosecution of these cases, however, the defendants had not offered any evidence whatsoever in the case, nor had they any duty to do so.

The necessity defense, authorized in New York by statute, is a subordinate classification within the broader justification defenses set out in Article 35 of the Penal Law.

[T]he opening phrase limits the defense of justification generally to cases where the otherwise admittedly criminal conduct of a defendant is "necessary as an emergency measure to avoid an imminent public or private injury which is about to occur by reason of a situation occasioned or developed through no fault of the actor . . . ," and where the injury [illegible] outweighs the injury the criminal statutes in question were calculated to prevent. Moreover, at the close of the subparagraph, the following sentence appears:

> "*Whenever evidence relating to the defense of justification under this subdivision is offered by the defendant,* the Court shall rule, as a matter of law, whether the claimed facts and circumstances would, if established, constitute a defense."

. . . .

For the reasons which follow, the Court denies the motion to preclude the defense of justification, and rules that, as a matter of law, if the claimed facts and circumstances are established, they will constitute a justification defense to the charges of Criminal trespass and Resisting Arrest.

1. Defense of Justification (Necessity Doctrine)

Whether justification is a defense to admittedly criminal behavior when the injury sought to be avoided is the abortion of unborn children is a question of first impression in New York. Our justification statute — mirroring the Model Penal Code which was its genesis — concerns itself primarily with the justifiable use of physical force in self-defense situations, or in situations where the protection of other persons or property from the imminent threat of direct injury or loss by third parties is the issue. New York has, however, enacted the justification defense generally for all criminal offenses under the Penal Code, "whenever the facts and circumstances of a criminal case force a choice between the lesser of two evils."

a. The New York Statutory Scheme of Justification as a Defense

New York's statutory defense of justification originated in 1965. Assemblyman Richard J. Bartless, Chairman of the Commission on Revision of the Penal Code, submitted the first preliminary draft of the proposed Revised Penal Code to the Legislature in 1964. This draft had derived from a principal reference source: the American Law Institute's proposed Model Penal Code. Between the 1964 and 1965 legislative sessions, however, the entire preliminary draft underwent substantial changes, particularly with respect to the justification defense.

. . . .

. . . Under the Model Code, whatever was legal, therefore, could not be evil. The Model Code, in other words, precluded the necessity defense whenever the Legislature had legalized conduct.

But what this Court must observe here is that both the Revisors of the New York Penal Law, and the Legislature itself, rejected this limiting language in the Model Code, and adopted, instead, a different standard. They wrote that the "injury . . . to be avoided must . . . *according to ordinary standards of intelligence and morality,* clearly outweigh the injury" the criminal law(s) in question were designed to prevent. The Revisors, therefore, deliberately chose to enlarge the categories of possible evils to include not simply illegal behavior, but any injury which existed "according to ordinary standards of intelligence and morality." In other words, despite the legality of behavior, that behavior could still constitute an "evil" or "injury" to be avoided, so long as, *according to ordinary standards of intelligence and morality,* it could reasonably be classified as such.

. . . .

In Nevada, for example, prostitution is legal, but still, immoral. Some type of gambling is almost everywhere legal, but many persons of ordinary intelligence and morality still consider it immoral. Traffic in alcoholic beverages is legal, but its by-product, drunkenness, remains immoral. Divorce is legal, but, in many cases, it is immoral, especially when it affects innocent children of the marriage. Thus the two ideas — morality and legality — are not the same. Morality is the standard of conduct to which, as good and decent people, we all aspire. Legality is the standard of conduct to which, as members of a civilized society, and under penalty of the criminal sanction, we must all adhere.

The question then, for this Court is whether, under this statutory test of "ordinary standards of intelligence and morality" a Jury may find that these nine abortions could have been an "injury to be avoided."

Abortion is still a crime under the New York Penal Code. Ironically (inasmuch as we are discussing the justification defense), the Legislature, in 1970, created the category of "Justifiable Abortional Act." That categorization became the method whereby any therapeutic abortion, and any abortion performed with consent within 24 weeks from the commencement of pregnancy, was absolved from criminal responsibility.

. . . .

This carefully crafted 1970 amendment to the penal abortion laws, therefore, was not authored to establish the morality of abortion. To the contrary, it was intended to alleviate a perceived social crisis of pernicious illegal abortions which were causing death and injury to hundred of thousands of child-bearing women every year. As Assemblywoman Cook said in her memorandum, "illegal abortions are the single largest cause of maternal death" and "hundreds of thousands of illegal abortions are done each year"; yet "virtually no deaths result when an abortion is conducted in accordance with proper medical procedures."

Her portrayals of the legislative purpose behind the 1970 amendment illuminate the complex social panorama that both surrounded and spawned the passage of these laws. In effect, because the Legislature could not stop illegal abortions, they capitulated to the social reality of it, rather than intensify the enforcement of the then current law. . . .

. . . .

In any event, if this change in the law did not propose to compel a citizen "to live in a moral or religious environment foreign to his upbringing," then that citizen remained free to adopt moral values in accordance with "ordinary standards of intelligence and morality," rather than in accordance with the tolerances of the Penal Law. Since that is so, abortion can still constitute a moral "injury to be avoided," because citizens of ordinary intelligence and morality remain free both as [illegible]standing the fact that the Legislature has made most abortions "justifiable" in relation to what would otherwise be a prohibited criminal act.

Moreover, from the evidence in this trial, the practice of abortion-on-demand has at this time — 18 years after the 1970 amendment — far transcended the narrow social evil of maternal deaths due to illegal and unsanitary abortion techniques. Abortion has become simply another birth-control device, or a way to overcome a social inconvenience, or an expedient remedy for conceiving a child of the "wrong" sex. These consequences of "justifying" the abortional act were not envisioned in any of the legislative history behind the 1970 amendment, and it is fair comment to say that these unforeseen and unfortunate circumstances can easily be thought of as "injuries to be avoided" according to ordinary standards of intelligence and morality.

For these reasons, the Court concludes that, despite the 1970 amendment, which made the abortion of a fetus twenty-four weeks or younger a "Justifiable Abortional Act," a jury of private citizens is free to decide, under § 35.05 of the Penal Law, that many of those abortions are immoral *"injuries to be avoided"* and that "the urgency of avoiding such injuries clearly outweighs the desirability of avoiding injuries such as Trespassing and Resisting Arrest" which the criminal statutes in issue here are designed to prevent. The jury may weigh the loss of the life of the developing fetus against the property rights the trespass statute protects, and the social order values the arrest statute supports. And if the jury finds that the value of these fetal lives clearly outweighs the competing values of private property and social order, then the Court shall instruct the jury, under § 35.05 of the Penal Law, that they may acquit the defendants.

. . . .

While the question is by no means free from doubt, there appears to be a body of judicial authority that requires courts to vindicate, in affirmative fashion, constitutionally protected rights of privacy and equality as contrasted with similarly protected due process property rights. For this reason, the Court holds that the decision of *Roe v. Wade*, making the first trimester abortion a constitutionally protected right of privacy, constrains the Court to instruct the Jury that § 35.05 cannot classify first trimester abortions as "injuries to be avoided" because neither the statute, nor the Court, nor the Jury itself, can intrude upon that constitutionally protected area of privacy. Accordingly, *Roe* prohibits the State statutory necessity defense whenever there are intentional interruptions which interfere with the performance of first trimester abortions.

. . . .

Thus, in cases of moral indignation, the flexibility of the New York statute avoids the chafing attrition of the eternal struggle between what is legal and what is moral. The statute allows a Jury to ventilate its displeasure at morally reprehensible conduct regardless of its legality by approving, in a verdict of not guilty, the behavior of those who try, even illegally, to prevent that conduct from happening.

Accordingly, the Court will instruct the Jury that the defendants can present and argue the defense of necessity so long as the Jury finds that the Highland Obstetrical Group was about to perform other than first trimester abortions on May 21, 1988.

. . . .

NOTES AND QUESTIONS

1. Under the foregoing instructions, and upon proof from Drs. Eisenberg and Wax that the nine abortions scheduled on May 21st were all during the first trimester, the Jury found the 42 defendants guilty of simple Trespass and Resisting Arrest.

2. It should be noted that *People v. Archer* is one of the very few cases to extend the defense of "necessity" or "choice of evils" to those who oppose abortion and do so by disrupting hospitals, doctors' offices or abortion clinics. Most trial judges, would decline to rule as Judge Regan did. In their view, there could be no justification or necessity for physically blocking access to a clinic or occupying the hallways of a wing of a hospital. Do you agree?

3. Note that the criminal law, at least since the drafting of the Model Penal Code in the 1960s, does create the affirmative defense of "necessity" or "choice of evils." In a typical case, a mother might kidnap her children and flee across state lines, committing the crime of kidnapping. Her defense, however, might be that she was seeking to save them from abuse by the father. Her argument, then, would be that of the two evils — kidnapping or abuse — she chose the lesser, that of kidnapping.

   Whether in the *Archer* context, in a kidnapping context or in a prison escape (to avoid being sexually abused or killed), does not the "choice of evils" defense mean that each person becomes judge and jury, able to act without responsibility to the community? Is this helpful to a sense of community?

4. If you were a member of the state legislature and knew of the facts of *Archer,* would you vote for the language as adopted or for the language as proposed by the Model Penal Code? If you were on the *Archer* jury, how would you vote?

5. What would Rawls say about the defense of choice of evils? Is not the conduct here the kind of individual imposition that he would condemn, as rejecting the burdens which come with the benefits of society? His definition of "morality" was accepting previously declared rules, even when they work to your disadvantage; were these protesters "immoral"?

6. In 1994, Paul Hill was convicted of killing a doctor and an escort at an abortion clinic. Another man did the same in 1995. Could either, under the reasoning of *Archer,* have offered a "choice of evils" defense?

7. There is a problem with being a conscientious objector in measuring the harm inflicted by the harm avoided. Stopping abortions may save "lives," but it harms the women seeking the abortions. And it displaces their judgment, overriding their choices and autonomy. The problem

is one of arrogance. Consider that in connection with the next case, *Dale v. Boy Scouts of America*.

DALE v. BOY SCOUTS OF AMERICA
530 U.S. 640 (2000)

Chief Justice **Rehnquist** delivered the opinion of the Court.

Petitioners are the Boy Scouts of America and the Monmouth Council, a division of the Boy Scouts of America (collectively, Boy Scouts). The Boy Scouts is a private, not-for-profit organization engaged in instilling its system of values in young people. The Boy Scouts asserts that homosexual conduct is inconsistent with the values it seeks to instill. Respondent is James Dale, a former Eagle Scout whose adult membership in the Boy Scouts was revoked when the Boy Scouts learned that he is an avowed homosexual and gay rights activist. The New Jersey Supreme Court held that New Jersey's public accommodations law requires that the Boy Scouts admit Dale. This case presents the question whether applying New Jersey's public accommodations law in this way violates the Boy Scouts' First Amendment right of expressive association. We hold that it does.

I

James Dale entered scouting in 1978 at the age of eight by joining Monmouth Council's Cub Scout Pack 142. Dale became a Boy Scout in 1981 and remained a Scout until he turned 18. By all accounts, Dale was an exemplary Scout. In 1988, he achieved the rank of Eagle Scout, one of Scouting's highest honors.

Dale applied for adult membership in the Boy Scouts in 1989. The Boy Scouts approved his application for the position of assistant scoutmaster of Troop 73. Around the same time, Dale left home to attend Rutgers University. After arriving at Rutgers, Dale first acknowledged to himself and others that he is gay. He quickly became involved with, and eventually became the copresident of, the Rutgers University Lesbian/Gay Alliance. In 1990, Dale attended a seminar addressing the psychological and health needs of lesbian and gay teenagers. A newspaper covering the event interviewed Dale about his advocacy of homosexual teenagers' need for gay role models. In early July 1990, the newspaper published the interview and Dale's photograph over a caption identifying him as the copresident of the Lesbian/Gay Alliance.

Later that month, Dale received a letter from Monmouth Council Executive James Kay revoking his adult membership. Dale wrote to Kay requesting the reason for Monmouth Council's decision. Kay responded by letter that the Boy Scouts "specifically forbid membership to homosexuals."

The New Jersey Supreme Court held that the Boy Scouts was a place of public accommodation subject to the public accommodations law, that the organization was not exempt from the law under any of its express exceptions, and that the Boy Scouts violated the law by revoking Dale's membership based on his avowed homosexuality. With respect to the right to intimate association, the court concluded that the Boy Scouts' "large size, nonselectivity, inclusive rather than exclusive purpose, and practice of inviting or allowing nonmembers to attend meetings, establish that the organization is not 'sufficiently personal or private to warrant constitutional protection' under the freedom of intimate association." With respect to the right of expressive association, the court "agreed that Boy Scouts expresses a belief in moral values and uses its activities to encourage the moral development of its members." But the court concluded that it was "not persuaded . . . that a shared goal of Boy Scout members is to associate in order to preserve the view that homosexuality is immoral." Accordingly, the court held "that Dale's membership does not violate the Boy Scouts' right of expressive association because his inclusion would not 'affect in any significant way [the Boy Scouts'] existing members' ability to carry out their various purposes.'" The court also determined that New Jersey has a compelling interest in eliminating "the destructive consequences of discrimination from our society," and that its public accommodations law abridges no more speech than is necessary to accomplish its purpose. Finally, the court addressed the Boy Scouts' reliance on *Hurley v. Irish-American Gay, Lesbian and Bisexual Group of Boston, Inc.,* 515 U.S. 557 (1995), in support of its claimed First Amendment right to exclude Dale. The court determined that *Hurley* did not require deciding the case in favor of the Boy Scouts because "the reinstatement of Dale does not compel Boy Scouts to express any message."

II

In *Roberts v. United States Jaycees,* 468 U.S. 609, 622 (1984), we observed that "implicit in the right to engage in activities protected by the First Amendment" is "a corresponding right to associate with others in pursuit of a wide variety of political, social, economic, educational, religious, and cultural ends." This right is crucial in preventing the majority from imposing its views on groups that would rather express other, perhaps unpopular, ideas. Government actions that may unconstitutionally burden this freedom may take many forms, one of which is "intrusion into the internal structure or affairs of an association" like a "regulation that forces the group to accept members it does not desire." Forcing a group to accept certain members may impair the ability of the group to express those views, and only those views, that it intends to express. Thus, "[f]reedom of association . . . plainly presupposes a freedom not to associate."

To determine whether a group is protected by the First Amendment's expressive associational right, we must determine whether the group engages in "expressive association." The First Amendment's protection of expressive association is not reserved for advocacy groups. But to come within its ambit, a group must engage in some form of expression, whether it be public or private.

The record reveals the following. The Boy Scouts is a private, nonprofit organization. According to its mission statement:

> "It is the mission of the Boy Scouts of America to serve others by helping to instill values in young people and, in other ways, to prepare them to make ethical choices over their lifetime in achieving their full potential.

"The values we strive to instill are based on those found in the Scout Oath and Law:

"Scout Oath

"On my honor I will do my best

To do my duty to God and my country and to obey the Scout Law;

To help other people at all times;

To keep myself physically strong, mentally awake, and morally straight.

"Scout Law

"A Scout is:

"Trustworthy Obedient

Loyal Cheerful

Helpful Thrifty

Friendly Brave

Courteous Clean

Kind Reverent." App. 184.

Thus, the general mission of the Boy Scouts is clear: "To instill values in young people." The Boy Scouts seeks to instill these values by having its adult leaders spend time with the youth members, instructing and engaging them in activities like camping, archery, and fishing. During the time spent with the youth members, the scoutmasters and assistant scoutmasters inculcate them with the Boy Scouts' values — both expressly and by example. It seems indisputable that an association that seeks to transmit such a system of values engages in expressive activity.

Given that the Boy Scouts engages in expressive activity, we must determine whether the forced inclusion of Dale as an assistant scoutmaster would significantly affect the Boy Scouts' ability to advocate public or private viewpoints. This inquiry necessarily requires us first to explore, to a limited extent, the nature of the Boy Scouts' view of homosexuality.

The New Jersey Supreme Court analyzed the Boy Scouts' beliefs and found that the "exclusion of members solely on the basis of their sexual orientation is inconsistent with Boy Scouts' commitment to a diverse and 'representative' membership . . . [and] contradicts Boy Scouts' overarching objective to reach 'all eligible youth.'" The court concluded that the exclusion of members like Dale "appears antithetical to the organization's goals and philosophy." But our cases reject this sort of inquiry; it is not the role of the courts to reject a group's expressed values because they disagree with those values or find them internally inconsistent.

The Boy Scouts asserts that it "teaches that homosexual conduct is not morally straight," and that it does "not want to promote homosexual conduct as a legitimate form of behavior." We accept the Boy Scouts' assertion. We need not inquire further to determine the nature of the Boy Scouts' expression with respect to homosexuality. But because the record before us contains written evidence of the Boy Scouts' viewpoint, we look to it as instructive, if only on the question of the sincerity of the professed beliefs.

A 1978 position statement to the Boy Scouts' Executive Committee, signed by Downing B. Jenks, the President of the Boy Scouts, and Harvey L. Price, the Chief Scout Executive, expresses the Boy Scouts' "official position" with regard to "homosexuality and Scouting":

> "Q. May an individual who openly declares himself to be a homosexual be a volunteer Scout leader?
>
> "A. No. The Boy Scouts of America is a private, membership organization and leadership therein is a privilege and not a right. We do not believe that homosexuality and leadership in Scouting are appropriate. We will continue to select only those who in our judgment meet our standards and qualifications for leadership."

Thus, at least as of 1978 — the year James Dale entered Scouting — the official position of the Boy Scouts was that avowed homosexuals were not to be Scout leaders.

A position statement promulgated by the Boy Scouts in 1991 (after Dale's membership was revoked but before this litigation was filed) also supports its current view: "We believe that homosexual conduct is inconsistent with the requirement in the Scout Oath that a Scout be morally straight and in the Scout Law that a Scout be clean in word and deed, and that homosexuals do not provide a desirable role model for Scouts." We must then determine whether Dale's presence as an assistant scoutmaster would significantly burden the Boy Scouts' desire to not "promote homosexual conduct as a legitimate form of behavior." As we give deference to an association's assertions regarding the nature of its expression, we must also give deference to an association's view of what would impair its expression. But here Dale, by his own admission, is one of a group of gay Scouts who have "become leaders in their community and are open and honest about their sexual orientation." Dale was the copresident of a gay and lesbian organization at college and remains a gay rights activist. Dale's presence in the Boy Scouts would, at the very least, force the organization to send a message, both to the youth members and the world, that the Boy Scouts accepts homosexual conduct as a legitimate form of behavior.

Hurley is illustrative on this point. There we considered whether the application of Massachusetts' public accommodations law to require the organizers of a private St. Patrick's Day parade to include among the marchers an Irish-American gay, lesbian, and bisexual group, GLIB, violated the parade organizers' First Amendment rights. We noted that the parade organizers did not wish to exclude the GLIB members because of their sexual orientations, but because they wanted to march behind a GLIB banner. We observed:

> "[A] contingent marching behind the organization's banner would at least bear witness to the fact that some Irish are gay, lesbian, or bisexual, and the presence of the organized marchers would suggest their view that people of their sexual orientations have as much claim to unqualified social acceptance as heterosexuals. . . . The parade's

> organizers may not believe these facts about Irish sexuality to be so, [illegible] or have some other reason for wishing to keep GLIB's message out of the parade. But whatever the reason, it boils down to the choice of a speaker not to propound a particular point of view, and that choice is presumed to lie beyond the government's power to control."

Here, we have found that the Boy Scouts believes that homosexual conduct is inconsistent with the values it seeks to instill in its youth members; it will not "promote homosexual conduct as a legitimate form of behavior." As the presence of GLIB in Boston's St. Patrick's Day parade would have interfered with the parade organizers' choice not to propound a particular point of view, the presence of Dale as an assistant scoutmaster would just as surely interfere with the Boy Scout's choice not to propound a point of view contrary to its beliefs.

The New Jersey Supreme Court determined that the Boy Scouts' ability to disseminate its message was not significantly affected by the forced inclusion of Dale as an assistant scoutmaster because of the following findings:

> "Boy Scout members do not associate for the purpose of disseminating the belief that homosexuality is immoral; Boy Scouts discourages its leaders from disseminating *any* views on sexual issues; and Boy Scouts includes sponsors and members who subscribe to different views in respect of homosexuality."

We disagree with the New Jersey Supreme Court's conclusion drawn from these findings.

First, associations do not have to associate for the "purpose" of disseminating a certain message in order to be entitled to the protections of the First Amendment. An association must merely engage in expressive activity that could be impaired in order to be entitled to protection. For example, the purpose of the St. Patrick's Day parade in *Hurley* was not to espouse any views [illegible], but we held that the parade organizers had a right to exclude certain participants nonetheless.

Second, even if the Boy Scouts discourages Scout leaders from disseminating views on sexual issues — a fact that the Boy Scouts disputes with contrary evidence — the First Amendment protects the Boy Scouts' method of expression. If the Boy Scouts wishes Scout leaders to avoid questions of sexuality and teach only by example, this fact does not negate the sincerity of its belief discussed above.

Third, the First Amendment simply does not require that every member of a group agree on every issue in order for the group's policy to be "expressive association." The Boy Scouts takes an official position with respect to homosexual conduct, and that is sufficient for First Amendment purposes.

Having determined that the Boy Scouts is an expressive association and that the forced inclusion of Dale would significantly affect its expression, we inquire whether the application of New Jersey's public accommodations law to require that the Boy Scouts accept Dale as an assistant scoutmaster runs afoul of the Scouts' freedom of expressive association. We conclude that it does.

State public accommodations laws were originally enacted to prevent discrimination in traditional places of public accommodation — like inns and trains. But the statute also includes places that often may not carry with them open invitations to the public, like summer camps and roof gardens. In this case, the New Jersey Supreme Court went a step further and applied its public accommodations law to a private entity without even attempting to tie the term "place" to a physical location. As the definition of "public accommodation" has expanded from clearly commercial entities, such as restaurants, bars, and hotels, to membership organizations such as the Boy Scouts, the potential for conflict between state public accommodations laws and the First Amendment rights of organizations has increased.

We recognized in cases such as *Roberts* and *[Board of Dirs. of Rotary Int'l v. Rotary Club of] Duarte*[, 481 U.S. 537 (1987),] that States have a compelling interest in eliminating discrimination against women in public accommodations. But in each of these cases we went on to conclude that the enforcement of these statutes would not materially interfere with the ideas that the organization sought to express. In *Roberts*, we said "indeed, the Jaycees has failed to demonstrate . . . any serious burden on the male members' freedom of expressive association." 468 U.S. at 626. In *Duarte*, we said:

> "Impediments to the exercise of one's right to choose one's associates can violate the right of association protected by the First Amendment. In this case, however, the evidence fails to demonstrate that admitting women to Rotary Clubs will affect in any significant way the existing members' ability to carry out their various purposes." 481 U.S. at 548.

We thereupon concluded in each of these cases that the organizations' First Amendment rights were not violated by the application of the States' public accommodations laws.

In *Hurley,* we said that public accommodations laws "are well within the State's usual power to enact when a legislature has reason to believe that a given group is the target of discrimination, and they do not, as a general matter, violate the First or Fourteenth Amendments." But we went on to note that in that case "the Massachusetts [public accommodations] law has been applied in a peculiar way" because "any contingent of protected individuals with a message would have the right to participate in petitioners' speech, so that the communication produced by the private organizers would be shaped by all those protected by the law who wish to join in with some expressive demonstration of their own."

In *Hurley,* we applied traditional First Amendment analysis to hold that the application of the Massachusetts public accommodations law to a parade violated the First Amendment rights of the parade organizers. Although we did not explicitly deem the parade in *Hurley* an expressive association, the analysis we applied there is similar to the analysis we apply here. We have already concluded that a state requirement that the Boy Scouts retain Dale as an assistant scoutmaster would significantly burden the organization's right to oppose or disfavor homosexual conduct. The state interests embodied in New Jersey's public accommodations law do not justify such a severe intrusion on the Boy Scouts' rights to freedom of expressive association. That being the case, we hold that the First Amendment prohibits the State from imposing such a requirement through the application of its public accommodations law.

We are not, as we must not be, guided by our views of whether the Boy Scouts' teachings with respect to homosexual conduct are right or wrong; public or judicial disapproval of a tenet of an organization's expression does not justify the State's effort to compel the organization to accept members where such acceptance would derogate from the organization's expressive message. "While the law is free to promote all sorts of conduct in place of harmful behavior, it is not free to interfere with speech for no better reason than promoting an approved message or discouraging a disfavored one, however enlightened either purpose may strike the government." *Hurley,* 515 U.S. at 579.

The judgment of the New Jersey Supreme Court is reversed, and the cause remanded for further proceedings not inconsistent with this opinion.

It is so ordered.

APPENDIX TO OPINION OF THE COURT

N.J. Stat. Ann. § 10:5-4 (West Supp. 2000). Obtaining employment, accommodations and privileges without discrimination; civil right

"All persons shall have the opportunity to obtain employment, and to obtain all the accommodations, advantages, facilities, and privileges of any place of public accommodation, publicly assisted housing accommodation, and other real property without discrimination because of race, creed, color, national origin, ancestry, age, marital status, affectional or sexual orientation, familial status, or sex, subject only to conditions and limitations applicable alike to all persons. This opportunity is recognized as and declared to be a civil right."

N.J. Stat. Ann. § 10:5-5 (West Supp. 2000). Definitions

"As used in this act, unless a different meaning clearly appears from the context:

. . . .

"*l*. 'A place of public accommodation' shall include, but not be limited to: any tavern, roadhouse, hotel, motel, trailer camp, summer camp, day camp, or resort camp, whether for entertainment of transient guests or accommodation of those seeking health, recreation or rest; any producer, manufacturer, wholesaler, distributor, retail shop, store, establishment, or concession dealing with goods or services of any kind; any restaurant, eating house, or place where food is sold for consumption on the premises; any place maintained for the sale of ice cream, ice and fruit preparations or their derivatives, soda water or confections, or where any beverages of any kind are retailed for consumption on the premises; any garage, any public conveyance operated on land or water, or in the air, any stations and terminals thereof; any bathhouse, boardwalk, or seashore accommodation; any auditorium, meeting place, or hall; any theatre, motion-picture house, music hall, roof garden, skating rink, swimming pool, amusement and recreation park, fair, bowling alley, gymnasium, shooting gallery, billiard and pool parlor, or other place of amusement; any comfort station; any dispensary, clinic or hospital; any public library; any kindergarten, primary and secondary school, trade or business school, high school, academy, college and university, or any educational institution under the supervision of the State Board of Education, or the Commissioner of Education of the State of New Jersey. Nothing herein contained shall be construed to include or to apply to any institution, bona fide club, or place of accommodation, which is in its nature distinctly private; nor shall anything herein contained apply to any educational facility operated or maintained by a bona fide religious or sectarian institution, and the right of a natural parent or one in loco parentis to direct the education and upbringing of a child under his control is hereby affirmed; nor shall anything herein contained be construed to bar any private secondary or post secondary school from using in good faith criteria other than race, creed, color, national origin, ancestry or affectional or sexual orientation in the admission of students."

Justice **Stevens**, with whom Justice **Souter**, Justice **Ginsburg** and Justice **Breyer** join, dissenting.

I

James Dale joined BSA as a Cub Scout in 1978, when he was eight years old. Three years later he became a Boy Scout, and he remained a member until his 18th birthday. Along the way, he earned 25 merit badges, was admitted into the prestigious Order of the Arrow, and was awarded the rank of Eagle Scout — an honor given to only three percent of all Scouts. In 1989, BSA approved his application to be an Assistant Scoutmaster.

To instill its shared values, BSA has adopted a "Scout Oath" and a "Scout Law" setting forth its central tenets. For example, the Scout Law requires a member to promise, among other things, that he will be "obedient." Accompanying definitions for the terms found in the Oath and Law are provided in the Boy Scout Handbook and the Scoutmaster Handbook. For instance, the Boy Scout Handbook defines "obedient" as follows:

> "A Scout is OBEDIENT. A Scout follows the rules of his family, school, and troop. He obeys the laws of his community and country. If he thinks these rules and laws are unfair, he tries to have them changed in an orderly manner rather than disobey them."

To bolster its claim that its shared goals include teaching that homosexuality is wrong, BSA directs our attention to two terms appearing in the Scout Oath and Law. The first is the phrase "morally straight," which appears in the Oath ("On my honor I will do my best . . . To keep myself . . . morally straight"); the second term is the word "clean," which appears in a list of 12 characteristics together comprising the Scout Law.

The Boy Scout Handbook defines "morally straight," as such:

> "To be a person of strong character, guide your life with honesty, purity, and justice. Respect and defend the rights of all people. Your

relationships with others should be honest and open. Be clean in your speech and actions, and faithful in your religious beliefs. The values you follow as a Scout will help you become virtuous and self-reliant."

As for the term "clean," the Boy Scout Handbook offers the following:

> "A Scout is CLEAN. *A Scout keeps his body and mind fit and clean. He chooses the company of those who live by these same ideals. He helps keep his home and community clean.*
>
> "You never need to be ashamed of dirt that will wash off. If you play hard and work hard you can't help getting dirty. But when the game is over or the work is done, that kind of dirt disappears with soap and water.
>
> "There's another kind of dirt that won't come off by washing. It is the kind that shows up in foul language and harmful thoughts.
>
> "Swear words, profanity, and dirty stories are weapons that ridicule other people and hurt their feelings. The same is true of racial slurs and jokes making fun of ethnic groups or people with physical or mental limitations. A Scout knows there is no kindness or honor in such mean-spirited behavior. He avoids it in his own words and deeds. He defends those who are targets of insults."

It is plain as the light of day that neither one of these principles — "morally straight" and "clean" — says the slightest thing about homosexuality. Indeed, neither term in the Boy Scouts' Law and Oath expresses any position whatsoever on sexual matters.

BSA's published guidance on that topic underscores this point. Scouts, for example, are directed to receive their sex education at home or in school, but not from the organization: "Your parents or guardian or a sex education teacher should give you the facts about sex that you must know." Boy Scout Handbook (1992) (reprinted in App. 211).

More specifically, BSA has set forth a number of rules for Scoutmasters when these types of issues come up:

> "You may have boys asking you for information or advice about sexual matters. . . .
>
> "How should you handle such matters?
>
> "Rule number 1: *You do not undertake to instruct Scouts, in any formalized manner, in the subject of sex and family life. The reasons are that it is not construed to be Scouting's proper area*, and that you are probably not well qualified to do this."

In light of BSA's self-proclaimed ecumenism, furthermore, it is even more difficult to discern any shared goals or common moral stance on homosexuality. Insofar as religious matters are concerned, BSA's bylaws state that it is "absolutely nonsectarian in its attitude toward . . . religious training." "The BSA does not define what constitutes duty to God or the practice of religion.

This is the responsibility of parents and religious leaders." In fact, many diverse religious organizations sponsor local Boy Scout troops.

II

The Court seeks to fill the void by pointing to a statement of "policies and procedures relating to homosexuality and Scouting" signed by BSA's President and Chief Scout Executive in 1978 and addressed to the members of the Executive Committee of the national organization.

[T]he 1978 policy was never publicly expressed — unlike, for example, the Scout's duty to be "obedient." It was an internal memorandum, never circulated beyond the few members of BSA's Executive Committee. It remained, in effect, a secret Boy Scouts policy. Far from claiming any intent to express an idea that would be burdened by the presence of homosexuals, BSA's *public* posture — to the world and to the Scouts themselves — remained what it had always been: one of tolerance, welcoming all classes of boys and young men. In this respect, BSA's claim is even weaker than those we have rejected in the past.

[I]t is apparent that the draftsmen of the policy statement foresaw the possibility that laws against discrimination might one day be amended to protect homosexuals from employment discrimination. Their statement clearly provided that, in the event such a law conflicted with their policy, a Scout's duty to be "obedient" and "obey the laws," even if "he thinks [the laws] are unfair" would prevail in such a contingency.

In 1991, BSA issued two statements both stating: "We believe that homosexual conduct is inconsistent with the requirement in the Scout Oath that a Scout be morally straight and in the Scout Law that a Scout be clean in word and deed, and that homosexuals do not provide a desirable role model for Scouts." A third statement issued in 1992 was substantially the same. By 1993, however, the policy had changed:

> "*BSA Position*
>
> "The Boy Scouts of America has always reflected the expectations that Scouting families have had for the organization.
>
> "We do not believe that homosexuals provide a role model consistent with these expectations. Accordingly, we do not allow for the registration of avowed homosexuals as members or as leaders of the BSA."

Aside from the fact that these statements were all issued after Dale's membership was revoked, there are four important points relevant to them. First, while the 1991 and 1992 statements tried to tie BSA's exclusionary policy to the meaning of the Scout Oath and Law, the 1993 statement abandoned that effort. Rather, BSA's 1993 homosexual exclusion policy was based on its view that including gays would be contrary to "the expectations that Scouting families have had for the organization."

Second, even during the brief period in 1991 and 1992, when BSA tried to connect its exclusion of homosexuals to its definition of terms found in the Oath and Law, there is no evidence that Scouts were actually taught anything about homosexuality's alleged inconsistency with those principles. Beyond the single sentence in these policy statements, there is no [illegible] goal of [illegible] homosexuality is incompatible with being "morally straight" and "clean."

. . . .

Fourth, at most the 1991 and 1992 statements declare only that BSA believed "homosexual *conduct* is inconsistent with the requirement in the Scout Oath that a Scout be morally straight and in the Scout Law that a Scout be clean in word and deed." But New Jersey's law prohibits discrimination on the basis of sexual *orientation*. And when Dale was expelled from the Boy Scouts, BSA said it did so because of his sexual orientation, not because of his sexual conduct.

III

BSA's claim finds no support in our cases. We have recognized "a right to associate for the purpose of engaging in those activities protected by the First Amendment — speech, assembly, petition for the redress of grievances, and the exercise of religion."

In *Roberts v. United States Jaycees,* we addressed just such a conflict. The Jaycees was a nonprofit membership organization " 'designed to inculcate in the individual membership . . . a spirit of genuine Americanism and civic interest, and . . . to provide . . . an avenue for intelligent participation by young men in the affairs of their community.' " But Minnesota's Human Rights Act, which applied to the Jaycees, made it unlawful to " 'deny any person the full and equal enjoyment of . . . a place of public accommodation because of . . . sex.' " The Jaycees, however, claimed that applying the law to it violated its right to associate — in particular its right to maintain its selective membership policy.

We rejected that claim. Cautioning that the right to associate is not "absolute," we held that "infringements on that right may be justified by regulations adopted to serve compelling state interests, unrelated to the suppression of ideas, that cannot be [illegible] means significantly less restrictive of associational freedoms." We found the State's purpose of eliminating discrimination is a compelling state interest that is unrelated to the suppression of ideas.

We took a similar approach in *Board of Directors of Rotary Int'l v. Rotary Club of Duarte.* "The exclusion of women," explained the group's General Secretary, "results in an 'aspect of fellowship . . . that is enjoyed by the present male membership.' " That policy also allowed the organization "to operate effectively in foreign countries with varied cultures and social mores." Though California's Civil Rights Act, which applied to Rotary International, prohibited discrimination on the basis of sex, the organization claimed a right to associate, including the right to select its members.

As in *Jaycees*, we rejected the claim, holding that "the evidence fails to demonstrate that admitting women to Rotary Clubs will affect in any significant way the existing members' ability to carry out their various purposes."

Finally, even if California's law worked a "slight infringement on Rotary members' right of expressive association, that infringement is justified because it serves the State's compelling interest in eliminating discrimination against women."

The evidence before this Court makes it exceptionally clear that BSA has, at most, simply adopted an exclusionary membership policy and has no shared goal of disapproving of homosexuality. BSA's mission statement and federal charter say nothing on the matter; its official membership policy is silent; its Scout Oath and Law — and accompanying definitions — are devoid of any view on the topic; its guidance for Scouts and Scoutmasters on sexuality declare that such matters are "not construed to be Scouting's proper area," but are the province of a Scout's parents and pastor; and BSA's posture respecting religion tolerates a wide variety of views on the issue of homosexuality. Moreover, there is simply no evidence that BSA otherwise teaches anything in this area, or that it instructs Scouts on matters involving homosexuality in ways not conveyed in the Boy Scout or Scoutmaster Handbooks. In short, Boy Scouts of America is simply silent on homosexuality. There is no shared goal or collective effort to foster a belief about homosexuality at all — let alone one that is significantly burdened by admitting homosexuals.

IV

An organization can adopt the message of its choice, and it is not this Court's place to disagree with it. But we must inquire whether the group is, in fact, expressing a message (whatever it may be) and whether that message (if one is expressed) is significantly affected by a State's antidiscrimination law. More critically, that inquiry requires our *independent* analysis, rather than deference to a group's litigating posture. Reflection on the subject dictates that such an inquiry is required.

Surely there are instances in which an organization that truly aims to foster a belief at odds with the purposes of a State's antidiscrimination laws will have a First Amendment right to association that precludes forced compliance with those laws. But that right is not a freedom to discriminate at will, nor is it a right to maintain an exclusionary membership policy simply out of fear of what the public reaction would be if the group's membership were opened up. It is an implicit right designed to protect the enumerated rights of the First Amendment, not a license to act on any discriminatory impulse. To prevail in asserting a right of expressive association as a defense to a charge of violating an antidiscrimination law, the organization must at least show it has adopted and advocated an unequivocal position inconsistent with a position advocated or epitomized by the person whom the organization seeks to exclude. If this Court were to defer to whatever position an organization is prepared to assert in its briefs, there would be no way to mark the proper boundary between genuine exercises of the right to associate, on the one hand, and sham claims that are simply attempts to insulate nonexpressive private discrimination, on the other hand. Shielding a litigant's claim from judicial scrutiny would, in turn, render civil rights legislation a nullity, and turn this important constitutional right into a farce. Accordingly, the Court's prescription of total deference will not do.

It is, of course, a valid concern that a court's independent review may run the risk of paying too little heed to an organization's sincerely held views. But unless one is prepared to turn the right to associate into a free pass out of antidiscrimination laws, an independent inquiry is a necessity. Though the group must show that its expressive activities will be substantially burdened by the State's law, if that law truly has a significant effect on a group's speech, even the subtle speaker will be able to identify that impact.

In this case, no such concern is warranted. It is entirely clear that BSA in fact expresses no clear, unequivocal message burdened by New Jersey's law.

V

Even if BSA's right to associate argument fails, it nonetheless might have a First Amendment right to refrain from including debate and dialogue about homosexuality as part of its mission to instill values in Scouts. It can, for example, advise Scouts who are entering adulthood and have questions about sex to talk "with your parents, religious leaders, teachers, or Scoutmaster," and, in turn, it can direct Scoutmasters who are asked such questions "not undertake to instruct Scouts, in any formalized manner, in the subject of sex and family life" because "it is not construed to be Scouting's proper area." See *supra*, at 7–8. Dale's right to advocate certain beliefs in a public forum or in a private debate does not include a right to advocate these ideas when he is working as a Scoutmaster. And BSA cannot be compelled to include a message about homosexuality among the values it actually chooses to teach its Scouts, if it would prefer to remain silent on that subject.

BSA has not contended, nor does the record support, that Dale had ever advocated a view on homosexuality to his troop before his membership was revoked. Accordingly, BSA's revocation could only have been based on an assumption that he would do so in the future. But the only information BSA had at the time it revoked Dale's membership was a newspaper article describing a seminar at Rutgers University on the topic of [illegible] teenagers that Dale [illegible]

Nothing in that article, however, even remotely suggests that Dale would advocate any views on homosexuality to his troop. The Scoutmaster Handbook instructs Dale, like all Scoutmasters, that sexual issues are not their "proper area," and there is no evidence that Dale had any intention of violating this rule. Indeed, from all accounts Dale was a model Boy Scout and Assistant Scoutmaster up until the day his membership was revoked, and there is no reason to believe that he would suddenly disobey the directives of BSA because of anything he said in the newspaper article.

As BSA itself puts it, its rights are "not implicated *unless* a prospective leader *presents himself* as a role model inconsistent with Boy Scouting's understanding of the Scout Oath and Law."

The majority, though, does not rest its conclusion on the claim that Dale will use his position as a bully pulpit. Rather, it contends that Dale's mere presence among the Boy Scouts will itself force the group to convey a message about homosexuality — even if Dale has no intention of doing so.

The majority's argument relies exclusively on *Hurley v. Irish-American Gay, Lesbian and Bisexual Group of Boston, Inc.*

Though *Hurley* has a superficial similarity to the present case, a close inspection reveals a wide gulf between that case and the one before us today.

First, it was critical to our analysis that GLIB was actually conveying a message by participating in the parade — otherwise, the parade organizers could hardly claim that they were being forced to include any unwanted message at all. Our conclusion that GLIB was conveying a message was inextricably tied to the fact that GLIB wanted to march in a parade, as well as the manner in which it intended to march.

Second, we found it relevant that GLIB's message "would likely be perceived" as the parade organizers' own speech. That was so because "parades and demonstrations . . . are not understood to be so neutrally presented or selectively viewed" as, say, a broadcast by a cable operator, who is usually considered to be "merely 'a conduit' for the speech" produced by others. Rather, parade organizers are usually understood to make the "customary determination about a unit admitted to the parade."

Dale's inclusion in the Boy Scouts is nothing like the case in Hurley. His participation sends no cognizable message to the Scouts or to the world. Unlike GLIB, Dale did not carry a banner or a sign; he did not distribute any fact sheet; and he expressed no intent to send any message. If there is any kind of message being sent, then, it is by the mere act of joining the Boy Scouts. Such an act does not constitute an instance of symbolic speech under the First Amendment.

Another difference between this case and *Hurley* lies in the fact that *Hurley* involved the parade organizers' claim to determine the content of the message they wish to give at a particular time and place. The standards governing such a claim are simply different from the standards that govern BSA's claim of a right of expressive association. Generally, a private person or a private organization has a right to refuse to broadcast a message with which it disagrees, and a right to refuse to contradict or garble its own specific statement at any given place or time by including the messages of others. An expressive association claim, however, normally involves the avowal and advocacy of a consistent position on some issue over time. This is why a different kind of scrutiny must be given to an expressive association claim, lest the right of expressive association simply turn into a right to discriminate whenever some group can think of an expressive object that would seem to be inconsistent with the admission of some person as a member or at odds with the appointment of a person to a leadership position in the group.

The State of New Jersey has decided that people who are open and frank about their sexual orientation are entitled to equal access to employment as school teachers, police officers, librarians, athletic coaches, and a host of other jobs filled by citizens who serve as role models for children and adults alike. Dozens of Scout units throughout the State are sponsored by public agencies, such as schools and fire departments, that employ such role models. BSA's affiliation with numerous public agencies that comply with New Jersey's law against discrimination cannot be understood to convey any particular message endorsing or condoning the activities of all these people.

VI

Unfavorable opinions about homosexuals "have ancient roots." *Bowers v. Hardwick.* Like equally atavistic opinions about certain racial groups, those roots have been nourished by sectarian doctrine.

That such prejudices are still prevalent and that they have caused serious and tangible harm to countless members of the class New Jersey seeks to protect are established matters of fact that neither the Boy Scouts nor the Court disputes. That harm can only be aggravated by the creation of a constitutional shield for a policy that is itself the product of a habitual way of thinking about strangers. As Justice Brandeis so wisely advised, "we must be ever on our guard, lest we erect our prejudices into legal principles."

If we would guide by the light of reason, we must let our minds be bold. I respectfully dissent.

Justice **Souter**, with whom Justice **Ginsburg** and Justice **Breyer** join, dissenting.

I join Justice Stevens's dissent but add this further word on the significance of Part VI of his opinion. There, Justice Stevens describes the changing attitudes toward gay people and notes a parallel with the decline of stereotypical thinking about race and gender. The legitimacy of New Jersey's interest in forbidding discrimination on all these bases by those furnishing public accommodations is, as Justice Stevens indicates, acknowledged by many to be beyond question. The fact that we are cognizant of this laudable decline in stereotypical thinking on homosexuality should not, however, be taken to control the resolution of this case.

The right of expressive association does not, of course, turn on the popularity of the views advanced by a group that claims protection. Whether the group appears to this Court to be in the vanguard or rearguard of social thinking is irrelevant to the group's rights. I conclude that BSA has not made out an expressive association claim therefore, not because of what BSA may espouse, but because of its failure to make sexual orientation the subject of any unequivocal advocacy, using the channels it customarily employs to state its message. As Justice Stevens explains, no group can claim a right of expressive association without identifying a clear position to be advocated over time in an unequivocal way. To require less, and to allow exemption from a public accommodations statute based on any individual's difference from an alleged group ideal, however expressed and however inconsistently claimed, would convert the right of expressive association into an easy trump of any antidiscrimination law.

If, on the other hand, an expressive association claim has met the conditions Justice Stevens describes as necessary, there may well be circumstances in which the antidiscrimination law must yield, as he says. It is certainly possible for an individual to become so identified with a position as to epitomize it publicly. When that position is at odds with a group's advocated position, applying an antidiscrimination statute to require the group's acceptance of the individual in a position of group leadership could so modify or muddle or frustrate the group's advocacy as to violate the expressive associational right. While it is not our business here to rule on any such hypothetical, it is at least clear that our estimate of the progressive character of the group's position will be irrelevant to the First Amendment analysis if such a case comes to us for decision.

NOTES AND QUESTIONS

1. In *Dale*, the New Jersey Supreme Court found the Boy Scouts were covered by New Jersey's public accommodation statutes (and hence could not discriminate). How could this be so? In what way are they akin to a restaurant or hotel? Or a church — which presumably may ban homosexuals? See appendix to Chief Justice Rehnquist's opinion.
2. Was the problem in *Dale* that the Boy Scouts had never really viewed homosexuality as immoral? Or that the view was not central to their set of beliefs and activities? Or that such a belief is impermissible (and, if so, why)? Or that the Boy Scouts did not engage in "expressive association?"
3. Given *Roberts* and *Hurley*, how could the Boy Scouts win in *Dale*?
4. Why might the Boy Scouts want to exclude homosexuals? Women? Atheists? Are these in some sense equal?
5. Would *Dale* have come out differently if the Boy Scouts excluded African-Americans, on the ground that God disfavors them? If your answer is yes, how would you square that conclusion with Justice Rehnquist's concluding comments, that the Court does not evaluate a group's beliefs?
6. Is Justice Stevens' dissent arguing that the Boy Scouts don't really believe that homosexuals are not "clean" or "morally straight"? Or is he arguing that it's a recent assertion by some Scout leaders, but not all? Is either of these permissible under the First Amendment? Or is it that they never implemented the policy?
7. What would the Boy Scouts have to do in order to persuade Justice Stevens of their "shared purpose" to discriminate? Even if they did, would he still (especially then) find a compelling state interest overrode the group's purpose?
8. And what does Justice Stevens envision the Boy Scouts must do in regard to "debate and dialogue about homosexuality"? Is the position consistent with his position on discrimination?
9. If you were James Dale, would you have brought this suit? Having won it, would you stay in the Scouts? Be openly gay at Scout functions? Proselytize? If the latter, would that then defeat Justice Stevens' attempt to distinguish *Hurley*?
10. Justice Stevens closes by equating discrimination against homosexuals with that against race. Justice Souter distances himself from this. Why?

And how would their (and the majority's) views be affected — if at all — by the later decision in *Lawrence v. Texas*?

11. Finally, at a national meeting of the Boy Scouts of America, how would you [illegible] your position (pro or con) on what the policy should be? Could you draw support from Rawls?

An ethical society must accommodate conscience and conduct related to it. Persons of principle are to be treasured. But when their principles conflict with those of others, the questions posed are how the accommodation must be effected, and what is the proper amount of dissent.

PLANNED PARENTHOOD OF THE COLUMBIA/ WILLAMETTE, INC. v. AMERICAN COALITION OF LIFE ACTIVISTS

290 F.3d 1058 (9th Cir. 2002)

Rymer, Circuit Judge.

For the first time we construe what the Freedom of Access to Clinics Entrances Act (FACE), 18 U.S.C. § 248, means by "threat of force." FACE gives aggrieved persons a right of action against whoever by "threat of force . . . intentionally . . . intimidates . . . any person because that person is or has been . . . providing reproductive health services." 18 U.S.C. § 248(a)(1) and (c)(1)(A). This requires that we define "threat of force" in a way that comports with the First Amendment, and it raises the question whether the conduct that occurred here falls within the category of unprotected speech.

Four physicians, Dr. Robert Crist, Dr. Warren M. Hern, Dr. Elizabeth Newhall, and Dr. James Newhall, and two health clinics that provide medical services to women including abortions, Planned Parenthood of the Columbia/ Willamette, Inc. (PPCW) and the Portland Feminist Women's Health Center (PFWHC), brought suit under FACE claiming that they were targeted with threats by the American Coalition of Life Activists (ACLA), Advocates for Life Ministries (ALM), and numerous individuals. Three threats remain at issue: the Deadly Dozen "GUILTY" poster which identifies Hern and the Newhalls among ten others; the Crist "GUILTY" poster with Crist's name, addresses and photograph; and the "Nuremberg Files," which is a compilation about those whom the ACLA anticipated one day might be put on trial for crimes against humanity. The "GUILTY" posters identifying specific physicians were circulated in the wake of a series of "WANTED" and "unWANTED" posters that had identified other doctors who performed abortions before they were murdered.

Although the posters do not contain a threat on their face, the district court held that context could be considered. It defined a threat under FACE in accordance with our "true threat" jurisprudence, as a statement made when "a reasonable person would foresee that the statement would be interpreted by those to whom the maker communicates the statement as a serious expression of intent to harm." Applying this definition, the court denied ACLA's motion for summary judgment in a published opinion. *Planned Parenthood of the Columbia/Willamette, Inc. v. ACLA (PPCW II)*, 23 F. Supp. 2d 1182 (D.Or.1998). The jury returned a verdict in physicians' favor, and the court enjoined ACLA from publishing the posters or providing other materials with the specific intent to threaten Crist, Hern, Elizabeth Newhall, James Newhall, PPCW, or the Health Center. *Planned Parenthood of the Columbia/Willamette, Inc. v. ACLA* (PPCW III), 41 F. Supp. 2d 1130 (D.Or.1999). *ACLA timely appealed.*

As we see no reversible error on liability or in the equitable relief that was granted, we affirm. However, we remand for consideration of whether the punitive damages award comports with due process.

I

The facts are fully set out in the district court's order granting injunctive relief, PPWC III, 41 F. Supp. 2d at 1131–1155, and we shall not belabor them. In sum:

On March 10, 1993, Michael Griffin shot and killed Dr. David Gunn as he entered an abortion clinic in Pensacola, Florida. Before this, a "WANTED" and an "unWANTED" poster with Gunn's name, photograph, address and other personal information were published. The "WANTED" poster describes Gunn as an abortionist and invites participation by prayer and fasting, by writing and calling him and sharing a willingness to help him leave his profession, and by asking him to stop doing abortions; the "unWANTED" poster states that he kills children at designated locations and "[t]o defenseless unborn babies Gunn in [sic] heavily armed and very dangerous." After Gunn's murder, Bray and Paul Hill (a non-party who was later convicted of murdering a different doctor) prepared a statement supporting Griffin's acquittal on a justifiable homicide theory, which ALM, Burnett, Crane, Dodds, Foreman, McMillan, Ramey and Stover joined.

On August 21, 1993, Dr. George Patterson, who operated the clinic where Gunn worked, was shot to death. A "WANTED" poster had been circulated prior to his murder, indicating where he performed abortions and that he had Gunn perform abortions for his Pensacola clinic.

In July 1994, Dr. John Bayard Britton was murdered by Paul Hill after being named on an "unWANTED" poster that Hill helped to prepare. One gives Britton's physical description together with his home and office addresses and phone numbers, and charges "crimes against humanity"; another also displays his picture and states that "he is considered armed and extremely dangerous to women and children. Pray that he is soon apprehended by the love of Jesus!!!" In addition to these items, a third version of the Britton "unWANTED" poster lists personal achievements and Britton's "crimes against humanity," also warning that "John Bayard Britton is considered armed and extremely dangerous, especialy [sic] to women and children." ALM, Bray, Burnett, Crane, McMillan, Ramey and Stover signed a petition supporting Hill.

Many pro-life activists in Operation Rescue condemned these acts of violence. As a result, ALM, Bray, Burnett, Crane, Foreman, McMillan, Ramey and Stover, who espoused a "pro-force" point of view, split off to form ACLA.

ACLA presented the Deadly Dozen poster during a January 25, 1995 press conference at the March for Life event in Washington, D.C. Bray, Burnett,

Crane, Dodds, Foreman, McMillan, Murch, Ramey, Stover, Treshman and Wysong were there; Dreste later ratified the poster's release. This poster is captioned "GUILTY" at the top (which meant the same thing to Crane, who drafted it, as "wanted"), beneath which in slightly smaller print the poster indicates "OF CRIMES AGAINST HUMANITY." The poster continues: "Abortion was provided as a choice for East European and Jewish women by the (Nazi) National Socialist Regime, and was prosecuted during the Nuremberg Trials (1945-46) under Allied Control Order No. 10 as a 'war crime.' " Under the heading "THE DEADLY DOZEN," the poster identifies thirteen doctors of whom James Newhall, Elizabeth Newhall, and Warren Hern are three. The poster provides Hern's residence and the home address of James Newhall and Elizabeth Newhall; it also lists the name and home address of Dr. George Kabacy, a doctor who provided abortions at PPCW. It offers a "$5,000 REWARD" "for information leading to arrest, conviction and revocation of license to practice medicine." At the bottom the poster bears the legend "ABORTIONIST" in large, bold typeface. The day after the Deadly Dozen poster was released, the FBI offered protection to doctors identified on it and advised them to wear bulletproof vests and take other security precautions, which they did. Knowing this, ALM reprinted the poster in the March 1995 edition of its magazine Life Advocate under a cover with the "grim reaper" holding a scythe; Murch printed it in his newsletter Salt & Light; and ACLA republished the Deadly Dozen poster at events in August 1995 and January 1996.

ACLA released the Crist poster along with five others in August 1995 at the old federal courthouse in St. Louis where the Dred Scott decision had been handed down. Burnett, Crane, Dreste, McMillan, Ramey, Stover and Wysong attended the event. Three of the posters identify doctors; the others identify reproductive health care clinics, one of which was a Planned Parenthood affiliate where Crist worked. The Crist poster has "GUILTY" in large bold letters at the top followed by "OF CRIMES AGAINST HUMANITY" in smaller font. It also gives his home and work addresses; states "Please write, leaflet or picket his neighborhood to expose his blood guilt"; offers a "$500 REWARD" "to any ACLA organization that successfully persuades Crist to turn from his child killing through activities within ACLA guidelines"; and has "ABORTIONIST" in large bold type at the bottom.

At its January 1996 conference, ACLA displayed the Deadly Dozen poster, held a "White Rose Banquet" to honor prisoners convicted of anti-abortion violence, and introduced ALM's Paul deParrie to unveil the "Nuremberg Files." ACLA sent a hard copy of some of the Files to Neal Horsley (a non-party) to post on the internet, and ACLA's name appeared on the Nuremberg Files website opened in January 1997. Approximately 200 people are listed under the label "ABORTIONISTS: the shooters," and 200 more are listed under Files for judges, politicians, law enforcement, spouses, and abortion rights supporters. Crist, Hern and the Newhalls are listed in the "abortionists" section, which bears the legend: "Black font (working); Greyed-out Name (wounded); Strikethrough (fatality)." The names of Gunn, Patterson and Britton are struck through.

By January 1995 ACLA knew the effect that "WANTED," "unWANTED," or "GUILTY" posters had on doctors named in them. For example, in a

September 1993 issue of Life Advocate which reported that an "unwanted" poster was being prepared for Britton, ALM remarked of the Gunn murder that it "sent shock waves of fear through the ranks of abortion providers across the country. As a result, many more doctors quit out of fear for their lives, and the ones who are left are scared stiff." Of another doctor who decided to quit performing abortions after circulation of a "Not Wanted" poster, Bray wrote that "it is clear to all who possess faculties capable of inductive analysis: he was bothered and afraid." Wysong also stated: "Listening to what abortionists said, abortionists who have quit the practice who are no longer killing babies but are now pro-life. They said the two things they feared the most were being sued for malpractice and having their picture put on a poster." And Burnett testified with respect to the danger that "wanted" or "guilty" posters pose to the lives of those who provide abortions: "I mean, if I was an abortionist, I would be afraid."

By January 1995 the physicians knew about the Gunn, Patterson and Britton murders and the posters that preceded each. Hern was terrified when his name appeared on the Deadly Dozen poster; as he put it: "The fact that wanted posters about these doctors had been circulated, prior to their assassination, and that the — that the posters, then, were followed by the doctor's assassination, emphasized for me the danger posed by this document, the Deadly Dozen List, which meant to me that — that, as night follows day, that my name was on this wanted poster . . . and that I would be assassinated, as had the other doctors been assassinated." Hern interpreted the poster as meaning "Do what we tell you to do, or we will kill you. And they do." Crist was "truly frightened," and stopped practicing medicine for a while out of fear for his life. Dr. Elizabeth Newhall interpreted the Deadly Dozen poster as saying that if she didn't stop doing abortions, her life was at risk. Dr. James Newhall was "severely frightened" in light of the "clear pattern" of a wanted poster and a murder when there was "another wanted poster with my name on it."

The jury found for plaintiffs on all claims except for Bray and Treshman on the RICO claims. The district court then considered equitable relief. It found that each defendant used intimidation as a means of interfering with the provision of reproductive health services; that each independently and as a co-conspirator published and distributed the Deadly Dozen poster, the Crist poster, and the Nuremberg Files; and that each acted with malice and specific intent in communicating true threats to kill, assault or do bodily harm to each of the plaintiffs to intimidate them from engaging in legal medical practices and procedures. The court found that the balance of hardships weighed "overwhelmingly" in plaintiffs' favor. It also found that the defendants' actions were not protected speech under the First Amendment. Accordingly, it issued a permanent injunction restraining defendants from threatening, with the specific intent to do so, any of the plaintiffs in violation of FACE; from publishing or distributing the Deadly Dozen poster and the Crist poster with specific intent to threaten the plaintiffs; from providing additional material concerning plaintiffs, with a specific intent to threaten, to the Nuremberg Files or similar web site; and from publishing or distributing the personally identifying information about the plaintiffs in the Files with a specific intent to threaten. The court also required defendants to turn over materials that are not in compliance with the injunction except for one copy of anything included in the record, which counsel was permitted [illegible]

III

ACLA argues that the First Amendment requires reversal because liability was based on political speech that constituted neither an incitement to imminent lawless action nor a true threat. It suggests that the key question for us to consider is whether these posters can be considered "true threats" when, in fact, the posters on their face contain no explicitly threatening language. Further, ACLA submits that classic political speech cannot be converted into non-protected speech by a context of violence that includes the independent action of others.

Physicians counter that this threats case must be analyzed under the settled threats law of this circuit. Following precedent, it was proper for the jury to take context into account. They point out that the district court limited evidence of anti-abortion violence to evidence tending to show knowledge of a particular defendant, and maintain that the objective standard on which the jury was instructed comports both with Ninth Circuit law and congressional intent. As the First Amendment does not protect true threats of force, physicians conclude, ACLA's speech was not protected.

A

We start with the statute under which this action arises. Section 248(c)(1)(A) gives a private right of action to any person aggrieved by reason of the conduct prohibited by subsection (a). Subsection (a)(1) provides:

> (a) . . . Whoever —
>
> (1) by force or threat of force or by physical obstruction, intentionally injures, intimidates or interferes with or attempts to injure, intimidate or interfere with any person because that person is or has been, or in order to intimidate such person or any other person or any class of persons from, obtaining or providing reproductive health services . . . shall be subject to the civil remedies provided in subsection (c). . . .

18 U.S.C. § 248(a)(1). The statute also provides that "[n]othing in this section shall be construed . . . to prohibit any expressive conduct (including peaceful picketing or other peaceful demonstration) protected from legal prohibition by the First Amendment to the Constitution." 18 U.S.C. § 248(d)(1).

FACE does not define "threat," although it does provide that "[t]he term 'intimidate' means to place a person in reasonable apprehension of bodily harm to him — or herself or to another." 18 U.S.C. § 248(e)(3). Thus, the first task is to define "threat" for purposes of the Act. This requires a definition that comports with the First Amendment, that is, a "true threat."

The Supreme Court has provided benchmarks, but no definition.

Brandenburg v. Ohio, 395 U.S. 444, 447 (1969), makes it clear that the First Amendment protects speech that advocates violence, so long as the speech is not directed to inciting or producing imminent lawless action and is not likely to incite or produce such action. So do *Hess v. Indiana*, 414 U.S. 105 (1973) (overturning disorderly conduct conviction of antiwar protestor who yelled "We'll take the fucking street later (or again)"), and *NAACP v. Claiborne Hardware Co.*, 458 U.S. 886 (1982). If ACLA had merely endorsed or encouraged the violent actions of others, its speech would be protected.

However, while advocating violence is protected, threatening a person with violence is not. In *Watts v. United States*, 394 U.S. 705 (1969), the Court explicitly distinguished between political hyperbole, which is protected, and true threats, which are not. Considering how to construe a statute which prohibited "knowingly and willfully . . . (making) any threat to take the life of or to inflict bodily harm upon the President," the Court admonished that any statute which criminalizes a form of pure speech "must be interpreted with the commands of the First Amendment clearly in mind. What is a threat must be distinguished from what is constitutionally protected speech." In that case, an 18-year old war protester told a discussion group of other young people at a public rally on the Washington Monument grounds: "They always holler at us to get an education. And now I have already received my draft classification as 1-A and I have got to report for my physical this Monday coming. I am not going. If they ever make me carry a rifle the first man I want to get in my sights is L.B.J." His audience laughed. Taken in context, and given the conditional nature of the statement and the reaction of the listeners, the Court concluded that the speech could not be interpreted other than as "a kind of very crude offensive method of stating a political opposition to the President." Accordingly, it ordered judgment entered for Watts.

ACLA's position is that the posters, including the Nuremberg Files, are protected political speech under Watts, and cannot lose this character by context. But this is not correct. The Court itself considered context and determined that Watts's statement was political hyperbole instead of a true threat because of context. Beyond this, ACLA points out that the posters contain no language that is a threat. We agree that this is literally true. Therefore, ACLA submits, this case is really an incitement case in disguise. So viewed, the posters are protected speech under *Brandenburg* and *Claiborne*, which ACLA suggests is the closest analogue. We disagree that *Claiborne* is closely analogous.

In March 1966 black citizens in Claiborne County made a list of demands for racial equality and integration. Unsatisfied by the response, several hundred black persons at a meeting of the local National Association for the Advancement of Colored People (NAACP) voted to place a boycott on white merchants in the area. The boycott continued until October 1969. During this period, stores were watched and the names of persons who violated the boycott were read at meetings of the NAACP at the First Baptist Church, and published in a local paper called "Black Times." These persons were branded as traitors to the black cause, were called demeaning names, and were socially ostracized. A few incidents of violence occurred. Birdshot was fired at the houses of two boycott violators; a brick was thrown through a windshield; and a flower garden was damaged. None of the victims ceased trading with white merchants. Six other incidents of arguably unlawful conduct occurred. White business owners brought suit against the NAACP and Charles Evers, its field secretary, along with other individuals who had participated in the boycott, for violating Mississippi state laws on malicious interference with a business, antitrust, and illegal boycott. Plaintiffs pursued several theories of liability: participating in management of the boycott; serving as an "enforcer" or monitor; committing or threatening acts of violence, which showed that the perpetrator wanted the boycott to succeed by coercion when it could not succeed by persuasion; and as to Evers, threatening violence against boycott breakers, and as to the NAACP because he was its field secretary when he committed tortious and constitutionally unprotected acts. Damages for business losses during the boycott and injunctive relief were awarded.

The Court held that there could be no recovery based on intimidation by threats of social ostracism, because offensive and coercive speech is protected by the First Amendment. "The use of speeches, marches, and threats of social ostracism cannot provide the basis for a damages award. But violent conduct is beyond the pale of constitutional protection." There was some evidence of violence, but the violence was not pervasive as it had been in *Milk Wagon Drivers Union Local 753 v. Meadowmoor Dairies, Inc.*, 312 U.S. 287 (1941). Accordingly, the Court made clear that only losses proximately caused by unlawful conduct could be recovered. Further, civil liability could not be imposed consistent with the First Amendment solely on account of an individual's association with others who have committed acts of violence; he must have incited or authorized them himself.

Claiborne, of course, did not arise under a threats statute. The Court had no need to consider whether Evers's statements were true threats of force within the meaning of a threats statute; it held only that his speeches did not incite illegal activity, thus could not have caused business losses and could not be the basis for liability to white merchants. As the opinion points out, there was no context to give the speeches (including the expression "break your neck") the implication of authorizing or directly threatening unlawful conduct. To the extent there was any intimidating overtone, Evers's rhetoric was extemporaneous, surrounded by statements supporting non-violent action, and primarily of the social ostracism sort.

Thus, *Watts* was the only Supreme Court case that discussed the First Amendment in relation to threats before we first confronted the issue. Apart from holding that Watts's crack about L.B.J. was not a true threat, the Court set out no standard for determining when a statement is a true threat that is unprotected speech under the First Amendment. Shortly after *Watts* was rendered, we had to decide in *Roy v. United States*, 416 F.2d 874 (9th Cir.1969), whether a Marine Corps private made a true threat for purposes of 18 U.S.C. § 871 against the President, who was coming to his base the next day, by saying: "I am going to get him." We adopted a "reasonable speaker" test. As it has come to be articulated, the test is:

> Whether a particular statement may properly be considered to be a threat is governed by an objective standard — whether a reasonable person would foresee that the statement would be interpreted by those to whom the maker communicates the statement as a serious expression of intent to harm or assault.

United States v. Orozco-Santillan, 903 F.2d 1262, 1265 (9th Cir.1990).

It is not necessary that the defendant intend to, or be able to carry out his threat; the only intent requirement for a true threat is that the defendant intentionally or knowingly communicate the threat. Nevertheless, we are urged to adopt a subjective intent requirement for FACE. In particular, amicus ACLU Foundation of Oregon, Inc., advocates a subjective intent component to "require evidence, albeit circumstantial or inferential in many cases, that the speaker actually intended to induce fear, intimidation, or terror; namely, that the speaker intended to threaten. If a person did not intend to threaten or intimidate (*i.e.*, did not intend that his or her statement be understood as a threat), then the speech should not be considered to be a 'true threat,' unprotected by the First Amendment." However, this much is subsumed within the statutory standard of FACE itself, which requires that the threat of force be made with the intent to intimidate.

Therefore, we hold that "threat of force" in FACE means what our settled threats law says a true threat is: a statement which, in the entire context and under all the circumstances, a reasonable person would foresee would be interpreted by those to whom the statement is communicated as a serious expression of intent to inflict bodily harm upon that person. So defined, a threatening statement that violates FACE is unprotected under the First Amendment.

B

Although ACLA does not believe we should reach this point, if we do it submits that no claim was made out even under "true threats" cases. First, it argues that other threats cases were criminal actions against someone who made a real threat directly to others, not political speech as is the case here.

ACLA also maintains that "context" means the direct circumstances surrounding delivery of the threat, or evidence sufficient to resolve ambiguity in the words of the statement — not two weeks of testimony as occurred here in the district court. Otherwise, ACLA submits, FACE is facially invalid. However, none of our cases has limited "context" to explaining ambiguous words, or to delivery. We, and so far as we can tell, other circuits as well, consider the whole factual context and "all of the circumstances."

Nor does consideration of context amount to viewpoint discrimination, as ACLA contends. ACLA's theory appears to be that because the posters did not contain any threat on their face, the views of abortion foes are chilled more than the views of abortion-right proponents because of the random acts of violence committed by some people against abortion providers. However, FACE itself is viewpoint neutral.

Because of context, we conclude that the Crist and Deadly Dozen posters are not just a political statement. Even if the Gunn poster, which was the first "WANTED" poster, was a purely political message when originally issued, and even if the Britton poster were too, by the time of the Crist poster, the poster format itself had acquired currency as a death threat for abortion providers. Gunn was killed after his poster was released; Britton was killed after his poster was released; and Patterson was killed after his poster was released. Knowing this, and knowing the fear generated among those in the reproductive health services community who were singled out for [illegible] tion on a "wanted"-type poster, ACLA [illegible] identified Crist on a "GUILTY" [illegible] intentionally put the names of Hern and the Newhalls on the Deadly Dozen "GUILTY" poster to intimidate them. This goes well beyond the political message (regardless of what one thinks of it) that abortionists are killers who deserve death too.

The Nuremberg Files are somewhat different. Although they name individuals, they name hundreds of them. The avowed intent is "collecting dossiers on abortionists in anticipation that one day we may be able to hold them on trial for crimes against humanity." The web page states: "One of the great tragedies of the Nuremberg trials of Nazis after WWII was that complete information and documented evidence had not been collected so many war criminals went free or were only found guilty of minor crimes. We do not want the same thing to happen when the day comes to charge abortionists with their crimes. We anticipate the day when these people will be charged in PERFECTLY LEGAL COURTS once the tide of this nation's opinion turns against child-killing (as it surely will)." However offensive or disturbing this might be to those listed in the Files, being offensive and provocative is protected under the First Amendment. But, in two critical respects, the Files go further. In addition to listing judges, politicians and law enforcement personnel, the Files separately categorize "Abortionists" and list the names of individuals who provide abortion services, including, specifically, Crist, Hern, and both Newhalls. Also, names of abortion providers who have been murdered because of their activities are lined through in black, while names of those who have been wounded are highlighted in grey. As a result, we cannot say that it is clear as a matter of law that listing Crist, Hern, and the Newhalls on both the Nuremberg Files and the GUILTY posters is purely protected, political expression.

Accordingly, whether the Crist Poster, the Deadly Dozen poster, and the identification of Crist, Hern, Dr. Elizabeth Newhall and Dr. James Newhall in the Nuremberg Files as well as on "wanted"-type posters, constituted true threats was properly for the jury to decide.

. . . .

D

ACLA joins in Treshman's assertion that the court erroneously admitted prejudicial evidence by permitting: an FBI agent and two federal marshals to testify that the FBI and the Justice Department considered ACLA's two posters to be "serious threats"; references to non-party violence; introduction of defendants' arrests; physicians' counsel to tell the jury about Bray's invocations of the Fifth Amendment through a summary of his deposition; references to actions of certain defendants and non-parties on the abortion debate and to such things as the signing of "Defensive Action petitions" by five or six of the individual defendants; an exhibit with Rev. Sullivan's hearsay opinion that ACLA is a "cancer" which prolifers must "cut out immediately" before it "destroys the pro-life movement" to remain in the exhibit books; and by permitting deposition summaries to be introduced. ACLA recognizes that evidentiary rulings are normally reviewed for an abuse of discretion, but argues that in cases raising First Amendment issues appellate courts must independently examine the record for evidentiary errors which penalize political speech or allow "a forbidden intrusion on the field of free expression." *Milkovich v. Lorain Journal Co.*, 497 U.S. 1, 17 (1990) (citation omitted).

Testimony about the law enforcement officers' response to the Crist and Deadly Dozen "GUILTY" posters had some tendency to show the physicians' state of mind when they found out they were named on "wanted"-type posters, as well as to show the knowledge and intent of ACLA in distributing the posters regardless of the reaction they precipitated. Both are nonhearsay purposes. No testimony was allowed about what officers thought the posters meant.

ACLA's knowledge of prior violence and its effect on reproductive health services providers bore directly on its intent to intimidate physicians, and was limited by the district court to that relevant purpose. Bray's invocation of the Fifth Amendment was not improperly admitted as to him in a civil trial. Coconspirator statements were admissible so long as they were connected to the conspiracy and the jury found that the statements were made in furtherance of it. The same is true of the Defensive Action petitions, which were clearly admissible against those defendants who signed them and as to others with whom the signatories were conspiring.

. . . .

F

As a direct result of having a "GUILTY" poster out on them, physicians wore bullet-proof vests and took other extraordinary security measures to protect themselves and their families. ACLA had every reason to foresee that its expression of intent to harm (the "GUILTY" poster identifying Crist, Hern, Elizabeth Newhall and James Newhall by name and putting them in the File that tracks hits and misses) would elicit this reaction. Physicians' fear did not simply happen; ACLA intended to intimidate them from doing what they do.

This is the point of the statute and is conduct that we are satisfied lacks any protection under the First Amendment.

Violence is not a protected value. Nor is a true threat of violence with intent to intimidate. ACLA may have been staking out a position for debate when it merely advocated violence as in Bray's A Time to Kill, or applauded it, as in the Defense Action petitions. Likewise, when it created the Nuremberg Files in the abstract, because the First Amendment does not preclude calling people demeaning or inflammatory names, or threatening social ostracism or vilification to advocate a political position. *Claiborne*, 458 U.S. at 903, 909–12. But, after being on "wanted"-type posters, Dr. Gunn, Dr. Patterson, and Dr. Britton can no longer participate in the debate. By replicating the poster pattern that preceded the elimination of Gunn, Patterson and Britton, and by putting Crist, Hern, and the Newhalls in an abortionists' File that scores fatalities, ACLA was not staking out a position of debate but of threatened demise. This turns the First Amendment on its head.

Like fighting words, true threats are proscribable. We therefore conclude that the judgment of liability in physicians' favor is constitutionally permissible.

CONCLUSION

A "threat of force" for purposes of FACE is properly defined in accordance with our long-standing test on "true threats," as "whether a reasonable person would foresee that the statement would be interpreted by those to whom the maker communicates the statement as a serious expression of intent to harm or assault." This, coupled with the statute's requirement of intent to intimidate, comports with the First Amendment.

We have reviewed the record and are satisfied that use of the Crist Poster, the Deadly Dozen Poster, and the individual plaintiffs' listing in the Nuremberg Files constitute a true threat. In three prior incidents, a "wanted" — type poster identifying a specific doctor who provided abortion services was circulated, and the doctor named on the poster was killed. ACLA and physicians knew of this, and both understood the significance of the particular posters specifically identifying each of them. ACLA realized that "wanted" or "guilty" posters had a threatening meaning that physicians would take seriously. In conjunction with the "guilty" posters, being listed on a Nuremberg Files scorecard for abortion providers impliedly threatened physicians with being next on a hit list. To this extent only, the Files are also a true threat. However, the Nuremberg Files are protected speech.

There is substantial evidence that these posters were prepared and disseminated to intimidate physicians from providing reproductive health services. Thus, ACLA was appropriately found liable for a true threat to intimidate under FACE.

Holding ACLA accountable for this conduct does not impinge on legitimate protest or advocacy. Restraining it from continuing to threaten these physicians burdens speech no more than necessary.

Therefore, we affirm the judgment in all respects but for punitive damages, as to which we remand.

Affirmed in Part; Vacated and Remanded in Part.

Reinhardt, Circuit Judge, with whom Kozinski, Kleinfeld, and

Berzon, Circuit Judges, join, dissenting:

I concur fully in both Judge Kozinski's and Judge Berzon's dissents. The differences between the majority and dissenting opinions with respect to the First Amendment are clear. I write separately to emphasize one point: the majority rejects the concept that speech made in a political forum on issues of public concern warrants heightened scrutiny. This rejection, if allowed to stand, would significantly weaken the First Amendment protections we now enjoy. It is a fundamental tenet of First Amendment jurisprudence that political speech in a public arena is different from purely private speech directed at an individual. See *NAACP v. Claiborne Hardware Co.*, 458 U.S. 886,

926–27 (1982); *Watts v. United States*, 394 U.S. 705, 708 (1969); *New York Times Co. v. Sullivan*, 376 U.S. 254, 270 (1964); *Terminiello v. City of Chicago*, 337 U.S. 1, 4 (1949). Political speech, ugly or frightening as it may sometimes be, lies at the heart of our democratic process. Private threats delivered one-on-one do not. The majority's unwillingness to recognize the difference is extremely troublesome. For this reason alone, I would be compelled to dissent.

Kozinski, Circuit Judge, with whom Circuit Judges **Reinhardt**, **O'Scannlain, Kleinfeld** and **Berzon** join, dissenting:

The majority writes a lengthy opinion in a vain effort to justify a crushing monetary judgment and a strict injunction against speech protected by the First Amendment. The apparent thoroughness of the opinion, addressing a variety of issues that are not in serious dispute, masks the fact that the majority utterly fails to apply its own definition of a threat, and affirms the verdict and injunction when the evidence in the record does not support a finding that defendants threatened plaintiffs.

After meticulously canvassing the case law, the majority correctly distills the following definition of a true threat: "a statement which, in the entire context and under all the circumstances, a reasonable person would foresee would be interpreted by those to whom the statement is communicated as a serious expression of intent to inflict bodily harm upon that person." The emphasized language is crucial, because it is not illegal — and cannot be made so-merely to say things that would frighten or intimidate the listener. For example, when a doctor says, "You have cancer and will die within six months," it is not a threat, even though you almost certainly will be frightened. Similarly, "Get out of the way of that bus" is not a threat, even though it is said in order to scare you into changing your behavior. By contrast, "If you don't stop performing abortions, I'll kill you" is a true threat and surely illegal.

The difference between a true threat and protected expression is this: A true threat warns of violence or other harm that the speaker controls. Thus, when a doctor tells a patient, "Stop smoking or you'll die of lung cancer," that is not a threat because the doctor obviously can't cause the harm to come about. Similarly, "If you walk in that neighborhood late at night, you're going to get mugged" is not a threat, unless it is clear that the speaker himself (or one of his associates) will be doing the mugging.

In this case, none of the statements on which liability was premised were overtly threatening. On the contrary, the two posters and the web page, by their explicit terms, foreswore the use of violence and advocated lawful means of persuading plaintiffs to stop performing abortions or punishing them for continuing to do so. Nevertheless, because context matters, the statements could reasonably be interpreted as an effort to intimidate plaintiffs into ceasing their abortion-related activities. If that were enough to strip the speech of First Amendment protection, there would be nothing left to decide. But the Supreme Court has told us that "[s]peech does not lose its protected character . . . simply because it may embarrass others or coerce them into action." *NAACP v. Claiborne Hardware Co.*, 458 U.S. 886, 910 (1982) (emphasis added). In other words, some forms of intimidation enjoy constitutional protection.

Buried deep within the long opinion is a single paragraph that cites evidence supporting the finding that the two wanted posters prepared by defendants constituted a true threat. The majority does not point to any statement by defendants that they intended to inflict bodily harm on plaintiffs, nor is there any evidence that defendants took any steps whatsoever to plan or carry out physical violence against anyone. Rather, the majority relies on the fact that "the poster format itself had acquired currency as a death threat for abortion providers. Gunn was killed after his poster was released; Britton was killed after his poster was released; and Patterson was killed after his poster was released." But neither Dr. Gunn nor Dr. Patterson was killed by anyone connected with the posters bearing their names.

The record reveals one instance where an individual — Paul Hill, who is not a defendant in this case — participated in the preparation of the poster depicting a physician, Dr. Britton, and then murdered him. All others who helped to make that poster, as well as those who prepared the other posters, did not resort to violence. There is therefore no pattern showing that people who prepare wanted-type posters then engage in physical violence. To the extent the posters indicate a pattern, it is that almost all people engaged in poster-making were non-violent.

The majority tries to fill this gaping hole in the record by noting that defendants "kn[ew] the fear generated among those in the reproductive health services community who were singled out for identification on a 'wanted'-type poster." But a statement does not become a true threat because it instills fear in the listener; as noted above, many statements generate fear in the listener, yet are not true threats and therefore may not be punished or enjoined consistent with the First Amendment. In order for the statement to be a threat, it must send the message that the speakers themselves — or individuals acting in concert with them — will engage in physical violence. The majority's own definition of true threat makes this clear. Yet the opinion points to no evidence that defendants who prepared the posters would have been understood by a reasonable listener as saying that they will cause the harm.

From the point of view of the victims, it makes little difference whether the violence against them will come from the makers of the posters or from unrelated third parties; bullets kill their victims regardless of who pulls the trigger. But it makes a difference for the purpose of the First Amendment. Speech — especially political speech, as this clearly was — may not be punished or enjoined unless it falls into one of the narrow categories of unprotected speech recognized by the Supreme Court: true threat, incitement, conspiracy to commit criminal acts, fighting words, etc.

Even assuming that one could somehow distill a true threat from the posters themselves, the majority opinion is still fatally defective because it contradicts the central holding of *Claiborne Hardware*: Where the speaker is engaged in public political speech, the public statements themselves cannot be the sole proof that they were true threats, unless the speech directly threatens actual injury to identifiable individuals. Absent such an unmistakable, specific threat, there must be evidence aside from the political statements themselves showing that the public speaker would himself or in conspiracy with others inflict unlawful harm. The majority cites not a scintilla of evidence — other than the posters themselves — that plaintiffs or someone associated with them would carry out the threatened harm.

Given this lack of evidence, the posters can be viewed, at most, as a call to arms for other abortion protesters to harm plaintiffs. However, the Supreme Court made it clear that under *Brandenburg*, encouragement or even advocacy of violence is protected by the First Amendment: "[M]ere advocacy of the use of force or violence does not remove speech from the protection of the First Amendment." *Claiborne Hardware*, 458 U.S. at 927 (citing *Brandenburg*, 395 U.S. at 447) (emphasis in the original). *Claiborne Hardware* in fact goes much farther; it cautions that where liability is premised on "politically motivated" activities, we must "examine critically the basis on which liability was imposed."

While set in a different time and place, and involving a very different political cause, *Claiborne Hardware* bears remarkable similarities to our case:

- Like *Claiborne Hardware*, this case involves a concerted effort by a variety of groups and individuals in pursuit of a common political cause. Some of the activities were lawful, others were not. In both cases, there was evidence that the various players communicated with each other and, at times, engaged in concerted action. The Supreme Court, however, held that mere association with groups or individuals who pursue unlawful conduct is an insufficient basis for the imposition of liability, unless it is shown that the defendants actually participated in or authorized the illegal conduct.
- Both here and in *Claiborne Hardware*, there were instances of actual violence that followed heated rhetoric. The Court made clear, however, that unless the violence follows promptly after the speeches, thus meeting the stringent *Brandenburg* standard for incitement, no liability could be imposed on account of the speech.
- The statements on which liability was premised in both cases were made during the course of political rallies and had a coercive effect on the intended targets. Yet the Supreme Court held in *Claiborne Hardware* that coercion alone could not serve as the basis for liability, because it had not been shown-by evidence aside from the political speeches themselves-that defendants or their agents were involved in or authorized actual violence.
- In *Claiborne Hardware*, the boycott organizers gathered facts — the identity of those who violated the boycott — and publicized them to the community by way of speeches and a newspaper. As in our case, this ostentatious gathering of information, and publication thereof, were intended to put pressure on those whose names were publicized, and perhaps put them in fear that they will become objects of violence by members of the community. Yet the Supreme Court held that this could not form the basis for liability.

The most striking difference between the two cases is that one of Evers's speeches in *Claiborne Hardware*, which expressly threatened violence against the boycott violators, was in fact followed by violence; he then made additional speeches, again referring to violence against boycott breakers. By contrast, the record here contains no evidence that violence was committed against [illegible] doctor after his name appeared [illegible] posters or web page.

Claiborne Hardware ultimately stands for the proposition that those who would punish or deter protected speech must make a very substantial showing that the speech stands outside the umbrella of the First Amendment. This message was reinforced recently by the Supreme Court in *Ashcroft v. Free Speech Coalition*, 535 U.S. 234 (2002), where the government sought to prohibit simulated child pornography without satisfying the stringent requirements of *Miller v. California*, 413 U.S. 15 (1973). The Court rejected this effort, even though the government had earnestly argued that suppression of the speech would advance vital legitimate governmental interests, such as avoiding the exploitation of real children and punishing producers of real child pornography. The evidence that, despite their explicitly nonthreatening language, the Deadly Dozen poster and the Nuremberg Files website were true threats is too "contingent and indirect" to satisfy the standard of Free Speech Coalition.

We have recognized that statements communicated directly to the target are much more likely to be true threats than those, as here, communicated as part of a public protest. Our case law also instructs that, in deciding whether the coercive speech is protected, it makes a big difference whether it is contained in a private communication-a face-to-face confrontation, a telephone call, a dead fish wrapped in newspaper — or is made during the course of public discourse. The reason for this distinction is obvious: Private speech is aimed only at its target. Public speech, by contrast, seeks to move public opinion and to encourage those of like mind. Coercive speech that is part of public discourse enjoys far greater protection than identical speech made in a purely private context.

Finally, a word about the remedy. The majority affirms a crushing liability verdict, including the award of punitive damages, in addition to the injunction. An injunction against political speech is bad enough, but the liability verdict will have a far more chilling effect. Defendants will be destroyed financially by a huge debt that is almost certainly not dischargeable in bankruptcy; it will haunt them for the rest of their lives [illegible] prevent them from ever again [illegible] financially self-sufficient. The Supreme Court long ago recognized that the fear of financial ruin can have a seriously chilling effect on all manner of speech, and will surely cause other speakers to hesitate, lest they find themselves at the mercy of a local jury. See *N.Y. Times Co. v. Sullivan*, 376 U.S. 254, 277–79 (1964). The lesson of what a local jury has done to defendants here will not be lost on others who would engage in heated political rhetoric in a wide variety of causes.

In that regard, a retrospective liability verdict is far more damaging than an injunction; the latter at least gives notice of what is prohibited and what is not. The fear of liability for damages, and especially punitive damages, puts the speaker at risk as to what a jury might later decide is a true threat, and how vindictive it might feel towards the speaker and his cause. In this case, defendants said nothing remotely threatening, yet they find themselves crucified financially. Who knows what other neutral statements a jury might imbue with a menacing meaning based on the activities of unrelated parties. In such circumstances, it is especially important for an appellate court to perform its constitutional function of reviewing the record to ensure that the speech in question clearly falls into one of the narrow categories that is unprotected by the First Amendment. The majority fails to do this.

While today it is abortion protesters who are singled out for punitive treatment, the precedent set by this court — the broad and uncritical deference to the judgment of a jury — will haunt dissidents of all political stripes for many years to come.

Berzon, Circuit Judge, with whom **Reinhardt, Kozinski**, and **Kleinfeld**, Circuit Judges, join, and **O'Scannlain**, Circuit Judge, joins as to Part III only, dissenting:

This case is proof positive that hard cases make bad law, and that when the case is *very* hard — meaning that competing legal and moral imperatives pull with impressive strength in opposite directions — there is the distinct danger of making *very* bad law.

I

The First Amendment and True Threats

1. *Clarifying the issue:* The reason this is a hard First Amendment case becomes somewhat obscured in all the factual detail and quotation of precedent that we as judges engage in. The essential problem — one that, as far as I am aware, is unique in the plethora of "threat" cases and perhaps more generally in First Amendment jurisprudence — is that the speech for which the defendants are being held liable in damages and are enjoined from reiterating in the future is, on its face, clearly, indubitably, and quintessentially the kind of communication that is fully protected by the First Amendment.

The point is not simply that the two posters and the Nuremberg files contain no *explicit* threats that take them outside the free speech umbrella. We are not talking simply about ambiguous or implicit threats that depend on context for their meaning, such as the Ryder trucks in *United States v. Hart*, 212 F.3d 1067 (8th Cir. 2000). Rather, the pivotal issue for me is that what the communications in this case do contain has all the attributes that numerous cases and commentators have identified as core factors underlying the special protection accorded communication under our Constitution.

The posters and website are all public presentations on a matter of current moral and political importance; they provide information to the public on that matter and propose a — peaceful, legal — course of action; and they were presented with explicit reference to great moral and political controversies of the past. Cases that are a virtual First Amendment "greatest hits" establish that these kinds of expressions — those that provide information to the public (particularly when directed at publicly-available media), publish opinions on matters of public controversy, and urge others to action — are the kinds of speech central to our speech-protective regime, and remain so even when the message conveyed is, in substance, form, or both, anathema to some or all of the intended audience.

The posters and website could not and would not have been proscribed, as "true threats" or otherwise, had there been no (1) history of similar — although not at all identical — publications [illegible] people that were followed [illegible] by other people, not members of either of the two defendant organizations — of health professionals who performed abortions; and (2) repeated advocacy by these defendants of the proposition that violence against abortion providers can be morally justified, advocacy that all concede was, standing alone, itself protected by the First Amendment.

2. *An analogy:* Stated in those terms, the issue bears a close resemblance to that faced by the courts with regard to First Amendment limitations on defamation actions, beginning with *New York Times Co. v. Sullivan*. Like "true threats," false speech has long been understood as a category of communication that contains few of the attributes that trigger constitutional speech protection and so great a likelihood of harming others that we refer to the speech as being beyond the protection of the First Amendment. See *R.A.V. v. City of St. Paul*, 505 U.S. 377 (1992). Like "true threats," false, defamatory speech can severely disrupt peoples' lives, both by affecting them emotionally (as does apprehension of danger) and by impairing their social ties, their professional activities, and their ability to earn a living (as does the perceived need to protect oneself from physical harm).

Under these circumstances, the question for me becomes devising standards that, like the constitutional defamation standards that vary with the strength of the protection of the communication, rely not on an unitary "true threats" standard, as does the majority, but on considerations that lessen the danger of mistaken court verdicts and resulting self-censorship to a greater or lesser degree depending upon the nature of the speech in question and the role of speech of that nature in the scheme of the First Amendment.

3. *Some constitutional parameters:* Judge Kozinski, in his dissent, makes one important suggestion toward this end with which, for all the reasons already canvassed, I fully agree: He suggests that "statements communicated directly to the target are much more likely to be true threats than those, as here, communicated as part of a public protest." As a first cut at separating out the kinds of allegedly threatening communications that are central to First Amendment values and therefore must be [illegible] particularly stringent criteria [illegible] they can be prohibited, these two criteria — the public nature of the presentation and content addressing a public issue (which can include matters of social or economic as well as political import for the individuals involved are critical).

In a rare instance, a threat uttered in the course of a public political protest might conceivably exceed the bounds of protected speech. *United States v. Kelner*, 534 F.2d 1020 (2d Cir.1976), is illustrative. In *Kelner*, a member of the Jewish Defense League stated at a press conference held in New York just before Yassir Arafat was scheduled to be in the city that "We have people who have been trained and who are out now and who intend to make sure that Arafat and his lieutenants do not leave this country alive. . . . We are planning to assassinate Mr. Arafat. . . . Everything is planned in detail. . . . It's going to come off." The press conference was broadcast on television that evening. The Second Circuit upheld the defendant's conviction for uttering the threat, over the objection that the speech was simply an extreme statement of opposition to Mr. Arafat, protected under the First Amendment as hyperbolic public discussion of a public issue.

The criteria the Second Circuit suggested to police the dividing line were that "the threat on its face and in the circumstances in which it is made is so unequivocal, unconditional, immediate and specific as to the person threatened, as to convey a gravity of purpose and imminent prospect of execution."

Kelner's criteria for adjudging the protection accorded alleged threats uttered in the course of public communications on public issues seem appropriate to me — and, as I show below, consistent with *NAACP v. C*laiborne Hardware Co., 458 U.S. 886 (1982) — with one exception, an addition, and some explication:

First, the exception: I would not include the imminence or immediacy of the threatened action as a prerequisite to finding a true threat delivered as part of a public speech, if all of the other factors were present. The immediacy requirement calls to mind the standard the Supreme Court erected for proscription of inciting speech in *Brandenburg*. But as the majority can be read to recognize and as Judge Kozinski well explains, the separate constitutional category of unprotected speech for threats does not include statements that induce fear of violence by third parties.

Where there is no threat, explicit or implicit, that the speaker or someone under his or her control intends to harm someone, a statement inducing fear of physical harm must be either (1) a prediction or warning of injury, or (2) an inducement or encouragement of someone else to cause the injury. The former is, as Judge Kozinski suggests, clearly entitled to protection under the First Amendment as either informative or persuasive speech. The latter kind of statement may or may not be protected. Whether it is or not must be governed by the strict inducement standard of *Brandenburg* if the more than fifty years of contentious development of the protection of advocacy of illegal action is not to be for naught.

One can, however, justify a somewhat different standard for judging the constitutionality of a restriction upon threats than for a restriction upon inducement of violence or other illegal action. There is a difference for speech-protective purposes between a statement that one oneself intends to do something and a statement encouraging or advocating that someone else do it. The latter will result in harmful action only if someone else is persuaded by the advocacy. If there is adequate time for that person to reflect, any harm will be due to another's considered act. The speech itself, in that circumstance, does not create the injury, although it may make it more likely. The Supreme Court has essentially decided that free expression would be too greatly burdened by anticipatory squelching of advocacy which can work harm only indirectly if at all.

A true threat, in contrast, implies a firmness of purpose by the person speaking, not mediated through anyone else's rational or emotional reaction to the speech. Threatening speech thereby works directly the harms of apprehension and disruption, whether the apparent resolve proves bluster or not and whether the injury is threatened to be immediate or delayed. Further, the social costs of a threat can be heightened rather than dissipated if the threatened injury is promised for some reasonably ascertainable time in the future — the "specific" prong — for then the apprehension and disruption directly caused by the threat will continue for a longer rather than a shorter period. So, while I would police vigorously the line between inducement and threats — as the jury instructions in this case did, although the majority opinion is less clear on this point — I would, where true threats are alleged, not require a finding of immediacy of the threatened harm.

Second, the addition: Although this court's cases on threats have not generally set any state of mind requirements, I would add to the *Kelner* requirements for proscribable threats in the public protest context the additional consideration whether the defendant subjectively intended the specific victims to understand the communication as an unequivocal threat that the speaker or his agents or coconspirators would physically harm them.

With regard to this subjective intent requirement, there is no meaningful distinction between incitement cases and threat cases such as this one — that is, cases involving public protest speech, especially where the alleged threat, on its face, consisted entirely of advocacy. The First Amendment protects advocacy statements that are likely to produce imminent violent action, so long as the statements are not directed at producing such action. To do otherwise would be to endanger the First Amendment protection accorded advocacy of political change by holding speakers responsible for an impact they did not intend.

Similarly, a purely objective standard for judging the protection accorded such speech would chill speakers from engaging in facially protected public protest speech that some might think, in context, will be understood as a true threat although not intended as such. Unsure of whether their rough and tumble protected speech would be interpreted by a reasonable person as a threat, speakers will silence themselves rather than risk liability.

Third, the explication: "unequivocal" means to me unambiguous, given the context. As such, the requirement is essentially a heightened burden of proof, requiring that a threatening meaning be clearly and convincingly apparent. And in determining whether that proof standard has been met, I would continue to apply the objective standard the majority embraces, based on our cases, in determining whether the speech in fact communicates an intent to harm specific individuals.

The first set of contextual evidence involves the poster/murder/ poster/ murder pattern the majority principally relies upon. Had the murders — or any murders, or any serious violence — been committed by the defendants and had the plaintiffs known that, the inference from the poster/murder pattern that the publication by them of posters similar to those previously followed by a murder might be a strong one. The inference would be stronger had the defendants also put out the earlier posters and had the plaintiffs known that. Neither is the case.

Plaintiffs' main submission to fill this gap was extensive evidence concerning the defendants' opinions condoning the use of violence against medical professionals who perform abortions, including general statements to that effect and particular statements concerning the people who murdered the doctors depicted on the previous posters, stating that their actions were justified and that they should be acquitted. Plaintiffs' closing argument, for example, went on for pages and pages about defendants' meetings and writings concerning the "justifiability of the use of force."

This evidence is certainly of some pertinence as to what the defendants may have intended to do. It is more likely that someone who believes in violence would intentionally threaten to commit it. It is also pertinent to what persons in the plaintiffs' position-that is, persons involved in the abortion controversy and alert to the division of opinion within it — would likely understand concerning defendants' communication. Individuals who believe in violence are not only more likely to threaten to commit it but also actually to commit it, and so defendants' views might well influence plaintiffs' perception of their speech. And since the defendants would know that, defendants' public statements approving the use of violence against doctors who perform abortion are relevant to whether reasonable speakers in defendants' position would expect their communications to be understood as threats.

At the same time, heavy reliance on evidence of this kind raises profound First Amendment issues of its own. One can not read plaintiffs' closing argument in this case without fearing that the jury was being encouraged to hold the defendants liable for their abstract advocacy of violence rather than for the alleged coded threats in the posters and website, the instructions to the jury to the contrary notwithstanding.

I would therefore hold that under the special rules I would apply to public protest speech such as that in this case, plaintiffs' judgment cannot stand because, after a proper review of the record, we would have to conclude that there was no unequivocal, unconditional and specific threat.

NOTES AND QUESTIONS

1. In the *Planned Parenthood v. American Coalition* decision, the Ninth Circuit confronts a clash of ideas between pro-life and pro-choice forces. It upholds an injunction and a crushing pecuniary award favoring the latter, remanding only as to punitive damages. In such a context, should the remedy be limited to compensating parties for injuries, or should it extend as well to silencing or suppressing one party in the debate?
2. Is it fair to say that ACLA's liability is based on statements which were carefully phrased *not* to constitute threats, yet are treated as "true threats" because criminal misconduct by *others* would cause physicians to be fearful? If so, isn't the Ninth Circuit allowing ACLA's right of expression to be forfeited by crimes of others. Is this just?
3. If not, should that freedom of expression, to advocate violence, lose its protection simply because the ACLA *knew* physicians would fear that others would interpret the expressions as threatening violence?
4. Of course, the Ninth Circuit requires even less. It states that the speaker's subjective intent and capacity do not control. Instead, liability

may be founded on a reasonable listener's perception or reasonable fear that the speaker intends bodily harm, even by others.

How [illegible] is this? How can free discourse prosper when a speaker cannot know, or need not know, how his words will be taken and by whom. And if the interpretation is affected by context, shouldn't there be a requirement that the speaker *know* the context, and that the listener know as well?

5. The dissents argue that a higher standard is required and the controlling authority, chiefly the *Claiborne Hardware* case, compels a contrary result. Are they correct? And how do the dissents of Judges Berzon and Kozinski differ? Which is better?
6. Finally, there is a clash between conscience and constitutional right. How should these cases be resolved? Was it done properly here?

PROBLEM 2–17 — Whistleblowers and Health Care

Carla Hausman was terminated as a neonatal intensive care unit nurse by Children's Hospital for "action inconsistent with continued employment." She had done three things: (a) testified before the legislature in opposition to tort reform of medical malpractice laws, urging instead a longer statute of limitations and continued use of contingent fee arrangements by plaintiffs' attorneys and injured patients of limited means; (b) she had appeared as an expert witness in medical malpractice cases; and (c) she first complained internally and then externally, to the Regional Ombudsman and the Bureau of Quality Compliance, Department of Health, that elder patients were falling out of bed, developing bedsores, being neglected and being placed inappropriately in soft restraints.

Nurse Hausman sued. The trial court dismissed on the basis that her employment was expressly "at will." The contract provided that Ms. Hausman could be terminated as an employee "with or without reason, at any time, in the sole discretion of the Executive Director." The trial court added that while Ms. Hausman may have been acting in good faith, none of her conduct was necessary to *her* patients. Indeed, the complaints [illegible] abuse had been [illegible] and simply complicated Children's Hospital's service to its patients. The public policy to limit at-will employment was thus inapplicable. What should the Court do on appeal?

See Carl v. Children's Hospital, 702 A.2d 159 (D.C. 1997), and *Hausman v. St Croix Care Center*, 571 N.W.2d 393 (Wis. 1997).

PROBLEM 2–18 — Capital Punishment: The Ethical Stakes of Stakeholders

When capital punishment is executed and a prisoner dies, many people contribute, other than simply the original judge and jury. Among these are the executioner, his (or her) staff, the attending physicians and those contributing logistical support, including equipment, heart, light and air. There are many such "stakeholders," including the victim's family and friends.

The basic justness of capital punishment in a specific case has been declared by a legislature and fixed by the sentencing judge and jury. But may/must a contributor, such as a physician, refuse to assist, upon personal, ethical grounds? Does it matter whether the grounds relate to doubts as to guilt of the individual prisoner, to questions about the method, or to objections about fairness and inequality of imposition? Many commentators have noted the racial inequality of capital punishment, as well as its unpredictability. Geographic disparities are stunning: As of January 1, 2006, there were 649 inmates on death row in California, but only one in New York. *See* 354 NESM 2525, 2526 (June 15, 2006). The greatest number of executions has been in Texas. *See* Gawande, *When Law and Ethics Collide — Why Physicians Participate in Executions*, New Eng. J. Med. 354:1221-9 (2006).

If a physician is entitled to object on these or other grounds (e.g., Hippocratic Oath — "first, do no harm"), what of other stakeholders?

A recent article in *The New England Journal of Medicine* (354 New Eng. J. Med. 2525 (June 15, 2006)) reported that an EEG machine had been used to measure an inmate's brain waves as he was being executed in North Carolina. It was a bispectral index monitor (BIS), manufactured by Aspect Medical Systems of Newton, Massachusetts. The device converts difficult to read information by means of a proprietary logarithm to an index of hypnotic level. It costs $5,000-6,000 dollars, compared to simpler machines costing 17 dollars, and is used in operating rooms and ICUs, to measure the effect of anesthetics. Use of the BIS reduces the dependency on physicians.

The Medical Director of Aspect, Scott Kelly, has refused to sell a BIS for execution purpose, blocking the execution of Michael Morales, in California. The sale to North Carolina was in ignorance of its purpose. Kelly's position is that use in an execution is incompatible with intended use and the company's mission "to improve lives." The American Society of Anesthesiologists considers participation in executions to be unethical.

May/Should Aspect take this position, and block executions? If the prison has an Aspect BIS and intends to proceed, should/may you as a physician refuse to assist? If they go ahead anyway, putting the patient/prisoner at risk, should you assist to minimize error and resulting harm?

[3] A Case in Point: Evolution, Creationism and the Origin of the Species

A profound and enduring debate exists as to the origins of life. For millenia, the prevailing view has been that humanity was created by a prior, superior being. In the western world, this view has been incorporated in the teachings of the major religions — Christianity, Judaism, and Mohammadism. Those who long held doubts about this view found support for challenging it in the studies of Charles Darwin, and in subsequent biological and anthropological research, confirming that homo sapiens evolved from lower, or lesser creatures by the interplay of random, unguided forces in nature.

The dispute over evolution becomes a matter of individual belief and dissent. In the *Scopes* case, the first case in this section, a high school teacher in 1927 was prosecuted in Tennessee for teaching the theory of evolution, contrary to state law. Subsequently, sixty years later, a similar law — mandating the teaching of the "science" of creationism along with evolution — was invalidated in *Edwards v. Aguillard*, which follows *Scopes* in this section. In the last case, a high school teacher was sanctioned for refusing to teach evolution.

Two issues arise. One concerns beliefs about the origin of the human species. The other concerns matters of conscience, in articulating those beliefs contrary to publicly adopted policy. In the early part of the 21st century, this debate has been re-born around the newly invented title of "Intelligent Design."

SCOPES v. STATE

289 S.W. 363 (Tenn. 1927)

Green, C. J.

Scopes was convicted of a violation of chapter 27 of the Acts of 1925, for that he did teach in the public schools of Rhea county a certain theory that denied the story of the divine creation of man, as taught in the Bible, and did teach instead thereof that man had descended from a lower order of animals. After a verdict of guilty by the jury, the trial judge imposed a fine of $100, and Scopes brought the case to this court by an appeal in the nature of a writ of error.

A motion to quash the indictment was seasonably made in the trial court raising several questions as to the sufficiency thereof and as to the validity and construction of the statute upon which the indictment rested. These questions appear on the record before us and have been presented and debated in this court with great elaboration.

Chapter 27 of the Acts of 1925, known as the Tennessee Anti-Evolution Act is set out in the margin.[1]

Evolution, like prohibition, is a broad term. In recent bickering, however, evolution has been understood to mean the theory which holds that man has developed from some pre-existing lower type.

Thus defining evolution, this act's title clearly indicates the purpose of the statute to be the prohibition of teaching in the schools of the state that man has developed or descended from some lower type or order of animals.

When the draftsman came to express this purpose in the body of the act, he first forbade the teaching of "any theory that denies the story of the divine

[1] "An act prohibiting the teaching of the evolution theory in all the Universities, normals and other public schools of Tennessee, which are supported in whole or in part by the public school funds of the state, and to provide penalties for the violations thereof.

Section 1. Be it enacted by the General Assembly of the state of Tennessee, that it shall be unlawful for any teacher in any of the Universities, normals and all other public schools of the state which are supported in whole or in part by the public school funds of the state, to teach any theory that denies the story of the divine creation of man as taught in the Bible and to teach instead that man has descended from a lower order of animals.

Sec. 2. Be it further enacted, that any teacher found guilty of the violation of this act, shall be guilty of a misdemeanor and upon conviction shall be fined not less than one hundred ($100.00) dollars nor more than five hundred ($500.00) dollars for each offense.

Sec. 3. Be it further enacted, that this act take effect from and after its passage, the public welfare requiring it."

creation of man, as taught in the Bible" — his conception evidently being that to forbid the denial of the Bible story would ban the teaching of evolution. To make the purpose more explicit, he added that it should be unlawful to teach "that man has descended from a lower order of animals."

So interpretated, the statute does not seem to be uncertain in its meaning nor incapable of enforcement for such a reason, notwithstanding the argument to the contrary.

It is contended that the statute violates section 8 of article 1 of the Tennessee Constitution, and section 1 of the Fourteenth Amendment of the Constitution of the United States — the law of the land clause of the state Constitution, and the due process of law clause of the federal Constitution, which are practically equivalent in meaning.

We think there is little merit in this contention. The plaintiff in error was a teacher in the public schools of Rhea county. He was an employee of the state of Tennessee or of a municipal agency of the state. He was under contract with the state to work in an institution of the state. He had no right or privilege to serve the state except upon such terms as the state prescribed. His liberty, his privilege, his immunity to teach and proclaim the theory of evolution, elsewhere than in the service of the state, was in no wise touched by this law.

The statute before us is not an exercise of the police power of the state undertaking to regulate the conduct and contracts of individuals in their dealings with each other. On the other hand, it is an act of the state as a corporation, a proprietor, an employer. It is a declaration of a master as to the character of work the master's servant shall, or rather shall not, perform. In dealing with its own employees engaged upon its own work, the state is not hampered by the limitations of section 8 of article 1 of the Tennessee Constitution, nor of the Fourteenth Amendment to the Constitution of the United States.

A leading case is *Atkins v. Kansas.* The court there considered and upheld a Kansas statute making it a criminal offense for a contractor for a public work to permit or require an employee to perform labor upon that work in excess of eight hours each day.

In *Ellis v. United States*, *Atkins v. Kansas* was followed, and an act of Congress sustained which prohibited, under penalty of fine or imprisonment, except in case of extraordinary emergency, the requiring or permitting laborers or mechanics employed upon any of the public works of the United States or of the District of Columbia to work more than eight hours each day.

These cases make it obvious that the state or government, as an incident to its power to authorize and enforce contracts for public services, "may require that they shall be carried out only in a way consistent with its views of public policy, and may punish a departure from that way." *Ellis v. United States*, supra.

Truaux v. Raich, supra, *Meyer v. Nebraska*, 262 U. S. 390, *Pierce v. Society of Sisters of the Holy Names of Jesus and Mary*, 268 U. S. 510, and other decisions of the Supreme Court of the United States, pressed upon us by counsel for the plaintiff in error, deal with statutes affecting individuals, corporations, and private institutions, and we do not regard these cases as in point.

But it is urged that chapter 27 of the Acts of 1925 conflicts with section 12 of article 11, the educational clause, and section 3 of article 1, the religious clause, of the Tennessee Constitution.

The relevant portion of section 12 of article 11 of the Constitution is in these words:

> "It shall be the duty of the General Assembly in all future periods of this government, to cherish literature and science."

The argument is that the theory of the descent of man from a lower order of animals is now established by the preponderance of scientific thought and that the prohibition of the teaching of such theory is a violation of the legislative duty to cherish science.

While this clause of the Constitution has been mentioned in several of our cases, these references have been casual, and no act of the Legislature has ever been held inoperative by reason of such provision. Although this court is loath to say that any language of the Constitution is merely directory, we are driven to the conclusion that this particular admonition must be so treated. It is too vague to be enforced by any court. To cherish science means to nourish, to encourage, to foster science.

If the Legislature thinks that, by reason of popular prejudice, the cause of education and the study of science generally will be promoted by forbidding the teaching of evolution in the schools of the state, we can conceive of no ground to justify the court's interference. The courts cannot sit in judgment on such acts of the Legislature or its agents and determine whether or not the omission or addition of a particular course of study tends "to cherish science."

The last serious criticism made of the act is that it contravenes the provision of section 3 of article 1 of the Constitution, "that no preference shall ever be given, by law, to any religious establishment or mode of worship."

We are not able to see how the prohibition of teaching the theory that man has descended from a lower order of animals gives preference to any religious establishment or mode of worship. So far as we know, there is no religious establishment or organized body that has in its creed or confession of faith any article denying or affirming such a theory. So far as we know, the denial or affirmation of such a theory does not enter into any recognized mode of worship. Since this cause has been pending in this court, we have been favored, in addition to briefs of counsel and various amici curiae, with a multitude of resolutions, addresses, and communications from scientific bodies, religious factions, and individuals giving us the benefit of their views upon the theory of evolution. Examination of these contributions indicates that Protestants, Catholics, and Jews are divided among themselves in their beliefs, and that there is no unanimity among the members of any religious establishment as to this subject. Belief or unbelief in the theory of evolution is no more a characteristic of any religious establishment or mode of worship than is belief or unbelief in the wisdom of the prohibition laws. It would appear that members of the same churches quite generally disagree as to these things.

Furthermore, chapter 277 of the Acts of 1925 requires the teaching of nothing. It only forbids the teaching of the evolution of man from a lower order of animals. Chapter 102 of the Acts of 1915 requires that ten verses from the Bible be read each day at the opening of every public school, without comment, and provided the teacher does not read the same verses more than twice during any session. It is also provided in this act that pupils may be excused from the Bible readings upon the written request of their parents.

As the law thus stands, while the theory of evolution of man may not be taught in the schools of the state, nothing contrary to that theory is required to be taught. It could scarcely be said that the statutory scriptural reading just mentioned would amount to teaching of a contrary theory.

Since a jury alone can impose the penalty this act requires, and as a matter of course no different penalty can be inflicted, the trial judge exceeded his jurisdiction in levying this fine, and we are without power to correct his error. The judgment must accordingly be reversed.

The court is informed that the plaintiff in error is no longer in the service of the state. We see nothing to be gained by prolonging the life of this bizarre case. On the contrary, we think the peace and dignity of the state, which all criminal prosecutions are brought to redress, will be the better conserved by the entry of a nolle prosequi herein. Such a course is suggested to the Attorney General.

Chambliss, J. (concurring).

I am of opinion that the constitutional objections urged do not apply for yet other reasons, and in another view. . . .

Two theories of organic evolution are well recognized, one the theistic, which not only concedes, but maintains, consistently with the Bible story, that "the Lord God formed man of the dust of the earth, and breathed into his nostrils the breath of life, and man became a living soul." This is the theory advanced eloquently by learned counsel for Scopes, and held to by numerous outstanding scientists of the world. The other theory is known as the materialistic, which denies that God created man, that He was the first cause, and seeks in shadowy uncertainties for the origin of life. The act before us, as I view it, prohibits the teaching in public schools of the state of this latter theory, inconsistent, not only with the common belief of mankind of every clime and creed and "religious establishment," even those that reject Christ or Judaism, and look through Buddha or Mohammed to God, but inconsistent also with our Constitution and the fundamental declaration lying back of it, through all of which runs recognition of and appeal to "God," and a life to come. The Declaration of Independence opens with a reference to "the laws of nature and nature's God," and holds this truth "to be self-evident, that all men are created equal, that they are endowed by their Creator," etc., and concludes "with a firm reliance on the protection of Divine Providence."

Now I find it conceded in an exceptionally able brief for Scopes, devoted exclusively to the question of uncertainty, that "the act might be construed as only aimed at materialists." This is my view of it. As I read it, the act makes no war on evolution, except in so far as the evolution theory conflicts with the recognition of the divine in creation.

. . . [I]t is clear that the act itself, as finally framed and passed, was expressly limited and restricted in its body to the prohibition of the teaching — not of any theory of evolution at all, but of any theory only that denies or controverts "the divine creation of man." Moreover, it would seem that, since "the story as taught in the Bible" of man's creation by God from the dust of the earth is readily susceptible of the construction given it by those known as liberalists, this language is consistent with the conclusion that what the act aims at and effects is the prohibition of the teaching of any such theory only as denies that man was divinely created according to the Bible story, however this story may be interpreted as to details.

The following statement of Dr. E. N. Reinke, professor of biology in Vanderbilt University, is repeatedly quoted in briefs of counsel for the defense:

> "The theory of evolution is altogether essential to the teaching of biology and its kindred sciences. To deny the teacher of biology the use of this most fundamental generalization of his science would make his teaching as chaotic as an attempt to teach astronomy without the law of gravitation or physics without assuming the existence of the ether."

Conceding that "the theory of evolution is altogether essential to the teaching of biology and its kindred sciences," it will not be contended by Dr. Reinke, or by learned counsel quoting from him, that the theory of evolution essentially involves the denial of the divine creation of man, and that, when construed to prohibit such a denial only, the act is objectionable as denying to "the teacher of biology the use of the most fundamental generalization of his science."

As was said by Chief Justice **Green**, the act gives no preference to any particular religious establishment. The doctrine or tenet of the instantaneous creation of man is not set forth or preferred over other conceptions. It is too well established for argument that "the story of the divine creation of man as taught in the Bible" is accepted — not "denied" — by millions of men and women who do not interpret it as teaching instantaneous creation, who hold with the Psalmist that "a thousand years in thy sight are but as yesterday when it is past," as but a day. It follows that to forbid the teaching of a denial of the biblical account of divine creation does not, expressly or by fair implication, involve acceptance or approval of instantaneous creation, held to by some literalists. One is not prohibited by this act from teaching, either that "days," as used in the book of Genesis, means days of 24 hours, the literalist view, or days of "a thousand years" or more, as held by liberalists, so long as the teaching does not exclude God as the author of human life.

In brief, as already indicated, I concur with the majority in the conclusion (1) that this case must be reversed for the error of the judge in fixing the fine; (2) that a nolle prosequi should be entered; and (3) that the act is constitutional as within the power of the Legislature as the employer of its teachers. However, I go further and find the act constitutional for additional reasons, rested upon the view that the act fairly construed is limited to the prohibition of the teaching of any theory of evolution only which denies the divine creation of man, without regard to details of religious belief, or differing interpretations of the story as taught in the Bible. In this view the constitutionality of the act is sustained, but the way is left open for such teaching of the pertinent sciences as is approved by the progressive God recognizing leaders of thought and life.

McKinney, J. (dissenting).

I am of the opinion that [the statute] is invalid for uncertainty of meaning. I therefore respectfully dissent from the contrary holding of my associates. . . .

NOTES AND QUESTIONS

1. The *Scopes* "Monkey Trial" is one of the famous trials of American history, attracting international attention in its day and generating an immense amount of popular and scholarly literature. The trial attorneys were Clarence Darrow and William Jennings Bryan (who had run for the United States presidency), two of the premier attorneys of their time. A fine movie, *Inherit the Wind*, portrays the case, recently discussed in a Pulitzer prize-winning book, *Summer for the Gods*, by Edward Larson.

2. The Tennessee Court treats this as a simple matter of employment law, distinguishing cases like *Meyer v. Nebraska* (and — by implication — many of the later cases discussed above, such as *Yoder* and *Moore*). Are you persuaded? Might it have instead invoked the State's authority to legislate for the public welfare, to prescribe the content of curriculum, "to cherish science"? Or is this simply a matter of contract law?

3. Does a public employee have a *right* to insist on personal belief? On asserting those beliefs? On *teaching* them? Why do you suppose Mr. Scopes raised the issue and then went to trial, facing a $100 fine (real money, back then) on a teacher's salary? What would the court in *Meyer v. Nebraska, supra,* say? Chief Judge Posner of the Seventh Circuit? See his opinion in the *Rodriguez* case, excerpted *infra,* at Problem 2-17.

4. Is the Tennessee Court correct in its assertion that the statute did not *favor* any religion? What about the argument that it did not require the *teaching* of anything, creationism or evolution? How then was Mr. Scopes hurt?

5. And what of the concurring opinion of Justice Chambliss, that the statute actually *permits* teaching evolution, so long as some place for the divine is conceded? And are you surprised that this was the view Mr. Scopes apparently held? Only materialism, denying God, was forbidden. Is this a fair reading of the statute? Why did the majority not adopt it? Would you?

6. And now, to ask how Tennessee's quaint statute would fare in the sophisticated 1990s, we turn to the *Edwards* case.

EDWARDS v. AGUILLARD

482 U.S. 578 (1987)

Justice **Brennan** delivered the opinion of the Court.

The question for decision is whether Louisiana's "Balanced Treatment for Creation-Science and Evolution-Science in Public School Instruction" Act (Creationism Act), is facially invalid as violative of the Establishment Clause of the First Amendment.

I

The Creationism Act forbids the teaching of the theory of evolution in public schools unless accompanied by instruction in "creation science." No school is required to teach evolution or creation science. If either is taught, however, the other must also be taught. The theories of evolution and creation science are statutorily defined as "the scientific evidences for [creation or evolution] and inferences from those scientific evidences."

Appellees, who include parents of children attending Louisiana public schools, Louisiana teachers, and religious leaders, challenged the constitutionality of the Act in District Court, seeking an injunction and declaratory relief. Appellants, Louisiana officials charged with implementing the Act, defended on the ground that the purpose of the Act is to protect a legitimate secular interest, namely, academic freedom. . . .

. . . .

II

The Establishment Clause forbids the enactment of any law "respecting an establishment of religion." The Court has applied a three-pronged test to determine whether legislation comports with the Establishment Clause. First, the legislature must have adopted the law with a secular purpose. Second, the statute's principal or primary effect must be one that neither advances nor inhibits religion. Third, the statute must not result in an excessive entanglement of government with religion. . . .

The Court has been particularly vigilant in monitoring compliance with the Establishment Clause in elementary and secondary schools. Families entrust public schools with the education of their children, but condition their trust on the understanding that the classroom will not purposely be used to advance religious views that may conflict with the private beliefs of the student and his or her family. Students in such institutions are impressionable and their attendance is involuntary. . . .

. . . .

III

. . . .

True, the Act's stated purpose is to protect academic freedom. This phrase might, in common parlance, be understood as referring to enhancing the freedom of teachers to teach what they will. The Court of Appeals, however, correctly concluded that the Act was not designed to further that goal. We find no merit in the State's argument that the "legislature may not [have] use[d] the terms 'academic freedom' in the correct legal sense. They might have [had] in mind, instead, a basic concept of fairness; teaching all of the evidence." Even if "academic freedom" is read to mean "teaching all of the evidence" with respect to the origin of human beings, the Act does not further this purpose. The goal of providing a more comprehensive science curriculum is not furthered either by outlawing the teaching of evolution or by requiring the teaching of creation science.

A

While the Court is normally deferential to a State's articulation of a secular purpose, it is required that the statement of such purpose be sincere and not a sham. . . .

It is clear from the legislative history that the purpose of the legislative sponsor, Senator Bill Keith, was to narrow the science curriculum. During the legislative hearings, Senator Keith stated: "My preference would be that neither [creationism nor evolution] be taught." Such a ban on teaching does not promote — indeed, it undermines — the provision of a comprehensive scientific education.

It is equally clear that requiring schools to teach creation science with evolution does not advance academic freedom. The Act does not grant teachers a flexibility that they did not already possess to supplant the present science curriculum with the presentation of theories, besides evolution, about the origin of life. Indeed, the Court of Appeals found that no law prohibited Louisiana public school teachers from teaching any scientific theory. . . .

. . . .

. . . While requiring that curriculum guides be developed for creation science, the Act says nothing of comparable guides for evolution. Similarly, resource services are supplied for creation science but not for evolution. Only "creation scientists" can serve on the panel that supplies the resource services. The Act forbids school boards to discriminate against anyone who "chooses to be a creation-scientist" or to teach "creationism," but fails to protect those who choose to teach evolution or any other non-creation science theory, or who refuse to teach creation science.

. . . .

B

. . . .

. . . There is a historic and contemporaneous link between the teachings of certain religious denominations and the teaching of evolution. . . .

These same historic and contemporaneous antagonisms between the teachings of certain religious denominations and the teaching of evolution are present in this case. The preeminent purpose of the Louisiana Legislature was clearly to advance the religious viewpoint that a supernatural being created humankind. The term "creation science" was defined as embracing this particular religious doctrine by those responsible for the passage of the Creationism Act. Senator [illegible] leading expert on creation science, Edward Boudreaux, testified at the legislative hearings that the theory of creation science included belief in the existence of a supernatural creator. . . .

Furthermore, it is not happenstance that the legislature required the teaching of a theory that coincided with this religious view. The legislative history documents that the Act's primary purpose was to change the science curriculum of public schools in order to provide persuasive advantage to a particular religious doctrine that rejects the factual basis of evolution in its entirety. . . .

. . . .

We do not imply that a legislature could never require that scientific critiques of prevailing scientific theories be taught. . . . But because the primary purpose of the Creationism Act is to endorse a particular religious doctrine, the Act furthers religion in violation of the Establishment Clause.

. . . .

Justice **Scalia**, with whom **The Chief Justice** joins, dissenting.

Even if I agreed with the questionable premise that legislation can be invalidated under the Establishment Clause on the basis of its motivation alone, without regard to its effects, I would still find no justification for today's decision. The Louisiana legislators who passed the "Balanced Treatment for Creation-Science and Evolution-Science Act", each of whom had sworn to support the Constitution, were well aware of the potential Establishment Clause problems and considered that aspect of the legislation with great care. After seven hearings and several months of study, resulting in substantial revision of the original proposal, they approved the Act overwhelmingly and specifically articulated the secular purpose they meant it to serve. Although the record contains abundant evidence of the sincerity of that purpose (the only issue pertinent to this case), the Court today holds, essentially on the basis of "its visceral knowledge regarding what must have motivated the legislators," that the members of the Louisiana Legislature knowingly violated their oaths and then lied about it. I dissent. . . .

. . . .

II

A

We have relatively little information upon which to judge the motives of those who supported the Act. About the only direct evidence is the statute itself and transcripts of the seven committee hearings at which it was considered. Unfortunately, several of those hearings were sparsely attended, and the legislators who were present revealed little about their motives. We have no committee reports, no floor debates, no remarks inserted into the legislative history, no statement from the Governor, and no postenactment statements or testimony from the bill's sponsor or any other legislators. . . .

. . . .

Most of the testimony in support of Senator Keith's bill came from the Senator himself and from scientists and educators he presented, many of whom enjoyed academic credentials that may have been regarded as quite impressive by members of the Louisiana Legislature. To a substantial extent, their testimony was devoted to lengthy, and, to the layman, seemingly expert scientific expositions on the origin of life. These scientific lectures touched upon, inter alia, biology, paleontology, genetics, astronomy, astrophysics, probability analysis, and biochemistry. The witnesses repeatedly assured committee members that "hundreds and hundreds" of highly respected, internationally renowned scientists believed in creation science and would support their testimony.

Senator Keith and his witnesses testified essentially as set forth in the following paragraphs: There are two and only two scientific explanations for the beginning of life — evolution and creation science. Both posit a theory of the origin of life and subject that theory to empirical testing. Evolution posits that life arose out of inanimate chemical compounds and has gradually evolved over millions of years. Creation science posits that all life forms now on earth appeared suddenly and relatively recently and have changed little. Since there are only two possible explanations of the origin of life, any evidence that tends to disprove the theory of evolution necessarily tends to prove the theory of creation science, and vice versa. For example, the abrupt appearance in the fossil record of complex life, and the extreme rarity of transitional life forms in that record, are evidence for creation science.

The body of scientific evidence supporting creation science is as strong as that supporting evolution. In fact, it may be stronger. The evidence for evolution is far less compelling than we have been led to believe. Evolution is not a scientific "fact," since it cannot actually be observed in a laboratory. . . .

Creation science is educationally valuable. Students exposed to it better understand the current state of scientific evidence about the origin of life. Those students even have a better understanding of evolution. . . .

Although creation science is educationally valuable and strictly scientific, it is now being censored from or misrepresented in the public schools. Evolution, in turn, is misrepresented as an absolute truth. Teachers have been brainwashed by an entrenched scientific establishment composed almost exclusively of scientists to whom evolution is like a "religion." These scientists discriminate against creation scientists so as to prevent evolution's weaknesses from being exposed.

The censorship of creation science has at least two harmful effects. First, it deprives students of knowledge of one of the two scientific explanations for the origin of life and leads them to believe that evolution is proven fact; thus, their education suffers and they are wrongly taught that science has proved their religious beliefs false. Second, it violates the Establishment Clause. The United States Supreme Court has held that secular humanism is a religion. . . .

Senator Keith repeatedly and vehemently denied that his purpose was to advance a particular religious doctrine. At the outset of the first hearing on the legislation, he testified: "We are not going to say today that you should have some kind of religious instructions in our schools.. . .We are not talking about religion today.. . .I am not proposing that we take the Bible in each science class and read the first chapter of Genesis." At a later hearing, Senator Keith stressed: "[T]o . . . teach religion and disguise it as creationism . . . is not my intent. My intent is to see to it that our textbooks are not censored." . . .

We have no way of knowing, of course, how many legislators believed the testimony of Senator Keith and his witnesses. But in the absence of evidence to the contrary, we have to assume that many of them did. Given that assumption, the Court today plainly errs in holding that the Louisiana Legislature passed the Balanced Treatment Act for exclusively religious purposes.

. . . .

NOTES AND QUESTIONS

1. Note that in *Edwards*, the complainants are teachers, parents and students, unlike in *Scopes*. Would that have made a difference in *Scopes*?
2. Are the statutes in *Scopes* and *Edwards* different? Both permit teaching *neither* evolution nor creationism, do they not? So is the Supreme Court saying evolution *must* be taught? That creationism may not be?
3. We are told the State sought to justify the statute on grounds of "academic freedom." How would this argument work? Could the argument succeed if the statute had been better drafted, in a balanced commitment of personnel and resources?
4. Could the legislature ban teaching *either* evolution or creationism?
5. Are you surprised that *Edwards* turns almost entirely on legislative *purpose*? Shouldn't it turn on content? Suppose a bill passed, mandating teaching *evolution,* at the insistence of *liberal* religious groups? Or enacting the death penalty, as part of conservative religious views held by members of the legislature? Would the *purpose* invalidate otherwise sound legislation?
6. Does Justice Scalia persuade you that a tenable case can be made for creation-science? At least as tenable as that for evolution? At least sufficiently so, as presented before the Louisiana Legislature, that the majority's remarkable attribution of duplicity and religious motive should be rejected?
7. And what of Justice Scalia's establishment and censorship points? Don't these support the Louisiana Legislature's concern for academic freedom? Isn't it fair to say that evolution represents a view of the universe which is of profound religious import, but presented as "fact"? And in public schools, isn't it fair to be concerned about the position and plight of teachers who take the contrary view — a mirror image of a latter-day *Scopes*? This is the situation in the third and last case in this section, *Peloza v. Capistrano Unified School District*.

PELOZA v. CAPISTRANO UNIFIED SCHOOL DISTRICT

37 F.3d 517 (9th Cir. 1994)

PER CURIAM:

John E. Peloza is a high school biology teacher. He sued the Capistrano Unified School District and various individuals connected with the school district under 42 U.S.C. § 1983. He alleges in his complaint that the school district requires him to teach "evolutionism" and that evolutionism is a religious belief system. . . .

. . . .

Peloza is a biology teacher in a public high school, and is employed by the Capistrano Unified School District. He is being forced by the defendants (the school district, its trustees and individual teachers and others) to proselytize his students to a belief in "evolutionism" "under the guise of [its being] a valid scientific theory." Evolutionism is an historical, philosophical and religious belief system, but not a valid scientific theory. Evolutionism is one of "two world views on the subject of the origins of life and of the universe." The other is "creationism" which also is a "religious belief system." "The belief system of evolutionism is based on the assumption that life and the universe evolved randomly and by chance and with no Creator involved in the process. The world view and belief system of creationism is based on the assumption that a Creator created all life and the entire universe." Peloza does not wish "to promote either philosophy or belief system in teaching his biology class." "The general acceptance of . . . evolutionism in academic circles does not qualify it or validate it as a scientific theory." Peloza believes that the defendants seek to dismiss him due to his refusal to teach evolutionism. His first amendment rights have been abridged by interference with his right "to teach his students to differentiate between a philosophical, religious belief system on the one hand and a true scientific theory on the other."

Peloza further alleges he has been forbidden to discuss religious matters with students the entire time that he is on the school campus even if a conversation is initiated by a student and the discussion is outside of class time.

He also alleges that the defendants have conspired to destroy and damage his professional reputation, career and position as a public school teacher. He has been reprimanded in writing for proselytizing students and teaching religion in the classroom. His inquiries as to whether he is being required to teach evolution as "fact" or"as the only valid scientific theory" have not been answered directly. He has not taught creationism in his classroom. . . .

. . . .

DISCUSSION

I

The Section 1983 Claim

A. The Establishment Clause

. . . .

Peloza's complaint is not entirely consistent. In some places he seems to advance the patently frivolous claim that it is unconstitutional for the school district to require him to teach, as a valid scientific theory, that higher life forms evolved from lower ones. At other times he claims the district is forcing him to teach evolution as fact. Although possibly dogmatic or even wrong, such a requirement would not transgress the establishment clause if "evolution" simply means that higher life forms evolved from lower ones.

Peloza uses the words "evolution" and "evolutionism" interchangeably in the complaint. This is not wrong or imprecise for, indeed, they are synonyms. Adding "ism" does not change the meaning nor magically metamorphose "evolution" into a religion. "Evolution" and "evolutionism" define a biological concept: higher life forms evolve from lower ones. The concept has nothing to do with how the universe was created; it has nothing . . . to do with whether or not there is a divine Creator (who did or did not create the universe or did or did not plan evolution as part of a divine scheme).

Charitably read, Peloza's complaint at most makes this claim: the school district's actions establish a state-supported religion of evolutionism, or more generally of "secular humanism." According to Peloza's complaint, all persons must adhere to one of two religious belief systems concerning "the origins of life and of the universe:" evolutionism, or creationism. Thus, the school district, in teaching evolutionism, is establishing a state-supported "religion."

We reject this claim because neither the Supreme Court, nor this circuit, has ever held that evolutionism or secular humanism are "religions" for Establishment Clause purposes. Indeed, both the dictionary definition of religion and the clear weight of the caselaw are to the contrary. The Supreme Court has held unequivocally that while the belief in a divine creator of the universe is a religious belief, the scientific theory that higher forms of life evolved from lower forms is not. *Edwards v. Aguillard.*

Peloza would have us accept his definition of "evolution" and "evolutionism" and impose his definition on the school district as its own, a definition that cannot be found in the dictionary, in the Supreme Court cases, or anywhere in the common understanding of the words. Only if we define "evolution" and "evolutionism" as does Peloza as a concept that embraces the belief that the universe came into existence without a Creator might he make out a claim. This we need not do. To say red is green or black is white does not make it so. Nor need we for the purposes of a 12(b)(6) motion accept a made-up definition of "evolution." Nowhere does Peloza point to anything that conceivably suggests that the school district accepts anything other than the common definition of "evolution" and "evolutionism." It simply required him as a biology teacher in the public schools of California to teach "evolution." Peloza nowhere says it required more.

. . . .

B. Free Speech

Peloza alleges the school district ordered him to refrain from discussing his religious beliefs with students during "instructional time," and to tell any students who attempted to initiate such conversations with him to consult their parents or clergy. He claims the school district, in the following official reprimand, defined "instructional time" as any time the students are on campus, including lunch break and the time before, between, and after classes. . . .

The school district's restriction on Peloza's ability to talk with students about religion during the school day is a restriction on his right of free speech. Nevertheless, "the Court has repeatedly emphasized the need for affirming the comprehensive authority of the States and of school officials, consistent with fundamental constitutional safeguards, to prescribe and control conduct in the schools." This principle applies in this case. The school district's interest in avoiding an Establishment Clause violation trumps Peloza's right to free speech.

. . . To permit him to discuss his religious beliefs with students during school time on school grounds would violate the Establishment Clause of the First Amendment. Such speech would not have a secular purpose, would have the primary effect of advancing religion, and would entangle the school with religion. . . .

The district court did not err in dismissing the part of Peloza's section 1983 claim that was predicated on an alleged violation of his right to free speech under the First Amendment.

. . . .

V

Affirmed in part; Reversed in part.

Poole, Circuit Judge, concurring in part and dissenting in part:

I am in agreement with the majority's resolution of John Peloza's Establishment Clause and Due Process Clause claims. However, because I believe we can dismiss Peloza's free speech claims only by turning a deaf ear to the procedural posture of this case, I respectfully dissent from parts I.B and II of the majority opinion.

I

Schoolteacher John Peloza seeks a declaratory judgment permitting him to "respond[] to student-initiated inquiries . . . regarding religion" during contract time. The majority opinion concludes that if Peloza's discussions would constitute an establishment of religion, the District may permissibly limit those discussions, even though such limitations restrict Peloza's free speech. With this I have no quarrel. But the majority's premise is that any discussions Peloza might have do constitute such an establishment, and I am unpersuaded that we may reach such a conclusion in the case's present posture.

. . . I can imagine a wide range of circumstances and questions "regarding religion" which Peloza could permissibly answer without violating the Establishment Clause. For example, a student might come to a teacher during lunch and ask about Malcolm X or Martin Luther King's religious beliefs, and how and why they evolved, or about the origins of Islam, or what the seven great religions of the world were. Such questions would certainly be "regarding religion," student-initiated, and during contract time. As such, [illegible] the class of [illegible] books to be permitted, yet it is hard to see how the descriptive role a teacher would have in responding to these questions would work any violation of the Establishment Clause.

The majority holding only makes sense if we presume that we know what kinds of questions are being asked and what kinds of answers Peloza would give. In the posture of this case, where we must reverse if there are any facts Peloza could conceivably prove which would entitle him to relief, this is a presumption we are forbidden from making. As a result, the majority holding means that any response to a student-initiated inquiry "regarding religion" during contract time, other than "Ask someone else," works a violation of the Establishment Clause. I cannot join in such a broad legal holding, and indeed the case law forbids it. . . .

. . . .

NOTES AND QUESTIONS

1. Is Mr. Peloza right — that evolutionism is "religion"? Would Justice Scalia agree? Would the *Scopes* court? Or is his complaint simply that evolution does not agree with *his* religion?
2. Should Peloza instead be arguing academic freedom? Relying on *Meyer v. Nebraska* ?
3. And what of his *own* religious freedom to speak and discuss his views? Are there no limits to the extent they may be sacrificed to political or educational orthodoxy? Even if the students initiate the inquiry or discussion? What of dissenting Judge Poole's views in this regard?
4. Is Mr. Peloza an updated equivalent of Mr. Scopes? Were they both treated badly?
5. For an excellent article, see H. Wayne House, *Darwinism and the Law: Can Non-Naturalistic Scientific Theories Survive Constitutional Challenge?*, 13 Regent U. L. Rev. 355 (2001), [illegible] George, *And [illegible] Created Kansas? The Evolution / Creationism Debate in America's Public Schools*, 149 U. Pa. L. Rev. 843 (2001).

PROBLEM 2–19 — Dissent, Conscience and Justice Scalia

The San Francisco Examiner, on Tuesday, July 7, 1998, reported that the administrative body that is responsible for disciplining state judges charged Justice J. Anthony Kline of San Francisco with misconduct.

Kline's alleged offense: flatly contradicting the state Supreme Court in a written opinion. The action by the state Commission on Judicial Performance could lead to Kline's ouster, according to the *Examiner.*

"It's an outrage," Boalt Hall law professor Stephen Barnett was quoted as saying. "It shows the commission doesn't know the difference between misconduct and an opinion."

"I'm amazed," said David Heilbron, former State Bar president. "There's never been a charge like this pursued by the commission."

The reason given by the San Francisco-based commission was that Kline, a member of the state Court of Appeal, had issued a dissenting opinion Dec. 2, 1997, in a San Mateo County landlord-tenant dispute centering on a point of law decided five years earlier by the state Supreme Court.

Kline said that he believed the state's highest court had been wrong and that he couldn't follow its ruling "as a matter of conscience." He said "stipulated reversals" wrongly permitted parties "with the necessary economic means to purchase the reversal of an adverse judgment" and undermined the integrity of the courts.

Such post-trial collaborations, he said, convert court judgments "into a commodity that can be bought and sold."

He protested that the commission was trying to punish him for "forthrightness and candor" in his attempt to persuade the state Supreme Court to revisit the issue.

But the 11-member commission, a politically appointed body composed mostly of non-lawyers named during the administration of Republican Gov. Wilson, said Kline had engaged in "willful misconduct . . . that brings the judicial office into disrepute."

It said he had violated canons of the state Code of Judicial Ethics barring actions that did not promote "public confidence" in the courts and requiring that a judge be "faithful to the law."

"Any attempt by any authority to muzzle a judge strikes at the independence of the judiciary and puts a dagger into the heart of our judicial system," said Court of Appeal Justice Arthur Gilbert of Ventura County. "And I'm not being overdramatic in saying that. This is really significant. Some of our great dissents turn into majority opinions."

Stanford legal ethicist William Simon said there was no legal compulsion for a California judge to follow precedent.

"There's no constitutional provision and no statute that requires judges to follow precedent," Simon said. "The practice is a custom that usually makes sense, but has not invariably been followed."

"It sometimes serves a useful role for judges to signal to a higher court that it ought to look at an issue again — which was what Kline was trying to do here. To treat it as an ethical violation borders on frivolousness."

Assume that Justice Scalia dissenting in the *Edwards* case was motivated by his profound Roman Catholic beliefs. Assume these also motivated his headstrong dissents in *Casey* and *Cruzan*. Can a case be made that he is disabled by his religious beliefs from serving as a judge? Suppose he were to state, as Judge Kline apparently has, explicitly, that as a matter of conscience he cannot and will not follow Supreme Court precedent in matters where his Church has an unqualified position.

Does Justice Scalia have a right to dissent, unlike Mssrs. Scopes and Peloza and Justice Kline? Would your view be different if Justice Scalia were on a Court of Appeals, expressing there the same views?

Change the problem a bit. Now suppose Justice Kline is running for re-election, is asked about the Supreme Court opinion, and gives exactly th[illegible] answer. Can he — should h[illegible] sanctioned by the Bar or Judiciary for violating a rule against a candidate's "announcing" how he or she would approach or decide an issue? *See Republican Party of Minnesota v. White*, 536 U.S. 765 (2002). (Before reading the *White* decision, try to predict how the liberal and conservative Justices align themselves on this issue.)

PROBLEM 2–20 — Saving Private Ryan

In the movie, *Saving Private Ryan,* a platoon goes in search of Pvt. James Ryan in the days following D-Day. He is the sole survivor of four sons. The Chief of the Army has ordered he should be brought back, to spare his mother the loss of all of her sons. The members of the platoon — in various ways — question the fairness of sacrificing them to save Pvt. Ryan. Were they right? When found, Ryan refuses to leave his own platoon, abandoning them as they defend a bridge. He thus puts the platoon in danger, defying orders. Was *he* right?

PROBLEM 2–21 — I Will Not Protect Abortion Clinics

Angelo Rodriguez is a patrol officer with the Chicago Police Department. He refuses, as a matter of religion, to provide protection to abortion clinics in his district. He refused an alternative assignment to another district because under the police contract he had freedom of choice. He was then fired. He claims he was subjected to discrimination on the ground of religion, contrary to law and the Constitution.

The Court upheld the City, saying it had made a reasonable accommodation to Mr. Rodriguez's beliefs. Chief Judge Posner, concurring, would affirm for different reasons. He wrote:

> The ground on which my colleagues have based decision is narrow — that the city made a reasonable effort to accommodate Officer Rodriguez's religious beliefs. It is convincing, but we would be doing a big favor for the bench and bar of this circuit, and for it[illegible] fire departm[illegible] little risk of error, if we made clear that police officers and firefighters have no right under Title VII of the Civil Rights Act of 1964 to recuse themselves from having to protect persons of whose activities they disapprove for religious (or any other) reasons. Mr. Rodriguez, a Chicago police officer, claims, I have no reason to doubt sincerely, that it violates his religious principles to guard abortion clinics. He is entitled to his view. He is not entitled to demand that his police duties be altered to conform to his view any more than a volunteer member of the armed forces is entitled to demand that he be excused from performing military duties that conflict with his religious faith (I specify "volunteer" because the claim of a conscripted soldier is stronger, see *Welsh v. United States*, 398 U.S. 333, 344, 90 S.Ct. 1792, 26 L.Ed.2d. 308 (1970); *United States v. Seeger* 380 U.S. 163, 185-87, 85 S.Ct. 850, 13 L.Ed.2d 733 (1965)), or than a firefighter is entitled to demand that he be entitled to refuse to fight fires in

places of worship of religious sects that he regards as Satanic. The objection to recusal in all of these cases is not the inconvenience to the police department, the armed forces, or the fire department, as the case may be, though that might be considerable in some instances. The objection is to the loss of public confidence in governmental protective services if the public knows that its protectors are at liberty to pick and choose whom to protect.

The public knows that its protectors have a private agenda; everyone does. But it would like to think that they leave that agenda at home when they are on duty — that Jewish policemen protect neo-Nazi demonstrators, that Roman Catholic policemen protect abortion clinics, that Black Muslim policemen protect Christians and Jews, that Fundamentalist Christian policemen protect noisy atheists and white-hating Rastafarians, that Mormon policemen protect Scientologists, and that Greek-Orthodox policemen of Serbian ethnicity protect Roman Catholic Croats. We judges certainly want to think that U.S. Marshals protect us from assaults and threats without regard to whether, for example, we vote for or against the pro-life position in abortion cases.

. . . .

Although the principle that public-safety officers have no right to pick and choose on religious or other personal grounds among the people whom they protect applies to all police officers employed by any public police force, including the U.S. Marshals Service, the FBI, and the Secret Service, and to all firefighters employed by public fire departments, I would reserve the case we put at argument, of a fire department paramedic who refuses on religious grounds to obey an order by his superiors to withdraw life support from a patient. That would be a case of a public-safety officer insisting on protecting all members of the public rather than refusing to protect some of them. It would thus be a different case from the present one and we need not decide today how it ought to be decided.

Do you agree with Judge Posner? (*See Rodriguez v. City of Chicago*, 156 F.3d 771.) *Shouldn't* society make a reasonable accommodation for religious beliefs or conscientious scruples? Or should Officer Rodriguez simply be a good soldier — like the Nazi S.S. prison camp guard in *United States v. Schmidt*, in Chapter 1 (or is that an unfair comparison)? Why would Posner impose a *lesser* burden on the paramedic — isn't there a right to die?

Chapter 3

BENEFICENCE: PHYSICIANS AND PATIENTS

§ 3.01 Introduction

The preceding chapters have surveyed two subjects: what are the essential qualities of community membership (and who is excluded) and what are the essential qualities of personhood for those who assume membership (with accompanying rights and responsibilities). This third chapter focuses more narrowly on physicians, patients and fiduciary relationships within an ethical community. It is that relationship between patient and provider, which is central to working out the principles and problems of health care within a framework of bioethics.

Bioethics, of course, affects much of society in many of its relationships. There are bioethical dimensions to the relationships between organ donor and recipient, surrogate mother and parents, wives seeking abortions and their husbands. When people speak of bioethics, however, they usually have in mind the unique relations between physicians (or other providers, such as nurses or psychologists) and patients, and the fiduciary obligations between them. These are relationships characterized by trust, imbalance of power and service.

In the main, the burden is upon the *physician,* but this is misleading. Patients have obligations as well, to physicians, hospitals and family. For example, when one addresses the "right to die," it is important to consider the patient's obligation to the physician who is being involved in what may offend the physician's fundamental ethical commitment to his or her profession. So also, a patient with AIDS may have an obligation of disclosure. This chapter therefore considers as an ethical matter the problems of conscience for the physician and the patient.

Different bioethicists analyze the subject differently, but most view the physician-patient relationship as somehow unique. The present text disagrees, relying on a traditional point of view to the effect that the essentials of a physician's obligation can be captured in three fiduciary concepts: fidelity, candor and competence. These are the obligations of *all* fiduciaries whether attorneys, clergy or physicians. Under these headings, the medical subjects of conflicts of interest, confidentiality, abuse of patients; informed consent, therapeutic privilege, experimentation; and best efforts, effectiveness and malpractice can all be effectively surveyed.

Three points of departure should be noted. First, a number of bioethical texts involve discussion of problems which are, at best, of infrequent occurrence and of interest principally for that very reason. The subjects presented here are — it is hoped — of more mainstream concern. Yet most bioethical texts avoid addressing these subjects, such as sexual abuse of patients, and managed care, which are, it is submitted, essential subjects in any bioethical review of the obligations of health care providers. Second, there is no effort to use the concepts of "beneficence," "nonmaleficence," "autonomy" and "justice," usually used by bioethicists. These four concepts seem unfortunately physician-based, poorly constructed and lacking in the content of patient experience. Most bioethical problems arise when candor is compromised, often by government dictate. Fidelity then fails and care suffers. These three organizing principles — fidelity, candor and care — provide the structure for most (but not all) obligations of providers to patients. The most important consideration is candor, including disclosure and informed consent.

Finally, a number of subjects which might be included in the physician-patient fiduciary relationship, such as ethical conception, DNR orders, prenatal screening, patient self-abuse (*e.g.*, tobacco or narcotics), maternal-fetal conflicts, organ transplants, vaccination, and physician-assisted death are all treated separately in Chapter IV. These, it is submitted, are instances of *ethical choices,* by both physicians and patients. It is the thesis of this text that ethics is less a set of rules than a structure for organization and a process of decision making. For that reason, the last chapter may be viewed as testing the principles developed in this and the preceding two chapters by applying them in particular contexts.

We begin with the first fiduciary principle, fidelity.

§ 3.02 Fiduciary Obligations: Fidelity

Fidelity is a beginning point for professional relations, whether for physicians, attorneys, accountants or priests. A patient does not buy a *product*; he or she seeks *care* and reposes *trust.* The professional should be free of (or — at minimum — disclose) conflicts of interest, should preserve the patient's confidences and not abuse or abandon the patient. These are the *sine qua non* for what follows — the candor and care the patient needs.

We therefore begin with conflicts of interest and the problem of competing loyalties.

[1] Conflicts of Interest

A physician's primary responsibility is to his or her patient. But conflicting demands may come from the patient's family or employer or HMO or from state licensing boards or legislatures. Too, the physician's own employer may impose demands, as may a physician's research agenda. We begin with this, in *Moore v. California.*

MOORE v. REGENTS OF UNIVERSITY OF CALIFORNIA

793 P.2d 479 (Cal. 1990)

I. Introduction

Panelli, Justice.

. . . .

II. Facts

. . . .

Moore first visited UCLA Medical Center on October 5, 1976, shortly after he learned that he had hairy-cell Leukemia. After hospitalizing Moore and "withdr[awing] extensive amounts of blood, bone marrow aspirate, and other bodily substances," Golde confirmed that diagnosis. At this time all defendants, including Golde, were aware that "certain blood products and blood components were of great value in a number of commercial and scientific efforts" and that access to a patient whose blood contained these substances would provide "competitive, commercial, and scientific advantages."

On October 8, 1976, Golde recommended that Moore's spleen be removed. Golde informed Moore "that he had reason to fear for his life, and that the proposed splenectomy operation . . . was necessary to slow down the progress of his disease." Based upon Golde's representations, Moore signed a written consent form authorizing the splenectomy.

Before the operation, Golde and Quan "formed the intent and made arrangements to obtain portions of [Moore's] spleen following its removal" and to take them to a separate research unit. Golde gave written instructions to this effect on October 18 and 19, 1976. These research activities "were not intended to have . . . any relation to [Moore's] medical . . . care." However, neither Golde nor Quan informed Moore of their plans to conduct this research or requested his permission. Surgeons at UCLA Medical Center, whom the complaint does not name as defendants, removed Moore's spleen on October 20, 1976.

Moore returned to the UCLA Medical Center several times between November 1976 and September 1983. He did so at Golde's direction and based upon representations "that such visits were necessary and required for his health and well-being, and based upon the trust inherent in and by virtue of the physician-patient relationship. . . ." On each of these visits Golde withdrew additional samples of "blood, blood serum, skin, bone marrow aspirate, and sperm." On each occasion Moore traveled to the UCLA Medical Center from his home in Seattle because he had been told that the procedures were to be performed only there and only under Golde's direction.

"In fact, [however,] throughout the period of time that [Moore] was under [Golde's] care and treatment, . . . the defendants were actively involved in a number of activities which they concealed from [Moore]. . . ." Specifically, defendants were conducting research on Moore's cells and planned to "benefit financially and competitively . . . [by exploiting the cells] and [their] exclusive access to [the cells] by virtue of [Golde's] ongoing physician-patient relationship. . . ."

Sometime before August 1979, Golde established a cell line from Moore's T-lymphocytes. On January 30, 1981, the Regents applied for a patent on the cell line, listing Golde and Quan as inventors. "[B]y virtue of an established policy . . . , [the] Regents, Golde, and Quan would share in any royalties or profits . . . arising out of [the] patent." The patent issued on March 20, 1984, naming Golde and Quan as the inventors of the cell line and the Regents as the assignee of the patent.

The Regent's patent also covers various methods for using the cell line to produce lymphokines. Moore admits in his complaint that "the true clinical potential of each of the lymphokines . . . [is] difficult to predict, [but] . . . competing commercial firms in these relevant fields have published reports in biotechnology industry periodicals predicting a potential market of approximately $3.01 Billion Dollars by the year 1990 for a whole range of [such lymphokines]. . . ."

With the Regents' assistance, Golde negotiated agreements for commercial development of the cell line and products to be derived from it. Under an agreement with Genetics Institute, Golde "became a paid consultant" and "acquired the rights to 75,000 shares of common stock." Genetics Institute also agreed to pay Golde and the Regents "at least $330,000 over three years, including a pro-rata share of [Golde's] salary and fringe benefits, in exchange for . . . exclusive access to the materials and research performed" on the cell line and products derived from it. On June 4, 1982, Sandoz "was added to the agreement," and compensation payable to Golde and the Regents was increased by $110,000. "[T]hroughout this period, . . . Quan spent as much as 70 [percent] of her time working for [the] Regents on research" related to the cell line.

Based upon these allegations, Moore attempted to state 13 causes of action.[1] Each defendant demurred to each purported cause of action. The superior court, however, expressly considered the validity of only the first cause of action, conversion. Reasoning that the remaining causes of action incorporated the earlier, defective allegations, the superior court sustained a general demurrer to the entire complaint with leave to amend. . . .

. . . .

III. Discussion

A. Breach of Fiduciary Duty and Lack of Informed Consent

Moore repeatedly alleges that Golde failed to disclose the extent of his research and economic interests in Moore' cells[2] before obtaining consent to the medical procedures by which the cells were extracted. These allegations,

[1] (1) "Conversion"; (2) "lack of informed consent"; (3) "breach of fiduciary duty"; (4) "fraud and deceit"; (5) "unjust enrichment"; (6) "quasi-contract"; (7) "bad faith breach of the implied covenant of good faith and fair dealing"; (8) "intentional infliction of emotional distress"; (9) "negligent misrepresentation"; (10) "intentional interference with prospective advantageous economic relationships"; (11) "slander of title"; (12) "accounting"; and (13) "declaratory relief."

[2] In this opinion we use the inclusive term "cells" to describe all of the cells taken from Moore's body, including blood cells, bone marrow, spleen, etc.

in our view, state a cause of action against Golde for invading a legally protected interest of his patient. This cause of action can properly be characterized either as the breach of a fiduciary duty to disclose facts material to the patient's consent or, alternatively, as the performance of medical procedures without first having obtained the patient's informed consent.

Our analysis begins with three well-established principles. First, "a person of adult years and in sound mind has the right, in the exercise of control over his own body, to determine whether or not to submit to lawful medical treatment." *Cobbs v. Grant, Schloendorff v. Society of New York Hospital.* Second, "the patient's consent to treatment, to be effective, must be an informed consent." Third, in soliciting the patient's consent, a physician has a fiduciary duty to disclose all information material to the patient's decision.

These principles lead to the following conclusions: (1) a physician must disclose personal interests unrelated to the patient's health, whether research or economic, that may affect the physician's professional judgment; and (2) a physician's failure to disclose such interests may give rise to a cause of action for performing medical procedures without informed consent or breach of fiduciary duty.

. . . .

[A] physician who treats a patient in whom he also has a research interest has potentially conflicting loyalties. This is because medical treatment decisions are made on the basis of proportionality — weighing the benefits *to the patient* against the risks *to the patient*. . . . A physician who adds his own research interests to this balance may be tempted to order a scientifically useful procedure or test that offers marginal, or no, benefits to the patient.[3] The possibility that an interest extraneous to the patient's health has affected the physician's judgment is something that a reasonable patient would want to know in deciding whether to consent to a proposed course of treatment.

Golde argues that the scientific use of cells that have already been removed cannot possibly affect the patient's medical interests. The argument is correct in one instance but not in another. If a physician has no plans to conduct research on a patient's cells at the time he recommends the medical procedure by which they are taken, then the patient's medical interests have not been impaired. In that instance the argument is correct. On the other hand, a physician who does have a preexisting research interest might, consciously or unconsciously, take that into consideration in recommending the procedure. In that instance the argument is incorrect: the physician's extraneous motivation may affect his judgment and is, thus, material to the patient's consent.

. . . .

Accordingly, we hold that a physician who is seeking a patient's consent for a medical procedure must, in order to satisfy his fiduciary duty[4] . . . and

[3] This is, in fact, precisely what Moore has alleged with respect to the postoperative withdrawals of blood and other substances.

[4] In some respects the term "fiduciary" is too broad. In this context the term "fiduciary" signifies only that a physician must disclose all facts material to the patient's decision. A physician is not the patient's financial adviser. As we have already discussed, the reason why a physician must disclose possible conflicts is not because he has a duty to protect his patient's financial interests, but because certain personal interests may affect professional judgment.

to obtain the patient's informed consent, disclose personal interests unrelated to the patient's health, whether research or economic, that may affect his medical judgment.

The superior court held that the lack of essential allegations prevented Moore from stating a cause of action based on the splenectomy. According to the superior court, Moore failed to allege that the operation lacked a therapeutic purpose or that the procedure was totally unrelated to therapeutic purposes. In our view, however, neither allegation is essential. Even if the splenectomy had a therapeutic purpose, it does not follow that Golde had no duty to disclose his additional research and economic interests. As we have already discussed, the existence of a motivation for a medical procedure unrelated to the patient's health is a potential conflict of interest and a fact material to the patient's decision.

. . . .

B. Conversion

Moore also attempts to characterize the invasion of his rights as a conversion — a tort that protects against interference with possessory and ownership interests in personal property. He theorizes that he continued to own his cells following their removal from his body, at least for the purpose of directing their use, and that he never consented to their use in potentially lucrative medical research. Thus, to complete Moore's argument, defendants' unauthorized use of his cells constitutes a conversion. As a result of the alleged conversion, Moore claims a proprietary interest in each of the products that any of the defendants might ever create from his cells or the patented cell line.

No court, however, has ever in a reported decision imposed conversion liability for the use of human cells in medical research. While that fact does not end our inquiry, it raises a flag of caution. In effect, what Moore is asking us to do is to impose a tort duty on scientists to investigate the consensual pedigree of each human cell sample used in research. To impose such a duty, which would affect medical research of importance to all of society, implicates policy concerns far removed from the traditional, two-party ownership disputes in which the law of conversion arose. Invoking a tort theory originally used to determine whether the loser or the finder of a horse had the better title, Moore claims ownership of the results of socially important medical research, including the genetic code for chemicals that regulate the functions of every human being's immune system.

. . . .

I. Moore's Claim Under Existing Law

. . . .

Since Moore clearly did not expect to retain possession of his cells following their removal, to sue for their conversion he must have retained an ownership interest in them. But there are several reasons to doubt that he did retain any such interest. . . .

. . . .

Lacking direct authority for importing the law of conversion into this context, Moore relies, as did the Court of Appeal, primarily on decisions addressing privacy rights. One line of cases involves unwanted publicity. These opinions hold that every person has a proprietary interest in his own likeness and that unauthorized, business use of a likeness is redressible as a tort. But in neither opinion did the authoring court expressly base its holding on property law. . . .

Not only are the wrongful-publicity cases irrelevant to the issue of conversion, but the analogy to them seriously misconceives the nature of the genetic materials and research involved in this case. Moore, adopting the analogy originally advanced by the Court of Appeal, argues that "[i]f the courts have found a sufficient proprietary interest in one's persona, how could one not have a right in one's own genetic material, something far more profoundly the essence of one's human uniqueness than a name or a face?" However, as the defendants' patent makes clear — and the complaint, too, if read with an understanding of the scientific terms which it has borrowed from the patent — the goal and result of defendants' efforts has been to manufacture lymphokines. Lymphokines, unlike a name or a face, have the same molecular structure in every human being and the same, important functions in every human being's immune system. Moreover, the particular genetic material which is responsible for the natural production of lymphokines, and which defendants use to manufacture lymphokines in the laboratory, is also the same in every person; it is no more unique to Moore than the number of vertebrae in the spine or the chemical formula of hemoglobin.

Another privacy case offered by analogy to support Moore's claim establishes only that patients have a right to refuse medical treatment. *Bouvia v. Superior Court*. . . . *Yet* one may earnestly wish to protect privacy and dignity without accepting the extremely problematic conclusion that interference with those interests amounts to a conversion of personal property. Nor is it necessary to force the round pegs of "privacy" and "dignity" into the square hole of "property" in order to protect the patient, since the fiduciary-duty and informed-consent theories protect these interests directly by requiring full disclosure.

The next consideration that makes Moore's claim of ownership problematic is California statutory law, which drastically limits a patient's control over excised cells. Pursuant to Health and Safety Code Section 7054.4, "[n]otwithstanding any other provision of law, recognizable anatomical parts, human tissues, anatomical human remains, or infectious waste following conclusion of scientific use shall be disposed of by interment, incineration, or any other method determined by the state department [of health services] to protect the public health and safety." . . . By restricting how excised cells may be used and requiring their eventual destruction, the statute eliminates so many of the rights ordinarily attached to property that one cannot simply assume that what is left amounts to "property" or "ownership" for purposes of conversion law.

. . . .

Finally, the subject matter of the Regents' patent — the patented cell line and the products derived from it — cannot be Moore's property. This is because the patented cell line is both factually and legally distinct from the cells taken from Moore's body. Federal law permits the patenting of organisms that represent the product of "human ingenuity," but not naturally occurring organisms. *Diamond v. Chakrabarty,* 447 U.S. 303, 309-10 (1980). Human cell lines are patentable because "[l]ong-term adaptation and growth of human tissues and cells in culture is difficult — often considered an art . . . ," and the probability of success is low. It is this *inventive effort* that patent law rewards, not the discovery of naturally occurring raw materials. Thus, Moore's allegations that he owns the cell line and the products derived from it are inconsistent with the patent, which constitutes an authoritative determination that the cell line is the production of invention. Since such allegations are nothing more than arguments or conclusions of law, they of course do not bind us.

2. Should Conversion Liability Be Extended?

. . . .

[T]o extend the conversion theory would utterly sacrifice the other goal of protecting innocent parties. Since conversion is a strict liability tort, it would impose liability on all those into whose hands the cells come, whether or not the particular defendant participated in, or knew of, the inadequate disclosures that violated the patient's right to make an informed decision. In contrast to the conversion theory, the fiduciary-duty and informed-consent theories protect the patient directly, without punishing innocent parties or creating disincentives to the conduct of socially beneficial research.

. . . .

The extension of conversion law into this area will hinder research by restricting access to the necessary raw materials. Thousands of human cell lines already exist in tissue repositories, such as the American Type Culture Collection and those operated by the National Institutes of Health and the American Cancer Society. These repositories respond to tens of thousands of requests for samples annually. Since the patent office requires the holders of patents on cell lines to make samples available to anyone, many patent holders place their cell lines in repositories to avoid the administrative burden of responding to requests. At present, human cell lines are routinely copied and distributed to other researchers for experimental purposes, usually free of charge.[5] This exchange of scientific materials, which still is relatively free and efficient, will surely be compromised if each cell sample becomes the potential subject matter of a lawsuit.

. . . .

. . . [T]he theory of liability that Moore urges us to endorse threatens to destroy the economic incentive to conduct important medical research. If the use of cells in research is a conversion, then with every cell sample a researcher purchases a ticket in a litigation lottery. Because liability for

5 "Under the current system of tissue banks, many firms have access to the tissue so the probability of efficient use of those tissues increases. . . . Presently, researchers need only ask for tissue samples, and their requests are usually granted by their own research facility, other research facilities, or tissue banks." (Note, *Source Compensation*, Notre Dame L. Rev. at 635.)

conversion is predicated on a continuing ownership interest, "companies are unlikely to invest heavily in developing, manufacturing, or [illegible] a product when uncertainty about [illegible] . . . .

For these reasons, we hold that the allegations of Moore's third amended complaint state a cause of action for breach of fiduciary duty or lack of informed consent, but not conversion.

IV. Disposition

The decision of the Court of Appeal is affirmed in part and reversed in part. . . .

Arabian, Justice, concurring.

I join in the views cogently expounded by the majority. I write separately to give voice to a concern that I believe informs much of that opinion but finds little or no expression therein. I speak of the moral issue.

Plaintiff has asked us to recognize and enforce a right to sell one's own body tissue *for profit.* He entreats us to regard the human vessel — the single most venerated and protected subject in any civilized society — as equal with the basest commercial commodity. He urges us to commingle the sacred with the profane. He asks much.

. . . .

Whether, as plaintiff urges, his cells should be treated as property susceptible to conversion is not, in my view, ours to decide. The question implicates choices which not only reflect, but which ultimately define our essence. A mark of wisdom for us as expositors of the law is the recognition that we cannot cure every ill, mediate every dispute, resolve every conundrum. Sometimes, as Justice Brandeis said, "the most important thing we do, is not doing."

. . . .

. . . First, plaintiff in this matter is not without a remedy; he remains free to pursue defendants on a breach-of-fiduciary-duty theory, as well as, perhaps, other tort claims not before us. Second, a judicial [illegible], while supple, is not without [illegible] Courts cannot and should not seek to [illegible] a remedy for every "heartache and the thousand natural shocks that flesh is heir to." Sometimes, the discretion of forbearance *is* the better part of responsive valor. This is such an occasion.

Broussard, Justice, concurring and dissenting.

. . . .

II

With respect to the conversion cause of action, I dissent from the majority's conclusion that the facts alleged in this case do not state a cause of action for conversion.

. . . Because plaintiff alleges that defendants wrongfully interfered with his right to determine, prior to the removal of his body parts, how those parts would be used after removal, I conclude that the complaint states a cause of action under traditional, common law conversion principles.

. . . .

The majority opinion fails to recognize, however, that, in light of the allegations of the present complaint, the pertinent inquiry is not whether a patient generally retains an ownership interest in a body part after its removal from his body, but rather whether a patient has a right to determine, before a body part is removed, the use to which the part will be put after removal. Although the majority opinion suggests that there are "reasons to doubt" that a patient retains "any" ownership interest in his organs or cells after removal, the opinion fails to identify any statutory provision or common law authority that indicates that a patient does not generally have the right, before a body part is removed, to choose among the permissible uses to which the part may be put after removal. On the contrary, the most closely related statutory scheme — the Uniform Anatomical Gift Act — makes it quite clear that patient does have this right.

. . . .

It is also clear, under traditional common law principles, that this right of a patient to control the future use of his organ is protected by the law of conversion. As a general matter, the tort of conversion protects an individual not only against improper interference with the right of possession of his property but also against unauthorized use of his property or improper interference with his right to control the use of his property. . . .

. . . .

III

. . . .

One of the majority's principal policy concerns is that "[t]he extension of conversion law into this area will hinder research by restricting access to the necessary raw materials" — the thousand of cell lines and tissues already in cell and tissue repositories. The majority suggests that the "exchange of scientific materials, which still is relatively free and efficient, will surely be compromised if each cell sample becomes the potential subject of a lawsuit."

This policy argument is flawed in a number of respects. First, the majority's stated concern does not provide any justification for barring plaintiff from bringing a conversion action against a party who does not obtain organs or cells from a cell bank but who directly interferes with or misappropriates a patient's right to control the use of his organs or cells. . . .

Second, even with respect to those persons who are not involved in the initial conversion, the majority's policy arguments are less than compelling. To begin with, the majority's fear that the availability of a conversion remedy will restrict access to existing cell lines is unrealistic. In the vast majority of instances the tissues and cells in existing repositories will *not* represent a potential source of liability because they will have come from patients who consented to their organ's use for scientific purposes under circumstances in which such consent was not tainted by a failure to disclose the known valuable nature of the cells. . . .

Furthermore, even in the [illegible] instance — like the present case — in which a conversion action might be successfully pursued, the potential liability is not likely "to destroy the economic incentive to conduct important medical research," as the majority asserts. If, as the majority suggests, the great bulk of the value of a cell line patent and derivative products is attributable to the efforts of medical researchers and drug companies, rather than to the "raw materials" taken from a patient, the patient's damages will be correspondingly limited, and innocent medical researchers and drug manufacturers will retain the considerable economic benefits resulting from their own work. Under established conversion law, a "subsequent innocent converter" does not forfeit the proceeds of his own creative efforts, but rather "is entitled to the benefit of any work or labor that he has expended on the [property]. . . ."

Finally, the majority's analysis of the relevant policy considerations tellingly omits a most pertinent consideration. In identifying the interests of the patient that are implicated by the decision whether to recognize a conversion cause of action, the opinion speaks only of the "patient's right to make autonomous medical decisions" and fails even to mention the patient's interest in obtaining the economic value, if any, that may adhere in the subsequent use of his own body parts. Although such economic value may constitute a fortuitous "windfall" to the patient, the fortuitous nature of the economic value does not justify the creation of a novel exception from conversion liability which sanctions the intentional misappropriation of that value from the patient.

. . . .

Mosk, Justice, dissenting.

I dissent.

. . . .

3.

The majority's third and last reason for their conclusion that Moore has no cause of action for conversion under existing law is that "the subject matter of the Regents' patent — the patented cell line and the products derived from it — cannot be Moore's property." The majority then offer a dual explanation: "This is because the patented cell line is *factually* and *legally* distinct from the cells taken from Moore's body." Neither branch of the explanation withstands analysis.

First, in support of their statement that the Mo cell line is "factually distinct" from Moore's cells, the majority assert that "Cells change while being developed into a cell line and continue to change over time," and in particular may acquire an abnormal number of chromosomes. No one disputes these assertions, but they are nonetheless irrelevant. For present purposes no distinction can be drawn between Moore's cells and the Mo cell line. It appears that the principal reason for establishing a cell line is not to "improve" the quality of the parent cells but simply to extend their life indefinitely, in order to permit long-term study and/or exploitation of the qualities already present in such cells. The complaint alleges that Moore's cells naturally produced certain valuable proteins in larger than normal quantities; indeed, that was why defendants were eager to culture them in the first place. Defendants do not claim that the cells of the Mo line are in any degree more productive of such proteins than were Moore's own cells. . . .

Second, the majority assert in effect that Moore cannot have an ownership interest in the Mo cell line because defendants patented it. The majority's point wholly fails to meet Moore's claim that he is entitled to compensation for defendants' unauthorized use of his bodily tissues *before* defendants patented the Mo cell line: defendants undertook such use immediately after the splenectomy on October 20, 1976, and continued to extract and use Moore's cells and tissue at least until September 20, 1983; the patent, however, did not issue until March 20, 1984, more than seven years after the unauthorized use began. Whatever the legal consequences of that event, it did not operate retroactively to immunize defendants from accountability for conduct occurring long before the patent was granted.

. . . .

4.

Having concluded — mistakenly, in my view — that Moore has no cause of action for conversion under existing law, the majority next consider whether to "extend" the conversion cause of action to this context. Again the majority find three reasons not to do so, and again I respectfully disagree with each.

. . . .

To begin with, if the relevant exchange of scientific materials was ever "free and efficient," it is much less so today. Since biological products of genetic engineering became patentable in 1980 (*Diamond v. Chakrabarty,* 447 U.S. 303 (1980)), human cell lines have been amenable to patent protection and, as the Court of Appeal observed in its opinion below, "The rush to patent for exclusive use has been rampant." . . .

. . . .

Secondly, to the extent that cell cultures and cell lines may still be "freely exchanged," *e.g.,* for purely research purposes, it does not follow that the researcher who obtains such material must necessarily remain ignorant of any limitations on its use: by means of appropriate recordkeeping, the researcher can be assured that the source of the material has consented to his proposed use of it, and hence that such use is not a conversion. . . .

. . . .

In any event, in my view whatever merit the majority's single policy consideration may have is outweighed by two contrary considerations, i.e., policies that are promoted by recognizing that every individual has a legally protectible property interest in his own body and its products. First, our society acknowledges a profound ethical imperative to respect the human body as the physical and temporal expression of the unique human persona. One manifestation of that respect is our prohibition against direct abuse of the body by torture or other forms of cruel or unusual punishment. Another is our prohibition against indirect abuse of the body by its economic exploitation for the sole benefit of another person. The most abhorrent form of such exploitation, of course, was the institution of slavery. Its lesser forms, such as indentured servitude or even debtor's prison, have also disappeared. Yet their specter haunts the laboratories and boardrooms of today's biotechnological research-industrial complex. It arises wherever scientists or industrialists claim, as defendants claim here, the right to appropriate and exploit a patient's tissue for their sole economic benefit — the right, in other words, to freely mine or harvest valuable physical properties of the patient's body. . . .

A second policy consideration adds notions of equity to those of ethics. Our society values fundamental fairness in dealings between its members, and condemns the unjust enrichment of any member at the expense of another. This is particularly true when, as here, the parties are not in equal bargaining positions. We are repeatedly told that the commercial products of the biotechnological revolution "hold the promise of tremendous profit." In the case at bar, for example, the complaint alleges that the market for the kinds of proteins produced by the Mo cell line was predicted to exceed $3 billion by 1990. These profits are currently shared exclusively between the biotechnology industry and the universities that support that industry. The profits are shared in a wide variety of ways, including "direct entrepreneurial ties to genetic-engineering firms" and "an equity interest in fledgling biotechnology firms." Thus the complaint alleges that because of his development of the Mo cell line defendant Golde became a paid consultant of defendant Genetics Institute and acquired the rights to 75,000 shares of that firm's stock at a cost of 1 cent each; that Genetics Institute further contracted to pay Golde and the Regents at least $330,000 over 3 years, including a pro rata share of Golde's salary and fringe benefits; and that defendant Sandoz Pharmaceuticals Corporation subsequently contracted to increase that compensation by a further $110,000.

There is, however, a third party to the biotechnology enterprise — the patient who is the source of the blood or tissue from which all these profits are derived. While he may be a silent partner, his contribution to the venture is absolutely crucial: as pointed out above, but for the cells of Moore's body taken by defendants there would have been no Mo cell line at all. Yet defendants deny that Moore is entitled to any share whatever in the proceeds of this cell line. This is both inequitable and immoral. . . .

. . . .

6.

The majority's final reason for refusing to recognize a conversion cause of action on these facts is that "there is no pressing need" to do so because the complaint also states another cause of action that is assertedly adequate to the task; that cause of action is "the breach of a fiduciary duty to disclose facts material to the patient's consent or, alternatively, . . . the performance of medical procedures without first having obtained the patient's informed consent." Although last, this reason is not the majority's least; in fact, it underlies much of the opinion's discussion of the conversion cause of action, recurring like a leitmotif throughout that discussion.

. . . .

. . . [I]t is not even enough for the plaintiff to prove that he personally would have refused consent to the proposed treatment if he had been fully informed; he must also prove that in the same circumstances *no reasonably prudent person* would have given such consent. . . .

. . . .

Third, the nondisclosure cause of action fails to reach a major class of potential defendants: all those who are outside the strict physician-patient relationship with the plaintiff. Thus the majority concede that here only defendant Golde, the treating physician, can be directly liable to Moore on a nondisclosure cause of action: "The Regents, Quan, Genetics Institute, and Sandoz are not physicians. In contrast to Golde, none of these defendants stood in a fiduciary relationship with Moore or had the duty to obtain Moore's informed consent to medical procedures." As to these defendants, the majority can offer Moore only a slim hope of recovery: if they are to be liable on a nondisclosure cause of action, say the majority, "it can only be on account of Golde's acts and on the basis of a recognized theory of secondary liability, such as respondeat superior." . . .

. . . .

In sum, the nondisclosure cause of action (1) is unlikely to be successful in most cases, (2) fails to protect patients' rights to share in the proceeds of the commercial exploitation of their tissue, and (3) may allow the true exploiters to escape liability. It is thus not an adequate substitute, in my view, for the conversion cause of action.

. . . .

NOTES AND QUESTIONS

1. The problem posed in *Moore* may seem sufficiently unusual so that it, at most, is of theoretical interest. The contrary is true. In many procedures and hospitals, patients are used instrumentally as research and teaching vehicles and human materials are appropriated by health care providers. This is true in every labor and delivery with respect to placental material. It is true also with every fertility procedure where multiple eggs are withdrawn from a woman, fertilized, with reimplantation of only a few. In many surgical and other procedures, multiple samples of tissue or blood are drawn, yet many are not used or required for serving the patient. And, of course, every time a patient dies, the body becomes a potential source of "harvesting."

2. What was different in *Moore* was that the doctors, *before* the operation, formed the intent and made arrangements to obtain portions of his spleen following its removal. Would the case have been decided differently if the physicians had formed their intent after the surgery? How?

   They then proceeded with a course of continuing contact and treatment which was designed, at least in part, to obtain further samples. Coupled with this conflict or motivation, the physicians also engaged in withholding of information *as to* their conflict, their profit motive and their activities. Thus, the physicians had a competing set of interests while serving Mr. Moore and then engaged in a pattern of deception. [illegible] the later deceptions [illegible] would *that* have made a difference?

3. In *Moore,* the plaintiff alleged thirteen separate theories of misconduct, from conversion to lack of informed consent to breach of fiduciary duty, plus fraud and deceit and unjust enrichment. The Court settled upon breach of fiduciary duty as the appropriate claim. It rejected conversion, which implies the taking of "property." Why? Was not the spleen the *property* of Mr. Moore? If so, did not the doctors take it improperly? Should he get it back? Or its equivalent?

4. Wouldn't a better argument be conflict of interests, not failure to disclose? Then the defense of intervening choice by the patient would be irrelevant, wouldn't it? And the conflict could reach well beyond the physicians to *their* employers, as well. Or would the problem of causation still remain?

5. Justice Mosk is concerned that the majority's reliance on fiduciary duty and informed consent will leave Mr. Moore without an adequate remedy. His reason is that Moore would have to show that, if he had been given full information, he — as a reasonable person — would have refused consent. (Informed consent itself will be treated separately in § 3.03.) Mosk's point is that no one would refuse. The doctors could then do what they want, unless the spleen is viewed as Moore's property. Do you agree with Justice Mosk's analysis?

6. The concurring Justice, Justice Arabian, argues that Mr. Moore believes that people should be able to sell their bodies for profit. He is offended by that. Is that, in fact, what Mr. Moore was arguing? And if so, what is wrong with that? The majority is concerned, according to concurring Justice Broussard, that a property approach to the case would impede the development of science and the products of science. Is this so? If so, is it a bad thing? Does Justice Mosk adequately respond to these concerns?

7. What *should* the measure of Mr. Moore's damages be? Assume that the cell line developed from his spleen is [illegible] billion dollars. Does [illegible] Assume that his spleen was worth $1.35. Is that what he should get? Or should he get one billion dollars, less the full capitalized value of the University's research facilities, as allocated to this project, plus the educational, research and career investments of the doctors involved? Should he get compensatory damages for breach of trust? Is not the pricing of the injury the best way really of settling on an ethical theory and determining responsibility and the extent of ethical departure?

8. In many settings, physicians have competing obligations. They may be employed by a university, by a hospital, by an HMO, by an employer, or an insurance company. The employment may be simply to examine, or it may be to do research (as to that, see *infra,* § 3.03[3]) or it may be to treat a patient. University hospitals engaged in education routinely use patients as vehicles for instruction. Employers and insurance

companies routinely hire physicians to examine patients *for them.* The patient's expectations nevertheless may simply be those of a conventional patient: seeking the best care. Institutionally, the physician may be prevented from meeting those expectations. What should the physician do?

The answer turns on whether a court finds a relationship exists between the patient and the physician. We begin with *Deramus v. Jackson Life.*

DERAMUS v. JACKSON NATIONAL LIFE INSURANCE COMPANY

92 F.3d 274 (5th Cir. 1996)

. . . .

Facts

In January, 1988, Mr. Doe had a life insurance policy with defendant which provided coverage of $500,000.00. Desiring additional life insurance, Mr. Doe applied for an increase of $300,000.00. Mrs. Doe simultaneously submitted an application for $250,000.00 of life insurance to replace a policy she held with another insurance company.

As part of its application process, JNL required its applicants to submit to medical examinations at Examination Management Services, Inc., (EMS), a paramedical facility designated by JNL. These examinations, which included blood and urine tests, were vital to JNL's underwriting procedure. JNL reserved the right to refuse coverage if an applicant failed the medical examination. No one disputes that it was JNL's policy at the time to deny life insurance coverage to any individual who tested positive for the Human Immunodeficiency Virus (HIV), also known as the Acquired Immune Deficiency Syndrome (AIDS) virus. So, as part of its medical examination, JNL tested the blood of its applicants to detect any presence of antibodies or antigens to HIV.

On April 19, 1988, EMS, JNL's contract laboratory for blood work, ran a variety of tests on the Does' blood. Mr. Doe's blood tested positive for HIV. Mrs. Doe's tested negative. Thereafter, on April 21, 1988, the laboratory sent a telecopy of the Does' results to Dr. Lewis L. Stewart, Jr., JNL's medical director. Five days later, Ed Keller, the JNL underwriter in charge of the Does' applications, received a copy of the laboratory results. Keller then rejected Mr. Doe's application.

The notice of rejection mailed to Mr. Doe on April 26, 1988, did not tell him that he had been rejected because of the HIV test. . . .

In May of 1988, Mr. Doe was hospitalized at the Mississippi Baptist Medical Center in Jackson, Mississippi. During his hospital stay, Dr. Eric McVey, a specialist in infectious diseases, visited Mr. Doe and asked him if he had ever exposed himself to any HIV risk factors. Mr. Doe answered in the negative. No blood test was conducted at that time to detect the existence of HIV.

Eighteen months after undergoing the medical examination in connection with his life insurance application, Mr. Doe was hospitalized at Johns-Hopkins

Medical Center ("Johns-Hopkins") in Baltimore, Maryland. While there, Mr. Doe was diagnosed as being HIV-positive. Immediately after Mr. D[illegible] positive for the HIV vi[illegible] took an HIV test. Her test, as had the blood test administered by JNL, indicated that she was not HIV-positive. Mrs. Doe has since taken additional tests and all of them have shown that she does not have HIV.

By April of 1991, Mr. Doe's condition had deteriorated and he was again hospitalized at Johns-Hopkins. At that time, Mr. Doe once more wrote to JNL requesting that JNL submit the results of his 1988 medical examination to his physician, Dr. Donald M. Poretz of Annadale [sic], Virginia. Nine days before Mr. Doe succumbed to AIDS, his doctor received a report from JNL. The report revealed that Mr. Doe had tested positive for HIV in 1988.

. . . .

Confidentiality of the Relationship

According to plaintiff, the occasion which brought her and her husband together with JNL created a confidential relationship because JNL demanded access to confidential information and retained exclusive control of Mr. Doe's medical test results. This confidential relationship, argues plaintiff, was special and placed on JNL certain duties, one of which was to disclose the adverse results of medical examinations. Plaintiff relies heavily upon the case of *Lowery v. Guaranty Bank and Trust Co.*, 592 So.2d 79(Miss.1991), as her authority. . . . *Lowery* involved a demonstrated course of conduct between the parties whereby the plaintiff was justified in relying on the defendant band to protect a particular interest which was at stake. The defendant bank had a history of dealing with the plaintiff and her husband whereby the bank would place certain notes on hold until the husband could come in and take care of them. During this course of dealings, the plaintiff's credit life insurance was allowed to lapse and this resulted in the plaintiff not having the benefit of such credit life insurance upon the death of her husband. The court held that because of the course of conduct between the parties the plaintiff and her husband had justifiably relied on the defendant bank to their detriment. . . .

The factual urgings here simply fail to allow plaintiff here to step into the status of the *Lowery* plaintiff. Unlike the defendant bank in *Lowery*, JNL in no way mislead [sic] the Does into any inaction. JNL never promised the Does that JNL would warn them of any medical risks to their health, nor did JNL ever advise the Does that its silence as to the specific result of the medical examination should be construed as a positive medical finding. To the contrary, JNL here specifically advised the Does that JNL undertook simply to determine for itself whether it would accept the risk of providing insurance coverage to the Does. This set of circumstances hardly shows any justifiable reliance by the Does that JNL would do anything other than perform the limited function of a life insurance business, i.e., consider their applications for life insurance and possibly extend life insurance coverage upon any acceptance of such applications. Moreover, there is absolutely no proof that the Does in any way relaxed the care and vigilance that they would normally have exercised in looking out after their own health conditions in reliance upon any finding by JNL.

Duty to Protect Life and Limb

Plaintiff says that by requiring her and her husband to submit to medical examinations, JNL undertook "the performance of an act" which required JNL to act reasonably and with due care . . .

[W]hile it is true that JNL had a duty to conduct its affairs reasonably and with due care, in this case that duty did not require JNL to protect plaintiff and her husband from harm from any force(s) that JNL did not set into motion. . . .

Plaintiff also cites several cases in which physicians have been found negligent for acts they performed even though no physician-patient relationship existed, the principal case of which is *Meena v. Wilburn* (holding that "a doctor may be held liable for negligence if the traditional elements — duty, breach of duty, causation, and injury — are evidenced, where such liability is not negated by the absence of a doctor-patient relationship.") *Meena,* however, is not applicable here.

In *Meena,* a physician negligently instructed his nurse to remove the staples from the wrong patient's leg. When the physician undertook the task to treat the patient, he commensurately undertook a duty to perform that task with care. As a result of the physician's negligence, the patient was injured.

The instant case is quite different. JNL is not a physician, but an insurance company. Additionally, there is no evidence here showing plaintiff to have been treated by a physician. Rather, plaintiff merely submitted blood samples that were later tested by a laboratory. This factual scenario hardly equates to that of *Meena,* which simply involved a physician, who, because of his special discipline, is under a special duty. Moreover, here there is no evidence that JNL acted or failed to act in such a way which facilitated Mr. Doe's contraction of and eventual death from A.I.D.S.

. . . .

. . . Here, there was no relationship (i.e., contract) between the plaintiff and her husband and JNL as it relates to their 1988 applications. The Does merely completed applications for life insurance coverage. JNL accepted the applications for processing. JNL, however, did not accept Mr. Doe's offer to sell him a policy. As such, [a significant] relationship between the parties [] is lacking here.

Additionally, plaintiff cites a litany of cases which plaintiff insist holds that an employer or prospective employer owes a duty to convey the results of medical exams it requires an employee or prospective employee to take. *See Daly v. United States*, 946 F.2d 1467 (9th Cir. 1991) (where employer was a hospital and pre-employment exam was conducted by hospital physician, court extended the physician's duty to disclose beyond the physician/patient relationship); *Green v. Walker*, 910 F.2d 291 (5th Cir. 1990) (court held when individual is required, as a condition of future or continued employment, to submit to medical examination, that examination creates a relationship between examining physician and examinee); *Wojcik v. Aluminum Co. of America*, 18 Misc.2d 740, 183 N.Y.S.2d 351, 356 (N.Y. 1959) (court held complaint stated cause of action [illegible] employer gratuitously provided medical examinations to its employees, had a policy of revealing any irregularities, discovered that plaintiff who relied upon the policy had a serious disease, but did not disclose same to him). . . . Upon close scrutiny of each of these cases, it becomes apparent that plaintiff's interpretation of these cases is either erroneous or that the case is clearly distinguishable. These cases deal either with the extension of the duty of a physician hired by a hospital employer, with employers which violated their own documented disclosure policy, or with circumstances where the courts did not even reach the issue of employer liability with regards to nondisclosure. As earlier stated, the instant case does not involve the violation of a documented disclosure policy nor treatment by a physician.

Where a physician is directly involved, people have a right to expect a certain degree of care and disclosure on their health and health related matters regardless of whether a doctor/patient relationship exists. Indeed, disclosure to, at least, the patient is essential to the treatment and retardation of diseases and other ailments. However, this court is not persuaded, nor does Mississippi law support such a conclusion, that an insurance company should bear the same burden of care as a physician, i.e., divulging the results of a medical examination. A physician and an insurance company, serve different purposes in our society. A physician is sworn to protect and respect human life. An insurance company, on the other hand, by insuring those individuals it perceives as "insurable," is here to soften the blow of natural and artificial disasters, be it death, fire or flood. To hold insurance companies to the same standard as physicians would be to expect expertise on health related matters from an entity which hasn't the knowledge or the resources.

. . . .

Duty of Good Faith and Fair Dealing

Plaintiff says that JNL owed a duty to her and her husband because of its contractual relationship with them — the Does were JNL policyholders and they applied for insurance with JNL in 1988. Consequently, [illegible] plaintiff, JNL owed them [illegible] of good faith and fair dealing. . . .

Any contractual relationship between Mr. Doe and JNL was based upon the life insurance policy already in existence at the time he applied for and was later denied additional coverage. There is no indication from the record that JNL did not fulfill its obligation to Mr. Doe under the first insurance policy. As for Mrs. Doe, although she and JNL had a contractual relationship via her own life insurance policy, there is no indication that the defendant, by not divulging Mr. Does condition to Mrs. Doe, interfered with Mrs. Doe's rights to receive the benefits of the agreement between Mrs. Doe and JNL.

Duty to Warn of Foreseeable Harm

Plaintiff says that this court should impose a duty of JNL in this case because it was foreseeable that harm would likely ensue from a given act or omission. . . .

. . . .

. . . There is no evidence here to show JNL's failure to disclose the results of its test proximately caused John Doe's damages. John Doe was stricken with the disease before he undertook application for additional insurance with JNL. Once JNL rejected his application on medical grounds, John Doe was on notice that JNL was of the opinion that he had some uninsurable medical ailment detected from tests on his urine or blood. It would have been a simple matter for John Doe to submit urine and blood samples to his own physician for further testing. JNL could reasonably have expected John Doe to follow this course. John Doe instead did not place his physician on notice of JNL's rejection and later even told his hospital physician that he had no reason to suspect he had AIDS, a statement which persuaded the hospital physician not to test for the disease. These facts simply fail to show any liability by JNL to plaintiff under any analysis. . . .

. . . .

NOTES AND QUESTIONS

1. As the *Deramus* Court notes, there are a number of courts which have held *physicians* liable for not disclosing examination results; here, the physician is not sued because he never met the patient. He just saw the result when it came back from the company's contract laboratory. Shouldn't that be enough to create an obligation to warn the "patient"?
2. Suppose Doctor Stewart had personally examined Mr. Doe and had drawn the blood sample. Suppose Mr. Doe had confided he had not been feeling well. Suppose that Doctor Stewart drew a sample of Mrs. Doe's blood and she said she was afraid her husband might be HIV positive. Would Doctor Stewart and/or the insurance company *then* have a duty to notify the Does of the lab results?
3. If you still find no liability, is it because there is no physician-patient relationship because the insurance company — and not the "patient" — hired the doctor? Or because there *was* a relationship, but with a conflict of interests? Or because liability here would be bad public policy in the world of insurance?
4. And what of the *existing* relationship between the patient/insured and the defendant insurer? Why do you suppose Mr. Doe went to *this* insurer and not another? Isn't there a fiduciary, continuing relationship on which Mr. Doe relied?
5. And what of Mrs. Doe? She experienced a real risk of infection and death because of the defendant's inaction. As to her, wasn't there reckless misconduct?
6. AIDS, in many ways is a special case. As to that reconsider this case when we come to § 4.03[3]. For now, we turn to a different question — when a duty is found, what is its scope and content?

PETTUS v. COLE*

49 Cal. App. 4th 402 (Cal. Ct. App. 1996)

. . . .

The material facts of this case are essentially undisputed. Appellant Pettus had been working for DuPont for 22 years when, in June 1988, he sought to take time off from work because he was suffering from a disabling stress-related condition. Before requesting disability leave, Pettus sought medical help for his stress condition from his personal physician and from an outpatient psychological counseling program at the Sierra Clinic. Both recommended to DuPont that Pettus's stress condition warranted a disability leave.

Under Du Pont's short-term disability leave policy, Pettus was required to submit to examination by a Du Pont-selected doctor for verification of his need for disability leave. The policy provided for up to six months' leave, with pay, for nonoccupational illnesses or injuries. Du Pont was "self-insured" for purposes of its short-term disability leave policy.

In the course of having his disability verified, Pettus submitted to three medical examinations arranged and paid for by Du Pont. The first examination was with Dr. Collins, a physician under contract with Du Pont to provide general medical services for Du Pont employees. Dr. Collins verified Pettus's stress condition, and his need for time off, but believed a psychiatric evaluation was necessary. She recommended to Du Pont that Pettus should see Dr. Cole. The second examination was a psychiatric evaluation conducted by Dr. Cole. Dr. Cole verified appellant's stress condition and agreed that appellant had a legitimate medical need for time off work. Finally, Pettus underwent another psychiatric evaluation by Dr. Unger. Du Pont arranged for Pettus to see Dr. Unger after Dr. Cole reported that Pettus's stress condition might be linked to an alcohol abuse problem. Dr. Cole recommended Dr. Unger to Du Pont because she is a specialist in chemical dependency cases.

Pettus was terminated from his job at Du Pont on September 21, 1988, because he refused to enter a 30-day inpatient alcohol rehabilitation program that Du Pont required as a condition of continued employment. Pettus's alcohol consumption became a matter of concern to Du Pont when Drs. Cole and Unger disclosed to Du Pont in their disability evaluation reports that his stress condition might be caused or exacerbated by misuse of alcohol. However, the trial court specifically found that, "From all of the evidence it is undisputed that plaintiff was not at any time an alcoholic, nor perhaps even an alcohol abuser in the more common lay use of the word." Drs. Unger and Cole also disclosed in their reports to Du Pont that Pettus believed his employers were racist, and that he had violent thoughts regarding a coworker. Pettus contends that he did not authorize the doctors to disclose the full contents of their evaluations to Du Pont, and that the unauthorized release of such information to his supervisors, and the subsequent use of that information as the basis for terminating his employment, violated the CMIA and his state constitutional right to privacy.

. . . .

* Most of the citation material has been omitted from this case.

The basic scheme of the CMIA, as amended in 1981, is that a provider of health care must not disclose medical information without a written authorization from the patient. Section 56.10, subdivision (a), provides that: "No provider of health care shall disclose medical information regarding a patient of the provider without first obtaining an authorization, except as provided in subdivision (b) or (c)." As our Supreme Court has observed, "Considered together, the statutory provisions require a health care provider to hold confidential a patient's medical information unless the information falls under one of several exceptions to the act."

. . . .

Dr. Cole contends that no health care services were provided to or received by Pettus, and that, therefore, he was not a "patient" under Section 56.10. In support of this contention Dr. Cole claims that the psychiatric evaluation he performed was for the sole purpose of advising Pettus's employer of his findings with respect to appellant's disability claim, not to advise Pettus. Though his report made explicit recommendations for treatment, he argues these recommendations were generated for Du Pont's information. He further contends that Pettus was not a "patient" because he saw Pettus on a single occasion, no care or treatment was contemplated, and no doctor/patient relationship existed between them.

When the definition of patient is construed in relation to the other statutory definitions and in view of the statute's purpose, respondent Cole's position is patently untenable. It is undisputed that Dr. Cole's meeting with Pettus generated highly sensitive medical information which was subsequently reported to Du Pont. According to statutory definitions, "medical information" is information "derived from a provider of health care" and a patient is someone who has received health care services from a provider of health care and to whom medical information pertains. Unfortunately, the term "health care services" is not defined by the Act. However, logic dictates that in order for a health care provider to gather medical information about a person, the provider must have dealt with the person at some level and performed professional services of some type. . . . The Legislature clearly intended for the statute to afford employees in Pettus's situation — i.e., where the employer has requested and paid for a medical examination to determine the validity of a claim for medical leave benefits — some protection by imposing a duty on health care providers involved in the procedure a duty to maintain, at least to a limited degree, the confidentiality of the employee's medical information. . . .

We do agree, however, that the traditional doctor/patient relationship, with the host of concomitant duties created by such a relationship, was not established between appellant and the respondent psychiatrists. This is the proposition for which both cases cited by Dr. Cole in his opening brief stand. In *Felton v. Schaeffer*, the defendant physician performed a preemployment physical on plaintiff and made an erroneous conclusion about the plaintiff's fitness which caused him to be rejected by the employer. The court held against the plaintiff in subsequent actions against the physician for negligence and medical malpractice, finding that defendant's sole function was to provide information to the prospective employer, that no doctor/patient relationship was created, and that, therefore, defendant owed no duty of care to the plaintiff. In *Keene v. Wiggins*, plaintiff [illegible] by his workers' compensation carrier for examination following an industrial accident. The doctor wrote a letter to the insurance carrier opining no treatment was necessary. Plaintiff received a copy of the report and allegedly relied on it to his detriment. The court held the doctor was not liable to the plaintiff for negligence or medical malpractice in making the report since the doctor conducted the examination only for the purpose of rating the plaintiff's injury for the insurance carrier. The court further held that there was no doctor/patient relationship of the sort giving rise to a duty of care owed to the plaintiff in connection with the medical report.

In the case before us, plaintiff is similarly situated in that he is bringing an action against a doctor who examined him at the request of a third party, his employer, Du Pont. If Pettus brought a professional negligence claim against Dr. Cole, or Dr. Unger, he would likely be defeated under the authority of *Keene* and *Felton*. Pettus, however, does not rely on common law theories of negligence of medical malpractice. Rather, he is seeking to enforce a duty of confidentiality codified in the CMIA. For purposes of that statute he is, clearly, a "patient."

. . . .

. . . The Legislature recognized in Section 56.10, subdivision (c)(8)(B), that the ability of employers to obtain some medical information without employee authorization may serve a legitimate purpose under some circumstances. At the same time it sought to preserve the employee's interest in maintaining the confidentiality of sensitive medical information in the employment context. To balance these interests, the Legislature restricted the information that may be disclosed without authorization to only that which is necessary to achieve the legitimate purpose. Where an employee has submitted to a medical examination to verify a disability that "may entitle the patient to leave from work for medical reasons," the Legislature determined that the information needed by the employer for verification is a description of the "functional limitations of the patient." Thus, this information may be disclosed to the employer without a written authorization from the patient. In contrast, in the absence of a written authorization from the employee, the Legislature explicitly prohibited disclosure of any "statement of medical cause" of the disability. This information is not necessary to achieve the legitimate purpose envisioned in subdivision (c)(8)(B) and, therefore, may not be disclosed without patient authorization. The trial court's conclusion that an employer that is entitled to have its doctors examine an employee is entitled to a "full and complete report" of the contents of the examination runs counter to the Legislature's attempt to balance the competing interests.

. . . .

Having concluded that the disclosure of detailed medical information by Drs. Cole and Unger to Pettus's employer violated his rights under the CMIA, we must decide whether Pettus has established that this conduct also constitutes a violation of his state constitutional right of privacy. Under standards enunciated by our Supreme Court while this matter was pending on appeal, the application of which has been fully briefed and argued by the parties, we conclude that Pettus, upon completion of his case-in-chief, made a prima facie showing of invasion of his constitutional right of privacy. . . .

. . . .

. . . The comparison and balancing of diverse interests is central to the privacy jurisprudence of both common and constitutional law. Invasion of a privacy interest is not a violation of the state constitutional right to privacy if the invasion is justified by a competing interest. Legitimate interests derive from the legally authorized and socially beneficial activities of government and private entities. Their relative importance is determined by their proximity to the central functions of a particular public or private enterprise. In general, where the privacy violation is alleged against a private entity, the defendant is not required to establish a "compelling interest" but, rather, one that is " 'legitimate' or 'important.' "

. . . .

"Legally recognized privacy interests are generally of two classes: (1) interests in precluding the dissemination or misuse of sensitive and confidential information ('informational privacy'); and (2) interests in making intimate personal decisions or conducting personal activities without observation, intrusion, or interference ('autonomy privacy')."

We have no doubt, and determine as a matter of law, that Pettus had a legally cognizable interest in maintaining the privacy of the detailed medical information he conveyed to Drs. Cole and Unger. . . .

A review of Dr. Cole's and Dr. Unger's written reports clearly demonstrates the private nature of the information transmitted to Du Pont. These reports were quite thorough and detailed in their discussion of: the rash that covered Pettus's body, the medication he was using to treat it, and his fears about that medication causing cancer; his sleep patterns and sex drive; his hostile feelings toward certain current and former coworkers and supervisors; past suicidal feelings; his smoking and drinking patterns; a social history of his life from the time of his birth, with his family of origin, through a marriage and divorce, to the present; and his anxious and highly emotional behavior during the interview (crying, wringing his hands, burying his face in his hands, jumping out of his chair and removing his shirt to reveal the marks on his skin from the rash medicine). Certainly, this is the type of "sensitive personal information" the California voters had in mind when they adopted the constitutional privacy guarantee, expressly limiting the freedom of both government and business entities to obtain, disseminate and use such data.

. . . .

. . . It is true, as a general matter, that Pettus put his mental condition in issue by requesting paid leave under Du Pont's disability policy. It is also true that Du Pont had a right to know whether Pettus was in fact disabled by stress and, perhaps, whether or not his disability was work related, before it was bound to provide Pettus with paid disability leave. But the detailed psychiatric information Du Pont requested and obtained from Drs. Cole and Unger, and ultimately used to make adverse personnel decisions about Pettus, was far more than the employer needed to accomplish its legitimate objectives. It also exceeded the scope of disclosure to which Pettus may be deemed to have consented either expressly or impliedly when he requested disability leave, submitted to psychiatric evaluation, and orally acknowledged that Dr. Cole would be reporting back to Du Pont.

. . . .

The final element of Pettus's prima facie case of invasion of privacy is the seriousness of the intrusion: . . . Anyone who has ever been an "employee" can relate to the Hill and Briscoe courts' discussion of the importance of protecting an individual's right to informational privacy, especially as against employers and others with whom the individual maintains only a business relationship. The "employee" mask is one that helps workers maintain an aura of competence, efficiency, professionalism, social propriety, seriousness of purpose, etc., allowing them to perform their duties to the satisfaction of their employers but simultaneously to protect their job security and, thus, their economic well-being. Many employees choose to conceal from their employers matters of disability, sexual orientation and conduct, political affiliation or activities, family or marital strife, unconventional life styles or avocations, etc., out of fear that, no matter how well they might perform in the workplace, revelations about these or other aspects of their private lives may cost them their jobs. . . .

. . . .

We turn next to an examination of the countervailing interests asserted by Drs. Cole and Unger to justify the invasion of Pettus's privacy, and determine whether Pettus has shown that there were equally effective, less intrusive means to serve those interests. Essentially, Drs. Cole and Unger explain that they gave Du Pont a full, detailed psychiatric report because that is what employers expect to receive when they retain a psychiatrist to evaluate an employee for disability leave. Respondents further assert that Du Pont "needed" the detailed report in order to evaluate Pettus's request for disability leave, and to formulate a plan forgetting him back to work as soon as possible. When balanced against the Pettus's privacy interests, and viewed in light of available alternatives, neither of these justifications carries the day.

. . . .

. . . [A] medical opinion by an employer-aligned physician as to the existence of "functional limitations," and [illegible] the industrial versus nonindustrial nature of the injury, is what the employer "needs" to know to make that eligibility determination. However, contrary to the respondents' argument, employers do not have a cognizable interest in dictating a course of medical treatment for employees who suffer nonindustrial injuries. That is a matter for the employees to decide, in consultation with their own health care providers — medical professionals who have their patients' best interests at heart.

Dr. Unger further contends that Du Pont had a legitimate interest in assessing Pettus's potential for violence, especially toward Judy Mendonca. While quite plausible on its face, this argument is too simplistic and sweeping in its implications. It is, of course, true that employers have a legitimate — indeed compelling — interest in maintaining a safe working environment for their employees. It is another matter altogether to say that an employer can require an employee to submit to examination by an employer-aligned psychiatrist whenever it learns that an employee is angry and resentful toward a coworker, and is thereafter entitled to the type of detailed report, including a full psychiatric history and evaluation, that Drs. Unger and Cole provided to Du Pont. Both of these psychiatrists, along with appellant's own therapist, Dr. Shervington, already had a common law duty to warn Mendonca, and possibly Du Pont, if they at any time determined that Pettus presented "a serious danger of violence" to her or any other reasonably identifiable Du Pont employee. (*Tarasoff v. Regents of University of California* [§ 3.02[2], *infra*]) Nothing we say today is intended to limit that duty in any way, but neither do we intend to expand it. If Pettus had indeed posed a danger of serious violence to Mendonca or any other identifiable Du Pont employee, Drs. Cole, Unger, and Shervington were at all times free to disclose that fact to the possible victim — but only that fact. . . .

In sum, based on the evidence presented in Pettus's case-in-chief, we hold that the disclosures by Drs. Cole and Unger of detailed medical and psychiatric information about Pettus to his direct supervisors were a serious violation of Pettus's reasonable expectations that the psychiatrists would maintain the confidentiality of such highly sensitive information. We further conclude that the justifications offered by respondents do not outweigh Pettus's informational privacy interests, and that there were less intrusive alternatives to full disclosure that would have equally well served the psychiatrists' and Du Pont's interests. . . .

. . . .

The trial court concluded that Du Pont was justified in discharging Pettus because he refused to enroll in an inpatient alcohol treatment program as directed by his employer as a condition of continued employment, and that Du Pont was not liable for either invasion of privacy or wrongful termination in violation of the public policy embodied in the privacy clause. It is these tort claims one arising from the California Constitution, the other from common law — that are at the heart of Pettus's appeal from the judgment in favor of Du Pont.

There has been a great deal of confusion about the role of the California constitutional right to privacy in the private workplace, especially when employees have resorted to the courts to claim that they have suffered some adverse personnel action for asserting or refusing to waive their constitutional privacy rights. The claims that have arisen in this context have typically involved employer-mandated drug-testing. . . .

Of course, a tort cause of action for wrongful termination in violation of public policy is now well established in California. The rule of these cases is an exception to the at-will employment doctrine. . . . The cases in which California courts have recognized a separate tort cause of action for wrongful termination in violation of public policy generally fall into four categories, where the employee is discharged for: (1) refusal to violate a statute; (2) performing a statutory obligation; (3) exercising (or refusing to waive) a statutory or constitutional right or privilege; or (4) reporting an alleged violation of a statute of public importance.

Of the existing wrongful termination cases, *Semore* and *Luck,* are most closely on point for purposes of evaluating Pettus's claim that he was discharged in violation of public policy. Like Pettus, the plaintiffs in *Semore* and

Luck claimed that they were discharged because they refused to waive or insisted that their employers honor their state constitutional right of privacy. *Semore* and *Luck* arrive at opposite conclusion[illegible] issue whether an employee can state [illegible] action for wrongful termination in violation of public policy against a private employer based on allegations that the employer somehow invaded the employee's state constitutional right of privacy. Both decisions were also accompanied by vigorous dissents.

. . . .

. . . What is really at stake in those cases, as well as in the instant case, is a violation of a fundamental state constitutional right that is directly and independently enforceable against both private and governmental entities where the threat of discharge is simply the means by which the employer applies economic coercion to the employee's decision whether to exercise (or waive) those rights, and/or where termination of employment is a form of punishment or retaliation for the employee's choice to exercise (or refusal to waive) those rights. Thus, in analyzing such a claim, courts must undertake a "careful consideration of reasonable expectations of privacy and employer, employee, and public interests arising in particular circumstances."

. . . .

Pettus had an "autonomy privacy" interest in making intimate personal decisions about an appropriate course of medical treatment for his disabling stress condition, without undue intrusion or interference from his employer. This "autonomy privacy" interest is at the heart of Pettus's privacy claim against Du Pont, and is plainly sufficient to satisfy the first element of his cause of action for violation of his constitutional right of privacy.

We turn next to the question whether Pettus's expectations that Du Pont would honor the identified informational and autonomy privacy interests were reasonable in the circumstances of this case. As we have already discussed, it is reasonable for an employee to expect that details of his personal life and thoughts, communicated in confidence to a psychiatrist, will be shielded against scrutiny by his employer. It is equally reasonable for an employee to expect that extraneous information about his personal life and thoughts, communicated in confidence to a psychiatrist in an [illegible] related examination, will not be used by [illegible] employer as the basis for adverse personnel [illegible].

As to Pettus's autonomy privacy interests, we are aware of no law or policy which suggests that a person forfeits his or her right of medical self-determination by entering into an employment relationship, or by requesting paid leave under a benefit plan that is voluntarily provided by the employer, or by submitting to a psychiatric examination by an employer-aligned physician. It is reasonable for the employee to believe that, notwithstanding the fact the employer is paying for the examination and will pay benefits upon adequate proof of disability, he or she will remain free to control both the information flow and the medical decisionmaking about a disabling medical condition. Indeed, it would be unprecedented for this court to hold that an employer may dictate to an employee the course of medical treatment he or she must follow, under pain of termination, with respect to a nonoccupational illness or injury. It is, thus, eminently reasonable for employees to expect that their employers will respect — i.e., not attempt to coerce or otherwise interfere with — their decisions about their own health care, including those which relate to drug or alcohol treatment.

. . . .

The third element of Pettus's prima facie case of invasion of privacy is the seriousness of the intrusion or interference by Du Pont with his identified privacy interests. We have already discussed at length how the disclosure of Pettus's private medical information by Drs. Cole and Unger may have seriously undermined his self-concept and image as a "responsible employee," and disrupted his employment relationship with Du Pont. That intrusion was greatly compounded when Messrs. Rotter and Montovino used information from the psychiatrists' reports to impose a new and extremely onerous condition on Pettus's continued employment with the company: enrollment in a 30-day inpatient alcohol treatment program. We have no doubt that this coercive course of conduct — involving both a misuse of the employee's private medical information and a penalty for his assertion of his autonomy privacy interests — was "an egregious breach of the social norms underlying the privacy right." Accordingly, we conclude that Pettus has established the third element of a prima facie claim for invasion of his constitutional right to privacy.

. . . .

For all the foregoing reasons, the judgments of the trial court are reversed and the causes remanded for further proceedings consistent with this opinion. Costs to appellant.

NOTES AND QUESTIONS

1. The two preceding cases came to opposite conclusions as to the patient's claim. Is it because in the second case there *was* a physician/patient relationship? Or because in the latter case the employer of the plaintiff — not an insurer — actually employed the physician to do the examination? Suppose it were a *potential* employer? *See Felton v. Schaeffer*, 229 Cal. App. 3d. 229 (1991) and *Green v. Walker*, 910 F.2d 291 (5th Cir. 1990).
2. Or is it that in this case a specific statute created an obligation of disclosure by the physician? The court says otherwise there would be no malpractice claim. Do you agree? And if so, is the statute wise? Here, unlike the preceding case, the physician(s) *saw* the patient; the requesting party was an *existing* employer; and harm was done — should these factors matter?
3. How *might* the employer have gained full disclosure of all information? *Should* it do so? And suppose the employer did *nothing* with the information. Would there still be an injury? A compensable one? What *should* DuPont have done once it got the information?
4. Note that Pettus posed a danger to a coworker, Judy Medonca. Does the the Court adequately analyze the psychiatrists' duty towards her?

The Court comments that the psychiatrists were already under a *Tarasoff* (*see infra*) duty to disclose to any potential victim the possibility that the employee might harm her. [illegible] could that duty be satisfied [illegible] means, with what content? Disclose to the *employer*?

5. In *Baer v. Regents of the University of California*, 884 P.2d 841 (N. Mex. Ct. App. 1994) an employer's physician failed to disclose a cancerous nodule discovered during an annual employment physical. Under the preceding cases, what result would there be in a suit against the employer, physician and physician's assistant?

6. Recall the facts of *Pettus* as we turn to the obligation of confidentiality and the *Humphers*and *Tarasoff* cases in the next section and then, subsequently, to the issue of informed consent in § 3.03[1], *infra.* But first consider two problems on a physician's conflict of interest in choosing among patients.

7. For an excellent article, see Jerome P. Kassirer, M.D., *Financial Conflict of Interest: An Unresolved Ethical Frontier*, 27 Am. J.L. & Med. 149 (2001); and see Robert A. Prentice, *Clinical Trial Results, Physicians, and Insider Trading*, 20 J. Legal Med. 195 (1999).

8. In *Clark v. Estate of Rice*, 653 N.W.2d 166 (Iowa 2002), a child, through his father, brings an action for loss of consortium against his now deceased mother. Is there a conflict of interest here? Why would a child want to bring an action against her now deceased mother? Should claims such as this be barred by a parental immunity? If not, does this weaken the notion or reality of "family"?

PROBLEM 3-1 — AIDS and the HMO Physician

Ralph Wells, age 22, has just come to you for the performance of a vasectomy. You have been the family doctor for Ralph and his wife, Eugenia, and their two children, Sam and Antonia. You explain that the procedure is considered minor surgery and that after blood samples you draw are tested at a nearby laboratory, the surgery can be performed in the Out[illegible] Clinic at Memorial Hospital next week. [illegible] is drawn, arrangements are made for [illegible] operating room and Ralph goes away. The next day, you receive three phone calls: the laboratory calls to say the blood has tested positive for AIDS; Ralph's wife calls to say she opposes the vasectomy; and the chief of surgery at the hospital calls to say that the hospital has just been selected to test a new method of vasectomy by means of internal cauterization through fiberoptic laser technology, eliminating the need for an external incision.

With whom do you have conversations? What is the content of those conversations? And what do you do upon learning today that a statute passed by the legislature has just become effective, requiring disclosure to the State Department of Public Health of the name of any person testing positive for AIDS? What if the HMO for which you work has just passed a protocol requiring immediate termination of service, without explanation, to patients diagnosed with AIDS — including *not* advising of the diagnosis?

PROBLEM 3–2 — Children, Parents and Abuse

Nicole Althaus was born in April 1975 to loving parents. In 1990, after a series of catastrophic illnesses struck the home, Nicole was referred by teacher Zappa to counselor Lappa. During their session Nicole alleged inappropriate touching by her father, and Lappa reported these allegations to Children and Youth Services. They removed Nicole from the home and set up counseling with a psychiatrist, Judith Cohen. Nicole's allegations of abuse became more extensive in character and soon came to include her mother and then others. The abuse included ritualistic torture and murder of babies Nicole claimed to have had by caesarian section.

Doctor Cohen never investigated these accusations. She accepted the CYS diagnosis of abuse. She testified in court that she believed Nicole, although she had doubts. She avoided confronting Nicole, to maintain a therapeutic relationship. Doctor Cohen refused contact with the parents or their retained psychologist. At trial, an independent psychiatrist — who had interviewed Nicole, family and friends — testified Nicole was lost in fantasy and incompetent to testify. Doctor Cohen testified to the contrary, then conceded *many* of Nicole's allegations were false, then advised Nicole not to testify.

Criminal charges against the parents were dismissed. They then sued Doctor Cohen for negligence. She maintained she had no obligation towards them and — moreover — she had not been negligent. Who should win?

See Althaus v. Cohen, 710 A.2d 1147 (Pa. Super. Ct. 1998).

LOWNSBURY v. VANBUREN

762 N.E.2d 354 (Ohio 2002)

Alice Robie **Resnick**, J.

This is an appeal from a summary judgment in favor of defendant-appellee Thomas Stover, M.D., in a medical malpractice action. The action was brought by plaintiffs-appellants Mary and Gerald Fabich, in their own right and as next friends of their adopted daughter, plaintiff-appellant Rebecca Fabich (formerly Rebecca Lownsbury), who was born severely brain damaged on January 10, 1995.

In their initial complaint, filed January 19, 1996, appellants asserted various claims of medical negligence against numerous defendants, all of which arise out of the prenatal care and treatment provided to Rebecca's biological mother, Cathy Lownsbury, at Akron City Hospital from January 6, 1995 through January 10, 1995. After extensive discovery, appellants settled with and/or dismissed all but two of the original defendants. As pertinent here, appellants alleged that on January 6, 1995, Lownsbury was given a nonstress test and an amniotic fluid index test at Akron City Hospital's perinatal testing center. Based on the results of these tests, George VanBuren, M.D., a defendant below, ordered that Lownsbury be taken to the hospital's labor and delivery unit for an induction of labor. However, rather than inducing labor as ordered, the obstetrics residents administered a contraction stress test, after which they discharged Lownsbury from the hospital the same day. The contraction stress test allegedly ran for two hours and twenty minutes and revealed repetitive late decelerations, suggesting fetal distress, but only an eighteen-minute portion of the fetal monitor tracing was reviewed, which showed no decelerations.

Appellants claimed, among other things, that Dr. Stover was negligent in failing to supervise the obstetrics residents who actually cared for Lownsbury on January 6, 1995, and that such failure was a proximate cause of Rebecca being born permanently brain damaged on January 10, 1995.

Dr. Stover moved for summary judgment on the sole ground that he owed no legal duty of supervision to Lownsbury or Rebecca because he and Lownsbury never had a physician-patient relationship. In his motion, Dr. Stover maintained that a physician-patient relationship cannot be found to exist between an on-call physician and a hospital patient unless it appears that the physician was either in direct contact with the patient or actively involved in the patient's care.

In response, appellants argued that regardless of whether Dr. Stover had any contact with Lownsbury or the residents who actually cared for her, he nevertheless assumed the duty to provide Lownsbury with supervisory care by contracting to serve as the on-premises attending and supervising obstetrician at Akron City Hospital on January 6, 1995.

Appellants' supporting evidence tended to show that Dr. Stover was employed by East Market Street Obstetrical-Gynecological Co., Inc. ("East Market") "to provide obstetrical and gynecological services to patients at Akron City Hospital in accordance with the working schedule promulgated by the Board of Directors of East Market from time to time." East Market had entered into an agreement with Akron City Hospital ("EMS-ACH contract") to "schedule sufficient PHYSICIANS to provide SERVICES on HOSPITAL premises twenty-four (24) hours per day, seven (7) days per week, consistent with accreditation requirements of the HOSPITAL Obstetrical and Gynecological Residency Program."

The EMS-ACH contract also required East Market to "provide sufficient PHYSICIANS in order to perform SERVICES required by this Agreement so as to insure high quality professional medical care will be provided to HOSPITAL'S obstetrical and gynecological patients," to provide physicians "to serve on such committees and in such similar positions as are necessary . . . to collaborate with the Medical Staff," and to "comply with all rules, regulations and bylaws of HOSPITAL and HOSPITAL'S professional staff."

The contract provided further that East Market physicians "must maintain membership on HOSPITAL'S Medical Staff and clinical privileges within HOSPITAL" and "shall be subject to HOSPITAL'S Articles of Incorporation, Code of Regulations, Professional Medical Staff Bylaws and Professional Rules and Regulations." In addition, both East Market and its physicians were obligated to "perform SERVICES to patients of HOSPITAL in accordance with currently approved medical standards, methods and practices."

Sometime between January 6 and January 10, 1995, Lownsbury signed a consent form setting forth conditions of admission to Akron City Hospital. This document explains that "the Hospital is a teaching institution . . . for undergraduate, graduate and post-graduate education," and that "students may participate in the care of the patient." It also confirms that these students are present for educational and instructional purposes "under appropriate supervision," that "the patient will be under the professional care of a Medical Doctor called the attending physician," and that "the patient . . . consents to hospital services as ordered by the attending physician . . . or . . . rendered under the general and specific instructions of the physician."

Appellants also presented affidavit and deposition testimony of two medical experts who stated that Dr. Stover had a responsibility as the supervising physician on January 6, 1995, to familiarize himself with Lownsbury's clinical condition and particularly to review the contraction stress test by the end of his scheduled working day and formulate a plan of management. They opined that Dr. Stover should have maintained an operational presence in the labor and delivery unit, rather than sitting in the hospital's staff room "wasting time" until his help was requested (as Dr. Stover claimed he could do), and that had Rebecca been delivered even a day earlier, she probably would not have suffered permanent neurological injury.

In *Tracy v. Merrell Dow Pharmaceuticals, Inc.*, we explained:

> "The physician-patient relationship arises out of an express or implied contract which imposes on the physician an obligation to utilize the requisite degree of care and skill during the course of the relationship. The relationship is a consensual one and is created when the physician performs professional services which another person accepts for the purpose of medical treatment.
>
> "The physician-patient relationship is a fiduciary one based on trust and confidence and obligating the physician to exercise good faith. As a part of this relationship, both parties envision that the patient will rely on the judgment and expertise of the physician. The relationship is predicated on the proposition that the patient seeks out and obtains the physician's services because the physician possesses special knowledge and skill in diagnosing and treating diseases and injuries which the patient lacks."

This court has not considered the application of these principles to the complicated institutional environment of a teaching hospital. Indeed, our development of these concepts has thus far been confined to the context of direct one-on-one, face-to-face relationships between physicians and patients. Accordingly, we find it helpful to review those cases in which other courts have considered whether, and under what circumstances, to recognize a duty of care owed by a supervisory physician to a patient actually cared for by a hospital resident.

In *Mozingo v. Pitt Cty. Mem. Hosp., Inc.* (1992), 331 N.C. 182, 415 S. E.2d 341, the Supreme Court of North Carolina held that a physician who undertook to provide on-call supervision of obstetrics residents at a teaching hospital owed the infant plaintiff and his parents a duty of reasonable care in supervising the residents who delivered plaintiff at his birth. In that case, Sandra Dee Mozingo was admitted to Pitt County Memorial Hospital on the afternoon of December 5, 1984, for the delivery of her second child, plaintiff

Alton Ray Mozingo, Jr. At 5:00 p.m. that same day, defendant Dr. Richard John Kazior began his assignment to provide on-call coverage for the obstetrics residents at the hospital. Dr. Kazior remained at his home available to take telephone calls from the residents until shortly before 9:45 p.m., when he received a call from one of the residents informing him of a problem with the delivery of Alton. Dr. Kazior immediately left his home, but when he arrived at the hospital the delivery of Alton had already been completed.

Specifically, plaintiffs submitted the affidavit of a medical expert who stated that Dr. Kazior had a responsibility as the supervising physician to call the hospital at the beginning of his coverage shift to find out what obstetrical patients had been admitted, their condition, and to formulate a plan of management, and also to call periodically thereafter to check on their status. Since it was undisputed that prior to receiving the phone call, Dr. Kazior was never in direct contact with the patient, consulted by the treating residents, or in any way involved in the patient's care, the issue presented in *Mozingo* is precisely the question confronting us in this case.

In resolving this issue, the court in *Mozingo* explained:

> "We conclude that the defendant's duty of reasonable care in supervising the residents was not diminished by the fact that his relationship with the plaintiffs did not fit traditional notions of the doctor-patient relationship.
>
> "The modern provision of medical care is a complex process becoming increasingly more complicated as medical technology advances. Large teaching hospitals, such as the Hospital in the present case, care for patients with teams of professionals, some of whom never actually come in contact with the treated patient but whose expertise is nevertheless vital to the treatment and recovery of patients.
>
> ". . .
>
> "Medical professionals may be held accountable when they undertake to care for a patient and their actions do not meet the standard of care for such actions as established by expert testimony. Thus, in the increasingly complex modern delivery of health care, a physician who undertakes to provide on-call supervision of residents actually treating a patient may be held accountable to that patient, if the physician negligently supervises those residents and such negligent supervision proximately causes the patient's injuries."

In *Maxwell v. Cole* (1984), 126 Misc.2d 597, 482 N.Y.S.2d 1000, the plaintiff, Diane Maxwell, entered New York Hospital in Manhattan for an elective tubal ligation. It was alleged that Maxwell's bladder was punctured during surgery and that the residents providing postoperative care failed to detect it. One of the defendants in the case was Dr. William Ledger, Chairman of the Department of Obstetrics and Gynecology at New York Hospital. Maxwell claimed that Dr. Ledger failed to adequately supervise the resident staff and to provide them with standards as to the necessity in certain circumstances to seek prompt consultation with attending physicians.

The court rejected "Dr. Ledger's narrow reading of a physician's responsibility," and explained:

> "In this case, it is claimed that the responsibility for supervision of the medical personnel lay in the hands of the chief of service, Dr. Ledger. With a broadened view of a hospital's role as a provider of health care services comes an expanded notion of its supervisory responsibilities over those who practice medical care on its premises. That supervisory responsibility, it is claimed was delegated to Dr. Ledger. If the chief of service fails to provide medically acceptable rules and regulations which would insure appropriate supervision of ill patients, then it is reasonable to find that a breach of the standards of medical care by that individual has occurred."

The basic underlying concept in these cases is that a physician-patient relationship, and thus a duty of care, may arise from whatever circumstances evince the physician's consent to act for the patient's medical benefit. The physician-patient relationship being consensual in nature, these courts recognize that physicians who practice in the institutional environment may be found to have voluntarily assumed a duty of supervisory care pursuant to their contractual and employment arrangements with the hospital. Unlike the traditional personalized delivery of health care, where the patient seeks out and obtains the services of a particular physician, the institutional environment of large teaching hospitals incorporates a myriad of complex and attenuated relationships. Here the presenting patient enters a realm of full-service coordinated care in which technical agreements and affiliations proliferate the specialized functions and designated obligations of various allied health professionals. In this reality, the responsibility for resident supervision that rests generally with the hospital is often delegated to or assumed by an individual physician or group of physicians. It is their level of skill and competence that ensures adequate patient care. When a patient enters this setting, he or she has every right to expect that the hospital and adjunct physicians will exercise reasonable care in fulfilling their respective assignments. So it is a logical and reasonable application of the principles set forth in *Tracy*, 58 Ohio St.3d 147, 569 N.E.2d 875, to find that a physician may agree in advance to the creation of a physician-patient relationship with the hospital's patients. According to Dr. Stover, however, the argument that a contract between a physician and hospital can be sufficient to form the basis for a physicianpatient relationship was rejected in *Hill v. Kokosky* (1990), 186 Mich. App. 300, 463 N.W.2d 265, and *St. John v. Pope* (Tex.1995), 901 S.W.2d 420. We disagree. In neither case was any such argument raised, nor any evidence of a contract presented.

While these cases can be interpreted to indicate that consultation without contract is insufficient to establish a physician-patient relationship, it does not follow that contract without consultation is also insufficient to form the relationship. These are two distinct questions, and these cases simply have nothing to do with the latter issue.

Dr. Stover also relies on *McKinney v. Schlatter* (1997), 118 Ohio App.3d 328, 692 N.E.2d 1045, and states in his brief the proposition that "direct contact and/or participation, or at the very least, knowledge regarding a patient, is necessary to establish a physician-patient relationship under any circumstances."

In *McKinney*, an on-call consulting physician allegedly misdiagnosed the condition of an emergency room patient during two telephone conversations with the emergency room physician. It was undisputed that the on-call physician had no personal contact with the patient. The court held that a physician-patient relationship can be found to exist under these circumstances, provided that the on-call physician "(1) participates in the diagnosis of the patient's condition, (2) participates in or prescribes a course of treatment for the patient, and (3) owes a duty to the hospital, staff or patient for whose benefit he is on call."

However, we now reject the *McKinney* test. In addition to the reasons stated above, we find that the test itself is incongruous, for it actually subsumes the ultimate question of duty. In order to satisfy what is merely the third of the three elements comprising the test, the plaintiff must prove the existence of the very duty that the test is ultimately designed to identify. Thus, even if a physician is shown to owe a duty of care to the patient, or to act for the patient's benefit, this duty is negated where the physician takes no affirmative action as provided in the other two elements of the test toward fulfilling his or her obligations. Simply put, the test allows a voluntarily assumed duty of care to be nullified by virtue of its very breach.

Of course, the physician-patient relationship cannot come into being without the physician's consent. Otherwise, the physician would be forced to provide care to anyone who desired medical attention. But there are many forms of consent, and the three elements of the *McKinney* test are, in reality, a compilation of the various possible ways in which the physician's consent can be manifested. The physician may consent to the relationship by explicitly contracting with the patient, treating hospital, or treating physician. Or the physician may take certain actions that indicate knowing consent, such as examining, diagnosing, treating, or prescribing treatment for the patient. The *McKinney* test essentially takes the sum total of these various possible forms of consent and converts them into a set of cumulative requirements. Consequently, the test requires not only proof of consent, actual or implied, but proof of consent in every conceivable form.

Under the *McKinney* test, as applied in the present context, a physician who explicitly accepts or voluntarily assumes the obligation to provide resident supervision, knowing full well that the fulfillment of these supervisory duties is vital to the interests of the hospital's patients, could escape his or her obligation simply by failing to provide any supervision at all. We find such a rigid, formalistic notion of consent to be both unrealistic and unjustified.

Accordingly, we hold that a physician-patient relationship can be established between a physician who contracts, agrees, undertakes, or otherwise assumes the obligation to provide resident supervision at a teaching hospital and a hospital patient with whom the physician had no direct or indirect contact.

This holding does not, however, end the inquiry in this case, but instead brings the pivotal issue into focus.

Thus, the determinative issue in this case is not whether Dr. Stover had any contact with Lownsbury or the residents treating her, but whether and to what extent Dr. Stover assumed the obligation to supervise the residents at Akron City Hospital. Specifically, did Dr. Stover assume only a limited and passive duty to remain in his call room until consulted by a resident with a problem, or did he assume an active duty to gauge the performance of the residents or familiarize himself with the condition of the patients at Akron City Hospital?

Having reviewed the entire record in this case, including the EMS-ACH contract, the consent form signed by Lownsbury, the agreement between Dr. Stover and EMS, and the various affidavits and depositions given by appellants' experts, EMS physicians and hospital residents, we conclude that there is sufficient evidence upon which the jury could decide this question either way. In so doing, we are aware that the EMS physicians and hospital residents testified that Dr. Stover had no responsibility to a hospital patient unless and until he was contacted by a resident. However, this testimony is disputed by the consent form and the testimony of appellants' experts.

Although it is not clear, as Dr. Stover points out, whether Lownsbury signed the consent form on January 6 or January 10, 1995, that form nevertheless establishes that Akron City Hospital considers the supervisory physician to be the patient's "attending physician" and expects that patient services will be ordered by or rendered under the general and specific instructions of such physician. Therefore, the consent form constitutes substantial evidence that Dr. Stover was required to take an active role in supervising the hospital's residents and caring for the hospital's patients.

We are also aware that the "RECITALS" portion of the EMS-ACH contract indicates that one of its objectives is to provide "for the ready availability of PHYSICIANS for the purpose of resident supervision." However, we cannot agree with Dr. Stover that this statement necessarily allows him to avoid all contact and communication with the resident staff except when consulted, or that it places the decision as to when supervision is needed into the hands of those who need to be supervised.

Accordingly, we find that summary judgment was inappropriately granted in favor of Dr. Stover, and the judgment of the court of appeals is hereby reversed. The cause, therefore, is remanded to the trial court for further proceedings.

Judgment reversed and cause remanded.

NOTES AND QUESTIONS

1. The *Lownsbury* case involves a suit for malpractice against a physician who never saw the patient. Doctor Stover was simply "on-call," providing coverage to the hospital if its residents needed help. They were sufficiently trained to call or not as circumstances dictated.
2. How then can liability exist? As a hospital supervisor? Third party contractor? Perhaps. But as a physician *to* Cathy Lownsbury? If so, what about all the other usual incidents of the fiduciary relationship — informed consent, confidentiality, privacy?

3. And what is the impact on the hospital's ability — in the future — to retain services of on-call physicians? How will they, *can* they limit liability?
4. Note there is a third party here, East Market Street OB-GYN, which contracted to provide services "on hospital premises." This is a standard arrangement. Throughout healthcare there are many such independent contractors (e.g., pharmacy managers, case managers). But how does *their* breach become *Stover's* breach? And how is it to be measured? As a contract violation? As medical malpractice? And how do the plaintiffs assert a claim under the contract?
5. Also, it appears that Rebecca's mother placed her for adoption with Mr. and Ms. Fabich. Does this affect Doctor Stover's liability? To whom do his obligations run?

[2] Confidentiality

A physician frequently learns of the most private aspects of a patient's life. Indeed, such information may be essential to diagnosis and treatment. Therefore in order to encourage open communication, it is important to maintain confidentiality. But competing with this is the public's need to know about private conduct as it affects public health, for example with epidemics such as AIDS. State statutes often require reports including patient indentities for infectious diseases or physical abuse.

There may also be a *private* need to know, as when a citizen may need information about a patient, and the professional has information which could help the inquiry. That is the problem in *Humphers,* where an adopted daughter wants to know her birth mother.

HUMPHERS v. FIRST INTERSTATE BANK OF OREGON
696 P.2d 527 (Ore. 1985)

Linde, Justice.

We are called upon to decide whether plaintiff has stated a claim for damages in alleging that her former physician revealed her identity to a daughter whom she had given up for adoption.

In 1959, according to the complaint, plaintiff, then known as Ramona Elwess or by her maiden name, Ramona Jean Peek, gave birth to a daughter in St. Charles Medical Center in Bend, Oregon. She was unmarried at the time, and her physician, Dr. Harry E. Mackey, registered her in the hospital as "Mrs. Jean Smith." The next day, Ramona consented to the child's adoption by Leslie and Shirley Swarens of Bend, who named her Leslie Dawn. The hospital's medical records concerning the birth were sealed and marked to show that they were not public. Ramona subsequently remarried and raised a family. Only Ramona's mother and husband and Dr. Mackey knew about the daughter she had given up for adoption.

Twenty-one years later the daughter, now known as Dawn Kastning, wished to establish contact with her biological mother. Unable to gain access to the confidential court file of her adoption (though apparently able to locate the attending physician), Dawn sought out Dr. Mackey, and he agreed to assist in her quest. Dr. Mackey gave Dawn a letter which stated that he had registered Ramona Jean Peek at the hospital, that although he could not locate his medical records, he remembered administering diethylstilbestrol to her, and that the possible consequences of this medication made it important for Dawn to find her biological mother. The latter statements were untrue and made only to help Dawn to breach the confidentiality of the records concerning her birth and adoption. In 1982, hospital personnel, relying on Dr. Mackey's letter, allowed Dawn to make copies of plaintiff's medical records, which enabled her to locate plaintiff, now Ramona Humphers.

Ramona Humphers was not pleased. The unexpected development upset her and caused her emotional distress, worry, sleeplessness, humiliation, embarrassment, and inability to function normally. She sought damages from the estate of Dr. Mackey, who had died, by this action against defendant as the personal representative. After alleging the facts recounted above, her complaint pleads for relief on five different theories: First, that Dr. Mackey incurred liability for "outrageous conduct"; second, that his disclosure of a professional secret fell short of the care, skill and diligence employed by other physicians in the community and commanded by statute; third, that his disclosure wrongfully breached a confidential or privileged relationship; fourth, that his disclosure of confidential information was an "invasion of privacy" in the form of an "unauthorized intrusion upon plaintiff's seclusion, solitude, and private affairs"; and fifth, that his disclosures to Dawn Kastning breached a contractual obligation of secrecy. We hold that if plaintiff has a claim, it arose from a breach by Dr. Mackey of a professional duty to keep plaintiff's secret rather than from a violation of plaintiff's privacy.

Privacy

Although claims of a breach of privacy and of wrongful disclosure of confidential information may seem very similar in a case like the present, which involves the disclosure of an intimate personal secret, the two claims depend on different premises and cover different ground. Their common denominator is that both assert a right to control information, but they differ in important respects. Not every secret concerns personal or private information; commercial secrets are not personal, and governmental secrets are neither personal nor private. Secrecy involves intentional concealment. "But privacy need not hide; and secrecy hides far more than what is private." Bok, Secrets 11 (1983).

For our immediate purpose, the most important distinction is that only one who holds information in confidence can be charged with a breach of confidence. If an act qualifies as a tortious invasion of privacy, it theoretically could be committed by anyone. In the present case, Dr. Mackey's professional role is relevant to a claim that he breached a duty of confidentiality, but he could be charged with an invasion of plaintiff's privacy only if anyone else who told Dawn Kastning the facts of her birth without a special privilege to do so would be liable in tort for invading the privacy of her mother.

Whether "privacy" is a usable legal category has been much debated in other English-speaking jurisdictions as well as in this country, especially since its use in tort law, to claim the protection of [illegible] against intrusions by oth[illegible] entangled with its use in constitutional law, to claim protection against rather different intrusions by government. No concept in modern law has unleashed a comparable flood of commentary, its defenders arguing that "privacy" encompasses related interests of personality and autonomy, while its critics say that these interests are properly identified, evaluated, and protected below that exalted philosophical level. Indeed, at that level, a daughter's interest in her personal identity here confronts a mother's interest in guarding her own present identity by concealing their joint past. But recognition of an interest or value deserving protection states only half a case. Tort liability depends on the defendant's wrong as well as on the plaintiff's interest, or "right," unless some rule imposes strict liability. One's preferred seclusion or anonymity may be lost in many ways; the question remains who is legally bound to protect those interests at the risk of liability.

Doubtless plaintiff's interest qualifies as a "privacy" interest. That does not require the judgment of a court or a jury; it is established by the statutes that close adoption records to inspection without a court order. ORS 7.211, 432.420. The statutes are designed to protect privacy interests of the natural parents, the adoptive parents, or the child. But as already stated, to identify an interest deserving protection does not suffice to collect damages from anyone who causes injury to that interest. Dr. Mackey helped Dawn Kastning find her biological mother, but we are not prepared to assume that Ms. Kastning became liable for invasion of privacy in seeking her out. Nor, we think, would anyone who knew the facts without an obligation of secrecy commit a tort simply by telling them to Ms. Kastning.

Dr. Mackey himself did not approach plaintiff or pry into any personal facts that he did not know; indeed, if he had written or spoken to his former patient to tell her that her daughter was eager to find her, it would be hard to describe such a communication alone as an invasion of privacy. The point of the claim against Dr. Mackey is not that he pried into a confidence but that he failed to keep one. If Dr. Mackey incurred liability for that, it must result from an obligation of confidentiality beyond any general duty of people at large not to invade one another's privacy. We there[illegible] plaintiff's claim that Dr. M[illegible] was liable for a breach of confidence, the third count of the complaint.

Breach of Confidence

In the case of the medical profession, courts in fact have found sources of a nonconsensual duty of confidentiality. Some have thought such a duty toward the patient implicit in the patient's statutory privilege to exclude the doctor's testimony in litigation, enacted in this state in OEC 504-1(2). More directly in point are legal duties imposed as a condition of engaging in the professional practice of medicine or other occupations.

As early as 1920, the Supreme Court of Nebraska, where a medical licensing statute defined professional misconduct to include "betrayal of a professional secret to the detriment of the patient," wrote in *Simonsen v. Swenson*, *supra*, 104 Neb. at 227, 177 N.W. 831:

"By this statute, it appears to us, a positive duty is imposed upon the physician, both for the benefit and advantage of the patient as well as in the interest of general public policy. The relation of physician and patient is necessarily a highly confidential one. It is often necessary for the patient to give information about himself which would be most embarrassing or harmful to him if given general circulation. This information the physician is bound, not only upon his own professional honor and the ethics of his high profession, to keep secret, but by reason of the affirmative mandate of the statute itself. A wrongful breach of such confidence, and a betrayal of such trust, would give rise to a civil action for the damages naturally flowing from such wrong."

This strikes us as the right approach to a claim of liability outside obligations undertaken expressly or implied in fact in entering a contractual relationship. The contours of the asserted duty of confidentiality are determined by a legal source external to the tort claim itself. A plaintiff asserting a breach of such a nonconsensual duty must identify its source and terms.

Because the duty of confidentiality is determined by standards outside the tort claim for its breach, so are the defenses of privilege or justification. Physicians, like members of many ordinarily confidential professions and occupations, also may be legally obliged to report medical information to others for the protection of the patient, of other individuals, or of the public. That was true of the defendant in *Simonsen v. Swenson*, *supra*, who reported a guest's contagious disease to a hotel. The court noted that this disclosure was legally required and affirmed a directed verdict for the defendant. Even without such a legal obligation, there may be a privilege to disclose information for the safety of individuals or important to the public in matters of public interest. In any event, defenses to a duty of confidentiality are determined in the same manner as the existence and scope of the duty itself. They necessarily will differ from one occupation to another and from time to time. A physician or other member of a regulated occupation is not to be held to a noncontractual duty of secrecy in a tort action when disclosure would not be a breach or would be privileged in direct enforcement of the underlying duty.

A physician's duty to keep medical and related information about a patient in confidence is beyond question.

It is less obvious whether Dr. Mackey violated ORS 677.190(5) when he told Dawn Kastning what he knew of her birth. She was not, after all, a stranger to that proceeding. Lord Mansfield, in denying a common law privilege against testimony of the Duchess of Kingston's surgeon concerning the birth of her child, said that "[i]f a surgeon was voluntarily to reveal these secrets, to be sure he would be guilty of a breach of honor, and of great indiscretion"; but he was not speaking of revealing them to the child. If Ms. Kastning needed information about her natural mother for medical reasons, as Dr. Mackey pretended, the State Board of Medical Examiners likely would find the disclosure privileged against a charge under ORS 677.190(5); but the statement is alleged to have been a pretext designed to give her access to the hospital records. If only ORS 677.190(5) were involved, we do not know how the Board would judge a physician who assists at the birth of a child and decades later reveals to that person his or her parentage. But as already noted other statutes specifically mandate [illegible] adoption records. ORS 7.211 provides that court records in adoption cases may not be inspected or disclosed except upon court order, and ORS 432.420 requires a court order before sealed adoption records may be opened by the state registrar. Given these clear legal constraints, there is no privilege to disregard the professional duty imposed by ORS 677.190(5) solely in order to satisfy the curiosity of the person who was given up for adoption.

NOTES AND QUESTIONS

1. What were Doctor Mackey's obligations to Dawn Kastning? Would/could they include lying (as he did) to help her? Was she a "patient," with a claim to ethical or professional or fiduciary performance by Doctor Mackey? Did this include protecting Dawn from her mother? And what of Doctor Mackey's obligation to Ramona Humphers? Didn't he discharge those in delivering the baby, Dawn? He was not (as far as we know) a party to the adoption; anyway, he never agreed to sealing the records. Was he obligated to Ramona not to communicate information to Dawn (who, as a baby, was also Mackey's patient)? Is *Humphers* a *confidentiality* case or a *conflict of interests* case, like *Moore*?

2. Note that Justice Linde rejects the privacy claim in favor of the breach of confidence claim. Why? Which would you favor? Are there other theories? To what extent are the answers to these questions resolved by the presence of a statute in Oregon? Suppose no statute existed; how should the case be resolved?

3. Justice Linde writes that even if Doctor Mackey violated the statute, he may escape liability if the violation was "privileged." This would apply, he writes, if Dawn needed the information for "medical reasons," but not "solely in order to satisfy the curiosity of the person given up for adoption." Why? Why is one reason more compelling or trivial than the other? And is it fair to describe Dawn Kastning's powerful, elemental need to know as casual "curiosity"?

4. And what of the statute here? Is it [illegible]. It permits a citizen to give up a child without reason and then invoke state authority to hide from that child, obscuring the child's identity from her, denying access to parentage and ancestry and history — essential elements of personhood. If the state could not do that to a criminal, why to a baby? Reconsider here the cases from § 2.02[1] and § 2.04[1].

5. Would your reaction to *Humphers* be different if the letter had spoken the truth: that is, that Dr. Mackey *had* administered DES to the mother? Would it matter if the mother had remained a patient of Dr. Mackey? If the daughter had *also* remained a patient? If Dr. Mackey could therefore undertaken a comparative assessment of the injury to mother and daughter from disclosure or nondisclosure?

6. On the facts as presented in court, how would you characterize the injury experienced by the mother and how would you measure damages? To the daughter?

TARASOFF v. REGENTS OF UNIVERSITY OF CALIFORNIA

551 P.2d 334 (Cal. 1976)

Tobriner, Justice.

On October 27, 1969, Prosenjit Poddar killed Tatiana Tarasoff. Plaintiffs, Tatiana's parents, allege that two months earlier Poddar confided his intention to kill Tatiana to Dr. Lawrence Moore, a psychologist employed by the Cowell Memorial Hospital at the University of California at Berkeley. They allege that on Moore's request, the campus police briefly detained Poddar, but released him when he appeared rational. They further claim that Dr. Harvey Powelson, Moore's superior, then directed that no further action be taken to detain Poddar. No one warned plaintiffs of Tatiana's peril.

. . . .

Plaintiffs' Complaints

. . . .

Plaintiffs' first cause of action, entitled "Failure to Detain a Dangerous Patient," alleges that on August 20, 1969, Poddar was a voluntary outpatient receiving therapy at Cowell Memorial Hospital. Poddar informed Moore, his therapist, that he was going to kill an unnamed girl, readily identifiable as Tatiana, when she returned home from spending the summer in Brazil. Moore, with the concurrence of Dr. Gold, who had initially examined Poddar, and Dr. Yandell, assistant to the director of the department of psychiatry, decided that Poddar should be committed for observation in a mental hospital. Moore orally notified Officers Atkinson and Teel of the campus police that he would request commitment. He then sent a letter to Police Chief William Beall requesting the assistance of the police department in securing Poddar's confinement.

Officers Atkinson, Brownrigg, and Hallernan took Poddar into custody, but, satisfied that Poddar was rational, released him on his promise to stay away from Tatiana. Powelson, director of the department of psychiatry at Cowell Memorial Hospital, then asked the police to return Moore's letter, directed that all copies of the letter and notes that Moore had taken as therapist be destroyed, and "ordered no action to place Prosenjit Poddar in 72-hour treatment and evaluation facility."

Plaintiffs' second cause of action, entitled "Failure to Warn on a Dangerous Patient," incorporates the allegations of the first cause of action, but adds the assertion that defendants negligently permitted Poddar to be released from police custody without "notifying the parents of Tatiana Tarasoff that their daughter was in grave danger from Prosenjit Poddar." Poddar persuaded Tatiana's brother to share an apartment with him near Tatiana's residence; shortly after her return from Brazil, Poddar went to her residence and killed her.

Plaintiffs' third cause of action, entitled "Abandonment of a Dangerous Patient," seeks $10,000 punitive damages against defendant Powelson. Incorporating the crucial allegations of the first cause of action, plaintiffs charge that Powelson "did the things herein alleged with intent to abandon a dangerous patient, and said acts were done maliciously and oppressively."

. . . .

. . . [W]hen the avoidance of foreseeable harm requires a def[illegible] control the conduct of [illegible], or to warn of such conduct, the common law has traditionally imposed liability only if the defendant bears some special relationship to the dangerous person or to the potential victim. Since the relationship between a therapist and his patient satisfies this requirement, we need not here decide whether foreseeability alone is sufficient to create a duty to exercise reasonable care to protect a potential victim of another's conduct.

Although, as we have stated above, under the common law, as a general rule, one person owed no duty to control the conduct of another the courts have carved out an exception to this rule in cases in which the defendant stands in some special relationship to either the person whose conduct needs to be controlled or in a relationship to the foreseeable victim of that conduct. Applying this exception to the present case, we note that a relationship of defendant therapists to either Tatiana or Poddar will suffice to establish a duty of care; as explained in Section 315 of the Restatement Second of Torts, a duty of care may arise from either "(a) a special relation . . . between the actor and the third person which imposes a duty upon the actor to control the third person's conduct, or (b) a special relation . . . between the actor and the other which gives to the other a right of protection."

Although plaintiffs' pleadings assert no special relation between Tatiana and defendant therapists, they establish, as between Poddar and defendant therapists the special relation that arises between a patient and his doctor or psychotherapist.[1] Such a relationship may support affirmative duties for the benefit of third persons. Thus, for example, a hospital must exercise reasonable care to control the behavior of a patient which may endanger other persons.[2] A doctor must also warn a patient if the patient's condition or medication renders certain conduct, such as driving a car, dangerous to others.

. . . .

Defendants contend, however, that imposition of a duty to exercise reasonable care to protect third persons is unworkable because therapists cannot accurately predict whether or not a patient [illegible] violence. In support [illegible] amicus representing the American Psychiatric Association and other professional societies cites numerous articles which indicate that therapists, in the present state of the art, are unable reliably to predict violent acts; their forecasts, amicus claims, tend consistently to overpredict violence, and indeed are more often wrong than right. Since predictions of violence are

---

[1] The pleadings establish the requisite relationship between Poddar and both Dr. Moore, the therapist who treated Poddar, and Dr. Powelson, who supervised that treatment. Plaintiffs also allege that Dr. Gold personally examined Poddar, and that Dr. Yandell, as Powelson's assistant, approved the decision to arrange Poddar's commitment. These allegations are sufficient to raise the issue whether a doctor-patient or therapist-patient relationship, giving rise to a possible duty by the doctor or therapist to exercise reasonable care to protect a threatened person of danger arising from the patient's mental illness, existed between Gold or Yandell and Poddar.

[2] When a "hospital has notice or knowledge of facts from which it might reasonably be concluded that a patient would be likely to harm himself *or others* unless preclusive measures were taken, then the hospital must use reasonable care in the circumstances to prevent such harm." . . .

often erroneous, amicus concludes, the courts should not render rulings that predicate the liability of therapists upon the validity of such predictions.

. . . .

We recognize the difficulty that a therapist encounters in attempting to forecast whether a patient presents a serious danger of violence. Obviously we do not require that the therapist, in making that determination, render a perfect performance; the therapist need only exercise "that reasonable degree of skill, knowledge, and care ordinarily possessed and exercised by members of [that professional specialty] under similar circumstances." Within the broad range of reasonable practice and treatment in which professional opinion and judgment may differ, the therapist is free to exercise his or her own best judgment without liability; proof, aided by hindsight, that he or she judged wrongly is insufficient to establish negligence.

In the instant case, however, the pleadings do not raise any question as to failure of defendant therapists to predict that Poddar presented a serious danger of violence. On the contrary, the present complaints allege that defendant therapists did in fact predict that Poddar would kill, but were negligent in failing to warn.

Amicus contends, however, that even when a therapist does in fact predict that a patient poses a serious danger of violence to others, the therapist should be absolved of any responsibility for failing to act to protect the potential victim. In our view, however, once a therapist does in fact determine, or under applicable professional standards reasonably should have determined, that a patient poses a serious danger of violence to others, he bears a duty to exercise reasonable care to protect the foreseeable victim of that danger. While the discharge of this duty of due care will necessarily vary with the facts of each case, in each instance the adequacy of the therapist's conduct must be measured against the traditional negligence standard of the rendition of reasonable care under the circumstances. . . .

. . . .

Defendants further argue that free and open communication is essential to psychotherapy; that "Unless a patient . . . is assured that . . . information [revealed by him] can and will be held in utmost confidence, he will be reluctant to make the full disclosure upon which diagnosis and treatment . . . depends." The giving of a warning, defendants contend, constitutes a breach of trust which entails the revelation of confidential communications.

We recognize the public interest in supporting effective treatment of mental illness and in protecting the rights of patients to privacy and the consequent public importance of safeguarding the confidential character of psychotherapeutic communication. Against this interest, however, we must weigh the public interest in safety from violent assault. The Legislature has undertaken the difficult task of balancing the countervailing concerns. In Evidence Code Section 1014, it established a broad rule of privilege to protect confidential communications between patient and psychotherapist. In Evidence Code Section 1024, the Legislature created a specific and limited exception to the psychotherapist-patient privilege: "There is no privilege . . . if the psychotherapist has reasonable cause to believe that the patient is in such mental or emotional condition as to be dangerous to himself or to the person or property of another and that disclosure of the communication is necessary to prevent the threatened danger."

We realize that the open and confidential character of psychotherapeutic dialogue encourages patients to express threats of violence, few of which are ever executed. Certainly a therapist should not be encouraged routinely to reveal such threats; such disclosures could seriously disrupt the patient's relationship with his therapist and with the persons threatened. To the contrary, the therapist's obligations to his patient require that he not disclose a confidence unless such disclosure is necessary to avert danger to others, and even then that he do so discreetly, and in a fashion that would preserve the privacy of his patient to the fullest extent compatible with the prevention of the threatened danger.

The revelation of a communication under the above circumstances is not a breach of trust or a violation of professional ethics; as stated in the Principles of Medical Ethics of the American Medical Association (1957), section 9: "A physician may not reveal the confidence entrusted to him in the course of medical attendance . . . *unless he is required to do so by law or unless it becomes necessary in order to protect the welfare of the individual or of the community.*" We conclude that the public policy favoring protection of the confidential character of patient-psychotherapist communications must yield to the extent to which disclosure is essential to avert danger to others. The protective privilege ends where the public peril begins.

Our current crowded and computerized society compels the interdependence of its members. In this risk-infested society we can hardly tolerate the further exposure to danger that would result from a concealed knowledge of the therapist that his patient was lethal. If the exercise of reasonable care to protect the threatened victim requires the therapist to warn the endangered party or those who can reasonably be expected to notify him, we see no sufficient societal interest that would protect and justify concealment. The containment of such risks lies in the public interest. For the foregoing reasons, we find that plaintiffs' complaints can be amended to state a cause of action against defendants Moore, Powelson, Gold, and Yandell and against the Regents as their employer, for breach of a duty to exercise reasonable care to protect Tatiana.

. . . .

Turning now to the police defendants, we conclude that they do not have any such special relationship to either Tatiana or to Poddar sufficient to impose upon such defendants a duty to warn respecting Poddar's violent intentions. Plaintiffs suggest no theory, and plead no facts that give rise to any duty to warn on the part of the police defendants absent such a special relationship. They have thus failed to demonstrate that the trial court erred in denying leave to amend as to the police defendants.

3. Defendant Therapists Are Not Immune From Liability for Failure to Warn

We address the issue of whether defendant therapists are protected by governmental immunity for having failed to warn Tatiana or those who reasonably could have been expected to notify her of her peril. We postulate our analysis on Section 820.2 of the Government Code. That provision declares, with exceptions not applicable here, that "a public employee is not liable for an injury resulting from his act or omission where the act or omission was the result of the exercise of the discretion vested in him, whether or not such discretion [was] abused."

. . . .

. . . [W]e conclude that defendant therapists in the present case are not immune from liability for their failure to warn of Tatiana's peril. *Johnson* held that a parole officer's determination whether to warn an adult couple that their prospective foster child had a background of violence "present[ed] no . . . reasons for immunity" was "at the lowest, ministerial rung of official action," and indeed constituted "a classic case for the imposition of tort liability." Although defendants in *Johnson* argued that the decision whether to inform the foster parents of the child's background required the exercise of considerable judgmental skills, we concluded that the state was not immune from liability for the parole officer's failure to warn because such a decision did not rise to the level of a "basic policy decision."

. . . .

We conclude, therefore, that the therapist defendant's failure to warn Tatiana or those who reasonably could have been expected to notify her of her peril does not fall within the absolute protection afforded by Section 820.2 of the Government Code. We emphasize that our conclusion does not raise the specter of therapists employed by the government indiscriminately being held liable for damage despite their exercise of sound professional judgment. We require of publicly employed therapists only that quantum of care which the common law requires of private therapists. The imposition of liability in those rare cases in which a public employee falls short of this standard does not contravene the language or purpose of Government Code Section 820.2.

. . . .

Mosk, Justice (concurring and dissenting).

I concur in the result in this instance only because the complaints allege that defendant therapists did in fact predict that Poddar would kill and were therefore negligent in failing to warn of that danger. Thus the issue here is very narrow: we are not concerned with whether the therapists, pursuant to the standards of their profession, "should have" predicted potential violence; they allegedly did so in actuality. Under these limited circumstances I agree that a cause of action can be stated.

Whether plaintiffs can ultimately prevail is problematical at best. As the complaints admit, the therapists *did* notify the police that Poddar was planning to kill a girl identifiable as Tatiana. While I doubt that more should be required, this issue may be raised in defense and its determination is a question of fact.

I cannot concur, however, in the majority's rule that a therapist may be held liable for failing to predict his patient's tendency to violence if other practitioners, pursuant to the "standards of the profession," would have done so. The question is, what standards? Defendants and a responsible amicus curiae demonstrate that psychiatric predictions of violence are inherently unreliable

I would restructure the rule designed by the majority to eliminate all reference to conformity to standards of the profession in predicting violence. If a psychiatrist does in fact predict violence, then a duty to warn arises. The majority's expansion of that rule will take us from the world of reality into the wonderland of clairvoyance.

Clark, Justice (dissenting).

Until today's majority opinion, both legal and medical authorities have agreed that confidentiality is essential to effectively treat the mentally ill, and that imposing a duty on doctors to disclose patient threats to potential victims would greatly impair treatment. Further, recognizing that effective treatment and society's safety are necessarily intertwined, the Legislature has already decided effective and confidential treatment is preferred over imposition of a duty to warn.

. . . .

Generally, a person owes no duty to control the conduct of another. Exceptions are recognized only in limited situations where (1) a special relationship exists between the defendant and injured party, or (2) a special relationship exists between defendant and the active wrongdoer, imposing a duty on defendant to control the wrongdoer's conduct. The majority does not contend the first exception is appropriate to this case.

. . . .

Overwhelming policy considerations weigh against imposing a duty on psychotherapists to warn a potential victim against harm. While offering virtually no benefit to society, such a duty will frustrate psychiatric treatment, invade fundamental patient rights and increase violence.

. . . .

Assurance of confidentiality is important for three reasons.

First, without substantial assurance of confidentiality, those requiring treatment will be deterred from [illegible]. It remains an unfortunate fact in our society that people seeking psychiatric guidance tend to become stigmatized. Apprehension of such stigma — apparently increased by the propensity of people considering treatment to see themselves in the worst possible light — creates a well-recognized reluctance to seek aid. This reluctance is alleviated by the psychiatrist's assurance of confidentiality.

Second, the guarantee of confidentiality is essential in eliciting the full disclosure necessary for effective treatment. The psychiatric patient approaches treatment with conscious and unconscious inhibitions against revealing his innermost thoughts. "Every person, however well-motivated, has to overcome resistances to therapeutic exploration. These resistances seek support from every possible source and the possibility of disclosure would easily be employed in the service of resistance." . . .

Third, even if the patient fully discloses his thoughts, assurance that the confidential relationship will not be breached is necessary to maintain his trust in his psychiatrist — the very means by which treatment is effected. "[T]he essence of much psychotherapy is the contribution of trust in the external world and ultimately in the self, modelled upon the trusting relationship established during therapy." Patients will be helped only if they can form a trusting relationship with the psychiatrist. . . .

. . . .

. . . [P]sychiatric patients are encouraged to discuss all thoughts of violence, and they often express such thoughts. However, unlike this court, the psychiatrist does not enjoy the benefit of overwhelming hindsight in seeing which few, if any, of his patients will ultimately become violent. Now, confronted by the majority's new duty, the psychiatrist must instantaneously calculate potential violence from each patient on each visit. The difficulties researchers have encountered in accurately predicting violence will be heightened for the practicing psychiatrist dealing for brief periods in his office with heretofore nonviolent patients. And, given the decision not to warn or commit must always be made at the psychiatrist's civil peril, one can expect most doubts will be resolved in favor of the psychiatrist protecting himself.

Neither alternative open to the psychiatrist seeking to protect himself is in the public interest. The warning itself is an impairment of the psychiatrist's ability to treat, depriving many patients of adequate treatment. It is to be expected that after disclosing their threats, a significant number of patients, who would not become violent if treated according to existing practices, will engage in violent conduct as a result of unsuccessful treatment. In short, the majority's duty to warn will not only impair treatment of many who would never become violent but worse, will result in a net increase in violence.

The second alternative open to the psychiatrist is to commit his patient rather than to warn. Even in the absence of threat of civil liability, the doubts of psychiatrists as to the seriousness of patient threats have led psychiatrists to overcommit to mental institutions. This overcommitment has been authoritatively documented in both legal and psychiatric studies. . . .

. . . .

The judgment should be affirmed.

. . . .

NOTES AND QUESTIONS

1. *Tarasoff* is a widely known case, since it has implications for professionals of all sorts. The obligation of confidentiality is implicit in any fiduciary relationship, whether that of a physician, psychologist, counselor, social worker, attorney, banker, real estate agent or teacher. Wherever someone acts on behalf of another, or counsels another, there is a relationship which may be characterized as being that of a "fiduciary." What would the result be in *Tarasoff* if the psychologist had been an attorney? A priest?
2. In *Tarasoff,* Mr. Poddar quite legitimately expected that Dr. Moore would protect his confidences. The Court, however, held that Dr. Moore had an obligation to tell Tatiana Tarasoff that Mr. Poddar might well

kill her. Do you agree or disagree? If Mr. Poddar had *known* Dr. Moore would tell, how would Poddar have changed his behavior?

3. The decision in *Tarasoff* leaves open a whole host of questions as to the implications and applications in other contexts. Among the questions are the following. *To whom* does the obligation of disclosure extend? *From whom*; that is, who besides Dr. Moore would be obligated to make disclosure? *When* does the obligation arise; that is, upon what dangers and how imminent must they be? And when is the obligation *satisfied*; that is, what warnings or communications, and to whom and when, would be sufficient? Finally, at what time does the obligation *arise*; that is, does the timing turn upon the formation of the relationship with the patient/client or upon the receipt of communications by the fiduciary?

4. Underlying all of these questions is a separate subset, significant in distinguishing ethics from law. *Tarasoff* is a malpractice case and so the *law* would say that Dr. Moore should be judged against the standard of the *reasonable* practitioner. Ethics might well pose a different standard: that of the *actual* person. Although relieved of legal obligation, ethics might well say that Dr. Moore, as a citizen in an ethical community, should do more (or, perhaps, under certain circumstances might do *less*) than the reasonable or average person. And if you opt for the ethical standard, does that mean disclosure or secrecy? What would Rawls say?

5. Are you satisfied with the Court's rather easy dismissal of the claim against the police? Are you not troubled by the rather equally easy way in which the Court finds the psychologist did not satisfy his obligations by notifying the police? And should not Dr. Moore have been relieved of any responsibility when he notified his employers, since, after all, the nature of his employment and of his relationship with Poddar was determined by Dr. Moore's superiors and, ultimately, by the University of California at Berkeley. What are the implications of your answer for a physician employed by an HMO or a hospital?

6. What will be the impact of *Tarasoff* [illegible] of fiduciaries (physicians, psychiatrists, psychologists, attorneys, clergy people)? The dissent in note 4 (omitted) illustrates the difficulty in making predictions. Will fiduciaries, in response to *Tarasoff,* engage in disclosures out of an excess of caution? Or will they engage in conduct concealing disclosures, all the while feeling they are acting unethically? Or will they, as the dissent suggests, commit patients rather than warn subjects? Whatever your conclusion, does it help to understand — and did the majority fail to understand — that rules of ethics are, in fact, *real world* rules of conduct?

7. What should be the amount of damages in *Tarasoff*? If there *had* been disclosure?

8. We will return to the obligation of physicians toward those other than their patients later, in § 3.03[2] in the *Reisner* case (boyfriend) and § 4.02[2] in the *Safer* case (daughter). For the present, however, we

shift our focus from the physician's obligation to the patient's obligation to drop the cloak of confidentiality, in *Head v. Colloton.*

HEAD v. COLLOTON
331 N.W.2d 870 (Iowa 1983)

McCormick, Justice.

. . . .

Plaintiff William Head is a leukemia victim who is currently undergoing chemotherapy in a Texas clinic. His illness is in relapse, and the prognosis is grim.

The University of Iowa Hospitals and Clinics include a bone marrow transplant unit. That unit maintains a bone marrow transplant registry, listing persons whose blood has been tissue-typed by the hospital. The tissue typing reveals blood antigen characteristics which must be known for determining whether a donor's bone marrow will be a suitable match-up for the bone marrow of a donee. A bone marrow transplant consists of removing bone marrow from a healthy person and infusing it into the body of a patient in the hope it will generate healthy white blood cells. The procedure is experimental between unrelated persons.

Late in 1982, plaintiff phoned the transplant unit and, through a series of conversations with a staff member, learned that the hospital's registry included the name of a woman who might, upon further testing, prove to be a suitable donor to him. Only one in approximately 6,000 persons would have blood with the necessary antigen characteristics.

The tissue typing of the woman, referred to in the record as "Mrs. X," had not been done for reasons of her own health but to determine her suitability as a blood platelet donor to a member of her family who was ill. The hospital subsequently placed her name in its platelet donor registry. Then, when it later established an experimental program involving bone marrow transplants between unrelated persons, the hospital, without Mrs. X's knowledge or consent, placed her name in the bone marrow transplant registry. When the hospital established the new program, its institutional review board approved a procedure for contacting persons listed on the registry to determine whether they would act as donors. The procedure involved sending a letter informing the person of the program, its nature and goals, and inviting the person's participation in it. If the letter was not answered, a staff member was authorized to telephone the person and ask a series of general questions designed to determine whether the person would volunteer as a donor.

After plaintiff's contact with the bone marrow unit, the unit staff on December 31, 1982, sent Mrs. X the general letter informing her about the program and encouraging her to participate in it. When no response to the letter was received, a staff member telephoned Mrs. X on January 10, 1983, and asked her the series of questions. In responding to those questions, Mrs. X said she was not interested in being a bone marrow donor. When asked if she might ever be interested in being a donor, she said, "Well, if it was for family, yes. Otherwise, no." Despite plaintiff's subsequent request that the hospital make a specific inquiry of Mrs. X in plaintiff's behalf or to disclose her or to disclose her identity to plaintiff. He then brought the present action.

Defendants John Colloton and Lloyd J. Filer are hospital employees with access to the bone marrow transplant registry. Plaintiff asked for a mandatory injunction to require them to disclose the name and identity of the potential donor either to the court or to his attorney. He proposed that the court or counsel then be permitted to write the woman to notify her of plaintiff's need and her possible suitability as a donor, asking her if she would consider being a donor to plaintiff.

After hearing evidence on the issue, the court ordered defendants to send the requested letter. This court sustained defendants' application for interlocutory review and issued a stay of the order.

This case involves application of the provisions of chapter 68A, Iowa's public records statute. Under Section 68A.1, "public records" include "all records and documents of or belonging to this state. . . ." § 68A.1. Defendants concede that the records of the University of Iowa hospital, a state hospital, are public records within the meaning of this provision. Thus the bone marrow donor registry is a public record. Section 68A.2 provides for public access to all public records "unless some other provision of the Code expressly limits such right or requires such records to be kept confidential."

Defendants contend that the registry is required to be kept confidential pursuant to Section 68A.7(2). In material part, Section 68A.7 provides:

> The following public records shall be kept confidential, unless otherwise ordered by a court, by the lawful custodian of the records, or by another person duly authorized to release information.
>
> . . . .

2. Hospital Records and Medical Records of the Condition, Diagnosis, Care, or Treatment of a Patient or Former Patient, Including Outpatient

Alternatively defendants seek an injunction against disclosure pursuant to Section 68A.8 which provides for such relief when a court finds upon a petition supported by affidavit "that such examination would clearly not be in the public interest and would substantially and irreparably injure any person or persons." In view of our disposition of the appeal, we do not reach defendant's alternative ground.

. . . .

Because Chapter 68A defines the right of the general public to access to public records, the exemptions in Section 68A.7 delineate exceptions only to the same general right. For example, they do not preclude access by an agency vested with investigative authority and subpoena power. Nor do they preclude access by a public officer granted subpoena authority pursuant to statute or rule. In the present case, however, plaintiff has no standing to seek access other than as a member of the public generally.

He contends Section 68A.7(2) is inapplicable on two bases. One is that a hospital record is not confidential unless it is a patient record. The other basis is that the tissue-typing record of Mrs. X is not a patient record. Defendants also offer a two-pronged argument. One prong is that a hospital record need not be a patient record to be confidential. The other is that the tissue-typing record is a hospital record of a patient within the meaning of the statute. We are thus confronted with a legal issue, requiring interpretation of Section 68A.7(2).

. . . .

. . . We agree with plaintiff that the only hospital records made confidential by the statute are those "of the condition, diagnosis, care, or treatment of a patient or former patient, including outpatient." Four considerations influence this interpretation. One is our duty to give the exemption a narrow interpretation. Limiting the kind of hospital records subject to the exemption gives effect to this duty. Another consideration is the use of the word "outpatient" in the qualifying language. The term ordinarily means a person treated at a clinic or dispensary connected with a hospital who is not a hospital inmate. Use of this word would be superfluous in Section 68A.7(2) unless the qualifying language modifies the term "hospital records" as well as "medical records." A third consideration is that in both ordinary and professional usage the term hospital record means the hospital's medical record relating to a patient. A final consideration is the unlikelihood that the legislature intended to create a blanket exemption to all records of a public hospital, whether they relate to patients or not. Accordingly we conclude that the only hospital records made confidential by Section 68A.7(2) are those "of the condition, diagnosis, care, or treatment of a patient or former patient, including outpatient."

We must next determine whether the record to which plaintiff seeks access is that kind of hospital record. In contending Mrs. X was not a patient, plaintiff relies on cases interpreting the physician-patient privilege in Section 622.10. Section 622.10 concerns only the circumstances under which certain persons including physicians are precluded from disclosing confidential communications in giving testimony. This court has said:

> The physician-patient privilege is intended to foster free and full communication between the physician and the patient in diagnosis or treatment of the patient's ills. This privilege is not designed, nor will it be so extended, to act as a shield behind which a patient may conceal information, though made to his physician, which is not necessary and proper to enable the physician to perform his profession skillfully. . . .

The critical issue is whether Mrs. X was a hospital patient for purposes of Section 68A.7(2) when she submitted to tissue typing as a potential platelet donor. The ordinary meaning of the word "patient" is "a person under medical or surgical treatment." . . .

The evidence shows the hospital believed Mrs. X became a patient when she submitted to tissue typing. Dr. Roger Gingrich, director of the hospital's bone marrow transplant program, testified she was a patient. He said: "I would regard any person who interfaces themselves with the medical profession and out of that interaction there's biologic information obtained about the . . . person, in fact to be a patient, to [have] established a doctor-patient relationship." Dr. James Armitage, former director of the unit, testified to the same effect. Although this testimony is not conclusive on the issue, it is consistent with the broad dictionary definition of a treatment concept.

It is also consistent with case law that recognizes the same duty between physician and donor as exists between physician and patient generally. . . .

Perhaps even more importantly the doctors' testimony is consistent with the reality of the situation. When a person submits to a hospital procedure, the hospital's duty should not depend on whether the procedure is for that person's benefit or the potential benefit of someone else. The fiduciary relationship is the same, and the standard of care is the same. In addition, just as with patients generally, a potential donor has a valuable right of privacy.

An individual's interest in avoiding disclosure of personal matters is constitutionally based. This right is also recognized at common law. A valuable part of the right of privacy is the right to avoid publicity concerning private facts. This right can be as important to a potential donor as to a person in ill health. The Hippocratic Oath makes no distinction based on how medical confidences are acquired. Nor does the American Medical Record Association make such a distinction in its model policy for maintenance of confidentiality of patient health information adopted in 1977.

. . . .

We conclude that the hospital record of Mrs. X is the hospital record of the "condition, diagnosis, care or treatment of a patient, or former patient" within the meaning of Section 68A.7(2). Therefore the record is confidential.

Plaintiff contends this does not necessarily decide the case. He points to the provision in the first paragraph of Section 68A.7 that provides for confidentiality "unless otherwise ordered by a court." He argues that this provision gives a court discretion to breach confidentiality otherwise required under the statute. We do not read the provision in that way nor do we understand that the trial court did so. To do so would undermine the careful legislative delineation of statutory exemptions. We hold, instead, that the power of a court is limited to ordering disclosure of otherwise confidential records only when a statute or rule outside of Chapter 68A gives a party a specific right of access superior to that of the public generally. Situations of that kind were presented and found to exist in the *City of Des Moines* and *Brown* cases.

Finally, plaintiff contends it is significant that the remedy he sought and the trial court awarded fell short of disclosure of Mrs. X's identity. He suggests the interests of the parties under chapter 68A are satisfied by this remedy. We find, instead, that the remedy the trial court fashioned was not authorized by the statute. If public access is available at all under chapter 68A, it is right of general public access. The statute does not permit the singling out of one member of the public for special access on special terms.

We have carefully considered all of plaintiff's contentions and arguments, whether expressly addressed in this opinion or not, and find they are without merit. The trial court order must be reversed.

Reversed.

NOTES AND QUESTIONS

1. One of the critical issues facing health care in the United States is the shortage of donors for organ transplants. These may include hearts, livers, kidneys and lungs, but the shortage extends as well to such commonplace materials as blood supplies. At issue in *Head v. Colloton*, of course, was bone marrow, frequently essential as a treatment option for leukemia and, like blood, a substance which a person can donate without injury or loss (other than the experience of the donating process itself). To expand the process of donation and the number of donors, maximum publicity is necessary. The rules of confidentiality, then, run counter to these public needs.

2. The donor's interest in *Head v. Colloton* in confidentiality, is different, is it not, from the interest of Mr. Poddar in *Tarasoff*? In the ordinary fiduciary relationship, the "purchaser" needs confidentiality to protect his or her interests, communications or privacy in past conduct. In *Head,* the potential donor really has no interest other than the minimalistic desire, however privileged, to be left alone as to *future* conduct. Is this a sufficient interest to be treated with the same dignity as the interests of patients, clients and penitents in the ordinary confidential relationship?

3. Is the Court's treatment of this issue superficial? It relies on Gingrich to say that "any person who interfaces themselves with the medical profession" becomes a patient; it then goes on to conclude that any "patient" is entitled to full-blown confidentiality within a fiduciary relationship. Is this not simply mixing and matching labels, without attention to the real interest and needs involved? *Why,* precisely, does the potential donor need to be protected from simply *knowing* there is someone out there who would benefit from her donation? Perhaps she *needs* to be protected from a direct approach; but is there truly a societal or personal need to protect her from *knowledge* of need?

4. How is Mrs. X different from Mr. Poddar in *Tarasoff*? Is not Ms. X in the position of bringing about the death of Mr. Head? If they are *both* patients, doesn't the hospital have an obligation *equally* to Mr. Head?

5. Ethically, what were Ms. X's responsibilities? What would *you* have done?

6. For an excellent article, see Steven Silverstein, *Medical Confidentiality In Israeli Law*, 30 J. Marshall L. Rev. 747 (1997); and see Michelle R. King, *Physician Duty to Warn a Patient's Offspring of Hereditary Genetic Defects: Balancing the Patient's Right to Confidentiality Against the Family Member's Right to Know — Can or Should Tarasoff Apply?*, 4 Quinnipiac Health L.J. 1 (2000).

PROBLEM 3–3 — *Tarasoff* on the Road

Ronald Peterson had an epileptic [illegible] driving. Another driver on [illegible], was struck and died as a result. Her husband and mother sued the family doctor, Raymond Johnson, who had treated Ronald for years. Although the medications controlling the epilepsy were prescribed by two other physicians, Dr. Johnson monitored the blood level of Dilantin.

Seven days before the accident Peterson saw Johnson; all appeared normal. But Johnson had reported a seizure to another physician, Wendenburg, ten months earlier. A neurologist, Dr. Waller, had told Peterson not to drive in 1986, but told him he could a year before the collision in 1990. By October of 1989, Peterson had been seizure-free for three years — except for the seizure reported to Wendenburg, after surgery for a ruptured disc and a myelogram.

Is there liability here under *Tarasoff*? What more do you need to know? *See Praesel v. Johnson*, 925 S.W. 2d 255 (Tex. Ct. App. 1996), *rev'd.* 967 S.W.2d 391 (Tex.) and *Myers v. Quesenberry*, 193 Cal. Rprtr. 733 (Cal. 1983).

As the *Tarasoff* case illustrates, therapists may harm third parties by failure to notify them of dangers posed by patients. Harm may also result by the therapy itself, as in reviving repressed memories of abuse. In either instance, the duty of confidentiality may collide with the obligation to warn.

PROBLEM 3–4 — Informing On the Patient

Ballensky is driving, swerves, and collides with an oncoming vehicle and his passenger dies. He pleads guilty to negligent homicide. Ballinsky then sues Jan-Marie Flattum-Riemers, M.D., for emotional distress. She treated him after the accident, running a blood screen, which tested positive for cannabinoids, which she disclosed to the highway patrol officer, telling the officer also the victim's family is interested in the results.

What result? Would it matter if Dr. Flattum-Riemers testified she did not think Ballensky was under the influence of drugs or alcohol at the time of the accident? Nor did the police officer?

Should there be a statute permitting such [illegible], should it [illegible] totally or just when acting in good faith — and what would that mean?

See Ballensky v. Flattum-Riemers, ___ N.D. ___ (6/5/06), 15 HL Rprtr. 700-701 (6/15/06).

DOE v. MCKAY

700 N.E.2d 1018 (Ill. 1998)

Justice **Miller** delivered the opinion of the court:

According to the allegations in the amended complaint, beginning in 1990 and continuing through October 1995, when the amended complaint was filed, the plaintiff's daughter, Jane Doe, underwent psychological treatment under the care of defendant Bobbie McKay, a licensed clinical psychologist. During the course of this treatment, Jane Doe supposedly discovered repressed memories of sexual abuse allegedly committed by the plaintiff. Jane Doe, who was born in 1964, had not been aware of these memories before beginning her treatment with Dr. McKay.

According to the amended complaint, during a counseling session attended by McKay, Jane Doe, and the plaintiff on February 6, 1992, Jane Doe accused the plaintiff of sexually abusing her when she was about 11 years old. Also during this session, McKay suggested to Jane Doe that the plaintiff might harm her further. At that time, McKay told the plaintiff that his daughter's memories of the alleged abuse had been repressed until they were retrieved during therapy, and that the plaintiff had repressed his own memories of the abuse. McKay recommended that the plaintiff commence treatment with another therapist; McKay spoke with the plaintiff the next day by telephone and recommended that he see Vicki Seglin, another psychologist employed by the McKay practice. The plaintiff saw Seglin individually until October 1992. The plaintiff further alleges that he later learned from his daughter that the February 6, 1992, session was arranged by the therapist to maximize the shock effect of his daughter's accusation and to force from the plaintiff a confession regarding the alleged abuse. The plaintiff denies that he ever sexually abused his daughter.

The amended complaint also alleges that at a counseling session on September 9, 1992, attended by McKay, Jane Doe, and the plaintiff, McKay told the plaintiff of the specific act of abuse he allegedly committed against his daughter. At that time, McKay again asserted that the plaintiff and his daughter had repressed their memories of the abuse. Later, at a session held on October 27, 1992, which was attended by McKay, Seglin, Jane Doe, and the plaintiff, McKay stated again that Jane Doe and the plaintiff had repressed their memories of the plaintiff's alleged sexual abuse. On this occasion, McKay said that the only explanation for Jane Doe's psychological condition was that she had been abused by the plaintiff.

Regarding the method of treatment employed in Jane Doe's case, the plaintiff alleges that McKay believes that mental or emotional problems in adults are often the result of childhood sexual abuse, the memory of which has been repressed. The plaintiff further asserts that McKay believes that previously repressed memories of abuse can be recalled with the techniques she uses, and that "healing" can occur when a patient recovers those memories and resolves the ensuing emotional turmoil. The plaintiff asserts that McKay's views regarding repression and the recovery of repressed memory are not supported by scientific evidence and are not generally accepted by the psychological community. The plaintiff further alleges that he paid a total of $ 3,208 for services rendered by McKay to his daughter from January through August 1992, and that he paid a total of $ 4,435 for services rendered to him by Vicki Seglin from February through October 1992. Jane Doe is not a party to this action, and she has not alleged any malpractice by the defendants.

I

To state a cause of action for negligence, a complaint must allege facts that are sufficient to show the existence of a duty, a breach of the duty, and an injury to the plaintiff proximately caused by the breach. Whether a duty exists is a question of law to be determined by the court. In deciding wh[illegible] case, a court will consider the foreseeability of the plaintiff's injury, the likelihood of the occurrence, the magnitude of the burden of guarding against it, and the consequences of placing that burden on the defendant.

In *Kirk v. Michael Reese Hospital & Medical Center*, 117 Ill. 2d 507, 111 Ill. Dec. 944, 513 N.E.2d 387 (1987), this court ruled that a third party injured by a patient could not bring a malpractice action against the patient's doctors, who allegedly failed to warn the patient that prescription drugs he was taking could impair his abilities. The plaintiff in that case was injured when the car in which he was riding struck a tree; the car was being driven by a recently discharged psychiatric patient who had received psychotropic drugs at a hospital and who had later consumed alcohol.

The plaintiff does not allege in counts I and XI, at issue here, that he was a patient of Dr. McKay. Elsewhere in the amended complaint the plaintiff separately alleges that he was a patient of Dr. McKay and seeks recovery on a malpractice theory, but those portions of the amended complaint are not involved in this appeal. Our only concern here is with the allegations in counts I and XI, which do not assert a therapist-patient relationship between Dr. McKay and the plaintiff. For the reasons expressed in *Kirk*, it would appear that these counts must therefore fail.

The appellate court below recognized that, as a general rule, a nonpatient may not bring a malpractice action against a healthcare professional. The court believed, however, that the present case fits within the concept of "transferred negligence," as illustrated by this court's decision in *Renslow v. Mennonite Hospital*, 67 Ill. 2d 348, 10 Ill. Dec. 484, 367 N.E.2d 1250 (1977).

In *Renslow* the plaintiff's mother had received incompatible blood during a transfusion, which had caused the mother's blood to become sensitized. The mother did not learn of the problem until a number of years later, when she was pregnant with the plaintiff, and the plaintiff was injured as a result of her mother's condition. The *Renslow* court concluded that the defendants owed the plaintiff a duty of due care, even though she had not been conceived at the time of the [illegible], and therefore permitted the plaintiff to bring a malpractice action against the defendants-a hospital and its laboratory director.

We do not believe that similarly compelling circumstances are present in this case, and thus we decline to apply *Renslow*'s concept of transferred negligence here. The relationship between a mother and a fetus is perhaps singular and unique, and it is demonstrably different from the relationship that exists between a parent and an adult child. Notably, the injury complained of in *Renslow* was physical, traceable to the negligent treatment of the mother. In the present case, in contrast, the injury is nonphysical and results from decisions made by the daughter. We also note that the interests of the mother and the fetus in *Renslow* were not adverse to each other, while in the present case the interests of the plaintiff and Jane Doe are different.

Nor is the present appeal like *O'Hara v. Holy Cross Hospital*, 137 Ill. 2d 332, 148 Ill. Dec. 712, 561 N.E.2d 18 (1990). In *O'Hara* the plaintiff accompanied her son to a hospital emergency room for treatment of a facial laceration. The plaintiff injured herself when she fainted during her son's treatment. The parties disputed whether the plaintiff was merely a bystander during her son's treatment or whether she was invited to assist in the treatment. This court concluded that the defendants did not have a duty to protect the plaintiff, a nonpatient, from physical injury if she was only a bystander during the treatment. If the plaintiff was invited to participate in her son's treatment, however, then the court believed that the defendants would owe her a duty to protect her from fainting.

A number of considerations relevant to the duty analysis strongly militate against imposition of a duty here, even when the asserted liability is characterized in terms of transferred negligence or a special relationship. Under the rule expressed in *Kirk*, the defendant therapist owed a duty of care to her patient only, and not to nonpatient third parties. Approval of the plaintiff's cause of action, however, would mean that therapists generally, as well as other types of counselors, could be subject to suit by any nonpatient third party who is adversely affected by personal decisions perceived to be made by a patient in response to counseling. This result would, we believe, place therapists in a difficult position, requiring them to answer to competing demands and to divide their loyalty between sharply different interests.

Moreover, recognition of the plaintiff's action could also be inconsistent with the duty of confidentiality that every therapist owes to his or her patients. The defendants point out that the therapist cannot properly defend the present action without revealing confidences revealed to her by Jane Doe. These communications are privileged and are subject to disclosure only in a limited range of circumstances, as in cases in which the patient has sued the therapist.

Allowing a nonpatient's action against another person's therapist to go forward would seriously intrude on the relationship between therapist and patient, jeopardizing the confidentiality necessary for the relationship to flourish. As this case illustrates, the patient would be faced with a difficult choice between preserving the confidentiality of patient-therapist communications and assisting the therapist in responding to what must, to the patient's eyes, be a meritless action. The patient could either waive the privilege and permit the therapist to defend the action, while suffering the public disclosure of communications originally intended to remain private, or assert the privilege and maintain the confidentiality of the therapy, but at the price of denying the therapist, presumably a valued friend, the use of potentially helpful evidence.

Thus, unless waived by the patient, the therapist's duty of confidentiality would restrict the therapist in the way in which she could respond here to the plaintiff's allegations. For example, the therapist could neither confirm nor deny that the patient told her certain things during the course of the patient's treatment. We note that the record in the present case contains an affidavit from defendant Bobbie McKay, in which she states that Jane Doe has declined to waive the statutory privilege. Thus, Dr. McKay could not easily answer the present action, for her patient has effectively forbidden her to respond to some of the central allegations of the plaintiff's complaint.

The considerations we have just discussed-the problem of divided loyalties, and the strong public interest in maintaining the confidentiality of therapist-patient com[illegible] strongly against imposing on therapists a duty of care toward nonpatients. Accordingly, we believe that the rule in *Kirk v. Michael Reese Hospital & Medical Center*, 117 Ill. 2d 507, 111 Ill. Dec. 944, 513 N.E.2d 387 (1987), barring malpractice actions by third parties must be applicable here and requires that no duty be extended to the plaintiff for psychic injuries allegedly arising from the therapist's treatment of Jane Doe. To be sure, the plaintiff may allege that he himself was a patient of Dr. McKay, and counts to that effect remain pending in the circuit court of Du Page County. They are not at issue in the present appeal, however.

In sum, we do not believe that the plaintiff has succeeded in stating a cause of action under the theories at issue in this appeal. Accordingly, the judgment of the appellate court is reversed, and the judgment of the circuit court of Du Page County is affirmed.

Appellate court judgment reversed; circuit court judgment affirmed.

Justice **Harrison**, dissenting:

My colleagues expound at length about the need to protect medical providers from liability to some indeterminate class of nonpatient third parties. They fail to see that that is not what this case is about at all. Plaintiff here was not a chance bystander or random member of the general public. He was a relative of the therapist's patient, he was the alleged cause of the patient's psychological difficulties, and, according to the complaint, the therapist specifically arranged to have him participate in the patient's therapy sessions as part of the patient's treatment program.

Where a third party has the kind of relationship with the patient that John Doe had here and the therapist chooses to make that third party an integral part of a patient's treatment, as the therapist in this case did, the majority's concerns about compromising patient confidentiality and divided loyalty make no sense. It was the therapist who orchestrated what happened here, she did so with the patient's consent, and once John Doe began participating in the sessions at the therapist's behest, protecting the patient's condition against disclosure to third [illegible] to be a consideration. Divulging the patient's complaints to John Doe was, in fact, the very foundation of the therapist's treatment plan. As the majority notes, the therapist hoped that the shock effect of the patient's disclosures would force Doe to confess.

As it turned out, no confession was forthcoming. The plan failed. The damage that John Doe allegedly sustained as a result was foreseeable by any meaningful standard. The likelihood of injury was great, the burden of guarding against that injury was slight, and there would be no significant adverse consequences from placing that burden on the therapist.

The majority claims that approving plaintiff's cause of action

> "would mean that therapists generally, as well as other types of counselors, could be subject to suit by any nonpatient third party who is adversely affected by personal decisions perceived to be made by a patient in response to counseling."

This is patently untrue. A cardinal principle of our common law system is that a holding can have no broader application than the facts of the case that gave rise to it. The case before us today does not involve "therapists generally," but a licensed clinical psychologist. As previously indicated, plaintiff was not simply "any third party," but a family member who was used as a tool in plaintiff's treatment program. Moreover, the harm alleged here did not result from "personal decisions perceived to be made by a patient," whatever that means. It was the product of a failed course of treatment formulated by a mental health professional.

In O'Hara v. Holy Cross Hospital, 137 Ill. 2d 332, 342, 148 Ill. Dec. 712, 561 N.E.2d 18 (1990), this court held that a hospital has a duty to protect a parent from harm where the parent is invited to participate in her child's care and treatment. I see no reason why we should not recognize a similar duty on the part of the psychologist who has been sued in this case. I would further hold that the plaintiff should be allowed to seek damages from that psychologist for lost society and companionship based on intentional and direct interference with a family relationship. The judgment of the appellate court should therefore be affirmed.

NOTES AND QUESTIONS

1. The question posed here is whether "John Doe" was harmed by the psychologist's use, indeed, deception of him. Is that the same as the question the Court answers: Did the psychologist owe a duty, in conventional therapeutic sense, to John Doe?
2. If the issue is what duty do therapists owe third parties, then the *Tarasoff* case becomes relevant. But there, the duty raised was to *warn*. As the majority observes, that poses problems of scope, predictability and confidentiality. But here, the duty would not be to use, abuse, or harm a third party as an instrument of, or while, treating one's patient. Isn't there a difference?
3. Perhaps the error here is the plaintiff's bringing a "malpractice" action — that implies negligence in discharging a duty. Might there be a better theory?
4. Finally, what about the *ethics* of the therapist? The initial course of treatment seems dubious at best. And the use made of "John Doe" seems abusive and dishonest. Are there, should there be, professional limits on such uses of third parties?

[3] Abandonment and Abuse

Fidelity to a patient requires not abusing the patient or that patient's trust. It also means not abandoning that patient. There is a paradox here. The patient is clearly in a position of need and oftentimes dependency. And so the professional may have to assume responsibility for the patient's decisionmaking. And yet he or she must be treated as autonomous, informed and respected as such.

Overreaching may be abuse; leaving the patient to make a decision within the normal range may be abandonment. This is the "flip" side of patient competence.

The terms "abuse" and "abandonment" are usually not concerned with such subtleties. As the next three cases — *Oswald*, *Burditt* and *Bragdon* — illustrate, abandonment means withdrawing care in a manner which leaves the patient in harm's way. To prevent "dumping" of patients, Congress passed the Emergency Medical Treatment and Active Labor Act. *See Burditt, infra.* "Abuse" usually means active, affirmative harm to patients. The most problematic is sexual abuse, involved in *Wall, infra*. But abuse can also mean acting without authority in a harmful way, as in many medical experimentation contexts. As for those, see *infra*, § § 3.03[3] & [4].

[a] Abandonment

OSWALD v. LEGRAND
453 N.W.2d 634 (Iowa 1990)

Neuman, Justice.

. . . .

Plaintiffs Susan and Larry Oswald have been married for ten years and are the parents of two healthy sons. During Susan's third pregnancy, she began experiencing bleeding and painful cramping just prior to her five-month checkup. At that time, she was under the care of a family practice physician, defendant Barry Smith. He ordered an ultrasound test and Susan was then examined in his office by one of his colleagues, defendant Larry LeGrand, an obstetrician. Neither the test nor the examination revealed an explanation for the bleeding and Susan was instructed to go home and stay off her feet. Later that day, however, Susan began to bleed heavily. She was taken by ambulance to defendant Mercy Health Center. The bleeding eventually stopped, Dr. Smith's further examination failed to yield a cause of the problem, and Susan was discharged the following day with directions to take it easy.

The following day, Susan's cramping and bleeding worsened. Susan thought she was in labor and feared a miscarriage. She was [illegible] reach Dr. Smith by teleph[illegible] so Larry drove her to the emergency room at Mercy. There Dr. Christopher Clark, another physician in association with Smith and LeGrand, examined her. He advised her there was nothing to be done and she should go home. Larry was angered by this response and insisted Susan be admitted to the hospital. Dr. Clark honored this request and Susan was transferred to the labor and delivery ward.

In considerable pain and anxious about her pregnancy, Susan's first contact on the ward was with a nurse who said, "What are you doing here? The doctor told you to stay home and rest." Susan felt like "a real pest." A short while later, while attached to a fetal monitor, Susan was told by another nurse that if she miscarried it would not be a baby, it would be "big blob of blood." Susan was scared.

The next morning, an argument apparently ensued over which physician was responsible for Susan's care. Standing outside Susan's room, Dr. Clark yelled, "I don't want to take that patient. She's not my patient and I am sick and tired of Dr. Smith dumping his case load on me." At the urging of Larry and a nurse, Dr. Clark apologized to Susan for this outburst. He assured her that he would care for her until he left for vacation at noon that day when he was scheduled to go "off call" and Dr. LeGrand would take over.

Around 9:00 a.m. Susan began experiencing a great deal of pain that she believed to be labor contractions. Dr. Clark prescribed Tylenol and scheduled her for an ultrasound and amniocentesis at 11:00 a.m. By that time, Susan was screaming in pain and yelling that she was in labor. Dr. Clark arrived in the x-ray department halfway through the ultrasound procedure and determined from viewing the sonogram that there was insufficient fluid in the amniotic sac to perform an amniocentesis. He told the Oswalds that the situation was unusual but did not reveal to them his suspicion that there was an infection in the uterus. He examined Susan abdominally but did not do a pelvic exam. By all accounts, Susan was hysterical and insisting she was about to deliver. Dr. Clark wanted her transferred upstairs for further monitoring. He told Larry to calm her down. Then he left on vacation, approximately one-half hour before the end of his scheduled duty.

Within minutes, Susan began delivering her baby in the hallway outside the x-ray lab. When Larry lifted the sheet covering Susan and "saw [his] daughter hanging from her belly" he kicked upon a glass door to get the attention of hospital personnel. Susan was quickly wheeled to the delivery room where two nurses delivered her one-pound baby girl at 11:34 a.m.

After visually observing neither a heartbeat nor any respiratory activity, one of the nurses announced that the baby was stillborn. The nurse wrapped the infant in a towel and placed her on an instrument tray. Ten minutes later, Dr. LeGrand arrived and delivered the placenta. At Susan's request, he checked the fetus for gender. He made no further examination of the infant, assuming it to be a nonviable fetus. After assuring himself that Susan was fine, and offering his condolences to the disappointed parents, he returned to his office.

Meanwhile, Larry called relatives to advise them of the stillbirth. Upon his return to Susan's room, he touched the infant's finger. Much to his surprise, his grasp was returned. Larry told a nurse in attendance that the baby was alive but the nurse retorted that it was only a "reflex motion." The nurses subsequently determined that the baby was alive. After having left her on an instrument tray for nearly half an hour, the nurses rushed the infant to the neonatal intensive care unit. The infant, registered on her birth certificate as Natalie Sue, received comfort support measures until she died about twelve hours later. Further facts will be detailed as they become pertinent to the issues on appeal.

In January 1987, the Oswalds sued the hospital and doctors Clark, Smith and LeGrand on theories of negligence, negligent loss of chance of survival, breach of implied contract and breach of implied warranty. . . .

. . . In September 1987, however, the defendants successfully moved to bar the plaintiffs from offering independent expert testimony on their malpractice claim due to plaintiffs' failure to designate an expert witness within the 180-day limit prescribed by Iowa Code Section 668.11. . . .

IV

The case boils down to whether the trial court [illegible] determined, as a matter of law, that the claims of negligence surrounding the Oswald family's care and treatment are so technical in nature as to require expert testimony to establish the applicable standard of care and its breach. In considering this question, we think it is useful to divide the case into three logical components: (1) the professional care and treatment accorded Susan prior to and during her delivery; (2) the professional care and treatment given Natalie Sue upon her birth; and (3) the emotional impact of (1) and (2) on Susan and Larry as expectant parents. Within these categories, we think the trial court correctly determined that certain conduct of the physicians and hospital could only be properly challenged through independent expert testimony, but that the principal conduct about which plaintiffs complain falls within the knowledge and experience of the average lay jury.

A

Evidence not within common knowledge. To begin, there is no evidence in this record that more prompt or heroic efforts to sustain Natalie Sue's life would have been successful. Such evidence, if it could be obtained, would be of a technical nature requiring expert testimony that plaintiffs cannot provide. Plaintiffs are unable, under this record, to rebut the affidavit of the attending pediatrician, Dr. Charles Winterwood, that stated "Baby Girl Oswald" was an "extremely immature fetus . . . not sufficiently developed to survive." Neither can they rebut his opinion that a gestational age of twenty-four weeks is medically accepted as the earliest point at which infants have been shown to have any chance of survival. Given this evidence, the trial court properly dismissed Susan and Larry's claim of emotional distress flowing from Natalie's lost chance of survival and all of count II of the petition relating to pecuniary loss sustained by Natalie's estate as a result of her wrongful death.

. . . .

B

Evidence within the "[illegible] knowledge" exception. Beyond these fundamental treatment issues, however, lie plaintiffs' claims that the care provided by defendants Clark, LeGrand, and Mercy Hospital fell below the standard of medical professionalism understood by laypersons and expected by them. Into this category fall Nurse Slater's unwelcoming remarks upon Susan's arrival at the birthing area; Nurse Gardner's deprecating description of a fetus as a "big blob of blood"; Dr. Clark's tirade outside Susan's door; Dr. Clark's insensitivity to Susan's insistence that she was in the final stage of labor, leaving her in a hysterical state minutes before her delivery in a hospital corridor while he went off call; Nurse Flynn's determination that the fetus was stillborn, only to discover it gasping for breath half-an-hour later; and Dr. LeGrand's admitted failure to make an independent determination of the viability of the fetus, conceding it was his obligation to do so. Larry and Susan contend that they have suffered severe emotional distress as a result of these alleged breaches of professional conduct.

We note preliminarily that because the Oswalds can sustain no claim of physical injury, they would ordinarily be denied recovery in a negligence action for emotional distress. An exception exists, however, where the nature of the relationship between the parties is such that there arises a duty to exercise ordinary care to avoid causing emotional harm. Such claims have been recognized in the negligent performance of contractual services that carry with them deeply emotional responses in the event of breach as, for example, in the transmission and delivery of telegrams announcing the death of a close relative, and services incident to a funeral and burial. Under the comparable circumstances demonstrated by this record, we think liability for emotional injury should attach to the delivery of medical services. . . .

. . . .

The first three incidents described above raise commonly understood issues of professional courtesy in communication regarding a patient's care and treatment. No expert testimony is needed to elaborate on whether the statements by the nurses and Dr. Clark were rude and uncaring; a lay fact finder could easily evaluate the statements in light of the surrounding circumstances to determine whether the language used or message conveyed breached the standard of care expected of medical professionals, and determine the harm, if any, resulting to the plaintiffs. In reaching this conclusion we hasten to emphasize that our decision in this case is closely limited to its facts. We in no way suggest that a professional person must ordinarily answer in tort for rudeness, even in a professional relationship. In order for liability to attach there must appear a combination of the two factors existing here: extremely rude behavior or crass insensitivity coupled with an unusual vulnerability on the part of the person receiving professional services.

We are similarly convinced that a lay jury is also capable of evaluating the professional propriety of Dr. Clark's early departure from the hospital, knowing that he had left Susan Oswald unattended in a hospital corridor screaming hysterically that she was about to give birth. In a strikingly similar case, a New Jersey court held that a woman claiming medical malpractice based on an "utter lack of attendance" at her delivery in a hospital need not produce expert testimony in order to overcome a motion for summary judgment. . . .

C

Evidence demonstrable through defendants' admissions. Falling outside the expert testimony exception applicable to the preceding claims are the delivery room nurse's failure to correctly determine that the fetus was alive, and Dr. LeGrand's uninformed acceptance of that determination. These facts seem to us to raise issues ordinarily beyond the common knowledge of laypersons. There is evidence in the summary judgment record, however, which could enable the plaintiffs to establish the applicable standard of care, and its breach, by the defendants' own statements. . . .

Defendant doctors Smith and Clark (along with Dr. Winterwood who is not named as a defendant) each testified that measurements of heartbeat and respiration should be taken, ordinarily with a stethoscope. Both Larry Oswald and Nurse Frommelt testified that Nurse Flynn performed no more than a brief visual examination of the fetus before pronouncing it stillborn. Dr. LeGrand conceded in deposition testimony th[illegible] no effort to determine wh[illegible] infant was alive. He also testified that the responsibility for examining a newborn's vital signs rests with the attending physician and that a nurse is not ultimately responsible for pronouncing a baby dead.

Defendants argue that because Natalie Sue's death was inevitable, the emotional distress suffered by the Oswalds is understandable but not compensable. What defendants overlook is the colorable claim of severe emotional distress proximately caused by the equivocation of those health care professionals on the very question of her life or death. Under this record, we think the plaintiffs have produced evidence minimally sufficient to overcome summary judgment on this claim of malpractice.

. . . .

In conclusion, we affirm in part, reverse in part, and remand this case for further proceedings not inconsistent with this opinion.

Affirmed in part, reversed in part, and remanded.

NOTES AND QUESTIONS

1. To repeat the comment made earlier, the nature of a fiduciary relationship is that the physician, psychologist or attorney acts *on behalf* of the person with whom he or she has contracted. What is purchased is judgment and fidelity, in the providing of continuing care. During the course of the relationship, that obligation continues and it cannot be terminated without due attention to the *impact* of termination. The patient, in other words, cannot simply be abandoned.
2. In *Oswald*, Dr. Clark, in effect, simply abandoned Susan by leaving on vacation half an hour before the end of his shift, following which — within minutes — Susan began delivering her baby. Quite apart from the other events, this would be sufficient to constitute a breach of the obligation of continuing care and fidelity.
3. Why did Dr. Clark behave as he did? For that matter, [illegible] did the nurses and [illegible] hospital staff behave as *they did* ? Could it be that they viewed Susan and Larry as troublesome and troublemaking? But, then, don't fiduciary obligations involve dealing with, and anticipating the needs of, "difficult" people?
4. Looking at the facts here, and slowly removing the more offensive ones, when would you conclude the plaintiffs' cause of action disappears? At that point would there still remain "rudeness" that must be tolerated?
5. Note that Larry and Susan encounter two procedural hurdles on their way to recovery. First, they could not produce expert testimony and therefore needed to rely on the common knowledge exception to the requirement of such testimony in malpractice cases. Does such a requirement make sense? Who does it protect? And then the plaintiffs sustained no physical injury, and so ordinarily would be denied recovery in a negligence action for emotional distress. They cleared this hurdle

only because the nature of the relationship involved a duty to avoid *causing* emotional harm.

But why should physical injury be necessary to recover for emotional distress? Again, who does such a requirement protect?

6. Does Larry have a claim separate from Susan's? On what theory? Was *he* a patient?
7. The Court never reached the issue of damages for the injuries sustained. What should they be and how should they be measured?

BURDITT v. U.S. DEPARTMENT OF HEALTH AND HUMAN SERVICES

934 F.2d 1362 (5th Cir. 1991)

Opinion: **Reavley**, Circuit Judge.

Hospitals that execute Medicare provider agreements with the federal government must treat all human beings who enter their emergency departments in accordance with the Emergency Medical Treatment and Active Labor Act (EMTALA), 42 U.S.C. § 1395dd. Hospitals and responsible physicians found to have violated EMTALA's requirements are subject to civil money penalties. The present appeal is from the order of an executive appeals board of the Department of Health and Human Services (DHHS) assessing a $20,000 fine against Dr. Michael L. Burditt. . . .

I. Background

A. Facts

Mrs. Rosa Rivera arrived in the emergency room of DeTar Hospital in Victoria, Texas at approximately 4:00 p.m. on December 5, 1986. At or near term with her sixth child, she was experiencing one-minute, moderate contractions every three minutes and her membranes had ruptured. Two obstetrical nurses, Tammy Kotsur and Donna Keining, examined her and found indicia of labor and dangerously high blood pressure. Because Rivera had received no prenatal care, and had neither a regular doctor nor means of payment, Kotsur telephoned Burditt, who was next on DeTar's rotating call-list of physicians responsible for such "unaligned" obstetrics patients. Upon hearing Rivera's history and condition, Burditt told Kotsur that he "didn't want to take care of this lady" and asked her to prepare Rivera for transfer to John Sealy Hospital in Galveston, Texas, 170 miles away. Burditt agreed to call back in five to ten minutes.

. . . .

Burditt arrived at approximately 4:50 to examine Rivera. He confirmed her blood pressure to be the highest he had ever seen, 210/130, and he assumed that she had been hypertensive throughout her pregnancy. As the experienced head of DeTar's obstetrics and gynecology department, Burditt knew that there was a strong possibility that Rivera's hypertension would precipitate complications which might kill both Rivera and her baby. He also knew that the infants of hypertensive mothers are at higher-than-normal risk of intrauterine growth retardation. He estimated that Rivera's baby was six pounds — less than normal weight — and [illegible] transfer to John Sealy, a [illegible] facility better equipped than DeTar to care for underweight infants. Burditt obtained telephonic acceptance of Rivera from a Dr. Downing at John Sealy, and, per Downing's request, instructed Keining to administer magnesium sulfate intravenously and have Rivera transported by ambulance.

At approximately 5:00, [Nursing Supervisor] Herman showed Burditt DeTar's guidelines regarding EMTALA, but he refused to read them. Burditt told Herman that Rivera represented more risk than he was willing to accept from a malpractice standpoint. Herman explained that Rivera could not be transferred unless Burditt signed a DeTar form entitled "Physician's Certificate Authorizing Transfer." Burditt asked for "that dang piece of paper" and signed his name under the following:

> I have examined the patient and have determined that, based upon the information available to me at this time, the medical benefits reasonably expected from the provision of appropriate medical treatment at another medical facility outweigh the increased risks to the patient's medical condition from effecting [the] transfer. The basis for my conclusion is as follows:

Burditt listed no basis for his conclusion and remarked to Herman that "until DeTar Hospital pays my malpractice insurance, I will pick and choose those patients that I want to treat."

Burditt then went to care for another unaligned patient, Sylvia Ramirez, while the nurses arranged Rivera's transfer. They found another obstetrical nurse, Anita Nichols, to accompany Rivera to John Sealy. . . .

Nichols delivered Rivera's healthy baby in the ambulance approximately 40 miles into the 170-mile trip to John Sealy. She directed the driver to nearby Ganado Hospital to get a drug called pitocin to staunch Rivera's bleeding. While there, Nichols telephoned Burditt, who ordered her to continue to John Sealy despite the birth. Instead, per Rivera's wishes, Nichols returned Rivera to DeTar, where Burditt refused to see her because she failed to proceed to John Sealy in accordance with his instructions. Burditt directed that Rivera be discharged if she was stable and not bleeding [illegible] DeTar official pressed [illegible] allow Dr. Shirley Pigott to examine Rivera. Rivera stayed at DeTar under Pigott's care for three days and left in good health.

. . . .

II. Discussion

. . . .

A. EMTALA Violations

1. Screening

Because Rivera presented herself to DeTar's emergency department and a request was made on her behalf for care, EMTALA required DeTar to provide for an *appropriate* medical screening examination *within the capability of the hospital's emergency department* to determine whether or not an emergency medical condition . . . exists or to determine if the individual is in active labor. . . .

The parties agree that DeTar appropriately screened Rivera and discovered that she had an "emergency medical condition" — severe hypertension — within the meaning of 42 U.S.C. § 1395dd(e)(1).[1]

2. Emergency Medical Condition and Active Labor

Patients diagnosed with an "emergency medical condition" or "active labor" must either be treated or be transferred in accordance with EMTALA. Burditt claims that Rivera received all of the care that she was due under EMTALA because he stabilized her hypertension sufficiently for transfer and she was not in active labor when she left DeTar for John Sealy.

a. Unstable Emergency Medical Condition

Rivera's blood pressure was 210/130 at 4:00 and 5:00. This was the last reading known to Burditt before he facilitated her transfer. Nurses also measured her blood pressure as 173/105 at 5:30, 178/103 at 5:45, 186/107 at 6:00, and 190/110 at 6:50. Experts testified that Rivera's hypertension put her at high risk of suffering serious complications, including seizures, heart failure, kidney dysfunction, tubular necrosis, stroke, intracranial bleeding, placental abruption, and fetal hypoxia. This is substantial, if not conclusive evidence that Rivera entered and exited DeTar with an emergency medical condition.

Burditt argues that he fulfilled EMTALA's requirements with respect to Rivera's hypertension by "stabilizing" it, or provid[ing] such medical treatment of the condition as may be necessary to assure, within reasonable medical probability, that no material deterioration of the condition is likely to result from [a] transfer. . . . He claims that the magnesium sulfate that he ordered for Rivera has an antihypertensive effect that complements its primary anticonvulsive purpose.

Development of any of the possible complications could have killed or seriously injured Rivera, her baby, or both, and thus would constitute a "material deterioration." Any deterioration would "result" from transfer in that Rivera would have received better care for any complication at DeTar than in the ambulance. Thus, Burditt could not have stabilized Rivera unless he provided treatment that medical experts agree would prevent the threatening and severe consequences of Rivera's hypertension while she was in transit. DAB could properly disregard Burditt's testimony and accept that of all other

---

[1] EMTALA defines "emergency medical condition" as a medical condition manifesting itself by acute symptoms of sufficient severity (including severe pain) such that the absence of immediate medical attention could reasonably be expected to result in —

(A) placing the patient's health in serious jeopardy,

(B) serious impairment to bodily functions, or

(C) serious dysfunction of any bodily organ or part.

testifying experts in holding that Burditt provided no such treatment, and thus did not stabilize Rivera's emergency medical condition.

b. Active Labor

EMTALA defines "active labor" as labor[2] at a time when . . .

(B) there is inadequate time to effect safe transfer to another hospital prior to delivery, or

(C) a transfer may pose a threat [to] the health and safety of the patient or the unborn child. . . .

. . . .

Read literally, clause B confers active labor status on any woman who delivers her baby in transit. But this interpretation enshrines the use of hindsight as a legal standard and in so doing, protects an irrationally selected group of women. We think that clause B allows hospitals to transfer at will women in uncomplicated labor who, within reasonable medical probability, will arrive at another hospital before they deliver their babies. A hospital that transfers a woman in labor when the timing call mandated by clause B is close risks a battle of experts regarding anticipated delivery time, distance, and safe transport speed.

Burditt challenges the ALJ's finding that, at approximately 5:00, there was inadequate time to safely transfer Rivera to John Sealy before she delivered her baby. Dr. Warren Crosby testified that, based on Burditt's own examination results,[3] Rivera would, more likely than not, deliver within three hours after Burditt spoke with Downing at John Sealy. This expert testimony constitutes substantial record evidence to sustain the ALJ's finding. Burditt does not challenge DAB's conclusion that the ambulance trip from DeTar to John Sealy takes approximately three hours. We therefore hold that DAB properly concluded that Rivera was in active labor.

. . . .

We believe that Congress intended clause C to extend EMTALA's "treat or transfer" protection to [illegible] who have any complication with their pregnancies regardless of delivery imminency. Because better medical care is available in a hospital than in an ambulance, whether a transfer "may pose a threat" depends on whether the woman in labor has any medical condition that could interfere with the normal, natural delivery of her healthy child. Under the statutory language, a woman in labor is entitled to EMTALA's treatment and transfer protections upon a showing of possible threat; it does not require proof of a reasonable medical probability that any threat will come to fruition. . . .

---

[2] All agree that labor begins with the onset of uterine contractions; Rivera began experiencing contractions before Burditt examined her at 4:50. Congress explicitly recognized this definition of "labor" in revising EMTALA. See 42 U.S.C.A. § 1395dd(e)(1)(B) (West Supp.1991).

[3] Burditt's 4:50 examination revealed that Rivera had carried several pregnancies to term and that she had ruptured membranes, contractions beginning at 7:00 a.m. and becoming regular before 4:00, a cervix dilated to 3 centimeters, and a smaller-than-usual fetus.

. . . .

3. Treat or Transfer

Upon discovery of active labor or an emergency medical condition, EMTALA usually requires hospitals to treat the discovered condition. Under certain circumstances, however, EMTALA allows hospitals to transfer patients instead of treating them. Because Burditt transferred Rivera without stabilizing her, whether he violated EMTALA depends on whether the manner in which he accomplished the transfer complies with the requirements of 42 U.S.C. § 1395dd(c).

a. Certification

A hospital may not legally transfer someone who has an emergency medical condition which has not been stabilized or who is in active labor unless the patient requests a transfer or

> a physician . . . has *signed* a *certification* that, *based upon* the reasonable risks and benefits to the patient, and *based upon* the information available at the time, the medical *benefits* reasonably expected from the provision of appropriate medical treatment at another medical facility *outweigh* the increased *risks* to the individual's medical condition from effecting the transfer.

. . . .

A hospital may violate this provision in four ways. First, before transfer, the hospital might fail to secure the required signature from the appropriate medical personnel on a certification form. But the statute requires more than a signature; it requires a signed certification. Thus, the hospital also violates the statute if the signer has not actually deliberated and weighed the medical risks and the medical benefits of transfer before executing the *certification*. Likewise, the hospital fails to make the certification if the signer makes an improper consideration a significant factor in the certification decision. Finally, a hospital violates the statute if the signer actually concludes in the weighing process that the medical risks outweigh the medical benefits of transfer, yet signs a certification that the opposite is true.

Whether a reasonable physician would have considered different medical factors than those considered by the signer, or would have weighted factors differently in reaching a certification decision, need not be considered in determining whether a hospital has violated 42 U.S.C. § 1395dd(c)(1)(A)(ii). The signer need not be correct in making a certification decision; the statute only requires a signed statement attesting to an actual assessment and weighing of the medical risks and benefits of transfer.

We find abundant record evidence to support DAB's finding that

> Burditt signed the "Physician's Certificate Authorizing Transfer" certifying that the risks of the transfer were outweighed by the

benefits without actually engaging in any meaningful weighing of the risks and benefits. . . .

Every reasonable adult, let alone physician, understands that labor evolves to delivery, that high blood pressure is dangerous, and that the desirability of transferring a patient with these conditions could well change over a two-hour period. Burditt's indifference to Rivera's condition for the two hours after he conducted his single examination demonstrates not that he unreasonably weighed the medical risks and benefits of transfer, but that he never made such a judgment. DAB's statement that Burditt certified "under circumstances where no reasonable [obstetrician] would have certified" means only that the facts of this case show certification to be so unacceptable that it is unlikely that Burditt actually made the required certification.

. . . .

b. Transfer Appropriateness

Besides certifying the medical need for transferring patients protected by EMTALA, hospitals must appropriately transfer these people. The statutory definition of appropriate transfer requires, *inter alia*, that the transfer [be] effected through qualified personnel and transportation equipment, as required including the use of necessary and medically appropriate life support measures during the transfer. . . .

As previously explained, 42 U.S.C. § 1395dd(c)(1)(A)(ii) does not require a physician to correctly ascertain all risks and benefits associated with transfer. For this reason, we think that Congress inserted "as required" to limit the scope of the requirement of qualified personnel and equipment to those conditions known to the transferring physician.

. . . .

. . . The record indicates that the obstetrical nurse and two emergency medical technicians who accompanied Rivera in transit were qualified to deliver Rivera's baby in the absence of complications. But it is undisputed that they were unqualified to perform a cesarean section or treat the other complications from Rivera's hypertension that could have developed

The ALJ could properly credit expert testimony to the effect that only a physician could have fulfilled the "qualified personnel" requirement in this case. Likewise, expert testimony substantially supports the ALJ's finding that because he did not order a fetal heart monitor for Rivera's ambulance, Burditt failed to effect the transfer through qualified transportation equipment.

. . . .

B. Civil Money Penalty

. . . .

3. Requisite Mental State

A responsible physician may be fined only if that person "knowingly violated [an EMTALA] requirement." By making the object of the knowing violation

EMTALA's requirements as opposed to EMTALA itself, Congress predicated liability on a physician's violative action or inaction undertaken with knowledge of facts such that the action or inaction constitutes a violation. Liability attaches regardless of the physician's understanding of the statute.

. . . .

DAB found that, in at least one manner, Burditt violated EMTALA because he actually knew all facts necessary to establish the violation. Thus, the ALJ's legal interpretation of "knowingly" was unnecessary to this case's outcome. Moreover, Congress has since amended EMTALA to allow the federal government to fine physicians who negligently violate EMTALA's requirements. Thus, it is not clear that the mental-state question posed by Burditt will ever need to be answered by a court.

. . . .

Burditt argues that he cannot be fined under EMTALA because he transferred Rivera in a good-faith effort to protect her underweight infant. But nothing in EMTALA admits the existence of a good-faith exception.

. . . .

4. Aggravating and Mitigating Circumstances

DAB's final $ 20,000 penalty assessment against Burditt comports with EMTALA's limit of $25,000 per knowing violation and our verification of at least one knowing violation. EMTALA provides no standard for deciding civil sanction amounts. . . .

As aggravating circumstances, the ALJ found that Burditt: 1) did not examine Rivera after his initial examination; 2) did not attempt to consult another doctor; 3) did not read the copy of the law given to him by Herman; and 4) did not treat Rivera upon her return to DeTar. As mitigating circumstances, the ALJ found that: 1) Rivera had received no prenatal care; 2) DeTar had no medical records of Rivera's health history; and 3) Burditt has instituted corrective measures to prevent future illegal transfers from DeTar.

We agree that substantial record evidence establishes the existence of all of the circumstances found to be aggravating or mitigating. We also agree that the ALJ properly characterized four of Burditt's acts as aggravating circumstances because they demonstrate flagrant disregard for the anti-dumping principles that Congress enshrined in EMTALA. Similarly, we think that DAB correctly held that a patient's lack of prenatal care or medical records cannot operate as a mitigating circumstance without undermining EMTALA's primary, though not exclusive, purpose of protecting the indigent. . . .

We find no error to the amount of Burditt's sanction.

. . . .

NOTES AND QUESTIONS

1. Note that EMTALA applies to hospitals, not individual physicians. Doctor Burditt is sanctioned because he was the ER physician on duty. Apart from that and EMTALA, was there liability? For abandonment

to arise, there must be a physician-patient relationship, wrongfully terminated. Did Doctor Burditt have a relationship/obligation to Ms. Rivera? *See Roberts v. Galen of Vi*[illegible] (6th Cir. 1997).

2. Because of difficulties in answering this question, especially in emergency room contexts, Congress adopted the Emergency Treatment and Active Labor Act invoked in *Burditt.* Is it good policy? And is it's application in *Burditt* clear? That is, was it an emergency? Wasn't her pregnancy stabilized? Couldn't it be argued that the fully staffed ambulance provided the necessary care?

3. Doctor Burditt, in some ways, is too easy a target. His conduct seems irresponsible, even arrogant or contemptuous. But what is the appropriate sanction: a fine higher than $20,000? Loss of license? Loss of admitting privileges? What are the appropriate criteria and desired outcome?

4. Important questions remain in any hospital (indeed, medical) context concerning the obligations of the other professionals. Did nurses Kotsur, Keining, and Nichols do all they should? What of Administrator Herman, the ambulance service, Dr. Downing at John Sealy — could/should they have opposed and blocked Dr. Burditt? Would *you* have?

5. Would EMTALA apply in the preceding case, *Oswald v. LeGrand* ? If not, does that illustrate shortcomings in the statute which should be corrected? And if so, who should be fined and how much?

6. Now we consider abandonment, not by a hospital but a dentist. In *Bragdon v. Abbott* the reason is AIDS.

BRAGDON v. ABBOTT*

524 U.S. 624 (1998)

Justice **Kennedy** delivered the opinion of the Court.

We address in this case the application of the Americans with Disabilities Act of 1990 (ADA), 42 U.S.C. § 12101 *et seq.*, to persons infected with the human immunodeficiency virus (HIV). . . .

I

Respondent Sidney Abbott has been infected with HIV since 1986. When the incidents we recite occurred, her infection had not manifested its most serious symptoms. On September 16, 1994, she went to the office of petitioner Randon Bragdon in Bangor, Maine, for a dental appointment. She disclosed her HIV infection on the patient registration form. Petitioner completed a dental examination, discovered a cavity, and informed respondent of his policy against filling cavities of HIV-infected patients. He offered to perform the work at a hospital with no added fee for his services, though respondent would be responsible for the cost of using the hospital's facilities. Respondent declined.

Respondent sued petitioner under state law and § 302 of the ADA, alleging discrimination on the basis of her disability. The state law claims are not before us. Section 302 of the ADA provides:

---

* Citation material has been omitted from this case.

> "No individual shall be discriminated against on the basis of disability in the full and equal enjoyment of the goods, services, facilities, privileges, advantages, or accommodations of any place of public accommodation by any person who . . . operates a place of public accommodation."

The term "public accommodation" is defined to include the "professional office of a health care provider."

A later subsection qualifies the mandate not to discriminate. It provides:

> "Nothing in this subchapter shall require an entity to permit an individual to participate in or benefit from the goods, services, facilities, privileges, advantages and accommodations of such entity where such individual poses a direct threat to the health or safety of others." § 12182(b)(3).

. . . .

II

We first review the ruling that respondent's HIV infection constituted a disability under the ADA. The statute defines disability as:

> "(A) a physical or mental impairment that substantially limits one or more of the major life activities of such individual;
>
> "(B) a record of such an impairment; or
>
> "(C) being regarded as having such impairment." § 12102(2).
>
> We hold respondent's HIV infection was a disability under subsection (A) of the definitional section of the statute. In light of this conclusion, we need not consider the applicability of subsections (B) or (C).

. . . .

1.

The first step in the inquiry under subsection (A) requires us to determine whether respondent's condition constituted a physical impairment. The Department of Health, Education and Welfare (HEW) . . . regulations, which appear without change in the current regulations issued by the Department of Health and Human Services, define "physical or mental impairment" to mean:

> "(A) any physiological disorder or condition, cosmetic disfigurement, or anatomical loss affecting one or more of the following body systems: neurological; musculoskeletal; special sense organs; respiratory, including speech organs; cardiovascular; reproductive, digestive, genitourinary; hemic and lymphatic; skin; and endocrine; or

> "(B) any mental or psychological disorder, such as mental retardation, organic brain syndrome, emotional or mental illness, and specific learning disabilities."

In issuing these regulations, HEW decided against including a list of disorders constituting physical or mental impairments, out of concern that any specific enumeration might not be comprehensive. The commentary accompanying the regulations, however, contains a representative list of disorders and conditions constituting physical impairments, including "such diseases and conditions as orthopedic, visual, speech, and hearing impairments, cerebral palsy, epilepsy, muscular dystrophy, multiple sclerosis, cancer, heart disease, diabetes, mental retardation, emotional illness, and . . . drug addiction and alcoholism."

. . . .

HIV infection is not included in the list of specific disorders constituting physical impairments, in part because HIV was not identified as the cause of AIDS until 1983. . . .

The disease follows a predictable and, as of today, an unalterable course. Once a person is infected with HIV, the virus invades different cells in the blood and in body tissues. Certain white blood cells, known as helper T-lymphocytes or CD4+ cells, are particularly vulnerable to HIV. The virus attaches to the CD4 receptor site of the target cell and fuses its membrane to the cell's membrane. HIV is a retrovirus, which means it uses an enzyme to convert its own genetic material into a form indistinguishable from the genetic material of the target cell. The virus' genetic material migrates to the cell's nucleus and becomes integrated with the cell's chromosomes. Once integrated, the virus can use the cell's own genetic machinery to replicate itself. Additional copies of the virus are released into the body and infect other cells in turn. . . .

. . . .

The initial stage of HIV infection is known as acute or primary HIV infection. In a typical case, this stage lasts three months. The virus concentrates in the blood. The assault on the immune system is immediate. The victim suffers from a sudden and serious decline in the number of white blood cells. There is no latency period. Mononucleosis-like symptoms often emerge between six days and six weeks after infection, at times accompanied by fever, headache, enlargement of the lymph nodes (lymphadenopathy), muscle pain (myalgia), rash, lethargy, gastrointestinal disorders, and neurological disorders. Usually these symptoms abate within 14 to 21 days. HIV antibodies appear in the bloodstream within 3 weeks; circulating HIV can be detected within 10 weeks. . . .

After the symptoms associated with the initial stage subside, the disease enters what is referred to sometimes as its asymptomatic phase. . . . The virus, however, thrives in the lymph nodes, which, as a vital point of the body's immune response system, represents an ideal environment for the infection of other CD4+ cells. . . .

. . . .

In light of the immediacy with which the virus begins to damage the infected person's white blood cells and the severity of the disease, we hold it is an impairment from the moment of infection. . . . HIV infection satisfies the statutory and regulatory definition of a physical impairment during every stage of the disease.

2.

The statute is not operative, and the definition not satisfied, unless the impairment affects a major life activity. Respondent's claim throughout this case has been that the HIV infection placed a substantial limitation on her ability to reproduce and to bear children. Given the pervasive, and invariably fatal, course of the disease, its effect on major life activities of many sorts might have been relevant to our inquiry. . . .

. . . .

. . . As the Court of Appeals held, "[t]he plain meaning of the word 'major' denotes comparative importance" and "suggest[s] that the touchstone for determining an activity's inclusion under the statutory rubric is its significance." Reproduction falls well within the phrase "major life activity." Reproduction and the sexual dynamics surrounding it are central to the life process itself.

While petitioner concedes the importance of reproduction, he claims that Congress intended the ADA only to cover those aspects of a person's life which have a public, economic, or daily character. The argument founders on the statutory language. Nothing in the definition suggests that activities without a public, economic, or daily dimension may somehow be regarded as so unimportant or insignificant as to fall outside the meaning of the word "major." The breadth of the term confounds the attempt to limit its construction in this manner.

As we have noted, the ADA must be construed to be consistent with regulations issued to implement the Rehabilitation Act. Rather than enunciating a general principle for determining what is and is not a major life activity, the Rehabilitation Act regulations instead provide a representative list, defining term to include "functions such as caring for one's self, performing manual tasks, walking, seeing, hearing, speaking, breathing, learning, and working." As the use of the term "such as" confirms, the list is illustrative, not exhaustive.

. . . [T]he Rehabilitation Act regulations support the inclusion of reproduction as a major life activity, since reproduction could not be regarded as any less important than working and learning. Petitioner advances no credible basis for confining major life activities to those with a public, economic, or daily aspect. In the absence of any reason to reach a contrary conclusion, we agree with the Court of Appeals' determination that reproduction is a major life activity for the purposes of the ADA.

3.

The final element of the disability definition in subsection (A) is whether respondent's physical impairment was a substantial limit on the major life activity she asserts. . . .

Our evaluation of the medical evidence leads us to conclude that respondent's infection substantially limited her ability to reproduce in two independent ways. Fi[illegible] who tries to conceive a child imposes on the man a significant risk of becoming infected. . . .

Second, an infected woman risks infecting her child during gestation and childbirth, i.e., perinatal transmission. Petitioner concedes that women infected with HIV face about a 25% risk of transmitting the virus to their children. . . .

Petitioner points to evidence in the record suggesting that antiretroviral therapy can lower the risk of perinatal transmission to about 8%. . . . We need not resolve this dispute in order to decide this case, however. It cannot be said as a matter of law that an 8% risk of transmitting a dread and fatal disease to one's child does not represent a substantial limitation on reproduction.

The Act addresses substantial limitations on major life activities, not utter inabilities. Conception and childbirth are not impossible for an HIV victim but, without doubt, are dangerous to the public health. This meets the definition of a substantial limitation. The decision to reproduce carries economic and legal consequences as well. There are added costs for antiretroviral therapy, supplemental insurance, and long-term health care for the child who must be examined and, tragic to think, treated for the infection. The laws of some States, moreover, forbid persons infected with HIV from having sex with others, regardless of consent.

In the end, the disability definition does not turn on personal choice. When significant limitations result from the impairment, the definition is met even if the difficulties are not insurmountable. . . .

B

Our holding is confirmed by a consistent course of agency interpretation before and after enactment of the ADA. Every agency to consider the issue under the Rehabilitation Act found statutory coverage for persons with asymptomatic HIV. . . .

One comprehensive and significant administrative precedent is a 1988 opinion issued by the Office of Legal Counsel of the Department of Justice (OLC) concluding that the Rehabilitation Act "protects symptomatic and asymptomatic HIV-infected individuals against discrimination in any covered program." . . .

The Opinion said:

> "Based on the medical knowledge available to us, we believe that it is reasonable to conclude that the life activity of procreation . . . is substantially limited for an asymptomatic HIV-infected individual. In light of the significant risk that the AIDS virus may be transmitted to a baby during pregnancy, HIV-infected individuals cannot, whether they are male or female, engage in the act of procreation with the normal expectation of bringing forth a healthy child."

. . . Without exception, the other agencies to address the problem before enactment of the ADA reached the same result.

Every court which addressed the issue before the ADA was enacted in July 1990, moreover, concluded that asymptomatic HIV infection satisfied the Rehabilitation Act's definition of a handicap. . . .

. . . .

C

. . . .

III

The petition for certiorari presented three other questions for review. [Q]uestion 5 state[s]:

> . . .
>
> "5. Did petitioner, Randon Bragdon, D. M. D., raise a genuine issue of fact for trial as to whether he was warranted in his judgment that the performance of certain invasive procedures on a patient in his office would have posed a direct threat to the health or safety of others?"
>
> . . . .

Again, we begin with the statute. Notwithstanding the protection given respondent by the ADA's definition of disability, petitioner could have refused to treat her if her infectious condition "pose[d] a direct threat to the health or safety of others." The ADA defines a direct threat to be "a significant risk to the health or safety of others that cannot be eliminated by a modification of policies, practices, or procedures or by the provision of auxiliary aids or services."

The ADA's direct threat provision stems from the recognition in *School Bd. of Nassau Cty. v. Arline*, [*infra,* § 4.03[2]], of the importance of prohibiting discrimination against individuals with disabilities while protecting others from significant health and safety risks, resulting, for instance, from a contagious disease. In *Arline*, the Court reconciled these objectives by construing the Rehabilitation Act not to require the hiring of a person who posed "a significant risk of communicating an infectious disease to others." Because few, if any, activities in life are risk free, *Arline* and the ADA do not ask whether a risk exists, but whether it is significant.

The existence, or nonexistence, of a significant risk must be determined from the standpoint of the person who refuses the treatment or accommodation, and the risk assessment must be based on medical or other objective evidence. As a health care professional, petitioner had the duty to assess the risk of infection based on the objective, scientific information available to him and others in his profession. His belief that a significant risk existed, even if maintained in good faith, would not relieve him from liability. To use the words of the question presented, petitioner receives no special deference simply because he is a health care professional. . . .

Our conclusion that courts should assess the objective reasonableness of the views of health care professionals without deferring to their individual judgments does not answer the implicit assumption in the question presented, whether petitioner's actions were reasonable in light of the available medical evidence. In assessing the reasonableness of petitioner's actions, the views of public health authorities, such as the U.S. Public Health Service, CDC, and the National Institutes of Health, are of special weight and authority. . . .

. . . .

A further illustration of a correct application of the objective standard is the Court of Appeals' refusal to give weight to the petitioner's offer to treat respondent in a hospital. Petitioner testified that he believed hospitals had safety measures, such as air filtration, ultraviolet lights, and respirators, which would reduce the risk of HIV transmission. Petitioner made no showing, however, that any area hospital had these safeguards or even that he had hospital privileges. His expert also admitted the lack of any scientific basis for the conclusion that these measures would lower the risk of transmission. Petitioner failed to present any objective, medical evidence showing that treating respondent in a hospital would be safer or more efficient in preventing HIV transmission than treatment in a well-equipped dental office.

We are concerned, however, that the Court of Appeals might have placed mistaken reliance upon two other sources. In ruling no triable issue of fact existed on this point, the Court of Appeals relied on the 1993 CDC Dentistry Guidelines and the 1991 American Dental Association Policy on HIV. This evidence is not definitive. As noted earlier, the CDC Guidelines recommended certain universal precautions which, in CDC's view, "should reduce the risk of disease transmission in the dental environment." . . .

Nor can we be certain, on this record, whether the 1991 American Dental Association Policy on HIV carries the weight the Court of Appeals attributed to it. The Policy does provide some evidence of the medical community's objective assessment of the risks posed by treating people infected with HIV in dental offices. It indicates:

> "Current scientific and epidemiologic evidence indicates that there is little risk of transmission of infectious diseases through dental treatment if recommended infection control procedures are routinely followed. Patients with HIV infection may be safely treated in private dental offices when appropriate infection control procedures are employed. Such infection control procedures provide protection both for patients and dental personnel."

We note, however, that the Association is a professional organization, which, although a respected source of information on the dental profession, is not a public health authority. . . .

. . . .

There are reasons to doubt whether petitioner advanced evidence sufficient to raise a triable issue of fact on the significance of the risk. Petitioner relied on two principal points: First, he asserted that the use of high-speed drills and surface cooling with water created a risk of airborne HIV transmission. The study on which petitioner relied was inconclusive, however, determining only that "[f]urther work is required to determine whether such a risk exists." . . .

Second, petitioner argues that, as of September 1994, CDC had identified seven dental workers with possible occupational transmission of HIV. It is now known that CDC could not ascertain whether the seven dental workers contracted the disease because they did not present themselves for HIV testing at an appropriate time after their initial exposure. It is not clear on this record, however, whether this information was available to petitioner in September 1994. If not, the seven cases might have provided some, albeit not necessarily sufficient, support for petitioner's position. Standing alone, we doubt it would meet the objective, scientific basis for finding a significant risk to the petitioner.

. . . .

We conclude the proper course is to give the Court of Appeals the opportunity to determine whether our analysis of some of the studies cited by the parties would change its conclusion that petitioner presented neither objective evidence nor a triable issue of fact on the question of risk. In remanding the case, we do not foreclose the possibility that the Court of Appeals may reach the same conclusion it did earlier. A remand will permit a full exploration of the issue through the adversary process.

Justice **Stevens**, with whom Justice **Breyer** joins, concurring.

The Court's opinion demonstrates that respondent's HIV infection easily falls within the statute's definition of "disability." . . .

There are not, however, five Justices who agree that the judgment should be affirmed. Nor does it appear that there are five Justices who favor a remand for further proceedings consistent with the views expressed in either Justice Kennedy's opinion for the Court or the opinion of The Chief Justice. Because I am in agreement with the legal analysis in Justice Kennedy's opinion, in order to provide a judgment supported by a majority, I join that opinion even though I would prefer an outright affirmance.

Justice **Ginsburg**, concurring.

HIV infection, as the description set out in the Court's opinion documents, has been regarded as a disease limiting life itself. . . .

I further agree, in view of the "importance [of the issue] to health care workers," that it is wise to remand, erring, if at all, on the side of caution. By taking this course, the Court ensures a fully informed determination whether respondent Abbott's disease posed "a significant risk to the health or safety of [petitioner Bragdon] that [could not] be eliminated by a modification of policies, practices, or procedures. . . ." 42 U.S.C. § 12182(b)(3).

Chief Justice **Rehnquist**, with whom Justice **Scalia** and Justice **Thomas** join, and with whom Justice **O'Connor** joins as to Part II, concurring in the judgment in part and dissenting in part.

I

[illegible] virus (HIV) but was asymptomatic at the time she suffered discriminatory treatment — a person with a "disability" as that term is defined in the Americans with Disabilities Act of 1990 (ADA)? . . .

Petitioner does not dispute that asymptomatic HIV-positive status is a physical impairment. I therefore assume this to be the case, and proceed to the second and third statutory requirements for "disability."

According to the Court, the next question is "whether reproduction is a major life activity." That, however, is only half of the relevant question. As mentioned above, the ADA's definition of a "disability" requires that the major life activity at issue be one "of such individual." The Court truncates the question, perhaps because there is not a shred of record evidence indicating that, prior to becoming infected with HIV, respondent's major life activities included reproduction (assuming for the moment that reproduction is a major life activity at all). At most, the record indicates that after learning of her HIV status, respondent, whatever her previous inclination, conclusively decided that she would not have children. There is absolutely no evidence that, absent the HIV, respondent would have had or was even considering having children. Indeed, when asked during her deposition whether her HIV infection had in any way impaired her ability to carry out any of her life functions, respondent answered "No." It is further telling that in the course of her entire brief to this Court, respondent studiously avoids asserting even once that reproduction is a major life activity to her. To the contrary, she argues that the "major life activity" inquiry should not turn on a particularized assessment of the circumstances of this or any other case.

But even aside from the facts of this particular case, the Court is simply wrong in concluding as a general matter that reproduction is a "major life activity." Unfortunately, the ADA does not define the phrase "major life activities." But the Act does incorporate by reference a list of such activities contained in regulations issued under the Rehabilitation Act. The Court correctly recognizes that this list of major life activities "is illustrative, not exhaustive," but then makes no attempt to demonstrate that reproduction is a major life activity in the same sense that "caring for one's self, performing manual tasks, walking, seeing, hearing, speaking, breathing, learning, and working" are.

. . . .

But even if I were to assume that reproduction is a major life activity of respondent, I do not agree that an asymptomatic HIV infection "substantially limits" that activity. The record before us leaves no doubt that those so infected are still entirely able to engage in sexual intercourse, give birth to a child if they become pregnant, and perform the manual tasks necessary to rear a child to maturity. While individuals infected with HIV may choose not to engage in these activities, there is no support in language, logic, or our case law for the proposition that such voluntary choices constitute a "limit" on one's own life activities.

. . . .

Respondent contends that her ability to reproduce is limited because "the fatal nature of HIV infection means that a parent is unlikely to live long enough to raise and nurture the child to adulthood." But the ADA's definition of a disability is met only if the alleged impairment substantially "limits" (present tense) a major life activity. Asymptomatic HIV does not presently limit respondent's ability to perform any of the tasks necessary to bear or raise a child. Respondent's argument, taken to its logical extreme, would render every individual with a genetic marker for some debilitating disease "disabled" here and now because of some possible future effects.

In my view, therefore, respondent has failed to demonstrate that any of her major life activities were substantially limited by her HIV infection.

II

While the Court concludes to the contrary as to the "disability" issue, it then quite correctly recognizes that petitioner could nonetheless have refused to treat respondent if her condition posed a "direct threat." . . .

"Direct threat" is defined as a "significant risk to the health or safety of others that cannot be eliminated by a modification of policies, practices, or procedures or by the provision of auxiliary aides or services." This statutory definition of a direct threat consists of two parts. First, a court must ask whether treating the infected patient without precautionary techniques would pose a "significant risk to the heath or safety of others." . . .

. . . .

Even if a significant risk exists, a health practitioner will still be required to treat the infected patient if "a modification of policies, practices, or procedures" (in this case, universal precautions) will "eliminat[e]" the risk.

. . . .

. . . In June 1994, the Centers for Disease Control and Prevention published a study identifying seven instances of possible transmission of HIV from patients to dental workers. While it is not entirely certain whether these dental workers contracted HIV during the course of providing dental treatment, the potential that the disease was transmitted during the course of dental treatment is relevant evidence. One need only demonstrate "risk," not certainty of infection. . . .

In addition, petitioner offered evidence of 42 documented incidents of occupational transmission of HIV to healthcare workers other than dental professionals. The Court of Appeals dismissed this evidence as irrelevant because these health professionals were not dentists. But the fact that the health care workers were not dentists is no more valid a basis for distinguishing these transmissions of HIV than the fact that the health care workers did not practice in Maine. At a minimum, petitioner's evidence was sufficient to create a triable issue on this question, and summary judgment was accordingly not appropriate.

Justice **O'Connor**, concurring in the judgment in part and dissenting in part.

I agree with **the Chief Justice** that respondent's claim of disability should be evaluated on an individualized basis and that she has not proven that her asymptomatic HIV status substantially limited one or more of her major life activities. In my view, the act of giving birth to a child, while a very important part of the lives of many women, is not generally the same as the representative major life activities of all persons — "caring for one's self, performing manual tasks, walking, seeing, hearing, speaking, breathing, learning, and working" — listed in regulations relevant to the Americans with Disabilities Act of 1990. Based on that conclusion, there is no need to address whether other aspects of intimate or family relationships not raised in this case could constitute major life activities; nor is there reason to consider whether HIV status would impose a substantial limitation on one's ability to reproduce if reproduction were a major life activity.

. . . .

NOTES AND QUESTIONS

1. Elsewhere, we deal with AIDS in other contexts. *See* § 3.02[3] *supra and* § 4.03[3] *infra*. We also deal with public accommodations/discrimination elsewhere, for example by the Boy Scouts against homosexuals. *See* § 2.05[2] *supra*. In comparing outcomes, attention to varying statutory language is crucial.
2. Why did Ms. Abbott not argue that her disability fit into the third "subset" — "regarded" as having an impairment. Would that be harder or easier than proving a substantial "limit" of a "major life activity?"
3. Should the Court have been so quick to hold, "simply" that HIV-positive status *is* a physical impairment? Why from the first moment of infection? People who are asymptomatic, receiving effective treatment, might disagree. Why?
4. And conversely, why is the Court so quick in finding reproduction is a "major life activity?" Is it *truly* "major," akin to eating, breathing, walking, working? Why are Justices Rehnquist, Scalia, Thomas, and O'Connor unpersuaded? Must there be a showing that *this* person found it "major," as the dissent argues? Would *that* be sufficient?
5. Of course, Ms. Abbott has *chosen* not to have children. *Is* that a "disability," or is it a matter of lifestyle? The elderly may choose not to drive; are they "disabled"? And since Ms. Abbott *could* have children, with only an 8% chance of transmitting HIV, is she *truly* "disabled"? If Doctor Bragdon's decision not to treat is irrational, is it more so than Ms. Abbott's decision not to have children?
6. The Court is concerned about deference to "public health authorities." But they are not the ones putting their hands in someone's mouth. If deference is due, shouldn't it at least be equal to providers and authorities? And which "authorities" should be consulted — researchers, infectious-disease administrators, or the American Dental Association? And what of a subjective standard; suppose a provider is so alarmed or offended by serving an HIV positive patient — or simply inept — that he or she is at unusual risk of needle pricks or drilling errors. . . .

7. If Doctor Bragdon contracts AIDS from Ms. Abbott, is she liable? If she did not make disclosure? If he pricks himself while in Ms. Abbott's mouth, should he close his practice until his tests show conclusively whether he contracted HIV? Should he make disclosure to his other patients?

8. Doctor Bragdon has three arguments available to him: first, Ms. Abbott was not a patient; second, she posed a "threat" to him; third, she declined reasonable terms as conditions of treatment that would reduce that threat. It appears the last argument was not made. Why? As to the second, note that the standard is "objective" as to the provider, but subjective as to the patient, and there is a remand. Why?

9. On the remand to the Court of Appeals. Suppose prior to the rehearing in the Court of Appeals new methods of treatment involving protease inhibitors now mean people will not die of AIDS or pass HIV along to children. Will that mean a different outcome? *Should* it?

10. What *should* Doctor Bragdon have done? What would *you* do? And suppose Doctor Bragdon disclosed to you, as a patient, that he was HIV positive; what do you do *then*?

11. For an excellent article, see Jerry Menikoff, *Demanded Medical Care*, 30 Ariz. St. L.J. 1091 (1998); and see Robert A. Clifford, *Physician's Liability in a Managed Care Environment*, 10 No. 2 Health Law 5 (1997).

PROBLEM 3–5 — Auto Abandonment

Doctor Sweetwater has seen Ann Accident twice, once for an employment physical, three years ago, and a second time, for a set of immunization shots prior to a trip to China, two years ago. Other than this, Ann's file contains only a standard intake and consent form, which has at the bottom, in boldface print, above Ann's signature line:

> *"Doctor Sweetwater does not treat conditions — such as automobile injuries — which may lead to litigation. She will not testify in court proceedings."*

Ten minutes ago, on Willamette Drive, directly outside Doctor Sweetwater's office, Ann was involved in a head-on collision, as she was turning into Sweetwater's parking lot, to bring her newborn baby for unscheduled emergency care for a swallowed safety pin.

Sweetwater hears the crash, looks outside the window and sees Ann, who has fallen out of the driver's sidedoor in the road, bleeding. She hears the sound of an ambulance, approaching in the distance. What should she do? If she does nothing, is there liability?

Would it matter if Doctor Sweetwater were at the Emergency Room of Willamette Falls Hospital and Ann was turning into the hospital parking lot, where Doctor Sweetwater was on duty as the ER physician?

PROBLEM 3-6 — Doctors and Torture

During the Iraq War, instances of torture by American troops were reported at Abu Ghraib Prison in Baghdad, as well as at the American Base at Guantanamo Bay, Cuba. Physical pounding, psychological infliction of terror by dogs, and sexual humiliation were all employed by military personnel. Some, or much, of this violated the Geneva Convention on treatment of prisoners, although arguably these were mere terrorists and not military personnel of a recognized government.

Doctors in Iraq stitched up prisoners and sent them back, suppressed information, shared medical records to facilitate interrogation, and assisted. Robert Lifton, in an article, *Doctors and Torture*, 351 New Eng. J. Med. 415, 416 (July 29, 2004), states:

> The doctors thus brought a medical component to what I call an "atrocity-producing situation" — one so structured, psychologically and militarily, that ordinary people can readily engage in atrocities. Even without directly participating in the abuse, doctors may have become socialized to an environment of torture and by virtue of their medical authority helped sustain it. In studying various forms of medical abuse, I have found that the participation of doctors can confer an aura of legitimacy and can even create an illusion of therapy and healing.
>
> . . . .
>
> Physicians are no more or less moral than other people. But as heirs to shamans and witch doctors, we may be seen by others — and sometimes by ourselves — as possessing special magic in connection with life and death. Various regimes have sought to harness that magic to their own despotic ends. Physicians have served as actual torturers in Chile and elsewhere; have surgically removed ears as punishment for desertion in Saddam Hussein's Iraq; have incarcerated political dissenters in mental hospitals, notably in the Soviet Union; have, as whites in South Africa, falsified medical reports on blacks who were tortured or killed; and have, as Americans associated with the Central Intelligence Agency, conducted harmful, sometimes fatal, experiments involving drugs and mind control.
>
> With the possible exception of the altering of death certificates, the recent transgressions of U.S. military doctors have apparently not been of this order. But these examples help us to recognize what doctors are capable of when placed in atrocity-producing situations. A recent statement by the Physicians for Human Rights addresses this vulnerability in declaring that "torture can also compromise the integrity of health professionals."

What should the role of doctors be in a military setting or hierarchy which practices torture? Are physicians' responsibilities different from lawyers' responsibilities? Is torture ever justified? *See Symposium: Fighting Terrorism with Torture*, 1 J. Natl. Security 187 (2005).

[b] Sexual Abuse

Physicians may often fail in their services to patients. One of the most frequently recurring failures is in the area of sexual relations and abuse. It is an unfortunately inevitable danger in any relation of trust and vulnerability. It is particularly troublesome because it may be private, arguably consensual and difficult to prove by an already vulnerable woman. The relationship may be extensive. Often it is not. We begin with *Smith v. Welch*, where the misconduct was brief, but outrageous.

SMITH v. WELCH*

265 Kan. 868, 967 P.2d 727 (1998)

. . . .

Plaintiff Peggy Smith was injured in an automobile accident and filed suit against Edward Williams, the other driver. During the litigation, plaintiff agreed to an independent medical examination by defendant's medical expert. Plaintiff alleges that during the examination, she was asked personal and inappropriate questions and was sexually battered by the examining doctor. . . . The purpose of the independent medical examination was to determine the extent, if any, of Smith's head and neck injuries.

During the examination at Dr. Welch's office, while Smith and Dr. Welch were alone, Welch asked Smith a series of questions about her medical history. While taking Smith's history, Dr. Welch would snap his fingers and tell her she was not answering fast enough. Numerous times Dr. Welch told Smith she was stupid or lying and she had better start cooperating or she would not receive her settlement.

Some of Welch's questions had obvious medical relevance to a head and neck injury and other questions required a detailed statement of Smith's sexual past. Although not a complete list, Dr. Welch asked Smith whether her parents and her sister were sexually active, whether Smith was having sex with someone else while dating her present boyfriend, what qualities about her boyfriend made her want to have sex with him, whether Smith had ever had sex with more than one person at a time, and whether she had ever had sex with her sister.

While asking Smith questions of a sexual nature, Dr. Welch told Smith numerous times that she had better answer his questions because he worked for the other side and a failure to answer would result in Smith not receiving a settlement in her personal injury action. Dr. Welch asked Smith if she knew what it meant to not "count your chickens before they hatch." He stated it meant she had better not count on her settlement because she was not doing what he required.

After Dr. Welch obtained Smith's medical history, he led her to an examination room where he threw a gown at Smith and told her to undress and put on the gown. Smith did. When Dr. Welch and his nurse entered the examination room, he untied the gown and exposed Smith's breasts. Smith crossed

* Most of the citation material has been omitted from this case.

her arms over her breasts. Welch grabbed Smith's arms and moved them away from her breasts. Dr. Welch began to examine Smith's breasts. Smith states it was unlike any other breast examination [illegible] previously. Smith [illegible] Dr. Welch fondled her nipples and placed a cold stethoscope on them.

During the course of the examination, Smith repeatedly placed her hands over her breasts. Dr. Welch continually removed her hands from her breasts. Welch told Smith not to be a "baby" about the examination.

After examining Smith's breasts, Dr. Welch moved his hands towards Smith's abdomen. Smith covered her pubic region with her hands. As Welch's hands reached Smith's pubic area, he attempted to move Smith's hands. At that point, Smith sat up and ended that portion of the examination.

. . . .

In a letter to Smith's counsel, Smith's expert, Dr. Janice M. Mullinix, wrote: "It is a departure from standard neurologic practice to do a breast examination or a gynecologic examination as part of assessment of head injury or of headaches. It is a further departure from standard neurologic practice to persuade a patient to consent to these procedures."

After significant discovery, Dr. Welch filed a motion for summary judgement. The district court stated in its conclusions of law:

> "20. That Dr. Janice Mullinix, who has been retained by Plaintiff's counsel to provide expert testimony, is not disqualified as an expert because she has not performed independent medical examinations, but is not qualified legally to usurp the function of the Court in directing the scope of the examination. Accordingly, the relevance of her opinions is questionable.
>
> . . . .
>
> "22. The nature and scope of questions about sexual activity is not within the province and understanding of laymen; rather, expert testimony is required on this issue. In light of the Plaintiff not having any expert testimony, on this issue, any alleged tort relating to the nature and scope of the sexual [illegible] as a matter of law.
>
> 23. Inasmuch as Plaintiff, by and through her counsel, consented to the examination, the invasion of privacy and assault and battery claims fail as a matter of law.
>
> . . . .
>
> "25. The Plaintiff's allegations, assuming the same to be true, would not cause a reasonable person to be outraged, and accordingly, the tort of outrage claim fails as a matter of law."
>
> . . . .

Smith admits she consented to an examination to ascertain the scope of her head and neck injuries. She asserts that Dr. Welch exceeded the scope of a medical examination for head and neck injuries. She argues that even if a breast examination were required, Welch did not conduct a medical exam; he groped and sexually fondled her.

A medical examination of the body of a person is a technical invasion of privacy, battery, or trespass, regardless of its results, unless the person or some authorized person consents to it. Ordinarily, as applied to a surgical operation, the distinction "between an unauthorized operation amounting to assault and battery on the one hand, and negligence such as would constitute malpractice on the other, is that the former is intentional while the latter is unintentional." The gravamen of a civil invasion of privacy, assault, batter, and sexual battery is grounded upon the actor's intention to inflict injury.

. . . .

The tort of outrage has two threshold requirements that the trial court must determine: (1) whether the defendant's conduct may reasonably be regarded as so extreme and outrageous as to permit recovery; and (2) whether the emotional distress suffered by the plaintiff was of such extreme degree the law must intervene because the distress inflicted was so severe that no reasonable person should be expected to endure it.

To prove the tort of outrage, a litigant must show: (1) the conduct of the defendant was intentional or in reckless disregard of the plaintiff; (2) the conduct was extreme and outrageous; (3) there was a causal connection between the defendant's conduct and the plaintiff's mental distress; and (4) the plaintiff's mental distress was extreme and severe.

. . . .

Dr. Welch presents several arguments in support of the district court's grant of summary judgement. Dr. Welch first claims that as the examining physician, his duty was not to Smith, but to the entity that retained him to examine Smith. In support of this argument, Dr. Welch cites cases that conclude that a physician performing an independent medical examination has no duty to treat the person examined for illnesses or to diagnose illnesses. *See Ervin v. American Guardian Life Assur.*, 376 Pa. Super. 132, 545 A.2d 354 (1988); *Elia v. Erie Ins. Exchange*, 398 Pa.Super. 433, 581 A.2d 209 (1990); *Henkemeyer v. Boxall*, 465 N.W.2d 437 (Minn. 1991).

These cases hold that no cause of action accrues when a physician, acting on behalf of the other party in litigation, failed to treat or to diagnose an illness in the opposing party examined. However, none of the cases cited by Dr. Welch discuss whether the physician conducting the independent medical examination may negligently or intentionally injure the person examined. *See Wilson v. Winsett*, 828 S.W.2d 231, 233 (Tex. App. 1992), which holds that in performing court-ordered examinations, the physician has a duty not to cause harm or injury to the examinee. . . .

. . . .

Dr. Welch's final argument is that he had qualified immunity insulating him from liability for injuries caused during the examination by his negligent or intentional acts. The basis of this argument is the historical protection afforded parties and witnesses from liability for damages arising from their testimony during court proceedings. The problem with this argument is obvious. The immunity Welch asserts is directed to the testimony of the witness.

If a witness testifying in open court leaped from the stand and battered the attorney questioning the witness, there is little doubt that there would be criminal and civil liability for the battery. Asking [illegible] personal questions during [illegible] of fondling Smith's breasts and attempting to grope her genitalia does not fit within the parameters of this historical privilege.

Even though Smith's claims are intentional torts, other courts have considered a physician's liability for negligence during an independent medical examination. *Greenberg v. Perkins*, 845 P.2d 530 (Co. 1993), involved a physician performing an independent medical examination who prescribed further tests to ascertain the extent of Perkins' injuries. Prior to the testing, Perkins told the physical therapist who was to perform the tests about previous back problems she had. Concerned that the testing would aggravate Perkins' problems, the physical therapist called Dr. Greenberg to tell him of the concerns. Dr. Greenberg replied that the physical therapist should do the best she could. During the course of the tests, Perkins' back problem was aggravated, ultimately requiring surgery to correct.

In determining the extent of Dr. Greenberg's liability, the Colorado court analyzed a physician's duty of care while performing independent medical examinations. The court noted:

> "Many courts set forth a 'general' rule that in the absence of a physician-patient relationship a physician owes no duty to an examinee. [Citations omitted.] Many of these same courts, however, recognize a duty of care if the examining physician undertakes in some way to act on behalf of the examinee [citations omitted] or induces reasonable reliance by the person examined. [Citations omitted.] Some courts conclude that medical malpractice standards govern, and recognize a duty of care simply on the basis of the relationship created by the referral and examination. [Citations omitted.] Others agree but temper this conclusion by expressly limiting the scope of the duty to the functions of the physician agrees to undertake. [Citations omitted.] Still others hold that the absence of a physician-patient relationship precludes a malpractice action, with the concomitant broad duty of care, but that an ordinary negligence action can be maintained in appropriate circumstances. [Citations omitted.] Some of th[illegible] cases are based [illegible] recognized principle that a person who assumes to act must act with care. [Citations omitted.]" 845 P.2d at 535.

. . . .

Dr. Welch was retained by the defendant to perform an examination and determine the extent of a head and neck injury. Although the examination was not court-ordered, it was agreed to by the parties' counsel. This agreement was in lieu of a court-ordered independent medical examination. Under either circumstances, Smith had every reason to believe she would be treated with dignity. She certainly had a right not to be criminally assaulted, battered, or sexually battered. If the allegations of such conduct are proven at trial, would an average person find a medical examination under those circumstances to be outrageous? Yes.

. . . .

Was there a physician-patient relationship between Dr. Welch and Smith? No. Dr. Welch was not treating Smith or examining her to recommend a course of treatment. The physician was retained to provide an expert medical opinion on an issue involved in civil litigation. Under such circumstances, the traditional physician-patient relationship does not exist.

Does a physician performing an independent medical examination have a duty not to negligently injure the person examined? Yes. A physician performing an independent medical examination has a duty to use reasonable and ordinary care and diligence in the examination the physician undertakes, to use his or her best judgment, and to exercise that reasonable degree of learning, skill, and experience which is ordinarily possessed by other physicians. The examining physician has a duty not to negligently cause harm or injury to the person examined.

Is the duty of a physician not to injure the person being examined affected by the fact that physician was employed by a third party? No. The duty of a physician conducting an independent medical examination not to injure the person being examined is not affected by the fact that the physician was employed to conduct the examination by a third party and no contractual relationship existed between the physician and the person being examined.

. . . .

Is the physician-patient relationship necessary for an intentional tort claim asserted by the person being examined? No. As to the intentional tort claims of invasion of privacy, assault, battery, and sexual battery, it makes no difference whether a physician-patient relationship exists.

. . . The facts alleged, if proven at trial, establish invasion of privacy, assault, battery, and sexual battery and those claims, in the context of a medical examination, are outrageous. The district court erred in granting summary judgment.

NOTES AND QUESTIONS

1. In *Smith v. Welch*, the woman is subjected to a physical examination which quickly exceeds bounds of medical necessity then propriety and then physical tolerance. Many women — but few men — submit the intimate parts of their bodies to physical examination on a recurring basis (to avoid, for example, cervical or breast cancer or to determine the status of a pregnancy). These are literally positions of trust and vulnerability, involving a relinquishment of privacy into the hands of another, often a male physician.

   All of the values developed in the preceding chapter — of identity, gender, bodily integrity, privacy and autonomy — are at risk during those minutes of vulnerability, as Peggy Smith — if she ever had any doubt — learned.

2. Ms. Smith has a number of theories in her lawsuit — battery, negligence, misrepresentation, invasion of privacy, violation of the right to

informed consent — outrage. Why so many? Which are the strongest? What would the defenses be?

3. In *Smith v. Welch*, why would the trial judge conclude that, as a matter of law, no reasonable person would be "outraged" by Doctor Welch's conduct? What are the elements of the tort of outrage? Were *you* outraged?

4. Doctor Welch argues that there *was* no physician-patient relationship. He was hired by the opposing side. He was openly hostile. Peggy Smith knew this — and *consented* to the examination. Isn't Welch right? If so, what is the significance of his argument?

5. Suppose Doctor Welch found symptoms of disease (say, AIDS) or a neurological disorder (say, MS or ALS) while doing the examination for the accident. What is his obligation to Peggy Smith? To defendant's attorney in the auto case? If that attorney is told, what is the *attorney's* obligation? *See* cases at § 3.02[1] *supra*.

6. How can women be protected from the misconduct Peggy Smith experienced? Medical Board rules of practice? Specialty guidelines? Legislatively mandated protocols? Treble damages in a tort action? And what should be done to Doctor Welch?

7. We now turn from abuse in a limited context to abuse in a continuing medical relationship in *Wall v. Fairview Hospital*. Note that there are multiple "patients" and caregivers — and they do not *all* share the same points of view.

WALL v. FAIRVIEW HOSPITAL AND HEALTHCARE SERVICES

584 N.W.2d 395 (1998)

Anderson, Paul H., Justice.

Respondents Sandra Slavik and Ruth Kay Wall suffer from multiple personality disorder, now known as dissociative identity disorder (DID). Slavik and Wall sued and won judgments against their psychiatrist, Dr. William Routt, for violations of the Vulnerable Adults Act (VAA), Minn. Stat. § 626.557 (1994), sexual exploitation, professional malpractice, battery, and intentional and negligent infliction of emotional distress. They also sued Routt's psychiatric nurse, appellant Kathy House, for malpractice, negligent permission, and failure to report Routt's abuse under the VAA, which requires that licensed health care professionals report abuse of a vulnerable adult when they know or have reasonable cause to believe that abuse has occurred or is occurring. Wall sued House for negligent and intentional infliction of emotional distress as well. The district court granted a directed verdict in favor of House on all claims, but the Minnesota Court of Appeals reversed as to the VAA and negligent infliction of emotional distress claims and remanded for a new trial.

The primary issue on appeal is the appropriateness of the directed verdict in favor of House. Therefore we begin with a thorough discussion of the record. The diagnostic manual used by mental health professionals, the DSM-IV, states that the essential feature of DID, the disorder that both Slavik and

Wall suffer from, is "the presence of two or more distinct identities or personality states . . . that recurrently take control of behavior." n1 American Psychiatric Ass'n, *Diagnostic and Statistical Manual of Mental Disorders* 484 (4th ed. 1994) (hereinafter DSM.IV). Both Slavik and Wall dissociate and manifest alternative identities, commonly known as alters. Slavik calls herself "Mary," and her alters include "Grandma," "Anne," "Elizabeth," "Kate," and "Amelia." Wall's alters include "Tootie Kay," "Kay," "Michael," "Daniel," "the Silent One," "the Destroyer," and "the Little Girls." When the women were dissociating, an alter spoke; conversely, when the alters spoke, the women were dissociating. Slavik and Wall have extensive histories of trauma, including sexual, physical, and emotional abuse. Both women have been through intensive psychiatric and mental health treatment for DID, as well as for post-traumatic stress disorder, depression, recurrent suicide attempts, and episodes of self-mutilation.

Routt began treating Slavik and Wall in 1988 and served as their psychiatrist until he committed suicide in June 1991. Routt had staff privileges at Fairview-Riverside Medical Center in Minneapolis and placed Slavik and Wall there when they needed to be hospitalized for psychiatric care. In addition to treating patients hospitalized at Fairview-Riverside, Routt held a medication clinic at his office once a week, during which he assessed his patients and adjusted their medications. Slavik and Wall visited Routt's office for appointments to manage their medications, and both women underwent psychotherapy with Routt as well as with other psychotherapists. Slavik had five office visits in 1990 and five in 1991. Wall had one office visit in 1988, three in 1989, one in 1990, and nine in 1991.

House worked as Routt's sole nurse and assistant for six years, beginning in 1985 and ending with Routt's death in 1991. When Routt saw his hospitalized patients, House went on rounds with him and attended treatment team meetings with him and hospital staff. She also acted as the liaison between Routt and his patients' outpatient psychotherapists. In Routt's office, House typically met with each patient for 20 minutes during each visit and did an assessment. Routt then joined House and the patient to review House's assessment and to adjust the patient's medications if necessary.

Several of Slavik's and Wall's alters testified at trial that Routt drank alcohol during appointments and offered them alcohol as well. The receptionist who worked for Routt during 1991 stated that Routt's office sometimes smelled like alcohol, although she never saw Routt drinking. In addition, House testified that Routt told her that a staff person at Fairview-Riverside reported Routt to the Impaired Physicians Committee, alleging that he had slurred speech and was disoriented when the staff person called him at home at 3:00 a.m. Routt responded to these allegations by stating that he had been taking medication for bronchitis that made him disoriented. Despite knowing about these allegations, House repeatedly testified that she never personally knew that Routt drank while on the job.

During the time that Routt treated Slavik and Wall, both women also received intensive psychotherapy with other psychotherapists. Both Slavik and Wall reported to their psychotherapists that they had positive relationships with Routt. Neither woman reported to House that Routt was abusing or had abused them. However, the women did report incidents of abuse by people other than Routt.

Both Slavik and Wall testified about personal information that Routt had told them about himself, including information about his daughter's suicide, his own experience of abuse as a child, and other personal problems he struggled with. An expert explained at trial that mental health professionals generally consider such confidences to be serious boundary violations and agreed that this behavior was inappropriate. Wall admitted that House was never present when Routt told her about his personal life and that she never told House about any of these discussions. Slavik also testified that she never told House about the things Routt confided in her. Slavik testified that only once was House present when Routt behaved unusually with Slavik. This occurred during the last time Slavik met with Routt, during which Routt looked "extremely awful, [and] scared." Slavik asked House what was wrong with Routt, but House did not respond. In contrast to Slavik's and Wall's testimony, House stated that she never overheard Routt discussing his own problems with any of his patients.

After Routt's death, Slavik and Wall revealed that Routt had sexually abused them. In both cases, an alter first reported the abuse. Slavik was an inpatient at a treatment center for dissociative disorders in Colorado during the fall of 1991 when her alter "Ann" told a counselor that Routt had sexually abused her. At trial, "Ann" testified that Routt had sexual intercourse with her between 10 and 20 times, with most of the incidents occurring while Slavik was an inpatient at Fairview-Riverside. Slavik herself does not remember the abuse, and she admitted that she and her alters never told House about Routt's abuse. Another alter, "Elizabeth," testified that House was not present when Routt had sex with Slavik.

The first record of Wall reporting Routt's abuse was in March 1992, while she was hospitalized at Fairview-Riverside. During a dissociative episode, one of Wall's alters told a hospital staff member that Routt abused her. Wall herself was unaware that Routt had abused her, and she testified that her alters have not told her exactly what Routt did to her. Wall's alter "Kay" testified at trial that she had sexual intercourse with Routt while she was hospitalized at Fairview-Riverside, but "Kay" did not know when this hospitalization occurred. Wall's alter "Michael" testified about having once talked to House, but did not know the content of the conversation.

Several witnesses presented critical testimony supporting the claims against House for failure to report Routt's abuse. Miles, whose affidavit was the basis for the court's denial of summary judgment on the VAA claims against House, testified about her relationship with Routt and House's knowledge of that relationship. Miles testified that House knew Miles and Routt went out for ice cream together because House asked Miles if she had enjoyed the ice cream; Routt told Miles in front of House that he had a drinking problem; Routt told Miles in front of House about his daughter's suicide and his problems with his wife; and House saw Routt cry in front of Miles. Contrary to the statement in her affidavit, however, at trial Miles denied that House had ever witnessed any sexual intercourse between Miles and Routt. But Miles testified that she saw House take a prescription pad out of a drawer in Routt's desk once when the drawer contained a vial of cocaine. She admitted on cross-examination, however, that the assertion in her affidavit stating that House saw Routt and Miles use cocaine together was incorrect.

James Konkler, a patient of Routt, claimed that during treatment sessions Routt smelled like alcohol and his speech was slurred. Konkler also testified that House was always present when he met with Routt. Carl Terwilliger, who worked at Fairview-Riverside, stated that he once had to help Routt find his way through the hospital because Routt appeared disoriented and hung over.

At the close of Slavik's and Wall's case, House moved for a directed verdict on all of the remaining claims against her, including their claims for failure to report abuse under the VAA and Wall's claims for negligent and intentional infliction of emotional distress. The district court granted House's motion in its entirety. The court also granted a directed verdict as to the claims for punitive damages against House, but this issue is not on appeal.

The district court found no evidence that House had actual knowledge of any abuse. Based on this finding, the court framed the VAA claim in terms of whether House had reasonable cause to know that abuse had occurred or was occurring. The court then reviewed the evidence presented that suggested that House had reasonable cause to believe Slavik and Wall were being abused. Taking as true Miles' testimony that House witnessed numerous boundary violations during Routt's treatment of Miles, the court determined that such information would alert House that Routt was a potential abuser, but would not by itself provide reasonable cause for House to know that Routt abused either Slavik or Wall. To hold otherwise, the court reasoned, would require that once the abuse of any patient occurred, a health care worker would be statutorily required to make a report of suspected abuse of every subsequent patient, regardless of whether she had any knowledge of abuse of that particular patient.

. . . .

III.

VAA Claims

We next address the court of appeals' reversal of the district court's grant of a directed verdict for House on Slavik's and Wall's claims under the VAA. House contends that the court of appeals misconstrued the VAA to require a lesser standard of suspicion to trigger its reporting requirement and that the district court properly interpreted the VAA and applied it to the facts elicited at trial.

The VAA creates a civil cause of action for negligent or intentional failure to report abuse of a vulnerable adult. Minn. Stat. § 626.557, subd. 7(b) (1994). At the time Routt abused Slavik and Wall, the VAA mandated that a licensed health care professional such as House "who has knowledge of the abuse or neglect of a vulnerable adult, [or] has *reasonable cause* to believe that a vulnerable adult is being or has been abused" immediately report the information. *Id.*, subd. 3 (emphasis added).

[illegible], we defined reasonable or probable cause as a "reasonable ground of suspicion supported by circumstances sufficiently strong in themselves to warrant a cautious man in believing the accused to be guilty."

Analogizing from this definition, reasonable cause requires grounds for belief beyond mere suspicion or foreseeability; mere suspicion or foreseeability must be supported by sufficiently strong circumstances. We thus conclude that the court of appeals erred in construing the VAA to require reporting based on suspicion alone. As the district court pointed out, the VAA's reporting requirement is particularized, extending to the abuse of individual vulnerable adults. *See* Minn. Stat. § 626.557, subd. 3. Therefore, the knowledge that gives rise to the reporting duty must be particularized or specific to each individual. Knowledge of abuse of a different individual, however, is a relevant factor for determining when there is reasonable cause to believe a vulnerable adult is being abused. In essence, knowledge of abuse of another person becomes a critical factor in reaching the reasonable cause threshold.

We must first determine precisely what information House had about Routt's abuse of other individuals. The only other person whom Routt allegedly abused is Erica Miles, and thus Miles' testimony is critical. Miles testified at trial only that House witnessed or knew about various boundary violations: Routt and Miles going out for ice cream; Routt telling Miles he had a drinking problem; Routt crying in front of Miles; and Routt telling Miles about his daughter's suicide and problems with his wife. Miles denied that House knew that she had sexual intercourse with Routt and testified that House knew only about Routt's hugging, kissing, and hand-holding. Thus, the record reflects only that House knew that Routt committed boundary violations in his treatment of Miles, but not that Routt sexually abused Miles.

Assuming here, as we must, the truth of Miles' testimony that House witnessed Routt's boundary violations with Miles, we hold that witnessing those boundary violations cannot on its own have provided reasonable cause for House to believe Routt had abused Slavik and Wall as well. If Miles' testimony alone created reasonable cause, House would have to make a report of suspected abuse for every [illegible] patients. Such a result would contradict the particularized or individualized nature of the statute and lead to an unworkable result. Nonetheless, we recognize that House's knowledge of Routt's abuse of Miles should have been a factor in her reasonable cause determination regarding abuse of Slavik and Wall. As a consequence of that knowledge, House should have required less information, albeit specific information about Slavik and Wall, to have reasonable cause to believe that Routt was abusing Slavik and Wall.

We next turn to what information House had about Routt's conduct with Slavik and Wall, particularly that information which, combined with her knowledge about Miles, would have created reasonable cause. The district court concluded that seeing Wall crying in the corner would not give House reasonable cause to believe Slavik and Wall were being abused. We agree. First, because the VAA's reporting requirement is individualized, Wall's conduct during treatment with Routt reveals nothing about Routt's actions with Slavik. More importantly, the record reveals that Wall was deeply psychologically troubled and the fact that Wall expressed her distress by crying in the corner was not inconsistent with her illness. Nor would House have reasonable cause to believe Routt was abusing either Slavik or Wall because Routt had jaundiced eyes and appeared overworked and sad. No person, not even a psychiatric nurse, could reasonably infer that a psychiatrist was abusing his patients from the fact that he looked tired, ill, and distressed.

Slavik and Wall testified that Routt drank in front of them. Given that House had a close working relationship with Routt, we believe a valid inference arises that House knew or should have known that Routt drank at work. Nonetheless, we agree with the district court that drinking in front of patients is not abuse under the VAA because it could not, in and of itself, as a matter of law produce or reasonably be expected to produce mental or emotional distress. *See* Minn. Stat. § 626.557, subd. 2(d)(2). Therefore, we conclude that House did not violate the VAA's reporting requirement solely by failing to report that Routt drank in front of Slavik and Wall.

Distilling these relevant facts produced at trial and linking them together, we must decide whether House's knowledge of Routt's boundary violations with Miles, together with our determination that House knew or should have known that Routt drank at work, created reasonable cause for House to believe Routt abused Slavik and Wall. Following the district court's adept and thoughtful analysis, we conclude that because the VAA requires particularized or individualized information to create reasonable cause to believe a specific vulnerable adult has been or is being abused, the evidence at trial fails to raise a sufficient question of fact to go to the jury. The most House knew about Routt's conduct with Slavik and Wall was that he drank in front of them. House never saw Routt abuse Slavik or Wall. Slavik and Wall did not present evidence that House knew or should have known about any of Routt's boundary violations with them, such as his statements to them about his daughter's suicide. There was no evidence that a third party told House about any boundary violations with Slavik and Wall. Without additional particularized or individualized information, the evidence Slavik and Wall presented at trial was insufficient to raise a fact question as to whether House had reasonable cause to believe that Routt abused them. We therefore reverse the court of appeals on this issue and reinstate the district court's directed verdict in favor of House on the VAA claims.

IV.

Negligent Infliction of Emotional Distress

The next issue we consider is the court of appeals' reversal of the district court's grant of a directed verdict on Wall's claim for negligent infliction of emotional distress. Wall's claim for negligent infliction of emotional distress rests on House's recurrent failure to prevent Routt's abuse, as well as a single incident when House failed to help Wall when informed that Wall's roommate, James Konkler, had a loaded gun and had threatened to commit suicide.

To establish a claim for negligent infliction of emotional distress, a plaintiff must show that she was within a zone of danger of physical impact, reasonably feared for her safety, and suffered severe emotional distress with accompanying physical manifestations. *Stadler v. Cross,* 295 N.W.2d 552, 553 (Minn. 1980). The zone of danger is limited to [illegible] physical danger caused by the defendant's negligence. *Langeland v. Farmers State Bank of Trimont,* 319 N.W.2d 26, 31 (Minn. 1982). In other words, a plaintiff presents a valid claim when she experiences a reasonable anxiety, with physical symptoms, "from being in a situation where it was abundantly clear that plaintiff was in grave personal peril for some specifically defined period of time. Fortune smiled and the imminent calamity did not occur." *K.A.C. v. Benson,* 527 N.W.2d 553, 558 (Minn. 1995). Due to concerns about unintended and unreasonable results, we have deliberately limited the zone of danger to the threat of personal physical danger. *Id.* at 559.

Wall's claim for negligent infliction of emotional distress does not fit the facts that emerged at trial. A plaintiff is in a zone of danger when physical harm might occur, but fortunately does not. Wall was not merely in a zone of danger with Routt — she was in fact physically harmed by his abuse. Furthermore, House could not have placed Wall in a zone of danger because she did not have reasonable cause to believe Routt abused Wall. Finally, House's alleged failure to prevent Wall from living in a potentially dangerous situation does not raise a valid claim for negligent infliction of emotional distress. Wall's own decisions regarding her living situation placed her in the zone of danger, if any, from her armed and suicidal roommate. We thus reverse the court of appeals on this issue and reinstate the district court's directed verdict in favor of House on Wall's claim for negligent infliction of emotional distress.

V.

Evidentiary Issues

Because we conclude that the district court correctly directed a verdict in favor of House, we need not review House's arguments that the district court erred in several of its evidentiary rulings and its denial of one of House's requested jury instructions, since those issues would be relevant only to a retrial. We nonetheless address [illegible] evidentiary questions because we wish to provide some direction as to how a district court should handle witnesses with DID and the testimony of their alters. House contends first that the court abused its discretion in concluding that Slavik and Wall were competent to testify while they were in a dissociative state, and second, that the court further abused its discretion in holding that it was a disputed question of fact whether Slavik and Wall had first related information about Routt's abuse while under hypnosis. We conclude that the court did not abuse its discretion regarding either of these determinations. In fact, after a thorough review of the voluminous transcript, we believe that the court's handling of these potentially difficult witnesses was entirely appropriate.

Determining the competency of a witness to testify is within a district court's sound discretion. *State ex rel. Dugal v. Tahash,* 278 Minn. 175, 177, 153 N.W.2d 232, 234 (1967). Typically, the district court conducts a preliminary examination to determine whether the witness understands the obligation of the oath and can correctly narrate the facts to which her testimony relates. *State v. Amos,* 347 N.W.2d 498, 501 (Minn. 1984). As long as the witness understands the obligation to tell the truth and can recall and relate relevant events, the witness is competent and should be permitted to testify. *Dugal,* 278 Minn. at 178, 153 N.W.2d at 234-35.

Here, the district court decided that Slavik and Wall were competent to testify while in a dissociative state, and thus the court permitted their alters to testify. The court reasoned that no legal authority prohibited such testimony, Slavik and Wall were rational and articulate, and defense counsel had the opportunity to cross-examine each alter concerning her understanding of the requirement to give truthful testimony and willingness to do so. Although the court did not do a preliminary competency determination on each of the alters, Slavik's and Wall's counsel and defense counsel questioned the alters about their ability to tell the truth. Presumably, if one of the alters said something indicating that she or he might not be competent to testify, the defense would have made a specific objection and the court would have made a ruling on the objection. Yet the record is void of objections based on the competency of specific alters, even though some of the alters who testified were only three or four years old. We conclude that the court did not abuse its discretion and, under the facts of this case, its decision to allow Slavik's and Wall's alters to testify was entirely appropriate.

The second evidentiary issue that House raises on appeal presents a more complex question: is dissociation a form of self-hypnosis or sufficiently similar to hypnosis so that our decision in *State v. Mack* [292 N.W.2d 764, 772 (Minn. 1980)] bars Slavik's and Wall's testimony about any issues that were first related while they were in a dissociative state. We concluded in *State v. Mack* that, under the facts in that case, testimony about information that was first adduced during hypnosis is inadmissible in a criminal proceeding

The court of appeals concluded that hypnosis and dissociation are fundamentally different because the nonvolitional nature of dissociation makes the information revealed during dissociative states inherently more reliable than information revealed during hypnosis. Therefore, the court of appeals held that *State v. Mack* did not bar any testimony about issues that first came to light during a dissociative episode. To reach this conclusion, the court of appeals adopted the reasoning of *Dorsey v. State*, [426 S.E.2d 224, 226–27 (Ga. Ct. App. 1992),] a Georgia Court of Appeals case with similar facts that analyzed the differences between hypnotic and dissociative testimony.

In *Dorsey*, a woman's alter personality told her psychologist that she was being sexually abused by a high school guidance counselor. 426 S.E.2d at 226. The district court permitted the woman to testify at the guidance counselor's trial about the sexual abuse, which first came to light while she was dissociating. The court also permitted the woman to testify while she was in a dissociative state, that is, to allow her alters to testify. The Georgia Court of Appeals affirmed the district court based on its articulation of the supposed fundamental difference between hypnosis and dissociation:

> The most important difference for our purposes is that hypnosis is a process a person voluntarily chooses to engage in yet which is externally imposed, while a dissociative state is involuntary and, although

> triggered by external stimuli, comes solely from within. We believe the non-volitional nature of a dissociative state itself makes statements made while in such a state inherently more reliable than statements made in a hypnotic trance.

Id. 426 S.E.2d at 227. The *Dorsey* court noted that questions about the inherent reliability of statements made under hypnosis did not arise in the case because the victim testified in a dissociative state and thus her statements' reliability could be tested on cross-examination and evaluated by the jury.

We specifically reject our court of appeals' uncritical reliance on Dorsey and its holding that dissociation is fundamentally different from hypnosis when considering the reliability of witness testimony. The *Dorsey* court never explained why the nonvolitional nature of dissociation makes the resulting statements more reliable than statements articulated during hypnosis; its reasoning may be grounded in the uncontradicted expert testimony at trial that "the victim in a dissociative state would not lie." Here, however, several of Slavik's and Wall's witnesses conceded that persons with DID can produce incomplete memories.

Moreover, the court of appeals failed to acknowledge that some of Slavik's and Wall's witnesses stated that dissociation may be related to self-hypnosis. One of Slavik's psychotherapists testified that many people with DID, including Slavik, engage in self-hypnosis and can induce a trance, a term she used interchangeably with hypnosis. This witness also described Slavik's presentation of alters at her therapist's request as involving hypnosis or trance. No witness stated that dissociation is fundamentally dissimilar from hypnosis for determining the reliability of witness testimony.

Finally, even if dissociation and hypnosis are not the same phenomena, many of the concerns we expressed in *Mack* about information elicited during hypnosis apply as well to statements produced during dissociation. Expert testimony revealed that persons with DID can be highly suggestible. To the extent that inaccurate information is "recalled" during dissociative episodes, the person's belief in the memory's validity is increased. The resulting inability to ferret out the truth through cross-examination about such memories is another of the concerns we articulated in *Mack* about hypnotically-recalled information. The court of appeals' reliance on Slavik's and Wall's testimony is misplaced if their testimony was based on inaccurate memories that they nonetheless unequivocally believed to be true.

We recognize, however, that there are compelling policy arguments against a per se rule that treats episodes of dissociation as equivalent to hypnosis. If testimony from a person in a dissociative state is never admissible, someone who is aware of the person's dissociative disorder could take advantage of that person with impunity. *See* 292 N.W.2d at 711-12. Excluding dissociative testimony would allow the mental state that led to the sexual abuse to become the shield of protection for the abuser.

In addition, there is considerable controversy in the psychiatric and psychotherapeutic communities about the diagnosis of DID. Experts cannot agree whether the occurrence of dissociation and the emergence of alters are sometimes encouraged or even produced by psychotherapy, and whether the disorder is overdiagnosed by a small number of psychotherapists. *See* DSM-IV, at 486-87. Coming to a reasoned conclusion on this issue is particularly difficult because the mental health community has not yet reached a consensus on the nature of the disorder. By allowing the jury to determine whether information had first emerged under hypnosis and thus was not admissible, the district court recognized that conflicting testimony on this issue would be presented at trial. This procedure thus allowed the jury to determine which side of the debate it found more credible — whether DID is or is not a form of hypnosis.

Because our understanding of DID is in flux, we decline to hold that *Mack* prohibits all testimony about events that first came to light while a witness was dissociating. Instead, we believe that the district courts are in the best position to determine how to handle witnesses with DID and whether their testimony is admissible. Therefore, we conclude that the district court did not abuse its discretion in allowing the jury to determine whether dissociation is sufficiently similar to hypnosis and whether any memories of abuse were actually first recalled during dissociation. Here, the court used appropriate discretion in allowing Slavik and Wall to testify, and we urge other courts to heed this example and to proceed thoughtfully and cautiously when witnesses with DID appear in their courtroom.

In sum, we hold that this appeal did not become moot while pending before the court of appeals. We affirm the part of the court of appeals decision addressing Slavik's and Wall's malpractice claim. Finally, we reinstate the district court's grant of a directed verdict to House on all of Slavik's and Wall's claims against her.

Affirmed in part and reversed in part.

Gilbert, J. (dissenting).

I respectfully dissent.

Subdivision 1 of the VAA clearly states the legislature's purpose in enacting the statute: "to protect adults who, because of physical or mental disability or dependency on institutional services, are particularly vulnerable to abuse or neglect." Minn. Stat. § 626.557, subd. 1. The legislature adds that the public policy of the state requires "the reporting of *suspected* abuse or neglect of vulnerable adults." *Id.* (emphasis added). The language from subdivision 1 mandating reporting of suspected abuse is repeated in subdivision 4, which describes the report that must be made:

> The written report shall be of sufficient content to identify the vulnerable adult, the caretaker, the nature and extent of the *suspected* abuse or neglect, any evidence of previous abuse or neglect, name and address of the reporter, and any other information that the reporter believes might be helpful in investigating the *suspected* abuse or neglect.

Id., subd. 4 (emphases added).

The legislature's repeated use of the term "suspected" is a sufficient indication that the legislature indeed intended for abuse to be reported when it was merely suspected. The majority focuses almost exclusively on the language of subdivision 3, which states that a health care professional must make a report when she either knows about the abuse or "has *reasonable cause to believe* that a vulnerable adult is being or has been abused or neglected." *Id.*, subd. 3 (emphasis added). While I tend to agree with the majority that the reasonable cause to believe standard may involve a higher standard than suspicion, suspicion must remain a part of the equation.

House knew of Routt's significant boundary violations with another female patient, and she knew or should have known that he committed the serious boundary violation of drinking in front of the plaintiffs while treating them. A pattern of abuse and neglect should have been apparent to House, an experienced psychiatric nurse possessing special training and understanding of such problems. A report would have initiated an inquiry or investigation by appropriate authorities and may have brought necessary help to these two vulnerable adults as well as to Routt.

Routt's drinking in front of the plaintiffs while treating them, which the majority concludes House should have known about, was all the more serious given the fact that one of the plaintiffs was chemically dependent. Abuse includes "any repeated conduct which produces or could reasonably be expected to produce mental or emotional distress," and neglect includes failure to provide the vulnerable adult with necessary health care. Minn. Stat. § 626.557, subd. 2(d)(2), 2(e). Routt's drinking in front of these patients fits the statutory definition of abuse.

Subdivision 7 of the VAA imposes liability on a mandated reporter who negligently fails to make a required report. If the jury were to find that House should have had reasonable cause to believe that Routt abused the plaintiffs and was negligent in failing to report the abuse, it would then decide the amount of damages as well. I would therefore uphold the court of appeals' decision to overturn the directed verdict in favor of House and to remand the case for a new trial of the plaintiffs' claims against House under the VAA.

NOTES AND QUESTIONS

1. Consider the various theories of the plaintiffs: malpractice, infliction of emotional distress, violation of the Vulnerable Adults Act. How do they differ? Which succeed? Given the availability of traditional theories for relief, why is the VAA necessary? Will it tend to encourage or discourage provision of Healthcare? Note the plaintiffs' case on the emotional distress claims — are you surprised? Do you disagree with the Court's conclusion?
2. What exactly *was* abusive about Doctor Routt's conduct:
   a) Exceeding "boundaries" (*e.g.,* consuming alcohol, touching patients)?
   b) Having sexual intercourse with patients? And does it matter whether that was "consensual"? *Could* it *be* consensual in this

context? Ever? Could it be consensual and yet abusive? Unprofessional?

c) Turning the "alter" personalities against each other and persuading them to withhold experiences/knowledge from each other?

d) Seeking help and comfort from his patients?

Would these be actionable as malpractice absent the VAA?

3. Note that Sandra Slavik and Ruth Wall are both afflicted with multiple personality disorders ("dissociative identity disorder") and the victims of past abuse as well as present emotional or psychiatric difficulties. They testified at trial to what happened during hypnosis or nonhypnotic therapy sessions to their various personalities; and — at trial — *their various personalities* testified. How, then, could a court accept such testimony or give it credit? The trial court, it is said, found the various witnesses "competent." What does that mean in the *Rock/Riggins*, FRE § 401 sense (*See supra,* § 2.02[1])?

4. It seems clear, doesn't it, that Sandra Slavik and Ruth Wall both felt genuine affection and concern for Doctor Routt, despite — perhaps because of — his abusive course of conduct. How is this significant?

5. Note that the jury returned a verdict of $4.4 million in damages. As plaintiff, how would you calculate this? As defendant, oppose it? And how would/should damages be apportioned between House and Routt? Are there other defendants possible: licensing boards, credentialing hospitals, insurance companies, HMOs and MCOs?

6. How could the injuries to Wall and Slavik have been prevented? Are there professional or administrative processes or bodies that could maintain professional oversight, screening, review? Should there be regular re-credentialing of providers, particularly mental health professionals? Should they, themselves, be subject to periodic mental health examinations? Should their services be rendered only in institutional — not private practice — settings?

7. The real defendant here, of course, is Nurse House. Traditionally, professionally and economically, nurses are given very little autonomy and accorded little professional independence by supervising employers, whether physicians or hospitals. Thus, isn't Nurse House being victimized by Doctor Routt, along with Slavik and Wall? To the extent that House *knew* (and she testified she *didn't*) about Routt's misconduct, what — fairly — can she be expected to do? Isn't she in the same position as Mr. Schmidt in the *Schmidt* case or Dr. Moore in the *Tarasoff* case: unfairly held to a standard imposed by hindsight?

8. If there was a duty on Nurse House, where will it be found — statutes, professional custom, contact (with Routt? Slavik? Wall?), training, agency regulation? And how will it be proven? Note the Court sustains dismissal of the malpractice claim *precisely* for the failure to prove the governing standard.

9. The issue of sexual relations between fiduciaries and their clients arises with unusual severity with physicians since the nature of the service

is physical and often private. Thus, whatever the rule may be for clergy or attorneys, the best rule with physicians may simply be to prohibit sexual relations or intimacy with [illegible] problems of definition and intent may be intractable, however.

Consider the following statute from California — is it wise? Should it create a civil claim for damages? How would you improve it?

Cal. Bus. & Prof. Code § 729 (1997)

§ 729. Sexual exploitation of patient or client by physician and surgeon, or psychotherapist

(a) Any physician and surgeon, psychotherapist, alcohol and drug abuse counselor or any person holding himself or herself out to be a physician and surgeon, psychotherapist, or alcohol and drug abuse counselor, who engages in an act of sexual intercourse, sodomy, oral copulation, or sexual contact with a patient or client, or with a former patient or client when the relationship was terminated primarily for the purpose of engaging in those acts, unless the physician and surgeon, psychotherapist, or alcohol and drug abuse counselor has referred the patient or client to an independent and objective physician and surgeon, psychotherapist, or alcohol and drug abuse counselor recommended by a third-party physician and surgeon, psychotherapist, or alcohol and drug abuse counselor for treatment, is guilty of sexual exploitation by a physician and surgeon, psychotherapist, or alcohol and drug abuse counselor.

(b) Sexual exploitation by a physician and surgeon, psychotherapist, or alcohol and drug abuse counselor is a public offense:

(1) An act in violation of subdivision (a) shall be punishable by imprisonment; in a county jail for a period of not more than six months, or a fine not exceeding one thousand dollars ($1,000), or by both that imprisonment and fine.

(2) Multiple acts in violation of subdivision (a) with a single victim, when the offender has no prior conviction for sexual exploitation, shall be punishable by imprisonment in a county [illegible] period of not more [illegible] months, or a fine not exceeding one thousand dollars ($1,000), or by both that imprisonment and fine.

. . . .

For purposes of subdivision (a), *in no instance shall consent of the patient or client be a defense.* However, physicians and surgeons shall not be guilty of sexual exploitation for touching any intimate part of a patient or client unless the touching is outside the scope of medical examination and treatment, or the touching is done for sexual gratification.

(c) For purposes of this section:

(1) "Psychotherapist" has the same meaning as defined in Section 728.

(2) "Alcohol and drug abuse counselor" means an individual who holds himself or herself out to be an alcohol or drug abuse professional or paraprofessional.

(3) "Sexual contact" means sexual intercourse or the touching of an intimate part of a patient for the purpose of sexual arousal, gratification, or abuse.

(4) "Intimate part" and "touching" have the same meanings as defined in Section 243.4 of the Penal Code.

(d) In the investigation and prosecution of a violation of this section, no person shall seek to obtain disclosure of any confidential files of other patients, clients, or former patients or clients of the physician and surgeon, psychotherapist, or alcohol and drug abuse counselor.

(e) This section does not apply to sexual contact between a physician and surgeon and his or her spouse or person in an equivalent domestic relationship when that physician and surgeon provides medical treatment, other than psychotherapeutic treatment, to his or her spouse or person in an equivalent domestic relationship.

(f) If a physician and surgeon, psychotherapist, or alcohol and drug abuse counselor in a professional partnership or similar group has sexual contact with a patient in violation of this section, another physician and surgeon, psychotherapist, or alcohol and drug abuse counselor in the partnership or group shall not be subject to action under this section solely because of the occurrence of that sexual contact.

Note that the statute permits referring a patient to another physician, *then* having sexual relations. Suppose the referral is for that very purpose? Isn't that a kind of abandonment? With the patient's "informed consent"? Is that worse?

And does the absolute ban on consent preclude terminating the professional relationship for the *agreed* purpose undertaking a personal relationship? Doesn't the absolute ban infringe the autonomy of the patient?

PROBLEM 3–7 — Privacy, Privilege and Personalities

Wanda Wall comes to Doctor Routt for psychiatric care, depressed, anxious, prey to recurring nightmares and obsessive fixations. In the course of therapy, several personalities emerge under hypnosis: Angela, a sweet child; Deirdre, a vengeful teenager; and Sonetta, a cocktail lounge singer. Each hate Wanda, who is a middle-aged, unattractive, unhappy woman. Each wants to become the dominant personality.

Each tells Doctor Routt that she is aware there are others; each wants to know about the others, to eclipse them; each wants her identity kept from the others and Wanda.

What should Doctor Routt tell them? Does your answer change if Doctor Routt's clinical judgment is that each is a part of a fifth personality, as yet unborn?

In resolving this problem, consider the dimensions of conflict of interests and patient abuse raised in *Wall v. Fairview Hospital*, § 3.02[3] *supra* and the applicability of the California statute, *supra*.

PROBLEM 3–8 — Chiropractic Manipulation

In *McCracken v. Walls-Kaufman*, 717 A.2d 346 (D.C. 1998), the court recited the following facts:

> Mrs. McCracken stated that during the course of Dr. Walls-Kaufman's chiropractic treatment she discussed personal matters with him and that he in turn offered advice and counseling, and that Dr. Walls-Kaufman sodomized her for the first time in December of 1994; then again on approximately a half dozen occasions through August 10, 1995. She had been addicted to Valium previously and became addicted again following her first sexual encounter with appellee. During the first encounter, Mrs. McCracken stated, she "froze up, and disassociated [herself] from the situation," although she had initially "pushed his hands away," and afterwards "told [him] that this was never to happen again." During the subsequent sexual encounters, Mrs. McCracken stated, she "did not know how to deal with this situation, [she] believe[d] in part because of the excessive doses of valium [she] was taking." The affidavits of both Mr. and Mrs. McCracken indicated that Mrs. McCracken's ability to live a normal life was impaired significantly for a period of time following her final sexual encounter with appellee.

In deciding whether the statute of limitation for malpractice (as opposed to assault) applied, the Court observed:

> To determine whether the McCrackens adequately alleged a breach of a duty owed them by Dr. Walls-Kaufman, we must consider whether, and if so under what circumstances, a chiropractor may be liable for professional malpractice based on negligence for engaging in sexual activity with a patient that results in injury to the patient. The issue is one of first impression in this jurisdiction. Many courts have taken the view that a person engaged in the healing arts, other than those practicing in psychiatry, psychology, and like fields, may be liable for medical malpractice based on a sexual relationship with a patient only if the doctor represents to the patient that sex is a part of the treatment. [not the case here].

In a separate category are professionals such as psychiatrists and psychologists whose role it is to counsel the patients, and who allegedly breached the standard of care applicable to their profession by engaging in sexual relations with a patient, resulting in injury to the patient.

In finding against the chiropractor, the Court said:

> Some courts have imposed liability, however, in a narrowly defined category of cases not involving mental health professionals in which, in addition to the physician-patient relationship, there was also a special relationship of trust and confidence between the doctor and the patient and the doctor abused that trust by engaging in sexual activity with the patient causing injury. In *Hoopes v. Hammargren*,

> 102 Nev. 425, 725 P.2d 238, 242-43 (1986), the Supreme Court of Nevada held that a neurosurgeon could be held liable, based on breach of fiduciary duty, for engaging in a sexual relationship with a patient, provided the patient could show that the neurosurgeon "held a superior authoritative position in the professional relationship," that he violated his fiduciary responsibilities by exploiting her vulnerabilities, and that the exploitation was the proximate cause of her claimed harm. *See also Dillon v. Callaway*, 609 N.E.2d 424 (Ind. Ct-.App.1993) (medical doctor, who began scheduling counseling sessions with patient after being unable to ascertain physical cause for her symptoms, could be found liable for medical malpractice for inducing patient to engage in sadomasochistic sexual relationship under guise of treatment).
>
> . . . .
>
> Therefore, as a medical professional, Dr. Walls-Kaufman can be found liable in tort for medical malpractice if it is found that he engaged in sexual acts with his patient, Mrs. McCracken; a relationship similar to a psychologist-patient relationship developed between the two; that it was a breach of the applicable standard of care for Dr. Walls-Kaufman to engage in sexual acts with Mrs. McCracken during the course of or attendant to that relationship; and that the breach of the standard of care by Dr. Walls-Kaufman proximately caused Mrs. McCraken's claimed injuries.

Evaluate the Court's reasoning. Why shouldn't *all* professionals simply be barred from sexual relations with clients or patients? Does the distinction between counselors and physicians make sense? And won't all (or many) professionals, as a part of the pattern of seduction, inquire about personal matters? Finally, by what standard will the chiropractor be judged — the reasonable chiropractor; the reasonable counselor; or some other standard?

Sexual relations between a physician or other fiduciary and the patient may be an abuse or imposition, or a "consensual" act. If the latter, the concept and content of "consent" must be carefully examined. Rarely does a patient seek sexual relations with a physician. Hence, informed consent, a prerequisite to care, is unlikely to encompass sexual services or relations by the physician or other fiduciary provider.

MACY v. BLATCHFORD

8 P.3d 204 (Or. 2000)

Gillette, J.

In this medical malpractice action, plaintiffs Danita and Lawrence Macy challenge a trial court ruling that prevented them from introducing evidence at trial that Dr. Blatchford (defendant) had a sexual relationship with Danita Macy at the time when the Macys assert that he negligently treated her for persistent and debilitating pelvic pain. We conclude that such evidence is relevant to one of the Macys' allegations, viz., that defendant was negligent in failing to obtain Macy's informed consent to recommended surgery. We therefore reverse the decision of the Court of Appeals on that ground.

In January 1992, Macy consulted [illegible], a gynecologist, about severe and [illegible] pelvic pain. Macy had complained to defendant about pelvic pain previously, in 1982 and in 1985. Dr. Alberts examined Macy and performed a laparoscopy in February 1992, in the course of which he removed an endometrioma (an abnormal growth of uterine tissue outside the uterus) from Macy's left ovary. After reviewing Dr. Alberts' report and a videotape made during the laparoscopic surgery, defendant diagnosed endometriosis, a condition marked by growth of uterine tissue outside the uterus.

In May 1992, Macy again complained to defendant about pelvic pain. Defendant recommended additional laparoscopic surgery, including removal of Macy's left ovary and fallopian tube. On June 3, 1992, defendant performed that surgery. Afterwards, Macy continued to suffer pelvic pain. Defendant then discussed with Macy the possibility of removing her right ovary and fallopian tube, along with her uterus. Macy agreed to the additional surgery, which defendant performed on August 20, 1992. Macy's pelvic pain did not subside after the second surgery. In fact, she began to suffer from new pain in her left side and back. Ultimately, Macy consulted a different physician, Dr. Ellis, about the latter pain. Ellis determined that Macy's left ureter — the tube connecting the kidney to the bladder — was obstructed, and performed surgery to correct the problem. Ellis believed that defendant inadvertently had stapled Macy's ureter during the June 1992 surgery, thereby causing the obstruction and related pain.

In 1994, the Macys filed the present malpractice action against defendant. In their complaint, they alleged four specifications of negligence — that defendant had been negligent in: (1) stapling Macy's ureter during the June 1992 surgery; (2) failing to ascertain that Macy's continuing pain after the June 1992 surgery arose from the obstructed ureter; (3) recommending the August 1992 surgery; and (4) failing to obtain Macy's informed consent for the August 1992 surgery. Defendant's answer denied all four specifications of negligence.

Shortly before trial, the Macys moved to amend their complaint to include a fifth specification — that defendant had been negligent [illegible] his physician-patient relationship [illegible] after entering into a personal, sex- [illegible] relationship with her.

The Macys argue that evidence of a sexual relationship between defendant and Macy is relevant to their third specification, because it supports an inference that, at the time that he recommended additional surgery, defendant lacked the objectivity that is required of physicians in their treatment of patients. They contend that, because defendant's conduct must be measured against a standard set by his own profession and because "everyone," including the medical profession as a whole, understands that physicians must be dispassionate and objective when making treatment decisions, maintaining an objective mental state is part of the standard of care that is applicable in this case. Thus, they conclude, any fact suggesting that defendant lacked objectivity in making his treatment recommendations to Macy is relevant and admissible to show that he was negligent.

We are not persuaded. The standard of care that is applicable to the medical profession requires physicians to "use that degree of care, skill and diligence that is used by ordinarily careful physicians . . . in the same or similar circumstances in the community of the physician . . . or a similar community." That standard is an objective one; it provides no ground for delving into a physician's subjective state of mind. Physicians may violate their ethical duties if they fail to maintain the requisite clear and objective state of mind — for example, if they work while intoxicated or while their judgment is clouded by a relationship with a patient. But if, despite their less than optimal mental and emotional condition, their actual treatment of a patient reflects the appropriate degree of care, they cannot be held liable in negligence.

In the present case, the jury had to determine in addressing the Macys' third specification of negligence whether defendant's recommendation for the August 1992 surgery was objectively reasonable, i.e., whether that recommendation departed from the treatment that other gynecologists in the community exercising ordinary care would have offered. Defendant's subjective frame of mind in making that recommendation was not relevant to that issue. Thus, at least insofar as the Macys sought to offer evidence of a sexual relationship to prove something about defendant's state of mind in the context of that specification, the trial court properly excluded it from the jury's consideration. In that respect, the trial court and Court of Appeals did not err.

The Macys next argue that the excluded evidence was relevant to their fourth specification, which alleged negligence:

> "in failing to obtain Plaintiff Danita Macy's informed consent to surgical removal of her uterus and right ovary, in that Defendant . . . did not advise her that there were medical and conservative surgical treatment options available as alternatives to sterilization and menopause, and he did not ask if she wanted detailed information about each of these alternatives."

The Macys contend that the duty of physicians to obtain informed consent includes a duty to explain that there may be alternative methods of treatment and that the duty presupposes that the patient is in a condition to understand the information that is being conveyed. In view of that presupposition, the Macys argue, evidence that shows that a physician was aware that a patient was not capable of understanding a physician's explanation is relevant to whether the physician's actions met the applicable standard of care. In the Macys' view, evidence of a sexual relationship between defendant and Macy thus is relevant, because it would support a conclusion that Macy lacked the state of mind that the standard of care implies, i.e., such evidence would tend to prove that Macy would trust defendant's treatment choice implicitly and would be incapable of listening objectively to any information about alternatives that defendant might have presented.

The Macys pleaded that defendant failed to "obtain Plaintiff Danita Macy's informed consent" — words that relate to Macy's state of mind when she consented to the second surgery. The issues were whether Macy "consented" and whether her consent was "informed." A physician's failure to "advise" of treatment alternatives may arise solely out of a physician's silence, but it also may arise in circumstances when the physician mouths the words to a patient who, for whatever reason, at that time lacks the capacity to listen to or to understand the significance of what is being said.

The standard of [illegible] respect to informed consent in medical malpractice cases is codified at ORS 677.097. ORS 677.097 provides, in part:

> "(1) In order to obtain the informed consent of a patient, a physician . . . shall explain the following:
>
> "(a) In general terms the procedure or treatment to be undertaken;
>
> "(b) That there may be alternative procedures or methods of treatment, if any; and,
>
> "(c) That there are risks, if any, to the procedure or treatment.
>
> "(2) After giving the explanation specified in subsection (1) of this section, the physician . . . shall ask the patient if the patient wants a more detailed explanation. If the patient requests further explanation, the physician . . . shall disclose in substantial detail the procedure, the viable alternatives and the material risks unless to do so would be materially detrimental to the patient."

In our view, it is significant that the statute requires a physician to "explain" the treatment, alternatives, and risks to his or her patient. "Explain" means "to make plain or understandable: clear of complexities or obscurity: . . . provide an understanding of [something]." Explanation implies more than a mere correct statement of the facts. An explanation clarifies an issue or makes it understandable to the recipient and, almost by definition, takes into account the mental state and capabilities of the recipient. For example, a physician can mouth words to an infant, or to a comatose person, or to a person who does not speak his or her language but, unless and until such patients are capable of understanding the physician's point, the physician cannot be said to have "explained" anything to any such person.

We also find it significant that the "explanation" requirement occurs in the context of describing what must be done to obtain a patient's informed consent. An "explanation" is "something that explains or that results from the act or process of explaining." In that context, it is clear that the whole point of explaining the required information is to ensure that patients have the information that they need to decide whether to agree to the recommended treatment. The concept presupposes that the patient is capable not only of understanding the risks of and alternatives to a proposed treatment, but of using that information in a rational decision-making process.

It follows that evidence that a patient did not, for whatever reason, have the capacity to understand and use what a physician told her would be relevant to show that the physician failed to obtain the patient's informed consent. That inquiry is not limited to evidence that purports to demonstrate an absolute inability to process a physician's words. In the context of the present case, for example, a reasonable juror might believe that a sexual relationship between defendant and Macy would undermine Macy's ability to listen objectively to and utilize information provided by the physician, in making an independent and informed decision about her health care.

For the foregoing reasons, we conclude that evidence of a sexual relationship between a physician and patient may be relevant to show that the physician failed to obtain the patient's informed consent for treatment, and that the evidence that the Macys offered here was relevant in that respect. The trial court therefore erred when it concluded that any evidence respecting a sexual relationship between defendant and Macy was irrelevant to the Macys' fourth specification of negligence.

NOTES AND QUESTIONS

1. Note that the *Macy* case involves sexual abuse, and so is included under § 3.02(3)(b). But the Court treats the issue as arising in an informed consent context. And so the case should be considered in § 3.03(1) as well, especially with reference to *Brown v. Dibbell* and *Perry v. Shaw*, *infra*. The Court in *Macy* treats sexual contact between doctor and patient as *part* of a cause of action, malpractice negligence, in obtaining informed consent. But can't it, shouldn't it, stand on its own? Ms. Macy went to seek treatment for pelvic pain; Doctor Blatchford delivered sex. Isn't that, *per se*, tortious? Say, a battery?
2. The Court says it is "unpersuaded" that physicians must use ordinary care and — even if drunk or in a "relationship with a patient" — if "actual treatment" reflects "the appropriate degree of care," there is no liability in negligence. Why? Isn't a sexual relationship *per se* contrary to appropriate care? The only remaining issue is not harm, but valuation.
3. Still, the Court admits evidence of the sexual relationship, but only as to failure to obtain informed consent. The patient might not think clearly; the doctor should have known; hence, negligence in having sex with her follows.

   But why, exactly? If *recommending* the surgery was objectively reasonable, then a reasonable patient would have accepted the recommendation. Hence, informed consent is presumed or irrelevant.
4. Finally, is it better to treat sexual relations as the wrong, or as *evidence* of a wrong? Are there defenses permissible one way, but not the other? Damages?
5. As to sexual abuse by other professionals, such as pastors, see *Jaqueline R. v. Household of Faith Family Church Inc.*, 118 Cal. Rptr. 2d 264 (Cal. App. 4 Dist. 2002). Should the standards be different?

§ 3.03 Fiduciary Obligations: Candor

For decades — perhaps centuries — physicians have communicated selectively with patients. This means — necessarily or not — they have withheld information from patients. They continue to do so today. But as medical procedures have become more standardized, diagnoses more certain and alternative treatments more numerous, better information has become *possible.* It has also become *obligatory,* as an ethical and legal matter, since evolving standards establish the choice of provider and service is the *patient's.* To enforce this, most jurisdictions now require a physician to advise as to procedures, alternatives and risks — at least to the limits of the understanding of both the [illegible] information, the patient can then give an "informed consent."

There are limits to candor and informed consent. For one thing, patients — in time of stress — realistically can understand only a limited amount of information. Also, much technical information is arcane and unnecessary. Moreover, a full understanding of risks, say with surgery, may be intimidating and disabling. Nevertheless, an ethical regard for a patient requires providing enough information so that his or her consent is "informed."

By consensus, the most significant court decision in this area is *Canterbury v. Spence*, to which we now turn. In so doing, however, we should note that since *Canterbury,* most jurisdictions have adopted statutes, varying greatly in elements, governing informed consent.

[1] Informed Consent

CANTERBURY v. SPENCE

464 F.2d 772 (D.C. Cir. 1972)

Spottswood W. **Robinson, III**, Circuit Judge.

I

The record we review tells a depressing tale. A youth troubled only by back pain submitted to an operation without being informed of a risk of paralysis incidental thereto. A day after the operation he fell from his hospital bed after having been left without assistance while voiding. A few hours after the fall, the lower half of his body was paralyzed, and he had to be operated on again. Despite extensive medical care, he has never been what he was before. Instead of the back pain, even years later, he hobbled about on crutches, a victim of paralysis of the bowels and urinary incontinence. In a very real sense this lawsuit is an understandable search for reasons.

At the time of the events which gave rise to this litigation, appellant was nineteen years of age, a clerk-typist employed by the Federal Bureau of Investigation. In December, 1958, he began to experience severe pain between his shoulder blades. He consulted two general practitioners, but the medications they prescribed failed to eliminate the pain. Thereafter, appellant secured an appointment with Dr. Spence, who is a neurosurgeon.

Dr. Spence examined appellant in his office at some length but found nothing amiss. On Dr. Spence's advice appellant was x-rayed, but the films did not identify any abnormality. Dr. Spence then recommended that appellant undergo a myelogram — a procedure in which dye is injected into the spinal column and traced to find evidence of disease or other disorder — at the Washington Hospital Center.

Appellant entered the hospital on February 4, 1959. The myelogram revealed a "filling defect" in the region of the fourth thoracic vertebra. Since a myelogram often does no more than pinpoint the location of an aberration, surgery may be necessary to discover the cause. Dr. Spence told appellant that he would have to undergo a laminectomy — the excision of the posterior arch of the vertebra — to correct what he suspected was a ruptured disc. Appellant did not raise any objection to the proposed operation nor did he probe into its exact nature.

Appellant explained to Dr. Spence that his mother was a widow of slender financial means living in Cyclone, West Virginia, and that she could be reached through a neighbor's telephone. . . . The testimony is contradictory as to whether during the course of the conversation Mrs. Canterbury expressed her consent to the operation. Appellant himself apparently did not converse again with Dr. Spence prior to the operation.

Dr. Spence performed the laminectomy on February 11 at the Washington Hospital Center. Mrs. Canterbury traveled to Washington, arriving on that date but after the operation was over, and signed a consent form at the hospital. The laminectomy revealed several anomalies: a spinal cord that was swollen and unable to pulsate, an accumulation of large tortuous and dilated veins, and a complete absence of epidural fat which normally surrounds the spine. A thin hypodermic needle was inserted into the spinal cord to aspirate any cysts which might have been present, but no fluid emerged. In suturing the wound, Dr. Spence attempted to relieve the pressure on the spinal cord by enlarging the dura — the other protective wall of the spinal cord — at the area of swelling.

For approximately the first day after the operation appellant recuperated normally, but then suffered a fall and an almost immediate setback. . . .

Several hours later, appellant began to complain that he could not move his legs and that he was having trouble breathing; paralysis seems to have been virtually total from the waist down. Dr. Spence was notified on the night of February 12, and he rushed to the hospital. Mrs. Canterbury signed another consent form and appellant was again taken into the operating room. The surgical wound was reopened and Dr. Spence created a gusset to allow the spinal cord greater room in which to pulsate.

Appellant's control over his muscles improved somewhat after the second operation but he was unable to void properly. As a result of this condition, he came under the care of an urologist while still in the hospital. In April, following a cystoscopic examination, appellant was operated on for removal of bladder stones, and in May was released from the hospital. He reentered the hospital the following August for a 10-day period, apparently because of his urologic problems. For several years after his discharge he was under the care of several specialists, and at all times was under the care of an urologist. At the time of the trial in April, 1968, appellant required crutches to walk, still suffered from urinal incontinence and paralysis of the bowels, and wore a penile clamp.

. . . .

III

. . . .

A physician is under a duty to treat his patient skillfully but proficiency in diagnosis and therapy is not the full measure of his responsibility. The cases demonstrate that the physician is under an obligation to [illegible] specific information to the [illegible] the exigencies of reasonable care call for it. Due care may require a physician perceiving symptoms of bodily abnormality to alert the patient to the condition. It may call upon the physician confronting an ailment which does not respond to his ministrations to inform the patient thereof. It may command the physician to instruct the patient as to any limitations to be presently observed for his own welfare, and as to any precautionary therapy he should seek in the future. It may oblige the physician to advise the patient of the need for or desirability of any alternative treatment promising greater benefit than that being pursued. Just as plainly, due care normally demands that the physician warn the patient of any risks to his well-being which contemplated therapy may involve.

. . . .

. . . [L]ong before the instant litigation arose, courts had recognized that the physician had the responsibility of satisfying the vital informational needs of the patient. More recently, we ourselves have found "in the fiducial qualities of [the physician-patient] relationship the physician's duty to reveal to the patient that which in his best interests it is important that he should know." We now find, as a part of the physician's overall obligation to the patient, a similar duty of reasonable disclosure of the choices with respect to proposed therapy and the dangers inherently and potentially involved.

IV

Duty to disclose has gained recognition in a large number of American jurisdictions, but more largely on a different rationale. The majority of courts dealing with the problem have made the duty depend on whether it was the custom of physicians practicing in the community to make the particular disclosure to the patient. If so, the physician may be held liable for an unreasonable and injurious failure to divulge, but there can be no recovery unless the omission forsakes a practice prevalent in the profession. We agree that the physician's noncompliance with a professional custom to reveal, [illegible] any other departure from prevailing [illegible] practice, may give rise to liability [illegible] patient. We do not agree that the patient's cause of action is dependent upon the existence and nonperformance of a relevant professional tradition.

. . . .

The majority rule, moreover, is at war with our prior holdings that a showing of medical practice, however probative, does not fix the standard governing recovery for medical malpractice. Prevailing medical practice, we have maintained, has evidentiary value in determinations as to what the specific criteria measuring challenged professional conduct are and whether they have been met, but does not itself define the standard. That has been our position in treatment cases, where the physician's performance is ordinarily to be adjudicated by the special medical standard of due care. We see no logic in a different rule for nondisclosure cases, where the governing standard is much more largely divorced from professional considerations. And surely in nondisclosure cases the factfinder is not invariably functioning in an area of such technical complexity that it must be bound to medical custom as an inexorable application of the community standard of reasonable care.

. . . .

V

Once the circumstances give rise to a duty on the physician's part to inform his patient, the next inquiry is the scope of the disclosure the physician is legally obliged to make. . . .

. . . .

In our view, the patient's right of self-decision shapes the boundaries of the duty to reveal. That right can be effectively exercised only if the patient possesses enough information to enable an intelligent choice. The scope of the physician's communications to the patient, then, must be measured by the patient's need, and that need is the information material to the decision. Thus the test for determining whether a particular peril must be divulged is its materiality to the patient's decision: all risks potentially affecting the decision must be unmasked. And to safeguard the patient's interest in achieving his own determination on treatment, the law must itself set the standard for adequate disclosure.

Optimally for the patient, exposure of a risk would be mandatory whenever the patient would deem it significant to his decision, either singly or in combination with other risks. Such a requirement, however, would summon the physician to second-guess the patient, whose ideas on materiality could hardly be known to the physician. That would make an undue demand upon medical practitioners, whose conduct, like that of others, is to be measured in terms of reasonableness. . . .

. . . .

From these considerations we derive the breadth of the disclosure of risks legally to be required. The scope of the standard is not subjective as to either the physician or the patient; it remains objective with due regard for the patient's informational needs and with suitable leeway for the physician's situation. In broad outline, we agree that "[a] risk is thus material when a reasonable person, in what the physician knows or should know to be the patient's position, would be likely to attach significance to the risk or cluster of risks in deciding whether or not to forego the proposed therapy."

The topics importantly demanding a communication of information are the inherent and potential hazards of the proposed treatment, the alternatives to that treatment, if any, and the results likely if the patient remains untreated. The factors contributing significance to the dangerousness of a medical technique are, of course, the incidence of injury and the degree of the harm threatened. A very small chance of death or serious disablement may well be significant; a potential disability which dramatically outweighs the potential benefit of the therapy or the detriments of the existing malady may summon discussion with the patient.

. . . .

VI

Two exceptions to the general rule of disclosure have been noted by the courts. Each is in the nature of a physician's privilege not to disclose, and the reasoning underlying them is appealing. Each, indeed, is but a recognition that, as important as is the patient's right to know, it is greatly outweighed by the magnitudinous circumstances giving rise to the privilege. The first comes into play when the patient is unconscious or otherwise incapable of consenting, and harm from a failure to treat is imminent and outweighs any harm threatened by the proposed treatment.

The second exception obtains when risk-disclosure poses such a threat of detriment to the patient as to become unfeasible or contraindicated from a medical point of view. It is recognized that patients occasionally become so ill or emotionally distraught on disclosure as to foreclose a rational decision, or complicate or hinder the treatment, or perhaps even pose psychological damage to the patient. Where that is so, the cases have generally held that the physician is armed with a privilege to keep the information from the patient, and we think it clear that portents of that type may justify the physician in action he deems medically warranted. The critical inquiry is whether the physician responded to a sound medical judgment that communication of the risk information would present a threat to the patient's well-being.

. . . .

VII

No more than breach of any other legal duty does nonfulfillment of the physician's obligation to disclose alone establish liability to the patient. An unrevealed risk that should have been made known must materialize, for otherwise the omission, however unpardonable, is legally without consequence. Occurrence of the risk must be harmful to the patient, for negligence unrelated to injury is nonactionable. And, as in malpractice actions generally, there must be causal relationship between the physician's failure to adequately divulge and damage to the patient.

. . . .

It has been assumed that the issue is to be resolved according to whether the factfinder believes the patient's testimony that he would not have agreed to the treatment if he had known of the danger which later ripened into injury. We think a technique which ties the factual conclusion on causation simply to the assessment of the patient's credibility is unsatisfactory. . . .

. . . .

Better it is, we believe, to resolve the causality issue on an objective basis: in terms of what a prudent person in the patient's position would have decided if suitably informed of all perils bearing significance. If adequate disclosure could reasonably be expected to have caused that person to decline the treatment because of the revelation of the kind of risk or danger that resulted in harm, causation is shown, but otherwise not. The patient's testimony is relevant on that score of course but it would not threaten to dominate the findings. And since that testimony would probably be appraised congruently with the factfinder's belief in its reasonableness, the case for a wholly objective standard for passing on causation is strengthened. Such a standard would in any event ease the fact-finding process and better assure the truth as its product.

. . . .

X

This brings us to the remaining question, common to all three causes of action: whether appellant's evidence was of such caliber as to require a submission to the jury. On the first, the evidence was clearly sufficient to raise an issue as to whether Dr. Spence's obligation to disclose information on risks was reasonably met or was excused by the surrounding circumstances. Appellant testified that Dr. Spence revealed to him nothing suggesting a hazard associated with the laminectomy. His mother testified that, in response to her specific inquiry, Dr. Spence informed her that the laminectomy was no more serious than any other operation. When, at trial, it developed from Dr. Spence's testimony that a paralysis can be expected in one percent of laminectomies, it became the jury's responsibility to decide whether that peril was of sufficient magnitude to bring the disclosure duty into play. There was no emergency to frustrate an opportunity to disclose, and Dr. Spence's expressed opinion that disclosure would have been unwise did not foreclose a contrary conclusion by the jury. There was no evidence that appellant's emotional makeup was such that concealment of the risk of analysis was medically sound. Even if disclosure to appellant himself might have bred ill consequences, no reason appears for the omission to communicate the information to his mother, particularly in view of his minority. The jury, not Dr. Spence, was the final arbiter of whether nondisclosure was reasonable under the circumstances.

. . . .

Reversed and remanded for a new trial.

NOTES AND QUESTIONS

1. *Canterbury* is widely regarded as the leading case on informed consent, along with *Cobbs v. Grant*, 8 Cal. 3d 229 (Cal. 1972), a California decision to the same effect. We have previously encountered the concept of informed consent in Rawls, where he discusses the ethical importance of an agreement between people as central to any relationship. Hence, slavery, in Rawls' point of view, could never be ethically justified. What would Rawls say about the principle of informed consent in general, or as articulated in *Canterbury*?
2. Physicians and health care providers frequently view "informed consent" as simply a hurdle or a form to be cleared. They speak of "taking" informed consent, by which they often mean assigning a subordinate or assistant the task of having the patient sign off on a form. Ethicists and other health care providers, particularly nurses, view "informed

consent" differently as a *process* in which information and understanding are exchanged and gained, providing the permission which an autonomous person may grant or deny for [illegible] consent, [illegible] relates directly to the constitutional and ethical concepts discussed in the preceding chapters.

3. Informed consent also relates directly to medical malpractice, as in *Canterbury v. Spence*. Here, there are two quite different concepts. First, *without* informed consent, any procedure is unauthorized and, by definition, malpractice. Indeed, it may even be an "unconsented touching," which constitutes a battery in the law of torts. Separately, the *administration* itself of the informed consent process may constitute malpractice, where, for example, the physician either fails to provide important information or, having done so, fails to recognize or abide by the patient's reservations, implicit or expressed.

4. In *Canterbury,* the Court holds that the information which must be provided is that which would be important (or "material") to the *specific patient* before the physician. Other courts have held that the physician only need provide the information required by a "reasonable" patient. The *Canterbury* standard is thus more demanding, requiring the physician to focus on the particular person in the position of the patient, with all of his or her anxieties, needs and reservations. Does this make sense in ethical terms? In legal terms? Is it a useful standard for organizing the delivery of health care? Which would you prefer — a subjective or objective standard — if you were a patient? Physician? Hospital administrator? Judge in a malpractice case?

5. *Canterbury* goes on to hold that nondisclosure can lead to liability only if the patient would have chosen against the treatment. One would expect the Court to be consistent and say that this measure of "causality" should be subjective and, since the advice is that required by the specific patient, the decision must belong to the specific patient as well. But the Court instead opts for an objective or reasonable patient standard; that is, the physician is liable only if a reasonable patient would have — properly informed — chosen against the treatment. [illegible] reasonable [illegible] gone forward, the physician is not liable, even if the *specific,* actual patient would have chosen — unreasonably, perhaps neurotically — to decline the treatment. Is this a good standard? Is it ethical? Does it ease or complicate the problems of proof at trial?

6. Note that some courts have opted against *Canterbury v. Spence.* In *Arena v. Gingrich*, 748 P.2d 547 (Or. 1988), the Oregon Supreme Court held that the standard of causation should be subjective. The court said that this opened the possibility that a patient moved by "bitterness or disillusion" might fabricate a claim that he or she would have declined treatment, but that issues of credibility are frequently determined by juries. It concluded that the issues of materiality and causality both should be determined in the light of the needs of the specific patient. Do you agree?

7. The concept of "informed consent" is embodied in the statutes of a number — perhaps the majority — of states. Although the formulations vary, they in general provide that a physician must advise a patient of the procedures the physician contemplates, the alternatives to them and the risks involved in each.

The next two cases *Carr v. Strode* and *Aden v. Younger* deal with statutory formulations in quite different settings. Evaluate those statutes — and cases — in the light of *Canterbury*.

CARR v. STRODE

904 P.2d 489 (Haw. 1995)

Opinion of the Court by **Moon,** C.J.

This case concerns a failed vasectomy operation that resulted in the unplanned birth of a healthy child. . . . Plaintiffs claim that defendants failed to obtain Carr's informed consent to perform the vasectomy operation.

I. Background

A. Facts

Carr and Sorrell are married, and, at the time of Carr's vasectomy, resided in Hawaii. During Sorrell's pregnancy with their second child, Carr and Sorrell decided not to have any more children because of financial and educational concerns. . . .

In November 1985, Carr had his first vasectomy consultation with Dr. Strode, a Straub employee. On December 5, 1985, Carr, accompanied by Sorrell, had a second vasectomy consultation with Dr. Strode. Dr. Strode performed the vasectomy operation on December 9, 1985, and subsequently saw Carr on December 12, 1985 for a follow-up examination. On January 13, 1986, Straub informed Carr that, because no live sperm had been found in the sperm sample analysis taken after the vasectomy, he was sterile.

In April 1986, Sorrell discovered that she was pregnant. On April 26, 1986, Carr gave Dr. Strode another sperm sample, which, upon analysis, revealed 340,000 dead sperm. At trial, Dr. Strode admitted that dead sperm could indicate that Carr was producing live sperm. On April 30, 1986, Carr submitted a second sperm sample which contained 21 sperm, six of which were live. Although Dr. Strode offered to perform a second vasectomy at no charge to Carr, Carr rejected this offer because he believed that Dr. Strode had performed the first vasectomy incorrectly.

. . . .

B. Prior Proceedings

On December 17, 1991, the jury returned a verdict in favor of plaintiffs, awarding them $75,000.00 in general damages on count II (lack of informed consent) only. Judgment was entered accordingly.

Post trial, defendants filed a motion for a JNOV, or, in the alternative, for a new trial. After a hearing on the matter, the trial court granted defendants' motion for a JNOV because the jury instructions had stated [illegible] must prove [illegible] legal cause based on medical expert evidence," noting that it had heard "no medical evidence presented by the plaintiff Robin Carr at all."

. . . .

II. Discussion

A. Plaintiffs' Appeal

In *Nishi v. Hartwell* [*infra* § 3.03[2]], this court acknowledged a common law cause of action for a physician's negligent failure "to disclose to [his or her] patient all relevant information concerning a proposed treatment, including the collateral hazards attendant thereto." . . .

. . . .

Despite our acknowledgment of the doctrine of informed consent, we nevertheless affirmed the trial court's dismissal of Nishi's complaint for two alternative reasons. First, the defendant-physicians' alleged failure to disclose the collateral risk of the thoracic aortography procedure that injured Nishi was justified by the therapeutic privilege exception to the physician's duty to disclose risk information. This exception recognizes that, under some circumstances, disclosure of certain risks would not be in the patient's best medical interests. Undisputed testimony was presented at trial that Nishi was apprehensive about his heart and circulatory system problems and that disclosure of information may have exacerbated his condition.

Second, and most importantly for the present case, under the "physician-oriented" or "professional" standard of disclosure, Nishi bore the burden to produce expert medical testimony "to establish a medical standard from which the jury could find that defendants deviated from their duty [of disclosure] to [the plaintiff]." . . .

Two years later, however, the United States Court of Appeals for the District of Columbia Circuit decided the seminal case of *Canterbury v. Spence* . . .

. . . .

Following *Canterbury*, the Hawaii legislature in 1976 enacted HRS Chapter 671, which deals specifically with informed consent and provides in pertinent part:

Informed Consent; Board of Medical Examiners Standards.

(a) The board of medical examiners, insofar as practicable, shall establish standards for health care providers to follow in giving information to a patient . . .

(b) If the standards established by the board of medical examiners include provisions which are designed to reasonably inform a patient, or a patient's guardian, of:

(1) The condition being treated;

(2) The nature and character of the proposed treatment or surgical procedure;

(3) The anticipated results;

(4) The recognized possible alternative forms of treatment; and

(5) The recognized serious possible risks, complications, and anticipated benefits involved in the treatment or surgical procedure, and in the recognized possible alternative forms of treatment, including nontreatment,

then the standards shall be admissible as evidence of the standard of care of the health care providers.

. . . .

2. The Patient-Oriented Standard Governs the Physician's Duty to Disclose Risk Information Prior to Treatment

Ideally, and in the abstract, the physician-oriented standard — i.e., what a reasonable physician believes should be disclosed to a patient prior to treatment in order for the patient to make an informed and intelligent decision regarding a course of treatment or surgery — and the patient-oriented standard — i.e., what a reasonable patient needs to hear from his or her physician in order to make an informed and intelligent decision regarding treatment or surgery — would dictate the same scope of disclosure, barring the applicability of any of the exceptions to a physician's duty to disclose. We must assume, for purposes of fashioning a prospective rule, that physicians seek to provide their patients with the same amount and quality of risk information prior to treatment that the patient would need to hear in order to make an informed and intelligent choice. Both standards, therefore, tempered by objectivity, seek to achieve the same goal, that is, to insure that the patient's decision to undergo a particular medical procedure is an informed and intelligent decision.

The dispositive issue, therefore, is one of proof; in other words, which party's viewpoint should dictate the standard against which the conduct in issue should be judged? The *Bernard* court provided the following rationale:

> Courts which apply [the patient-oriented] standard emphasize what the patient needs to know to make an informed decision, rather than what the medical community thinks the patient should be told. . . . [The patient-oriented] standard provides the patient with effective protection against a possible conspiracy of silence wherever it may exist among physicians. Moreover, since the patient must suffer the consequences, and since he or she bears all the expenses of the medical treatment, fundamental fairness requires that the patient be allowed to know what risks a proposed treatment entails, what the alternatives thereto are and the relative probabilities of success. . . .

We believe that the patient-oriented standard of disclosure better respects the patient's right of self-determination and affixes the focus of the inquiry regarding the standard of disclosure on the motivating force and purpose of the doctrine of informed consent — aiding the individual patient in making an important decision regarding medical care. It also protects against the pitfalls of proof associated with the physician-oriented standard discussed in *Canterbury*. Moreover, not only should the patient's decision [illegible] the physician's disclosure to his or her patient in each case, but we also believe that, barring situations where the therapeutic privilege exception to the physician's duty to disclose is applicable, what the *medical community* believes the patient needs to hear in order for the patient to make an informed decision is insufficient, without more, to resolve the question of what an *individual patient* reasonably needs to hear in order for that patient to make an informed and intelligent choice regarding the proposed medical treatment.

. . . .

The dispositive inquiry regarding the physician's duty to disclose in an informed consent case, therefore, is not what the physician believes his or her patient needs to hear in order for the patient to make an informed and intelligent decision; the focus should be on what a reasonable person objectively needs to hear from his or her physician to allow the patient to make an informed and intelligent decision regarding proposed medical treatment.

We strongly caution, however, as did the ICA in Bernard, that our adoption of the patient-oriented standard does not relieve plaintiffs of their burden to provide expert medical testimony as to the "materiality" of the risk; to the contrary, a plaintiff maintains the burden of adducing expert medical testimony to establish "the nature of risks inherent in a particular treatment, the probabilities of therapeutic success, the frequency of the occurrence of particular risks, and the nature of available alternatives to treatment." . . .

Therefore, the net prospective effect of our holding today is that a plaintiff's case will not fail for lack of expert medical testimony regarding the prevailing standard of disclosure in the medical community for a particular medical procedure or treatment.

. . . .

. . . [A] plaintiff is not required to prove the standard of disclosure required for informed consent with medical expert evidence, but is required to prove by expert medical evidence the materiality of the risk of harm to which the plaintiff was subjected. It is clear that a [illegible] testimony may [illegible] this burden. . . .

. . . .

However, Dr. Strode testified that "a urologist is required, in the general setting of informed consent, to indicate to the patient that the procedure is not guaranteed to succeed." Dr. Strode explained that "medicine is not an exact science and no procedure can be guaranteed, of any kind, vasectomy included." Although indicating a requirement to disclose that a procedure was "not guaranteed," Dr. Strode also stated that the exact wording was a matter within the urologist's discretion. Based on Dr. Strode's testimony, we hold that plaintiffs met their burden of establishing the materiality of the risk of the vasectomy failing through the defendant-physician's expert medical testimony.

. . . .

Defendants retort by asserting that, although Dr. Strode may not have uttered certain specific words, his discussions with plaintiffs prior to performing the vasectomy on Carr constituted a "statement" that the procedure might fail. Defendants claim that Dr. Strode informed Carr about the failure rates associated with vasectomies and told Carr that he could not guarantee his permanent sterility. Additionally, defendants note that Carr himself admitted that Dr. Strode informed him that the surgery had a ninety-nine percent success rate, which necessarily implies that Carr was made aware that the procedure had at least a one percent failure rate. . . .

. . . .

The inquiry before the jury for resolution was whether Dr. Strode provided Carr with sufficient information so as to insure that Carr's consent to submit to the vasectomy procedure was "informed." The circuit court's finding that Dr. Strode failed to specifically state to Carr that "the vasectomy procedure might fail, and if such failure were to occur, that it would or could cause Carr to remain fertile or become fertile again in the future" not only foreclosed the jury's consideration of one of, if not the most, effective means of informing Carr of an important recognized risk associated with the vasectomy procedure, but closely paralleled the ultimate issue before the jury. Under the narrow circumstances surrounding the informed consent inquiry and, because of the similarity between the issue resolved by the circuit court's finding and the ultimate issue in the case, we believe the circuit court's finding amounted to reversible error due to the likelihood that it prejudiced the jury's consideration and resolution of the issue of Dr. Strode's liability on the informed consent claim.

. . . .

NOTES AND QUESTIONS

1. In *Carr v. Strode*, the Hawaii Supreme Court reverses *Nishi* (which appears *infra* at § 3.03[2]), finding that the subsequent developments in *Canterbury* and Hawaii statutes, compel a "patient-oriented" standard of informed consent. The Court, in reversing *Nishi,* notes that it partially turned on the "therapeutic privilege" principle, which is carefully preserved as an exception to informed consent. But does the exception, in reality, survive *Canterbury* and *Carr*?
2. No expert is needed, the *Carr* court says, to prove the standard of disclosure required of a physician. But an expert *is* required as to what risks are "material." Does the distinction make sense? And, how do you prove causation? If the husband had known of the 1% possibility of recanalization, would he (as a reasonable patient) have chosen against a vasectomy?
3. Is the Hawaii statute consistent with *Canterbury* ? Is the *Carr* court's interpretation? What effect should a court give official standards of practice?
4. What would you advise the physician to tell people in *the future*?

5. How would *you* draft a general purpose informed consent statute for a specific context such as psycho-surgery and electro-convulsive therapy, as in the next case, *Aden v. Younger*?

ADEN v. YOUNGER*

57 Cal. App. 3d 662 (Ca. 1976)

Gerald **Brown**, Presiding Justice.

Petitioners Jane Doe and Betty Roe are mentally ill. Doe has had electroconvulsive therapy (ECT) and may need further voluntary treatments. Roe wants a surgical "multiple target procedure," or psychosurgery. Petitioner Aden, a licensed California physician is certified by the American Board of Psychiatry and Neurology as a specialist in the treatment of psychiatric illnesses. Dr. Aden is Jane Doe's attending physician. Dr. Brown who is a California licensed surgeon and physician, is Betty Roe's treating physician and surgeon. He specializes in neurosurgery and is a member of the American Board of Neurological Surgeons and the American College of Surgeons. Petitioner Campbell is a licensed California physician and surgeon, with a specialty in neurology and psychiatry for over 30 years, but he is not certified by the American Board of Psychiatry and Neurology.

The Attorney General, the Director of Health, and the Board of Medical Examiners are respondents.

The law involved in this petition is part of the Lanterman-Petris-Short Act. The law changes conditions under which psychosurgery and shock treatment can be performed. The changes applicable to persons involuntarily detained and persons voluntarily admitted to state hospitals, private mental institutions, county psychiatric hospitals and certain mentally retarded persons, are:

Psychosurgery.

Patients have the right to refuse psychosurgery and the professional person in charge of the facility may not deny them that right. If a patient refuses consent, it must be entered on the record.

If a patient wants psychosurgery, then the conditions for performing such surgery include:

(a) The patient [illegible] consent, dated, witnessed and entered in his record. The consent may be withdrawn at any time. An oral explanation by the doctor is necessary.

(b) The patient must have capacity to consent.

. . .

(d) The reasons for surgery must be in the patient's treatment record, other treatments must be exhausted and surgery must be critically needed.

(e) Three appointed physicians (two board-certified psychiatrists or neurosurgeons), must examine the patient and unanimously agree with the treating physician's determinations and that the patient has capacity to consent. There must be a 72-hour wait after the patient's written consent before surgery.

* Most of the citation material has been omitted from this case.

Shock Treatment

If the treating physician feels shock treatments are necessary, he must give an extensive oral explanation to the patient and his relative, guardian, or conservator.

Shock treatments shall be performed only after:

(a) The patient gives written informed consent.

(b) The patient has capacity to consent.

(c) A relative, guardian or conservator has been given a thorough oral explanation.

(d) "Adequate documentation" has been entered in the patient's record. All other treatments have been exhausted and the treatment is critically needed.

(e) There has been a review by three appointed physicians (two board-certified) who agree with the treating physician that the patient has capacity to consent.

If the patient does not have the capacity to consent, shock treatments can be given if conditions (c), (d) and (e) are met.

No shock treatments may be given if the patient is able to give informed consent and refuses.

. . . .

Petitioners assert the changes are unconstitutional in certain respects and want a peremptory writ of mandate permanently preventing respondents from enforcing the amendments.

. . . .

Perhaps the most striking feature of authorities (and case law) in the area dealt with by this legislation is they are quite uniform in acknowledging that the processes by which electroconvulsive therapy and psychosurgery induce therapeutic effects are not fully understood. The two modes of treatment are quite different in several aspects and their relevant characteristics will be considered briefly and separately.

Psychosurgery . . . includes those operations "referred to as lobotomy, psychiatric surgery, and behavioral surgery. . . ." Instructive and persuasive in this area is the case of *Kaimowitz v. Department of Mental Health for the State of Michigan*, 2 Prison L. Rptr. 433. . . .

The distinctive feature of such psychosurgical procedures is the destruction, removal, or disconnection of brain tissue in order to modify or control "thoughts, feelings, actions, or behavior" when the tissue is normal or when there is no evidence any abnormality has caused the behavioral disorder.[1] Psychosurgery is also distinguished from "shock" therapy by its experimental nature. Psychosurgery is an irreversible alteration of the brain and its

[1] The lack of tissue abnormality, or causal relation between an abnormality and character or behavior disorder is the primary feature of the definition. . . . This characteristic is emphasized in the definitions adopted by the court in Kaimowitz v. Department of Mental Health for the State of Michigan. . . .

functions that presents serious risks to patients, some of which risks are unknown. . . .

"Shock" treatment, more [illegible] electroconvulsive therapy" (ECT), is the name given to a group of therapies which involves passing electrical currents through the brain in order to induce convulsions. The therapeutic effects of ECT are generally believed to be obtained by the seizure produced by the stimulation of the central nervous system. The risks attending such treatment have been greatly reduced by the use of muscle relaxants and general anesthetics, which greatly reduce the body convulsions that led to bone fractures in the past. The mechanism by which ECT confers its benefits is still unknown, but two facts stand out in almost every discussion of the treatment: first, ECT does relieve symptoms of certain mental illnesses, most notably acute depression, and is widely recognized therapy for obtaining remission of those symptoms; second, ECT has several adverse effects, including memory loss and intellectual disorientation. The extent of memory loss and the risk of permanent memory loss are not fully known or agreed upon, but the fact of memory loss is not questioned. The risk of other adverse effects is possible, since the procedure is still so little understood. Those possible risks include permanent brain damage in the local area of the electrodes and a slowing of brain waves. The outstanding features of ECT, then, are the acknowledged benefits in the treatment of certain illnesses, and the intrusive and possibly hazardous character of the treatment.

. . . .

A. Equal Protection

. . . .

. . . The objective of the challenged law is to ensure certain medical procedures are not performed on unwilling patients. The classifications that single out mental patients and two specific procedures are rationally related to that objective.

Mental patients are distinct from other ill patients in two special circumstances. First, their competence to accede to treatment is more questionable than that of other patients. Mental [illegible] may not be presumed solely by their hospitalization, but it is common knowledge mentally-ill persons are more likely to lack the ability to understand the nature of a medical procedure and appreciate its risks. Second, their ability to voluntarily accept treatment is questionable. "Voluntary" patients, newly included within the protection of the "Patients' Bill of Rights" (§ 5325) are susceptible to many of the pressures placed on involuntary patients. The Legislature's inclusion of these "voluntary" patients recognizes the fact the "voluntary" label is a creation of the Legislature, and often only means the patient did not formally protest hospitalization. These circumstances make the separate treatment of mental patients clearly rationally related to the objective of ensuring their rights to refuse treatment. The special regulation of psychosurgery and ECT is also a reasonable classification because these procedures, associated with mental illness, present a great danger of violating the patient's rights.

Petitioners and amici in support of the petition assert Section 5326.4 conflicts with California law and violates patients' constitutional rights as declared in *Cobbs v. Grant*. Petitioners object to the requirement "[a]ll of the possible risks and possible side effects to the patient should he consent" to ECT, be disclosed to the patient as an element of the "informed consent" necessary before treatment. Petitioners do not object to the almost identical language of Section 5326.3 referring to the elements of informed consent for psychosurgery. Petitioners rely on *Cobbs v. Grant*, contending that decision gives patients the right to refuse information.

The court in *Cobbs* was concerned with the patient's right to express an informed consent before medical treatment. The petitioners rely on language which concerns a doctor's defenses to tort actions for batter or negligence. In the context of a malpractice suit, the patient's request to be left uninformed would be a defense to the doctor's nondisclosure. The court also said the only time a patient should be "denied the opportunity to weigh the risks" is "where it is evident he cannot evaluate the data, as for example, where there is an emergency or the patient is a child or incompetent."

Thus, a patient's request to be left uninformed may provide a doctor a defense to a tort action, but it does not obligate or constitutionally coerce the doctor into acceding to the patient's wishes. The Legislature has determined ECT and psychosurgery are such intrusive and hazardous procedures that informed consent is a mandatory prerequisite to treatment. *Cobbs v. Grant* does not prevent such a determination; it provides that, except in the instances of simple procedures, or where the patient is incompetent to make a decision, there is a right to full information. The right to fully informed consent protects the patient's constitutional rights.

B. Vagueness

. . . .

Petitioners contend various provisions of the new statute are so ambiguous they cannot be constitutionally enforced: first, the terms "private mental institution," "psychosurgery" and "shock treatment;" second, the terms which establish elements of informed consent; and third, the terms which refer to the criteria for approval by a review committee.

. . . .

Contrary to petitioners' contentions "psychosurgery" and "shock treatment" have established technical meanings. The meaning of "psychosurgery" is evident on the face of the statute. It clearly does not refer to surgical procedures other than those used for modification of behavior, thought, or feelings, in the treatment of mental illnesses. "Shock treatment" is an inexact term since it refers to the characteristics of "shock" rather than "convulsion," which is the primary feature of that form of treatment. It is clear, however, the Legislature intended to include electroconvulsive therapy (ECT) within the term "shock treatment" and did not intend to include "defibrillation of the heart" which is not associated with the treatment of mental disorders. It is less clear whether convulsive therapies based on drug-induced convulsions are properly included within the term. "Shock treatment" does not necessarily include all convulsive therapies, although the intention of the Legislature to so include them may be inferred from their similarity to ECT in almost every respect. Because certain drug therapies are [illegible] therapies, it is reasonable to conclude "shock treatment" is not restricted to ECT, and includes both insulin coma therapy and other drug-induced convulsion therapies.

. . . .

The contention the subsections requiring explanations of all of the possible risks, possible side effects, and the degree of uncertainty of the benefits and hazards associated with the procedure, are void for vagueness is also unmeritorious. Whatever may be the wisdom of such a strict standard of disclosure, the statutory language calls for a full explanation to the patient of all relevant information. Thus, the requirement of all possible risks and possible side effects must be read to mean the disclosure of all risks and side effects thought to be associated with these procedures. . . .

There is, however, one criterion which is so imprecise this Court is compelled to conclude it as impermissibly vague: the requirement a procedure be "critically" needed for the patient's welfare. While the "welfare" of a patient is arguably imprecise, it encompasses the patient's physical well-being, psychological health, ability to function in his society, and ability to attain happiness — a broad range of interests to be considered and protected. The requirement of a procedure be "critically" needed for the patient's welfare, however, provides no guide to the degree of need required.

. . . .

"Critically" means "in a critical manner." "Critical" means "crucial, decisive;" "in or approaching a crisis;" "of doubtful issue; attended by risk or uncertainty" (Webster's 3d New Internat. Dict., Unabridged). "Critical" is also defined as "fraught with danger or risk; perilous." A patient with acute depression and suicidal tendencies would come within the standard if the form of treatment were essential to protect his life. But what of the patient who does not have self-destructive tendencies and is completely dysfunctional psychologically? Does an inability to remain employed [illegible] a critical condition? Must there be a danger of deterioration, or is a stable condition of severe psychosis critical? If all other forms of appropriate therapies have been attempted, has a "critical" need for ECT or psychosurgery been established?

It seems probable the legislative intent was to require a compelling need for these forms of treatment beyond the mere existence of a behavioral or mental disorder. There seems to be a tacit assumption by the Legislature that the cure is sometimes more harmful than the disease, and only the most dangerous and harmful conditions should be so treated. Some persons of "common intelligence" may agree an assessment of impending injury, absent prompt treatment, gives rise to a critical need. Others of like intelligence may demand considerably more, or somewhat less. We conclude on its face the "critically needed" criterion is impermissibly vague.

C. Due Process

The regulation of ECT and psychosurgery is a legitimate exercise of the state's inherent policy power. The state has an interest in seeing that these procedures, like other medical procedures, are performed under circumstances ensuring maximum safety for the patient. These two procedures are not identical in their effect on the patient, nor in their acceptance by the medical community, and may be regulated in different ways and to differing extents. The state has an interest in protecting patients from unwarranted, unreasonable and unconsented-to invasions of body and mind. Arrayed against these legitimate state interests are equally valid considerations of rights of privacy, freedom of speech and thought, and the right to medical treatment.[2]

. . . .

The right to be free in the exercise of one's own thoughts is essential to the exercise of other constitutionally guaranteed rights. First Amendment rights of free speech would mean little if the state were to control thought. "Our whole constitutional heritage rebels at the thought of giving government the power to control men's minds. . . ." (*Stanley v. Georgia.*) Here the state has sought to control neither what is thought by mental patients, nor how they think. Rather, the state is attempting to regulate the use of procedures which touch upon thought processes in significant ways, with neither the intention nor the effect of regulating thought processes, per se. Yet despite the lack of any showing the state has attempted to regulate freedom of thought, this legislation may diminish this right. If so, the legislation can only be sustained by showing (1) it is necessary to further a "compelling state interest" and (2) the least drastic means has been employed to further those interests.

Freedom of thought is intimately touched upon by any regulation of procedures affecting thought and feelings. In an effort to protect freedom of thought, the state has put procedural and substantive obstacles in the path of those who both need and desire certain forms of treatment, and in that way their freedom of thought remains impaired because they cannot get treatment. The means of alleviating mental disorders generate their own kinds of fear and misunderstanding. This attitude touches our public affairs; the fact of treatment alone may impair our confidence in people of unquestioned talent and industry. Psychosurgery and ECT are viewed, rightly or wrongly, as drastic, radical forms of treatment compared to psychotherapy or drug therapy, and indicative of more severe illness. Public exposure, or even disclosure to limited numbers of government representatives, may have a chilling effect on patients' efforts to undergo these treatments, thereby restricting their freedom of thought. Some patients will be denied treatment as a natural and intended result of this legislation. Although the reasons for such denials may be the patients' own best interests, such regulation must be justified by a compelling state interest.

---

[2] On the one hand, out of deference to personal autonomy, the state prohibits involuntary treatment. On the other hand, again out of deference to personal autonomy, the state promotes access to voluntary treatment which restores functionality and thus enhances future autonomy. (See Shapiro, *Legislating the Control of Behavior Control: Autonomy and the Coercive Use of Organic Therapies*, 47 S. Cal. L. rev. 237.)

As previously explained, there are three changes because of the new legislation: First, voluntary patients as well as institutionalized mentally-retarded persons are included within the mental [illegible] the Lanterman-Petris-Short Act. This change recognizes the fact that "voluntary" and "involuntary" labels do not always indicate the voluntariness of a specific patient. Second, the denial of patients' rights for good cause was made inapplicable to psychosurgery and "shock treatment" by requiring the informed consent of the patient prior to treatment. To this end, the Legislature defined the contents of informed consent. The purpose was to ensure consent was competent, informed, and voluntary. Third, a review procedure was established to determine the patient's competence and the necessity and appropriateness of the proposed treatment. The review procedure was also established to approve the administration of "shock treatment" to patients who were found incompetent to give or withhold consent.

Additionally, the new law requires informing a "responsible relative," as well as the patient, of the risks of treatment to obtain informed consent. In order to control abuse of denials of patients' rights, a system of reporting is established.

. . . .

The provision that a "responsible relative" be informed of the eight items constituting "informed consent" before the treatment be administered is a violation of the patient's right of privacy and the right to confidentiality. The disclosure of the nature and seriousness of the patient's disorder is a clear infringement of the patient's right of privacy and no countervailing state interest is apparent. Because no standing to assert the patient's rights is granted to the relative, it is doubtful this disclosure furthers the protection of patients' rights or prevents unnecessary treatment. Thus, the requirement of such disclosure is an unconstitutional invasion of the patient's right to privacy.

The establishment of a reporting system seeking to control possible abuses of patients' rights would be a clear invasion of the patients' privacy if the patients' identities were disclosed. The state has a valid interest in the prevention of denials of patients' rights without good cause, and such a reporting system is [illegible] achieving that end. To further that end, it must be possible to identify which patients' rights are denied, both to correct individual wrongs and to correct general patterns of abuse. Thus, the report to the Director of Health must provide for identification of individual treatment records. . . .

. . . .

. . . [L]isting items of information that must be orally explained to the patient in order to get his informed consent before treatment, constitutes a minimal invasion of privacy. An oral explanation only invades the patient's privacy to the extent the treating physician would not otherwise be in possession of such information. The information is not recorded in the patient's record and is not made available to any review committee. The explanation does ensure the patient gives consent in a knowing, intelligent, and voluntary manner. The state's interest in protecting the patient's right to refuse treatment could not be accomplished by any measure short of such disclosure, and the procedure is constitutional.

The most difficult aspects of this legislation involve the mandatory review of proposed treatments by a review committee. As discussed above, the two forms of treatment are distinct and may be regulated to differing degrees. An analysis of the review procedures involved in each form of treatment will be considered separately.

Consent to psychosurgery is regulated and applied differently to three groups of patients: incompetent, involuntary, and all others. The state's interest in protecting patients from unconsented-to and unnecessary administrations of psychosurgery clearly justifies a review procedure which ensures the competence of the patient and the truly voluntary nature of his consent. The incompetent patient is incapable of consenting to such a procedure, and the state's interest in protecting him from such procedures fully justifies the attendant invasion of privacy. Although there are substantial problems of procedural due process involved, a review of a patient's competence by a review committee is constitutional where, as here, there is reason to suspect incompetence.

The involuntary patient presents the dilemma of either prohibiting the administration of psychosurgery to such patients or providing for a substitute decisionmaking process. Because the voluntariness of such a patient's consent can never be adequately confirmed, the establishment of a review committee to make the treatment decision for the patient is justified by the state's compelling interest in preventing involuntary administration of psychosurgery.

The substantive review of proposed treatments for competent and voluntary patients is a different problem. Once the competency of the patient and voluntariness of the consent is confirmed, what interest of the state can justify the substitution of the review committee's decision for that of the patient and his physician?

The hazardous, experimental nature of psychosurgery is a legitimate reason for the state to regulate its use as a treatment of last resort. Requiring unanimity by the review committee ensures each approved treatment is an appropriate use of an experimental procedure. The importance of assuring that consents to psychosurgery be voluntarily given by informed, competent mental patients, plus the need to regulate an experimental procedure, justify the Legislature's decision to remove these considerations from the sole discretion of the treating physician. . . .

The new regulatory scheme as it applies to "shock treatment" is almost identical to the regulatory system for psychosurgery. . . . In the case of incompetent patients, the substitute decisionmaking process permits the use of this form of treatment for patients who cannot consent for themselves. These applications of Section 5326.4 are constitutional for the reasons previously discussed.

The thorny question concerns the application of the review system to voluntary competent patients. As already noted, the state has a compelling interest in assuring the competency and voluntariness of patients who undergo this form of treatment. To this end, the review system is compatible with due process. However, once the competency of a voluntary patient has been confirmed, and the truly voluntary nature of his consent is determined, the state has little excuse to invoke the substitute [illegible] treatment," or more precisely ECT, is not an experimental procedure, nor are its hazards as serious as those of psychosurgery. Where informed consent is adequately ensured, there is no justification for infringing upon the patient's right to privacy in selecting and consenting to the treatment. The state has varied interests which are served by the regulation of ECT, but these interests are not served where the patient and his physician are the best judges of the patient's health, safety and welfare.

Therefore, insofar as Section 5326.4 applies to competent and voluntary patients who have given competent, voluntary and informed consent, it is unconstitutional. Substantive review is proper for involuntary or incompetent patients because there is a need for a substitute decision maker. Any possible need which exists for the voluntary and competent patient cannot prevail in the face of the serious infringement to the patient's right to privacy as guaranteed by *Roe v. Wade.*

. . . .

NOTES AND QUESTIONS

1. Electroshock therapy and psychosurgery have a disquieting history. Both were practiced in the 1920s and 1930s at a time when techniques and consequences were little understood. In the 1950s and 1960s, a better understanding was achieved, but the likelihood of "cure" of mental illness was never established. Since the subjects were frequently institutionalized and often incompetent, public concern and awareness were slow to arise, but the 1970s finally generated protective legislation of the kind reflected in *Aden*.

2. It is perhaps paradoxical that legislation designed to protect patients was challenged, as in *Aden,* on the grounds that the legislation denied equal protection of the laws and due process to those patients. The argument that the patient's rights to informed consent were violated [illegible] too *much* information is, at best, incongruous. As subsequent materials in Chapter 3 establish, the usual problem is that too little information is given for informed consent. Why would those interested in the welfare of mental patients attack the giving of full information? Recall the argument here — that vulnerable patients may be hurt by legislation — when we consider physician-assisted death in § 4.05[2]. It returns there, in *Lee v. Oregon*, but with a different spin.

3. It seems likely that opposition came from physician and professional, or institutional, constituencies. Why? Is the effectiveness of — or need for — psychosurgery and electroconvulsive therapy so well established that these modes of treatment should not be singled out? Put somewhat differently, why would the legislature single out these therapies and restrict their use to situations in which a compelling need is required and shown?

4. Should the legislation have provided that before psychosurgery or electroconvulsive is undertaken, there must be a showing that medication — as in *State of Washington v. Harper*, § 1.03[1] — cannot be effective? Should there be, as a policy or constitutional matter, in other words, a requirement that the least intrusive alternative be employed? Was this what was meant by the requirement that a procedure by "critically needed"? What was *wrong* with that?

5. Why — and how — did the opponents differentiate psychosurgery from ECT? Competent patients from incompetent?

6. And what of the patient's "right to be left uninformed"? Should there — can there — be such a right? It is usually referred to as a right of "therapeutic privilege" *in the physician* — the subject of the next section.

7. Note that the legislation applies to both voluntary and involuntary patients, to both competent and incompetent patients. Should it? Are the concerns different for these groups?

8. The court is concerned with the "experimental" nature of ECT and psychosurgery. Is that a misnomer, or is it *really* that no one knows the workings or predictable outcomes of these approaches? Either way, should "experiments" be performed on people who cannot consent? See § 3.03[3] as to medical experimentation and § 4.04[2] as to "investigational" treatments.

9. The Supreme Court of Illinois in *In re Branning*, 1998 Ill. LEXIS 6 (1998) reversed a trial judge's order, which had authorized electroconvulsive therapy. The statutes did not require a finding that the ward lacked capacity to reject ECT; did not specify criteria for such treatment; and did not set time limits or require a hearing at which the ward could be present. Nor was counsel required. The Court found ECT to be invasive and subject to abuse, distinguishing an earlier case where it held psychotropic drugs could be administered, pursuant to a guardian's consent, with appropriate, narrowly tailored procedures.

10. For an excellent article, see Paula Berg, *Toward a First Amendment Theory of Doctor-Patient Discourse and the Right to Receive Unbiased Medical Advice*, 74 B.U. L. Rev. 201 (1994); and see Frances H. Miller, *Trusting Doctors: Tricky Business When It Comes to Clinical Research*, 81 B.U. L. Rev. 423 (2001).

11. Can an ER doctor be held liable for failure to obtain informed consent when a violent, hallucinating patient is brought in and the physician gives antipsychotic medications which lead to an adverse reaction and then death? What would you advise the physician to do? *Barcai v. Betwee*, 98 Haw. 470 (Haw. 2002).

12. Informed consent is a prerequisite to medical services. Most states have statutes so requiring. Two issues (among many others) are raised. One is whether a physician may raise a defense that the patient was contributorily negligent in relying on advice given in the informed consent process. The second is whether the tort reform limits on damages

applied to negligence malpractice cases (including negligence in informed consent contexts) should also apply to battery cases.

BROWN v. DIBBELL
595 N.W.2d 358 (Wis. 1999)

Shirley S. **Abrahamson**, Chief Justice

These are the relevant facts for review. At age 36, Marlene Brown sought the advice of her doctor, Dr. R.P. Alfuth of the Midelfort Clinic, for his opinion about a lump in her right breast. Dr. Alfuth examined Ms. Brown and felt a possible cyst in her right breast. He decided to obtain a mammogram and, because Ms. Brown had saline breast implants, sent her for a consultation with Dr. David Dibbell, a reconstructive surgeon at the Midelfort Clinic who was familiar with examining patients with breast implants.

On June 17, 1993, Dr. Perry L. Kyser, a radiologist at the Midelfort Clinic, reported that Ms. Brown's mammogram showed a possible density in her right breast, that clinical confirmation was recommended, and that if clinical examination revealed no palpable abnormality in the right breast, then "follow-up of the right breast only in 6 months [was] suggested."

On August 30, 1993, Ms. Brown consulted with Dr. Dibbell. At trial, Dr. Dibbell testified that at this first consultation with Ms. Brown he reassured her that the lump she detected was actually a portion of her implant. Ms. Brown told him that her twin sister had died three years previously from breast cancer, that her mother also had breast cancer, and that she had multiple other female relatives with the disease. He testified that he explained to Ms. Brown that she was at "high risk" for developing breast cancer because of her family history, but that there was nothing to indicate that she had cancer. Dr. Dibbell also testified that Ms. Brown repeatedly asked about treatment options despite his insistence that the discussion was premature until after he had consulted with the radiologists. Dr. Dibbell stated that he reluctantly discussed with Ms. Brown the option of elective bilateral mastectomies because of her remarkable fear of developing breast cancer, her significant family history of the disease and the difficulty of assessing the lump because of her breast implants.

Dr. Dibbell testified that shortly after this first consultation with Ms. Brown, he consulted with Dr. Kyser and another radiologist at the Midelfort Clinic. According to Dr. Dibbell's testimony, the radiologists told him that they did not consider the lesion to be suspicious and that therefore it was reasonable to wait six months and take another mammogram of her right breast. He also testified that the radiologists told him that biopsy by "needle localization" was not medically indicated because the needle might puncture her implant and that the procedure was otherwise futile because the lesion could not be localized by touch.

On September 9, 1993, Dr. Dibbell saw Ms. Brown for a follow-up examination. Dr. Dibbell physically re-examined Ms. Brown's right breast and again concluded that he felt nothing particularly suspicious. Dr. Dibbell testified that he spent 40 minutes at the September 9, 1993, consultation and discussed treatment options with Ms. Brown. He stated that these discussions included the radiologists' opinions that it was reasonable to wait for six months and that needle localization was not appropriate. Dr. Dibbell also testified that Ms. Brown refused the option of waiting for six months and then taking another mammogram because of her intense fear of developing breast cancer. He explained to her that if she felt she had to do something, prophylactic bilateral mastectomies made better sense than many inconclusive biopsies.

Ms. Brown testified that Dr. Dibbell never informed her that the radiologists had found nothing wrong with her right breast and that they had recommended a treatment plan of a follow-up mammogram in six months. She also testified that Dr. Dibbell never discussed with her the option of seeking a biopsy by needle localization or any other alternative treatment plan. Ms. Brown also testified that neither Dr. Dibbell nor Dr. Johnson could tell her whether she had breast cancer, but that they did tell her there was a high risk of her developing breast cancer and that bilateral mastectomies were the best way to reduce the risk.

Following surgery, Ms. Brown experienced several problems including scarred breasts, asymmetrical nipples and areola, loss of sensation in her breasts, and other problems requiring additional surgeries.

II

The first issue is whether the circuit court erred in instructing the jury that Ms. Brown may be found contributorily negligent in this informed consent action under Wis. Stat. § 448.30 (1993-94). Contributory negligence is conduct by an injured party that falls below the standard to which a reasonably prudent person in that injured party's position should conform for his or her own protection and that is a legally contributing cause of the injured party's harm.

To answer the question presented about the role of contributory negligence in an informed consent action, we turn first to the informed consent statute, Wis. Stat. § 448.30, which provides that "any physician who treats a patient shall inform the patient about the availability of all alternate viable medical modes of treatment and about the benefits and risks of these treatments." Wisconsin Stat. § 448.30 in its entirety provides as follows:

> 448.30 Information on alternate modes of treatment. Any physician who treats a patient shall inform the patient about the availability of all alternate, viable medical modes of treatment and about the benefits and risks of these treatments. The physician's duty to inform the patient under this section does not require disclosure of:
>
> (1) Information beyond what a reasonably well-qualified physician in a similar medical classification would know.
>
> (2) Detailed technical information that in all probability a patient would not understand.
>
> (3) Risks apparent or known to the patient.
>
> (4) Extremely remote possibilities that might falsely or detrimentally alarm the patient.

(5) Information in emergencies where failure to provide treatment would be more harmful to the patient than [illegible]

(6) Information in cases where the patient is incapable of consenting.

The informed consent statute is silent about contributory negligence. An action alleging a doctor's failure to adequately inform a patient is, however, grounded on a negligence theory of liability. Contributory negligence is generally a defense in an action based on a negligence theory of liability.

The doctrine of informed consent focuses on the reasonableness of a doctor's disclosure. The standard regarding what a doctor must disclose is described as "the prudent patient standard." To fulfill the doctor's duty under Wis. Stat. § 448.30 a doctor must provide information that a reasonable person in the patient's position would want to know in order to make an informed decision with respect to the alternative choices of treatments or procedures. That information includes "an assessment of and communication regarding 'the gravity of the patient's condition, the probabilities of success, and any alternative treatment or procedures if such are reasonably appropriate.' "

We agree with the defendants that patients have a duty to exercise ordinary care for their own health and well-being; that contributory negligence, as a general rule, is an available defense in suits based on negligence; and that contributory negligence may, under certain circumstances, be a defense in an informed consent action because the action is based on negligence. We thus recognize that a patient bringing an informed consent action is not exempt from the duty to exercise ordinary care for his or her own health and well-being. We also agree, however, with the court of appeals that the very patient-doctor relation assumes trust and confidence on the part of the patient and that it would require an unusual set of facts to render a patient guilty of contributory negligence when the patient relies on the doctor.

(1)

The defendants [illegible] in an informed consent action includes the patient's telling the truth to the doctor and giving complete and accurate information when the doctor asks about material personal, family and medical histories. They contend that the jury could have concluded that Ms. Brown falsely told the doctors that her mother had breast cancer; that Dr. Dibbell's advice to Ms. Brown that she had a high risk of developing breast cancer was based at least in part on Ms. Brown's misrepresentation; and that therefore the misrepresentation constituted negligence contributing to her injury.

A patient is usually the primary source of information about the patient's material personal, family and medical histories. If a doctor is to provide a patient with the information required by Wis. Stat. § 448.30, it is imperative that in response to a doctor's material questions a patient provide information that is as complete and accurate as possible under the circumstances. We therefore conclude that for patients to exercise ordinary care, they must tell the truth and give complete and accurate information about personal, family and medical histories to a doctor to the extent possible in response to the doctor's requests for information when the requested information is material to a doctor's duty as prescribed by § 448.30 and that a patient's breach of that duty might, under certain circumstances, constitute contributory negligence.

We therefore conclude that the circuit court in the present case should have given the jury an instruction on contributory negligence tailored to Ms. Brown's duty to exercise ordinary care in providing complete and accurate information to her doctors in response to their questions concerning personal, family and medical histories material to their duties prescribed in Wis. Stat. § 448.30.

(2)

The defendants contend that the jury could have found Ms. Brown contributorily negligent because she failed to ask for brochures about mastectomies or photographs showing what patients look like after this kind of surgery. According to the defendants, the jury could have found that a reasonable person in Ms. Brown's position would take these measures to ensure that she had enough information to make an informed decision. The defendants also assert that the jury could have found Ms. Brown contributorily negligent for failing to ask the doctor for more information about her risk of developing cancer. They contend that a reasonable person in Ms. Brown's position who had been told she had a high risk of developing breast cancer would have asked about the statistical chance of developing breast cancer so she could make an informed decision.

We agree with the plaintiffs and the court of appeals that in most cases it is illogical and contrary to the concept of informed consent to place on patients the burden of asking questions of their doctors or engaging in their own independent research. It is the doctor who possesses medical knowledge and skills and who has the affirmative duty under Wis. Stat. § 448.30 both to determine what a reasonable patient in the position of Ms. Brown would want to know and to provide that material information. The informed consent statute speaks solely in terms of the doctor's duty to disclose and discuss information related to treatment options and risks. The informed consent statute recognizes that a patient is not in a position to know treatment options and risks and, if unaided, is unable to make an informed decision.

For these reasons, we conclude that as a general rule a jury should not be instructed that a patient can be found contributorily negligent for failing to ask questions or for failing to undertake independent research. A patient's duty to exercise ordinary care generally does not encompass a duty to ascertain the truth or the completeness of the information presented by a doctor. Requiring patients either to ask questions or to independently seek information would erode a doctor's duty to obtain informed consent.

We do not conclude, however, that a patient may never be contributorily negligent for failing to seek information. It would, however, require a very extraordinary fact situation to render a patient contributorily negligent when the patient accepts and trusts the information a doctor provides, because ordinarily a patient may rely on the knowledge and skills of a doctor. The [illegible] the present case in the realm of the extraordinary.

(3)

The defendants urge that a patient's duty to exercise ordinary care in an informed consent action requires that a patient make a reasonable choice among the alternative viable medical modes of treatment presented by a doctor. According to the defendants, a jury may find a patient contributorily negligent for choosing a viable mode of treatment presented by a doctor when that treatment contravenes the patient's concerns.

In this case, the defendants argue that Ms. Brown was presented with two viable medical modes of treatment: surgery or periodic mammograms. The surgery was highly disfiguring; periodic mammograms would involve no disfigurement. Thus the defendants contend that Ms. Brown was contributorily negligent for proceeding with bilateral mastectomies, the most disfiguring and cosmetically displeasing treatment alternative, when she was very concerned about her appearance and placed tremendous importance on the size and shape of her breasts. According to the defendants, the jury could have concluded that, on these facts, Ms. Brown's choice of surgery constituted contributory negligence.

The plaintiffs respond that a patient cannot be held contributorily negligent simply for consenting to a viable medical mode of treatment presented by a doctor. They argue that the focus in an informed consent action is on a doctor's failure to provide the information that would permit a patient to choose among the viable medical modes of treatment and that a patient cannot, as a matter of law, be negligent for choosing a mode of medical treatment presented by a doctor as viable.

We agree with the plaintiffs and hold, as did the court of appeals, that except in a very extraordinary fact situation, a patient is not contributorily negligent for choosing a viable medical mode of treatment presented by a doctor. See *Brown* [v. Dibbell, 220 Wis. 2d 200, 582 N.W.2d 134 (Ct. App. 1998)], 220 Wis. 2d at 20[illegible]. The evidence [illegible] this [illegible] in the realm of the extraordinary.

III

The plaintiffs assert that the court of appeals erred in holding that the circuit court should have given jury instructions on defenses asserted by the defendants.

Wisconsin Stat. § 448.30 sets forth six types of information that a doctor does not have the duty to disclose to a patient. The defendants assert that the jury should have been instructed that Dr. Dibbell was not required to disclose the following four types of information set forth in the statute. Their proposed jury instruction read as follows:

> The physician's duty to inform the patient . . . does not require disclosure of:

(1) Information beyond what a reasonably well qualified physician in a similar medical classification would know;

(2) Detailed technical information that in all probability a patient would not understand;

(3) Risks apparent or known to the patient;

(4) Extremely remote possibilities that might falsely or detrimentally alarm the patient.

This requested jury instruction correctly states the law; it repeats verbatim four of the express exceptions to disclosure listed in Wis. Stat. § 448.30. The circuit court rejected these proposed jury instructions on the ground that none of the statutory exceptions would apply to the facts as presented at trial.

At trial, Dr. Dibbell and other doctors testified that they did not provide Ms. Brown with statistical information on her risk of developing cancer because this information is confusing and misleading to patients. The defendants contend that Dr. Dibbell presented an arguably reasonable explanation for his failure to disclose such statistics to Ms. Brown and that this evidence was sufficient for the circuit court to give the jury the requested statutory instruction that a doctor need not disclose detailed technical information that a patient would not likely understand.

Further, Dr. Dibbell testified at trial that the description he gave Ms. Brown of the mastectomy procedure-removal of all breast tissue, the nipple and part of the areola-would convey to her that breast sensation would be diminished. According to the defendants, Ms. Brown must have been aware that she would suffer diminished breast sensation because after the surgery virtually none of her breast tissue would remain.

We hold, as did the court of appeals, that the defense that the risk was apparent or known to Ms. Brown is a defense the jury could consider. As discussed previously, the plaintiffs assert that Dr. Dibbell had failed in his duty of disclosure by not advising Ms. Brown that after undergoing bilateral mastectomies she would have diminished breast sensation. We hold, as did the court of appeals, that the evidence raised the issue of whether this was a risk apparent or known to Ms. Brown. See Wis. Stat. § 448.30(3). We hold, as did the court of appeals, that the circuit court erred in not instructing the jury on one or more of the statutory defenses requested by the defendants and that this error was prejudicial because the jury was probably misled about the scope of the defendants' duty under the informed consent statute.

At the close of evidence at trial, the defendants also asked the circuit court to include in the jury instructions the optional fourth paragraph of the standard Wisconsin informed consent instruction, Wis JI-Civil 1023.2. This paragraph explains that a doctor may be justified in failing to make disclosures to a patient and reads as follows:

> If the doctor comes forward and offers to you an explanation as to why the doctor did not make a particular disclosure or disclosures to the plaintiff, and if such explanation satisfies you that it was reasonable for the doctor not to have made such disclosures, then you will find

> that the defendant did not fail in the duties owed by the doctor to the patient.

The plaintiffs appear to contend that the six statutory exceptions listed in Wis. Stat. § 448.30 are the only explanations a doctor may offer for not disclosing information to a patient and therefore the optional fourth paragraph should not have been given.

The defendants assert that an instruction on a non-statutory defense should have been given in this case. They point out, for example, that the jury could have found that Dr. Dibbell's explanation of his failure to provide Ms. Brown with statistical information on her risk of developing breast cancer because the information would be misleading and confusing was a reasonable explanation for nondisclosure from the perspective of a patient, even if this court were to conclude that the explanation does not fit within the express exceptions set forth in Wis. Stat. § 448.30.

We agree with the plaintiffs that the optional fourth paragraph of Wis JI-Civil 1023.2 is misleading. The instruction does not make clear, as it should, that the reasonableness of a doctor's explanation for failure to disclose information must be measured from the perspective of what a reasonable person in the patient's position would want to know. A doctor has an affirmative duty to disclose information that a reasonable person in the patient's position would want to know.

In other words, the optional fourth paragraph is misleading because it can be construed as stating that the question of a doctor's failure to disclose information is to be answered from the doctor's perspective. The paragraph states that "if such explanation [provided by the doctor] satisfies you that it was reasonable for the doctor not to have made such disclosures, you will find that the defendant did not fail in the duties owed by the doctor to the patient." Wis JI-Civil 1023.2. Determining the reasonableness of the nondisclosure from the perspective of what a doctor believes should be disclosed, instead of what a reasonable patient wants to know, is an erroneous statement of the law of informed consent.

The instruction should make clear that for a jury to find that a doctor did not fail in the duty of disclosure owed by the doctor to the patient, a doctor must satisfy the jury that a reasonable patient under the circumstances then existing would not want to know the information the doctor failed to disclose.

In summary, we agree with the defendants, as did the court of appeals, that the circuit court erred in refusing to grant the defendants' motion to instruct the jury about defenses set forth in Wis. Stat. § 448.30, when evidence suggesting such defenses was presented. We also conclude that the language of the optional fourth paragraph of the informed consent jury instruction, Wis JI-Civil 1023.2, is misleading and should not have been given in the form proposed by the defendants.

For the reasons set forth, we affirm the decision of the court of appeals and remand the cause for a new trial.

NOTES AND QUESTIONS

1. *Brown v. Dibbell* builds on the informed consent cases in the text and seems consistent with the basic principles of *Canterbury v. Spence*. Note that those principles, by negative implication, are validated constitutionally in *Ferguson v. City Of Charleston*, 532 U.S. 67 (2001), *supra* § 2.03[2], the Supreme Court decision dealing with the South Carolina hospital policy of testing pregnant women, without their consent, for drugs.

2. *Brown*, however, addresses issues not reached in *Canterbury*. For example, the Court notes the statutory elements of advice imposed on a physician, then concludes a claimed breach of duty is essentially a claim of negligence; hence, contributory negligence by the patient may be a defense.

   But isn't the essence of informed consent that a patient is not competent, or at least capable of effective decision making? And the physician is in a fiduciary position? If so, isn't a claim of contributory negligence incompatible with informed consent?

3. Or does it turn on the precise misconduct of the patient, such as lying about medical history or failing to follow advice? It is at least clear, after *Brown*, that accepting — without more — the physician's advice can rarely be contributory negligence. But in the age of ample information, and second opinions, why not?

4. *Brown* also deals with the content and outer limits of the information the physician must provide, by specifying four kinds that need not be included. Is this wise? Listing four factors implicitly excludes others, although the Court disagrees. And listing *no* factors leaves the jury free to impose a reasonableness standard, which is, after all, the essence of the negligence standard.

5. And what do you think of the statutory list, especially items 3 and 4? Would you add others, such as the physician's "won/loss" ratio?

6. How does intent fit into a claim of battery for lack of informed consent? For an excellent article, see Craig M. Lawson, *The Puzzle of Intended Harm in the Tort of Battery*, 74 Temp. L. Rev. 355 (Summer 2001).

7. Would the statutory provisions in *Brown* make a difference in *Canterbury* or *Truman v. Thomas, infra* § 3.04[1], or in the next case, *Perry v. Shaw*?

PERRY v. SHAW

88 Cal. App. 4th 658, 106 Cal. Rptr. 2d 7 (2001)

Vogel (Miriam A.), J.

In 1972, our Supreme Court held that when a patient gives permission to a doctor to perform one type of surgical procedure but the doctor performs a substantially different operation, "the requisite element of deliberate intent to deviate from the consent given is present" and a battery has been committed. (*Cobbs v. Grant* (1972), 8 Cal. 3d 229, 239-240 [104 Cal. Rptr. 505, 502 P.2d 1].)

In 1975, our Legislature enacted the Medical Injury Compensation Reform Act (MICRA), substantially changing the law governing medical malpractice actions. Among other things, the Legislature imposed a $250,000 limitation on noneconomic damages in any action "based on professional negligence," with "professional negligence" defined as "a negligent act or omission to act by a health care provider in the rendering of professional services. . . ." (Civ. Code, § 3333.2, subds. (a), (c)(2).)

In 1985, our Supreme Court held that when a plaintiff proceeds on both non-MICRA and MICRA causes of action and obtains a recovery that may be based on a non-MICRA theory, another MICRA statutory limitation does not apply.

In 1987, Division Five of our court held that the MICRA definition of "professional negligence" in another MICRA statute was "a deliberate choice" by the Legislature to exclude intentional torts, including battery.

In other contexts, the Supreme Court has applied an expansive definition to the MICRA definition of "professional negligence," but it has not done so in the context of section 3333.2. To the contrary, our high court has said that the meaning of " 'based on professional negligence' [may] vary depending upon the legislative history and 'the purpose underlying each of the individual statutes.' " We take the Supreme Court at its word and hold in this case that where, as here, a common law battery — something more than a "technical battery" — has been proved, the limitation imposed by section 3333.2 does not apply.

Facts

Following a very substantial loss of weight, Sandra Perry asked William Shaw, M.D., to surgically remove excess skin from her arms, back, thighs and stomach. During one office visit, they discussed a breast enlargement procedure in which muscle is moved from the back to the breasts, but Ms. Perry told Dr. Shaw she did not want that procedure. During another office visit, they talked about a breast-lifting procedure designed to lift but not enlarge the breasts, but Ms. Perry told Dr. Shaw she "had definitely decided not to have any breast surgery at that time." At the hospital, Ms. Perry was asked to sign a form that included [illegible] to the breast-lifting procedure. Ms. Perry twice refused to sign the form and only changed her mind after she was medicated, taken to the operating room, and reassured by Dr. Shaw that he would not perform breast surgery.[2]

Ms. Perry awoke to discover that, in addition to the skin removal procedures, Dr. Shaw had performed a breast enlargement procedure by moving tissue flaps from the sides of her chest into her breasts. To her shock and dismay, Dr. Shaw had substantially augmented her breasts (from a 34B to a 40DD), making them "many, many times bigger" than they had been. When Ms. Perry questioned Dr. Shaw, he told her that although she might then be upset, she would be happy within a year — after one or two additional surgeries for minor revisions.

---

[2] In the context of this case, it is unnecessary for us to decide whether "consent" obtained under these circumstances could ever constitute informed consent.

Ms. Perry sued Dr. Shaw and the Regents of the University of California (collectively Dr. Shaw), alleging both medical negligence and battery. Dr. Shaw answered, alleging that Ms. Perry's noneconomic damages for both claims were limited to $ 250,000 by section 3333.2. A jury rejected Dr. Shaw's testimony and returned special verdicts in favor of Ms. Perry, finding that Dr. Shaw was negligent, that he had committed a battery, and that both had caused Ms. Perry's injury (but that Ms. Perry was not entitled to punitive damages). The jury awarded Ms. Perry $ 59,000 for medical expenses (past and future) and $ 1,030,000 for her noneconomic damages (past and future). The trial court denied Dr. Shaw's motion to reduce the noneconomic damage award to $ 250,000 (and later denied his motion for a new trial made on the same ground) and entered judgment in favor of Ms. Perry. Dr. Shaw appeals.

Discussion

Dr. Shaw contends section 3333.2 applies to Ms. Perry's entire noneconomic damage award "because both her medical malpractice and battery claims were based on a single course of conduct constituting professional negligence as defined by that statute." We disagree.

A.

As relevant, section 3333.2 provides: "(a) In any action for injury against a health care provider *based on professional negligence*, the injured plaintiff shall be entitled to recover noneconomic losses to compensate for pain, suffering, inconvenience, physical impairment, disfigurement and other nonpecuniary damage. In no action shall the amount of damages for noneconomic losses exceed . . . $ 250,000. . . . 'Health care provider' [includes doctors and hospitals]. *'Professional negligence' means a negligent act or omission to act by a health care provider in the rendering of professional services*, which act or omission is the proximate cause of a personal injury or wrongful death, provided that such services are within the scope of services for which the provider is licensed and which are not within any restriction imposed by the licensing agency or licensed hospital."

B.

In *Cobbs v. Grant*, supra, 8 Cal. 3d 229, our Supreme Court held that where

> "a doctor obtains consent of the patient to perform one type of treatment and subsequently performs a substantially different treatment for which consent was not obtained, there is a clear case of battery. . . . [W]hen an undisclosed potential complication results, the occurrence of which was not an integral part of the treatment procedure but merely a known risk, the courts are divided on the issue of whether this should be deemed to be a battery or negligence. . . . California authorities have favored a negligence theory. . . . Dean Prosser surveyed the decisions in this area and concluded, 'The earliest cases treated this as a matter of vitiating the consent, so that there was liability for battery. Beginning with a decision in Kansas

in 1960 . . ., it began to be recognized that this was really a matter of the standard of professional conduct. . . . [T]he prevailing view now is that the action . . . is in reality [illegible] failing to conform to the proper standard. . . .'

"Although this is a close question, either prong of which is supportable by authority, the trend appears to be towards categorizing failure to obtain informed consent as negligence. That this result now appears with growing frequency is of more than academic interest; it reflects an appreciation of the several significant consequences of favoring negligence over a battery theory. . . . [M]ost jurisdictions have permitted a doctor in an informed consent action to interpose a defense that the disclosure he omitted to make was not required within his medical community. *However, expert opinion as to community standard is not required in a battery count, in which the patient must merely prove failure to give informed consent and a mere touching absent consent. Moreover a doctor could be held liable for punitive damages under a battery count, and if held liable for the intentional tort of battery he might not be covered by his malpractice insurance. . . .*

"*We agree with the majority trend. The battery theory should be reserved for those circumstances when a doctor performs an operation to which the patient has not consented. When the patient gives permission to perform one type of treatment and the doctor performs another, the requisite element of deliberate intent to deviate from the consent given is present.* However, when the patient consents to certain treatment and the doctor performs that treatment but an undisclosed inherent complication with a low probability occurs, no intentional deviation from the consent given appears; rather, the doctor in obtaining consent may have failed to meet his due care duty to disclose pertinent information. *In that situation the action should be pleaded in negligence.*"

In our case, Dr. Shaw performed an operation to which Ms. Perry did not consent. He committed a battery. We agree [illegible] as a result, Dr. Shaw's liability is greater than it would have been for the sort of "technical battery" distinguished by the court in *Cobbs v. Grant*.

. . . .

D.

In the declining economy of the early 1970's, California was in the middle of a medical malpractice crisis. Insurance carriers were concerned that fewer policies would be written and, at the same time, that the number of medical malpractice claims was escalating (as was the amount awarded for those claims). When the carriers increased their rates, doctors and other health care providers cancelled or reduced their coverage. Some limited their practices by abandoning high-risk specialties and others moved out of state. There were concerns that doctors who continued in practice would increase the fees charged to their patients, that injured patients would be unable to collect judgments, and that the availability of affordable medical care was threatened.

MICRA was our Legislature's response to this crisis. As adopted in 1975, the idea was to reduce malpractice judgments in order to reduce insurance rates, thereby ensuring available and affordable health care. To those ends, several substantial changes were made in the law governing medical malpractice actions. The period of limitations during which a medical malpractice action could be brought was limited. (Code Civ. Proc., § 340.5.) The collateral source rule was abolished. (§ 3333.1.) Periodic payments of future damages were allowed without the plaintiff's consent. (Code Civ. Proc., § 667.7.) Contingency fee arrangements were regulated. (Bus. & Prof. Code, § 6146.) Arbitration clauses in medical services contracts were authorized. (Code Civ. Proc., § 1295.) And, "perhaps most significantly," a $ 250,000 cap was placed on noneconomic losses by the enactment of section 3333.2.

The cap on noneconomic damages is an integral part of MICRA. In medical malpractice litigation, noneconomic damages typically account for a large part of a total damage award and, therefore, a large part of the insurance carriers' expense. Accordingly, the Legislature adopted section 3333.2 "to calm insurance companies and assure them that they would not have to face huge pain and suffering payments[,] . . . to induce insurance companies to reduce their premiums[, and] to prevent plaintiffs and their lawyers from inflating damage awards." (Finkelstein, [*California Civil Code Section 3333.2 Revisited: Has it Done Its Job?* (July 1994) [67 So. Cal. L. Rev. [1609,] 1614; see also Arentz, [*Defining "Professional Negligence" After Central Pathology Service Medical Clinic v. Superior Court: Should California's Medical Injury Compensation Reform Act Cover Intentional Torts?* (Spring 1994)] 30 Cal. Western L. Rev. 221–222.) As one commentator has summed it up, "the Legislature's intended goal was to bring down premiums so that doctors could continue to practice medicine in California, and charge reasonable prices." (Finkelstein, *supra*, at p. 1614.)

E.

But there is nothing in the legislative history generally, or with regard to section 3333.2 specifically, to suggest that the Legislature intended to extend the $ 250,000 limitation to intentional torts. n4 As noted at the outset, *Cobbs v. Grant* was decided *three years before MICRA was enacted*, and the Legislature therefore knew when it defined "professional negligence" that there existed a species of battery that our highest court had said was *not negligence*. In that context, the only rational conclusion is "that the words 'negligent' and 'negligence' were carefully chosen to apply only to causes of action based upon negligence."

If section 3333.2 is in fact the most significant limitation created by MICRA, it is also one of the most Draconian. When as a matter of legislative fiat the courts are required to reduce awards of noneconomic damages to $ 250,000 without regard to the result of a health care provider's negligence — notwithstanding brain damage, paralysis, and other equally devastating injury — the scope of that fiat must be limited to its terms. By its plain language, the cap imposed by section 3333.2 applies only in actions "based on professional negligence," not (like Code of Civil Procedure section 425.13) [illegible] arising out of professional negligence." Whatever argument there may be to support a broad construction of "arising out of," we do not think it applies to a statute in which those words were not used.

We reject Dr. Shaw's suggestion that our distinction between battery and negligence defeats MICRA's policy of cost containment and threatens its broader purpose by resurrecting the pre-MICRA instability associated with unlimited noneconomic damages, thereby increasing the overall cost of malpractice insurance to account for these larger recoveries. The fact that this issue comes before us for the first time in 2001 speaks volumes against such a conclusion — in the 26 years that MICRA has been on the books, this is apparently the first time this issue has reached this level. If the floodgates are there, they are holding back droplets, not a deluge.[6]

The jury believed that Dr. Shaw performed the breast enlargement without Ms. Perry's consent and contrary to her express wishes or, in legal terms, that Dr. Shaw is liable for the intentional tort of battery. Based on those findings, the jury awarded about $ 1 million in noneconomic damages. We see no reason to reduce that amount and therefore affirm the judgment.

Disposition

The judgment is affirmed. Ms. Perry is entitled to her costs of appeal.

NOTES AND QUESTIONS

1. *Perry v. Shaw* is a useful case for summarizing the standard "tort reform" package adopted by the majority of state legislatures during the 1970s and 1980s to reduce the impact of medical malpractice judgments on medical practice and insurance. The Court gives an overview in the second paragraph of Part D of its opinion, noting perhaps the most significant element is the $250,000 cap on noneconomic damages. Evaluate generally the need for, and fairness of, this package of legislation. Are there [illegible] omit, reforms you would add?
2. Note that the cap on damages has been held unconstitutional in some states. What might be the appropriate theory?
3. The cap only applies to negligence actions, and so the plaintiff in *Perry* argues that this is a case in *battery*. Does the distinction make sense? Should the legislation be broadened?
4. And what *is* the difference? In a sense, aren't all malpractice cases in battery, since no one *consents* to negligent care. How do you suppose

[6] As the trial court put it: "This court is persuaded that there . . . has never been a problem of runaway jury verdicts in battery actions. Just never heard of it. It isn't on the scene. It doesn't present itself as an item to be addressed by the Legislature, so I think it was not addressed by the Legislature. I think battery was simply not considered as the kind of action that falls within the coverage of the MICRA cap."

it has happened that most malpractice actions are in negligence? Shouldn't they rest on contract theory?

5. There are advantages to a battery theory. Expert testimony is not required (why?). Punitive damages are available (why?). Damages are not capped (why?).

   This, of course, raises the issue of the damages to which Ms. Perry might be entitled. What are the elements? How much? The Court let stand a judgment of $1,000,000. If you had been on the jury, would you have voted for more or less?

PROBLEM 3-9 — How Long Do I Have to Live?

Miklos Arato was 42, a successful real estate contractor, and had pancreatic cancer. Mr. Arato filled out a 150-question form, one part of which asked whether he wanted "the truth" or wanted the physician "to bear the burden." Arato wanted the truth. The oncologists explained his course of treatment — F.A.M. chemotherapy, coupled with surgery. They never explained the high rate of mortality with pancreatic cancer — partly because Mr. Arato exhibited great anxiety about his condition; partly because he wanted the truth, "not a cold shower"; partly because it might deprive him of hope ("a medically inadvisable state"); and partly because statistical data is misleading in particular cases. They did advise Mr. Arato that most patients, upon recurrence, die; but they never estimated his chances — partly because during his 70 visits he never asked "How long do I have to live?"

Mr. Arato chose the chemotherapy. He died a year later. Only one to two percent of patients diagnosed with pancreatic cancer live as long as five years. His widow maintained that if Mr. Arato had known his death would be certain despite the chemotherapy, he would have declined, avoided the pain, arranged his affairs, and lived his last days in peace. Instead, his business failed and he incurred extensive tax liabilities.

Should the trial court have instructed the jury that the doctrine of informed consent requires physicians to advise on:

(a) *all* facts which materially affect the patient's rights and interests, including;

(b) the knowledge the patient needs to make an informed choice, including;

(c) life expectancy, as it bears on the futility of care and financial or familial considerations?

How would damages be measured? *See Arato v. Avedon*, 11 Cal. Rptr. 2d 169, *rev'd,* 23 Cal. Rptr 2d 131 (Cal. 1993). Consider the problem under the case law in the next section, dealing with therapeutic privilege.

PROBLEM 3-10 — Placentas R Us

In February of 2006, the Portland Oregonian reported that several medical malpractice insurance companies had formed a laboratory, Cascadia lab, to examine placentas from problem pregnancies and deliveries at hospitals in the Northwest. The mothers were not told of this, their consent was not sought, they were not told the results of the tests. They learned only if they ultimately brought a lawsuit.

The purpose was not healthcare. It was to defend against possible malpractice by establishing causes other than provider negligence.

Analyze this practice in terms of law relating to informed consent, fiduciary relations, conversion, and the tort of outrage.

What relief is available if the tests revealed a defect in the mother, and she — in ignorance — has other (defective) children? If the test shows physician abuse and neglect, and he repeats this on subsequent patients?

For a brief discussion, see LaFrance, *Patients, Placentas, and Ethics,* Oregonian (Feb. 17, 2006).

PROBLEM 3–11 — Emergency Consent

In February of 2006, the Wall Street Journal reported that Northfield Labs was testing a blood substitute on emergency patients at accident scenes. Some got the substitute, Polyheme, while others got the standard treatment, saline. This division was continued after the patients arrived at the Emergency department, with those on saline getting blood. No consent was sought or obtained. In a prior study, on heart surgery patients, ten got heart attacks. The study has been approved under a federal "informed Consent" regulation, with an exemption for "emergency" research; instead communities may opt out, by having residents wear plastic bracelets. *See* King et al, American Journal of Bioethics (website) (Mar. 10, 2006).

Does this experiment qualify as "emergency" research? Even if so, does the "community opt out" qualify as informed consent"?

And, anyway, how does the federal government have authority to suspend the effect or operation of state informed consent laws? (As to that, consider the *Raich* and *Gonzalez* cases, *infra.*)

PROBLEM 3–12 — Informed Consent by Community

Usually, informed consent must be obtained prior to a medical experiment. But suppose the patient is unconscious? May the "community" consent? Consider the following three experiments:

(a) The Resuscitation Outcomes Consortium, with federal and private funding of $50,000,000, proposed in eleven cities to compare the normal saline solution given in ambulances with a saltier solution, one which also contains a sugary substance. The recipients would usually be unconscious, needing blood as soon as they arrive at the hospital. One hundred thousand people die annually en route.

(b) An earlier, similar experiment with a blood substitute was discontinued in 2004 because of deaths from the artificial blood.

(c) A separate trial of an automated CPR band on 1071 out-of-hospital cardiac patients, to compare efficacy with manual CPR, was halted after a "trend toward worse survival" and "worse neurological outcomes" was observed. *See Portland Oregonian*, B-1 (May 2006); JAMA 295: 2620, 2629 (June 14, 2006).

In all three instances, the experiments were conducted without informed consent, pursuant to 45 CFR § 46.116 (1997) and 21 CFR § 50.23 (1979), but were preceded by community informational meetings and IRB and IEC clearances. Those meetings were sparsely attended and, since no one can predict or know in advance who will suffer trauma or cardiac arrest, specific notice to affected patients could not be given.

The provisions cited above from the Code of Federal Regulations are part of a rule common to most federal agencies, including Agriculture, Food and Drug, Agency for International Development, Defense, Veterans Affairs, Environmental Protection, National Science Foundation and Transportation. After defining the content of informed consent, this common rule provides for the Department of Agriculture that. . . . (7 CFR § 1c.116 *Protection of Human Subjects*):

> (c) An IRB may approve a consent procedure which does not include, or which alters, some or all of the elements of informed consent set forth above, or waive the requirement to obtain informed consent provided the IRB finds and documents that:
>
> (1) The research or demonstration project is to be conducted by or subject to the approval of state or local government officials and is designed to study, evaluate, or otherwise examine: (i) Public benefit of service programs; (ii) procedures for obtaining benefits or services under those programs; (iii) possible changes in or alternatives to those programs or procedures; or (iv) possible changes in methods or levels of payment for benefits or services under those programs; and
>
> (2) The research could not practicably be carried out without the waiver or alteration.
>
> (d) An IRB may approve a consent procedure which does not include, or which alters, some or all of the elements of informed consent set for the in this section, or waive the requirements to obtain informed consent provided the IRB finds and documents that:
>
> (1) The research involves no more than minimal risk to the subjects;
>
> (2) The waiver or alteration will not adversely affect the rights and welfare of the subjects;
>
> (3) The research could not practicably be carried out without the waiver or alteration; and
>
> (4) Whenever appropriate, the subjects will be provided with additional pertinent information after participation.
>
> (e) The informed consent requirements in this policy are not intended to preempt any applicable federal, state, or local laws which require additional information to be disclosed in order for informed consent to be legally effective.

However, the provisions for the FDA are more extensive and rigorous (21 CFR § 50.24 et seq):

§ 50.24 Exception from informed consent requirements for emergency research.

(a) The IRB responsible for the review, approval, and continuing review of the clinical investigation described in this section may approve that investigation without requiring that informed consent of all research subjects be obtained if the IRB (with the concurrence of a licensed physician who is a member of or consultant to the IRB and who is not otherwise participating in the clinical investigation) finds and documents each of the following:

(1) The human subjects are in a life-threatening situation, available treatments are unproven or unsatisfactory, and the collection of valid scientific evidence, which may include evidence obtained through randomized placebo-controlled investigations, is necessary to determine the safety and effectiveness of particular interventions.

(2) Obtaining informed consent is not feasible because:

(i) The subjects will not be able to give their informed consent as a result of their medical condition;

(ii) The intervention under investigation must be administered before consent from the subjects' legally authorized representatives is feasible; and

(iii) There is no reasonable way to identify prospectively the individuals likely to become eligible for participation in the clinical investigation.

(3) Participation in the research holds out the prospect of direct benefit to the subjects because:

(i) Subjects are facing a life-threatening situation that necessitates intervention;

(ii) Appropriate animal and other preclinical studies have been conducted, and the information derived from those studies and related evidence support the potential for the intervention to provide a direct benefit to the individual subjects; and

(iii) Risks associated with the investigation are reasonable in relation to what is known about the medical condition of the potential class of subjects, the risks and benefits of standard therapy, if any, and what is known about the risks and benefits of the proposed intervention or activity.

(4) The clinical investigation could not practicably be carried out without the waiver.

(5) The proposed investigational plan defines the length of the potential therapeutic window based on scientific evidence, and the investigator has committed to attempting to contact a legally authorized representative for each subject within that window of time and, if feasible, to asking the legally authorized representative contacted for consent within that window rather than proceeding without consent. The investigator will summarize efforts made to contact legally

authorized representatives and make this information available to the IRB at the time of continuing review.

(6) The IRB has reviewed and approved informed consent procedures and an informed consent document consistent with § 50.25. These procedures and the informed consent document are to be used with subjects or their legally authorized representatives in situations where use of such procedures and documents is feasible. The IRB has reviewed and approved procedures and information to be used when providing an opportunity for a family member to object to a subject's participation in the clinical investigation consistent with paragraph (a)(7)(v) of this section.

(7) Additional protections of the rights and welfare of the subjects will be provided, including, at least:

(i) Consultation (including, where appropriate, consultation carried out by the IRB) with representatives of the communities in which the clinical investigation will be conducted and from which the subjects will be drawn;

(ii) Public disclosure to the communities in which the clinical investigation will be conducted and from which the subjects will be drawn, prior to initiation of the clinical investigation, of plans for the investigation and its risks and expected benefits;

(iii) Public disclosure of sufficient information following completion of the clinical investigation to apprise the community and researchers of the study, including the demographic characteristics of the research population, and its results;

(iv) establishment of an independent data monitoring committee to exercise oversight of the clinical investigation; and

(v) If obtaining informed consent is not feasible and a legally authorized representative is not reasonably available, the investigator has committed, if feasible, to attempting to contact within the therapeutic window the subject's family member who is not a legally authorized representative, and asking whether he or she objects to the subject's participation in the clinical investigation. The investigator will summarize efforts made to contact family members and make this information available to the IRB at the time of continuing review.

(b) The IRB is responsible for ensuring that procedures are in place to inform, at the earliest feasible opportunity, each subject, or if the subject remains incapacitated, a legally authorized representative of the subject, or if such a representative is not reasonably available, a family member, of the subject's inclusion in the clinical investigation, the details of the investigation and other information contained in the informed consent document. The IRB shall also ensure that there is a procedure to inform the subject, or if the subject remains incapacitated, a legally authorized representative of the subject, or if such a representative is not reasonably available, a family member, that he or she may discontinue the subject's participation at any time without penalty or loss of benefits to which the subject is otherwise entitled.

> If a legally authorized representative or family member is told about the clinical investigation and the subject's condition improves, the subject is also to be informed [illegible] a subject is entered into a clinical investigation with waived consent and the subject dies before a legally authorized representative or family member can be contacted, information about the clinical investigation is to be provided to the subject's legally authorized representative or family member, if feasible.
>
> (c) The IRB determinations required by paragraph (a) of this section and the documentation required by paragraph (e) of this section are to be retained by the IRB for at least 3 years after completion of the clinical investigation, and the records shall be accessible for inspection and copying by FDA in accordance with § 56.115(b) of this chapter.
>
> (d) Protocols involving an exception to the informed consent requirement under this section must be performed under a separate investigational new drug application (IND) or investigational device exemption (IDE) that clearly identifies such protocols as protocols that may include subjects who are unable to consent. The submission of those protocols in a separate IND/IDE is required even if an IND for the same drug product or an IDE for the same device already exists. Applications for investigations under this section may not be submitted as amendments under § § 312.30 or 812.35 of this chapter.
>
> (e) If an IRB determines that it cannot approve a clinical investigation because the investigation does not meet the criteria in the exception provided under paragraph (a) of this section or because of other relevant ethical concerns, the IRB must document its findings and provide these findings promptly in writing to the clinical investigator and to the sponsor of the clinical investigation. The sponsor of the clinical investigation must promptly disclose this information to FDA and to the sponsor's clinical investigators who are participating or are asked to participate in this or a substantially equivalent clinical investigation of the sponsor, and to other IRB's that have been, or are, asked to review this or a substantially equivalent investigation by that sponsor.

Are these provisions satisfactory? In theory? In practice? If not, how could they be improved?

Or should the concept and authorization of "community consent" simply be abandoned?

[2] Therapeutic Privilege

An important limitation on informed consent is that only "material" information need be given. A related concept is that "harmful" information may be withheld. In the 1960s, 80% of physicians surveyed said they would not tell a patient of a cancer diagnosis; it would be too upsetting. In the 1990s, the figures were reversed — 90% *would* tell.

The question still remains: may a physician, ethically or legally, withhold information which might adversely affect a patient? And what if the adverse effect is simply to discourage a particularly timorous patient from needed surgery?

We have encountered this issue previously in the *Arato* problem, *supra*. We now turn to a discussion of the right to withhold information, under the rubric of the "therapeutic privilege."

NISHI v. HARTWELL
473 P.2d 116 (Haw. 1970)

Marumoto, Justice.

. . . .

The action was originally brought by Dr. Paul Nishi, a Honolulu dentist, and his wife Frances. Dr. Nishi sought to recover damages for the physical disability he suffered from undergoing a diagnostic surgical procedure known as thoracic aortography, which was recommended by Dr. Hartwell and performed by Dr. Scully. . . .

. . . .

The purpose of thoracic aortography is to determine the existence of aneurysm. The procedure involves an exposure of an artery in the inguinal region, followed by an injection of radio-opaque contrast medium through a catheter so that the concentration of the contrast medium will outline the aorta under X-ray.

Dr. Scully performed the procedure pursuant to consent signed by Dr. Nishi and Mrs. Nishi, concededly with professional competence. However, after the procedure was completed, Dr. Nishi was paralyzed from the waist down and had no control of his bowel and bladder. It is admitted that this condition occurred as a side effect of Urokon, the contrast medium which Dr. Scully used in the procedure. Neither Dr. Hartwell nor Dr. Scully apprised Dr. Nishi of the danger before he submitted himself to the procedure, although both were aware of the existence of such collateral hazard.

. . . .

The doctrine of informed consent imposes upon a physician a duty to disclose to his patient all relevant information concerning a proposed treatment, including the collateral hazards attendant thereto, so that the patient's consent to the treatment would be an intelligent one based on complete information.

However, the doctrine recognizes that the primary duty of a physician is to do what is best for his patient and that a physician may withhold disclosure of information regarding any untoward consequences of a treatment where full disclosure will be detrimental to the patient's total care and best interest.

. . . .

. . . Dr. Hartwell explained the procedure to Dr. Nishi but said nothing to him about the attendant collateral hazard. Dr. Hartwell's reasons for the omission appear in the following excerpts of his testimony:

. . . .

"Each person is different. This man was very well-educated, a fine man, but in [illegible] very frightened about his condition, he was apprehensive, and this actually guided our hand in much of what we did because if a man has a serious heart disease, with hypertension, and you thereupon frighten him further, you have a problem which you have created. . . .

"I mentioned he had high blood pressure, he had pain in his chest which we were trying to find an answer to, and if I had sat down with Dr. Nishi and said,'We are about to inject something into you which has a remote chance of causing you to be paralyzed, you may get an immediate reaction which will cost you your life,' if I had said these things to Dr. Nishi, I think it would have been a terrible mistake. . . .

. . . .

. . . "You will recall, also, that Dr. Nishi is a professional man, he's a dentist. I would dare say he's given thousands of injections of novocaine and he knows, as well as I . . . that every time you inject anything into somebody, a hazard exists, so that it didn't seem necessary to tell this professional man,'Now it is a hazard.' He knows it. And, therefore, not very much was said to him by me about the dangers of the procedure. I wished to reassure him that we were doing everything we could to find the cause of his pain and so I think, in talking to him, I said,'This is a fairly simple procedure, it simply is an injection of material into your circulation so we can outline the swelling or widening of your aorta.' "

Dr. Scully also explained the procedure to Dr. Nishi. He did so independently of Dr. Hartwell. In his explanation, he went into the technical aspects of the procedure in greater detail than he would have done with average laymen; but, as in the case of Dr. Hartwell, omitted any mention of attendant collateral hazard. He gave two reasons for the omission. One was that he thought that full disclosure would not be in Dr. Nishi's best medical interest in view of the psychological condition of Dr. Nishi alluded to in Dr. Hartwell's testimony. The other was that [illegible] the only satisfactory contrast medium then available for the procedure and he was of the opinion that the chance of the collateral hazard materializing from its use was relatively minimal. The procedure here was performed on November 3, 1959.

. . . .

The evidence recited above was uncontradicted. It brought defendants' omission to disclose clearly within the exception to the duty of full disclosure which excuses the withholding of information for therapeutic reasons. Under the showing made, we do not think that reasonable minds can differ on this point. Consequently, we hold that the circuit court properly granted defendants' motion to dismiss.

. . . .

Here, Mrs. Nishi testified that she heard Dr. Hartwell say to her husband: "You have nothing to worry about, the procedure was going to take just a few minutes and when you get out of the anesthetic, you'll be just as good as new." It is admitted that Dr. Hartwell made some statement to the effect that the procedure was a fairly simple one, in the course of reassuring Dr. Nishi that everything was being done to locate source of his pain, which he desperately wanted to know. Dr. Nishi did not consider Dr. Hartwell's statement to be a warranty, for he answered very definitely in the negative to the question whether defendants made any promises regarding the outcome of the procedure.

Plaintiffs' purpose . . . was not to claim a warranty but to emphasize their contention that Mrs. Nishi should have been told, if Dr. Nishi could not be told. This is clear from the following argument: "Thus, in the case at bar defendants' assertion that Dr. Nishi would be 'as good as new' placed upon him [sic] a correspondingly greater duty to inform Mrs. Nishi of risks and hazards."

. . . .

We are of the opinion that defendants owed no duty of disclosure to Mrs. Nishi under the law. The duty of a physician to make full disclosure is one that arises from physician-patient relationship. It is owed to the patient himself and not to his spouse or any other member of his family.

If it should be the law that, if the patient could not be told, his spouse should be told, the necessary corollary of that requirement would be that the spouse could refuse her consent to the proposed treatment. A spouse has no such right. . . .

. . . .

Dr. Nishi was mentally competent and had the legal capacity to act. Mrs. Nishi was not his guardian.

It is true that a statement is frequently made that, in a situation where withholding of some information from a patient is called for by therapeutic considerations, full disclosure should be made to his spouse. But we are aware of no case which imposes a legal duty to do so upon the physician. . . .

On this point, reference may be made to two law review articles written by Professor Hubert Winston Smith, a noted authority on legal medicine. . . .

In the first article, Professor Smith stated: "The surgeon should always disclose the full facts to the immediate family and gain help in these dangerous and delicate cases from their knowledge of the patient's reaction patterns."

The statement in the second article is as follows: "There is another principle to be borne in mind from a legal point of view: in all such cases, the physician should make it a practice, wherever possible, to communicate the true facts immediately to near relatives. This will enable special arrangements to be made in respect to financial affairs, property matters or family dispositions, almost as effectually as if the individual himself knew the truth."

Professor Smith's statements show the real reason underlying the injunction that a physician should make full disclosure to the patient's spouse, when disclosure could not be made to the patient. The reason is not that the law enjoins a physician to do so. It is that to apprise the patient's immediate family, not necessarily limited to the spouse, is a considerate act on the part of the physician to the spouse and the family; it is good public relations; and in some cases, the discussion which follows the disclosure will be helpful to the physician in deciding his course of action.

. . . .

Affirmed.

Abe, Justice (dissenting).

As I see it, the sole issue of this case may be framed thus: where a patient suffers injuries as an after effect of thoracic aortography performed with his consent, such consent having been obtained without the disclosure of attendant collateral hazards, which party has the burden to prove that such nondisclosure was or was not according to reasonable standard of medical practice and therefore was or was not actionable?

. . . .

I

If the decision of this court is that all claims for relief under the doctrine of informed consent shall be tried under the negligence theory, I question the soundness of such holding. It appears to me that the only difference in the trial of such action under the battery theory and the negligence theory is as follows: (a) under the battery theory a physician must prove that withholding the information was justified under reasonable standard of medical practice; and (b) under the negligence theory a patient must prove it was negligent under established standard of medical practice for a physician to have withheld the information.

Fundamentally, the claim for relief under the doctrine of informed consent is founded on the theory of battery. And as I have noted above, this doctrine is based on the concept that consent unless intelligently given is not a consent, and thus, consent obtained by fraud or without reasonable disclosure is void — a nullity. In other words, fraud or misrepresentation or failure on the part of a doctor to reasonably inform a patient vitiates the consent that he may have obtained from a patient and, therefore, whatever was done by a doctor, even with the utmost skill, is battery and a patient would have a claim for relief. Thus it is no defense for a doctor that the treatment or diagnostic procedure was conducted with utmost skill, because the claim for relief is not the unskillful nor negligent act of a physician, but the unconsented touching of a patient which is battery.

The plaintiffs correctly tried this case under this theory. The evidence is uncontradicted that Dr. Hartwell and Dr. Scully failed to fully disclose to the patient the collateral hazards of the injection of Urokon in the diagnostic procedure of thoracic aortography. Thereby, I believe, the plaintiffs had proven a prima facie case of battery and liability on the part of the doctors. The burden was not on the plaintiffs to show that under reasonable standard of medical practice the doctors should have been required to make full disclosure.

. . . .

Here, there was no such standard established, nor was there an attempt to do so because the trial judge dismissed the case after the plaintiffs rested, though they had proven a prima facie case. The dismissal was based on an erroneous theory that the plaintiffs had the burden to prove that under reasonable standard of medical practice, Dr. Hartwell and Dr. Scully were under a duty to make reasonable disclosure to Dr. Nishi. As I have noted above that was not the case, and the plaintiffs by showing that Dr. Hartwell and Dr. Scully failed to reasonably inform Dr. Nishi, had proven a prima facie case for recovery against and liability on the part of Dr. Hartwell and Dr. Scully.

. . . .

III

Further, if the decision of this court means that all cases under the doctrine of informed consent shall be tried under the negligence theory, it may amount to nullification of all such claims because it may be almost impossible, if not absolutely impossible in many cases, to prove damages under the generally recognized rule of proximate cause.

Now let us assume that in this case it was proven that under established standard of medical practice Dr. Hartwell and Dr. Scully should have made full disclosure of the collateral hazards attendant, and therefore, their failure to do so was negligence. Now, will they be liable for damages to Dr. Nishi for the injuries he suffered because of this negligence? Not under the generally recognized rule of proximate cause because the injuries he suffered were not the proximate result of the negligence of the physicians — their failure to make full disclosure. The injuries were the result of the injection of Urokon into his bloodstream and its aftereffect.

. . . .

Here, Dr. Nishi in his deposition stated that he would not have consented to undergo thoracic aortography if he had been fully informed of the collateral hazards attendant and thus, the plaintiffs would have been able to prove damages under the "but for" rule. However, how is a plaintiff, who sues a physician in a representative capacity for a deceased person, to show causal relation even under the "but for" rule where the patient dies during a surgery or immediately thereafter before he learns of the nondisclosure?

Also to require a patient-plaintiff to show that his mental and emotional condition at the time of the treatment or prior thereto did not justify a physician from withholding certain information, I believe, would be placing almost an insurmountable burden of proof upon a plaintiff. In many cases a patient may have had one family doctor and he alone would have the specific knowledge regarding plaintiff's condition that would justify nondisclosure.

I believe logic and reason dictate that courts should permit the trial of cases involving informed consent under the battery theory for the reasons I have stated above, unless the basic ground for requiring such cases to be tried only under the negligence theory is to discourage such actions by making proof difficult for patients.

IV

I would reverse and remand for a new trial.

NOTES AND QUESTIONS

1. Note that *Nishi* was reversed by *Carr v. Strode*, *supra* § 3.0[illegible] not as to therapeutic privi[illegible] also that it is this privilege — or at least its corollary — which is characterized as the *patient's* right "to be left uninformed." Is this a better way of looking at it? Why?

2. Note that the so-called "therapeutic privilege" may be "therapeutic" in three different ways. First, by withholding information, the physician may bring the patient to needed treatment and therapy. Second, by withholding information, the physician may avoid upsetting the patient and improve chances of recovery. Third, by withholding information, or actively misrepresenting the nature of the diagnosis or injury, the physician may protect other professionals as to the fault or responsibility for the condition. Are these different? Is one more valid than the others?

3. The problem is how to measure *what* may be withheld, since the usual rules of informed consent — by definition — are not working and are suspended. If we say that the physician may withhold only information which is not "material," then nothing is achieved, since that is true with conventional informed consent. Therapeutic privilege, to be effective, *must* mean that a physician may withhold *material* information. Thus, arises the problem: *how* material may be the information and who shall determine, other than the physician, whether or not to go forward if the admittedly competent judgment of the patient is being deliberately disabled by the deception?

4. Frequently, physicians will inform the family and seek their assistance and rely upon their guidance. This will, in many cases, relieve them of liability, negligence, or malpractice. Should it? And if it does, is it ethical?

5. Of course, in *Nishi*, Dr. Hartwell did not explain the risk from the injection to *either* the patient or his wife. Nor did Dr. Scully. Why did the majority not find this significant?

6. And do you agree with the dissenting Justice, that nondisclosure is fatal to the physician in a battery case, as opposed [illegible] negligence/malpractice case? D[illegible] agree with his analysis of the causation problems posed by informed consent under a negligence theory? Was *that* the theory in *Canterbury v. Spence*?

REISNER v. REGENTS OF UNIVERSITY OF CALIFORNIA

31 Cal. App. 4th 1195 (Cal. Ct. App. 1995)

Miriam A. **Vogel**, Associate Justice.

. . . .

Facts

On April 18, 1985, during surgery performed at the UCLA Medical Center by Jennifer's physician, Eric Fonklesrud, M.D., Jennifer received blood and plasma transfusions. The next day, Dr. Fonklesrud and UCLA learned the blood given to Jennifer was contaminated with human immunodeficiency virus (HIV) antibodies and the donor of the blood was notified — but neither Dr. Fonklesrud nor UCLA told Jennifer or her parents about the contaminated blood, either at that time or at any time during the next five years of Jennifer's continuing treatment. More specifically, no one told Jennifer or her parents that Jennifer might develop acquired immune deficiency syndrome (AIDS) or warned them about the dangers of contagion or counseled them about precautionary measures to prevent the spread of the disease to others.

About three years later, Jennifer started dating Daniel and, at some point, they became intimate. Obviously, since Jennifer did not know she had been exposed to AIDS, she could not warn Daniel about the risk he was taking.

On March 7, 1990, Jennifer "was diagnosed as having AIDS and it was determined that she had become infected as a result of the blood transfusion received in 1985 at UCLA." Jennifer and her parents told Daniel and Daniel was immediately tested for AIDS. A month later, Jennifer died. Shortly thereafter, Daniel was told he was HIV positive.

. . . .

Discussion

When the avoidance of foreseeable harm to a third person requires a defendant to control the conduct of a person with whom the defendant has a special relationship (such as physician and patient) or to warn the person of the risks involved in certain conduct, the defendant's duty extends to a third person with whom the defendant does not have a special relationship. (*Tarasoff v. Regents of University of California* [*supra* § 3.02[2]) Dr. Fonklesrud and UCLA concede as much but contend this rule does not create a duty where, as here, the third person is both unknown and unidentifiable. We disagree.[1]

In Tarasoff, a therapist who knew his patient intended to kill a young woman failed to warn the woman or her parents and the patient later killed the woman. When the woman's parents sued the therapist and others for her wrongful death, the therapist claimed the only duty he owed was to his patient. . . .

For several reasons, it is immaterial that, in Tarasoff, the therapist knew the identity of his patient's intended victim whereas, in this case, Defendants did not know Daniel or even that he existed.

[1] This was the only issue raised in the trial court and it is the only issue properly before us on this appeal. Accordingly, we treat Dr. Fonklesrud and UCLA in the same manner, without regard to whether, for other purposes, they may stand in different positions vis-a-vis their liability to Daniel. (*See, e.g.*, Derrick v. Ontario Community Hospital (1975) 47 Cal. App. 3d 145, 154, 120 Cal.Rptr. 566 [a hospital does not owe a duty to warn a patient that she had contracted a contagious, communicable disease when the patient has an attending physician who has undertaken to treat and advise her].) For similar reasons, we do not reach Defendants' causation issues. Causation was not raised below and could not, in any event, be determined at the pleading stage in a case such as this.

A

First, Tarasoff dictates the result in our case by holding that [illegible] duty includes the duty to [illegible] likely to apprise the victim of the danger . . . or to take whatever . . . steps are reasonably necessary under the circumstances." Daniel does not claim Defendants had to warn him, only that they had to warn Jennifer or her parents, "others [who were] likely to apprise [him] of the danger" (and, of course, did just that when they learned of it).

B

Second, there is the case of *Myers v. Quesenberry* (1983) 193 Cal. Rptr. 733. In Myers, two physicians (Quesenberry and Beaumont) were treating a pregnant patient (Hansen) for diabetes. During an examination at Quesenberry's office, the doctor concluded the fetus had died. When Quesenberry told Hansen to have the dead fetus removed within 18 hours, Hansen became emotionally upset. "The doctors then directed Hansen to drive immediately to [a local hospital] for preliminary laboratory tests. Hansen lost control of her car due to a diabetic attack and struck Myers as he was standing by the side of the road." Myers sued the doctors. The trial court sustained the doctors' demurrer . . .

The Court of Appeal reversed, holding (among other things) that "the fact that Myers was a foreseeable but not a readily identifiable victim of Hansen's driving does not preclude him from stating an action against the doctors for negligently failing to warn her not to drive in an irrational and uncontrolled diabetic condition. As a practical matter, the doctors here could not have effectively warned Myers of the danger presented by Hansen's driving. . . . However, they could easily have warned Hansen not to drive because of her irrational and uncontrolled diabetic condition. Under the facts as alleged here, this probably would not have been a futile act. Having otherwise complied with her doctors' professional recommendations, Hansen presumably would have continued to follow their advice had they warned her not to drive. . . . On these pleadings, we cannot factually presume Hansen would have ignored the doctors' warning. Thus, under these circumstances where warning the actor is a reasonable step to take in the exercise of the standard of [illegible] applicable to physicians, [illegible] liability [illegible] conditioned on potential victims [illegible] identifiable as well as foreseeable."

Similarly, on the pleadings before us, where warning Jennifer would have been a reasonable step to take in the exercise of the standard of care applicable to physicians, Defendants' liability is not conditional upon Daniel's identity being known or ascertainable, and we cannot factually presume Jennifer or her parents would have ignored Defendants' warning. According to Daniel's complaint, as soon as Jennifer and her parents discovered Jennifer had AIDS, Daniel was immediately notified. As a result, it appears a timely warning to Jennifer probably would have prevented Daniel's injury.

We reject Defendants' efforts to distinguish Myers by suggesting there is no "immediate temporal connection" here as there was in Myers (where the doctors told their patient to immediately drive to the hospital) — because Defendants did not tell Jennifer to become intimate with Daniel and because at least three years "elapsed between the negligent act and [Daniel's] injury." This analysis begs the question. Dr. Fonklesrud maintained a physician-patient relationship with Jennifer until she died, which was after Daniel's injury. Just as Dr. Fonklesrud knew or reasonably should have known that Jennifer was likely to get AIDS as a result of the contaminated blood, he knew or reasonably should have known that, as she matured, Jennifer was likely to enter an intimate relationship. What happened to Daniel as a result of Defendants' failure to warn Jennifer was just as foreseeable as what happened to Mr. Myers — which is why we reject Defendants' euphemistic effort to limit liability on an artificial and immaterial basis.

C

. . . .

3.

We summarily reject Defendants' alternative suggestion that a physician ought not to owe any duty to a third person because such a duty could adversely affect the doctor's treatment of his patient, to whom his primary duty is owed. As explained above, existing California law already imposes a duty to third persons and the only arguably "new" issue in this case is whether that duty is the same when the third person's identity is unknown to the physician and not readily ascertainable. And, contrary to Defendants' contention, the duty involved in this case — a duty to warn a contagious patient to take steps to protect others — has nothing to do with a physician's decision about how to treat his patient or with a physician's potential liability for the unauthorized disclosure of AIDS test results. (Health & Saf. Code, § 199.20 et seq.) Once the physician warns the patient of the risk to others and advises the patient how to prevent the spread of the disease, the physician has fulfilled his duty — and no more (but no less) is required.

4.

We also reject Defendants' suggestion that we ought not to find a duty is owed to Daniel because it would necessarily follow that a duty would be owed to "other persons with whom [Daniel] had sex, and the persons with whom they had sex," and so on ad infinitum. Why? Because "insurance premiums would soar and, quite likely, coverage at any price would not exist long." There are at least two reasons for rejecting this argument.

First, it presumes too much. Arguments premised on opened floodgates and broken dams are not persuasive where, as here, we suspect that only a few drops of water may spill onto a barren desert. To actually recover in this case, Daniel will be required to prove (not merely allege) that a physician and a teaching hospital, knowing they had inadvertently infected a patient with a contagious disease that is almost always deadly, failed to tell her what had happened and failed to warn her about the danger in infecting her loved ones. Daniel will also have to prove causation — not just that Jennifer would have told him about her illness and that he would then have refrained from intimate contact with her but also that he could not have acquired the disease elsewhere. We recognize the sympathetic nature of Daniel's case and the probability that jurors might be inclined to construe the [illegible] against those whose negligence probably sentenced him to death. But the very facts which favor Daniel in this case show how unlikely it is that there are dozens of other Daniels waiting in the wings.

Second, the argument goes too far. We need not decide in this case what the result would be if someone infected by Daniel sued the doctor who failed to warn Jennifer, and the fact that a duty is owed to Daniel does not mean it will be extended without limitation. However, the possibility of such an extension does not offend us, legally or morally. Viewed in the abstract (and not with reference to Jennifer or Daniel), we believe that a doctor who knows he is dealing with the 20th Century version of Typhoid Mary[2] ought to have a very strong incentive to tell his patient what she ought to do and not do and how she ought to comport herself in order to prevent the spread of her disease. In any event, the doctor's liability to fourth and fifth persons would by its nature be limited by traditional causation principles.

In short, we see no reason to limit duty in this particular case.

Disposition

The judgment is reversed and the matter is remanded to the trial court with directions to set the case for trial. Daniel is awarded his costs of appeal.

NOTES AND QUESTIONS

1. Why did Jennifer's doctor, Dr. Fonklesrud, not tell her and her parents when he discovered she received contaminated blood? Could there be a reason, ethical or otherwise? Is therapeutic privilege a possibility?

2. Suppose he *had* told them and then learned that Jennifer was dating Daniel. Would Dr. Fonklesrud have an obligation to tell Daniel? See *Tarasoff*, *supra* § 3.02[2] and the *Safer* case, *infra* § 4.02[2]. If Jennifer said not to? If she said she would, but the Doctor had reason to believe she would not? What if Daniel was also Dr. Fonklesrud's patient (as in a small town, he might well be)?

3. And note footnote 1. Does UCLA Medical Center escape liability by blaming the Doctor? What about the reverse? Is it a matter of causation or contract or ethics?

4. How will Daniel prove Jennifer *would* have warned him? She did, later, of course, but then she was dying. Or is it *necessary* to show she would have or just that she *couldn't* warn him if she didn't know?

5. What of confidentiality? The defendants argue disclosure will hurt the physician/patient relationship, which — under different facts — may

---

[2] In the early 1900's, Mary Mallon, an Irish cook working in the United States, was a typhoid carrier who, herself immune to the typhoid bacilli, unwittingly infected virtually everyone with whom she came in contact (51 original cases were directly attributed to her). (Webster's Third New International Dictionary (1981) p. 2476; 12 New Encyclopaedia Britannica (15th ed. 1988) p. 88.)

well be true. Indeed, some statutes prohibit disclosure of conditions without patient permission. Isn't the result in *Reisner* (and *Tarasoff*) in direct conflict with basic policies on privilege and confidentiality?

6. What must the plaintiff prove at trial? What will be the damages? How measured?
7. And what of Dr. Fonklesrud's license? What, exactly, was his ethical/professional misconduct?

PROBLEM 3–13 — Asbestos, Conflicts of Interest and the Therapeutic Privilege

Workers in the asbestos industry from 1920 through 1970 were almost certain to contract a unique form of lung cancer. If they worked for ten years or more, statistically death was certain. Deaths from asbestos exposure are predicted to be as many as 265,000 by 2015. Over 100,000 asbestos-related lawsuits cost over $7 billion dollars for the American legal system to process in the 1980s and 1990s. Victims received only 40% of recoveries. The danger to workers was known in the 1930s, but covered up by manufacturers well into the 1970s. See Edley, *Asbestos: A Multi-Billion Dollar Crisis,* 30 Harv. J. on Legisl. 383 (1993); Lilienfield, *The Silence: The Asbestos Industry,* 81 Am. J. Pub. Hlth. 791 (1991); Broderer, *Outrageous Misconduct: The Asbestos Industry on Trial* (1985); and *Borel v. Fibreboard Paper Products Corp.*, 493 F.2d 1076 (5th Cir. 1973). *See also Amchem Products v. Windsor*, 521 U.S. 591 (1997). Litigation has caused 16 corporate bankruptcies.

Company doctors delayed telling workers of their asbestosis/cancer diagnosis as long as possible, to reduce benefits and claims, possibly until after retirement. Doctor Kenneth Smith, corporate physician for John Manville said:

> It must be remembered that although these men have the X-ray evidence of asbestosis, they are working today and definitely are not disabled from asbestosis. . . . They have not been told of this diagnosis for it is felt that as long as the man feels well, is happy at home and at work, and his physical condition remains good, nothing should be said. When he becomes disabled and sick, then the diagnosis should be made and the claim submitted by the Company. The fibrosis of this disease is irreversible and permanent so that eventually compensation will be paid to each of these men. But as long as the man is not disabled it is felt that he should not be told of his condition so that he can live and work in peace and the Company can benefit by his many years of experience. Should the man be told of his condition today there is a very definite possibility that he would become mentally and physically ill, simply through the knowledge that he has asbestosis.

How could Doctor Smith justify not telling the workers of their conditions? Was it truly an instance of therapeutic privilege, as in the *Nishi* case? Or was it due to a conflict of interests, akin to *Moore v. California*, *supra* § 3.02[1]? Or was it simply that there was no physician-patient relationship and Doctor

Smith owed no obligation of disclosure to Manville's employees? As to that see the *Pettus* and *Deramus* cases, *supra* § 3.02[1].

[illegible] Experimentation

Experimentation is a necessary part of modern medicine, to test new drugs and new procedures or therapies. It is an essential part of the teaching mission of university hospitals. We are here concerned, however, with basic medical experimentation, where outcomes are unknown and people — usually patients — participate knowing there may be no benefit from the new technique. Indeed, they may be in a "control group" and not even get the new technique or product.

The question is often, *when* is a technique (*e.g.*, autologous bone marrow transplant or peripheral stem cell rescue) so new as to be experimental as a technique or in a new application (*e.g.*, for treatment of breast cancer)? And if it is deemed experimental, what are the implications — for consent, funding and regulation? This issue arises often in the context of prior authorization for reimbursement by managed care organizations. *See* § 4.04[2], *infra*. Or in the law of medical malpractice.

For us, in this text on bioethics, where autonomy is important, the principal issue recurring in experimentation is one concerning consent. Partly this is because "good science" requires control groups — those not receiving the tested therapy — for comparison with the subject group. Thus all of the participants know that some are not being "helped" (or *hurt*), but they do not know who. Partly, too, there is a confusion of roles and responsibilities where experiments are performed on patients, who came seeking help. Ethical issues are compounded where the researchers fill *two* roles — physician/healer and researcher/scientist. Most troublesome, however, are those cases where consent is simply not even sought.

We begin with the *Burton* case, which in 1953 involved the first multi-center medical investigation in the United States. Nearly 30 years later, young master Burton brings suit.

BURTON v. BROOKLYN DOCTORS HOSPITAL

452 N.Y.S.2d 875 (Sup. Ct. 1982)

Sullivan, Justice.

Plaintiff, blind since infancy from a disease known as retrolental fibroplasia (RLF), caused by his exposure to a prolonged liberal application of oxygen, has recovered a substantial judgment for medical malpractice against New York Hospital, where he was treated as a premature infant, and two of its physicians, all of whom appeal.

Born five to six weeks premature at Brooklyn Doctors Hospital on July 3, 1953, plaintiff, who weighed only 1362 grams or three pounds at birth, was transferred the next day to New York Hospital, which had been designated by the City of New York as a premature nursery care center. Transfer was automatic in cases where an infant weighed less than 1550 grams. At the time, more than half of all premature babies of plaintiff's size died in infancy; many of the survivors either sustained brain damage or were blinded by RLF, a disease which, first identified in 1942, reached epidemic proportions in this country in the late 1940s and early 1950s. The increase in the incidence of RLF coincided with the widespread advances in the development of life-saving techniques in treating premature infants, all of which revolved around the liberal use of oxygen.

. . . .

In the summer of 1953 a significant segment of the medical community continued to believe that the liberal administration of oxygen to prematures was important in preventing death or brain damage. Yet, a respected body of medical opinion believed that oxygen contributed to RLF. Thus, the medical profession was confronted with a terrible dilemma — the antidote to two problems, death and brain damage, appeared to be the cause of another, blindness. One court, commenting on the perplexity of the problem, spoke of the anxiety of those physicians who "tried to steer their tiny patients between the Scylla of blindness and the Charybdis of brain damage."

On July 1, 1953, just two days before plaintiff's birth and after years of uncoordinated and inconclusive independent investigation, a national human research study known as the Cooperative Study of Retrolental Fibroplasia and the Use of Oxygen was undertaken in an attempt to determine the role of oxygen in RLF and the effect of its withdrawal or curtailment. The Cooperative Study, whose conclusions were announced on September 19, 1954 and published in October of 1956, found that prolonged liberal use of oxygen was the critical factor in the development of RLF, and that curtailment of the supply of oxygen to premature infants after 48 hours to clinical need decreased the incidence of RLF without increasing the risk of death or brain damage.

While liberal exposure to oxygen continued to be routine treatment for premature babies at the time of plaintiff's birth, the view that increased oxygen was a necessary life saver had, as already noted, become suspect. New York Hospital, for instance, had, from January 1952 to June 1953, conducted its own study of the effects of oxygen on premature infants and concluded "that prolonged oxygen therapy may be related to the production of RLF. . . ." The results of that 18-month study were announced by the hospital on June 16, 1953 at a meeting attended by its pediatricians and ophthalmologists. Because the preliminary results of its investigation were considered to be insufficient, however, the hospital decided to become a participant in the Cooperative Study. This was the situation that existed on July 4, 1953 when plaintiff entered New York Hospital.

At the time of his transfer plaintiff's condition was recorded as "good" and, except for his prematurity, no abnormal conditions were noted. From the time of birth until his arrival at New York Hospital around noon, he was being administered four liters of oxygen continuously. Upon his arrival he was placed under the care of Dr. Lawrence Ross, a pediatric resident, who examined him and found his condition "good, his color pink, cry vigorous and clear lungs throughout." He concluded that plaintiff was "a vigorous premature infant, in good condition with no abnormalities or anamolies [sic]." A loss of 62 grams in his weight was noted, however, and plaintiff was placed on the "serious list." Dr. Ross directed that plaintiff be placed in an incubator with oxygen at three to four liters. At 11:15 that evening Dr. Ross, aware that oxygen had been implicated as a cause of RLF, ordered that oxygen be "reduced . . . as tolerated." Dr. Ross testified that [illegible] oxygen was good medical practice and in accordance with [my] judgment." The following day he noted that plaintiff appeared "to be doing well."

The hospital records indicate that, in compliance with Dr. Ross' order, the nurses did reduce the oxygen flow from three to two and one-half liters, and the concentration of oxygen in the incubator from 35% to 30%. Plaintiff's condition throughout remained good, and no problems necessitating an increase in the oxygen flow were reported.

On July 6th at 2:10 p.m., Dr. Mary Engle, a member of the hospital staff and an instructor in pediatrics at New York Hospital's affiliate, the Cornell University Medical College, on instructions from Dr. Levine, the Chairman of the Department of Pediatrics, entered an order in the hospital record, "Oxygen study: In prolonged oxygen at concentration greater than 50%." At the time Dr. Engle was serving as Dr. Levine's assistant for purposes of coordinating the hospital's participation in the Cooperative Study. Dr. Engle conceded that she countermanded Dr. Ross' order without examining plaintiff and without ever speaking to his parents. She testified further that she had no responsibility for the care and treatment of premature infants or the supervision of residents.

The Cooperative Study's methodology was to enter and observe prematures of 1500 grams or less at birth after 48 hours. Its protocol provided that one out of every three such premature infants be placed in an increased oxygen environment, while two out of three be placed in reduced oxygen. This method of distribution was designed to subject the least number of babies to the risk of blindness that statistics would permit. Of the approximately 760 babies who were placed in the Study throughout the United States, only 68 were placed in increased oxygen.

As a result of Dr. Engle's order the concentrations of oxygen went from 2 to 5 liters in one day, and, over a span of 28 days in increased dosages up to a high of 9 liters, and from an environment of 30% oxygen to a high of 82%. Dr. Engle testified that at the time of plaintiff's birth the medical community [illegible] whether premature babies were better or worse off in routine (increased) oxygen, but conceded that the doctors familiar with the earlier New York Hospital study, of which she was a co-author, had concluded that increased oxygen might be unnecessary for premature babies. Nevertheless, she stated, prolonged oxygen was the routine practice. New York Hospital's manual on the "Management of Premature Infants," which set forth the hospital's rules relating to premature care, provided for the liberal administration of oxygen.

. . . .

Except for faint light perception in his left eye plaintiff is totally blind. He suffers daily pain and irritation, which has worsened in recent years and which he eases by rubbing and pressing his eyes. Except for a brief stint in his family's business answering phones, and a part time job as an interviewer with the Blind Guild he has been unable to find employment. Eventually, because his eyes are shrinking, they will have to be enucleated and replaced with plastic ones.

. . . .

We believe that the evidence supports a finding that Dr. Engle and the hospital failed in their duty to plaintiff in both respects and, thus, the verdict of liability against them should stand. We further find that Dr. Ross, who did not order the increase in oxygen, and whose own order to reduce oxygen was countermanded, should not have been found liable at all.

. . . .

Although the conventional medical wisdom at the time believed that increased oxygen was essential to the survival of premature babies, the hospital and Dr. Engle cannot avail themselves of the shield of acceptable medical practice when a number of studies, including their own, had already indicated that increased oxygen was both unnecessary and dangerous, particularly for an otherwise healthy baby, and especially when the attending physician, who had primary responsibility for the patient's health, had recommended a decrease. "[A] physician should use his best judgment and whatever superior knowledge, skill and intelligence he has." Moreover, "his judgment must be founded upon his intelligence."

. . . .

Moreover, that increased oxygen was the only accepted practice at the time of the study is belied to an extent by the hospital's own involvement in the Cooperative Study. Two out of three premature babies were given curtailed oxygen, while only one out of three was placed in increased oxygen. Thus, by testing two out of three babies, the hospital was acting contrary to its own routine. Without in any way challenging the legitimacy of the debate within the medical community as to the effect of the curtailment of oxygen on premature infants, we find it difficult to believe that any reputable institution would permit two out of three of its patients to receive unusual treatment, which might result in death or brain damage, unless it was fairly convinced that the conventional wisdom no longer applied.

. . . .

In the factual context in which it is presented, the issue of informed consent is, to an extent, virtually inseparable from the malpractice question. Both parents testified that they were unaware that their child had been placed in a study concerning the effects of oxygen on RLF or of Dr. Engle's order directing that their baby receive prolonged, high concentrations of oxygen. Plaintiff's father testified that he was given a consent form from a nurse which he signed without any elaboration or elucidation as to the risks of the treatment plaintiff was to receive. The consent was general in nature and authorized "the doctors of the New York Hospital to give such treatment and medication to my son which in their judgment becomes necessary while he is a patient in the New York Hospital." In the consent plaintiff's father also waived all claim to prior notification of any treatment. As was customary at the time the consent form itself did not recite any of the risks involved or indeed that the individual signing it had ever been apprised of the existence of such risks.

Defendants contend that in 1953 no legal duty to obtain informed consent based upon broad disclosure of the proposed procedure, its risks and other factors existed in New York or, for that matter, in any oth[illegible] the [illegible] consent was not recognized in New York until 1965. . . . Plaintiff's expert, Dr. Abramson, although not a physician in 1953, stated that the practice for "centuries" had been to inform patients of the type and risks of treatment, and to obtain their consent.

While the law in New York at that time did not require the detailed imparting of information such as has been statutorily mandated since 1975, either with respect to treatment or the conduct of research, doctors were never free to expose their patients to unwarranted risks without first obtaining their consent. As the Court of Appeals noted in 1914 in *Schloendorff v. New York Hospital*, "[e]very human being of adult years and sound mind has a right to determine what shall be done with his own body. . . ."

. . . .

We have examined defendants' other contentions and find that they are without merit, except that we agree that the damage award of $2,887,000 is disproportionate to plaintiff's damages, to the extent that it exceeded $1,500,000.

. . . .

NOTES AND QUESTIONS

1. In bioethical circles, *Burton* is a famous case. It was the first time in America that a multi-center, scientifically disciplined investigation was undertaken in hospital settings to evaluate treatment using subject groups and control groups. The stature of the undertaking stems partly from its seeming success: by the 1950s, premature children were no longer being treated with high levels of oxygen, and the rate of blindness seemed to drop. Later, the success of the experimentation was subjected to doubt and review, as other causes of blindness in premature infants were identified and as the age at which premature infants could be sustained was advanced to earlier weeks in pregnancy. *See* Silverman, Human [illegible] (1980).

   Human experimentation has been the subject of a number of reform movements, beginning with the Nuremberg Code incorporated in the judgment of the war crimes tribunal in convicting 13 Nazi physicians for experiments on concentration camp prisoners. Among the Nazi "experiments" were sexual mutilation, cold water immersions and exposure to toxic gases. Certain central principles were articulated at Nuremberg, that no human experimentation would be possible without the consent of the subject, without first exhausting animal alternatives, without the prospect of developing therapy for the subject or others, and without maximum scientific training and safeguards. Also, no experiments would be tolerated if they involved a high likelihood of death. In subsequent national conferences at Helsinki and Tokyo during the 1970s, these principles were in the main confirmed, although the politics of these conferences — seeking to enlarge the role of experimentation — led to a dilution of the standards. *See* Silverman, *supra*.

Why then would the experiments in *Burton* have proceeded, only eight years after Nuremberg?

2. Standards governing human experimentation are now reflected in a number of federal governmental guidelines. The National Institute of Health provides funding for experimentation on humans, subject to guidelines similar to the Nuremberg Code, enforced by review through institutional review boards required in each hospital receiving such funds. Similarly, the Department of Health and Human Services and the Department of the Army have, over the last three decades, from time to time, set guidelines of experimentation on human beings. Nevertheless, during the past two decades, with increasing frequency, the Secretaries of Health and Human Services, Defense and Energy, have all revealed documentation with respect to human experimentation during the 1950s, 1960s and 1970s, particularly concerning radiation and either institutionalized or military personnel.

3. An issue in the background of *Burton* is what a physician should do, or is obligated to do, when the results of an experimental protocol begin to materialize midway through its time frame. So, with *Burton*, it was fairly clear that his oxygen should be reduced well before the national experiment was concluded. Should the physician respond to the ethics of experimentation or the ethics of the physician-patient relationship? Does it matter whether the experimental physician *has* any relationship with the patient?

4. The experiments in *Burton* would have passed the requirements for what constitutes "good science," at least as understood in the 1950s. But the *selection* and *treatment* of experimental subjects would have failed then and now. What is your judgment on the ethics of Dr. Ross, Dr. Engle, Dr. Levine and of the hospital? What should their liability be? Suppose you had been a nurse or a hospital administrator and had learned of the treatment of young master Burton, what would you have done? What would you be ethically obligated to do?

5. As with other cases we have discussed, the true measure of ethics and their worth comes in assigning damages for breach. The Court reduces the damage award from $2,800,000 to $1,500,000. What is your evaluation of these two figures? How should damages be measured?

6. Whether the need for treatment should override the science of experimentation became a hotly debated controversy during the 1980s and 1990s as national research was undertaken to find a cure for AIDS. AIDS advocates sought to have results published early and treatments released prematurely and control groups dissolved prior to completion. In many instances, they were successful. Both NIH and FDA acceded to demand and so AIDS victims in areas where experimental opportunities did not exist were deemed qualified to receive the medicines being tested in the experiments. As a result, the FDA withdrew its requirement that any drug first be tested on human beings and shown to be

safe *and effective* before being made available to the general community. The argument was advanced that AIDS victims were, after all, facing death. Why not let them take untested medicines and [illegible] compassionate use"?

Is this fair or unfair to AIDS victims? Reconsider Chief Justice Bird's dissent in *Privitera*, *infra* § 3.04[1].

7. One of the recurring problems in medical experimentation is the use of vulnerable populations — children, as in *Burton*, *supra*; mental patients, as in *Barrett*, our next case; prisoners as in the infamous Tuskegee syphilis experiments; and the poor, as in the *Cincinnati Radiation Litigation*, the case after *Barrett.* As to research on vulnerable populations, see generally, *Conducting Medical Research on the Decisionally Impaired,* I.J. Health Care L. & P. 1 (1998); *T.D. v. New York State Office of Mental Health*, 626 N.Y.S.2d 1015 (Sup. Ct. 1995), *aff'd* 650 N.Y.S.2d 173 (App. Div. 1996), *appeal dismissed* 680 N.E. 2d 617 (N.Y. 1997), *appeal dismissed,* 1997 W.L. 785461; Annas & Grodin, The Nazi Doctors and the Nuremberg Code (1992); Jay Katz, *Human Experimentation and Human Rights,* 38 St. Louis U.L.J. 7, 12-18 (1993); Jay Katz, *Informed Consent: A Fairy Tale?,* 39 Pitt. L. Rev. 137 (1997); Garrett, *Why Informed Consent? Human Experimentation and Autonomy,* 36 Cath. Law 455 (1996); Beecher, *Ethics and Clinical Research,* 274 New Eng. J. Med. 1354 (1966).

   Why, after seventy years of scandal, codes, legislation, and litigation are vulnerable populations still at risk of medical experimental imposition? See most recently *Ethics Officials to Investigate Experiments on Children, New York Times,* April 15, 1998, A25. Is an answer — or solution — to be found in the next cases, on military experimentation and the Cincinnati radiation experiments?

8. In considering the history, law and ethics of human experimentation one recurring theme over the decades is that abuses are the product of *evil* men and women. In contrast, the participants — at least at the time — asserted the highest of motivation: the need for knowledge, to cure dread disease. And they tap the grand traditions of public health. *See* Robert Lifton, The Nazi Doctors [illegible]

   In considering the cases in this section, the most difficult questions are not philosophical or ethical, but personal: would *you* have done better? Better than Doctor Mary Engle in *Burton*. Better than Private Schmidt in the *Schmidt* case, § 1.02[2] *supra*? Better than Attorney Marcus or Doctor Hoch in the next case, *Barrett v. United States*?

BARRETT v. UNITED STATES

798 F.2d 565 (1986)

Mansfield, Circuit Judge.

. . . .

. . . In December 1952, Blauer, 42 years old, was admitted voluntarily to the New York State Psychiatric Institute (NYSPI) for psychotherapeutic treatment for depression. Shock therapy at another hospital had been unsuccessful in treating the illness. On January 8, 1953, after being injected by NYSPI personnel with a synthetic mescaline derivative, which was one of a series of injections administered to him during his stay at NYSPI, he died. The mescaline derivative had been supplied by the United States Army Chemical Corps pursuant to contracts between its procurement agency and NYSPI. NYSPI undertook to test the psychiatric effect of the compound on human subjects so that the Chemical Corps could determine its suitability as a chemical warfare agent. The contracts prohibited NYSPI from disclosing any information developed by it in the performance of its obligations thereunder.

The New York City Medical Examiner's death certificate listed the cause of Blauer's death as "Coronary arteriosclerosis; sudden death after intravenous injection of a mescaline derivative, January 8, 1953." A NYSPI medical record, which was disclosed to Blauer's estate, stated that the drug administered to Blauer was "for diagnostic and therapeutic purposes," and resulted in an "unexpected and total atypical response." This information as to the cause of death was conveyed shortly after Blauer's death to his estranged wife, Amy Blauer, and to the law firm which she retained for the purpose of investigating the matter and taking appropriate legal action. In this action the estate claims that in fact the injections of the synthetic mescaline derivative were not for a therapeutic purpose but were performed pursuant to the experimental program conducted under NYSPI's contracts with the Army Chemical Corps to determine the clinical effect of the agent on Blauer's behavior. It is also asserted that, if the Medical Examiner had been apprised of the true facts, his autopsy report would have read, "Convulsive seizures, hypotension and cardiorespiratory arrest immediately following and due to intravenous injection of a mescaline compound for investigative purposes."

In April 1953 Amy Blauer, then Administratrix of Blauer's estate, brought an action for damages against the State of New York in the New York Court of Claims, alleging that Blauer's death was caused by negligence of the NYSPI in injecting him with a toxic and dangerous compound. Defendant David Marcus, then Assistant Attorney General of the State of New York, was assigned to defend the case. His investigation uncovered the Army Chemical Corps' involvement in furnishing the mescaline derivative and arranging for its administration. . . .

After the matter was brought to the attention of the Department of Justice a conference of federal counsel and medical personnel was held in early July 1954. . . . Another conference was held on July 12, 1954, in Washington, attended by various government officials including Marcus and appellant Harris J. North, then an attorney with the U.S. Army Judge Advocate General Corps; appellant Herbert K. Greer, then Legal Advisor to the Chief Chemical Officer, Army Chemical Corps; and appellant George S. Lenard, then first assistant to the Assistant Attorney General for the Civil Division, United States Department of Justice.

. . . Dr. Hoch stated that he would not have used the new compound for experimental purposes but for the NYSPI's contract with the Army and that the experimental nature of the treatment made it a departure from accepted medical practice, which, if disclosed, would support a finding of negligence and an award of damages. According to the report of the meeting by the Judge Advocate General, Mr. Leonard "forcibly informed Mr. M[illegible] and any further proceedings should be limited to the medical aspects of the case" and that disclosure of the Army-NYSPI contract, its purpose and the results of the experiments would be objectionable. . . . Appellant North later recommended to appellant Greer that the Chemical Corps' contracts with NYSPI be removed from New York to the Chemical Corps Procurement Agency in Maryland where "they would be beyond subpoena power of the plaintiff [Amy Blauer] in this action [in the New York State Court of Claims]."

In recognition of the Army's interest in not disclosing the Chemical Corps' involvement in the administration of its mescaline derivatives to Blauer, Marcus repeatedly postponed the pretrial examinations of NYSPI doctors by Amy Blauer's counsel. . . . It is claimed by the estate that the State of New York, however, did not turn over NYSPI classified records that would have revealed that the injections were part of an Army Chemical Corps experimental drug program conducted for chemical warfare research. The estate contends that it was misled by the State into the belief that it had received all relevant hospital records with respect to Blauer. Marcus pursued settlement negotiations with the Blauer estate's counsel, arriving at a tentative figure of $15,000. Marcus requested an assurance from the Army that one-half of his figure would be reimbursed by the Department of the Army, which thereupon requested the Chemical Corps to draw a check for $7,500 to be used for that purpose.

At no time was the estate or its counsel ever informed of the involvement of the United States Army Chemical Corps in the administration of the mescaline derivative to Blauer, that it was part of a Chemical Corps experimental program, that the injection causing his death was the fifth in a series to which he had reacted unfavorably, and that but for the NYSPI's contract with the Army the mescaline derivative would not have been administered to Blauer. If his estate had pursued its right to examine the relevant NYSPI files and witnesses it probably would have uncovered all or most of these facts or have been met with a refusal to answer or make a disclosure on grounds of executive [illegible], allegedly in the belief that it faced the risk of not proving its negligence claim against the state since mescaline (as distinguished from the experiment compound) was recognized as sometimes used for diagnostic or therapeutic purposes, the estate agreed, in 1955 negotiations with Marcus, to settle its claim of wrongful death for $15,000.

Under procedures in effect in 1955 the State of New York could not settle the case without presenting evidence of prima facie liability to the Court of Claims, which would then make a finding of liability and award damages in the amount agreed upon by the parties. Before following this procedure Marcus revealed the Army's involvement to the judge in an *ex parte* conference. The Judge thereupon increased the settlement figure to $18,000. At the court proceeding that followed, Marcus introduced certain NYSPI medical records (the exact scope of which is not shown in the record) by handing them directly to the judge but did not turn them over to the estate's counsel. Nor did the latter insist on examining them, allegedly for the reason that the amount of the settlement had already been agreed upon and the court proceeding was viewed as a formality. Dr. Hoch testified that Blauer's death was caused by the injection of a mescaline compound and that the administration of the drug was not in accordance with generally accepted medical practice. However, at no time was the estate made aware of the Army's involvement in the injections. . . .

The Army's involvement in the injections and the fact that the mescaline derivatives were furnished as part of its chemical warfare testing program remained secret for 20 years and would have continued to do so but for the public disclosure of these facts by the Secretary of the Army on August 12, 1975. . . .

. . . .

Discussion

Since the principal issue on this appeal is what immunity, if any, may properly be asserted as a defense by each of the defendants, a brief review of the principles governing immunity is essential. Two kinds of immunity have been recognized under certain circumstances, absolute and qualified. Absolute immunity from liability has been accorded to a few types of government officials whose duties are deemed as a matter of public policy to require such protection to enable them to function independently and effectively, without fear or harassment. These include the President of the United States . . ., although the Attorney General of the United States is accorded absolute immunity in his direction or conduct of litigation involving the government, in view of the risk that disappointed litigants will seek to relitigate a lost case by suing him, he is not entitled to such immunity for his performance of national security tasks since they do not pose the same risks. . . .

. . . .

With these principles in mind, we turn to the present case in which, upon the undisputed facts, the district court upheld defendant Marcus' defense of absolute immunity and rejected the absolute immunity defense asserted by the federal attorneys. With respect to Marcus, little discussion is needed. It is beyond dispute that his sole involvement was at all times as Assistant Attorney General of the State of New York representing that state as its attorney in the action brought by Blauer's estate against it in the Court of Claims for damages caused by the negligence of the NYSPI, a state institution, in the treatment of Blauer. Under the governing principles we have outlined, the district court's decision upholding his claim of absolute immunity must be upheld. The fact that he may or may not have engaged in questionable or harmful conduct during the course of his representation of the State in that litigation is irrelevant. The immunity attaches to his function, not to the manner in which he performed it.

On the other hand, upon the present record, the claim of the federal-attorney appellants to absolute immunity must just as surely be rejected. They contend that all federal attorneys acting "in anticipation of a lawsuit" are cloaked with absolute immunity. We need not define the outer boundary of the absolute protection granted to government lawyers defending civil suits, because the conduct of the federal appellants clearly falls outside it. The federal attorneys did not act as counsel for any of the parties in litigation relating to the [illegible] On the contrary, their efforts were devoted mainly to avoiding involvement of the federal government or federal officials in such proceedings by keeping the estate ignorant of the role played by the United States Government. Their conduct was not public and was unknown to those affected by it. Indeed, the open conflict of a court battle, which creates the need for protective immunity to enable the government attorney to perform his duty fearlessly, was totally absent. Finally, acceptance of the view urged by the federal appellants would result in a blanket grant of absolute immunity to government lawyers acting to prevent exposure of the government to liability. Given the "rare and exceptional character" of absolute immunity, *Cleavinger,* we must reject this proposed wide-ranging immunity.

. . . .

The federal-attorney appellants' entitlement to qualified immunity by reason of their status as government officials depends on whether reasonable persons would have recognized at the time that their conduct violated any clearly established statutory or constitutional norms. Appellees claim that the federal attorneys unconstitutionally deprived the estate of a property interest in its causes of action against the United States Government and various federal officials. . . .

It is readily apparent that knowledge of the government's role in Blauer's death would have been critically important to the estate's assessment of its legal rights. There can be no doubt that the Army Chemical Corps' alleged instigation of and participation in the experimental administration of the mescaline derivative to Blauer without his consent (indeed, it is claimed that the hospital records show it to have been over his objection) would have provided the basis for a valid claim of violation of Blauer's underlying right to be free from unjustified and unconsented to invasion of his person, amounting to a battery. The alleged conduct would in 1953 have amounted to both a tort and a violation of Blauer's constitutional rights. Although the availability of a damages remedy against the government under the Federal Tort Claims may, because of sovereign immunity principles [illegible] in 1953, Blauer's right to be free from a battery at the instigation of Army Chemical Corps officials could hardly be questioned at that time. . . .

. . . .

In the 1953-1955 period it was well settled that the estate's underlying right to sue the alleged Army Chemical Corps wrongdoers for damages for causing Blauer's death constituted a property right protected by the Constitution from arbitrary governmental interference. Indeed the Supreme Court as far back as 1882 had stated, "a vested right of action is property in the same sense in which tangible things are property, and is equally protected from arbitrary interference." . . .

Whether the alleged "cover-up" conduct of the federal-attorney defendants violated the estate's foregoing property right presents a closer question. The federal-attorney defendants were neither parties to the ongoing litigation between the estate and the State of New York nor the subjects of discovery in that action. They therefore were not under any duty to volunteer to the estate information that would alert it to the existence of a claim against the federal government and certain of its officials for Blauer's wrongful death. On the other hand, the government officials were not free to arbitrarily interfere with the estate's vindication of its claims. . . . Thus, the officials owed a duty to the estate under currently prevailing law not to suborn perjury by any witness in the ongoing litigation and not to induce Marcus to evade disclosure to the estate, in the course of discovery in the Court of Claims case, of the Army Chemical Corps' complicity in Blauer's death.

. . . .

In the present case the estate claims that the federal-attorney defendants crossed the line from mere silence to active interference with the estate's rights in its pending Court of Claims action. Dr. Paul Hoch, for instance, is alleged to have been counseled by the federal-attorney defendants not to reveal the Army Chemical Corps' involvement in supplying the mescaine derivative or the purpose of the injections. Instead, while conceding that the injections were not in accordance with generally accepted medical routine, he testified falsely before the New York Court of Claims that the drug was a derivative compound used quite commonly by the profession for purposes of diagnosing certain types of psychiatric ills, that it had been administered "for diagnostic purposes to Mr. Blauer," and that "Mr. Blauer's condition could best be diagnosed and treatment thereafter given if he could be observed during a psychotic state under controlled conditions." In fact, according to the estate, Dr. Hoch was well aware that the mescaline derivative was a new compound not being administered for diagnostic or therapeutic purposes but as an experiment to study its effect for chemical warfare purposes.

The estate further claims that the federal-attorney defendants violated its rights in its pending litigation by inducing Marcus to improperly conceal the Army Chemical Corps' involvement in NYSPI's collaborative chemical warfare experiment. It is alleged that the concealment was further effectuated by Marcus' knowing participation in an alleged fraud upon the estate through his elicitation of Dr. Hoch's false testimony at the New York Court of Claims hearing, his dexterous handling of the NYSPI medical records at that hearing so that they would not be examined by the estate's counsel, his submission of findings of fact that concealed the Army Chemical Corps' involvement, his misrepresentation of the administration of the drug as for "therapy," and his inducement of the estate to sign a release prepared by him which barred claims against the "government body" supplying the lethal derivative with which Blauer was injected without revealing that the "government" supplier was not the State of New York, as the estate assumed, but the Army Chemical Corps.

. . . .

In our view, proof of the foregoing conduct on the part of the federal-attorney defendants would preclude their resort to qualified immunity as a defense in the present action. Their alleged conduct would amount not only to active participation in a conspiracy to deceive the estate by concealing material evidence in its pending actin in the New York Court of Claims, for which they could be held liable under currently effective law, but a violation of the estate's constitutional rights in a potential action against both the Army Chemical Corps and the federal officials participating in the unconsented-to lethal [illegible], which was currently recognized as a property right entitled to protection.

. . . .

NOTES AND QUESTIONS

1. The Second Circuit Court of Appeals affirmed the trial court's decision in 1986. The principal issue on appeal was what immunity could be asserted as a defense by each of the defendants. Absolute immunity was extended to Marcus, the Assistant Attorney General for the state of New York. However, the federal attorneys were denied immunity, because their efforts were devoted mainly to avoiding involvement of the federal government by keeping the estate ignorant of the role played by the United States government. They were thus seeking to avoid open litigation, the very reason for granting immunity. The court did, however, hold open the possibility of "qualified" immunity, if the federal attorneys could show they acted in "good faith." On the facts of the case, the Second Circuit concluded that proof of the conduct of active interference with the estate's rights would preclude the resort to qualified immunity.

2. Institutionalized people, as in *Harper*, *Skinner*, *Hayes*, *Northern*, and *Strunk* (*see* Chapter 1), and in *Barrett*, are particularly subject to abuse. Generally, they have been involuntarily committed. Moreover, if restrained in a psychiatric institution, they have not only been determined amenable to psychological incursions but also may be attractive targets for the testing of innovative therapies or theories. *See*, *Aden v. Younger*, *supra,* § 3.03[1]. In lieu of laboratory animals or volunteers, inmates and patients may be viewed as targets of opportunity. For this reason, also, a national bill of rights for those institutionalized has been adopted by Congress. What should such a bill of rights provide?

3. In the world of bioethics, the important ethical limitations are usually those of physicians or other health care providers. However, as the *Barrett* case establishes, the ethics of [illegible] may also become important. In the *Barrett* case, how could the attorneys there justify their misconduct and cover-up? The state and federal attorneys were charged with protecting the public interest — did that not include Mr. Barrett? With telling the truth in court — did that not include the whole truth? With respecting opposing counsel — did they do so?

4. And *should* Mr. Marcus get *absolute* immunity? *Any* immunity?

5. How could the physicians involved in the *Barrett* case justify *their* misconduct? They had obligations of fidelity, candor and care with respect to Mr. Blauer; was there any way they could rationalize their behavior as fitting their obligations? If the rationalization somehow was that these "experiments" were necessary in the national interest, would not the physicians still be found wanting because of the scientific deficiencies in their practices, as well as the cover-up and the failure to obtain

informed consent (Mr. Blauer, after all, *was* a voluntary patient)? How different was the doctors' performance from that of the medical doctors in Nazi Germany? As to that see Lifton, The Nazi Doctors (Basic Books 1986). And reconsider here the statutes in *Aden v. Younger, supra.*

6. What of the damages awarded? In the world of bioethics, the concept of "damages" is seldom used. However, when bioethics become implemented through legal processes, the necessity of translating abstractions into dollars and cents is a useful method for apportioning responsibility and for measuring the gravity of misconduct, as well as the extent of injury. In varying ways, these become surrogates for foreseeability and culpability. The *Barrett* court thus seeks to measure lost support, parental nurture, and pain and suffering, working through to $500,000 in compensatory damages and an ultimate total of $700,000. Should there have been punitive damages for outrageous misconduct?

7. *Burton* and *Barrett* involved experiments conducted nearly fifty years ago. Lest we think such conduct is behind us and cannot recur, we now turn to two more contemporary experiments, the Cincinnati Radiation Experiments of the 1970s and The Africa AZT tests of the 1990s. This time, the victims are the poor, in hospitals or foreign countries.

IN RE CINCINNATI RADIATION LITIGATION

874 F. Supp. 796 (S.D. Ohio 1995)

Beckwith, District Judge.

. . . .

A. Factual Allegations

. . . From 1960 to 1972 experiments were conducted at the University of Cincinnati College of Medicine and Cincinnati General Hospital on at least 87 people. The subjects of the experiments were exposed to total or partial body irradiation. The primary purpose of the experiments was to test the psychological and physical effects of radiation on humans. Indeed, a report prepared for the Department of Defense by the individual Defendants who conducted the Human Radiation Experiments during the period 1960 to 1966 indicated that the goal was "to develop a baseline for determining how much radiation exposure was too much, and to determine how shielding could decrease the deleterious effect of the radiation," and to determine what a single dose of whole or partial radiation could do to "cognitive or other functions mediated through the central nervous system."

Patients were selected to be subjects in the experiments because they had cancer. The patients were not, however, in the final stages of their disease, nor were they close to death. Each patient selected was deemed in reasonably good clinical condition. Further, Dr. Saenger is alleged to have noted that the patients selected had life expectancies of up to two years. Those patients selected were primarily indigent, poorly educated, and of lower than average intelligence. A majority of the patients selected were African-Americans.

The patients selected for the experiments were told that they were receiving radiation for their cancer, although the radiation tests were designed to benefit the Human Radiation Experiments rather than the patient[illegible] individual Defendants on the Human Radiation Experiments indicates that the patients were told that they were to receive treatment to help their sickness.

No consent forms were used for the first five years of the Human Radiation Experiments. Beginning in 1965, the Complaint alleges, consent forms were used but failed to state the real risk of the radiation exposure to the patients. Further, the Complaint alleges that the consent forms did not indicate to the Plaintiffs that they were part of experiments funded by the Department of Defense or that the primary purpose of the experiments was to test the effect of radiation on soldiers in the event that they would encounter a nuclear attack. Rather, the consent forms indicated only that the patients were participating in scientific experiments. Thus, the Plaintiffs allege, all risks and hazards of the Human Radiation Experiments were not made known and, indeed, were intentionally concealed from the Plaintiffs. Specifically, none of the consent forms indicated that there was a risk of death from bone marrow infection within 40 days of irradiation. Likewise, none of the consent forms indicated that nausea and vomiting would likely be experienced by the subjects following irradiation. Finally, the long-term carcinogenic and genetic hazards associated with massive doses of radiation were also concealed.

. . . .

Radiation exposure from the Human Radiation Experiments either led to the patients' death, seriously shortened their life expectancies, and/or led to radiation injury resulting in bone marrow failure or suppression, nausea, vomiting, burns on the patients' bodies, severe and permanent pain, and/or suffering and emotional distress.

The Plaintiffs allege that the Human Radiation Experiments were designed and conducted by Defendant Saenger and the other individual Defendants with callous indifference to the effects such experiments would have on the physical and mental health of the subjects, and with conscious disregard for the rights and safety of the subjects in situations where there was a [illegible] substantial harm. The Human Radiation Experiments were also designed and conducted by Defendant Saenger and the other individual Defendants in direct contravention of the Helsinki Declaration Mandate regarding nontherapeutic clinical research. The Helsinki Declaration requires that the doctor "remain the protector of the life and health of that person on whom clinical research is being carried out." Instead, the Human Radiation Experiments were conducted recklessly and willfully without due regard for the rights of the subjects of the research under the United States Constitution and laws, the laws of the State of Ohio, and international law.

B. Legal Claims

Based upon the foregoing factual allegations, Plaintiffs set forth the following claims for relief:

(1) Plaintiffs' participation in the Human Radiation Experiments without informed consent resulted in a violation of their rights, privileges and immunities secured by the First and Fourteenth Amendments to the United States Constitution, including, but not limited to, the right of access to the courts, the rights to procedural and substantive due process of law, the right to equal protection under the law, and the right to privacy under 42 U.S.C. § 1983.

. . . .

(10) By intentionally exposing Plaintiffs or their decedents to harmful or fatal doses of radiation without informed consent, the Defendants committed a battery.

(11) By intentionally concealing from the Plaintiffs the full extent, potential consequences, and true purposes of the Human Radiation Experiments, the Defendants perpetrated a fraud upon Plaintiffs.

. . . .

IV. Due Process

A. Right to Bodily Integrity

. . . .

The Plaintiffs' substantive due process claim in this case is grounded upon the premise that individuals have a liberty interest in their bodily integrity that is protected by the Due Process Clause of the Fourteenth Amendment, and particularly upon the premise that nonconsensual experiments involving extremely high doses of radiation, designed and supervised by military doctors and carried out by City hospital physicians violate that right.

The right to be free of state-sponsored invasion of a person's bodily integrity is protected by the Fourteenth Amendment guarantee of due process. . . .

As a threshold matter, the individual and *Bivens* Defendants raise the issue of voluntariness. Voluntariness pertains to this case on two levels. First is the question of whether the Plaintiffs were voluntary patients at Cincinnati General Hospital, and if so, what effect that voluntary presence has on their ability to assert this claim. Second, the Court must determine whether the Plaintiffs in this case sufficiently allege that they were involuntary participants in the Human Radiation Experiments, and, if so, what effect that involuntary participation has on their ability to assert this claim.

Many of the cases recognizing constitutional causes of action for nonconsensual medical treatment involve plaintiffs who were either prisoners or were involuntarily committed to psychiatric institutions. In their various memoranda and at oral argument, the Defendants argue that Plaintiffs were voluntarily present at Cincinnati General Hospital when the Human Radiation Experiments were performed. The Defendants argue that all of the Plaintiffs came to the hospital of their own volition and could have left the hospital at any time they chose. Since the liberty interest at issue has only been extended to prison inmates and patients involuntarily confined in psychiatric institutions, the Defendants argue that Plaintiffs cannot base their cause of action on this liberty interest.

. . . .

This argument fails at this stage of the litigation for several reasons. First, it is not at all clear that Plaintiffs were voluntary patients at Cincinnati General Hospital. The Plaintiffs in this case are all alleged to have been poor. Discovery may demonstrate that the only hospital in the city to treat indigent patients was Cincinnati General Hospital. If this is so, the Court would be reluctant to hold that a person with only one hospital from which to choose voluntarily enters that hospital when he becomes ill. Regardless of that factual uncertainty, Defendants argument still fails for the following reasons.

The Plaintiffs allege that they were purposefully misled in several respects. First, Plaintiffs allege that they were specifically not informed that the radiation they were receiving was for a military experiment rather than treatment of their cancer. Further, Plaintiffs allege that they were never informed that the amount of radiation they were to receive would cause burns, vomiting, nausea, bone marrow failure, severe shortening of life expectancy, or even death. When a person is purposefully misled about such crucial facts as these, he can no longer be said to exercise that degree of free will that is essential to the notion of voluntariness.

To manipulate men, to propel them toward goals which we see but they may not, is to deny their human essence, to treat them as objects without wills of their own, and therefore to degrade them. This is why to lie to men, or to deceive them, that is, to use them as means for our not their own, independently conceived ends, even if it is to their own benefit, is, in effect to treat them as sub-human, to behave as if their ends are less ultimate and sacred than our own. . . . For if the essence of men is that they are autonomous beings — authors of values, of ends in themselves . . . — then nothing is worse than to treat them as if they were not autonomous but natural objects whose choices can be manipulated.

. . . .

When an individual's bodily integrity is at stake, a determination that the state has accorded adequate procedural protection should not be made lightly. Since bodily invasions often [illegible] after the fact through damage awards in the way that most deprivations of property can, the state must precede any deliberate invasion with formalized procedures. . . .

In applying the criterion of needless severity, the crucial factors are the presence of physical pain, the permanence of any disfigurement or ensuing complication, the risk of irreversible injury to health, and the danger to life itself. However, an intrusion otherwise sufficiently minimal to pass this test is, nevertheless, beyond the boundaries of due process if less severe means could achieve the state's purpose with the same effectiveness. . . .

The allegations in the Complaint indicate that procedural regularity was absent and that the invasion of bodily integrity was severe. In essence, the allegations in the Complaint amount to a claim that the individual Defendants blatantly lied to the Plaintiffs. Unlike in *Washington v. Harper*, a decision was not made by the treating physician that Plaintiffs' medical condition required drastic doses of radiation. Rather, the allegations give rise to the question of whether Plaintiffs were receiving medical treatment at all. This absence of procedural safeguards alone is sufficient to trigger the protections of the Due Process Clause. However, the allegations contained even more.

The allegations also indicate that the Plaintiffs received needlessly severe invasions of their bodily integrity. Unlike in *Schmerber*, where the invasion was minimal and had no lasting side effects, the invasion Plaintiffs allege in this case was total and partial body radiation, which caused burns, vomiting, diarrhea and bone marrow failure, and resulted in death or severe shortening of life. These allegations are more than sufficient to trigger Fifth Amendment protection.

Thus, in accord with *Barrett v. United States*, the Court is compelled to hold that the individual and *Bivens* Defendants may not assert the defense of qualified immunity. The qualified immunity defense is reserved to those officials who are sued for their exercise of discretionary responsibilities delegated to them by the government. There can be no doubt that the individual and *Bivens* Defendants' alleged instigation of and participation in the Human Radiation Experiments were acts far beyond the scope of their delegated powers. The individual and *Bivens* Defendants, many of whom were physicians, were not acting as physicians when they conducted experiments on unwitting subjects at Cincinnati General Hospital. Rather, the Defendants were acting as scientists interested in nothing more than assembling cold data for use by the Department of Defense. While many government officials are authorized to conduct research, the individual and *Bivens* Defendants were hired by the City to care for the sick and injured. The Constitution never authorizes government officials, regardless of their specific responsibilities, to arbitrarily deprive ordinary citizens of liberty and life.

. . . .

B. Clearly Established Law

The Court must next determine whether the conduct alleged by Plaintiffs was clearly unconstitutional when the Human Radiation Experiments were performed. As the Court indicated previously, the right that Plaintiffs assert must have been sufficiently clear during the period between 1960 and 1972 that a reasonable official would have understood that his actions violated that right. . . .

. . . .

If the Constitution were held to permit the acts alleged in this case, the document would be revealed to contain a gaping hole. This is so in part because the alleged conduct is so outrageous in and of itself, and also because a constitution inadequate to deal with such outrageous conduct would be too feeble in method and doctrine to deal with a very great amount of equally outrageous activity. Indeed, virtually all of the rights that we as a nation hold sacred would be subject to the arbitrary whim of government.

Respect for an individual's right to bodily integrity is central to American constitutional history and tradition. The Constitution's Framers were heavily influenced by the enlightened views of popular sovereignty and limited government. For John Locke, the ideological father of the American Revolution, liberty was freedom from restraint, and the exercise of coercive power by the [illegible] suspect. The function of the law, in Locke's view, was to protect individual liberty from restraint by government or others. A central principle in Locke's thinking was the essential need for a certain minimum area of personal freedom which must on no account be violated; for if it is overstepped, the individual will find himself in an area too narrow for even that minimum development of his natural faculties which alone make it possible to pursue, and even to conceive, the various ends which men hold good or right, or sacred. . . .

An individual's autonomy was, thus, the primary value in revolutionary idealism that led to colonial independence. Then, when the first ten amendments to the Constitution were ratified in 1791, six amendments made clear that the newly created national government was a government of limited authority. Our entire history has been a continuous effort to safeguard that concept of ordered liberty. Respect for individual autonomy by the government is a central principle within that ideal.

. . . .

In the Human Radiation Experiments, it is alleged that the individual and *Bivens* Defendants designed and implemented experiments to study the effect of massive doses of radiation on military personnel during a nuclear war. To facilitate their experiments, the individual and *Bivens* Defendants are alleged to have targeted low income and African-American cancer patients from Cincinnati General Hospital. Plaintiffs allege that the Defendants did not even explain to their decedents that experiments were being' conducted, what the purposes of the experiments were, or that the high doses of radiation could result in their death, shorten their lives substantially, or cause burns, nausea, vomiting, or bone marrow failure.

The invasions of bodily integrity alleged in this case are *more* extreme than those at issue in either *Skinner* or *Rochin*. Unlike the cases of *Jacobson* and *Schmerber*, the invasion of bodily integrity alleged to have occurred in this case had extreme consequences, among them the most permanent of all possible consequences. Thus, had this set of facts [illegible] the Court would have found that Plaintiffs had stated a valid claim under the Due Process Clause of the Constitution. The right at issue and its contours were sufficiently well-defined by the Supreme Court prior to 1972 such that the individual and *Bivens* Defendants should have known that their conduct would violate the Constitution.

C. The Nuremberg Code

The preceding demonstrates that the constitutional law controlling the invasion of an individual's bodily integrity was clearly established between 1960 and 1972. Indeed, the prevailing law detailing the right was sufficiently clear that a reasonable official would have known that the Human Radiation Experiments violated constitutional law. Accordingly, that law provides an independent basis for the Plaintiffs' Section 1983 action. Nevertheless, it is impossible for the Court to ignore the historical context in which the Human Radiation Experiments were conducted.

After World War II, the United States and its allies were involved in a succession of criminal trials. The trials have commonly become known as the Nuremberg trials. Perhaps the best known Nuremberg trial involved the military officers of the Third Reich. The doctors' trial, *United States of America v. Carl Brandt*, et al., I Trials of War Criminals, Vol. 11 at 181 (1949); 6 F.R.D. 305 (1949), also known as the "Medical Case", was tried at the Palace of Justice in postwar Nuremberg, Germany. The trial was conducted under U.S. military auspices according to the Moscow Declaration on German Atrocities (November 1, 1943), Executive Order 9547 (May 2, 1945), and the London Agreement (August 8, 1945).

. . . .

The Nuremberg tribunal was asked to determine the culpability of twenty-three (23) German physicians under "the principles of the law of nations as they result from the usages established among civilized peoples, from the laws of humanity, and from the dictates of public conscience." The charges against the physicians included human experimentation involving nonconsenting prisoners. The experiments included studies of the limits of human tolerance to high altitudes and freezing temperatures. Medically-related experiments included inoculation of prisoners with infectious disease pathogens and tests of new antibiotics. Various experiments involving the mutilation of bone, muscle and nerve were also performed on nonconsenting prisoner subjects.

Throughout the trial, the question of what were or should be the universal standards for justifying human experimentation recurred. The lack of a universally accepted principle for carrying out human experimentation was the central issue pressed by the defendant physicians throughout their testimony.

The final judgment of the court was delivered on July 19, 1947. The judgment has since become known as the "Nuremberg Code." The first provision of the Code states as follows:

The voluntary consent of the human subject is absolutely essential. This means that the person involved should have legal capacity to give consent; should be so situated as to be able to exercise free power of choice without the intervention of any element of force, fraud, deceit, duress, overreaching, or other ulterior form of constraint or coercion and should have sufficient knowledge and comprehension of the elements of the subject matter involved as to enable him to make an understanding and enlightened decision. This latter element requires that before the acceptance of an affirmative decision by the experimental subject there should be made known to him the nature, duration, and purpose of the experiment; the method and means by which it is to be conducted; all inconveniences and hazards reasonably to be expected; and the effects upon his health and person which may possibly come from his participation in the experiment.

The duty and responsibility for ascertaining the quality of the consent rests upon each individual who initiates, directs, or engages in the experiment. It is a personal duty and responsibility which may not be delegated to another with impunity.[3]

Only five years later, in recognition of these [illegible] directed that human experimentation for the Department of Defense could only be conducted where there was full and voluntary consent of the subject. The directive issued by the Secretary of Defense is a mirror of the Nuremberg Code. In 1954, the World Medical Association adopted five general principles for those engaged in research and experimentation. Also in the mid-1950's, the Clinical Center of the National Institutes of Health ("NIH") adopted guidelines that applied to the use of human subjects in experimental medical research. The NIH Guidelines state:

> The rigid safeguards observed at NIH are based on the so-called "ten commandments" of human medical research which were adopted at the Nuremberg War Crimes Trials after the atrocities performed by Nazi doctors had been exposed. Every subject must give his full consent to any test, and he must be told exactly what it involves so that he goes into it with his eyes open. Among other things, the experiment must be designed to yield "fruitful results for the good of society," unnecessary "physical and mental suffering and injury" must be avoided, the test must be conducted by "scientifically qualified" persons, and the subject must be free to end it at any time he feels unable to go on.

. . . .

The Nuremberg Code is part of the law of humanity. It may be applied in both civil and criminal cases by the federal courts in the United States. At the very least, by the time the Human Radiation Experiments were designed, the Nuremberg Code served as a tangible example of conduct that "shocked the conscience," as contemplated in *Rochin, supra*. Rochin came only five years after the Nuremberg trials. Certainly Justice Frankfurter and the other members of the Court were influenced by the state-sponsored atrocities delineated in the Medical Case. Thus, even were the Nuremberg Code not afforded precedential weight in the courts of the United States, it cannot be readily dismissed from its proper context in this case. The individual and *Bivens* Defendants, as physicians and other health professionals, must have been aware of the Nuremberg Code, the Hippocratic Oath, and the several pronouncements by both world and American medical organizations [illegible] inconceivable to the Court that the individual and *Bivens* Defendants, when allegedly planning to perform radiation experiments on unwitting subjects, were not moved to pause or rethink their procedures in light of the forceful dictates of the Nuremberg Tribunal and the several medical organizations.

. . . .

VII. Equal Protection

Plaintiffs have made a Section 1983 claim alleging that they have been denied equal protection of the laws under the Fourteenth Amendment of the Constitution. . . .

[3] United States of America v. Brandt (the Medical Case), II Trials of War Criminals Before The Nuremberg Military Tribunals Under Control Council Law No. 10, p.181 (1949).

. . . .

Plaintiffs allege that the Human Radiation Experiments were directed predominantly at African-Americans. Plaintiffs also allege that the individual Defendants intentionally discriminated against them by purposefully targeting African-Americans as subjects. In an inartful passage of their Complaint, Plaintiffs assert that the disparity between the racial composition of the general population of patients at General Hospital vis-a-vis patients selected for the Human Radiation Experiments demonstrates that one purpose of the experiments was to subject African-Americans to high levels of radiation.

. . . .

. . . [E]vidence of intent in addition to disparate impact (where the disparate impact was not extreme) was necessary to state an equal protection claim. To satisfy this additional pleading, Plaintiffs assert that the predominance of African-Americans in the Human Radiation Experiments was not coincidental. Rather, Plaintiffs assert that African-American cancer patients were purposefully targeted as subjects for the Human Radiation Experiments. That allegation of intent, Plaintiffs contend, is sufficient to meet the pleading requirements of *Washington* and *Arlington Heights.*

The individual Defendants, on the other hand, contend that the Court need not examine the disparity in racial composition of the subject groups of the Human Radiation Experiments because Plaintiffs have failed to meet the threshold requirement that similarly situated persons were treated differently. Indeed, at oral argument, liaison counsel for the Defendants argued that the similarly situated persons at issue are the subjects of the Human Radiation Experiments. Thus, counsel contended, the Plaintiffs must demonstrate that African-American subjects were treated differently from the Caucasian subjects of the Human Radiation Experiments. Defense counsel's universe is simply too small. Plaintiffs allege that when the Defendants determined who would become subjects in the Human Radiation Experiments, they did so with racial animus. Obviously, then, the similarly situated group at issue is that universe of people from which the individual Defendants could have chosen their subjects. This fact reveals in part why the Court does not today dismiss the Plaintiffs' equal protection claim. The record in this case must be developed in order to determine what the universe of patients was and whether the racial composition of that group was similar to the racial composition of the subjects of the Human Radiation Experiments. . . .

. . . .

NOTES AND QUESTIONS

1. Recall, in connection with the Cincinnati Radiation experiments, earlier cases: *Barrett v. United States*, *Moore v. California*, *Canterbury v. Spence*, and *Oswald v. Le Grand*. Each case involved a breach of fiduciary duty. Is there something different here? Suppose all of the concerns of abuse and disclosure and fidelity and informed consent had been satisfied, would there *still* be something objectionable about the Cincinnati radiation experiments? If so, what? Is a return to the *Casey* decision, *supra* § 1.04[1] helpful?

2. In a portion of the opinion which is omitted, Judge Beckwith held the plaintiffs had a right to access to the courts and to fair procedure, and these had been denied by defendants' fraud and [illegible]; there had been a violation of due process and the right to petition for redress. What is the value of such theories — were they simply alternatives? Do they add anything legally? Ethically?

3. The defendants argue consent. How could a credible argument be made, when the patients knew nothing? Was it that, being poor, they *had no choice?* And can a person *consent* to his or her own abuse or death? What would Rawls say? The Council of Europe Convention, *supra,* Ch. 1? Also see Problem 3-12, *supra*, for consent by community. Would that work here?

4. The Court considered whether the various defendants might have acted in good faith, objectively measured. *See Harlow v. Fitzgerald*, 457 U.S. 800 (1982). What should its answer have been? Even if the answer is yes, should the plaintiffs succeed on some of their claims (*e.g.,* battery)?

5. Is it likely the defendants set out to target African-Americans? Indeed, isn't the opposite more likely: they would want a random sample for valid scientific results? What, then, is the plaintiffs' Equal Protection theory?

6. The Court refers, cogently, to the Nuremberg Code. But what is its legal status and relevance? And what of the Code itself? As a judgment on wrongdoing, it may have been necessary and appropriate. But is it adequate to regulate and guide legitimate, complex research?

THE NUREMBERG CODE*

The great weight of evidence before us is to the effect that certain types of medical experiments on human beings, when kept within reasonable well-defined bounds, conform to the ethics of the medical profession generally. The protagonists of the practice of human experimentation justify their views on the basis that such experiments yield results for the good of society that are unprocurable by other methods or means of study. All agree, however, that certain basic principles must be observed in order [illegible] and legal concepts:

1. The voluntary consent of the human subject is absolutely essential.

This means that the person involved should have legal capacity to give consent; should be so situated as to be able to exercise free power of choice, without the intervention of any element of force, fraud, deceit, duress, overreaching, or other ulterior form of constraint or coercion; and should have sufficient knowledge and comprehension of the elements of the subject matter involved as to enable him to make an understanding and enlightened decision. This latter element requires that before the acceptance of an affirmative decision by the experimental subject there should be made known to him the nature, duration, and purpose of the experiment; the

* From H.J. Steiner & P. Alston, *International Human Rights in Context*, at 102 (Oxford Univ. Press, 1996).

method and means by which it is to be conducted; all inconveniences and hazards reasonably to be expected; and the effects upon his health or person which may possibly come from his participation in the experiment.

The duty and responsibility for ascertaining the quality of the consent rests upon each individual who initiates, directs or engages in the experiment. It is a personal duty and responsibility which may not be delegated to another with impunity.

2. The experiment should be such as to yield fruitful results for the good of society, unprocurable by other methods or means of study, and not random and unnecessary in nature.

3. The experiment should be so designed and based on the results of animal experimentation and a knowledge of the natural history of the disease or other problem under study that the anticipated results will justify the performance of the experiment.

4. The experiment should be so conducted as to avoid all unnecessary physical and mental suffering and injury.

5. No experiment should be conducted where there is an *a priori* reason to believe that death or disabling injury will occur; except, perhaps, in those experiments where the experimental physicians also serve as subjects.

6. The degree of risk to be taken should never exceed that determined by the humanitarian importance of the problem to be solved by the experiment.

7. Proper preparations should be made and adequate facilities provided to protect the experimental subject against even remote possibilities of injury, disability, or death.

8. The experiment should be conducted only by scientifically qualified persons. The highest degree of skill and care should be required through all stages of the experiment of those who conduct or engage in the experiment.

9. During the course of the experiment the human subject should be at liberty to bring the experiment to an end if he has reached the physical or mental state where continuation of the experiment seems to him to be impossible.

10. During the course of the experiment the scientist in charge must be prepared to terminate the experiment at any stage, if he has probable cause to believe, in the exercise of the good faith, superior skill and careful judgment required of him that a continuation of the experiment is likely to result in injury, disability, or death to the experimental subject.

DECLARATION OF HELSINKI*

I. Basic Principles

1. Biomedical research involving human subjects must conform to generally accepted scientific principles and should be based on adequately performed laboratory animal experimentation and on a thorough knowledge of the scientific literature.

2. The design and performance of each experimental procedure involving human subjects should be clearly formulated in an experimental protocol which should be transmitted to a specially appointed independent committee for consideration, comment and guidance.

3. Biomedical research involving human subjects should be conducted only by scientifically qualified persons and under the supervision of a clinically competent medical person. The responsibility for the human subject must always rest with a medically qualified person and never rest on the subject of the research, even though the subject has given his or her consent.

4. Biomedical research involving human subjects cannot be legitimately be carried out unless the importance of the objectives is in proportion to the inherent risk to the subject.

5. Every biomedical research project involving human subjects should be preceded by careful assessment of predictable risks in comparison with foreseeable benefits to the subject or to others. Concern for the interests of the subject must always prevail over the interest of science and society.

6. The right of the research subject to safeguard his or her integrity must always be respected. Every precaution should be taken to respect the privacy of the subject and to minimize the impact of the study on the subject's physical and mental integrity and on the personality of the subject.

7. Doctors should abstain from engaging in research projects involving human subjects unless they are satisfied that the hazards involved are believed to be predictable. Doctors should cease any investigation if the hazards are found to outweigh the potential benefits.

8. In publication of the results of his or her research, the doctor is obliged to preserve the accuracy of the results. Reports of experimentation not in accordance with the principles laid down in this Declaration should not be accepted for publication.

9. In any research on human beings, each potential subject must be adequately informed of the aims, methods, anticipated benefits and potential hazards of the study and the discomfort it may entail. He or she should be informed that he or she is at liberty to abstain from participation in the study and that he or she is free to withdraw his or her consent to participation at any time. The doctor should then obtain the subject's freely given informed consent, preferably in writing.

* From W.A. Silverman, Human Experimentation, at 156 (Oxford Univ. Press 1985).

10. When obtaining informed consent for the research project the doctor should be particularly cautious if the subject is in a dependent relationship to him or her or may consent under duress. In that case the informed consent should be obtained by a doctor who is not engaged in the investigation and who is completely independent of this official relationship.

11. In case of legal incompetence, informed consent should be obtained from the legal guardian in accordance with national legislation. Where physical or mental incapacity makes it impossible to obtain informed consent, or when the subject is a minor, permission from the responsible relative replaces that of the subject in accordance with national legislation.

12. The research protocol should always contain a statement of the ethical considerations involved and should indicate that the principles enunciated in the present Declaration are complied with.

II. Medical Research Combined with Professional Care (Clinical Research)

1. In the treatment of the sick person, the doctor must be free to use a new diagnostic and therapeutic measure, if in his or her judgment it offers hope of saving life, reestablishing health, or alleviating suffering.

2. The potential benefits, hazards and discomforts of a new method should be weighed against the advantages of the best current diagnostic and therapeutic methods.

3. In any medical study, every patient — including those of a control group, if any — should be assured of the best proven diagnostic and therapeutic method.

4. The refusal of the patient to participate in a study must never interfere with the doctor-patient relationship.

5. If the doctor considers it essential not to obtain informed consent, the specific reasons for this proposal should be stated in the experimental protocol for transmission to the independent committee (I, 2).

6. The doctor can combine medical research with professional care, the objective being the acquisition of new medical knowledge, only to the extent that medical research is justified by its potential diagnostic or therapeutic value for the patient.

III. Nontherapeutic Biomedical Research Involving Human Subjects (Nonclinical Biomedical Research)

1. In the purely scientific application of medical research carried out on a human being, it is the duty of the doctor to remain the protector of the life and health of that person on whom biomedical research is being carried out.

2. The subjects should be volunteers — either healthy persons or patients for whom the experimental design is not related to the patient's illness.

3. The investigator or the investigating team should discontinue the research if in his/her or their judgment it may, if continued, be harmful to the individual.

4. In research on man, the interest of science and society should never take precedence over considerations related to the well-being of the subject.

NOTES AND QUESTIONS

1. Following Nuremberg there was a vast expansion in medical experimentation around the world. After Nuremberg, *Burton*, *Barrett*, and *The Cincinnati Experiments*, the World Medical Association met at Helsinki and adopted the Helsinki Declaration. Contrast it to the Nuremberg Code — was it a retreat? What are its implications for the decisions in *Burton, Barrett,* and *Cincinnati*?
2. Consider at this point the Council of Europe Convention reproduced in Ch. 1, in the Introduction, and the materials on fetal research, in § 4.02 *infra*. Are these consistent with the *Nuremberg* and *Helsinki* protocols? What are their implications for the Cincinnati Experiments?
3. Consider now the following summary of the report of the Advisory Committee on Human Radiation Experiments, convened by President Clinton, as it appeared in the Journal of the American Medical Association. Are its conclusions and criticisms strong enough; are its recommendations sufficient? Could similar experiments be undertaken in the future and a similar Commission meet in the year 2020?

RESEARCH ETHICS AND THE MEDICAL PROFESSION
*Report of the Advisory Committee on Human Radiation Experiments**

The Advisory Committee on Human Radiation Experiments was convened by President Clinton in January 1994 in response to allegations of abuses of human subjects in radiation research conducted or sponsored by the US government during the Cold War. The suspect research included experiments in which hospitalized patients had been administered plutonium and other atomic bomb materials, nontherapeutic research with prisoners, and total-body irradiation research with cancer patients. The Advisory Committee also investigated nontherapeutic research with children, human experimentation conducted in conjunction with nuclear weapons testing, intentional environmental releases of radiation, and observational research involving uranium miners and residents of the Marshall Islands.

Part 2: Rules, Norms, and Practices of Human Research

A central task for the Advisory Committee was reconstruction of the rules, norms, and practices of research involving human subjects in the decades immediately following World War II. We found evidence of discussion of the conduct of human research in the highest reaches of government as well as within the medical profession, particularly including concerns about risk. These discussions also addressed questions of consent and voluntary participation. Questions of subject selection, as in the case of seriously ill patients, emerged only in the context of discussions about risk. There is no evidence that issues of fairness or concerns about exploitation in the selection of subjects figured in policies or practices of the period.

One of the more striking features of the history we uncovered was the extent to which rules, norms, and practices differed when the subjects of research were patients and when they were not. In both federal policy and professional practice, requirements of consent and disclosure were much more likely to apply to so-called healthy subjects or normal volunteers than to patient-subjects.

U.S. Government Rules on Consent and Disclosure

Evidence of sustained attention on the part of U.S. government agencies to questions of voluntariness and consent in the conduct of human research dates from at least the 1920s, when the army promulgated a regulation concerning the use of "volunteers" for medical research. In 1932, the secretary of the navy required that subjects of a proposed experiment be "informed volunteers." In 1942 the requirement that healthy subjects be informed volunteers was also articulated (if not always followed) by the Committee on Medical Research, which oversaw war-related research for the Executive Office of the President. In 1953, the principle of consent articulated in the Nuremberg Code was adopted by the Department of Defense in a top-secret memorandum from Secretary of Defense Charles Wilson (the Wilson Memorandum) regarding human research related to atomic, biological, and chemical warfare. In 1954, this application of the Nuremberg Code was expanded by the Army Office of the Surgeon General as an unclassified policy for all research with "human volunteers."

The significance and meaning attached to these regulations at the time are difficult to ascertain. Generally, these requirements did not stipulate what was meant by consent, nor did they indicate whether investigators were obligated to disclose specific information to potential subjects. The scope of the requirements was also often unclear, although supporting evidence suggests that they focused on "healthy volunteers" and were not intended to apply to research with patient-subjects.

The histories of other federal agencies also demonstrate that healthy subjects were privileged in government rule making. In 1953 the National Institutes of Health (NIH) opened the Clinical Center, a state-of-the-science research hospital. The center adopted a policy requiring "voluntary agreement based on informed understanding" from all research subjects. Although consent was required to be obtained in writing from all healthy, "normal" subjects of research, written consent was required from patient-subjects only when the research was believed by the physician to be unusually hazardous. The NIH Clinical Center approach adopted by the mid 1950s — written consent from healthy subjects but from only certain patient-subjects — persisted through the early 1960s and was paralleled in policies of the Department of Defense and the AEC. The government did not have comprehensive policies requiring the consent of all subjects of research, including both healthy subjects and patient-subjects, in both intramural and extramural research, until 1974.

Professional Rules and Practices

Government rules distinguishing healthy subjects from [illegible] paralleled the [illegible] of the biomedical community. As early as 1944, it was conventional for physicians and other biomedical scientists to obtain consent from healthy subjects of research. By contrast, at least through the early 1960s, physicians engaged in clinical research generally did not obtain consent from patient-subjects for whom the research was intended to offer a prospect of medical benefit. Even when there was no such prospect, it was common for physicians to conduct research on patients without their consent. There also is evidence, however, that it was common for physicians to be concerned about risk in conducting research on patient-subjects and, in the absence of a prospect for medical benefit, to restrict research uses of patients to what physicians considered to be lower minimal-risk interventions.

By contrast, various sources confirm that it was not conventional to obtain consent from patient-subjects. These sources include documents from the period as well as the Advisory Committee's Ethics Oral History Project, in which physicians active in research in the 1940s and 1950s agreed that consent played little or no role in research with patient-subjects, even when there was no expectation that the patient would benefit medically from the research.

The Committee's Ethical Framework

The committee's response to this task was to adopt an ethical framework for judgment that identified 3 types of ethical standards as relevant to the evaluation of the human radiation experiments:

1. Basic ethical principles that are widely accepted and generally regarded as so fundamental as to be applicable to the past as well as the present;
2. The policies of government departments and agencies at the time; and
3. Rules of professional ethics that were widely accepted at the time.

The committee's findings with respect to standard 2, government policies, and standard 3, rules of professional ethics, are summarized in part 2 of this article. The following discussion [illegible] 1, basic ethical principles.

Basic ethical principles are general standards or rules that all morally serious individuals accept. The Advisory Committee identified 6 basic ethical principles as particularly relevant to our work:

1. One ought not to treat people as mere means to the ends of others.
2. One ought not to deceive others.
3. One ought not to inflict harm or risk of harm.
4. One ought to promote welfare and prevent harm.
5. One ought to treat people fairly and with equal respect.
6. One ought to respect the self-determination of others.

Every principle on this list has exceptions, because all basic moral principles can justifiably be overridden by other basic principles in circumstances when they conflict. To give priority to 1 principle over another is not a moral mistake; it is a reality of moral judgment. The justifiability of such judgments depends on many factors in the circumstance; it is not possible to assign priorities to these principles in the abstract.

The validity of basic moral principles is not typically thought of as limited by time. We commonly judge agents in the past by these standards — for example, the passing of 50 years in no way changes the fact that Hitler's extermination of millions of people was wrong, nor does it erase or even diminish his culpability. Nor would the passing of 100 years or 1000 years do so.

While basic ethical principles do not change, interpretations and applications of basic ethical principles as they are expressed in more specific rules of conduct do evolve over time through processes of cultural change. Recognizing that more specific moral rules do change has implications for how we judge the past. For example, the current requirement of informed consent is the result of evolution. Acceptance of the simple idea that medical treatment or research intervention requires the consent of the patient (at least in the case of competent adults) seems to have preceded by a considerable interval the more complex belief that informed consent is required. Furthermore, the concept of informed consent itself has undergone refinement and development through common law rulings, analyses and explanations of these rulings in the scholarly legal literature, philosophical treatments of the key concepts emerging from legal analyses, and guidelines in reports by government and professional bodies, such as *The Belmont Report of the National Commission for the Protection of Human Subjects of Biomedical and Behavioral Research.*

Thus, it is probably fair to say that the current understanding of informed consent is more sophisticated, and what is required of physicians and scientists more demanding, than both the preceding requirement of consent and earlier interpretations of what counts as informed consent. As the content of the concept has evolved, so has the scope of the corresponding obligation on the part of these professionals. For this reason, it would be inappropriate to blame clinicians or researchers of the 1940s and 1950s for not adhering to the details of a standard that has emerged through a complex process of cultural change spanning decades. At the same time, however, it remains appropriate to hold them to the general requirements of the basic moral principles that underlie informed consent — not treating others as mere means, promoting the welfare of others, and respecting self-determination.

The Committee's Evaluation

The Advisory Committee believes that this historical context properly affects judgments about the moral blameworthiness of physician-investigators of the period following World War II who violated the basic moral principle of respect for the self-determination of others by enrolling patients in research without their knowledge or consent. Physicians were less blameworthy in cases in which the physician took this decision based on a considered and informed assessment that involvement in research was in the patient's best medical interests. In such cases, the blameworthiness for failing to respect self-determination by obtaining consent was lessened by the physician's fidelity to the profession's primary moral commitment to promote the welfare of the patient, as this commitment was understood at the time. [illegible] physicians were more [illegible] for failing to obtain consent in cases in which involvement in research less clearly served the medical interests of the patient. The less likely the patient-subject would benefit medically from the research and the greater the research-related risks, the greater the moral burden on physicians for failing to obtain consent.

The Advisory Committee reserved its harshest criticism for those cases in which physicians used patients without their consent as subjects in research from which the patients could not possibly benefit medically. These cases included a series of experiments in which 18 patients, some but not all of whom were terminally ill, were injected with plutonium at Oak Ridge Hospital in Tennessee, the University of Rochester in New York, the University of Chicago, and the University of California, San Francisco, as well as 2 experiments in which seriously ill patients were injected with uranium, 6 at the University of Rochester and 11 at Massachusetts General Hospital, Boston.

The medical profession could and should have seen that healthy subjects and patient-subjects in nontherapeutic experiments were in similar moral positions — neither was expected to benefit medically. Just as physicians had no moral license to determine an "acceptable risk" for healthy subjects without their voluntary consent, they had no moral license to do so in the case of patient-subjects who also could not benefit from being in research. Indeed, it is arguably the case that physicians could and should have seen that using patients in this way was morally less justifiable than using healthy people, for in so doing the basic ethical principles not to use people as a mere means and to treat people fairly and with equal respect would be violated. Moreover, physicians who used patients in this manner violated a trust and exploited the dependency of others. The use of patients in nontherapeutic experiments without their consent was also a violation of the Hippocratic principle that enjoins physicians to act in the best interests of their patients, which would seem to prohibit subjecting patients to experiments from which they could not benefit.

The fact that neither the profession's practices [illegible] policies [illegible] the rights of all subjects of research does not excuse the moral failure each represents. The Advisory Committee criticized the government as well as the medical profession for these failures and recommended that the government pay compensation to subjects or their families under specific criteria. In addition, we recommended that the government make an official, formal apology, again under specific criteria. The president extended such an apology in his remarks on October 3, 1995.

Part 4: Human Research Today

In tandem with our evaluation of the past, we undertook 3 projects to examine the current state of human research. The numerous findings of these projects are presented elsewhere. We summarize herein those findings relevant to the discussion in this article.

Compared with what we have learned about human subject research in the 1940s, 1950s, and 1960s, in more recent decades there have been many changes in the climate and conduct of research with human subjects. The most obvious change is the existence of federal regulations governing human subject research, now known as the Common Rule, which was not in place in that earlier time. The rules of research ethics are also more clearly articulated today than they were then, as exemplified by the evolution of the concept of, and requirements for, informed consent. Although the basic moral principles that serve as the underpinning for research ethics are the same now as they were then, some of the issues of greatest concern to us today are different, or have taken on a different cast, from those of earlier decades.

In our historical inquiry, for example, we concentrated on cases that offered subjects no prospect of medical benefit; these were instances of nontherapeutic research in the strictest sense. That is, these were experiments in which there was never any basis or expectation that subjects could benefit medically — both the design and the objectives precluded such a possibility. Most of the human radiation experiments that were public controversies when the Advisory Committee was appointed, including the plutonium injections, were of this type. The basic moral concern they raised was whether people had been used as mere means to the ends of scientists and the government; this would have occurred if the subjects could not possibly have benefited medically from being in the research and they had not consented to this use of their persons.

As we noted in part 3, the ethical issues raised by research that is nontherapeutic in this strict sense are stark and straightforward. Because risks to subjects cannot be offset by the possibility that they might benefit medically, nontherapeutic research that puts subjects at significant risk is rarely justifiable. Much research involving human subjects does not, however, fit this nontherapeutic paradigm. Many of today's most pressing ethical questions concern research that raises at least the hope of potential medical benefit to the patient-subject. For example, in the modern phase 1 trial, which is conducted to establish doses that cause toxic effects, there is at least the possibility of therapeutic benefit, however slim. Thus, although phase 1 trials often impose significant burden and risk on subjects, they are not always nontherapeutic in the strict sense. And, in contrast with phase 1 trials, in some research involving patient-subjects there is a real prospect that subjects will benefit medically from their participation. In many of these cases, being a research subject is clearly in the best medical interests of the patient.

Based on our review, it appears that much of current human subject research poses only minimal risk of harm to subjects and is largely ethically sound. At the same time, however, we also found evidence suggesting serious deficiencies in the current system for the protection of the rights and interests of human subjects. Committee member Jay Katz, JD, in his independent review of contemporary research proposals and documents, expressed in a separate statement even more serious concerns than did the committee report about current informed consent review and practices. Many of the committee's most serious concerns centered on research involving patient-subjects with poor prognoses, people who are particularly vulnerable to confusion about the relationship of research to treatment.

The findings of the SIS underscore what other, smaller studies also have identified — that many patient-subjects decide to participate in medical research because they believe that being in research is th[illegible] improve their medi[illegible] To say that there is no prospect that the patients in phase 1 trials might benefit medically is questionable. Beneficial effects of phase 1 trials have a very low probability, but do occur. For example, it is estimated that among 5% of subjects enrolled in phase 1 chemotherapy studies, tumors respond to the experimental drug, although it is unclear what clinical significance such response has or what the tumor response means from a patient's point of view. Any suggestion of the possibility of benefit, however, has the potential to be magnified many times over by patients with a lack of good medical alternatives. It is understandable that physicians, faced with the prospect of little or nothing to offer seriously ill patients, may sometimes impart more hope than the clinical facts warrant. At the same time, however, desperate hopes are easily manipulated.

One of the most powerful themes to emerge from the SIS is the role of trust in patients' decisions to participate in research, a finding that has been observed in other studies as well. Patients in the SIS who participated in the in-depth interviews frequently commented that they had joined a research project at the suggestion of their physicians and that they trusted that their physicians would never endorse options that were not in their best interests. This trust underscores the tension in the role of physician-investigator, whose duties as a healer and as a scientist inherently conflict. This trust that patients place in their physicians often is generalized to the medical and research community as a whole. Some patients expressed faith not only in their physicians but also in the institutions where they were receiving medical care. These patients believed that hospitals would never permit research to be conducted that was not good for the patient-subjects.

Conclusions and Recommendations

Many of the Advisory Committee's recommendations are directed toward the future. We call, for example, for changes in the current federal system for the protection of the rights and interests of human subjects, including changes in IRBs; in the interpretation of ethics rul[illegible]; in oversight, [illegible], and sanctions for ethics violations; and in compensation for research injuries. Specifically, we recommend that the IRB component of the federal system be altered in the following 5 ways:

1. Institutional review boards should be permitted to appropriately allocate their time so they can adequately review studies that pose more than minimal risk to human subjects.
2. The information provided to potential subjects should clearly distinguish research from treatment, realistically portray the likelihood that subjects may benefit medically from their participation and the nature of the potential benefit, and clearly explain the potential for discomfort and pain that may accompany participation in the research.
3. The information provided to potential subjects should clearly identify the federal agency or agencies sponsoring or supporting the research

project and all purposes for which the research is being conducted or supported.

4. The information provided to potential subjects should clearly identify the financial implications of deciding to consent to, or refuse, participation in research.

5. Institutional review boards should have the responsibility to determine that the science is of a quality to warrant the imposition of risk or inconvenience on human subjects and, in the case of research that purports to offer a prospect of medical benefit to subjects, to determine that participating in the research affords patient-subjects at least as good an opportunity of securing this medical benefit as would be available to them without participating in research.

NOTES AND QUESTIONS

1. Is the Commission excusing the defendants in the Cincinnati Radiation experiments? If not totally, then to the extent they might be held personally liable in damages? In reviewing history and finding six basic principles does the Commission take a stand which it then abandons by saying that understanding of those principles has only slowly evolved?

2. What of the distinctions between research on patients and nonpatients? Therapeutic and nontherapeutic research? Research where harm is not probable and where it (perhaps death) is certain? Does the Commission deal adequately with these? Consistently with the Nuremberg and Helsinki protocols?

3. Should the Commission — in view of its findings that patients trust their physicians and hope (against advice) for a cure — have concluded that physicians should simply *never* be researchers? That *patients* simply cannot be research subjects?

4. And in its recommendations, does the Commission agree with the Nuremberg Code, that responsibility rests with *every* participant in experimentation? If not there, where?

5. There had been an earlier Commission, with a similar charge and report, to investigate the Tuskegee Syphilis Study, perhaps this nation's darkest chapter in human experimentation. The final report of the Ad Hoc Advisory Panel in 1973 is available from the Government Printing Office and the experiments are detailed in Jones, *Bad Blood* (Free Press 1981). From 1932 to 1972 African American prisoners were left — to varying degrees — untreated for syphilis, long after routine treatment became available, in an experiment under the aegis of the United States Public Health Service. Every conceivable principle and standard of research and treatment was violated. The Panel's criticisms and recommendations remain largely unanswered — contrary to the Cincinnati Report and in contrast thereto.

6. For an excellent article, see Jay Katz, *Human Sacrifice And Human Experimentation: Reflections At Nuremberg*, 22 Yale J. Int'l L. 401

(1997); and see Jonathan Todres, *Can Research Subjects of Clinical Trials in Developing Countries Sue Physician-Investigators for Human Rights Violations?*, 16 N.Y.L. Sch. J. Hum. [illegible].

7. Most cases of medical experimentation involve testing new therapies or products, raising issues of consent and risk. These issues become acute and compelling when the experiment involves non-therapeutic investigation, and the subjects are children. And subsidies are provided to place or keep the children at risk.

GRIMES v. KENNEDY KRIEGER INSTITUTE, INC.
782 A.2d 807 (Md. 2001)

Opinion by **Cathell**, J.

Prologue

We initially note that these are cases of first impression for this Court. For that matter, precious few courts in the United States have addressed the issues presented in the cases at bar. In respect to nontherapeutic research using minors, it has been noted that "consent to research has been virtually unanalyzed by courts and legislatures." Robert J. Katerberg, *Institutional Review Boards, Research on Children, and Informed Consent of Parents: Walking the Tightrope Between Encouraging Vital Experimentation and Protecting Subjects' Rights,* 24 J.C. & U.L. 545, 562, quoting National Commission for the Protection of Human Subjects of Biomedical and Behavioral Research, Report and Recommendations [National Commission]: Research Involving Children 79-80 (1977). Our research reveals this statement remains as accurate now as it was in 1977.

In these present cases, a prestigious research institute, associated with Johns Hopkins University, based on this record, created a nontherapeutic research program[2] whereby it required certain classes of homes to have only partial lead paint abatement modifications performed, and in at least some instances, including at least one of the cases at bar, arranged for the landlords to receive public funding by way of grants or loans [illegible] modifications. [illegible] institute then encouraged, and in at least one of the cases at bar, required, the landlords to rent the premises to families with young children. In the event young children already resided in one of the study houses, it was contemplated that a child would remain in the premises, and the child was encouraged to remain, in order for his or her blood to be periodically analyzed. In other words, the continuing presence of the children that were the subjects of the study was required in order for the study to be complete. Apparently, the children and their parents involved in the cases *sub judice* were from a lower economic strata and were, at least in one case, minorities.

---

[2] At least to the extent that commercial profit motives are not implicated, therapeutic research's purpose is to directly help or aid a patient who is suffering from a health condition the objectives of the research are designed to address — hopefully by the alleviation, or potential alleviation, of the health condition.

Nontherapeutic research generally utilizes subjects who are not known to have the condition the objectives of the research are designed to address, and/or is not designed to directly benefit the subjects utilized in the research, but, rather, is designed to achieve beneficial results for the public at large (or, under some circumstances, for profit).

The purpose of the research was to determine how effective varying degrees of lead paint abatement procedures were. Success was to be determined by periodically, over a two-year period of time, measuring the extent to which lead dust remained in, or returned to, the premises after the varying levels of abatement modifications, and, as most important to our decision, by measuring the extent to which the theretofore healthy children's blood became contaminated with lead, and comparing that contamination with levels of lead dust in the houses over the same periods of time.

The same researchers had completed a prior study on abatement and partial abatement methods that indicated that lead dust remained and/or returned to abated houses over a period of time.

Apparently, it was anticipated that the children, who were the human subjects in the program, would, or at least might, accumulate lead in their blood from the dust, thus helping the researchers to determine the extent to which the various partial abatement methods worked. There was no complete and clear explanation in the consent agreements signed by the parents of the children that the research to be conducted was designed, at least in significant part, to measure the success of the abatement procedures by measuring the extent to which the children's blood was being contaminated. It can be argued that the researchers intended that the children be the canaries in the mines but never clearly told the parents. (It was a practice in earlier years, and perhaps even now, for subsurface miners to rely on canaries to determine whether dangerous levels of toxic gasses were accumulating in the mines. Canaries were particularly susceptible to such gasses. When the canaries began to die, the miners knew that dangerous levels of gasses were accumulating.)

The researchers and their Institutional Review Board apparently saw nothing wrong with the search protocols that anticipated the possible accumulation of lead in the blood of otherwise healthy children as a result of the experiment, or they believed that the consents of the parents of the children made the research appropriate. Institutional Review Boards (IRB) are oversight entities within the institutional family to which an entity conducting research belongs. In research experiments, an IRB can be required in some instances by either federal or state regulation, or sometimes by the conditions attached to governmental grants that are used to fund research projects. Generally, their primary functions are to assess the protocols of the project to determine whether the project itself is appropriate, whether the consent procedures are adequate, whether the methods to be employed meet proper standards, whether reporting requirements are sufficient, and the assessment of various other aspects of a research project. One of the most important objectives of such review is the review of the potential safety and the health hazard impact of a research project on the human subjects of the experiment, especially on vulnerable subjects such as children. Their function is *not* to help researchers seek funding for research projects.

In the instant case, as is suggested by some commentators as being endemic to the research community as a whole, *infra,* the IRB involved here, the Johns Hopkins University Joint Committee on Clinical Investigation, in part, abdicated that responsibility, instead suggesting to the researchers a way to miscast the characteristics of the study in order to avoid the responsibility inherent in nontherapeutic research involving children. In a letter dated May 11, 1992, the Johns Hopkins University Joint Committee on Clinical Investigation (the RB for the University), charged with insuring the safety of the subjects and compliance with federal regulations, wrote to Dr. Farfel, the person in charge of the research:

> "A number of questions came up. . . . Please respond to the following points[:]
>
> . . .
>
> 2. The next issue has to do with drawing blood from the control population, namely children growing up in modern urban housing. *Federal guidelines are really quite specific regarding using children as controls in projects in which there is no potential benefit* [to the particular children]. To call a subject a normal control is to indicate that there is no real benefit to be received [by the particular children]. . . . So, we think it would be much more acceptable to indicate that the 'control group' is being studied to determine what exposure outside the home may play in a total lead exposure; thereby, indicating that these control individuals are gaining some benefit, namely learning whether safe housing alone is sufficient to keep the blood-lead levels in acceptable bounds. We suggest that you modify . . . consent form[s] . . . accordingly." [Emphasis added.]

While the suggestion of the IRB would not make this experiment any less nontherapeutic or, thus, less regulated, this statement shows two things: (1) that the IRB had a partial misperception of the difference between therapeutic and nontherapeutic research and the IRB's role in the process and (2) that the IRB was willing to aid researchers in getting around federal regulations designed to protect children used as subjects in nontherapeutic research. An IRB's primary role is to assure the safety of human research subjects — not help researchers avoid safety or health-related requirements. The IRB, in this case, misconceived, at least partially, its own role.

Otherwise healthy children, in our view, should not be enticed into living in, or remaining in, potentially lead-tainted housing and intentionally subjected to a research program, which contemplates the probability, or even the possibility, of lead poisoning or even the accumulation of lower levels of lead in blood, in order for the extent of the contamination of the children's blood to be used by scientific researchers to assess the success of lead paint or lead dust abatement measures. Moreover, in our view, parents, whether improperly enticed by trinkets, food stamps, money or other items, have no more right to intentionally and unnecessarily place children in potentially hazardous nontherapeutic research surroundings, than do researchers. In such cases, parental consent, no matter how informed, is insufficient.

While the validity of the consent agreement and its nature as a contract, the existence or nonexistence of a special relationship, and whether the researchers performed their functions under that agreement pursuant to any special relationships are important issues in these cases that we will address, the very inappropriateness of the research itself cannot be overlooked.

The research relationship proffered to the parents of the children the researchers wanted to use as measuring tools, should never have been presented in a nontherapeutic context in the first instance. Nothing about the research was designed for treatment of the subject children. They were presumed to be healthy at the commencement of the project. As to them, the research was clearly nontherapeutic in nature. The experiment was simply a "for the greater good" project.[6] The specific children's health was put at risk, in order to develop low-cost abatement measures that would help all children, the landlords, and the general public as well.

In *Olmstead v. United States*, 277 U.S. 438 (1928), Justice Brandeis, dissenting, noted:

> "Experience should teach us to be most on our guard to protect liberty when the Government's purposes are beneficent. Men born to freedom are naturally alert to repel invasion of their liberty by evil-minded rulers. The greatest dangers to liberty lurk in insidious encroachment by men of zeal, well-meaning but without understanding."

The research project at issue here, and its apparent protocols, differs in large degree from, but presents similar problems as those in the Tuskegee Syphilis Study conducted from 1932 until 1972 *(The Tuskegee Syphilis Study,* 289 New England Journal of Medicine 730 (1973)), the intentional exposure of soldiers to radiation in the 1940s and 50s (*Jaffee v. United States*, 663 F.2d 1226 (3d Cir. 1981), the tests involving the exposure of Navajo miners to radiation (*Begay v. United States*, 591 F. Supp. 991 (1984), aff'd, 768 F.2d 1059 (9th Cir. 1985)),[7] and the secret administration of LSD to soldiers by the CIA and the Army in the 1950s and 60s (*United States v. Stanley*, 483 U.S. 669 (1987); *Central Intelligence.*

The tenants involved, presumably, would be from a lower rent-urban class. At least one of the consenting parents in one of these cases was on public assistance, and was described by her counsel as being a minority. The children of middle class or rich parents apparently were not involved.

---

[6] The ultimate goal was to find the cost of the minimal level of effective lead paint or lead dust abatement costs so as to help landlords assess, hopefully positively, the commercial feasibility of attempting to abate lead dust in marginally profitable, lower rent-urban housing, in order to help preserve such housing in the Baltimore housing market. One of the aims was to evaluate low-cost methods of abatement so that some landlords would not abandon their rental units. For those landlords, complete abatement was not deemed economically feasible. The project would be able to assess whether a particular level of partial abatement caused a child's blood lead content to be elevated beyond a level deemed hazardous to the health of children.

[7] The Navajo miners had been already working in the uranium mines when the study commenced. Unlike the present case, the Navajos were not recruited by the researchers to be placed in the environment being tested for unhealthy substances.

> "Indeed, the literature on the law and ethics of human experimentation is replete with warnings that all subjects, but especially vulnerable subjects, are at risk of abuse by inclusion [as research subjects]. Those vulnerable subjects included prisoners, who are subject to coercion [see The Prisoner's Cases: *Clay v. Martin*, 509 F.2d 109 (1975); *Bailey v. Lally*, 481 F. Supp. 203 (1979); *Valenti v. Prudden*, 58 A.D.2d 956, 397 N.Y.S.2d 181 (1997)]; children and the elderly . . . and racial minorities, ethnic minorities, and women [see the silicone injections/ informed consent case of *Retkwa v. Orentreich*, 154 Misc. 2d 164, 584 N.Y.S.2d 710 (1992)],whom history shows to be the most frequent victims of abuses in human experimentation."

R. Alta Charo, *Protecting us to Death: Women, Pregnancy and Clinical Research Trials,* 38 St. Louis U. L.J. 135, 135 (Fall, 1993); see also *In Re Cincinnati Radiation Litigation*, 874 F. Supp. 796, 800 (1995) ("The experiments utilized terminal cancer patients. . . . The Complaint alleges that most of the patients selected were African-American and, in the vernacular of the time, charity patients."); Lainie Ross, *Children as Research Subjects: A Proposal to Revise the Current Federal Regulations Using a Moral Framework,*8 Stan. L. & Policy Rev. 159, 164 (Winter, 1997) ("The failures in the informed consent process lead to serious inequities in research, specifically for the poor and less educated who bear most of the research burden. Studies show that the process of informed consent serves as a social filter: Better educated and wealthier individuals are more likely to refuse to participate and are underrepresented in most research. The problem is perpetuated in pediatrics, where parents who volunteer their children were found to be significantly less educated and underrepresented in the professional and managerial occupations compared to their nonvolunteering counterparts." (footnote omitted)). *Agency v. Sims*, 471 U.S. 159 (1985).

The research experiments that follow were also prior instances of research subjects being intentionally exposed to infectious or poisonous substances in the name of scientific research. They include the Tuskegee Syphilis Study, aforesaid, where patients infected with syphilis were not subsequently informed of the availability of [illegible] illness, in order for the scientists and researchers to be able to continue research on the effects of the illness, the Jewish Hospital study,[8] and several other post-war research projects. Then there are the notorious use of "plague bombs" by the Japanese military in World War II where entire villages were infected in order for the results to be "studied";[9] and perhaps most notorious, the deliberate use of infection in a nontherapeutic project in order to study the degree of infection and the rapidity of the course of the disease in the Rose and Mrugowsky

[8] Generally known as the Jewish Chronic Disease Hospital study where chronically ill and debilitated patients were injected with cancer cells without their consent. *See Zeleznik v. Jewish Chronic Disease Hosp.*, 47 A.D.2d 199, 366 N.Y.S.2d 163 (1975); *Application of Hyman*, 42 Misc. 2d 427, 248 N.Y.S.2d 245, rev'd, *Hyman v. Jewish Chronic Disease Hospital*, 21 A.D.2d 495, 251 N.Y.S.2d 818 (1964), rev'd, 15 N.Y.2d 317, 206 N.E.2d 338, 258 N.Y.S.2d 397 (1965).

[9] *See generally,* A. Brockman, *The Other Nuremberg: The Untold Story of the Tokyo War Crime Trials* (1987); P. Williams & D. Wallace, *Unit 731: Japan's Secret Biological Warfare in World War II* (1989).

typhus experiments at Buchenwald concentration camp during World War II. These programs were somewhat alike in the vulnerability of the subjects; uneducated African American men, debilitated patients in a charity hospital, prisoners of war, inmates of concentration camps and others falling within the custody and control of the agencies conducting or approving the experiments. In the present case, children, especially young children, living in lower economic circumstances, albeit not as vulnerable as the other examples, are nonetheless, vulnerable as well.

It is clear to this Court that the scientific and medical communities cannot be permitted to assume sole authority to determine ultimately what is right and appropriate in respect to research projects involving young children free of the limitations and consequences of the application of Maryland law. The Institutional Review Boards, IRBs, are, primarily, inhouse organs. In our view, they are not designed, generally, to be sufficiently objective in the sense that they are as sufficiently concerned with the ethicality of the experiments they review as they are with the success of the experiments. This has been the subject of comment in a constitutional context, in dissent, in a case involving the use of psychiatric medication on mental patients without their consent. In *Washington v. Harper*, 494 U.S. 210, 238, Justice Stevens said:

> "The Court has undervalued respondent's liberty interest; has misread the Washington involuntary medication Policy . . ., and has concluded that a mock trial before an institutionally biased tribunal constitutes 'due process of law.'" [Citation omitted.]

In footnote two of his dissent, Justice Stevens noted:

> "(The Constitution's promise of due process of law guarantees at least compensation for violations of the principle stated by the Nuremberg Military Tribunals 'that the "voluntary consent of the human subject is absolutely essential . . . to satisfy moral, ethical and legal concepts[.]'");
>
> (The Fourteenth Amendment protects the 'freedom to care for one's health and person[.]')"

As can be seen from the letter from the Johns Hopkins University Joint Committee on Clinical Investigation, *supra,* to the researchers in this case, Justice Steven's doubts as to the effectiveness of such in-house review to assess the ethics of research were warranted. Here, the IRB, whose primary function was to insure safety and compliance with applicable regulations, encouraged the researchers to misrepresent the purpose of the research in order to bring the study under the label of "therapeutic" and thus under a lower safety standard of regulation. The IRB's purpose was ethically wrong, and its understanding of the experiment's benefit incorrect.

The conflicts are inherent. This would be especially so when science and private industry collaborate in search of material gains. Moreover, the special relationship between research entities and human subjects used in the research will almost always impose duties.

In respect to examining that special relationship, we are obliged to further examine its nature and its ethical constraints. In that regard, when contested [illegible] the legal effect of research on human subjects must always be subject to judicial evaluation. One method of making such evaluations is the initiation of appropriate actions bringing such matters to the attention of the courts, as has been done in the cases at bar. It may well be that in the end, the trial courts will determine that no damages have been incurred in the instant cases and thus the actions will fail for that reason. In that regard, we note that there are substantial factual differences in the Higgins and in the Grimes cases. But the actions, themselves, are not defective on the ground that no legal duty can, according to the trial courts, possibly exist. For the reasons discussed at length in the main body of the opinion, a legal duty normally exists between researcher and subject and in all probability exists in the cases at bar. Moreover, as we shall discuss, the consents of the parents in these cases under Maryland law constituted contracts creating duties. Additionally, under Maryland law, to the extent parental consent can ever be effective in research projects of this nature, the parents may not have been sufficiently informed and, therefore, the consents ineffective and, based on the information contained in the sparse records before this court, the research project, may have invaded the legal rights of the children subjected to it.

I. The Cases

We now discuss more specifically the two cases before us, and the relevant law.

II. Facts & Procedural Background

A. The Research Study

In 1993, The Environmental Protection Agency (EPA) awarded Contract 68-D4-0001, entitled "Evaluation of Efficacy of Residential Lead Based Paint Repair and Maintenance Interventions" to KKI. KKI was to receive $ 200,000 for performing its responsibilities under the contract. It was thus a [illegible] researcher. The purpose of this research study was "to characterize and compare the short and long-term efficacy of comprehensive lead-paint abatement and less costly and potentially more cost-effective Repair and Maintenance interventions for reducing levels of lead in residential house dust which in turn should reduce lead in children's blood." As KKI acknowledged in its Clinical Investigation Consent Form, "Lead poisoning in children is a problem in Baltimore City and other communities across the country. Lead in paint, house dust and outside soil are major sources of lead exposure for children. Children can also be exposed to lead in drinking water and other sources." Lead poisoning poses a distinct danger to young children. It adversely effects cognitive development, growth, and behavior. Extremely high levels have been known to result in seizures, coma, and even death. *See* Centers for Disease Control and Prevention. *Recommendations for Blood Lead Screening of Young Children Enrolled in Medicaid: Targeting a Group at High Risk,* 49 Morbidity and Mortality Weekly Report 1 (Dec. 8, 2000).

The research study was sponsored jointly by the EPA and the Maryland Department of Housing and Community Development (DHCD). It was thus a joint federal and state project. The Baltimore City Health Department and Maryland Department of the Environment also collaborated in the study. It appears that, because the study was funded and sponsored in part by a federal entity, certain federal conditions were attached to the funding grants and approvals.

The research study included five test groups, each consisting of twenty-five houses The first three groups consisted of houses with a considerable amount of lead dust present therein and each group received assigned amounts of maintenance and repair. The fourth group consisted of houses, which at one time had lead present in the form of lead based paint but had since received a supposedly complete abatement of lead dust. The fifth group consisted of modern houses, which had never had a presence of lead dust. The aim of the research study was to analyze the effectiveness of different degrees of partial lead paint abatement in reducing levels of lead dust present in these houses. The ultimate aim of the research was to find a less than complete level of abatement that would be relatively safe, but economical, so that Baltimore landlords with lower socio-economical rental units would not abandon the units.

The research study was to collect data from all five groups over a period of two years.

If the children were to leave the houses upon the first manifestation of lead dust, it would be difficult, if not impossible, to test, over time, the rate of the level of lead accumulation in the blood of the children attributable to the manifestation. In other words, if the children were removed from the houses before the lead dust levels in their blood became elevated, the tests would probably fail, or at least the data that would establish the success of the test — or of the abatement results, would be of questionable use. Thus, it would benefit the accuracy of the test, and thus KKI, the compensated researcher, if children remained in the houses over the period of the study even after the presence of lead dust in the houses became evident.

B. Case No. 128

Appellant, Ericka Grimes, resided at 1713 N. Monroe Street in Baltimore, Maryland (the Monroe Street property) with members of her family from the time of her birth on May 30, 1992, up until the summer of 1994. Her mother, Viola Hughes, had lived in the property since the Summer of 1990. In March 1993, representatives of KKI came to Ms. Hughes's home and successfully recruited her to participate in the research study. After a discussion regarding the nature, purpose, scope, and benefits of the study, Ms. Hughes agreed to participate and signed a Consent Form dated March 10, 1993.

Nowhere in the consent form was it clearly disclosed to the mother that the researchers contemplated that, as a result of the experiment, the child might accumulate lead in her blood, and that in order for the experiment to succeed it was necessary that the child remain in the house as the lead in the child's blood increased or decreased, so that it could be measured. The Consent Form states in relevant part:

"PURPOSE OF STUDY:

As you may know, lead poisoning in children is a problem in Baltimore City and oth[illegible] across the country. Lead in paint, house dust and outside soil are major sources of lead exposure for children. Children can also be exposed to lead in drinking water and other sources. We understand that your house is going to have special repairs done in order to reduce exposure to lead in paint and dust. On a random basis, homes will receive one of two levels of repair. We are interested in finding out how well the two levels of repair work. The repairs are not intended, or expected, to completely remove exposure to lead.

We are now doing a study to learn about how well different practices work for reducing exposure to lead in paint and dust. We are asking you and over one hundred other families to allow us to test for lead in and around your homes up to 8 to 9 times over the next two years provided that your house qualifies for the full two years of study. Final eligibility will be determined after the initial testing of your home. We are also doing free blood lead testing of children aged 6 months to 7 years, up to 8 to 9 times over the next two years. We would also like you to respond to a short questionnaire every 6 months. This study is intended to monitor the effects of the repairs and is not intended to replace the regular medical care your family obtains.

BENEFITS

To compensate you for your time answering questions and allowing us to sketch your home we will mail you a check in the amount of $ 5.00. In the future we would mail you a check in the amount of $ 15 each time the full questionnaire is completed. The dust, soil, water, and blood samples would be tested for lead at the Kennedy Krieger Institute at no charge to you. *We would provide you with specific blood-lead results. We would contact you to discuss a summary of house test results and steps that you could take to reduce any risks of exposure.*" [Emphasis added.]

Pursuant to the plans of the research study, KKI collected dust samples in the Monroe Street property on March 9, 1993, August 23, 1993, March 9, 1994, September 19, 1994, April 18, 1995, and November 13, 1995. The March 9, 1993 dust testing revealed what the researchers referred to as "hot spots" where the level of lead was "higher than might be found in a completely renovated [abated] house." This information about the "hot spots" was not furnished to Ms. Hughes until December 16, 1993, more than nine months after the samples had been collected and, as we discuss, *infra,* not until after Ericka Grimes's blood was found to contain elevated levels of lead.

KKI drew blood from Ericka Grimes for lead content analysis on April, 9, 1993, September 15, 1993, and March 25, 1994. Unlike the lead concentration analysis in dust testing, the results of the blood testing were typically available to KKI in a matter of days. KKI notified Ms. Hughes of the results of the blood tests by letters dated April 9, 1993, September 29, 1993, and

March 28, 1994, respectively. The results of the April 9, 1993 test found Ericka Grimes blood to be less than 9 [mu] g/dL, which placed her results in the "normal" range according to classifications established by the Centers for Disease Control (CDC). However, on two subsequent retests, long after KKI had identified "hot spots," but before KKI informed Ms. Hughes of the "hot spots," Ericka Grimes's blood lead level registered Class III — 32 [mu] g/dL on September 15, 1993 and 22 [mu] g/dL on March 25, 1994. Ms. Hughes and her daughter vacated the Monroe Street property in the Summer of 1994, and, therefore, no further blood samples were obtained by KKI after March 25, 1994.

C. Case No. 129

Appellant, Myron Higgins, was born on December 23, 1989. According to Ms. Catina Higgins's deposition testimony, during the Spring of 1994 she was looking for a home in which to reside with her several small children. She located the property known as 1906 East Federal Street (the Federal Street property) in an advertisement in the local newspaper listing the property as a rental for $ 315 per month. She rented the property from CFOD-2 Limited Partnership. She signed a lease for the property on May 13, 1994 and moved in shortly thereafter.

Pursuant to the protocols of the research study, KKI collected dust samples in the Federal Street property on May 17, 1994, July 25, 1994, and November 3, 1994. KKI informed Ms. Higgins of the dust sample results by letters dated June 24, 1994, September 14, 1994, and February 7, 1995, respectively. Although KKI had recorded high levels of lead concentration in the dust samples collected by the Cyclone vacuum during the May 17, 1994 visit, KKI failed to disclose this information to Ms. Higgins in the letter dated June 24, 1994. Instead, KKI relied on the results obtained from the dust wipe samples collected and informed her that there was no area in her house where the lead level was higher than what might have been found in a completely renovated house. The dust samples collected by dust wipe methodology in July and November showed areas above the clearance levels and KKI did inform Ms. Higgins of these elevated levels in the subsequent letters. Ms. Higgins contends that KKI knew of the presence of high levels of lead-based paint and dust in the Federal Street property as early as December of 1993, that even after Level II intervention it still had high levels as of June 24, 1994, and that it was not until she received a letter dated September 14, 1994 that KKI specifically informed Ms. Higgins of the fact that her house had elevated lead levels.

KKI drew blood from Myron Higgins for lead content analysis on June 8, 1994, July 29, 1994, and November 9, 1994. KKI notified Ms. Higgins of the results of the blood tests by letters dated July 18, 1994, August 2, 1994, and December 6, 1994, respectively. The results of the tests were 17.5 [mu] g/dL, 21 [mu] g/dL, and 11 [mu] g/dL, respectively. The first and third tests placed him in the CDC Class IIA while the second test placed him in CDC Class III. KKI told Ms. Higgins that it had informed the BCHD of the second result and that she "should provide the test result to [her] child's primary health care provider right away."

Ms. Higgins contends that KKI was negligent in its failure to inform her of its knowledge of the high levels of lead dust recorded by both XRF testing in December 1993, prior to her moving into th[illegible] abatement [illegible], and from the samples collected via the Cyclone vacuum in May 1994. Ms. Higgins asserts that this withholding of information combined with KKI's letter dated June 24, 1994 informing her solely of the lower results of the samples collected by dust wipe methodology was misleading to her as a participant in the study. She implies that it gave her a false sense of security that there were no potential lead-based paint or dust hazards in her house.

. . . .

B. General Discussion

[W]e, at the very least, hold that, under the particular circumstances testified to by the parties, there are genuine disputes of material fact concerning whether a special relationship existed between KKI and Ericka Grimes, as well as between KKI and Ms. Higgins and Myron Higgins. Concerning this issue, the granting of the summary judgment motions was clearly inappropriate. When a "special relationship" can exist as a matter of law, the issue of whether, given certain facts, a special relationship does exist, when there is a dispute of material fact in that respect, is a decision for the finder of fact, not the trial judge. We shall hold initially that the very nature of nontherapeutic scientific research on human subjects can, and normally will, create special relationships out of which duties arise. Since World War II the specialness or nature of such relationships has been frequently of concern in and outside of the research community.

As a result of the atrocities performed in the name of science during the Holocaust, and other happenings in the World War II era, what is now known as The Nuremberg Code evolved. Of special interest to this Court, the Nuremberg Code, at least in significant part, was the result of legal thought and legal principles, as opposed to medical or scientific principles, and thus should be the preferred standard for assessing the legality of scientific research on human subjects. Under it, duties to research subjects arise.

Just recently the research community has been [illegible] as a [illegible] experimentation on a Pennsylvania citizen. Jesse Gelsinger consented to participate in a research project at the University of Pennsylvania's Institute of Human Gene Therapy. After Gelsinger's death, the U.S. Food and Drug Administration ordered a halt to eight human gene therapy experiments at the Institute. Additionally, other similar projects were halted elsewhere. The FDA took the action after a "discovery of a number of serious problems in the Institute's informed consent procedures and, more generally, a lapse in the researchers' ethical responsibilities to experimental subjects." Jeffrey H. Barker, *Human Experimentation and the Double Facelessness of a Merciless Epoch,* 25 New York University Review of Law and Social Change 603, 616 (1999).

Gelsinger had a different type of ornithine transcarbamylase deficiency (OTC) disease, than that addressed by the research. His particular brand of the disease was under control. There was no possibility that the research being conducted would directly benefit him. It was thus, as to him, as it was to the children in the case at bar, nontherapeutic; a way to study the affects on the subjects (in the present case, the children) in order to measure the success of the experiment. In Gelsinger's case, the research was to test the efficiency of disease vectors. In other words, weakened adenovirus (common-cold viruses) were used to deliver trillions of particles of a particular OTC gene into his artery and thus to his liver. Gelsinger experienced a massive and fatal immune system reaction to the introduction of the common-cold virus.

There were problems with the extent of the informed consent there obtained. Barker noted that:

> "Is this just a case of rogue experimenters giving a bad name to all genetic research? Not at all. The program in Philadelphia is (or at least was) one of the most prestigious in the world and the researchers there were first-rate. Rather, the problems with that program are indicative of systemic problems with genetic research and informed consent as a protection of the autonomy of research subjects.
>
> . . . Researchers, under competitive pressure and also financial pressure from corporate backers, operate under a paternalistic approach to research subjects, asserting professional expertise and arguing experimental necessity while minimizing the right to self-determination — a key aspect of the exercise of autonomy — of their subjects. The result is a greater or lesser degree of ethical effacement."

Id. at 617-620.

C. Negligence

It is important for us to remember that appellants allege that KKI was negligent. Specifically, they allege that KKI, as a medical researcher, owed a duty of care to them, as subjects in the research study, based on the nature of the agreements between them and also based on the nature of the relationship between the parties. They contend specifically that KKI was negligent because KKI breached its duty to: (1) design a study that did not involve placing children at unnecessary risk; (2) inform participants in the study of results in a timely manner; and (3) to completely and accurately inform participants in the research study of all the hazards and risks involved in the study.

In order to establish a claim for negligence under Maryland law, a party must prove four elements: "(1) that the defendant was under a duty to protect the plaintiff from injury, (2) that the defendant breached that duty, (3) *that the plaintiff suffered actual injury or loss* and (4) that the loss or injury proximately resulted from the defendant's breach of the duty." Because this is a review of the granting of the two summary judgments based solely on the grounds that there was no legal duty to protect the children, we are primarily concerned with the first prong — whether KKI was under a duty to protect appellants from injury.

The relationship that existed between KKI and both sets of appellants in the case at bar was that of medical researcher and research study subject.

Though not expressly recognized in the Maryland Code or in our prior cases as a type of relationship which creates a duty of care, evidence in the record suggests that such a relationship involving a duty or duties would ordinarily exist, and certainly could exist, based on the facts and circumstances of each of these individual cases. Once we have determined that the facts and circumstances of the present cases, considered in a light most favorable to the nonmoving parties, are susceptible to inferences supporting the position of the party opposing summary judgment, we are mandated to hold that the granting of summary judgment in the lower court was improper. In addition to the trial courts' erroneous conclusions on the law, the facts and circumstances of both of these cases are susceptible to inferences that a special relationship imposing a duty or duties was created in the arrangements in the cases *sub judice,* and, ordinarily, could be created in similar research programs involving human subjects.

IV. The Special Relationships

A. The Consent Agreement Contract

Both sets of appellants signed a similar Consent Form prepared by KKI in which KKI expressly promised to: (1) financially compensate (however minimally) appellants for their participation in the study; (2) collect lead dust samples from appellants' homes, analyze the samples, discuss the results with appellants, and discuss steps that could be taken, which could reduce exposure to lead; and (3) collect blood samples from children in the household and provide appellants with the results of the blood tests. In return, appellants agreed to participate in the study, by: (1) allowing KKI into appellants' homes to collect dust samples; (2) periodically filling out questionnaires; and (3) allowing the children's blood to be drawn, tested, and utilized in the study if consent agreements contain such provisions, and the trial court did not find otherwise, and we hold from our own examination of the record that such provisions were so contained, mutual assent, offer, acceptance, and consideration existed, all of which created contractual relationships imposing duties by reason of the consent agreement themselves (as well, as we discuss elsewhere, by the very nature of such relationships).

By having appellants sign this Consent Form, both KKI and appellants expressly made representations, which, in our view, created a bilateral contract between the parties. At the very least, it suggests that appellants were agreeing with KKI to participate in the research study with the expectation that they would be compensated, albeit, more or less, minimally, be informed of all the information necessary for the subject to freely choose whether to participate, and continue to participate, and receive promptly any information that might bear on their willingness to continue to participate in the study. This includes full, detailed, prompt, and continuing warnings as to all the potential risks and hazards inherent in the research or that arise during the research. KKI, in return, was getting the children to move into the houses and/or to remain there over time, and was given the right to test the children's blood for lead. As consideration to KKI, it got access to the houses and to the blood of the children that had been encouraged to live in a "risk" environment. In other words, KKI received a measuring tool — the children's blood. Considerations existed, mainly money, food coupons, trinkets, bilateral promises, blood to be tested in order to measure success. "Informed consent" of the type used here, which imposes obligation and confess consideration on both researcher and subject (in these cases, the parents of the subjects) may differ from the more onesided "informed consent" normally used in actual medical practice. Researcher/ subject consent in nontheraputical research can, and in this case did, create a contract.

B. The Sufficiency of the Consent Form

The consent form did not directly inform the parents of the fact that it was contemplated that some of the children might ingest lead dust particles, and that one of the reasons the blood of the children was to be tested was to evaluate how effective the various abatement measures were.

A reasonable parent would expect to be clearly informed that it was at least contemplated that her child would ingest lead dust particles, and that the degree to which lead dust contaminated the child's blood would be used as one of the ways in which the success of the experiment would be measured. The fact that if such information was furnished, it might be difficult to obtain human subjects for the research, does not affect the need to supply the information, or alter the ethics of failing to provide such information. A human subject is entitled to *all* material information. The respective parent should also have been clearly informed that in order for the measurements to be most helpful, the child needed to stay in the house until the conclusion of the study. Whether assessed by a subjective or an objective standard, the children, or their surrogates, should have been additionally informed that the researchers anticipated that, as a result of the experiment, it was possible that there might be some accumulation of lead in the blood of the children. The "informed" consent was not valid because full material information was not furnished to the subjects or their parents.

C. Special Relationship

In Case Number 128, Ms. Hughes signed a Consent Form in which KKI agreed to provide her with "specific blood-lead results" and discuss with her "a summary of house test results and steps that [she] could take to reduce any risks of exposure." She contends that this agreement between the parties gave rise to a duty owed by KKI to provide her with that information in a timely manner.

In Case Number 129, Ms. Higgins also signed a Consent Form in which KKI agreed to provide her with "specific blood-lead results" in respect to her child and to discuss with her "a summary of house test results and steps that [she] could take to reduce any risks of exposure." She contends that this agreement between the parties gave rise to a duty owed by KKI to provide her with complete and accurate information.

Specifically, Ms. Higgins contends that KKI was negligent in its failure to inform her of its knowledge of the high levels of lead dust recorded by both XRF testing in December 1993 and from the samples collected via the Cyclone vacuum in May 1994 and that this withholding of information combined with KKI's letter dated June 24, 1993, informing her solely of the lower results of the samples collected by dust wipe methodol[illegible] to her as a participant in the study. KKI does not argue the facts as appellant presents them. Instead, it argues that no duty to inform existed because although the Cyclone readings were high, they were not an indication of a potential hazard because the clearance levels were based on dust wipe methodology and the dust wipe results were not above the clearance levels. Looking at the relevant facts of Case Number 129, they are susceptible to inferences supporting the position of appellant, Ms. Higgins. Accordingly, for this reason alone, the grant of summary judgment was improper.

It is of little moment that an entity is an institutional volunteer in a community. If otherwise, the legitimacy of the claim to noble purpose would always depend upon the particular institution and the particular community it is serving in a given case. As we have indicated, history is replete with claims of noble purpose for institutions and institutional volunteers in a wide variety of communities.

D. The Federal Regulations

A duty may be prescribed by a statute, or a special relationship creating duties may arise from the requirement for compliance with statutory provisions. Although there is no duty of which we are aware prescribed by the Maryland Code in respect to scientific research of the nature here present, federal regulations have been enacted that impose standards of care that attach to federally funded or sponsored research projects that use human subjects. *See* 45 C.F.R. Part 46 (2000). 45 C.F.R. Part 46, Subpart A, is entitled "Basic HHS Policy for Protection of Human Research Subjects" and Subpart D of the regulation is entitled "Additional Protections for Children Involved as Subjects in Research." 45 C.F.R. section 46.101(a) (2000) provides:

> "Sec. 46.101
>
> (a) Except as provided in paragraph (b) of this section, this policy applies to all research involving human subjects conducted, supported or otherwise subject [illegible] any federal department or agency *which takes appropriate administrative action to make the policy applicable to such research.* This includes research conducted by federal civilian employees or military personnel, except that each department or agency head may adopt such procedural modifications as may be appropriate from an administrative standpoint. It also includes research conducted, supported, or otherwise subject to regulation by the federal government outside the United States."

[Emphasis added.]

As we discussed, *supra,* this study was funded, and co-sponsored, by the EPA and presumably was therefore subject to these federal conditions. These conditions, if appropriate administrative action has been taken, require fully informed consent in any research using human subjects conducted, supported, or otherwise subject to any level of control or funding by any federal department or agency. 45 C.F.R. section 46.116 provides in relevant part:

> "Sec. 46.116 General requirements for informed consent. Except as provided elsewhere in this policy, no investigator may involve a human being as a subject in research covered by this policy unless the investigator has obtained the *legally effective* informed consent of the subject or the subject's legally authorized representative. *An investigator shall seek such consent only under circumstances that provide the prospective subject or the representative sufficient opportunity to consider whether or not to participate and that minimize the possibility of coercion or undue influence.* The information that is given to the subject or the representative shall be in language understandable to the subject or the representative. No informed consent, whether oral or written, may include any exculpatory language through which the subject or the representative is made to waive or appear to waive any of the subject's legal rights, or releases or appears to release the investigator, the sponsor, the institution or its agents from liability for negligence.
>
> (a) Basic elements of informed consent. Except as provided in paragraph (c) or (d) of this section, in seeking informed consent the following information shall be provided to each subject:
>
> (2) A description of any reasonably foreseeable *risks* or discomforts to the subject;
>
> (4) A disclosure of appropriate alternative procedures or courses of treatment, if any, that might be advantageous to the subject;
>
> (6) For research involving more than minimal *risk,* an explanation as to whether any compensation and an explanation as to whether any medical treatments are available if injury occurs and, if so, what they consist of, or where further information may be obtained;
>
> (b) Additional elements of informed consent. When appropriate, one or more of the following elements of information shall also be provided to each subject:
>
> (1) A statement that the particular treatment or procedure may involve risks to the subject (or to the embryo or fetus, if the subject is or may become pregnant) which are currently unforeseeable;
>
> *(5) A statement that significant new findings developed during the course of the research which may relate to the subject's willingness to continue participation will be provided to the subject. . . .*" [Emphasis added.]

Subpart D of the regulation concerns children involved as subjects in research. 45 C.F.R. section 46.407 therefore additionally provides:

"Sec. 46.407 Research not otherwise approvable which presents an opportunity to understand, prevent, or alleviate a serious problem affecting the health or welfare of children. HHS will conduct or fund research that the IRB does not believe meets the requirements of Sec. 46.404, Sec. 46.405, or Sec. 46.406 only if:

(a) The RB finds that the research presents a reasonable opportunity to further the understanding, prevention, or alleviation of a serious problem affecting the health or welfare of children; *and*

(b) *The Secretary, after consultation with a panel of experts in pertinent disciplines (for example: science, medicine, education, ethics, law) and following opportunity for public review and comment, has determined either:*

(1) That the research in fact satisfies the conditions of Sec. 46.404, Sec. 46.405, or Sec. 46.406, as applicable, or

(2) The following:

(i) The research presents a reasonable opportunity to further the understanding, prevention, or alleviation of a serious problem affecting the health or welfare of children;

(ii) *The research will be conducted in accordance with sound ethical principles;*

(iii) Adequate provisions are made for soliciting the assent of children and the permission of their parents or guardians, as set forth in Sec. 46.408." [Emphasis added.]

These federal regulations, especially the requirement for adherence to sound ethical principles, strike right at the heart of KKI's defense of the granting of the Motions for Summary Judgment. *Fully informed* consent is lacking in these cases. The research did not comply with the regulations. There clearly was more than a minimal risk involved. Under the regulations, children should not have been used for the purpose of measuring how much lead they would accumulate in their blood while living in partially abated houses to which they were recruited initially or encouraged to remain, because of the study.

Clearly, KKI, as a research institution, is required to obtain a human participant's fully informed consent, using sound ethical principles. It is clear from the wording of the applicable federal regulations that this requirement of informed consent continues during the duration of the research study and applies to new or changing risks. In this case, a special relationship out of which duties might arise might be created by reason of the federally imposed regulations. The question becomes whether this duty of informed consent created by federal regulation, as a matter of state law, translates into a duty of care arising out of the unique relationship that is researcher-subject, as opposed to doctor-patient. We answer that question in the affirmative. In this State, it may, depending on the facts, create such a duty.

Additionally, the Nuremberg Code, intended to be applied internationally, and never expressly rejected in this county, inherently and implicitly, speaks strongly to the existence of special relationships imposing ethical duties on researchers who conduct nontherapeutic experiments on human subjects. The Nuremberg Code specifically requires researchers to make known to human subjects of research "all inconveniences and hazards reasonably to be expected; and the effects upon his health or person which may *possibly* come from his participation in the experiment." (Emphasis added.) The breach of obligations imposed on researchers by the Nuremberg Code, might well support actions sounding in negligence in cases such as those at issue here. We reiterate as well that, given the facts and circumstances of both of these cases, there were, at the very least, genuine disputes of material facts concerning the relationship and duties of the parties, and compliance with the regulations.

V. The Ethical Appropriateness of the Research

The World Medical Association in its Declaration of Helsinki[39] included a code of ethics for investigative researchers and was an attempt by the medical community to establish its own set of rules for conducting research on human subjects. The Declaration states in relevant part:

> "III. Non-therapeutic biomedical research involving human subjects (Non-clinical biomedical research)
>
> 1. *In the purely scientific application of medical research carried out on a human being, it is the duty of the physician to remain the protector of the life and health of that person on whom biomedical research is being carried out.*
>
> 2. The subjects should be volunteers — either healthy persons or patients for whom the experimental design is not related to the patient's illness.
>
> 3. The investigator or the investigating team should *discontinue the research if in his/her or their judgment it may, if continued, be harmful to the individual.*
>
> 4. *In research on man, the interest of science and society should never take precedence over considerations related to the well being of the subject."* [Emphasis added.]

Adopted in Declaration of Helsinki, World Medical Assembly (WMA) 18th Assembly (June 1964), amended by 29th WMA Tokyo, Japan (October, 1975),

[39] The Declaration of Helsinki was crafted by the international medical profession, as preferable to the Nuremberg Code crafted by lawyers and judges and adopted right after the Second World War. The Declaration, or, for that matter, the Nuremberg Code, have never been formally adopted by the relevant governmental entities, although the Nuremberg Code was intended to apply universally. The medical profession, and its ancillary research organs, felt that the Nuremberg Code was too restrictive because of its origins from the Nazi horrors of that era. Serious questions arise in this case under either code, even under the more general provisions of the Declaration of Helsinki apparently favored by doctors and scientists.

35th WMA Venice, Italy (October 1983), and the 41st WMA Hong Kong (September 1989).

The determination of whether a duty exists under Maryland law is the ultimate function of various policy considerations as adopted by either the Legislature, or, if it has not spoken, as it has not in respect to this situation, by Maryland courts. In our view, otherwise healthy children should not be the subjects of nontherapeutic experimentation or research that has the potential to be harmful to the child. It is, first and foremost, the responsibility of the researcher and the research entity to see to the harmlessness of such nontherapeutic research. Consent of parents can never relieve the researcher of this duty.

In a recent report, the National Bioethics Advisory Commission recognized that this conflict between pursuit of scientific knowledge and the wellbeing of research participants requires some oversight of scientific investigators:

> "However noble the investigator's intentions, when research involves human participants, the uncertainties inherent in any research study raise the prospect of unanticipated harm. In designing a research study an investigator must focus on finding or creating situations in which one can test important scientific hypotheses. *At the same time, no matter how important the research questions, it is not ethical to use human participants without appropriate protections.* Thus, there can be a conflict between the need to test hypotheses and the requirement to respect and protect individuals who participate in research. This conflict and the resulting tension that can arise within the research enterprise suggest a need for guidance and oversight."

National Bioethics Advisory Commission, *Ethical and Policy Issues in Research Involving Human Participants,* 2-3 (Dec. 19, 2000) (emphasis added). When human subjects are used in scientific research, the rights of the human subjects are afforded the protection of the courts when such subjects seek redress for any wrongs committed.

A special relationship giving rise to duties, the breach of which might constitute negligence, might also arise because, generally, the researchers are in a better position to anticipate, discover, and understand the potential risks to the health of their subjects. Practical inequalities exist between researchers, who have superior knowledge, and participants "who are often poorly placed to protect themselves from risk." "Given the gap in knowledge between investigators and participants and the inherent conflict of interest faced by investigators, participants cannot and should not be solely responsible for their own protection."

This duty requires the protection of the research subjects from unreasonable harm and requires the researcher to completely and promptly inform the subjects of potential hazards existing from time to time because of the profound trust that participants place in investigators, institutions, and the research enterprise as a whole to protect them from harm. "Faced with seemingly knowledgeable and prestigious investigators engaged in a noble pursuit, participants may simply assume that research is socially important or of benefit to them individually; they may not be aware that participation could be harmful to their interests." *Id.*

The study, by its design, placed and/or retained children in areas where they might come into contact with elevated levels of lead dust. Clearly, KKI contemplated that at least some of the children would develop elevated blood lead levels while participating in the study. At 45 C.F.R. section 46.111 *Criteria for IRB approval of research,* the regulations require IRBs to encourage the safety aspects of research rather than encouraging noncompliance with regulations: "(b) When some or all of the subjects . . . such as children . . ., [are] economically or educationally disadvantaged persons, *additional* safeguards have been included . . . to protect the rights and welfare of these subjects." (Emphasis added.)

While we acknowledge that foreseeability does not necessarily create a duty, we recognize that potential harm to the children participants of this study was both foreseeable and potentially extreme. A "special relationship" also exists in circumstances where such experiments are conducted.

VI. Parental Consent for Children to Be Subjects of Potentially Hazardous Nontherapeutic Research

It is not in the best interest of a specific child, in a nontherapeutic research project, to be placed in a research environment, which might possibly be, or which proves to be, hazardous to the health of the child. We have long stressed that the "best interests of the child" is the overriding concern of this Court in matters relating to children. Whatever the interests of a parent, and whatever the interests of the general public in fostering research that might, according to a researcher's hypothesis, be for the good of all children, this Court's concern for the particular child and particular case, over-arches all other interests. It is, simply, and we hope, succinctly put, not in the best interest of any healthy child to be intentionally put in a nontherapeutic situation where his or her health may be impaired, in order to test methods that may ultimately benefit all children.

One simply does not expose otherwise healthy children, incapable of personal assent (consent), to a nontherapeutic research environment that is known at the inception of the research, might cause the children to ingest lead dust. It is especially troublesome, when a measurement of the success of the research experiment is, in significant respect, to be determined by the extent to which the blood of the children absorbs, and is contaminated by, a substance that the researcher knows can, in sufficient amounts, whether solely from the research environment or cumulative from all sources, cause serious and long term adverse health effects. Such a practice is not legally acceptable.

In the case sub judice, no impartial judicial review or oversight was sought by the researchers or by the parents. Additionally, in spite of the RB's improper attempt to manufacture a therapeutic value, there was absolutely no such value of the research in respect to the minor subjects used to measure the effectiveness of the study. In the absence of a requirement for judicial review, in such a circumstance, the researchers, and their scientific based review boards would be, if permitted, the sole judges of whether it is appropriate to use children in nontherapeutic research of the nature here present, where the success of an experiment is to be measured in substantial [illegible] research environments cause the absorption of poisons into the blood of children. Science cannot be permitted to be the sole judge of the appropriateness of such research methods on human subjects, especially in respect to children. We hold that in these contested cases, the research study protocols, those of which we are aware, were not appropriate.

Additionally, there are conflicting views in respect to nontherapeutic research, as to whether consent, even of a person capable of consenting, can justify a research protocol that is otherwise unjustifiable.

Based on the record before us, no degree of parental consent, and no degree of furnished information to the parents could make the experiment at issue here, ethically or legally permissible. It was wrong in the first instance.

VII. Conclusion

We hold that in Maryland a parent, appropriate relative, or other applicable surrogate, cannot consent to the participation of a child or other person under legal disability in nontherapeutic research or studies in which there is any risk of injury or damage to the health of the subject.

We hold that informed consent agreements in nontherapeutic research projects, under certain circumstances can constitute contracts; and that, under certain circumstances, such research agreements can, as a matter of law, constitute "special relationships" giving rise to duties, out of the breach of which negligence actions may arise. We also hold that, normally, such special relationships are created between researchers and the human subjects used by the researchers. Additionally, we hold that governmental regulations can create duties on the part of researchers towards human subjects out of which "special relationships" can arise. Likewise, such duties and relationships are consistent with the provisions of the Nuremberg Code.

The determination as to whether a "special relationship" actually exists is to be done on a case by case basis. The determination as to whether a special relationship exists, if properly pled, lies with the trier of fact. We hold that there was ample [illegible] at bar to support a fact finder's determination of the existence of duties arising out of contract, or out of a special relationship, or out of regulations and codes, or out of all of them, in each of the cases.

We hold that on the present record, the Circuit Courts erred in their assessment of the law and of the facts as pled in granting KKI's motions for summary judgment in both cases before this Court. Accordingly, we vacate the rulings of the Circuit Court for Baltimore City and remand these cases to that court for further proceedings consistent with this opinion.

Raker, J., concurring in result only:

I concur in the Court's judgment because I find that appellants have alleged sufficient facts to establish that there existed a special relationship between the parties in these cases, which created a duty of care that, if breached, gives rise to an action in negligence.

I have some concern with the mixed message sent by the majority as to whether the existence of a tort duty arising from a special relationship existed is a question of law for the court or a question to be determined by the trier of fact.

I cannot join in the majority's sweeping factual determinations that the risks associated with exposing children to lead-based paint were foreseeable and well known to appellees and that appellees contemplated lead contamination in participants' blood, that the children's health was put at risk; that there was no complete and clear explanation in the consent agreements that the research to be conducted was designed to measure the success of the abatement procedures by measuring the extent to which the children's blood was being contaminated and that a certain level of lead accumulation was anticipated; that the parental consent was ineffective; that the consent form was insufficient because it lacked certain specific warnings; that the consent agreements did not provide that appellees would provide repairs in the event of lead dust contamination subsequent to the original abatement measures; that the Institutional Review Board involved in these cases abdicated its responsibility to protect the safety of the research subjects by misconstruing the difference between therapeutic and nontherapeutic research and aiding researchers in circumventing federal regulations; that Institutional Review Boards are not sufficiently objective to regulate the ethics of experimental research; that it is never in the best interest of any child to be placed in a nontherapeutic research study that might be hazardous to the child's health; that there was no therapeutic value in the research for the child subjects involved; that the research did not comply with applicable regulations; or that there was more than a minimal risk involved in this study. I do not here condone the conduct of appellee, and it may well be that the majority's conclusions are warranted by the facts of these cases, but the record before us is limited. Indeed, the majority recognizes that the record is "sparse." The critical point is that these are questions for the jury on remand and are not properly before this Court at this time.

I cannot join the majority in holding that, in Maryland, a parent or guardian cannot consent to the participation of a minor child in a nontherapeutic research study in which there is *any* risk of injury or damage to the health of the child without prior judicial approval and oversight. Nor can I join in the majority's holding that the research conducted in these cases was *per se* inappropriate, unethical, and illegal. Such sweeping holdings are far beyond the question presented in these appeals, and their resolution by the Court, at this time, is inappropriate. I also do not join in what I perceive as the majority's wholesale adoption of the Nuremberg Code into Maryland state tort law. Finally, I do not join in the majority's comparisons between the research at issue in this case and extreme historical abuses, such as those of the Nazis or the Tuskegee Syphilis Study.

Accordingly, I join the majority only in the judgment to reverse the Circuit Courts' granting of summary judgments to appellees.

NOTES AND QUESTIONS

1. The *Grimes* case is unique in its categorical condemnation, banning, non-therapeutic research on children and its declaration that parents

simply lack authority to grant consent to such research. It is also unique in its condemnation of the procedures and participants involved in human research generally. While it contains [illegible] form (160 pages), an exhaustive, comprehensive review of the literature and case law criticizing the abuses of human experimentation, it is the first case to suggest those abuses are *inherent* in the system.

2. A thoughtful preliminary commentary on the *Grimes* case is Ross, *Defense of the Hopkins Lead Abatement Studies*, 30 JLME 50 (2002). The author herself conducts experiments on children pursuant to NIH grants. Her criticisms of the Court are thus substantial and her criticisms of the Hopkins researchers are muted. Nevertheless, Doctor Ross notes that the IRB did not do its job, and the researchers should have known that the children had blood levels of lead that posed risk to them (one had a peak level of 21 (g/dL, the other 32; the CDC "poison" level was 25 (g/dL in 1985, reduced to 10 (g/dL in 1991.) Doctor Ross argues unconvincingly that the research *was* therapeutic, valuable and ethical, and that parents *have* moral authority to expose their children to the risks of non-therapeutic experimentation.

3. The *Grimes* court reviews the sorry history of human experimentation and the abuses attending it from Nuremberg to the Cincinnati Radiation Cases to the year 2000 *Gelsinger* case at the University of Pennsylvania involving gene therapy. Some factors appear: imbalance in power, disadvantaged subjects, profit motive. Are there others? The pattern of abuses is so pervasive and persistent that one seeks for deeper causes, of historic tenacity. What might these be?

4. Given the pattern noted above, should human experimentation be totally banned? Or limited to circumstances where no harm can result, and no imposition is possible, and therapeutic potential is clear? When might that be? And how would you police the system? (The IRBs?)

5. In *Grimes*, the Court found the research itself was inappropriate. Why? Was it, truly, akin to the Tuskegee Syphilis Study, and the past instances of abuse?

6. The *Grimes* court also found that the scientific and medical communi- [illegible] permitted to assume sole authority for what is right and the IRBs are inadequate for the task. Why? Was there sufficient evidence to justify this sweeping conclusion? Who then should do the job?

7. The research study sorted housing into five groups of twenty-five units, encouraging families to be exposed to lead, to be determined by testing for lead in the blood of the children. What could/would be learned from this?

8. Note that there were incentives for families to remain in, or enter upon, housing at increased risk. Note also that there was (some) deception and (some) withholding of information (see the "Consent Form"). Suppose these two factors were absent; would/should the case be decided differently? Is *Grimes* about harm in fact, abuse in fact, or systemic inevitability?

9. If this was "medical," did a patient/physician relationship emerge? Was one necessary? And if this was "treatment," was informed consent (in the sense developed in the preceding cases) necessary? Obtained? How should these questions be resolved — by contract? perception? custom?

10. The plaintiffs sued in negligence. This required a duty of care. The Court found a "special relationship" between subject and researcher. Why? What is its source, content, limit? If it is created by contract, can it ever be *more* than the contract? And if by tort law, then what/where are the elements? And who is liable? If by federal regulations, what/where are the remedies? And if by international standards of ethical conduct, such as those articulated in Nuremberg, Helsinki or the European Human Rights Convention (*see In Re A (Children) (Conjoined Twins: Medical Treatment)* No. 1, [2000] H.R.L.R. 721, 2000 WL 1274054 *supra,* § 1.04[2][b]), how do these become a part of American law?

11. The *Grimes* court relied heavily upon federal regulations, mandating ethical conduct, informed consent, IRB oversight and minimal risk. But what is their status under American, particularly state, law in a negligence action?

12. The Court also held parental consent was simply not possible/ permissible in Maryland under these circumstances. How and where does the Court get the authority for that declaration? And under *what* circumstances (and by what procedures) might consent become permissible?

13. Note that there is a remand here. What are the issues for the trial court — whether duties arose, were violated, causing harm, subject to contributory negligence, as well as a duty to minimize harm, with what cost(s) in dollars and sense? Note also that these (at least some) are for the jury. Why?

14. What damages should be awarded here? Are they subject to a cap on noneconomic damages?

15. What are the implications of *Grimes* for human experimentation in the United States? What would your advice be if you were counsel to: (a) NIH; (b) Johns Hopkins; (c) Kennedy-Krieger; (d) the Maryland legislature?

16. Sometimes, the experimental treatments are very successful. In that case, may they be compelled to continue beyond the length of the experimental trial? *Suthers v. Amgen*, Inc., 2005 U.S. Dist. LEXIS 11119 (S.D.N.Y. 2005).

17. Finally, what are the duties to third persons in experimental settings? In *Doe v. Pharmacia & Upjohn*, 122 Fed. Appx. 20 (4th Cir. 2005), the wife of a former employee of Pharmacia & Upjohn brought suit against the company for her contraction of HIV from her husband, who contracted it at work due to the employers' lack of reasonable care and negligent methods of testing. Should the former employer owe a duty to Mrs. Doe? If no duty is found to exist, is Mrs. Doe out of options, or might there be other causes of action for her to bring?

PROBLEM 3–14 — Nazi Data

In the 1980s, ETA and OSHA both became concerned about establishing safety standards for the manufacture of phosgene, a gas used in the commercial manufacture of fertilizer in the United States. The gas is extremely dangerous and had been used as a vehicle in gas warfare in the first World War. A storm of controversy was generated when the draft safety report of the consultant was disclosed to rely upon data from the 1930s, derived from experiments on concentration camp prisoners by Nazi doctors. Those who opposed use of the data argued that it was a product of inhuman barbarism and should be eliminated. Those who favored use of the data argued that it was scientifically valid and, in fact, the only *possible* data showing the actual impact of phosgene on human beings.

Should the report reflecting the data have been accepted in final form and safety standards based thereon?

PROBLEM 3–15 — Deception and Experimentation

In the 1960s, an experiment was conducted at an east coast university. A psychologist recruited undergraduates and paid them an hourly wage to administer electric shocks to a subject in a chair. They were told that they were testing the tolerance level of the person receiving the shocks. With each jolt, the subject in the chair reacted with increasingly dramatic symptoms of pain. Finally, in most instances, the students administering the electrical shocks refused to continue raising the level of current, upset and appalled by the pain they were inflicting.

In reality, the purpose of the testing was to determine the extent to which average citizens, when paid a minimum wage, would be willing to inflict pain on another citizen. In many instances, the students who inflicted pain experienced psychological trauma after reflecting on the extent to which they were willing to be cruel and abusive to another person. They also felt manipulated and deceived upon learning that *they* had been the unwitting subjects of the experiment.

The psychologist conducting the experiments defended on the grounds that oftentimes psychological experiments *must* involve deception if they are to simulate reality successfully. An example given in support of this view is the illegal, surreptitious wiretapping of jury rooms to learn what juries actually discuss in a criminal case.

A similar experiment was conducted at an academic center in California. There, recruits were cast in roles of inmates and guards at a jail. Although free to leave at any time, they played their roles over a period of time, leading to harassment and brutality. Years later, several remained upset by the experiment, terminated only by the objection of another faculty member (who subsequently married the principal investigator).

Evaluate these two experiments in the light of the foregoing cases and materials

PROBLEM 3–16 — Injury to Research Volunteers

A small German immuno-therapeutics firm tested TGN1412 on eight humans (two receiving placebos). The monoclonal antibody, it was hoped, might be useful in fighting auto immune diseases, such as MS, by agonizing CD28 receptors on T lymphocytes. Six of the volunteers became profoundly ill. *See* Wood & Darbyshire, *Injury to Research Volunteers*, 354 New Eng. J. Med. 1869 (May 4, 2006). The authors comment that safety and risks are affected by the trend towards shifting experimentation to smaller companies.

One might also note the increasing trend in the United States to move experimentation out of medical centers and into physicians' offices. . . .

The authors recommend keeping numbers small, and prolonging observation periods. What else will protect volunteers? Insurance? It is rarely used in the United States, but required in Europe. *See* Steinbrook, 354 New Eng. J. Med. 1871 (May 4, 2006). Are there other measures to protect or compensate volunteers, or are informed consent and IRB review enough?

PROBLEM 3–17 — The Constant Gardener

In the movie *The Constant Gardener,* pharmaceutical companies test unproven drugs on African women and children. There is confusion and concern and unclear consent. But they are going to die anyway, so perhaps they (or someone) will be helped. Is this ethical?

See generally Brown Medical Group Condemns U.S., Washington Post A-10 (Apr. 23, 1997); Unethical Trials, 337 New Eng. J. Med. 853 (1997); Angell, *The Ethics of Clinical Research In the Third World,* 337 New Eng. J. Med. (Sep. 18, 1997); Msamanga & Fawzi, *The Double Burden of HIV Infection,* 337 New Eng. J. Med. (Sep. 18, 1997).

PROBLEM 3–18 — Play for Pay

On November 23, 2005, CMS announced that Medicare would not cover bariatric surgery for beneficiaries over the age of 65, because evidence of risks was inconclusive. However, coverage would be extended if they enrolled in clinical trials. This was pursuant to CMS' policy of "coverage with evidence development," which has also been applied in dealing with PET scans in Alzheimer's treatment, some chemotherapy in colon cancer, and implantable defribrillators. In these instances, payment would be mad only for beneficiaries who "volunteer" for clinical trials. Is this ethical? *See*, Pearson et al., *Medicare's Requirement for Research Participation as a Condition of Coverage*, 296 JAMA 988 (Aug. 23, 2006).

§ 3.04 Fiduciary Obligations: Competence

Patients not only seek treatment and care, but they choose as well the skills of specific physicians. To that extent, they are seeking not the *norm* of performance in the profession, but the best (in their judgment) person and the best services. In varying ways, this obligates the physician or other provider to use his or her best efforts to care for a patient. We have already seen this in the *Burton* case, *supra* § 3.03[3]. The duty of best efforts poses problems for physicians. For example, in the *Tarasoff* context (*supra* § 3.02[2]) where they may have to disobey orders, or in *Burton* where new technology is not yet "standard of care" but *is* "state of the art." Most often a lesser standard, based on community practice or the reasonable practitioner, is sufficient, but even then issues of resource and definition arise.

A different issue is *scope* of service, as opposed to *level*. This is the question of *what* the physician is responsible *for*. Where patients fail to follow advice, what is the physician's responsibility? Where an HMO denies coverage, does the physician have an obligation of advocacy? In a rapidly changing environment of managed care, fiduciary ethics may be subordinated to corporate ethics or population — based ethics.

We begin with the duty of competence, requiring a healthcare provider's "best efforts."

[1] Best Efforts

TRUMAN v. THOMAS
611 P.2d 902 (Cal. 1980)

Bird, Chief Justice.

This court must decide whether a physician's failure to inform a patient of the material risks of not consenting to a recommended pap smear, so that the patient might make an informed choice, may have breached the physician's duty of due care to his patient, who died from cancer of the cervix.

I

Respondent, Dr. Claude R. Thomas, is a family physician engaged in a general medical practice. He was first contacted in April 1963 by appellants' mother, Rena Trumen, in connection with her second pregnancy. He continued to act as the primary physician for Mrs. Truman and her two children until March 1969. During this six-year period, Mrs. Truman not only sought his medical advice, but often discussed personal matters with him.

In April 1969, Mrs. Truman consulted Dr. Casey, a urologist, about a urinary tract infection which had been treated previously by Dr. Thomas. While examining Mrs. Truman, Dr. Casey discovered that she was experiencing heavy vaginal discharges and that her cervix was extremely rough. Mrs. Truman was given a prescription for the infection and advised to see a gynecologist as soon as possible. When Mrs. Truman did not make an appointment with a gynecologist, Dr. Casey made an appointment for her with a Dr. Ritter.

In October 1969, Dr. Ritter discovered that Mrs. Truman's cervix had been largely replaced by a cancerous tumor. Too far advanced to be removed by surgery, the tumor was unsuccessfully treated by other methods. Mrs. Truman died in July 1970 at the age of 30.

Appellants are Rena Truman's two children. They brought this wrongful death action against Dr. Thomas for his failure to perform a pap smear test on their mother. At the trial, expert testimony was presented which indicated that if Mrs. Truman had undergone a pap smear at any time between 1964 and 1969, the cervical tumor probably would have been discovered in time to save her life. There was disputed expert testimony that the standard of medical practice required a physician to explain to women patients that it is important to have a pap smear each year to "pick up early lesions that are treatable rather than having to deal with [more developed] tumor[s] that very often aren't treatable. . . ."[1]

Although Dr. Thomas saw Mrs. Truman frequently between 1964 and 1969, he never performed a pap smear test on her. Dr. Thomas testified that he did not "specifically" inform Mrs. Truman of the risk involved in any failure to undergo the pap smear test. Rather, "I said, 'You should have a pap smear.' We don't say by now it can be Stage Two [in the development of cervical cancer] or go through all of the different lectures about cancer. I think it is a widely known and generally accepted manner of treatment and I think the patient has a high degree of responsibility. We are not enforcers, we are advisors." However, Dr. Thomas' medical records contain no reference to any discussion or recommendation that Mrs. Truman undergo a pap smear test.

For the most part, Dr. Thomas was unable to describe specific conversations with Mrs. Truman. For example, he testified that during certain periods he "saw Rena very frequently, approximately once a week or so, and I am sure my opening remark was, 'Rena, you need a pap smear,' . . . I am sure we discussed it with her so often that she couldn't [have] fail[ed] to realize that we wanted her to have a complete examination, breast examination, ovaries and pap smear." Dr. Thomas also testified that on at least two occasions when he performed pelvic examinations of Mrs. Truman she refused him permission to perform the test, stating she could not afford the cost. Dr. Thomas offered to defer payment, but Mrs. Truman wanted to pay cash.

Appellants argue that the failure to give a pap smear test to Mrs. Truman proximately caused her death. Two instructions requested by appellants described alternative theories under which Dr. Thomas could be held liable for this failure. First, they asked that the jury be instructed that it "is the duty of a physician to disclose to his patient all relevant information to enable the patient to make an informed decision regarding the submission to or refusal to take a diagnostic test.

Failure of the physician to disclose to his patient all relevant information including the risks to the patient if the test is refused renders the physician liable for any injury legally resulting from the patient's refusal to take the test if a reasonably prudent person in the patient's position would not have refused the test if she had been adequately informed of all the significant perils." Second, they requested that the jury be informed that "as a matter of law . . . a physician who fails to perform a Pap smear test on a female patient over the age of 23 and to whom the patient has entrusted her general

[1] Dr. Thomas conceded at the trial that it is the accepted standard of practice for physicians in his community to recommend that women of child-bearing age undergo a pap smear each year. His records indicate that during the period in which he acted as Mrs. Truman's family physician he performed between 10 and 20 pap smears per month.

physical care is liable for injury or death proximately caused by the failure to perform the test." Both instructions were refused.

The jury rendered [illegible] Dr. Thomas free of any negligence that proximately caused Mrs. Truman's death. This appeal followed.

II

The central issue for this court is whether Dr. Thomas breached his duty of care to Mrs. Truman when he failed to inform her of the potentially fatal consequences of allowing cervical cancer to develop undetected by a pap smear.

In *Cobbs v. Grant,* 8 Cal.3d 229 (1972), this court considered the scope of a physician's duty to disclose medical information to his or her patients in discussing proposed medical procedures. Certain basic characteristics of the physician-patient relationship were identified. "The first is that patients are generally persons unlearned in the medical sciences and therefore, except in rare cases, courts may safely assume the knowledge of patient and physician are not in parity. The second is that a person of adult years and in sound mind has the right, in the exercise of control over his own body, to determine whether or not to submit to lawful medical treatment. The third is that the patient's consent to treatment, to be effective, must be an informed consent. And the fourth is that the patient, being unlearned in medical sciences, has an abject dependence upon and trust in his physician for the information upon which he relies during the decisional process, thus raising an obligation in the physician that transcends arms-length transactions."

In light of these factors, the court held that "as an integral part of the physician's overall obligation to the patient there is a duty of reasonable disclosure of the available choices with respect to proposed therapy and of the dangers inherently and potentially involved in each." The scope of a physician's duty to disclose is measured by the amount of knowledge a patient needs in order to make an informed choice. All information material to the patient's decision should be given.

Material information is that which the physician knows or should know would be regarded as significant by a reasonable person in the patient's position [illegible] or reject the recommended medical procedure. To be material, a fact must also be one which is not commonly appreciated. If the physician knows or should know of a patient's unique concerns or lack of familiarity with medical procedures, this may expand the scope of required disclosure.[2]

Applying these principles, the court in *Cobbs* stated that a patient must be apprised not only of the "risks inherent in the procedure [prescribed, but also] the risks of a decision not to undergo the treatment, and the probability of a successful outcome of the treatment." This rule applies whether the procedure involves treatment or a diagnostic test. On the one hand, a physician recommending a risk-free procedure may safely forego discussion beyond that

[2] The scope of a physician's duty to disclose is set by law rather than by the custom of physicians. The physician must also provide "such additional information as a skilled practitioner of good standing would provide under similar circumstances." . . .

necessary to conform to competent medical practice and to obtain the patient's consent. . . .

Nevertheless, Dr. Thomas contends that *Cobbs* does not apply to him because the duty to disclose applies only where the patient *consents* to the recommended procedure. He argues that since a physician's advice may be presumed to be founded on an expert appraisal of the patient's medical needs, no reasonable patient would fail to undertake further inquiry before rejecting such advice. Therefore, patients who reject their physician's advice should shoulder the burden of inquiry as to the possible consequences of their decision.

This argument is inconsistent with *Cobbs*. The duty to disclose was imposed in *Cobbs* so that patients might meaningfully exercise their right to make decisions about their own bodies. The importance of this right should not be diminished by the manner in which it is exercised. Further, the need for disclosure is not lessened because patients reject a recommended procedure. Such a decision does not alter "what has been termed the 'fiducial qualities' of the physician-patient relationship," since patients who reject a procedure are as unskilled in the medical sciences as those who consent. . . . It must be remembered that Dr. Thomas was not engaged in an arms-length transaction with Mrs. Truman. Clearly, under *Cobbs,* he was obligated to provide her with all the information material to her decision.

The record indicates that the pap smear test is an accurate detector of cervical cancer. Although the probability that Mrs. Truman had cervical cancer was low, Dr. Thomas knew that the potential harm of failing to detect the disease at an early stage was death. This situation is not analogous to one which involves, for example, "relatively minor risks inherent in [such] common procedures" as the taking of blood samples. These procedures are not central to the decision to administer or reject the procedure. In contrast, the risk which Mrs. Truman faced from cervical cancer was not only significant, it was the principal reason why Dr. Thomas recommended that she undergo a pap smear.

. . . .

Dr. Thomas testified he never specifically informed her of the purpose of a pap smear test. There was no evidence introduced that Mrs. Truman was aware of the serious danger entailed in not undergoing the test. However, there was testimony that Mrs. Truman said she would not undergo the test on certain occasions because of its cost or because "she just didn't feel like it." Under these circumstances, a jury could reasonably conclude that Dr. Thomas had a duty to inform Mrs. Truman of the danger of refusing the test because it was not reasonable for Dr. Thomas to assume that Mrs. Truman appreciated the potentially fatal consequences of her conduct. Accordingly, this court cannot decide as a matter of law that Dr. Thomas owed absolutely no duty to Mrs. Truman to make this important disclosure that affected her life.

The instruction proposed by appellants . . . correctly indicated that a physician has a duty to disclose all material information to a patient. The instruction also stated that breach of duty renders the physician liable for any "legally resulting [injury] . . . if a reasonably prudent person in the patient's position would not have refused the test if she had been adequately informed of all the significant perils."

. . . .

Refusal to give the requested instruction meant that the jury was unable to consider whether Dr. Thomas breached a duty by not disclosing the danger of failing to undergo a pap smear. Since this theory finds support in the record, it was error for the court to refuse to give the requested instruction. . . .

III

The other contentions of instructional and evidentiary error urged by appellants are considered because these matters probably will arise at any retrial of the case.

First, the trial court refused to instruct the jury that "as a matter of law . . . a physician who fails to perform a Pap smear test on a female patient over the age of 23 and to whom the patient has entrusted her general physical care is liable for injury or death proximately caused by the failure to perform the test." In support of this instruction plaintiffs relied on the decision of the Supreme Court of Washington in *Helling v. Carey.*

That decision involved a suit against two physicians specializing in ophthalmology who failed to recommend a test for glaucoma. The court held as a matter of law that the exercise of due care required the administration of that test. That holding has no application to this case since the evidence presented showed that the physician recommended the appropriate test but failed to inform the patient of the risks entailed in refusing to follow his advice. The suggestion that a physician must perform a test on a patient, who is capable of deciding whether to undergo the proposed procedure, is directly contrary to the principle that it is the patient who must ultimately decide which medical procedures to undergo. Accordingly, the trial court did not err in refusing this instruction.

. . . .

The judgment is reversed.

. . . .

Clark, Justice, dissenting.

I dissent.

. . . .

I. Duty

. . . .

The burden of explaining the purposes of a pap smear and the potential risks in failing to submit to one may not appear to be great, but the newly imposed duty upon physicians created by today's majority opinion goes far beyond. The instruction requires disclosure of all "relevant information to enable the patient to make an informed decision regarding the submission to or refusal to take a diagnostic test." In short, it applies not only to pap smears, but to all diagnostic procedures allegedly designed to detect illness which could lead to death or serious complication if not timely treated.

Carried to its logical end, the majority decision requires physicians to explain to patients who have not had a recent general examination the intricacies of chest examinations, blood analyses, X-ray examinations, electrocardiograms, urine analyses and innumerable other procedures. In short, today's ruling mandates doctors to provide each such patient with a summary course covering most of his or her medical education. Most medical tests — like pap smears — are designed to detect illness which might prove fatal absent timely treatment. Explaining the purposes of each procedure to each such patient will obviously take hours if not days.

. . . .

When a patient chooses a physician, he or she obviously has confidence in the doctor and intends to accept proffered medical advice. When the doctor prescribes diagnostic tests, the patient is aware the tests are intended to discover illness. It is therefore reasonable to assume that a patient who refuses advice is aware of potential risk.

Moreover, the physician-patient relationship is based on trust, and forcing the doctor in a hard sell approach to his services can only jeopardize that relationship.

. . . .

II. The Instruction

A trial court has no duty to modify or edit an instruction offered by either side in a civil case. If the instruction is incomplete or erroneous the trial judge may, as he did here, properly refuse it. . . .

. . . .

Before refusing the instruction, the trial judge indicated he was sympathetic to its theory but felt it confusing. He pointed out that a duty to disclose "all relevant" information was too broad, substituted "proximate cause" for "legally resulting," and made an effort to rewrite the last portion of the instruction to avoid confusing the jury. When his attempts at simplification failed, he advised counsel he would consider a revised version of the instruction. However, counsel presented no revision. The trial judge also pointed out that the jury would be instructed on general negligence and proximate cause principles, including the community standard of medical care.

. . . .

. . . [C]onflicting evidence exists as to whether community medical standards required explanation of the risks inherent in refusing a pap smear. As noted above, the majority recognize that whether such explanation is required depends upon factual circumstances. Clearly, the issue was properly before the jury under standard negligence instructions, including instructions on community medical standards.

Refusal to give the requested instruction does not warrant reversal. I would affirm the judgment.

. . . .

NOTES AND QUESTIONS

1. The issue here is informed consent, reviewed earlier at § 3.03[1]. But this is different, isn't it, from *Canterbury*? Here, the patient *resists* the proposed service. Somehow, the physician is required to do a "hard sell." Is this wise? And if most patients or physicians would disagree, should there be liability in the case?

2. Does it not appear here that the physician did all that a reasonable physician could be expected to do? Put somewhat differently, should the patient not be required to assume some care and some responsibility for his or her own health care? Pap smears are designed to find cancer; cancer kills; everybody knows this. Should the physician have to explain all of this? How many times?

3. If you conclude that Dr. Thomas discharged his obligations, you must then consider why. That is, was it because he had successfully performed all of his treatment of Mrs. Truman? Or was it because his failure to perform was because of Mrs. Truman's own failure? Or was it because under the PAR (procedure, alternative, risk) analysis, Dr. Thomas had adequately informed Mrs. Truman?

4. Or is it that, even with the information that failure to get a pap smear might cause death, Mrs. Truman would nevertheless have declined? On this last point, does it matter whether California follows an objective or subjective standard as to causality?

5. With respect to informed consent, should testing be treated differently than other services, such as surgery or radiation therapy? Is that the point of the dissent?

6. Note that generally, permission is not required for routine testing within the course of broader care, with the exception of blood tests for HIV. Halperin, *HIV Testing Without Consent,* 294 JAMA 734 (2005). Of course in *Truman v. Thomas*, the problem wasn't giving a test, but failing to do so. Should the same standards of informed consent apply?

7. *Truman v. Thomas* involves, arguably, a physician's failure to use his best efforts. The next case, *Privitera,* involves the reverse: physicians whose view is that their best efforts require unorthodox — indeed, illegal — therapy.

PEOPLE v. PRIVITERA

591 P.2d 919 (Cal. 1979)

Clark, Justice.

Under California Health and Safety Code, it is a misdemeanor to sell, deliver, prescribe or administer any drug or device to be used in the diagnosis, treatment, alleviation or cure of cancer which has not been approved by the designated federal agency or by the state board.

Defendants James Robert Privitera, Jr., a medical doctor, William David Turner, Phyllis Blanche Disney, Winifred Agnes Davis, and Carroll Ruth Leslie were convicted by jury of the felony of conspiracy to sell and to prescribe an unapproved drug, laetrile intended for the alleviation or cure of cancer. Davis and Turner were also convicted of selling laetrile for the alleviation or cure of cancer.

Viewed in the light most favorable to the judgments, the evidence amply supports the jury's conclusion that defendants were involved in a common plan to import, prescribe, sell and distribute laetrile (also referred to as amygdalin or vitamin B-17) to cancer patients. Dr. Privitera prescribed laetrile for cancer patients and referred his patients to Turner and Disney as suppliers of laetrile. Disney referred patients to Dr. Privitera for treatment. Leslie and Disney worked as distributors in various residential areas. Defendants told prospective users that laetrile is an effective treatment or cure for cancer. Laetrile has not been approved for that purpose by one of the designated governmental agencies.

Defendants appeal on the ground the statute is unconstitutional. They contend the *right of privacy* protected by the federal and California Constitutions includes a right to obtain laetrile or, more generally, a right of access to drugs not recognized by the government as effective. Fundamental rights, defendants point out, may be regulated only to the extent necessary to achieve a compelling state interest. Defendants argue the purported right to obtain laetrile is fundamental and therefore the regulation challenged here must be reviewed under the compelling state interest standard. Section 1707.1 is found to be unconstitutional, defendants conclude, when measured against that standard.

. . . .

However, a fundamental privacy right is not at stake here. The interest defendants allege is, apparently, "the interest in independence in making certain kinds of important decisions." (*Whalen v. Roe.*) But the kinds of "important decisions" recognized by the high court to date as falling within the right of privacy involve "matters relating to marriage, procreation, contraception, family relationships, and child rearing and education," but do not include medical treatment.

. . . .

Significantly, when danger to health exists *Roe v. Wade* indicates that state regulation shall be tested under the rational basis standard. Indeed, the High Court held in *Roe v. Wade* that a state may without encroaching upon any right of privacy further its important interests "in the areas of health and safety" by requiring abortions be performed at licensed institutions which "insure maximum safety for the patient" and prohibiting performance of abortion by a person not a physician as defined by state law. The lesson of *Roe v. Wade* for our case is that a requirement that a drug be certified effective for its intended use is a reasonable means to "insure maximum safety for the patient."

. . . .

The legitimate state interest expressed in the challenged statute is set forth in the legislative findings recited in Section 1700. "The effective diagnosis, care, treatment or cure of persons suffering from [illegible] public importance. Vital statistics indicate that approximately 16 percent of the total deaths in the United States annually result from one or another of the forms of cancer. It is established that accurate and early diagnosis of many forms of cancer, followed by prompt application of methods of treatment which are scientifically proven, either materially reduces the likelihood of death from cancer or may materially prolong the useful life of individuals suffering therefrom. Despite intensive campaigns of public education, there is a lack of adequate and accurate information among the public with respect to presently proven methods for the diagnosis, treatment and cure of cancer. Various persons in this State have represented and continue to represent themselves as possessing medicines, methods, techniques, skills, or devices for the effective diagnosis, treatment, or cure of cancer, which representations are misleading to the public, with the result that large numbers of the public, relying on such representations, needlessly die of cancer, and substantial amounts of the savings of individuals and families relying on such representations are needlessly wasted."

These findings were recently echoed by the Commissioner of the federal Food and Drug Administration with specific reference to laetrile. "In the Commissioner's opinion, the use of Laetrile in the United States has become a genuine public health problem. Increasingly, doctors dealing with cancer patients are finding that the patients are coming to legitimate therapy too late, having delayed while trying Laetrile. It seems clear that another substantial group of persons afflicted with cancer is avoiding effective therapy altogether and using Laetrile instead. The question has become one of life and death for these patients and for others who may be convinced to use Laetrile in the future."

. . . .

Because of defendants' reliance on it, subsequent developments in the *Rutherford* case will now be considered. In *Rutherford v. United States*, the district court set aside the commissioner's action and enjoined federal authorities from interfering with distribution of laetrile in [illegible] with use of laetrile for the treatment of cancer. The decision was based on two grounds: First, contrary to the conclusion reached by the commissioner, the court held that laetrile is exempt from the premarket approval requirement for new drugs by virtue of compliance with the 1962 grandfather clause. Second, contrary to the conclusion we reach today, the court concluded the federal right of privacy encompasses a "right to use a nontoxic substance in connection with one's own personal health-care."

On appeal by the government, the Court of Appeals addressed neither the grandfather clause question nor the right of privacy issue. Instead, the court held that "the 'safety' and 'effectiveness' terms used in the statute have no reasonable application to terminally ill cancer patients." "We are considering only cancer patients who are terminally ill and only their intravenous use of Laetrile. Thus in this context, what can 'generally recognized' as 'safe' and 'effective' mean as to such persons who are so fatally stricken with a disease for which there is no known cure? What meaning can 'effective' have in the absence of anything which may be used as a standard? Under this record Laetrile is as effective as anything else. What can 'effective' mean if the person, by all prevailing standards . . . is going to die of cancer regardless of what may be done." The permanent injunction granted by the district court was continued but limited only to permit procurement of intravenous injections of laetrile administered by a licensed medical practitioner to persons who are certified by a licensed medical practitioner to be terminally ill of cancer in some form.

Defendants can take no comfort in the Court of Appeals' decision for, unlike Rutherford, this case is not an action on behalf of the class of terminally ill cancer patients. Whatever may be said in favor of permitting "terminal" cancer patients access to laetrile, there is no indication in the record that defendants sought to restrict their activities to that class when prescribing, distributing and administering laetrile. Indeed, the record reflects that Dr. Privitera sometimes neither took a medical history from nor personally examined the patients for whom he prescribed laetrile. The lay defendants, of course, were not qualified to diagnose cancer, much less to determine whether a cancerous condition was "terminal."

Moreover, we are not prepared to reject as unreasonable the explanation given by the commissioner for the Food and Drug Administration's refusal to approve laetrile for use by "terminal" cancer patients. The commissioner concluded: "[A]pproval of Laetrile restricted to 'terminal' patients would lead to needless deaths and suffering among (1) patients characterized as 'terminal' who could actually be helped by legitimate therapy and (2) patients clearly susceptible to the benefits of legitimate therapy who would be misled as to Laetrile's utility by the limited approval program or who would be able to obtain the drug through the inevitable leakage in any system set up to administer such a program." Substantial evidence in the administrative record appears to support the conclusion reached by the commissioner. Certainly the record in this case does not inspire one with confidence that advocates of laetrile would cooperate with a regulation restricting it to "terminal" cancer patients. In studied defiance of current law, Dr. Privitera prescribed and administered the drug as a cancer cure, advised his patients to discontinue conventional treatment, and warned them not to let their regular physicians know they were taking laetrile.

In conclusion, we emphasize we are not taking sides on the fiercely contested medical questions regarding laetrile's safety or efficacy as a cancer drug. Laetrile advocates may yet be vindicated in the court of scientific opinion, for even as this is being written the National Cancer Institute is seeking approval from the Food and Drug Administration to test laetrile on advanced cancer patients. Nor are we endorsing the decision the Legislature has made on the basis of existing scientific evidence. Whether cancer patients especially advanced cancer patients who have unsuccessfully sought relief from conventional therapy and who are fully informed as to the consensus of scientific opinion concerning the drug should have access to laetrile is clearly a question about which reasonable persons may differ. It is not our function to render scientific or legislative judgments. Rather, we must resolve a narrow question:

Does the challenged legislation bear a reasonable relationship to the achievement of the legitimate state interest in the health and safety of its citizens? We conclude Section 1707.1 [illegible] it therefore does not encroach upon the federal constitutional right of privacy.

. . . .

The judgments of conviction are affirmed.

Tobriner, Mosk, Richardson and **Manuel**, J.J., concur.

Bird, Chief Justice, dissenting.

I respectfully dissent.

I do not question for a moment that the effective treatment of persons suffering from cancer is a matter of paramount public importance. However, we are dealing here with a disease whose causes and treatment continue to baffle the medical community. Among physicians and scientists themselves there remains legitimate dispute as to what is truly an effective program of treatment for cancer. So long as there is no clear evidence that laetrile is unsafe to the user, I believe each individual patient has a right to obtain the substance from a licensed physician who feels it appropriate to prescribe it to him.

. . . .

II. The Patient's Right to Privacy

. . . .

We examine first the right of the patient and determine this right is of such fundamental nature its free exercise may be impinged upon or forbidden only by such state interest as may be a "compelling interest."

The "fundamental" nature of this right derives from its source. It flows from the very nature of man. *Justice Brandeis in Olmstead v. United States* states: "The makers of our Constitution undertook to secure conditions favorable to the pursuit of happiness. They recognized the significance of man's spiritual nature, of his feelings and of his intellect. They knew that only a part of the pain, pleasure and [illegible] in material things. They sought to protect Americans in their beliefs, their thoughts, their emotions and their sensations. They conferred, as against the government, the right to be let alone the most comprehensive of rights and the right most valued by civilized men. To protect, that right, every unjustifiable intrusion by the government upon the privacy of the individual, whatever the means employed, must be deemed a violation. . . ."

Judge Cardozo in *Schloendorff v. Society of New York Hospital* stated: "Every human being of adult years and sound mind has a right to determine what shall be done with his own body; . . . "

. . . .

This right-of-choice-of-medical-treatment concept reached its quintessence in the *Matter of Quinlan*. The New Jersey Supreme Court was called upon to determine whether the father, as guardian of Karen Quinlan, a 21-year-old girl existing in a "persistent vegetative state," could be authorized to discontinue the extraordinary procedures sustaining the daughter's vital processes. The first question was: Did the comatose Karen Quinlan or her father have a right of choice to choose death or life? And secondly, could the father, through the court guardianship procedures, be authorized on her behalf to make such a choice. The court authorized, through the father-guardian, the withdrawal of the life support processes. The right of privacy inherent in the exceptional circumstances of that case authorized the rejection of the life support systems. Reasoned the court: "The claimed interests of the State in this case are essentially the preservation and sanctity of human life and defense of the right of the physician to administer medical treatment according to his best judgment. In this case the doctors say that removing Karen from the respirator will conflict with their professional judgment."

Yet, the court affirmed Karen's right to choice, had she been competent to assert it, and authorized the father to exercise it on her behalf: "there would be no criminal homicide in the circumstances of this case. . . . even if it were to be regarded as homicide, it would not be unlawful." Concerning the interests of the state in preservation of human health and life the court said: "We have no hesitancy in deciding, in the instant diametrically opposite case, that no external compelling interest of the State could compel Karen to endure the unendurable."

III. The Doctor's Zone of Privacy

. . . .

Dr. Privitera additionally asserts an *independent* right to treat, not derived from or measured by his patient's right of choice, without first obtaining approval of the procedure or drug prescribed from a governmental board. He argues Health and Safety Code Section 1707.1 invades this right. Again, as in the right of the patient, the doctor's asserted right must be first examined to determine its nature and thereby select the test, the degree of scrutiny to which the state interference will be put. The right found must be balanced against the — state the public interest protected.

Dr. Privitera's right, in relation to the patient, has been viewed traditionally as a species of economic interest rather than as "fundamental" akin to the privacy right. If a rational basis was found to support an encroachment, the statute was sustained.

While a dispassionate reading of the physician's licensing requirements raises some question concerning the total rationality of the licensing scheme, such standards are generally upheld as reasonable and necessary means of protecting the public health.

The more recent cases hint at the more profound right in the doctor. It is postulated: There exists in the doctor licensed to practice medicine a right, constitutional in nature, as yet ill-defined, to treat and to treat by unorthodox modalities as yet unapproved by the state board an informed consenting patient.

. . . .

Reason, based on history, experience, supports the doctor's premise. To require prior state approval before advising — prescribing-administering — a new treatment modality for an [illegible] innovation by the person best qualified to make medical progress. The treating doctor, the clinician, is at the cutting edge of medical knowledge.

To require the doctor to use only orthodox "state sanctioned" methods of treatment under threat of criminal penalty for variance is to invite a repetition in California of the Soviet experience with "Lysenkoism."[1] The mention of a requirement that licensed doctors must prescribe, treat, within "state sanctioned alternatives" raises the specter of medical stagnation at best, statism, paternalistic Big Brother at worst. It is by the alternatives to orthodoxy that medical progress has been made. A free, progressive society has an enormous stake in recognizing and protecting this right of the physician.

. . . .

VI. Conclusions

We turn now to the final, the pivotal question: Does the imposition of criminal sanction on the doctor for prescribing amygdalin as a cancer treatment for an informed consenting cancer victim, without first seeking governmental approval of its safety and effectiveness, serve a compelling state interest?

. . . .

The doctor in California is licensed to practice only after meeting long rigid education, experience qualifications. He is bound by oath to preserve, to prolong, the life of his patient. He is under a legal duty, under threat of malpractice suit, to act in accordance with the generally accepted standards of medical practice in his community in this state. He is required under threat of malpractice to treat only after receiving the informed consent of the patient. These are the "rational means" society through law has imposed to insure a high standard of performance by the California doctor. It follows after such rigid standards are met, the matter of choice of treatment of the informed consenting patient becomes "a purely medical determination, which is within a doctor's professional judgment." "Reliance must be placed upon the assurance given by his license, . . . that he possesses the requisite qualifications."

. . . .

The statute must be measured against the legislative purpose of frustrating cancer quacks, and for the promotion of the early effective care, diagnosis and cure of cancer. Instead, the immediate and most direct effect of the prohibition of Section 1707.1 is to chill, to prevent, innovative treatment by a licensed doctor, the person or in the class of persons most likely to make the hoped-for breakthrough against dreaded cancer. How logically this threat to the

[1] Soviet geneticist T.D. Lysenko, controversial dictator of "communistic" biology during the Stalin period, stultified the science of genetics in the U.S.S.R. for at least a generation. He imposed the "state sanctioned alternative," the curious idea that environmentally acquired characteristics of an organism could be transmitted to the offspring through inheritance. Thus, the Stalinist concept of ideological conformity politically implanted in genetics paralyzed this important branch of Soviet science.

innovative physician will increase early effective diagnosis and cure of cancer is difficult to perceive.

. . . .

We conclude not only is there no compelling reason shown to override the patient's or the doctor's fundamental right of choice in the treatment setting but that the statute when sought to be applied to a licensed medical doctor does not pass the test as a rational means of accomplishment of the announced legislative purpose.

. . . .

The nineteen witnesses testifying for Dr. Privitera conveyed a felt imminency of death. One senses a mortal fear of both the disease and the orthodox alternatives. This is a desperate utterly human seeking to avoid the pain and to prolong life. These elements form the unspoken rationale of the *Rutherford* and *Carnohan* decisions. Matter of Quinlan states the premise eloquently: i.e., . . . "no external compelling interest of the State could compel Karen to endure the unendurable, only to vegetate a few measurable months with no realistic possibility of returning to any semblance of cognitive or sapient life. We perceive no thread of logic distinguishing between such a choice on Karen's part and a similar choice which, under the evidence in this case, could be made by a competent patient terminally ill, riddled by cancer and suffering great pain; such a patient would not be resuscitated or put on a respirator and *a fortiori* would not be kept *against his will* on a respirator."

To these nineteen cancer victims the enforcement of Health and Safety Code Section 1707.1, the denial to them of medical treatment, albeit unorthodox, albeit unapproved by a state agency, must surely take on a Kafkaesque, a nightmare, quality. No demonstrated public danger, no compelling interest of the state, warrants an Orwellian intrusion into the most private of zones of privacy.

. . . .

Newman, Justice, dissenting.

I join in the Chief Justice's dissent, except that I would not rely on the federal Constitution. What the majority of my colleagues condone here is action that appears to me to constitute cruel and inhuman treatment. . . .

By selective quotation the majority opinion downgrades the right of privacy in California, which "relates, of course, to a enormously broad and diverse field of personal action and belief. . . ." What the California Constitution in article I, Section 1, guarantees is an inalienable right of "pursuing and obtaining safety, happiness, and privacy." By no means do those words merely mirror United States Supreme Court opinions. In *White v. Davis*, Justice Tobriner's opinion for a unanimous court noted approvingly these statements from the official election brochure that help illuminate privacy's full scope: "The right of privacy is the right to be left alone. It is a fundamental and compelling interest. It protects our homes, our families, our thoughts, our emotions, our expressions, our personalities, our freedom of communion and our freedom to associate with the people we choose. . . ." "The right of privacy is an important American heritage and essential to the fundamental rights guaranteed by the First, Third, Fourth, Fifth and Ninth Amendments to the U.S. Constitution. This right should be abridged only when there is a compelling public need . . . ." In this case I [illegible]

. . . .

NOTES AND QUESTIONS

1. Note that *Privitera* was decided before the Supreme Court's decisions in *Casey*, *Washington v. Glucksberg*, and *Vacco v. Quill*. What impact would these decisions have on the criminal prosecution in *Privitera*?
2. *Whose* rights are at issue in *Privitera*? The court seems to imply that if patients — not physicians — were the plaintiffs, the case might come out differently. Should it? Recall *Griswold v. Connecticut* and *Roe v. Wade*, where both patients and physicians sued. Are their rights independent, or are the physician's rights derivative of the patient's rights? Does it matter?
3. What professional right or latitude does a physician enjoy in deviating from the norm of the profession to offer to patients, with their consent, care and treatment which in the physician's view is effective and needed? See, as to medical uses of marijuana, § 4.04[1] *infra*. Should this be a matter of the criminal law? Would *not* prescribing laetril ordinarily be malpractice?
4. Of course, the physicians here do not seem to be practicing medicine very carefully. Doctor Privitera frequently took no medical history and sometimes never met his patients. This may hurt *his* case, but shouldn't it *help* theirs?
5. And what of the point in the *Rutherford* case: they *are* dying anyway, so laetrile *is* "as effective as anything else"?
6. Ultimately, isn't the issue in *Privitera* about *who* decides what is safe — the federal government, states, physicians or patients? And more basically, what is the *standard*: effectiveness or no harm. And still further, whether harm *can* be done to someone who is dying. Put that way, is a dying patient *less* of a "person" to be protected by society? Or given greater choices? See § 4.05[2] *infra,* and the preceding section on experimentation.
7. This issue of physician latitude is of vital importance today. Even as late as 1998, the French contraception pill, RU486, was unavailable in the United States because of abortion politics. As of September 1, 2006, "Plan B," a morning after pill, had only just been approved by the FDA for OTC purchase, and only by women over the age of 18. Similarly, of a quite different order, the availability of acupuncture, a Chinese form of treatment of centuries, was sharply limited by conventional licensing throughout the United States. And the right of a physician to assist in the death of another person remains very much in controversy, despite the passage of the physician-assisted death legislation in Oregon. *See infra,* § 4.05[2].

8. In *United States v. Rutherford*, 442 U.S. 544 (1979) the Supreme Court considered laetrile. The Court did not directly rule on a patient's right to laetrile, but on remand the Tenth Circuit rejected the constitutional claim. To the same effect was *Cannohan v. United States*, 616 F.2d 1120 (9th Cir. 1980). *Contra, Suennam v. Society Valley Hospital,* 383 A.2d 143 (N.J. Super. 1977) (recognizing a constitutional right of privacy for cancer patient to take laetril).
9. *Privitera* involved government's efforts to bar a physician's best efforts in using unorthodox therapy. The next case involves a barrier to conventional therapy — abortion.

RUST v. SULLIVAN
500 U.S. 173 (1991)

Chief Justice **Rehnquist** delivered the opinion of the Court.

. . . .

I

A

In 1970, Congress enacted Title X of the Public Health Service Act (Act), which provides federal funding for family-planning services. . . .

In 1988, the Secretary promulgated new regulations designed to provide "'clear and operational guidance' to grantees about how to preserve the distinction between Title X programs and abortion as a method of family planning." The regulations clarify, through the definition of the term "family planning," that Congress intended Title X funds "to be used only to support preventive family planning services." . . .

The regulations attach three principal conditions on the grant of federal funds for Title X projects. First, the regulations specify that a "Title X project may not provide counseling concerning the use of abortion as a method of family planning or provide referral for abortion as a method of family planning." Because Title X is limited to preconceptional services, the program does not furnish services related to childbirth. Only in the context of a referral out of the Title X program is a pregnant woman given transitional information. . . . The Title X project is expressly prohibited from referring a pregnant woman to an abortion provider, even upon specific request. One permissible response to such an inquiry is that "the project does not consider abortion an appropriate method of family planning and therefore does not counsel or refer for abortion."

Second, the regulations broadly prohibit a Title X project from engaging in activities that "encourage, promote or advocate abortion as a method of family planning." Forbidden activities include lobbying for legislation that would increase the availability of abortion as a method of family planning, developing or disseminating materials advocating abortion as a method of family planning, providing speakers to promote abortion as a method of family planning, using legal action to make abortion available in any way as a method of family planning, and paying dues to any group that advocates abortion as a method of family planning as a substantial part of its activities.

Third, the regulations require that Title X projects be organized so that they are "physically and financially separate" from prohibited abortion activities. To be deemed physically and financially separate, "a Title X project must have an objective integrity and independence from prohibited activities. Mere bookkeeping separation of Title X funds from other monies is not sufficient." . . .

. . . .

III

Petitioners contend that the regulations violate the First Amendment by impermissibly discriminating based on viewpoint because they prohibit "all discussion about abortion as a lawful option — including counseling, referral, and the provision of neutral and accurate information about ending a pregnancy — while compelling the clinic or counselor to provide information that promotes continuing a pregnancy to term." They assert that the regulations violate the "free speech rights of private health care organizations that receive Title X funds, of their staff, and of their patients" by impermissibly imposing "viewpoint-discriminatory conditions on government subsidies" and thus penaliz[e] speech funded with non-Title X monies." . . .

There is no question but that the statutory prohibition is constitutional. In *Maher v. Roe*, we upheld a state welfare regulation under which Medicaid recipients received payments for services related to childbirth, but not for nontherapeutic abortions. The Court rejected the claim that this unequal subsidization worked a violation of the Constitution. We held that the government may "make a value judgment favoring childbirth over abortion, and . . . implement that judgment by the allocation of public funds." . . .

The challenged regulations implement the statutory prohibition by prohibiting counseling, referral, and the provision of information regarding abortion as a method of family planning. They are designed to ensure that the limits of the federal program are observed. The Title X program is designed not for prenatal care, but to encourage family planning. A doctor who wished to offer prenatal care to a project patient who became pregnant could properly be prohibited from doing so because such service is outside the scope of the federally funded program. The regulations prohibiting abortion counseling and referral are of the same ilk; "no funds appropriated for the project may be used in programs where abortion is a method of family planning," and a doctor employed by the project may be prohibited in the course of his project duties from counseling abortion or referring for abortion. This is not a case of the Government "suppressing a dangerous idea," but of a prohibition on a project grantee or its employees from engaging in activities outside of its scope.

To hold that the Government unconstitutionally discriminates on the basis of viewpoint when it chooses to fund a program dedicated to advance certain permissible goals, because the program in advancing those goals necessarily discourages alternate goals, would render numerous government programs constitutionally suspect. . . .

. . . .

Petitioners rely heavily on their claim that the regulations would not, in the circumstance of a medical emergency, permit a Title X project to refer a woman whose pregnancy places her life in imminent peril to a provider of abortions or abortion-related services. This case, of course, involves only a facial challenge to the regulations, and we do not have before us any application by the Secretary to a specific fact situation. On their face, we do not read the regulations to bar abortion referral or counseling in such circumstances. Abortion counseling as a "method of family planning" is prohibited, and it does not seem that a medically necessitated abortion in such circumstances would be the equivalent of its use as a "method of family planning." . . .

. . . .

The same principles apply to petitioners' claim that the regulations abridge the free speech rights of the grantee's staff. Individuals who are voluntarily employed for a Title X project must perform their duties in accordance with the regulation's restrictions on abortion counseling and referral. The employees remain free, however, to pursue abortion-related activities when they are not acting under the auspices of the Title X project. The regulations, which govern solely the scope of the Title X project's activities, do not in any way restrict the activities of those persons acting as private individuals. The employees' freedom of expression is limited during the time that they actually work for the project; but this limitation is a consequence of their decision to accept employment in a project, the scope of which is permissibly restricted by the funding authority.

. . . It could be argued by analogy that traditional relationships such as that between doctor and patient should enjoy protection under the First Amendment from government regulation, even when subsidized by the Government. We need not resolve that question here, however, because the Title X program regulations do not significantly impinge upon the doctor-patient relationship. Nothing in them requires a doctor to represent as his own any opinion that he does not in fact hold. Nor is the doctor-patient relationship established by the Title X program sufficiently all-encompassing so as to justify an expectation on the part of the patient of comprehensive medical advice. The program does not provide post-conception medical care, and therefore a doctor's silence with regard to abortion cannot reasonably be thought to mislead a client into thinking that the doctor does not consider abortion an appropriate option for her. The doctor is always free to make clear that advice regarding abortion is simply beyond the scope of the program. In these circumstances, the general rule that the Government may choose not to subsidize speech applies with full force.

IV

We turn now to petitioners' argument that the regulations violate a woman's Fifth Amendment right to choose whether to terminate her pregnancy. We recently reaffirmed the long-recognized principle that " 'the Due Process

Clauses generally confer no affirmative right to governmental aid, even where such aid may be necessary to secure life, liberty, or property interests of which [illegible]

That the regulations do not impermissibly burden a woman's Fifth Amendment rights is evident from the line of cases beginning with *Maher* and *McRae* and culminating in our most recent decision in *Webster*. Just as Congress' refusal to fund abortions in *McRae* left "an indigent woman with at lest the same range of choice in deciding whether to obtain a medically necessary abortion as she would have had if Congress had chosen to subsidize no health care costs at all," and "Missouri's refusal to allow public employees to perform abortions in public hospitals leaves a pregnant woman with the same choices as if the State had chosen not to operate any public hospitals," Congress' refusal to fund abortion counseling and advocacy leaves a pregnant woman with the same choices as if the government had chosen not to fund family-planning services at all. The difficulty that a woman encounters when a Title X project does not provide abortion counseling or referral leaves her in no different position than she would have been if the government had not enacted Title X.

. . . .

Petitioners contend, however, that most Title X clients are effectively precluded by indigency and poverty from seeing a health care provider who will provide abortion-related services. But once again, even these Title X clients are in no worse position than if Congress had never enacted Title X. "The financial constraints that restrict an indigent woman's ability to enjoy the full range of constitutionally protected freedom of choice are the product not of governmental restrictions on access to abortion, but rather of her indigency." *McRae, supra.*

The Secretary's regulations are a permissible construction of Title X and do not violate either the First or Fifth Amendments to the Constitution. Accordingly, the judgment of the Court of Appeals is

Affirmed.

Justice **Blackmun**, with whom Justice **Marshall** joins, with whom Justice [illegible] as to Part I, dissenting.

Casting aside established principles of statutory construction and administrative jurisprudence, the majority in these cases today unnecessarily passes upon important questions of constitutional law. In so doing, the Court, for the first time, upholds viewpoint-based suppression of speech solely because it is imposed on those dependent upon the Government for economic support. Under essentially the same rationale, the majority upholds direct regulation of dialogue between a pregnant woman and her physician when that regulation has both the purpose and the effect of manipulating her decision as to the continuance of her pregnancy. I conclude that the Secretary's regulation of referral, advocacy, and counseling activities exceeds his statutory authority, and, also, that the Regulations violate the First and Fifth Amendments of our Constitution. Accordingly, I dissent and would reverse the divided-vote judgment of the Court of Appeals.

. . . .

II

I also strongly disagree with the majority's disposition of petitioners' constitutional claims, and because I feel that a response thereto is indicated, I move on to that issue.

A

Until today, the Court never has upheld viewpoint-based suppression of speech simply because that suppression was a condition upon the acceptance of public funds. Whatever may be the Government's power to condition the receipt of its largess upon the relinquishment of constitutional rights, it surely does not extend to a condition that suppresses the recipient's cherished freedom of speech based solely upon the content or viewpoint of that speech. *Speiser v. Randall*. . . . This rule is a sound one, for, as the Court often has noted: "'A regulation of speech that is motivated by nothing more than a desire to curtail expression of a particular point of view on controversial issues of general interest is the purest example of a "law . . . abridging the freedom of speech, or of the press.'" League of Women Voters. "[A]bove all else, the First Amendment means that government has no power to restrict expression because of its message, its ideas, its subject matter, or its content." *Police Department of Chicago v. Mosley.*

. . . .

It cannot seriously be disputed that the counseling and referral provisions at issue in the present cases constitute content-based regulation of speech. Title X grantees may provide counseling and referral regarding any of a wide range of family planning and other topics, save abortion. *Cf. Consolidated Edison Co.,* 447 U.S. at 537, ("The First Amendment's hostility to content-based regulation extends not only to restrictions on particular viewpoints, but also to prohibition of public discussion of an entire topic").

The regulations are also clearly viewpoint based. While suppressing speech favorable to abortion with one hand, the Secretary compels anti-abortion speech with the other. For example, the Department of Health and Human Services' own description of the Regulations makes plain that "Title X projects are *required* to facilitate access to prenatal care and social services, including adoption services, that might be needed by the pregnant client to promote her well-being and that of her child, while making it abundantly clear that the project is not permitted to promote abortion by facilitating access to abortion through the referral process."

Moreover, the regulations command that a project refer for prenatal care each woman diagnosed as pregnant, irrespective of the woman's expressed desire to continue or terminate her pregnancy. If a client asks directly about abortion, a Title X physician or counselor is required to say, in essence, that the project does not consider abortion to be an appropriate method of family planning. Both requirements are antithetical to the First Amendment. *See Wooley v. Maynard.*

. . . .

Remarkably, the majority concludes that "the Government has not discriminated on the basis of viewpoint; it has merely chosen to fund one activity to the exclusion of another." But the majority's claim that the Regulations merely limit a Title X project's speech to preventive or preconceptional services, rings hollow in light of the broad range of nonpreventive services that the Regulations authorize Title X projects to provide. By refusing to fund those family-planning projects that advocate abortion because they advocate abortion, the Government plainly has targeted a particular viewpoint. The majority's reliance on the fact that the Regulations pertain solely to funding decisions simply begs the question. Clearly, there are some bases upon which government may not rest its decision to fund or not to fund. For example, the Members of the majority surely would agree that government may not base its decision to support an activity upon considerations of race. . . .

. . . .

B

The Court concludes that the challenged Regulations do not violate the First Amendment rights of Title X staff members because any limitation of the employees' freedom of expression is simply a consequence of their decision to accept employment at a federally funded project. But it has never been sufficient to justify an otherwise unconstitutional condition upon public employment that the employee may escape the condition by relinquishing his or her job. It is beyond question "that a government may not require an individual to relinquish rights guaranteed him by the First Amendment as a condition of public employment." . . .

. . . Under the majority's reasoning, the First Amendment could be read to tolerate *any* governmental restriction upon an employee's speech so long as that restriction is limited to the funded workplace. This is a dangerous proposition, and one the Court has rightly rejected in the past.

. . . .

In the cases at bar, the speaker's interest in the communication is both clear and vital. In addressing the family-planning needs of their clients, the physicians and counselors who staff Title X projects seek to provide them with the full range of information and options regarding their health and reproductive freedom. Indeed, the legitimate expectations of the patient and the ethical responsibilities of the medical profession demand no less. "The patient's right of self-decision can be effectively exercised only if the patient possesses enough information to enable an intelligent choice. . . . The physician has an ethical obligation to help the patient make choices from among the therapeutic alternatives consistent with good medical practice." Current Opinions, the Council on Ethical and Judicial Affairs of the American Medical Association ¶ 8.08 (1989). See also President's Commission for the Study of Ethical Problems in Medicine and Biomedical and Behavioral Research, Making Health Care Decisions 70 (1982); American College of Obstetricians & Gynecologists, Standards for Obstetric-Gynecologic Services 62 (7th ed. 1989). When a client becomes pregnant, the full range of therapeutic alternatives includes the abortion option, and Title X counselors' interest in providing this information is compelling.

The Government's articulated interest in distorting the doctor/patient dialogue — ensuring that federal funds are not spent for a purpose outside the scope of the program — falls far short of that necessary to justify the suppression of truthful information and professional medical opinion regarding constitutionally protected conduct. Moreover, the offending Regulation is not narrowly tailored to serve this interest. For example, the governmental interest at stake could be served by imposing rigorous bookkeeping standards to ensure financial separation or adopting content-neutral rules for the balanced dissemination of family-planning and health information. By failing to balance or even to consider the free speech interests claimed by Title X physicians against the Government's asserted interest in suppressing the speech, the Court falters in its duty to implement the protection that the First Amendment clearly provides for this important message.

C

Finally, it is of no small significance that the speech the Secretary would suppress is truthful information regarding constitutionally protected conduct of vital importance to the listener. One can imagine no legitimate governmental interest that might be served by suppressing such information. Concededly, the abortion debate is among the most divisive and contentious issues that our Nation has faced in recent years. "But freedom to differ is not limited to things that do not matter much. That would be a mere shadow of freedom. The test of its substance is the right to differ as to things that touch the heart of the existing order." *West Virginia Board of Education v. Barnette.*

III

. . . .

The substantial obstacles to bodily self-determination that the Regulations impose are doubly offensive because they are effected by manipulating the very words spoken by physicians and counselors to their patients. In our society, the doctor/patient dialogue embodies a unique relationship of trust. The specialized nature of medical science and the emotional distress often attendant to health-related decisions requires that patients place their complete confidence, and often their very lives, in the hands of medical professionals. One seeks a physician's aid not only for medication or diagnosis, but also for guidance, professional judgment, and vital emotional support. Accordingly, each of us attaches profound importance and authority to the words of advice spoken by the physician.

. . . .

NOTES AND QUESTIONS

1. *Rust v. Sullivan* extends government regulation to the exchange of information betwen physician and patient. This, of course, is true of the informed consent statutes, which mandate *inclusion* of information

about procedures, alternatives and risks. Recall *Aden v. Younger* and *Canterbury v. Spence*, *supra*. It is also true of a number of other statutes which mandate testing (for example, for PKU at birth) or reporting (for example, of suspected child abuse). But here, the regulations mandate *exclusion* of information a woman might be want (or might *expect*) to receive. Is there a kind of misrepresentation here? Deception? Should not the clinic at least have a sign that says "federal law forbids counseling you about abortion"?

2. We have seen other legislation regulating informed consent, for example in *Casey*, or in the *Aden v. Younger* case, concerning psychosurgery. But in each instance, the objective was to *expand* knowledge. Here, it is to impede or censor. Is not the limiting of knowledge in the physician-patient relationship like doing so in an academic setting? Should not both settings be protected?

3. And *is not* this "viewpoint-based" legislation, suppressing speech which would otherwise occur? And supporting a competing point of view? And are these not *linked* ?

4. As to the employees' interests, it is true that they must abide by an employer's limits. But here, the government is imposing the limits, and they are central to the employees' medical/professional ethics. Is this a separate area for concern? Does the majority seem to care?

5. *Rust* was decided prior to *Casey.* Would it be decided the same way today? Are not these regulations a burden on the right to choose an abortion? To conduct a relationship with a physician? *Rust* was also decided after *Employment Div. v. Oregon* where the majority rewrote and limited *Sherbert v. Verner*. Can you see why?

6. Can you think of other, comparable limitations on communication between physician and patient? Between an attorney and client? Priest and communicant?

PROBLEM 3–19 — Gag Rules and Managed Care

The leading HMO in your State, Fidelity Health Care, has developed a profile of services needed by average patients by age, gender and diagnosis. It has then developed a standard array of procedures for the average patient by diagnosis, with a budgetary allocation per enrolled patient. Based on its patient population and projected enrollment for the upcoming year, the HMO has developed an annual budget, established its premium based on that budget and from these calculated the allowable reimbursement rate per physician.

Each physician participating with the HMO is paid a capitated rate per enrollee. If the physician incurs costs in excess of the budgeted amount, for example, by ordering tests or conducting procedures beyond "the profile," the physician is viewed as an "outlier." He or she may be decertified and dropped as a participating physician in the following year. On the other hand, if a physician stays within the profile and incurs costs due to treatment or testing *below* the allocated amount, then the amount saved goes into a "pool." At the end of the year, those who have contributed to the pool receive a percentage share, based on the amount *by which* that physician was below the expected incurred costs.

You are Jane Smith. You are in your mid-40s and have been experiencing fatigue, showing some blood spotting and have experienced bouts of nausea and dizziness. A lump has also appeared upon your breast. You consult your primary care physician who conducts a pelvic and breast examination, concludes the tumor is benign and declines to order x-rays or to order a full blood screen. It has been two years since your last visit to a physician. You ask for a referral to a gynecologist or an oncologist, which the physician declines in her capacity as your "gatekeeper." She tells you that the best approach in these cases is "watchful waiting" and suggests you return in two months.

You have been told nothing about the financial arrangements detailed above. Your physician last year was deemed an "outlier" and told she would be decertified if that happened again. She was also told not to tell this to any patient.

Is there a conflict of interest? What is the physician's fiduciary obligation with respect to you? What is the fiduciary obligation of the HMO itself to you, since your coverage is through your employer, whose employees are a group served by the HMO?

See Weiss v. Cigna Healthcare, 972 F. Supp. 748 (S.D.N.Y. 1997); Martin & Bjerknes, *The Legal and Ethical Implications of Gag Clauses,* 22 Am. J. L. & Med. 433 (1996); *Ethics in Managed Care,* Report, American Medical Association (1994).

[2] Standard of Care

The preceding section dealt with when health care providers may be required to use their best efforts in providing care. Usually, liability for malpractice imposes a lesser standard — that of the reasonable physician in the community. That standard, as with the tort standard of negligence generally, looks to what a reasonable person would have done and thereby defines the duty of care.

The debate over medical malpractice liability frequently focuses on whether frivolous claims are filed, driving up the cost of medical practice insurance. A study in the New England Journal of Medicine concluded that there is only limited merit to these claims. Studdert, et al., *Claims Errors and Compensation Payments in Medical Malpractice Litigation*, 354 New Eng. J. Med. 2024 (May 11, 2006).

Trained physicians reviewed a random sample of 1452 closed cases from five liability insurers. They concluded that 3% showed no injuries, and 37% involved no errors. In 70% to 80% of cases, the result was appropriate — that is, liability or freedom from liability *should* have been found. But non-payment of deserved claims was higher than payment of undeserving claims, and payment of the latter amounted to only 13% to 16% of the system's total monetary cost. For every dollar spent on compensation, 54% went to administrative costs, including attorney's fees, prompting the conclusion that "the overhead costs of malpractice litigation are exorbitant."

Does the study support tort reform — caps on damages, limits on attorneys' fees and the like? What are the implications for healthcare; the judicial system; a workers' compensation approach to medical injury?

Problems arise when legislatures in courts attempt to practice medicine, as in the next two cases. And the practice of medicine becomes ever more problematic when patients fail to follow advice. We begin with a statutory mandate for what is arguably bad medicine.

MARGARET S. v. TREEN

597 F. Supp. 636 (E.D. La. 1984)

Robert F. **Collins**, District Judge.

This is an individual and class action brought by two representatives of the class of pregnant women desiring abortions, three physicians who perform abortions, and five clinics offering facilities for the performance of abortions. . . .

. . . .

In approaching this inquiry into the constitutionality of the Louisiana abortion statute, the Court is of the opinion that it is appropriate to preface its discussion of the challenged sections with a statement of the legislative intent motivating the enactment of the provisions regulating abortion:

> [i]t is the intention of the Legislature of the State of Louisiana to regulate abortion to the extent permitted by the decisions of the United States Supreme Court. The Legislature does solemnly declare and find in reaffirmation of the longstanding policy of this State, that the unborn child is a human being from the time of conception and is, therefore, a legal person for purposes of the unborn child's right to life and is entitled to the right to life from conception under the laws and Constitution of this State. Further, the Legislature finds and declares that the longstanding policy of this State is to protect the right to life of the unborn child from conception by prohibiting abortion impermissible only because of the decisions of the United States Supreme Court and that, therefore, if those decisions of the United States Supreme Court are ever reversed or modified or the United States Constitution is amended to allow protection of the unborn then the former policy of this State to prohibit abortions shall be enforced.

The Court finds this expression of legislative intent particularly significant in view of the Supreme Court's specific holding in *Roe v. Wade*, that "the word 'person,' as used in the Fourteenth Amendment, does not include the unborn," and the Court's refusal to decide "the difficult question of when life begins." . . .

. . . .

The Ultra-Sound Testing Requirement

La. Rev. Stat. Ann. § 40:1299.35.2(B) (West Supp. 1981) requires the attending physician in an abortion procedure to perform an ultra-sound test upon the pregnant woman before carrying out the abortion procedure.[2] The ultra-sound procedure, which involves the use of sound waves to produce fetal pictures, enables the physician to estimate fetal age. The constitutionality of this section is an issue of first impression since it is the first law of this nature to be enacted by a state legislature.

The plaintiffs contend that the ultra-sound requirement violates the due process and equal protection clauses of the Fourteenth Amendment in that it impedes women's access to abortions. Specifically, the plaintiffs charge that the ultra-sound requirement directly interferes with the abortion right because it increases the cost of abortions and lessens the availability of the procedure in Louisiana. The plaintiffs also contend that this provision creates an illegal classification by imposing the ultra-sound testing requirement only upon pregnant women seeking abortions, while it is not required in comparable medical procedures.

. . . .

The task before the Court, then, is to determine whether the plaintiffs have demonstrated that the ultra-sound testing requirement interferes directly with a woman's fundamental right to obtain an abortion. The plaintiffs contend that this requirement interferes directly with the abortion right since it would raise the cost of abortions by imposing an unnecessary test. The plaintiffs further maintain that the ultra-sound testing requirement would lessen the availability of abortion services in Louisiana because physicians would be able to perform fewer abortions if the test were required.

The Court finds credible evidence in the record to support the plaintiffs' claim that the ultra-sound testing requirement would impose additional costs on women seeking abortions in Louisiana. The evidence reveals that the ultra-sound testing requirement would increase the cost of each abortion in Louisiana by at least $100.00, given current rates. This significant increase in the cost of an abortion would be likely to occur for several reasons. First, the current cost of an ultra-sound test administered on an outpatient basis in Louisiana ranges from $60.00 to $195.00. Additionally, the testimony adduced at trial indicates that relatively few obstetricians and gynecologists in private practice own ultra-sound machines. If required to perform an ultra-sound test on each abortion patient, these physicians would incur substantial costs in purchasing and maintaining such machines, and in hiring or training technicians to assist with the administration of the test. Further, since the ultra-sound test is a relatively new technique which most physicians are not familiar with, they would be required to secure additional training in order to properly administer the test and interpret the results.

---

[2] This section provides: B. In order to preserve the health of the mother by insuring the use of the method of abortion most likely to preserve the health of the mother and to enable the physician to exercise his best medical judgment, each physician who performs or induces any abortion at any time during pregnancy shall perform an ultra-sound test in order to facilitate the determination of the state of development of the unborn child.

The requirement that the attending physician in the abortion procedure also administer the ultra-sound test is an additional factor which would raise the cost of abortion. Currently, a first trimester abortion can be performed in approximately five minutes, and a second trimester procedure in approximately ten minutes. The performance of an ultra-sound test requires approximately twenty minutes. Thus, the statutorily imposed requirement that the attending physician perform the ultra-sound test would require the physician to spend an additional twenty minutes with each patient. Two physicians, as well as the administrator of an abortion clinic in Louisiana, stated at trial that this additional expenditure of time occasioned by the ultra-sound testing requirement would result in higher costs for abortion services. . . .

. . . .

The plaintiffs also demonstrated at trial that because of the increased amount of time the ultra-sound testing provision would require of physicians performing abortions, the law would decrease the availability of abortion services in Louisiana. Testimony revealed that currently, in a typical Louisiana abortion clinic, approximately 24 abortions can be performed in four hours. If the ultra-sound testing requirement were operative, only eight abortions could be performed in a comparable period of time. This is particularly significant in a state that is already under-signed in terms of the availability of abortion services. Approximately 17,680 abortions were performed in Louisiana in 1980. The projected number of abortions which would have been performed in 1978 had there been good availability is 48,680. Thus, only 35.4 percent of the need for abortion services in Louisiana was met. . . .

The Court concluded that Louisiana's ultra-sound testing requirement constitutes a direct burden on the abortion right. Accordingly, the State must demonstrate a compelling state interest which justifies this requirement. Louisiana offers in support of the requirement that such testing is necessary in order to accurately determine gestational age and the correct method of abortion, and to determine life-threatening conditions such as atopic pregnancies. The Court will analyze each of these contentions.

As to the first claim, that ultra-sound testing is necessary in order to accurately determine gestational age, the state has failed to demonstrate that such testing is medically necessary. Louisiana does not argue that the most common method of determining gestational age, a pelvic examination coupled with the patient's menstrual history, is inaccurate or otherwise unreliable. The range of error in estimating gestational age by this method is approximately plus or minus one week during the first trimester, and plus or minus 10 days to two weeks during the second trimester. By contrast, ultra-sound testing does not measure gestational age with any reliability until the eighth week of pregnancy. By the eighth week of pregnancy, approximately 60 percent of all abortions in Louisiana have already been performed. Ultra-sound testing achieves its greatest accuracy in approximately the twelfth week of pregnancy, when it is possible to determine gestational age to within plus or minus three to four days, that is, assuming skilled personnel and high quality equipment. Starting with the eighteenth week of pregnancy, however, the accuracy of ultra-sound testing declines to plus or minus one week by the 20th week of pregnancy, and, by the 24th week, to plus or minus 10 days.

The testimony of several physicians indicated that overall, that is, throughout the course of a pregnancy, the clinical examination method and ultrasound testing are comparable in their levels of accuracy and reliability as to gestational age. . . .

. . . .

This Court is of the opinion that La. Rev. Stat. Ann., which requires the attending physician to perform an ultra-sound examination on abortion patients, must fall. This result is dictated by the jurisprudence since the statute commands a physician to perform a specific diagnostic procedure which imposes significant costs upon the exercise of a woman's constitutionally protected right to obtain an abortion, and it is apparent that there is no legitimate, compelling state interest justifying the requirement of such a test. Indeed the evidence indicates that this test would be useless in the vast majority of abortions performed in Louisiana. Accordingly, this section of the statute cannot survive the constitutional attack launched by the plaintiffs in this matter. In view of the Court's disposition of this issue, it is unnecessary to consider the plaintiffs' challenge to this section on equal protection grounds.

. . . .

NOTES AND QUESTIONS

1. With the reasoning of the Supreme Court in the more recent *Casey* decision, would not the state's interest early on in the pregnancy be greater than it was under the *Roe* analysis? If so, would *Casey* require a different result in *Margaret S.*? Recall here the cases from the earlier section on privacy and bodily integrity. Should the Court in *Margaret S.* have grounded its opinion on privacy and liberty interests? They, at least, would not require a showing of a "burden," as is required by *Casey.*
2. While the Court may be correct in saying that ultrasound testing is not, in many instances, more accurate than clinical examination, does it not appear that in some instances ultrasound testing is more effective? Also, administration of an ultrasound leaves an objective record, in the event that the state has a regulatory interest or an investigatorial interest. Is *that* a sufficient reason for requiring ultrasound?
3. How persuasive is the Court's conclusion that the cost of an ultrasound would drive up the cost of abortions and deter the obtaining of abortions? Would the additional cost be distributed across all insured persons and amount to a minimal deterrent to an individual patient?
4. Should not the Court have reasoned that requiring a test which is clinically unnecessary or contrary to the course of treatment chosen by a woman's physician impermissibly interferes with the physician's relationship with the patient? Indeed, the physician becomes an *agent* for the state, conducting a course of treatment not dictated by the patient's needs or interest. The physician, then, is serving someone other than his or her patient.
5. Of course, states regularly mandate physician services and control physician behavior. Tests required at birth (*e.g.*, PKU), and reporting

of AIDS or abuse are two examples. But in *Margaret S.,* a form of practice was mandated. Is that different? If so, is it dissimilar to the [illegible]

HELLING v. CAREY

519 P.2d 981 (Wa. 1974)

Hunter, Associate Justice.

This case arises from a malpractice action instituted by the plaintiff (petitioner), Barbara Helling.

The plaintiff suffers from primary open angle glaucoma. . . . The disease usually has few symptoms and, in the absence of a pressure test, is often undetected until the damage has become extensive and irreversible.

The defendants (respondents), Dr. Thomas F. Carey and Dr. Robert C. Laughlin, are partners who practice the medical specialty of ophthalmology. Ophthalmology involves the diagnosis and treatment of defects and diseases of the eye.

The plaintiff first consulted the defendants for myopia, nearsightedness, in 1959. At that time she was fitted with contact lenses. She next consulted the defendants in September, 1963, concerning irritation caused by the contact lenses. Additional consultations occurred in October, 1963; February, 1967; September, 1967; October, 1967; May, 1968; July, 1968; August, 1968; September, 1968; and October, 1968. Until the October 1968 consultation, the defendants considered the plaintiff's visual problems to be related solely to complications associated with her contact lenses. On that occasion, the defendant, Dr. Carey, tested the plaintiff's eye pressure and field of vision for the first time. This test indicated that the plaintiff had glaucoma. The plaintiff, who was then 32 years of age, had essentially lost her peripheral vision and her central vision was reduced to approximately 5 degrees vertical by 10 degrees horizontal.

Thereafter, in August of 1969, after consulting other physicians, the plaintiff filed a complaint against the defendants alleging, among other things, that she sustained severe and permanent damage to her eyes as a proximate result of the defendants' negligence. During trial, the testimony of the medical experts for both the plaintiff and the defendants established that the standards of the profession for that specialty in the same or similar circumstances do not require routine pressure tests for glaucoma upon patients under 40 years of age. The reason the pressure test for glaucoma is not given as a regular practice to patients under the age of 40 is that the disease rarely occurs in this age group. Testimony indicated, however, that the standards of the profession do require pressure tests if the patient's complaints and symptoms reveal to the physician that glaucoma should be suspected.

. . . .

We find this to be a unique case. The testimony of the medical experts is undisputed concerning the standards of the profession for the specialty of ophthalmology. It is not a question in this case of the defendants having any greater special ability, knowledge and information than other ophthalmologists which would require the defendants to comply with a higher duty of care than that "degree of care and skill which is expected of the average practitioner in the class to which he belongs, acting in the same or similar circumstances." . . .

The defendants argue that the standard of the profession, which does not require the giving of a routine pressure test to persons under the age of 40, is adequate to insulate the defendants from liability for negligence because the risk of glaucoma is so rare in this age group. . . .

The incidence of glaucoma in one out of 25,000 persons under the age of 40 may appear quite minimal. However, that one person, the plaintiff in this instance, is entitled to the same protection, as afforded persons over 40, essential for timely detection of the evidence of glaucoma where it can be arrested to avoid the grave and devastating result of this disease. The test is a simple pressure test, relatively inexpensive. There is no judgment factor involved, and there is no doubt that by giving the test the evidence of glaucoma can be detected. The giving of the test is harmless if the physical condition of the eye permits. The testimony indicates that although the condition of the plaintiff's eyes might have at times prevented the defendants from administering the pressure test, there is an absence of evidence in the record that the test could not have been timely given.

Justice Holmes stated in *Texas & Pac. Ry. v. Behymer*:

What usually is done may be evidence of what ought to be done, but what ought to be done is fixed by a standard of reasonable prudence, whether it usually is complied with or not.

In The T. J. Hooper, Justice Hand stated:

[I]n most cases reasonable prudence is in fact common prudence; but strictly it is never its measure; a whole calling may have unduly lagged in the adoption of new and available devices. It never may set its own tests, however persuasive be its usages. *Courts must in the end say what is required; there are precautions so imperative that even their universal disregard will not excuse their omission.*

Under the facts of this case reasonable prudence required the timely giving of the pressure test to this plaintiff. The precaution of giving this test to detect the incidence of glaucoma to patients under 40 years of age is so imperative that irrespective of its disregard by the standards of the ophthalmology profession, it is the duty of the courts to say what is required to protect patients under 40 from the damaging results of glaucoma.

We therefore hold, as a matter of law, that the reasonable standard that should have been followed under the undisputed facts of this case was the timely giving of this simple, harmless pressure test to this plaintiff and that, in failing to do so, the defendants were negligent, which proximately resulted in the blindness sustained by the plaintiff for which the defendants are liable.

. . . .

The judgment of the trial court and the decision of the Court of Appeals is reversed, and the case is remanded for a new trial on the issue of damages only.

. . . .

Utter, Associate Justice (concurring).

I concur in the result reached by the majority. I believe a greater duty of care could be imposed on the [illegible] established by their profession. The duty could be imposed when a disease, such as glaucoma, can be detected by a simple, well-known harmless test whose results are definitive and the disease can be successfully arrested by early detection, but where the effects of the disease are irreversible if undetected over a substantial period of time.

The difficulty with this approach is that we as judges, by using a negligence analysis, seem to be imposing a stigma of moral blame upon the doctors who, in this case, used all the precautions commonly prescribed by their profession in diagnosis and treatment. Lacking their training in this highly sophisticated profession, it seems illogical for this court to say they failed to exercise a reasonable standard of care. It seem to me we are, in reality, imposing liability, because, in choosing between an innocent plaintiff and a doctor, who acted reasonably according to his specialty but who could have prevented the full effects of this disease by administering a simple, harmless test and treatment, the plaintiff should not have to bear the risk of loss. As such, imposition of liability approaches that of strict liability.

. . . .

. . . There are many similarities in this case to other cases of strict liability. Problems of proof have been a common feature in situations where strict liability is applied. Where events are not matters of common experience, a juror's ability to comprehend whether reasonable care has been followed diminishes. There are few areas as difficult for jurors to intelligently comprehend as the intricate questions of proof and standards in medical malpractice cases.

In applying strict liability there are many situations where it is imposed for conduct which can be defined with sufficient precision to insure that application of a strict liability principle will not produce miscarriages of justice in a substantial number of cases. If the activity involved is one which can be defined with sufficient precision, that definition can serve as an accounting unit to which the costs of the activity may be allocated with some certainty and precision. With this possible, strict liability serves a [illegible] situations where the defendant is, through the use of insurance, the financially more responsible person.

If the standard of a reasonably prudent specialist is, in fact, inadequate to offer reasonable protection to the plaintiff, then liability can be imposed without fault. To do so under the narrow facts of this case does not offend my sense of justice. The pressure test to measure intraocular pressure with the Schiotz tonometer and the Goldman applanometer takes a short time, involves no damage to the patient, and consists of placing the instrument against the eyeball. An abnormally high pressure requires other tests which would either confirm or deny the existence of glaucoma. It is generally believed that from 5 to 10 years of detectable increased pressure must exist before there is permanent damage to the optic nerves.

Although the incidence of glaucoma in the age range of the plaintiff is approximately one in 25,000, this alone should not be enough to deny her a claim. Where its presence can be detected by a simple, well-known harmless test, where the results of the test are definitive, where the disease can be successfully arrested by early detection and where its effects are irreversible if undetected over a substantial period of time, liability should be imposed upon defendants even though they did not violate the standard existing within the profession of ophthalmology.

. . . .

NOTES AND QUESTIONS

1. The majority in *Helling* says, that the "reasonable" standard that should have been followed was the giving of a test and that, without more, failure to do so leads to liability. They reach this conclusion even though the standard of care in the community and in the profession, even among experts, did not dictate giving a test in these circumstances. Is this a reasonableness standard or is this a strict liability standard? How could the defendant physicians anticipate such a requirement or conclusion?

2. Is this dangerously close to a court practicing medicine? Is it dangerously close to substituting itself for a legislature, a hospital board of trustees or an HMO? In the proceeding case, mandating a particular test (an ultra-sound) was invalidated in *Margaret S. v. Treen, supra.* It would have burdened obtaining health care, adding to costs and delays. Should not the Court here engage in similar analysis, and then leave the decision to another body? Say, an HMO? As to this issue, see *infra,* § § 4.04[2] and [3].

3. Or is this case closer to *Truman v. Thomas* ? If so, why is the analysis different?

4. If a physician cannot reasonably rely upon either the standard of care in the community or the highest standard of care dictated by the board certified specialists of the nation, then how *is* a physician to determine what he or she should do? In this case, Drs. Carey and Laughlin deviated from *no* known norm. What should they have done: propose a pointless test to their patient? Or should specialties develop "practice guidelines"? Would one have helped here? What would it have said?

5. We now turn from the demands of legislatures and judges to those of patients. When may a physician — as in *Truman v. Thomas* — assume the patient is a reasonable person? And if the physician understands the contrary, what is his or her ethical reponsibility?

OSTROWSKI v. AZZARA, D.P.M.

545 A.2d 148 (N.J. 1988)

The opinion of the Court was delivered by **O'Hern**, J.

This case primarily concerns the legal significance of a medical malpractice claimant's pre-treatment health habits. . . .

I

As noted, the parties do not dispute that a physician must exercise the degree of care commensurate with the needs of the patient as she presents herself. This is but another way of saying that a defendant takes the plaintiff as she finds her. The question here, however, is much more subtle and complex. The complication arose from the plaintiff's seemingly routine need for care of an irritated toe. The plaintiff had long suffered from diabetes attributable, in unfortunate part perhaps, to her smoking and to her failure to adhere closely to her diet. . . .

On May 17, 1983, plaintiff, a heavy smoker and an insulin-dependent diabetic for twenty years, first consulted with defendant, Lynn Azzara, a doctor of podiatric medicine, a specialist in the care of feet. Plaintiff had been referred to Dr. Azzara by her internist whom she had last seen in November 1982. Dr. Azzara's notes indicated that plaintiff presented a sore left big toe, which had troubled her for approximately one month, and calluses. She told Dr. Azzara that she often suffered leg cramps that caused a tightening of the leg muscles or burning in her feet and legs after walking and while lying in bed. She had had hypertension (abnormally high blood pressure) for three years and was taking a diuretic for this condition.

. . . .

Plaintiff next saw Dr. Azzara three days later, on May 20, 1983. . . . At this second visit, Dr. Azzara concluded that plaintiff had peripheral vascular disease, poor circulation, and diabetes with a very high sugar elevation. She discussed these conclusions with plaintiff and explained the importance of better sugar maintenance. She also explained that a complication of peripheral vascular disease and diabetes is an increased risk of losing a limb if the diabetes is not controlled. . . .

In any event, plaintiff came back to Dr. Azzara on May 31, 1983, and according to the doctor, reported that she had seen her internist and that the internist had increased her insulin and told her to return to Dr. Azzara for further treatment because of her continuing complaints of discomfort about her toe. However, plaintiff had not seen the internist. Dr. Azzara contends that she believed plaintiff's representations. . . .

Dr. Azzara says that prior to performing the removal procedure she reviewed with Mrs. Ostrowski both the risks and complications of the procedure, including nonhealing and loss of limb, as well as the risks involved with not treating the toe. Plaintiff executed a consent form authorizing Dr. Azzara to perform a total removal of her left big toenail. The nail was cut out. (Defendant testified that she cut out only a portion of the nail, although her records showed a total removal.)

. . . .

During the time plaintiff was being treated by her internist and by Dr. Azzara, she continued to smoke despite advice to the contrary. Her internist testified at the trial that smoking accelerates and aggravates peripheral vascular disease and that a diabetic patient with vascular disease can by smoking accelerate the severity of the vascular disease by as much as fifty percent. By mid-July, plaintiff's toe had become more painful and discolored.

. . . As a result, plaintiff had to undergo immediate bypass surgery to prevent the loss of the extremity. If left untreated, the pre-gangrenous toe condition resulting from the defendant's nail removal procedure would have spread, causing loss of the leg. The plaintiff's first bypass surgery did not arrest the condition, and she underwent two additional bypass surgeries which, in the opinion of her treating vascular surgeon, directly and proximately resulted from the unnecessary toenail removal procedure on May 31, 1983. In the third operation a vein from her right leg was transplanted to her left leg to increase the flow of blood to the toe.

At trial, defense counsel was permitted to show that during the pre-treatment period before May 17, 1983, the plaintiff had smoked cigarettes and had failed to maintain her weight, diet, and blood sugar at acceptable levels. The trial court allowed this evidence of the plaintiff's pre-treatment health habits to go to the jury on the issue of proximate cause. Defense counsel elicited admissions from plaintiff's internist and vascular surgeon that some doctors believe there is a relationship between poor self-care habits and increased vascular disease, perhaps by as much as fifty percent. But no medical expert for either side testified that the plaintiff's post-treatment health habits could have caused her need for bypass surgery six weeks after defendant's toenail removal. Nevertheless, plaintiff argues that defense counsel was permitted to interrogate the plaintiff extensively on her post-avulsion and post-bypass health habits, and that the court allowed such evidence of plaintiff's health habits during the six weeks after the operation to be considered as acts of comparative negligence that could bar recovery rather than reduce her damages. The jury found that the doctor had acted negligently in cutting out the plaintiff's toenail without adequate consideration of her condition, but found plaintiff's fault (fifty-one percent) to exceed that of the physician (forty-nine percent). She was therefore disallowed any recovery. We are told that since the trial, the plaintiff's left leg has been amputated above the knee. This was foreseen, but not to a reasonable degree of medical probability at the time of trial.

II

Several strands of doctrine are interwoven in the resolution of this matter. The concepts of avoidable consequences, the particularly susceptible victim, aggravation of preexisting condition, comparative negligence, and proximate cause each play a part. It may be useful to unravel those strands of doctrine for separate consideration before considering them in the composite.

Comparative negligence is a legislative amelioration of the perceived harshness of the common-law doctrine of contributory negligence. In a fault-based system of tort reparation, the doctrine of contributory negligence served to bar any recovery to a plaintiff whose fault contributed to the accident. Whatever its conceptual underpinnings, its effect was to serve as a "gatekeeper." Any fault kept a claimant from recovery under the system. Fault in that context meant a breach of a legal duty that was comparable to the duty of the other actors to exercise such care in the circumstances as was necessary to avoid the risk of injury incurred. Its prototype was the carriage driver who crossed the train tracks as the train was approaching the crossing.

Comparative negligence was intended to ameliorate the harshness of contributory negligence but should not blur its clarity. It was designed only to leave the door open to those plaintiffs whose fault was [illegible] the defendant's, not to create an independent gate-keeping function. Comparative negligence, then, will qualify the doctrine of contributory negligence when that doctrine would otherwise be applicable as a limitation on recovery. . . .

Related in effect, but not in theory, to the doctrine of contributory negligence is the doctrine of avoidable consequences. . . . The doctrine proceeds on the theory that a plaintiff who has suffered an injury as the proximate result of a tort cannot recover for any portion of the harm that by the exercise of ordinary care he could have avoided. It has a simple thesis of public policy:

> . . . [I]t is not true that the injured person has a duty to act, nor that the conduct of the tortfeasor ceases to be a legal cause of the ultimate harm; but recovery for the harm is denied because it is in part the result of the injured person's lack of care, and public policy requires that persons should be discouraged from wasting their resources, both physical or economic. [Restatement (Second) of Torts § 918 at 500, comment a.]

Avoidable consequences, then, normally comes into action when the injured party's carelessness occurs after the defendant's legal wrong has been committed. . . .

A counterweight to the doctrine of avoidable consequences is the doctrine of the particularly susceptible victim. This doctrine is familiarly expressed in the maxim that "defendant 'must take plaintiff as he finds him.' " . . . Like contributory negligence, this doctrine is harsh but clear in the opposite tendency. It is ameliorated by the doctrine of aggravation of a preexisting condition. While it is not entirely possible to separate the doctrines of avoidable consequence and preexisting condition, perhaps the simplest way to distinguish them is to understand that the injured person's conduct is irrelevant to the consideration of the doctrine of aggravation of a preexisting condition. Negligence law generally calls for an apportionment of damages when a plaintiff's antecedent negligence is "found not to contribute in any way to the original accident or injury, but to be a substantial contributing factor in increasing the harm which ensues." *Restatement (Second) of Torts* § 465 at 510-11, comment c. Courts recognize that a [illegible] aggravate a plaintiff's preexisting condition is liable only for the amount of harm actually caused by the negligence. . . .

Finally, underpinning all of this is that most fundamental of risk allocators in the tort reparation system, the doctrine of proximate cause.

We have sometimes melded proximate cause with foreseeability of unreasonable risk. "When negligent conduct creates such a risk, setting off foreseeable consequences that lead to plaintiff's injury, the conduct is deemed the proximate cause of the injury." More traditionally:

> . . . plaintiff must prove that defendant's conduct constituted a cause in fact of his injuries and loss. An act or omission is not regarded as a cause of an event if the event would have occurred without it. If the injury or loss were to occur in the absence of a physician's negligence or malpractice, then before responsibility may be visited upon the defendant the negligent conduct

or malpractice must have been shown to have been a substantial factor in causing the harm.

We have been candid in New Jersey to see this doctrine, not so much as an expression of the mechanics of causation, but as an expression of line-drawing by courts and juries, an instrument of "overall fairness and sound public policy." Juries, like courts, should understand the doctrine to be based on " 'logic, common sense, justice, policy and precedent.' " . . .

III

Each of these principles, then, has some application to this case. Plaintiff obviously had a preexisting condition. It is alleged that she failed to minimize the damages that she might otherwise have sustained due to mistreatment. Such mistreatment may or may not have been the proximate cause of her ultimate condition.

But we must be careful in reassembling these strands of tort doctrine that none does double duty or obscures underlying threads. In particular, we must avoid the indiscriminate application of the doctrine of comparative negligence (with its fifty percent qualifier for recovery) when the doctrines of avoidable consequences or preexisting condition apply.

The doctrine of contributory negligence bars any recovery to the claimant whose negligent action or inaction before the defendant's wrongdoing has been completed has contributed to cause actual invasion of plaintiff's person or property. By contrast,

> "[t]he doctrine of avoidable consequences comes into play at a later stage. Where the defendant has already committed an actionable wrong, whether tort or breach of contract, then this doctrine [avoidable consequences] limits the plaintiff's recovery by disallowing only those items of damages which could reasonably have been averted . . . [.]"
>
> "[C]ontributory negligence is to be asserted as a complete defense, whereas the doctrine of avoidable consequences is not considered a defense at all, but merely a rule of damages by which certain particular items of loss may be excluded from consideration. . . ."

Hence, it would be the bitterest irony if the rule of comparative negligence, designed to ameliorate the harshness of contributory negligence, should serve to shut out any recovery to one who would otherwise have recovered under the law of contributory negligence. Put the other way, absent a comparative negligence act, it would have never been thought that "avoidable consequences" or "mitigation of damages" attributable to post-accident conduct of any claimant would have included a shutout of apportionable damages proximately caused by another's negligence. Negligent conduct is not "immunized by the concept of 'avoidable consequences.' " . . .

. . . .

In this context of post-injury conduct by a claimant, given the understandable complexity of concurrent causation, expressing mitigation of damages as a percentage of fault which reduces plaintiff's damages may aid juries in their just apportionment of damages, provided that the jury understands that neither mitigation of damages nor avoidable consequences will bar the plaintiff from recovery if the defendant's conduct was a substantial factor without which the ultimate condition would not have arisen.

IV

As noted, in this case the parties agree on certain fundamentals. The pre-treatment health habits of a patient are not to be considered as evidence of fault that would have otherwise been pled in bar to a claim of injury due to the professional misconduct of a health professional. This conclusion bespeaks the doctrine of the particularly susceptible victim or recognition that whatever the wisdom or folly of our life-styles, society, through its laws, has not yet imposed a normative life-style on its members; and, finally, it may reflect in part an aspect of that policy judgment that health care professionals have a special responsibility with respect to diseased patients. . . .

This does not mean, however, that the patient's poor health is irrelevant to the analysis of a claim for reparation. While the doctor may well take the patient as she found her, she cannot reverse the frames to make it appear that she was presented with a robust vascular condition; likewise, the physician cannot be expected to provide a guarantee against a cardiovascular incident. All that the law expects is that she not mistreat such a patient so as to become a proximate contributing cause to the ultimate vascular injury.

However, once the patient comes under the physician's care, the law can justly expect the patient to cooperate with the health care provider in their mutual interests. Thus, it is not unfair to expect a patient to help avoid the consequences of the condition for which the physician is treating her. While the conduct on the part of the patient is not "similar in scope and in nature to that of the defendant," we can at the same time recognize that the principles of comparative negligence may be of assistance to a jury in determining the just allocation of responsibility for damages. As noted, expressing mitigation of damages as a percentage of fault reducing a plaintiff's damages has been found to be a proper method for fairly accounting for failure to mitigation. See *Brant v. United States* (plaintiff's fault contributed to cause fifty-five percent of his total damages. He recovers only forty-five percent).

Hence, we approve in this context of post-treatment conduct submission to the jury of the question whether the just mitigation or apportionment of damages may be expressed in terms of the patient's fault. If used, the numerical allocation of fault should be explained to the jury as a method of achieving the just apportionment of the damages based on their relative evaluation of each actor's contribution to the end result — that the allocation is but an aspect of the doctrine of avoidable consequences or of mitigation of damages. In this context, plaintiff should not recover more than she could have reasonably avoided, but the patient's fault will not be a bar to recovery except to the extent that her fault caused the damages.

. . . .

V

. . . .

We find that the instructions to the jury in this case did not adequately separate or define the concepts that were relevant to the disposition of the plaintiff's case.

First, we note that the jury interrogatories did not specifically cordon off the jury's consideration of health habits to either the pre-treatment period or the post-treatment period. The interrogatories asked only whether plaintiff's failure "to exercise that [reasonable] degree of care for her own safety and well-being" was "a proximate cause of her injuries and damages."

. . . .

Second, the instruction did not distinguish between the patient's pre-operative and post-operative conduct. In melding the causation of "injuries and damages," the charge did not separate the post-treatment conduct that could serve to avoid any recovery (was her failure to consult with her internist a prior or concurrent cause of the contraindicated toenail removal) and her post-treatment conduct that would serve only to mitigate her damages (was the extent of her vascular damage an avoidable consequence of her continued failure to follow dietary and smoking rules).

Defense counsel had emphasized from his opening that plaintiff was a "19-year noncompliant diabetic who admitted neglecting her diet and maintaining her appropriate sugar and acetone test as instructed by her doctors." And he wound up his summation by reminding the jury that the plaintiff didn't pay any attention to her diet, her testing, her smoking for years prior to the time that she ever saw Dr. Azzara.

She persistently failed to honor her dietary restrictions to control her weight, to test the blood sugar, to eliminate the smoking even after having experienced first hand significant consequences of that failure to act.

Now, admittedly exercising such control is not always easy. The simple fact is, ladies and gentlemen, unless one endeavors to do so, one cannot, one should not be permitted in fairness, to blame another to the consequences of one's own inaction. I ask you to return a verdict in Lynn Azzara's favor.

Given the limited role that pre-treatment health habits have in such a case, i.e., being limited to causation, not fault, there is potential for jury misunderstanding of the repeated reference to plaintiff's failings in her health habits.

Finally, the court's instruction permitted the jury to bar the plaintiff entirely from recovery of damages that were justly attributable to the physician. It did not explain that the portion of fault attributable to plaintiff's failure to mitigate damages would not serve to bar recovery entirely. On the motion for new trial, the trial court set forth its understanding of its own charge: "It was not error to submit comparative negligence as a complete defense based on the actions with regard to mitigation of damages."

It is this point that we now clarify with respect to the relationship between the doctrine of comparative negligence and mitigation of damages. The doctrine of comparative negligence, although a useful method for apportioning damages in the mitigation/avoidance context, does not transform those doctrines into "gatekeeper" doctrines that preclude any recovery. Of course, just as at common law, there can be cases of mitigation or avoidance [illegible] through comparative fault where the plaintiff will have no recovery or almost no recovery.

. . . .

Plaintiff argues that any retrial be limited to damages, with the jury's finding of malpractice and proximate cause binding on the retrial. We believe that the interwoven facts of this case do not permit such a partial retrial.

The judgment of the Appellate Division is reversed and the case is remanded to the Law Division for a new trial.

. . . .

NOTES AND QUESTIONS

1. The narrow question here, is how to apportion responsibility for injury. The plaintiff put herself at risk prior to the surgery and after. But the more fundamental, ethical question is whether the physician is responsible for such conduct by the patient? Could the physician have insisted upon a waiver of any claim as protection from the patient's own self-abuse? (*See infra,* § 4.03.)
2. The Court says that several strands of doctrine are interwoven in this case: the "concepts of avoidable consequences, the particularly susceptible victim, aggravation of preexisting condition, comparative negligence and proximate cause . . . " Which of these is determinative and in what way? Which of these, if you were the legislature, would you repeal?
3. On remand and retrial, how should the judge's instructions differ? Why can the remand *not* be limited to damages? What result?
4. In a world in which most Americans drink too much, smoke too much, eat too much, and exercise too little, is it fair to say that the complexity of the doctrine in this case (which fairly represents the American norm) is a good argument for abolishing the "fault" system of funding health care? Should not the results simply be that the plaintiff, having incurred costs, should have them paid for, with perhaps a contribution or co-payment, from her own funds?
5. We will return to these issues in the next chapter, under the heading of self-abuse. There the question will not concern the physician's obligation but society's.
6. For an excellent article, see Jessica W. Berg, *Ethics and E-Medicine*, 46 St. Louis U. L.J. 61 (2002); and see Jacob B. Nist, *Liability for Overprescription of Controlled Substances*, 23 J. Legal Med. 85 (2002).

PROBLEM 3–20 — A Healing Hell

A recent *New Yorker* article* describes the experience of a cancer patient,

* Jerome Groopman, *A Healing Hell*, New Yorker, October, 1998 at 34.

Courtney, undergoing chemotherapy preparatory to bone marrow/stem cell transplant therapy. Groopman wrote as follows:

> "It was a complete nightmare," she recalled. "For days, I'd be on all fours and just retch and retch." Her skin was badly burned by the total-body radiation, and the drugs made her delirious. "I looked like a lobster, and thought I had bugs crawling on me. I'd hit myself and scream." The hardest part for her, though, was being removed from human contact. Visitors are strictly limited, and those who enter must wear special masks, gloves, and tight-fitting gowns. "I was in that sterile bubble, and forgot what skin against skin felt like. That was lost. I just wanted to hold on to my mom and dad, like a two-year-old and I couldn't."

A second patient, Tamar, "was brought as close to death as was clinically sustainable." Goodman described the chemotherapy this way:

> "It's getting worse every hour," she said miserably, several days after the last dose; the maximum impact of chemotherapy comes about a week after its administration. Her lips were so blistered that even speaking was painful. Her eyes were sunken, and her body trembled. She turned to the side of the bed, searching for what's politely called the emesis basin. I found it on her night table, and held it under her quivering chin. A fetid mix of bile and bloody tissue gushed forth. I reached over to help wipe her face. "Be careful," she said, in a small voice. Even the lightest touch was like a searing iron on her burned lips.
>
> I swabbed the vomit first from her chin and from the area around her lips, avoiding the oozing blisters. I then applied a thin layer of Vaseline over her mouth; even through the latex of my gloves I could feel the heat.
>
> Tamar had a raging fever, reaching 104 degrees F. at times during the day. The extraordinary amounts of chemotherapy had produced a chemical burn throughout her gastrointestinal tract, from mouth to rectum. Then, taking advantage of her lack of immunity, a fungus began to grow in her macerated gut.
>
> Carol, a nurse specialist on the transplant team, came into the room and told Tamar it was time for her Amphotericin infusion. Amphotericin is a potent antifungal, but it has toxic effects, too. Each infusion caused Tamar to shake with painful rigors and further raised her temperature.
>
> Tamar closed her eyes as a sedative that the nurse had given her prior to the Amphotericin began to take effect. I gripped Tamar's hand and watched the Amhotericin run slowly into her vein.
>
> In less than a minute, Tamar began to shake violently, her teeth audibly gnashing. I gripped her hand harder, but she had no strength for returning the gesture. The nurse gave her more of the sedative, and then began to bathe her skin with alcohol. This was an effort to

stem the rising temperature, but it worsened the rigors, and Tamar began to moan.

"I wish I hadn't done it," she breathed. "It [illegible]"

"You'll get through this, Tamar," I told her. "This will pass."

"How long?"

I said I didn't know exactly. "Soon, I hoped."

Tamar went without eating for five weeks, because her mouth and stomach were so severely burned that she regurgitated even clear consomme and jello. Her weight dropped by forty-six pounds, and her form became skeletal.

Assume that both Tamar and Courtney survived and would go through this experience again. (Indeed, Courtney returned to high school, graduated, and met her anonymous donor on the stage at graduation). Still, the issues posed throughout this chapter are all embraced in this one problem:

What should/can the physician tell the patient before the chemotherapy to help her prepare herself and make an informed choice?

What may/should the physician choose not to tell?

If the patient — midway through the chemotherapy — begs to end the therapy, should the physician assent? Or leave it to the family?

What if the family insists on ending the chemotherapy? Over the patient's objection? While the patient has been rendered incompetent?

And what of the care, the course of treatment, itself? Is it so brutal and painful and dehumanizing as to be beyond permissible limits of care? Recall here the *Rochin* case from § 2.03. Or is consent enough? Reconsider here the provisions of the Nuremberg Code, the Helsinki Declaration, and the *Cincinatti Radiation Case* and Report, *supra*.

We will return to this subject in Chapter 4, when we review cases on "experiemental" or "investigational" therapies, for which managed care organizations will not make reimbursement. Among these is bone marrow/stem cell therapy, like that experienced by Courtney and Tamar. Should MCO's revise reimbursement and prior authorization simply on the grounds that the brutality of chemotherapy "shocks the conscience"?

PROBLEM 13–21 — The Power of Prayer

Doctor Feldstein wrote of praying with a patient after giving a cancer diagnosis, in JAMA in 2001. Upon seeing a large crucifix, the doctor asked the patient if she would like him to pray with her. He was concerned about the ethics of this and later reviewed it with an ethicist, who said:

"To tell the truth and to provide comfort, what physicians pledge to do. Mrs. Martinez asked you specifically for the test results. You answered truthfully. You were aware how your pronouncement could provide harm and suffering and you followed the Hippocratic principle First, do no harm. Conventional medical, psychological, or philosophical explanations were insufficient or problematic, so you considered a spiritual approach. Prayer is a tremendous source of comfort for people who are prayerful. Although new for you, in the world of spiritual care, offering a prayer is as straightforward as recommending an antibiotic.

"A physician praying with a patient may not be standard practice," he went on, "but this does not make it unethical unless you do not have the permission of the patient or if you conducted your prayer in an unethical way. You identified a cue — the cross — that it would be appropriate to offer a prayer and trusted your deep intuition and judgment. You could have called a cleric if one was available, but then there is the question of timing, to make the right intervention in the right moment. You asked her first if she was a prayerful person. She said yes. Only then did you ask her if she wanted to have a prayer together. She could have said no. You found a common language. You did not tell her what faith to have and did not pray for a miracle."

286 JAMA 1291 (Sep. 19, 2001).

Is this correct, or was it an imposition on the patient? And if prayer is appropriate, which and when and why?

See also Post et al., *Physicians and Patient Spirituality*, 132 Annals of Internal Medicine 578 (2004).

Chapter 4

ETHICS, CHOICES, AND BIOETHICAL CONTEXTS

§ 4.01 Introduction

This chapter involves ethical choices. It focuses on contexts in which people — patients, physicians, nurses, judges, family members or others — make choices which involve — or should involve — ethical values. The emphasis is on "choices," because ethics is above all a system for decision-making. The contexts chosen are bioethical contexts with inevitably competing values and outcomes. For the same reason, there are frequently competing agents and agencies. Also, there may be a dispute not as to *what* a decision should be, but *who* has the right — or duty — to make it.

As a society, we may expect and indeed insist upon an adherence to ethical values within a sense of community responsibility when making choices about, for example, prenatal screening, or the use of fetal tissue; self-abuse, as with tobacco and alcohol; commercial hazard in employment or product development; and death, whether by choice or through capital punishment. Both legislatively and individually, respect for autonomy and for community must be regarded equally. The role of courts and legislatures is to assure both justice and fairness.

This chapter introduces us more fully to the world of public health. In many contemporary ethical discussions, particularly those of a *bioethical* nature, the debate and issues are frequently framed as matters of competing individual choices. This, however, ignores a centuries-old tradition in this country and in Europe of community concern for health. Contagion is an example, whether of the ages-old plagues of leprosy and cholera, or of the more recent contagions of diphtheria, polio and AIDS. The AIDS epidemic has highlighted the continuing vitality of traditional values in the arena of public health, even while challenging their impingement on individual rights. Focusing exclusively on those rights would mean ignoring and losing an important body of thought, which — at its best — has eliminated some of the ancient scourges of humanity.

In the last decade, important ethical questions have also been raised in the delivery of health services with the advent of managed care, cost containment and rationing of health care. These are addressed in some of the problems in earlier sections of this text and, as well, in some of the materials in the present chapter. This Chapter is concerned, for example, with how we should deal — as a community — with self-abuse or maternal-fetal conflict. The complex issues raised by AIDS are here dealt with, including how to balance community and individual interests. This chapter also covers treatment issues — medical uses of marijuana, for example, and autologous bone marrow transplants which have been deemed 'experimental' for breast cancer.

The present chapter thus reaches beyond individual autonomy and ethics to community concerns, but staying well within a focus on individual health care. We begin with birth, and maternal-fetal conflict.

§ 4.02 Birth

The choice of having children is usually (it may be hoped) accompanied by joy and optimism. But we have already dealt with cases involving abortion, sterilization and impaired children. In these instances, parental interests are burdened by — and may be antagonistic to — the interests of children. This section deals with that context, where the parent's interests may be so hostile, or capabilities so inadequate, that his or her judgment may be questioned or challenged in the best interests of the child.

[1] Maternal-Fetal Conflict

IN RE FETUS BROWN
689 N.E.2d 397 (Ill. Ct. App. 1997)

Opinion by: **Theis.**

The issue before this court is whether a competent, pregnant woman's right to refuse medical treatment, which, in this case involves religiously offensive blood transfusions, may be overridden by the State's substantial interest in the welfare of the viable fetus.

. . . .

On June 26, 1996, Darlene Brown, then 26 years old, was 34-3/7 weeks pregnant. After consulting with her treating physician, Dr. Robert Walsh, Brown was admitted into Ingalls Memorial Hospital in Harvey, Illinois, to have a cystoscopy and then to remove a urethral mass. Brown was anticipated to lose 100 cubic centimeters of blood due to the procedure. Before the surgery, Brown did not discuss with Dr. Walsh that she was a Jehovah's Witness.

During the surgery, Brown lost more blood than anticipated. After Brown lost approximately 700 cubic centimeters of blood, Dr. Walsh ordered three units of blood for transfusion. Once the blood arrived in the operating room, Brown, who was fully conscious and alert during the procedure, refused the blood, explaining that she was a Jehovah's Witness. The doctors believed Brown was competent to refuse the blood and they completed the surgery using other techniques to control her bleeding. By the end of the surgery, Brown had lost almost 1,500 cubic centimeters of blood.

. . . .

On June 28, 1996, the State filed a petition for adjudication of wardship and a motion for temporary custody of Baby Doe, a fetus. . . .

At the hearing, the State called Dr. Robert Walsh, Darlene's treating physician, and Kurt Johnson, the hospital administrator. Dr. Walsh testified to the facts of Darlene Brown's condition as indicated above. Dr. Walsh also stated that, from the blood transfusion, Darlene Brown had a 1 in 1,000 risk of contracting hepatitis and a 1 in 5,000 or 10,000 risk of contracting HIV. Dr. Walsh explained that the blood transfusion was necessary, not to get blood to the fetus, but rather to get oxygen to the placenta via the mother's blood. Dr. Walsh explained that, while there were other methods of oxygenation, the problem was that the maternal blood was the only medium for transporting the oxygen to the placenta.

. . . .

The parties stipulated that, if called to testify, Lester Brown would confirm that Darlene Brown understood the risks to herself and the fetus if she did not accept the blood transfusion. The parties further stipulated that Lester Brown supported Darlene Brown's decision not to accept the blood transfusion. . . .

The trial court granted the State's petition and appointed the hospital administrator as "temporary custodian of Fetus Brown, with the right to consent to one or more blood transfusions for Darlene Brown, when advised of such necessity by any attending physician." . . . As alleged in the Browns' later pleadings, Darlene Brown was transfused with six units of packed red blood cells beginning on the night of June 28 and continuing to approximately noon on June 29. Further, Darlene Brown tried to resist the transfusion and the doctors "yelled at and forcibly restrained, overpowered and sedated" her.

. . . .

Illinois recognizes a common law right of competent adults to refuse medical treatment. . . .

. . . .

The right to refuse medical treatment, however, is not absolute. The State may intervene in a given case if the State's interests outweigh the interests of the patient in refusing medical treatment. This is true whether the refusal is based on common law or constitutional principles. Generally, courts consider four State interests — the preservation of life, the prevention of suicide, the protection of third parties, and the ethical integrity of the medical profession — when deciding whether to override competent treatment decisions. *Application of the President & Directors of Georgetown College, Inc.,* [see next case, *infra*]. . . .

. . . .

. . . The circuit court found that the State had an interest in preserving both the life of the mother and the fetus. Typically, however, this factor concerns only preservation of the life of the decision maker. . . .

Most cases concern competent adults who are not pregnant. Of the cases concerning a pregnant woman, most concern the woman's refusal of medical treatment after the birth of the child, and, thus, the woman's wishes are respected. . . . Only in the instant case are we confronted with a situation in which both the pregnant mother and the viable fetus were to benefit from the proposed blood transfusions. We determine that the State's interest in preservation of life continues to concern the life of the decision maker.

Illinois public policy values the sanctity of life. Illinois statutorily recognizes a competent adult's decision to refuse medical treatment. Construing the State's interest in preserving life in conjunction with its interest in protecting the autonomy of the individual, we find that the State's interest in preserving Darlene Brown's life is not determinative in this case.

Thus, the final State interest is the impact upon third parties. Most cases have considered this interest in the context of the impact upon the minor children of a woman refusing medical treatment. *Application of the President & Directors of Georgetown College, Inc.* . . .

. . . .

Here, the record does not indicate evidence of abandonment of the minor children. Lester Brown, the natural father of the three-year-old, supported Darlene's decision to refuse consent. While there is no evidence in the record regarding the eight-year-old's natural father, Lester Brown as well as his and Darlene's parents all were willing to help support both minor children. Thus, the State's interest in protecting the living minor children is not determinative.

We therefore encounter the ultimate issue, the State's interest in protecting the viable fetus. In the abortion context, the state's important and legitimate interest becomes compelling at viability. . . . At that point, the state may restrict abortion, except when necessary to preserve the life or health of the mother.

. . . .

In examining the State's interest in the viable fetus, we note the distinct circumstances of this case. This is not an abortion case in which a pregnant woman seeks to terminate an unwanted pregnancy. Likewise, this case does not involve substance abuse or other abuse by a pregnant woman. And while refusal to consent to a blood transfusion for an infant would constitute neglect without a determination by the Illinois legislature that a fetus is a minor for purposes of the Juvenile Court Act, we cannot separate the mother's valid treatment refusal from the potential adverse consequences to the viable fetus.

Consequently, in this case balancing the mother's right to refuse medical treatment against the State's substantial interest in the viable fetus, we hold that the State may not override a pregnant woman's competent treatment decision, including refusal of recommended invasive medical procedures, to potentially save the life of the viable fetus. We disagree with the *Baby Boy Doe* court's suggestion that a blood transfusion constitutes a "relatively noninvasive and risk-free procedure" (*Baby Boy Doe,* 260 Ill. App. 3d at 402), and find that a blood transfusion is an invasive medical procedure that interrupts a competent adult's bodily integrity. We thus determine that the circuit court erred in ordering Brown to undergo the transfusion on behalf of the viable fetus.

In reaching this difficult conclusion, we note the mother's apparent disparate ethical and legal obligations. Under the law of this State, however, we cannot impose a legal obligation upon a pregnant woman to consent to an invasive medical procedure for the benefit of her viable fetus. . . .

From a practical standpoint, this court questions the enforcement of such court orders, even assuming their validity. . . . Such an order would be in the nature of an injunction, issued by the court and requiring the mother to consent. The only enforcement of such injunctive orders is a contempt citation issued against the mother for willfully violating an order of the court. Contempt is punishable by the imposition of a fine, imprisonment, or other sanction." We question the efficacy of a court order requiring a blood transfusion for someone who is facing death.

As a final matter, the public guardian's appeal argues that, in light of *In re Baby Boy Doe*, the circuit court erred in appointing a guardian *ad litem* to represent the alleged interests of the viable fetus in opposition to the express wishes of its mother. Invoking the provision in the Illinois Abortion Law of 1975 stating that an unborn child is a human being from the time of conception and a legal person, the circuit court determined that it had authority to appoint a guardian *ad litem* for Fetus Brown.

Although the public guardian is correct that *Baby Boy Doe* held that the mother's rights and the fetus' rights may not be balanced, this case did not involve such a balancing. Instead, the issue as framed in this case involved the mother's right to refuse medical treatment as considered against the State's interest in the viable fetus. The asserted legal interests did not require the public guardian's representation of the separate, putative interests of the viable fetus. Thus, the circuit court erred in appointing the public guardian to represent the interests of the viable fetus in this case.

In conclusion, the circuit court erred in appointing a temporary custodian for Fetus Brown with the authority to consent to blood transfusions for Darlene Brown and erred in appointing the public guardian as guardian *ad litem* for Fetus Brown.

Reversed.

Greiman and **Zwick,** JJ., concur.

NOTES AND QUESTIONS

1. Note that this is a *custody* proceeding, but of a fetus, not (yet) a person. Usually, taking custody means removing the child from the parent. Here, is the proceeding a fiction? Tenable? Consistent with the mother's right to abort?
2. What interests is the mother asserting? Autonomy, as in *Casey*? The right to refuse treatment, as in *Cruzan*? A First Amendment right, as in *Yoder*? What of the ethics of becoming pregnant, conceiving a child, when doing so puts the child at risk from the outset?
3. If you were the public guardian, what would your position be? How would you decide that? And do you agree that a public guardian should *not* have been appointed?
4. Could the case have come out the other way? Would you agree with such a result? Would Rawls? What would the Council of Europe's Convention say?
5. Note that this decision comes *after* the transfusions have already occurred. Could/should an expedited opinion have been possible? What relief is *now* available — damages?

6. How would damages be measured? Note that there was a struggle, overcome by force. Note also that blood transfusions *are* "invasive procedures." So there *is* injury to *more* than religious and personal values. How is all of this relevant to the damages? And dos the husband have a claim?

7. Consider the next case involving Georgetown University and compare the reasoning and outcome. Which is more satisfactory to you?

APPLICATION OF THE PRESIDENT AND DIRECTORS OF GEORGETOWN COLLEGE, INC.

331 F.2d 1000 (D.C. Cir. 1964)

J. Skelly **Wright**, Circuit Judge.

Attorneys for Georgetown Hospital applied for an emergency writ at 4:00 P.M., September 17, 1963 seeking relief from the action of the United States District Court for the District of Columbia denying the hospital's application for permission to administer blood transfusions to an emergency patient. The application recited that "Mrs. Jesse E. Jones is presently a patient at Georgetown University Hospital," "she is in extremis," according to the attending physician "blood transfusions are necessary immediately in order to save her life," and "consent to the administration thereof can be obtained neither from the patient nor her husband." The patient and her husband based their refusal on their religious beliefs as Jehovah's Witnesses. The order sought provided that the attending physicians "may" administer such transfusions to Mrs. Jones as might be "necessary to save her life." After the proceedings detailed in Part IV of this opinion, I signed the order at 5:20 P.M.

I.

. . . The treatment proposed by the hospital in its application was not a single transfusion, but a series of transfusions. The hospital doctors sought a court determination before undertaking either this course of action or some alternative. The temporary order issued was more limited than the order proposed in the original application, in that the phrase "to save her life" was added, thus limiting the transfusions in both time and number. Such a temporary order to preserve the life of the patient was necessary if the cause were not to be mooted by the death of the patient.

At any time during the series of transfusions which followed, the cause could have been brought on for hearing by motion before the motions division of this court, and the order either vacated, continued, or superseded by an order of a more permanent nature, such as an interlocutory injunction. Neither the patient, her husband, nor the hospital, however, undertook further proceedings in this court or in the District Court during the succeeding days while blood was being administered to the patient.

. . . .

IV.

Let us now reconstruct the narrative of events through the medium of the [illegible] Memorandum of Facts filed in this cause, the substance of which is as follows:

> Mrs. Jones was brought to the hospital by her husband for emergency care, having lost two thirds of her body's blood supply from a ruptured ulcer. She had no personal physician, and relied solely on the hospital staff. She was a total hospital responsibility. It appeared that the patient, age 25, mother of a seven-month-old chid, and her husband were both Jehovah's Witnesses, the teachings of which sect, according to their interpretation, prohibited the injection of blood into the body. When death without blood became imminent, the hospital sought the advice of counsel, who applied to the District Court in the name of the hospital for permission to administer blood. Judge Tamm of the District Court denied the application, and counsel immediately applied to me, as a member of the Court of Appeals, for an appropriate writ.
>
> . . . .
>
> I asked permission of Mr. Jones to see his wife. This he readily granted. Prior to going into the patient's room, I again conferred with Dr. Westura and several other doctors assigned to the case. All confirmed that the patient would die without blood and that there was a better than 50 percent chance of saving her life with it. Unanimously they strongly recommended it. I then went inside the patient's room. Her appearance confirmed the urgency which had been represented to me. I tried to communicate with her, advising her again as to what the doctors had said. The only audible reply I could hear was "against my will." It was obvious that the woman was not in a mental condition to make a decision. I was reluctant to press her because of the seriousness of her condition and because I felt that to suggest repeatedly the imminence of death without blood might place a strain on her religious convictions. I asked her whether she would oppose the blood transfusion if the court allowed it. She indicated, as best I could make out, that it would not then be her responsibility.
>
> I returned to the doctors' room where some 10 to 12 doctors were congregated, along with the husband and counsel for the hospital. The President of Georgetown University, Father Bunn, appeared and pleaded with Mr. Jones to authorize the hospital to save his wife's life with a blood transfusion. Mr. Jones replied that the Scriptures say that we should not drink blood, and consequently his religion prohibited transfusions. The doctors explained to Mr. Jones that a blood transfusion is totally different from drinking blood in that the blood physically goes into a different part and through a different process in the body. Mr. Jones was unmoved. I thereupon signed the order allowing the hospital to administer such transfusions as the doctors should determine were necessary to save her life.

V.

This opinion is being written solely in connection with the emergency order authorizing the blood transfusions "to save her life." It should be made clear that no attempt is being made here to determine the merits of the underlying controversy. . . .

Before proceeding with this inquiry, it may be useful to state what this case does not involve. This case does not involve a person who, for religious or other reasons, has refused to seek medical attention. It does not involve a disputed medical judgment or a dangerous or crippling operation. Nor does it involve the delicate question of saving the newborn in preference to the mother. Mrs. Jones sought medical attention and placed on the hospital the legal responsibility for her proper care. In its dilemma, not of its own making, the hospital sought judicial direction.

It has been firmly established that the courts can order compulsory medical treatment of children for any serious illness or injury. . . .

The child cases point up another consideration. The patient, 25 years old, was the mother of a seven-month-old child. The state, as parens patriae, will not allow a parent to abandon a child, and so it should not allow this most ultimate of voluntary abandonments. The patient had a responsibility to the community to care for her infant. Thus the people had an interest in preserving the life of this mother.

Apart from the child cases, a second range of factors may be considered. It is suggested that an individual's liberty to control himself and his life extends even to the liberty to end his life. . . .

. . . But whether attempted suicide is a crime is in doubt in some jurisdictions, including the District of Columbia.

The Gordian knot of this suicide question may be cut by the simple fact that Mrs. Jones did not want to die. Her voluntary presence in the hospital as a patient seeking medical help testified to this. Death, to Mrs. Jones, was not a religiously-commanded goal, but an unwanted side effect of a religious scruple. There is no question here of interfering with one whose religious convictions counsel his death, like the Buddhist monks who set themselves afire. Nor are we faced with the question of whether the state should intervene to reweigh the relative values of life and death, after the individual has weighed them for himself and found life wanting. Mrs. Jones wanted to live.

A third set of considerations involved the position of the doctors and the hospital. Mrs. Jones was their responsibility to treat. The hospital doctors had the choice of administering the proper treatment or letting Mrs. Jones die in the hospital bed, thus exposing themselves, and the hospital, to the risk of civil and criminal liability in either case. It is not certain that Mrs. Jones had any authority to put the hospital and its doctors to this impossible choice. The normal principle that an adult patient directs her doctors is based on notions of commercial contract which may have less relevance to life-or-death emergencies. It is not clear just where a patient would derive her authority to command her doctor to treat her under limitations which would produce death. The patient's counsel suggests that this authority is part of constitutionally protected liberty. But neither the principle that life and liberty are inalienable rights, nor the principle of liberty of religion, provides an easy answer to the question whether the state can prevent martyrdom. Moreover, Mrs. Jones had no wish to be a martyr. And her religion merely prevented her consent to a transfusion. If the law undertook the responsibility of authorizing the transfusion without her consent, no problem would be raised with respect to her religious practice. Thus, the effect of the order was to preserve for Mrs. Jones the life she wanted without sacrifice of her religious beliefs.

The final, and compelling, reason for granting the emergency writ was that a life hung in the balance. There was no time for research and reflection. Death could have mooted the cause in a matter of minutes, if action were not taken to preserve the status quo. To refuse to act, only to find later that the law required action, was a risk I was unwilling to accept. I determined to act on the side of life.

NOTES AND QUESTIONS

1. In cases such as this, as well as the *Brown* case, the *Mary Northern* case or the case of *In re A.C.*, an important question always is, how does the case get into court? Who brings it? Why? In cases where a person is in an institution, such as a hospital or a nursing home, what is the custodial obligation to respect the person's wishes, without subjecting her to the indignity of court processes? This, ultimately, was the focus of the New Jersey Supreme Court in the *Karen Quinlan* case, § 1.04[2][c]: courts simply are not well adapted to resolving bioethical questions of life and death. Would the New Jersey Supreme Court's view dictate a different result in the *Georgetown College* case?

2. The decision in the *Georgetown College* case to proceed with the transfusion goes against the belief of Jehovah's Witnesses that introduction of blood to their bodies is contrary to Biblical teaching and affects their soul and chance of immortality. The objection is well-established, well-considered, and rests upon fundamental concepts of freedom of religion and freedom of personhood, all of which are supported by cases earlier in this text. *See In Re Est*[illegible] Wright was certainly familiar with all of this. Did he simply disagree with the Jehovah Witnesses' faith?

3. Or was it that Judge Wright was not persuaded that the patient wanted to die? As in *Mary Northern*, there is a fundamental ambiguity: one may not want to die, but one may still not want to be subjected to a proposed medical procedure. Which desire must be respected? If the answer is the one in which the patient *herself* chooses, then did Judge Wright act correctly?

4. Or was it that Judge Wright concluded the patient was not competent at the end? Even so, had not the patient made her choice when she *was competent*? Should it not be enough that she had joined a church and adopted doctrine designed precisely to govern the situation which Judge Wright confronted?

5. What of Judge Wright's actions, concerns and expressions? Is there an element of patronizing condescension here? Or, like a good physician, is he observing the first rule of ethics: first, do no harm? What would you have done?

BOWEN v. AMERICAN HOSPITAL ASSOCIATION
476 U.S. 610 (1986)

Justice **Stevens** announced the judgment of the Court and delivered an opinion, in which Justice **Marshall**, Justice **Blackmun**, and Justice **Powell** join.

This case presents the question whether certain regulations governing the provision of health care to handicapped infants are authorized by § 504 of the Rehabilitation Act of 1973. That section provides, in part:

> "No otherwise qualified, handicapped individual . . . shall, solely by reason of his handicap, be excluded from the participation in, be denied the benefits of, or be subjected to discrimination under any program or activity receiving Federal financial assistance."[1]

I

. . . .

Although the Final Rules comprise six parts, only the four mandatory components are challenged here.[2] Subsection (b) is entitled "Posting of informational notice" and requires every "recipient health care provider that provides health care services to infants in programs or activities receiving Federal financial assistance" — a group to which we refer generically as "hospitals" — to post an informational notice in one of two approved forms. Both forms include a statement that § 504 prohibits discrimination on the basis of handicap, and indicate that because of this prohibition "nourishment and medically beneficial treatment (as determined with respect for reasonable

[1] "Handicapped individual" is defined in § 7(7)(B) of the Act, as amended, as "any person who (i) has a physical or mental impairment which substantially limits one or more of such person's major life activities, (ii) has a record of such an impairment, or (iii) is regarded as having such an impairment."

[2] Although they do not contain any definition of "discrimination," they do state that § 504 is not applicable to parents and that the regulation applies to only two categories of activities of hospitals: (1) refusals to provide treatment or nourishment to handicapped infants whose parents have consented to, or requested, such treatment; and (2) the failure or refusal to take action to override a parental decision to withhold consent for medically beneficial treatment or nourishment. With respect to the second category, the guidelines state that the hospital may not "solely on the basis of the infant's present or anticipated future mental or physical impairments, fail to follow applicable procedures on reporting such incidents to the child protective services agency or to seek judicial review."

With respect to the first category, the guidelines do not state that § 504 categorically prohibits a hospital from withholding requested treatment or nourishment "solely on the basis of present or anticipated physical or mental impairments of an infant." In general, the guidelines seem to make a hospital's liability under § 504 dependent on proof that (1) it refused to provide requested treatment or nourishment solely on the basis of an infant's handicapped condition, and (2) the treatment or nourishment would have been medically beneficial. . . .

medical judgments) should not be withheld from handicapped infants solely on the basis of their present or anticipated mental or physical impairments." The notice's statement of the legal requirement does not distinguish between medical care for which parental consent has been obtained and that for which it has not. . . .

Subsection (c), which contains the second mandatory requirement, sets forth "Responsibilities of recipient state child protective services agencies." Subsection (c) does not mention § 504 (or any other federal statute) and does not even use the word "discriminate." It requires every designated agency to establish and maintain procedures to ensure that "the agency utilizes its full authority pursuant to state law to prevent instances of unlawful medical neglect of handicapped infants." Mandated procedures must include (1) "[a] requirement that health care providers report on a timely basis . . . known or suspected instances of unlawful medical neglect of handicapped infants," (4) protection of "medically neglected handicapped infants" including, where appropriate, legal action to secure "timely court order[s] to compel the provision of necessary nourishment and medical treatment," and (5) "[t]imely notification" to HHS of every report of "suspected unlawful medical neglect" of handicapped infants. The preamble to the Final Rules makes clear that this subsection applies "where a refusal to provide medically beneficial treatment is a result, not of decisions by a health care provider, but of decisions by parents."

. . . .

II

The Final Rules represent the Secretary's ultimate response to an April 9, 1982, incident in which the parents of a Bloomington, Indiana infant with Downs syndrome and other handicaps refused consent to surgery to remove an esophageal obstruction that prevented oral feeding. On April 10, the hospital initiated judicial proceedings to override the parents' decision, but an Indiana trial court, after holding a hearing the same evening, denied the requested relief. On April 12 the court asked the local Child Protection Committee to review its decision. After conducting its own hearing, the Committee found no reason to disagree with the court's ruling. The infant died six days after its birth.

. . . .

III

On October 11, 1983, after the Department's Interim Final Rule had been declared invalid but before it had promulgated the Final Rules challenged here, a child with multiple congenital defects known as "Baby Jane Doe" was born in Long Island, New York, and was promptly transferred to University Hospital for corrective surgery. After consulting with physicians and other advisers, the parents decided to forgo corrective surgery that was likely to prolong the child's life, but would not improve many of her handicapping conditions.

. . . .

. . . .HHS on October 22, 1983, made repeated requests of the hospital to make its records available for inspection in order to determine whether the hospital was in compliance with § 504. The hospital refused the requests and advised HHS that the parents had not consented to a release of the records.

Subsequently, on November 2, 1983, the Government filed suit in Federal District Court invoking a regulation broadly authorizing access to information necessary to ascertain compliance. The District Court allowed the parents to intervene as defendants, expedited the proceeding, and ruled against the Government. It reasoned that the Government had no right of access to information because the record clearly established that the hospital had not violated the statute. Since the uncontradicted evidence established that the hospital "ha[d] at all times been willing to perform the surgical procedures in question, if only the parents . . . would consent," the hospital "failed to perform the surgical procedures in question, not because Baby Jane Doe [wa]s handicapped, but because her parents ha[d] refused to consent."

. . . .

IV

The Solicitor General is correct that "handicapped individual" as used in § 504 includes an infant who is born with a congenital defect. If such an infant is "otherwise qualified" for benefits under a program or activity receiving federal financial assistance, § 504 protects him from discrimination "solely by reason of his handicap." It follows, under our decision in *Alexander v. Choate* that handicapped infants are entitled to "meaningful access" to medical services provided by hospitals, and that a hospital rule or state policy denying or limiting such access would be subject to challenge under § 504.

However, no such rule or policy is challenged, or indeed has been identified in this case. Nor does this case, in contrast to the University Hospital litigation, involve a claim that any specific individual treatment decision violates § 504. This suit is not an enforcement action, and as a consequence it is not necessary to determine whether § 504 ever applies to individual medical treatment decisions involving handicapped infants. Respondents brought this litigation to challenge the four mandatory components of the Final Rules on their face. The specific question presented by this case, then, is whether the four mandatory provisions of the Final Rules are authorized by § 504.

V

It is an axiom of administrative law that an agency's explanation of the basis for its decision must include "a 'rational connection between the facts found and the choice made.' " . . . [W]ithout the consent of the parents or a surrogate decision maker the infant is neither "otherwise qualified" for treatment nor has he been denied care "solely by reason of his handicap." Indeed, it would almost certainly be a tort as a matter of state law to operate on an infant without parental consent. This analysis makes clear that the Government's heavy reliance on the analogy to race-based refusals which violate § 601 of the Civil Rights Act is misplaced. If, pursuant to its normal practice, a hospital refused to operate on a black child whose parents had withheld their consent to treatment, the hospital's refusal would not be based on the race of the child even if it were assumed that the parents based *their decision* entirely on a mistaken assumption that the race of the child made the operation inappropriate.

. . . .

The Secretary's belated recognition of the effect of parental nonconsent is important, because the supposed need for federal monitoring of hospitals' treatment decisions rests *entirely* on instances in which parents have refused their consent. Thus, in the Bloomington, Indiana case that precipitated the Secretary's enforcement efforts in this area, as well as in the University Hospital case that provided the basis for the summary affirmance in the case now before us, the hospital's failure to perform the treatment at issue rested on the lack of parental consent. The Secretary's own summaries of these cases establish beyond doubt that the respective hospitals did not withhold medical care on the basis of handicap and therefore did not violate § 504; as a result, they provide no support for his claim that federal regulation is needed in order to forestall comparable cases in the future.

The Secretary's initial failure to recognize that withholding of consent by *parents* does not equate with discriminatory denial of treatment by *hospitals* likewise undermines the Secretary's findings in the preamble to his proposed rulemaking. In that statement, the Secretary cited four sources in support of the claim that "Section 504 [is] not being uniformly followed." None of the cited examples, however, suggests that recipients of federal financial assistance, as opposed to parents, had withheld medical care on the basis of handicap.

. . . .

In sum, there is nothing in the administrative record to justify the Secretary's belief that "discriminatory withholding of medical care" in violation of § 504 provides any support for federal regulation: In two of the cases (Robinson, Illinois, and Daytona Beach, Florida), the hospital's refusal was based on the absence of parental consent, but the parents' decision was overridden by state authorities and the operation was performed; in the third case (Colorado Springs, Colorado) it is not clear whether the parents would have given their consent or not, but the corrective surgery was in fact performed.

VII

As a backstop to his manifestly incorrect perception that withholding of treatment in accordance with parental instructions necessitates federal regulation, the Secretary contends that a hospital's failure to report parents' refusals to consent to treatment violates § 504, and that past breaches of this kind justify federal oversight.

By itself, § 504 imposes no duty to report instances of medical neglect — that undertaking derives from state-law reporting obligations or a hospital's own voluntary practice. Although a hospital's selective refusal to report medical neglect of handicapped infants might violate § 504, the Secretary has failed to point to any specific evidence that this has occurred. . . . Even assuming that cases in which parents have withheld consent to treatment for handicapped infants have gone unreported, that fact alone would not prove that the hospitals involved had discriminated on the basis of handicap rather than simply failed entirely to discharge their state-law reporting obligations, if any, a matter which lies wholly outside the nondiscriminatory mandate of § 504.

The particular reporting mechanism chosen by the Secretary — indeed the entire regulatory framework imposed on state child protective services agencies — departs from the nondiscrimination mandate of § 504 in a more fundamental way. . . . The Rules effectively make medical neglect of handicapped newborns a state investigative priority, possibly forcing state agencies to shift scarce resources away from other enforcement activities — perhaps even from programs designed to protect handicapped children outside hospitals. The Rules also order state agencies to "immediate[ly]" review reports from hospitals, to conduct "on-site investigation[s]," and to take legal action "to compel the provision of necessary nourishment and medical treatment," — all without any regard to the procedures followed by state agencies in handling complaints filed on behalf of nonhandicapped infants. These operating procedures were imposed over the objection of several state child protective services agencies that the requirement that they turn over reports to HHS "conflicts with the confidentiality requirements of state child abuse and neglect statutes," thereby requiring under the guise of nondiscrimination a service which state law denies to the nonhandicapped.

. . . .

The Final Rules, however, impose just the sort of absolute obligation on state agencies that the Secretary had previously disavowed. The services state agencies are required to make available to handicapped infants are in no way tied to the level of services provided to similarly situated nonhandicapped infants. Instead, they constitute an "*absolute* right to receive particular services or benefits" under a federally assisted program. Even if a state agency were scrupulously impartial as between the protection it offered handicapped and nonhandicapped infants, it could still be denied federal funding for failing to carry out the Secretary's mission with sufficient zeal.

. . . .

VIII

Section 504 authorizes any head of an Executive Branch agency — regardless of his agency's mission or expertise — to promulgate regulations prohibiting discrimination against the handicapped. . . .

Even according the greatest respect to the Secretary's action, however, deference cannot fill the lack of an evidentiary foundation on which the Final Rules must rest. The Secretary's basis for federal intervention is perceived discrimination against handicapped infants in violation of § 504, and yet the Secretary has pointed to no evidence that such discrimination occurs. Neither the fact that regulators generally may rely on generic information in a particular field or comparable experience gained in other fields, nor the fact that regulations may be imposed for preventative or prophylactic reasons, can substitute for evidence supporting the Secretary's own chosen rationale. . . .

. . . .

. . . [N]othing in the statute authorizes the Secretary to dispense with the law's focus on discrimination and instead to employ federal resources to save the lives of handicapped newborns, without regard to whether they are victims of discrimination by recipients of federal funds or not. Section 504 does not authorize the Secretary to give unsolicited advice either to parents, to hospitals, or to state officials who are faced with difficult treatment decisions concerning handicapped children. We may assume that the "qualified professionals" employed by the Secretary may make valuable contributions in particular cases, but neither that assumption nor the sincere conviction that an immediate "on-site investigation" is "necessary to protect the life or health of a handicapped individual" can enlarge the statutory powers of the Secretary.

The judgment of the Court of Appeals is affirmed.

NOTES AND QUESTIONS

1. The Baby Doe regulations in *Bowen* were invalidated on the ground that they were beyond the statutory authority of the agency issuing them. Suppose the statute was amended, so that Congress either authorized such regulations or adopted them as a statute itself. Would they withstand constitutional challenge? How would you use the case law presented in earlier chapters?

2. As they stood, the regulations invalidated in *Bowen* were justified on the grounds that children born with massive limitations or disabilities might be allowed to die by their parents and denying them life-saving health care was a form of discrimination. What is wrong with this analysis? In terms of the relevant statutes, was it not clearly true that letting the handicapped die *was* impermissible discrimination under existing federal legislation?

3. Quite apart from the legalities, what are the ethical issues here? The competing values are society's interest in "life" versus the parental interest in autonomous decision-making. Is the latter entitled to a certain irreducible minimum of respect, either in Rawls' view or in the view of the Court in *Casey*? Or may a court look at the parents' reasons, rejecting some, for example their desire to avoid a life-long burden? And is there a separate set of issues, concerning whether there are "lives" not worth living? As to that, see the cases in the next section.

4. The debate in *Bowen* impacts the physician-patient relationship. This relationship has received constitutional attention in such cases as *Griswold*, *Roe* and *Casey*. It was central to Justice Bird's dissent in *Privitera*. What is the constitutional status of that relationship? Since it is a creature of state law, should the federal government intrude or preempt it? Or is it a part of the 14th Amendment's "liberty"?

5. Indeed, since health and welfare are largely left to state law, and since the practices prohibited by the regulations in *Bowen* were *permitted* by state law, should the federal government even have been interfering? Is this an ethical question? Is it a constitutional one?

6. For an excellent article, see Linda Farber Post, *Bioethical Consideration of Maternal-Fetal Issues,* 24 Fordham Urb. L.J. 757 (1997); Christa J. Richer, *Fetal Abuse Law: Punitive Approach and the Honorable Status of Motherhood*, 50 Syracuse L. Rev. 1127 (2000).

PROBLEM 4–1 — Crack Babies

Your state Senate Judiciary Committee is considering how to deal with the problem of drug addiction and usage by pregnant women. Four possibilities are suggested: placing women in drug-free custody until after labor and delivery; prosecuting them for criminal neglect and abuse after delivery, for the addiction, withdrawal, and suffering experienced by the newborn child; terminating their parental rights (and transferring these rights to the State); and forced sterilization.

The Chair of the Committee asks you to write a memo on these alternatives, and any others that might suggest themselves.

In so doing, consider the decisions in *Whitner v. South Carolina*, 492 S.E.2d 777 (S.C. 1997) (holding a mother could be prosecuted for ingesting cocaine during the third trimester of pregnancy for child abuse and endangerment); *State ex rel Angela M.W. v. Kruzicki*, 561 N.W.2d 729 (Wis. 1997) (holding the term "child" did not include an unborn fetus and a court could not commit a drug-abusing mother until after delivery) and *Collens v. Texas*, 890 S.W.2d 893 (Tex. Ct. App. 1994) holding that a woman could not be prosecuted for reckless injury to her child, born drug-addicted, due to the ingestion of cocaine during pregnancy. As the three courts note, other courts have reached different results on similar language.

Consider, in your memorandum to the Committee Chair, the care and reporting obligations of obstetricians treating pregnant, addicted women as well as the implications for tort and inheritance laws.

PROBLEM 4–2 — Doing Good

Mrs. Harris has set up a charitable foundation and travels from state to state, paying $300 to encourage long-term birth control by female drug addicts. Harris, herself, has adopted four children born to addicts. Government involvement may be through Medicaid provision of the services such as Norplant or tubal ligation. Some 2000 women have chosen the funding and the services. Harris' approach and funding are private.

Is this consistent with the reproductive freedom of women? Does it respect their autonomy, particularly in light of the economic plight (and often minority status) of most addicts? Does the foundation meet federal requirements as a 501(c)(3) non-profit?

See Paltrow, *Why Caring Communities Must Oppose. . .*, 5 J.L. & Soc'y 11 (2003).

[2] Prenatal Screening and Wrongful Birth

It is now possible to test for a range of diseases or defects during a pregnancy, to determine the health and prospects of the unborn child. Amniocentesis can determine whether, for example, a child will be afflicted with Downs syndrome. Genetic testing may determine whether the child will have Tay-Sachs. With such information, the parents may make an informed choice of whether to conceive a pregnancy or allow a pregnancy to continue.

At least two questions arise. One is *what* should we test (and presumably terminate a pregnancy) for, and *when* must testing be undertaken? The other question is what is the measure of damages when an unwanted — or defective — child is born?

We begin with the first question.

PHILLIPS v. UNITED STATES
575 F. Supp. 1309 (D.S.C. 1983)

Blatt, District Judge.

Introduction

This matter is before the court for final disposition of the issue of damages in plaintiffs' consolidated medical malpractice actions against the United States, which were brought pursuant to the Federal Tort Claims Act. This court has previously addressed certain aspects of these claims in considerable detail. . . .[1]

Briefly, plaintiffs have shown that the staff of the Naval Regional Medical Center (NRMC) in Charleston, South Carolina, breached the applicable standards of medical care by failing to advise, counsel, and test the parents concerning the risk that their offspring would be afflicted with Downs syndrome, commonly known as mongolism, and by failing to diagnose and treat a cardiac disorder in the newborn child. . . .

Findings of Fact

A. Filial Claim for Neonatal Medical Malpractice

This court has previously found that "the pediatric care received by William Randall Phillips at the NRMC did not conform to the applicable standard of medical care."

> [A] pediatric or family practice specialist or resident should refer an infant patient to a pediatric cardiologist at the first sign of congestive heart failure. Although Randy showed clear signs of congestive heart failure in December, 1977, he was not referred to Dr. Riopel until June 19, 1978. This clearly constituted a breach of medical care.

[1] For the sake of brevity, as well as clarity, and to avoid extensive citations to these previous opinions, the general discussions concerning medical background and terminology contained therein are incorporated by reference in this order. *See Phillips v. United States*, 508 F. Supp. 544, 545-46 (D.S.C. 1981); *Phillips v. United States*, 508 F. Supp. 537, 538-39 (D.S.C. 1980).

"During this period, Randy exhibited numerous signs and symptoms related to his heart condition. These included cyanosis, retarded growth, emesis, lack of muscle force, depressed body temperature and pale or clammy skin." According to the testimony of his mother,

> He did a lot of crying. He was real limp. He used to turn blue around the lips and just be splotchy blue. I'd have to sit up at night in a rocking chair holding him up to get him to sleep. I couldn't lay him down because when I laid him down he would start crying again. And like feeding him, his sucking the bottle, he would start turning blue; so I would have to take the bottle away from him every couple of sips. He would get mad and start crying. He would usually throw up three or four times a day at least because he would get so mad crying because I took the bottle away from him that he gagged himself and started throwing up. He was just a miserable little baby is what he was.
>
> On June 23, 1978, shortly after Dr. Riopel's diagnosis of plaintiff's cardiac problem, "Randy underwent a surgical ligation of the heart defect by Dr. Ashby Taylor. . . ."

. . . .

Parental Claim for Wrongful Birth

Plaintiffs presented expert testimony on the issue of damages in the wrongful birth claim; additionally, both of the plaintiffs testified in their own behalf. . . .

Dr. Marion testified that, based on his examination of plaintiffs' child, as well as his review of the clinical history and pertinent medical literature, Randy had a life expectancy of approximately 50 years. . . .

The expert medical testimony of Dr. Marion, which was uncontradicted, establishes that "Randy is going to need twenty-four hour care and supervision." Moreover, Randy will require physical therapy, hearing and speech therapy, and extensive medical services, including ongoing pediatric, ENT, orthopedic, neurological, ophthalmological, and dental care, as well as frequent medication and periodic hospitalization.

Dr. Marion referred plaintiffs' child to Dr. Horowitz for psychological testing and evaluation. The various tests she administered, including the Stanford-Binet Intelligence Scale, indicated that Randy had an I.Q. of fifty-six, which is in the bottom of the mildly retarded range, that "his language skills were somewhat depressed," particularly his receptive language skills, and that he had the "most difficulty in areas of responsibility and ideation." Dr. Horowitz states that Randy's test results indicated a current mental age of approximately two to three years,[2] and that his mental age was never expected to exceed seven years.

[2] As an example of Randy's developmental problems, Dr. Horowitz testified that he was not yet toilet trained.

Dr. Horowitz also testified that Randy needs special schooling, commencing immediately, but that he could eventually be placed in a special public school class. She reiterated that he [illegible] could be expected to enter a group home with vocational training or a sheltered workshop sometime between the ages of eighteen and twenty-one.

. . . .

After thoroughly reviewing the historical rise in medical and maintenance costs, Dr. Wood testified extensively concerning the costs attributable to Randy's condition.

> Because of the child's condition, the child will need the following care: A, twenty-four hours per day care for life. B, therapy in the form of, one, physical therapy, thirty-five dollars per visit, current cost, two times per week for one month, one time per week for the following month, one time per month for the next three years. With respect to speech therapy, current cost is thirty-six dollars an hour. It's needed for one-half hour, five days a week to age seven. Two times per week to age nine. One time per week to age twelve. With respect to schooling, parental training is needed at seven hundred fifty dollars . . . on a one time basis. Nursery training, seventy dollars per month now, a hundred twenty dollars per month beginning in September of '82 for ten months a year to age seven. With respect to physicians first, regular physicians' current cost of eighteen dollars per visit, eight times per year to life expectancy. Lab fees thirty dollars one time per year to life expectancy. ENT specialists, thirty dollars per visit every two years to life expectancy. Ophthalmologist, thirty-five dollars per visit every eight months to life expectancy. Dentist, two hundred dollars per year every year, approximately two to three visits to life expectancy. Orthopedist, sixty dollars per visit every two years to life expectancy. Neurologist, eighty-five dollars per visit every four years to life expectancy. Medications, a hundred fifty dollars per year every year to life expectancy. Hospitalization four times during his lifetime, current cost two hundred dollars per day, five days per stay. Diagnostic tests, one hundred fifty dollars per stay. Physicians' costs, twenty dollars per day during these stays. The mother spends at present approximately a hundred dollars per month on food for the child, three hundred dollars per year on clothing for the child; two hundred dollars per month for rent on a trailer and a lot; eighty-five dollars per month for utilities. The mother lives thirty-seven miles from Charleston and provides transportation for the child. The current cost of institutional care at the residential group home is fifty-three dollars, forty-six cents per day and at the Coastal Center fifty-eight dollars and thirty-two cents per day.

After taking into account inflation and discounting the future expenses to present cash value, Dr. Wood testified concerning the costs of providing the aforementioned services until Randy is approximately eighteen years old, the costs of providing these services from age eighteen to age thirty, forty, or fifty,[3] and the economic costs from Randy's birth until the date of trial.

. . . .

After a careful and circumspect review of the evidence, this court finds that plaintiffs, Dwight A. Phillips and Kathleen E. Phillips, are entitled to damages for the extraordinary expenses, medical, custodial, and otherwise, necessitated by their child's condition from birth to an estimated life expectancy of forty years. They are also entitled to damages for emotional distress, as discussed more fully hereinafter.

Conclusions of Law

Filial Claim for Neonatal Medical Malpractice

Although the medical testimony in this case has established that plaintiff, William Randall Phillips, did not incur any permanent injury by virtue of defendant's failure to refer him to a pediatric cardiologist at the first sign of congestive heart failure, plaintiff is clearly entitled to damages for his pain, suffering, and loss of enjoyment of life during the six-month period between the first indication of congestive heart failure and his eventual referral to Dr. Riopel. Plaintiff's infancy and inability to articulate the pain and anguish he has suffered do not diminish this court's duty to fully compensate him for his injuries; of course, money damages provide the only allowable medium for such compensation. Taking these factors into account, this court finds that an appropriate amount for the child's damages is Five Thousand and no/100 ($5,000.00) Dollars.

C. Parental Claim for Wrongful Birth

1. Generally

As previously noted by this court, "the question of damages has presented a difficult and troublesome problem to the courts that have considered "wrongful birth" claims, with that difficulty engendering widely divergent approaches. . . ." Courts generally allow the extraordinary expenses relating to the child's condition that must be borne by the parents, and some courts have also compensated the parents for their pain and suffering or mental anguish. One court has allowed all expenses incident to the care of the child, without discounting those expenses not directly related to the child's condition that would be necessary for a normal child. *Robak v. United States.*

2. Economic Damages

The jurisdictions that have considered wrongful birth claims are currently unanimous in their allowance of damages for the parent's economic or pecuniary loss due to the child's condition. After a thorough review of those

[3] These calculations incorporated three different proposals: private sitter, Coastal Center (Ladson), and residential group home.

cases in light of the general law of South Carolina concerning damages, this court holds that plaintiffs are entitled to damages for all of the extraordinary expenses necessitated by their child's condition.

This court disagrees with plaintiffs' contention that defendant should be liable for all of the expenses incident to raising their child, whether or not those expenses are directly attributable to the child's condition. While some courts have allowed child-rearing expenses in "wrongful pregnancy" cases, involving children born after negligently performed contraceptive procedures, those cases are distinguishable from the present one because " 'wrongful pregnancy' actions typically involve a[n] . . . unwanted child; '[w]rongful birth' actions, on the other hand, usually involve planned children who, coincidentally, were born with congenital defects." To the extent that this conclusion is inconsistent with the opinion of the United States Court of Appeals for the Seventh Circuit in *Robak*, this court expressly declines to follow that opinion.

. . . .

Dr. Wood provided the court with several alternative options with respect to the calculations concerning the parents' economic damages. His calculation of the reasonable value of attendant care, food, clothing, housing and other necessary items from birth to age 4.42 years, which coincides with the date of trial, February 22, 1982, was essentially uncontradicted by the defendant. This amount is One Hundred Twenty-Four Thousand, Six Hundred Sixty-Nine and no/100 ($124,669.00) Dollars.

Dr. Wood established the present value of the economic costs subsequent to trial with several different scenarios. These calculations incorporated three different care proposals: home care with private sitter, institutional care at the Coastal Center (Ladson), and institutional care in a residential group home. After a careful and circumspect review of all the evidence, this court finds that Randy's condition will necessitate that he remain at home and receive attendant care there until he reaches age 18.42, this being fourteen years from the date of trial. The present economic value of this element of damages is Four Hundred Fifty Thousand, Two Hundred Two and no/100 ($450,202.00) Dollars. This element must be reduced by the cost of raising a "normal" child until the same age. This cost is calculated to be Sixty-Two Thousand, Five Hundred and no/100 $62,500.00) Dollars. Thus, the net allowable economic loss from birth to age 18.42 is Five Hundred Twelve Thousand, Three Hundred Seventy-One and no/100 ($512,371.00) Dollars.

Having found that Randy Phillips will need attendant care at home until age 18.42 years and that he has a prospective life expectancy of forty years, this court finds that his condition will necessitate his transfer to a residential group home, where he will remain from age 18.42 years to age forty years. Dr. Wood calculated the present value of this element of damages to be Seven Hundred Seventy-One Thousand, Three Hundred Ninety-Four and no/100 ($771,394.00) Dollars. Thus, the total economic damages from Randy's birth to his life expectancy of forty years is One Million, Two Hundred Eighty-Three Thousand, Seven Hundred Sixty-Five and no/100 ($1,283,765.00) Dollars.

3. Emotional Damages

. . . .

Generally speaking, "emotional distress is a proper element of tort damage as long as such distress encompasses some physical manifestation." . . .

The testimony of Mrs. Phillips vividly depicts the anguish she experienced as a result of her child's condition. She described sitting up with Randy at night when he would "turn blue around the lips," her reaction when he would throw up three to four times a day, and the marital stress created by his condition. Furthermore, Mrs. Phillips testified: "It upsets me knowing that he'll never be able to do the things that normal kids can do and not being able to do anything to change it."

Mrs. Phillips gave up all social activity, became nervous and resorted to over-eating. Clearly, Mrs. Phillips is not able to live a normal life because of the special care required by Randy. Finally, she observed that, although she loved her child, "[h]e's also a source of heartache because I know I always had dreams of a little boy playing ball and doing things in school which I know he will never be able to do. So at times, he brings me sadness." Aside from the marital difficulties, Mr. Phillips described feelings of anger, outrage, and disappointment, as well as gastrointestinal problems requiring medication.

. . . .

Thus, since the plaintiffs' emotional distress has been and continues to be accompanied by physical symptoms, this court can confidently predict that the South Carolina Supreme Court would follow those jurisdictions which permit wrongful birth plaintiffs to recover emotional distress damages. Moreover, the caesarean section performed at Randy's birth provided the "contact" required under the older case law.

. . . .

In the present case, the economic damages suffered by plaintiffs are sufficient to remove the case from the category in which the sole damages alleged are those of mental anguish. Thus, damages for emotional distress would be permissible even assuming arguendo that there was no physical manifestation of those damages. After careful and circumspect consideration of the evidence, this court finds that an appropriate amount for this element of plaintiffs' damages is Five Hundred Thousand and No/100 ($500,000.00) Dollars.

4. "Benefits Rule"

Much of the confusion apparent in the area of damages has been created by the "benefits rule." *See* Restatement (second) of Torts § 920 (1977). Admittedly, the physician's negligence may result in both benefits and detriments to the parents; despite the affliction of the child, the "parents may yet experience a love that even an abnormality cannot fully dampen." *Becker v. Schwartz*. Indeed, Mrs. Phillips readily admitted that she loved her child, and that Randy was, in the words of counsel for defendant, "the sunshine of [her] life."

This argument has been used in other cases to deny, as a matter of law, recovery for both pecuniary loss and emotional anguish. *Becker v. Schwartz.* The principle underlying the [illegible] complete bar to any element of plaintiffs' damages, with the possible exception of emotional distress. Although the benefits rule was originally propounded as a theoretical barrier to the recognition of wrongful pregnancy claims involving healthy children, its application even in that context has gradually been restricted; it would be "myopic to declare today that the benefits [of parenthood] exceed the costs as a matter of law." Moreover, the benefits derived by the parents in a wrongful birth case are generally distinguishable from the benefits in a wrongful pregnancy case because the benefits in a wrongful birth case depend at least partially on the extent of the child's affliction. *Becker v. Schwartz.*

Thus, although the benefits rule is a legitimate factor in the calculation of damages, it should not improperly restrict the scope of permissible damages. "In calculating plaintiffs' damages, any benefits they derive from defendant's negligence may properly be offset against the detriments which flow from that conduct, in accordance with traditional tort principles." Because the benefits at issue are essentially emotional in nature, the principle applies to the parents' mental suffering and emotional distress. The court finds that the "benefits" flowing from the child's birth despite his condition amount to fifty per cent of the damages for plaintiffs' mental anguish and emotional distress. Accordingly, the damages attributable to plaintiffs' emotional distress is reduced to Two Hundred Fifty Thousand and No/100 ($250,000.00) Dollars. . . .

. . . .

NOTES AND QUESTIONS

1. We have previously encountered failure to screen following birth as actionable in cases involving PKU. The present case involves screening *prior* to birth. Here, the problem is that the child was born with Downs syndrome. The *Procanik* case (below) involves congenital rubella syndrome. In all of these cases, as well [illegible] tests of high accuracy which, given certain circumstances or symptoms, should always be conducted prior to birth.
2. In *Phillips*, the Court considers a "wrongful birth" claim; that is, the tests would have revealed the condition of Mongolism and the birth would then have been avoided. May the defendant show that, even with the information, the parents would have proceeded to a live birth?
3. Note the precision of the testimony and accounting concerning the services, costs and life which will be experienced by a child born with Mongolism (or Downs syndrome). How precise is it possible to be in such a case? If dealing with averages, and the child dies early, should monies be repaid? If the child lives *longer* than the average, who pays then?
4. And how does a court value emotional distress? The figure of $500,000 is awarded; would it be less if the defendant were not the federal

government? *Should it be less* in light of the "benefit" conferred by Randy who was, in the words of counsel for defendant, "the sunshine of [her] life"?

5. Ultimately, the underlying issue is whether life is *ever* "wrongful." The United Nations Declaration, the European Convention and virtually all of the case law under the United States Constitution place prime value on life. Is it fair to ask whether Randy would prefer life to death or nonexistence?

PROCANIK v. CILLO*

97 N.J. Super. 339, 478 A.2d 755 (1984)

Pollock, J.

The primary issue on this appeal is the propriety of a grant of a partial summary judgment dismissing a "wrongful life" claim brought by an infant plaintiff through his mother and guardian ad litem. . . .

The infant plaintiff, Peter Procanik, alleges that the defendant doctors, Joseph Cillo, Herbert Langer, and Ernest P. Greenberg, negligently failed to diagnose that his mother, Rosemary Procanik, had contracted German measles in the first trimester of her pregnancy. As a result, Peter was born with congenital rubella syndrome. Alleging that the doctors negligently deprived his parents of the choice of terminating the pregnancy, he seeks general damages for his pain and suffering and for "his parents' impaired capacity to cope with his problems." He also seeks special damages attributable to the extraordinary expenses he will incur for medical, nursing, and other health care. . . .

. . . .We now conclude that an infant plaintiff may recover as special damages the extraordinary medical expenses attributable to his affliction, but that he may not recover general damages for emotional distress or for an impaired childhood. Consequently, we affirm in part and reverse in part the judgment of the Appellate Division, and remand the matter to the Law Division.

. . . .

The defendant doctors, Joseph Cillo, Herbert Langer, and Ernest P. Greenberg, are board-certified obstetricians and gynecologists who apparently conduct a group practice. On June 9, 1977, during the first trimester of her pregnancy with Peter, Mrs. Procanik consulted the defendant doctors and informed Dr. Cillo "that she had recently been diagnosed as having measles but did not know if it was German measles." Dr. Cillo examined Mrs. Procanik and ordered "tests for German Measles, known as Rubella Titer Test." The results "were 'indicative of past infection of Rubella.'" Instead of ordering further tests, Dr. Cillo negligently interpreted the results and told Mrs. Procanik that she "had nothing to worry about because she had become immune to German Measles as a child." In fact, the "past infection" disclosed by the tests was the German measles that had prompted Mrs. Procanik to consult the defendant doctors.

* Citation material has been omitted from this case.

Ignorant of what an accurate diagnosis would have disclosed, Mrs. Procanik allowed her pregnancy to continue, and Peter was born on December 26, 1977. Shortly thereafter, on January 16, 1978, he was diagnosed as suffering from congenital rubella syndrome. As a result of the doctors' negligence, Mr. and Mrs. Procanik were deprived of the choice of terminating the pregnancy, and Peter was "born with multiple birth defects," including eye lesions, heart disease, and auditory defects. The infant plaintiff states further that "he has suffered because of his parents' impaired capacity to cope with his problems," and seeks damages for his pain and suffering and for his "impaired childhood."

. . . .

III

The terms "wrongful birth" and "wrongful life" are but shorthand phrases that describe the causes of action of parents and children when negligent medical treatment deprives parents of the option to terminate a pregnancy to avoid the birth of a defective child. In the present context, "wrongful life" refers to a cause of action brought by or on behalf of a defective child who claims that but for the defendant doctor's negligent advice to or treatment of its parents, the child would not have been born. "Wrongful birth" applies to the cause of action of parents who claim that the negligent advice or treatment deprived them of the choice of avoiding conception or, as here, of terminating the pregnancy.

. . . .

Analysis of the infant's cause of action begins with the determination whether the defendant doctors owed a duty to him. The defendant doctors do not deny they owed a duty to the infant plaintiff, and we find such a duty exists. In evaluating the infant's cause of action, we assume, furthermore, that the defendant doctors were negligent in treating the mother. Moreover, we assume that their negligence deprived the parents of the choice of terminating the pregnancy and of preventing the birth of the infant plaintiff.

Notwithstanding recognition of the existence of a duty and its breach, policy considerations have led this Court in the past to decline to recognize any cause of action in an infant for his wrongful life. The threshold problem has been the assertion by infant plaintiffs not that they should not have been born without defects, but that they should not have been born at all. The essence of the infant's cause of action is that its very life is wrongful. . . .

. . . .

Recently we recognized that extraordinary medical expenses incurred by parents on behalf of a birth-defective child were predictable, certain, and recoverable. *Schroeder v. Perkel.* In reaching that conclusion, we discussed the interdependence of the interests of parents and children in a family tort:

> The foreseeability of injury to members of a family other than one immediately injured by the wrongdoing of another must be viewed in light of the legal relationships among family members. A family is woven of the fibers of life; if one strand is damaged, the whole structure may suffer. The filaments of family life, although individually spun, create a web of interconnected legal interests. This Court

has recognized that a wrongdoer who causes a direct injury to one member of the family may indirectly damage another.

. . . .

Law is more than an exercise in logic, and logical analysis, although essential to a system of ordered justice, should not become an instrument of injustice. Whatever logic inheres in permitting parents to recover for the cost of extraordinary medical care incurred by a birth-defective child, but in denying the child's own right to recover those expenses, must yield to the inherent injustice of that result. The right to recover the often crushing burden of extraordinary expenses visited by an act of medical malpractice should not depend on the "wholly fortuitous circumstance of whether the parents are available to sue." *Turpin v. Sortini.*

The present case proves the point. Here, the parents' claim is barred by the statute of limitations. Does this mean that Peter must forego medical treatment for his blindness, deafness, and retardation? We think not. His claim for the medical expenses attributable to his birth defects is reasonably certain, readily calculable, and of a kind daily determined by judges and juries. We hold that a child or his parents may recover special damages for extraordinary medical expenses incurred during infancy, and that the infant may recover those expenses during his majority.

. . . .

We find, however, that the infant's claim for pain and suffering and for a diminished childhood presents insurmountable problems. The philosophical problem of finding that such a defective life is worth less than no life at all has perplexed not only Justice Schreiber, but other distinguished members of this Court. We need not become preoccupied, however, with these metaphysical considerations. Our decision to allow the recovery of extraordinary medical expenses is not premised on the concept that non-life is preferable to an impaired life, but is predicated on the needs of the living. We seek only to respond to the call of the living for help in bearing the burden of their affliction.

. . . .

The crux of the problem is that there is no rational way to measure non-existence or to compare non-existence with the pain and suffering of his impaired existence. Whatever theoretical appeal one might find in recognizing a claim for pain and suffering is outweighed by the essentially irrational and unpredictable nature of that claim. Although damages in a personal injury action need not be calculated with mathematical precision, they require at their base some modicum of rationality.

. . . .

As speculative and uncertain as is a comparison of the value of an impaired life with non-existence, even more problematic is the evaluation of a claim for diminished childhood. . . .

Several considerations lead us to decline to recognize a cause of action for impaired childhood. At the outset, we note the flaw in such a claim in those instances in which the parents assert not that the information would have prepared them for the birth of the defective child, but that they would have [illegible] recognize that a claim for "the kind of injury suffered by the child in this context may not be readily divisible from that suffered by her wronged parents." We believe the award of the cost of the extraordinary medical care to the child or the parents, when combined with the right of the parents to assert a claim for their own emotional distress, comes closer to filling the dual objectives of a tort system: the compensation of injured parties and the deterrence of future wrongful conduct.

. . . .

Handler, J., concurring in part and dissenting in part.

. . . .

We should recognize that the wrongful deprivation of the individual choice either to bear or to not bear a handicapped child is a tort — to the infant as well as the parents — and embark upon the important task of defining the infant's damages.

I

. . . .

The essence of the injury of a diminished childhood is that it can be a mirror reflection of the diminished ability of the parents to care for their child. This does not involve only, or even, a lack of love, as suggested by the majority. In truth, parental love in this tragic scene may be blocked by overwhelming dark emotions, as the sun's light can be eclipsed by the moon. The psychological trauma is much deeper and the impairment more pernicious than a seeming lack of love. As the authorities have come to recognize, the parental condition is characterized not by diminished love for the child. Rather, such parents "are consumed with an awful sorrow. Not the surgical sorrow of death, but an hourly, daily, yearly sorrow — an agonizing, shattering, tearing sorrow." G. Stigen, Heartaches and Handicaps 6 (1976).

The emotional trauma associated with a delayed, confusing or mishandled communication of diagnosis is particularly relevant in this case, in that the parents' fears that their unborn child would suffer rubella syndrome had initially been assuaged by defendant's negligent genetic counseling. The parents were led to believe prior to birth that their child was healthy and normal, only to discover at birth that the very fears they had laid to rest as a result of defendants' alleged malpractice had now materialized. Thus, the "delayed" diagnosis they received was likely to result in greater shock and disbelief. This perception of "novelty shock," underlies the injury of diminished parenthood.

. . . .

In sum, the resultant adverse consequences to the parents — the mental and emotional suffering — are now acknowledged by the Court and accepted as an element in its award of damages. Experience teaches us that persons suffering in this way may be significantly impaired in their capacity as parents. Consequently, the adverse impact to the child in the form of a diminished childhood is equally real and undeniable. I am, thus, disheartened by this Court's refusal to permit plaintiffs in an appropriate case — and this case is assuredly that — to develop through competent evidence the diminished childhood of the infant plaintiff as an element of compensable damages.

II

I would also invite the Court to consider both the soundness and fairness of more general damages on behalf of the afflicted child. The majority awards extraordinary medical expenses as an element of damages of the parents, which it then transfers to the infant child. It makes a point of stressing that its damages award "is not premised on the concept that non-life is preferable to an impaired life. . . ." . . . The Court appears to assume that to justify any award of damages to the infant, the infant's injury must be defined as having been born with birth defects, with any resultant damages necessitating a preference of nonlife to life itself.

. . . .

This Court has recognized that an individual may in certain circumstances have the right to make a decision that favors nonexistence over existence. The Court, it is to be emphasized, can recognize that individual right without itself expressing a preference. There is a right of personal autonomy and self-determination with respect to an individual's control of his or her own body and destiny. This can implicate the fundamental choice of life itself. In some situations, the Court has accepted the substituted judgment of a surrogate, guardian or family as the only means of preserving the right of personal choice or self-determination on the part of an individual otherwise unable to exercise that right. Some people may be helpless or incompetent and devoid of the means to express their will on matters concerning their own care, including survival. This does not mean, however, that they lack a right of individual autonomy that involves personal choice and self-determination. When the right exists but the ability or will to exercise it does not, courts will struggle to find a way to effectuate that right. *In re Quinlan.*

. . . .

Clearly then what confronts the Court is not divining a standard by which one can know whether nonexistence is to be preferred over existence. It is, rather, identifying the damages that flow from the denial of parental choice. . . .

. . . .

I respectfully suggest therefore that no "insurmountable problems" thwart the formulation of fair redress for the infant himself. To reiterate, the Court itself need not engage in the prospect of valuing life but only recognize that this is an individual right, the wrongful loss of which justifies redress.

III

In vindicating this individual right, the Court does not arrogate to itself the individual's choice. Rather, it allows the individual's guardian or surrogate to make that choice, recognizing not only the legitimacy of a personal right to opt for nonexistence, but also the necessity of protecting that choice in order to preserve a basic right of personal autonomy and self-determination. . . .

Concededly, the difficulties in formulating standards to assess damages for an infant plaintiff who asserts wrongful life, claiming he was denied the choice of nonexistence over an impaired life, are manifold. . . .

Although the infant plaintiff's injury consists of the deprivation of his parents' choice of whether to bring him into an afflicted existence, his damages need not be assessed by expressing a preference of nonexistence over existence. There are alternative standards that may be used feasibly in appropriate cases. One such approach can be a balancing test, comparing the severity of the child's defects against the benefits of his life; when the burden outweighs the benefits, the difference between the burden of life with defects and the benefits of that impaired existence can be the measure of damages. Another alternative can permit a recovery involving a consideration of the quality of life for the child, had the infant's parents not suffered a diminished parenthood with the resultant diminished childhood visited on the infant. Further, in appropriate circumstances, diminished or impaired childhood can also constitute an element of damages.

. . . .

Schreiber, J., dissenting in part.

I join in substantially all of Justice Pollock's sensitive opinion concerning the infant's claim of general damages for wrongful life. However, I cannot agree that the defendant doctors must pay the infant the costs of medical and other health-care expenses that were not incurred as a result of any breach of duty owed by the doctors to the infant.

The majority recognizes, as do I, that the child's wrongful life action for general damages is fundamentally flawed. . . .

. . . .

Once one acknowledges, as the majority has, that the child has no cause of action for general damages stemming from wrongful life, it is unfair and unjust to charge the doctors with the infant's medical expenses. The position that the child may recover special damages despite the failure of his underlying theory of wrongful life violates the moral code underlying our system of justice from which the fundamental principles of tort law are derived.

An essential element of negligence law is that the defendant's conduct must proximately cause the plaintiff's damages. Most significant is the fact here that the defendant doctors did not injure the child. The doctors did not cause or fail to do something to prevent the multiple birth defects. Yet the damages with which the doctors are being charged are the costs of the medical expenses necessitated by those birth defects.

. . . .

There are two circumstances in which monetary awards unrelated to the plaintiff's injury may be justifiable. The first is when punishment is in order, that is, when the defendant should be punished civilly for wanton and willful misconduct to the plaintiff. However, there is no allegation that the defendants' conduct approached that level and, indeed, the majority accepts the proposition that the defendants did not direct any improper conduct toward the infant plaintiff.

The second circumstance in which awarding such damages may be justified is when the award would help to deter doctors from negligently failing to advise parents of significant possible defects in their future children. How realistic is that contention? First, doctors carry malpractice insurance, and the costs seemingly imposed on the defendants will actually be borne by those members of the public using the services of obstetricians or whatever grouping of doctors occurs for insurance purposes. Second, under existing law, parents have a malpractice claim for the identical misconduct. Thus, the possible deterrent effect is already there.

. . . .

On balance I do not believe the Court is justified in discarding the concept that defendants ordinarily pay as damages only those expenses that are incurred as a result of the defendants' action or inaction. To make the leap from negligence to noncausally-related damages is unwarranted in this case. I, too, am sensitive to the difficulties with which this family must grapple. However, sympathy for a handicapped child and his parents should not lead us to ignore the notions of responsibility, causation, and damage that underlie the entire philosophy of our system of justice. It would be unwise — and, what is more, unjust — to permit the plaintiff to recover damages from persons who caused him no injury. I cannot concur in such a result.

NOTES AND QUESTIONS

1. Here, the mother was afflicted with German Measles in the first trimester of her pregnancy. The impact on a fetus, and subsequently a child, is devastating. During the 1960s, there was a little publicized epidemic of German Measles. Thus, by the 1970s, the defendants knew the importance of testing for German Measles and the relative ease of doing so. There are today, now, thousands of adult children, in their 30s and moving into middle age, who are profoundly disabled neurologically. Their hearing, vision, speech and movement may be so severely limited that they cannot earn a living or live independently.
2. Note that, unlike the preceding case, this is a "wrongful *life*" case. That is, it is the child who is suing to say that he should never have been born. The basic paradox is plain: Peter says death is better than life and he should be compensated for being brought into life. How do you value life? Death?
3. The Court holds that a child may recover in a "wrongful life" case. To what extent is that holding influenced by the fact that the parents'

claim for wrongful *birth* is barred by the statute of limitations? Constitutionally or ethically, could a state deny recovery totally in circumstances such as this?

4. Note the disagreement between the majority and Justice Handler, who would allow recovery of general damages. Do you agree? Or do you agree with Justice Schreiber, who would allow even narrower damages? As has been said elsewhere in this text, the measure of damages — both in terms of elements and amounts — is a crucial test for validating (or rejecting) those values and ethical principles which are so important that they cannot be denied without compensating the citizen.

5. *Phillips* and *Procanik* deal with failure to screen *prior* to birth. The next case involving Donna Safer dealt with failure to tell a child of her father's hereditary form of cancer, with implications for her. As you read *Safer,* compare it to *Phillips* and *Procanik,* but recall as well the *Tarasoff* case in § 3.02[2].

DRAPER v. JASIONOWSKI

858 A.2d 1141 (N.J. Super. 2004)

Holston, Jr., J.A.D.

The issue on this appeal is one of first impression. We decide there exists an independent cause of action for an infant, on reaching his majority, against his mother's obstetrician, for prenatal injuries caused by his vaginal delivery when the physician failed to obtain his mother's informed consent prior to delivery. We reverse and remand for trial.

The facts are not in dispute. Plaintiff, Patrick Draper, was born on April 18, 1982 at St. Peter's Hospital in New Brunswick. His mother, Valerie Cissou, was age twenty at the time of his birth.

Plaintiff was in a "frank breech" position with a large cranial vault while in his mother's womb. The delivering physician, defendant, Dr. Edward Jasionowski, was aware of his presentation prior to the delivery. Cissou signed consent forms for both vaginal and cesarean deliveries. She gave birth to plaintiff by vaginal breech delivery.

Plaintiff alleges defendant neither informed his mother of the option to do a cesarean section rather than a vaginal delivery, nor left the decision of his manner of delivery to his mother's choice. The delivery was complicated by a torn umbilical cord. According to the medical report of plaintiff's board certified obstetrics expert, Dr. Richard L. Luciani, plaintiff suffered from anemia, hypoxia and neurological damage, indicating a tremendous loss of blood secondary to the torn umbilical cord. Plaintiff was born with bilateral Erb's Palsy, an injury to the shoulders.

Plaintiff asserts that birth by cesarean section would have prevented his bilateral Erb's Palsy. Plaintiff initiated suit in 2002, twenty years after his birth. Plaintiff alleges that defendant had a duty to discuss the possibility of a caesarean delivery with his mother. Because defendant did not inform his mother of the cesarean section option for delivery, he failed to obtain her informed consent.

Defendant filed a motion for summary judgment on the informed consent issue alone. Plaintiff cross-moved for summary judgment on the same issue. On December 5, 2003, the Law Division judge granted defendant's motion for summary judgment and denied plaintiff's motion. The judge concluded that because a fetus does not have the ability to consent to a medical procedure, plaintiff could not sustain an independent cause of action arising out of his mother's alleged failure to consent to the method of delivery. We granted plaintiff's motion for leave to appeal.

This appeal involves a purely legal issue. Because "[a] trial court's interpretation of the law and the legal consequences that flow from established facts are not entitled to any special deference," our scope of review is de novo.

Defendant argues that the obligation to disclose the risks and alternatives to obstetric care runs solely to the mother and not the child. Defendant contends that plaintiff's informed consent claim is strictly derivative of the mother and time-barred. Defendant argues that no New Jersey case permits an individual, on his own behalf, to file a claim for informed consent for a procedure performed on someone else's body.

Plaintiff argues that New Jersey law recognizes that a doctor owes a duty to an infant in utero when treating his expectant mother. A doctor who fails in the duty of securing informed consent violates a duty owed to both the mother and the child. Plaintiff asserts that his claim is for his own injuries and is not derivative of any claim of his mother for her own injuries. The parties have stipulated that any cause of action which plaintiff's mother may have had is time-barred.

In *Smith v. Brennan,* 31 N.J. 353, 157 A.2d 497 (1960), our Supreme Court recognized a cause of action on behalf of an infant, born alive, for injuries suffered in utero. Sean Smith, while in the womb of his mother, was injured on July 25, 1956 in an automobile accident caused by the defendant's negligence.

Our Supreme Court, in overruling *Stemmer v. Kline,* held that a surviving child should have a right of action in tort for prenatal injuries. The Court found that there was no reason to deny recovery for a prenatal injury because it occurred before the child was capable of separate existence. The Court reasoned that medical authority recognizes that an unborn child is a distinct biological entity and many branches of the law afford an unborn child protection during various periods of gestation.

The Court stated:

> Justice requires that . . . a child has a legal right to begin life with a sound mind and body. If the wrongful conduct of another interferes with that right, and it can be established . . . that there is a causal connection between the wrongful interference and the harm suffered by the child when born, damages for such harm should be recoverable by the child.

The existence of a viable cause of action on behalf of an infant for injuries sustained as a result of a physician's failure to adequately inform his mother of the risks of a medical procedure was established in *Niemiera v. Schneider,*

114 N.J. 550, 555 A.2d 1112 (1989). Gregory Niemiera suffered a disabling convulsive episode that left him brain damaged when he was age two months. Through his [illegible] from an adverse reaction to the pertussis component of DPT vaccine administered by a nurse under Dr. Schneider's direction.

The child developed severe brain damage resulting from acute encephalopathy, which was diagnosed eight days after the DPT inoculation. Gregory suffered convulsive seizures. As a result of his nervous system injury, he will have impaired vision and suffer from cerebral palsy. He will be mentally defective for the rest of his life.

The Supreme Court recognized the cause of action, which Gregory's mother was asserting on her son's behalf, in addition to the cause of action asserted on behalf of herself and her husband. A child of two-months is in no better position to personally give an informed consent than plaintiff, Patrick Draper, was in utero. Indeed, a child in any stage of minority would require informed consent obtained by a parent or guardian before submitting to a medical procedure or treatment. Clearly, New Jersey law grants a child the right to assert a cause of action by the parent, as guardian ad litem, if the parent was not warned by way of informed consent of the dangers of treatment.

Procanik v. Cillo, 97 N.J. 339, 478 A.2d 755 (1984), is also instructive. There, the Supreme Court approved a cause of action for wrongful birth. The Court declined to sanction a cause of action for general damages for wrongful life. However, the Court recognized a wrongful life cause of action, whereby a child may recover special damages. The Court held that Peter Procanik could recover extraordinary medical expenses caused by his mother's physician's negligent failure to inform his parents that his mother had contracted German measles during the first trimester of her pregnancy. The physician's failure to inform deprived Peter's mother of the right to make an informed decision as to whether or not to continue her pregnancy. Peter Procanik was born with congenital rubella syndrome.

Explaining the rationale for its decision, the Court noted:

> The foreseeability of injury to members of a family other than one immediately injured by the [illegible] light of the legal relationships among family members. A family is woven of the fibers of life; if one strand is damaged, the whole structure may suffer. . . . When a child requires extraordinary medical care, the financial impact is felt not just by the parents, but also by the injured child. As a practical matter, the impact may extend beyond the injured child to his brothers or sisters."

The same rationale applies here. The Court in *Procanik* permitted recovery only for extraordinary medical expenses, since such damages are "predictable, certain and recoverable." The Court refused to permit a claim for damages for a "diminished childhood," noting the difficulty in quantifying the damages. Significantly, the Court expressed its awareness of "the cost of the extraordinary medical care to the child or the parents, when combined with the right of the parents to assert a claim for their own emotional distress, . . . [fulfills] the dual objectives of a tort system: the compensation of injured parties and the deterrence of future wrongful conduct."

Plaintiff alleges that his mother would have opted for delivery by cesarean section had she been fully informed of the medical dangers. Had he been delivered by cesarean section, plaintiff contends he would have been born without deformities and experienced a normal childhood.

Thus, *Brennan* and *Procanik* recognize the infant's own cause of action for damages proximately caused by the negligence of another while in utero. *Niemiera* recognizes a cause of action brought by a parent on behalf of an infant for the infant's own damages based on the inability of the parent to give informed consent. *Procanik* reaffirmed judicial recognition of the duty owed by a mother's obstetrician to her unborn child, as well as to the mother. Unlike *Procanik*, however, the judicial comparison here is not between existence and non-existence of life, but between existence and nonexistence of injury. Plaintiff alleges he did not have to suffer Erb's Palsy. He suffers as a result of his vaginal delivery, which could have been avoided.

Gregory Niemiera, age two, could not have given informed consent. Similarly, no minor or incompetent person could bring suit on their own behalf for their own injuries, on reaching majority, or on return to competency, as a result of the violation of the duty of informed consent, if the law were to bar such an action because the informed consent could only be given to a parent or guardian. No sound public policy reason exists for such a restriction. The law of this State recognizes the viability of such a cause of action.

No case has been presented from any jurisdiction which precludes a child's claim for birth injuries suffered as a result of a pre-birth violation of the duty of informed choice and consent. *Hughson v. St. Francis Hosp. of Port Jervis,* 92 A.D.2d 131, 459 N.Y.S. 2d 814 (App. Div. 1983), addressed the precise issue before us. The court held that an independent cause of action on behalf of an infant may be sustained against a physician for prenatal injuries due to the physician's alleged failure to obtain the informed consent of the mother. As here, the appeal in *Hughson* arose from a dismissal of the complaint. The pleadings were devoid of any facts concerning the nature of the infant's injuries, although it was clear plaintiff's mother was time-barred from asserting her own claim.

The court assumed that damages could be readily ascertained and that causation existed. Defendant's duty to the infant was the sole issue. Defendant argued that the "obligation to disclose the risks and alternatives of obstetric care runs to the mother," and since she must consent for both her and the child, the child's cause of action must be "derivative" of the mother's time-barred cause of action. Rejecting this argument, the *Hughson* court found the infant's cause of action to be "viable and independent." Significantly, the court noted that "it is now beyond dispute that in the case of negligence resulting in prenatal injuries, both the mother and the child in utero may each be directly injured and are each owed a duty, independent of the other." Plaintiffs cannot be denied protection against incompetent medical advice or treatment simply because they are incapable of giving legal consent. The court found further support for its holding in the recognition by the New York Legislature that an infant in utero is as much a "patient" as the expectant mother.

Addressing public policy concerns, the court observed that denying relief to the infant-patient would be tantamount to ignoring "the realities of modern obstetrical practice" [illegible] against incompetent medical advice." Indeed, since the failure to disclose risks and alternatives to the mother may result in "direct physical injury to the fetus alone," the court found it necessary that the infant be able to sustain an independent cause of action. To illustrate the potentially detrimental results of a contrary holding, the court pointed to the Thalidomide litigation, where mothers who used the drug were not affected but the consequences to their children were devastating. Denying relief to the children in those cases, for example, would have been grossly unfair.

Defendant in the case before us asserted that the decision of whether to perform a caesarean section is a medical judgment, not an option for the patient, and consequently, he was not required to obtain plaintiff's mother's informed consent regarding the method of delivery. If this were true, plaintiff's informed consent claim would be moot. The flaw in defendant's reasoning, is that, regardless of how the decision to perform a caesarean is made, any birthing method is an "invasion" of the mother's body which gives her the right to refuse treatment.

Reversed and remanded.

NOTES AND QUESTIONS

1. In *Draper*, who was the patient — the mother, Valerie Cissou, or Patrick Draper, the unborn child? How do you reconcile your answer with *Roe* and *Casey*?
2. If Doctor Jasionowski had a duty towards the fetus, was it as a "patient" or as a third party, as in *Tarasoff* et al? How expansive was the duty — in content or relationship?
3. What role does foreseeability play in this decision? Is it congruent with the decision in *Procanik, supra*? How does this decision weaken the Doctor's role in decisionmaking? Could it actually strengthen the relationship between Doctor and Patient? How?
4. Suppose Valerie *had* been fully informed and chose against a Cesarean, but the Doctor knew this would wrongly expose Draper to risk? What should the Doctor do? Can the mother waive or abandon the fetus' right to proper care? Could the child sue the mother?
5. Would the analysis here be different or easier if the claim rested in negligence and not informed consent?
6. Isn't there a substantial issue of causation here? How can Draper prove his mother would have chosen differently? Need he? Consider the next case, *Canesi v. Wilson*.
7 Do the children in *Kennedy-Kreiger* (*supra*, § 3.03) have a claim against experimenters? The parents? The builders and painters?
8. As of 2005, the States of Maryland, Connecticut, and California supported wrongful birth suits. South Carolina and Michigan do not. For

interesting articles on this topic and emerging fetal protection legislation, see Thomas Burns, *When Life is an Injury: An Economic Approach to Wrongful Life*, 52 Duke L.J. 807 (February, 2003), and see Michelle Haynes, *Inner Turmoil: Redefining the Individual and the Conflict of Rights between Woman and Fetus Created by the Prenatal Protection Act*, 11 Tex. Wesleyan L. Rev. 131 (Fall 2004).

SAFER v. ESTATE OF T. PACK

677 A.2d 1188 (N.J. Super. A.D. 1996)

Before Judges A.M. **Stein**, **Kestin** and **Cuff**.

The opinion of the court was delivered by **Kestin,** J.A.D.

. . . .

Donna Safer's claim arises from the patient-physician relationship in the 1950s and 1960s between her father, Robert Batkin, a resident of New Jersey, and Dr. George T. Pack, also a resident of New Jersey, who practiced medicine and surgery in New York City and treated Mr. Batkin there. It is alleged that Dr. Pack specialized in the treatment and removal of cancerous tumors and growths.

In November 1956, Mr. Batkin was admitted to the hospital with a preoperative diagnosis of retroperitoneal cancer. A week later, Dr. Pack performed a total colectomy and an ileosigmoidectomy for multiple polyposis of the colon with malignant degeneration in one area. The discharge summary noted the finding in a pathology report of the existence of adenocarcinoma developing in an intestinal polyp, and diffuse intestinal polyposis "from one end of the colon to the other." Dr. Pack continued to treat Mr. Batkin postoperatively.

In October 1961, Mr. Batkin was again hospitalized. Dr. Pack performed an ileoabdominal perineal resection with an ileostomy. The discharge summary reported pathology findings of "ulcerative adenocarcinoma of colon Grade II with metastases to Levels II and III" and "adenomatous polyps." Dr. Pack again continued to treat Mr. Batkin postoperatively. He also developed a physician-patient relationship with Mrs. Batkin relative to the diagnosis and treatment of a vaginal ulcer.

In December 1963, Mr. Batkin was hospitalized once again at Dr. Pack's direction. The carcinoma of the colon had metastasized to the liver with secondary jaundice and probable retroperitoneal disease causing pressure on the sciatic nerve plexus. After some treatment, Mr. Batkin died on January 3, 1964, at forty-five years of age. Donna was ten years old at the time of her father's death. Her sister was seventeen.

In February 1990, Donna Safer, then thirty-six years of age and newly married, residing in Connecticut, began to experience lower abdominal pain. Examinations and tests revealed a cancerous blockage of the colon and multiple polyposis. In March, Ms. Safer underwent a total abdominal colectomy with ileorectal anastamosis. A primary carcinoma in the sigmoid colon was found to extend through the serosa of the bowel and multiple polyps were seen throughout the entire bowel. Because of the detection of additional metastatic adenocarcinoma and carcinoma, plaintiff's left ovary was also removed. Between April 1990 and mid-1991, Ms. Safer underwent chemother- [illegible]

In September 1991, plaintiffs obtained Robert Batkin's medical records, from which they learned that he had suffered from polyposis. Their complaint was filed in March 1992, alleging a violation of duty (professional negligence) on the part of Dr. Pack in his failure to warn of the risk to Donna Safer's health.

Plaintiffs contend that multiple polyposis is a hereditary condition that, if undiscovered and untreated, invariably leads to metastatic colorectal cancer. They contend, further, that the hereditary nature of the disease was known at the time Dr. Pack was treating Mr. Batkin and that the physician was required, by medical standards then prevailing, to warn those at risk so that they might have the benefits of early examination, monitoring, detection and treatment, that would provide opportunity to avoid the most baneful consequences of the condition.

. . . .

Whether a legal duty exists is, however, a matter of law. We see no impediment, legal or otherwise, to recognizing a physician's duty to warn those known to be at risk of avoidable harm from a genetically transmissible condition. In terms of foreseeability especially, there is no essential difference between the type of genetic threat at issue here and the menace of infection, contagion or a threat of physical harm. The individual or group at risk is easily identified, and substantial future harm may be averted or minimized by a timely and effective warning.

. . . .

Although an overly broad and general application of the physician's duty to warn might lead to confusion, conflict or unfairness in many types of circumstances, we are confident that the duty to warn of avertible risk from genetic causes, by definition a matter of familial concern, is sufficiently narrow to serve the interests of justice. Further, it is appropriate, for reasons already expressed by our Supreme Court, that the duty be seen as owed not only to the patient himself but that it also "[illegible] to members of the immediate family of the patient who may be adversely affected by a breach of that duty." We need not decide, in the present posture of this case, how, precisely, that duty is to be discharged, especially with respect to young children who may be at risk, except to require that reasonable steps be taken to assure that the information reaches those likely to be affected or is made available for their benefit. . . .

We decline to hold as the Florida Supreme Court did in *Pate v. Threlkel*, that, in all circumstances, the duty to warn will be satisfied by informing the patient. It may be necessary, at some stage, to resolve a conflict between the physician's broader duty to warn and his fidelity to an expressed preference of the patient that nothing be said to family members about the details of the disease. We cannot know presently, however, whether there is any likelihood that such a conflict may be shown to have existed in this matter or, if it did, what its qualities might have been. As the matter is currently constituted, it is as likely as not that no such conflict will be shown to have existed and that the only evidence on the issue will be Mrs. Batkin's testimony, including that she received no information, despite specific inquiry, that her children were at risk. We note, in addition, the possible existence of some offsetting evidence that Donna was rectally examined as a young child, suggesting that the risk to her had been disclosed.

This case implicates serious and conflicting medical, social and legal policies. For example, if evidence is produced that will permit the jury to find that Dr. Pack received instructions from his patient not to disclose details of the illness or the fact of genetic risk, the court will be required to determine whether, as a matter of law, there are or ought to be any limits on physician-patient confidentiality, especially after the patient's death where a risk of harm survives the patient, as in the case of genetic consequences.

Issues of fact remain to be resolved, as well. What was the extent of Donna's risk, for instance? We are led to understand from the experts' reports that the risk of multiple polyposis was significant and that, upon detection, an early full colectomy, i.e., an excision of her entire colon, may well have been the treatment of choice to avoid resultant cancer — including metastasis, the loss of other organs and the rigors of chemotherapy. Full factual development may, however, cast a different light on these issues of fact and others.

Difficult damage issues portend also. Not the least of these will involve distinguishing between the costs of the medical surveillance that would have followed a timely and effective warning, and the costs of medical care attributable to any breach of duty that may be found to have occurred.

Because of the necessarily limited scope of our consideration, we have highlighted only a few of the potentially troublesome issues presented by this case. Such questions are best conceived and considered in the light of a fully developed record rather than in the abstract.

. . . .

The order of the trial court dismissing the complaint is reversed. For similar reasons, the trial court's order denying plaintiffs' motion for summary judgment on liability is affirmed. The matter is remanded to the trial court for further proceedings.

NOTES AND QUESTIONS

1. In the *Safer* case, *why* would Doctor Pack have deliberately misrepresented Mr. Batkin's cancer as a "blockage" or "infection"? Was this an instance of therapeutic privilege — to withhold information in the physician's best judgment? *See* § 3.03[2], *supra*.
2. Did Doctor Pack *have* any obligation — as in *Tarasoff* — to those other than his patient? Is the obligation with genetic conditions, which a patient may choose to pass on to children (indeed, already *have* passed on) different from the obligation with infectious diseases such as AIDS? *See* cases at § 3.02[2], *supra* and § 4.03[3], *infra*.
3. Suppose Mr. Batkin did not *want* his daughter to be told? The Court leaves this issue open — how should it be resolved?

4. *Who* should Doctor Pack have told? Donna Safer, at a young age? Her mother? A court?

5. For an excellent article, see *Section II: Testing — Prenatal*, 29 J.L. Med. & Ethics 30 (2001); and see Wendy E. Roop, *Not in My Womb: Compelled Prenatal Genetic Testing*, 27 Hastings Const. L.Q. 397 (2000).

6. Parents may choose to terminate a pregnancy and may seek prenatal screening to assure a healthy birth. If misinformed, a negligence action is appropriate. What is unclear, however, is what risks must be warned against and whether, to recover, the parents must show causation, that is, not simply failure to warn, but that the risks actually caused the harm which resulted.

CANESI v. WILSON, M.D.

730 A.2d 805 (N.J. 1999)

Handler, J.

In this medical malpractice case, parents brought suit against two obstetricians after their child was born with the congenital defect of bilateral limb reduction. The parents' principal allegation was that the doctors were negligent in failing to warn them that a drug prescribed for the plaintiff mother posed the specific risk of fetal limb reduction and that the prescribed drug caused this defect. They also alleged other acts of negligence, including the failure to warn of general, unspecified fetal risks posed by the prescribed drug, and to take diagnostic measures during the mother's pregnancy that would have disclosed the presence of a fetal defect. They assert that as a result of defendants' negligence they were deprived of their right as parents to decide whether or not to terminate the pregnancy, they would have terminated the pregnancy had they been warned, and they are entitled to the damages allowable in a wrongful birth cause of action. The doctors, focusing on the parents' allegation that the prescribed drug caused their child's birth defect, characterize plaintiffs' claims as based on the doctrine of informed consent and contend, accordingly, that they cannot be found liable because the parents cannot prove medical causation, that is, that the drug was the medical cause of the child's congenital impairment.

In light of the contentions of the parties and the determinations of the lower courts, the basic issue that must be addressed is whether it is necessary to establish medical causation in a wrongful birth action that involves the prescription of drugs without adequate warning of the fetal risks posed by those drugs.

I

On July 1, 1991, plaintiff Melissa Canesi, then twenty-nine years old, consulted defendant Dr. James A. Wilson, a specialist in obstetrics and gynecology, concerned that she might be pregnant because she had been amenorrheic for eleven days. A urinalysis yielded the same results as a home pregnancy test had: plaintiff was not pregnant. Thereafter, Dr. Wilson prescribed for plaintiff Provera, a progestational agent designed to induce menstruation. Dr. Wilson did not provide any information to plaintiff concerning the potential side effects and contraindications of the drug. At the time, the Physicians' Desk Reference (PDR) warned that if a woman was or became pregnant while taking Provera, she should be advised that there was a risk that the fetus would suffer from congenital anomalies, including limb reduction, and a risk that she would retain a defective ovum instead of spontaneously aborting it.

Provera did not succeed in inducing menstruation and, on July 15, Dr. Wilson gave plaintiff a blood serum test to determine if she was pregnant. This time, the test was positive. Upon learning that she was pregnant with twins, plaintiff asked Dr. Wilson if her ingestion of Provera would have a deleterious impact on the fetuses or the course of her pregnancy. Dr. Wilson told plaintiff not to worry.

Because Dr. Wilson was not a participating physician in plaintiff's health insurance plan, she needed to look elsewhere for pregnancy care. On July 25, she saw Dr. Ronald Loewe for the first time and informed him both of her pregnancy and of the fact that she had taken Provera. Dr. Loewe told her that she should not be concerned that she had taken the drug.

Plaintiff's pregnancy was not without incident. She began spotting, one of the fetal twins died, and an amniocentesis revealed excessive amniotic fluid, an indication that the remaining fetus might be suffering from an abnormality. On March 18, 1992, plaintiff gave birth to a boy, Brandon, who had the congenital impairment of bilateral limb reduction.

Plaintiff, together with her husband Sebastian, sued Drs. Wilson and Loewe, alleging that Dr. Wilson was negligent for failing to diagnose her pregnancy in a timely manner, and that both doctors were negligent for failing to inform her of the effect her ingestion of Provera would have on her fetus and for "otherwise" negligently caring for and treating her. Plaintiff claimed that had she known of the risk of congenital defects generally, or limb reduction specifically, that Provera posed to her remaining fetus, or had she been told that she was at an increased risk of retaining a defective ovum, she would have terminated her pregnancy. Being kept ignorant of these risks, she asserted, deprived her of the personal choice of determining whether or not to terminate her pregnancy. The complaint also included a claim brought on behalf of Brandon. That claim alleged that Provera caused his bilateral limb reduction and that defendants were negligent in prescribing the drug to his mother without warning of this risk.

II

A.

A wrongful birth cause of action is predicated on a woman's right to determine for herself whether or not to continue or terminate her pregnancy. Persons "have a right of their own either to accept or reject a parental relationship, and the deprivation of that right by the negligent misconduct of another creates a cause of action in the parents." *Schroeder v. Perkel*, 87 N.J. 53, 66, 432 A.2d 834 (1981). The right protects a distinctively personal interest.

Because the patient's protectable interest is the personal right of self-determination, the doctor's duty of disclosure must be sufficient to enable her to make an informed and meaningful decision concerning whether or not to continue the pregnancy.

Compensable damages in a wrongful birth case include the emotional injury of the parents caused by the deprivation of "the option to accept or reject a parental relationship with the child. . . ." These damages also include the special medical expenses attributable to raising a child with a congenital impairment. Damages, however, do not encompass the birth defect or congenital impairment itself. See *Berman [v. Allen]*, 80 N.J. [421,] 429–30 (stating that plaintiff may not recover compensable damages for existence per se of child in impaired state).

Because in a wrongful birth action damages for the birth defect itself are not recoverable, the parents are not required to prove that the doctor's negligence caused the defect. Because the cognizable harm is the emotional and economic injury suffered by the parents, they must prove that these injuries were proximately caused by the doctor's negligence in depriving them of the opportunity to decide whether or not to become parents of a child with a congenital defect.[2]

Like a cause of action for wrongful birth, a claim based on the doctrine of informed consent is predicated on the patient's right to selfdetermination. The doctrine of informed consent is rooted in the premise that "every human being of adult years and sound mind has a right to determine what shall be done with his own body." *Canterbury v. Spence*. Informed consent doctrine requires a plaintiff to prove that the undisclosed risk was medically accepted and material, that a reasonably prudent person in the patient's condition would not have undergone the treatment if aware of the risk, and that the risk came to fruition.

In sum, the informed consent and wrongful birth causes of action are similar in that both require the physician to disclose those medically accepted risks that a reasonably prudent patient in the plaintiff's position would deem material to her decision. What is or is not a medically accepted risk is informed by what the physician knows or ought to know of the patient's history and condition. These causes of action, however, have important differences. They encompass different compensable harms and measures of damages. In both causes of action, the plaintiff must prove not only that a reasonably prudent patient in her position, if apprised of all material risks, would have elected a different course of treatment or care. In an informed consent case, the plaintiff must additionally meet a twopronged test of proximate causation: she

[2] Closely related to a claim for wrongful birth is one for "wrongful life." A wrongful life cause of action is "brought by or on behalf of" a child with a defect when negligent medical treatment deprived his parents of the option to terminate the pregnancy and avoid his birth. Procanik, *supra*, 97 N.J. at 347–48. The infant does "not allege that the negligence of defendant doctors caused" the defect from which he suffers, or even that he "ever had a chance to be a normal child." Rather, the "essence of the infant's claim is that the defendant doctors wrongfully deprived his mother of information that would have prevented his birth." Damages for wrongful life, like those for wrongful birth, consist of "the medical expenses attributable to [the infant's] birth defects." Expressly excepted from compensable damages is a valuation of the nonexistence of the child as compared to the child's existence in an impaired state.

must prove that the undisclosed risk actually materialized and that it was medically caused by the treatment. In a wrongful birth case, on the other hand, a plaintiff need not prove that the doctor's negligence was the medical cause of her child's birth defect. Rather, the test of proximate causation is satisfied by showing that an undisclosed fetal risk was material to a woman in her position; the risk materialized, was reasonably foreseeable and not remote in relation to the doctor's negligence; and, had plaintiff known of that risk, she would have terminated her pregnancy. The emotional distress and economic loss resulting form this lost opportunity to decide for herself whether or not to terminate the pregnancy constitute plaintiff's damages.

B.

The question remains, however, whether summary judgment was properly entered on the wrongful birth claim. Plaintiffs tried unsuccessfully at the hearings on the summary judgment motion to argue that they had a wrongful birth claim apart from and in addition to their claims based on the allegation that Provera posed the specific risk of bilateral limb reduction and in fact caused that defect. They asserted that they did not restrict their claims only to the specific fetal risk of bilateral limb reduction allegedly posed by Provera and that they did not seek damages only for the impairment suffered by their child; therefore, they were entitled to recover on other grounds that were not dependent on medical causation between the prescribed drug and the resulting birth defect.

Among those "other independent grounds of liability" was defendants' negligent failure "to inform and warn" plaintiffs "that the drug manufacturers issued clear warnings that Provera should not be taken during the first four months of pregnancy" and that the PDR required warnings of general "congenital anomalies, and that this negligence, together with other negligent acts, deprived them of the opportunity to terminate the pregnancy. Plaintiffs' attorney summarized this position. While acknowledging that he had "some big problems on the causation" issue, he contended, citing the wrongful-birth decisions of *Berman* and *Procanik, supra*, that he need not prove causation because he was alleging wrongful birth arising from the failure to warn and other negligent acts. He expressly argued that the doctors should have warned plaintiffs and that in failing to do so they didn't give her her chance, all[] they had to do was say, "Provera has the possibility of (a) causing fetal abnormalities, generically; (b) of retaining an abnormal fetus rather than spontaneously aborting it; (c) [and] that [there were] indications of mild polyhydramnios[] an indication of fetal abnormality," and [their] failure to tell her [of those things] deprived her of her right to abort.

"This particular claim," plaintiffs insisted, "is not the more typical case of a failure to obtain informed consent." Although aware of this argument, the trial court did not determine whether plaintiffs' contentions based on a wrongful birth claim fell beyond the scope of defendants' motion for summary judgment and whether the evidence was sufficient to support a wrongful birth claim. The record provides an adequate basis for making that determination.

The initial analysis based on the record must focus on whether defendants breached a duty. As previously noted, the duty of disclosure in a wrongful birth case is grounded in the right of self-determination. The test of "materiality" in a wrongful birth case is "whether a 'reasonable patient,' in what the physician knows or should know to be the patient's position, would be likely to attach significance to the risk or cluster of risks' in deciding whether to forego the [pregnancy or to bring the fetus to term]."

Although the duty of disclosure in wrongful birth cases serves to protect the individual's right of self-determination and personal autonomy, because that duty is premised on principles of civil tort law, the scope of disclosure in a wrongful birth context is not coextensive with or measured by the woman's constitutional right to decide the fate of her pregnancy. Cf. *Roe v. Wade*, 410 U.S. 113 (1973) (holding that woman has constitutionally protected right to determine for any reason or no reason to terminate her pregnancy). The physician's duty to warn is thus limited by what risks a reasonably prudent patient in the plaintiff's position would consider material to her decision.[5] These constraints serve to place reasonable bounds on the extent of disclosure required by doctors and, so bounded, the standard comports with basic considerations of fairness and public policy that are relevant in determining the scope of a duty of care and the extent of liability that may be placed on the medical profession. *E.g., Carey v. Lovett*, 132 N.J. 44, 58–60, 622 A.2d 1279 (1993).

Plaintiffs contend that the PDR, which contained specific warnings that Provera could cause bilateral limb reduction, the retention of a defective ovum, and general genetic anomalies, constituted evidence of the standard of care governing the doctors' duty of disclosure. In determining what constitutes a medically accepted risk when defining a doctor's duty to warn, we have recognized that the PDR, standing alone, is not and should not be the touchstone of what risks a physician must reveal to his or her patient. Thus, the fact that the PDR contained warnings of the general and specific risks Provera posed to the fetus is not, of itself, sufficient evidence to establish a standard of care.

Plaintiffs, however, do not rely solely on the PDR to establish the standard of care. They present additional evidence that fetal deformity was a medically accepted risk of which they should have been informed. Dr. William Vilensky, one of plaintiffs' experts, noted in his report that the standard of care required that, under circumstances such as were present in this case, the patient be informed of the PDR warnings. Similarly, Dr. Deborah Consoli, plaintiffs' second expert, testified that in 1991 the medical community was split concerning whether Provera caused limb reduction and that she, therefore, informed

[5] The medical probability of the risk manifesting in the patient is highly relevant to whether a reasonably prudent patient would consider the risk material or not. A number of factors, referred to as "maternal indicators," have been recognized and accepted as material in determining whether a risk should be disclosed to a particular pregnant patient. Sylvia Schild & Rita Beck Black, *Social Work and Genetics: A Guide for Practice* 40 (1984). Accepted maternal indicators include exposure to drugs, irradiation, or infection; diabetes, mental retardation, or PKU; a familial pattern of inherited disorders; metabolic or biochemical disorders; known or suspected chromosomal abnormalities; multiple miscarriages or still births; infertility; consanguinity or incest; previous child with any kind of genetic abnormality; age over 35; possession of a recessive gene; and membership in an ethnic group at risk for a certain defect (i.e., African-Americans and sickle cell anemia; Ashkenazi Jews and Tay Sachs Syndrome).

her patients of the risk. Moreover, both defendant doctors had actual knowledge of plaintiff's personal concern about having taken Provera while pregnant. The doctors, however, did not explain to plaintiff whether there were any risks posed by or associated with the ingestion of Provera that were recognized by the medical community or a substantial segment thereof, or whether those risks were remote or likely, or could result in severe or mild impairments. Instead, the doctors dismissed her personal concerns and told her "not to worry."

In addition, plaintiff exhibited other "maternal indicators." The record discloses evidence that plaintiff was spotting, one of the fetal twins died in utero, and an amniocentesis revealed polyhydramnios, which is a possible indicator of fetal abnormality. Defendants' own expert admitted that there were signs that "suggested that this was an abnormal pregnancy." Plaintiffs' evidence also showed that a diagnostic procedure that could have detected whether the potential defect had in fact materialized was available and yet was not utilized until so late in the pregnancy that detection was unlikely. Defendants did not inform plaintiffs of the availability of this diagnostic test nor did they administer that test during the critical period of her pregnancy. As her pregnancy progressed and more maternal risks appeared, the evidence would sustain the determination that Dr. Loewe, instead of keeping plaintiff properly apprised of the status of her pregnancy, chose to keep her in the dark. Given these maternal indicators, the doctors should have known that a reasonable prudent patient in this woman's position would have likely attached significance to the risks associated with Provera. In sum, there was sufficient evidence to enable a jury to determine that defendants breached their duty of disclosure.

The evidence, we find, was also sufficient to establish proximate cause. The dissent accuses the Court of "eliminating proximate cause" altogether, or, alternatively, "redefining it beyond recognition." That simply is not the case.

Legal or proximate cause is clearly an essential element of a wrongful birth cause of action. Medical causation, however, is not.

The appropriate proximate cause question, therefore, is not whether the doctor's negligence caused the fetal defect; the congenital harm suffered by the child is expressly not compensable. Rather, the determination to be made is whether the doctors' inadequate disclosure deprived the parents of their deeply personal right to decide for themselves whether to give birth to a child who could possibly be afflicted with a physical abnormality. There is sufficient evidence in the record of this case to enable a jury to make that determination.

The dissent suggests, therefore, that these cases require that the malpractice be a medical cause or a cause-in-fact of the child's birth defect. These decisions, however, do not require proof that the doctor's malpractice constitutes the medical cause of the child's defect, only that the defect was a foreseeable risk posed by the malpractice. These cases present the circumstance of a factual similarity or parallel between the unwarned or undetected risk and the birth defect that eventuated. That circumstance serves only to support the finding that the resulting birth defect was not too remote in relation to the doctor's omission as an element of proximate cause. These cases do not require that the omission be causally related to the defect. The circumstance of the similarity between the unwarned and undetected risk and the ultimate defect was not used to establish medical causation, which, we acknowledge, it does not do; nor was it invoked as a substitute for medical causation, which, we repeat, is not required. Rather, the circumstance is one that is relevant to the jury's determination of legal or proximate cause: whether the birth of a child with a defect was a material risk that was reasonably foreseeable and was itself a result that was not too remote in relation to the doctor's failure to apprise the parents of that risk during the pregnancy.

Finally, we turn to the issue of the sufficiency of the evidence relating to damages. As noted, a woman asserting a wrongful birth claim who proves that she herself would have had an abortion if apprised of the risk of fetal defect is entitled to damages consisting of both the special medical expenses attributable to raising a child with a congenital impairment, see *Schroeder*, *supra*, 87 N.J. at 70, and the emotional injury attributable to the deprivation of "the option to accept or reject a parental relationship with the child[,]" *Berman*, *supra*, 80 N.J. at 433. Defendants' motion for summary judgment and the rulings of the lower court sustaining that motion did not purport to determine or foreclose those claims for damages.

III

We affirm in part and reverse in part and remand to the trial court to proceed in accordance with this opinion.

Chief Justice **Poritz** and Justices **O'Hern, Garibaldi, Stein**, and **Coleman** join in Justice **Handler**'s opinion. Justice **O'Hern** has filed a separate concurring opinion. Justice **Pollock** has filed a separate dissenting opinion.

Pollock, J., dissenting.

The majority holds that a physician who fails to warn a pregnant woman of a potential adverse effect of a prescribed drug virtually insures that her child will be born without birth defects from any cause. I respectfully dissent.

Under the majority opinion, the parents of a child born with congenital defects may maintain a wrongful birth action against physicians who failed to warn the mother of the potential adverse [illegible] the defects. The import of the holding is that the parents need not prove that the drug was the proximate cause of the birth defects that give rise to the action. All the mother need prove is that she would have aborted the fetus if apprised of potential risks, even if the risks never materialized. Both the reasoning and the result of the majority opinion are flawed.

. . . .

II

A.

The majority acknowledges that proximate cause is an essential element of an action based on a physician's failure to obtain a patient's informed consent. It also acknowledges the strong similarities between an action based on lack of informed consent and a wrongful birth action based on a physician's failure to warn. Specifically, the majority recognizes that wrongful birth claims, as well as those based on lack of informed consent, stem from a patient's right of self-determination. With both claims, a cause of action accrues when a physician denies a patient information necessary to make an informed decision.

Contrary to the majority opinion, nothing in this dissent requires proof that the doctor's failure caused the child's defect. The dissent recognizes that a wrongful birth action based on the doctor's failure to warn requires only the occurrence of the unwarned risk. In this case, the unwarned risk was that Provera might cause birth defects. Provera, however, was not the cause of Brandon Canesi's limb reduction, the only defect that materialized. In fact, Provera did not cause any birth defects.

The majority opinion identifies different elements of proof of proximate cause for informed consent and wrongful birth actions.

According to the majority, "medical causation" is not an element of proximate cause in a wrongful birth action. Thus, the majority finds irrelevant the fact that Provera did not cause Brandon's limb reduction. For the majority, it suffices that the doctors failed to warn of the risk of birth defects that Provera did not cause or of other risks that did not result in defects.

B.

Depending on one's interpretation, the majority either eliminates proximate cause, a result that the opinion disavows, or redefines it beyond recognition. Either alternative, in my opinion, is wrong.

The majority's result is unprecedented in any jurisdiction. In every previous failure-to-warn case, the harm about which the doctors failed to warn was the harm that in fact occurred.

The majority opinion in effect eliminates the requirement of proximate cause. As the majority explains, a causal connection between the doctors' breach and the plaintiffs' injury is not essential.

Initially, the majority acknowledges the absence of any causal connection between Provera and Brandon's birth defect. Later, however, the majority relies on the "factual similarity or parallel between the unwarned or detected risk and the birth defect that eventuated." The majority concludes, "This record clearly demonstrates a sufficient connection or parallel between the various allegations of physician negligence and the resulting harm to the infant, and warrants submission of plaintiff's wrongful birth claim to a jury." In effect, the majority has substituted parallelism for proximate cause.

For the majority, proximate cause is satisfied in a wrongful birth action because the PDR once included an inaccurate warning of a correlation between Provera and limb reduction defects. Rejected by the majority in its causation analysis is the fact that medical science now accepts that the drug does not cause the defect. That rejection also informs the majority's conclusion that "the risk materialized." For the purposes of determining causation, however, the risk did not "materialize." The unwarned risk was that Provera would cause limb reduction. Nothing in the record establishes that Provera caused Brandon's limb reduction. It follows that the risk did not materialize. The majority is left, as it expressly acknowledges, with a risk that paradoxically, [illegible] is not the proximate cause of Brandon's birth defect.

The role of foreseeability in the analysis of proximate cause, however, is determined by looking back, with full knowledge of all that has transpired since the breach of duty. Thus, an actor's conduct is not the proximate cause of harm "where after the event and looking back from the harm to the actor's negligent conduct, it appears . . . highly extraordinary that it should have brought about the harm."

The medical profession knows now, as distinguished from what some believed in 1991, that Provera does not cause limb reduction defects. Furthermore, the PDR no longer warns that Provera may cause those defects. Indeed, the Canesis' own experts no longer warn their patients about limb reduction defects. As a matter of law, the defects cannot be considered the foreseeable result of the doctors' failure to warn. The doctors should not be held liable for medical expenses arising from those defects. By conflating the role of foreseeability in determining the physician's duty to warn with its role in determining causation, the majority imposes liability for an injury unrelated to the breach of the doctor's duty to the patient.

By creating a cause of action for defects unrelated to the doctor's omission, the majority eliminates the requirement that the resulting injury be precisely the one about which the physician failed to warn.

The result is that the majority has constituted physicians virtual insurers of the health of every baby born to women whom they fail to warn of all relevant risks. Miss any warning and the physician runs the risk of liability for any defect, even if unconnected with the omitted warning. Everything that follows from the child's birth is "caused by" the doctor's negligence.

Identifying relevant public policy considerations is crucial when considering such sensitive claims as those for wrongful birth or wrongful life. Those claims implicate understandable compassion both for the child and for the child's parents. Accompanying that compassion is concern for the financial costs that the parents and child must bear because of the child's birth defects. Another consideration is the woman's constitutional right to choose whether to abort a fetus or to carry it to term. A countervailing consideration is the fairness of imposing liability on a physician for a result unrelated to the physician's act. Childbearing and childbirth, moreover, pose inherent risks for both mother and child. Finally, if physicians are to ensure the birth of perfect babies, the cost of that insurance will be spread among all pregnant woman. Thus, the majority opinion also implicates concerns about the undue escalation of the cost of health care. Until today, courts have struck the balance in failure-to-warn wrongful birth actions by requiring the unwarned risk to be the one that eventuates. From my perspective, that conclusion still represents the appropriate balance.

NOTES AND QUESTIONS

1. What is the injury here in *Canesi v. Wilson*: failure to warn as required by informed consent doctrine or causing a birth defect? Isn't the first

a duty and an independent injury to the parents? And weren't they thereby denied their right to abort? Why inquire further as to causation?

2. The Court draws a distinction between an informed consent case and a "wrongful birth" case. What is the difference, and which is this. Does the distinction make sense?

3. Why weren't the warnings contained in the PDR sufficient to establish the duty to warn about Provera. Of course, the Court finds other clinical symptoms created that duty, but standard reference works should be sufficient for warning, if not treatment, shouldn't they?

4. In the end, the Court reverses, finding there may be liability although the risk not warned of is *not* the risk that caused the harm. How much sense does this make? Turn it around — suppose the warning was given, the child was aborted, and it turns out later (as it did) that Provera does not/could not cause the bilateral deformity. Would the doctors *then* be liable for giving the warning whose absence creates liability here?

5. Doesn't Justice Pollock have it right? The majority virtually eliminates proximate cause and unfairly makes physicians insurers against *all* defects. Or does he overstate the matter?

6. In the end, isn't this case really about the inadequacies of our tort, fault-based system as a way of providing costly healthcare for those who need it. We are thus forced to find "fault" to divert insurance monies. In the process, do we distort logic and ethics, and cripple the willingness (and capacity) of providers to provide the very care needed?

7. Should a defendant doctor in a wrongful birth action be allowed to defend based on the joy, pride, and love the "wrongfully birthed" baby has brought to the family? Should damages be reduced by this amount? Who receives the windfall in either scenario — the doctor or the parents? *See Lodato v. Kappy*, 803 A.2d 160 (N.J. Super. 2002).

8. For an excellent article discussing responsibility of the ethical practitioner (written by a pediatrician), see Jeffrey R. Botkin, *Genes and Disability: Defining Health and the Goals of Medicine: Prenatal Diagnosis and the Selection of Children*, 30 Fla. St. U. L. Rev. 265 (Winter, 2003).

PROBLEM 4–3 — Birmingham's Disease

Laurie and Clark Welch go to Carrie Nation, an obstetrician/gynecologist, for pregnancy counseling. Laurie is two months pregnant with their first child. Dr. Nation does a standard history of both Laurie and Clark, including a genetic family tree to determine whether they are at risk of any genetically transmitted conditions or diseases. It appears that in the family tree of the as yet unborn child, there are, for the preceding three generations, adults who have developed and died of Birmingham's disease. Birmingham's is a condition, genetically transmitted, which does not manifest symptoms until middle age, and which leads inevitably to a wasting away and — ultimately — to a difficult death. There is now, because of the human genome project, a relatively simple and certain genetic test to see whether a fetus has inherited the gene which causes Birmingham's.

Dr. Nation does not tell either Laurie and Clark that Birmingham's is genetically transmitted or that there is a test for it. She does tell them that she has ordered the conventional tests which would reveal whether other defects are present which would cause the fetus to be born defective (*e.g.,* Down Syndrome) and the tests have all come back negative. The child will be born, in all probability, healthy and fully functioning. Dr. Nation does not advise concerning Birmingham's or conduct the test for Birmingham's because Laurie and Clark might terminate the pregnancy, depriving the child of four decades of healthy, functioning life. For ethical and religious reasons, Dr. Nation believes that aborting such a child would be immoral.

Comment on the ethics and legal liability attending such conduct, with particular reference to Justice Souter's concurring opinion in *Smith v. Cote,* 513 A.2d 341 (N.H. 1986).

Would your answer be different if either Laurie or Clark had prevailed upon Dr. Nation not to conduct a test for Birmingham's, in order to keep the other spouse from knowing of this?

PROBLEM 4–4 — The Right to an Open Future

You are a genetic counselor. Among your clients are the following:

1. A young deaf couple who desire a deaf child, in the belief that their parenting of a nondeaf child would be inferior and that a deaf child would succeed in the deaf community and culture;
2. A middle aged couple who have initiated a pregnancy in the hope of conceiving a fetus who will be a genetic match for their teenaged daughter who has leukemia. Stem cells would be withdrawn from the fetus as transplant material for the teenaged daughter. The fetus would then be aborted;
3. A couple of mixed race who want a dark skinned child.

Do you assist these couples in learning whether their pregnancies involve fetuses having the desired qualities?

Do you go further — advise about or employ techniques of genetic engineering designed to create the characteristics in the fetuses?

See generally, Davis, *Genetic Dilemmas And The Child's Right To An Open Future,* 27 Hast. Cent. Rep. 7 (1997); McGee, *Parenting In An Era Of Genetics,* 27 Hast. Cent. Rep. 16 (1997). And consider here the Council of Europe Convention in Chapter 1.

[3] Transplants and Fetal Tissue

Fetal tissue may be of medical value in at least two ways: treatment (as with Parkinson's or transplants) and experimentation. Indeed, it is routinely, if inadvertently, available with every abortion and delivery (where placental material is regularly gathered and sometimes sold). Controversy has arisen concerning systematic use of fetal tissue for experimentation, since the experiments may be the very nature of life. And, indeed, if commercially extensive such research might lead to the deliberate creation of fetal material *for the purpose* of experimentation.

For these and other, nonpolitical, reasons NIH withdrew funding during the 1980s for research using fetal tissue. Some states sought to ban it altogether. We begin with one such effort, in Illinois.

LIFCHEZ v. HARTIGAN
735 F. Supp. 1361 (N.D. Ill. 1990)

Ann C. **Williams** District Judge.

Dr. Lifchez represents a class of plaintiff physicians who specialize in reproductive endocrinology and fertility counseling. Physicians with these medical specialties treat infertile couples who wish to conceive a child. Dr. Lifchez is suing the Illinois Attorney General and the Cook County State's Attorney, seeking a declaratory judgment that a provision of the Illinois Abortion Law is unconstitutional. The court finds that § 6(7) of the Illinois Abortion Law violates the Constitution in two ways: (1) it offends Fourteenth Amendment principles of due process by being so vague that persons such as Dr. Lifchez cannot know whether or not their medical practice may run afoul of the statute's criminal sanctions, and (2) the statute impinges upon a woman's right of privacy and reproductive freedom as established in *Roe v. Wade*, *Carey v. Population Services International* and their progeny. . . .

Vagueness

Section 6(7) of the Illinois Abortion law provides as follows:

> (7) No person shall sell or experiment upon a fetus produced by the fertilization of a human ovum by a human sperm unless such experimentation is therapeutic to the fetus thereby produced. Intentional violation of this section is a Class A misdemeanor. Nothing in this subsection (7) is intended to prohibit the performance of in vitro fertilization.

Dr. Lifchez claims that the Illinois legislature's failure to define the terms "experimentation" and "therapeutic" renders the statute vague, thus violating his due process rights under the Fourteenth Amendment. The court agrees.

. . . .

A. Experiment or Routine Test?

The Illinois legislature's failure to define "experimentation" and "therapeutic" in § 6(7) means that persons of common intelligence will be forced to guess at whether or not their conduct is unlawful. As Dr. Lifchez points out in his briefs, there is no single accepted definition of "experimentation" in the scientific and medical communities. Dr. Lifchez identifies four referents for the term. One meaning of experiment is pure research, where there is no direct [illegible] experimented on, and the only goal of the research is to increase the researcher's knowledge. This definition describes the defendants' "Orwellian nightmare" of laying out fetuses in a laboratory and exposing them to various harmful agents "just for the scientific thrill" of it. A second meaning of experiment includes any procedure that has not yet been sufficiently tested so that the outcome is predictable, or a procedure that departs from present-day practice. This is the kind of definition adhered to by insurance companies, which often deny coverage for procedures whose effectiveness is not generally recognized. Dr. Lifchez also cites to the definition of experiment by the American Fertility Society, which includes as "experimental" even standard techniques when those techniques are performed by a practitioner or clinic for the first time. Finally, any medical therapy where the practitioner applies what he learns from one patient to another, could be described as an "experiment." *See, e.g., Margaret S. v. Edwards* (medical treatment can be described as both a test and an experiment "whenever the results of the treatment are observed, recorded, and introduced into the data base that one or more physicians use in seeking better therapeutic methods"). This definition of experiment is in line with that apparently contemplated by the federal regulations on protection of human research subjects: " 'Research' means a systematic investigation designed to develop or contribute to generalizable knowledge." 45 C.F.R. § 46.102(e) (1989).

The legislative history of § 6(7) is unenlightening as far as nailing down a particularized meaning of "experiment" to counter the vagueness that Dr. Lifchez claims is inherent in the statutory language. The bill's sponsor, Representative O'Connell, responded as follows to the governor's veto of the bill (due to what the governor saw as unconstitutional vagueness in the word "experimentation"): "I would submit that the word experiment is quite clear and does not have a vague connotation to it. In fact, the American Heritage dictionary is quite clear in defining experiments as a test made to demonstrate a known truth; to examine the validity of a hypothesis or to determine the efficacy of something previously untried." It is hard to imagine two more opposed definitions of "experiment" than, on the one hand, "a test made to demonstrate a known [illegible] other hand, a test "to determine the efficacy of something previously untried." That the bill's sponsor could offer such wildly different definitions of "experiment" as if they both meant the same thing offers little help to persons of common intelligence who want to know what the state forbids.[1]

It is difficult to know where along this broad spectrum of possible meanings for "experiment" to fit the medical procedures performed by Dr. Lifchez and his colleagues. These procedures can be roughly divided into three kinds: diagnostic, in vitro fertilization and related technologies, and procedures

[1] Defendant Daley claims that "experiment" and "therapeutic" have common definitions which, for some reason he does not explain, keep § 6(7) from being too vague. But the problem of vagueness here derives not so much from lack of a common definition of "experiment" as from the fact that there are several "common definitions," some of which oppose each other. A "test" to demonstrate something already known and a "test" to determine something as yet untried are very different kinds of tests. Vagueness can arise as much from coupling a concept with its antithesis as from a single, imprecise definition.

performed exclusively for the benefit of the pregnant woman. The statute's vagueness affects all three kinds of procedures, but in different ways.

Diagnostic Procedures

One of the more common procedures performed by reproductive endocrinologists is amniocentesis. Amniocentesis involves withdrawing a portion of the amniotic fluid in order to test it for genetic anomalies. It is performed on women considered to be at risk for bearing children with serious defects. The purpose of the procedure is to provide information about the developing fetus; this information is often used by women in deciding whether or not to have an abortion. Although now routinely performed, amniocentesis could be considered experimental under at least two of Dr. Lifchez' definitions: it could be classified as pure research, since there is no benefit to the fetus, the subject being "experimented" on; it could also be experimental (as defined by the American Fertility Society) if the particular practitioner or clinic were doing it for the first time.

Amniocentesis illustrates well the problem of deciding at what point a procedure graduates from "experimental" to routine. Does this occur the fifth time a procedure is performed? the fiftieth? the five hundredth? the five thousandth? Shortly before the Illinois Abortion Law was first passed in 1975, amniocentesis was considered an experimental procedure by most definitions of the term. . . . Dr. Lifchez can hardly be expected to know which of his medical activities would be illegal now if he were to look back on the quick evolution of amniocentesis from (very likely) illegal experiment in 1975 to explicitly endorsed "process" in 1985. Statutory language that embraces both of these possibilities simply "has no core" of meaning and forces people of common intelligence to guess at what the law forbids. For this reason, it is unconstitutionally vague.

. . . .

The development of chorionic villi sampling further illustrates this problem. Chorionic villi sampling involves inserting a catheter through the cervix in order to take a biopsy of the chorionic tissue, tissue surrounding the fetus. As with amniocentesis, it is a diagnostic procedure designed to give information about the developing fetus; this information is often used by a pregnant woman in deciding whether or not to have an abortion. Chorionic villi sampling differs from amniocentesis in that it yields different genetic information, it can be performed earlier in the pregnancy, and, at least at present, it is riskier to the fetus. There is also little dispute that it is experimental. Considering all this, and especially given that chorionic villi sampling would only rarely be therapeutic to the fetus (if, for example it led to in utero surgery). . . . [E]ven if he were to study the statute and read the legislative debates, Dr. Lifchez could not know with any certainty what conduct is being forbidden. . . .

In Vitro Fertilization and Related Technologies

Many other procedures that Dr. Lifchez performs on his patients could fall within the ambit of § 6(7). Among these are in vitro fertilization and the many techniques spawned through research into in vitro fertilization. The difficulty [illegible] by these procedures is not just whether or not they are "experimental," but whether they are "therapeutic to the fetus." The statute's failure to [illegible] this phrase contributes to its vagueness. In vitro fertilization itself involves removal of a mature ovum, placing it in a petri dish or test tube (in glass, that is, in vitro), fertilizing it, and returning the embryo to the woman's uterus where it matures into a fetus. In vitro fertilization itself is explicitly permitted by the statute. Related reproductive technologies are less certain. Embryo transfer, for example, involves removal of an embryo from one woman's uterus and placing it in the uterus of a second woman. The variations on this basic technique are considerable. A donated egg could be fertilized in vitro (with a partner's or a donor's sperm), be placed in a second woman's uterus to gestate for five days, and then be flushed out for implantation in the woman trying to get pregnant. . . .

Perhaps this particular technique is protected by § 6(7)'s exception for in vitro fertilization. ("Nothing in this subsection (7) is intended to prohibit the performance of in vitro fertilization.") But consider a slight variation on the procedure, where fertilization occurs in vivo, that is, in the uterus of the second woman. There is ample evidence in the legislative debates that the legislature did not intend to prohibit technologies that might result in the birth of healthy children: "The in vitro fertilization process will improve but it will still remain in vitro fertilization and it is not this intent . . . the intent of this Bill to, in any way, diminish that very valuable medical wonder. . . . We're not trying to, in any way, jeopardize the legitimate purposes of in vitro fertilization or amniocentesis or anything designed to enhance the birth of children by parents who otherwise could not have had those children." However, in vivo fertilization is not the same as in vitro fertilization, and the legislature chose to exempt only the latter from its ban on experimental procedures on the embryo.

. . . Since *in vivo* fertilization and other non-in vitro variations on embryo transfer are not explicitly exempted by § 6(7), they are subject to the same objection mentioned above: they are therapeutic for the woman trying to get pregnant and unnecessarily risky for the developing embryo.

Other procedures give rise to this and similar objections. In g[illegible]ing of *in vitro* embryos, one cell of an eight-cell embryo is removed for testing, while the rest are frozen. If the genetic screening on the single cell is negative, the remaining seven cells can be gestated to produce a child. This experimental procedure is undisputedly non-therapeutic to the embryo, and although it could fall within the statute's *in vitro* exception, that exception speaks to fertilization, not genetic testing. A failed implantation following *in vitro* fertilization genetic screening could subject Dr. Lifchez to criminal liability.

Two other *in vitro* fertilization-related procedures have a similarly uncertain status. Super-ovulation involves administering various hormones to induce ovulation, resulting in multiple ova. However, the hormones that are used for super-ovulation may have two negative effects on a woman's ability to get pregnant: lower-quality ova are produced and the uterus becomes less receptive to the embryo being implanted. In order to improve the chances of super-ovulation resulting in a pregnancy, Dr. Lifchez may need to experiment with particular elements in the procedure to achieve a more receptive uterine lining or better quality embryos. Not all such attempts will be successful, and any particular one might not be therapeutic to the embryos, thus violating § 6(7).

. . . .

Procedures for the Pregnant Woman

A third class of procedures that Dr. Lifchez performs for his patients are those that are exclusively for the benefit of the pregnant woman. In order to discover correal carcinoma, for example, Dr. Lifchez would need to take a sample of fetal tissue for testing. Correal carcinoma originates with the fetus and is capable of killing pregnant women. Any experimental therapy designed to detect or treat this condition is necessarily a non-therapeutic experiment upon the fetus.

. . . .

What happens when a physician wishes to try a new therapy on his pregnant patient which may have an unknown effect upon the fetus? What happens when he is virtually certain of a deleterious effect upon the fetus? Such a procedure could certainly be classified as "experimental" as to the fetus. And to the extent the physician chooses to treat primarily, or exclusively, his pregnant patient, it is doubtful that such treatment could be called "therapeutic to the fetus." By not adequately defining the terms "experiment" and "therapeutic," § 6(7) not only makes it difficult to know what conduct is forbidden, it also creates a situation where the pregnant woman and her fetus are in competition for the physician's therapy.

. . . .

B. Therapeutic Intent

The defendants claim that the scienter requirement in § 6(7), "Intentional violation of this section is a Class A misdemeanor," saves it from being unconstitutionally vague. It is true that a scienter requirement can do this for a statute. . . .

. . . If a practitioner is unable to tell whether a procedure he is about to perform is an experiment or a test, grafting on a requirement that he intend it to be one or the other does not mitigate the vagueness of what is being forbidden. In other words, while the physician may take comfort in the fact that he is administering a test in good faith, he still does not know which tests are tests and which are experiments. . . .

The intent requirement is more complicated with regard to the second class of procedures that Dr. Lifchez performs, procedures such as in vitro fertilization which are designed to produce an embryo. Dr. Lifchez argues that § 6(7) requires his experiments to be successful. Unless a procedure "is therapeutic to the fetus," he fears, he will be criminally liable. The defendants argue that the only thing inhibiting Dr. Lifchez in his efforts to improve in vitro fertilization through experimentation is his own unreasonable interpretation of § 6(7): as long as a practitioner intends his procedure to help the fetus, § 6(7) [illegible]

. . . However, it is equally plausible to interpret the removal of a gestating embryo from one uterus to another, exposing it to the considerable risk associated with embryo transfer, as evidence of therapeutic intent directed only toward the woman who wishes to bear her own child. A therapeutic intent (or at least the most therapeutic intent) toward the embryo would leave it alone to develop in the uterus in which it was fertilized.

. . . .

Reproductive Privacy

Section 6(7) of the Illinois Abortion Law is also unconstitutional because it impermissibly restricts a woman's fundamental right of privacy, in particular, her right to make reproductive choices free of governmental interference with those choices. . . .

Section 6(7) intrudes upon this "cluster of constitutionally protected choices." Embryo transfer and chorionic villi sampling are illustrative. Both procedures are "experimental" by most definitions of that term. Both are performed directly, and intentionally, on the fetus. Neither procedure is necessarily therapeutic to the fetus. In embryo transfer, it is not therapeutic to remove the embryo from a woman's uterus after it has been fertilized and expose it to the high risk associated with trying to implant it in the infertile woman. In chorionic villi sampling, it is not therapeutic to the fetus to invade and snip off some of its surrounding tissue. Both embryo transfer and chorionic villi sampling violate any reasonable interpretation of § 6(7).

Both procedures, however, fall within a woman's zone of privacy as recognized in *Roe v. Wade*, *Carey v. Population Services International*, and their progeny. *See also* John A. Robertson, The Right To Procreate and In Utero Fetal Therapy, 3 J. LEG. MED. 333, 339 (1982). Embryo transfer is a procedure designed to enable an infertile woman to bear her own child. It takes no great leap of logic to see that within the cluster of constitutionally protected choices that includes the right to have access to contraceptives, there must be included within that cluster the right to submit to a medical procedure that may bring about, rather than prevent, pregnancy. Chorionic villi sampling is similarly protected. The cluster of constitutional choices that includes the right to abort a fetus within the first trimester must also include the right to submit to a procedure designed to give information about that fetus which can then lead to a decision to abort. Since there is no compelling state interest sufficient to prevent a woman from terminating her pregnancy during the first trimester, there can be no such interest sufficient to intrude upon these other protected activities during the first trimester. By encroaching upon this protected zone of privacy, § 6(7) is unconstitutional.

. . . .

NOTES AND QUESTIONS

1. Note that the problem of what to do with fetal tissue has arisen earlier, for example, with anencephalic babies in § 1.04[2][b] and with test tube babies in § 1.04[1][b]. In both instances, the generation or the use of fetal materials was a secondary by-product of the principal concern. In the world of ethics, it raises the principle of "double effect": if an undertaking, for example, *in vitro* fertilization, has a good effect and a bad effect (creating fetal material), it is ethical to proceed if the intended purpose is acceptable and is not outweighed by the secondary effect.

2. Experimentation with fetal tissue has chilling implications, since it is no longer merely science-fiction to believe that fertilized eggs may be developed to a multi-cell level in the laboratory. At the present time, at least as far as published literature is concerned, laboratories have been unable to develop pre-embryos to the embryo stage. But the literature already reflects the ability to stimulate eggs to behave as though they have been fertilized in the *absence of sperm.* Indeed, as reflected elsewhere in these materials, that is the essence of cloning. *See supra,* § 2.03[3]. Thus, it is a legitimate concern to worry about the development of fetuses in the laboratory and experimentation thereon, which might include harvesting organs for transplant from them or, indeed, might include transgenic manipulation.

3. Of more therapeutic value, it is now possible to use fetal materials for treatment of certain diseases, most notably Parkinson's disease. Placing fetal cells in close proximity to areas of the brain which have deteriorated due to Parkinsons brings them back to vitality, at least for a period of time. Stem cells in the embryo (or pre-embryo) particularly have great potential for treatment, including transplantation. Research on this and other applications of fetal material is promising, yet, as the *Lifchez* case indicates, also highly controversial.

4. During the 1970s, the National Institutes of Health funded research into the development and uses of fetal tissue. During the 1980s, such funding was considered politically unacceptable and withdrawn. Funding has been restored in the 1990s, but with the limitation that research cannot include efforts to "grow" fetuses in the laboratory. Why? Is this good policy? Does it implicate ethical principles developed in the first or second chapters of this book? Does it collide with academic freedom? Consider here the Council of Europe's Convention, presented in the Introduction to the first chapter.

5. Is Judge Williams being disingenuous in criticizing the use of such terms as "experimentation" and "therapeutic"? Would it not be *possible* for her to find precise meanings and to import clarity to the statute? See elsewhere, in these materials, for accepted definitions of experimentation, § 3.03[3] and § 4.04[2]. Indeed, given the troubling history of experimentation over the past 80 years, should she not ethically have attempted to save the Illinois statute? Similarly, given the desirability of promoting "therapeutic" abortions, should Judge Williams not have

attempted — again, ethically — to give common sense meaning to that [illegible]?

6. Are chorionic villi sampling, amniocentesis and embryo transfer "experimental," or are they simply new, developing treatment techniques? Is there a difference for insurance? Ethics? The Constitution?

7. Is Judge Williams correct, that the statute "burdens" reproductive freedom under the *Casey* opinion. Does it burden reproductive freedom in the same way? To the same extent?

Report and Recommendations: Research on the Fetus

National Commission for Protection of Human Subjects of Biomedical and Behavioral Research (1975)[*]

The Commission has considered the principles proposed by ethicists in relation to the exigencies of scientific inquiry, the requirements and present limitations of medical practice, and legal commentary. Among the general principles for research on human subjects judged to be valid and binding are: (1) to avoid harm whenever possible, or at least to minimize harm; (2) to provide for fair treatment by avoiding discrimination between classes or among members of the same class; and (3) to respect the integrity of human subjects by requiring informed consent. An additional principle pertinent to the issue at hand is to respect the human character of the fetus.

To this end, the Commission concludes that in order to be considered ethically acceptable, research involving the fetus should be determined by adequate review to meet certain general requirements:

(1) Appropriate prior investigations using animal models and nonpregnant humans must have been completed.

(2) The knowledge to be gained must be important and obtainable by no reasonable alternative means.

(3) Risks and benefits to both the mother and the fetus must have been fully evaluated and described.

(4) Informed consent must be sought and granted under proper conditions.

(5) Subjects must be selected so that risks and benefits will not fall inequitably among economic, racial, ethnic and social classes.

These requirements apply to all research on the human fetus. In the application of these principles, however, the Commission found it helpful to consider the following distinctions: (1) therapeutic and nontherapeutic research; (2) research directed toward the pregnant woman and that directed toward the fetus; (3) research involving the fetus-going-to-term and the fetus-to-be-aborted; (4) research occurring before, during or after an abortion procedure; and (5) research which involves the nonviable fetus ex utero and that which involves the possibly viable infant. The first two distinctions encompass the

[*] United States Dept. of Health, Education, and Welfare (1975). DHEW Publication No. (OS) 76-127.

entire period of the pregnancy through delivery; the latter three refer to different portions of the developmental continuum.

The Commission observes that the fetus is sometimes an unintended subject of research when a woman participating in an investigation is incorrectly presumed not to be pregnant. Care should be taken to minimize this possibility.

. . . .

The Deliberations and Conclusions of the Commission regarding the application of general principles to the use of the fetus as a human subject in scientific research are as follows:

1. In therapeutic research directed toward the fetus, the fetal subject is selected on the basis of its health condition, benefits and risks accrue to that fetus, and proxy consent is directed toward that subject's own welfare. Hence, with adequate review to assess scientific merit, prior research, the balance of risks and benefits, and the sufficiency of the consent process, such research conforms with all relevant principles and is both ethically acceptable and laudable. In view of the necessary involvement of the woman in such research, her consent is considered mandatory; in view of the father's possible ongoing responsibility, his objection is considered sufficient to veto.

2. Therapeutic research directed toward the pregnant woman may expose the fetus to risk for the benefit of another subject and thus is at first glance more problematic. Recognizing the woman's priority regarding her own health care, however, the Commission concludes that such research is ethically acceptable provided that the woman has been fully informed of the possible impact on the fetus and that other general requirements have been met. Protection for the fetus is further provided by requiring that research put the fetus at minimum risk consistent with the provision of health care for the woman. Moreover, therapeutic research directed toward the pregnant woman frequently benefits the fetus, though it need not necessarily do so. In view of the woman's right to privacy regarding her own health care, the Commission concludes that the informed consent of the woman is both necessary and sufficient.

In general, the Commission concludes that therapeutic research directed toward the health condition of either the fetus or the pregnant woman is, in principle, ethical. Such research benefits not only the individual woman or fetus but also women and fetuses as a class, and should therefore be encouraged actively.

The Commission, in making recommendations on therapeutic and nontherapeutic research directed toward the pregnant woman, (Recommendations 2 and 3), in no way intends to preclude research on improving abortion techniques otherwise permitted by law and government regulation.

3. Nontherapeutic research directed toward the fetus *in utero* or toward the pregnant woman poses difficult problems because the fetus may be exposed to risk for the benefit of others.

Here, the Commission concludes that where no additional risks are imposed on the fetus (e.g., where fluid withdrawn during the course of treatment is used additionally for nontherapeutic research), or where risks are so minimal [illegible] consent by the parent(s) is sufficient to provide protection. (Hence, the consent of the woman is sufficient provided the father does not object.) The Commission recognizes that the term "minimal" involves a value judgement and acknowledges that medical opinion will differ regarding what constitutes "minimal risk." Determination of acceptable minimal risk is a function of the review process.

When the risks cannot be fully assessed, or are more than minimal, the situation is more problematic. The Commission affirms as a general principle that manifest risks imposed upon nonconsenting subjects cannot be tolerated. Therefore, the Commission concludes that only minimal risk can be accepted as permissible for nonconsenting subjects in nontherapeutic research.

The Commission affirms that the woman's decision for abortion does not, in itself, change the status of the fetus for purposes of protection. Thus, the same principles apply whether or not abortion is contemplated; in both cases, only minimal risk is acceptable.

Differences of opinion have arisen in the Commission, however, regarding the interpretation of risk to the fetus-to-be-aborted and thus whether some experiments that would not be permissible on a fetus-going-to-term might be permissible on a fetus-to-be aborted. Some members hold that no procedures should be applied to a fetus-going-to-term. Indeed, it was also suggested that any research involving fetuses-to-be-aborted must also involve fetuses-going-to-term. Others argue that, while a woman's decision for abortion does not change the status of the fetus per se, it does make a significant difference in one respect — namely, in the risk of harm to the fetus. For example, the injection of a drug which crosses the placenta may not injure the fetus which is aborted within two months after injection. There is always, of course, the possibility that a woman might change her mind about the abortion. Even taking this into account, however, some members argue that risks to the fetus-to-be-aborted may be considered "minimal" in research which would entail more than minimal risk for a fetus-going-to-term.

The question of consent is a complicated one in this area of research. The Commission holds that [illegible] part of the research design should be fully disclosed and clearly distinguished from those which are dictated by the health care needs of the pregnant woman or her fetus. Questions have been raised regarding the validity of parental proxy consent where the parent(s) have made a decision for abortion. The Commission recognizes that unresolved problems both of law and of fact surround this question. It is the considered opinion, however, that women who have decided to abort should not be presumed to abandon thereby all interest in and concern for the fetus. In view of the close relationship between the woman and the fetus, therefore, and the involvement of the woman in the research process, the woman's consent is considered necessary. The Commission is divided on the question of whether her consent alone is sufficient. Assignment of an advocate for the fetus was proposed as an additional safeguard; this issue will be thoroughly explored in connection with the Commission's review of the consent process. Most of the Commissioners agree that in view of the father's possible responsibility for the child, should it be brought to term, the objection of the father should be sufficient to veto. Several Commissioners, however, hold that for nontherapeutic research directed toward the pregnant woman, the woman's consent alone should be sufficient and the father should have no veto.

4. Research on the fetus during the abortion procedure or on the nonviable fetus *ex utero* raises sensitive problems because such a fetus must be considered a dying subject. By definition, therefore, the research is nontherapeutic in that the benefits will not accrue to the subject. Moreover, the question of consent is complicated because of the special vulnerability of the dying subject.

The Commission considers that the status of the fetus as dying alters the situation in two ways. First, the question of risk becomes less relevant, since the dying fetus cannot be "harmed" in the sense of "injured for life." Once the abortion procedure has begun, or after it is completed, there is no chance of a change of mind on the woman's part which will result in a living, injured subject. Second, however, while questions of risk become less relevant, considerations of respect for the dignity of the fetus continue to be of paramount importance, and require that the fetus be treated with the respect due to dying subjects. While dying subjects may not be "harmed" in the sense of "injured for life," issues of violation of integrity are nonetheless central. The Commission concludes, therefore, that out of respect for the dying subjects, no nontherapeutic interventions are permissible which would alter the duration of life of the nonviable fetus *ex utero*.

. . . .

Furthermore, it is possible that, due to mistaken estimation of gestational age, an abortion may issue in a possibly viable infant. If there is any danger that this might happen, research which would entail more than minimal risk would be absolutely prohibited. In order to avoid that possibility the Commission recommends that, should research during abortion be approved by national review, it be always on condition that estimated gestational age below 20 weeks. There is, of course, a moral and legal obligation to attempt to save the life of a possibly viable infant.

Finally, the Commission has been made aware that certain research, particularly that involving the living nonviable fetus, has disturbed the moral sensitivity of many persons. While it believes that its Recommendations would preclude objectionable research by adherence to strict review processes, problems of interpretation or application of the Commission's Recommendations may still arise. In that event, the Commission proposes ethical review at a national level in which informed public disclosure and assessment of the problems, the type of proposed research and the scientific and public importance of the expected results can take place.

NOTES AND QUESTIONS

1. The Commission's views pre-date the *Casey* decision and so must be evaluated in the light of that case as well as the other cases on autonomy and reproductive rights and family associations reflected in this book.
2. In Section 9, the Commission went on to recommend that fetal research be funded, whether therapeutic or nontherapeutic, consistent with the views excerpted above. Dissenting Commissioner David Louisell wrote:

I am compelled to disagree with the Commission's Recommendations (and the reasoning and definitions on which they are based) insofar as they succumb to the error of sacrificing the interests of innocent human life to a postulated social need. I fear this is the inevitable result of Recommendations 5 and 6. These would permit nontherapeutic research on the fetus in anticipation of abortion and during the abortion procedure, and on a living infant after abortion when the infant is considered nonviable, even though such research is precluded by recognized norms governing human research in general. Although the Commission uses adroit language to minimize the appearance of violating standard norms, no facile verbal formula can avoid the reality that under these Recommendations the fetus and nonviable infant will be subjected to nontherapeutic research from which other humans are protected.

. . .

A shorthand way, developed during the Commission's deliberations, of stating the principle that would adhere to recognized human experimentation norms and that should be recommended in place of Recommendation (5) is: No research should be permitted on a fetus-to-be-aborted that would not be permitted on one to go to term. This principle is essential if all of the unborn are to have the protection of recognized limits on human experimentation. Any lesser protection violates the autonomy and integrity of the fetus, and even a decision to have an abortion cannot justify ignoring this fact. There is not only the practical problem of a possible change of mind by the pregnant woman. For me, the chief vice of Recommendation 5 is that it permits an escape hatch from human experimentation principles merely by decision of a national ethical review body. No principled basis for an exception has been, nor in my judgement can be, formulated. The argument that the fetus-to-be-aborted "will die anyway" proves too much. All of us "will die anyway." A woman's decision to have an abortion, however protected by *Roe* and *Doe* in the interests of her privacy or freedom of her own body, does not change the nature or quality of fetal life.

Recommendation 6 concerns what is now called the "nonviable fetus *ex utero*" but which up to now has been known by the law, and I think by society generally, as an infant, however premature. This Recommendation is unacceptable to me because, on approval of a national review body, it makes certain infants up to five months gestational age potential research material, provided the mother who has of course consented to the abortion, also consents to the experimentation and the father has not objected. In my judgment all infants, however premature or inevitable their death, are within the norms governing human experimentation generally. We do not subject the aged dying to unconsented experimentation, nor should we the youthful dying.

Commissioner Karen Lebacqs, with the concurrence of Commissioner Albert Jonsen, wrote:

> [T]he establishment of criteria for "no risk" or "minimal risk" is obviously related to the interpretation of "harm." In general, the Commission has discussed "harm" in terms of two indices: (1) injury or diminished faculty, and (2) pain. A third commonly accepted definition of "harm" is "offense against right or morality"; this meaning of harm has been subsumed under the rubric of violation of dignity or integrity of the fetus, and thus is separated out of the Commission's deliberations on acceptable levels of risk. In establishing acceptable levels of risk, therefore, the Commission has been concerned with injury and pain to the fetus.
>
> Several ethicists argued cogently before the Commission that the ability to experience pain is morally relevant to decisions regarding research. Indeed, the argument was advanced that the ability to experience pain is a more appropriate consideration than is viability for purposes of establishing the limits of intervention into fetal life.
>
> However, scientific opinion is divided on the question of whether the fetus can experience pain — and on the appropriate indices on which to measure the experience of pain. Several experts argue that the fetus does not feel pain.
>
> I believe that the Commission has implicitly accepted this view in making Recommendation (6) regarding research on the fetus during the abortion procedure and on the nonviable fetus *ex utero*. Should this view not be correct, and should the fetus indeed be able to experience pain before the twentieth week of gestation, I would modify Recommendation (6) in two ways:
>
> First, the Recommendation as it now stands does not specify an acceptable level of risk. The reason for this omission is essentially as follows: in a dying subject prior to viability, "diminution of faculties" does not appear to be a meaningful index of harm since this index refers largely to future life expectations. Therefore, the critical meaning of "harm" for such a subject lies in the possibility of experiencing pain. If the fetus does not feel pain it cannot be "harmed" in this sense, and thus there is no risk of harm for such a fetus. It is for this reason that the Commission has not specified an acceptable level of "risk" for fetuses in this category, although it has been careful to protect the dignity of the fetus.
>
> Clearly, however, if the fetus does indeed feel pain, then it can be "harmed" by the above definition of harm. If so, then I would argue that an acceptable level of risk should be established at the same level as that considered acceptable for fetuses *in utero* — namely, "no risk" or "minimal risk."

Do you agree or disagree with the concerns expressed by Commissioners Louisell and Lebacqz?

3. Subsequently, the Department of Health and Human Services established a [illegible] Human Embryo Research Panel, pursuant to the AIH Revitalization Act of 1993, 42 U.S.C. § 289 a-1, removing many obstacles to fetal research. On September 27, 1994 the Panel filed its report. The pre-existing moratorium on federal funding for fetal research was lifted by President Clinton on January 22, 1993.

4. Evaluate the reasoning of the Commission, in terms of its view of the fetus and the roles of the mother and the father. Are they consistent with cases discussed earlier? If not, why not? Consider as well The Council of Europe Convention in Chapter 1 of this book — Is the Convention consistent with the Commission's views?

5. In particular, are you bothered by the Commissioner's view of tolerable risks; balancing of the interests of mother and fetus; according a veto to the father; treating the fetus as "dying"; permitting nontherapeutic research; providing for "proxy consent"? Are your objections matters of definition or substance?

6. For an excellent article, see Jose L. Gonzalez, M.D., Esq., *The Legitimization Of Fetal Tissue Transplantation Research Under* Roe v. Wade, 34 Creighton L. Rev. 895 (2001); and see Jason H. Casell, *Lengthening the Stem: Allowing Federally Funded Researchers to Derive Human Pluripotent Stem Cells from Embryos*, 34 U. Mich. J.L. Ref. 547 (2001).

PROBLEM 4–5 — Fetal Material and State Regulation

You are staff counsel to the Chair of the California State Senate Committee on Health Care, Medicine and Ethics. She is concerned about commercial development and exploitation of fetuses for fetal material. She is particularly concerned about two technologies, surrogate parenting and cloning, both of which might be used to generate anencephalic babies for the precise purpose of commercial sale of fetal material or organs. She asks you to draft a state regulatory code concerning these issues, and to do so while avoiding the pitfalls of the Illinois statute invalidated in [illegible]

What will the regulatory scheme look like? What weight must you give, if any, to federal law permitting fetal experimentation? Prohibiting it? Consider here the state statutes cited in footnote 7 of the *Lifchez* opinion.

Consider as well the recommendations of The National Commission for Protection of Human Subjects of Biomedical Research, in its *Report and Recommendation: Research on the Fetus* (1975) and the language of the Uniform Anatomical Gift Act (adopted by all fifty states) and Comment, *Playing God or Playing Scientist: State Laws Banning Embryological Procedures*, 27 Pac. L.J. 1331 (1996).

And finally, consider the reports that primordial cells had been isolated from pre-implantion embryos for the first time (without the use of federal funds) and that fetal stem cells could be used to grow organs, being "totipotent." (New York Times, November 10 and 12, 1998.)

§ 4.03 Health and Hazard

By the year 2000, major health problems have become very different from those at the dawn of the 20th century, when the principal concerns were infectious diseases, such as tuberculosis, diphtheria, malaria and, later, polio. The principal diseases now are degenerative, such as cancer, stroke, heart disease, and Alzheimers. And many of the principal health problems in the U.S. — both degenerative and traumatic — are a product of self-imposed hazard or abuse, by consumption of alcohol, drugs, tobacco or improper diet. Hazards of the environment, such as auto accidents, employment, spousal abuse and gun ownership or use, continue also having an effect on health.

To the extent that people "choose" such hazards, they harm not only themselves but those dependent upon them. As to this recall *Helling v. McKinney*, *supra,* § 1.03[1]. They also impose daunting burdens of cost and care upon society. Ethical issues arise when a clear connection can be drawn between tobacco use and illnesses such as lung cancer and coronary disease. Among the questions are those of response, of intervention and sanction, or of abandonment of the individual.

"Curing" these diseases may involve some of the public health concepts of the 1890s (such as quarantine and vaccination) but these collide with more recently developed concepts of autonomy and privacy. These in turn are of dubious value when the individual's "choice" is overborne by advertising and government subsidy. We begin with tobacco, and the *Cipollone* case.

[1] Self-Abuse: Tobacco and Alcohol

[a] Tobacco

The following cases have in common the ethical issues of whether a person may inflict harm on him or herself; whether others may or should intervene; and whether society should or must support the self-abuse. Central to these questions is the issue of autonomy of a competent person — may she later be heard to complain that she was in error? That was the dilemma posed by Rose Cipollone, now dead.

CIPOLLONE v. LIGGETT GROUP, INC.
893 F.2d 541 (3d Cir. 1990)

Becker, Circuit Judge.

I. Introduction

This appeal is from a final judgment in a protracted products liability case in which the plaintiff, Antonio Cipollone, seeks to hold Liggett Group, Inc., Lorillard, Inc., and Philip Morris, Inc., three of the leading firms in the tobacco industry, liable for the death from lung cancer of his wife, Rose Cipollone, who smoked cigarettes from 1942 until her death in 1984. . . .

. . . At the conclusion of the trial, the jury, answering a series of special interrogatories, returned a verdict in the sum of $400,000.00 for the plaintiff in his individual capacity on the breach of express warranty claim. The jury [illegible] strictly liable for failing to warn adequately of the hazards of their products, but returned a verdict in their favor on that claim because Mrs. Cipollone's comparative fault. More precisely, the jury apportioned 80% of the responsibility for Mrs. Cipollone's injuries to her because of its finding that she knew and appreciated the damages of cigarette smoking and voluntarily chose to smoke.

. . . .

II. The Relevant Facts Adduced at Trial

Rose Cipollone was born in 1925 and began to smoke in 1942. She smoked Chesterfield brand cigarettes, manufactured by Liggett, until 1955. In her deposition, introduced into evidence at the trial, she stated that she smoked the Chesterfield brand to be "glamorous," to "imitate" the "pretty girls and movie stars" depicted in Chesterfield advertisements, and because the advertisements stated that Chesterfield cigarettes were "mild." Mrs. Cipollone stated that she understood the description of Chesterfield cigarettes as "mild" to mean that the cigarettes were safe.

Mrs. Cipollone also testified that she was an avid reader of a variety of magazines, frequently listened to the radio, and often watched television during the years that she smoked the Chesterfield brand. Although she could not specifically remember which Chesterfield advertisements she saw or heard during those years, Chesterfield advertisements appeared continuously in those media during that period. Several of these advertisements were introduced into evidence. The following copy appeared commonly in Chesterfield magazine advertisements during the year 1952:

> PLAY SAFE Smoke Chesterfield.
>
> NOSE, THROAT, and Accessory Organs not Adversely Affected by Smoking Chesterfields. First such report ever published about any cigarette. A responsible consulting organization has reported the results of a continuing study by a competent medical specialist and his staff on the effects of smoking Chesterfield cigarettes. A group of people from various walks of life was organized to smoke only Chesterfields. For six months this group of men and women smoked their normal amount of Chesterfields — 10 to 40 a day. 45% of the group have smoked Chesterfields continually from one to thirty years for an average of 10 years each. At the beginning and at the end of the six-month period each smoker was given a thorough examination, including X-ray pictures, by the medical specialist and his assistants. The examination covered the sinuses as well as the nose, ears and throat. The medical specialist, after a thorough examination of every member of the group, stated: 'It is my opinion that the ears, nose, throat and accessory organs of all participating subjects examined by me were not adversely affected in the six-month period by smoking the cigarettes provided." . . .[1]

[1] Chesterfield magazine advertisements during this period also contained the following messages: Chesterfield contains only ingredients that give you the Best Possible Smoke — as

Television advertisements for the Chesterfield brand were also introduced into evidence. The Chesterfield cigarette was described as having "ingredients that make Chesterfield the best possible smoke as tested and approved by scientists from leading universities," and being manufactured with "electronic miracle" technology that makes "cigarettes . . . more better [sic] and safer for you." One advertisement stated "[n]ow Chesterfield is the first cigarette to present this scientific evidence on the effects of smoking — a medical specialist making regular bi-monthly examinations of a group of people from various walks of life — 45% of this group have smoked Chesterfield's for an average of over 10 years — after 8 months, the medical specialist reports that he observed no adverse effects to the nose, throat and sinuses of the group who were smoking Chesterfield. I'd say that means real mildness."

Mrs. Cipollone testified that she frequently listened to the radio show "Arthur Godfrey and His Friends," sponsored by the Chesterfield brand. The Chesterfield brand was marketed on the show as follows (text read by Mr. Godfrey):

> [Y]ou saw me read this last week but a lot of folks didn't and it's a very important message — especially those of you who smoke Chesterfields — you probably been wonderin' about this. You hear stuff all the time about "cigarettes are harmful to you" this and that and the other thing. . . .
>
> Here's an ad, you've seen it in the papers — please read it when you get it. If you smoke it will make you feel better, really.
>
> "Nose, throat and accessory organs not adversely affected by smoking Chesterfield. This is the first such report ever published about any cigarette. A responsible consulting organization has reported the results of a continuing study by a competent medical specialist and his staff on the effects of smoking Chesterfield cigarettes.
>
> "A group of people from various walks of life was organized to smoke only Chesterfields. For six months this group of men and women smoked their normal amount of Chesterfields — 10 to 40 a day. 45% of the group have smoked Chesterfields continually from one to thirty years for an average of 10 years each.
>
> "At the beginning and at the end of the six months period each smoker was given a thorough examination, including X-Ray pictures, by the medical specialist and his assistants. The examination covered the sinuses as well as the nose, ears and throat."
>
> Now — here's the important thing. "The medical specialist, after a thorough examination of every member of the group, stated: 'It is my opinion that the ears, nose, throat and accessory organs of all

tested and approved by scientists from leading universities. [Chesterfield cigarettes contain] PURE, COSTLY MOISTENING proved by over 40 years of continuous use in U.S.A. tobacco products as entirely safe for use in the mouth — chemically pure, far most costly glycerol and pure sugars which are natural to tobacco — nothing else. . .. Scientists from Leading Universities Make Sure that Chesterfield Contains Only Ingredients that Give You the Best Possible Smoke. AND NOW — CHESTERFIELD FIRST TO GIVE YOU SCIENTIFIC FACTS IN SUPPORT OF SMOKING. . . .

> participating subjects examined by me were not adversely affected in [illegible] the period by smoking the Chesterfield cigarettes provided.' "
>
> Now that ought to make you feel better if you've had any worries at all about it. I never did. I smoke two or three packs of these things every day. I feel pretty good. I don't know, I never did believe they did you any harm and now, we've got the proof. So — Chesterfields are the cigarette for you to smoke, be they regular size or king-size.[2]

In 1955, Mrs. Cipollone stopped smoking Chesterfield cigarettes and began to smoke L&M filter cigarettes, also made by Liggett. In response to a question as to why she switched to the L&M brand, Mrs. Cipollone stated that "[w]ell, they were talking about the filter tip, that it was milder and a miracle it would keep the stuff inside a trap, whatever." When asked why she desired the filter tip, she testified that "it was the new thing and I figured, well, go along[, and that] it was better [because t]he bad stuff would stay in the filter then." When asked whether concern about the "bad stuff" was due to a concern about her health, she stated "[n]ot really. . . . It was the trend. Everybody was smoking the filter cigarettes and I changed, too."

. . . .

Mr. Cipollone also introduced evidence as to how the L&M brand was marketed during the years that Mrs. Cipollone smoked that brand. One series of advertisements that appeared on television and in magazines at the outset of L&M's introduction to the public stated that L&M "miracle tip" filters were "just what the doctor ordered!"; the "just what the doctor ordered" phrase often appeared in a large bold typescript in magazine advertisements. The "miracle tip" was advertised as "remov[ing] the heavy particles, leaving you a Light and Mild smoke."

In 1968, Mrs. Cipollone stopped smoking the L&M brand and started smoking the Virginia Slims brand, manufactured by Philip Morris. She stated that she switched "because it was very glamorous and very attractive ads and [illegible] looking cigarette. That persuaded me." In the 1970s, Mrs. Cipollone switch to the Parliament brand, also manufactured by Philip [illegible] She testified that this brand was advertised as having a "recessed" filter and that she thought that this made it healthier. In 1974, she changed from the Parliament to the True brand, a cigarette manufactured by Lorillard, Inc. ("Lorillard") and advertised as low tar, upon the advice of her doctor, who had told her son to stop smoking.

---

[2] Many similar Arthur Godfrey advertisements were also introduced into evidence, including the following three: "You know you hear all this applesauce about — you'd better quit smoking, pal, or you won't be here long and stuff. Listen to this. [At this point Mr. Godfrey told his listeners about the same 'medical' study that he had related on September 24.] There's the story. Were not adversely affected. Chesterfield is the right — [now addressing Tony Marvin, the announcer] Will you hold that over there for me? — Chesterfield — you've been smoking'em, gosh, Tony, how many do you smoke a day?" [Mr. Marvin:] I run about 2½ packs a day, Arthur. [Mr. Godfrey:] "2½ packs a day. If he wasn't so tight, he'd smoke 3. LAUGHTER. They're wonderful cigarettes, in either size, you know, king-size, this size here, or the regular size, they're the same tobacco. Go ahead and smok'em and enjoy'em, they're wonderful." (Oct. 1, 1952).

From 1942 until the early 1980s, Mrs. Cipollone smoked between one pack and two packs of cigarettes per day. The only exception to this pattern was that, at the urging of her husband, Mrs. Cipollone substantially reduced her smoking during her first pregnancy in the 1940s. In 1981, Mrs. Cipollone was diagnosed as having lung cancer, but even though her doctors advised her to stop smoking, she was unable to do so. Mrs. Cipollone continued to smoke until June of 1982 when her lung was removed. Even after that, she smoked occasionally, in secret. She testified that she was "addicted" to cigarette smoking and that it was terribly difficult for her to give it up. She stopped smoking in 1983 after her cancer had spread widely and she had become terminally ill. Mrs. Cipollone died on October 21, 1984.

. . . .

There is also evidence that Mrs. Cipollone feared that her cigarette smoking would damage her health. When she developed a bad cough, her concern about the possible effect of smoking on her health led her, apparently prior to 1966, to make novenas to Saint Jude asking his intercession on her behalf to prevent her from developing cancer. There is also evidence, however, that Mrs. Cipollone disbelieved the reports linking cigarette smoking to cancer and other health problems. As explained above, there is evidence that she read the cigarette companies' advertisements, understood them as representing that the cigarettes were safe, and thus, as she put it, "was led to assume that [the cigarettes that I purchased] wouldn't harm me." She stated that she had often read cigarette company or Tobacco Institute statements, reported in articles about the health consequences of smoking or reproduced in advertisements, stating that the link between smoking and disease has not been proven. She also testified that because she found it so difficult to stop smoking, she "[m]aybe . . . didn't want to believe" the reports that she heard that smoking caused cancer or other diseases and that she "didn't believe" that her smoking would cause her to contract lung cancer. In addition, Mrs. Cipollone stated that she believed that "[t]obacco companies wouldn't do anything that was really going to kill you."

Procedural History

On August 1, 1983, Mr. and Mrs. Cipollone filed a complaint in the district court for the District of New Jersey, founded on diversity of citizenship, seeking damages against Liggett, Philip Morris, and Lorillard for the suffering and monetary losses resulting from Mrs. Cipollone's lung cancer. The complaint alleged that the lung cancer resulted from Mrs. Cipollone's smoking of cigarettes manufactured by the named defendants.

On May 31, 1985, following Mrs. Cipollone's death, and suing in his capacity as Mrs. Cipollone's executor and on his own behalf, Mr. Cipollone filed a third amended complaint, upon which the case was tried. The third amended complaint included damages claims against each defendant based on the following theories of liability:

1. Strict liability in tort (and negligence) on the theory that the defendants failed to warn adequately (or negligently failed to warn adequately) of the health effects of smoking ("the failure to warn claim");

2. Strict liability in tort on the theory that the defendants marketed [illegible] cigarettes rather than alternatively designed, safer cigarettes ("The design defect claim");

3. Strict liability in tort on the theory that the health risks of the defendants' cigarettes exceeded their social utility ("the generic risk-utility claim");

4. Breach of express warranty regarding the health effects of smoking ("the express warranty claim");

5. Fraud and misrepresentation in the advertising and promotion of cigarettes from 1940 to 1983 ("the fraudulent misrepresentation claim");

6. Conspiracy to defraud the public regarding the health effects of smoking ("the conspiracy to defraud claim").

. . . .

After a four-month trial, the jury deliberated for four and one half days and returned its verdict in the form of answers to special interrogatories.

. . . .

As the answers to the interrogatories indicate, the jury rejected the fraudulent misrepresentation claims and the conspiracy to defraud claims against all defendants. As to the failure to warn claim against Liggett, the jury concluded that Liggett breached its duty to warn of the health hazards of smoking before 1966, that this breach was a proximate cause of Mrs. Cipollone's smoking, and that Mrs. Cipollone's smoking was a proximate cause of her death. No damages were awarded on the failure to warn claim, however, because New Jersey's comparative fault law bars a plaintiff from recovering damages if she is more than 50% at fault for the injury, and the jury found that Mrs. Cipollone "voluntarily and unreasonably encounter[ed] a known danger by smoking cigarettes" and in so doing bore 80% of the responsibility for her injuries. As to the express warranty claim, the jury found that Liggett had breached an express warranty made to consumers. The jury awarded Mr. Cipollone $400,000 to compensate him for damages that he sustained from Liggett's breach of warranty; the jury awarded Mrs. Cipollone's estate no damages on the breach of warranty claim.

. . . .

V. Did the District Court Otherwise Err in Instructing the Jury on the Failure to Warn Claim?

. . . .

First, Liggett contends that it was under no duty to warn of the dangers of cigarettes because their dangers were commonly understood. We find that there is no basis for so holding as a matter of law, and that as a matter of fact the jury found otherwise.

. . . .

Liggett's more substantial contention has to do with the district court's instruction on causation, which defines proximate cause as follows:[3] a cause which necessarily set the other causes in motion and was a substantial contributing factor in bringing about the injury. Proximate cause is defined as a cause which naturally and probably led to and might have been expected to produce the result complained of.

The district court also instructed the jury that "there may be two or more concurrent and directly cooperative and efficient proximate causes of an injury" if the defendant was "a substantial contributing factor" in the plaintiff's injuries.

. . . .

As a substantive matter, Liggett is liable if its behavior proximately caused Mrs. Cipollone's cancer. For pleading purposes, Mr. Cipollone divided Liggett's conduct up into different preestablished legal categories, i.e., a tort-based failure to warn claim and a contract-based express warranty claim. Although the elements of proof necessary to prove liability under these two legal theories differ, the procedural pleading and proof requirements do not transform Mr. Cipollone's allegations into two completely different lawsuits. Thus, Mr. Cipollone does not have to prove that each legal violation proximately caused his wife's cancer. He need only prove that the totality of Liggett's wrongful behavior, which as doctrinal matter is divided into a tort and contract claim, proximately caused her cancer.

Second, Liggett may be arguing that Mrs. Cipollone's conduct would have caused her cancer no matter what Liggett did, and that therefore Liggett's conduct cannot be considered the cause of Mrs. Cipollone's injury. This argument is plainly inconsistent with the established jurisprudence of concurrent causation. The "substantial factor" test has traditionally been used in concurrent cause cases, i.e., cases in which there are two or more causes each of which is sufficient to cause the injury. Our preemption decision makes this case quite comparable to a concurrent cause situation. Liggett's pre-1966 behavior might have been enough, by itself, to cause Mrs. Cipollone's cancer, and its post-1965 behavior might also have been enough to cause the cancer. Thus, just as it is unfair to let one tortfeasor completely escape liability for his fire merely because another tortfeasor caused another fire, so it is unfair to let Liggett completely escape liability for its pre-1966 behavior merely because its post-1965 behavior (or that of its codefendants), which was immunized from scrutiny at the trial, might also have caused enough damage, by itself, to kill her.

Third, Liggett may be arguing that Mr. Cipollone had to prove, to a greater degree of certainty than the district court's instruction required, that Liggett's failure to warn caused her injuries. Under this theory, the fact that defendant's conduct might have been a substantial factor in causing Mrs. Cipollone's cancer would not be enough; rather, Mr. Cipollone would have had to prove, by a preponderance of the evidence, that if Liggett had not breached

[3] As the district court carefully instructed, this case involves two distinct causal inquiries: first, whether Liggett's violation of legal norms caused Mrs. Cipollone to smoke, and second, whether the cigarettes that Mrs. Cipollone smoked as a result of Liggett's violations proximately caused her cancer.

its warranty and if it had warned consumers of the dangers of smoking, Mrs. Cipollone would not have contracted cancer. In other words, Liggett argues that plaintiff had to prove that "but for" Liggett's conduct, the injury would not have occurred. We find this argument to be inconsistent with New Jersey law.

. . . .

Did the District Court Err in Failing to Instruct the Jury That Mrs. Cipollone's Nonreliance on Liggett's Safety Advertisements Would Prevent Her From Recovering on Her Express Warranty Claim?

We turn now to another major area of dispute between the parties, one that implicates the conceptual basis of express warranty law. Mr. Cipollone brought his express warranty claim under U.C.C. § 2-313(1), which provides:

(1) Express warranties by the seller are created as follows:

(a) Any affirmation of fact or promise made by the seller to the buyer which relates to the goods and becomes *part of the basis of the bargain* creates an express warranty that the goods shall conform to the affirmation or promise.

(b) Any description of the goods which is made *part of the basis of the bargain* creates an express warranty that the goods shall conform to the description.

N.J.S.A. § 12A:2-313(1). With respect to this issue, the district court gave the following instructions to the jury:

> [P]laintiff must prove . . . that Liggett, made one or more of the statements claimed by the plaintiff and that such statements were affirmations of fact or promises by Liggett . . . [and] that such statements were part of the basis of the bargain between Liggett and consumers like Rose Cipollone. . . .
>
> The law does not require plaintiff to show that Rose Cipollone specifically relied on Liggett's warranties.
>
> Ordinarily a guarantee or promise in an advertisement or other description of the goods becomes part of the basis of the bargain if it would naturally induce the purchase of the product and no particular reliance by the buyer on such statement needs to be shown. However, if the evidence establishes that the claimed statement cannot fairly be viewed as entering into the bargain, that is, that the statement would not naturally induce the purchase of a product, then no express warranty has been created.

4 J.A. at 232-34.

Liggett contends that this interpretation of "part of the basis of the bargain" is flawed because the jury should also have been instructed that Mrs. Cipollone's nonreliance on the advertisements would preclude those advertisements from becoming "part of the basis of the bargain." Liggett argues that the express warranty verdict must therefore be set aside. Although our interpretation of the precise meaning of "reliance" differs somewhat from Liggett's, we agree.[4]

A.

Authority on the question whether reliance is a necessary element of section 2-313 is divided. Although a few courts have held that reliance is not a necessary element of section 2-313, the more common view has been that it is, and that either a buyer must prove reliance in order to recover on an express warranty or the seller must be permitted to rebut a presumption of reliance in order to preclude recovery. Some treatise writers support this interpretation. No New Jersey court or panel of this court has squarely addressed the question.

The history of section 2-313(1)(a), although informative, fails to give a clear answer as to whether reliance is required. . . .

. . . .

. . . Without a reliance requirement, one runs the risk of draining the term "basis of the bargain" of all meaning, because the buyer's subjective state of mind becomes completely irrelevant. The district court instructed the jury that a statement could be considered part of the basis of the bargain if it "would naturally induce the purchase of the products." This instruction is completely objective and would permit a buyer to sue for breach of express warranty even if the seller's warranties were advertisements made in another state or country, and even if the buyer did not hear of the claims in these advertisements until the day that she walked into an attorney's office to bring suit for personal injury. It strains the language to say that a statement is part of the "basis" of the buyer's "bargain," when that buyer had no knowledge of the statement's existence.

The above arguments notwithstanding, it is possible to read the "basis of the bargain" requirement as requiring some subjective inducement of the buyer, without requiring a reliance finding. Requiring that the buyer rely on an advertisement, whether by imposing this burden initially on the buyer bringing suit, or by allowing the seller to rebut a presumption of reliance, puts a heavy burden on the buyer — a burden that is arguably inconsistent with the U.C.C. as a whole, with other comments to section 2-313 in particular, and with several commentators' suggestions in this area.

---

[4] Initially, we emphasize that a representation made by a seller is not an express warranty if it is made in such a manner that both the seller and the buyer should understand to be a representation upon which the buyer will not rely. "[A]ll descriptions by merchants must be read against the applicable trade usages. . . ." N.J.S.A. § 12A:2-313 U.C.C. Comment 5. A representation made in a manner that is generally recognized not to be a basis upon which purchasers make a decision to purchase goods cannot be a warranty when read against "applicable trade usages." This requirement is in accord with the traditional common law "puffing" exception in the law of contracts. But Liggett has not contended, and we do not think it could, that its advertisements to consumers are generally recognized as not forming the basis upon which cigarette purchasing decisions are made. If such were the case, Liggett would not have spent millions of dollars on advertising.

. . . .

. . . We believe [illegible] construction of section 2-313 is neither Liggett's reliance theory, which fails to explain how reliance can be relevant to "what a seller agreed to sell," or the district court's purely objective theory, which fails to explain how an advertisement that a buyer never even saw becomes part of the "basis of the bargain." Instead, we believe that the New Jersey Supreme Court would hold that a plaintiff effectuates the "basis of the bargain" requirement of section 2-313 by proving that she read, heard, saw or knew of the advertisement containing the affirmation of fact or promise. Such proof will suffice "to weave" the affirmation of fact or promise "into the fabric of the agreement," U.C.C. Comment 3, and thus make it part of the basis of the bargain. We hold that once the buyer has become aware of the affirmation of fact or promise, the statements are presumed to be part of the "basis of the bargain" unless the defendant, by "clear affirmative proof," shows that the buyer knew that the affirmation of fact or promise was untrue. We believe that by allowing a defendant to come forward with proof that the plaintiff did not believe in the warranty,[5] we are reconciling, as the New Jersey Supreme Court would want us to, the U.C.C. comments, the U.C.C. case law, and traditional contract principles, which serve as the background rules to the U.C.C.

As indicated above, Comment 4 and Comment 7, as well as the largely dominant objective theory of contracts, militate in favor of an interpretation of express warranty that ignores the buyer's subjective state of mind. Under the extreme version of this theory apparently adopted by the district court, all the buyer should have to show is what the seller agreed to sell. In other words, an express warranty would be created when a seller makes statements to the public at large that would induce a reasonable buyer to purchase the product, even if the actual buyer never heard those statements. We find this result untenable, however. . . .

Much of the case law supports this "belief" principle. A statement in the bill of sale that the goods are new does not constitute an express warranty [illegible] the buyer and the seller knew that the statement was false. When a buyer has operated trucks before and knows that they need [illegible] cannot sue in express warranty on the seller's statement that the trucks were in good condition. "The same representation that could have constituted an express warranty early in the series of transactions, might not have qualified as an express warranty in a later transaction if the buyer had acquired independent knowledge as to the fact asserted." . . .

. . . .

[5] If the defendant proves that the buyer did not believe in the warranty, the plaintiff should then be given the opportunity to show that the buyer nonetheless relied on the warranty. It is possible to disbelieve, but still rely on, the existence of a warranty. In this sense, the buyer can "buy" a lawsuit. Thus, if the buyer disbelieved the warranty, but could prove that she was relying on it when she bought the product, she could return the product for stipulated damages — for example, a refund — or economic damages — the difference between "the value of the goods accepted and the value of the goods would have had if they had been warranted," U.C.C. § 2-714. Such a buyer could not recover consequential damages, however. . . .

B.

Applying our interpretation of section 2-313 to the case at bar, we conclude that the district court's jury instructions were erroneous for two reasons. First, they did not require the plaintiff to prove that Mrs. Cipollone had read, seen, or heard the advertisements at issue. Second, they did not permit the defendant to prove that although Mrs. Cipollone had read, seen, or heard the advertisements, she did not believe the safety assurances contained therein. We must therefore reverse and remand for a new trial on this issue.

There is ample evidence from which a jury could conclude that Mrs. Cipollone saw, read, or heard the advertisements. She frequently listened to the Arthur Godfrey show, and frequently read magazines that contained the advertisements. Thus, the awareness question is not problematic. However, there is also evidence that family members brought the hazards of smoking to her attention. Thus Liggett might be able to prove that she did not believe the advertisements that she saw.

. . . .

VII. A. Did the District Court Err in Failing to Instruct the Jury That Comparative Fault Principles Apply to an Express Warranty Claim?

Liggett contends that New Jersey law permits a manufacturer to assert a comparative fault defense to an express warranty products liability suit and that the district court consequently erred in failing to so instruct the jury. We agree that comparative fault principles may be applicable in some express warranty cases, but we do not believe that they are applicable here.

. . . .

As discussed in Part VI, in order to make out a *prima facie* express warranty claim, Mr. Cipollone must show that Liggett's affirmations were part of the basis of the bargain. As long as the plaintiff can show that Mrs. Cipollone knew of Liggett's affirmations of fact, those affirmations are presumed to be a basis of the bargain unless Liggett can prove that she did not believe those advertisements. Arthur Godfrey referred to the fears about smoking as "applesauce." If Mrs. Cipollone believed him, she could not have had the subjective knowledge about the harms of smoking that would permit a jury to conclude that she voluntarily assumed a known risk.[6]

. . . .

If she bought some cigarettes while believing in the advertisements and then learned that the advertisements were false and smoked those previously purchased cigarettes anyway, then she would have been assuming a known risk when she smoked the previously purchased, warranted cigarettes. We conclude that under such circumstances, she could be barred, by reason of

[6] Defendants could prevent Mr. Cipollone's recovery on the express warranty claim if, despite finding the warranty, the jury finds that the plaintiff misused or abused the cigarettes. There is no evidence of misuse or abuse in this record, however. Plaintiff was using the cigarettes just as Liggett advertised that she should.

contributory fault, from recovering on an express warranty claim. But that [illegible] finding that it was those specific cigarettes, bought while believing the advertisements but smoked after she knew that the ads were false, that caused her cancer. No reasonable jury could find this unless Mrs. Cipollone bought vast amounts of cigarettes in bulk, and there is no evidence in the record that she did.

Liggett's defense is thus more appropriate in the more typical U.C.C. case. For instance, if a tire purchaser relied on the affirmations of the seller, then discovered that the seller's affirmation was false, and then used the tire anyway, she could be barred from recovering on an express warranty claim under an assumption for risk theory. Because the purchaser believed the affirmations when she purchased the tire, the tire would be warranted. Still the law would not allow her to collect on that warranty if she used the tire after she learned that the seller's affirmations were false. This scenario is inapplicable in the cigarette context because the few cigarettes used after learning of a warranty's falsity cannot cause the kind of harm that one defective tire can.

In sum, we find that a comparative fault defense is available in an express warranty action, but only to the extent that the defendant can show that the buyer misused or abused the product or used the product after learning that the warranty was false. We do not think that that would be possible in this case. . . .

. . . .

B.

The same rationale that overcomes Liggett's comparative fault defense overcomes Liggett's contention that Mrs. Cipollone's knowledge of the advertisements' falsity breaks the chain of causation linking Liggett's breach to Mrs. Cipollone's injury. Liggett contends that the district court erred in failing to instruct the jury that if a buyer uses a product with knowledge of its warranty-breaching defect, any personal injuries arising from that use did not proximately result from the breach of warranty. . . .

Like the comparative fault defense, however, the knowing [illegible] cause argument applies in the kind of case represented in the tire hypothetical outlined above, not the cigarette sales at issue in this case. If a buyer uses a tire after having discovered a warranty-breaching condition that makes use of that tire unreasonable, then she cannot collect consequential damages under the warranty. In the instant case, however, once the plaintiff discovered that Liggett's advertisements were false, the cigarettes she purchased after that time must, as a matter of law, have been unwarranted, and therefore would not be considered by a jury asked to determine whether the cigarettes she smoked that were in breach of Liggett's warranty proximately caused her lung cancer.

Thus, both the comparative fault and the causal chain arguments fail to defeat the express warranty claim because both contentions depend on Liggett's proving that Mrs. Cipollone knew that the advertisements were false. But the basis of the bargain provision in N.J.S.A. § 12A:2-313 requires that the buyer believe the advertisements. If Liggett proves that she did not believe their advertisements, then there is no warranty in the first place. . . .

Liggett must be given the opportunity at the outset to prove that at some point prior to January 1, 1966, Mrs. Cipollone ceased to believe, or never believed, Liggett's advertisements. If the jury finds such disbelief, they must be instructed to find that the advertisements could not have formed the basis of the bargain for cigarettes she purchased after that date. As to cigarettes purchased and smoked before that date, however, for which the advertisements would constitute a basis of the bargain, Liggett should not be given another opportunity to prove what they failed to prove in the first instance, i.e., that Mrs. Cipollone did not believe the advertisements.

Was There Sufficient Evidence to Support a Jury Finding That Mrs. Cipollone's Injury Was Caused by Liggett's Breach of Express Warranty?

. . . .

Many Chesterfield and L&M advertisements were submitted to the jury. Liggett contends that "[n]one of them could constitute to a reasonable person a warranty covering serious health effects in the future from long term use of cigarettes." We disagree.

One Chesterfield advertisement stated, without qualification, that "NOSE, THROAT, and Accessory Organs [are] not Adversely Affected by Smoking Chesterfields." The advertisement discussed a "study by a competent medical specialist and his staff on the effects of smoking Chesterfield cigarettes" on a study group that included "men and women" who had "continually" smoked "10 to 40" cigarettes per day for "one to thirty years." Members of the study group were "given a thorough examination, including X-ray pictures" at "the beginning and at the end of" a "six-month []period." According to the advertisement, "[t]he medical specialist, after a thorough examination of every member of the group," concluded that "the ears, nose, throat and accessory organs of all participating subjects examined . . . were not adversely affected in the six-month period by smoking the cigarettes provided."

In a radio commercial, Arthur Godfrey related the story of another of these "six-month[] period" studies involving thirty-year chain smokers and stated that the study was "proof" of the proposition that Chesterfield cigarettes "never . . . did you any harm." Mr. Godfrey also told his listeners that he could not remember ever seeing a "gravestone" stating that the buried individual had "[s]moked [t]oo [m]uch." One magazine advertisement declared in a bold typescript that the consumer should "PLAY SAFE" and "Smoke Chesterfield." A series of television and magazine advertisements for the L&M brand stated that the cigarettes were "just what the doctor ordered."

We hold that a reasonable jury could conclude from these advertisements, and the many others entered into evidence, that Liggett had represented to the consumer that the long-term smoking of Chesterfield or L&M cigarettes would not endanger the consumer's health, and that these warranties were untrue. . . .

. . . .

The Risk-Utility Claim

The District Court ruled that the New Jersey Products Liability Act, N.J.S.A. § 2A:58C [hereinafter "The Act"] operated in this case to bar plaintiff's risk-utility claim.[7] Section 3(a)(2) of the Act provides that if the plaintiff asserts a design defect claim against a manufacturer, the manufacturer shall not be liable if:

> The characteristics of the product are known to the ordinary consumer or user, and the harm was caused by an unsafe aspect of the product that is an inherent characteristic of the product and that would be recognized by the ordinary person who uses or consumes the product with the ordinary knowledge common to the class of persons for whom the product is intended. . . .

. . . .

We cannot affirm the district court's decision to deny, as a matter of law, plaintiff's generic risk-utility claim because, applying the language of the Act, we cannot find, and we do not think that there was sufficient evidence for the district court to find, that the "inherent[ly] [dangerous] characteristic[s]" of cigarettes were known to the "ordinary consumer or user," prior to 1966. This is an issue of fact for the jury.[8]

. . . Therefore we will remand on this issue, and, if the New Jersey Supreme Court has not written expansively enough to dispose of this issue before the case is retried, the plaintiff should be allowed to proceed on his generic risk-utility claim.

. . . .

Did the District Court Err in Holding That Federal Law Preempted Plaintiff's Intentional Tort Claims?

Mr. Cipollone contends that the district court misconstrued our decision on the preemptive effect of the Federal Cigarette Labeling and Advertising Act ("Labeling Act") by holding that it preempts post-1966 intentional tort claims. As amended, the Labeling Act states:

> It is . . . the purpose of this chapter . . . to establish a comprehensive Federal program to deal with cigarette labeling and advertising with respect to any relationship between smoking and health, whereby —
>
> (1) the public may be adequately informed about any adverse health effects of cigarette smoking by inclusion of warning notices on each package of cigarettes and in each advertisement of cigarettes; and

[7] The risk-utility claim alleged that the risk of cigarettes outweighed their social utility.

[8] The district court (in an unpublished opinion of October 27, 1987) apparently relied on comment i to Section 402A of the RESTATEMENT (SECOND) OF TORTS, which the drafters of the Product Liability Act meant to incorporate. *See* N.J.S.A. § 2A:58C-1, Senate Judiciary Committee Statement at 465. Comment i says that "[g]ood tobacco is not unreasonably dangerous merely because the effects of smoking may be harmful." We reject the applicability of comment i in this situation. The fact that the New Jersey Legislature endorsed comment i in 1987 does not mean that the ordinary consumer must have known about the harms of smoking in, for example, 1958.

(2) commerce and the national economy may be (A) protected to the maximum extent consistent with this declared policy and (B) not impeded by diverse, nonuniform, and confusing cigarette labeling and advertising regulations with respect to any relationship between smoking and health.

In our preemption decision, we applied the doctrine of implied preemption and held that in light of section 1331's declaration of congressional purpose

the Act preempts . . . state law damage actions relating to smoking and health that challenge either the adequacy of the warning on cigarette packages or the propriety of a party's actions with respect to the advertising and promotion of cigarettes. . . .

. . . Mr. Cipollone contends on appeal that the district court erred in construing our preemption decision to stand for "the extreme and untenable proposition that all of plaintiff's claims based on intentional tort, fraud and misrepresentation were preempted for the post-1966 period." Mr. Cipollone contends that "there is obviously a logical distinction between failure to warn, which derives from a breach of existing duty, and intentional misrepresentation, which emanates from defendants' affirmative and gratuitous undertaking to misrepresent facts to the public" because "[l]iability imposed for intentional tort would not impose requirements on defendants with respect to the warnings contained on the label or in cigarette advertisements."

We disagree. Plaintiff's intentional tort claim is founded on an allegation that defendants "intentionally, wil[l]fully, and wantonly, through their advertising, attempted to neutralize the [federally mandated] warnings that were given regarding the adverse effects of cigarette smoking." The plaintiff's claim manifestly "challenge[s] . . . the propriety" of the defendants' "actions with respect to the advertising and promotion of cigarettes." The district court did not err in construing our preemption decision.[9]

Conclusion

For the foregoing reasons we will:

(1) affirm the district court's order dismissing plaintiff's post-1965 failure to warn, express warranty, and intentional tort claims against the defendants Liggett, Lorillard, and Philip Morris;

(2) reverse the district court's order in favor of defendants Liggett, Lorillard, and Philip Morris, barring plaintiff's generic risk-utility claim as a matter of law;

(3) reverse the district court's judgment in favor of defendant, Liggett, and against plaintiff on plaintiff's failure to warn claim;

(4) reverse the district court's judgment in favor of plaintiff and against defendant, Liggett, on plaintiff's express warranty claim;

[9] Lorillard argues in its brief that Mr. Cipollone's risk-utility claim is also barred, impliedly, by the Labeling Act. As the language quoted in text indicates, however, the Labeling Act was meant to apply to cigarette companies' actions with respect to the advertising and promotion of cigarettes. The risk-utility claim involves the basic decision to market the product. As we held in our earlier preemption decision, "we cannot say that the scheme created by the Act is 'so pervasive' or 'so dominant' as to eradicate all of the Cipollone's claims. . . .

(5) reverse the district court's order granting plaintiff's motion for summary judgment striking defendants' affirmative defenses based on the statute of limitations; and

(7) remand for a new trial.

Gibbons, Chief Judge, concurring:

I join in the opinion of the court. I write separately to observe that the enormous complications which arose during the trial of this complex case are largely due to the interlocutory ruling of this court to the effect that some state law claims were preempted by the Federal Cigarette Label and Advertising Act (Labeling Act). . . . When a case involves multiple theories of liability, the application of which depends on what facts are found, it will rarely be true that an interlocutory appeal will "materially advance the ultimate termination of the litigation." . . .

More fundamentally, I believe that our interlocutory ruling on the preemptive effect of the Labeling Act, to the extent that we reached a definitive ruling, was wrong as a matter of law, and should be overruled by the court in banc. . . .

Thus, while I join in Part XII of the opinion of the court, I do so only because this panel is bound by what I believe to be an erroneous opinion of the Court.

NOTES AND QUESTIONS

1. The United States Supreme Court reviewed the Court of Appeals' opinion, 505 U.S. 504 (1992). In an opinion by Justice Stevens, it held that Congress' 1969 Act preempted state law, but only "with respect to advertising or promotion" of cigarettes. It held the Act did not affect the claims based on fraud, conspiracy or express warranty.

2. In the 1990s, a number of states sued tobacco manufacturers for increased costs to healthcare programs, leading to several multi-billion dollar settlements. Two news items from 1998 were of particular interest. British tobacco firms, chiefly B.A.T., developed an especially potent nicotine leaf called Y-1 during the 1960s and 1970s, marketed by American firms in the 1980s and 1990s. Executives denied manipulating nicotine or that it was addictive. Secondly, on September 22, 1998, DNA Plant Technology pleaded guilty and was fined $100,000 in Washington, D.C. for exporting Y-1 seeds developed for Brown & Williamson.

3. Self-abuse, depending upon one's definition, is perhaps the leading cause of health care problems in the United States. Obesity, for example, is a crippling affliction, affecting one's ability to work, associate with others and even ultimately to survive. Consumption of alcohol and narcotics is a main contributing factor in the proliferation of automobile deaths and property thefts. Far more than all of these — overeating, consumption of alcohol, usage of drugs — tobacco consumption causes death and disability from cancer, heart attacks, emphysema and other systemic or organ disorders.

4. Mrs. Cipollone therefore represents an important figure in the law and ethics of health care. By most standards, she was a perfectly competent woman who made a knowing and informed choice over decades to abuse her body and destroy herself. Did she have an ethical obligation — to herself or others — not to do so? Did *others* have an ethical obligation to prevent her from abusing herself: husband, children, physicians, manufacturers of cigarettes, their suppliers or advertising agencies, the physicians who did research for them, Arthur Godfrey?

5. Congress, of course, in the 1960s addressed the health problems of tobacco and provided that there should be federal cigarette labeling. It also pre-empted state law claims. Was this to help the industry or the consumer? Should it, at the same time, have continued agricultural subsidies to tobacco growers of two billion dollars annually?

6. What of the comparative fault analysis? Are not the manufacturers on good ground in saying that, although they presented their products as safe and healthful, Mrs. Cipollone simply did not believe them? And, more significantly, that she chose to smoke despite this?

7. Does the warranty mode of analysis in effect amount to a strict liability imposition? Are cigarettes, by definition, "dangerous instrumentalities"?

8. Finally, what of the risk-utility claim? As a legal concept or instrument, how effective or fair is it? The Restatement of Torts recognizes that there may be legitimate consumer products that are inherently unsafe, yet marketable. Does tobacco qualify? As an ethical concept, would Rawls approve? For more on risk-utility analysis and tobacco, *see Horton v. American Tobacco*, 667 So. 2d 1289 (Miss. 1995); *Dewey v. R. J. Reynolds Tobacco Co.,* 577 A. 2d 1239 (D.J. 1990); *Gilbey v. American Tobacco*, 582 So. 2d 1263 (Louis. 1991); *Forster v. R. J. Reynolds*, 437 N.W.2d 655 (Minn. 1989); *American Tobacco v. Grinnell*, 951 S.W.2d 420 (Tex. 1997).

BUCKINGHAM v. R.J. REYNOLDS TOBACCO CO.*
142 N.H. 822, 713 A.2d 381 (1998)

Horton, Justice.

. . . .

Count I of the plaintiff's writ of summons is a strict liability claim based on the Restatement (Second) of Torts § 402A. The plaintiff alleged that Ms. Ramsey-Buckingham was diagnosed with terminal lung cancer resulting from her exposure to environmental tobacco smoke (ETS) from cigarettes manufactured or sold by the defendants. Although Ms. Ramsey-Buckingham did not smoke cigarettes or use tobacco products, the plaintiff asserts that it was foreseeable by the defendants that bystanders, like Ms. Ramsey-Buckingham, would be exposed to ETS. The plaintiff contends that the cigarettes made or sold by the defendants were defective because they were in an unreasonably dangerous condition, in that the cigarettes were dangerous beyond the

* Citation material has been omitted from this case.

expectations of the ordinary consumer and the utility of smoking did not outweigh the risk caused by ETS. The plaintiff did not allege a defect in the cigarettes other than their dangerous character.

Count II of the plaintiff's claim is based on the Restatement (Second) of Torts § 389. The plaintiff additionally alleged that the defendants knew or should have known that it was unlikely that their products would be made reasonably safe prior to their customary and intended use, and that it was foreseeable that Ms. Ramsey-Buckingham would be endangered by ETS from the defendants' cigarettes.

. . . .

I. Strict Liability Under Section 402A

With regard to count I of the plaintiff's writ, we hold that the plaintiff has failed to state a claim upon which relief may be granted because the complaint does not allege that the product was "defective" and "unreasonably dangerous" as separate elements. Instead, the plaintiff alleges only that "[t]he cigarettes sold by the defendants were defective or unsuitable at the time of sale in that they were in an unreasonably dangerous condition for innocent bystanders such as the plaintiff." The plaintiff's argument that "defect" is not a "separate and distinct element of proof" from the "unreasonably dangerous" element is not borne out by the language of section 402A, the history of its adoption, or our case law.

We have adopted the tort of strict liability as set out in the Restatement (Second) of Torts § 402A. Section 402A imposes liability for selling "any product in a defective condition unreasonably dangerous to the user or consumer" when the product causes injury to the user or consumer. In other words, "the basis of any claim involving products liability, is an allegation of a defect associated with the product, which makes the product unreasonably dangerous, and causes the injury for which recovery is sought."

If the plaintiff were correct that a product is per se defective if it is unreasonably dangerous, then it would be redundant for section 402A to include both the terms "defective" and "unreasonably dangerous." The operative phrase used in § 402A of the Restatement (Second) of T[illegible] defective condition unreasonably dangerous' was deliberately chosen to make it clear that the product must be defective, and that the manufacturer of a product that may involve some danger, but that is not defective, will not be held liable.

. . . .

When the plaintiff cannot allege that something is "wrong" with the product, strict liability should not be used as a tool of social engineering to mandate that manufacturers bear the entire risk and costs of injuries caused by their products. . . .

II. Restatement (Second) of Torts § 389

Count II of the plaintiff's writ was based on the Restatement (Second) of Torts § 389. The trial court dismissed this count on the grounds that New

Hampshire law does not recognize a claim based on section 389, which provides:

Chattel Unlikely to be Made Safe for Use.

> One who supplies directly or through a third person a chattel for another's use, knowing or having reason to know that the chattel is unlikely to be made reasonably safe before being put to a use which the supplier should expect it to be put, is subject to liability for physical harm caused by such use to those whom the supplier should expect to use the chattel or to be endangered by its probable use, and who are ignorant of the dangerous character of the chattel or whose knowledge thereof does not make them contributorily negligent, although the supplier has informed the other for whose use the chattel is supplied of its dangerous character. Restatement (Second) of Torts § 389.

The scope of liability under section 389 has been summarized as follows:

> Under section 389 a supplier of a chattel who has informed the persons to whom he supplied the chattel of its dangerous condition may be held liable to persons ignorant of the dangerous condition of the chattel if he knows or has reason to know that the chattel is unlikely to be made reasonably safe before being put to its expected use. If the supplier of a chattel knows or has information from which a person of reasonable intelligence would infer that it is unlikely that the chattel will be made reasonably safe, the fact that he has informed the person through whom the chattel is supplied does not absolve him from liability. However, a supplier has no duty under section 389 to determine whether the chattel will be made reasonably safe — liability arises only when the supplier knows or has information from which he should know that there is a substantial probability that the chattel will not be made safe before it is used. Among the circumstances which render it unlikely that it will be made safe are knowledge of the fact that the chattel will be used so soon after it is turned over that it is substantially certain that no change will be made or that the person through whom it is supplied is financially incapable of making it safe, or is notoriously careless. There are also some chattels which are so unsafe for the use for which they are likely to be put that the supplier cannot reasonably assume that the warning will be effective. Section 389 imposes liability upon the supplier in those situations.

As the plaintiff correctly argues, section 389 is not a form of strict liability because it requires the defendant's knowledge of the product's dangerous condition and does not require that the product be defective. . . .

Section 389 is simply a statement of basic negligence principles of foreseeability and fault in the supplier context. . . .

We accept the plaintiff's invitation and adopt section 389 as a proper statement of the law of supplier negligence. . . .

The comments to section 389 make it clear that a bystander, assuming he is within the scope of foreseeability of risk, is owed a duty under law and may recover on a showing of breach, damage, and causation. . . .

. . . .

A review of the pleadings in this case discloses sufficient allegations to support a cause of action in negligence based on the principles stated in section 389 of the Restatement (Second) of Torts. Accordingly, we reverse the trial court's ruling on count II.

This case should proceed to discovery as a negligence case. Through this process, the parties may learn the extent of the suppliers' knowledge of the hazards of the products they supplied, the suppliers' expectations as to the use of the product and those that might reasonably be affected, the extent of the plaintiff's knowledge of the hazards involved in the product's use, any actual causation of the damage alleged, and any conduct of the plaintiff material to comparative negligence.

Affirmed in part; reversed in part; remanded.

NOTES AND QUESTIONS

1. Procedurally, what difference does it make whether the case goes forward on a strict liability or a negligence theory? On remand, what will the plaintiffs have to prove? Will they succeed?

   Is there something paradoxical, indeed perverse, in denying liability because cigarettes — in causing cancer — are not "defective"; they are simply functioning as *designed*? *Would* allowing liability under § 402 constitute "social engineering"?

3. In fairness, how can the manufacturers foresee and control the harm posed to those other than the purchaser/consumer? If they cannot, should they still be held liable? And how widely can the circle of victims be drawn? As to this, see *Helling v. McKinney*, *supra* § 1.03[1].

4. And what of the issues raised in the *Cipollone* case, of assumption of risk, reliance, duty to avoid? Do those operate against the victim of [illegible]

5. In addition to self-abuse through consuming tobacco, Americans injure themselves and others — by the tens of thousands — through consuming alcohol. This may rise to the level of a disease, alcoholism, and it may — arguably — lead to insanity. The latter issue is raised in the *Egelhoff* case.

6. Some 400,000 deaths in America annually are attributable to tobacco consumption. Ethical issues abound in the public's support of tobacco production and the legal limits on the liability of producers. What follows are three brief excerpts of recent efforts to respond to these issues — the FDA attempt to regulate nicotine as a "drug," the efforts by Massachusetts to regulate cigarette advertising, and the participation of Rhode Island in the 1999 Multi-State Settlement Agreement, ending suits brought by 40 states to recover healthcare expenses resulting from tobacco consumption.

FOOD & DRUG ADMIN. v. BROWN & WILLIAMSON TOBACCO CORP.

529 U.S. 120 (2000)

Justice **O'Connor** delivered the opinion of the Court.

This case involves one of the most troubling public health problems facing our Nation today: the thousands of premature deaths that occur each year because of tobacco use. In 1996, the Food and Drug Administration (FDA), after having expressly disavowed any such authority since its inception, asserted jurisdiction to regulate tobacco products. See 61 Fed. Reg. 44619-45318. The FDA concluded that nicotine is a "drug" within the meaning of the Food, Drug, and Cosmetic Act (FDCA or Act), 52 Stat. 1040, as amended, 21 U.S.C. § 301 *et seq.*, and that cigarettes and smokeless tobacco are "combination products" that deliver nicotine to the body. Pursuant to this authority, it promulgated regulations intended to reduce tobacco consumption among children and adolescents. *Id.*, at 44615–44618. The agency believed that, because most tobacco consumers begin their use before reaching the age of 18, curbing tobacco use by minors could substantially reduce the prevalence of addiction in future generations and thus the incidence of tobacco-related death and disease.

Regardless of how serious the problem an administrative agency seeks to address, however, it may not exercise its authority "in a manner that is inconsistent with the administrative structure that Congress enacted into law." And although agencies are generally entitled to deference in the interpretation of statutes that they administer, a reviewing "court, as well as the agency, must give effect to the unambiguously expressed intent of Congress." In this case, we believe that Congress has clearly precluded the FDA from asserting jurisdiction to regulate tobacco products. Such authority is inconsistent with the intent that Congress has expressed in the FDCA's overall regulatory scheme and in the tobacco-specific legislation that it has enacted subsequent to the FDCA. In light of this clear intent, the FDA's assertion of jurisdiction is impermissible.

I

On August 11, 1995, the FDA published a proposed rule concerning the sale of cigarettes and smokeless tobacco to children and adolescents. The rule, which included several restrictions on the sale, distribution, and advertisement of tobacco products, was designed to reduce the availability and attractiveness of tobacco products to young people. A public comment period followed, during which the FDA received over 700,000 submissions, more than "at any other time in its history on any other subject."

On August 28, 1996, the FDA issued a final rule entitled "Regulations Restricting the Sale and Distribution of Cigarettes and Smokeless Tobacco to Protect Children and Adolescents." The FDA determined that nicotine is a "drug" and that cigarettes and smokeless tobacco are "drug delivery devices," and therefore it had jurisdiction under the FDCA to regulate tobacco products as customarily marketed — that is, without manufacturer claims of therapeutic benefit. First, the FDA found that tobacco products " 'affect the structure or any function of the body' " because nicotine "has significant pharmacological effects." Specifically, nicotine "exerts psychoactive, or mood-altering, effects on the brain" that cause and sustain addiction, have both tranquilizing and stimulating effects, and control weight. Second, the FDA determined that these effects were "intended" under the FDCA because they "are so widely known and foreseeable that [they] may be deemed to have been intended by the manufacturers," consumers use tobacco products "predominantly or nearly exclusively" to obtain these effects; and the statements, research, and actions of manufacturers revealed that they "have 'designed' cigarettes to provide pharmacologically active doses of nicotine to consumers." Finally, the agency concluded that cigarettes and smokeless tobacco are "combination products" because, in addition to containing nicotine, they include device components that deliver a controlled amount of nicotine to the body.

Having resolved the jurisdictional question, the FDA next explained the policy justifications for its regulations, detailing the deleterious health effects associated with tobacco use. It found that tobacco consumption was "the single leading cause of preventable death in the United States." According to the FDA, "more than 400,000 people die each year from tobacco-related illnesses, such as cancer, respiratory illnesses, and heart disease." The agency also determined that the only way to reduce the amount of tobacco-related illness and mortality was to reduce the level of addiction, a goal that could be accomplished only by preventing children and adolescents from starting to use tobacco. The FDA found that 82% of adult smokers had their first cigarette before the age of 18, and more than half had already become regular smokers by that age. It also found that children were beginning to smoke at a younger age, that the prevalence of youth smoking had recently increased, and that similar problems existed with respect to smokeless tobacco. The FDA accordingly concluded that if "the number of children and adolescents who begin tobacco use can be substantially diminished, tobacco-related illness can be correspondingly reduced because data suggest that anyone who does not begin smoking in childhood or adolescence is unlikely ever to begin."

Based on these findings, the FDA promulgated regulations concerning tobacco products' promotion, labeling, and accessibility to children and adolescents. The access regulations prohibit the sale of cigarettes or smokeless tobacco to persons younger than 18; require retailers to verify through photo identification the age of all purchasers younger than 27; prohibit the sale of cigarettes in quantities smaller than 20; prohibit the distribution of free samples; and prohibit sales through self-service displays and vending machines except in adult-only locations. The promotion regulations require that any print advertising appear in a black-and-white, text-only format unless the publication in which it appears is read almost exclusively by adults; prohibit outdoor advertising within 1,000 feet of any public playground or school; prohibit the distribution of any promotional items, such as T-shirts or hats, bearing the manufacturer's brand name; and prohibit a manufacturer from sponsoring any athletic, musical, artistic, or other social or cultural event using its brand name. The labeling regulation requires that the statement, "A Nicotine-Delivery Device for Persons 18 or Older," appear on all tobacco product packages.

We granted the Government's petition for certiorari, to determine whether the FDA has authority under the FDCA to regulate tobacco products as customarily marketed.

II

The FDA's assertion of jurisdiction to regulate tobacco products is founded on its conclusions that nicotine is a "drug" and that cigarettes and smokeless tobacco are "drug delivery devices." Again, the FDA found that tobacco products are "intended" to deliver the pharmacological effects of satisfying addiction, stimulation and tranquilization, and weight control because those effects are foreseeable to any reasonable manufacturer, consumers use tobacco products to obtain those effects, and tobacco manufacturers have designed their products to produce those effects.

A

Viewing the FDCA as a whole, it is evident that one of the Act's core objectives is to ensure that any product regulated by the FDA is "safe" and "effective" for its intended use.

In its rulemaking proceeding, the FDA quite exhaustively documented that "tobacco products are unsafe," "dangerous," and "cause great pain and suffering from illness."

These findings logically imply that, if tobacco products were "devices" under the FDCA, the FDA would be required to remove them from the market. Consider, first, the FDCA's provisions concerning the misbranding of drugs or devices. The Act prohibits "the introduction or delivery for introduction into interstate commerce of any food, drug, device, or cosmetic that is adultered or misbranded." In light of the FDA's findings, two distinct FDCA provisions would render cigarettes and smokeless tobacco misbranded devices.

[T]he FDCA requires the FDA to place all devices that it regulates into one of three classifications. Given the FDA's findings regarding the health consequences of tobacco use, the agency would have to place cigarettes and smokeless tobacco in Class III because, even after the application of the Act's available controls, they would "present a potential unreasonable risk of illness or injury." Thus, once the FDA fulfilled its statutory obligation to classify tobacco products, it could not allow them to be marketed.

The FDCA's misbranding and device classification provisions therefore make evident that were the FDA to regulate cigarettes and smokeless tobacco, the Act would require the agency to ban them.

Congress, however, has foreclosed the removal of tobacco products from the market. A provision of the United States Code currently in force states that "the marketing of tobacco constitutes one of the greatest basic industries of the United States with ramifying activities which directly affect interstate and foreign commerce at every point, and stable conditions therein are necessary to the general welfare."

The FDA apparently recognized this dilemma and concluded, somewhat ironically, that tobacco products are actually "safe" within the meaning of the

FDCA. In promulgating its regulations, the agency conceded that "tobacco products are unsafe, as that term is conventionally understood." Nonetheless, the FDA reasoned that, in determining whether a device is safe under the Act, it must consider "not only the risks presented by a product but also any of the countervailing effects of use of that product, including the consequences of not permitting the product to be marketed." Applying this standard, the FDA found that, because of the high level of addiction among tobacco users, a ban would likely be "dangerous."

Applied to tobacco products, the inquiry is whether their purported benefits — satisfying addiction, stimulation and sedation, and weight control — outweigh the risks to health from their use. To accommodate the FDA's conception of safety, however, one must read "any probable benefit to health" to include the benefit to public health stemming from adult consumers' continued use of tobacco products, even though the *reduction* of tobacco use is the *raison d'etre* of the regulations. In other words, the FDA is forced to contend that the very evil it seeks to combat is a "benefit to health." This is implausible.

B

In determining whether Congress has spoken directly to the FDA's authority to regulate tobacco, we must also consider in greater detail the tobacco-specific legislation that Congress has enacted over the past 35 years.

Congress has enacted six separate pieces of legislation since 1965 addressing the problem of tobacco use and human health. Those statutes, among other things, require that health warnings appear on all packaging and in all print and outdoor advertisements; prohibit the advertisement of tobacco products through "any medium of electronic communication" subject to regulation by the Federal Communications Commission (FCC); require the Secretary of Health and Human Services (HHS) to report every three years to Congress on research findings concerning "the addictive property of tobacco," and make States' receipt of certain federal block grants contingent on their making it unlawful "for any manufacturer, retailer, or distributor of tobacco products to sell or distribute any such product to any individual under the age of 18."

Congress ultimately decided in 1965 to subject tobacco products to the less extensive regulatory scheme of the FCLAA, which created a "comprehensive Federal program to deal with cigarette labeling and advertising with respect to any relationship between smoking and health." The FCLAA rejected any regulation of advertising, but it required the warning, "Caution: Cigarette Smoking May Be Hazardous to Your Health," to appear on all cigarette packages.

Not only did Congress reject the proposals to grant the FDA jurisdiction, but it explicitly preempted any other regulation of cigarette labeling: "No statement relating to smoking and health, other than the statement required by . . . this Act, shall be required on any cigarette package."

Between 1987 and 1989, Congress considered three more bills that would have amended the FDCA to grant the FDA jurisdiction to regulate tobacco products. See H. R. 3294, 100th Cong., 1st Sess. (1987); H. R. 1494, 101st Cong., 1st Sess. (1989); S. 769, 101st Cong., 1st Sess. (1989). As before,

Congress rejected the proposals. In 1992, Congress instead adopted the Alcohol, Drug Abuse, and Mental Health Administration Reorganization Act, Pub. L. 102-321, § 202, 106 Stat. 394 (codified at 42 U.S.C. § 300x *et seq.*), which creates incentives for States to regulate the retail sale of tobacco products by making States' receipt of certain block grants contingent on their prohibiting the sale of tobacco products to minors.

Taken together, these actions by Congress over the past 35 years preclude an interpretation of the FDCA that grants the FDA jurisdiction to regulate tobacco products.

C

By no means do we question the seriousness of the problem that the FDA has sought to address. The agency has amply demonstrated that tobacco use, particularly among children and adolescents, poses perhaps the single most significant threat to public health in the United States. Nonetheless, no matter how "important, conspicuous, and controversial" the issue, and regardless of how likely the public is to hold the Executive Branch politically accountable, an administrative agency's power to regulate in the public interest must always be grounded in a valid grant of authority from Congress. Reading the FDCA as a whole, as well as in conjunction with Congress' subsequent tobacco-specific legislation, it is plain that Congress has not given the FDA the authority that it seeks to exercise here. For these reasons, the judgment of the Court of Appeals for the Fourth Circuit is affirmed.

It is so ordered.

Justice **Breyer**, with whom Justice **Stevens**, Justice **Souter**, and Justice **Ginsburg** join, dissenting.

In its own interpretation, the majority nowhere denies the following two salient points. First, tobacco products (including cigarettes) fall within the scope of this statutory definition, read literally. Cigarettes achieve their mood-stabilizing effects through the interaction of the chemical nicotine and the cells of the central nervous system. Both cigarette manufacturers and smokers alike know of, and desire, that chemically induced result. Hence, cigarettes are "intended to affect" the body's "structure" and "function," in the literal sense of these words.

Second, the statute's basic purpose — the protection of public health — supports the inclusion of cigarettes within its scope.

Despite the FDCA's literal language and general purpose (both of which support the FDA's finding that cigarettes come within its statutory authority), the majority nonetheless reads the statute as *excluding* tobacco products for two basic reasons:

(1) the FDCA does not "fit" the case of tobacco because the statute requires the FDA to prohibit dangerous drugs or devices (like cigarettes) outright, and the agency concedes that simply banning the sale of cigarettes is not a proper remedy; and

(2) Congress has enacted other statutes, which, when viewed in light of the FDA's long history of denying tobacco-related jurisdiction and

> considered together with Congress' failure explicitly to grant the agency tobacco-specific authority, demonstrate that Congress did not intend for the FDA to exercise jurisdiction over tobacco.

In my view, neither of these propositions is valid. Rather, the FDCA does not significantly limit the FDA's remedial alternatives. And the later statutes do not tell the FDA it cannot exercise jurisdiction, but simply leave FDA jurisdictional law where Congress found it.

And the fact that the FDA changed its mind about the scope of its own jurisdiction is legally insignificant because (as Part IV establishes) the agency's reasons for changing course are fully justified. Finally, as I explain in Part V, the degree of accountability that likely will attach to the FDA's action in this case should alleviate any concern that Congress, rather than an administrative agency, ought to make this important regulatory decision.

. . . .

II

A

The tobacco companies contend that the FDCA's words cannot possibly be read to mean what they literally say. The statute defines "device," for example, as "an instrument, apparatus, implement, machine, contrivance, implant, in vitro reagent, or other similar or related article . . . intended to affect the structure or any function of the body. . . ." Taken literally, this definition might include everything from room air conditioners to thermal pajamas. The companies argue that, to avoid such a result, the meaning of "drug" or "device" should be confined to *medical* or *therapeutic* products, narrowly defined.

The companies may well be right that the statute should not be read to cover room air conditioners and winter underwear. But I do not agree that we must accept their proposed limitation. For one thing, such a cramped reading contravenes the established purpose of the statutory language.

Most importantly, the statute's language itself supplies a different, more suitable, limitation: that a "drug" must be a *chemical* agent. The FDCA's "device" definition states that an article which affects the structure or function of the body is a "device" only if it "does *not* achieve its primary intended purposes through chemical action within . . . the body," and "is *not* dependent upon being metabolized for the achievement of its primary intended purposes." One can readily infer from this language that at least an article that *does* achieve its primary purpose through chemical action within the body and that *is* dependent upon being metabolized is a "drug," provided that it otherwise falls within the scope of the "drug" definition. And one need not hypothesize about air conditioners or thermal pajamas to recognize that the chemical nicotine, an important tobacco ingredient, meets this test.

B

The tobacco companies' principal definitional argument focuses upon the statutory word "intended." The companies say that "intended" in this context is a term of art.

The FDCA, however, does not use the word "claimed"; it uses the word "intended." And the FDA long ago issued regulations that say the relevant "intent" can be shown not only by a manufacturer's "expressions," *but also* "by the circumstances surrounding the distribution of the article."

The companies also cannot deny that the evidence of their intent is sufficient to satisfy the statutory word "intended" as the FDA long has interpreted it. In the first place, there was once a time when they actually *did* make express advertising claims regarding tobacco's mood-stabilizing and weight-reducing properties — and historical representations can portend present expectations. In the late 1920's, for example, the American Tobacco Company urged weight-conscious smokers to " 'Reach for a Lucky instead of a sweet.' " Kluger, Ashes to Ashes, at 77–78. The advertisements of R J Reynolds (RJR) emphasized mood stability by depicting a pilot remarking that " 'It Takes Steady Nerves To Fly the Mail At Night. . . . That's why I smoke Camels. And I smoke plenty!' " RJR also advertised the stimulating quality of cigarettes, stating in one instance that " 'You get a Lift with a Camel,' " and, in another, that Camels are " 'A Harmless Restoration of the Flow of Natural Body Energy.' " And claims of medical proof of mildness (and of other beneficial effects) once were commonplace. (Brown & Williamson advertised Kool-brand mentholated cigarettes as "a tonic to hot, tired throats"); (Phillip Morris contended that "recognized laboratory tests have conclusively proven the advantage of Phillip Morris"); (RJR proclaimed " 'For Digestion's sake, smoke Camels! . . . Camels make mealtime more pleasant — digestion is stimulated — alkalinity increased' "). Although in recent decades cigarette manufacturers have stopped making express health claims in their advertising, consumers have come to understand what the companies no longer need to express — that through chemical action cigarettes stabilize mood, sedate, stimulate, and help suppress appetite.

Second, even though the companies refused to acknowledge publicly (until only very recently) that the nicotine in cigarettes has chemically induced, and habit-forming, effects, see, *e.g.,* Regulation of Tobacco Products (Part 1): Hearings before the House Subcommittee on Health and the Environment, 103d Cong., 2d Sess., 628 (1994) (hereinafter 1994 Hearings) (heads of seven major tobacco companies testified under oath that they believed "nicotine is *not* addictive" (emphasis added)), the FDA recently has gained access to solid, documentary evidence proving that cigarette manufacturers have long *known* tobacco produces these effects within the body through the metabolizing of chemicals, and that they have long *wanted* their products to produce those effects in this way.

For example, in 1972, a tobacco-industry scientist explained that " 'smoke is beyond question the most optimized vehicle of nicotine,' " and " 'the cigarette is the most optimized dispenser of smoke.' " That same scientist urged company executives to " 'think of the cigarette pack as a storage container for a day's supply of nicotine. . . . Think of the cigarette as a dispenser for a dose unit of nicotine [and] think of a puff of smoke as a vehicle of nicotine.' " (Philip Morris).

That same year, other tobacco industry researchers told their superiors that " 'in different situations and at different dose levels, nicotine appears to act as a stimulant, depressant, tranquilizer, psychic energizer, appetite reducer, anti-fatigue agent, or energizer. . . . Therefore, [tobacco] products may, in a sense, compete with a variety of other products with certain types of drug action.' "

A draft report prepared by authorities at Philip Morris said that nicotine " 'is a physiologically active, nitrogen containing substance [similar to] quinine, cocaine, atropine and morphine. [And] while each of these [other] substances can be used to affect human physiology, nicotine has a particularly broad range of influence.' "

And a 1980 manufacturer's study stated that " 'the pharmacological response of smokers to nicotine is believed to be responsible for an individual's smoking behaviour, providing the motivation for and the degree of satisfaction required by the smoker.' " (Brown & Williamson).

With such evidence, the FDA has more than sufficiently established that the companies "intend" their products to "affect" the body within the meaning of the FDCA.

C

The majority nonetheless reaches the "inescapable conclusion" that the language and structure of the FDCA as a whole "simply do not fit" the kind of public health problem that tobacco creates. That is because, in the majority's view, the FDCA requires the FDA to ban outright "dangerous" drugs or devices (such as cigarettes); yet, the FDA concedes that an immediate and total cigarette-sale ban is inappropriate.

This argument is curious because it leads with similarly "inescapable" force to precisely the opposite conclusion, namely, that the FDA *does* have jurisdiction but that it must ban cigarettes. More importantly, the argument fails to take into account the fact that a statute interpreted as requiring the FDA to pick a more dangerous over a less dangerous remedy would be a perverse statute, *causing*, rather than preventing, unnecessary harm whenever a total ban is likely the more dangerous response. And one can at least imagine such circumstances.

Suppose, for example, that a commonly used, mildly addictive sleeping pill (or, say, a kind of popular contact lens), plainly within the FDA's jurisdiction, turned out to pose serious health risks for certain consumers. Suppose further that many of those addicted consumers would ignore an immediate total ban, turning to a potentially more dangerous black-market substitute, while a less draconian remedy (say, adequate notice) would wean them gradually away to a safer product. Would the FDCA still *force* the FDA to impose the more dangerous remedy? For the following reasons, I think not.

The Court points to other statutory subsections which it believes require the FDA to ban a drug or device entirely, even where an outright ban risks more harm than other regulatory responses. But the cited provisions do no such thing. It is true, as the majority contends, that "the FDCA requires the FDA to place all devices" in "one of three classifications" and that Class III devices require "premarket approval." But it is not the case that the FDA *must* place cigarettes in Class III because tobacco itself "presents a potential unreasonable risk of illness or injury." In fact, Class III applies *only* where *regulation* cannot otherwise "provide reasonable assurance of . . . safety." (placing a device in Class I or Class II when regulation can provide that assurance). Thus, the statute plainly allows the FDA to consider the relative, overall "safety" of a device in light of its regulatory alternatives, and where the FDA has chosen the least dangerous path, *i.e.*, the safest path, then it can — and does — provide a "reasonable assurance" of "safety" within the meaning of the statute. A good football helmet provides a reasonable assurance of safety for the player even if the sport itself is still dangerous. And the safest regulatory choice by definition offers a "reasonable" assurance of safety in a world where the other alternatives are yet more dangerous.

In any event, it is not entirely clear from the statute's text that a Class III categorization would require the FDA affirmatively to *withdraw* from the market dangerous devices, such as cigarettes, which are already widely distributed.

And nothing in the statute prevents the agency from adopting a view of "safety" that would avoid such harm. Indeed, the FDA already seems to have taken this position when permitting distribution of toxic drugs, such as poisons used for chemotherapy, that are dangerous for the user but are not deemed "dangerous to health" in the relevant sense.

The tobacco companies point to another statutory provision which says that if a device "would cause serious, adverse health consequences or death, the Secretary *shall* issue" a cease distribution order. But that word "shall" in this context cannot mean that the Secretary must resort to the recall remedy *whenever* a device would have serious, adverse health effects. Rather, that language must mean that the Secretary "shall issue" a cease distribution order in compliance with the section's procedural requirements *if* the Secretary chooses *in her discretion* to use that particular subsection's recall remedy. Otherwise, the subsection would trump and make meaningless the same section's provision of other lesser remedies such as simple "notice" (which the Secretary similarly can impose if, but only if, she finds that the device "presents an unreasonable risk of substantial harm to the public"). Section 360h(a)(1). And reading the statute to compel the FDA to "recall" every dangerous device likewise would conflict with that same subsection's statement that the recall remedy "shall be *in addition to* [the other] remedies provided" in the statute. Section 360h(e)(3) (emphasis added).

The statute's language, then, permits the agency to choose remedies consistent with its basic purpose — the overall protection of public health.

I concede that, as a matter of logic, one could consider the FDA's "safety" evaluation to be different from its choice of remedies. But to read the statute to forbid the agency from taking account of the realities of consumer behavior either in assessing safety or in choosing a remedy could increase the risks of harm — doubling the risk of death to each "individual user" in my example above. Why would Congress insist that the FDA ignore such realities, even if the consequent harm would occur only unusually, say, where the FDA evaluates a product (a sleeping pill; a cigarette; a contact lens) that is already on the market, potentially habit forming, or popular? III

In the majority's view, laws enacted since 1965 require us to deny jurisdiction, whatever the FDCA might mean in their absence. But why? Do those laws contain language barring FDA jurisdiction? The majority must concede that they do not. Do they contain provisions that are inconsistent with the FDA's exercise of jurisdiction? With one exception, the majority points to no such provision.

Consider, for example, Congress' failure to provide the FDA with express authority to regulate tobacco — a circumstance that the majority finds significant. In fact, Congress *both* failed to grant express authority to the FDA when the FDA denied it had jurisdiction over tobacco *and* failed to take that authority expressly away when the agency later asserted jurisdiction. Consequently, the defeat of various different proposed jurisdictional changes proves nothing. This history shows only that Congress could not muster the votes necessary either to grant or to deny the FDA the relevant authority. It neither favors nor disfavors the majority's position.

IV

I now turn to the final historical fact that the majority views as a factor in its interpretation of the subsequent legislative history: the FDA's former denials of its tobacco-related authority.

What changed? For one thing, the FDA obtained evidence sufficient to prove the necessary "intent" despite the absence of specific "claims." This evidence, which first became available in the early 1990's, permitted the agency to demonstrate that the tobacco companies *knew* nicotine achieved appetite-suppressing, mood-stabilizing, and habituating effects through chemical (not psychological) means, even at a time when the companies were publicly denying such knowledge.

Moreover, scientific evidence of adverse health effects mounted, until, in the late 1980's, a consensus on the seriousness of the matter became firm. That is not to say that concern about smoking's adverse health effects is a new phenomenon. It is to say, however, that convincing epidemiological evidence began to appear mid-20th century; that the First Surgeon General's Report documenting the adverse health effects appeared in 1964; and that the Surgeon General's Report establishing nicotine's addictive [illegible] in 1988. At each stage, the health conclusions were the subject of controversy, diminishing somewhat over time, until recently — and only recently — has it become clear that there is a wide consensus about the health problem.

Finally, administration policy changed. Earlier administrations may have hesitated to assert jurisdiction for the reasons prior Commissioners expressed. Commissioners of the current administration simply took a different regulatory attitude.

Nothing in the law prevents the FDA from changing its policy for such reasons.

V

One might nonetheless claim that, even if my interpretation of the FDCA and later statutes gets the words right, it lacks a sense of their "music."

First, one might claim that, despite the FDA's legal right to change its mind, its original statements played a critical part in the enactment of the later statutes and now should play a critical part in their interpretation. But the FDA's traditional view was largely premised on a perceived inability to prove the necessary statutory "intent" requirement.

Second, one might claim that courts, when interpreting statutes, should assume in close cases that a decision with "enormous social consequences," 1994 Hearings 69, should be made by democratically elected Members of Congress rather than by unelected agency administrators. If there is such a background canon of interpretation, however, I do not believe it controls the outcome here.

I do not believe that an administrative agency decision of this magnitude — one that is important, conspicuous, and controversial — can escape the kind of public scrutiny that is essential in any democracy. And such a review will take place whether it is the Congress or the Executive Branch that makes the relevant decision.

According to the FDA, only 2.5% of smokers successfully stop smoking each year, even though 70% say they want to quit and 34% actually make an attempt to do so. The fact that only a handful of those who try to quit smoking actually succeed illustrates a certain reality — the reality that the nicotine in cigarettes creates a powerful physiological addiction flowing from chemically induced changes in the brain. The FDA has found that the makers of cigarettes "intend" these physical effects. Hence, nicotine is a "drug"; the cigarette that delivers nicotine to the body is a "device"; and the FDCA's language, read in light of its basic purpose, permits the FDA to assert the disease-preventing jurisdiction that the agency now claims.

The upshot is that the Court today holds that a regulatory statute aimed at unsafe drugs and devices does not authorize regulation of a drug (nicotine) and a device (a cigarette) that the Court itself finds unsafe. Far more than most, this particular drug and device risks the life-threatening harms that administrative regulation seeks to rectify. The majority's conclusion is counter-intuitive. And, for the reasons set forth, I believe that the law does not require it.

Consequently, I dissent.

LORILLARD TOBACCO CO. v. REILLY

533 U.S. 525 (2001)

Justice **O'Connor** delivered the opinion of the Court.

I

In November 1998, Massachusetts, along with over 40 other States, reached a landmark agreement with major manufacturers in the cigarette industry. The signatory States settled their claims against these companies in exchange for monetary payments and permanent injunctive relief. At the press conference covering Massachusetts' decision to sign the agreement, then-Attorney General Scott Harshbarger announced that as one of his last acts in office, he would create consumer protection regulations to restrict advertising and sales practices for tobacco products. He explained that the regulations were necessary in order to "close holes" in the settlement agreement and "to stop Big Tobacco from recruiting new customers among the children of Massachusetts."

The regulations have a broader scope than the master settlement agreement, reaching advertising, sales practices, and members of the tobacco industry not covered by the agreement. The regulations place a variety of restrictions on outdoor advertising, point-of-sale advertising, retail sales transactions, transactions by mail, promotions, sampling of products, and labels for cigars.

The cigarette and smokeless tobacco regulations being challenged before this Court provide:

> "(2) Retail Outlet Sales Practices. Except as otherwise provided in [§ 21.04(4)], it shall be an unfair or deceptive act or practice for any person who sells or distributes cigarettes or smokeless tobacco products through a retail outlet located within Massachusetts to engage in any of the following retail outlet sales practices:
>
> . . . .
>
> "(c) Using self-service displays of cigarettes or smokeless tobacco products;
>
> "(d) Failing to place cigarettes and smokeless tobacco products out of the reach of all consumers, and in a location accessible only to outlet personnel." §§ 21.04(2)(c)–(d).
>
> "(5) Advertising Restrictions. Except as provided in [§ 21.04(6)], it shall be an unfair or deceptive act or practice for any manufacturer, distributor or retailer to engage in any of the following practices:
>
> "(a) Outdoor advertising, including advertising in enclosed stadiums and advertising from within a retail establishment that is directed toward or visible from the outside of the establishment, in any location that is within a 1,000 foot radius of any public playground, playground area in a public park, elementary school or secondary school;
>
> "(b) Point-of-sale advertising of cigarettes or smokeless tobacco products any portion of which is placed lower than five feet from the floor of any retail establishment which is located within a one thousand foot radius of any public playground, playground area in a public park, elementary school or secondary school, and which is not an adult-only retail establishment." §§ 21.04(5)(a)–(b).

The term "advertisement" is defined as:

> "any oral, written, graphic, or pictorial statement or representation, made by, or on behalf of, any person who manufactures, packages, imports for sale, distributes or sells within Massachusetts [tobacco products], the purpose or effect of which is to promote the use or sale of the product. Advertisement includes, without limitation, any picture, logo, symbol, motto, selling message, graphic display, visual

image, recognizable color or pattern of colors, or any other indicia of product identification identical or similar to, or identifiable with, those used for any brand of [tobacco product]. This includes, without limitation, utilitarian items and permanent or semi-permanent fixtures with such indicia of product identification such as lighting fixtures, awnings, display cases, clocks and door mats, but does not include utilitarian items with a volume of 200 cubic inches or less." §§ 21.03, 22.03.

II

Before reaching the First Amendment issues, we must decide to what extent federal law pre-empts the Attorney General's regulations. The cigarette petitioners contend that the FCLAA, 15 U.S.C. § 1331 *et seq.*, preempts the Attorney General's cigarette advertising regulations.

A

In the FCLAA, Congress has crafted a comprehensive federal scheme governing the advertising and promotion of cigarettes. The FCLAA's preemption provision provides:

> "(a) Additional statements
>
> "No statement relating to smoking and health, other than the statement required by section 1333 of this title, shall be required on any cigarette package.
>
> "(b) State regulations
>
> "No requirement or prohibition based on smoking and health shall be imposed under State law with respect to the advertising or promotion of any cigarettes the packages of which are labeled in conformity with the provisions of this chapter."

The FCLAA's pre-emption provision does not cover smokeless tobacco or cigars.

In this case, our task is to identify the domain expressly pre-empted, because "an express definition of the pre-emptive reach of a statute . . . supports a reasonable inference . . . that Congress did not intend to preempt other matters." See *Freightliner Corp. v. Myrick.*

The FTC has continued to report on trade practices in the cigarette industry. In 1999, the first year since the master settlement agreement, the FTC reported that the cigarette industry expended $ 8.24 billion on advertising and promotions, the largest expenditure ever. Substantial increases were found in point-of-sale promotions, payments made to retailers to facilitate sales, and retail offers such as buy one, get one free, or product giveaways. Substantial decreases, however, were reported for outdoor advertising and transit advertising. Congress and federal agencies continue to monitor advertising and promotion practices in the cigarette industry.

The scope and meaning of the current pre-emption provision become clearer once we consider the original pre-emption language and the amendments to the FCLAA. Without question, "the plain language of the preemption provision in the 1969 Act is much broader." Rather than preventing only "statements," the amended provision reaches all "requirements or prohibitions . . . imposed under State law." And, although the former statute reached only statements "in the advertising," the current provision governs "with respect to the advertising or promotion" of cigarettes. Congress expanded the pre-emption provision with respect to the States, and at the same time, it allowed the FTC to regulate cigarette advertising. Congress also prohibited cigarette advertising in electronic media altogether. Viewed in light of the context in which the current pre-emption provision was adopted, we must determine whether the FCLAA pre-empts Massachusetts' regulations governing outdoor and point-of-sale advertising of cigarettes.

B

Before this Court, the Attorney General focuses on a different phrase in the pre-emption provision: "based on smoking and health." The Attorney General argues that the cigarette advertising regulations are not "based on smoking and health," because they do not involve health-related content in cigarette advertising but instead target youth exposure to cigarette advertising. To be sure, Members of this Court have debated the precise meaning of "based on smoking and health," but we cannot agree with the Attorney General's narrow construction of the phrase.

At bottom, the concern about youth exposure to cigarette advertising is intertwined with the concern about cigarette smoking and health. Thus the Attorney General's attempt to distinguish one concern from the other must be rejected.

The Attorney General next claims that the State's outdoor and point-of-sale advertising regulations for cigarettes are not pre-empted because they govern the location, and not the content, of advertising. This is also Justice Stevens' main point with respect to pre-emption.

Justice Stevens finds it ironic that we conclude that "federal law precludes States and localities from protecting children from dangerous products within 1,000 feet of a school," in light of our prior conclusion that the "Federal Government lacks the constitutional authority to impose a similarly-motivated ban" in *United States v. Lopez*, 514 U.S. 549 (1995). Our holding is not as broad as the dissent states; we hold only that the FCLAA pre-empts state regulations targeting cigarette advertising. States remain free to enact generally applicable zoning regulations, and to regulate conduct with respect to cigarette use and sales.

C

Although the FCLAA prevents States and localities from imposing special requirements or prohibitions "based on smoking and health" "with respect to the advertising or promotion" of cigarettes, that language still leaves significant power in the hands of States to impose generally applicable zoning regulations and to regulate conduct.

For instance, the FCLAA does not restrict a State or locality's ability to enact generally applicable zoning restrictions. We have recognized that state interests in traffic safety and esthetics may justify zoning regulations for advertising. [T]here is no indication that Congress intended to displace local community interests in general regulations of the location of billboards or large marquee advertising, or that Congress intended cigarette advertisers to be afforded special treatment in that regard. Restrictions on the location and size of advertisements that apply to cigarettes on equal terms with other products appear to be outside the ambit of the pre-emption provision. Such restrictions are not "based on smoking and health."

The FCLAA also does not foreclose all state regulation of conduct as it relates to the sale or use of cigarettes.

III

By its terms, the FCLAA's pre-emption provision only applies to cigarettes. Accordingly, we must evaluate the smokeless tobacco and cigar petitioners' First Amendment challenges to the State's outdoor and point-of-sale advertising regulations. The cigarette petitioners did not raise a preemption challenge to the sales practices regulations. Thus, we must analyze the cigarette as well as the smokeless tobacco and cigar petitioners' claim that certain sales practices regulations for tobacco products violate the First Amendment.

A

For over 25 years, the Court has recognized that commercial speech does not fall outside the purview of the First Amendment. See, *e.g.*, *Virginia Bd. of Pharmacy v. Virginia Citizens Consumer Council, Inc.*. Instead, the Court has afforded commercial speech a measure of First Amendment protection " 'commensurate' " with its position in relation to other constitutionally guaranteed expression. See, *e.g.*, *Florida Bar v. Went For It, Inc.*, 515 U.S. 618, 623 (1995) (quoting *Board of Trustees of State Univ. of N. Y. v. Fox*, 492 U.S. 469 (1989)). In recognition of the "distinction between speech proposing a commercial transaction, which occurs in an area traditionally subject to government regulation, and other varieties of speech," we developed a framework for analyzing regulations of commercial speech that is "substantially similar" to the test for time, place, and manner restrictions. The analysis contains four elements:

> "At the outset, we must determine whether the expression is protected by the First Amendment. For commercial speech to come within that provision, it at least must concern lawful activity and not be misleading. Next, we ask whether the asserted governmental interest is substantial. If both inquiries yield positive answers, we must determine whether the regulation directly advances the governmental interest asserted, and whether it is not more extensive than is necessary to serve that interest."

Focusing on the third and fourth steps of the *Central Hudson Gas & Elec. Corp. v. Public Serv. Comm'n of N.Y.*, 447 U.S. 557 (1980), analysis, we first address the outdoor advertising and point-of-sale advertising regulations for smokeless tobacco and cigars. We then address the sales practices regulations for all tobacco products.

B

The outdoor advertising regulations prohibit smokeless tobacco or cigar advertising within a 1,000-foot radius of a school or playground. The District Court and Court of Appeals concluded that the Attorney General had identified a real problem with underage use of tobacco products, that limiting youth exposure to advertising would combat that problem, and that the regulations burdened no more speech than necessary to accomplish the State's goal. The smokeless tobacco and cigar petitioners take issue with all of these conclusions.

1

The smokeless tobacco and cigar petitioners contend that the Attorney General's regulations do not satisfy *Central Hudson*'s third step. They maintain that although the Attorney General may have identified a problem with underage cigarette smoking, he has not identified an equally severe problem with respect to underage use of smokeless tobacco or cigars. The smokeless tobacco petitioner emphasizes the "lack of parity" between cigarettes and smokeless tobacco. The petitioners finally contend that the Attorney General cannot prove that advertising has a causal link to tobacco use such that limiting advertising will materially alleviate any problem of underage use of their products.

The Attorney General relies in part on evidence gathered by the Food and Drug Administration (FDA) in its attempt to regulate the advertising of cigarettes and smokeless tobacco.

In its rulemaking proceeding, the FDA considered several studies of tobacco advertising and trends in the use of various tobacco products.

For instance, children smoke fewer brands of cigarettes than adults, and those choices directly track the most heavily advertised brands, unlike adult choices, which are more dispersed and related to pricing. Another study revealed that 72% of 6 year olds and 52% of children ages 3 to 6 recognized "Joe Camel," the cartoon anthropomorphic symbol of R. J. Reynolds' Camel brand cigarettes. After the introduction of Joe Camel, Camel cigarettes' share of the youth market rose from 4% to 13%. The FDA also identified trends in tobacco consumption among certain populations, such as young women, that correlated to the introduction and marketing of products geared toward that population.

Researchers tracked a dramatic shift in patterns of smokeless tobacco use from older to younger users over the past 30 years. Smokeless tobacco brand preference and brand switching among US adolescents and young adults. In particular, the smokeless tobacco industry boosted sales tenfold in the 1970s and 1980s by targeting young males. Another study documented the targeting of youth through smokeless tobacco sales and advertising techniques.

The Attorney General presents different evidence with respect to cigars. There was no data on underage cigar use prior to 1996 because the behavior was considered "uncommon enough not to be worthy of examination."

More recently, however, data on youth cigar use has emerged. The National Cancer Institute concluded in its 1998 Monograph that the rate of cigar use by minors is increasing and that, in some States, the cigar use rates are higher than the smokeless tobacco use rates for minors.

Studies have also demonstrated a link between advertising and demand for cigars. After Congress recognized the power of images in advertising and banned cigarette advertising in electronic media, television advertising of small cigars "increased dramatically in 1972 and 1973," "filled the void left by cigarette advertisers," and "sales . . . soared." Smoking and Tobacco Control Monograph No. 9, at 24. In 1973, Congress extended the electronic media advertising ban for cigarettes to little cigars.

Our review of the record reveals that the Attorney General has provided ample documentation of the problem with underage use of smokeless tobacco and cigars. In addition, we disagree with petitioners' claim that there is no evidence that preventing targeted campaigns and limiting youth exposure to advertising will decrease underage use of smokeless tobacco and cigars. On this record and in the posture of summary judgment, we are unable to conclude that the Attorney General's decision to regulate advertising of smokeless tobacco and cigars in an effort to combat the use of tobacco products by minors was based on mere "speculation [and] conjecture."

2

Whatever the strength of the Attorney General's evidence to justify the outdoor advertising regulations, however, we conclude that the regulations do not satisfy the fourth step of the *Central Hudson* analysis. The final step of the *Central Hudson* analysis, the "critical inquiry in this case," requires a reasonable fit between the means and ends of the regulatory scheme. The Attorney General's regulations do not meet this standard.

The outdoor advertising regulations prohibit any smokeless tobacco or cigar advertising within 1,000 feet of schools or playgrounds. In the District Court, petitioners maintained that this prohibition would prevent advertising in 87% to 91% of Boston, Worchester, and Springfield, Massachusetts. The 87% to 91% figure appears to include not only the effect of the regulations, but also the limitations imposed by other generally applicable zoning restrictions. The Attorney General disputed petitioners' figures but "conceded that the reach of the regulations is substantial." Thus, the Court of Appeals concluded that the regulations prohibit advertising in a substantial portion of the major metropolitan areas of Massachusetts.

In some geographical areas, these regulations would constitute nearly a complete ban on the communication of truthful information about smokeless tobacco and cigars to adult consumers. The breadth and scope of the regulations, and the process by which the Attorney General adopted the regulations, do not demonstrate a careful calculation of the speech interests involved.

In addition, the range of communications restricted seems unduly broad. For instance, it is not clear from the regulatory scheme why a ban on oral communications is necessary to further the State's interest. Apparently that restriction means that a retailer is unable to answer inquiries about its tobacco products if that communication occurs outdoors. Similarly, a ban on all signs of any size seems ill suited to target the problem of highly visible billboards, as opposed to smaller signs. To the extent that studies have identified particular advertising and promotion practices that appeal to youth, tailoring would involve targeting those practices while permitting others. As crafted, the regulations make no distinction among practices on this basis.

In addition, a retailer in Massachusetts may have no means of communicating to passersby on the street that it sells tobacco products because alternative forms of advertisement, like newspapers, do not allow that retailer to propose an instant transaction in the way that onsite advertising does. The ban on any indoor advertising that is visible from the outside also presents problems in establishments like convenience stores, which have unique security concerns that counsel in favor of full visibility of the store from the outside. It is these sorts of considerations that the Attorney General failed to incorporate into the regulatory scheme.

A careful calculation of the costs of a speech regulation does not mean that a State must demonstrate that there is no incursion on legitimate speech interests, but a speech regulation cannot unduly impinge on the speaker's ability to propose a commercial transaction and the adult listener's opportunity to obtain information about products. After reviewing the outdoor advertising regulations, we find the calculation in this case insufficient for purposes of the First Amendment.

C

Massachusetts has also restricted indoor, point-of-sale advertising for smokeless tobacco and cigars. Advertising cannot be "placed lower than five feet from the floor of any retail establishment which is located within a one thousand foot radius of" any school or playground.

We conclude that the point-of-sale advertising regulations fail both the third and fourth [illegible] of the Central Hud[illegible] above, the State's goal is to prevent minors from using tobacco products and to curb demand for that activity by limiting youth exposure to advertising. The 5 foot rule does not seem to advance that goal. Not all children are less than 5 feet tall, and those who are certainly have the ability to look up and take in their surroundings.

D

The Attorney General also promulgated a number of regulations that restrict sales practices by cigarette, smokeless tobacco, and cigar manufacturers and retailers. Among other restrictions, the regulations bar the use of self-service displays and require that tobacco products be placed out of the reach of all consumers in a location accessible only to salespersons. 940 Code of Mass. Regs. §§ 21.04(2)(c)–(d), 22.06(2)(c)–(d) (2000). The cigarette petitioners do not challenge the sales practices regulations on pre-emption grounds. Two of the cigarette petitioners (Brown & Williamson Tobacco Corporation and Lorillard Tobacco Company), petitioner U.S. Smokeless Tobacco Company, and the cigar petitioners challenge the sales practices regulations on First Amendment grounds. The cigar petitioners additionally challenge a provision that prohibits sampling or promotional giveaways of cigars or little cigars. 940 Code of Mass. Regs. § 22.06(1)(a).

The District Court concluded that these restrictions implicate no cognizable speech interest.

The cigarette and smokeless tobacco petitioners contend that "the same First Amendment principles that require invalidation of the outdoor and indoor advertising restrictions require invalidation of the display regulations at issue in this case."

Massachusetts' sales practices provisions regulate conduct that may have a communicative component, but Massachusetts seeks to regulate the placement of tobacco products for reasons unrelated to the communication of ideas. We conclude that the State has demonstrated a substantial interest in preventing access to tobacco products by minors and has adopted an appropriately narrow means of advancing that interest.

Unattended displays of tobacco products present an opportunity for access without the proper age verification required by law. Thus, the State prohibits self-service and other displays that would allow an individual to obtain tobacco products without direct contact with a salesperson. It is clear that the regulations leave open ample channels of communication. The regulations do not significantly impede adult access to tobacco products. Moreover, retailers have other means of exercising any cognizable speech interest in the presentation of their products. We presume that vendors may place empty tobacco packaging on open display, and display actual tobacco products so long as that display is only accessible to sales personnel. As for cigars, there is no indication in the regulations that a customer is unable to examine a cigar prior to purchase, so long as that examination takes place through a salesperson.

IV

We have observed that "tobacco use, particularly among children and adolescents, poses perhaps the single most significant threat to public health in the United States." *FDA v. Brown & Williamson Tobacco Corp.*, 529 U.S. at 161. From a policy perspective, it is understandable for the States to attempt to prevent minors from using tobacco products before they reach an age where they are capable of weighing for themselves the risks and potential benefits of tobacco use, and other adult activities. Federal law, however, places limits on policy choices available to the States.

In this case, Congress enacted a comprehensive scheme to address cigarette smoking and health in advertising and pre-empted state regulation of cigarette advertising that attempts to address that same concern, even with respect to youth. The First Amendment also constrains state efforts to limit advertising of tobacco products, because so long as the sale and use of tobacco is lawful for adults, the tobacco industry has a protected interest in communicating information about its products and adult customers have an interest in receiving that information.

To the extent that federal law and the First Amendment do not prohibit state action, States and localities remain free to combat the problem of underage tobacco use by appropriate means. The judgment of the United States Court of Appeals for the First Circuit is therefore affirmed in part and reversed in part, and the cases are remanded for further proceedings consistent with this opinion.

It is so ordered.

Justice **Kennedy**, with whom Justice **Scalia** joins, concurring in part and concurring in the judgment.

The obvious overbreadth of the outdoor advertising restrictions suffices to invalidate them under the fourth part of the test in *Central Hudson Gas & Elec. Corp.*

Justice **Thomas**, concurring in part and concurring in the judgment.

I join the opinion of the Court (with the exception of Part III-B-1) because

I agree that the Massachusetts cigarette advertising regulations are preempted by the Federal Cigarette Labeling and Advertising Act. I also agree with the Court's disposition of the First Amendment challenges to the other regulations at issue here, and I share the Court's view that the regulations fail even the intermediate scrutiny of *Central Hudson Gas & Elec. Corp. v. Public Serv. Comm'n of N.Y.* At the same time, I continue to believe that when the government seeks to restrict truthful speech in order to suppress the ideas it conveys, strict scrutiny is appropriate, whether or not the speech in question may be characterized as "commercial." See *44 Liquormart, Inc. v. Rhode Island*, 517 U.S. 484, 518. (Thomas, J., concurring in part and concurring in judgment). I would subject all of the advertising restrictions to strict scrutiny and would hold that they violate the First Amendment.

. . . .

III

Underlying many of the arguments of respondents and their *amici* is the idea that tobacco is in some sense *sui generis* — that it is so special, so unlike any other object of regulation, that application of normal First Amendment principles should be suspended. Smoking poses serious health risks, and advertising may induce children (who lack the judgment to make an intelligent decision about whether to smoke) to begin smoking, which can lead to addiction. The State's assessment of the urgency of the problem posed by tobacco is a policy judgment, and it is not this Court's place to second-guess it. Nevertheless, it seems appropriate to point out that to uphold the Massachusetts tobacco regulations would be to accept a line of reasoning that would permit restrictions on advertising for a host of other products.

The effect of advertising on children's eating habits is significant for two reasons. First, childhood obesity is a serious health problem in its own right.

Troiano & Flegal, *Overweight Children and Adolescents*, 101 Pediatrics 497 (1998). Second, eating preferences formed in childhood tend to persist in adulthood. Birch & Fisher, *Development of Eating Behaviors Among Children and Adolescents*, 101 Pediatrics 539 (1998). So even though fast food is not addictive in the same way tobacco is, children's exposure to fast food advertising can have deleterious consequences that are difficult to reverse.

To take another example, the third largest cause of preventable deaths in the United States is alcohol. McGinnis & Foege, *Actual Causes of Death in the United States*, 270 JAMA 2207, 2208 (1993). Alcohol use is associated with tens of thousands of deaths each year from cancers and digestive diseases. And the victims of alcohol use are not limited to those who drink alcohol. In 1996, over 17,000 people were killed, and over 321,000 people were injured, in alcohol-related car accidents. Each year, alcohol is involved in several million violent crimes, including almost 200,000 sexual assaults.

. . . .

Justice **Souter**, concurring in part and dissenting in part.

I join Parts I, II-C, II-D, III-A, III-B-1, III-C, and III-D of the Court's opinion. I join Part I of the opinion of Justice **Stevens** concurring in the judgment in part and dissenting in part. I respectfully dissent from Part III-B-2 of the opinion of the Court, and like Justice **Stevens** would remand for trial on the constitutionality of the 1,000-foot limit.

Justice **Stevens**, with whom Justice **Ginsburg** and Justice **Breyer** join, and with whom Justice **Souter** joins as to Part I, concurring in part, concurring in the judgment in part, and dissenting in part.

This suit presents two separate sets of issues. The first — involving preemption — is straightforward. The second — involving the First Amendment — is more complex. Because I strongly disagree with the Court's conclusion that the Federal Cigarette Labeling and Advertising Act of 1965 (FCLAA or Act). as amended, precludes States and localities from regulating the location of cigarette advertising, I dissent from Parts II-A and II-B of the Court's opinion. On the First Amendment questions, I agree with the Court both that the outdoor advertising restrictions imposed by Massachusetts serve legitimate and important state interests and that the record does not indicate that the measures were properly tailored to serve those interests. Because the present record does not enable us to adjudicate the merits of those claims on summary judgment, I would vacate the decision upholding those restrictions and remand for trial on the constitutionality of the outdoor advertising regulations. Finally, because I do not believe that either the point-of-sale advertising restrictions or the sales practice restrictions implicate significant First Amendment concerns, I would uphold them in their entirety.

I

This task, properly performed, leads inexorably to the conclusion that Congress did not intend to preempt state and local regulations of the location of cigarette advertising when it adopted the provision at issue in this suit. In both 1965 and 1969, Congress made clear the purposes of its regulatory endeavor, explaining with precision the federal policies motivating its actions. According to the acts, Congress adopted a "comprehensive Federal program to deal with cigarette labeling and advertising with respect to any relationship between smoking and health," for two reasons: (1) to inform the public that smoking may be hazardous to health and (2) to ensure that commerce and the interstate economy not be "impeded by diverse, nonuniform, and confusing cigarette labeling and advertising regulations with respect to any relationship between smoking and health."

In order to serve the second purpose it was necessary to preempt state regulation of the content of both cigarette labels and cigarette advertising. If one State required the inclusion of a particular warning on the package of cigarettes while another State demanded a different formulation, cigarette manufacturers would have been forced into the difficult and costly practice of producing different packaging for use in different States. To foreclose the waste of resources that would be entailed by such a patchwork regulatory system, Congress expressly precluded other regulators from requiring the placement on cigarette packaging of any "statement relating to smoking and health."

There was, however, no need to interfere with state or local zoning laws or other regulations prescribing limitations on the location of signs or billboards. Laws prohibiting a cigarette company from hanging a billboard near a school in Boston in no way conflict with laws permitting the hanging of such a billboard in other jurisdictions. Nor would such laws even impose a significant administrative burden on would-be advertisers, as the great majority of localities impose general restrictions on signage, thus requiring advertisers to examine local law before posting signs whether or not cigarette-specific laws are preempted. Hence, it is unsurprising that Congress did not include any provision in the 1965 Act preempting location restrictions.

The Public Health Cigarette Smoking Act of 1969 (1969 Act), § 2, 84 Stat. 87, made two important changes in the preemption provision. First, it limited the applicability of the advertising prong to States and localities, paving the way for further federal regulation of cigarette advertising. FCLAA., § 4. Second, it expanded the scope of the advertising preemption provision. Where previously States were prohibited from requiring particular statements in cigarette advertising based on health concerns, they would henceforth be prohibited from imposing any "requirement or prohibition based on smoking and health . . . with respect to the advertising or promotion" of cigarettes.

I am firmly convinced that, when Congress amended the preemption provision in 1969, it did not intend to expand the application of the provision beyond content regulations. I, therefore, find the conclusion inescapable that the zoning regulation at issue in this suit is not a "requirement or prohibition . . . with respect to . . . advertising" within the meaning of the 1969 Act.

II

On the First Amendment issues raised by petitioners, my disagreements with the majority are less significant. I would, however, reach different dispositions as to the 1,000-foot rule and the height restrictions for indoor advertising, and my evaluation of the sales practice restrictions differs from the Court's.

The 1,000-Foot Rule

I am in complete accord with the Court's analysis of the importance of the interests served by the advertising restrictions.

To my mind, the 1,000-foot rule does not present a tailoring problem of the first type. For reasons cogently explained in our prior opinions and in the opinion of the Court, we may fairly assume that advertising stimulates consumption and, therefore, that regulations limiting advertising will facilitate efforts to stem consumption.

However, I share the majority's concern as to whether the 1,000-foot rule unduly restricts the ability of cigarette manufacturers to convey lawful information to adult consumers. This, of course, is a question of linedrawing. While a ban on all communications about a given subject would be the most effective way to prevent children from exposure to such material, the state cannot by fiat reduce the level of discourse to that which is "fit for children."

Because I do not think the record contains sufficient information to enable us to answer that question, I would vacate the award of summary judgment upholding the 1,000-foot rule and remand for trial on that issue. Therefore, while I agree with the majority that the Court of Appeals did not sufficiently consider the implications of the 1,000-foot rule for the lawful communication of adults, I dissent from the disposition reflected in Part III-B-2 of the Court's opinion.

More importantly, the Court lacks sufficient qualitative information as to the areas where cigarette advertising is prohibited and those where it is permitted. The fact that 80% or 90% of an urban area is unavailable to tobacco advertisements may be constitutionally irrelevant if the available areas are so heavily trafficked or so central to the city's cultural life that they provide a sufficient forum for the propagation of a manufacturer's message. One electric sign in Times Square or at the foot of the Golden Gate Bridge may be seen by more potential customers than a hundred signs dispersed in residential neighborhoods.

I note, moreover, that the alleged "overinclusivity" of the advertising regulations, (Thomas, J., concurring in part and concurring in judgment), while relevant to whether the regulations are narrowly tailored, does not "belie" the claim that tobacco advertising imagery misleads children into believing that smoking is healthy, glamorous, or sophisticated. For purposes of summary judgment, the State conceded that the tobacco companies' advertising concerns lawful activity and is not misleading. Under the Court's disposition of the case today, the State remains free to proffer evidence that the advertising is in fact misleading. I would vacate the grant of summary judgment to respondents on this issue and remand for further proceedings.

After addressing petitioners' challenge to the sales practice restrictions imposed by the Massachusetts statute, the Court concluded that these provisions did not violate the First Amendment. I concur in that judgment, but write separately on this issue to make two brief points.

Second, though I admit the question is closer, I would, for similar reasons, uphold the regulation limiting tobacco advertising in certain retail establishments to the space five feet or more above the floor. When viewed in isolation, this provision appears to target speech. Further, to the extent that it does target speech it may well run into constitutional problems, as the connection between the ends the statute purports to serve and the means it has chosen are dubious. Nonetheless, I am ultimately persuaded that the provision is unobjectionable because it is little more than an adjunct to the other sales practice restrictions. As the Commonwealth of Massachusetts can properly legislate the placement of products and the nature of displays in its convenience stores, I would not draw a distinction between such restrictions and height restrictions on related product advertising. I would accord the Commonwealth some latitude in imposing restrictions that can have only the slightest impact on the ability of adults to purchase a poisonous product and may save some children from taking the first step on the road to addiction.

III

Because I strongly disagree with the Court's conclusion on the preemption issue, I dissent from Parts II-A and II-B of its opinion. Though I agree with much of what the Court has to say about the First Amendment, I ultimately disagree with its disposition or its reasoning on each of the regulations before us.

GREENLESS v. ALMOND

277 F.3d 601 (1st Cir. 2002)

Lynch, Circuit Judge.

This case concerns claims made on the allocation of monies to the states, specifically Rhode Island, from the 1998 Master Settlement Agreement in the tobacco litigation.

Blanche E. Greenless appeals the dismissal of her suit under 42 U.S.C. [illegible] Island and various other state officials, all in their official capacities. Greenless seeks to represent all of Rhode Island's Medicaid recipients who have suffered damages from the use of tobacco. She claims that federal law requires Rhode Island to pay that class a portion of the proceeds from the settlement of its claims against the tobacco industry, and that Rhode Island is wrongfully converting what are essentially Medicaid recovery collections.

The district court dismissed Greenless's suit without a hearing as barred by the doctrine of state sovereign immunity embodied in the Eleventh Amendment. We affirm the dismissal of the action, but on different grounds, holding that Greenless has failed to state a claim on which relief can be granted due to a recent amendment of the Medicaid statute. We do not reach the difficult question whether a claim of the sort Greenless asserts, if provided by federal law, would be barred by the Eleventh Amendment.

I.

A. Facts

During the 1990s, more than forty of the fifty states, including Rhode Island, filed suits against the major manufacturers of tobacco products. See *State v. Brown & Williamson Tobacco Corp.*, No. 97-3058 (R.I. Sup. Ct. Dec. 17, 1998) (consent decree and final judgment). The exact theories of recovery varied from state to state. Generally, the states alleged that the tobacco industry had misled the public by concealing the risks of cigarette smoking and had therefore caused the states to spend vast sums of public money on providing health care for those made ill by tobacco. Unlike prior attempts to hold tobacco manufacturers liable for smoking-related illnesses or deaths, the states' suits resulted in a lucrative settlement, recorded by the Master Settlement Agreement. See National Association of Attorneys General, Master Settlement Agreement, at www.naag.org/tobac/cigmsa.rtf (Nov. 23, 1998). According to Greenless, under the Agreement Rhode Island will receive approximately $ 1.408 billion.[1]

The expenditures on health care on which the state's suits relied arose in significant part through the Medicaid program. The Medicare and Medicaid programs are the two largest sources of public funding for health care in the United States. Medicare, which provides health care primarily to the elderly and to some individuals with disabilities, receives funds exclusively from the federal government. Medicaid, which provides health care primarily to the indigent, receives funds from both the federal government and the states. State Medicaid expenditures consume large portions of states' budgets; in fiscal year 2000, Rhode Island spent 22.6% of its budget on Medicaid. When the states sought to recover funds spent on health care made necessary by smoking, some of their alleged damages were Medicaid expenditures. So stated Rhode Island's complaint at the time.

The recovery of Medicaid expenditures from the tobacco industry arguably brought into play certain aspects of the federal Medicaid statute. When a state agrees to participate in Medicaid by enacting a statute, it must create a plan that meets requirements specified by Congress. That state Medicaid plan must "provide that, as a condition of eligibility for medical assistance under the State plan . . . the individual is required — (A) to assign the State any rights . . . to payment for medical care from any third party."

Moreover, when a state, acting on an individual's assignment of his or her rights, has recovered from a third party compensation for state expenditures to provide health care via Medicaid, the state may not necessarily keep all of the money. Instead, such part of any amount collected by the State under an assignment made under the provisions of this section shall be retained by the State as is necessary to reimburse it for medical assistance payments made

[1] Payments under the Agreement are contingent on many factors, and assigning values to a state's right to payment is therefore difficult. See *Floyd v. Thompson*, 227 F.3d 1029, 1038 (7th Cir. 2000) ("The final amount to be paid . . . is unknown and unknowable at this point. . . ."). The question presented by this appeal is not quantitative, so exact amounts are not material. Rhode Island stands to receive a great deal of money.

on behalf of an individual with respect to whom such assignment was executed (with appropriate reimbursement of the Federal Government to the extent of its participation in the financing of such medical assistance), and the remainder of such amount collected shall be paid to such individual.

After the state and federal governments are reimbursed, any excess is paid to the individual, "who is usually a person of limited resources."

If these provisions apply to the Master Settlement Agreement (Rhode Island claims they do not because the suit was brought not as a § 1396k assignment but under different theories) then at least some of the money that the tobacco industry paid the states under the Agreement belongs to the federal government as appropriate reimbursement within the meaning of § 1396k(b). If, as well, the states received more money from the tobacco industry under the Agreement than was necessary to reimburse both the state and federal governments for medical assistance payments made on behalf of smokers, then the remainder belongs to the smokers on whose behalf those payments were made. Greenless's claim rests on this theory.

Congress has recently amended the statute. The 1999 Emergency Supplemental Appropriations Act exempts from the normal procedures by which the federal government takes its share of state recoveries "any amount recovered or paid to a State as part of the comprehensive settlement of November 1998 between manufacturers of tobacco products . . . and State Attorneys General." Pub. L. No. 106-31, § 3031, 113 Stat. 57, 103–04 (1999) (codified at 42 U.S.C. § 1396b (d)(3)(B)(i) (Supp. V 1999)). It furthermore provides, with an exception irrelevant to this case, that "a State may use amounts recovered or paid to the State as part of a comprehensive . . . settlement . . . described in [the prior] clause . . . for any expenditures determined appropriate by the State." *Id.*, 113 Stat. at 104 (codified at 42 U.S.C. § 1396b (d)(3)(B)(ii)).

The parties agree that this new language removes any claim to the states' tobacco settlement money by the federal government. The question presented by this appeal is whether the language also removes any possible claim to that money under federal law by the individuals whose illnesses caused the states to spend the money.

B. History

Greenless filed this suit in the District of Rhode Island against the various defendants in their official capacities, claiming that Rhode Island must pay her and the members of her class the amount by which the tobacco settlement exceeds its actual costs. She alleged this amount to be substantial. For her cause of action she relied on 42 U.S.C. § 1983 and its broadranging remedies for violations of federal rights under color of state law. She asked for declaratory and injunctive relief to compel Rhode Island's officials to pay her the alleged excess.

The defendants moved to dismiss on two grounds. First, they argued that Greenless's suit is barred under the Eleventh Amendment by state sovereign immunity as a suit for, in effect, money damages against the treasury of a state. Second, they argued that Greenless has no cause of action under § 1983 because her rights under the Medicaid statute have not been and will not be violated. Greenless in response claimed that her suit does not run afoul of the Eleventh Amendment because the state is not a party, only state officials, and because she seeks only prospective relief permissible under the doctrine of *Ex parte Young*, 209 U.S. 123 (1908), as explained in *Edelman v. Jordan*, 415 U.S. 651 (1974). She also responded to the defendants' statutory arguments. On February 26, 2001, the district court dismissed the case in a seven-page opinion addressing only the question of state sovereign immunity. *Greenless v. Almond,* C.A. No. 00-037ML (D.R.I. Feb. 26, 2001). This appeal followed. The defendants make on appeal both sets of arguments presented to the district court in support of the judgment.

II.

A. Eleventh Amendment and constitutional avoidance

Other plaintiffs have brought cases similar to this one against numerous other states. None have yet succeeded. The only circuit courts to address the Eleventh Amendment question, the Fifth and Tenth Circuits, have held that the Amendment would not prevent the plaintiffs in a case such as this one from obtaining the relief they seek, if that relief were available under federal law.

Every court to consider the question has, however, decided that § 1396k(b) does not apply to the state tobacco settlements, either because the settlements are not recoveries of the sort governed by that section as a general matter or because § 1396b(d)(3)(B)(ii) specifically exempts the settlements.

We do not decide any question of state sovereign immunity today. We will, however, sketch the outlines of the question on the facts of this case in order to explain our reasons for avoiding it. As a general matter the several states are immune under the Eleventh Amendment from private suit in the federal courts, absent their consent. Among the exceptions to this rule is the doctrine of *Ex parte Young*, which allows a plaintiff to enforce a claim of federal right by obtaining injunctive or declaratory relief against a state officer in the officer's official capacity. In *Edelman v. Jordan*, the Supreme Court explained that the purpose of this exception is to prevent continuing violations of federal law, but not to remedy past violations.

Greenless claims to seek a prospective remedy for an allegedly ongoing violation of federal law that will recur each time the state actually receives an installment payment of the tobacco settlement. The defendants claim she seeks retrospective compensation for the alleged violation that the state committed when it reached agreement with the tobacco industry without providing that a portion of the proceeds would go to Greenless and her class. Because of the Supreme Court's recent reinvigoration of the doctrine of state sovereign immunity, see*, e.g*., *Seminole Tribe v. Florida*, 517 U.S. 44 (1996); *Alden v. Maine*, 527 U.S. 706 (1999), private plaintiffs' ability to enforce congressionally enacted restraints on the states' use of many types of funds may well turn on just such questions to a degree few readers of *Edelman* would have predicted when that case was decided.

It is not, however, the role of the federal courts to answer legal questions unless specific cases need answers. This principle applies with special force to complex questions of constitutional law, so that courts often avoid such questions by choosing to focus on other aspects of a case that adequately dispose of the controversy between the parties. In this case, the constitutional question is difficult; but, as we discuss below, at least one statutory question is easy and disposes completely of Greenless's suit. We therefore bypass the constitutional question, as have the Second, Seventh, and Eleventh Circuits, in favor of the easier question whether plaintiffs have stated a claim on which relief may be granted. We recommend this course to the district courts of this circuit as the wiser approach.

B. Statutory interpretation

There are two reasons to doubt whether the amended Medicaid statute will support Greenless's claim. The first reason is that it is not clear whether any of the money recovered by Rhode Island is money to which Greenless and her class can stake a claim under § 1396k(b) as it stood at the time of the settlements. The second reason, and the one on which we base our holding, is § 1396b(d)(3)(B)(ii), added by the Emergency Supplemental Appropriations Act of 1999, Pub. L. No. 106-31, 113 Stat. 57, 103–04 (1999). We find persuasive the reasoning of *Tyler* [*v. Douglas,* 280 F.3d 116 (2d Cir. 2001)], in which the Second Circuit held that § 1396b(d)(3)(B)(ii) was plain and foreclosed a suit similar to the present one. We agree with the Second Circuit that the funds described in that section as available "for any expenditures determined appropriate by the State" cannot simultaneously be owed to Medicaid recipients.

Greenless makes two arguments against this reading of § 1396b(d)(3)(B)(ii) based on traditional principles of statutory interpretation. First, she claims that the reading violates the presumption against implied repeal. Second, she claims that the reading violates the presumption against giving legislation retroactive effect. Although these two presumptions are wellknown landmarks of this area of the law, neither applies to this case.

The "implied repeal" argument is an odd one because at issue is not whether Congress totally repealed § 1396k, but whether it intended to carve out tobacco settlement monies from the reach of that provision. But we will use Greenless's terminology. She argues that the amendment only waives the federal government's share of the settlement and does not affect any rights of individuals. Not so. The presumption against implied repeal, although of particular force when, as here, applied to appropriations riders, nevertheless turns on legislative intent. Indeed, the presumption results from certain assumptions that courts make about the legislative process:

> Courts do not lightly assume that one statute has implicitly repealed another. This principle is a product of a set of beliefs about the legislative process — in particular, a belief that Congress, focused as it usually is on a particular problem, should not be understood to have eliminated without specific consideration another program that was likely the product of sustained attention. C. R. Sunstein, *Interpreting Statutes in the Regulatory State*, 103 Harv. L. Rev. 405, 475 (1989) (footnote omitted). These concerns have less force where, as here,

> Congress was responding to a recent event, the Master Settlement Agreement, and was clear in its language. The only even arguable doubt is whether that repeal covered Medicaid recipients' possible claims as well as the federal government's. In our view the plain statutory language means both.

The presumption against retroactivity also does not affect the result in this case. It is true that as a general matter Congress must speak clearly to make its legislation retroactive. *Landgraf v. USI Film Prods.*, 511 U.S. 244, 280 (1994). Whatever the proper characterization of the relief Greenless seeks in this case, Congress made its intent clear in the amendment, which "applies to all funds received under the Master Settlement Agreement, whether past, present, or future." *Harris [v. Owens]*, 264 F.3d 1282, 1296 [10th Cir. 2001].

III.

To avoid the unnecessary resolution of a difficult constitutional question, we have assessed the merits of Greenless's case and have found that she has failed to state a claim upon which relief may be granted. Therefore, although we do not reach the reasoning of the district court's opinion, its judgment dismissing the case is affirmed.

NOTES AND QUESTIONS

1. The three preceding cases, *FDA v. Brown and Williamson*, *Lorillard Tobacco v. Reilly* and *Greenless v. Almond* all flow from the same appalling paradox: This nation spends billions to subsidize production and consumption of a substance — tobacco — that annually kills 400,000 Americans. That is ten times the number of Americans killed in the Vietnam War; it is 100 times the number killed in the bombing of the World Trade Towers in New York City on September 11, 2001; it is exceeded only by the total killed in America's bloodiest war, the Civil War of 1860-1865. And that number is repeated every year.
2. In *Brown & Williamson*, the Supreme Court rejects the FDA's finding that tobacco is a "drug" subject to regulation. Partly, Justice O'Connor writes, this is because Congress has in the past declined to authorize regulation. Partly, it is because FDA regulation is to make products "safe," which is impossible with tobacco. Partly, it is because the FDA's only course of action would be to remove tobacco products from the market, which Congress has chosen not to do, and the FDA also chose — inconsistently with O'Connor's view — not to do.

   What are Justice Breyer's responses? And isn't he right — the majority's own reasoning leads to the conclusion that the FDA *has* jurisdiction and must ban tobacco as unsafe? What should Congress do now?
3. In *Lorillard Tobacco*, at issue is the 1998-99 agreement between "Big Tobacco" and forty-five states, settling their "Medicaid" suits, in which they sought billion in damages for the healthcare expenses they incurred while caring for the injury inflicted by smoking. The Agreement

obligates the major producers to pay some 200 billion dollars over 20 years, pro-rated by sales in each state (Oregon will get 50–70 million dollars per year). In return, all RICO and consumer fraud and product liability claims — known and unknown — were dropped against the tobacco companies, their suppliers, advertisers, accountants and attorneys. As a result, states now have a financial interest in *increasing* sales.

Several attorneys representing the states claimed (and received) billions in fees.

Subsequently, some states sought to regulate tobacco sales and advertising, as in Massachusetts. In the *Lorillard* case, the multi-state agreement was raised in bar. Justice O'Connor (again) wrote an opinion favoring the tobacco companies, holding that federal law precludes regulating cigarette advertising, and that while state laws on zoning are nevertheless permissible, the Massachusetts statutes were not narrowly tailored and violated "Big Tobacco's" First Amendment rights — as to outdoor advertising near schools and indoor placement of store displays.

Justice Stevens disagrees on both points. Why? And why isn't the usual deference paid to state primacy in health matters in our federal system?

4. *Greenless* also involves the multi-state agreement. Here, a class of citizens want some of Rhode Island's share paid directly to them for injuries from smoking. The District Court dismissed for sovereign immunity reasons. The First Circuit affirms, but because a subsequent amendment to the Medicaid statutes barred such suits, "carving out" tobacco settlement monies from those otherwise available to Medicaid recipients.

   The question thus posed is how could states' attorneys forfeit the future claims of citizens by the multi-state agreement? And how, ethically, may they do so for people whom they do not represent? Moreover, as a "legislative" resolution of taxing and health interests of citizens, what is the authority of courts to impose the Multi-State Tobacco Agreement on states and their citizens.

5. On a different level, what has this to do with bioethics? Individually, people may choose to harm themselves by smoking, may they not? Societally, we may choose to tolerate this, and the revenues it generates for farmers and manufacturers and state budges, yes? Is the concern that, ethically, these are impermissible choices, or that the balance has simply been struck in the wrong direction, at the wrong point?

6. Finally, is there an ethical issue for professionals in all of this? Doctors did research for tobacco companies, enhancing the additive properties of their products. Attorneys hid company documents from discovery, and buried litigants who sued for injuries from smoking. Attorneys-general negotiated away legislative and litigational checks on tobacco marketing. In all of this, are there issues of professional ethics? Of broader ethical significance, would you do, for hire, what they did?

7. As this casebook went into final printing, Judge Gladys Kessler, of the United States District Court for the District of Columbia, on August 17, 2006, ruled in a 1700 page opinion that Big Tobacco has engaged in decades of deception, aided by attorneys, to the detriment of the public. However, she failed to impose the extensive relief the government had sought. The opinion and commentary are just appearing on the web, as of this printing.

PROBLEM 4–6 — The Health Care Costs of Smoking

Consider the following excerpts from Barendregt, Bonneux & Van Der Maas, *The Health Care Costs of Smoking*, which appeared in *The New England Journal of Medicine.*[*]

> Smoking is a major health hazard, and since nonsmokers are healthier than smokers, it seems only natural that not smoking would save money spent on health care. Yet in economic studies of health care it has been difficult to determine who uses more dollars — smokers, who tend to suffer more from a large variety of diseases, or nonsmokers, who can accumulate more health care costs because they live longer. The Surgeon General reported in 1992 that the estimated average lifetime medical costs for a smoker exceed those for a nonsmoker by more than $6,000. On the other hand, Lippiatt estimated that a 1 percent decline in cigarette sales increases costs for medical care by $405 million among persons 25 to 79 years old. Manning et al. argued that although smokers incur higher medical costs, these are balanced by tobacco taxes and by smokers' shorter life spans (and hence their lower use of pensions and nursing homes). Leu and Schaub showed that even when only health care expenditures are considered, the longer life expectancy of nonsmokers more than offsets their lower annual expenditures.
>
> We have analyzed comprehensively the health care costs of smoking. In doing so we have distinguished between the assessment of differences between smokers and nonsmokers and the assessment of what would happen after interventions that changed smoking behavior. Would a nonsmoking population have lower health care costs than one in which some people smoke? Are antismoking interventions economically attractive? We sought to answer these questions and to determine the consequences for health policy.
>
> . . .
>
> [The] dynamic analysis produces a projection of future health care costs. To assess the economic attractiveness of an intervention that would make smokers quit, these costs are compared with those expected when no intervention is made. One difficulty in such an evaluation is the fact that most people prefer to receive benefits as

[*] Barendrengt et al., *The Health Care Costs of Smoking*, 337 New. Eng. J. Med. 1052-57 (1997).

soon as possible and to postpone payments. Economists call this phenomenon "time preference,"[16] [17] and it is taken into account by discounting the future benefits and costs — that is, those further away in time are given lower weights in the overall evaluation.

Per capita costs rise sharply with age, increasing almost 10 times from persons 40 to 44 years of age to those 85 to 89 years of age. In each age group, smokers incur higher costs than nonsmokers. The difference varies with the age group, but among 65-to-74-year-olds the costs for smokers are as much as 40 percent higher among men and as much as 25 percent higher among women.

However, the annual cost per capita ignores the differences in longevity between smokers and nonsmokers. These differences are substantial: for smokers, the life expectancies at birth are 69.7 years in men and 75.6 years in women; for nonsmokers, the life expectancies are 77.0 and 81.6 years. This means that many more nonsmokers than smokers live to old age. At age 70, 78 percent of male nonsmokers are still alive, as compared with only 57 percent of smokers (among women, the figures are 86 percent and 75 percent); at age 80, men's survival is 50 percent and 21 percent, respectively (among women, 67 percent and 43 percent).

These differences in the numbers of elderly people have a profound effect on the health care costs for the population. In the younger age groups, in which mortality even among smokers is quite low, a population of smokers has higher health care costs than a population of nonsmokers, but in the groups of men 70 to 74 and over (and those of women 75 to 79 and over), the lower per capita cost of the nonsmokers is outweighed by the greater number of people remaining alive.

[T]he nonsmoking population as a whole is more expensive than the smoking population.

. . .

The risk of the diseases not related to smoking is considered equal for smokers and nonsmokers, but the nonsmoking population lives longer and therefore incurs more costs due to those diseases, particularly in old age, when the costs are highest [illegible] for male and female nonsmokers are 7 percent and 4 percent higher, respectively, than for a mixed population, whereas for smokers the total costs are 7 percent and 11 percent lower.

[I]f all smokers stopped smoking. . . , the total health care costs for men would initially be lower than they would have been (by up to 2.5 percent), because the incidence of smoking-related diseases among the former smokers would decline to the level among nonsmokers. Prevalence rates start to decline, costs decline, and the intervention shows

[16] Drummond MP, Stoddart GL, Torrance GW. Methods for the economic evaluation of health care programmes. Oxford, England: Oxford University Press, 1990.

[17] Murray CJL. Rethinking DALYs. In: Murray CJL, Lopez AD, eds. The global burden of disease; a comprehensive assessment of mortality and disability from diseases, injuries, and risk factors in 1990 and projected to 2010. Vol. 1 of Global burden of disease and injury series. Boston: Harvard School of Public Health, 1996;1-96.

a benefit. With time, however, the benefit reverses itself to become a cost. The reason is that along with incidence and prevalence, smoking-related mortality declines and the population starts to age. Growing numbers of people in the older age groups mean higher costs for health care. By year 5, the benefit derived from the presence of the new nonsmokers starts to shrink, and by year 15 these former smokers are producing excess costs. Eventually a new steady state is reached in which costs are about 7 percent higher — the difference between the mixed and the nonsmoking populations.

. . .

This study shows that although per capita health care costs for smokers are higher than those of nonsmokers, a nonsmoking population would have higher health care costs than the current mixed population of smokers and nonsmokers. Yet given a short enough period of follow-up and a high enough discount rate, it would be economically attractive to eliminate smoking.

Other studies of this subject estimate lifetime health care costs, taking the differences in life expectancy into account, and find that smokers have higher medical costs.[3] [21] [22] In our study, lifetime costs for smokers can be calculated as $72,700 among men and $94,700 among women, and lifetime costs among nonsmokers can be calculated as $83,400 and $111,000, respectively. This amounts to lifetime costs for nonsmokers that are higher by 15 percent among men and 18 percent among women.

. . .

Finally, with respect to public health policy, how important are the costs of smoking? Society clearly has an interest in this matter, now that several states are trying to recoup Medicaid expenditures from tobacco firms and the tobacco companies have agreed to a settlement. Yet we believe that in formulating public health policy, whether or not smokers impose a net financial burden ought to be of very limited importance. Public health policy is concerned with health. Smoking is a major health hazard, so the objective of a policy on smoking should be simple and clear: smoking should be discouraged.

Since we as a society are clearly willing to spend money on added years of life and on healthier years, the method of choice in evaluating medical interventions is cost-effectiveness analysis, which yields costs per year of life gained. Decision makers then implement the interventions that yield the highest return in health for the budget.[28] We have no doubt that an effective antismoking policy fits the bill.

---

[3] Manning WG, Keeler EB, Newhouse JP, Sloss EM, Wasserman J. The taxes of sin: do smokers and drinkers pay their way? JAMA 1989;261:1604-9.

[21] Hodgson TA. Cigarette smoking and lifetime medical expenditures. Milbank Q 1992;70:81-125.

[22] Viscusi WK. Cigarette taxation and the social consequences of smoking: Working paper no. 4891. Cambridge, Mass.: National Bureau of Economic Research, 1994.

[28] Murray CJ, Kreuser J, Whang W. Cost-effectiveness analysis and policy choices: investing in health systems. Bull World Health Organ 1994;72:663-74.

Questions

1. Does the conclusion of the study — that a nonsmoking population would have higher healthcare costs — surprise you? Does it seem valid?
2. What are the implications of this study legislatively? Ethically? Under the European Council Convention? For litigation against tobacco companies?
3. During late 1998 and early 1999, 46 states settled their litigation with the major tobacco companies for health care costs to Medicaid, and for fraud and misconduct. The companies are to pay approximately $8 billion dollars per year for 25 years. What more do you need to know to evaluate the adequacy and fairness of that settlement? A number of cities, foreign countries and the federal government are contemplating litigation. How would you evaluate the wisdom and desirability of such actions?
4. For an excellent article, see Mitchell L. Lathrop, *Tobacco-Related Litigation: How It May Impact The World's Insurance Industry*, 3 Conn. Ins. L.J. 305 (1997); and see Lucien J. Dhooge, *Smoke Across the Waters: Tobacco Production and Exportation as International Human Rights Violations*, 22 Fordham Int'l L.J. 355 (1998).

PROBLEM 4–7 — Federal Tobacco Quotas

Consider the following excerpts from an article from *The Newhouse News Service*, September 1998.*

> PEMBROKE, N.C. — Zebbie Pipkin looks out over acres of lush, yellow-green tobacco leaves and remembers the days when a few acres of dirt and a big family were all it took to run a tobacco farm.
>
> He also remembers kids like the McArthur brothers, who spent their summers planting, picking and playing in the sandy tobacco fields of this rural Robeson County town not far from the South Carolina border.
>
> But, like most people of Pipkin's generation, the McArthur brothers left Pembroke for even greener pastures. And, when they left, they took along their Southern heritage and a valuable commodity known as a federal tobacco quota.
>
> . . .
>
> Tobacco quotas were first given out by the federal government 60 years ago and are, in essence, a license to grow tobacco. While 82,000 people hold quotas to grow tobacco in North Carolina — which produces about one-third of the nation's cigarette tobacco — many of those quotas have been bought, sold, leased, inherited and, in many cases, moved far from the tobacco country land to which they are attached. The quota system is part of a complicated and arcane set of controls put in place during the Great Depression to protect tobacco farmers. Today, some in Congress want to abolish the entire program.

Each year, the U.S. Department of Agriculture calculates the amount of tobacco supply that is needed to meet the demands of cigarette producers here and abroad. The quotas are then set based on that figure and farmers are told how much of the leaf they can grow.

. . .

McArthur is more typical of the tobacco quota holders that left rural South and moved to New Jersey and just about every other state over the past several decades. He and his siblings own seven quotas totaling 7,980 pounds that were passed on to a generation that had little interest in raising the labor-intensive crop. "No one in my generation was willing to take on the farm; most of us left the area," McArthur said. Of his seven siblings, only two sisters still live in Pembroke, and they don't farm.

"We rent out our farm along with the quota, but it is still in the family. You rent it out to someone who does the planting and the harvesting and all the other work and when it comes time to sell the crop, you split the money. The tobacco still sells in your name since you hold the quota," he explained.

. . .

In Washington, where the debate on a mammoth tobacco bill has been raging for more than a year, Congress is considering scrapping the quota system and spending as much as $13 billion to compensate farmers and quota holders. One plan, offered by Sen. Richard Lugar, R-Ind., the chairman of the Senate Agriculture Committee, would buy off quota holders at $8 per pound.

At the same time, there are those in Washington who think the quota system should end, along with price supports, with out paying quota holders a dime.

"Growing tobacco is against the public interest," said Sen. Frank Lautenberg, D-N.J., one of Capitol Hill's fiercest anti-tobacco advocates.

"We want to try and whittle away at tobacco production. I'm sorry that it would mean less value to these quotas, but it happens when there is a product that is against the human and social interests," he said.

That attitude does not sit too well with growers in Robeson County, or with quota holders living in far-flung regions of the country. Without quotas, they say, farmland in these parts would be practically worthless.

"That would be terrible. That would be the end of farming in this area," said Larry Sampson, a Robeson County tobacco farmer and president of the Tobacco Growers Association of North Carolina." A lot of these farms would just dry up and blow away," said Sampson, a 46-year-old who traces his heritage to the Lumbee Native Americans.

> Sampson, who leases about 90 percent of the quota he needs to grow 1 million pounds of tobacco a year on his 550-acre farm, said such a move would devastate a regional economy that is inextricably hooked to tobacco.

In light of the preceding case law, (a) do the tobacco growers have any liability to the ultimate consumers? (b) does the policy of subsidies and quotas make sense? (c) can that policy be squared with the national costs to Medicaid and Medicare of smoking? (d) should those holding quotas be compensated if the federal program is terminated?

[b] Alcohol

As with tobacco, society must confront the dilemma of social and health costs inflicted by alcohol use, a use explicitly allowed by law and supported by custom. The result is an inconsistent pattern of tolerance and intolerance. We begin with the question — ethical, fully as much as biological — of whether intoxication may excuse crime.

MONTANA v. EGELHOFF*
518 U.S. 37 (1996)

Justice **Scalia** announced the judgment of the Court and delivered an opinion, in which the **Chief Justice**, Justice **Kennedy**, and Justice **Thomas** join.

We consider in this case whether the Due Process Clause is violated by Montana Code Annotated § 45-2-203, which provides, in relevant part, that voluntary intoxication "may not be taken into consideration in determining the existence of a mental state which is an element of [a criminal] offense."

I

In July 1992, while camping out in the Yaak region of northwestern Montana to pick mushrooms, respondent made friends with Roberta Pavola and John Christenson, who were doing the same. On Sunday, July 12, the three sold the mushrooms they had collected and spent the rest of the day and evening drinking, in bars and at a private party in Troy, Montana. Some time after 9 p.m., they left the party in Christenson's 1974 Ford Galaxy station wagon. The drinking binge apparently continued, as respondent was seen buying beer at 9:20 p.m. and recalled "sitting on a hill or a bank passing a bottle of Black Velvet back and forth" with Christenson.

At about midnight that night, officers of the Lincoln County, Montana, sheriff's department, responding to reports of a possible drunk driver, discovered Christenson's station wagon stuck in a ditch along U.S. Highway 2. In the front seat were Pavola and Christenson, each dead from a single gunshot to the head. In the rear of the car lay respondent, alive and yelling obscenities. His blood-alcohol content measured .36 percent over one hour later. On the

* Citation material has been omitted from this case.

floor of the car, near the brake pedal, lay respondent's .38 caliber handgun, with four loaded rounds and two empty casings; respondent had gunshot residue on his hands.

Respondent was charged with two counts of deliberate homicide, a crime defined by Montana law as "purposely" or "knowingly" causing the death of another human being. . . . Respondent's defense at trial was that an unidentified fourth person must have committed the murders; his own extreme intoxication, he claimed, had rendered him physically incapable of committing the murders, and accounted for his inability to recall the events of the night of July 12. Although respondent was allowed to make this use of the evidence that he was intoxicated, the jury was instructed, pursuant to Mont. Code Ann. § 45-2-203 (1995), that it could not consider respondent's "intoxicated condition . . . in determining the existence of a mental state which is an element of the offense." The jury found respondent guilty on both counts, and the court sentenced him to 84 years' imprisonment.

. . . .

The historical record does not leave room for the view that the common law's rejection of intoxication as an "excuse" or "justification" for crime would nonetheless permit the defendant to show that intoxication prevented the requisite mens rea. Hale, Coke and Blackstone were familiar, to say the least, with the concept of mens rea, and acknowledged that drunkenness "deprive[s] men of the use of reason," It is inconceivable that they did not realize that an offender's drunkenness might impair his ability to form the requisite intent; and inconceivable that their failure to note this massive exception from the general rule of disregard of intoxication was an oversight. . . .

Against this extensive evidence of a lengthy common-law tradition decidedly against him, the best argument available to respondent is the one made by his amicus and conceded by the State: Over the course of the 19th century, courts carved out an exception to the common law's traditional across-the-board condemnation of the drunken offender, allowing a jury to consider a defendant's intoxication when assessing whether he possessed the mental state needed to commit the crime charged, where the crime was one requiring a "specific intent." The emergence of this new rule is often traced to an 1819 English case, in which Justice Holroyd is reported to have held that "though voluntary drunkenness cannot excuse from the commission of crime, yet where, as on a charge of murder, the material question is, whether an act was premeditated or done only with sudden heat and impulse, the fact of the party being intoxicated [is] a circumstance proper to be taken into consideration." . . .

. . . .

. . . [F]ully one-fifth of the States either never adopted the "new common-law" rule at issue here or have recently abandoned it.

It is not surprising that many States have held fast to or resurrected the common-law rule prohibiting consideration of voluntary intoxication in the determination of mens rea, because that rule has considerable justification — which alone casts doubt upon the proposition that the opposite rule is a "fundamental principle." A large number of crimes, especially violent crimes, are committed by intoxicated offenders; modern studies put the numbers as high as half of all homicides, for example. Disallowing consideration of voluntary intoxication has the effect of increasing the punishment for all unlawful acts committed in that state, and thereby deters drunkenness or irresponsible behavior while drunk. The rule also serves as a specific deterrent, ensuring that those who prove incapable of controlling violent impulses while voluntarily intoxicated go to prison. And finally, the rule comports with and implements society's moral perception that one who has voluntarily impaired his own faculties should be responsible for the consequences.

There is, in modern times, even more justification for laws such as § 45-2-203 than there used to be. Some recent studies suggest that the connection between drunkenness and crime is as much cultural as pharmacological — that is, that drunks are violent not simply because alcohol makes them that way, but because they are behaving in accord with their learned belief that drunks are violent. . . .

. . . .

Justice **Ginsburg**, concurring in the judgment.

. . . .

. . . [C]an a State, without offense to the Federal Constitution, make the judgment that two people are equally culpable where one commits an act stone sober, and the other engages in the same conduct after his voluntary intoxication has reduced his capacity for self-control? . . .

. . . .

As urged by Montana and its amici, § 45-2-203 "extract[s] the entire subject of voluntary intoxication from the mens rea inquiry," thereby rendering evidence of voluntary intoxication logically irrelevant to proof of the requisite mental state. Thus, in a prosecution for deliberate homicide, the State need not prove that the defendant "purposely or knowingly cause[d] the death of another," in a purely subjective sense. To obtain a conviction, the prosecution must prove only that (1) the defendant caused the death of another with actual knowledge or purpose, or (2) that the defendant killed "under circumstances that would otherwise establish knowledge or purpose 'but for' [the defendant's] voluntary intoxication . . .

Comprehended as a measure redefining mens rea, § 45-2-203 encounters no constitutional shoal. States enjoy wide latitude in defining the elements of criminal offenses, particularly when determining "the extent to which moral culpability should be a prerequisite to conviction of a crime," . . . Defining mens rea to eliminate the exculpatory value of voluntary intoxication does not offend a "fundamental principle of justice," given the lengthy common-law tradition, and the adherence of a significant minority of the States to that position today. . . .

. . . .

Justice **O'Connor**, with whom Justice **Stevens**, Justice **Souter**, and Justice **Breyer** join, dissenting.

The Montana Supreme Court unanimously held that Mont. Code Ann. § 45-2-203 (1995) violates due process. I agree. Our cases establish that due process sets an outer limit on the restrictions that may be placed on a defendant's ability to raise an effective defense to the State's accusations. Here, to impede the defendant's ability to throw doubt on the State's case, Montana has removed from the jury's consideration a category of evidence relevant to determination of mental state where that mental state is an essential element of the offense that must be proved beyond a reasonable doubt. Because this disallowance eliminates evidence with which the defense might negate an essential element, the State's burden to prove its case is made correspondingly easier. The justification for this disallowance is the State's desire to increase the likelihood of conviction of a certain class of defendants who might otherwise be able to prove that they did not satisfy a requisite element of the offense. In my view, the statute's effect on the criminal proceeding violates due process.

I

This Court's cases establish that limitations placed on the accused's ability to present a fair and complete defense can, in some circumstances, be severe enough to violate due process. . . . It is true that a defendant does not enjoy an absolute right to present evidence relevant to his defense. But none of the "familiar" evidentiary rules operates as Montana's does. The Montana statute places a blanket exclusion on a category of evidence that would allow the accused to negate the offense's mental-state element. In so doing, it frees the prosecution, in the face of such evidence, from having to prove beyond a reasonable doubt that the defendant nevertheless possessed the required mental state. In my view, this combination of effects violates due process.

. . . .

A State's placement of a significant limitation on the right to defend against the State's accusations "requires that the competing interest be closely examined." Montana has specified that to prove guilt, the State must establish that the defendant acted purposely or knowingly, but has prohibited a category of defendants from effectively disputing guilt through presentation of evidence relevant to that essential element. And the evidence is indisputably relevant: The Montana Supreme Court held that evidence of intoxication is relevant to proof of mental state, and furthermore, § 45-2-203's exception for involuntary intoxication shows that the legislature does consider intoxication relevant to mental state. . . . Montana has barred the defendant's use of a category of relevant, exculpatory evidence for the express purpose of improving the State's likelihood of winning a conviction against a certain type of defendant. The plurality's observation that all evidentiary rules that exclude exculpatory evidence reduce the State's burden to prove its case, is beside the point. The purpose of the familiar evidentiary rules is not to alleviate the State's burden, but rather, to vindicate some other goal or value — e.g., to ensure the reliability and competency of evidence or to encourage effective communications within certain relationships. Such rules may or may not help the prosecution, and when they do help, do so only incidentally. While due process does not "ba[r] States from making changes . . . that have the effect of making it easier for the prosecution to obtain convictions," an evidentiary rule whose sole purpose is to boost the State's likelihood of conviction distorts the adversary process. . . .

. . . .

. . . [The Court] acknowledges that a reduction of the State's burden through disallowance of exculpatory evidence is unconstitutional if it violates a principle of fairness. I believe that such a violation is present here. Montana's disallowance of consideration of voluntary-intoxication evidence removes too critical a category of relevant, exculpatory evidence from the adversarial process by prohibiting the defendant from making an essential argument and permitting the prosecution to benefit from its suppression. Montana's purpose is to increase the likelihood of conviction of a certain class of defendants, who might otherwise be able to prove that they did not satisfy a requisite element of the offense. The historical fact that this disallowance once existed at common law is not sufficient to save the statute today. I would affirm the judgment of the Montana Supreme Court.

Justice **Souter**, dissenting.

I have no doubt that a State may so define the mental element of an offense that evidence of a defendant's voluntary intoxication at the time of commission does not have exculpatory relevance and, to that extent, may be excluded without raising any issue of due process. I would have thought the statute at issue here had implicitly accomplished such a redefinition, but I read the opinion of the Supreme Court of Montana as indicating that it had no such effect, and I am bound by the state court's statement of its domestic law.

. . . .

. . . Montana had at least one way to give effect to its judgment that defendants should not be permitted to use evidence of their voluntary intoxication to defeat proof of culpable mental state, and perhaps a second. First, it could have defined culpable mental state so as to give voluntary intoxication no exculpatory relevance. While the Due Process Clause requires the government to prove the existence of every element of the offense beyond a reasonable doubt, within fairly broad limits the definition of those elements is up to the State. . . .

While I therefore find no apparent constitutional reason why Montana could not render evidence of voluntary intoxication excludable as irrelevant by redefining "knowledge" and "purpose," as they apply to the mental state element of its substantive offenses, or by making some other provision for mental state, I do not believe that I am free to conclude that Montana has done so here. Our view of state law is limited by its interpretation in the State's highest court, and I am not able to square the State Supreme Court's opinion in this case with the position advanced by the State here (and supported by the United States, as amicus curiae), that Montana's legislature changed the definition of culpable mental states when it enacted § 45-2-203.

. . . .

A State (though not necessarily Montana) might, for example, argue that admitting intoxication evidence on the issue of culpable mental state but not on a defense of incapacity (as to which it is widely assumed to be excludable) as generally irrelevant would be irrational since both capacity to obey the law and purpose to accomplish a criminal result presuppose volitional ability. See Model Penal Code § 4.01 ("A person is not responsible for criminal conduct if at the time of such conduct as a result of mental disease or defect he lacks substantial capacity . . . to conform his conduct to the requirements of law") and Model Penal Code § 2.02(2)(a)(i) ("A person acts purposely with respect to a material element of an offense when . . . it is his conscious object to engage in conduct of that nature or to cause such a result"). And quite apart from any technical irrationality, a State might think that admitting the evidence in question on culpable mental state but not capacity (when each was a jury issue in a given case) would raise too high a risk of juror confusion. While Thomas Reed Powell reportedly suggested that "learning to think like a lawyer is when you learn to think about one thing that is connected to another without thinking about the other thing it is connected to," Teachout, *Sentimental Metaphors,* 34 UCLA L. Rev. 537, 545 (1986), a State might argue that its law should be structured on the assumption that its jurors typically will not suffer from this facility.

Quite apart from the fact that Montana has made no such arguments for justification here, however, I am not at all sure why such arguments would go any further than justifying redefinition of mental states (the first option above). I do not understand why they would justify the state in cutting the conceptual corner by leaving the definitions of culpable mental states untouched but excluding evidence relevant to this proof. Absent a convincing argument for cutting that corner, Chambers and the like constrain us to hold the current Montana statute unconstitutional. I therefore respectfully dissent.

Justice **Breyer**, with whom Justice **Stevens** joins, dissenting.

. . . A statute that makes voluntary intoxication the legal equivalent of purpose or knowledge *but only where external circumstances would establish purpose or knowledge in the absence of intoxication,* is a statute that turns guilt or innocence not upon state of mind, but upon irrelevant external circumstances. An intoxicated driver stopped at an intersection who unknowingly accelerated into a pedestrian would likely be found guilty, for a jury unaware of intoxication would likely infer knowledge or purpose. An identically intoxicated driver racing along a highway who unknowingly sideswiped another car would likely be found innocent, for a jury unaware of intoxication would likely infer negligence. Why would a legislature want to write a statute that draws such a distinction, upon which a sentence of life imprisonment, or death, may turn? If the legislature wanted to equate voluntary intoxication, knowledge, and purpose, why would it not write a statute that plainly says so, instead of doing so in a roundabout manner that would affect, in dramatically different ways, those whose minds, deeds, and consequences seem identical? I would reserve the question of whether or not such a hypothetical statute might exceed constitutional limits.

NOTES AND QUESTIONS

1. Alcohol abuse, as Justice Scalia notes, is involved in the majority of crimes. It is, independently, a legitimate matter of societal concern. Mr.

Egelhoff's blood alcohol level of .36 was *four times* the level established by many states for presuming intoxication in the operation of a motor vehicle.

2. A full reading of the Justices' opinions would suggest a state may make intoxication irrelevant in establishing guilt of homicide. Should a state do so? *Should* it do so while imposing the maximum penalty for *knowing* misconduct? And for what reason — to define culpability? Deter excessive drinking?

3. If your answer is in the affirmative, what of § 4.01 of the Model Penal Code? *Must* a state provide for a defense of insanity?

   And what of repetitive, compulsive drinking, so pathological as to resemble (indeed, *constitute*) a disease? Should such a condition, denominated alcoholism, excuse Mr. Egelhoff? On what theory — insanity? Excuse totally, or simply reduce the *degree* of culpability? *See Powell v. Texas*, 392 U.S. 514 (1968). Alcoholism as a disease or disability has received mixed acceptance in society. The next case may illustrate why.

TRAYNOR v. TURNAGE
485 U.S. 535 (1988)

Justice **White**, J., delivered the opinion of the Court.

These cases arise from the Veterans' Administration's refusal to grant two recovered alcoholics extensions of time in which to use their veterans' educational benefits. We must decide whether the Veterans' Administration's decision is subject to judicial review and, if so, whether that decision violates § 504 of the Rehabilitation Act of 1973, U.S.C. § 794, which requires that federal programs not discriminate against handicapped individuals solely because of their handicap.

I

Veterans who have been honorably discharged from the United States Armed Forces are entitled to receive educational assistance benefits under the Veterans' Readjustment Benefit Act of 1966 ("GI Bill") to facilitate their readjustment to civilian life. These benefits generally must be used within 10 years following discharge or release from active duty. Veterans may obtain an extension of the 10-year delimiting period, however, if they were prevented from using their benefits earlier by "a physical or mental disability which was not the result of [their] own willful misconduct."

Petitioners are honorably discharged veterans who did not exhaust their educational benefits during the decade following their military service. They sought to continue to receive benefits after the expiration of the 10-year delimiting period on the ground that they had been disabled by alcoholism during much of that period. The Veterans' Administration determined that petitioners' alcoholism constituted "willful misconduct"[1] and accordingly

[1] The applicable regulation, 38 C.F.R. § 3.301(c)(2) (1987), provides: "Alcoholism: The simple drinking of alcoholic beverage is not of itself willful misconduct. The deliberate drinking of a

denied the requested extensions.

III

. . . .

Congress historically has imposed time limitations on the use of "G.I. Bill" educational benefits. Veterans of World War II were required to use their benefits within nine years after their discharge from military service, while Korean Conflict veterans had eight years in which to use their benefits. The delimiting period under the current "G.I. Bill" was raised from 8 years to 10 years in 1974. In 1977, Congress created an exception to this 10-year delimiting period for veterans who delayed their education because of "a physical or mental disability which was not the result of [their] own willful misconduct."

Congress did not use the term "willful misconduct" inadvertently. The same term had long been used in other veterans' benefits statutes. For example, veterans are denied compensation for service-connected disabilities that are "the result of the veteran's own willful misconduct." The Veterans' Administration had long construed the term "willful misconduct" for purposes of these statutes as encompassing primary alcoholism (i.e., alcoholism that is not "secondary to and a manifestation of an acquired psychiatric disorder").

. . . [W]e must assume that Congress was aware of the Veterans' Administration's interpretation of "willful misconduct" at the time that it enacted § 1662(a)(1), and that Congress intended that the term receive the same meaning for purposes of that statute as it had received for purposes of other veterans' benefits statutes. The legislative history confirms that Congress intended that the Veterans' Administration apply the same test of "willful misconduct" in granting extensions of time under § 1662(a)(1) as the agency already was applying in granting disability compensation. . . .

. . . .

It was the same Congress that one year later extended § 504's prohibition against discrimination on the basis of handicap to "any program or activity conducted by any Executive agency." Yet, in enacting the 1978 Rehabilitation Act amendments, Congress did not affirmatively evince any intent to repeal or amend the "willful misconduct" provision of § 1662(a)(1). Nor did Congress anywhere in the language or legislative history of the 1978 amendments expressly disavow its 1977 determination that primary alcoholism is not the sort of disability that warrants an exemption from the time constraints of § 1662(a)(1).

. . . .

. . . Moreover, the 1978 legislation is not rendered meaningless, even with respect to those who claim to have been handicapped as a result of alcoholism,

known poisonous substance or under conditions which would raise a presumption to that effect will be considered willful misconduct. If, in the drinking of a beverage to enjoy its intoxicating effects, intoxication results proximately and immediately in disability or death, the disability or death will be considered the result of the person's willful misconduct. Organic diseases and disabilities which are a secondary result of the chronic use of alcohol as a beverage, whether out of compulsion or otherwise, will not be considered of willful misconduct origin."

. . . .

if the "willful misconduct" provision of § 1662(a)(1) is allowed to retain the import originally intended by Congress.

First, the "willful misconduct" provision does not undermine the central purpose of § 504, which is to assure that handicapped individuals receive "evenhanded treatment" in relation to nonhandicapped individuals. Rather, petitioners challenge a statutory provision that treats disabled veterans more favorably than able-bodied veterans: The former may obtain extensions of time in which to use their educational benefits so long as they did not become disabled as a result of their own "willful misconduct"; the latter are absolutely precluded from obtaining such extensions regardless of how compelling their reasons for having delayed their schooling might be. In other words, § 1662(a)(1) merely provides a special benefit to disabled veterans who bear no responsibility for their disabilities that is not provided to other disabled veterans or to any able-bodied veterans.

. . . .

Furthermore, § 1662(a)(1) does not deny extensions of the delimiting period to all alcoholics but only to those whose drinking was not attributable to an underlying psychiatric disorder. It is estimated by some authorities that mental illness is responsible for 20% to 30% of all alcoholism cases. Each veteran who claims to have been disabled by alcoholism is entitled to an individualized assessment of whether his condition was the result of a mental illness.

Petitioners, however, perceive an inconsistency between § 504 and the conclusive presumption that alcoholism not motivated by mental illness is necessarily "willful." They contend that § 504 mandates an individualized determination of "willfulness" with respect to each veteran who claims to have been disabled by alcoholism. It would arguably be inconsistent with § 504 for Congress to distinguish between categories of disabled veterans according to generalized determinations that lack any substantial basis. If primary alcoholism is not always "willful," as that term has been defined by Congress and the Veterans' Administration, some veterans denied benefits may well be [illegible] Congress failed to act in accordance with § 504 in this instance, however, given what the District of Columbia Circuit accurately characterized as "a substantial body of medical literature that even contests the proposition that alcoholism is a disease, much less that it is a disease for which the victim bears no responsibility." Indeed, even among many who consider alcoholism a "disease" to which its victims are genetically predisposed, the consumption of alcohol is not regarded as wholly involuntary. As we see it, § 504 does not demand inquiry into whether factors other than mental illness rendered an individual veteran's drinking so entirely beyond his control as to negate any degree of "willfulness" where Congress and the Veterans' Administration have reasonably determined for purposes of the veterans' benefits statutes that no such factors exist.

. . . .

IV

Justice **Blackmun**, with whom Justice **Brennan** and Justice **Marshall** join, concurring in part and dissenting in part.

. . . .

My dispute with the Court centers in its upholding of the regulation, whereby the Veterans' Administration (VA) presumes, irrebuttably, that primary alcoholism always is the result of the veteran's "own willful misconduct." This is the very kind of broad social generalization that § 504 of the Rehabilitation Act is intended to eliminate. The petitioners in these cases ask only that their situations be given individualized evaluation. Because I think this is what the Rehabilitation Act clearly requires, I dissent from the Court's conclusion to the contrary.[2]

I

Petitioner Eugene Traynor began drinking when he was eight or nine years old. He drank with increasing frequency throughout his teenage years, and was suffering alcohol-related seizures by the time he was on active military duty in Vietnam. During the four years following his honorable discharge in 1969, Mr. Traynor was hospitalized repeatedly for alcoholism and related illnesses.

By the end of 1974, however, petitioner Traynor had conquered his drinking problem. He attended college part-time beginning in 1977, and continued working toward his degree until the 10-year period for using his veteran's educational benefits expired for him in 1979. Mr. Traynor applied for the extension of time available to one whose disability had prevented him from completing a program of education within the 10-year period. Because he was unable to establish that his alcoholism was due to an underlying psychiatric disorder, his condition was labeled "primary alcoholism." Pursuant to the regulation cited above, Mr. Traynor was presumed to have brought his alcoholism upon himself through "willful misconduct." The requested extension therefore was denied.

Petitioner James P. McKelvey also started drinking as a child. He was 13 when he began to develop the alcohol dependency that was common among members of his family. His drinking problem plagued him while he was in the Army, and he was hospitalized frequently during the nine years that followed his honorable discharge in 1966. Despite his disability, however, McKelvey managed, between hospital stays, to attend two educational institutions under the veterans' educational-benefits program.

Mr. McKelvey took his last drink in 1975, only a year and a half before his 10-year delimiting period expired. Like Traynor, McKelvey sought an extension on the ground that his alcoholism had prevented him from using, within the period, the benefits to which he was entitled. And, like Traynor, McKelvey was denied the extension because his disability, primary alcoholism, was conclusively presumed to have been caused by his "own willful misconduct." the

[2] It perhaps is worth noting that, despite much comment in the popular press, these cases are not concerned with whether alcoholism, simplistically, is or is not a "disease."

VA's regulation deprived each of these veterans of any opportunity to establish that, in his particular case, disabling alcoholism was not willfully incurred.

II

The VA's reliance on its irrebuttable presumption that all primary alcoholism is attributable to willful misconduct cannot be squared with the mandate against discrimination contained in § 504 of the Rehabilitation Act. . . .

In these cases, the Court is called upon, not to make its own medical judgments about the causes of alcoholism, but to interpret § 504. That statute sets forth a simple rule:

> "No otherwise qualified individual with handicaps . . . shall, solely by reason of his handicap, be excluded from the participation in, be denied the benefits of, or be subjected to discrimination under any program or activity receiving Federal financial assistance or under any program or activity conducted by any Executive agency. . . ."

It is beyond dispute that petitioners, as alcoholics, were handicapped individuals covered by the Act. [T]he VA, by its regulation, has established an irrebuttable presumption that primary alcoholism is the result of willful misconduct. This presumption appears to be a clear violation of § 504's mandate requiring individualized assessment of each claimant's qualifications.

. . . .

III

. . . .

In order to escape § 504's requirements, the majority must conclude that in 1977 Congress defined a primary alcoholic as not "otherwise qualified," within the meaning of § 504, for the extension of time available under § 1662(a)(1). The language of § 1662(a)(1) itself merely establishes that a willfully incurred disability, as a general matter, does not [illegible] the extension of time. And the Senate Report, upon which the Court exclusively relies, makes only passing reference to the relevant regulations — regulations which encompass the VA's entire policy on the applicability of the willful-misconduct provisions, not just the application of that term to alcoholism. Finally, even those portions of the regulations expressly addressed to alcoholism do not state that primary alcoholism is to be equated with willful misconduct. . . .

. . . .

IV

I am reluctant to conclude that anything short of a congressional determination linking all primary alcoholism to willful misconduct could justify the VA's substitution of its generic rule for the individualized assessment generally required under § 504.b. It is conceivable that an agency legitimately could eschew individualized assessments of disabled individuals' qualifications if it were evident, as a matter of medical fact, that a particular disqualifying characteristic always is associated with a particular disability.[3] But it is not at all evident that an absolute correlation exists between the condition of primary alcoholism and the disqualifying factor of willful misconduct, as defined by the VA. Nor has the VA successfully demonstrated that such an absolute correlation is medically justified. The VA suggests that it is enough that "although the policy may not produce in an individual case the same conclusion another arbiter might reach, the VA policy provides a reasonable and workable accommodation of modern medico-psychological evidence."

A

The VA seems to suggest that generalizations about attributes associated with individuals suffering from a particular disability can be relied upon to assess those individuals' qualifications, as long as the generalizations are shown to be reasonable. But reliance on generalizations, even "reasonable" ones, is clearly prohibited under *Arline*. In that case, the Court ruled that § 504 prevented the Nassau County School Board from generalizing about the contagiousness of tuberculosis. Acknowledging that in some cases contagiousness would justify altering or perhaps terminating a tuberculosis sufferer's employment in order to avoid infecting others, the Court nevertheless found impermissible a generalization built on that less-than-perfect correlation between disability and qualification. The Court explained:

> "The fact that some persons who have contagious diseases may pose a serious health threat to others under certain circumstances does not justify excluding from the coverage of the Act all persons with actual or perceived contagious diseases. Such exclusion would mean that those accused of being contagious would never have the opportunity to have their condition evaluated in light of medical evidence and a determination made as to whether they were otherwise qualified. Rather, they would be vulnerable to discrimination on the basis of mythology — precisely the type of injury Congress sought to prevent."

The myth to which the Court was referring was not that some tuberculosis sufferers were contagious, but that they all were. The parallel myth in the present cases, of course, is that all primary alcoholics became disabled as a result of their own willful misconduct. Just as § 504 entitles each person suffering from tuberculosis to an individualized determination, based on sound medical evidence, as to whether that person is contagious and therefore not "otherwise qualified" for a job, the statute entitles each alcoholic veteran to an individualized determination, based on the medical evidence in his own

[3] For example, a blind person, by definition, cannot see. While the Rehabilitation Act does not expressly recognize the absolute correlation between the qualification of seeing and the condition of blindness, it seems appropriate for an employer to rely on that absolute correlation in making certain hiring decisions. Presumably, an employer subject to § 504 could refuse to hire blind individuals for jobs clearly requiring sighted employees without first conducting an individualized assessment of each blind applicant's qualifications.

case, of the causes of his disability. If this individualized assessment leads the adjudicator to conclude that the particular veteran's alcoholism was brought on by willful misconduct, that veteran will have been adjudicated to be not "otherwise qualified" to collect the education benefits. But only after this individualized inquiry has been conducted, can the VA deprive him of benefits available to all whose disabilities were not caused by willful misconduct.

B

. . . .

In contrast, ample evidence supports petitioners' contrary contention that the degree of willfulness associated with the onset of alcoholism varies from case to case. Recent medical research indicates that the causes of primary alcoholism[4] are varied and complex, only some of which conceivably could be attributed to a veteran's will.[5] Indeed, even the VA acknowledges that "alcoholism is not a unitary condition [but rather] has multiple forms and ranges of severity." A sensitivity to this case-to-case variation is precisely what § 504 requires of employers and federal agencies in their assessments of the qualifications for employment or benefits of an individual with handicaps. As the medical community's understanding of the causes of alcoholism continues to develop, § 504 requires the VA to take these new developments into account in making "sound medical judgments" about the source of a particular veteran's alcoholism. Presumably, evidence concerning the circumstances surrounding a veteran's development of alcohol dependence — including his age, home environment, and psychological health — always will be relevant to this assessment.

C

Finally, in asserting that its automatic association of primary alcoholism with willful misconduct is supported by medical evidence, the VA adopts, perhaps for purposes of this litigation alone, a definition of willful misconduct which is inconsistent with the definition articulated in the VA's own regulations and practices. According to the VA, primary alcoholism is appropriately

[4] The American Medical Association and American Psychiatric Association (AMA/APA) and the National Council on Alcoholism, Inc. (NCA), emphasize in their respective *amicus* briefs that the primary/secondary distinction is a crude one. A diagnosis of alcoholism as primary or secondary may depend as much on the nature of the facility in which the diagnosis is made as it does on the alcoholic's true clinical history. *See* Brief for NCA as *Amicus Curiae* 18-19, n.9. The primary/secondary distinction is particularly difficult to apply to an alcoholic who, like petitioners, began drinking as a child before underlying psychiatric disorders could be diagnosed. *See* Brief for AMA/APA as *Amici Curiae* 7. AMA/APA also emphasizes that the distinction between the two kinds of alcoholism was developed, and is properly used, only for treatment purposes and reveals little about the degree of willfulness involved in the onset of the alcoholism.

[5] Notable among the studies are those that suggest that heredity plays a significant role in the development of primary, but not secondary, alcoholism. *See, e.g.*, Schuckit, *Genetic Aspects of Alcoholism*, 15 Annals Emergency Medicine 991, 992 (1986). Some evidence suggests that the genetic predisposition to alcoholism can be attributed to a biochemical abnormality that prevents proper metabolism of alcohol. From this it would appear that there may be a more purely physiological explanation for the onset of some cases of primary alcoholism than there is for most cases of secondary alcoholism.

attributed to willful misconduct because medical evidence suggests that "many alcoholics are not completely helpless," in controlling their disability. But a "not completely helpless" test is not the standard the VA has established for determining whether other disabilities are incurred willfully.

The VA defines willful misconduct as "an act involving conscious wrongdoing or known prohibited action," and "the intentional doing of something either with the knowledge that it is likely to result in serious injury or with a wanton and reckless disregard of its probable consequences."[6] This definition of willful misconduct is a far cry from a "not completely helpless" standard. While some primary alcoholics may well owe their disability to willful misconduct, as delineated by the regulation, the VA has failed to demonstrate that *all* primary alcoholics had any awareness that their initial drinking was likely to result in serious injury. Nor, in many cases, would it be appropriate to describe one's gradual development of alcohol dependency as evidence of "wanton and reckless disregard of [drinking's] probable consequences." Indeed, I wonder how one meaningfully can ascribe such intent and appreciation of long-range consequences to a 9-or 13-year-old boy who follows the lead of his adult role models in taking his first drinks.

. . . .

Individuals suffering from a wide range of disabilities, including heart and lung disease and diabetes, usually bear some responsibility for their conditions. And the conduct that can lead to this array of disabilities, particularly dietary and smoking habits, is certainly no less voluntary than the consumption of alcohol. Nevertheless, the VA has expressed an unwillingness to extend the definition of willful misconduct to all voluntary conduct having some relation to the development of a disability. In justifying the exclusion of secondary organic effects of alcoholism, such as cirrhosis of the liver, from the reach of the willful-misconduct presumption, the VA has explained:

> "[H]istorically, the question of willful misconduct has never been raised in other related situations where personal habits or neglect are possible factors in the incurrence of disability. For example, the harmful effects of tobacco smoking on circulation and respiration were known long before tobacco was incriminated as a causative factor in the high incidence of cancer, emphysema and heart disease. Yet smoking has not been considered misconduct. It is unreasonable and illogical to apply one set of rules with respect to alcohol and a different one in a situation closely analogous."

In deferring to the VA's "reasonable" determination that all primary alcoholism is attributable to willful misconduct, the Court obscures the meaning of "willful misconduct" in a similar fashion. The Court discusses the propriety of denying benefits to those who "bear some responsibility for their disabilities," and suggests that the attribution of all primary alcoholism to

[6] Outside the alcoholism context, the Board of Veterans Appeals has found willful misconduct when, for example, a veteran "placed [a] gun to his head and pulled the trigger," or intentionally put his arm through window glass, or attempted to ride his motorcycle on one wheel, or engaged in an altercation, or drove about 100 miles per hour in a 25-mile-per-hour zone on a wet road at dusk.

willful misconduct is justified because "the consumption of alcohol is not regarded as wholly involuntary." The degree of personal responsibility for their disability attributed to alcoholics by the VA in its brief and echoed by the Court in its opinion is clearly not of the magnitude contemplated by the VA's general definition of willful misconduct.

V

Section 504 guarantees Eugene Traynor and James P. McKelvey federal benefits absent a demonstration that they, as individuals, fail to satisfy the legitimate qualifications Congress has imposed upon receipt of those benefits. The VA has failed to demonstrate that any legislative or medical determinations justify its conclusive presumption that Mr. Traynor's and Mr. McKelvey's alcoholism was incurred willfully. Both cases therefore should be remanded to the VA for individualized determinations, based on "sound medical judgments" whether these men are "otherwise qualified" to receive veterans' education benefits beyond the 10-year period.

I dissent.

NOTES AND QUESTIONS

1. What of the term "disease" itself? It suggests an organic grounding for a condition or behavior. It also suggests irresponsibility as to causes or consequences. It may also invite intervention by others or legitimate societal intrusions that would otherwise be impermissible. With such thoughts in mind, is it desirable to label alcoholism a disease? Ethically, which is the preferable view: that alcoholism is a disease or that it is a pattern of repeated behavior for which the individual is responsible?
2. Was Rose Cipollone suffering from a disease? Was Mr. Egelhoff? Would it have mattered in either case?
3. Is not the dissent in any event correct, that lumping *all* alcoholics and *all* alcoholism together, is impermissible? Or does administrative convenience justify so doing? If so, where does such a conclusion fit in a scheme of ethics?
4. And regardless of characterization, what was the ethical sense in making alcohol available, but withholding education, in *Traynor*? Is the focus on willfulness important for other reasons, such as excess weight or sexual predation, as earlier cases suggest?
5. Consider now the treatment of alcohol and drug usage and addiction under the Americans With Disabilities Act, in a case involving a recovering addict, Dan Buckley.

BUCKLEY v. CONSOLIDATED EDISON COMPANY OF NEW YORK, INC.

127 F.3d 270 (2nd Cir. 1997)

Calabresi, Circuit Judge:

This is an appeal from a judgment of the United States District Court for the Southern District of New York (Parker, J.) dismissing the plaintiff's complaint for failure to state a claim under the Americans with Disabilities Act ("ADA"), 42 U.S.C. § 12101-12213.

. . . .

I

. . . .

The plaintiff, Dan Buckley, is a recovering drug and alcohol addict. He was employed by defendant Con Edison from February 1976 until July 1994. Buckley was identified as an alcohol and substance abuser in 1991, and he underwent treatment at a residential facility on two occasions, in March 1991 and February 1993. As a result of his status as a former addict, he was required by Con Edison to submit to random drug testing approximately once a month. Con Edison employees who are not former alcohol and substance abusers are randomly tested about once every five years.

. . . .

Buckley also suffers from a medical condition known as a neurogenic bladder, which makes it difficult for him to urinate in public or on command. As a result, it usually takes him several hours to produce a urine sample. On June 24, 1994, Buckley was ordered to report to Con Edison's medical facility for a drug test. Though he did provide a blood sample (which, in the current posture of the case, we must assume is as good as a urine sample for detecting drug use), Buckley was unable to produce a urine specimen in the time allotted. He asked for additional time, but his request was denied. Shortly after, he went on his own to Beth Israel Hospital and paid to have a urine sample taken. He then had the results of the test forwarded to Con Edison. Nevertheless, on July 1, 1994, Buckley was fired by Con Edison because he was a former drug and alcohol addict who had failed to provide a urine sample in the time allotted.

. . . .

II

The ADA prohibits employers from discriminating "against a qualified individual with a disability because of the disability of such individual." 42 U.S.C. § 12112(a). To state a claim under the ADA, therefore, Buckley must allege facts sufficient to support a finding that: a) he is a qualified individual with an ADA-covered disability; and b) Con Edison discriminated against him because of his disability.

A. The ADA's Definition of Disability Includes Recovering Drug Addicts

The statute defines "disability" as: "(A) a physical or mental impairment that substantially limits one or more of the major life activities of such individual; (B) a record of such impairment; or (C) being regarded as having such an impairment." Buckley concedes that his neurogenic bladder condition is not a disability under the ADA. He argues, however, that being a recovering drug addict is a disability. We agree.

Section 12114 addresses the status of drug and alcohol users, providing that "the term 'qualified individual with a disability' shall not include any employee or applicant who is currently engaging in the illegal use of drugs, when the covered entity acts on the basis of such use." The statute, however, expressly states that individuals who formerly used illegal drugs, but who have completed a drug rehabilitation program and are no longer using drugs, are not excluded from its coverage. But while former drug users are not barred from invoking the Act's protection, they, like everyone else making a claim under the ADA, are required to demonstrate that they have a "disability" covered by the Act. They must, for example, show that they have an impairment that "substantially limits one or more . . . major life activities." And the mere status of being a recovering alcohol or substance abuser does not, on its face, appear to amount to such a limitation. That does not dispose of Buckley's claim, however, because under § 12102(2)(B), a plaintiff may also demonstrate a disability by proving that he has a "record of such an impairment." Thus, if drug or alcohol addiction is an impairment, recovering addicts, so long as they are not currently using drugs, will automatically be covered for having a record of drug addiction.

Other circuits have deemed alcohol or drug addiction to be an impairment that "substantially limits one or more . . . major life activities" and therefore qualifies as a disability under the ADA. . . .

We, moreover, have previously held that "substance abuse is a 'handicap' for purposes of the Rehabilitation Act," *Teahan v. Metro-North Commuter R.R. Co.* Similarly, in another case, we assumed that alcoholism was a covered disability under the ADA when we held that a hospital's offer of a position with reduced responsibilities to an alcoholic physician was a reasonable accommodation of his disability under the ADA.

. . . .

In this respect, it is important to emphasize that past drug addiction, not merely past use, is required to make out a claim under the ADA. The references in Buckley's complaint to his history of "dependence" on drugs and alcohol can fairly be read to allege such a past addiction. Accordingly, Buckley has successfully made out the first prong of his claim for the purposes of this Rule 12(b)(6) motion: he has alleged that he is a qualified individual with an ADA-covered disability, namely a record of past drug and alcohol addiction that impaired one or more of his major life activities.

B. Differential Frequency in Drug Testing of Recovering Addicts Is Unlawful Under the ADA in the Absence of Reasonable Accommodations

Buckley's complaint, however, is not yet out of the woods, for in it he must also allege facts sufficient to support a finding that he was discriminated against on the basis of his disability. We believe that he has done so.

. . . .

. . . Con Edison's policy treats those employees who have neurogenic bladders and who are recovering drug addicts differently from those employees who have neurogenic bladders and who are not recovering drug addicts. Recovering addicts are, appropriately, required to take a drug test approximately once a month, while employees without a record of addiction are only tested, on average, once every five years. Given the test that Con Edison uses, the neurogenic bladder employees who are recovering addicts will be fired after one month, regardless of drug use. The neurogenic bladder employees who are not recovering addicts will also be fired regardless of drug use, but only after an average of five years. This differential treatment discriminates on the basis of an ADA-covered disability (being a recovering addict) and therefore constitutes a prima facie violation of the ADA if a reasonable accommodation for the "known physical or mental limitations of an otherwise qualified individual with a disability" is available.

. . . In this case, plaintiff suggests that there is an alternative. Employees with neurogenic bladders who are recovering addicts can be accommodated either by allowing them more time to urinate or by permitting them to submit blood rather than urine samples. In evaluating the reasonableness of this accommodation, it is important to note that Buckley is subject to dismissal some five years earlier than others who suffer from the same bladder condition only because of his ADA-covered disability (being a recovering addict). For it is this disability that makes frequent public urination on command a condition of his employment. As a result, although the remedy might seem to respond to his bladder condition, what is truly being accommodated is Buckley's disability that derives from his status as a recovering addict. It follows that Con Edison's refusal to make this type of accommodation is a violation of the ADA.

. . . .

Kearse, Circuit Judge, dissenting:

. . . .

The ADA prohibits an employer from discriminating in, inter alia, terms or conditions of employment, against "a qualified individual with a disability because of the disability of such individual." Even assuming the correctness of the majority's ruling that "being a recovering drug addict is a disability" within the meaning of the ADA, I see two critical flaws in the majority's conclusion that Buckley stated a valid claim under the Act.

. . . .

In the present case, Buckley, a recovering substance abuser, alleged that he was discharged because he failed to produce a urine sample during a supervised drug test. . . . There is no suggestion that Buckley's inability to produce a urine sample under supervision was related to his recovering-substance-abuser status; and his amended complaint states expressly that his neurogenic bladder condition "is not claimed as a disability pursuant to the [ADA]."

Thus, Buckley's claim was that he was discharged not because he was a recovering addict but because his neurogenic bladder condition prevented his compliance with Con Edison's drug testing program; he claimed not that his status as a recovering addict was not accommodated, but that his unrelated bladder condition was not accommodated. Since the inability to urinate under supervision or in public neither is nor results from a disability within the meaning of the ADA, and it is that inability that Con Edison refused to accommodate and that caused the termination of Buckley's employment, I would conclude that Buckley has not stated a claim under the Act.

Second, the majority implicitly rules that Con Edison discriminated against Buckley because of his recovering-substance-abuser status because it tests such employees more frequently than it tests employees who have neurogenic bladder conditions but who are not recovering substance abusers. The ADA provides, however, that "reasonable policies or procedures, including . . . drug testing, designed to ensure that a former substance abuser is no longer engaging in the illegal use of drugs" "shall not be a violation of [the Act]." Since it is not an ADA violation for an employer to administer reasonable drug tests to former substance abusers without administering any tests to other employees, it logically cannot be a violation for employers to administer such tests to both former abusers and nonabusers, but simply to test the former more frequently.

. . . .

NOTES AND QUESTIONS

1. Mr. Buckley is a *recovering* addict. How is *that* a "disability"? Presumably, whatever impairment his condition posed is now gone.
2. Suppose Buckley were *still* an addict. *Would* that condition be a "disability" under the ADA? *Should* it be? If the ADA excludes drug or alcohol consumption as a disability, should it be more protective of *diseases* related to those substances?
3. As the *Traynor* and *Buckley* cases indicate, a disability may be the basis of discrimination if it affects job performance. But here the effect was on the ability to perform a *test*. Should that be treated differently?
4. [illegible] alternatives of hospital based urine and blood samples?
5. We will return to the ADA in the context of AIDS, below, § 4.03[3]. There, the concern is as much for AIDS as a cause of public opprobrium as for actual performance impairment. Here, in the *Buckley* case, it was the *past record* of the condition which created the disability. *Should* that qualify?
6. For an excellent article, see Blane Workie, *Chemical Dependency And The Legal Profession: Should Addiction To Drugs And Alcohol Ward Off Heavy Discipline?*, 9 Geo. J. Legal Ethics 1357 (1996); and see Janet Golden, *"A Tempest in a Cocktail Glass": Mothers, Alcohol, and Television, 1977-1996*, 25 J. Health Pol. Pol'y & L. 473 (2000).
7. The use of alcohol presents a troublesome ethical dilemma. The consumer may harm others — a fetus, a co-worker, a patient. But the use

itself may be the product of a disease or addiction. And so society has an obligation to guard against discrimination, as with any disability.

BEKKER v. HUMANA HEALTH PLAN, INC.

229 F.3d 662 (7th Cir. 2000)

Ripple, Circuit Judge.

Dr. Stephanie Bekker worked as a physician for Humana Health Plan, Inc. ("Humana") until Humana discharged her because it had received numerous reports that Dr. Bekker had smelled of alcohol and had exhibited other signs of alcohol use when seeing her patients. After her discharge, Dr. Bekker filed this action against Humana; she alleged that Humana discriminated against her on account of her perceived disability of alcoholism in violation of the Americans with Disabilities Act ("ADA"), 42 U.S.C. § 12101 et seq. The district court granted summary judgment for Humana. For the reasons set forth in the following opinion, we affirm the judgment of the district court.

I

BACKGROUND

A. Facts

Dr. Stephanie Bekker began practicing as an internist at Humana's Lincoln Park Center in 1983. She worked weekdays and every other Saturday. She also had on-call duty, which required her to work 24-hour shifts three to five times a month. At times, she was the only physician on the premises at the Lincoln Park Center.

1.

In 1990, a nurse at Humana informed the Clinical Director for the Lincoln Park Center, Dr. Thomas, that a rumor was circulating that Dr. Bekker smelled of alcohol while working. Dr. Thomas discussed the rumor with Dr. Bekker. That discussion led to the conclusion that the odor probably was Dr. Bekker's mouthwash.

In 1995, a patient reported that she had smelled alcohol on Dr. Bekker during her appointment. Dr. Bekker, at Humana's request, thereafter agreed to undergo an independent clinical evaluation to determine whether she suffered from an alcohol disorder. This evaluation was conducted at Rush-Presbyterian-St. Luke's Medical Center ("Rush") and was headed by Dr. Paul Feldman, a physician who specializes in the diagnosis and treatment of substance abuse, particularly substance abuse by physicians. At the completion of the evaluation, Dr. Feldman did not diagnose Dr. Bekker with alcohol abuse or dependence.

2.

In 1996, another patient complained that Dr. Bekker had smelled of alcohol during her appointment. When advised of the complaint, Humana's Director of Employee Health Services/Risk Management, Diane Dusek, initiated an investigation and suspended Dr. Bekker pending the resolution of the investigation.

In her investigation, Dusek spoke first with the patient who had made the complaint. The patient confirmed that Dr. Bekker had smelled of alcohol during her appointment. Also, the patient stated that Dr. Bekker may have smelled of alcohol on a previous visit. Dusek then spoke with Dr. Bekker. In their conversation, Dr. Bekker denied drinking before or during working hours or while she was on call.

Dusek interviewed other staff members at Humana during the course of her investigation. A medical assistant reported that she had smelled alcohol on Dr. Bekker at least once a week, that Dr. Bekker had glassy eyes when the odor was present, and that both patients and employees had commented to her about the odor. A nurse reported that she had smelled alcohol on Dr. Bekker two or three times a week over the previous two years and that patients had commented to her that Dr. Bekker or her examination room had smelled of alcohol. Another employee also reported that Dr. Bekker had smelled of alcohol on at least a weekly basis, that Dr. Bekker's face was flushed and her eyes were dilated when the odor was present, and that a patient had commented to her that Dr. Bekker smelled of alcohol. Two triage nurses confirmed that they had smelled alcohol on Dr. Bekker and that other employees had spoken of the situation. Another physician reported that a week or two before the investigation, she had smelled an unusual odor on Dr. Bekker and had wondered if it was alcohol.

Dusek stated that she found no evidence that Dr. Bekker consumed alcohol while at work, that she reported to work while impaired by alcohol, or that her professional care was diminished as a result of alcohol impairment. Dusek also admits that she never found evidence that Dr. Bekker actually provided poor patient care or exercised poor medical judgment. Also, Dr. Bekker's colleague, Dr. Thomas, stated that she did not think that Dr. Bekker ever drank alcohol at work.

Humana's Vice-President and Medical Director for Chicago, Dr. Ernest Weis, determined that, although Dr. Bekker could be discharged under her employment contract for cause, he would continue her employment if she agreed to certain terms.

Dr. Bekker again denied drinking on the job or reporting to work under the influence of alcohol. She offered to undergo daily testing, but Dr. Weis declined her offer. She told Dr. Weis that she would seek a second independent evaluation to prove that she was not under the influence of alcohol while at work. Finally, Dr. Bekker stated that she wanted to seek the advice of counsel before agreeing to Dr. Weis' conditions. Dr. Weis agreed. He did not set, at that time, a deadline by which Dr. Bekker needed to accept his conditions before he would discharge her.

The next day, December 10, Dr. Bekker called Dusek to inform her that she had contacted counsel regarding Dr. Weis' conditions. She told Dusek that her attorney would not be available until Monday, December 16; Dusek did not object to the delay.

In a letter to Dusek dated December 16, Dr. Feldman wrote that he believed Dr. Bekker met the criteria for alcohol abuse. He wrote that, although Dr. Bekker did not appear to drink in the workplace, she drank heavily the night before and that the odor lingered into the next day. He also recommended that Dr. Bekker refrain from practicing medicine and enter a treatment program for chemically dependent healthcare professionals. Neither Dusek nor Dr. Weis spoke with Dr. Feldman after receiving this letter.

Dr. Weis sent a letter to Dr. Bekker on December 17 that informed her of her discharge. Dr. Weis later stated that he had terminated Dr. Bekker because he believed that she was an alcoholic and because she would not agree to the conditions he proposed at the December 6 meeting. He stated that Dr. Bekker presented a risk to her patients because, as an alcoholic, she might make bad clinical decisions. He also stated that she was a business threat because patients would not like seeing a physician who smelled of alcohol. He admitted that he did not know of any bad clinical decisions that she had made or of any patients who had stopped coming to her because of her problem.

B. Discrimination

The ADA prohibits an employer from discriminating against a qualified individual with a disability.[3] The term "qualified individual with a disability" "means an individual with a disability who, with or without reasonable accommodation, can perform the essential functions of the employment position that such individual holds or desires."[4] To establish disability discrimination, therefore, Dr. Bekker must show that (1) she is disabled within the meaning of the ADA, (2) she is qualified to perform the essential functions of her job either with or without reasonable accommodation, and (3) she suffered from an adverse employment decision because of her disability. In order to prevail, Dr. Bekker must establish all three elements of her claim.

First, Dr. Bekker must establish that she is disabled. To be disabled within the meaning of the ADA, Dr. Bekker must demonstrate that she (1) has "a physical or mental impairment that substantially limits one or more of the major life activities of such individual"; (2) has "a record of such an impairment"; or (3) is "regarded as having such an impairment." Dr. Bekker claims, and Humana admits, that she comes within the third definition of disability because Humana regarded her as an alcoholic.

---

[3] The ADA prescribes that:

> No covered entity shall discriminate against a qualified individual with a disability because of the disability of such individual in regard to job application procedures, the hiring, advancement, or discharge of employees, employee compensation, job training, and other terms, conditions, and privileges of employment.

42 U.S.C. § 12112 (a).

[4] The term "reasonable accommodation" may include:

> job restructuring, part-time or modified work schedules, reassignment to a vacant position, acquisition or modification of equipment or devices, appropriate adjustment or modifications of examinations, training materials or policies, the provision of qualified readers or interpreters, and other similar accommodations for individuals with disabilities.

42 U.S.C. § 12111 (9).

Humana nevertheless posits that, even if Dr. Bekker is an alcoholic, she is not a qualified individual with a disability because she presents a direct threat to the health and safety of her patients. "The term 'direct threat' means a significant risk to the health or safety of others that cannot be eliminated by reasonable accommodation." The district court agreed with Humana's assessment when it granted summary judgment to Humana. We have no disagreement with the analysis of the district court, which we already have set forth at length. Nevertheless, even assuming that Dr. Bekker is a qualified individual with a disability, Humana was justified in discharging her.

1.

Under the ADA, an employee has available two methods for establishing that her employer discriminated against her based on her disability. First, the employee "may present direct or circumstantial evidence that the employment decision was motivated by the employer's discriminatory animus." Second, the employee may use the burden-shifting method set forth in *McDonnell Douglas Corporation v. Green*, 411 U.S. 792 (1973), to prove by indirect evidence that her employer intentionally discriminated against her.

2.

We focus for now on the first of these methods. "Evidence of discrimination may be direct or circumstantial." Direct evidence is evidence that " 'in and of itself suggests' that someone with managerial authority was 'animated by an illegal employment criterion.' " "When the employee has presented evidence that the employer was motivated in part by discrimination, the defendant may then avoid a finding of liability by proving that *it would have made the same decision absent discrimination.*" To survive a motion for summary judgment, therefore, Dr. Bekker must present sufficient evidence to allow a rational jury to reasonably conclude that, but for her disability of alcoholism, Humana would not have discharged her.

We note that an employer:

> (1) may prohibit the illegal use of drugs and the use of alcohol at the workplace by all employees;
>
> (2) may require that employees shall not be under the influence of alcohol or be engaging in the illegal use of drugs at the workplace;
>
> . . . .
>
> (4) may hold an employee who engages in the illegal use of drugs or who is an alcoholic to the same qualification standards for employment or job performance and behavior that such entity holds other employees, even if any unsatisfactory performance or behavior is related to the drug use or alcoholism of such employee. . . .

Dr. Bekker claims that Humana terminated her because it believed she was an alcoholic and not because it believed she was working while under the influence of alcohol. Humana submits that it was justified in terminating Dr.

Bekker based on the complaints it received about her. Humana claims that it may hold an alcoholic employee to the same standards as a non-alcoholic employee. Because a non-alcoholic employee would be terminated if Humana concluded she was under the influence of alcohol while working, Humana contends that Dr. Bekker could be terminated under the same circumstances. Due to the serious risks to patients of being treated by a physician under the influence of alcohol, Humana states that it would be justified in terminating Dr. Bekker merely because she smelled of alcohol.

The risks of harm when a patient is seen by a physician under the influence of alcohol are many and serious. A physician under the influence of alcohol could prescribe the wrong medication or an incorrect dosage of medication. She could misdiagnose the patient's condition or could miss an important symptom indicative of a more serious condition, possibly one needing immediate attention or posing a threat to life. Moreover, a physician under the influence of alcohol might be clumsy with her instruments and cause serious harm to the patient because of a slip of the hand or a second of inattention. Furthermore, the confidence of a patient in the capabilities of the physician understandably would be undermined if the patient became aware that the physician was under the influence of alcohol.

Humana has presented sufficient evidence to show that it had good reason to believe that Dr. Bekker was under the influence of alcohol while seeing patients. During Dusek's investigation, she received reports from employees and patients who had smelled alcohol on Dr. Bekker while she was working. Moreover, several of the employees had observed her with glassy or dilated eyes and a flushed face, signs of alcohol use. Reports stating that Dr. Bekker smelled of alcohol were filed in 1990, 1995, and 1996; the number of reports regarding Dr. Bekker were substantial and appeared to be increasing. In short, all of the reports indicating that Dr. Bekker was seeing her patients while under the influence of alcohol substantiate Humana's decision to discharge Dr. Bekker.

Furthermore, the persistent nature of the problem, despite Humana's intervention, substantiates the need for concern on the part of Humana. After the first patient reported that she had smelled alcohol on Dr. Bekker, Humana required her to undergo treatment, but, despite this treatment, Dr. Bekker continued to appear at work smelling of alcohol. The large number of reports of Dr. Bekker's symptoms also indicate the repetitious and long-term nature of Dr. Bekker's problem. With a suggestion of such pervasive alcohol use while Dr. Bekker was seeing patients, Humana was justified in terminating Dr. Bekker. A physician in such a patient-oriented practice, whether or not she is an alcoholic, justifiably could be discharged by her employer if the employer received numerous reports that suggested that the doctor was seeing patients under the influence of alcohol. Moreover, Humana has, and the ADA explicitly allows for, a policy prohibiting the use of alcohol in the workplace. Dr. Bekker, therefore, failed to present direct proof of intentional discrimination by Humana on account of a perceived disability of alcoholism. Indeed, Humana has offered substantial proof that it was justified in discharging her on the ground that she posed an immediate risk to patients.

3.

Dr. Bekker's case would fare no better under the *McDonnell Douglas* burden-shifting approach. The Supreme Court established the burden-shifting method of proving intentional discrimination "because employers usually are careful not to offer smoking gun remarks indicating intentional discrimination. . . ." Under this method, a plaintiff first must establish a prima facie case of discrimination by her employer, which creates a presumption of intentional discrimination. The burden of production then shifts to the employer to articulate a legitimate, nondiscriminatory reason for the adverse employment action. Once the employer has proffered a legitimate reason, the inference of discrimination disappears, and the plaintiff must prove by a preponderance of the evidence that the employer's proffered reason was a pretext for intentional discrimination. The ultimate burden to prove intentional discrimination remains with the plaintiff.

Assuming for the sake of argument that Dr. Bekker could establish a prima facie case of discrimination, Humana has proffered a legitimate nondiscriminatory reason for her discharge: the belief that she was under the influence of alcohol while seeing patients. Dr. Bekker has not presented any evidence to show that Humana's legitimate reason for her discharge was pretextual. By failing to rebut Humana's legitimate, nondiscriminatory reason, Dr. Bekker cannot meet her burden to show that she was a victim of intentional discrimination by Humana.

NOTES AND QUESTIONS

1. The *Bekker* case is yet another ADA case balancing the needs of the disabled against the needs (or intolerance) of society to ignore disabilities. How should that balance or accommodation be struck? Does it depend on the "disability"?
2. A disability, as in *Bekker*, may in some degree be voluntarily incurred — as with alcohol, drug usage, obesity, sports injuries. Does that factor distinguish the disability and society's obligations from nonvoluntary disabilities, such as cerebral palsy, age or blindness. And how shall we classify pregnancy?
3. To some extent these questions are resolved under the ADA by defining "disability" as affecting a "major life activity" or capacity, and discrimination as being directed at that or the perception of that — both involved in Doctor Bekker's alcohol use, which may not have affected her work, but greatly concerned her co-workers. Was she, in fact, "disabled"?
4. And the accommodation is also affected by creating defenses — discrimination is permissible if the disability affects the job and if reasonable accommodations are offered. Did it; were they?
5. To shift analysis, what of Doctor Bekker's ethical obligation? Suppose she *is* an alcoholic with a disability? Should she nevertheless insist on employment? Would your answer be different if she were epileptic? HIV positive? And would your answer change if you were her patient? Should she *tell* you? Would you go to a different doctor?

[2] Employment

Historically, the second leading cause of health problems — after infectious diseases — was injury in the workplace. Mines, construction, docks, manufacturing, all involved hazardous duty and materials, in unhealthful settings, under long hours.

In our own century, one of the major environmental health scandals, still unfolding, is that involving asbestosis — in which major asbestos manufacturers suppressed medical research and individual diagnoses by company doctors during the first three decades of the century, to hide the fact that asbestos fibers cause a deadly cancer in the lung. During the 1960s and 1970s, they fought — with considerable success — to beat back a badly funded and organized group of litigants and attorneys. Similar stories exist in other industries, now thankfully subject to regulation as to wages, hours, safety and working environment.

It was not always so. We begin with *Lochner v. New York*.

LOCHNER v. NEW YORK
198 U.S. 45 (1905)

Mr. Justice **Peckham** delivered the opinion of the court:

The indictment charges that the plaintiff wrongfully and unlawfully required and permitted an employee working for him to work more than sixty hours in one week. . . . The mandate of the statute, that 'no employee shall be required or permitted to work,' is the substantial equivalent of an enactment that 'no employee shall contract or agree to work,' more than ten hours per day; and, as there is no provision for special emergencies, the statute is mandatory in all cases. It is not an act merely fixing the number of hours which shall constitute a legal day's work, but an absolute prohibition upon the employer permitting, under any circumstances, more than ten hours' work to be done in his establishment. The employee may desire to earn the extra money which would arise from his working more than the prescribed time, but this statute forbids the employer from permitting the employee to earn it.

The statute necessarily interferes with the right of contract between the employer and employees, concerning the number of hours in which the latter may labor in the bakery of the employer. The general right to make a contract in relation to his business is part of the liberty of the individual protected by the 14th Amendment of the Federal Constitution. Under that provision no state can deprive any person of life, liberty, or property without due process of law. The right to purchase or to sell labor is part of the liberty protected by this amendment, unless there are circumstances which exclude the right. There are, however, certain powers, existing in the sovereignty of each state in the Union, somewhat vaguely termed police powers, the exact description and limitation of which have not been attempted by the courts. . . .

. . . .

It must, of course, be conceded that there is a limit to the valid exercise of the police power by the state. In every case that comes before this court, therefore, where legislation of this character is concerned, and where the protection of the Federal Constitution is sought, the question necessarily arises: Is this a fair, reasonable, and appropriate exercise of the police power of the state, or is it an unreasonable, unnecessary, and arbitrary interference with the right of the individual to his personal liberty, or to enter into those contracts in relation to labor which may seem to him appropriate or necessary for the support of himself and his family? Of course the liberty of contract relating to labor includes both parties to it. The one has as much right to purchase as the other to sell labor.

. . . .

. . . One of the judges of the court of appeals, in upholding the law, stated that, in his opinion, the regulation in question could not be sustained unless they were able to say, from common knowledge, that working in a bakery and candy factory was an unhealthy employment. The judge held that, while the evidence was not uniform, it still led him to the conclusion that the occupation of a baker or confectioner was unhealthy and tended to result in diseases of the respiratory organs. . . .

We think that there can be no fair doubt that the trade of a baker, in and of itself, is not an unhealthy one to that degree which would authorize the legislature to interfere with the right to labor, and with the right of free contract on the part of the individual, either as employer or employee. In looking through statistics regarding all trades and occupations, it may be true that the trade of a baker does not appear to be as healthy as some other trades, and is also vastly more healthy than still others. To the common understanding the trade of a baker has never been regarded as an unhealthy one. Very likely physicians would not recommend the exercise of that or of any other trade as a remedy for ill health. . . . But are we all, on that account, at the mercy of legislative majorities? A printer, a tinsmith, a locksmith, a carpenter, a cabinetmaker, a dry goods clerk, a bank's, a lawyer's, or a physician's clerk, or a clerk in almost any kind of business, would all come under the power of the legislature, on this assumption. No trade, no occupation, no mode of earning one's living, could escape this all-pervading power, and the acts of the legislature in limiting the hours of labor in all employments would be valid, although such limitation might seriously cripple the ability of the laborer to support himself and his family. . . .

. . . We mention these extreme cases because the contention is extreme. We do not believe in the soundness of the views which uphold this law. . . . These several sections provide for the inspection of the premises where the bakery is carried on, with regard to furnishing proper wash rooms and water-closets, apart from the bake room, also with regard to providing proper drainage, plumbing, and painting; the sections, in addition, provide for the height of the ceiling, the cementing or tiling of floors, where necessary in the opinion of the factory inspector, and for other things of that nature; alterations are also provided for, and are to be made where necessary in the opinion of the inspector, in order to comply with the provisions of the statute. These various sections may be wise and valid regulations, and they certainly go to the full extent of providing for the cleanliness and the healthiness, so far as possible, of the quarters in which bakeries are to be conducted. Adding to all these requirements a prohibition to enter into any contract of labor in a bakery for more than a certain number of hours a week is, in our judgment, so wholly beside the matter of a proper, reasonable, and fair provision as to run counter to that liberty of person and of free contract provided for in the Federal Constitution.

. . . .

. . . It seems to us that the real object and purpose were simply to regulate the hours of labor between the master and his employees (all being men, sui juris), in a private business, not dangerous in any degree to morals, or in any real and substantial degree to the health of the employees. Under such circumstances the freedom of master and employee to contract with each other in relation to their employment, and in defining the same, cannot be prohibited or interfered with, without violating the Federal Constitution.

. . . .

Reversed.

Mr. Justice **Holmes** dissenting:

I regret sincerely that I am unable to agree with the judgment in this case, and that I think it my duty to express my dissent.

This case is decided upon an economic theory which a large part of the country does not entertain. If it were a question whether I agreed with that theory, I should desire to study it further and long before making up my mind. But I do not conceive that to be my duty, because I strongly believe that my agreement or disagreement has nothing to do with the right of a majority to embody their opinions in law. It is settled by various decisions of this court that state constitutions and state laws may regulate life in many ways which we as legislators might think as injudicious, or if you like as tyrannical, as this, and which, equally with this, interfere with the liberty to contract. Sunday laws and usury laws are ancient examples. A more modern one is the prohibition of lotteries. The liberty of the citizen to do as he likes so long as he does not interfere with the liberty of others to do the same, which has been a shibboleth for some well-known writers, is interfered with by school laws, by the post office, by every state or municipal institution which takes his money for purposes thought desirable, whether he likes it or not. The 14th Amendment does not enact Mr. Herbert Spencer's Social Statistics. The other day we sustained the Massachusetts vaccination law. *Jacobson v. Massachusetts.* United States and state statutes and decisions cutting down the liberty to contract by way of combination are familiar to this court. Two years ago we upheld the prohibition of sales of stock on margins, or for future delivery, in the Constitution of California. The decision sustaining an eight-hour law for miners is still recent. *Holden v. Hardy.* Some of these laws embody convictions or prejudices which judges are likely to share. Some may not. But a Constitution is not intended to embody a particular economic theory, whether of paternalism and the organic relation of the citizen to the state or of laissez faire. It is made for people of fundamentally differing views, and the accident of our finding certain opinions natural and familiar, or novel, and even shocking, ought not to conclude our judgment upon the question whether statutes embodying them conflict with the Constitution of the United States.

. . . .

Mr. Justice **Harlan** (with whom Mr. Justice **White** and Mr. Justice **Day** concurred) dissenting:

. . . .

. . . It must be remembered that this statute does not apply to all kinds of business. It applies only to work in bakery and confectionery establishments, in which, as all know, the air constantly breathed by workmen is not as pure and healthful as that to be found in some other establishments or out of doors.

Professor Hirt in his treatise on the 'Diseases of the Workers' has said: 'The labor of the bakers is among the hardest and most laborious imaginable, because it has to be performed under conditions injurious to the health of those engaged in it. It is hard, very hard, work, not only because it requires a great deal of physical exertion in an overheated workshop and during unreasonably long hours, but more so because of the erratic demands of the public, compelling the baker to perform the greater part of his work at night, thus depriving him of an opportunity to enjoy the necessary rest and sleep, — a fact which is highly injurious to his health.' Another writer says: 'The constant inhaling of flour dust causes inflammation of the lungs and of the bronchial tubes. The eyes also suffer through this dust, which is responsible for the many cases of running eyes among the bakers. The long hours of toil to which all bakers are subjected produce rheumatism, cramps, and swollen legs. The average age of a baker is below that of other workmen; they seldom live over their fiftieth year, most of them dying between the ages of forty and fifty. During periods of epidemic diseases the bakers are generally the first to succumb to the disease, and the number swept away during such periods far exceeds the number of other crafts in comparison to the men employed in the respective industries. . . .

. . . .

Statistics show that the average daily working time among workingmen in different countries is, in Australia, eight hours; in Great Britain, nine; in the United States, nine and three-quarters; in Denmark, nine and three-quarters; in Norway, ten; Sweden, France, and Switzerland, ten and one-half; Germany, ten and one-quarter; Belgium, Italy, and Austria, eleven; and in Russia, twelve hours.

We judicially know that the question of the number of hours during which a workman should continuously labor has been, for a long period, and is yet, a subject of serious consideration among civilized peoples, and by those having special knowledge of the laws of health. Suppose the statute prohibited labor in bakery and confectionery establishments in excess of eighteen hours each day. No one, I take it, could dispute the power of the state to enact such a statute. . . .

We also judicially know that the number of hours that should constitute a day's labor in particular occupations involving the physical strength and safety of workmen has been the subject of enactments by Congress and by nearly all of the states. Many, if not most, of those enactments fix eight hours as the proper basis of a day's labor.

. . . .

I take leave to say that the New York statute, in the particulars here involved, cannot be held to be in conflict with the 14th Amendment, without enlarging the scope of the amendment far beyond its original purpose, and without bringing under the supervision of this court matters which have been supposed to belong exclusively to the legislative departments of the several states when exerting their conceded power to guard the health and safety of their citizens by such regulations as they in their wisdom deem best. Health laws of every description constitute, said Chief Justice Marshall, a part of that mass of legislation which 'embraces everything within the territory of a state, not surrendered to the general government; all which can be most advantageously exercised by the states themselves.' A decision that the New York statute is void under the 14th Amendment will, in my opinion, involve consequences of a far-reaching and mischievous character; for such a decision would seriously cripple the inherent power of the states to care for the lives, health, and well-being of their citizens. Those are matters which can be best controlled by the states. The preservation of the just powers of the states is quite as vital as the preservation of the powers of the general government.

. . . .

NOTES AND QUESTIONS

1. *Lochner* has acquired a bad reputation, as a case in which the United States Supreme Court imposed its own philosophy of economics on the nation. Is that fair? Would it not be more accurate to say that it simply reflected the philosophy of a bygone era, out of tune with the needs of the 20th century? Those needs would become irresistible and the legislation responding to them overwhelming, during the depression and the New Deal of the 1930s. But in 1905, was not Justice Peckham acting responsibly and with restraint?

2. Moreover, may not *Lochner* properly be viewed as a civil rights case? Equally important, within the world of ethics, did it not *affirm* individual autonomy and dignity? Or were the agreements with the bakers of a kind which Rawls would say is illegitimate because both parties did not, could not, actually be said to have agreed on the working conditions?

3. Note that the dissents seek to avoid economics by arguing from the perspective and tradition of public health. We will see more of this below. Why did they make that choice and was it valid? And should public health considerations override individual economic needs or ethical choices? Consider that question in connection with the next case.

4. What would the various justices in *Lochner* think of the Americans with Disabilities Act? Of Title VII of the Civil Rights Act of 1964, the subject of the next case, *Johnson Controls*?

5. May a company refuse to hire an individual whose disability will be worsened by his working conditions, even if that individual wishes to work at that establishment? *See Chevron USA v. Echazabal*, 536 U.S.

73 (2002). Should it matter what the disability is? (In this case, the disability claimed by Chevron, not the plaintiff, was liver damage from Hepatitis C.)

6. Contrast: *Everson v. Mich Dept of Corrections*, 391 F.3d 737 (6th Cir. 2004) where the Michigan department was able to use gender as a "BFOQ" for prison guards at a female-only facility. Whose protection is at stake in this case? What standards (do you think) are enough to allow gender discrimination? Should there be different standards depending on who is being discriminated against?

UAW v. JOHNSON CONTROLS, INC.
499 U.S. 187 (1991)

Justice **Blackmun** delivered the opinion of the Court.

In this case we are concerned with an employer's gender-based fetal-protection policy. May an employer exclude a fertile female employee from certain jobs because of its concern for the health of the fetus the woman might conceive?

I

Respondent Johnson Controls, Inc., manufactures batteries. In the manufacturing process, the element lead is a primary ingredient. Occupational exposure to lead entails health risks, including the risk of harm to any fetus carried by a female employee.

Before the Civil Rights Act of 1964 became law, Johnson Controls did not employ any woman in a battery-manufacturing job. In June 1977, however, it announced its first official policy concerning its employment of women in lead-exposure work: . . .

. . . .

Five years later, in 1982, Johnson Controls shifted from a policy of warning to a policy of exclusion. Between 1979 and 1983, eight employees became pregnant while maintaining blood lead levels in excess of 30 micrograms per deciliter. This appeared to be the critical level noted by the Occupational Health and Safety Administration (OSHA) for a worker who was planning to have a family. The company responded by announcing a broad exclusion of women from jobs that exposed them to lead:

> "[I]t is [Johnson Controls'] policy that women who are pregnant or who are capable of bearing children will not be placed into jobs involving lead exposure or which could expose them to lead through the exercise of job bidding, bumping, transfer or promotion rights."

The policy defined "women . . . capable of bearing children" as "[a]ll women except those whose inability to bear children is medically documented." It further stated that an unacceptable work station was one where, "over the past year," an employee had recorded a blood lead level of more than 30 micrograms per deciliter or the work site had yielded an air sample containing a lead level in excess of 30 micrograms per cubic meter.

. . . .

III

The bias in Johnson Controls' policy is obvious. Fertile men, but not fertile women, are given a choice as to whether they wish to risk their reproductive health for a particular job. Section 703(a) of the Civil Rights Act of 1964 prohibits sex-based classifications in terms and conditions of employment, in hiring and discharging decisions, and in other employment decisions, and in other employment decisions that adversely affect an employee's status. Respondent's fetal-protection policy explicitly discriminates against women on the basis of their sex. The policy excludes women with childbearing capacity from lead-exposed jobs and so creates a facial classification based on gender. . . .

Nevertheless, the Court of Appeals assumed, as did the two appellate courts who already had confronted the issue, that sex-specific fetal-protection policies do not involve facial discrimination. . . . The court assumed that because the asserted reason for the sex-based exclusion (protecting women's unconceived offspring) was ostensibly benign, the policy was not sex-based discrimination. That assumption, however, was incorrect.

First, Johnson Controls' policy classifies on the basis of gender and childbearing capacity, rather than fertility alone. Respondent does not seek to protect the unconceived children of all its employees. Despite evidence in the record about the debilitating effect of lead exposure on the male reproductive system, Johnson Controls is concerned only with the harms that may befall the unborn offspring of its female employees. Johnson Controls' policy is facially discriminatory because it requires only a female employee to produce proof that she is not capable of reproducing.

Our conclusion is bolstered by the Pregnancy Discrimination Act of 1978 (PDA), in which Congress explicitly provided that, for purposes of Title VII, discrimination "on the basis of sex" includes discrimination "because of or on the basis of pregnancy, childbirth, or related medical conditions." . . . Under the PDA, such a classification must be regarded, for Title VII purposes, in the same light as explicit sex discrimination. Respondent has chosen to treat all its female employees as potentially pregnant; that choice evinces discrimination on the basis of sex.

. . . .

IV

Under § 703(e)(1) of Title VII, an employer may discriminate on the basis of "religion, sex, or national origin in those certain instances where religion, sex, or national origin is a bona fide occupational qualification reasonably necessary to the normal operation of that particular business or enterprise." We therefore turn to the question whether Johnson Controls' fetal-protection policy is one of those "certain instances" that come within the BFOQ exception.

. . . .

Johnson Controls argues that its fetal-protection policy falls within the so-called safety exception to the BFOQ. Our cases have stressed that discrimination on the basis of sex because of safety concerns is allowed only in narrow circumstances. In *Dothard v. Rawlinson*, this Court indicated that danger to a woman herself does not justify discrimination. We there allowed the employer to hire only male guards in contact areas of maximum-security male penitentiaries only because more was at stake than the "individual woman's decision to weigh and accept the risks of employment." We found sex to be a BFOQ inasmuch as the employment of a female guard would create real risks of safety to others if violence broke out because the guard was a woman. Sex discrimination was tolerated because sex was related to the guard's ability to do the job — maintaining prison security. We also required in *Dothard* a high correlation between sex and ability to perform job functions and refused to allow employers to use sex as a proxy for strength although it might be a fairly accurate one.

. . . .

. . . The concurrence attempts to transform this case into one of customer safety. The unconceived fetuses of Johnson Controls' female employees, however, are neither customers nor third parties whose safety is essential to the business of battery manufacturing. No one can disregard the possibility of injury to future children; the BFOQ, however, is not so broad that it transforms this deep social concern into an essential aspect of battery making.

Our case law, therefore, makes clear that the safety exception is limited to instances in which sex or pregnancy actually interferes with the employee's ability to perform the job. This approach is consistent with the language of the BFOQ provision itself, for it suggests that permissible distinctions based on sex must relate to ability to perform the duties of the job. Johnson Controls suggests, however, that we expand the exception to allow fetal-protection policies that mandate particular standards for pregnant or fertile women. We decline to do so. Such an expansion contradicts not only the language of the BFOQ and the narrowness of its exception but the plain language and history of the [Pregnancy Discrimination Act].

. . . .

We conclude that the language of both the BFOQ provision and the PDA which amended it, as well as the legislative history and the case law, prohibit an employer from discriminating against woman because of her capacity to become pregnant unless her reproductive potential prevents her from performing the duties of her job. We reiterate our holdings in *Criswell* and *Dothard* that an employer must direct its concerns about a woman's ability to perform her job safely and efficiently to those aspects of the woman's job-related activities that fall within the "essence" of the particular business.

V

We have no difficulty concluding that Johnson Controls cannot establish a BFOQ. Fertile women, as far as appears in the record, participate in the manufacture of batteries as efficiently as anyone else. Johnson Controls' professed moral and ethical concerns about the welfare of the next generation do not suffice to establish a BFOQ of female sterility. Decisions about the welfare of future children must be left to the parents who conceive, bear, support, and raise them rather than to the employers who hire those parents. Congress has mandated this choice through Title VII, as amended by the Pregnancy Discrimination Act. Johnson Controls has attempted to exclude women because of their reproductive capacity. Title VII and the PDA simply do not allow a woman's dismissal because of her failure to submit to sterilization.

Nor can concerns about the welfare of the next generation be considered a part of the "essence" of Johnson Controls' business. Judge Easterbrook in this case pertinently observed: "It is word play to say that 'the job' at Johnson [Controls] is to make batteries without risk to fetuses in the same way 'the job' at Western Air Lines is to fly planes without crashing."

. . . Even on this sparse record, it is apparent that Johnson Controls is concerned about only a small minority of women. Of the eight pregnancies reported among the female employees, it has not been shown that any of the babies have birth defects or other abnormalities. The record does not reveal the birth rate for Johnson Controls' female workers but national statistics show that approximately nine percent of all fertile women become pregnant each year. The birthrate drops to two percent for blue collar workers over age 30. Johnson Controls' fear of prenatal injury, no matter how sincere, does not begin to show that substantially all of its fertile women employees are incapable of doing their jobs.

VI

A word about tort liability and the increased cost of fertile women in the workplace is perhaps necessary. . . .

More than 40 States currently recognize a right to recover for a prenatal injury based either on negligence or on wrongful death. According to Johnson Controls, however, the company complies with the lead standard developed by OSHA and warns its female employees about the damaging effects of lead. It is worth noting that OSHA gave the problem of lead lengthy consideration and concluded that "there is no basis whatsoever for the claim that women of childbearing age should be excluded from the workplace in order to protect the fetus or the course of pregnancy." Without negligence, it would be difficult for a court to find liability on the part of the employer. If, under general tort principles, Title VII bans sex-specific fetal-protection policies, the employer fully informs the woman of the risk, and the employer has not acted negligently, the basis for holding an employer liable seems remote at best.

. . . .

The tort-liability argument reduces to two equally unpersuasive propositions. First, Johnson Controls attempts to solve the problem of reproductive health hazards by resorting to an exclusionary policy. Title VII plainly forbids illegal sex discrimination as a method of diverting attention from an employer's obligation to police the workplace. Second, the specter of an award of damages reflects a fear that hiring fertile women will cost more. The extra cost of employing members of one sex, however, does not provide an affirmative Title VII defense for a discriminatory refusal to hire members of that gender.

. . . .

The judgment of the Court of Appeals is reversed and the case is remanded for further proceedings consistent with this opinion.

It is so ordered.

Justice **White**, with whom the **Chief Justice** and Justice **Kennedy** join, concurring part and concurring in the judgment.

. . . .

. . . A fetal protection policy would be justified under the terms of the statute if, for example, an employer could show that exclusion of women from certain jobs was reasonably necessary to avoid substantial tort liability. Common sense tells us that it is part of the normal operation of business concerns to avoid causing injury to third parties, as well as to employees, if for no other reason than to avoid tort liability and its substantial costs. This possibility of tort liability is not hypothetical; every State currently allows children born alive to recover in tort for prenatal injuries caused by third parties, and an increasing number of courts have recognized a right to recover even for prenatal injuries caused by torts committed prior to conception.

. . . [I]t is far from clear that compliance with Title VII will preempt state tort liability, and the Court offers no support for that proposition. Second, although warnings may preclude claims by injured employees, they will not preclude claims by injured children because the general rule is that parents cannot waive causes of action on behalf of their children, and the parents' negligence will not be imputed to the children. Finally, although state tort liability for prenatal injuries generally requires negligence, it will be difficult for employers to determine in advance what will constitute negligence. Compliance with OSHA standards, for example, has been held not to be a defense to state tort or criminal liability. . . .

. . . .

Prior decisions construing the BFOQ defense confirm that the defense is broad enough to include considerations of cost and safety of the sort that could form the basis for an employer's adoption of a fetal protection policy. . . .

. . . .

The Pregnancy Discrimination Act (PDA), contrary to the Court's assertion, did not restrict the scope of the BFOQ defense. The PDA was only an amendment to the "Definitions" section of Title VII, and did not purport to eliminate or later the BFOQ defense. Rather, it merely clarified Title VII to make it clear that pregnancy and related conditions are included within Title VII's antidiscrimination provisions. As we have already recognized, "the purpose of the PDA was simply to make the treatment of pregnancy consistent with general Title VII principles."

. . . .

II

Despite my disagreement with the Court concerning the scope of the BFOQ defense, I concur in reversing the Court of Appeals because that court erred in affirming the District Court's grant of summary judgment in favor of Johnson Controls. First, the Court of Appeals erred in failing to consider the level of risk-avoidance that was part of Johnson Controls' "normal operation." Although the court did conclude that there was a "substantial risk" to fetuses from lead exposure in fertile women, it merely meant that there was a high risk that some fetal injury would occur absent a fetal protection policy. That analysis, of course, fails to address the extent of fetal injury that is likely to occur. If the fetal protection policy insists on a risk-avoidance level substantially higher than other risk levels tolerated by Johnson Controls such as risks to employees and consumers, the policy should not constitute a BFOQ.[1]

Second, even without more information about the normal level of risk at Johnson Controls, the fetal protection policy at issue here reaches too far. This is evident both in its presumption that, absent medical documentation to the contrary, all women are fertile regardless of their age, and in its exclusion of presumptively fertile women from positions that might result in a promotion to a position involving high lead exposure. There has been no showing that either of these aspects of the policy is reasonably necessary to ensure safe and efficient operation of Johnson Controls' battery-manufacturing business. Of course, these infirmities in the company's policy do not warrant invalidating the entire fetal protection program.

Finally, the Court of Appeals failed to consider properly petitioners' evidence of harm to offspring caused by lead exposure in males. Thus, the court should have analyzed whether the evidence was sufficient for petitioners to survive summary judgment in light of respondent's burden of proof to establish a BFOQ. Moreover, the court should not have discounted the evidence as "speculative" merely because it was based on animal studies. We have approved the use of animal studies to assess risks, and OSHA uses animal studies in establishing its lead control regulations. It seems clear that if the Court of Appeals had properly analyzed that evidence, it would have concluded that summary judgment against petitioners was not appropriate because there was a dispute over a material issue of fact.

. . . .

NOTES AND QUESTIONS

1. Three-quarters of a century elapsed between *Lochner* and *Johnson Controls*. During that time, both the states and the federal government adopted sweeping legislation concerning maximum hours, minimum wages, working conditions and collective bargaining in the workplace. Some of these could be justified in public health terms.
2. However, the legislation in *Johnson Controls* prohibited employment discrimination against women generally. The Constitution itself, of

[1] It is possible, for example, that alternatives to exclusion of women, such as warnings combined with frequent bloodtestings, would sufficiently minimize the risk such that it would be comparable to other risks tolerated by Johnson Controls.

course, would prohibit discrimination along the lines of gender but only by government. Title VII of the 1964 Act reached into the workplace under the interstate commerce clause, including *private* employers. Ethically, was this wise? Did it not intrude upon the autonomy of both employers and employees?

Absent the Pregnancy Discrimination Act, would the policy in *Johnson Controls* have survived challenge under Title VII?

3. One of the ethical issues in workplace settings is the extent to which individuals may choose to place themselves at risk. Workers on high rise construction projects in Manhattan know that for each building floor, on the average, a life is lost. May they still choose to undertake such work? Coal miners understand that mines collapse; long haul truckers understand that cars crash; on September 11, 2001, in New York City, over 300 fire fighters and police personnel lost their lives in volunteer service in the aftermath of the World Trade Center bombings.

   In each instance, the worker may have dependents or family who will be harmed if he or she is harmed. Are there ethical principles involved in such risks and, if so, how should they be measured and by whom?

4. In *Johnson Controls,* of course, there were competing ethical concerns: one for equal opportunity in the workplace and the other for protecting the potentiality for human life. Does not the Court dismiss the latter by slight of hand, simply saying that ethical concerns are not part of the "essence" of Johnson Controls' business. Is not this the exact *opposite* of what we want: ethical business, functioning under ethical principles and assuring ethical results?

5. Or is it that, while professing an adherence to ethical principles, Johnson Controls did not tailor its rules appropriately. If so, how would *you* so tailor the rules? Should not there be some way for an employer to protect unborn generations? To protect employees from their own mistakes or bad judgments? Should not the community require this?

6. And what of the ethical obligation of the women (and men) working at Johnson Controls, toward their unborn children? Are you as sanguine as the Court that there is no tort liability or duty owing to them?

SCHOOL BOARD OF NASSAU COUNTY, FLORIDA v. ARLINE

480 U.S. 273 (1987)

Justice **Brennan** delivered the opinion of the Court.

Section 504 of the Rehabilitation Act of 1973 prohibits a federally funded state program from discriminating against a handicapped individual solely by reason of his or her handicap. This case presents the questions whether a person afflicted with tuberculosis, a contagious disease, may be considered a "handicapped individual" within the meaning of § 504 of the Act, and, if so, whether such an individual is "otherwise qualified" to teach elementary school.

I

From 1966 until 1979, respondent Gene Arline taught elementary school in Nassau County, Florida. She was discharged in 1979 after suffering a third relapse of tuberculosis within two years. After she was denied relief in state administrative proceedings, she brought suit in federal court, alleging that the school board's decision to dismiss her because of her tuberculosis violated § 504 of the Act.

A trial was held in the District Court, at which the principal medical evidence was provided by Marianne McEuen, M.D., an assistant director of the Community Tuberculosis Control Service of the Florida Department of Health and Rehabilitative Services. According to the medical records reviewed by Dr. McEuen, Arline was hospitalized for tuberculosis in 1957. For the next 20 years, Arline's disease was in remission. Then, in 1977, a culture revealed that tuberculosis was again active in her system; cultures taken in March 1978 and in November 1978 were also positive.

The superintendent of schools for Nassau County, Craig Marsh, then testified as to the school board's response to Arline's medical reports. After both her second relapse, in the spring of 1978, and her third relapse in November 1978, the school board suspended Arline with pay for the remainder of the school year. At the end of the 1978-1979 school year, the school board held a hearing, after which it discharged Arline, "not because she had done anything wrong," but because of the "continued reoccurence [sic] of tuberculosis."

. . . .

II

In enacting and amending the (Rehabilitation) Act, Congress enlisted all programs receiving federal funds in an effort "to share with handicapped Americans the opportunities for an education, transportation, housing, health care, and jobs that other Americans take for granted." To that end, Congress not only increased federal support for vocational rehabilitation, but also addressed the broader problem of discrimination against the handicapped by including § 504, an antidiscrimination provision patterned after Title VI of the Civil Rights Act of 1964. Section 504 of the Rehabilitation Act reads in pertinent part:

> "No otherwise qualified handicapped individual in the United States, as defined in section 706(7) of this title, shall, solely by reason of his handicap, be excluded from participation in, be denied the benefits of, or be subjected to discrimination under any program or activity receiving Federal financial assistance. . . ."

In 1974 Congress expanded the definition of "handicapped individual" for use in § 504 to read as follows:

> "[A]ny person who (i) has a physical or mental impairment which substantially limits one or more of such person's major life activities,

(ii) has a record of such an impairment, or (iii) is regarded as having such an impairment."

The amended definition reflected Congress' concern with protecting the handicapped against discrimination stemming not only from simple prejudice, but also from "archaic attitudes and laws" and from "the fact that the American people are simply unfamiliar with and insensitive to the difficulties confront[ing] individuals with handicaps." To combat the effects of erroneous but nevertheless prevalent perceptions about the handicapped, Congress expanded the definition of "handicapped individual" so as to preclude discrimination against "[a] person who has a record of, or is regarded as having, an impairment [but who] may at present have no actual incapacity at all."

. . . "Physical impairment" is defined as follows:

> "[A]ny physiological disorder or condition, cosmetic disfigurement, or anatomical loss affecting one or more of the following body systems: neurological; musculoskeletal; special sense organs; respiratory, including speech organs; cardiovascular; reproductive, digestive, genito-urinary; hemic and lymphatic; skin; and endocrine."

In addition, the regulations define "major life activities" as

> "functions such as caring for one's self, performing manual tasks, walking, seeing, hearing, speaking, breathing, learning, and working."

III

. . . .

We do not agree with petitioners that, in defining a handicapped individual under § 504, the contagious effects of a disease can be meaningfully distinguished from the disease's physical effects on a claimant in a case such as this. Arline's contagiousness and her physical impairment each resulted from the same underlying condition, tuberculosis. It would be unfair to allow an employer to seize upon the distinction between the effects of a disease on others and the effects of a disease on a patient and use that distinction to justify discriminatory treatment.

Nothing in the legislative history of § 504 suggests that Congress intended such a result. That history demonstrates that Congress was as concerned about the effect of an impairment on others as it was about its effect on the individual. Congress extended coverage to those individuals who are simply "regarded as having" a physical or mental impairment. The Senate Report provides as an example of a person who would be covered under this subsection "a person with some kind of visible physical impairment which in fact does not substantially limit that person's functioning."[2] Such an impairment

[2] Congress' desire to prohibit discrimination based on the effects a person's handicap may have on others was evident from the inception of the Act. For example, Representative Vanik, whose remarks constitute "a primary signpost on the road toward interpreting the legislative history of § 504," cited as an example of improper handicap discrimination a case in which "a court ruled that a cerebral palsied child, who was not a physical threat and was academically competitive, should be excluded from public school, because his teacher claimed his physical appearance "produced a nauseating effect" on his classmates."

might not diminish a person's physical or mental capabilities, but could nevertheless substantially limit that person's ability to work as a result of the negative reactions of others to the impairment.[3]

Allowing discrimination based on the contagious effects of a physical impairment would be inconsistent with the basic purpose of § 504, which is to ensure that handicapped individuals are not denied jobs or other benefits because of the prejudiced attitudes or the ignorance of others. By amending the definition of "handicapped individual" to include not only those who are actually physically impaired, but also those who are regarded as impaired and who, as a result, are substantially limited in a major life activity, Congress acknowledged that society's accumulated myths and fears about disability and disease are as handicapping as are the physical limitations that flow from actual impairment. Few aspects of a handicap give rise to the same level of public fear and misapprehension as contagiousness. Even those who suffer or have recovered from such noninfectious diseases as epilepsy or cancer have faced discrimination based on the irrational fear that they might be contagious. The Act is carefully structured to replace such reflexive reactions to actual or perceived handicaps with actions based on reasoned and medically sound judgments: the definition of "handicapped individual" is broad, but only those individuals who are both handicapped *and* otherwise qualified are eligible for relief. . . .

IV

The remaining question is whether Arline is otherwise qualified for the job of elementary schoolteacher. To answer this question in most cases, the district court will need to conduct an individualized inquiry and make appropriate findings of fact. Such an inquiry is essential if § 504 is to achieve its goal of protecting handicapped individuals from deprivations based on prejudice, stereotypes, or unfounded fear, while giving appropriate weight to such legitimate concerns of grantees as avoiding exposing others to significant health and safety risks.[4] The basic factors to be considered in conducting this inquiry are well established. In the context of the employment of a person handicapped with a contagious disease, we agree with amicus American Medical Association that this inquiry should include "[findings of] facts, based on reasonable medical judgments given the state of medical knowledge, about (a) the nature of the risk (how the disease is transmitted), (b) the duration of the risk (how long is the carrier infectious), (c) the severity of the risk (what is the potential harm to third parties) and (d) the probabilities the disease will be transmitted and will cause varying degrees of harm." In making these

[3] The Department of Health and Human Services regulations, which include among the conditions illustrative of physical impairments covered by the Act "cosmetic disfigurement," lend further support to Arline's position that the effects of one's impairment on others is as relevant to a determination of whether one is handicapped as is the physical effect of one's handicap on oneself. . . .

[4] A person who poses a significant risk of communicating an infectious disease to others in the workplace will not be otherwise qualified for his or her job if reasonable accommodation will not eliminate that risk. The Act would not require a school board to place a teacher with active, contagious tuberculosis in a classroom with elementary schoolchildren. Respondent conceded as much at oral argument.

findings, courts normally should defer to the reasonable medical judgments of public health officials. The next step in the "otherwise-qualified" inquiry is for the court to evaluate, in light of these medical findings, whether the employer could reasonably accommodate the employee under the established standards for that inquiry.

. . . .

Affirmed.

NOTES AND QUESTIONS

1. It is, of course, demeaning to an individual to be subject to discrimination either because of gender or handicap when the person is otherwise qualified for service. Thus, in *Cleveland Board of Education v. LaFleur*, 414 U.S. 632 (1974) the Supreme Court held that it denied due process for a school board to terminate *all* teachers in their third month of pregnancy. The point of the Rehabilitation Act is essentially to bar such irrationality from both the public and the private workplace.
2. But is there not a risk here of injuring the rights of other workers? That is, requiring that handicapped individuals be given a hearing, a job or be permitted to bring litigation complicates the workplace and drives up the cost of business. It may put other workers at risk. Since handicapped individuals are not distributed equally throughout an industry, some employers will be placed at a competitive disadvantage. Their rights, and the rights of their other employees, will therefore be jeopardized. How is it, as a society, that we can make such choices?
3. The important point about Gene Arline is that she was suffering from tuberculosis which had been in remission for 20 years and then became active before relapsing several times. How does this fall within the statute? Congress defines a handicapped person as one having an impairment "which substantially limits one or more of such person's major life activities." If Ms. Arline meets that definition, how could she teach? On the other hand, if she does not (as she asserts), and if she is able to teach, then is she not handicapped? Or does this miss the point?
4. The Court says there must be an individualized inquiry avoiding "prejudice, stereotypes, or unfounded fear." Why? If your children were being taught by a teacher with tuberculosis, would you want to hear that your fears were "unfounded"? What if Ms. Arline were a convicted pedophile, but the pedophilia "was in remission"? Same question, as to AIDS.
5. One of the issues left open after *Arline* was whether AIDS would qualify as a disability or handicap under federal legislation. That question was resolved in the *Bragdon* decision, presented in the next section on AIDS.
6. For an excellent article, see *Employer Liability for Domestic Violence in the Workplace: Are Employers Walking a Tightrope Without a Safety Net?*, 31 Tex. Tech L. Rev. 139 (2000); and see Michelle Gorton, *Intentional Disregard: Remedies for the Toxic Workplace*, 30 Envtl. L. 811 (2000).

PROBLEM 4-8 — Pregnancy and Disability

The State of California has a disability insurance program for private employees temporarily disabled from work-related injury or illnesses not covered by the conventional workers' compensation program. An employee pays up to $85 annually for coverage, which covers no more than 8 days per year. Excluded disabilities include dipsomania, drug addiction, sexual psychopathology, and pregnancy. Applicants are four pregnant women, only one with a normal pregnancy. Administrative regulations exclude only normal pregnancies.

The program is administered so that risks and population covered will never require funding above one percent annual level of contribution.

Under the preceding cases dealing with the Rehabilitation Act, the Americans with Disabilities Act and the Pregnancy Discrimination Act, are the exclusions valid? (Consider here as well the cases in the next section, dealing with AIDS). What of the constitutionality of such a program? And what of the ethics? *See Geduldig v. Aiello*, 417 U.S. 484 (1974).

[3] AIDS: Discrimination, Fear, Disclosure, Punishment

The following materials are representative of the intensive attention directed toward AIDS and the issues it posed as it burst upon the health and legal scenes in the early 1980s. In each instance, consider how the reasoning might change by the year 2010, when AIDS is no longer absolutely fatal and is largely treatable. *See* Palella, *Declining Morbidity,* 338 New Eng. J. Med. 853 (1998). The reader should also recall the decision in *Bragdon v. Abbott* presented *supra,* § 3.02[3], and the cases concerning disability in the preceding section, in analyzing the following cases.

Throughout there is a tension between the privacy interests of those who are HIV positive and others with whom they may have contact. How should this tension, between the individual and society be resolved?

[a] Discrimination and Disclosure

MAURO v. BORGESS MEDICAL CENTER
137 F.3d 398 (6th Cir. Ct. App.)

John R. **Gibson**, Circuit Judge.

William C. Mauro brought an action against his former employer, Borgess Medical Center, alleging violations of the Americans with Disabilities Act, 42 U.S.C. §§ 12101-12213 (1994), and the Rehabilitation Act, 29 U.S.C. §§ 701-796 (1994). . . .

Borgess employed Mauro from May 1990 through August 24, 1992 as an operating room technician. In June of 1992, an undisclosed source telephoned Robert Lambert, Vice President of Human Resources for Borgess Medical Center and Borgess Health Alliance, and informed Lambert that Mauro had "full blown" AIDS. Because of Borgess's concern that Mauro might expose a patient to HIV, Georgiann Ellis, Vice President of Surgical, Orthopedic and Clinical Services at Borgess, and Sharon Hickman, Mauro's supervisor and Operating Room Department Director, created a new full-time position of case cart/instrument coordinator, a position that eliminated all risks of transmission of the HIV virus. In July of 1992, Borgess officials offered Mauro this position, which he refused.

After Mauro's refusal of the case cart/instrument coordinator position, Borgess created a task force to determine whether an HIV-positive employee could safely perform the job responsibilities of a surgical technician. Lambert and Ellis informed Mauro by a letter dated August 10, 1992, that the task force had determined that a job requiring an HIV-infected worker to place his or her hands into a patient's body cavity in the presence of sharp instrumentation represented a direct threat to patient care and safety. Because the task force had concluded that an essential function of a surgical technician was to enter a patient's wound during surgery, the task force concluded that Mauro could no longer serve as a surgical technician. Lambert and Ellis concluded by offering Mauro two choices: to accept the case cart/instrument coordinator position, or be laid off. Mauro did not respond by the deadline stated in the letter, and Borgess laid him off effective August 24, 1992. Mauro filed this suit in January 1994.

. . . .

To prevail under his Americans with Disabilities Act claim, Mauro must show that he is "otherwise qualified" for the job at issue. A person is "otherwise qualified" if he or she can perform the essential functions of the job in question. A disabled individual, however, is not "qualified" for a specific employment position if he or she poses a "direct threat" to the health or safety of others which cannot be eliminated by a reasonable accommodation.

The "direct threat" standard applied in the Americans With Disabilities Act is based on the same standard as "significant risk" applied by the Rehabilitation Act. Our analysis under both Acts thus merges into one question: Did Mauro's activities as a surgical technician at Borgess pose a direct threat or significant risk to the health or safety of others?

. . . .

. . . The Centers for Disease Control has released a report discussing its recommendations regarding HIV-positive health care workers. *See* Centers for Disease Control, U.S. Dep't of Health & Human Servs., *Recommendations for Preventing Transmission of Human Immunodeficiency Virus and Hepatitis B Virus to Patients During Exposure-Prone Invasive Procedures*, 40 Morbidity & Mortality Weekly Report, 1, 3-4 (July 12, 1991).

The Report states that the risk of transmission of HIV from an infected health care worker to a patient is very small, and therefore recommends allowing most HIV-positive health care workers to continue performing most surgical procedures, provided that the workers follow safety precautions outlined in the Report. The Report, however, differentiates a limited category of invasive procedures, which it labels exposure-prone procedures, from general invasive procedures. General invasive procedures cover a wide range of procedures from insertion of an intravenous line to most types of surgery.

Exposure-prone procedures, however, involve those that pose a greater risk of percutaneous (skin-piercing) injury. Though the Centers for Disease Control did not specifically identify which types of procedures were to be labeled exposure-prone, it supplies a general definition: "Characteristics of exposure-prone procedures include digital palpation of a needle tip in a body cavity or the simultaneous presence of the [health care worker's] fingers and a needle or other sharp instrument or object in a poorly visualized or highly confined anatomic site." The Report advises that individual health care institutions take measures to identify which procedures performed in their hospital should be labeled exposure-prone and recommends that HIV-infected health care workers should not perform exposure-prone procedures unless they have sought counsel from an expert review panel and have been advised under what circumstances they may continue to perform these procedures. The Report further recommends that those health care workers who engage in exposure-prone procedures notify prospective patients of their condition.

We must defer to the medical judgment expressed in the Report of the Centers for Disease Control in evaluating the district court's ruling on whether Mauro posed a direct threat in the essential functions of his job.

Mauro stated in his deposition that during surgery his work did not include assisting in surgery, but instead handing instruments to the surgeon and helping the surgeon with whatever else he or she needed. . . .

The continued questioning led to a distinction between the wound and the body cavity. Mauro was asked if he ever had his hands in a body cavity, described as being past the wound area, and Mauro stated that he personally never had his hand in a body cavity because the small size of the surgical incision prevented too many hands from being placed inside the body cavity.

. . . .

Mauro explained that during his training, discussion had occurred indicating that nicks and cuts were always a possibility for a surgical technician. In fact, the record included two incident reports involving Mauro. One report indicated that Mauro had sliced his right index finger while removing a knife blade from a handle on June 25, 1991, and another report indicated that he had scratched his hand with the sharp end of a dirty needle while threading it on June 8, 1990.

. . . .

Dr. Davenport testified in his deposition that even if HIV-infected health care workers followed universal precautions, methods designed to ensure that health care workers do not come into contact with blood, some risk of exposure existed when HIV-infected health care workers come into contact with patients. Dr. Davenport stated that this can happen because of human error, as health care workers would not completely follow the precautions; through needle injuries; and because there was always potential for blood exposure in situations that could not be controlled, such as when surgical gloves tore.

Dr. Davenport identified the Centers for Disease Control Report as one of the best resources available on preventing transmission of the HIV virus. He stated that he was familiar with the theoretical model estimating that the risk of a patient being infected by an HIV-positive surgeon during a single operation as being somewhere between one in 42,000, and one in 420,000. He further stated that any patient who comes in contact with the HIV-infected blood of a health care worker has some risk of the virus being transferred to that patient. Though a few people infected with HIV suffer no consequences, Dr. Davenport stated that in general most people consider HIV a uniformly lethal disease. . . .

Sharon Hickman, a registered nurse, was the interim director of operating rooms at Borgess in June and July of 1992. While serving as interim director Hickman supervised the surgical technicians at Borgess, including Mauro. In her affidavit Hickman described a meeting of the Ad Hoc HIV Task Force for the hospital on July 23, 1992 and the statements she made at that meeting. Hickman stated that she told the task force that the duties of a surgical technician include preparing and maintaining the equipment used during surgery, but that:

> On an infrequent basis, the Surgical Technician is required to assist in the performance of surgery by holding back body tissue, with the use of either retractors or the Technician's hands, to assist the surgeon in visualizing the operative site. The Surgical Technician also may assist the surgeon with suturing and other duties related to the performance of the operation.

She also advised the task force that, although the need for a surgical technician's assistance in the performance of a surgical procedure arises infrequently, it is not possible to restructure the job to eliminate the surgical technician from performing such functions because this need arises on an emergency basis and cannot be planned in advance. . . .

. . . .

. . . The district judge recognized, based on Mauro's testimony, that he occasionally was required to place his hands "upon and into the patient's surgical incision to provide room and visibility to the surgeon." The testimony we have outlined above demonstrates that the district court did not err in so quoting Mauro's direct statement that: "Usually if I had my hands near the wound, it would be to like, on an abdominal incision, to kind of put your finger in and hold — kind of pull down on the muscle tissue and . . . pull that back." The material issue as to whether Mauro was a direct threat or significant risk to the health and safety of others turns on whether his job duties require him, even on rare occasions, to have his hands in or near an operative site in the presence of sharp instrumentation where visibility is poor. Mauro's statement above, that at times he would place his finger in an incision in order to pull down on and pull back the muscle tissue, is consistent with Hickman's uncontradicted statement that the duties of a surgical technician require a surgical technician, on an infrequent basis, to hold back body tissue with a retractor or his or her hands to assist the surgeon in visualizing the operative site. . . .

. . . .

We conclude that the district court did not err in determining that Mauro's continued employment as a surgical technician posed a direct threat to the health and safety of others. The district court based this conclusion on both the description of a Borgess surgical technician's duties indicating the necessity for a surgical technician to place his or her hands upon and into the surgical incision to provide room and visibility for the surgeon, and the risk of sustaining a needle stick or minor laceration which Mauro had in the past sustained. All the evidence, together with the uncontradicted fact that a wound causing an HIV-infected surgical technician to bleed while in the body cavity could have catastrophic results and near certainty of death, indicates that Mauro was a direct threat.

. . . .

Accordingly, we affirm the judgment of the district court.

Boggs, Circuit Judge, dissenting.

There are two difficult legal issues in this case, somewhat intertwined with issues of political theory that are not for us to determine. The ADA, a statute duly enacted by Congress, demands that patient sovereignty and informed consent, normally paramount considerations (*see, e.g., Washington v. Glucksberg,*) not be respected. The ADA thus requires employers to employ people they would rather not employ, and by whom they believe, rightly or wrongly, their patients would prefer not to be ministered to.

. . . .

. . . At bottom, the only relevant question is this:

Could reasonable minds differ on whether Mauro poses a "significant risk" based on the interpretative standards laid down by Arline and the CDC and AMA guidelines? Based on my analysis of this case, I believe the answer must be yes. Although there are some people who believe that the Three Mile Island accident caused cancer all over the Northeast and some people who believe that the tiniest trace of dioxin will cause bladder cancer in anyone who ingests it, reasonable minds can, and do, differ from these beliefs, and over the "significance" of those risks.

In the same way, Mauro poses some risk. It is not ontologically impossible for him to transmit a disease of very great lethality. However, the chance that he will do so to any given patient is "small." Whether we call the risk "extremely small," "vanishingly small," "negligible," or whatever, assessing the risk remains a judgment that must be made by considering both the actual probability of harm and the degree of the consequences, just as the Supreme Court instructed us.

That is what the District Court did not do, and that is why I would reverse its decision and remand for reconsideration under the correct standard — a full assessment of both the risk and the consequence. The court agrees that some change is needed, but then jumps directly to the second difficult question, the application of the rules for more dangerous, "exposure-prone" procedures as opposed to merely "invasive" procedures. As a person uneducated in this particular area, I might have thought that "invasive" procedures, with the implication of intrusion into the body, and the absence of any qualifier, would be more dangerous than "exposure-prone" ones, with the contingent meaning of "prone" and the hopeful sound of mere "exposure."

However, we must live with the language given us, and we must try to make sense of it. Whatever the words mean, it is clear that "invasive" procedures, under the CDC guidelines, require no special precautions (beyond the quite considerable “universal” ones) and do not contemplate patient notification, while performance of exposure-prone procedures permits special restrictions on an infected employee and even, under some circumstances, the removal of an employee who performs those procedures. As set out at greater length below, the exact nature of Mauro’s duties are a matter of considerable dispute, especially when the record is read, as we must read it, in a light most favorable to him. Whether the procedures he may perform cross the line from the merely “invasive” to the actionable “exposure-prone” is a genuine and material issue, on which reasonable minds can differ.

I

In *School Bd. of Nassau County v. Arline*, the Supreme Court considered whether a tubercular teacher was “otherwise qualified” under the Rehabilitation Act of 1973, 29 U.S.C. § 794, which she would not be if she unavoidably presented “a significant risk to the health and safety of others.” Observing that “[a] person who poses a significant risk of communicating an infectious disease to others in the workplace will not be otherwise qualified for his or her job if reasonable accommodation will not eliminate that risk,” the Court stated that the district court, in determining whether a person poses a significant risk, must “conduct an individualized inquiry and make appropriate findings of fact.” In the context of an employee with a communicable disease, this “individualized inquiry” should include “appropriate findings of fact,” including four “basic factors” suggested to the Court by the American Medical Association in its amicus brief in that case: “(a) the nature of the risk (how the disease is transmitted), (b) the duration of the risk (how long is the carrier infectious), (c) the severity of the risk (what is the potential harm to third parties), and (d) the probabilities the disease will be transmitted and will cause varying degrees of harm.” . . .

In the case before us, the district court held that “a real possibility of transmission, however small” constituted a significant risk, “because the consequence of [HIV] transmission is invariably death.” In so holding, the court effectively negated the Supreme Court’s instruction to consider, as one of the “basic factors,” the probability of transmission of contagious disease

On appeal, it appears that this court recognizes that the district court erred in this way, for the court’s opinion states, instead, that “our analysis . . . must not consider the possibility of HIV transmission, but rather focus on the probability of transmission weighed with the other three factors of the Arline test.” This recognition by the court offered the promise of a correct solution. Unfortunately, rather than proceeding to analyze the factor of probability of transmission, the court immediately moves on to the proxy question of the risk associated with surgical procedures that are described by the CDC as either “exposure prone” or merely “invasive.” . . .

A

The CDC “has estimated that the risk to a single patient from an HIV-positive surgeon ranges from.0024% (1 in 42,000) to.00024% (1 in 417,000).”

This estimate, of course, is for surgeons, who by the very nature of their work enter surgical wounds with sharp instruments during virtually every procedure they perform. Common sense — and, of course, the court's obligation to interpret the evidence in the light most favorable to the nonmovant — requires us to suppose, in the absence of contrary information, that the activities of a surgical technician such as Mauro who touched only the margin of the wound, and that only very rarely, would pose an even smaller risk. So may the resulting coefficients of risk — numbers somewhat smaller than .0024% to .00024% — still be deemed "significant?"

. . . .

My view is that, where the absence of a definite standard leaves the matter almost wholly subjective, "significant risk" should be found to exist — or not to exist — as a matter of law, thus supporting an order of summary judgment, only if reasonable minds could not differ as to that conclusion. It is not before the court whether the risk was so small as to be insignificant as a matter of law, but it is clear to me that Borgess failed to eliminate a genuine issue of fact as to whether the risk Mauro posed was "significant." It is obvious that reasonable people routinely and voluntarily submit to medical care (including non-essential medical care) and undertake non-medical activities that have a comparable or greater risk of causing grave injuries, including death, than the risk Mauro seems to have posed, based on the record we have. Consequently, a jury might well find that Mauro's work as a surgical technician did not create a significant risk.

There is another reason for entrusting this question to a jury. The degree of risk a person with a communicable disease poses to others likely depends on specific facts or other assessments about that person, not just on aggregate data about the person's contagious disease — which is why the Court in Arline insisted upon an "individualized inquiry." If surgeons whom the surgical technician assisted were to testify, for instance, that the assistant had a record of impeccable reliability, technical skills, and professionalism, and that they themselves were not concerned about risks they incurred by performing surgery with him, then a fact-finder could easily conclude that an employee with a contagious blood-borne disease did not pose a significant risk. On the other hand, if the testimony showed that the employee's co-workers found him to be inattentive, careless, and physically clumsy, then the jury might well conclude that, however small the theoretical risk of transmission, it would not be a safe bet for this particular person to continue working in surgery, and that he was not, therefore, "otherwise qualified."

. . . .

D

The court today effectively announces that HIV seropositivity renders surgical workers not otherwise qualified as a matter of law. Among its other failings, that rule is based on earlier clinical information. It is true that Borgess's liability in the immediate case turns upon the state of medical knowledge at the time of its conduct. *See Abbott v. Bragdon*, 107 F.3d at 944. However, rules of law may be hard to dislodge despite changes in underlying circumstances. The court should not announce this decision without careful qualification that it is based upon older and incomplete medical information. For example, the CDC has reported that immediate treatment with antiviral medications after percutaneous exposure to HIV appears to reduce the rate of infection by approximately 80%. Needles and other surgical implements have been redesigned to reduce risk. And, as has been understood for almost two years now, combinations of protease inhibitors with nucleoside analogues can combat HIV in some patients with remarkable success. It is not yet clear whether these drug therapies will be permanently effective, and even with them, HIV infection remains a grave condition. Nonetheless, HIV infection today may not entail the "inevitable death" assumed by the district court. In the weighing of the probabilities of transmission against the gravity of harm, such medical progress could well affect the determination of whether the risk of HIV transmission is "significant."

. . . .

II

Rather than directly evaluating the probabilities, the court instead reaches its holding by relying on the Centers for Disease Control Guidelines regarding the participation of HIV-positive health-care workers in surgery. . . . The Guidelines identified two categories of surgical procedures: those that are merely "invasive," and for which no restrictions (other than "universal precautions") on HIV-positive health-care workers are appropriate; and the subset of invasive procedures that are "exposure-prone," and for which restrictions, including exclusion from participation, may be warranted. In a general way, it might be thought that, for seropositive health-care workers who perform merely invasive procedures, there is a rebuttable presumption that the worker does not pose a significant risk; while seropositive health-care workers who perform exposure-prone procedures face a rebuttable presumption that they *do* create significant risk.

. . . .

There is a glaringly obvious reason why the court must be wrong in its interpretation. Mauro occasionally placed his fingertip at the *margin* of the surgical wounds. Surgeons, by comparison, must constantly place their fingers *inside* such wounds. Yet the CDC Guidelines are perfectly clear that many, if not most, invasive procedures such as surgeons perform are not regarded as exposure-prone. So how could the peripherally invasive work Mauro sometimes did be classified as exposure-prone? For the court to interpret Mauro's activity as being exposure-prone means *a fortiori* that virtually every procedure any *surgeon* ever performs must be deemed exposure-prone.

In addition to that reason, the descriptions in the record of what Mauro's job entailed simply do not suggest that his work had the characteristics of exposure-proneness, the relevant ones here being "the simultaneous presence of the HCW's fingers and a needle or other sharp instrument or object in a poorly visualized or highly confined anatomic site." Guidelines at 4. I presume that working with sharp instruments in a space that is cramped or shielded from view makes cuts or jabs more likely because the health-care worker cannot see the relative positions of fingers and instruments, or because the fingers and instruments are forced to be very close together.

. . . .

On the basis of this record, there is a genuine issue of material fact whether any of Mauro's activities, as described by him, Nurse Hickman, and Dr. Ross and Dr. Tolchin, were "exposure-prone" as the CDC Guidelines use that term. Recall that under the Guidelines, a health-care worker's "surgical entry into tissues, cavities, or organs" does not, without more, constitute an exposure-prone procedure. The Guidelines clearly regard such entry into wounds as acceptable, absent particularly hazardous conditions. There is simply no solid evidence that Mauro's job, as he had performed it in the past or would be required to perform it in the future, included those dangerous conditions. There are only unsubstantiated allegations that such conditions would or might exist.

In concluding either as a matter of fact or of law that Mauro's retraction of surgical wounds constituted an "exposure-prone" procedure, the court has erred. If the outcome of the case is to turn on whether what Mauro did was "exposure prone" or not, as defined by the CDC, summary judgment was not warranted because there is a genuine issue of fact as to whether it was.

. . . .

NOTES AND QUESTIONS

1. Note that Mr. Mauro (actually, his estate) relies on two separate statutes: The Americans with Disabilities Act and the Rehabilitation Act. How do these Acts, and his theories, differ. In elements? Defenses? Relief?
2. Was the offer of case cart/instrument coordinator a fair one? If the salary and rank remained the same, how could Mr. Mauro complain? Wasn't it a "reasonable accommodation?"
3. The key issue is the likelihood of transmission of AIDS. The Court says Mauro needn't eliminate all possibility. Why not? Isn't that the point? The "sterile field" approach to surgery? If you were the patient, wouldn't you want to reduce risk to a minimum?
4. Does Mr. Mauro, as a healthcare provider, have an ethical obligation to his patient to remove himself from the operating room?
5. If Mauro continued in the operating room, should he, or the surgeon, or the hospital, notify the patient? If not, is there liability under the doctrine of informed consent? If so, may patients reject Mr. Mauro?
6. The risk of transmission is statistically small, between 1:42,000 and 1:420,000. Yet the *fear* of transmission is great, well beyond the statistics. Could a hospital legitimately defer to patient fear as an independent reason for excluding Mr. Mauro? Or is that pandering to prejudice?
7. Judge Boggs, dissenting, says that the ADA is counter to "patient sovereignty and informed consent," demanding that they not be

"rejected." Is this true of the legislation? Of the result in this case? And if so, is suspending patient sovereignty and autonomy a good thing?

8. What is the exact point of Judge Bogg's disagreement with the majority: that the risk of transmission is insignificant; that reasonable minds might differ on this; that the trial court focused on the procedure and not Mauro's role; on the roles and not Mauro himself? How can a hospital run an operating room if it must individually assess each professional's individual chance of pricking him or herself?
9. Is Judge Boggs correct? Does the majority's view mean that virtually every procedure a surgeon performs must be "exposure-prone"? And HIV positive surgeons must therefore be barred from all operating rooms?
10. Judge Boggs makes the point that medical science is rapidly changing the treatment and outcome of AIDS. What is the significance of this? And how should courts process this information?

DOE v. NORTHWESTERN UNIVERSITY

682 N.E.2d 145 (Ill. App. Ct. 1997)

McNulty, J.

. . . .

The six fictitiously named plaintiffs received various treatments from several students in Northwestern's dental clinic during 1990 and 1991. On July 22, 1991, Northwestern sent a letter to all six plaintiffs, along with numerous other patients, stating:

> "Recently we learned that a dental student involved in providing care to you in the Dental Clinic has tested positive for HIV.
>
> . . . .
>
> We believe, based on the most current and reliable scientific evidence, that the likelihood that you were infected with the HIV virus as a result of contact with this student is extremely low. All persons providing dental care are required to follow precautions designed to prevent the communication of diseases, including HIV. These precautions have been taken. However, *we strongly recommend that you be tested for the presence of the virus.*
>
> The Northwestern University Dental School is offering free testing for HIV."

Because defendants did not in the letter identify the infected student, plaintiffs feared that any of the students may have been infected. Plaintiffs' attorneys later determined the identity of the infected student, whom they then sued under the fictitious name of John Noe. Noe worked in Northwestern's dental clinic from June 1990 until July 1991. He participated in electrosurgery to reduce Anita Doe's gums and in a root canal performed on her in July and August 1990. He diagnosed Laurel Doe's fractured tooth and participated in a tooth extraction in September 1990. He took X rays of Bertha Doe's teeth in March 1991. Noe treated John Doe several times over the course of his year in the clinic. The last treatment was a tooth cleaning Noe performed on May 23, 1991. Anita, Laurel and John bled during Noe's treatments. Noe cemented a loose tooth for Brian Doe in August 1990, and he took Carol Doe's blood pressure while discussing oral hygiene with her in February 1991.

. . . .

Plaintiffs brought a complaint in 12 counts. . . . Plaintiffs separated those whom Noe invasively treated from plaintiffs who received no such treatment. According to plaintiffs, Anita, Laurel, Bertha and John Doe received invasive treatment, while Noe never invasively treated Brian or Carol Doe. The invasively treated plaintiffs charged defendants with breach of fiduciary duty (count II), intentional infliction of emotional distress (count IV), battery (count VI), common law fraud (count VII), consumer fraud (count XII), breach of contract (count VIII), and negligent malpractice (count X). Brain and Carol sued for breach of fiduciary duty (count III), intentional infliction of emotional distress (count V), breach of contract (count IX), and dental malpractice (count XI).

In counts II through XII, plaintiffs alleged they "suffered physical distress and discomfort and mental pain and anguish upon learning of the possibility of infection with HIV." Plaintiffs do not allege that any of them have ever tested positive for HIV, and in response to defendants' request, the named plaintiffs admitted that they never tested positive for HIV. Defendants also presented the conclusions of studies which found only a very small chance of transmission of HIV in the course of medical treatment. Although plaintiffs in their complaint emphasized that researchers could not rule out the possibility of HIV transmission from health care providers to patients, they did not allege any particular level of probability of transmission. . . .

The trial court dismissed counts II through XII for failure to allege actual exposure to HIV, finding that allegation necessary for recovery of damages for fear of contracting AIDS. . . .

Plaintiffs seek reversal of the judgment as to all counts. They argue that they have stated a cause of action for battery because they never consented to treatment by a student infected with HIV. . . .

Plaintiffs here consented to all of the dental procedures; they did not know about risks associated with the procedures when Dr. Noe performed them. In *Faya v. Almaraz,* 329 Md. 435, 620 A.2d 327 (1993), the plaintiff sued a doctor for performing surgery on him without disclosing that the doctor was HIV positive. The court rejected the battery claim, holding that "the cause of action for lack of informed consent is one in tort for negligence, as opposed to battery or assault." We agree. Plaintiffs separately stated their cause of action for negligence and dental malpractice based on the failure to obtain informed consent. Therefore we affirm dismissal of count VI, in which plaintiffs sought recovery for battery.

. . . .

The plaintiff must allege legally cognizable damages to plead a cause of action for common law fraud. For all of these counts, we assume that plaintiffs have adequately alleged facts establishing defendants' duties to plaintiffs and showing that defendants breached those duties. We confine our discussion to the adequacy of the allegations of damages.

Emotional distress constitutes legally cognizable damage only where the distress is particularly severe. "The law intervenes only where the distress inflicted is so severe that no reasonable man could be expected to endure it." Plaintiffs suggest that AIDS causes such severe panic that any reasonable fear of AIDS should be compensable, even without proof of "actual exposure. Defendants cite more numerous cases requiring "actual exposure." . . .

In *Williamson* the court criticized the reasoning of cases requiring proof of actual exposure. . . .

The plaintiff in *Williamson* punctured herself on a sharp instrument improperly left in the trash. She did not know whether the instrument had been in contact with an HIV-positive person, but she feared that she contracted HIV. The court held:

> "[AIDS] is a disease universally dreaded by the lay public. Under those circumstances, it cannot be concluded as a matter of law that the plaintiff reacted unreasonably or unforeseeably. Fearing that she faced serious injury as a result of exposure to HIV, it was not unreasonable that she would be greatly upset during the period of time that was necessary to obtain medical assurance that she was not infected. It may very well be that there is some period of time after receiving a puncture wound from medical waste during which any person would experience a range of mental reactions, from mere anxiety to actionable emotional distress, and ought to be eligible for compensation therefor if she meets the required tests, including the serious injury standard applying to all claims based upon infliction of emotional distress."

Although we are persuaded by the reasoning of *Williamson* that a reasonable person in plaintiffs' situation would foreseeably fear that he or she might have contracted HIV, we disagree with that court's conclusion that the complaint must, therefore, state a compensable claim. *Williamson*, in effect, creates a special rule for fear of AIDS as opposed to other fears: that decision allows compensation for any reasonable fear of AIDS, regardless of the remoteness of the medically verifiable possibility of contracting the disease. This creates a special AIDS exception to the general rule that not all reasonable fears are compensable. . . .

. . . .

We find that plaintiffs who fear that they have contracted AIDS because of a defendant's negligence should recover damages for the time in which they reasonably feared a substantial, medically verifiable possibility of contracting AIDS. The reasonable, compensable fear does not include the augmentation of that fear due to ignorance concerning AIDS and its transmission. We believe this reasoning is compatible with the results of most cases requiring proof of "actual exposure": while any person stuck with a used needle should, reasonably, fear the possibility of contracting AIDS, this reasonable fear is not of a sufficient degree to be compensable, unless the plaintiff faces a particularly substantial risk of HIV infection, as, for instance, when the plaintiff learns that the used needle probably held bodily fluids of a person who had HIV. . . .

The concurrence accuses us of "stopping short" and adopting a "lesser standard" than the "actual exposure" requirement the concurrence espouses. The standard adopted herein is distinct from, not lesser than, the "actual exposure" requirement. Under the standard stated herein, a plaintiff who has proved an "actual exposure" will recover no damages if she presents insufficient evidence that she feared a substantial, medically verifiable possibility of contracting AIDS. Under the standard the concurrence espouses, a plaintiff may recover damages for an "actual exposure," even without evidence that she knew facts showing a substantial possibility of contracting the disease.

. . . As the concurrence correctly points out, under the standard we adopt, litigation will focus on differing opinions as to what level of medically verified risk qualifies as a substantial possibility of contracting AIDS. We believe that this is precisely the proper focus for litigation. The parties should marshal medical evidence of the possibility of contracting the disease and argue as to whether that possibility is so substantial as to merit compensation. The rhetoric of the concurrence would instead focus the attention of litigants and the courts on the less informative issue of whether the occurrence qualifies as an "actual" exposure.

. . . .

Defendants' letter itself shows that plaintiffs had reason to fear that they might have been infected with HIV. However, not all reasonable fears of AIDS are compensable. Plaintiffs have not alleged facts that could support a finding that they faced more than an extremely remote possibility of contracting AIDS. In the absence of a particularly substantial risk of HIV infection, plaintiffs' reasonable fears were not severe enough to warrant tort compensation. Plaintiffs have not suffered legally cognizable damages due to defendants' alleged malpractice, fraud, intentional infliction of emotional distress, or breaches of fiduciary duty or contract. We affirm the trial court's decision dismissing those counts of the complaint. . . .

. . . .

Affirmed.

Presiding Justice **Divito** specially concurring:

Although I agree with the result reached by the majority and with much of its analysis, I disagree with the standard it applies to determine whether a fear of HIV infection is compensable. According to the majority, plaintiffs may recover damages "for the time in which they reasonably feared a substantial, medically verifiable possibility of contracting AIDS." The majority states that this standard is compatible with cases requiring plaintiffs to prove actual exposure to the virus in order to recover damages based on a fear of HIV infection, but it stops short of requiring actual exposure. I write separately because I believe that an actual exposure requirement is preferable.

. . . .

To establish actual exposure, a plaintiff must show that HIV was present in the alleged disease-transmitting agent and that a medically-accepted channel of transmission for the virus existed. . . .

. . . .

The court in *K.A.C. v. Benson*, 527 N.W.2d 553 (Minn. 1995), listed a number of policy considerations that support an actual exposure requirement:

> "Proliferation of fear of AIDS claims in the absence of meaningful restrictions would run an equal risk of compromising the availability and affordability of medical, dental and malpractice insurance, medical and dental care, prescription drugs, and blood products. Juries deliberating in fear of AIDS lawsuits would be just as likely to reach inconsistent results, discouraging early resolution or settlement of such claims. Last but not least, the coffers of defendants and their insurers would risk being emptied to pay for the emotional suffering of the many plaintiffs uninfected by exposure to HIV or AIDS, possibly leaving inadequate compensation for plaintiffs to whom the fatal AIDS virus was actually transmitted."

. . . For these reasons, I would require proof of actual exposure as a prerequisite to recovery in cases based on a fear of HIV infection.

In this case, plaintiffs alleged breach of contract, breach of fiduciary duty, fraud, intentional infliction of emotional distress, and medical negligence. For all of these claims, the damages plaintiffs alleged were their fears of HIV infection. For breach of contract and tort actions, such as these, however, a defendant is liable only for consequences that were the proximate result of its conduct and is not liable for speculative damages. Because plaintiffs failed to allege actual exposure, their fears were based on speculation and cannot be said to have resulted from defendants' conduct. Consequently, their damages are not legally cognizable. . . .

. . . .

The actual exposure requirement is particularly helpful to controlling litigation in cases such as this, where much of the damages plaintiffs allege arise from the letter they received. We should commend health care providers for taking the initiative to advise patients of a risk of HIV infection, not penalize them for doing so. By requiring proof of actual exposure, courts establish a principle of law that encourages timely notification, which is critical in controlling further spread of the virus. . . .

For these reasons, I specially concur.

NOTES AND QUESTIONS

1. In the *Northwestern University* case, if the defendants *had* known the dental student were HIV positive, what should they have done? Remove the student from patient contact? Notify the patients? Dismiss the student from school? Would these steps have violated the Americans with Disabilities Act?
2. What is the plaintiff's theory, exactly? That they were denied material information under the doctrine of informed consent? If so, *material* to what (treatment, danger, choice of provider)? Or was it risk of harm? Battery? Negligence? What was the fiduciary duty that was breached?

Was the duty not to inflict emotional distress (no matter how remote, irrational or prejudiced)?

3. Is the Court on sound ground in rejecting the *Williamson* rule, that fear of AIDS is sufficiently well-founded to be actionable, on the ground that it creates an exception to the rule that the cause of fear must be "severe"? *Isn't* AIDS "severe"?

4. Wasn't part of the plaintiff's claim the irresponsibility (alleged) of the defendants in knowingly (alleged) putting them in contact with the infected student? Is that fairly part of an intentional infliction of emotional distress claim?

5. Does the majority hold that actual exposure plus fear of a "substantial, medically verifiable possibility of contracting AIDS" are both necessary for recovery? Didn't the plaintiffs plead these? Which is missing? As to the latter, since the statistical possibility of contracting AIDS in any single exposure is very low, will plaintiffs *ever* recover? When?

6. The Court finds plaintiffs' fears too remote to allow recovery for a number of plaintiffs' theories: fraud, fiduciary duty, intentional infliction of emotional distress, contract. Is that analysis equally applicable to each of these theories? And what of the battery claim coupled with the informed consent — *wasn't* there an unconsented touching?

7. Does the concurring opinion make a good case that "actual exposure" should be required? Is that, in fact, different from the majority? And wouldn't it still be necessary to evaluate the probability of infection from the exposure? Or would it be sufficient to show actual exposure, regardless of probable consequences?

8. The concurrence argues that an 'actual exposure' standard will encourage responsible reporting. But wouldn't the threat of damages — denied here — do more, including increase screening and vigilance to reduce infection possibilities?

9. Would the answers to any of the preceding questions be different if the plaintiffs had actually contracted AIDS? If AIDS, as the *Maùro* dissent argues, is now shown to be no longer certainly fatal, due to medical advances?

FAYA v. ALMAREZ

620 A.2d 327 (Md. 1993)

Opinion by **Murphy**, C.J.

These companion cases present the important question whether a surgeon infected with the AIDS virus has a legal duty to inform patients of that condition before operating upon them and, failing that, whether a patient's fear of having contracted the AIDS virus from the infected surgeon constitutes a legally compensable injury where the patient has not shown HIV-positive status.

. . . .

II

Dr. Rudolf Almaraz, an oncological surgeon specializing in breast cancer with operative privileges at the Johns Hopkins Hospital (Hopkins) in Baltimore, knew himself to be HIV-positive, i.e. a carrier of the HIV virus, since 1986. On October 7, 1988, Almaraz performed a partial mastectomy and axiliary dissection on Sonja Faya at Hopkins. He removed an axillary hematoma from Faya the following March. On November 14, 1989, again at Hopkins, Almaraz surgically excised a benign lump from the breast of Perry Mahoney Rossi. The therapeutic outcome of these operations is not in dispute.

On October 27, 1989, Almaraz was first diagnosed as suffering from cytomegalovirus retinitis, the eye infection signaling full-blown AIDS. That diagnosis was confirmed by a second ophthalmologist on November 17, 1989. Thus, as well as knowing his HIV-positive status throughout the period in question, Almaraz knew that he had AIDS prior to the Rossi operation.

Almaraz gave up his practice of medicine on March 1, 1990. He terminated his association with Hopkins in June of that year. He died of AIDS on November 16, 1990. Faya and Rossi learned of their physician's illness for the first time from a local newspaper on or about December 6, 1990, well over a year after Rossi's operation and twenty months after Faya's last contact with Almaraz. Both Faya and Rossi immediately underwent blood tests for the AIDS virus, which came back negative for both. Nevertheless, by December 11 Sonja Faya, Perry Mahoney Rossi, and her husband, Dennis T. Rossi (appellants), filed suit against Almaraz's estate, his Maryland professional association business entity, and Hopkins (appellees) for compensatory and punitive damages.

. . . .

IV

A

. . . .

. . . HIV is a fragile virus that can survive only in the habitat of bodily fluids. While others can carry HIV, the only fluids that can transmit the virus are blood, semen, vaginal fluids and breast milk. For the virus to pass from one person to another, at least one such fluid of the carrier must enter the body of the other. HIV is primarily transmitted through unprotected sexual intercourse, the sharing of contaminated syringes among intravenous drug users, and blood transfusions, although transmission by the latter route has greatly decreased since the Red Cross began testing the blood supply in 1985.

The virus is only transmitted if it reaches the bloodstream of the transmittee. That is, the fluid of the carrier must pass through some channel to the transferee's blood system. Hence unprotected sex, needle-sharing, pregnancy and nursing are relatively efficient modes of transfer, while others are not; for HIV to pass in non-sexual, non-needle-sharing contexts, blood must pass both through a wound in the carrier and into a wound in the transferee. In short, the two parties' blood must commingle. Thus there have been no reports of HIV transmission through casual contact.

We take notice of one other fact regarding HIV. While there is often a long latency period between infection with HIV and the onset of AIDS, at least 95% of HIV carriers will test positive for the virus (though not manifest AIDS) within six months of acquiring it. . . .

. . . .

B

While the appellants allege many counts of misconduct by the appellees, the core of their complaints is that Dr. Almaraz was negligent in failing to disclose his HIV-positive status before operating on Faya and Rossi. Appellants assert that a physician's duty of care must encompass disclosure that an operating surgeon's HIV-positive status poses the risk, however minimal, of transmission of the AIDS virus during surgery. Appellants maintain that, having properly pleaded this issue, the trial court erred in not allowing a jury to evaluate Almaraz's conduct and its consequences. We agree.

. . . .

. . . Under the allegations of the appellants' complaints, taken as true, it was foreseeable that Dr. Almaraz might transmit the AIDS virus to his patients during invasive surgery. Thus, we are unable to say, as a matter of law, that Dr. Almaraz owed no duty to the appellants, either to refrain from performing the surgery or to warn them of his condition. This is so even though the medical literature indicates that, with proper barrier techniques, the risk of HIV transmission during surgery is extremely low, for legal scholars have long agreed that the seriousness of potential harm, as well as its probability, contributes to a duty to prevent it. Restatement, Second, Torts, § 293(c), comment c; Prosser and Keeton, Torts, § 31 (5th ed. 1984); while it may be unlikely that an infected doctor will transmit the AIDS virus to a patient during surgery, the patient will almost surely die if the virus is transmitted.

The House of Delegates of the American Medical Association (AMA) has adopted the following policy statement on HIV-infected physicians:

> "It should be noted that transmission of HIV from an infected physician to a patient has not yet been reported, but it is a theoretical possibility during invasive procedures. It is longstanding AMA policy that when the scientific basis for patient protection policy decisions are unclear, the physician must err on the side of protecting patients.
>
> "That being the case, the following recommendations should be followed in the management of an HIV-infected health care worker:
>
> "HIV-infected physicians should disclose their HIV seropositivity to a public health officer or a local review committee, and should refrain from doing procedures that pose a significant risk of HIV transmission or perform these procedures only with the consent of the patient and the permission of a local review committee. This committee will determine the activities the physician can continue to perform."

AMA "Digest of HIV/AIDS Policy," September 14, 1992. Similarly, the AMA's Code of Medical Ethics provides:

> "A physician who knows that he or she has an infectious disease, which if contracted by the patient would pose a significant risk to the patient, should not engage in any activity that creates a risk of transmission of that disease to the patient. The precautions taken to prevent the transmission of a contagious disease to a patient should be appropriate to the seriousness of the disease and must be particularly stringent in the case of a disease that is potentially fatal.
>
> "A physician who knows that he or she is [HIV] seropositive should not engage in any activity that creates a risk of transmission of the disease to others. A physician who has HIV disease or who is seropositive should consult colleagues as to which activities the physician can pursue without creating a risk to patients."

AMA Council on Ethical and Judicial Affairs, "Current Opinions, Code of Medical Ethics," 1992.

Thus, in evaluating the well-pleaded allegations of the complaints with respect to the duty component of the tort of negligence, we cannot conclude that they are legally insufficient to survive the appellees' motions to dismiss; in other words, we cannot say as a matter of law that no duty was imposed upon Dr. Almaraz to warn the appellants of his infected condition or refrain from operating upon them.

The appellants pleaded that as a result of Dr. Almaraz's breach of duty, they were put in fear of having contracted HIV and thereby suffered the derivative consequences of that fear, which were manifested by emotional and mental distress, headaches, sleeplessness, and, in addition, the pain and expense associated with repeated blood tests. We turn now to the question of whether these are legally compensable injuries where the appellants have not alleged in their complaints an actual transmission of the HIV virus into their bodies during the surgical procedures. Instead, appellants allege only that because of Dr. Almaraz's HIV positive status, he exposed them to the virus during the surgery. In this regard, the complaints do not allege that subsequent blood tests have revealed that the appellants have, in fact, shown HIV positive status.

C

Courts have differed on the question of recovery of damages for the fear of AIDS and attendant physical consequences absent an HIV-positive test. In *Burk v. Sage Products, Inc.*, the court rejected a paramedic's claim based on fear of contracting AIDS after he suffered a needle-stick from a discarded syringe. The paramedic could not demonstrate that the needle had been used on an AIDS patient, and he himself had tested HIV-negative no fewer than five times during the thirteen months after the incident. The court held first that, in the absence of any allegation that the syringe harbored HIV, the plaintiff had failed to establish an exposure to the AIDS virus sufficient to support a cause of action. Moreover, the court found no compensable injury:

"Plaintiff here has alleged no injury which arises out of his exposure to the AIDS virus. Rather, plaintiff's only injuries stem from his fear that he has been exposed to the disease." . . .

Other courts have concurred with *Burk* in denying recovery where the plaintiff can demonstrate neither a channel of exposure to the AIDS virus nor demonstrable injury in the form of an HIV-positive test. . . .

On the other hand, some courts have reasoned differently. In *Johnson v. W. Va. University Hospitals*, the court affirmed a judgment for a police officer attacked in a hospital by an AIDS-infected patient who had first bitten himself on the arm, thereby drawing his own infected blood into his mouth, and then bitten the officer. There, the officer sued the hospital, claiming that it negligently failed to advise him that the patient had AIDS, and that as a result of his exposure to AIDS, the officer had suffered from emotional distress. Although regularly tested for the HIV virus after having been bitten by the patient, the tests were negative for the disease. The officer's treating psychologist testified that the officer suffered from post traumatic stress disorder and was unable to sleep. The court noted that, absent physical injury, there would be no recovery for emotional distress. It held, however, that there was evidence of physical injury because of the officer's having been bitten and that his physical injury included sleeplessness, loss of appetite, and other physical manifestations accompanying the emotional distress. The officer's physical injury, the court said, was a factor going to the reasonableness of the officer's fear of contracting AIDS for which he could recover damages for emotional distress, even though he tested HIV-negative. . . .

. . . .

In the instant case, we cannot say that appellants' alleged fear of acquiring AIDS was initially unreasonable as a matter of law, even though the averments of the complaints did not identify any actual channel of transmission of the AIDS virus. But Burk's requirement that plaintiffs must allege actual transmission would unfairly punish them for lacking the requisite information to do so.

Appellants' continued fear of contracting AIDS may, however, be unreasonable after they tested HIV-negative upon learning of Dr. Almaraz's illness, which was well over a year after their last contacts with the physician. As we noted above, there is current credible evidence of a 95% certainty that one will test positive for the AIDS virus, if at all, within six months after exposure to it. Once appellants learned of their HIV-negative status more than a year after their respective surgeries, the possibility of their contracting AIDS from Dr. Almaraz became extremely unlikely and thus, as a matter of law, might be deemed unreasonable. Therefore, appellants may only recover for their fear and its physical manifestations which may have resulted from Almaraz's alleged negligence for the period constituting their reasonable window of anxiety — the period between which they learned of Almaraz's illness and received their HIV-negative results.

. . . .

D

We next consider whether the appellants have stated a cause of action in negligence against appellee Hopkins Hospital. Like any other employer, a hospital is responsible under agency principles for the negligence of its servants or employees; this vicarious liability extends to any apparent agents whom a hospital represents as its employees. The existence of an agency relationship is a question of fact which must be submitted to the factfinder if any legally sufficient evidence tending to prove the agency is offered.

Appellants here alleged that Hopkins represented that Dr. Almaraz was its agent; that they believed that he was its agent; and that they relied on this representation and Hopkins' excellent medical reputation in selecting Almaraz as their surgeon. Because it is undisputed that Almaraz enjoyed "operative privileges" at Hopkins, we cannot say as a matter of law that the facts alleged in the appellants' complaints are legally insufficient on their face to aver an agency relationship. Thus, the trial court erred in dismissing appellants' basic negligence complaints against Hopkins.

. . . .

NOTES AND QUESTIONS

1. *Faya v. Almarez* is similar to the preceding case against Northwestern University. Both involve failure to tell patients that a provider has AIDS. But the outcomes are different; the plaintiffs in *Faya* state a successful claim. Why the difference? For facts and outcome similar to those in *Faya*, *see Doe v. Noe*, 690 N.E.2d 1012 (Ill. App. Ct. 1997).
2. Since the plaintiffs state a successful claim against Johns Hopkins Hospital and the now deceased surgeon, what should Hopkins have done in 1986? Tell the patients? Discharge or decertify the physician? Remove him from the operating room? What of the Americans with Disabilities Act, discussed in *Mauro*?
3. Note that the *Faya* court says a duty arises not just from *probability* of harm but *severity*. Is this different from the analysis in *Northwestern*? Note that the *Faya* decision is based on treatment possibilities *circa* 1993; within the ensuing 10 years, combinations of AZT and protease inhibitors substantially reduced the likelihood of AIDS and death from HIV positive patients. Would/should such matters be a matter of evidence before a jury? Or would they lead, now, to a dismissal of the complaint in *Faya*?
4. Note the policy of the American Medical Association that a physician should consult colleagues and avoid risk of exposure to patients. Are you surprised that the AMA did not enjoin the physician to consult the patient(s)? Doesn't the presence of this policy settle the case, at least as to the doctor's duty, if not damages?
5. In considering damages, does the *Faya* court use a different standard from the *Northwestern* court, which required actual exposure and a risk of infection? Here, there *was* surgery, but does that amount to 'actual exposure' sufficient for the majority in *Northwestern*? The concurrence?

6. The Court creates a narrow "window" when fear might be reasonable: six months after the exposure by which time testing negative eliminates almost all possibility of infection.
7. What was Doctor Almarez's ethical obligation to his patients? Did he violate it?
8. Would the answers to any of the preceding questions be different if the plaintiffs had contracted AIDS?
9. Because of its political structure, Cuba has been able to take steps to control the transmission of HIV that the United States has not, such as mandatory testing and segregation. Does the end result (success) of these efforts make the process any more palatable?

PROBLEM 4-9 — AIDS and Doctor Acer

During the 1990s, much publicity was extended to the case of Dr. David Acer, a dentist who — it was said — had infected five of his patients with AIDS. One of the patients, Kimberly Berghalis, a young woman in her early 20s, appeared in a number of public forums and before Congress to testify in support of mandatory disclosure by health care professionals when they are HIV positive. An article in Science Magazine, examining the evidence, found it persuasive — but not to a legal standard — that Acer had in fact infected his patients. However, most professional bodies, including the American Medical Association, concluded that compulsory disclosure would be unnecessary, since the likelihood of infection was from patient to physician and not the reverse, and that it would be unwise, since patients would leave their physicians or dentists out of an irrational fear of becoming infected with AIDS.

Ethically, *should* a health care provider notify patients that he or she is HIV positive? If so, should such a provider — say, a surgeon — be denied hospital privileges, board certification, or reimbursement status by an HMO or insurance company? Should we *test* all doctors, dentists, nurses, teachers, prison guards, attorneys, law students?

Two final questions: If your dentist disclosed to you that he or she was HIV positive, would you go to another dentist? And if *you* were HIV positive, and your dentist asked, what would you say?

[b] Duty to Report

MIDDLEBROOKS v. STATE BOARD OF HEALTH
710 So. 2d 891 (Ala. 1998)

Maddox, Justice.

This case presents the issue whether § 22-11A-2, Ala. Code 1975, which requires physicians, dentists, and certain other persons to report cases or suspected cases of "notifiable diseases" and health conditions, such as HIV infections and AIDS cases, to the Alabama State Board of Health, is discriminatory and therefore violates the Equal Protection Clause of the Fourteenth Amendment to the Constitution of the United States.

Dr. Mark Middlebrooks, a physician practicing in Jefferson County, specializes in infectious diseases. Through his practice, Dr. Middlebrooks diagnoses and treats patients who are infected with HIV and AIDS. Under the provisions of § 22-11A-2, Dr. Middlebrooks is within the class of persons required to report all cases of HIV infection and AIDS to the State Board of Health. The required reports are to include the names and addresses of persons infected.[1]

The rules of the State Board of Health define HIV and AIDS as "notifiable diseases" and require the reporting person to give the patient's name and address and certain laboratory data. Alabama Administrative Code, Chapter 420-4-1 et seq.

In July 1993, Dr. Middlebrooks was contacted by officials of the Jefferson County Health Department, who requested that he comply with the reporting mandate of the statute and with the rules of the State Board of Health. (*See* note 1.) Dr. Middlebrooks provided certain statistical data, as the statute and regulatory rules required, but he refused to provide the names and addresses of his patients.

On September 8, 1994, the State Board of Health filed this action against Dr. Middlebrooks, seeking to compel him to disclose the names and addresses of his HIV and AIDS patients, as required by statute and rule. On March 13, 1996, the trial court entered an order compelling disclosure; Dr. Middlebrooks appealed.

Dr. Middlebrooks primarily contends that the statutory and regulatory scheme violates the Equal Protection Clause of the Fourteenth Amendment because persons or entities not listed in the statute are authorized by regulations adopted by the Federal Food and Drug Administration to sell confidential HIV-testing kits and the sellers of those kits are not required to report the names and addresses of the purchasers. Dr. Middlebrooks argues that he is subjected to discriminatory treatment because he is required to report the names and addresses of his HIV and AIDS patients while those who sell the testing kits and out-of-state testing laboratories that evaluate the test results are not required to report the names and addresses of those persons who test positive.

In order to address Dr. Middlebrooks's arguments, we believe it essential to discuss briefly the right of privacy in regard to disclosure of medical information relating to diseases such as HIV and AIDS.

---

[1] Section 22-11A-2 provides, in part:

"Each physician, dentist, nurse, medical examiner, hospital administrator, nursing home administrator, laboratory director, school principal, and day care center director shall be responsible to report cases or suspected cases of notifiable diseases and health conditions. The report shall contain such information, and be delivered in such a manner, as may be provided for from time to time by the rules of the state board of health. All medical and statistical information and reports required by this chapter shall be confidential and shall not be subject to the inspection, subpoena, or admission into evidence in any court, except proceedings brought under this chapter to compel the examination, testing, commitment or quarantine of any person or upon the written consent of the patient, or if the patient is a minor, his parent or legal guardian. Any physician or other person making any report required by this chapter or participating in any judicial proceeding resulting therefrom shall, in doing so, be immune from any civil or criminal liability, that might otherwise be incurred or imposed."

The United States Supreme Court has stated:

> "Disclosures of private medical information to doctors, to hospital personnel, to insurance companies, and to public health agencies are often an essential part of modern medical practice even when the disclosure may reflect unfavorably on the character of the patient. Requiring such disclosures to representatives of the State having responsibility for the health of the community, does not automatically amount to an impermissible invasion of privacy."

Whalen v. Roe, 429 U.S. 589, 602 (1977). In *United States v. Westinghouse Electric Corp.*, 638 F.2d 570, 578 (3d Cir. 1980), the United States Court of Appeals for the Third Circuit established factors for a court to consider when determining "whether an invasion into an individual's records is justified." Those factors are:

> "The type of record requested, the information it does or might contain, the potential for harm in any subsequent nonconsensual disclosure, the injury from disclosure to the relationship in which the record was generated, the adequacy of safeguards to prevent unauthorized disclosure, the degree of need for access, and whether there is an express statutory mandate, articulated public policy, or other recognizable public interest militating toward access."

After weighing the *Westinghouse* factors, we hold that the prevention of the spread of HIV and AIDS is a legitimate governmental interest, and that, even in regard to HIV and AIDS, where, in some situations, the disclosure may reflect unfavorably on the character of the patient, the State can require disclosure to representatives of the State having responsibility for the health of the community, and that the disclosure required by § 22-11A-2 does not amount to an impermissible invasion of privacy. The statute and the regulatory rules adopted pursuant thereto have adequate safeguards to protect the medical records from unauthorized disclosure.

Now that we have determined that § 22-11A-2 does not violate the right to privacy, we must decide whether Dr. Middlebrooks's constitutional right to equal protection is violated by the fact that § 22-11A-2 does not apply to the stores that market and sell at-home HIV testing kits and out-of-state testing labs that analyze the results of the tests.

The purpose of the Equal Protection Clause is to prevent states from enacting legislation that treats persons "similarly situated" differently. *City of Cleburne v. Cleburne Living Center, Inc.*, 473 U.S. 432, 439 (1985). "It does not, however, require that a statute necessarily apply equally to all persons or require that things different in fact be treated in law as though they were the same."

We conclude that the State has made a reasonable classification in this instance. It appears to us that the out-of-state testing labs that analyze the results of the testing kits are not, as to those required to report HIV and AIDS cases under § 22-11A-2, similarly situated.

We conclude that the trial judge properly ordered Dr. Middlebrooks to disclose to the State Board of Health the names of his patients infected with HIV and AIDS. The judgment is, therefore, affirmed.

Affirmed.

NOTES AND QUESTIONS

1. The Alabama statute in *Middlebrooks* is similar to public health statutes in most states, where mandated reporting is usually justified as a public health measure. Communicable diseases are dealt with by vaccination, quarantine and isolation. These, and other measures, have historically justified overriding individual interests in privacy and association.
2. Is AIDS different? Note that in *Middlebrooks,* no patients appear to assert privacy or due process interests? Why not? Would they succeed? Are names and addresses, in fact, necessary?
3. Does Dr. Middlebrooks' argument surprise you? Wouldn't/shouldn't he have made a due process argument? Invoking *Casey,* isn't there an argument to be made that the physician/patient relation is compromised by mandatory reporting? That a person's autonomy requires leaving that choice to him or her?
4. Does the reporting requirement in *Middlebrooks* conflict with the Americans with Disabilities Act?
5. Contrast Alabama's basic policy judgements with those in the next case, from New Jersey, where far greater protection is accorded physician/patient privacy. Why?

NEW JERSEY v. J.E.

606 A.2d 1160 (N.J. Super. Ct. 1992)

Costello, J.S.C.

The State has moved before this court for an order permitting the State to obtain any and all medical records from The Harbor, a drug abuse clinic, regarding the testing for the presence of AIDS (Acquired Immune Deficiency Syndrome) and other related illnesses in the defendant. The State has also moved for the release of any records in the possession of the warden of the Hudson County Jail on this same subject. The defense opposes both motions. The Hudson County Counsel, appearing on behalf of the warden, takes no position.

On February 21, 1991 the defendant was arrested and later indicted for two counts of kidnaping and two counts of aggravated sexual assault, all first degree offenses. The crimes allegedly occurred on January 25, 1991 and January 27, 1991 and involved two victims, C.R. and M.B. respectively.

The defendant posted bail and was released on March 1, 1991. On June 27, 1991 he entered into a drug rehabilitation program at The Harbor in Hoboken, N.J. . . .

. . . .

The State has filed an affidavit from an assistant prosecutor in support of its motion which states that in October of 1991, a Hudson County probation officer advised the Hudson County prosecutor's office that the defendant (one of his probationers) had tested positive for the HIV virus while enrolled in The Harbor drug program. Since defendant is charged with committing acts of sexual penetration against C.R. and M.B., the State theorizes that it is possible that C.R. and M.B. have been infected with the HIV virus from defendant. For the above reasons the State asks for the release of the blood test results ". . . so that it may inform C.R. and M.B. of the results."

The applicable statute for the release of AIDS records is N.J.S.A. 26:5C-5 et seq. The purpose of the statute is". . . . to protect the confidentiality of individual AIDS records while assuming their limited availability for essential health, scientific and other legitimate purposes." Although the State's papers do not rely on any specific subsection there are several methods through which records can be disclosed.

The defendant in this case has refused to consent to the release of the records so NJ.S.A. 26:5C-8(a) is not relevant. N.J.S.A. 26:5C-9 sets out the two situations in which a court may order disclosure of test results without the consent of the defendant. First, under N.J.S.A. 26:5C-9(b):

> A court may authorize disclosure of a person's record *for the purpose of conducting an investigation of or a prosecution for a crime of which the person is suspected*, only if the crime is of a first degree crime and there is a reasonable likelihood that the record in question will disclose material information or evidence of substantial value in connection with the investigation or prosecution (emphasis added).

As stated in the supporting affidavit, the State's sole purpose in seeking this information is so that the victims can be informed of the fact that they may have contracted the HIV virus. There has been no claim by the State that the information sought is needed to investigate or prosecute the defendant. Indeed he has already been indicted and with the exception of this motion and a pending defense motion to sever, both sides are ready for trial. In spite of the State's claim at oral argument of reliance on this section, there is no basis to grant relief under § 9(b).[1]

Second, N.J.S.A. 26:5C-9(a) provides that records "may be disclosed by an order of a court of competent jurisdiction which is granted pursuant to an application showing good cause therefor." The statute also outlines factors [that] are to be considered at a good cause hearing:

> the Court shall weigh the public interest and need for disclosure against the injury to the person who is the subject of the record, to the physician-patient relationship, and to the services offered by the program.

[1] Parenthetically, three states have recently enacted legislation compelling AIDS testing for rape suspects. Two of these three statutory schemes provide that the test results may not be used against the suspect in any criminal prosecution.

. . . .

There is a strong, even compelling general public interest in preventing the spreading of AIDS and in encouraging those infected to seek treatment. There is also a specific public interest in preserving the health of a rape victim and her sexual partners. Those two public interests are clearly in conflict here, because if confidentiality of AIDS records is not maintained, inmates may elect not to report their HIV status to correctional authorities. This reluctance to seek treatment and counseling can logically result in the disease being spread further either within an institution or beyond.

The emotional appeal of a request to quell the fears of a rape victim is undeniable. Individual victims and the lay public will surely be frustrated by any analysis which balances the rights of a suspect against those of a victim. But, by valuing the public interest in a small number of identifiable rape victims over the public interest in the larger anonymous population, the effect may very well be to do more harm to a greater number.

The need for disclosure must be evaluated: is it as compelling as the State indicates in its affidavit? The crimes here are alleged to have occurred on January 25, 1991 and January 27, 1991. In October of 1991, more than eight months later, a Hudson County probation officer gave the prosecutor's office the information which is the basis for this motion. This is significant because the period of time between infection and the appearance of HIV antibodies creates a two-to-six month "window period" in which an infected person may still test negative for the virus. Therefore, taking into account the fact that the earliest the State had its information was two months after the "window" had closed then the public's need for the information is considerably decreased, since the victims can now have themselves tested to see if they have contracted the HIV virus. Indeed, this is presumably the same action the alleged victims will take even if the court orders disclosure of records confirming the State's supposition that the defendant has AIDS.

The above must then be balanced first against the injury to the person who is the subject of the record. In this case J. E. is currently lodged in the Hudson County jail. This is not a setting where the information to be disclosed could have some negative affect on his standing in the social community (i.e. loss of employment, damage to family relationships, etc.) Defense counsel cannot be allowed to speculate that there will be some negative impact on his standing within the jail community, because if the results were released they would only be released to the State and the victims.

The next countervailing factor to consider is the effect disclosure will have on the physician-patient relationship. It should be noted that none of the counsel involved gives any more than passing mention to this factor.

New Jersey has a long tradition of honoring the physician-patient privilege. Ordinarily an exception to this rule occurs when third parties have been or may be exposed to infectious conditions. In those cases, a physician may have a duty to warn those third parties they are at risk. Historically, the contagious diseases referred to have been tuberculosis and venereal diseases. AIDS has now joined the list. In New Jersey, even this duty to warn third parties has been abrogated in the case of AIDS by N.J.S.A. 26:5C-5 et seq. To that extent the passage of this statute strengthens the already firm policy in this State of honoring the physician-patient privilege.

. . . .

In conclusion, the window period during which the victims would have faced uncertainty has long since passed. Indeed it had already passed when the State received its initial tip that the defendant had AIDS. The tip, although not substantiated as yet, certainly seems sufficiently specific to be the catalyst for the State to warn its victims, without disclosing the basis for their action, of their potential exposure to AIDS. If the defendant's medical records were released and it was determined that he is HIV positive, the next logical step would be for the victims to have themselves tested and treated, the same course of action available to them now without any violation of the privacy of medical records.

Therefore, a balancing of factors compels the conclusion that under these circumstances the physician/patient relationship outweighs the public interest and need for disclosure. Accordingly, the State's motion for disclosure of the defendant's medical records from The Harbor and the Hudson County jail is hereby denied.

NOTES AND QUESTIONS

1. The preceding cases have concluded healthcare providers may have a duty to disclose HIV status to third parties. There are statutes to the contrary, however, as that involved in *New Jersey v. J.E.*
2. Why doesn't the State simply require J.E. to provide a blood sample, rather than seeking the records of the clinic and the jail? There is suggestion that J.E. has not cooperated in prison and the jail can not force him to give a jailhouse blood sample. *Should* it? *See Schmerber* and *Rochin*, *supra*, § 2.03[1], and *Johnetta v. Municipal Court*, the next case.
3. The Court chooses not to value the interests of a few victims over those of a "larger anonymous population." What does this mean? Wouldn't disclosure in all instances help everyone? In fact, aren't the numbers of interest exactly the reverse of those the Court indentifies?
4. Note that the *Tarasoff* duty to warn discussed in the preceding cases is rejected in New Jersey, favoring the physician/patient relationship. Would you agree this is a desirable outcome? Is it helpful to physicians or patients or the public for medical doctors to withhold HIV positive results?
5. Couldn't the victims sue the defendants for infecting them or raping them while HIV positive, even if they aren't infected? And wouldn't the HIV status be relevant then? Indeed, wouldn't it be relevant at sentencing in the pending criminal case? So, why not disclose it now?
6. Finally, there are a number of players in the scenario underlying the New Jersey case. Evaluate the professional ethics and performance of the unidentified probation officer, the prosecutor, the county jail warden, the county counsel and the director of the Harbor.

PROBLEM 4-10 — Mothers and AIDS

On September 20, 1998, *The New York Times* ran the following story:*

> BANGOR, Maine — As 4-year-old Nikolas Emerson ran across the grass in a public park on Friday, he spun like a top and shrieked with glee.
>
> Watching him, his mother, Valerie Emerson, said that Nikolas, who is infected with HIV, has never been happier or healthier.
>
> She attributed his good condition to her refusal to treat him with the drug therapy recommended by infectious-disease specialists in Maine and Boston as the way to suppress HIV and prevent the infection from progressing to AIDS.
>
> Emerson, who also is infected with HIV and has stopped her own drug therapy, contends that the devastating side effects of the drugs could kill her child.
>
> "I think the medication on the market now will be unheard of in five years," Emerson said. "Why should we be guinea pigs?"
>
> Last week, a Maine District Court judge agreed with her reasoning and turned down a request by the state's Department of Human Services for custody of the boy, if his mother continued her refusal, so that he could have the treatment. The state contends that withholding drugs is child abuse and neglect.
>
> . . . .
>
> The case raised questions about appropriate medical treatment for HIV-infected youngsters and the degree to which states should intervene in parents' decisions on medical care for their children.
>
> **Battle draws attention**
>
> Emerson's battle has drawn the attention of a group that does not think that HIV causes AIDS, said her lawyer, Hilary Billings. Billings identified the organization as the Group for the Reappraisal of the AIDS Hypothesis.
>
> . . . .
>
> Emerson said she gave AZT to Nikolas for 10 weeks in 1997, but in that time he became fussy, whimpered in his sleep and suffered from continuous stomach aches.
>
> "Within two months after I stopped the AZT, he was on the road back," she said.
>
> The state became involved in the case about a year ago, soon after Emerson's family physician referred Nikolas to Dr. John Milliken, a Bangor pediatrician who specializes in infectious diseases. When Emerson refused the aggressive drug treatment he recommended, Milliken referred the case to the state. He suggested that Emerson

* *Boy is Healthy Without Drug for H.I.V, Mother Says* (Sep. 20, 1998).

could not adequately manage her son's medical care, according to court records. Milliken has declined to comment.

The state solicited a third opinion, from Dr. Kenneth McIntosh, a professor of pediatrics at Harvard Medical School, chief of the Division of Infectious Diseases at Children's Hospital in Boston and head of a trial on aggressive drug therapy for HIV-infected children. McIntosh testified that although he recommended enrolling Nikolas in his drug trial, he also supported the mother's decision to withhold treatment.

On appeal, what result? Consider here the earlier cases on the family and reproductive rights. Consider as well the ethics of intervention by a state agency in this family's home and by Doctor Milliken, a physician who while caring for Nikolas invoked that intervention.

[c] Misconduct

People with AIDS pose a threat of transmitting the disease to others, with deadly consequences. One mode of transmission is sexual intercourse but there are others. In the AIDS hysteria of the 1980s, the criminal law was invoked in response to concerns this posed.

JOHNETTA v. THE MUNICIPAL COURT*

218 Cal. App. 3d 1255, 267 Cal. Rptr. 666 (1990)

Haning, Associate Justice.

. . . .

Petitioner allegedly became disruptive while attending a child dependency hearing in San Francisco Superior Court, and her conduct required her physical removal from the courtroom by the bailiff, a San Francisco Sheriff's Deputy. Petitioner became violent and assaulted the deputy, inflicting a deep bite on the deputy's arm which penetrated the skin and drew blood. As a result of the fracas, a complaint was filed in respondent court charging petitioner with felony assault with force likely to produce great bodily injury, felony assault on a peace officer, and misdemeanor interference with an officer.

These charges triggered applicability of Proposition 96. . . .

Proposition 96 covers three distinct situations involving possible transmission of AIDS: to the victim of a sex crime; to an assaulted peace officer, firefighter or emergency medical technician; and to an employee of a custodial facility.

The initiative measure begins with a purpose clause: "The people of the State of California find and declare that AIDS, AIDS-related conditions, and other communicable diseases pose a major threat to the public health and safety. The health and safety of the public, victims of sexual crimes, and peace officers, firefighters and custodial personnel who may come into contact with infected persons, have not been adequately protected by law. . . .

* Citation material has been omitted from this case.

. . . .

Section 199.97 reads, in pertinent part: "Any person charged in any criminal complaint filed with a magistrate or court . . . in which it is alleged in whole or in part that the defendant . . . interfered with the official duties of a peace officer . . . by biting . . . or transferring blood or other bodily fluids on, upon, or through the skin or membranes of a peace officer . . . shall in addition to any penalties provided by law be subject to an order of a court having jurisdiction of the complaint . . . requiring testing as provided in this chapter. The peace officer, . . . or the employing agency, officer, or entity may petition the court for an order authorized under this section. The court shall promptly conduct a hearing upon any such petition. If the court finds that probable cause exists to believe that a possible transfer of blood, saliva, semen, or other bodily fluid took place between the defendant . . . and the peace officer . . . the court shall order that the defendant . . . provide two specimens of blood for testing as provided in this chapter. . . ."

. . . .

Dr. Maring's report described the bite as "a deep puncture type bite." It stated "[t]here was no blood in the mouth of [petitioner] at the time; but certainly saliva was transferred." It further stated that the AIDS virus "is in all bodily fluids, although in low concentrations in saliva. Theoretically, a transmission of the AIDS virus (HIV) could have occurred. No such transmission has been reported in the medical literature without blood present — but it is theoretically possible."

. . . .

At the first hearing, in addition to articles from medical journals petitioner presented the declarations of three experts on AIDS and its treatment: Dr. Marcus Conant, M.D.; Dr. Nancy Padian, Ph.D.; and Dr. Paul Volberding, M.D. Each declarant states that AIDS is spread three ways: "[1] sexually, [2] through blood or blood products, and [3] directly from mother to child [in utero and during parturition]." Given Dr. Maring's observation that none of petitioner's blood entered the deputy's bloodstream, the experts focused on the question whether saliva alone could transmit HIV. The experts declared that no case of HIV transmission by [illegible] infections have been found in individuals exposed to the saliva of an infected person. . . .

The declarations also note there have been no documented cases of AIDS transmission through biting. Categorical statements are again avoided, but Dr. Volberding goes so far as to state "there is no reason to think HIV is transmitted by biting."

. . . .

Dr. Gerberding declared that "the number of cases to date involving incidents of bites is not sufficient to enable me to conclude that HIV cannot be transmitted by a bite that breaks the skin. Similarly while the risk of such transmission is clearly low, there is insufficient information to determine precisely how low." Both Dr. Gerberding and Dr. Sande agreed that the possibility of saliva transfer is greater when the saliva is placed in contact with broken skin, as in a bite. In Dr. Sande's words:

"The possibility of transmitting HIV through a bite is probably greater than the possibility of its transmission through touching, eating off the same plate, or sharing a toothbrush. . . . The possibility of transmission would likely increase if the bite is deep. . . . Studies to date indicate that the risk of transmission is highly remote. However, it cannot be said, based on currently available information, that HIV could not be transmitted through a bite. The possibility that HIV could be transmitted continues to be a subject of inquiry in the medical community."

. . . .

Discussion

Petitioner contends that section 199.97 violates her right under the Fourth Amendment to the United States Constitution and article I, section 13 of the California Constitution to be free from unreasonable searches and seizures. She begins with the premise that a blood test is an intrusion of the body, however minimal, and like other bodily intrusions is governed by Fourth Amendment strictures. She concludes that the mandatory scheme of court-ordered testing falls afoul of the Fourth Amendment (1) because it permits a bodily intrusion for removal of blood for testing without probable cause that the AIDS virus will be found, and (2) because it fails to provide for a balancing test to determine whether the character of the intrusion is appropriate to the circumstances.

. . . .

Petitioner argues that the blood testing in this case is not minimal because it is more intrusive than that in Skinner or in the typical driving-under-the-influence case in that (1) the psychological impact of receiving a positive AIDS test result "has been compared to receiving a death sentence"; and (2) the Proposition 96 confidentiality measures are in petitioner's view insufficient and likely to lead to substantial disclosure of the test result and possible discrimination and opprobrium. The former factor is indeed significant, and prompted the Doe court to rule that mandatory AIDS testing in the context of civil litigation conducted absent explicit statutory authority can only be ordered on "a showing of compelling need." As will be seen below, however, the governmental interests behind Proposition 96, including the assaulted officer's fear that he or she has in fact been infected, outweighs the psychological impact of the assailant's receipt of a positive test for HIV.

The confidentiality argument merits consideration although, strictly speaking, it is not a Fourth Amendment issue. Proposition 96 permits disclosure of petitioner's test results to herself, the deputy she assaulted, real party as the deputy's employer and, if HIV-positive, the State Department of Health Services. After testing, "[T]he court shall order all persons, other than the test subject, who receive test results" pursuant to section 199.97, "to maintain the confidentiality of personal identifying data relating to the test results except for disclosure which may be necessary to obtain medical or psychological care or advice."

Petitioner fears this disclosure is too widespread. She argues that the exemption for disclosure necessary to obtain medical or psychological care or advice would allow disclosure to persons not before the court and thus not subject to contempt sanctions to enforce nondisclosure. Although petitioner's concerns are well-grounded in the light of the problem of AIDS discrimination, she reads the disclosure provisions too narrowly. The voters clearly intended that the test results be kept in maximum secrecy and disclosed only to those directly involved and those to whom information must be disclosed to obtain needed medical or psychological treatment — and to no others. . . .

. . . .

. . . Medical opinion expresses considerable uncertainty concerning AIDS and cannot rule out the possibility that a bitten police officer, whose blood is commingled with saliva, may be infected by the AIDS virus. Dr. Gerberding's words echo here: that the bitten public safety employee "finds little solace or comfort in medical opinion that the chances of infection are extremely remote." We reiterate that the law authorizes the minimal intrusion of a blood test only by court order after a noticed hearing and a finding that the prohibited assault occurred. The test must be performed in a medically approved manner, and the results are subject to highly limited disclosure. These circumstances support the electorate's reasonable determination that society's interest in the health and safety of its peace officers, on balance, justify the intrusion without the additional probable cause that the assailant is infected. Cases in which officers would have probable cause or some individualized suspicion that their assailants were AIDS-infected are rare, in the vast majority of cases the officers will have no way of knowing the infection status of the person who has bitten them. Thus, a requirement of probable cause that the assailant is an HIV-carrier would not be practical; a reasonable solution is to test those persons who assault peace officers if there is probable cause to believe the officer has been exposed to the assailant's bodily fluids.

Petitioner also asserts that mandatory testing of the assailant serves no useful governmental purpose because the assaulted officer is free to have his or her own blood tested and that test should be dispositive. This contention cannot withstand the numerous statements of medical opinion in this record, which detail the medical usefulness of testing the person who has assaulted an officer. The experts believe test results from the potential source of infection, while not dispositive, provide some useful information. If the results are negative, the chances of HIV infection are believed to be smaller, and a negative result will diminish the officer's anxiety, a factor pertinent to treatment. The experts suggest that a bitten officer would be well advised to have a blood test for clearer information, but HIV antibodies generally would not develop for three to six months after the bite. Proposition 96 provides a prompt mechanism to obtain some information pertinent to the officer's health and therefore to the governmental special need. The fact that the test of the assailant's blood would not be conclusive does not defeat the government's interest. . . .

. . . .

We also note that petitioner is not a random, innocent victim of an uncontrolled testing scheme. Under the statutory procedure at issue, testing is permitted only on persons formally accused of assaults or other offenses against peace officers, firefighters and emergency medical personnel resulting in the transfer of bodily fluids. Persons committing criminal offenses are generally forewarned that they are subject to some intrusions on their civil liberties. For example, even prior to any conviction they are subject to arrest, to pretrial incarceration (subject to having to post reasonable bail if they can do so, or release on their own recognizance if they qualify), to compulsory court appearances, and to reasonable searches and seizures of their persons, houses, papers and effects. In appropriate cases, blood samples may be obtained from the accused. Petitioner initiated the operation of the statute by her assault upon the deputy, thus voluntarily placing herself in a different category than the innocent or unsuspecting person she hypothecates as a potential victim of a renegade testing scheme.

Accordingly, we hold that with regard to public safety employees suffering subcutaneous bites in the course of their duties, Proposition 96's mandatory scheme of blood testing does not violate the Fourth Amendment or the California right of privacy.

. . . .

NOTES AND QUESTIONS

1. Would you have voted for Proposition 96 in 1988? In 1998? How would you change its language or scope? Would you add victims in addition to peace officers, firefighters, emergency medical technicians, or employees of a custodial facility? Why not include everyone? Why limit disclosure to the victim? What about others, such as jail or probation or court officials or employees? What if any other diseases should be tested for?
2. What is the countervailing interest? Why does the defendant oppose giving blood? The medical technology is safe and commonplace. If the use of the sample is limited to testing for disease, the defendant's rights are protected. Indeed, as *Schmerber* held, there is no Fifth Amendment interest in exemplars, such as blood or hair clippings. So a court order could be obtained for evidence. What then is the issue here?
3. The defendant asserts a Fourth Amendment privacy claim. But she is already in custody. And the protection is only against "unreasonable" searches and seizures — here, easily resolved against the defendant. What is unreasonable about drawing blood?
4. Was there a due process/equal protection issue in the background of *Johnetta*? The testing really was required only because she was arrested and charged, and this was dependent solely on prosecutorial discretion. Even probable cause and a warrant were not required. Suppose she were ultimately found not guilty. It is rare indeed for a defendant to be sanctioned prior to trial.
5. Would the Court in *Johnetta* reach a different result if, ten years later, it were to learn that no reported cases existed of AIDS/HIV transmission by saliva and new tests could determine within days of a bite

whether the victim had been infected? Would this bear on the *Skinner v. Railway Labor Exec. Ass'n* special needs analysis?

6. For other decisions, see *In Re Donald P. v. Palmieri*, 668 N.Y.S.2d 218 1998 (denying a test) and *Adams v. State*, 498 S.E.2d 268 (Ga. 1998) (ordering tests).

7. Now that common knowledge of HIV and AIDS has progressed so that we know that it is exceptionally unlikely to be transferred through saliva to skin contact or through sweat, does this rule seem punitive?

JKB v. ARMOUR PHARMACEUTICAL COMPANY

660 N.E.2d 602 (Ind. Ct. App. 1996)

Robertson, Judge.

. . . .

Facts

The dispositive facts are not disputed. JKB was born on February 21, 1977. He had hemophilia. From 1980 through 1986, JKB received blood clotting factor products, known as Factor VIII, produced and sold by the pharmaceutical companies to treat his hemophilia. Unfortunately, the products used by JKB had been contaminated by the virus that causes AIDS. JKB contracted AIDS from the blood products and died on December 31, 1991. Medical and technological advances since the advent of AIDS have now made such blood products safe.

The Factor VIII blood products produced by the pharmaceutical companies are derived from human blood and are produced by a process called "plasmapheresis." Blood is taken from a donor and spun in a centrifuge to separate the plasma from the red blood cells and the red blood cells are then returned to the donor. Because these extra steps are involved, giving blood for plasmapheresis is much more time consuming than the donation of whole blood and donors must be compensated accordingly. The plasma is then pooled with plasma from other donors and various chemical and physical processes are employed to extract the Factor VIII clotting factor from the plasma. Factor VIII is then concentrated, sterile filtered, placed into vials, and freeze-dried. It is sold, by prescription, in this freeze-dried, powdered form.

The pharmaceutical companies filed a motion to dismiss (which was later converted into a motion for summary judgment) with respect to the count in JKB's complaint alleging strict liability in tort arguing that, under Indiana's blood shield statute, the provision of Factor VIII constituted a rendition of a service and not the sale of a product and thus could not give rise to a product liability action. The pharmaceutical companies did not challenge the remaining counts in JKB's complaint which include allegations of negligent manufacture and the negligent failure to warn of the dangers associated with the blood products.

The trial court granted the pharmaceutical companies' motion. This discretionary, interlocutory appeal ensued.

Decision

. . . .

The Blood Shield Statute, Ind.Code 16-41-12-11, reads as follows:

> (a) The: (1) procurement, processing, distribution, or use of whole blood, plasma, blood products, blood derivatives, or other human tissue, such as corneas, bones, or organs, by a bank, storage facility, or hospital; . . .
>
> is the rendition of a service and not the sale of a product. Such services do not give rise to an implied warranty of merchantability or fitness for a particular purpose, nor do the services give rise to strict liability in tort. . . .
>
> (a) "Bank or storage facility" means a facility licensed, accredited or approved under the laws of any state for storage of human bodies or parts thereof.
>
> (d) "Hospital" means a hospital licensed, accredited or approved under the laws of any state [including] a hospital operated by the United States government, a state or a subdivision thereof, although not required to be licensed under state laws.
>
> (h) "State" includes any state, district, commonwealth, territory, insular possession and any other area subject to the legislative authority of the United States of America.

The cause of action for strict liability in tort arose under common law. Thus, the blood shield statute, which limits the ability to bring such a cause of action, is in derogation of the common law. As such, two rules of statutory construction apply:

First, a statute . . . which is in derogation of the common law must be strictly construed against limitations on a claimant's right to bring suit. Secondly, when the legislature enacts a statute in derogation of the common law, this Court presumes that the legislature is aware of the common law, and does not intend to make any change therein beyond what it declares either in express terms or by unmistakable implication. . . . Thus, courts must consider the goals of the statute and the reasons and policy underlying the statute's enactment. . . . The specific inclusion of one entity usually precludes the implication of another entity's inclusion in the same statutory provision. When certain items or words are specified or enumerated in a statute, then, by implication, other items or words not so specified or enumerated are excluded.

Blood shield statutes, effected in nearly every state, have the purpose of ensuring an adequate supply of life-saving and essential blood products. To achieve this end, such statutes generally provide for liability only in cases of negligence. As the *Zichichi* court noted: "[t]o require providers to serve as insurers of the safety of these materials might impose such an overwhelming burden as to discourage the gathering and distribution of blood."

In the present case, the pharmaceutical companies sought (and obtained) refuge under Indiana's blood shield statute by arguing that they each constituted a "storage facility". The pharmaceutical companies argued further that they satisfied the requirement that they be licensed "under the laws of any state for storage of human bodies or parts thereof" by virtue of their licenses issued by the United States Federal Drug Administration [FDA] for the manufacture of blood products because their licenses authorize them to store plasma and other blood products.

However, under a strict construction analysis, we simply cannot conclude that our legislature intended to include a pharmaceutical company, which commercially produces blood products for mass distribution, as an entity within the same class described as an organ or a blood "[b]ank or storage facility." The manufacture and distribution of blood products by pharmaceutical companies is better characterized as the sale of a product rather than the provision of a service. It is quite unlikely that our legislature intended to include pharmaceutical companies in its definition of "[b]ank or storage facility" simply because the manufacture or production of blood products incidentally involves their storage.

Pharmaceutical companies are not included in the class of entities protected under the blood shield statute either expressly or by unmistakable implication. Had our legislature intended to include pharmaceutical companies under the statute scrutinized, it could have done so expressly. For example, our legislature expressly listed "pharmaceutical companies" along with "blood centers" when it named the types of facilities subject to regulation under I.C. 16-41-16-1 for the disposal of medical waste.

As the blood shield statute does not insulate pharmaceutical companies from product liability under the present circumstances, the trial court's entry of summary judgment against JKB on this issue was erroneous. Therefore, we must reverse.

. . . .

Chezem, Judge, concurring in result.

I concur in result. While I agree that summary judgment should not have been granted against JKB, I arrive at this conclusion for reasons different than the majority's.

The pharmaceutical companies argue that they are protected by the Blood Shield Statute, Ind.Code § 16-41-12-11, because they fall within the definition of a "storage facility." "As used in the Blood Shield Statute, 'storage facility' means "a facility licensed, accredited or approved under the laws of any state for storage of human bodies or parts thereof." The pharmaceutical companies assert that their FDA licenses qualify them as being licensed for storage "under the laws of any state." I do not believe that the legislature was referring to an FDA license when it drafted that language.

Indiana Code outlines what it means to be licensed in Indiana, and, I believe, provides guidance for the resolution of the present issue. That section states:

> It is unlawful to operate a blood center in Indiana without a license issued by the state department under this chapter. *A blood center that applies for a license in Indiana must also be licensed or appropriately*

registered by the federal Food and Drug Administration and remain in compliance with all applicable federal regulations.

Therefore, merely having an FDA license or registration is not enough to operate a blood center in Indiana; a blood center must have a registration or license from the FDA and a license issued by the State of Indiana. . . .

The appellees have not designated any evidence which would indicate that they are licensed to store blood, blood products, etc., in Indiana, or in any other state. They have only produced the licenses from the FDA. These are not enough to bring them within the protection of the Blood Shield Statute.

NOTES AND QUESTIONS

1. AIDS is — or at least until recently has been — invariably fatal. Transmission of AIDS then, if negligent or otherwise actionable, leads to liability in considerable damages. Special legislation has been sought to avoid exposure in a number of contexts. *JKB* represents an instance, a so-called "blood shield" statute.
2. Is such legislation wise? What public policies does it advance? Whom does it protect? Does it encourage negligence or care? Are there other instances than the AIDS context where such immunity is extended?
3. It is widely understood, or at least believed, that the manufacturers of Factor VIII knew by the early 1980's that their product was contaminated, yet did nothing to warn recipients, to screen their product, or pull it out of circulation. How does this — if true — influence your answer to Question 2?
4. If Armour had been successful, it would have avoided strict liability for distributing a "product," while remaining liable for negligence in distributing a "service." Quite apart from statutory language, does this result make sense? Could it lead to a higher, more profound liability as a fiduciary — or would/could Armour avoid that as well, since it never dealt directly with the patient?
5. What was Armour's statutory argument? That it was a "storage facility"? Wasn't a better argument that it was engaged in "procurement, processing, distribution . . . "? Wasn't it really engaged in manufacture? Why wasn't that *included* in the statute? Wouldn't that help ensure "an adequate supply of lifesaving and essential blood products?"
6. Suppose the blood had been contaminated whole blood, distributed by the Red Cross and used at a local hospital. Would *that* be covered by the blood shield laws? *Should* it be?

PEOPLE v. DEMPSEY

610 N.E. 2d 208 (Ill. 1993)

Justice **Welch** delivered the opinion of the court:

. . . .

The following evidence was adduced at defendant's trial. The victim testified that he was nine years old and his birthday was July 18. He resides with his mother and father. The victim stated he has two brothers, and he stated their names. The victim identified one of his brothers, Randy, the defendant, in the courtroom. . . .

. . . Using the doll, he demonstrated that Randy had touched his penis. . . .

When asked whether Randy had put anything in his mouth, the victim stated, "He put that in my mouth", pointing to the penis on the doll. With his finger, the victim demonstrated that Randy's penis was erect when Randy put it in his mouth. . . .

Randy indicated that he would give the victim a turtle. Randy told the victim not to tell his mom. The incident occurred when Randy and the victim were in bed in Randy's room at their mother's house. The victim talked to his mother, about what had happened, on the porch and in the car when they went for a drive. He told her the truth in the car, and he was telling the truth in court. He testified that he still loved Randy.

. . . .

Randy's physician, Dr. Thomas P. Hyde, was called to testify. Prior to his testimony, the prosecutor filed a petition with the court asking that Dr. Hyde be authorized to give testimony regarding the medical condition and treatment of defendant. The prosecutor indicated that Dr. Hyde's testimony was necessary to prove that defendant had knowledge that he was infected with HIV, an essential element of the offense of criminal transmission of HIV. The prosecutor also argued that the physician-patient privilege should not bar Dr. Hyde's testimony in that the case arose out of a report of child abuse, one of the statutory exceptions to the privilege. Defendant argued that he had not waived the privilege and that the statutory exception did not apply. The court found that there was a compelling need for Dr. Hyde's testimony to prove defendant's knowledge of his infection and authorized his testimony, overruling defendant's objection.

. . . .

On cross-examination, defendant testified that he had been advised by Dr. Hyde that he had tested positive for HIV. At the end of December, Hyde prescribed AZT for defendant. Defendant took the AZT in January but over the next few months took less and less of it. In April he was hardly taking any of it. At the time of trial, defendant was taking AZT while incarcerated in jail. Defendant testified that on the date of the offense, he was feeling so good, he did not actually believe that he was infected with HIV. Dr. Hyde had never told defendant that he was cured of the infection. . . .

. . . .

Defendant's fourth argument on appeal is that his conviction for criminal transmission of HIV must be vacated because the statute upon which it is based, is unconstitutionally vague and therefore invalid. Section 12-16.2 provides in pertinent part as follows:

> Criminal Transmission of HIV.
>
> (a) A person commits criminal transmission of HIV when he or she, knowing that he or she is infected with HIV:
>
> (1) engages in intimate contact with another;
>
> (b) For purposes of this Section:
>
> 'HIV' means the human immunodeficiency virus or any other identified causative agent of acquired immunodeficiency syndrome.
>
> 'Intimate contact with another' means the exposure of the body of one person to a bodily fluid of another person in a manner that could result in the transmission of HIV.
>
> (c) Nothing in this Section shall be construed to require that an infection with HIV has occurred in order for a person to have committed criminal transmission of HIV.

Defendant argues that the statute is unconstitutionally vague because the term "bodily fluid" is insufficiently defined and that, because the word "could" in the definition of intimate contact encompasses such a broad range of conduct, it fails to clearly indicate what behavior is prohibited. As a result, the term "intimate contact with another" is not adequately defined and is vague. Defendant argues that because the term "bodily fluid" is not defined, the jury could conclude that saliva and tears could transmit the virus, when experts in the field assert that these are not bodily fluids capable of transmitting the virus. Furthermore, because the word "could" encompasses such a broad range of conduct, a jury could conclude that some sexual act short of penetrative oral, anal or vaginal intercourse could transmit the virus when experts assert that only these penetrative sexual acts could transmit the virus. Defendant further argues that one must speculate whether biting or spitting on another while knowingly infected with HIV constitutes criminal transmission of HIV because the statute does not define what bodily fluids are possible transmitters of the virus. Defendant argues that these uncertainties in the statute render it unconstitutionally vague in that it fails to give adequate notice to as to what acts are prohibited and allows arbitrary and discriminatory application.

Defendant's argument must fail because, not only does he lack standing to raise the constitutionality of the statute as applied to other acts and actors, the statute is not vague and unconstitutional as applied to him. It is well settled that vagueness challenges to statutes which do not involve first amendment freedoms must be examined in light of the facts of the case at hand. . . .

. . . .

Defendant's next argument on appeal is that the testimony of defendant's physician, Dr. Hyde, was improperly admitted in that the physician-patient privilege barred his testimony and no exception to that privilege applied. The State sought to introduce Dr. Hyde's testimony to establish that defendant had knowledge that he was infected with HIV, an essential element of the offense of criminal transmission of HIV. The court allowed Dr. Hyde to testify over defendant's objection, finding that there was a compelling need for the testimony. Defendant argues that the trial court improperly allowed Dr. Hyde to testify over defendant's assertion of the physician-patient privilege. The statute sets forth several exceptions to the privilege, among them the following:

> "(4) in all actions brought by or against the patient, his or her personal representative, a beneficiary under a policy of insurance, or the executor or administrator of his or her estate wherein the patient's physical or mental condition is an issue, . . ., (7) in actions, civil or criminal, arising from the filing of a report in compliance with the 'Abused and Neglected Child Reporting Act."

Neither party argues that Dr. Hyde's testimony does not fall within the scope of the physician-patient privilege. At trial, however, the State argued that exception (7) to the privilege applies because the prosecution arose from the filing of a report of child abuse in compliance with the Abused and Neglected Child Reporting Act. On appeal, the State argues that not only does exception (7) apply but exception (4) also applies in that defendant's physical condition is in issue. The State also argues on appeal that, in any event, defendant had waived the privilege prior to trial in that, with defendant's consent, several of his relatives, including his mother and sister, had been present when Dr. Hyde discussed with defendant his HIV status, his condition and his treatment.

We find it unnecessary to decide whether defendant had waived the privilege or whether any exceptions to the privilege apply because we find that any error in the admission of the testimony was harmless. Dr. Hyde's testimony regarding defendant's medical condition and treatment was essentially cumulative to that given by defendant's mother and sister and by the defendant himself. . . .

Dr. Hyde's testimony did not differ from that of the other witnesses and did not add anything that was not otherwise in evidence. Accordingly, we find that his testimony was essentially cumulative, and its admission, if error, was harmless and did not deprive [illegible]

Defendant's sixth argument on appeal is that his conviction for criminal transmission of HIV must be vacated because it is based on the same physical act as is his conviction for aggravated criminal sexual assault. Defendant argues that his conviction for criminal transmission of HIV is based upon the defendant having placed his penis in the victim's mouth knowing he was HIV positive, thereby exposing the victim to the virus. That act, defendant argues, is the same act which resulted in his conviction for aggravated criminal sexual assault. Defendant is wrong. Defendant's conviction for criminal transmission of HIV is not based on his having put his penis in the victim's mouth but on his act of exposing the body of the victim to his own bodily fluid, in this case either through ejaculation of semen or emission of preejaculatory fluid containing semen into the victim's mouth, while knowing he was infected with HIV. Neither ejaculation of semen nor emission of preejaculatory fluid is required for defendant's conviction for aggravated criminal sexual assault, but either act is an exposure to a bodily fluid, which is required for defendant's conviction for criminal transmission of HIV. Aggravated criminal sexual assault may be committed without the exposure to any bodily fluid. Criminal transmission of HIV can be committed without the commission of sexual assault. Accordingly, the two convictions are not based upon the same physical act, and both convictions can stand.

Defendant's final argument on appeal is that the trial judge's reliance on improper factors in sentencing led him to abuse his discretion in imposing defendant's sentences. We agree. . . .

. . . .

The trial judge discussed the presentence investigation report, indicating he had reviewed and considered it. The judge then made the following comments which we find demonstrate that he abused his discretion in sentencing defendant as he did:

> . . . .
>
> "You know, we have a lot of laws with respect to this HIV virus that the legislature makes, and we have those that try to surround information — even if a person takes a test, the doctor or who knows about it, unless it's in the line of duty, he should not even reveal that he went to take the test or she went to take the test. So it is in a sense, this HIV virus is a hidden disease. The general trend of the law and all the requirements seems to be that they try to take a person with this HIV virus and hide him in a closet and don't tell the world about it, but let him go on out and get his girlfriend, and she's not allegedly supposed to know about it apparently because — unless he tells her or somebody tells her. It's a hidden disease. What's the public going to do about it? What are these innocent people who don't have HIV going to do about people roaming the streets making dates and fooling around with little boys? What is the world going to do with that sort of a person?
>
> . . . .
>
> You know, what did we do with a mad dog, dog that was alleged to be rabid, mad dog? He would probably be put in a cage, as I understand the way they're handled, for about ten days or two weeks to see if he acts kind of like he's got rabies to see if he really comes through with it. In the meantime, you're sitting there having been bitten, and you don't know what to do. But if he comes through and he has to be done away with because he exhibits a slobbering or whatever the reaction is of a rabid dog, they kill that dog and have his head examined. . . . But if a little child even got scarlet fever or the measles, the child would probably be confined by quarantine until the child had healed to the extent that the child could again mingle with the public. But with a virus, you can't discriminate. The law protects them. They can't even refuse to hire them. I suppose they can work in a restaurant and serve food to us, work as a cook. If you don't hire them, even though you know they've got the HIV virus, there might be a suit of discrimination.

> I suppose there's been too many big wheels in this world who have had this virus. It may be sometimes called a political disease. Be it as it may, it has the publicity of being a very serious ailment, and I'm not a doctor, and I don't know how serious it is, but that's what I hear.
>
> . . . .
>
> But you have a conviction by a jury after a long trial, and I'm trying to obey some of these rules that hide the evidence, hide the evidence, don't reveal to the public about your position. Let everybody be innocent bystanders while you run through the crowd at will, and wherever you find a possibility spread your sperm or body fluids maybe in a way to cause a spread of this horrible disease.
>
> . . . .
>
> I hope that people who hear of this will think it's best if they have the HIV virus that they start protecting the public and not be like a mad dog out in the wilds biting anything that comes along or stands still or falls over backwards."

. . . Where the sentencing judge relies on improper factors, including prejudice, speculation, and conjecture, to the exclusion of the requisite statutory factors, the sentence should be vacated and the cause remanded for resentencing. . . .

. . . In the instant case, it appears to us that the trial judge relied on unfounded fear and prejudice relating to HIV infection and on speculation and conjecture. The sentencing judge speculated that because defendant reportedly had a girl friend prior to his arrest, he likely engaged in activity which could infect her, without any evidence in the record that this was so. The judge compared HIV sufferers with scarlet fever victims, suggesting the need for quarantine. He suggested, with no evidentiary support, that HIV sufferers receive some protection under the law, because of political considerations, that they do not deserve. He made comparisons of HIV sufferers to rabid dogs, mad dogs, and lepers, dwelling on the danger of allowing defendant to "run through the crowd at will": "wherever you find a possibility spread your sperm or body fluids maybe in a way to cause a spread of this horrible disease." Th[illegible] absolutely no evidence in the record that defendant had had any type of contact with any individual other than the victim which could result in transmission of HIV. Finally, the judge stated that he hoped the sentence imposed would tell HIV sufferers that they should "start protecting the public and not be like a mad dog out in the wilds biting anything that comes along or stands still or falls over backwards." Indeed, we are unable to determine whether the judge gave any consideration to the rehabilitative potential of the defendant, as required by our constitution. Clearly, these improper factors were significant elements in the defendant's sentences.

We do not believe that this sentencing judge made a reasoned and dispassionate determination as to the appropriate sentences to be imposed on defendant. He clearly abused his discretion in sentencing defendant. Accordingly, we vacate defendant's sentences and remand this case for resentencing with directions that the case be assigned to a different judge on remand.

. . . .

NOTES AND QUESTIONS

1. In the 1990s, a number of men were prosecuted for homicide in circumstances where they had intercourse with a woman without disclosure that they were HIV positive. Evidentiary problems concerning knowledge, consent and causation proved difficult, but were not insurmountable. The statute adopted in Illinois, and involved in *People v. Dempsey*, was designed to avoid such problems. It made criminal transmission of HIV a felony by itself. Should such legislation be adopted?

2. Mr. Dempsey argues that the statute is unconstitutionally vague, an argument we have seen elsewhere, for example, with respect to the Illinois abortion statute bearing on fetal tissue, *supra* § 4.02. Why does the Court reject the argument here, when it was persuasive there? *See also, Guevera v. Superior Court*, 73 Cal. Rptr. 2d 421 (Cal. 1998).

3. And what of the testimony of Dr. Hyde? Ordinarily, a physician is under a legal and ethical obligation of confidentiality. This becomes translated into a "privilege" in the patient to object to testimony breaching that confidentiality. However, in a whole array of public health statutes, physicians are required to either notify the state when they find certain facts to be true (*e.g.*, child or spousal abuse) or to testify in certain cases, such as the present one. What do you think of such statutes? Under what circumstances do they make sense? *Not* make sense?

4. It should be noted that most states have adopted statutes which specifically provide for confidentiality and nondisclosure of the identity of a person testing HIV positive. This has become crucial in a range of litigation involving the American Red Cross, where people received tainted transfusions sought to establish negligence in screening the donors, by seeking the identities of the donors. In the main, where the donors are still alive, disclosure has been denied. Do you think this is wise?

5. And finally, what about the sentencing judge's "eloquence"? When the AIDS epidemic first became public in the early-and mid-1980s, there was a backlash, critical of those who had the disease. The trial judge seems to be expressing that hysteria. Subsequently, public officials and legislation distinguished between those afflicted with the disease and those irresponsibly imposing it upon others in a criminal fashion. Mr. Dempsey obviously qualifies as the latter. On remand and resentencing, what should his sentence be?

6. For an excellent article, see Benjamin F. Neidl, *The Lesser of Two Evils: New York's New HIV/AIDS Partner Notification Law and Why the Right of Privacy Must Yield to Public Health*, 73 St. John's L. Rev. 1191 (1999); and see *State Statutes Dealing with HIV and AIDS: A Comprehensive State-by-State Summary (1999 Edition)*, 8 Law & Sex. 1 (1998).

PROBLEM 4-11 — AIDS and Fundamentalist Christians

The Plymouth Brethren are a devoutly religious group of Irish Christians established in the 1820s. They number 35,000 worldwide, with 2000 in your state. They are a fundamentalist, separatist community. They object to a recent curricular mandate by the State Commission of Education, requiring education in the elementary schools on the mechanism of sexual intercourse and prophylactic measures to combat AIDS. They seek to exempt their children from such instruction.

What result? *See Ware v. Valley Stream High School District*, 551 N.Y.S.2d 167 (N.Y. 1989).

[4] Female Genital Mutilation

People may alter their bodies for many purposes and in many ways. They may undertake comprehensive alterations, such as a change in gender (*see* § 2.02[2], *supra*), or lesser changes, such as body piercing or coloring hair. Similarly, society may impose physically upon people, as with testing or extraction of bodily materials. *See* § 2.03[2] and § 4.03[3], *supra*. Families may support this, for example, with vaccinations against infectious diseases. Deference is ordinarily due the family in such decisions.

But normal considerations become distorted or lost in the context of female genital mutilation. The United Nations estimates this practice affects 130 million women worldwide, most of them in Africa. The practice is a part of the cultural and ritual fabric of many tribal groups, imposed upon girls at a very young age, oftentimes by their own mothers. The surgery is accompanied by pain and often infection, and is performed by tribal lay midwives. There is extensive literature on the subject, but little legal product, perhaps because the practice is widespread in the nations where it exists. *See* Gloria Steinem, Outrageous Acts and Everyday Rebellions (1984); Alice Walker, Possessing the Secret of Joy (1992); Comment, *In Re Kasinga*, 24 New Eng. J. on Crime and Civ. Commitment 89 (1998); Hope Lewis, *Between IRVA and Female Genital Mutilation*, 8 Harv. Hum. Rts. J., 1 (1995); Patricia Rudloff, *In Re Oluloro*, 26 St. Mary's L.J. 877 (1995). In her article,* Rudloff described the practice of female genital mutilation.

> Approximately forty Middle Eastern and African countries engage in the practice of ritual female genital mutilation, a custom that originated more than 2500 years ago. Estimates suggest that eighty to one-hundred million women and young girls know the trauma of having their external genitalia removed. Experts predict that this mutilation affects half the women and girls in Nigeria. While the tradition of removing external female genitalia varies from culture to culture, generally, a tribe will practice only one of three types of FGM. The first and mildest form of FGM is somewhat similar to male circumcision in that the procedure removes the top of a woman's clitoris, just as circumcision removes the foreskin from a man's penis.

* Patricia Rudloff, *In Re Oluloro*, 26 St. Mary's L.J. 877 (1995).

Muslim cultures refer to this FGM procedure as sunna, which, in English, translates to "tradition". The second form, excision, is the removal of a woman's clitoris and labia minora. Infibulation is the third and most drastic form of genital mutilation: after removal of all a woman's external female genitalia, thorns are used to stitch together the raw edges of the labia majora. A small piece of wood is inserted into the resultant incision to prevent the wound from closing, and the woman's legs are temporarily bound together to allow scar tissue to form.

The age at which ritual FGM occurs is as varied as the procedure. Teens, women on wedding nights, and women about to give birth to their first child may be victims of this painful procedure. The normal practice, however, is to perform the ritual on babies or young girls. While men are responsible for the procedure in some cultures, more typically, the tribal women and midwives make the cuts necessary to bring a "high bride price". Of course, these "surgeons" have no medical training, and true surgical instruments, sterile conditions, and anesthesia are unknown to the practitioners. Crude knives, pieces of glass, or razor blades are often used to make the incision, while kerosene, motor oil, or native soaps are used to cleanse the wound.

The consequences of genital mutilation can be severe: shock, intense pain, infections, hemorrhaging, and death are often the immediate results. Urinary and menstrual problems can also occur when the body is unable to rid itself of fluids in the normal manner. To have sexual intercourse or give birth, an infibulated woman may be opened and then refibulated afterwards. Moreover, infibulated women often give birth to stillborn or brain-damaged babies because scar tissue, which can block the baby's oxygen supply during birth, develops around the vagina. Infant mortality rates are highest in countries allowing genital mutilation — a result of the stillbirths as well as the mutilation itself.

Westerners view FGM as persecution, torture, abuse, and, as its name suggests, mutilation. The practitioners of this procedure, however, have no such intent; they believe that their respective cultures are merely continuing a traditional rite of passage that provides females with a sense of identity and tribal recognition. Some practitioners further believe their religion requires the surgery, and many others see the procedure as virginity insurance for a future husband or as a method of controlling a woman's sex drive to prevent marital infidelity. Enhanced fertility, aesthetics, and cleanliness are other justifications offered by practitioners for the continuation of FGM.

To date, international disdain and condemnation of FGM has not forced these communities to abandon their deeply rooted tradition. In light of the continuation of this practice, the international community must offer a safe refuge to the women and girls who attempt to escape the trauma of FGM. In the United States, refuge is theoretically possible under the Immigration and Naturalization Act when the circumstances of those who fear atrocities like FGM merit such relief.

An overview of the practices, responses, and legislature of many countries is provided in a report, Warzazi, *Final Report of the Special Rapporteur on Traditional Practices Affecting the Health of Women and Children,* U.N. Economic and Social Council C/CN.4/Sub.2/1996. The practice reportedly is prosecuted, among western nations, only in France. However, in 1996, the United States Congress provided as follows at 18 USC § 116:

§ 116. Female genital mutilation

(a) Except as provided in subsection (b), whoever knowingly circumcises, excises, or fibulates the whole or any part of the labia majora or labia minora or clitoris of another person who has not attained the age of 18 years shall be fined under this title or imprisoned for not more than 5 years, or both.

(b) A surgical operation is not a violation of this section if the operation is —

  (1) necessary to the health of the person on whom it is performed, and is performed by a person licensed in the place of its performance as a medical practitioner; or

  (2) performed on a person in labor or who has just given birth and is performed for medical purposes connected with that labor or birth by a person licensed in the place it is performed as a medical practitioner, midwife, or person in training to become such a practitioner or midwife.

(c) In applying subsection (b)(1), no account shall be taken of the effect on the person on whom the operation is to be performed of any belief on the part of that person, or any other person, that the operation is required as a matter of custom or ritual.

Based upon the following findings:

"(1) the practice of female genital mutilation is carried out by members of certain cultural and religious groups within the United States;

"(2) the practice of female genital mutilation often results in the occurrence of physical and psychological health effects that harm the women involved;

"(3) such mutilation infringes upon the guarantees of rights secured by Federal and State law, both statutory and constitutional;

"(4) the unique circumstances surrounding the practice of female genital mutilation place it beyond the ability of any single State or local jurisdiction or control;

"(5) the practice of female genital mutilation can be prohibited without abridging the exercise of any rights guaranteed under the first amendment to the Constitution or under any other law; and

"(6) Congress has the affirmative power under section 8 of article I, the necessary and proper clause, section 5 of the fourteenth Amendment, as well as under the treaty clause, to the Constitution to enact such legislation."

In a case which drew national publicity, an immigration judge in Portland, Oregon reversed a deportation order against a Nigerian national, Lydia Oluloro. The case was reported as follows, with commentary by nationally syndicated columnist Ellen Goodman.

Ellen Goodman, *Redefining Abuse of Women One Step at a Time* *

BOSTON They are safe now. The two girls, 6-year-old Shade and 5-year-old Lara, will stay with their mother and stay in their country. The mother, Lydia Oluloro, will be spared the choice she described between leaving her daughters with an abusive father or taking them with her to an abusive culture.

An immigration judge resolved Lydia's choice. On Wednesday, he lifted the order to deport the Nigerian woman who had been married, had given birth, and been divorced in the United States. He ruled that sending her back would, in the jargon of immigration law, cause "extreme hardship" to her children who were U.S. citizens.

The hardship in this case wasn't economic nor was it political. The threat was not from a government nor a leader. The danger was something that is almost never claimed in the immigration court proceedings: genital mutilation.

There was the probability, the virtual certainty, that if these girls were relocated from Portland, Ore., to their mother's homeland, they would be assaulted the way she had been at 4 years old. Indeed, they would be assaulted the way their mother's mother's mothers had been for perhaps a thousand years.

Shade and Lara would have their genitals attacked with a blade. One and then the other would have her clitoris cut out along with her labia minor. One and then the other would be stitched together with barely room for urinating and menstruating. They would be mutilated in the name of tradition.

But Judge Kendall Warren ruled to protect them, saying, "This court attempts to respect traditional cultures, but this is cruel and serves no known medical purpose."

So, two girls were saved from a ritual that maims two million a year across the world. And another small step was taken toward redefining abuse of women.

Until these last few years, the abuse of women never quite made the world's agenda. Rape was a private assault. Wife-battering was a family affair. Sexual slavery was about sex, not slavery. Gender discrimination was considered a matter of tradition — rather like music or dress.

Now our eyes are opened and our vocabulary has increased. From Bosnia, we saw rape as a deliberate political act. From Thailand, we heard from thousands of Burmese girls tricked into sexual slavery while the officials winked. From Pakistan and India we learned of bride-burning. And from Africa we bore witness to genital mutilation and the fight to end it.

---

* Ellen Goodman, *Redefining Abuse of Women One Step at a Time*, Boston Globe, March 27, 1994.

Slowly the terrible things that happen to women are being understood as human rights abuses. At the United Nations Conference on Human Rights last summer, women's groups from every culture signed the same petition saying: "We demand gender violence to be recognized as a violation of human rights." And at last, the U.S. State Department includes women's rights when tallying the world's records of human rights abuses.

In our own country, the policy of offering refuge or asylum on these grounds has been slow to change. In theory, anyone who has been severely harassed, persecuted, can ask for asylum here. But in practice, it's granted mostly to people fleeing communism or to men in political cases.

As Deborah Anker of Harvard's Immigrant and Refugee Program said, "The kinds of harm women face have been traditionally trivialized and considered private." Slowly, gender claims have begun to appear — claims by women's rights advocates fleeing governments, claims by victims of political rape, claims by wives battered in countries that don't protect them, and now by women fearing this female ritual.

Lydia Oluloro's claims were made for her daughters' sake. The judge sidestepped the issue of asylum. She won the right to stay here on humanitarian grounds — to protect two young U.S. citizens. But for the first time a case was won on the need to protect females from forced genital mutilation.

Will this open some vast new floodgate of refugees? Most girls are cut by this blade while they are as young as Shade and Lara. Few 5-year-olds will find their way here to beg refuge. The struggle to uproot this "tradition" will have to continue on its own home turf.

But if we are to take mutilation seriously in the world, and in our foreign policy, we have to take it seriously in our own rules about refugees and asylum. They are one way we show our values to the world, one way we define persecution and offer protection.

The forced genital mutilation of young girls fits all the definitions of persecution we apply to any refugee. The brutal assault by a knife on the sexual organ is persecution of the most extreme — and the most female — sort.

Last week, two girls were [illegible] by their mother and by a judge. Just two out of two million. Sometimes you have to defend human rights two at a time.

Officially recorded decisions or opinions in cases concerning female genital mutilation (FGM) are difficult to find. Summaries of two cases are *In Re K-*, 72 Interpreter Releases 1188 (9/95) and *Matter of J*, 72 Interpreter Releases 1375 (4/95). In the former case, a native of Sierra Leone was allowed to remain in the United States, based upon the risk of female genital mutilation, beating by her husband, and the absence of a means for political challenge to FGM. In the latter case, asylum was denied another resident of Sierra Leone, who feared FGM of her daughters, the summary stating:

> The respondent also testified that she has a well-founded fear of persecution because of membership in a particular social group

> relating to the issue of genital mutilation. She stated that she was opposed to genital mutilation, which had been forced upon her at the age of 13, and that if returned to Sierra Leone, she along with her daughters would be persecuted for not allowing themselves to be mutilated and/or for opposing tribal customs.

Noting that respondent's fears were not primarily politically based, IJ Gossart said:

> Her greatest fear is of the tribes back in Sierra Leone. She disagrees with FGM [female genital mutilation], refuses to submit her children to it and fears retribution and isolation from her tribe because of her differing views. The court does not find this to be an adequate showing of fear of political persecution.
>
> IJ Gossart asserted that respondent's fears of her tribe's customs with regard to genital mutilation did not grant her any advantage with respect to her persecution claim, since there was no evidence that a social group exists of persons in Sierra Leone who do not practice female genital mutilation, or that the government is aware of such a group's opinions. Moreover, he said, a social group for asylum purposes must share some common characteristic that is beyond the respondent's power to change, or is so fundamental to the individual's identity or conscience that he or she ought not to be required to change:
>
> In this situation, respondent cannot change the fact that she is female, but she can change her mind with regards to her position towards the FGM practices. It is not beyond the respondent's control to acquiesce to the tribal position on FGM. Therefore, the respondent does not fit into the category of a particular social group as delineated by case law.

IJ Gossart noted, among other things, that "while some cultures view FGM as abhorrent and/or even barbaric, others do not. To constitute persecution, motive and purpose must be considered as well as consequence." He also stated that the definition of persecution requires that the persecutors either be the government or a group that the government cannot control, but that in this case, the persecutors would be the tribe.

IJ Gossart said that although he sympathized with the respondent's fears, they did not constitute persecution under the INA. He therefore denied her asylum claim, but granted her request for voluntary departure. *Matter of J*, 72 Interpreter Releases 1375 (April 1995).

The issue thus posed is how one society may judge the practices of another, when those practices are widespread, culturally grounded and time-honored. To re-phrase the question, within the criteria for granting asylum, when does a practice — here, female genital mutilation — amount to political persecution, gender abuse or humanitarian affront sufficient to warrant granting asylum? And how much might we expect a person to endure upon return to her community of origin?

We now turn to *In Re Fauziya Kasinga.*

IN RE FAUZIYA KASINGA, APPLICANT*

Interim Decision (BIA) 3278 (1996)
1996 BIA Lexis 15

Schmidt, Chairman:

. . . .

The applicant is a 19-year-old native and citizen of Togo. She attended 2 years of high school. She is a member of the Tchamba-Kunsuntu Tribe of northern Togo. She testified that young women of her tribe normally undergo FGM at age 15. However, she did not because she initially was protected from FGM by her influential, but now deceased, father.

The applicant stated that upon her father's death in 1993, under tribal custom her aunt, her father's sister, became the primary authority figure in the family. The applicant's mother was driven from the family home, left Togo, and went to live with her family in Benin. The applicant testified that she does not currently know her mother's exact whereabouts.

The applicant further testified that her aunt forced her into a polygamous marriage in October 1994, when she was 17. The husband selected by her aunt was 45 years old and had three other wives at the time of marriage. The applicant testified that, under tribal custom, her aunt and her husband planned to force her to submit to FGM before the marriage was consummated.

The applicant testified that she feared imminent mutilation. With the help of her older sister, she fled Togo for Ghana. However, she was afraid that her aunt and her husband would locate her there. Consequently, using money from her mother, the applicant embarked for Germany by airplane.

. . . .

The applicant further stated that in December 1994, while on her way to a shopping center, she met a young Nigerian man. He was the first person from Africa she had spoken to since arriving in Germany. They struck up a conversation, during which the applicant told the man about her situation. He offered to sell the applicant his sister's British passport so that she could seek asylum in the United States, where she has an aunt, an uncle, and a cousin. The applicant followed the man's suggestion, purchasing the passport and the ticket with money given to her by her sister.

The applicant did not attempt a fraudulent entry into the United States. Rather, upon arrival at Newark International Airport on December 17, 1994, she immediately requested asylum. She remained in detention by the Immigration and Naturalization Service ("INS") until April 1996.

The applicant testified that the Togolese police and the Government of Togo were aware of FGM and would take no steps to protect her from the practice. She further testified that her aunt had reported her to the Togolese police. Upon return, she would be taken back to her husband by the police and forced

* Citation material has been omitted from this decision.

to undergo FGM. She testified at several points that there would be nobody to protect her from FGM in Togo.

In her testimony, the applicant referred to letters in the record from her mother. Those letters confirmed that the Togolese police were looking for the applicant and that the applicant's father's family wanted her to undergo FGM.

. . . .

4. Description of FGM

According to the applicant's testimony, the FGM practiced by her tribe, the Tchamba-Kunsuntu, is of an extreme type involving cutting the genitalia with knives, extensive bleeding, and a 40-day recovery period. The background materials confirm that the FGM practiced in some African countries, such as Togo, is of an extreme nature causing permanent damage, and not just a minor form of genital ritual. *See, e.g.,* Nahid Toubia, Female Genital Mutilation: A Call for Global Action 9, 24-25 (Gloria Jacobs ed., Women Ink. 1993).

The record material establishes that FGM in its extreme forms is a practice in which portions of the female genitalia are cut away. In some cases, the vagina is sutured partially closed. This practice clearly inflicts harm or suffering upon the girl or woman who undergoes it.

FGM is extremely painful and at least temporarily incapacitating. It permanently disfigures the female genitalia. FGM exposes the girl or woman to the risk of serious, potentially life-threatening complications. These include, among others, bleeding, infection, urine retention, stress, shock, psychological trauma, and damage to the urethra and anus. It can result in permanent loss of genital sensation and can adversely affect sexual and erotic functions.

. . . .

The record also contains two reports compiled by the United States Department of State. The first of these, dated January 31, 1994, 1) confirms that FGM is practiced by some ethnic groups in Togo; 2) notes that while some reports indicate that the practice may be diminishing, an expert indicates that as many as 50% of Togolese females may have been mutilated; and 3) notes that various acts of violence against women occur in Togo with little police intervention.

. . . .

While a number of descriptions of persecution have been formulated in our past decisions, we have recognized that persecution can consist of the infliction of harm or suffering by a government, or persons a government is unwilling or unable to control, to overcome a characteristic of the victim.

As observed by the INS, many of our past cases involved actors who had a subjective intent to punish their victims. However, this subjective "punitive" or "malignant" intent is not required for harm to constitute persecution.

. . . .

To be a basis for a grant of asylum, persecution must relate to one of five categories described in section 101(a)(42)(A) of the Act. The parties agree that the relevant category in this case is "particular social group."

In the context of this case, we find the particular social group to be the following: young women of the Tchamba-Kunsuntu Tribe who have not had FGM, as practiced by that tribe, and who oppose the practice. This is very similar to the formulations suggested by the parties.

. . . .

In accordance with Acosta, the particular social group is defined by common characteristics that members of the group either cannot change, or should not be required to change because such characteristics are fundamental to their individual identities. The characteristics of being a "young woman" and a "member of the Tchamba-Kunsuntu Tribe" cannot be changed. The characteristic of having intact genitalia is one that is so fundamental to the individual identity of a young woman that she should not be required to change it.

. . . .

The burden of proof is upon an applicant for asylum to establish that a "reasonable person" in her circumstances would fear persecution upon return to Togo. The applicant has met this burden through a combination of her credible testimony and the introduction of documentary evidence and background information that supports her claim.

. . . .

To be eligible for asylum, the applicant must establish that her well-founded fear of persecution is "on account of" one of the five grounds specified in the Act, here, her membership in a "particular social group."

. . . .

Record materials state that FGM "has been used to control woman's sexuality," It also is characterized as a form of "sexual oppression" that is "based on the manipulation of women's sexuality in order to assure male dominance and exploitation." During oral argument before us, the INS General Counsel agreed with the latter characterization. He also stated that the practice is a "severe bodily invasion" that should be regarded as meeting the asylum standard even if done with "subjectively benign intent".

We agree with the parties that, as described and documented in this record, FGM is practiced, at least in some significant part, to overcome sexual characteristics of young women of the tribe who have not been, [illegible] be, subjected to FGM. We therefore find that the persecution the applicant fears in Togo is "on account of" her status as a member of the defined social group.

. . . .

VII. Discretion

We have determined that the applicant is eligible for asylum because she has a well-founded fear of persecution on account of her membership in a particular social group in Togo. A grant of asylum to an eligible applicant is discretionary. The final issue is whether the applicant merits a favorable exercise of discretion. The danger of persecution will outweigh all but the most egregious adverse factors. The type of persecution feared by the applicant is very severe.

To the extent that the Immigration Judge suggested that the applicant had a legal obligation to seek refuge in Ghana or Germany, the record does not support such a conclusion. The applicant offered credible reasons for not seeking refuge in either of those countries in her particular circumstances.

The applicant purchased someone else's passport and used it to come to the United States. However, upon arrival, she did not attempt to use the false passport to enter. She told the immigration inspector the truth.

We have weighed the favorable and adverse factors and are satisfied that discretion should be exercised in favor of the applicant. Therefore, we will grant asylum to the applicant.

. . . .

CONCURRING OPINION: Lauri **Steven Filppu**, Board Member, joined by Michael J. **Heilman**, Board Member, joined.

I respectfully concur. I write separately in part to respond more completely to several arguments advanced by the Immigration and Naturalization Service.

I. Introduction

The questions necessarily presented to the Board by virtue of the positions advanced by the parties in this case are narrow. The majority resolves the case on those grounds, and properly declines to address issues raised by the Service that go well beyond those essential to the disposition of this appeal.

. . . .

Despite the absence of any major dispute between the parties in this case, the Service requests that we adopt its broad "framework of analysis" for claims of this type. Its suggestion candidly is aimed at addressing issues it sees arising in relation to claims that may be made by women from other "parts of the world where FGM is practiced" and by those "who have been subjected to it in the past."

. . . .

The Service then offers its "framework of analysis." That framework includes a new "shocks the conscience" test for persecution. The advantages seen by the Service of this test evidently include: 1) the ability to define FGM as "persecution" notwithstanding any lack of intent to "punish" FGM victims on the part of the victims' parents or tribe members who may well "believe that they are simply performing an important cultural rite that bonds the individual to the society"; 2) the ability to exclude other cultural practices, such as "body scarring," from the definition of persecution as these do not shock the conscience; and 3) the ability to exclude past victims of FGM from asylum eligibility if "they consented" to it or "at least acquiesced," as in the case of a woman who experienced FGM as "a small child," since FGM would not shock the conscience unless inflicted on "an unconsenting or resisting individual."

. . . .

The Board certainly is not oblivious to immigration policy considerations in the disposition of cases falling within our jurisdiction. But we are not fundamentally a policy-making body. There may be some unsettling or unsatisfying aspects to the slower and less predictable development of legal guidelines that inures in the Board's case adjudication system. But there are alternatives if resort to the Board's issuance of precedent is not satisfactory in a particular context. The Service can seek to have the Attorney General issue regulations that comprehensively address competing concerns, or it can work within the Administration for appropriate legislative action by Congress. The Service should not, however, expect the Board to endorse a significant new framework for assessing asylum claims in the context of a single novel case, especially when that framework seems intended primarily to address cases that are not in fact before the Board yet.

CONCURRING OPINION: Lory D. **Rosenberg**, Board Member

Today, in the specific case before us, this Board decides that a young woman of a particular tribe in Togo, who opposes being subjected to female genital mutilation as practiced by that tribe, is a member of a particular social group, and that on account of that membership, a reasonable person could fear persecution as defined in the Immigration and Nationality Act. I join the majority decision in its entirety.

. . . .

The social group category within the refugee definition incorporated into the Act has been recognized as having deliberately been included as a "catch-all" for individuals not falling into the first four specifically enumerated categories of political opinion, race, religion, or ethnicity.

. . . .

It may be true that sometimes an individual woman's political opinion may overlap or coexist with her membership in a group designated as a particular social group; however, that does not detract from the fact that social group membership is a status-based ground protected under the Act, just as is religion or ethnicity. While it is not impossible that a political or social opinion, [illegible] or imputed, may be shared by persons whom, as a result, we would characterize as constituting a particular social group within the meaning of the Act, that is not the case here. As I have stated, the applicant's political or social views — her attitude or intent — is not relevant to our definition of the social group to which she belongs, but rather to whether the harm or abuse she faces constitutes persecution.

. . . .

The only distinguishing characteristic about this case that I can perceive to set it apart from others we already have decided is that it involves a woman. Reliance upon such a distinction to support a separate category for treatment of women's asylum claims, to my mind, would be impermissible. Here, the applicant is a member of a group: girls and women of a given tribe, some perhaps of marriageable age, whose members are routinely subjected to the harm which the majority finds to constitute persecution. The applicant's opposition (which happens to be present in this case) or the lack of it, is neither determinative, nor necessary to define the social group in accordance with the statutory language.

. . . .

NOTES AND QUESTIONS

1. Are *Kasinga* and *Matter of J* consistent? How might they be? Which is the better result?
2. Compare the issues, procedures and result in *Kasinga* with those in *United States v. Schmidt, supra,* § 1.02[2]. Are they totally dissimilar? Are there aspects in common? Is such a comparison helpful?
3. What *exactly* about the practice of female genital mutilation is offensive? Suppose the procedures were performed by trained medical personnel, in modern medical facilities, unaccompanied by risk of infection, spousal brutality or political repression? Suppose it was delayed until the age of consent? If all these were true would the objection remain that a society may not deprive women of the organs of sexual experience, expression and pleasure? How should such a judgment be made, and would it then be severe enough to warrant asylum?
4. Note that FGM is persecution only if directed at a "particular social group". In Togo, it seems directed at all females. Is there, then, persecution? And who shall decide whether intact genitalia are so "fundamental to identity" that a society may not require changes? *See* § 1.03[1][b], *supra,* as to sterilization and § 2.03[1], [2] as to the importance of gender to identity.
5. Is the Board of Immigration Appeals saying that "control of sexuality" is *not* a proper societal objective? That it is always "sexual oppression"?
6. What of Board Members Filppu and Heilman's concurring opinion, and the INS proposal of a "shock the conscience" framework for analysis? Why *not* adopt that framework? Is there a better one? What should it provide?
7. And do you agree or disagree with the concurring opinion of Member Rosenberg? Do you see his point?
8. For an excellent article, see Khadijah F. Sharif, *Female Genital Mutilation: What Does The New Federal Law Really Mean?*, 24 Fordham Urb. L.J. 409 (1997); and see Amy Stern, *Female Genital Mutilation: United States Asylum Laws Are in Need of Reform*, 6 Am. U. J. Gender & L. 89 (1997).

PROBLEM 4–12 — All in the Family

The daughter of Fauziya Kasinga, born in the United States, is brought to you by her Aunt who is visiting from Togo. They ask you — a Board certified obstetrician/gynecologist, with surgical credentialing — to perform the extreme traditional Togo genital ritual surgery upon the daughter. The reason is threefold:

(1) the daughter intends to return to Togo, where the surgery will be enforced upon her, under dangerous conditions, badly done;

(2) Fauziya and the daughter have been shunned by their entire family and ritual surgery is the only way to bring the daughter back into the fold;

(3) the Aunt has brokered a traditional marriage with the son of a prominent family, but traditional surgery is a precondition to marriage with the daughter, who is now twelve.

In the light of the fiduciary obligations discussed in Chapter 3, *may* you perform this surgery? What circumstances or conditions would be necessary? And are you concerned about criminal liability under 18 USC § 116? Does the daughter have a valid claim under *Roe v. Wade* or *Casey* that the criminal prohibition on FGM infringes her right to autonomy and reproductive choice?

§ 4.04 Treatments

The subject of treatments has been previously explored in Chapter 3, in terms of the provider's fiduciary obligations. Here the focus is on three specific objects — medical uses of marijuana, investigational therapies, and medical futility.

[1] Medical Marijuana

Marijuana has medical applications from treating glaucoma to easing post-traumatic disorders. For some patients, it is the treatment of choice, yet it is banned. This raises important issues of patient autonomy and physician prerogative. Ethically and legally, the marijuana cases provide a testing ground for many of the principles in the preceding chapters.

SEELEY v. WASHINGTON
940 P.2d 604 (Wash. 1996)

Madsen, J.

The Respondent, Mr. Seeley, was diagnosed with chordoma, a rare form of bone cancer, in 1986. Mr. Seeley has undergone numerous surgeries including the removal of his right lung and a removal of part of the lower lobe of his left lung. Mr. Seeley also suffers from "Severe Obstructive Airway Disease." Mr. Seeley's condition is diagnosed as terminal.

Throughout his battle with cancer, Mr. Seeley has received radiation therapy and chemotherapy. Mr. Seeley was treated with various chemotherapeutic agents which commonly produce nausea and vomiting. He was treated with synthetic tetrahydrocannabinal (THC) (Marinol or dronabinol) and other antiemetic drugs for the nausea and vomiting which resulted from the chemotherapy. Mr. Seeley has also smoked marijuana during chemotherapy. Mr. Seeley prefers smoking marijuana to control these side effects. Mr. Seeley's states that smoking marijuana has been more effective in relieving his symptoms than other antiemetics.

Marijuana is a hallucinogen derived from the Indian hemp plant. One of the principle active ingredients in marijuana is delta-9-tetrahydrocannabinal (THC). The amount of THC present in marijuana varies in the plant depending on the origin of the plant, growing conditions, and cultivation. In addition to THC, marijuana contains over 400 other chemical substances including 61 identified cannabinoids, the active ingredients in marijuana, including THC. In 1986, the pure synthetic form of THC (Marinol or Dronabinol) was approved by the federal Food and Drug Administration (FDA) and is used as an antiemetic. The FDA has not approved marijuana for medical treatment.

Marijuana is regulated by both the state and federal government. Washington adopted the Uniform Controlled Substances Act. . . . Substances on schedule I are illegal under all circumstances except for research. Substances on schedules II to V are legal to possess only under a valid prescription. . . .

Both federal and state statutes list marijuana in schedule I of controlled substances. . . .

. . . .

II. Equal Protection Analysis

In an equal protection analysis this court must first determine the standard of review against which to test the challenged legislation. Respondent contends that the legislative decision placing marijuana in schedule I threatens a fundamental right and is therefore entitled to strict scrutiny. If governmental action threatens a "fundamental right," the classification will be upheld only if it is necessary to accomplish a compelling state interest.

. . . .

Here, Respondent asserts a constitutionally protected interest in having his physician prescribe marijuana, an unapproved drug which is regulated as a Schedule I controlled substance, for medical treatment. In an equally compelling case, the United States Supreme Court recently held that terminally ill patients do not have a constitutionally protected right to physician assisted suicide nor did they constitute a suspect class for purposes of and equal protection analysis. *Vacco v. Quill. Thus*, it is apparent from the case law that although the Respondent is facing a terminal illness, he is not part of a suspect class nor does he have a fundamental right to have marijuana prescribed as his preferred treatment over the legitimate objections of the state.

. . . .

To support his argument that marijuana's classification is purely arbitrary, Respondent cites to an opinion and recommended ruling by Administrative Law Judge (ALJ) Young in response to a petition by NORML before the Drug Enforcement Administration (DEA) to reschedule marijuana, asserting that the drug had an accepted medical use.[1] Judge Young heard testimony and reviewed evidence on both sides of the issue. In September 1988, Judge Young issued his ruling and concluded:

---

1 Like its state counterpart, a substance will be classified in Schedule I under the federal scheme if the substance has (1) a high potential for abuse, (2) no currently accepted medical use in treatment in the United States, and (3) no accepted safety for use in treatment under medical supervision. 21 U.S.C. 812(b)(1) (1981).

The evidence in this record clearly shows that marijuana has been accepted as capable of relieving the distress of great numbers of very ill people, and doing so with safety under medical supervision. It would be unreasonable, arbitrary and capricious for the DEA to continue to stand between those sufferers and the benefits of this substance in light of the evidence in this record. . . .

The Administrator of the DEA, however, did not follow the ALJ's recommended ruling and retained marijuana on schedule I. The ALJ determined that a respectable minority of physicians who advocated marijuana's medical use was sufficient to show that marijuana had an "accepted medical use." The Administrator declined to follow the ALJ's standard for "accepted medical use" because it lacked scientific credibility. . . .

Furthermore, scientifically reliable evidence showed that currently available therapies are more effective and do not carry with them the same risks which are attributable to marijuana. The Administrator's decision to retain marijuana in schedule I was upheld by the United States Court of Appeals for the District of Columbia. For this court to rely on the recommended ruling by the Administrative Law Judge would be the equivalent of relying on a decision by a trial court which has been reversed on appeal.

. . . .

The State maintains that placing marijuana in schedule I is rationally related to the state's dual interest in controlling potential drug abuse and assuring efficacy and safety in medicines. Respondent argues that placing marijuana in schedule I is not rationally related to the states purpose of preventing drug abuse. Respondent maintains that placing marijuana in schedule II could not possibly contribute to the drug abuse problem because marijuana would be available only by prescription. However, the Legislature could reasonably consider marijuana's widespread availability and its pattern of abuse as requiring a different legislative response than to other substances. "It is enough that there is an evil at hand for correction, and that it might be thought that the particular legislative measure was a rational way to correct it."

Respondent also contends that the placement of marijuana in schedule I is irrational because it is a safe and effective medicine for controlling the vomiting and nausea associated with cancer chemotherapy. He argues that marijuana has an "accepted medical use" and, therefore, cannot be placed in schedule I. Respondent relies primarily on the testimony of Dr. Lester Grinspoon, associate clinical professor of psychiatry at Harvard Medical School and specialist in psychoactive drugs, and Dr. Ernest Conrad, an orthopedic physician at the University of Washington School of Medicine and Mr. Seeley's treating physician for nine years.

Dr. Grinspoon offered testimony advocating the safety and benefits of using marijuana as a medicine. He contends that marijuana is one of the safest drugs available, stating there has never been a documented overdose. Based on anecdotal testimony from cancer patients, Dr. Grinspoon contends that marijuana is more effective than other new generation antiemetic drugs such as ondansetron. Dr. Grinspoon admits that smoking marijuana carries the same risks associated with smoking cigarettes and that marijuana may even contain more particulate matter than cigarettes. However, he notes that a cigarette smoker smokes in far greater quantities than a cancer chemotherapy patient, who will smoke a marijuana cigarette only until the nausea symptoms subside.

The Respondent also offered testimony of his physician, Dr. Ernest Conrad, who stated that he would prescribe marijuana if it were legally available. Dr. Conrad maintained that for some of his patients, including Mr. Seeley, smoking marijuana is an effective means to control the nausea and vomiting associated with cancer chemotherapy. He admits that his opinions are not based on scientific evidence but, rather, on claims of patients who have found that it alleviates their symptoms.

In response, the State provided testimony of several physicians who do not advocate the use of marijuana as a medicine. Dr. Janet Lapey, a pathologist and executive director of Concerned Citizens for Drug Prevention, has also studied the scientific research and medical literature regarding marijuana's potential use as a medicine. However, unlike Dr. Grinspoon, she has concluded that marijuana has no currently accepted use in the treatment of any medical condition. Dr. Lapey notes that marijuana is a complex mixture of over 400 chemicals, which increases to 2,000 when smoked. Among those 400 chemicals, there are at least 61 identified cannabinoids, the active ingredients in marijuana. The amount of the active ingredients, including THC, can vary depending on the growing condition of the plant. Dr. Lapey explains that to gain approval as a medicine a substance must be capable of precise chemical quantification of all ingredients. Dr. Barry Logan, a toxicologist for the State of Washington, explains that with a marijuana plant there is no way to create a standardized dosing system because there is no singularly identifiable and/or chemically consistent plant. Thus, he concludes this quality renders the plant form of marijuana incapable of establishment of standards for the accepted safety for use in treatment under medical supervision.

Dr. Lapey also notes that marijuana has been rejected as a medicine by the American Medical Association, the American Cancer Society, the National Multiple Sclerosis Society, the American Glaucoma Society, the Food and Drug Administration, and the American Academy of Opthamology. Dr. Lapey states that no scientifically credible evidence exists which supports the conclusion that marijuana is an effective medicine. Dr. Lapey maintains that when compared against other currently available medications there is no support for using marijuana as a medicine.

Dr. Daniel Brookoff, a specialist in medical oncology, also testified that marijuana is not an effective medication. He states that in the last 15 years other drugs, such as ondansetron, have been developed that have proved to be safer and far more effective in treating the nausea and vomiting associated with chemotherapy. . . .[2]

Dr. Brookoff stated that for physicians the issue of whether inhaled marijuana should be used as an anti-emetic was settled in 1984 when Dr.

[2] This report is published in 3 Proceedings of the American Society of Clinical Oncology 91 (1984).

Levitt and colleagues conducted a randomized, double-blind comparison of synthesized THC and marijuana for the treatment of nausea and vomiting associated with chemotherapy. The study found that neither substance was particularly effective in treating nausea and vomiting with 75 percent of patients in both groups still suffering significant nausea and vomiting. Moreover, among those who found the substances to be effective, the majority preferred the synthesized form of THC as opposed to marijuana. . . .

. . . .

Additionally, Washington's Uniform Controlled Substances Act contains a mechanism by which evidence may be presented to the board of pharmacy to determine whether a drug should be reclassified. The very existence of this statutory scheme indicates that the Legislature intended flexibility and receptivity to the latest scientific information. This scheme is a sensible mechanism for dealing with a field in which factual claims are conflicting and the state of scientific knowledge is still growing. This is the antithesis of irrationality which the Respondent attributes to the Legislature. Thus, the determination of whether new evidence regarding marijuana's potential medical use should result in the reclassification of marijuana is a matter for legislative or administrative, not judicial, judgment.

. . . .

In light of this policy of legislative freedom when confronting social problems, the exclusion of other potentially more harmful drugs from schedule I does not render the scheme unconstitutional. That cocaine or morphine have adverse health effects does not mean that placing these substances in schedule I is the best means of regulating these substances, or that marijuana should be treated similarly. The fact that cocaine, morphine, and methanphetamines have all been approved for medical use and marijuana has not is sufficient reason for treating the substances differently. Likewise, the synthesized form of THC has been approved for medical use. Marijuana, unlike synthesized THC contains over 400 different chemicals and there is no way to create a standardized dosing system because there are no chemically consistent plants. The differences between marijuana and synthesized THC, in addition to the health risks associated with inhaled marijuana, justify the Legislature's decision to treat the substances differently.

. . . .

Because substantial evidence is available to support the Legislature's action, we decline to interfere with the broad judicially recognized prerogative of the Legislature particularly where the challenged legislation involves a myriad of complicated medical, physiological, and moral issues and substantial evidence is available to support the Legislature's action. The debate over the proper classification of marijuana belongs in the political arena.

. . . .

Sanders, J. (dissenting)

. . . .

The trial court, and the majority here, analyze Mr. Seeley's claim under the privileges and immunities clause of article I, section 12, of the Washington

Constitution as well as the equal protection clause of the Fourteenth Amendment to the United States Constitution. Notwithstanding, I prefer the due process clause of the Fourteenth Amendment, as argued by amicus American Civil Liberties Union of Washington Foundation because the problem is how the government treats Mr. Seeley, not that Mr. Seeley is treated differently from others. Equalizing injustice does not cure it. I dissent.

This dissent relies primarily on recent Supreme Court precedent in two abortion cases, *Roe v. Wade* and *Planned Parenthood v. Casey*, wherein the Supreme Court majority credited the state's interest to preserve the life of the fetus as "important" but nevertheless insufficient to prohibit the practice when measured against the liberty interests of the mother. The majority cannot distinguish these cases. If the state cannot prohibit abortions consistent with due process, it can hardly constitutionally prohibit drug use as its interest to do so is arguably much less important. I further rely on *Ravin v. State*, 537 P.2d 494 (Alaska 1975) which construes a comparable provision in the Alaska constitution to immunize persons who smoke marijuana in the privacy of their home from criminal prosecutions, as well as *Washington v. Glucksberg*, which rejects the claim that due process protects the asserted right of physician assisted suicide however still provides much comfort to Mr. Seeley, who claims due process protection against "arbitrary impositions and purposeless restraints."

. . . .

As to Mr. Seeley's claim that inhalation of leaf form marijuana subsequent to chemotherapy relieves symptoms of nausea, the State admitted during oral argument it "cannot dispute Mr. Seeley's beliefs about marijuana and how it affects him. . . ." Seeley's medical doctor filed an affidavit attesting that in his medical judgment Mr. Seeley would benefit from the use of marijuana.

But the State purports to justify this total prohibition of marijuana by taking a "larger focus." It asserts absolute criminal prohibition, even as applied to Mr. Seeley, promotes legitimate governmental objectives associated with discouraging drug abuse and otherwise protecting the citizenry from itself by curtailing what it alleges to be the unknown consequences associated with the inhalation of marijuana. But these reasons even if valid have no particular application to Seeley who is terminally ill, admittedly finds relief in smoking marijuana, and seeks to follow the advice of his own physician who attests marijuana is medically advisable. From the perspective of one writhing in nausea on the tiled floor of an oncological recovery room, the State's justifications to withhold the blessings of relief are more sophomoric than substantive.[3]

. . . .

Let us recall both *Roe* and *Casey*, like the case before us, focus upon an individual's claim that the State lacks sufficient justification to dictate to a woman matters associated with her bodily integrity, abortion specifically. A

3 The record is replete with uncontroverted evidence that Seeley and many similarly situated cancer patients undergo unbearable pain and digestive unrest as a result of chemotherapy and radiation treatments and that they claim leaf marijuana is one of the only efficacious agents available to ease their suffering.

majority in Roe recognized that the State "may properly assert important interests in safeguarding health, in maintaining medical standards, and in protecting potential life." Similarly, a majority in *Casey* recognized these same legitimate interests, yet held "legitimate interests are not enough."

. . . .

. . . *Roe* and *Casey* clarify that the more personal the individual interest, the more that interest concerns bodily autonomy, the more that interest centers on purely personal concerns such as the avoidance of pain through a medical procedure, the less likely the governmental restraint will be upheld. The rationale behind *Glucksberg* is much the same. An absolute criminal bar to the use of marijuana includes specifically personal concerns of bodily autonomy coupled with the personal desire to mitigate if not alleviate needless physical suffering. These are grave interests which favor the individual.

On the other hand, the claimed interests of the State are insubstantial. There is little relation between the ingestion of marijuana by Mr. Seeley and the specter of drug abuse by others, other than the desire to make a political statement that marijuana in leaf form has no legitimate use under any conceivable circumstance.[4] But the government's argument that the ingestion of marijuana may have uncertain medical consequences seems unpersuasive when, at the same time, the government concedes that it cannot dispute Mr.

[4] Historically, marijuana has been used in a variety of ways. The original Declaration of Independence (July 4, 1776) was written on hemp as was Thomas Paine's *Common Sense*. Jack Herer, *The Emperor Wears No Clothes* 7 (1995). George Washington and Thomas Jefferson grew it, and Benjamin Franklin used it in an early papermill. Marty Bergoffen & Roger Lee Clark, *Hemp as an Alternative to Wood Fiber in Oregon,* 11 J. Envtl. L. & Litig. 119, 120 (1996).

Throughout the nineteenth century marijuana was used as an anticonvulsant, as an analgesic and in the treatment of rheumatism, epilepsy and tetanus. Lester Grinspoon, M.D., and James B. Bakalar, *Marihuana, the Forbidden Medicine* 5-6 (1993) (included in part in CP at 92-119). Marijuana was administered to Queen Victoria by her court physician. *Id.* at 4. In nineteenth century America marijuana was listed in the *United States Dispensatory* (1854), was generally available in drug stores, and was characterized in an early medical study as "a drug that has a special value in some morbid conditions and the intrinsic merit and safety of which entitles it to a place once held in therapeutics." Dr. J. B. Mattison, *Cannabis indica as an Anodyne and Hypnotic*, St. Louis Medical Surgical Journal 61, 266 (1891), quoted in Grinspoon & Bakalar, *supra* at 6.

However, marijuana was repressed by the federal government in 1937 through a stamp tax so burdensome both financially and procedurally that it virtually eliminated any legal medicinal, industrial or recreational use of marijuana. 26 U.S.C. 4741, *repealed by* Comprehensive Drug Abuse Prevention and Control Act of 1970, tit. III, 1101(b)(3)(A), 84 Stat. 1292. The purpose of the tax was prohibition although it was effectuated in the form of a revenue measure because of constitutional limits still enforced against federal lawmaking power. Grinspoon & Bakalar, *supra* at 8. The elimination of marijuana came from pressures exerted by newly created "Federal drug control agencies, cotton and timber interests, and chemical industries." Bergoffen & Clark, *supra* at 122 n.20. Marijuana was removed from the United States Pharmacopoeia and National Formulary in 1941.

Shortly after the Marijuana Tax Act was held unconstitutional in 1969, in a failed attempt to prosecute Dr. Timothy Leary for possession of untaxed marijuana (*Leary v. United States*, 395 U.S. 6, 89 S. Ct. 1532, 23 L. Ed. 2d 57 (1969) (marijuana tax unconstitutional as violative of the Fifth Amendment's guarantee against self-incrimination), Congress passed the Controlled Substances Act, placing marijuana in schedule I and directly criminalizing any use of it. Washington followed suit in 1971 and adopted an identical regime also placing marijuana in schedule I. Laws of 1971, 1st Ex. Sess., ch. 308 at 1794 (Uniform Controlled Substances Act).

Seeley's testimony about how its ingestion affects him, the tragic medical fact that he is terminally ill, nor the fact that Seeley's doctor states on the record it is in Seeley's interest to use marijuana for medical reasons.

. . . .

Necessary Means

Even assuming the interests of the public are sufficient to require such interference, the means [must] be reasonably necessary to accomplish the purpose. But the means employed here, total and absolute prohibition, are anything but that. Under our statute marijuana in leaf form is not even available through medical prescription, unlike PCP angel dust, cocaine, opium, and morphine. . . .

A recent study conducted amongst the members of the Washington State Medical Association found 80 percent of its doctors favored controlled availability of marijuana for medical purposes. Another recent study found that 44 percent of oncologists surveyed had already recommended the illegal use of marijuana to at least one patient and half would prescribe it to other patients if doing so was legal. Individuals anecdotally praise the successful use of medical marijuana for a variety of ailments. California and Arizona voters recently approved physician prescription of marijuana in their states. The New England Journal of Medicine, the premier authority in this country on medical developments, editorialized in January 1997 against prohibition. After cataloging the medical benefits, the journal's editor opined government authorities are "out of step with the public" and the medical community and urged the government "to rescind their prohibition of the medical use of marijuana for seriously ill patients and allow physicians to decide which patients to treat." The editorial concluded that depriving seriously ill patients medical marijuana is "inhumane."

. . . .

. . . I find our criminal prohibition on marijuana unduly oppressive in every sense of the word. Offensive, in the extreme, is the proposition that the government may restrict ingestion of a substance found by a licensed physician to be medically advisable to comfort a terminal patient. Such right is as fundamental as any. *Compare, e.g., Cruzan* (fundamental right to refuse life support by exercising personal control of medical treatment).

. . . .

I wonder how many minutes of Seeley's agony the Legislature and/or the majority of this court would endure before seeing the light. Words are insufficient to convey the needless suffering which the merciless State has imposed.

. . . .

NOTES AND QUESTIONS

1. Earlier cases have developed the special, protected relationship between patient and physician. This has been particularly true with reproductive rights (*see Roe v. Wade* and *Casey*, *supra* § 1.04[1]) and communicative aspects of care, such as informed consent (*see Canterbury v. Spence*,

supra § 3.03[1]; *Rust v. Sullivan*, *supra* § 3.04[1] and *People v. Privitera supra* § 3.04[1]). Shouldn't it be equally true with prescribing medication, at least those — such as marijuana — which are not demonstrably harmful and *do* have recognized benefits?

2. Are you surprised to learn marijuana is banned as a matter of administrative law? Shouldn't the decision be subject to judicial review under conventional principles of administrative procedure? *See* 5 U.S.C. § 701 et seq. If so, would the result in *Seeley* be different? Are you helped in this by the actions of Administrative Law Judge Young in 1988? *See District of Columbia in Alliance for Cannabis Therapeutic v. Drug Enforcement Administration*, 15 F.3d 1131 (D.C. Cir. 1994).

3. What exactly is Mr. Seeley's equal protection argument? Who are the class members? Those who are ill and need marijuana, versus those who are *not* ill? Those who will use marijuana carefully versus those who will not?

4. Note the difference, in equal protection terms between "over-inclusive" arguments and those which argue regulations are "under-inclusive", that is, leave out even more dangerous substances. Why does the latter argument fail, when it seems so clearly accurate?

5. Note also that the parties did not make a due process argument. Why not? Would it have been procedural or substantive? What would it have added to the equal protection argument? Are you persuaded by the dissent of Justice Sanders, relying on *Casey* and *Roe v. Wade* and the privacy cases which protect people in their own homes? Is the dissent more effective in relying upon *Cruzan*?

6. What of the medical testimony. If it is in equipoise who should win? And does it matter that Mr. Seeley only wanted to move marijuana from schedule I to schedule II, not to de-criminalize it for public use?

7. Note that the dissent musters its own medical evidence. Is it different in kind or quality from that relied upon by the majority? More persuasive? And what of the dissent's emphasis upon Mr. Seeley's own perception of his pain and response to marijuana? Is it relevant?

8. If Mr. Seeley had won, what would the relief be? The Court concedes that federal legislation would override state authority to prescribe marijuana. Should it?

9. Other cases have dealt with the right of people in their own homes to consume marijuana, most resulting in a negative finding. For a recent, thorough analysis with extensive dissenting views, see *Hawaii v. Mallan*, 86 Haw. 440, 950 P.2d 178 (Sup. Ct. 1998).

CONANT v. MCCAFFREY*

172 F.R.D. 681 (N.D. Cal. 1997)

Fern M. **Smith**, District Judge.

. . . .

In November 1996, the citizens of California passed an initiative known as Proposition 215 or the Compassionate Use Act. The initiative took legal effect at 12:01 a.m. on Wednesday, November 6, 1996. It provides, in pertinent part, that

> [S]eriously ill Californians have the right to obtain and use marijuana for medical purposes where that medical use is deemed appropriate and has been recommended by a physician who has determined that the person's health would benefit from the use of marijuana in the treatment of cancer, anorexia, AIDS, chronic pain, spasticity, glaucoma, arthritis, migraine, or any other illness for which marijuana provides relief.

Cal. Health & Safety Code § 11362.5(a) (1997).

Under the Act, neither patients nor physicians may be punished or denied any right or privilege for conduct relating to medical use of marijuana.

. . . .

According to the complaint, prior to passage of the Compassionate Use Act, the federal government had neither punished nor threatened physicians in any way for recommending the medical use of marijuana to seriously ill patients. As the election approached, however, and polls indicated that Proposition 215 would likely pass, defendant Barry McCaffrey, the director of the United States Office of Drug Control Policy, first suggested that the federal government would take action against physicians for conduct protected by the Act. Soon after Proposition 215's enactment, the government confirmed that it would prosecute physicians, revoke their prescription licenses, and deny them participation in Medicare and Medicaid for recommending medical marijuana. In the months since the election, federal officials have made at least fifteen separate statements verifying the government's intent.

On February 14, 1997, plaintiffs — ten physicians, five patients, and two nonprofit organizations — filed this case, contending that the government's medical marijuana policy infringes on the First Amendment rights of both physicians and patients. Plaintiffs proffered declarations indicating that some physicians are sufficiently worried by the government's threats that they are afraid to offer patients their best medical judgment regarding the use of marijuana to treat disease, and have begun to censor their communications with patients. Plaintiffs claim that physicians' self-censoring threatens the integrity of the physician-patient relationship and prevents proper patient care. Equally important, plaintiffs contend that the "chilling" of physician-patient communication violates the First Amendment rights of physicians and patients alike. . . .

* Some of the citation material has been omitted from this case.

. . . .

Subsequent to the filing of plaintiffs' law suit, the Department of Health and Human Services ("DHHS") and the Department of Justice ("DOJ") issued a joint letter to "clarify" the scope of the Administration Response and eliminate misperceptions that had developed regarding the federal government's interpretation of federal drug laws ("Clarification to Administration Response" or "Clarification"). The Clarification states that federal law does not prohibit physicians from discussing the risks and benefits of marijuana, and that the federal government did not intend to establish a "gag rule" to prevent physicians from communicating their professional judgments regarding the risks and benefits of any course of treatment. The Clarification also states, however, that "[p]hysicians may not intentionally provide their patients with oral or written statements in order to enable them to obtain controlled substances in violation of federal law. Physicians who do so risk revocation of their DEA prescription authority, criminal prosecution, and exclusion from participation in the Medicare and Medicaid programs."

. . . .

2. Analysis of Plaintiffs, Claims

. . . .

b. Plaintiffs, Hardships

Because they fear prosecution or administrative sanction, plaintiff physicians contend they have censored their medical advice to patients, refusing to provide guidance regarding the risks and benefits of medical marijuana. Despite defendants' alleged clarification of federal policy, the physicians remain unsure as to whether bona fide discussions regarding medical marijuana will result in federal punishment. Their fears are corroborated by the testimony of Robert Mastroianni, M.D. ("Dr. Mastroianni"). Dr. Mastroianni has been interrogated by DEA agents who questioned his medical education and training, confronted a pharmacist regarding prescriptions he has dispensed, and informed him that it was illegal to "recommend or prescribe" marijuana.

. . . .

c. First Amendment

Plaintiffs assert, and defendants appear to concede, that the government's policy implicates First Amendment rights. In seeking to restrict what doctors may legally say to their patients concerning the use of medical marijuana, the government seeks to regulate physician-patient dialogue based on the content of that dialogue. "It is axiomatic that the government may not regulate speech based on its substantive content or the message it conveys." *Rosenberger v. Rector & Visitors of Univ. of Va.*, 515 U.S. 819 (1995). This proposition is even stronger in situations in which the government targets particular views of the speaker on a given subject. This case presents just that situation. Finding itself in disagreement with plaintiff physicians' views about the efficacy of medical marijuana, the government has announced a policy which significantly inhibits communication of those views.

The government concedes that it may not prohibit "discussion" of marijuana, but the government attempts to justify its policy of sanctioning physicians on the unremarkable and undisputed proposition that the government can regulate distribution and possession of drugs. The government's statutory authority to regulate that conduct, however, does not allow the government to quash protected speech about it. *See NAACP v. Alabama*, 377 U.S. 288, 307, 84 S.Ct. 1302, 1314, 12 L.Ed.2d 325 (1964) ("[A] governmental purpose to control or prevent activities constitutionally subject to state regulation may not be achieved by means which sweep unnecessarily broadly and thereby invade the area of protected freedoms."). The government's fear that frank dialogue between physicians and patients about medical marijuana might foster drug use does not justify infringing First Amendment freedoms.[1]

Plaintiffs argue that the First Amendment protects the sanctity of physician-patient dialogue, and, in fact, that physician-patient communications receive heightened First Amendment protection. Although the Supreme Court has never held that the physician-patient relationship, as such, receives special First Amendment protection, its case law assumes, without so deciding, that the relationship is a protected one. *See. e.g., Planned Parenthood of Southeastern Pa. v. Casey*, *City of Akron v. Akron Ctr. for Reprod. Health, Inc.*, (discussing relationship of trust between patient and doctor). Thus, the Court has discussed the physician's right to exercise her best medical judgment, *see Casey,* and the patient's right to rely on the medical advice of her physician.

. . . Although the practice of medicine is subject to state regulation, it does not automatically follow that speech that would otherwise be protected if between two ordinary citizens somehow loses that protection when it occurs in the context of the physician-patient relationship. At the very least, courts confronted with the issue of regulation of physician speech have presupposed that speech between physicians and their patients is protected by the First Amendment. Moreover, sound policy reasons justify special protection of open and honest communication between those groups.

. . . .

For the foregoing reasons, the broad reaches of the government's policy implicate speech that is protected by the First Amendment. Having so found, the Court must now determine whether plaintiffs have raised serious questions as to whether the government's policy violates the First Amendment and whether the balance of hardships tips in favor of plaintiffs.

Plaintiffs argue that the ambiguities in the government's policy render that policy facially invalid and therefore justify entry of a preliminary injunction. Plaintiffs seem to argue both that the government's policy is void for vagueness and that it is overbroad. The Supreme Court views the doctrines of vagueness and overbreadth as related and similar doctrines. Because plaintiffs have met their burden of showing that there are serious questions as to

[1] Moreover, the government's fears in this case are exaggerated and without evidentiary support. It is unreasonable to believe that use of medical marijuana by this discrete population for this limited purpose will create a significant drug problem.

whether the government's policy is unconstitutionally vague, no analysis of the overbreadth doctrine need be done at this time.

. . . .

Plaintiffs argue that the government's policy sweeps too broadly, leaving physicians confused as to the boundaries of the conduct it prohibits. This vagueness allegedly has led physicians to censor otherwise protected speech in order to ensure that they do not run afoul of conduct for which the government has threatened criminal prosecution and/or administrative sanctions. As discussed above, the government has issued numerous statements regarding its position on medical marijuana since Proposition 215 was passed. Several of those statements indicate that the government means to take action against physicians who simply recommend marijuana to treat disease. In other statements, the government has conceded that physicians may discuss the risks and alleged benefits of medical marijuana, in the context of a bona fide physician-patient relationship, but has stated that they may not recommend marijuana "in order to enable [patients] to obtain controlled substances in violation of federal law." The government's statements range from suggesting that the government will use informers and surveillance to detect physicians who recommend medical marijuana to assuring that simple advice about the risks and benefits of marijuana for a specific patient will not subject physicians to government sanctions.

. . . .

. . . [W]hen faced with the fickle iterations of the government's policy, physicians have been forced to suppress speech that would not rise to the level of that which the government constitutionally may prohibit. Plaintiffs therefore have raised at least serious questions as to whether the government's policy is unconstitutionally vague.

. . . .

Because plaintiffs have alleged deprivation of a First Amendment right, irreparable injury is presumed: "The loss of First Amendment freedoms, for even minimal periods of time, unquestionably constitutes irreparable injury." . . .

. . . .

Because plaintiffs have shown both that there are serious questions as to the constitutionality of the government's policy and that the balance of hardships tips sharply in their favor, the Court may properly enter a preliminary injunction enjoining the government's policy, but only to the extent that such policy is likely unconstitutional. . . .

The First Amendment does not protect speech that is itself criminal because too intertwined with illegal activity. . . .

In addition to threatening criminal prosecution, defendants have threatened to take administrative action under the Controlled Substances Act and the Medicare statute against physicians for recommending medical marijuana. . . .

. . . .

Plaintiffs contend that the Controlled Substances Act ("CSA") gives the DEA authority to revoke a physician's license only if that physician commits an illegal act related to the distribution, dispensing, or manufacture of controlled substances. Defendants counter that the CSA provides broad authority to the DEA to revoke a physician's license for any act that violates the public interest. Defendants argue that a physician who recommends marijuana violates the public interest, making such a recommendation grounds for revocation of that physician's license.

. . . .

In the abstract, the term "public interest" is broad and may allow the DEA wide latitude to revoke licenses for "recommending" marijuana; however, in the context of sections 823 and 824, the term public interest may be reasonably interpreted to encompass only actual violations of state and federal drug law. The Court has found no case, and defendants submit none, in which a court has concluded that sections 823 and 824 empower the DEA to revoke a physician's license for underlying conduct that did not violate federal, state, or local law, or state licensing guidelines. For these reasons, plaintiffs have raised serious questions as to whether the CSA can be interpreted in a manner that would allow the DEA to revoke a physician's license for merely recommending marijuana. As discussed above, see supra part II.C, the balance of harms weighs in favor of plaintiffs, making entry of a preliminary injunction appropriate.

. . . .

2. Medicare Statute

Section 1320(a)-7 of Title 42 provides that individuals can be excluded from participation in Medicare and state health care programs under certain circumstances. The circumstances pertinent to this analysis include: (1) conviction for Medicare-related crimes, (2) conviction of a criminal offense relating to neglect or abuse of patients, (3) conviction relating to fraud, (4) conviction relating to obstruction of an investigation of Medicare fraud, (5) conviction relating to the manufacture, distribution, prescription, or dispensing of a controlled substance, and (6) claims for fraud or excess charges. Nothing in the text of this section supports defendants' argument that the DEA has the authority to exclude physicians from participation in Medicare or Medicaid programs for merely recommending marijuana to their patients without criminal intent.

. . . .

For the foregoing reasons, the Court PRELIMINARILY ENJOINS defendants, their agents, employees, assigns, and all persons acting in concert or participating with them, from threatening or prosecuting physicians, revoking their licenses, or excluding them from Medicare/Medicaid participation based upon conduct relating to medical marijuana that does not rise to the level of a criminal offense. . . .

. . . .

NOTES AND QUESTIONS

1. The *Conant* case addresses the issues avoided in *Seeley*: may a state override federal opposition to prescribing marijuana? May it be prescribed while illegal to possess or produce? Is there a right in the physicians apart from the patient?

2. Note the sanctions the DEA posed against physicians: prosecution, revocation of prescription licenses, exclusion from Medicaid and medical reimbursement. These are very severe penalties. Why not simply prosecute the user/buyer/patient, as previously? In *United States v. Cannabis Cultivators Club*, 5 F. Supp. 2d 1086 (N.D. Cal. 1998), federal injunctions were granted against marijuana cooperatives operating under Proposition 215. The court rejected the constitutional argument accepted in *Conant* but reserved a possible defense of medical necessity.

3. The Court finds the government policies are unclear, hence, the case is ripe for review. But aren't the defendants correct, they are being *perfectly* clear — they will prosecute physicians who prescribe marijuana? If so, do the plaintiffs lose their constitutional claim?

4. If this case is ultimately about freedom of speech, does it really matter since — after all — the government may continue to withhold marijuana despite a physician's prescription? But, may the government prosecute a person (say a physician) for inciting an illegal act (say, making a bomb or buying marijuana)? Isn't content regulation, to that extent, permitted under the First Amendment?

5. The Court does not reach the overbreath argument, finding the Government's policy void for vagueness. What is the difference between the two concepts? Isn't this really a case of overbreadth?

6. What may the government do? What may it prevent *physicians* from doing? Can you tell from the content of the injunction issued by the Court? Would your answer be different if the California voters not only authorized discussion of marijuana but prescription and sale?

7. California and Arizona approved state ballot initiatives approving marijuana for medicinal uses in 1996. Oregon and Washington were to vote on similar initiatives in 1998. On September 15, 1998 the House of Representatives in Congress passed a resolution, 310-93, opposing such use.

8. For an excellent article, see Erik R. Neusch, *Medical Marijuana's Fate in the Aftermath of the Supreme Court's New Commerce Clause Jurisprudence*, 72 U. Colo. L. Rev. 201 (2001).

PROBLEM 4–13 — Uncle Sam's Pot Farm

According to a 1997 article in *George* magazine, *Uncle Sam's Pot Farm,* the National Institute on Drug Abuse, a unit within NIH, has conducted a Marijuana Project since 1970. The project provides marijuana to pharmacies, which provide it to thirteen users, of which eight remained active in 1997. The marijuana is grown at the University of Mississippi, on a seven acre plot.

The Food and Drug Administration grants "compassionate investigational new drug" waiver so that the eight may receive the drug for treatment. The U.S. Public Health Service closed the program to new entrants in 1992, due to a flood of AIDS applicants.

The research from the project suggests marijuana may be helpful in treating epilepsy, multiple sclerosis, migraines, depression, menstrual cramping, glaucoma and nausea from chemotherapy and AIDS treatments. The budget is $300,00 per year; some 500 to 1000 pounds is produced annually.

You represent a grandmother who has glaucoma, multiple sclerosis and AIDS (acquired through a blood transfusion). Does this information help you in seeking marijuana as a means of treatment, as recommended by her primary care physician (but not her HMO)? What will you do?

Medical treatment evolves with time, as knowledge and mores change. What was once ineffective or unethical may become permissible, indeed orthodox. How this is to be done is a question posed with respect to marijuana as a medical treatment.

U.S. v. OAKLAND CANNABIS BUYERS' COOPERATIVE

532 U.S. 483 (2001)

Justice **Thomas** delivered the opinion of the Court.

The Controlled Substances Act, 84 Stat. 1242, 21 U.S.C. § 801 *et seq.*, prohibits the manufacture and distribution of various drugs, including marijuana. In this case, we must decide whether there is a medical necessity exception to these prohibitions. We hold that there is not.

I

In November 1996, California voters enacted an initiative measure entitled the Compassionate Use Act of 1996. Attempting "to ensure that seriously ill Californians have the right to obtain and use marijuana for medical purposes," the statute creates an exception to California laws prohibiting the possession and cultivation of marijuana. These prohibitions no longer apply to a patient or his primary caregiver who possesses or cultivates marijuana for the patient's medical purposes upon the recommendation or approval of a physician. In the wake of this voter initiative, several groups organized "medical cannabis dispensaries" to meet the needs of qualified patients. Respondent Oakland Cannabis Buyers' Cooperative is one of these groups.

The Cooperative is a not-for-profit organization that operates in downtown Oakland. A physician serves as medical director, and registered nurses staff the Cooperative during business hours. To become a member, a patient must provide a written statement from a treating physician assenting to marijuana therapy and must submit to a screening interview. If accepted as a member, the patient receives an identification card entitling him to obtain marijuana from the Cooperative.

In January 1998, the United States sued the Cooperative and its executive director, respondent Jeffrey Jones (together, the Cooperative), in the United

States District Court for the Northern District of California. Seeking to enjoin the Cooperative from distributing and manufacturing marijuana, the United States argued that, whether or not the Cooperative's activities are legal under California law, they violate federal law. Specifically, the Government argued that the Cooperative violated the Controlled Substances Act's prohibitions on distributing, manufacturing, and possessing with the intent to distribute or manufacture a controlled substance. Concluding that the Government had established a probability of success on the merits, the District Court granted a preliminary injunction.

The Cooperative did not appeal the injunction but instead openly violated it by distributing marijuana to numerous persons. To terminate these violations, the Government initiated contempt proceedings. In defense, the Cooperative contended that any distributions were medically necessary. Marijuana is the only drug, according to the Cooperative, that can alleviate the severe pain and other debilitating symptoms of the Cooperative's patients.

II

The Controlled Substances Act provides that, "except as authorized by this subchapter, it shall be unlawful for any person knowingly or intentionally . . . to manufacture, distribute, or dispense, or possess with intent to manufacture, distribute, or dispense, a controlled substance." The subchapter, in turn, establishes exceptions. For marijuana (and other drugs that have been classified as "schedule I" controlled substances), there is but one express exception, and it is available only for Government-approved research projects, § 823(f). Not conducting such a project, the Cooperative cannot, and indeed does not, claim this statutory exemption.

The Cooperative contends, however, that notwithstanding the apparently absolute language of § 841(a), the statute is subject to additional, implied exceptions, one of which is medical necessity. According to the Cooperative, because necessity was a defense at common law, medical necessity should be read into the Controlled Substances Act. We disagree.

As an initial matter, we note that it is an open question whether federal courts ever have authority to recognize a necessity defense not provided by statute. A necessity defense "traditionally covered the situation where physical forces beyond the actor's control rendered illegal conduct the lesser of two evils."

We need not decide, however, whether necessity can ever be a defense when the federal statute does not expressly provide for it. In this case, to resolve the question presented, we need only recognize that a medical necessity exception for marijuana is at odds with the terms of the Controlled Substances Act. The statute, to be sure, does not explicitly abrogate the defense. But its provisions leave no doubt that the defense is unavailable.

Under any conception of legal necessity, one principle is clear: The defense cannot succeed when the legislature itself has made a "determination of values." In the case of the Controlled Substances Act, the statute reflects a determination that marijuana has no medical benefits worthy of an exception (outside the confines of a Government-approved research project). Whereas some other drugs can be dispensed and prescribed for medical use, the same is not true for marijuana. Indeed, for purposes of the Controlled Substances Act, marijuana has "no currently accepted medical use" at all. § 811.

The structure of the Act supports this conclusion. The statute divides drugs into five schedules, depending in part on whether the particular drug has a currently accepted medical use. The Act then imposes restrictions on the manufacture and distribution of the substance according to the schedule in which it has been placed. Schedule I is the most restrictive schedule. The Attorney General can include a drug in schedule I only if the drug "has no currently accepted medical use in treatment in the United States," "has a high potential for abuse," and has "a lack of accepted safety for use . . . under medical supervision." §§ 812(b)(1)(A)–(C). Under the statute, the Attorney General could not put marijuana into schedule I if marijuana had any accepted medical use.

The Cooperative points out, however, that the Attorney General did not place marijuana into schedule I. Congress put it there, and Congress was not required to find that a drug lacks an accepted medical use before including the drug in schedule I. We are not persuaded that this distinction has any significance to our inquiry. Under the Cooperative's logic, drugs that Congress places in schedule I could be distributed when medically necessary whereas drugs that the Attorney General places in schedule I could not. Nothing in the statute, however, suggests that there are two tiers of schedule I narcotics, with drugs in one tier more readily available than drugs in the other.

The Cooperative further argues that use of schedule I drugs generally — whether placed in schedule I by Congress or the Attorney General — can be medically necessary, notwithstanding that they have "no currently accepted medical use." According to the Cooperative, a drug may not yet have achieved general acceptance as a medical treatment but may nonetheless have medical benefits to a particular patient or class of patients. We decline to parse the statute in this manner. It is clear from the text of the Act that Congress has made a determination that marijuana has no medical benefits worthy of an exception. The statute expressly contemplates that many drugs "have a useful and legitimate medical purpose and are necessary to maintain the health and general welfare of the American people," § 801(1), but it includes no exception at all for any medical use of marijuana. Unwilling to view this omission as an accident, and unable in any event to override a legislative determination manifest in a statute, we reject the Cooperative's argument.

Finally, the Cooperative contends that we should construe the Controlled Substances Act to include a medical necessity defense in order to avoid what it considers to be difficult constitutional questions. In particular, the Cooperative asserts that, shorn of a medical necessity defense, the statute exceeds Congress' Commerce Clause powers, violates the substantive due process rights of patients, and offends the fundamental liberties of the people under the Fifth, Ninth, and Tenth Amendments. As the Cooperative acknowledges, however, the canon of constitutional avoidance has no application in the absence of statutory ambiguity. Because we have no doubt that the Controlled Substances Act cannot bear a medical necessity defense to distributions of marijuana, we do not find guidance in this avoidance principle. Nor do we consider the underlying constitutional issues today. Because the Court of Appeals did not address these claims, we decline to do so in the first instance.

For these reasons, we hold that medical necessity is not a defense to manufacturing and distributing marijuana.[7] The Court of Appeals erred when it held that medical necessity is a "legally cognizable defense." It further erred when it instructed the District Court on remand to consider "the criteria for a medical necessity exemption, and, should it modify the injunction, to set forth those criteria in the modification order."

III

C

In this case, the Court of Appeals erred by considering relevant the evidence that some people have "serious medical conditions for whom the use of cannabis is necessary in order to treat or alleviate those conditions or their symptoms," that these people "will suffer serious harm if they are denied cannabis," and that "there is no legal alternative to cannabis for the effective treatment of their medical conditions." As explained above, in the Controlled Substances Act, the balance already has been struck against a medical necessity exception. Because the statutory prohibitions cover even those who have what could be termed a medical necessity, the Act precludes consideration of this evidence. It was thus error for the Court of Appeals to instruct the District Court on remand to consider "the criteria for a medical necessity exemption, and, should it modify the injunction, to set forth those criteria in the modification order."

. . . .

The judgment of the Court of Appeals is reversed, and the case is remanded for further proceedings consistent with this opinion.

It is so ordered.

Justice **Breyer** took no part in the consideration or decision of this case.

Justice **Stevens**, with whom Justice **Souter** and Justice Ginsburg join, concurring in the judgment.

---

[7] Lest there be any confusion, we clarify that nothing in our analysis, or the statute, suggests that a distinction should be drawn between the prohibitions on manufacturing and distributing and the other prohibitions in the Controlled Substances Act. Furthermore, the very point of our holding is that there is no medical necessity exception to the prohibitions at issue, even when the patient is "seriously ill" and lacks alternative avenues for relief. Indeed, it is the Cooperative's argument that its patients are "seriously ill," see, *e.g.*, Brief for Respondents 11, 13, 17, and lacking "alternatives," see, *e.g.*, id. at 13. We reject the argument that these factors warrant a medical necessity exception. If we did not, we would be affirming instead of reversing the Court of Appeals.

Finally, we share Justice Stevens' concern for "showing respect for the sovereign States that comprise our Federal Union." *Post*, at 3 (opinion concurring in judgment). However, we are "construing an Act of Congress, not drafting it." Because federal courts interpret, rather than author, the federal criminal code, we are not at liberty to rewrite it. Nor are we passing today on a constitutional question, such as whether the Controlled Substances Act exceeds Congress' power under the Commerce Clause.

Lest the Court's narrow holding be lost in its broad dicta, let me restate it here: "We hold that medical necessity is not a defense to *manufacturing* and *distributing* marijuana."

Accordingly, in the lower courts as well as here, respondents have raised the medical necessity defense as a justification for distributing marijuana to cooperative members, and it was in that context that the Ninth Circuit determined that respondents had "a legally cognizable defense." The Court is surely correct to reverse that determination. Congress' classification of marijuana as a schedule I controlled substance — that is, one that cannot be distributed outside of approved research projects, — makes it clear that "the Controlled Substances Act cannot bear a medical necessity defense to *distributions* of marijuana."

Apart from its limited holding, the Court takes two unwarranted and unfortunate excursions that prevent me from joining its opinion. First, the Court reaches beyond its holding, and beyond the facts of the case, by suggesting that the defense of necessity is unavailable for anyone under the Controlled Substances Act. Because necessity was raised in this case as a defense to distribution, the Court need not venture an opinion on whether the defense is available to anyone other than distributors. Most notably, whether the defense might be available to a seriously ill patient for whom there is no alternative means of avoiding starvation or extraordinary suffering is a difficult issue that is not presented here.

Second, the Court gratuitously casts doubt on "whether necessity can ever be a defense" to *any* federal statute that does not explicitly provide for it, calling such a defense into question by a misleading reference to its existence as an "open question." By contrast, our precedent has expressed no doubt about the viability of the common-law defense, even in the context of federal criminal statutes that do not provide for it in so many words. The Court's opinion on this point is pure dictum.

The overbroad language of the Court's opinion is especially unfortunate given the importance of showing respect for the sovereign States that comprise our Federal Union. That respect imposes a duty on federal courts, whenever possible, to avoid or minimize conflict between federal and state law, particularly in situations in which the citizens of a State have chosen to "serve as a laboratory" in the trial of "novel social and economic experiments without risk to the rest of the country." In my view, this is such a case. By passing Proposition 215, California voters have decided that seriously ill patients and their primary caregivers should be exempt from prosecution under state laws for cultivating and possessing marijuana if the patient's physician recommends using the drug for treatment. This case does not call upon the Court to deprive *all* such patients of the benefit of the necessity defense to federal prosecution, when the case itself does not involve *any* such patients.

An additional point deserves emphasis. This case does not require us to rule on the scope of the District Court's discretion to enjoin, or to refuse to enjoin, the possession of marijuana or other potential violations of the Controlled Substances Act by a seriously ill patient for whom the drug may be a necessity. Whether it would be an abuse of discretion for the District Court to refuse to enjoin those sorts of violations, and whether the District Court may consider the availability of the necessity defense for that sort of violator, are questions that should be decided on the authority of cases such as *Hecht Co. v. Bowles* and *Weinberger v. Romero-Barcelo*, and that properly should be left "open" by this case.

I join the Court's judgment of reversal because I agree that a distributor of marijuana does not have a medical necessity defense under the Controlled Substances Act. I do not, however, join the dicta in the Court's opinion.

NOTES AND QUESTIONS

1. The *Oakland Cannabis* case is as close as the Supreme Court has come to dealing with the "right to treatment" if patients might benefit from using marijuana. As Justice Stevens carefully notes, however, the issue narrowly confined relates only to *manufacturing* and *distributing* marijuana. Suppose it were *consuming*? Prescribing? What result? Is the *Raich* case, *infra*, any help?
2. The Court finds no "necessity" defense in the Congressional language or history underlying the Controlled Substances Act. Should there be one? If so, how would it be met? What would its limits be? And what of Justice Stevens' observation concerning the common law defense?
3. What about the constitutional principles reflected in such cases as *Casey, Cruzan,* and *Quinlan*? Is there a right to treatment? Or a right to be free from arbitrary *interference* with treatment? A right to association or privacy in consulting physicians? How would this bear on the medical use of marijuana? And how, as well, on physician-assisted death, the subject of *Gonzales v. Oregon,* § 4.05[2] *infra* ?
4. Also, as the next case illustrates, a fair question may be raised as to whether Congress, through the Controlled Substances Act, may preempt state legislation, authorizing medical uses of marijuana or physician-assisted death. What are the outer limits of the interstate commerce clause? *See Lopez v. United States*, 514 U.S. 549 (1995).

GONZALES v. RAICH

125 S. Ct. 2195 (2005)

Justice **Stevens** delivered the opinion of the Court.

California is one of at least nine States that authorize the use of marijuana for medicinal purposes.[1] The question presented in this case is whether the

[1] See Alaska Stat. §§ 11.71.090, 17.37.010–17.37.080 (Lexis 2004); Colo. Const., Art. XVIII, § 14, Colo. Rev. Stat. § 18-18-406.3 (Lexis 2004); Haw. Rev. Stat. §§ 329-121 to 329-128 (2004 Cum. Supp.); Me. Rev. Stat. Ann., Tit. 22, § 2383-B(5) (West 2004); *Nev.* Const., Art. 4, § 38, Nev. Rev. Stat. §§ 453A.010–453A.810 (2003); Ore. Rev. Stat. §§ 475.300–475.346 (2003); *Vt.* Stat. Ann., Tit. 18, §§ 4472–4474d (Supp. 2004); Wash. Rev. Code §§ 69.51.010–69.51.080 (2004); see also *Ariz.* Rev. Stat. Ann. § 13-3412.01 (West Supp. 2004) (voter initiative permitting physicians to prescribe Schedule I substances for medical purposes that was purportedly repealed in 1997, but the repeal was rejected by voters in 1998). In November 2004, Montana voters approved Initiative 148, adding to the number of States authorizing the use of marijuana for medical purposes.

power vested in Congress by Article I, § 8, of the Constitution "to make all Laws which shall be necessary and proper for carrying into Execution" its authority to "regulate Commerce with foreign Nations, and among the several States" includes the power to prohibit the local cultivation and use of marijuana in compliance with California law.

I

California has been a pioneer in the regulation of marijuana. In 1913, California was one of the first States to prohibit the sale and possession of marijuana, and at the end of the century, California became the first State to authorize limited use of the drug for medicinal purposes. In 1996, California voters passed Proposition 215, now codified as the Compassionate Use Act of 1996. The proposition was designed to ensure that "seriously ill" residents of the State have access to marijuana for medical purposes, and to encourage Federal and State Governments to take steps towards ensuring the safe and affordable distribution of the drug to patients in need. The Act creates an exemption from criminal prosecution for physicians, as well as for patients and primary caregivers who possess or cultivate marijuana for medicinal purposes with the recommendation or approval of a physician. A "primary caregiver" is a person who has consistently assumed responsibility for the housing, health, or safety of the patient.

Respondents Angel Raich and Diane Monson are California residents who suffer from a variety of serious medical conditions and have sought to avail themselves of medical marijuana pursuant to the terms of the Compassionate Use Act. They are being treated by licensed, board-certified family practitioners, who have concluded, after prescribing a host of conventional medicines to treat respondents' conditions and to alleviate their associated symptoms, that marijuana is the only drug available that provides effective treatment. Both women have been using marijuana as a medication for several years pursuant to their doctors' recommendation, and both rely heavily on cannabis to function on a daily basis. Indeed, Raich's physician believes that forgoing cannabis treatments would certainly cause Raich excruciating pain and could very well prove fatal.

Respondent Monson cultivates her own marijuana, and ingests the drug in a variety of ways including smoking and using a vaporizer. Respondent Raich, by contrast, is unable to cultivate her own, and thus relies on two caregivers, litigating as "John Does," to provide her with locally grown marijuana at no charge. These caregivers also process the cannabis into hashish or keif, and Raich herself processes some of the marijuana into oils, balms, and foods for consumption.

On August 15, 2002, county deputy sheriffs and agents from the federal Drug Enforcement Administration (DEA) came to Monson's home. After a thorough investigation, the county officials concluded that her use of marijuana was entirely lawful as a matter of California law. Nevertheless, after a 3-hour standoff, the federal agents seized and destroyed all six of her cannabis plants.

Respondents thereafter brought this action against the Attorney General of the United States and the head of the DEA seeking injunctive and declaratory relief prohibiting the enforcement of the federal Controlled Substances Act (CSA), 84 Stat. 1242, 21 U.S.C. § 801 et seq., to the extent it prevents them from possessing, obtaining, or manufacturing cannabis for their personal medical use. In their complaint and supporting affidavits, Raich and Monson described the severity of their afflictions, their repeatedly futile attempts to obtain relief with conventional medications, and the opinions of their doctors concerning their need to use marijuana. Respondents claimed that enforcing the CSA against them would violate the Commerce Clause, the Due Process Clause of the Fifth Amendment, the Ninth and Tenth Amendments of the Constitution, and the doctrine of medical necessity.

II

Shortly after taking office in 1969, President Nixon declared a national "war on drugs." As the first campaign of that war, Congress set out to enact legislation that would consolidate various drug laws on the books into a comprehensive statute, provide meaningful regulation over legitimate sources of drugs to prevent diversion into illegal channels, and strengthen law enforcement tools against the traffic in illicit drugs. That effort culminated in the passage of the Comprehensive Drug Abuse Prevention and Control Act of 1970, 84 Stat. 1236.

Marijuana itself was not significantly regulated by the Federal Government until 1937 when accounts of marijuana's addictive qualities and physiological effects, paired with dissatisfaction with enforcement efforts at state and local levels, prompted Congress to pass the Marihuana Tax Act, Pub. L. 75-238, 50 Stat. 551 (repealed 1970). Like the Harrison Act, the Marihuana Tax Act did not outlaw the possession or sale of marijuana outright. Rather, it imposed registration and reporting requirements for all individuals importing, producing, selling, or dealing in marijuana, and required the payment of annual taxes in addition to transfer taxes whenever the drug changed hands. Moreover, doctors wishing to prescribe marijuana for medical purposes were required to comply with rather burdensome administrative requirements. Noncompliance exposed traffickers to severe federal penalties, whereas compliance would often subject them to prosecution under state law. Thus, while the Marihuana Tax Act did not declare the drug illegal *per se*, the onerous administrative requirements, the prohibitively expensive taxes, and the risks attendant on compliance practically curtailed the marijuana trade.

Then in 1970, after declaration of the national "war on drugs," federal drug policy underwent a significant transformation. A number of noteworthy events precipitated this policy shift. First, in *Leary v. United States,* 395 U.S. 6 (1969), this Court held certain provisions of the Marihuana Tax Act and other narcotics legislation unconstitutional. Second, at the end of his term, President Johnson fundamentally reorganized the federal drug control agencies. The Bureau of Narcotics, then housed in the Department of Treasury, merged with the Bureau of Drug Abuse Control, then housed in the Department of Health, Education, and Welfare (HEW), to create the Bureau of Narcotics and Dangerous Drugs, currently housed in the Department of Justice. Finally, prompted by a perceived need to consolidate the growing number of piecemeal drug laws and to enhance federal drug enforcement powers, Congress enacted the Comprehensive Drug Abuse Prevention and Control Act.

Title II of that Act, the CSA, repealed most of the earlier anti-drug laws in favor of a comprehensive regime to combat the international and interstate traffic in illicit drugs. The main objectives of the CSA were to conquer drug abuse and to control the legitimate and illegitimate traffic in controlled substances. Congress was particularly concerned with the need to prevent the diversion of drugs from legitimate to illicit channels.

In enacting the CSA, Congress classified marijuana as a Schedule I drug. 21 U.S.C. § 812(c). This preliminary classification was based, in part, on the recommendation of the Assistant Secretary of HEW "that marihuana be retained within schedule I at least until the completion of certain studies now underway." Schedule I drugs are categorized as such because of their high potential for abuse, lack of any accepted medical use, and absence of any accepted safety for use in medically supervised treatment. § 812(b)(1). These three factors, in varying gradations, are also used to categorize drugs in the other four schedules.

The CSA provides for the periodic updating of schedules and delegates authority to the Attorney General, after consultation with the Secretary of Health and Human Services, to add, remove, or transfer substances to, from, or between schedules. § 811. Despite considerable efforts to reschedule marijuana, it remains a Schedule I drug.[23]

III

Respondents in this case do not dispute that passage of the CSA, as part of the Comprehensive Drug Abuse Prevention and Control Act, was well within Congress' commerce power. Nor do they contend that any provision or section of the CSA amounts to an unconstitutional exercise of congressional authority. Rather, respondents' challenge is actually quite limited; they argue that the CSA's categorical prohibition of the manufacture and possession of marijuana as applied to the intrastate manufacture and possession of marijuana for medical purposes pursuant to California law exceeds Congress' authority under the Commerce Clause.

Our case law firmly establishes Congress' power to regulate purely local activities that are part of an economic "class of activities" that have a substantial effect on interstate commerce. See, *e.g*, *Perez v. United States,* 402

---

[23] Starting in 1972, the National Organization for the Reform of Marijuana Laws (NORML) began its campaign to reclassify marijuana. Grinspoon & Bakalar, [*Marihuana, the Forbidden Medicine*] 13–17 (1993). After some fleeting success in 1988 when an Administrative Law Judge (ALJ) declared that the DEA would be acting in an "unreasonable, arbitrary, and capricious" manner if it continued to deny marijuana access to seriously ill patients, and concluded that it should be reclassified as a Schedule III substance, *Grinspoon v. DEA,* 828 F.2d 881, 883–884 (CA1 1987), the campaign has proved unsuccessful. The DEA Administrator did not endorse the ALJ's findings, 54 Fed. Reg. 53767 (1989), and since that time has routinely denied petitions to reschedule the drug, most recently in 2001. 66 Fed. Reg. 20038 (2001). The Court of Appeals for the District of Columbia Circuit has reviewed the petition to reschedule marijuana on five separate occasions over the course of 30 years, ultimately upholding the Administrator's final order. See *Alliance for Cannabis Therapeutics v. DEA,* 304 U.S. App. D.C. 400, 15 F.3d 1131, 1133 (1994).

U.S. 146, 151 (1971); *Wickard v. Filburn,* 317 U.S. 111, 128–129 (1942). As we stated in *Wickard*, "even if appellee's activity be local and though it may not be regarded as commerce, it may still, whatever its nature, be reached by Congress if it exerts a substantial economic effect on interstate commerce." We have never required Congress to legislate with scientific exactitude. When Congress decides that the " 'total incidence' " of a practice poses a threat to a national market, it may regulate the entire class.

Our decision in *Wickard,* 317 U.S. 111, is of particular relevance. In *Wickard*, we upheld the application of regulations promulgated under the Agricultural Adjustment Act of 1938, 52 Stat. 31, which were designed to control the volume of wheat moving in interstate and foreign commerce in order to avoid surpluses and consequent abnormally low prices. The regulations established an allotment of 11.1 acres for Filburn's 1941 wheat crop, but he sowed 23 acres, intending to use the excess by consuming it on his own farm.

The similarities between this case and *Wickard* are striking. Like the farmer in *Wickard*, respondents are cultivating, for home consumption, a fungible commodity for which there is an established, albeit illegal, interstate market. Just as the Agricultural Adjustment Act was designed "to control the volume [of wheat] moving in interstate and foreign commerce in order to avoid surpluses . . ." and consequently control the market price, a primary purpose of the CSA is to control the supply and demand of controlled substances in both lawful and unlawful drug markets.

More concretely, one concern prompting inclusion of wheat grown for home consumption in the 1938 Act was that rising market prices could draw such wheat into the interstate market, resulting in lower market prices. The parallel concern making it appropriate to include marijuana grown for home consumption in the CSA is the likelihood that the high demand in the interstate market will draw such marijuana into that market.

The fact that *Wickard's* own impact on the market was "trivial by itself" was not a sufficient reason for removing him from the scope of federal regulation. That the Secretary of Agriculture elected to exempt even smaller farms from regulation does not speak to his power to regulate all those whose aggregated production was significant, nor did that fact play any role in the Court's analysis. Moreover, even though *Wickard* was [illegible] farmer, the activity he was engaged in — the cultivation of wheat for home consumption — was not treated by the Court as part of his commercial farming operation.

Respondents nonetheless insist that the CSA cannot be constitutionally applied to their activities because Congress did not make a specific finding that the intrastate cultivation and possession of marijuana for medical purposes based on the recommendation of a physician would substantially affect the larger interstate marijuana market. Be that as it may, we have never required Congress to make particularized findings in order to legislate.

IV

To support their contrary submission, respondents rely heavily on two of our more recent Commerce Clause cases. In their myopic focus, they overlook the larger context of modern-era Commerce Clause jurisprudence preserved by those cases. Moreover, even in the narrow prism of respondents' creation, they read those cases far too broadly. Those two cases, of course, are *Lopez v. United States,* 514 U.S. 549 (1995), and *United States v. Morrison,* 529 U.S. 598 (2000). As an initial matter, the statutory challenges at issue in those cases were markedly different from the challenge respondents pursue in the case at hand. Here, respondents ask us to excise individual applications of a concededly valid statutory scheme. In contrast, in both *Lopez* and *Morrison*, the parties asserted that a particular statute or provision fell outside Congress' commerce power in its entirety. This distinction is pivotal for we have often reiterated that "where the class of activities is regulated and that class is within the reach of federal power, the courts have no power 'to excise, as trivial, individual instances' of the class." *Perez.*

At issue in *Lopez*, was the validity of the Gun-Free School Zones Act of 1990, which was a brief, single-subject statute making it a crime for an individual to possess a gun in a school zone. The Act did not regulate any economic activity and did not contain any requirement that the possession of a gun have any connection to past interstate activity or a predictable impact on future commercial activity. Distinguishing our earlier cases holding that comprehensive regulatory statutes may be validly applied to local conduct that does not, when viewed in isolation, have a significant impact on interstate commerce, we held the statute invalid.

The statutory scheme that the Government is defending in this litigation is at the opposite end of the regulatory spectrum. As explained above, the CSA, enacted in 1970 as part of the Comprehensive Drug Abuse Prevention and Control Act, was a lengthy and detailed statute creating a comprehensive framework for regulating the production, distribution, and possession of five classes of "controlled substances." Most of those substances — those listed in Schedules II through V — "have a useful and legitimate medical purpose and are necessary to maintain the health and general welfare of the American people." 21 U.S.C. § 801(1). The regulatory scheme is designed to foster the beneficial use of those medications, to prevent their misuse, and to prohibit entirely the possession or use of substances listed in Schedule I, except as a part of a strictly controlled research project.

The Violence Against Women Act of 1994, 108 Stat. 1902, created a federal civil remedy for the victims of gender-motivated crimes of violence. 42 U.S.C. § 13981. The remedy was enforceable in both state and federal courts, and generally depended on proof of the violation of a state law. Despite congressional findings that such crimes had an adverse impact on interstate commerce, we held the statute unconstitutional because, like the statute in *Lopez*, it did not regulate economic activity. We concluded that "the noneconomic, criminal nature of the conduct at issue was central to our decision" in *Lopez*, and that our prior cases had identified a clear pattern of analysis: " 'Where economic activity substantially affects interstate commerce, legislation regulating that activity will be sustained.' "

Unlike those at issue in *Lopez* and *Morrison*, the activities regulated by the CSA are quintessentially economic. "Economics" refers to "the production, distribution, and consumption of commodities." Webster's Third New

International Dictionary 720 (1966). The CSA is a statute that regulates the production, distribution, and consumption of commodities for which there is an established, and lucrative, interstate market. Prohibiting the intrastate possession or manufacture of an article of commerce is a rational (and commonly utilized) means of regulating commerce in that product. Such prohibitions include specific decisions requiring that a drug be withdrawn from the market as a result of the failure to comply with regulatory requirements as well as decisions excluding Schedule I drugs entirely from the market. Because the CSA is a statute that directly regulates economic, commercial activity, our opinion in *Morrison* casts no doubt on its constitutionality.

First, the fact that marijuana is used "for personal medical purposes on the advice of a physician" cannot itself serve as a distinguishing factor. The CSA designates marijuana as contraband for *any* purpose; in fact, by characterizing marijuana as a Schedule I drug, Congress expressly found that the drug has no acceptable medical uses. Moreover, the CSA is a comprehensive regulatory regime specifically designed to regulate which controlled substances can be utilized for medicinal purposes, and in what manner. Indeed, most of the substances classified in the CSA "have a useful and legitimate medical purpose." 21 U.S.C. § 801(1). Thus, even if respondents are correct that marijuana does have accepted medical uses and thus should be redesignated as a lesser schedule drug, the CSA would still impose controls beyond what is required by California law.

Second, limiting the activity to marijuana possession and cultivation "in accordance with state law" cannot serve to place respondents' activities beyond congressional reach. The Supremacy Clause unambiguously provides that if there is any conflict between federal and state law, federal law shall prevail. It is beyond peradventure that federal power over commerce is " 'superior to that of the States to provide for the welfare or necessities of their inhabitants,' " however legitimate or dire those necessities may be.

Respondents acknowledge this proposition, but nonetheless contend that their activities were not "an essential part of a larger regulatory scheme" because they had been "isolated by the State of California, and [are] policed by the State of California," and thus remain "entirely separated from the market." The dissenters fall prey to similar reasoning. See n. 38, *supra* this page. The notion that California law has surgically excised a discrete activity that is hermetically sealed off from the larger interstate marijuana market is a dubious proposition, and, more importantly, one that Congress could have rationally rejected.

Indeed, that the California exemptions will have a significant impact on both the supply and demand sides of the market for marijuana is not just "plausible" as the principal dissent concedes, (**O'Connor**, J., dissenting), it is readily apparent. The exemption for physicians provides them with an economic incentive to grant their patients permission to use the drug. In contrast to most prescriptions for legal drugs, which limit the dosage and duration of the usage, under California law the doctor's permission to recommend marijuana use is open-ended.

The exemption for cultivation by patients and caregivers can only increase the supply of marijuana in the California market.[41] The likelihood that all such production will promptly terminate when patients recover or will precisely match the patients' medical needs during their convalescence seems remote; whereas the danger that excesses will satisfy some of the admittedly enormous demand for recreational use seems obvious.

V

Respondents also raise a substantive due process claim and seek to avail themselves of the medical necessity defense. These theories of relief were set forth in their complaint but were not reached by the Court of Appeals. We therefore do not address the question whether judicial relief is available to respondents on these alternative bases. We do note, however, the presence of another avenue of relief. As the Solicitor General confirmed during oral argument, the statute authorizes procedures for the reclassification of Schedule I drugs. But perhaps even more important than these legal avenues is the democratic process, in which the voices of voters allied with these respondents may one day be heard in the halls of Congress. Under the present state of the law, however, the judgment of the Court of Appeals must be vacated. The case is remanded for further proceedings consistent with this opinion.

It is so ordered.

Justice **Scalia**, concurring in the judgment.

I agree with the Court's holding that the Controlled Substances Act (CSA) may validly be applied to respondents' cultivation, distribution, and possession of marijuana for personal, medicinal use. I write separately because my understanding of the doctrinal foundation on which that holding rests is, if not inconsistent with that of the Court, at least more nuanced.

Since *Perez v. United States* our cases have mechanically recited that the Commerce Clause permits congressional regulation of three categories: (1) the channels of interstate commerce; (2) the instrumentalities of interstate commerce, and persons or things in interstate commerce; and (3) activities that "substantially affect" interstate commerce. The third category, however, is different in kind, and its recitation without explanation is misleading and incomplete.

[41] The state policy allows patients to possess up to eight ounces of dried marijuana, and to cultivate up to 6 mature or 12 immature plants. Cal. Health & Safety Code Ann. § 11362.77(a) (West Supp. 2005). However, the quantity limitations serve only as a floor. Based on a doctor's recommendation, a patient can possess whatever quantity is necessary to satisfy his medical needs, and cities and counties are given *carte blanche* to establish more generous limits. Indeed, several cities and counties have done just that. For example, patients residing in the cities of Oakland and Santa Cruz and in the counties of Sonoma and Tehama are permitted to possess up to 3 pounds of processed marijuana. Reply Brief for United States 19 (citing Proposition 215 Enforcement Guidelines). Putting that quantity in perspective, 3 pounds of marijuana yields roughly 3,000 joints or cigarettes. Executive Office of the President, Office of National Drug Control Policy, What America's Users Spend on Illegal Drugs 24 (Dec. 2001), www.whitehousedrugpolicy.gov/publications/pdf/american_users_spend_2002.pdf. And the street price for that amount can range anywhere from $900 to $24,000. DEA, Illegal Drug Price and Purity Report (Apr. 2003) (DEA-02058).

It is *misleading* because, unlike the channels, instrumentalities, and agents of interstate commerce, activities that substantially affect interstate commerce are not themselves part of interstate commerce, and thus the power to regulate them cannot come from the Commerce Clause alone. Rather, as this Court has acknowledged since at least *United States v. Coombs,* 37 U.S. 72 (1838), Congress's regulatory authority over intrastate activities that are not themselves part of interstate commerce (including activities that have a substantial effect on interstate commerce) derives from the Necessary and Proper Clause. And the category of "activities that substantially affect interstate commerce," *Lopez, supra,* at 559, is *incomplete* because the authority to enact laws necessary and proper for the regulation of interstate commerce is not limited to laws governing intrastate activities that substantially affect interstate commerce. Where necessary to make a regulation of interstate commerce effective, Congress may regulate even those intrastate activities that do not themselves substantially affect interstate commerce.

I

As we implicitly acknowledged in *Lopez*, however, Congress's authority to enact laws necessary and proper for the regulation of interstate commerce is not limited to laws directed against economic activities that have a substantial effect on interstate commerce. Though the conduct in *Lopez* was not economic, the Court nevertheless recognized that it could be regulated as "an essential part of a larger regulation of economic activity, in which the regulatory scheme could be undercut unless the intrastate activity were regulated." 514 U.S., at 561. This statement referred to those cases permitting the regulation of intrastate activities "which in a substantial way interfere with or obstruct the exercise of the granted power."

II

Lopez and *Morrison* affirm that Congress may not regulate certain "purely local" activity within the States based solely on the attenuated effect that such activity may have in the interstate market. But those decisions do not declare noneconomic intrastate activities to be categorically beyond the reach of the Federal Government. Neither case involved the power of [illegible] control over intrastate activities in connection with a more comprehensive scheme of regulation.

III

The application of these principles to the case before us is straightforward. In the CSA, Congress has undertaken to extinguish the interstate market in Schedule I controlled substances, including marijuana. The Commerce Clause unquestionably permits this. The power to regulate interstate commerce "extends not only to those regulations which aid, foster and protect the commerce, but embraces those which prohibit it." To effectuate its objective, Congress has prohibited almost all intrastate activities related to Schedule I substances — both economic activities (manufacture, distribution, possession with the intent to distribute) and noneconomic activities (simple possession).

See 21 U.S.C. § 841(a), 844(a). That simple possession is a noneconomic activity is immaterial to whether it can be prohibited as a necessary part of a larger regulation. Rather, Congress's authority to enact all of these prohibitions of intrastate controlledsubstance activities depends only upon whether they are appropriate means of achieving the legitimate end of eradicating Schedule I substances from interstate commerce.

By this measure, I think the regulation must be sustained. Not only is it impossible to distinguish "controlled substances manufactured and distributed intrastate" from "controlled substances manufactured and distributed interstate," but it hardly makes sense to speak in such terms. Drugs like marijuana are fungible commodities. As the Court explains, marijuana that is grown at home and possessed for personal use is never more than an instant from the interstate market — and this is so whether or not the possession is for medicinal use or lawful use under the laws of a particular State.

Justice **O'Connor**, with whom **The Chief Justice** and Justice **Thomas** join as to all but Part III, dissenting.

We enforce the "outer limits" of Congress' Commerce Clause authority not for their own sake, but to protect historic spheres of state sovereignty from excessive federal encroachment and thereby to maintain the distribution of power fundamental to our federalist system of government. One of federalism's chief virtues, of course, is that it promotes innovation by allowing for the possibility that "a single courageous State may, if its citizens choose, serve as a laboratory; and try novel social and economic experiments without risk to the rest of the country."

This case exemplifies the role of States as laboratories. The States' core police powers have always included authority to define criminal law and to protect the health, safety, and welfare of their citizens. Today the Court sanctions an application of the federal Controlled Substances Act that extinguishes that experiment, without any proof that the personal cultivation, possession, and use of marijuana for medicinal purposes, if economic activity in the first place, has a substantial effect on interstate commerce and is therefore an appropriate subject of federal regulation. In so doing, the Court announces a rule that gives Congress a perverse incentive to legislate broadly pursuant to the Commerce Clause — nestling questionable assertions of its authority into comprehensive regulatory schemes — rather than with precision. That rule and the result it produces in this case are irreconcilable with our decisions in *United States v. Lopez,* and *United States v. Morrison.*

Accordingly I dissent.

. . . .

II

A

Today's decision allows Congress to regulate intrastate activity without check, so long as there is some implication by legislative design that regulating intrastate activity is essential (and the Court appears to equate "essential" with "necessary") to the interstate regulatory scheme. Seizing upon our language in *Lopez* that the statute prohibiting gun possession in school zones was "not an essential part of a larger regulation of economic activity, in which the regulatory scheme could be undercut unless the intrastate activity were regulated," the Court appears to reason that the placement of local activity in a comprehensive scheme confirms that it is essential to that scheme. If the Court is right, then *Lopez* stands for nothing more than a drafting guide: Congress should have described the relevant crime as "transfer or possession of a firearm anywhere in the nation" — thus including commercial and noncommercial activity, and clearly encompassing some activity with assuredly substantial effect on interstate commerce. Had it done so, the majority hints, we would have sustained its authority to regulate possession of firearms in school zones.

A number of objective markers are available to confine the scope of constitutional review here. Both federal and state legislation — including the CSA itself, the California Compassionate Use Act, and other state medical marijuana legislation — recognize that medical and nonmedical (*i.e.*, recreational) uses of drugs are realistically distinct and can be segregated, and regulate them differently. Respondents challenge only the application of the CSA to medicinal use of marijuana. Moreover, because fundamental structural concerns about dual sovereignty animate our Commerce Clause cases, it is relevant that this case involves the interplay of federal and state regulation in areas of criminal law and social policy, where "States lay claim by right of history and expertise."

B

Having thus defined the relevant conduct, we must determine whether, under our precedents, the conduct is economic and, in the aggregate, substantially affects interstate commerce. Even if intrastate cultivation and possession of marijuana for one's own medicinal use can properly be characterized as economic, and I question whether it can, it has not been shown that such activity substantially affects interstate commerce. Similarly, it is neither self-evident nor demonstrated that regulating such activity is necessary to the interstate drug control scheme.

The Court suggests that *Wickard*, which we have identified as "perhaps the most far reaching example of Commerce Clause authority over intrastate activity," established federal regulatory power over any home consumption of a commodity for which a national market exists. I disagree. *Wickard* involved a challenge to the Agricultural Adjustment Act of 1938 (AAA), which directed the Secretary of Agriculture to set national quotas on wheat production, and penalties for excess production. The AAA itself confirmed that Congress made an explicit choice not to reach — and thus the Court could not possibly have approved of federal control over — smallscale, noncommercial wheat farming. In contrast to the CSA's limitless assertion of power, Congress provided an exemption within the AAA for small producers.

Even assuming that economic activity is at issue in this case, the Government has made no showing in fact that the possession and use of homegrown marijuana for medical purposes, in California or elsewhere, has a substantial effect on interstate commerce. Similarly, the Government has not shown that regulating such activity is necessary to an interstate regulatory scheme. Whatever the specific theory of "substantial effects" at issue (*i.e.*, whether the activity substantially affects interstate commerce, whether its regulation is necessary to an interstate regulatory scheme, or both), a concern for dual sovereignty requires that Congress' excursion into the traditional domain of States be justified.

There is simply no evidence that homegrown medicinal marijuana users constitute, in the aggregate, a sizable enough class to have a discernable, let alone substantial, impact on the national illicit drug market — or otherwise to threaten the CSA regime. Explicit evidence is helpful when substantial effect is not "visible to the naked eye." And here, in part because common sense suggests that medical marijuana users may be limited in number and that California's Compassionate Use Act and similar state legislation may well isolate activities relating to medicinal marijuana from the illicit market, the effect of those activities on interstate drug traffic is not self-evidently substantial.

The Government has not overcome empirical doubt that the number of Californians engaged in personal cultivation, possession, and use of medical marijuana, or the amount of marijuana they produce, is enough to threaten the federal regime. Nor has it shown that Compassionate Use Act marijuana users have been or are realistically likely to be responsible for the drug's seeping into the market in a significant way. The Government does cite one estimate that there were over 100,000 Compassionate Use Act users in California in 2004, but does not explain, in terms of proportions, what their presence means for the national illicit drug market.

III

We would do well to recall how James Madison, the father of the Constitution, described our system of joint sovereignty to the people of New York: "The powers delegated by the proposed constitution to the federal government are few and defined. Those which are to remain in the State governments are numerous and indefinite. . . . The powers reserved to the several States will extend to all the objects which, in the ordinary course of affairs, concern the lives, liberties, and properties of the people, and the internal order, improvement, and prosperity of the State." The Federalist No. 45, pp. 292–293 (C. Rossiter ed. 1961).

Justice **Thomas**, dissenting.

Respondents Diane Monson and Angel Raich use marijuana that has never been bought or sold, that has never crossed state lines, and that has had no demonstrable effect on the national market for marijuana. If Congress can regulate this under the Commerce Clause, then it can regulate virtually anything — and the Federal Government is no longer one of limited and enumerated powers.

I

Respondents' local cultivation and consumption of marijuana is not "Commerce . . . among the several States." U.S. Const., Art. I, § 8, cl. 3. By holding that Congress may regulate activity that is neither interstate nor commerce under the Interstate Commerce Clause, the Court abandons any attempt to enforce the Constitution's limits on federal power. The majority supports this conclusion by invoking, without explanation, the Necessary and Proper Clause. Regulating respondents' conduct, however, is not "necessary and proper for carrying into Execution" Congress' restrictions on the interstate drug trade. Art. I, § 8, cl. 18. Thus, neither the Commerce Clause nor the Necessary and Proper Clause grants Congress the power to regulate respondents' conduct.

. . . .

B

On its face, a ban on the intrastate cultivation, possession and distribution of marijuana may be plainly adapted to stopping the interstate flow of marijuana. Unregulated local growers and users could swell both the supply and the demand sides of the interstate marijuana market, making the market more difficult to regulate. But respondents do not challenge the CSA on its face. Instead, they challenge it as applied to their conduct. The question is thus whether the intrastate ban is "necessary and proper" as applied to medical marijuana users like respondents.

Respondents are not regulable simply because they belong to a large class (local growers and users of marijuana) that Congress might need to reach, if they also belong to a distinct and separable subclass (local growers and users of state-authorized, medical marijuana) that does not undermine the CSA's interstate ban.

California's Compassionate Use Act sets respondents' conduct apart from other intrastate producers and users of marijuana. The Act channels marijuana use to "seriously ill Californians," Cal. Health & Safety Code Ann. § 11362.5(b)(1)(A) (West Supp. 2005), and prohibits "the diversion of marijuana for nonmedical purposes," § 11362.5(b)(2). California strictly controls the cultivation and possession of marijuana for medical purposes. To be eligible for its program, California requires that a patient have an illness that cannabis can relieve, such as cancer, AIDS, or arthritis, § 11362.5(b)(1)(A), and that he obtain a physician's recommendation or approval, § 11362.5(d). Qualified patients must provide personal and medical information to obtain medical identification cards, and there is a statewide registry of cardholders. §§ 11362.715-.76. Moreover, the Medical Board of California has issued guidelines for physicians' cannabis recommendations, and it sanctions physicians who do not comply with the guidelines. See, *e.g., People v. Spark,* 121 Cal. App. 4th 259, 263, 16 Cal.Rptr. 3d 840, 843 (2004).

This class of intrastate users is therefore distinguishable from others. We normally presume that States enforce their own laws.

These controls belie the Government's assertion that placing medical marijuana outside the CSA's reach "would prevent effective enforcement of the interstate ban on drug trafficking." Enforcement of the CSA can continue as it did prior to the Compassionate Use Act. Only now, a qualified patient could avoid arrest or prosecution by presenting his identification card to law enforcement officers. In the event that a qualified patient is arrested for possession or his cannabis is seized, he could seek to prove as an affirmative defense that, in conformity with state law, he possessed or cultivated small quantities of marijuana intrastate solely for personal medical use.

But even assuming that States' controls allow some seepage of medical marijuana into the illicit drug market, there is a multibillion-dollar interstate market for marijuana. Executive Office of the President, Office of Nat. Drug Control Policy, Marijuana Fact Sheet 5 (Feb. 2004), www.whitehousedrugpolicy.gov/publications/factsht/marijuana/index.html. It is difficult to see how this vast market could be affected by diverted medical cannabis, let alone in a way that makes regulating intrastate medical marijuana obviously essential to controlling the interstate drug market.

. . . .

2

Even assuming the CSA's ban on locally cultivated and consumed marijuana is "necessary," that does not mean it is also "proper." The means selected by Congress to regulate interstate commerce cannot be "prohibited" by, or inconsistent with the "letter and spirit" of, the Constitution. *McCulloch v. Maryland,* 4 Wheat. 316, 421 (1819).

Here, Congress has encroached on States' traditional police powers to define the criminal law and to protect the health, safety, and welfare of their citizens. Further, the Government's rationale — that it may regulate the production or possession of any commodity for which there is an interstate market — threatens to remove the remaining vestiges of States' traditional police powers. Cf. Ehrlich, *The Increasing Federalization of Crime*, 32 Ariz. St. L. J. 825, 826, 841 (2000) (describing both the relative recency of a large percentage of federal crimes and the lack of a relationship between some of these crimes and interstate commerce). This would convert the Necessary and Proper Clause into precisely what Chief Justice Marshall did not envision, a "pretext . . . for the accomplishment of objects not intrusted to the government." *McCulloch, supra,* at 423.

II

If the majority is correct that *Lopez* and *Morrison* are distinct because they were facial challenges to "particular statutes or provisions," then congressional power turns on the manner in which Congress packages legislation. Under the majority's reasoning, Congress could not enact — either as a single-subject statute or as a separate provision in the CSA — a prohibition on the intrastate possession or cultivation of marijuana. Nor could it enact an intrastate ban simply to supplement existing drug regulations. However, that same prohibition is perfectly constitutional when integrated into a piece of legislation that reaches other regulable conduct.

Finally, the majority's view — that because *some* of the CSA's applications are constitutional, they must *all* be constitutional — undermines its reliance on the substantial effects test. The intrastate conduct swept within a general regulatory scheme may or may not have a substantial effect on the relevant interstate market. "One *always* can draw the circle broadly enough to cover an activity that, when taken in isolation, would not have substantial effects on commerce." The breadth of legislation that Congress enacts says nothing about whether the intrastate activity substantially affects interstate commerce, let alone whether it is necessary to the scheme. Because medical marijuana users in California and elsewhere are not placing substantial amounts of cannabis into the stream of interstate commerce, Congress may not regulate them under the substantial effects test, no matter how broadly it drafts the CSA.

. . . .

NOTES AND QUESTIONS

1. After the *Raich* decision, what options remain for those who seek to apply marijuana for healing purposes?
2. Is the case closer to *Wickard* or *Lopez* and *Morrison*? The former was regulating economic activity, the latter criminal misconduct. Which is the interstate commerce clause aimed at? Which is involved with the Controlled Substances Act?
3. And anyway, the *Raich* case involves a compelling argument for personal health and liberty, not present in *Lopez* or *Morrison* or *Wickard*. The Fifth and Fourteenth Amendments might properly be viewed as limiting the Interstate Commerce Clause. . . this was not reached by the Supreme Court or the Ninth Circuit — why? And what will/should be the outcome?
4. Why is marijuana so strictly banned? And used?
5. And what are the implications of *Raich* for *Gonzales v. Oregon*, § 4.05[2], *infra,* involving a challenge to Oregon's assisted suicide law, under the Controlled Substances Act involved in *Raich*?

§ 4.05 Death

For millennia, death was accepted as a natural part of life. People commonly died relatively young, of trauma or infectious disease. Until the 20th century, dying and death usually occurred in a familial context, ushered in and understood through ritual integration into everyday life. In some cultures, the elderly chose the time and place of their deaths by simply removing themselves from the group.

Today, people can expect to live much longer. Death now comes with age and is isolated from life and the living. Those who are dying are isolated by treatment procedures, machines and personnel. For many, the fear is no longer the *fact* of death but the awful process.

The following materials deal with death in the 21st century. We begin with the right of hospitals to refuse to treat a dying person, through a Do Not

Resuscitate Order. For decades, hospitals — without notice or participation — decided to withhold treatment, because it was futile, and let people die. We follow with the right of an individual to refuse treatment, the converse of the first concern. And we close with case law on legislation concerning assisting a person to die; first prohibiting it (held constitutional) and elsewhere authorizing it (also to be held constitutional).

We have dealt, of course, with death earlier in this text. Those prior cases and discussions should be recalled now. Thus, in § 1.04, the abortion cases are concerned with a kind of "death," as are the partial abortion cases in § 4.02. The definition of a "person" is bounded by birth and death, which itself is a special matter for definition in § 1.04, particularly with reference to brain death and anencephalic babies or adults in a persistent vegetative state. And the value of a life prematurely terminated by death was a subject within the compass of § 3.05.

What is missing from this treatment of death is capital punishment. While a legislative problem does appear in the following materials, the extensive case law, literature and debate concerning capital punishment are noticeably absent. Early drafts of this casebook included dozens of pages on capital punishment, and appropriately so, since the question of when and why society may kill its members is a fundamental bioethical issue. Still, the subject is largely gone from this volume for three reasons: other subjects (such as DNR orders) have recently acquired sufficient "law" to warrant treatment; the "medical" element is largely missing from capital punishment (although clearly pervasive in this text); and adequate treatment is given elsewhere to capital punishment.

With this, we turn first to the subject of when a hospital or physician may refuse to treat a patient; specifically, when it may choose not to resuscitate a patient.

[1] Do Not Resuscitate (DNR) Orders and Medical Futility

For decades physicians have entered "DNR" orders on patient charts in hospitals. The meaning was well understood and the practice was widely followed — the patient was to die, not be saved, when the next episode (*e.g.,* cardiac arrest) occurred. Often the notation was made without patient or family consent. Even with such consent, profound ethical issues arise.

The *reason* for not resuscitating a patient may be that doing so is "futile." But the meaning of that term is hardly self-evident. And the possibility of other, less tenable reasons (*e.g.,* cost), or of *no* reason at all — other than error — calls the practice into serious question. Any discussion of the ethics of entering DNR orders must address not only the reason but the methodology — the pain, the active involvement of staff, the patient's consciousness.

DNR orders should be considered against the backdrop of earlier cases, particularly the *Quinlan* and *Cruzan* cases, § 1.04[2][c], *supra,* dealing with removal of life support from a patient in a persistent vegetative state.

IN RE INTEREST OF RILEY, STATE OF NEBRASKA v. D'ETTA H.*

1997 Neb. App. Lexis 49 (Neb. Ct. App. 1997)

Factual and Procedural Background

Sievers, Judge.

Riley M., who will be 2 years of age on April 5, 1997, sustained profound brain injury within the first month of his life as a result of "shaken baby syndrome." He has continuously been in the custody of the Nebraska Department of Social Services (DSS) since May 4, 1995. On December 22, 1995, an adjudication hearing was held upon a second amended petition which alleged that Timothy M., Riley's father, had shaken Riley, resulting in the injury to his brain. The second amended petition further alleged that neither D'Etta H., Riley's mother, nor his father was capable or trained to provide for the special needs of Riley without the assistance of DSS. . . .

In March 1996, Riley's doctors rendered a diagnosis that Riley was in a persistent vegetative state and recommended a do-not-resuscitate (DNR) order. A DNR order would mean that in the event Riley suffered cardiac or respiratory arrest, there would be no rescue breathing, chest compressions, suction, intubation, or medication to revive him. In short, Riley would be allowed to die if he suffered cardiac or respiratory arrest.

DSS included the recommendation of the DNR order in its plan for Riley's medical care and sought, in conjunction with Riley's guardian ad litem, review and approval of such plan by the separate juvenile court. At a hearing to review the proposed plan on March 14, 1996, medical records and affidavits of physicians were introduced, and Michael Kripal, the DSS case manager for Riley, testified. Kripal testified that DSS endorsed the DNR order. . . .

. . . .

The undisputed evidence before the juvenile court, when the DNR order was entered, was that Riley was in a persistent vegetative state and that a DNR order was medically appropriate. Dr. Mary Kay Bowen, a specialist in pediatric and developmental medicine, opined on March 1, 1996, that a DNR order was in Riley's best interest and also that the NG [nasal gastric] tube should be withdrawn and attempts to nipple should be continued as long as he is able. . . .

. . . .

The supplemental transcript and bill of exceptions reveal that by July 16, 1996, Dr. Bowen had changed her opinion because of marked changes in Riley's condition. She concluded that Riley was no longer in a persistent vegetative state and that a DNR order for Riley was inappropriate. This is not to say that Riley does not have severe injuries as a result of being shaken by his father. Dr. Bowen makes it clear that Riley has been profoundly injured. But Riley has made significant progress and no longer meets the diagnostic criteria for persistent vegetative state. The record does not reveal how long

* Citation material has been omitted from this case.

DSS had Dr. Bowen's new opinion in hand before acting, but that opinion is in evidence via a letter dated July 16, 1996, from Dr. Bowen. . . .

. . . .

On September 16, the juvenile court signed an order specifically withdrawing its March DNR order.

. . . .

. . . .The legal appropriateness of the original DNR order is something we do not need to discuss or decide in this appeal. This is so because the evidence adduced at the August 29, 1996, hearing, which is now before us by way of the supplemental bill of exceptions, shows that Riley is not in a persistent vegetative state and that a DNR order is medically inappropriate. This is not a matter of a different opinion being rendered by a different medical expert. Instead, the same physicians who previously declared Riley to be in a persistent vegetative state and recommended entry of the DNR order, now say that he is not in a persistent vegetative state and that the DNR order is inappropriate.

Under these circumstances, leaving the DNR order in place is obviously unacceptable and untenable, but it is unnecessary to engage in the legal analysis of the original DNR order when all now agree that it is medically inappropriate. However, our standard of review allows us to act to correct the situation. In the instant case, the evidence offered in support of the stipulation to vacate the DNR order was through written reports, letters, and affidavits, to which there were no objections. And, there is no conflict in this evidence. Therefore, this is not a situation where we give deference to the juvenile court's findings of fact. Accordingly, applying our de novo review of the entire record now before us, we conclude that the order of the juvenile court providing that Riley not be resuscitated in the event of cardiac or respiratory arrest, as well as prohibiting invasive procedures, is no longer appropriate, and we therefore vacate the DNR order of March 15, 1996, in its entirety, effective immediately.

. . . .

NOTES AND QUESTIONS

1. Recall the record from the *Quinlan* and *Cruzan* cases in Chapter 1, to the effect that a persistent vegetative state is nonreversible. Yet there *was* a reversal here, for little Riley M. What does that suggest (if anything) about decisionmaking in this area?
2. Who is to represent Riley M? His parents inflicted the brain damage; the State Department of Social Services has no incentive to protect him; the hospital and its physicians will lose money on him. And if someone *is* appointed, what should that person's position be as to the DNR order? What would *yours* be?
3. Months after the original DNR order, the Nebraska Court of Appeals reverses, but not because the DNR order was void, but because *now* it appears inappropriate. Was it appropriate when entered?

4. Given Riley's continuing condition, could/should/might a DNR order be continued, if all parties consented?

ESTATE OF LUCILLE AUSTWICK v. MURPHY, COOK COUNTY PUBLIC GUARDIAN

656 N.E.2d 773 (Ill. App. Ct. 1995)

Justice Sheila M. **O'Brien** delivered the opinion of the court:

The Cook County Public Guardian (hereinafter Public Guardian) appeals from the trial court's order removing a Do Not Resuscitate Order (DNR) from the medical chart of the Public Guardian's ward, Lucille Austwick. Mrs. Austwick cross-appeals from the trial court's order denying her petition to remove the Public Guardian for cause. We affirm.

On October 18, 1991, the probate court adjudicated 81-year-old Lucille Austwick a disabled person and appointed the Public Guardian as plenary guardian of Mrs. Austwick's person and estate. In July 1992, Mark Broaddus, an attorney employed by the Public Guardian, visited Mrs. Austwick at her nursing home and asked whether she wanted a DNR in her medical chart. Broaddus explained to Mrs. Austwick the DNR would direct nursing home staff not to administer artificial ventilation, endotracheal intubation, closed chest cardiac massage, and emergency paramedic resuscitation. Mrs. Austwick stated she wanted the DNR. On January 7, 1993, the Public Guardian gave his consent to Mrs. Austwick's attending physician to place the DNR in Mrs. Austwick's nursing home medical chart.

On January 14, 1994, Mrs. Austwick, through the Legal Advocacy Service of the Illinois Guardianship and Advocacy Commission, petitioned the probate court to terminate the DNR. She also requested the removal of the Public Guardian as her plenary guardian because he failed to comply with the procedures set forth in the Health Care Surrogate Act when consenting to the DNR. Under the HCSA, an adult patient who is able to make and communicate an informed decision to forgo life-sustaining treatment may do so without judicial involvement. When a person lacks such "decisional capacity" and suffers from a "qualifying condition", that is, a "terminal condition", "permanent unconsciousness", or "irreversible condition", the HCSA authorizes a surrogate decision maker to decide whether to forgo life-sustaining treatment on that person's behalf. Mrs. Austwick argued she did not lack decisional capacity or have a qualifying condition, and therefore the Public Guardian had no authority to consent to a DNR for her.

Mrs. Austwick also argued for the removal of the Public Guardian because he had authorized the administration of psychotropic medication for her without court approval. . . . This decision contradicted the advice of S.B.'s surgeon, David C. Johnson, M.D. ("Dr. Johnson"), and her referring physician, Richard Jonas, M.D.

At the hearing on the petition, Mark Broaddus testified about his conversation with Mrs. Austwick in July 1992 when she told him she wanted the DNR. Broaddus also testified that on January 17, 1994, three days after Mrs. Austwick filed her petition to terminate the DNR and remove the Public Guardian, he again spoke with Mrs. Austwick and she told him she still desired the DNR. Broaddus believed Mrs. Austwick had decisional capacity during both conversations.

Dr. Steven Fox, an expert in geriatric medicine, testified he had reviewed Mrs. Austwick's medical records and found no physician's statement saying she lacked decisional capacity. However, Dr. Fox noted since Mrs. Austwick had been adjudicated disabled under the Probate Act, "that's [an] indication . . . capacity is lacking somewhere." Dr. Fox also determined Mrs. Austwick was not suffering from one of the qualifying conditions as defined in the HCSA.

Mrs. Austwick's sister, Geraldine Champlain, testified in her evidence deposition that Mrs. Austwick stated prior to her adjudication as a disabled adult she would not want to be kept alive by machines. However, Mrs. Champlain testified Mrs. Austwick might not object to closed chest cardiac massage, one of the procedures prohibited under the DNR. Mrs. Austwick did not testify at the hearing.

The trial court ordered the DNR be removed. After hearing testimony that Mrs. Austwick's medical records did not indicate psychotropic medication had been administered against her will, the trial court denied her petition to remove the Public Guardian. On appeal, the Public Guardian argues (a) Mrs. Austwick had decisional capacity when she informed Broaddus in July 1992 and January 1994 she wanted the DNR, and (b) the HCSA authorized the Public Guardian to consent to the DNR for her. Therefore, the trial court erred when it ordered the removal of the DNR from Mrs. Austwick's medical chart.

. . . The Act defines as disabled a person 18 years or older who lacks the ability to fully manage her person or estate. Dr. Fox concluded because Mrs. Austwick was disabled under the Probate Act she must lack decisional capacity. We disagree. Although a petition for adjudication of disability must be accompanied by a doctor's evaluation of the patient's mental and physical condition, the doctor is not required to determine the patient's decisional capacity. Nor is a concurring determination of the patient's condition required. Thus, the adjudication of Mrs. Austwick as a disabled person under the Probate Act, of itself, does not overcome the presumption under the HCSA that she has decisional capacity.

However, we do not agree with the Public Guardian that the HCSA authorized him to give his consent to Mrs. Austwick's attending physician to place the DNR in her nursing home medical chart. The HCSA authorizes a surrogate decision maker to forgo life-sustaining treatment for a patient only when the patient lacks decisional capacity and has a qualifying condition. Where, as here, the patient has decisional capacity, she must herself give consent to the appropriate medical personnel to forgo life-sustaining treatment.

. . . .

Next, we address Mrs. Austwick's cross-appeal from the trial court's order denying her petition to remove the Public Guardian for "good cause." . . .

. . . .

Mrs. Austwick first contends the Public Guardian should be removed for good cause because he improperly consented to the DNR for her. We disagree.

At the hearing on Mrs. Austwick's removal petition, the Public Guardian presented evidence he consented to the DNR because (a) Mrs. Austwick stated she wanted it; (b) he believed it was in Mrs. Austwick's best interest to effectuate her wishes; and (c) he thought the HCSA authorized him to give his consent on Mrs. Austwick's behalf. Although the Public Guardian misinterpreted the HCSA, and in fact he has no authority to consent to a DNR for Mrs. Austwick while she retains decisional capacity, there is no indication his error was anything other than a well-intentioned mistake that will not be repeated. Under these circumstances, the trial court's finding that the Public Guardian's consent to the DNR did not constitute "good cause" sufficient to remove him as Mrs. Austwick's plenary guardian was not against the manifest weight of the evidence.

Second, Mrs. Austwick argues the Public Guardian should be removed for good cause because he authorized the administration of psychotropic drugs for her on January 7, 1993, without seeking court approval. . . .

The Public Guardian interpreted section 2-107.1 then in effect as requiring court approval only if he sought to authorize psychotropic medication against Mrs. Austwick's will. Since Mrs. Austwick did not refuse consent, the Public Guardian did not go to court before authorizing the administration of psychotropic medication for her. However, in In re Guardianship of Austin, the Fourth District of the Illinois Appellate Court held section 2-107.1(g) then in effect required a petition, hearing, and court order before the guardian can authorize psychotropic medication, even where, as here, the ward does not refuse consent. Thus, the Public Guardian technically violated Austin when he authorized psychotropic medication for Mrs. Austwick without seeking prior court approval. As with the Public Guardian's consent to the DNR, though, there is no indication his authorization of psychotropic medication was anything other than a well-intentioned effort to act in Mrs. Austwick's best interests. Accordingly, the trial court's denial of Mrs. Austwick's petition to remove the Public Guardian for authorizing psychotropic medication without court approval was not against the manifest weight of the evidence.

. . . .

NOTES AND QUESTIONS

1. With DNR orders, or simple removal of life support, the question of who assists the patient is crucial. That was unclear in *Riley*, the preceding case. Here, it *is* clear — the "Public Guardian," which arranged for Mrs. Austwick to *consent* to a DNR, which she now opposes. Why would the Public Guardian initially solicit Mrs. Austwick's consent? Why does it now oppose her objection?
2. Did the attending physician have an obligation independent of the Public Guardians? Of Mrs. Austwick's wishes?
3. How does yet *another* agency — the Legal Advocacy Service — get into the picture in opposition to the Public Guardian? How does the Service get to speak for Mrs. Austwick?

4. And how can the Court make *any* decision without hearing testimony from Mrs. Austwick, who after all, claims she is competent?
5. As to the DNR order, apparently the Public Guardian argues *both* that Mrs. Austwick is not competent (and so the Guardian can act *for* her) and *is* competent (and so her decision stands). Which is the better argument? And if the latter, does the Guardian mean to claim that she cannot *revoke* a competent decision? Would you agree?
6. *Shouldn't* the Public Guardian be removed, as Mrs. Austwick argues? How can she have confidence in him? How can he represent her when he has consistently advocated her death?

FIRST HEALTHCARE CORPORATION v. RETTINGER*

456 S.E.2d 347 (N.C. Ct. App. 1995)

. . . .

Lawrence Rettinger (hereinafter Mr. Rettinger) cared for his first wife during her prolonged illness and eventual death from cancer. Mr. Rettinger married his second wife, Nell Rettinger (hereinafter Mrs. Rettinger), in November 1985. Prior to marrying Mrs. Rettinger, Mr. Rettinger was diagnosed with Parkinson's Disease. On 18 August 1983, Mr. Rettinger executed a "Declaration Of A Desire For A Natural Death" pursuant to G.S. 90-321. In that document, Mr. Rettinger stated that he did not wish his life to be prolonged by "extraordinary means if [his] condition [was] determined to be terminal and incurable."

Mr. Rettinger was placed in the Winston-Salem Convalescent Center (hereinafter Hillhaven) on 11 January 1990. Mrs. Rettinger signed a document entitled "Standard Nursing Facility Services Agreement" in which she agreed to be financially responsible for services provided by Hillhaven to her husband. Hillhaven was aware that Mr. Rettinger had executed a living will and retained a copy of it in Mr. Rettinger's medical file at Hillhaven.

On 4 February 1991, Dr. Fredric J. Romm, Mr. Rettinger's attending physician, transferred Mr. Rettinger to North Carolina Baptist Hospital for treatment of pneumonia. Dr. Mark Knudson, Mr. Rettinger's primary physician at Baptist Hospital, inserted a nasogastric tube to facilitate administration of his pneumonia medications. On 4 March 1991, Mr. Rettinger was returned to Hillhaven. Mrs. Rettinger stated in her affidavit that when Mr. Rettinger was returned to Hillhaven, he was "bedridden, lying in a fetal position, unable to move and unable to communicate." She further stated that the family was informed that "he had little mental functioning, suffered from dementia, was in the late stages of irreversible Parkinson's Disease, and would die." Mrs. Rettinger alleged that Dr. Knudson had assured her that the tube would be removed within ten days of her husband's return to Hillhaven. The tube was not removed.

Mrs. Rettinger prepared a "No Code Blue" form for Mr. Rettinger in March 1991, requesting that the staff not resuscitate her husband. Because she amended the form to request that no nasogastric tube be used, Hillhaven

* Citation material has been omitted from this case.

returned the form as invalid. Mrs. Rettinger then attempted to move her husband to another facility, but could not find another facility. She stated that she wanted to take him home but the Hillhaven staff told her she could not, "apparently because they felt [she] was not able to care for him." In March 1991, Dr. Romm informed Mrs. Rettinger that Hillhaven had a policy of not removing nasogastric tubes "if to do so would likely cause a patient to starve or dehydrate to death." . . .

On 4 May 1993, Hillhaven filed a complaint against Mrs. Rettinger, individually and as personal representative of Mr. Rettinger's estate, for $14,458.43 for services rendered to Mr. Rettinger from 26 June 1991 to 22 October 1991. . . .

Eagles, Judge.

I.

. . . .

Mrs. Rettinger argues that [summary judgment should not have been granted because] genuine issues of material fact exist as to whether the requirements of G.S. 90-321 were met before the nasogastric tube was removed by court order in September 1991. G.S. 90-321(b) provides:

> If a person has declared . . . a desire that his life not be prolonged by extraordinary means or by artificial nutrition or hydration, and the declaration has not been revoked . . . ; and
>
> (1) It is determined by the attending physician that the declarant's present condition is
>
> a. Terminal and incurable; or
>
> . . . .
>
> c. Diagnosed as a persistent vegetative state; and
>
> (2) There is confirmation of the declarant's present condition as set out above in subdivision (b)(1) by a physician other than the attending physician; then extraordinary means or artificial nutrition or hydration, as specified by the declarant, may be withheld or discontinued upon the direction and under the supervision of the attending physician. . . .

Here, Dr. Romm stated in his affidavit that he signed a form sent by Norman Sloan, Mr. Rettinger's attorney, "which stated that Mr. Rettinger's condition was terminal and incurable and ordered removal of the nasogastric tube." The form, signed by Dr. Romm on 25 June 1991, provided:

> I have examined Lawrence John Rettinger and have determined that his medical condition is terminal and incurable. Nutrition and hydration provided to Mr. Rettinger through a nasogastric tube constitutes life-prolonging extraordinary means. Consistent with the Declaration of a Desire for a Natural Death executed by Lawrence J. Rettinger, I order the removal of the nasogastric tube. The family

recognizes that implementation of Mr. Rettinger's Declaration of a Desire for a Natural Death will result in Mr. Rettinger's death within a relatively short period of time.

The language of this form conforms to the requirement in G.S. 90-321(b) that the attending physician determine that the declarant is terminal and incurable.

Hillhaven argues that Dr. Romm never told Hillhaven to remove the tube after he signed the form. However, the statute does not specify that the attending physician has to personally direct the facility to remove the tube. The statute simply provides that "extraordinary means . . . may be withheld or discontinued upon the direction and under the supervision of the attending physician." Therefore, there is a genuine issue of material fact as to whether Dr. Romm's order to remove the nasogastric tube in the 25 June 1991 form he signed satisfies the language of G.S. 90-321(b) that the attending physician direct the removal of the nasogastric tube and whether his order was communicated to Hillhaven.

G.S. 90-321(b) requires a physician other than the attending physician to confirm the attending physician's conclusion that the declarant's condition is terminal and incurable. Dr. Romm stated in his affidavit that "[t]he findings in the [25 June 1991] form were . . . never confirmed by another physician." However, Norman Sloan stated in his affidavit that a second doctor was willing to confirm Dr. Romm's findings at the time Dr. Romm signed the form. Judge Reingold's September 1991 order, attached as Exhibit C to Hillhaven's May 1993 complaint, included a finding of fact that "Dr. Michael Adler, a colleague of Dr. Romm, saw and observed Mr. Rettinger in July, 1991, and it is Dr. Adler's opinion, which this court accepts, that Mr. Rettinger has severe Parkinson's disease and dementia and there is confirmation of Mr. Rettinger's present condition by Dr. Adler." Judge Reingold's finding of fact, combined with Mr. Sloan's assertion in his affidavit, creates a material issue of fact as to whether the statute's requirement of confirmation by a second doctor was met in July 1991. If the requirements of the statute were met in July 1991, then according to Hillhaven's own policy, set out in its 20 June 1991 letter to Mr. Sloan, Hillhaven should have removed the nasogastric tube in July 1991.

. . . .

III.

Mrs. Rettinger also argues that summary judgment was not appropriate because she is not obligated to pay for medical services rendered by Hillhaven after 26 June 1991. Mrs. Rettinger argues that she had previously requested removal of the nasogastric tube and if her late husband's declaration and her expressed wishes for the nasogastric tube to be removed had been honored, no other medical services would have been necessary. The plain language of the "Standard Nursing Facility Services Agreement" that Mrs. Rettinger signed when Mr. Rettinger was admitted to Hillhaven provided that Mrs. Rettinger agreed to pay for all services rendered to her husband. The agreement contains no language stating that Mrs. Rettinger would only pay for services she authorized. However, we have concluded above that there are genuine issues of material fact as to whether and when the requirements of G.S. 90-321(b), the living will statute, were met. If a jury determines that the requirements of the living will statute were complied with in July 1991, then the nasogastric tube should have been removed at that time. If the nasogastric tube had been removed in July 1991, it is likely that Mr. Rettinger would not have survived until 22 October 1991 and Mrs. Rettinger's alleged financial obligation to Hillhaven would have been substantially less.

Accordingly, we reverse the summary judgment order and remand for trial. . . .

. . . .

V

Walker, Judge dissenting.

. . . .

Plaintiff submitted the affidavit of Dr. Frederic L. Romm and Lawrence Rettinger's medical chart with its motion for summary judgment. In his affidavit, Dr. Romm states that:

> 12. Between March 1991 and June 1991, I never made the necessary findings nor documented any findings in the medical record that Mr. Rettinger was terminal or incurable or that the nasogastric tube constituted extraordinary means.
>
> 13. In June 1991, Hillhaven's policy was not the reason that I did not order withdrawal of Mr. Rettinger's nasogastric tube or make the findings required under the North Carolina Right to Natural Death Act. Given my understanding of the law and the advice of my attorney, I was not comfortable withdrawing the nasogastric tube from Mr. Rettinger without a court order.
>
> 14. In July 1991, I took a one-month leave of absence. Just prior to this leave of absence, I received a form from the Rettingers' attorney, Mr. Norman Sloan, which stated that Mr. Rettinger's condition was terminal and incurable and ordered removal of the nasogastric tube.
>
> 15. On June 25, 1991, I signed the form and returned it to Mr. Sloan . . . I did not send a copy of the form to Hillhaven or ever communicate to Hillhaven that I had signed it. This form was never entered into Mr. Rettinger's medical record. The findings in the form were also never confirmed by another physician.
>
> . . . .
>
> 17. As a result of the court's order, I made findings in Mr. Rettinger's medical record that his condition was terminal and incurable and that the nasogastric tube was extraordinary means. The findings were confirmed by another physician in the medical record. I then ordered removal of the tube and personally removed the nasogastric tube from

Mr. Rettinger. Per my orders, Hillhaven fed Mr. Rettinger by mouth a liquid and then a puree diet.

. . . The medical chart confirms Dr. Romm's statement that he made no findings in the chart pursuant to N.C. Gen. Stat. § 90-321 until 4 October 1991, after the court's order, and that on 5 October 1991, another physician confirmed Dr. Romm's findings in the medical chart.

This evidence establishes that the three requirements of N.C. Gen. Stat. § 90-321 were not met until 5 October 1991, after the court ordered that the tube be removed. Assuming that the language of the form signed by Dr. Romm on 25 June 1991 conforms to the requirement of N.C. Gen. Stat. § 90-321(b)(1), defendant produced no evidence tending to show that defendant or her attorney informed plaintiff that Dr. Romm had made the requisite findings. . . .

Since defendant failed to produce any evidence to contradict plaintiff's evidence that the requirements were not met until 5 October 1991, there were no genuine issues of material fact as to whether the requirements of N.C. Gen. Stat. § 90-321 were met before the nasogastric tube was removed on 5 October 1991 pursuant to the court's order in September 1991. Thus, summary judgment was properly granted in plaintiff's favor.

NOTES AND QUESTIONS

1. The Court of Appeals decision in *First Healthcare* was reversed by the North Carolina Supreme Court, at 467 S.E.2d 243 (N.C. 1996), for the reasons stated in Judge Walker's dissent.
2. Mrs. Rettinger wanted two things: a DNR order entered (called a "no code blue") and a nasogastric tube removed by Hillhaven. She got neither. Why would Hillhaven refuse? Why did Doctor Knudsen not remove the tube? Why didn't Doctor Romm?
3. The nursing home sues for four months of care. Could the estate of Mr. Rettinger or Mrs. Rettinger countersue for misconduct? On what theory?
4. How, in the future, can a patient or the family ensure that their wishes will be respected? And how should the distinction be drawn between the patient's wishes and the family's? As to DNRs? Withdrawal of nutrition and hydration?
5. Note that here Mr. Rettinger executed a "living will," directing that nutrition and hydration be withheld. The other option in many states is a "durable power of attorney," appointing — let us say, Mrs. Rettinger — to make decisions when a patient becomes incompetent. Would that have worked better here? Note that, by state statute, a durable power may not include removing life support. If it does, it may not include nutrition and hydration. Why? Should it?
6. The use of Do Not Resuscitate orders leads inevitably to considering the rights of patients and families to insist that such orders be entered and that other forms of healthcare (such as NG tubes and life support)

be withdrawn. For recent case law from two state supreme courts, see *Tabitha R. v. Ronde R.*, 564 N.W.2d 598 (Neb. 1997) (State could not withdraw life support from three-year-old who is in a persistent vegetative state, over parental objection, without the same procedure as in termination of parental rights) and *In Re Daniel Fiori,* 673 A.2d 1061 (Del. 1995) (guardian's petition to remove nasogastric tube from 88-year-old patient granted).

7. Compare the issues and procedures discussed in this section on DNR orders with those in the next section, on physician assisted death. Why is the latter so much more controversial and contentious?

8. For an excellent article, see Charles P. Sabatino, *Survey of State EMSDNR Laws and Protocols*, 27 J.L. Med. & Ethics 297 (1999); and see Vassyl A. Lonchyna, *To Resuscitate or Not . . . In the Operating Room: The Need for Hospital Policies for Surgeons Regarding DNR Orders*, 6 Annals Health L. 209 (1997).

PROBLEM 4–14 — Goodbye, Conor Shamus McInnerney

On February 23, 1998, the following article* appeared in the Portland, Oregon *Oregonian*:

James Burke, *State Investigates Newborn's Death*

Nurses say a doctor obstructed a 3-day old's breathing after declaring the child "brain dead" in a Washington E.R.

Snow swirled thickly outside when 3-day old Conor Shamus McInnerney, snuggling at his mother's breast, suddenly stopped breathing and went still.

Thirty-nine minutes after his frantic parents summoned paramedics on the night of Jan. 12, emergency room doctors had the baby's heart pumping again. But he still lay limply on the table, his pupils fixed and dilated. After so long with no detectable pulse, his chances for survival were considered "dismal," according to a subsequent report by the hospital executive committee.

[illegible] to halt life support, and Conor was pronounced dead in their arms at 9:54 p.m.

Martin and Michelle McInnerney tearfully departed Olympic Memorial Hospital along with Dr. Eugene Turner, the baby's pediatrician, who had overseen the emergency room heroics.

But half an hour later, a nurse returning to the emergency room found the infant gasping on a hospital cart, his skin turning pink.

Turner hastened back but told a nurse not to call the McInnerneys, saying it would be too much for them to endure their child's dying twice, hospital reports say.

Working with another emergency room doctor and then on his own, Turner spent close to two hours more trying to revive the infant.

---

* James Burke, *State Investigates Newborn's Death*, The Oregonian (Feb. 23, 1994).

But what he did then confounded nurses and put him under scrutiny by local police and state medical authorities, with the parents considering a lawsuit. According to reports, Turner declared the baby brain dead, then "manually obstructed the airway of the child." A nurse described the doctor as "plugging off the infant's nose."

A declaration of brain death is usually made only with the sophisticated equipment that Olympic Memorial, the only hospital in Port Angeles, a logging town of 18,300, does not have.

"It felt awful to us, like it was a done deal," said an unidentified nurse quoted in records compiled by the committee. "I felt like he was hurrying this along; I felt like it was taking a life."

The nurse added:

"Dr. Turner said, 'I can't stand it, I can't have this go on anymore.' I . . . felt that he was feeling great compassion for the infant, that he felt the death was inevitable, let's expedite it."

. . . .

Turner, 62, has a reputation for integrity and fine medical judgment and has treated multiple generations of families. He has surrendered his hospital privileges pending completion of the investigations, but he still is treating children at Peninsula Children's Clinic.

Normally, a child brought in to Olympic Memorial with breathing distress would receive preliminary treatment, then be airlifted 63 miles southeast to Children's Hospital and Medical Center in Seattle, the region's premier child-care facility, said Raedell Warren, an Olympic Memorial spokeswoman.

But the snowstorm that night had grounded medical flights and fouled attempts to arrange ground transportation.

. . . .

According to minutes of the committee's four-hour meeting, members questioned why Turner felt he should "assist the infant in stopping breathing" and decided not to go to the police for fear "the local community may not be able to cope with such a report."

The Medical Quality Assurance Commission holds its next regular meeting March 4 and may announce its intent then. Police have declined to comment on their investigation.

The McInnerneys declined to be interviewed.

The baby's paternal grandmother, Diane Anderson, calls Turner a "wonderful physician" who made two mistakes — failing to tell the family their "dead" baby was showing signs of life to allow them to join in the decision-making, and assuming Conor was brain-dead without EEG confirmation.

"I have no animosity toward Dr. Turner," she said, "but he took my grandson's life — and that should have been God's choice."

* * *

Consider Dr. Turner's conduct, and that of Shamus' parents, under the New York legislation in the preceding problem. If you were the district attorney in Port Angeles, would you prosecute? And, consider this case under the Oregon assisted death legislation, in the next section. Would it be covered? Should it be?

On August 31, 1998, the Clallam County Prosecutor, David Bruneau, charged Doctor Turner with murder in the second degree.

[2] Physician Assisted Suicide

The preceding cases dealt with withdrawal of life support and nutrition and hydration and the withholding of heroic measures, such as CPR, via DNR orders. All of this would lead, sooner or later, to death. And so it may be called passive euthanasia.

Active euthanasia would mean taking affirmative steps to end a person's life. A bullet, an overdose of insulin, gas — all of these may kill a person, with attendant criminal consequences. And yet the reasons and justifications may be identical with those in "passive euthanasia" cases. Is there, ethically or morally, a difference?

We begin with a case, *Bouvia v. Superior Court*, which is usually viewed as a case simply involving the right to refuse treatment — at most a passive euthanasia case. As you read it, ask whether taking affirmative steps to end Elizabeth's life (as she wished) would not have been a kindness, as it might have been in the *Quinlan* and *Cruzan* cases, *supra,* § 1.04[2][c]. We then consider the case law banning and authorizing assisted suicide; in each instance consider why it is that society resists — in an age of medical sophistication — applying modern technology to the age-old problem of how we die.

BOUVIA v. SUPERIOR COURT*

225 Cal. Rptr. 297 (Cal. App. 2d 1986)

Beach, Associate Justice.

Petitioner, Elizabeth Bouvia, a patient in a public hospital seeks the removal from her body of a nasogastric tube inserted and maintained against her will and without her consent by physicians who so placed it for the purpose of keeping her alive through involuntary forced feeding.

. . . .We have heard oral argument from the parties and now order issuance of a peremptory writ, granting petitioner, Elizabeth Bouvia, the relief for which she prayed.

. . . .

To petitioner it is a dismal prospect to live with this hated and unwanted device attached to her, through perhaps years of the law's slow process. She has the right to have it removed immediately. This matter constitutes a perfect paradigm of the axiom: "Justice delayed is justice denied."

. . . .

In explanation of its ruling, the trial court stated that it considered petitioner's "motives" to be indicative of an attempt to commit suicide with

* Most citation material has been omitted from this case.

the State's help rather than a bona fide exercise of her right to refuse medical treatment. No evidence supports this conclusion.

. . . .

Petitioner is a 28-year-old woman. Since birth she has been afflicted with and suffered from severe cerebral palsy. She is quadriplegic. She is now a patient at a public hospital maintained by one of the real parties in interest, the County of Los Angeles. Other parties are physicians, nurses and the medical and support staff employed by the County of Los Angeles. Petitioner's physical handicaps of palsy and quadriplegia have progressed to the point where she is completely bedridden. Except for a few fingers of one hand and some slight head and facial movements, she is immobile. She is physically helpless and wholly unable to care for herself. She is totally dependent upon others for all of her needs. These include feeding, washing, cleaning, toileting, turning, and helping her with elimination and other bodily functions. She cannot stand or sit upright in bed or in a wheelchair. She lies flat in bed and must do so the rest of her life. She suffers also from degenerative and severely crippling arthritis. She is in continual pain. Another tube permanently attached to her chest automatically injects her with periodic doses of morphine which relieves some, but not all of her physical pain and discomfort.

She is intelligent, very mentally competent. She earned a college degree. She was married but her husband has left her. She suffered a miscarriage. She lived with her parents until her father told her that they could no longer care for her. She has stayed intermittently with friends and at public facilities. A search for a permanent place to live where she might receive the constant care which she needs has been unsuccessful. She is without financial means to support herself and, therefore, must accept public assistance for medical and other care.

She has on several occasions expressed the desire to die. . . .

Petitioner must be spoon fed in order to eat. Her present medical and dietary staff have determined that she is not consuming a sufficient amount of nutrients. Petitioner stops eating when she feels she cannot orally swallow more, without nausea and vomiting. As she cannot now retain solids, she is fed soft liquid-like food. Because of her previously announced resolve to starve herself, the medical staff feared her weight loss might reach a life-threatening level. Her weight since admission to real parties' facility seems to hover between 65 and 70 pounds. Accordingly, they inserted the subject tube against her will and contrary to her express written instructions.[1]

Petitioner's counsel argue that her weight loss was not such as to be life threatening and therefore the tube is unnecessary. However, the trial court found to the contrary as a matter of fact, a finding which we must accept. Nonetheless, the point is immaterial, for, as we will explain, a patient has the right to refuse any medical treatment or medical service, even when such treatment is labeled "furnishing nourishment and hydration." This right exists even if its exercise creates a "life threatening condition."

[1] Her instructions were dictated to her lawyers, written by them and signed by her by means of her making a feeble "x" on the paper with a pen which she held in her mouth.

. . . .

The right to refuse medical treatment is basic and fundamental. It is recognized as a part of the right of privacy protected by both the state and federal constitutions. Its exercise requires no one's approval. It is not merely one vote subject to being overridden by medical opinion.

. . . .

For example, addressing one part of the problem, California passed the "Natural Death Act," Health and Safety Code sections 7185 et seq. Although addressed to terminally ill patients, the significance of this legislation is its expression as state policy "that adult persons have the fundamental right to control the decisions relating to the rendering of their own medical care . . . " (Health & Saf. Code, § 7186.) Section 7188 provides the method whereby an adult person may execute a directive for the withholding or withdrawal of life-sustaining procedures. Recognition of the right of other persons who may not be terminally ill and may wish to give other forms of direction concerning their medical care is expressed in section 7193: "Nothing in this chapter shall impair or supersede any legal right or legal responsibility which any person may have to effect the withholding or withdrawal of life-sustaining procedures in any lawful manner. In such respect the provisions of this chapter are cumulative."

. . . .

In large measure the courts have sought to protect and insulate medical providers from criminal and tort liability. (*E.g., Barber v. Superior Court.*) The California Natural Death Act also illustrates this approach. Nonetheless, as indicated it too recognizes, even if inferentially, the existence of the right, even in a non-terminal patient, which overrides the concern for protecting the medical profession.

This right is again reflected in the statute concerning execution of a power of attorney for health care (Civ. Code, § 2500), which states in pertinent part: "Notwithstanding this document, you have the right to make medical and other health care decisions for yourself so long as you can give informed consent with respect to the particular decision. In addition, no treatment may be given to you over your objection at the time. . . ."

. . . .

A recent Presidential Commission for the Study of Ethical Problems in Medicine and Biomedical and Behavioral Research concluded in part: "The voluntary choice of a competent and informed patient should determine whether or not life-sustaining therapy will be undertaken, just as such choices provide the basis for other decisions about medical treatment. Health care institutions and professionals should try to enhance patients' abilities to make decisions on their own behalf and to promote understanding of the available treatment options. . . . Health care professionals serve patients best by maintaining a presumption in favor of sustaining life, while recognizing that competent patients are entitled to choose to forgo any treatments, including those that sustain life." (*Deciding to Forgo Life-Sustaining Treatment,* at pp. 3, 5 (U.S. Gov't Printing Office 1983) (Report of the President's Commission for the Study of Ethical Problems in Medicine and Biomedical and Behavioral Research).)

. . . .

Significant also is the statement adopted on March 15, 1986, by the Council on Ethical and Judicial Affairs of the American Medical Association. It is entitled "Withholding or Withdrawing Life Prolonging Medical Treatment." In pertinent part, it declares: "The social commitment of the physician is to sustain life and relieve suffering. Where the performance of one duty conflicts with the other, the choice of the patient, or his family or legal representative if the patient is incompetent to act in his own behalf, should prevail. Life prolonging medical treatment includes medication and artificially or technologically supplied respiration, nutrition or hydration. In treating a terminally ill or irreversibly comatose patient, the physician should determine whether the benefits of treatment outweigh its burdens. At all times, the dignity of the patient should be maintained."

We do not believe that all of the foregoing case law and statements of policy and statutory recognition are mere lip service to a fictitious right. . . .

It is indisputable that petitioner is mentally competent. She is not comatose. She is quite intelligent, alert and understands the risks involved.

4. The Claimed Exceptions to the Patient's Right to Choose are Inapplicable.

. . . .[T]he real parties in interest, a county hospital, its physicians and administrators, urge that the interests of the State should prevail over the rights of Elizabeth Bouvia to refuse treatment. Advanced by real parties under this argument are the State's interests in (1) preserving life, (2) preventing suicide, (3) protecting innocent third parties, and (4) maintaining the ethical standards of the medical profession, including the right of physicians to effectively render necessary and appropriate medical service and to refuse treatment to an uncooperative and disruptive patient. Included, whether as part of the above or as separate and additional arguments, are what real parties assert as distinctive facts not present in other cases, i.e., (1) petitioner is a patient in a public facility, thereby making the State a party to the result of her conduct, (2) she is not comatose, nor incurably, nor terminally ill, nor in a vegetative state, all conditions which have justified the termination of life-support system in other instances, (3) she has asked for medical treatment, therefore, she cannot accept a part of it while cutting off the part that would be effective, and (4) she is, in truth, trying to starve herself to death and the State will not be a party to a suicide.

. . . .

At bench the trial court concluded that with sufficient feeding petitioner could live an additional 15 to 20 years; therefore, the preservation of petitioner's life for that period outweighed her right to decide. In so holding the trial court mistakenly attached undue importance to the amount of time possibly available to petitioner, and failed to give equal weight and consideration for the quality of that life; an equal, if not more significant, consideration.

All decisions permitting cessation of medical treatment or life-support procedures to some degree hastened the arrival of death. In part, at least, this was permitted because the quality of life during the time remaining in those cases had been terribly diminished. In Elizabeth Bouvia's view, the quality of her life has been diminished to the point of hopelessness, uselessness, unenjoyability and frustration. She, as the patient, lying helplessly in bed, unable to care for herself, may consider her existence meaningless. She cannot be faulted for so concluding. If her right to choose may not be exercised because there remains to her, in the opinion of a court, a physician or some committee, a certain arbitrary number of years, months, or days, her right will have lost its value and meaning.

. . . .

Here, if force fed, petitioner faces 15 to 20 years of a painful existence, endurable only by the constant administrations of morphine. Her condition is irreversible. There is no cure for her palsy or arthritis. Petitioner would have to be fed, cleaned, turned, bedded, toileted by others for 15 to 20 years! Although alert, bright, sensitive, perhaps even brave and feisty, she must lie immobile, unable to exist except through physical acts of others. Her mind and spirit may be free to take great flights but she herself is imprisoned and must lie physically helpless subject to the ignominy, embarrassment, humiliation and dehumanizing aspects created by her helplessness. We do not believe it is the policy of this State that all and every life must be preserved against the will of the sufferer. It is incongruous, if not monstrous, for medical practitioners to assert their right to preserve a life that someone else must live, or, more accurately, endure, for "15 to 20 years." We cannot conceive it to be the policy of this State to inflict such an ordeal upon anyone.

It is, therefore, immaterial that the removal of the nasogastric tube will hasten or cause Bouvia's eventual death. . . .

Real parties assert that what petitioner really wants is to "commit suicide" by starvation at their facility. . . .

Overlooking the fact that a desire to terminate one's life is probably the ultimate exercise of one's right to privacy, we find no substantial evidence to support the court's conclusion. Even if petitioner had the specific intent to commit suicide in 1983, while at Riverside, she did not carry out that plan. Then she apparently had the ability without artificial aids to consume sufficient nutrients to sustain herself, now she does not. That is to say, the trial court here made the following express finding, "Plaintiff, when she chooses, can orally ingest food by masticating 'finger food' though additional nutritional intake is required intravenously and by nasogastric tube. . . ." As a consequence of her changed condition, it is clear she has now merely resigned herself to accept an earlier death, if necessary, rather than live by feedings forced upon her by means of a nasogastric tube. Her decision to allow nature to take its course is not equivalent to an election to commit suicide with real parties aiding and abetting therein.

Moreover, the trial court seriously erred by basing its decision on the "motives" behind Elizabeth Bouvia's decision to exercise her rights. If a right exists, it matters not what "motivates" its exercise. We find nothing in the law to suggest the right to refuse medical treatment may be exercised only if the patient's motives meet someone else's approval. It certainly is not illegal or immoral to prefer a natural, albeit sooner, death than a drugged life attached to a mechanical device.

. . . .

Petitioner is without means to go to a private hospital and, apparently, real parties' hospital as a public facility was required to accept her. Having done so it may not deny her relief from pain and suffering merely because she has chosen to exercise her fundamental right to protect what little privacy remains to her.

Personal dignity is a part of one's right of privacy. Such a right of bodily privacy led the United States Supreme Court to hold that it shocked its conscience to learn that a state, even temporarily, had put a tube into the stomach of a criminal defendant to recover swallowed narcotics. *Rochin v. California*, [*supra,* § 2.03[1]]. Petitioner asks for no greater consideration.

. . . .

Compton, Associate Justice, concurring opinion.

Although I have concurred in the very well-reasoned and superbly-crafted opinion of my colleague Justice Beach, I feel compelled to write separately and reflect on what I consider to be one of the real tragedies of this case which is that Elizabeth Bouvia has had to go to such ends to obtain relief from her suffering.

Fate has dealt this young woman a terrible hand. Can anyone blame her if she wants to fold her cards and say "I am out"? Yet medical personnel who have had charge of her case have attempted to force Elizabeth to continue in the game. In their efforts they have been abetted by two different trial courts.

This is not to say that those members of the medical profession and those courts were not well motivated. In each instance the persons involved have expressed a concern for the sanctity of life and a desire to avoid any conduct that could be characterized as aiding in a suicide. Undoubtedly, those persons were, in no small way, influenced by the presence in our law of Penal Code section 401 which imposes penal sanctions on persons who aid and abet in a suicide.

In my opinion, as I shall point out, the application of that statute to circumstances such as are present here is archaic and inhumane.

I have no doubt that Elizabeth Bouvia wants to die; and if she had the full use of even one hand, could probably find a way to end her life — in a word — commit suicide. In order to seek the assistance which she needs in ending her life by the only means she sees available — starvation — she has had to stultify her position before this court by disavowing her desire to end her life in such a fashion and proclaiming that she will eat all that she can physically tolerate. Even the majority opinion here must necessarily "dance" around the issue.

. . . .

The right to die is an integral part of our right to control our own destinies so long as the rights of others are not affected. That right should, in my opinion, include the ability to enlist assistance from others, including the medical profession, in making death as painless and quick as possible.

. . . .

The Hippocratic Oath reads in pertinent part:

> ". . . I will follow that method of treatment which, according to my ability and judgment, I consider for the benefit of my patients. . . . I will give no deadly medicine to anyone if asked. . . ."

Surely, adherence to that oath would yet admit of a reasonable balancing between the doctor's obligation to alleviate suffering and his obligation to preserve life, remembering that the term "life" has itself recently undergone substantial redefinition.

It is also worth noting that the original oath also contained the phrase ". . . I will not give to a woman an instrument to produce abortion. . . ." Obviously, the profession has already accommodated a deviation from that part of the oath.

Whatever choice Elizabeth Bouvia may ultimately make, I can only hope that her courage, persistence and example will cause our society to deal realistically with the plight of those unfortunate individuals to whom death beckons as a welcome respite from suffering.

If there is ever a time when we ought to be able to get the "government off our backs" it is when we face death — either by choice or otherwise.

NOTES AND QUESTIONS

1. Elizabeth Bouvia attracted national attention during the 1980s, as she sought to end her life. On television, she appeared to be an articulate, attractive, intelligent and intense individual, facing a horrible death from cerebral palsy. As the disease progressed, she went from a person who was a successful student, participating in a successful marriage, to a person who was increasingly alone, immobilized and dependent. Ultimately, she [illegible] die essentially through starvation rather than being kept alive and imprisoned in her own body, possibly for decades.
2. Note that *Bouvia* was decided before *Cruzan* and *Quinlan* — how would those cases affect the analysis here? Compare this case to the *Georgetown College* case. Are they similar in the problem posed? The resolution? And consider the same questions as to the case of *In Re A.C.*
3. Cases such as *Cruzan, Quinlan* and *Bouvia* are fairly uniformly clear that a person may decline treatment. In that sense, the *Georgetown College* case and the case of *In Re A.C.* are departures, possibly on the ground that they were dealing with incompetent people. But even incompetent people may decline treatment if the court finds that was their choice or, on a principle of substituted judgment, *would be* their choice. Why, then, should Elizabeth Bouvia have been rejected from hospitals and nursing homes as she sought to die?

4. One dimension raised in the *Bouvia* case, not adequately raised elsewhere, is the question of what weight to ascribe to the ethics and scruples of health care providers. The *Bouvia* Court says the patient's wishes are not subject to being overridden by medical opinion — there is only one vote. But there is a contrary view. Rawls indicates, in terms echoed in the case law, that a proper appreciation for autonomy includes the autonomy of *both* parties to an agreement and a respect for *each* of them. The New York legislation in the preceding section seeks to assure this. A physician should not be allowed to impose his or her ideas on a patient, but the reverse is also true.

   How can these colliding interests *all* be protected? *Should* they be?

5. And what of the right to die? It is a far more broadly shared concern than that of abortion, since all of us *will* die. If patients cannot choose the mode and circumstances, because of scruples of health care providers, then a broadly-based interest is compromised. Thus, the issue in *Bouvia* was not necessarily whether she had a right to die, but whether she could require others to assist her. *Should* she?

6. If the court in *Bouvia* really means there is a right to refuse treatment, should the poor quality of life remaining matter? Is the court implicitly second-guessing the rationality of the decision? *See* cases *supra* at § 1.03[2].

7. *Bouvia* also raises the principle of "double effect." This principle involves conduct or action with two consequences, one of which is primary and the other of which is either unintended or unavoidable. Thus, it seems clear that Elizabeth Bouvia wanted to decline treatment, which was her right. But her purpose was to bring about her death. That, in states which prohibit suicide, is not her right, as Justice Scalia, dissenting in *Cruzan* said. Should we, as did the trial court, consider her "real" motives? What if the appellate court had been forced to conclude that her declared intent *was* suicide?

8. Of course, Elizabeth Bouvia does not seek to be put to death, just to have life support withdrawn. This is the distinction between active and passive euthanasia. Does it make sense? Does it turn on *who you are* — a nurse who turns the body for bedsores, a physician who unplugs the ventilator, the hospital administrator who deals with litigation, the Catholic chaplain, the parent/child/brother/sister? The patient?

9. Of course, Elizabeth Bouvia was not simply seeking to refuse treatment. She was seeking assistance in dying, the subject of the next cases.

IN RE CHRISTOPHER I

131 Cal. Rptr. 2d 122 (Cal. App. 4th 2003)

Fybel, J.

Christopher I., born in September 2001, is a dependent of the juvenile court as a result of suffering severe physical abuse. In an unpublished opinion, *Tamara S. v. Superior Court*, we described the abuse. We concluded there was substantial evidence to support the juvenile court's findings by clear and convincing evidence that on December 17, 2001, Christopher was violently shaken and thrown against his crib railing by his biological father, who had shaken Christopher on prior occasions; and Christopher's biological mother was unable or unwilling to protect Christopher.

In our earlier opinion, we concluded that the juvenile court was permitted to order continuation of life-sustaining medical treatment pending a court hearing. In October 2002, the juvenile court held a four-day evidentiary hearing to determine whether removal of life-sustaining medical treatment was in Christopher's best interests. Six medical doctors who were familiar with Christopher and his condition testified in detail. Three of these doctors were Christopher's treating physicians, two were independent pediatric neurologists, and one was an independent pediatrician who specializes in care for children in hospitals and hospices.

Evidence at the hearing showed that since December 2001, Christopher has been comatose, hospitalized in intensive care, and dependent on a ventilator to breathe. Christopher is neurologically devastated, is in a persistent vegetative condition, and has no cognitive function. Christopher has received heroic medical care in a continuous effort to sustain his life. Future medical treatment will be futile. Even if life-sustaining efforts by machine continue, Christopher will succumb to complications of treatment.

Counsel appointed for Christopher as well as counsel for Christopher's biological mother and father (Tamara S. and Moises I., respectively) participated fully in the hearing. Written reports of the Orange County Social Services Agency (SSA) were presented, and a social worker was cross-examined.

Tamara sought withdrawal of Christopher's life-sustaining medical treatment; Moises opposed this request. Counsel for Christopher, relying on the unanimous views of the testifying doctors, agreed that withdrawal of treatment was in Christopher's best interests. SSA took no position and submitted the issue to the court.

The juvenile court determined that it had the authority to consider withdrawal of Christopher's life-sustaining medical treatment pursuant to the Welfare and Institutions Code. The juvenile court concluded there was clear and convincing evidence that it would be in Christopher's best interests to withdraw life-sustaining medical treatment, except for nutrition, hydration and pain medication. Moises appeals.

We hold (1) the juvenile court has jurisdiction to determine whether life-sustaining medical treatment for a dependent child should be withdrawn; (2) a decision regarding whether withdrawal of life-sustaining medical treatment is in the best interests of a dependent child requires consideration of the factors identified in this opinion; (3) the standard of proof for such determination is clear and convincing evidence; (4) an evidentiary hearing with live testimony must be held; and (5) the juvenile court must state its findings on the record, either orally in open court or in a written order. We conclude that in this case the juvenile court applied the correct legal standards and considered the appropriate factors. Substantial evidence supports its decision. Therefore, we affirm.

Moises does not challenge the sufficiency of the evidence, the clear and convincing standard of proof, or that the issue before the juvenile court was the best interests of the child. Instead, Moises argues the juvenile court did not have the authority to order removal of life-sustaining medical treatment from a dependent child. Moises further contends the juvenile court did not have the authority to make medical decisions concerning a dependent child, for whom counsel had been appointed, absent the appointment of a guardian. Next, Moises contends for the first time on appeal that we should reverse the juvenile court's order because of SSA's alleged inadequacies in giving notice pursuant to the federal Indian Child Welfare Act (25 U.S.C. § 1901). Finally, Moises contends the juvenile court erred in failing to conduct an examination of Tamara's competency or to appoint a guardian ad litem for her. For the reasons explained below, and based on the relevant authorities, we reject all of Moises's arguments as being without merit.

We appreciate the significance of our decision to Christopher, now one and a half years old. We reach our conclusions with his fate in our minds and our hearts. In making his ruling in the juvenile court, Judge Behn said, "I would ask you to keep Christopher in your prayers and thoughts, as I have done for these last three or four months." We join in Judge Behn's sentiments, and wish Christopher peace and serenity.

I. FACTS

A. *Procedural history*

In December 2001, when Christopher was three months old, SSA took him into protective custody. SSA filed a juvenile dependency petition pursuant to Welfare and Institutions Code section 300, subdivisions (a), (b) and (e), alleging that: Moises had thrown Christopher against a crib, causing serious brain damage; Moises had been arrested for child endangerment; Moises had violently shaken Christopher on more than one previous occasion; Tamara witnessed Moises throw Christopher into the crib and inflict physical abuse on Christopher; Tamara was unable or unwilling to protect Christopher from harm; and Christopher was on life support and would be neurologically devastated if he survived. (All further statutory references are to the Welfare and Institutions Code, unless otherwise indicated.)

B. *Evidence regarding Christopher's condition adduced at the hearing*

Christopher is not brain dead. "An individual who has sustained either (1) irreversible cessation of circulatory and respiratory functions, or (2) irreversible cessation of all functions of the entire brain, including the brain stem, is dead." The testifying doctors agreed that Christopher has some lower and mid-brain-stem activity, and therefore he is not brain dead.

Christopher's life is sustained by a ventilator that operates 24 hours a day to cause his lungs to fill with and then expel air, and by a gastrointestinal tube (G-tube) that provides nutrition. His numerous medications include medications to reduce pain or discomfort. Christopher's physical existence is

"100 percent" dependent on technology. Christopher has no gag reflex, no cough reflex, no sucking reflex, and no swallowing reflex.

The testifying doctors all agreed that Christopher is in a persistent vegetative state, with no cognitive functioning.

The consensus among the testifying doctors was that Christopher will likely die as a result of some type of collateral problem, such as lung damage caused by repeated bouts of pneumonia and bronchitis, which in turn are caused by an inability to effectively clear Christopher's bronchial tubes and "chronic contamination of the airway." The use of life-sustaining medical treatment over an extended period of time has created complications for Christopher, and these complications will increase and worsen as time goes on. Dr. Amlie testified, "He will have complications to some of the treatment that's been given and that is supporting him. And he will eventually succumb to the complications of the treatment."

Long-term use of artificial respiration through a tracheostomy has potential side effects such as secretions plugging the tube, which may lead to pneumonia and bacterial infections. The use of the ventilator may also result in barotrauma, or the increase in pressure on the chest wall resulting in air being forced out of the lungs and into the surrounding tissue.

Long-term use of the G-tube to provide nutrition increases Christopher's risk of liver and kidney damage. Nutrition passing through the G-tube can cause aspiration pneumonia.

Christopher's lack of any mobility has resulted in hip dysplasia. His bones have become osteopenic, and acts as seemingly simple as changing his diaper have resulted in bone fractures.

Christopher also stores fluid in his skin and has experienced abnormal weight gain. Christopher's edema is indicative of his body's inability to effectively utilize the nutrition being provided by his G-tube. He also suffers from pulmonary edema, and increasingly needs his lungs suctioned.

C. *Medical conclusions*

[illegible] doctors and two of the three independent doctors agreed that continued life-sustaining medical treatment will not benefit Christopher. The third independent doctor (Dr. Lott) had no opinion regarding whether maintenance of life-sustaining medical treatment will benefit Christopher. All the testifying doctors supported removal of lifesustaining medical treatment or at least a DNR order.

Dr. Hicks testified: "I think it's important for us to decide what is in Christopher's best interest. Not in anybody else's best interest, but Christopher's best interest. And right now I do not believe in his condition, that remaining on a ventilator, remaining in a level of possibl[e] discomfort for his whole life would be in his best interest."

Dr. Umnas testified: "I don't see any improvements in [Christopher's] status. He is just being maintained with the mechanical ventilator. He has no quality of life. He can't do any activities of daily living. His eyes are fixed and very sluggish pupils. He cannot track. He cannot speak. He cannot eat or drink on his own or maintain his own bowel functions on his own. And I think he is just being maintained by the ventilator."

Dr. Lubens. . . testified that continuing Christopher's life-sustaining medical treatment would be pointless. "From a medical standpoint, it's as a doctor, there should be a point to treatment. Treatment should have some goal. Treatment should be to make the person getting the treatment better. And doctors treat diseases and disorders in order to make sick people well. And I think there is — the only thing we are doing with Christopher is in a very heroic way maintaining his life. But again a life where there is virtually no consciousness. . . . And it's not a question, I think, in this situation of can it be done, but should it be done. I don't think it should be done."

When questioned about what would be the harm in maintaining Christopher on life-sustaining medical treatment, Dr. Sine replied: "I feel that that goes completely against the Hippocratic Oath for physicians on a physician level in that the number one clause for the Hippocratic Oath is to do no harm. Clearly we're doing harm with Christopher. We are allowing him to be in pain. We are allowing him to continue to have complications with harm and further medical interventions that cause pain. On a layman's perspective, I would say anyone who feels that we are not causing him harm just needs to go into the room and look at him and watch him for five minutes. And in five minutes, it becomes quite clear that he is suffering."

Christopher's social worker had no recommendation regarding whether life-sustaining medical treatment should be maintained or withdrawn.

II. APPLICABLE STANDARDS

. . . .

(2) There is no reported case in which a California court has set forth the standards to apply when deciding whether to withhold or withdraw life-sustaining medical treatment from a child who is a dependent of the juvenile court.[2] In reaching our decision in this case, we have analyzed California statutes, case law from California and other states, federal case law, including cases from the United States Supreme Court, treatises and commission reports.

A. *What constitutes life-sustaining medical treatment?*

(3) Reference to life-sustaining medical treatment includes not only treatments that might be considered extraordinary, such as machines to maintain breathing or circulation, but also the provision of nutrition, hydration and medication.

This distinction is not at issue in this case because the juvenile court did not authorize withdrawal of nutrition, hydration or medication from

---

[2] Withdrawal of life-sustaining medical treatment is not the same as physician-assisted suicide. California courts have correctly observed that the "decision to allow nature to take its course is not equivalent to an election to commit suicide with [medical professionals] aiding and abetting therein." (Bouvia v. Superior Court (1986) 179 Cal. App. 3d 1127, 1144–1145 [225 Cal. Rptr. 297]; *see also* Bartling v. Superior Court (1984) 163 Cal. App. 3d 186 [209 Cal. Rptr. 220].)

Christopher. The analysis that follows, however, would apply equally to another court's decision to withdraw nutrition, hydration or medication from a dependent child.

B. *The decision to withhold or withdraw life-sustaining medical treatment is governed by consideration of the dependent child's best interests.*

Courts deciding whether to withhold or withdraw life-sustaining medical treatment from persons not legally competent to make their own medical decisions have employed one of two decision-making models: the substituted judgment test and the best interests test. The substituted judgment test permits a surrogate to make decisions regarding medical care based on what the patient would have chosen had he or she been competent.

The best interests model is the correct one to use in this case. (*Barber v. Superior Court,* 147 Cal. App. 3d 1006, 1021.) Under this model, the decision maker is guided by a determination of what medical treatment is in the patient's best interests.

C. *The factors to consider when determining whether to withhold or withdraw life-sustaining medical treatment from a dependent child.*

(4) What factors should the juvenile court consider in determining whether it is in a dependent child's best interests to withhold or withdraw life-sustaining medical treatment? In *Barber v. Superior Court,* the Second Appellate District identified the following factors to be considered in determining whether to withdraw life-sustaining medical treatment from a previously competent adult who had become comatose: "the relief of suffering, the preservation or restoration of functioning and the quality as well as the extent of life sustained." *Barber v. Superior Court* emphasized that a court must consider the burdens treatment may cause to the patient in proportion to the benefits it may provide. "A more rational approach involves the determination of whether the proposed treatment is proportionate or disproportionate in terms of the benefits to be gained versus the burdens caused."

The California Legislature has recognized that medical technology may prolong the process of dying and that "continued health care [that] does not improve the prognosis for recovery may violate patient dignity and cause unnecessary pain and suffering, while providing nothing medically necessary or beneficial to the person." (Prob. Code, § 4650, subd. (b).) Although this statute addresses the right of adult patients to make their own decisions regarding their health care, including the right to refuse life-sustaining medical treatment, it also provides us with further guidance regarding the information a court should consider in deciding whether life-sustaining medical treatment should be withheld or withdrawn from a dependent child.

The Superior Court of Los Angeles County enacted a series of rules listing factors to consider when determining whether continuance or withdrawal of life-sustaining medical treatment is in the best interests of a dependent child, as follows: "(a) Evidence about the minor's present level of physical, sensory, emotional and cognitive functioning; (b) The degree of physical pain resulting from the medical condition, treatment, and termination; (c) The degree of humiliation, dependence and loss of dignity probably resulting from the condition and treatment; (d) The quality of life, life expectancy and prognosis for recovery with and without treatment; (e) The various treatment options, and the risks, side effects and benefits of each of those options; (f) Whether the minor's preference has been or can be ascertained." (Super. Ct. L.A. County, Local Rules, rule 17.4(h).)

We conclude that a court making the decision of whether to withhold or withdraw life-sustaining medical treatment from a dependent child should consider the following factors: (1) the child's present levels of physical, sensory, emotional and cognitive functioning; (2) the quality of life, life expectancy and prognosis for recovery with and without treatment, including the futility of continued treatment; (3) the various treatment options, and the risks, side effects, and benefits of each; (4) the nature and degree of physical pain or suffering resulting from the medical condition; (5) whether the medical treatment being provided is causing or may cause pain, suffering, or serious complications; (6) the pain or suffering to the child if the medical treatment is withdrawn; (7) whether any particular treatment would be proportionate or disproportionate in terms of the benefits to be gained by the child versus the burdens caused to the child; (8) the likelihood that pain or suffering resulting from withholding or withdrawal of treatment could be avoided or minimized; (9) the degree of humiliation, dependence and loss of dignity resulting from the condition and treatment; (10) the opinions of the family, the reasons behind those opinions, and the reasons why the family either has no opinion or cannot agree on a course of treatment; (11) the motivations of the family in advocating a particular course of treatment; and (12) the child's preference, if it can be ascertained, for treatment.

This list is not meant to be exclusive, but is intended to provide a set of factors to be considered, analyzed and weighed. Not all of these factors may be applicable in a given case. The court is not limited to consideration of only these factors, and may take other factors into account when appropriate, especially as medical science and technology develop.

D. *The court's decision to withhold or withdraw lifesustaining medical treatment must be supported by clear and convincing evidence.*

E. *A court deciding whether to withhold or withdraw lifesustaining medical treatment from a dependent child must hear live testimony, evaluate and weigh the relevant factors, and make its findings on the record.*

III. DISCUSSION

A. *Substantial evidence supported the juvenile court's determination that withdrawal of life-sustaining medical treatment was in Christopher's best interests.*

. . . .

(6b) The juvenile court correctly determined that continuation of life-sustaining medical treatment would not be in Christopher's best interests. The juvenile court considered the applicable factors and found by clear and convincing evidence that: Christopher has no cognitive function, and is in a persistent vegetative state; Christopher's current treatment is of no benefit to him; no treatment will change his current condition; Christopher is 100 percent dependent on the ventilator and the G-tube; immobility caused by Christopher's brain damage is leading to other medical problems, which will increase over time; Christopher may live for many years in his current vegetative condition, if life-sustaining treatment continues; and circumstantial evidence indicates Christopher is in "substantial" pain, and is suffering. The juvenile court's oral recitation of its findings on the record did not refer to the opinions of Christopher's family members. Those opinions, however, are clear from the record, given that counsel for both Moises and Tamara set forth their respective clients' positions regarding withdrawal of life-sustaining medical treatment.

The juvenile court weighed and balanced the factors. The testimony from Christopher's treating physicians and the independent physicians who examined him was both compelling and consistent.

Based on clear and convincing evidence, the juvenile court determined that continuation of Christopher's life-sustaining medical treatment would not be in his best interests. We hold this determination was supported by substantial evidence, and the juvenile court did not err in reaching its conclusion.

B. *The juvenile court had the authority to consider and rule on withdrawal of Christopher's life-sustaining medical treatment.*

1. *The juvenile court has the statutory authority to consider matters relating to life-sustaining medical treatment for dependent children within its jurisdiction.*

C. *Indian Child Welfare Act (ICWA) — Title 25 United States Code section 1901 et seq.*

1. *Facts relevant to ICWA analysis.*

(a). *The original record on appeal*

When the dependency petition was initially filed on December 21, 2001, SSA did not state that Christopher might be a member of, or eligible for membership in, a federally recognized Indian tribe, or that he was of Indian ancestry. In an interview with a social worker, however, Tamara had previously stated "she was part Indian from the Puma Tribe." Moises indicated he had no information as to Christopher's American Indian heritage.

In the permanency hearing report, filed August 26, 2002, SSA indicated that notice had been sent to the Puma Indian tribe and the Bureau of Indian Affairs (the BIA), but that no response had yet been received. A search by SSA of the listings of federally recognized tribes did not locate a tribe by the name of Puma. The BIA confirmed that such a tribe was unknown to that agency.

At that point, SSA had attempted to communicate with the tribe identified by Tamara, and had notified the BIA. Tamara then came up with another possible name of the tribe she claimed to belong to — Pima. SSA then checked with the Gila River Indian Community in Sacaton, Arizona, which maintains the records for the Pima tribe. On September 9, 2002, the Gila River Indian Community wrote to SSA, stating, "Base[d] on my research for a Christopher I[.] with date of birth as . . . and Social Security #. . . , the son of Tamara S[.], which I find no person on the Gila River Indian Community roll book, base[d] on the information you provided." The actual notification from SSA to the Gila River Indian Community was not included in the record on appeal.

(b). *Request for judicial notice; augmentation of record*

(9) SSA filed a request for judicial notice with this court on February 11, 2003, to add documents to the record showing SSA's additional notices to the BIA and the Pima tribes sent in January 2003, and the responses of the BIA and the tribes. All of the documents attached to the request for judicial notice were filed in the case in the juvenile court. (Cal. Rules of Court, rule 12(a)(1)(A).) Christopher, through his counsel, joined in the request on February 18, 2003. Moises had never raised the issue of ICWA compliance by the time the deadline (absent extraordinary circumstances) for augmenting the record on appeal passed. Therefore, SSA could not have known additional

material would be necessary in the appellate record. It appears from the documents attached to the request for judicial notice that SSA moved promptly to remedy any alleged deficiencies in the record.

(c). *The augmented record*

On January 22, 2003, SSA sent notice of the proceedings and a request for confirmation of Christopher's status as an Indian child to the BIA, the Gila River Indian Community Council, and the Salt River Pima-Maricopa Indian Community Council. These documents identified the names and birthdates (if known) of Christopher, Tamara, Tamara's parents, and Tamara's grandfather. The documents further indicated that Tamara's father and grandfather might be affiliated with the Arizona Pima Indian tribe, although it was unknown whether they were enrolled in the tribe.

On January 27, 2003, the Salt River Pima-Maricopa Indian Community confirmed in writing that Christopher, Tamara, and Tamara's parents were not enrolled as members of the community, and that Christopher was "not eligible for enrollment through any relative listed in the inquiry."

On February 3, 2003, the Gila River Indian Community confirmed in writing that Christopher was not listed as an enrolled member of the community. It also confirmed that Tamara, her parents and her grandfather were not listed as enrolled members, meaning that Christopher was not eligible for membership.

ICWA was enacted in response to " 'rising concern in the mid-1970's over the consequences to Indian children, Indian families, and Indian tribes of abusive child welfare practices that resulted in the separation of large numbers of Indian children from their families and tribes through adoption or foster care placement, usually in non-Indian homes.' " (*In re Alexandria Y.* (1996) 45 Cal. App. 4th 1483, 1488–1489 [53 Cal. Rptr. 2d 679].) The policy of ICWA is set forth in section 1902 of title 25 of the United States Code: "The Congress hereby declares that it is the policy of this Nation to protect the best interests of Indian children and to promote the stability and security of Indian tribes and families by the establishment of minimum Federal standards for the removal of Indian children from their families and the placement of such children in foster or adoptive homes which will reflect the unique values of Indian culture, and by providing for assistance to Indian tribes in the operation of child and family service programs."

No one proposes to separate Christopher from an Indian family and place him with a non-Indian family. Whether the juvenile court ruled that withdrawal of life-sustaining medical treatment from Christopher was or was not in his best interests, the stability and security of any Indian tribe or Indian family would not be served. Christopher will never be able to appreciate his alleged Indian ancestry, nor will he procreate and advance the lineage or culture of any Indian tribe.

4. *Application of the usual ICWA analysis.*

D. *The juvenile court's refusal to appoint a guardian ad litem for Tamara or to order a psychological evaluation of her was not in error.*

(10) Moises also contends that the court's failure to grant his request to appoint a guardian ad litem for Tamara or order a psychological evaluation of her constitutes reversible error. We initially question whether Moises may raise this issue on appeal. "The statutes regarding appointment of guardians *ad litem* were enacted to protect minors and insane and incompetent persons." (*Briggs v. Briggs* (1958) 160 Cal. App. 2d 312, 319 [325 P.2d 219].) Moises does not cite, and we have not located, any case in which a competent party challenges a court's order granting the relief sought by an allegedly incompetent party on the ground that the winning party was incompetent. We see no need to "protect" Tamara from the relief she herself sought in this case. If Moises was really arguing that Christopher needed protection from Tamara, the juvenile court's decision to hold an evidentiary hearing before life-sustaining medical treatment could be withdrawn, a decision we agreed with, provided whatever protection was needed.

In support of his request that a guardian ad litem be appointed to represent Tamara, Moises argued that Tamara did not cook, could not navigate the public transportation system, and had been referred to the county for social services.

The juvenile court appears to have based its decision not to grant Moises's request to appoint a guardian ad litem for Tamara on the standards of *Penal Code section 1367*, subdivision (a), which provides in part: "A defendant is mentally incompetent for purposes of this chapter if, as a result of mental disorder or developmental disability, the defendant is unable to understand the nature of the criminal proceedings or to assist counsel in the conduct of a defense in a rational manner."

The juvenile court did not abuse its discretion in determining whether a guardian ad litem for Tamara was required. The juvenile court had significant opportunities to consider Tamara's competence and her ability to understand the dependency court proceedings and to assist her counsel, having considered her testimony at the jurisdiction hearing. The court made a factual finding that Tamara's mental disability was not sufficiently severe that she would be unable to understand the proceedings or assist her counsel. Tamara's counsel supported that conclusion. The juvenile court and Tamara's counsel were in a far better position than we are to analyze Tamara's competence.

In any event, the determination for the juvenile court was whether Tamara could understand the nature of the proceedings *against her* and cooperate with counsel in protecting *her interests*. The evidentiary hearing regarding withdrawal of Christopher's life-sustaining medical treatment was not a proceeding against Tamara, and her best interests were not at issue. The juvenile court did not abuse its discretion in denying Moises's request on this ground.

DISPOSITION

The order of the juvenile court is affirmed.

Rylaarsdam, Acting P. J., and **Bedsworth**, J., concurred.

A petition for a rehearing was denied March 10, 2003, and the opinion was modified to read as printed above. Appellant's petition for review by the Supreme Court was denied April 23, 2003.

NOTES AND QUESTIONS

1. In *In Re Christopher I*, how could his own attorney accede to withdrawing life support? Shouldn't there have been a guardian ad litem? Do they have different functions? Responsibilities? Does one answer to the other?
2. As the perpetrator of the crime leading to Christopher's death, should Moises be barred from the proceeding? And what of his challenge to Tamara's competence — what is the relevance of that?
3. In discontinuing care, does it matter whether the care
   a. Will not effect a cure;
   b. May inflict pain;
   c. May continue pain;
   d. May itself produce complications leading to death?
4. When the doctors say treatment is "futile," what do they mean? *Can* it be futile if it keeps Christopher alive?
5. Do you agree with the Court's conclusion (note 2) that withdrawing treatment is "not the same" as physician assisted suicide?
6. In defining what factors to be considered "in the best interests" of a comatose child, how adequate are the lists in the *Barber* and *L.A. County* cases? Are there other factors in the list the Court itself articulates? What about death?
7. The Court discussed whether the Indian Child Welfare Act had been met, concluding notice had been given — albeit defective — and two Puma tribes found no evidence that Christopher was a Native American. Moreover, his case was helpless anyway, right?

   But suppose he had been Indian and the Puma view was clear, that life support should be continued. Which view controls?
8. And what of Tamara's need for a guardian, since she seems clearly incompetent?

WASHINGTON v. GLUCKSBERG*

521 U.S. 702 (1997)

Chief Justice **Rehnquist** delivered the opinion of the Court.

The question presented in this case is whether Washington's prohibition against "caus[ing]" or "aid[ing]" a suicide offends the Fourteenth Amendment to the United States Constitution. We hold that it does not.

It has always been a crime to assist a suicide in the State of Washington. In 1854, Washington's first Territorial Legislature outlawed "assisting another in the commission of self-murder." Today, Washington law provides: "A person is guilty of promoting a suicide attempt when he knowingly causes or aids another person to attempt suicide." "Promoting a suicide attempt" is a felony, punishable by up to five years' imprisonment and up to a $10,000 fine. At the same time, Washington's Natural Death Act, enacted in 1979, states that the "withholding or withdrawal of life-sustaining treatment" at a patient's direction "shall not, for any purpose, constitute a suicide."[1]

Petitioners in this case are the State of Washington and its Attorney General. respondents Harold Glucksberg, M.D., Abigail Halperin, M.D., Thomas A. Preston, M.D., and Peter Shalit, M.D., are physicians who practice in Washington. These doctors occasionally treat terminally ill, suffering patients, and declare that they would assist these patients in ending their lives if not for Washington's assisted-suicide ban. In January 1994, respondents, along with three gravely ill, pseudonymous plaintiffs who have since died and Compassion in Dying, a nonprofit organization that counsels people considering physician-assisted suicide, sued in the United States District Court, seeking a declaration that Wash. Rev. Code § 9A.36.060(1) (1994) is, on its face, unconstitutional.

The plaintiffs asserted "the existence of a liberty interest protected by the Fourteenth Amendment which extends to a personal choice by a mentally competent, terminally ill adult to commit physician-assisted suicide." Relying primarily on *Planned Parenthood v. Casey*, and *Cruzan v. Director, Missouri Dept. of Health*, the District Court agreed and concluded that Washington's assisted-suicide ban is unconstitutional because it "places an undue burden on the exercise of [that] constitutionally protected liberty interest." . . .

. . . .The Ninth Circuit reheard the case en banc, and affirmed the District Court. *Compassion in Dying v. Washington*, 79 F.3d 790, 798 (1996). . . . The court did not reach the District Court's equal-protection holding.[2]

---

* Some citation material has been omitted from this case.

[1] Under Washington's Natural Death Act, "adult persons have the fundamental right to control the decisions relating to the rendering of their own health care, including the decision to have life-sustaining treatment withheld or withdrawn in instances of a terminal condition or permanent unconscious condition." In Washington, "[a]ny adult person may execute a directive directing the withholding or withdrawal of life-sustaining treatment in a terminal condition or permanent unconscious condition," and a physician who, in accordance with such a directive, participates in the withholding or withdrawal of life-sustaining treatment is immune from civil, criminal, or professional liability.

[2] The Court of Appeals did note, however, that "the equal protection argument relied on by [the District Court] is not insubstantial," 79 F.3d at 838, n.139, and sharply criticized the opinion in a separate case then pending before the Ninth Circuit, *Lee v. Oregon*, 891 F. Supp. 1429 (Ore.

I

We begin, as we do in all due-process cases, by examining our Nation's history, legal traditions, and practices. . . . In almost every State — indeed, in almost every western democracy — it is a crime to assist a suicide.[3] The States' assisted-suicide bans are not innovations. Rather, they are longstanding expressions of the States' commitment to the protection and preservation of all human life. . . . Indeed, opposition to and condemnation of suicide — and, therefore, of assisting suicide — are consistent and enduring themes of our philosophical, legal, and cultural heritages.

More specifically, for over 700 years, the Anglo-American common-law tradition has punished or otherwise disapproved of both suicide and assisting suicide. . . .

. . . .

The earliest American statute explicitly to outlaw assisting suicide was enacted in New York in 1828, and many of the new States and Territories followed New York's example. . . . In this century, the Model Penal Code also prohibited "aiding" suicide, prompting many States to enact or revise their assisted-suicide banks. The Code's drafters observed that "the interests in the sanctity of life that are represented by the criminal homicide laws are threatened by one who expresses a willingness to participate in taking the life of another, even though the act may be accomplished with the consent, or at the request, of the suicide victim."

Though deeply rooted, the States' assisted-suicide bans have in recent years been reexamined and, generally, reaffirmed. Because of advances in medicine and technology, Americans today are increasingly likely to die in institutions, from chronic illnesses. Public concern and democratic action are therefore sharply focused on how best to protect dignity and independence at the end of life, with the result that there have been many significant changes in state laws and in the attitudes these laws reflect. Many States, for example, now permit "living wills," surrogate health-care decisionmaking, and the withdrawal or refusal of life-sustaining medical treatment. At the same time, however, voters and legislators continue for the most part to reaffirm their States' prohibitions on assisting suicide.

The Washington statute at issue in this case was enacted in 1975 as part of a revision of that State's criminal code. Four years later, Washington passed its Natural Death Act, which specifically stated that the "withholding or withdrawal of life-sustaining treatment . . . shall not, for any purpose,

1995) (Oregon's Death With Dignity Act, which permits physician-assisted suicide, violates the Equal Protection Clause because it does not provide adequate safeguards against abuse), vacated, *Lee v. Oregon*, 107 F.3d 1382 (C.A.9 1997) (concluding that plaintiffs lacked Article III standing). Lee, of course, is not before us, any more than it was before the Court of Appeals below, and we offer no opinion as to the validity of the Lee courts' reasoning. In *Vacco v. Quill*, post, however, decided today, we hold that New York's assisted-suicide ban does not violate the Equal Protection Clause.

[3] Since the Ninth Circuit's decision, Louisiana, Rhode Island, and Iowa have enacted statutory assisted-suicide bans. For a detailed history of the States' statutes, *see* Marzen, O'Dowd, Crone & Balch, *Suicide: A Constitutional Right?*, 24 Duquesne L. Rev. 1, 148-242 (1985) (Appendix) (hereinafter Marzen).

constitute a suicide" and that "[n]othing in this chapter shall be construed to condone, authorize, or approve mercy killing. . . ." In 1991, Washington voters rejected a ballot initiative which, had it passed, would have permitted a form of physician-assisted suicide.[4] Washington then added a provision to the Natural Death Act expressly excluding physician-assisted suicide. 1992 Wash. Laws, ch. 98, § 10; Wash. Rev. Code § 70.122.100 (1994).

California voters rejected an assisted-suicide initiative similar to Washington's in 1993. On the other hand, in 1994, voters in Oregon enacted, also through ballot initiative, that State's "Death With Dignity Act," which legalized physician-assisted suicide for competent, terminally ill adults.[5] Since the Oregon vote, many proposals to legalize assisted-suicide have been and continue to be introduced in the States' legislatures, but none has been enacted. And just last year, Iowa and Rhode Island joined the overwhelming majority of States explicitly prohibiting assisted suicide. Also, on April 30, 1997, President Clinton signed the Federal Assisted Suicide Funding Restriction Act of 1997, which prohibits the use of federal funds in support of physician-assisted suicide. Pub. L. 105-12, 111 Stat. 23 (codified at 42 U.S.C. § 14401 et seq.)[6] . . . .

. . . .

Attitudes toward suicide itself have changed since Bracton, but our laws have consistently condemned, and continue to prohibit, assisting suicide. Despite changes in medical technology and notwithstanding an increased emphasis on the importance of end-of-life decisionmaking, we have not

[4] Initiative 119 would have amended Washington's Natural Death Act, Wash. Rev. Code § 70.122.010 et seq. (1994), to permit "aid-in-dying," defined as "aid in the form of a medical service provided in person by a physician that will end the life of a conscious and mentally competent qualified patient in a dignified, painless and humane manner, when requested voluntarily by the patient through a written directive in accordance with this chapter at the time the medical services is to be provided."

[5] Ore. Rev. Stat. §§ 127.800 et seq. (1996); *Lee v. Oregon*, 891 F. Supp. 1429 (Ore. 1995)(Oregon Act does not provide sufficient safeguards for terminally ill persons and therefore violates the Equal Protection Clause), vacated, *Lee v. Oregon*, 107 F.3d 1382 (9th Cir. 1997).

[6] Other countries are embroiled in similar debates: The Supreme Court of Canada recently rejected a claim that the Canadian Charter of Rights and Freedoms establishes a fundamental right to assisted suicide, Rodriguez v. British Columbia (Attorney General), 107 D.L.R. (4th) 342 (1993); the British House of Lords Select Committee on Medical Ethics refused to recommend any change in Great Britain's assisted-suicide prohibition, House of Lords, Session 1993-94 Report of the Select Committee on Medical Ethics, 12 Issues in Law & Med. 193, 202 (1996) ("We identify no circumstances in which assisted suicide should be permitted"); New Zealand's Parliament rejected a proposed "Death With Dignity Bill" that would have legalized physician-assisted suicide in August 1995, Graeme, MPs Throw Out Euthanasia Bill, *The Dominion* (Wellington), Aug. 17, 1995, p.1; and the Northern Territory of Australia legalized assisted suicide and voluntary euthanasia in 1995. *See* Shenon, Australian Doctors Get Right to Assist Suicide, *N.Y. Times*, July 28, 1995, p.A8. As of February 1997, three persons had ended their lives with physician assistance in the Northern Territory, Mydans, Assisted Suicide: Australia Faces a Grim Reality, *N.Y. Times*, Feb. 2, 1997, p.A3. On March 24, 1997, however, the Australian Senate voted to overturn the Northern Territory's law. Thornhill, Australia Repeals Euthanasia Law, *Washington Post*, March 25, 1997, p. A14; *see* Euthanasia Laws Act 1977, No. 17, 1997 (Austl.). On the other hand, on May 20, 1997, Colombia's Constitutional Court legalized voluntary euthanasia for terminally ill people. Sentencia No. C-239/97 *(Corte Constitutional*, Mayo 20, 1997); *see* Colombia's Top Court Legalizes Euthanasia, *Orlando Sentinel*, May 22, 1997, p. A18.

retreated from this prohibition. Against this backdrop of history, tradition, and practice, we now turn to respondents' constitutional claim.

II

The Due Process Clause guarantees more than fair process, and the "liberty" it protects includes more than the absence of physical restraint. *Collins v. Harker Heights*. The Clause also provides heightened protection against government interference with certain fundamental rights and liberty interests. *Reno v. Flores*; *Casey*. In a long line of cases, we have held that, in addition to the specific freedoms protected by the Bill of Rights, the "liberty" specially protected by the Due Process Clause includes the rights to marry, *Loving v. Virginia*; to have children; to direct the education and upbringing of one's children, *Meyer v. Nebraska, Pierce v. Society of Sisters;* to marital privacy, *Griswold v. Connecticut*; to use contraception; to bodily integrity, *Rochin v. California*; and to abortion, *Casey, supra*. We have also assumed, and strongly suggested, that the Due Process Clause protects the traditional right to refuse unwanted lifesaving medical treatment. *Cruzan*. . . .

. . . .

Turning to the claim at issue here, the Court of Appeals stated that "[p]roperly analyzed, the first issue to be resolved is whether there is a liberty interest in determining the time and manner of one's death," or, in other words, "[i]s there a right to die?" Similarly, respondents assert a "liberty to choose how to die" and a right to "control of one's final days," and describe the asserted liberty as "the right to choose a humane, dignified death," and "the liberty to shape death." As noted above, we have a tradition of carefully formulating the interest at stake in substantive-due-process cases. . . .

We now inquire whether this asserted right has any place in our Nation's traditions. Here, as discussed above, we are confronted with a consistent and almost universal tradition that has long rejected the asserted right, and continues explicitly to reject it today, even for terminally ill, mentally competent adults. To hold for respondents, we would have to reverse centuries of legal doctrine and practice, and strike down the considered policy choice of almost every State.

. . . .

The right assumed in *Cruzan* . . . , was not simply deduced from abstract concepts of personal autonomy. Given the common-law rule that forced medication was a battery, and the long legal tradition protecting the decision to refuse unwanted medical treatment, our assumption was entirely consistent with this Nation's history and constitutional traditions. The decision to commit suicide with the assistance of another may be just as personal and profound as the decision to refuse unwanted medical treatment, but it has never enjoyed similar legal protection. Indeed, the two acts are widely and reasonably regarded as quite distinct.

Respondents also rely on *Casey*. . . .

. . . .

[R]respondents emphasize the statement in *Casey* that:

> "At the heart of liberty is the right to define one's own concept of existence, of meaning, of the universe, and of the mystery of human life. Beliefs about these matters could not define the attributes of personhood were they formed under compulsion of the State."

By choosing this language, the Court's opinion in *Casey* described, in a general way and in light of our prior cases, those personal activities and decisions that this Court has identified as so deeply rooted in our history and traditions, or so fundamental to our concept of constitutionally ordered liberty, that they are protected by the Fourteenth Amendment.[7] The opinion moved from the recognition that liberty necessarily includes freedom of conscience and belief about ultimate considerations to the observation that "though the abortion decision may originate within the zone of conscience and belief, it is more than a philosophic exercise." That many of the rights and liberties protected by the Due Process Clause sound in personal autonomy does not warrant the sweeping conclusion that any and all important, intimate, and personal decisions are so protected, and *Casey* did not suggest otherwise.

. . . .

First, Washington has an "unqualified interest in the preservation of human life." . . . This interest is symbolic and aspirational as well as practical:

> "While suicide is no longer prohibited or penalized, the ban against assisted suicide and euthanasia shores up the notion of limits in human relationships. It reflects the gravity with which we view the decision to take one's own life or the life of another, and our reluctance to encourage or promote these decisions."

New York Task Force 131-132.

. . . .

Those who attempt suicide — terminally ill or not — often suffer from depression or other mental disorders. *See* New York Task Force 13-232, 126-128 (more than 95% of those who commit suicide had a major psychiatric illness at the time of death; among the terminally ill, uncontrolled pain is a "risk factor" because it contributes to depression). Research indicates, however, that many people who request physician-assisted suicide withdraw that

---

[7] *See Moore v. East Cleveland*, 431 U.S. 494, 503 (1977) ("[T]he Constitution protects the sanctity of the family precisely because the institution of the family is deeply rooted in this Nation's history and tradition") (emphasis added); *Griswold v. Connecticut*, 381 U.S. 479, 485-486 (1965)(intrusions into the "sacred precincts of marital bedrooms" offend rights "older than the Bill of Rights"); id., at 495-496 (Goldberg, J., concurring) (the law in question "disrupt[ed] the traditional relation of the family — a relation as old and as fundamental as our entire civilization"); *Loving v. Virginia*, 388 U.S. 1, 12 (1967) ("The freedom to marry has long been recognized as one of the vital personal rights essential to the orderly pursuit of happiness"); *Turner v. Safley*, 482 U.S. 78, 95 (1987) ("[T]he decision to marry is a fundamental right"); *Roe v. Wade*, 410 U.S. 113, 140 (1973) (stating that at the Founding and throughout the 19th century, "a woman enjoyed a substantially broader right to terminate a pregnancy"); *Skinner v. Oklahoma* ex rel. Williamson, 316 U.S. 535, 541 (1942) ("Marriage and procreation are fundamental"); *Pierce v. Society of Sisters*, 268 U.S. 510, 535 (1925); *Meyer v. Nebraska*, 262 U.S. 390, 399 (1923) (liberty includes "those privileges long recognized at common law as essential to the orderly pursuit of happiness by free men").

request if their depression and pain are treated. H. Hendin, Seduced by Death: Doctors, Patients and the Dutch Cure 24-25 (1997) (suicidal, terminally ill patients "usually respond well to treatment for depressive illness and pain medication and are then grateful to be alive"). . . .

The State also has an interest in protecting the integrity and ethics of the medical profession. In contrast to the Court of Appeals' conclusion that "the integrity of the medical profession would [not] be threatened in any way by [physician-assisted suicide]," 79 F.3d. at 827, the American Medical Association, like many other medical and physicians' groups, has concluded that "[p]hysician-assisted suicide is fundamentally incompatible with the physician's role as healer." American Medical Association, Code of Ethics § 2.211 (1994); *see* Council on Ethical and Judicial Affairs, *Decisions Near the End of Life,* 267 JAMA 2229, 2233 (1992) ("[T]he societal risks of involving physicians in medical interventions to cause patients' deaths is too great"); New York Task Force 103-109 (discussing physicians' views). And physician-assisted suicide could, it is argued, undermine the trust that is essential to the doctor-patient relationship by blurring the time-honored line between healing and harming.

Next, the State has an interest in protecting vulnerable groups — including the poor, the elderly, and disabled persons — from abuse, neglect, and mistakes. . . .

The State's interest here goes beyond protecting the vulnerable from coercion; it extends to protecting disabled and terminally ill people from prejudice, negative and inaccurate stereotypes, and "societal indifference." The State's assisted-suicide ban reflects and reinforces its policy that the lives of terminally ill, disabled, and elderly people must be no less valued than the lives of the young and healthy, and that a seriously disabled person's suicidal impulses should be interpreted and treated the same way as anyone else's.

Finally, the State may fear that permitting assisted suicide will start it down the path to voluntary and perhaps even involuntary euthanasia. The Court of Appeals struck down Washington's assisted-suicide ban only "as applied to competent, terminally ill adults who wish to hasten their deaths by obtaining medication prescribed by their doctors." Washington insists, however, that the impact of [illegible] decision will not and cannot be so limited. If suicide is protected as a matter of constitutional right, it is argued, "every man and woman in the United States must enjoy it." Thus, it turns out that what is couched as a limited right to "physician-assisted suicide" is likely, in effect, a much broader license, which could prove extremely difficult to police and contain. Washington's ban on assisting suicide prevents such erosion.

This concern is further supported by evidence about the practice of euthanasia in the Netherlands. The Dutch government's own study revealed that in 1990, there were 2,300 cases of voluntary euthanasia (defined as "the deliberate termination of another's life at his request"), 400 cases of assisted suicide, and more than 1,000 cases of euthanasia without an explicit request. In addition to these latter 1,000 cases, the study found an additional 4,941 cases where physicians administered lethal morphine overdoses without the patients' explicit consent. *Physician-Assisted Suicide and Euthanasia in the Netherlands: A Report of Chairman Charles T. Canady,* at 12-13 (citing Dutch study). This study suggests that, despite the existence of various reporting procedures, euthanasia in the Netherlands has not been limited to competent, terminally ill adults who are enduring physical suffering, and that regulation of the practice may not have prevented abuses in cases involving vulnerable persons, including severely disabled neonates and elderly persons suffering from dementia. *Id.*, at 16-21; *see generally* C. Gomez, Regulating Death: Euthanasia and the Case of the Netherlands (1991); H. Hendin, Seduced By Death: Doctors, Patients, and the Dutch Cure (1997).

We need not weigh exactingly the relative strengths of these various interests. They are unquestionably important and legitimate, and Washington's ban on assisted suicide is at least reasonably related to their promotion and protection. We therefore hold that Wash. Rev. Code § 9A.36.060(1) (1994) does not violate the Fourteenth Amendment, either on its face or "as applied to competent, terminally ill adults who wish to hasten their deaths by obtaining medication prescribed by their doctors."

Justice **O'Connor**, concurring.[8]

Death will be different for each of us. For many, the last days will be spent in physical pain and perhaps the despair that accompanies physical deterioration and a loss of control of basic bodily and mental functions. Some will seek medication to alleviate that pain and other symptoms.

The Court frames the issue in this case as whether the Due Process Clause of the Constitution protects a "right to commit suicide which itself includes a right to assistance in doing so," and concludes that our Nation's history, legal traditions, and practices do not support the existence of such a right. I join the Court's opinions because I agree that there is no generalized right to "commit suicide." But respondents urge us to address the narrower question whether a mentally competent person who is experiencing great suffering has a constitutionally cognizable interest in controlling the circumstances of his or her imminent death. I see no need to reach that question in the context of the facial challenges to the New York and Washington laws at issue here. . . . The parties and amici agree that in these States a patient who is suffering from a terminal illness and who is experiencing great pain has no legal barriers to obtaining medication, from qualified physicians, to alleviate that suffering, even to the point of causing unconsciousness and hastening death. In this light, even assuming that we would recognize such an interest, I agree that the State's interests in protecting those who are not truly competent or facing imminent death, or those whose decisions to hasten death would not truly be voluntary, are sufficiently weighty to justify a prohibition against physician-assisted suicide.

Every one of us at some point may be affected by our own or a family member's terminal illness. There is no reason to think the democratic process will not strike the proper balance between the interests of terminally ill, mentally competent individuals who would seek to end their suffering and the State's interests in protecting those who might seek to end life mistakenly or under pressure. As the Court recognizes, States are presently undertaking

[8] Justice **Ginsburg** concurs in the Court's judgments substantially for the reasons stated in this opinion. Justice **Breyer** joins this opinion except insofar as it joins the opinions of the Court.

extensive and serious evaluation of physician-assisted suicide and other related issues.

. . . .

Justice **Stevens**, concurring in the judgments.

. . . .

I

. . . .

Today, the Court decides that Washington's statute prohibiting assisted suicide is not invalid "on its face," that is to say, in all or most cases in which it might be applied. That holding, however, does not foreclose the possibility that some applications of the statute might well be invalid.

. . . .

But just as our conclusion that capital punishment is not always unconstitutional did not preclude later decisions holding that it is sometimes impermissibly cruel, so is it equally clear that a decision upholding a general statutory prohibition of assisted suicide does not mean that every possible application of the statute would be valid. A State, like Washington, that has authorized the death penalty and thereby has concluded that the sanctity of human life does not require that it always be preserved, must acknowledge that there are situations in which an interest in hastening death is legitimate. Indeed, not only is that interest sometimes legitimate, I am also convinced that there are times when it is entitled to constitutional protection.

II

. . . .

. . . .[T]he source of Nancy Cruzan's right to refuse treatment was not just a common-law rule. Rather, this right is an aspect of a far broader and more basic concept of freedom that is even older than the common law.[9] This freedom embraces, not merely a person's right to refuse a particular kind of unwanted treatment, but also her interest in dignity, and in determining the character of the memories that will survive long after her death. In recognizing that the State's interests did not outweigh Nancy Cruzan's liberty interest in refusing medical treatment, Cruzan rested not simply on the common-law right to refuse medical treatment, but — at least implicitly — on the even

[9] "[N]either the Bill of Rights nor the laws of sovereign States create the liberty which the Due Process Clause protects. The relevant constitutional provisions are limitations on the power of the sovereign to infringe on the liberty of the citizen. The relevant state laws either create property rights, or they curtail the freedom of the citizen who must live in an ordered society. Of course, law is essential to the exercise and enjoyment of individual liberty in a complex society. But it is not the source of liberty, and surely not the exclusive source.

"I had thought it self-evident that all men were endowed by their Creator with liberty as one of the cardinal unalienable rights. It is that basic freedom which the Due Process Clause protects, rather than the particular rights or privileges conferred by specific laws or regulations." *Meachum v. Fano*, 427 U.S. 215, 230 (1976) (**Stevens**, J., dissenting).

more fundamental right to make this "deeply personal decision" (**O'Connor**, J., concurring).

Thus, the common-law right to protection from battery, which included the right to refuse medical treatment in most circumstances, did not mark "the outer limits of the substantive sphere of liberty" that supported the Cruzan family's decision to hasten Nancy's death. Whatever the outer limits of the concept may be, it definitely includes protection for matters "central to personal dignity and autonomy." . . .

. . . .

. . . The liberty interest at stake in a case like this differs from, and is stronger than, both the common-law right to refuse medical treatment and the unbridled interest in deciding whether to live or die. It is an interest in deciding how, rather than whether, a critical threshold shall be crossed.

III

The state interests supporting a general rule banning the practice of physician-assisted suicide do not have the same force in all cases. First and foremost of these interests is the " 'unqualified interest in the preservation of human life.' " Properly viewed, however, this interest is not a collective interest that should always outweigh the interests of a person who because of pain, incapacity, or sedation finds her life intolerable, but rather, an aspect of individual freedom.

. . . .

Similarly, the State's legitimate interests in preventing suicide, protecting the vulnerable from coercion and abuse, and preventing euthanasia are less significant in this context. I agree that the State has a compelling interest in preventing persons from committing suicide because of depression, or coercion by third parties. But the State's legitimate interest in preventing abuse does not apply to an individual who is not victimized by abuse, who is not suffering from depression, and who makes a rational and voluntary decision to seek assistance in dying. . . .

Relatedly, the State and amici express the concern that patients whose physical pain is inadequately treated will be more likely to request assisted suicide. Encouraging the development and ensuring the availability of adequate pain treatment is of utmost importance; palliative care, however, cannot alleviate all pain and suffering. An individual adequately informed of the care alternatives thus might make a rational choice for assisted suicide. For such an individual, the State's interest in preventing potential abuse and mistake is only minimally implicated.

The final major interest asserted by the State is its interest in preserving the traditional integrity of the medical profession. The fear is that a rule permitting physicians to assist in suicide is inconsistent with the perception that they serve their patients solely as healers. But for some patients, it would be a physician's refusal to dispense medication to ease their suffering and make their death tolerable and dignified that would be inconsistent with the healing role. . . .

. . . .Unlike the Court of Appeals, I would not say as a categorical matter that these state interests are invalid as to the entire class of terminally ill, mentally competent patients. I do not, however, foreclose the possibility that an individual plaintiff seeking to hasten her death, or a doctor whose assistance was sought, could prevail in a more particularized challenge. Future cases will determine whether such a challenge may succeed.

Justice **Souter**, concurring in the judgment.

. . . .

II

When the physicians claim that the Washington law deprives them of a right falling within the scope of liberty that the Fourteenth Amendment guarantees against denial without due process of law, they are not claiming some sort of procedural defect in the process through which the statute has been enacted or is administered. Their claim, rather, is that the State has no substantively adequate justification for barring the assistance sought by the patient and sought to be offered by the physician. Thus, we are dealing with a claim to one of those rights sometimes described as rights of substantive due process and sometimes as unenumerated rights, in view of the breadth and indeterminacy of the "due process" serving as the claim's textual basis. . . .

. . . .

After the ratification of the Fourteenth Amendment, with its guarantee of due process protection against the States, interpretation of the words "liberty" and "property" as used in due process clauses became a sustained enterprise, with the Court generally describing the due process criterion in converse terms of reasonableness or arbitrariness. . . .

The theory became serious, however, beginning with *Allgeyer v. Louisiana*, 165 U.S. 578 (1897), where the Court invalidated a Louisiana statute for excessive interference with Fourteenth Amendment liberty to contract, and offered a substantive interpretation of "liberty," that in the aftermath of the so-called *Lochner* era has been scaled back in some respects, but expanded in others, and never repudiated in principle. The Court said that Fourteenth Amendment liberty includes "the right of the citizen to be free in the enjoyment of all his faculties; to be free to use them in all lawful ways; to live and work where he will; to earn his livelihood by any lawful calling; to pursue any livelihood or avocation; and for that purpose to enter into all contracts which may be proper, necessary and essential to his carrying out to a successful conclusion the purposes above mentioned."

. . . Allgeyer was succeeded within a decade by *Lochner v. New York*, 198 U.S. 45 (1905), and the era to which that case gave its name, famous now for striking down as arbitrary various sorts of economic regulations that post-New Deal courts have uniformly thought constitutionally sound. . . .

. . . [H]owever, the more durable precursors of modern substantive due process were reaffirming this Court's obligation to conduct arbitrariness review, beginning with *Meyer v. Nebraska*, 262 U.S. 390 (1923). Without referring to any specific guarantee of the Bill of Rights, the Court invoked precedents from the Slaughter-House Cases through Adkins to declare that the Fourteenth Amendment protected "the right of the individual to contract, to engage in any of the common occupations of life, to acquire useful knowledge, to marry, establish a home and bring up children, to worship God according to the dictates of his own conscience, and generally to enjoy those privileges long recognized at common law as essential to the orderly pursuit of happiness by free men." The Court then held that the same Fourteenth Amendment liberty included a teacher's right to teach and the rights of parents to direct their children's education without unreasonable interference by the States, with the result that Nebraska's prohibition on the teaching of foreign languages in the lower grades was, "arbitrary and without reasonable relation to any end within the competency of the State." *See also Pierce v. Society of Sisters* (finding that a statute that all but outlawed private schools lacked any "reasonable relation to some purpose within the competency of the State"). . . .

. . . .

The second major opinion leading to the modern doctrine was Justice Harlan's Poe dissent, the conclusion of which was adopted in *Griswold v. Connecticut*, and the authority of which was acknowledged in *Planned Parenthood of Southeastern Pa. v. Casey.* The dissent is important for three things that point to our responsibilities today. The first is Justice Harlan's respect for the tradition of substantive due process review itself, and his acknowledgment of the Judiciary's obligation to carry it on. For two centuries American courts, and for much of that time this Court, have thought it necessary to provide some degree of review over the substantive content of legislation under constitutional standards of textual breadth. The obligation was understood before Dred Scott and has continued after the repudiation of *Lochner*'s progeny. . . .

. . . The second of the dissent's lessons is a reminder that the business of such review is not the identification of extratextual absolutes but scrutiny of a legislative resolution (perhaps unconscious) of clashing principles, each quite possibly worthy in and of itself, but each to be weighed within the history of our values as a people. . . . Part III, below, deals with this second point, and also with the dissent's third, which takes the form of an object lesson in the explicit attention to detail that is no less essential to the intellectual discipline of substantive due process review than an understanding of the basic need to account for the two sides in the controversy and to respect legislation within the zone of reasonableness.

III

. . . .

. . . Exact analysis and characterization of any due process claim is critical to the method and to the result.

. . . .

. . . [H]ere we are faced with an individual claim not to a right on the part of just anyone to help anyone else commit suicide under any circumstances, but to the right of a narrow class to help others also in a narrow class under a set of limited circumstances. And the claimants are met with the State's assertion, among others, that rights of such narrow scope cannot be recognized without jeopardy to individuals whom the State may concededly protect through its regulations.

IV

A

Respondents claim that a patient facing imminent death, who anticipates physical suffering and indignity, and is capable of responsible and voluntary choice, should have a right to a physician's assistance in providing counsel and drugs to be administered by the patient to end life promptly. They accordingly claim that a physician must have the corresponding right to provide such aid, contrary to the provisions of Wash. Rev. Code § 9A.36.060 (1994). I do not understand the argument to rest on any assumption that rights either to suicide or to assistance in committing it are historically based as such. Respondents, rather, acknowledge the prohibition of each historically, but rely on the fact that to a substantial extent the State has repudiated that history. The result of this, respondents say, is to open the door to claims of such a patient to be accorded one of the options open to those with different, traditionally cognizable claims to autonomy in deciding how their bodies and minds should be treated. They seek the option to obtain the services of a physician to give them the benefit of advice and medical help, which is said to enjoy a tradition so strong and so devoid of specifically countervailing state concern that denial of a physician's help in these circumstances is arbitrary when physicians are generally free to advise and aid those who exercise other rights to bodily autonomy.

. . . .

2

The argument supporting respondents' position thus progresses through three steps of increasing forcefulness. First, it emphasizes the decriminalization of suicide. Reliance on this fact is sanctioned under the standard that looks not only to the tradition retained, but to society's occasional choices to reject traditions of the legal past. While the common law prohibited both suicide and aiding a suicide, with the prohibition on aiding largely justified by the primary prohibition on self-inflicted death itself, *see, e.g.,* American Law Institute, Model Penal Code § 210.5, Comment 1, pp. 92-93, and n.7 (1980), the State's rejection of the traditional treatment of the one leaves the criminality of the other open to questioning that previously would not have been appropriate. The second step in the argument is to emphasize that the State's own act of decriminalization gives a freedom of choice much like the individual's option in recognized instances of bodily autonomy. One of these, abortion, is a legal right to choose in spite of the interest a State may legitimately invoke in discouraging the practice, just as suicide is now subject to choice, despite a state interest in discouraging it. The third step is to emphasize that respondents claim a right to assistance not on the basis of some broad principle that would be subject to exceptions if that continuing interest of the State's in discouraging suicide were to be recognized at all. Respondents base their claim on the traditional right to medical care and counsel, subject to the limiting conditions of informed, responsible choice when death is imminent, conditions that support a strong analogy to rights of care in other situations in which medical counsel and assistance have been available as a matter of course. There can be no stronger claim to a physician's assistance than at the time when death is imminent, a moral judgment implied by the State's own recognition of the legitimacy of medical procedures necessarily hastening the moment of impending death.

In my judgment, the importance of the individual interest here, as within that class of "certain interests" demanding careful scrutiny of the State's contrary claim, cannot be gainsaid. Whether that interest might in some circumstances, or at some time, be seen as "fundamental" to the degree entitled to prevail is not, however, a conclusion that I need draw here, for I am satisfied that the State's interests described in the following section are sufficiently serious to defeat the present claim that its law is arbitrary or purposeless.

B

The State has put forward several interests to justify the Washington law as applied to physicians treating terminally ill patients, even those competent to make responsible choices: protecting life generally, discouraging suicide even if knowing and voluntary, and protecting terminally ill patients from involuntary suicide and euthanasia, both voluntary and nonvoluntary.

It is not necessary to discuss the exact strengths of the first two claims of justification in the present circumstances, for the third is dispositive for me. . . . The State claims interests in protecting patients from mistakenly and involuntarily deciding to end their lives, and in guarding against both voluntary and involuntary euthanasia. Leaving aside any difficulties in coming to a clear concept of imminent death, mistaken decisions may result from inadequate palliative care or a terminal prognosis that turns out to be error; coercion and abuse may stem from the large medical bills that family members cannot bear or unreimbursed hospitals decline to shoulder. Voluntary and involuntary euthanasia may result once doctors are authorized to prescribe lethal medication in the first instance, for they might find it pointless to distinguish between patients who administer their own fatal drugs and those who wish not to, and their compassion for those who suffer may obscure the distinction between those who ask for death and those who may be unable to request it. The argument is that a progression would occur, obscuring the line between the ill and the dying, and between the responsible and the unduly influenced, until ultimately doctors and perhaps others would abuse a limited freedom to aid suicides by yielding to the impulse to end another's suffering under conditions going beyond the narrow limits the respondents propose. The State thus argues, essentially, that respondents' claim is not as narrow as it sounds, simply because no recognition of the interest they assert could be limited to vindicating those interests and affecting no others. The State says that the claim, in practical effect, would entail consequences that the State could, without doubt, legitimately act to prevent.

. . . .

The State, however, goes further, to argue that dependence on the vigilance of physicians will not be enough. First, the lines proposed here (particularly the requirement of a knowing and voluntary decision by the patient) would be more difficult to draw than the lines that have limited other recently recognized due process rights. limiting a state from prosecuting use of artificial contraceptives by married couples posed no practical threat to the State's capacity to regulate contraceptives in other ways that were assumed at the time of Poe to be legitimate; the trimester measurements of Roe and the viability determination of Casey were easy to make with a real degree of certainty. But the knowing and responsible mind is harder to assess. Second, this difficulty could become the greater by combining with another fact within the realm of plausibility, that physicians simply would not be assiduous to preserve the line. . . .

. . . .

. . . Respondents' proposals, as it turns out, sound much like the guidelines now in place in the Netherlands, the only place where experience with physician-assisted suicide and euthanasia has yielded empirical evidence about how such regulations might affect actual practice. Dutch physicians must engage in consultation before proceeding, and must decide whether the patient's decision is voluntary, well considered, and stable, whether the request to die is enduring and made more than once, and whether the patient's future will involve unacceptable suffering. *See* C. Gomez, Regulating Death 40-43 (1991). There is, however, a substantial dispute today about what the Dutch experience shows. Some commentators marshall evidence that the Dutch guidelines have in practice failed to protect patients from involuntary euthanasia and have been violated with impunity. *See, e.g.,* H. Hendin, Seduced By Death 75-84 (1997). This evidence is contested The day may come when we can say with some assurance which side is right, but for now it is the substantiality of the factual disagreement, and the alternatives for resolving it, that matter. They are, for me, dispositive of the due process claim at this time.

. . . .

Justice **Ginsburg**, concurring in the judgments.

I concur in the Court's judgments in these cases substantially for the reasons stated by Justice **O'Connor** in her concurring opinion.

Justice **Breyer**, concurring in the judgments.

I believe that Justice **O'Connor**'s views, which I share, have greater legal significance than the Court's opinion suggests. I join her separate opinion, except insofar as it joins the majority. And I concur in the judgments. I shall briefly explain how I differ from the Court.

I agree with the Court in *Vacco v. Quill*, that the articulated state interests justify the distinction drawn between physician assisted suicide and withdrawal of life-support. I also agree with the Court that the critical question in both of the cases before us is whether "the 'liberty' specially protected by the Due Process Clause includes a right" of the sort that the respondents assert. I do not agree, however, with the Court's formulation of that claimed "liberty" interest. The Court describes it as a "right to commit suicide with another's assistance." But I would not reject the respondents' claim without considering a different formulation, for which our legal tradition may provide greater support. That formulation would use words roughly like a "right to die with dignity." But irrespective of the exact words used, at its core would lie personal control over the manner of death, professional medical assistance, and the avoidance of unnecessary and severe physical suffering — combined.

. . . .

I do not believe, however, that this Court need or now should decide whether or a not such a right is "fundamental." That is because, in my view, the avoidance of severe physical pain (connected with death) would have to comprise an essential part of any successful claim and because, as Justice **O'Connor** points out, the laws before us do not force a dying person to undergo that kind of pain. . . .

. . . .

Were the legal circumstances different — for example, were state law to prevent the provision of palliative care, including the administration of drugs as needed to avoid pain at the end of life — then the law's impact upon serious and otherwise unavoidable physical pain (accompanying death) would be more directly at issue. And as Justice **O'Connor** suggests, the Court might have to revisit its conclusions in these cases.

VACCO v. QUILL
117 S.Ct. 2293 (1997)

Chief Justice **Rehnquist** delivered the opinion of the Court.

In New York, as in most States, it is a crime to aid another to commit or attempt suicide,[1] but patients may refuse even lifesaving medical treatment. The question presented by this case is whether New York's prohibition on assisting suicide therefore violates the Equal Protection Clause of the Fourteenth Amendment. We hold that it does not.

. . . .

The Equal Protection Clause commands that no State shall "deny to any person within its jurisdiction the equal protection of the laws." This provision creates no substantive rights. *San Antonio Independent School Dist. v. Rodriguez*. Instead, it embodies a general rule that States must treat like cases alike but may treat unlike cases accordingly. *Plyler v. Doe*. If a legislative classification or distinction "neither burdens a fundamental right nor targets

[1] N.Y. Penal Law § 125.15 (McKinney 1987) ("Manslaughter in the second degree") provides: "A person is guilty of manslaughter in the second degree when . . . (3) He intentionally causes or aids another person to commit suicide. Manslaughter in the second degree is a class C felony." Section 120.30 ("Promoting a suicide attempt") states: "A person is guilty of promoting a suicide attempt when he intentionally causes or aids another person to attempt suicide. Promoting a suicide attempt is a class E felony."

a suspect class, we will uphold [it] so long as it bears a rational relation to some legitimate end." *Romer v. Evans.*

. . . .

On their faces, neither New York's ban on assisting suicide nor its statutes permitting patients to refuse medical treatment treat anyone differently than anyone else or draw any distinctions between persons. Everyone, regardless of physical condition, is entitled, if competent, to refuse unwanted lifesaving medical treatment; no one is permitted to assist a suicide. Generally speaking, laws that apply evenhandedly to all "unquestionably comply" with the Equal Protection Clause. . . .

The Court of Appeals, however, concluded that some terminally ill people — those who are on life-support systems — are treated differently than those who are not, in that the former may "hasten death" by ending treatment, but the latter may not "hasten death" through physician-assisted suicide. This conclusion depends on the submission that ending or refusing lifesaving medical treatment "is nothing more nor less than assisted suicide." Unlike the Court of Appeals, we think the distinction between assisting suicide and withdrawing life-sustaining treatment, a distinction widely recognized and endorsed in the medical profession[2] and in our legal traditions, is both important and logical; it is certainly rational.

The distinction comports with fundamental legal principles of causation and intent. First, when a patient refuses life-sustaining medical treatment, he dies from an underlying fatal disease or pathology; but if a patient ingests lethal medication prescribed by a physician, he is killed by that medication. . . .

Furthermore, a physician who withdraws, or honors a patient's refusal to begin, life-sustaining medical treatment purposefully intends, or may so intend, only to respect his patient's wishes and "to cease doing useless and futile or degrading things to the patient when [the patient] no longer stands to benefit from them." Assisted Suicide in the United States, Hearing before the Subcommittee on the Constitution of the House Committee on the Judiciary, 104th Cong., 2d Sess., 368 (1996) (testimony of Dr. Leon R. Kass). The same is true when a doctor provides aggressive palliative care; in some cases, painkilling drugs may hasten a patient's death, but the physician's purpose and intent is, or may be, only to ease his patient's pain. A doctor who

[2] The American Medical Association emphasizes the "fundamental difference between refusing life-sustaining treatment and demanding a life-ending treatment." American Medical Association, Council on Ethical and Judicial Affairs, *Physician-Assisted Suicide*, 10 Issues in Law & Medicine 91, 93 (1994); *see also* American Medical Association, Council on Ethical and Judicial Affairs, *Decisions Near the End of Life*, 267 JAMA 2229, 2230-2231, 2233 (1992) ("The withdrawing or withholding of life-sustaining treatment is not inherently contrary to the principles of beneficence and nonmaleficence," but assisted suicide "is contrary to the prohibition against using the tools of medicine to cause a patient's death"); New York State Task Force on Life and the Law, *When Death is Sought: Assisted Suicide and Euthanasia in the Medical Context* 108 (1994) ("[Professional organizations] consistently distinguish assisted suicide and euthanasia from the withdrawing or withholding of treatment, and from the provision of palliative treatments or other medical care that risk fatal side effects"); Brief for the American Medical Association et al. as Amici Curiae 18-25. Of course, as respondents' lawsuit demonstrates, there are differences of opinion within the medical profession on this question. *See* New York Task Force, *When Death is Sought, supra,* at 104-109.

assists a suicide, however, "must, necessarily and indubitably, intend primarily that the patient be made dead." Similarly, a patient who commits suicide with a doctor's aid necessarily has the specific intent to end his or her own life, while a patient who refuses or discontinues treatment might not.

The law has long used actors' intent or purpose to distinguish between two acts that may have the same result. Put differently, the law distinguishes actions taken "because of" a given end from actions taken "in spite of" their unintended but foreseen consequences. *Compassion in Dying v. Washington*, 79 F.3d 790, 858 (C.A.9 1996) (Kleinfeld, J., dissenting) ("When General Eisenhower ordered American soldiers onto the beaches of Normandy, he knew that he was sending many American soldiers to certain death. . . . His purpose, though, was to . . . liberate Europe from the Nazis"). . . .

Given these general principles, it is not surprising that many courts, including New York courts, have carefully distinguished refusing life-sustaining treatment from suicide. . . .

Similarly, the overwhelming majority of state legislatures have drawn a clear line between assisting suicide and withdrawing or permitting the refusal of unwanted lifesaving medical treatment by prohibiting the former and permitting the latter. And "nearly all states expressly disapprove of suicide with durable powers of attorney in health-care situations, or in 'living will' statutes." Thus, even as the States move to protect and promote patients' dignity at the end of life, they remain opposed to physician-assisted suicide. . . .

This Court has also recognized, at least implicitly, the distinction between letting a patient die and making that patient die. In *Cruzan v. Director, Mo. Dept. of Health*, we concluded that "[t]he principle that a competent person has a constitutionally protected liberty interest in refusing unwanted medical treatment may be inferred from our prior decisions," and we assumed the existence of such a right for purposes of that case. But our assumption of a right to refuse treatment was grounded not, as the Court of Appeals supposed, on the proposition that patients have a general and abstract "right to hasten death," but on well established, traditional rights to bodily integrity and freedom from unwanted touching. *Cruzan* therefore provides no support for the notion that refusing life-sustaining medical treatment is "nothing more nor less than suicide."

For all these reasons, we disagree with respondents' claim that the distinction between refusing lifesaving medical treatment and assisted suicide is "arbitrary" and "irrational." . . .

. . . .

The judgment of the Court of Appeals is reversed.

It is so ordered.

Justice **Souter**, concurring in the judgment.

Even though I do not conclude that assisted suicide is a fundamental right entitled to recognition at this time, I accord the claims raised by the patients and physicians in this case and *Washington v. Glucksberg* a high degree of importance, requiring a commensurate justification. The reasons that lead me to conclude in *Glucksberg* that the prohibition on assisted suicide is not arbitrary under the due process standard also support the distinction between assistance to suicide, which is banned, and practices such as termination of artificial life support and death-hastening pain medication, which are permitted. I accordingly concur in the judgment of the Court.

NOTES AND QUESTIONS

1. Note that the lower courts in *Glucksberg* and *Quill* invalidated similar statutes on different grounds, *Glucksberg* using a due process rationale and *Quill* relying on equal protection. Are these really different? How? As counsel for the doctors and patients, which rationale would you prefer to advance?

2. With the equal protection analysis in *Quill,* the Court emphasizes the role of physicians' intent to *help* in withdrawing support or administering painkillers, as compared to the intent to *kill* in prescribing lethal medications (the difference between "passive" and "active" euthanasia). This, the Court says, is a real distinction meeting equal protection requirements. Is it? Is it consistent with analysis in *Glucksberg,* to the effect that doctors cannot be trusted to protect patients and so, as a matter of due process, assistance may be banned?

3. With the due process analysis, none of the Justices finds an explicit guarantee in the Constitution of a "right" in patients; hence, a balancing analysis follows. The choice for assistance is rejected in part because palliative care is available and because some patients might choose death on error. Is this consistent with the autonomy focus adopted in *Cruzan* and *Casey*? And what of the Fourth Amendment's guarantee that people shall be "secure in their persons" from unreasonable searches and seizures? Isn't that a specific guarantee; if so, is balancing analysis still appropriate?

4. Similarly, there is agreement on individual interests in managing one's own death, but the "right" itself is variously characterized. What — exactly — is it? Is it a right to commit suicide or simply to control the time, place and manner of death? And how can such a right be squared with centuries of prohibition on suicide? As the plaintiffs' att[illegible] would you *characterize* the right?

5. All of the Justices agree that there are three or four state interests in preventing assisted death. What are they and are they of equal dignity? And does it matter that they might be protected without a total ban on assisted death? Or that they are also endangered by Washington's Natural Death Act, also adopted by a majority of states?

6. The challenges in the trial courts were to the statutes "on their faces." Was this a wise litigational strategy? Could a challenge to the statutes "as applied" have been mounted and, if so, would it have made a difference? Several Justices — Souter, O'Connor, Stevens and Breyer — seem to think actual practice is important in evaluating the constitutionality of a ban on assisting suicide. Could actual practice be shown in a courtroom, or is that best left to legislative inquiry?

7. In that connection, what of the debate and uncertainty concerning the Netherlands experience? How is that experience relevant? And why is the legislative practice of other states or nations relevant? And how can/should a trial or appellate court inform itself of such matters?
8. Contrast the styles and analyses of the Chief Justice and concurring Justice Souter. Both appeal to history. Rehnquist emphasizes more the history of suicide in this country, developing at length the prohibited status of assisting another to die and the states' interests in such a ban. Souter concedes those interests and that history, but does so while emphasizing a different tradition, that of the Supreme Court's obligation to closely scrutinize state legislation under the Due Process Clause. Which approach is more faithful to constitutional traditions and such values as federalism, separation of powers, and individual rights? Which insists on tight, close analysis?
9. What of Chief Justice Rehnquist's concern for imposition on the vulnerable and his discussion of depression among those seeking assistance in dying? Is he — in essence — saying that such people simply aren't competent? Or — at least — not capable of autonomy and rationality? See cases at § 1.03[2] *supra,* and the *Bouvia* case in the preceding Section Do Justices Souter and O'Connor agree? And why does Justice Stevens concur, rather than dissent?
10. How significant, really, is the nearly universal criminal prohibition on assisting suicide? Physicians are rarely prosecuted. As the opinion in *Barber v. Superior Court of the State of California*, 195 Cal. Rptr. 484 (1983), indicates, the intent requirements of a criminal conviction are usually missing. Indeed, that was part of the analysis in *Glucksberg* and *Quill*. Moreover, the cases on DNR practices in the preceding section make it clear that physicians have been assisting patients to die for decades. If states *really* do not *mean* to *prosecute,* does the *prohibition* lose all significance; indeed, become a kind of fraud and tool for harassment of physicians such as Michigan's Jack Kevorkian?
11. After the decision in *Glucksberg* and *Quill,* is there room for another, better constructed challenge to the statutory bars to assisting suicide?

LEE v. STATE OF OREGON

69 F. Supp. 1491 (D. Oregon 1994)

Hogan, District Judge.

Before the court is Measure 16, passed by Oregon voters on November 8, 1994. This law, for the first time in the history of this country, authorizes physician assisted suicide for the terminally ill. The law invokes profound questions of constitutional dimension. The narrow issue presented at this juncture is whether those questions justify a brief delay in the implementation of this law. For the reasons set forth below, I find that the balancing of the important factors in this case merits a postponement of the implementation of the legislation until the constitutional concerns are fully heard and analyzed, which will be scheduled as soon as practicable.

Plaintiffs are two physicians, four terminally ill or potentially terminally ill patients, a residential care facility, and individual operators of residential care facilities. Plaintiffs claim Measure 16 violates the Equal Protection and Due Process Clauses of the Fourteenth Amendment, the First Amendment rights of freedom to exercise religion and to associate, and the Americans with Disabilities Act. I granted plaintiffs' motion for a temporary restraining order on December 7, 1994. I heard oral arguments and took evidence on plaintiffs' motion for a preliminary injunction on December 19, 1994. The following are my findings of fact and conclusions of law concerning that motion, in accordance with Fed. R. Civ. P. 52(a).

. . . .

Plaintiff Weinkauf is a diabetic who argues that diabetes may fit within the definition of "terminal disease" under Measure 16, if he ceases taking insulin. It is undisputed that plaintiffs Dutson, Elsner, and Stotler have terminal illnesses. All claim that they would not choose assisted suicide while exercising sound judgment. The record does not reveal whether any have contemplated suicide in the past. The gist of their claims is that they may, at some future time, request physician assisted suicide due to undue influence caused by judgment-impairing depression, or other inappropriate influence.

Hopefully, these plaintiffs will never experience the severe, judgment-impairing, undiagnosed depression which concerns them. If they do not, they will not benefit from a ruling in their favor. However, I must consider the unique facts presented by this action. Interpreting the "imminence" requirement too strictly may lead to claims becoming moot on account of plaintiffs' deaths. One may ask, if a terminal patient does not have standing, who does? However, because this court finds that both the physician and residential care provider plaintiffs have standing (see below), it is not necessary to decide at this time whether these plaintiffs have standing.

. . . .

Plaintiff Dr. Lee specializes in oncology and hematology, and is a medical director of the Sacred Heart Hospital Hospice. Plaintiff Dr. Petty specializes in gynecologic oncology. A majority of their caseloads are cancer patients who are expected to die. Dr. Lee states that some of his patients fall into such severe depression that they become dysfunctional. Several have approached him requesting assistance in ending their lives. He claims that almost no one chooses suicide if their physical, emotional, social, and spiritual needs are met. He states that he does not have specialized training in identifying debilitating depression or suicidal tendencies. Both physician plaintiffs state that significant numbers of their patients will seek physician assistance in ending their lives prematurely due to severe depression or undue influence, if Measure 16 takes effect.

. . . .

Equal Protection

Plaintiffs allege that Measure 16 violates the rights of the terminally ill to equal protection under the law. Under Oregon law, a person may be convicted of manslaughter in the second degree for intentionally causing or aiding another to commit suicide. In addition, a person acting with a reasonable belief, is justified in using physical force on another to thwart a suicide attempt. Oregon law also provides for commitment proceedings for a person who, because of a mental disorder is "dangerous to self." Measure 16 arguably creates exceptions to coverage of these statutes for terminally ill patients. It prohibits criminal liability for anyone who participates in good faith within its terms, and provides that a patient's request for assistance cannot be the sole basis for the appointment of a guardian or conservator.

The Equal Protection Clause of the Fourteenth Amendment states that no state shall "deny to any person within its jurisdiction the equal protection of the laws." This means that all persons similarly situated should be treated alike. "The general rule is that legislation is presumed to be valid and will be sustained if the classification drawn by the statute is rationally related to a legitimate state interest." The Equal Protection Clause allows states wide latitude when social legislation is at issue. However, the rational basis test does not apply where a state law impinges on personal rights protected by the Constitution or involves a suspect class. In such a case, the state law must be suitably tailored to serve a compelling state interest.

Among the questions concerning whether plaintiffs' rights to equal protection under Oregon law will be violated are the following:

. . . .

3. Is there a rational basis for the classification of "terminally ill" patient if, as plaintiffs claim:

   a. Physicians often misdiagnose terminal illness, or

   b. A physician's prognosis of six months to live is often fallible, i.e., plaintiff Stotler claims she was given 6 months to live in 1992, or,

   c. It may be contrary to reasoned medical judgment to include a patient who can live a normal life span with medication, i.e., a diabetic taking insulin, but not without it.

5. Are persons who have a terminal disease disabled for purposes of the Americans With Disabilities Act and if so, does this mean they are a suspect class?

6. Must Measure 16 serve a compelling state interest, and does it?

7. Does Measure 16 "deny" terminally ill patients the protections of Oregon's criminal and civil commitment statutes or does it give them the benefit of opting out of coverage under those laws?

Due Process

The Due Process Clause of the Fourteenth Amendment provides that "[n]o State shall . . . deprive any person of life, liberty, or property, without due process of law." Plaintiffs allege that Measure 16 unconstitutionally deprives persons who have the disability of a terminal disease of protections for their right to live. They also claim that Measure 16 violates plaintiffs' liberty interests because it does not sufficiently guarantee that the choice to end life will be both informed and voluntary.

. . . .

There are serious questions on the merits of the due process claims, because Measure 16 is the first of its kind and the Supreme Court has expressly limited its holdings on related issues. Among the serious questions raised and which require further briefing and argument are:

1. Does Measure 16 deprive a person of constitutional rights? Before a state can allow an individual to waive a federal constitutional right, must it also ensure that the waiver is voluntary and informed?[1]

2. A state does not have a constitutional duty to protect members of the general public, with a few exceptions. *DeShaney v. Winnebago County DSS*. Does this rule of law apply when the state enacts a law and allows a state operated facility, Oregon Health Sciences University, to implement the law on its premises?

. . . .

4. If Measure 16 implicates a terminally ill person's liberty interest, does that interest outweigh that of the state?

Americans with Disability Act

Plaintiffs allege that "Ballot Measure 16 unlawfully deprives persons who have the disability of a terminal disease of protection afforded other persons under Oregon law in violation of the Americans with Disabilities Act (ADA) and to the extent the statute applies to federally funded programs, Section 504 of the Rehabilitation Act of 1973."

. . . .

The parties arguments about the application of the ADA to Measure 16 involve whether the "option" of assisted suicide is a "benefit" or a "deprivation" under the law. It may be necessary to decide whether the parties positions are based on philosophical, moral, or religious beliefs or whether they are subject to statutory analysis.

Plaintiffs' ADA claims raise interesting questions. It is unnecessary to decide whether these questions are "serious" because a preliminary injunction may issue based on my earlier findings.

---

[1] Among the questions raised by plaintiffs are the following: Are there sufficient "due process" safeguards to ensure that a judgment-impaired, or unduly influenced patient is not allowed to request assisted death? Section 3.03 of Measure 16, provides that a requesting patient is referred to a licensed psychologist or psychiatrist only if the attending or consulting physician believes the patient may not be able to make a voluntary choice. Should these physicians also be deciding whether "a patient may be suffering from a psychiatric or psychological disorder, or depression causing impaired judgment"? According to Dr. Carol Gill, research indicates that up to 95% of persons who wish to commit suicide are suffering from depression or other emotional disorders that could be eased or eliminated through support, therapy, or medication. According to Dr. Patricia Wesley, a recent suicide study in Cook County, Illinois, indicates that 88-94% had a psychiatric disorder at the time they committed suicide, 25% had seen a physician within 24 hours of death, 41% within one week of death, and 70% within one month of death. The contacts were for vague physical complaints. "The general practice physician did not, and probably could not have picked up either the psychiatric condition or the suicidal intention." . . .

Vagueness

Plaintiffs allege that the definition of "terminal illness" in Measure 16 is unconstitutionally vague, and, therefore, violates the due process and/or equal protection clause of the Fourteenth Amendment.

Defendants argue that "regardless of the 'vagueness' of the definition, Measure 16 does not mandate or prohibit any particular conduct."

. . . .

Ballot Measure 16 defines "terminal illness" as "an incurable and irreversible disease that has been medically confirmed and will, within reasonable medical judgment, produce death within six months."

Plaintiffs argue that some diseases, such as diabetes, are terminal absent regular medication and that the "statutory definition of this key term is unclear as to whether it sweeps in this class of persons or not." Therefore, the argument goes, doctors and health care facilities are exposed to liability because they cannot know whether to advise people with such illnesses of the alternative of assisted suicide under the requirements of the federal Patient Self-Determination Act, 42 U.S.C. § 1395cc(a)(1).

. . . .

However, the "flip side" of what is prohibited by a statute is what is permitted. Since Measure 16 creates an exception to other Oregon criminal laws (*see e.g.*, § 4.01, "Immunities"), it may be illogical to hold that the vagueness doctrine is not applicable simply because the conduct permitted under the measure is "voluntary."

. . . .

However, the rights and liabilities of a physician requested to intentionally provide a lethal prescription to an individual with a medically controlled terminal condition which may not involve great pain and suffering raises serious questions.

First Amendment

Plaintiffs allege that certain provisions of Measure 16 require complicity of physicians and health care providers that is contrary to plaintiffs' religious and moral convictions and violates the Free Exercise Clause and freedom of association protections of the First Amendment and the Religious Freedom Restoration Act.

Plaintiffs contend that the following aspects of Measure 16 infringe on their freedom of association and freedom to exercise their religious beliefs:

1. Measure 16 requires health care providers to transfer records at a patient's request if a facility is unwilling to comply with the patient's wishes;

2. Oregon's "informed consent" law requires physicians to discuss available treatment options with patients. "As a result, Plaintiffs will be required to advise patients of their right to assisted suicide."

3. The federal Patient Self-Determination Act, 42 U.S.C. § 1395cc(a)(1) *et seq.*, requires health care facilities to inform patients of their rights under

state law. "As a result, medical care facilities will be required in Oregon to advise patients of their right to assisted suicide and to appoint a witness to witness written requests for assisted suicide."

4. Measure 16 prohibits facilities from denying staff privileges to or otherwise disciplining physicians who choose to honor a patient's request for medication.

If a health care provider or physician is required to perform acts to facilitate or accommodate a request for assisted suicide and based on sincerely held religious convictions, reasonably believes that their participation constitutes "complicity" in the suicide, there is a serious question regarding an infringement on religious beliefs against such conduct.

Defendants also argue that the issue whether a physician may be disciplined or denied staff privileges for complying with a patient's request for medication under Measure 16 "is more properly litigated when and if that issue arises in a live dispute between a physician and a health care facility." However, as noted in the section regarding "irreparable harm," the loss of First Amendment freedoms even for "minimal periods of time" may constitute an irreparable injury.

Irreparable Harm

. . . .

Dr. Lee alleges that many of his patients suffer from depression, "although physicians are not well-trained in depression so the problem is generally undertreated." Dr. Lee further alleges that depression and the debilitating effects of the disability of a terminal disease make his patients highly susceptible to the suggestion that their lives are not worth living.

. . . .

Death is overwhelmingly final and not subject to reversal, mitigation, or correction. Although death may be viewed as a release from suffering, it is nevertheless the end of life and, therefore, the legal equivalent to an injury to life. Death constitutes an irreparable injury and I find that the possibility of unnecessary death by assisted suicide has been sufficiently raised to satisfy the irreparable harm requirement for a preliminary injunction.

. . . .

Another hardship claimed by plaintiffs is the risk that suicide attempts by lethal drug overdose may fail to cause death and result instead in serious physical impairments and protracted suffering.

The possible hardships created by the complications associated with failed suicide attempts and the public interest in protecting against misdiagnosed "terminal" (within six months) illness should be considered when evaluating the public interest.

. . . .

A preliminary injunction in this case results in the maintenance of the status quo for a limited period of time to thoroughly consider the constitutionality of Measure 16. Although the status quo will be regarded as a hardship by some terminally ill patients who want the "option" of physician assisted suicide to be immediately available, the public interest in protecting vulnerable citizens from the irreparable harm of death is greater. Surely, the first assisted suicide law in this country deserves a considered, thoughtful constitutional analysis.

I find that the balance of hardships favors plaintiffs and that the issuance of the preliminary injunction sought by plaintiffs is in the public interest.

. . . .

NOTES AND QUESTIONS

1. As Chief Justice Rehnquist noted — and implicitly criticized — in *Glucksberg*, the decision in *Lee v. Oregon* was vacated and remanded by the Ninth Circuit Court of Appeals. As of September 22, 1998, the case was dismissed by the District Court of Oregon. The Oregon statute, ORS §§ 127.800 *et seq.*, remains operative. According to the Oregon Health Division, as of 2006, an average of forty to fifty people annually had received medications under the Oregon statute to assist them in dying. One quarter of patients do not use the prescriptions. Different physicians wrote the prescriptions; they were usually oncologists, internists, or family doctors. Typically, the patients have cancer or AIDS; die at home or in hospice; are in their mid-sixties; and are better educated than the average citizen. There are now (2006) seven Annual Reports of the Oregon Department of Health, which may be accessed at their website. (egov.oregon.gov/DHS/ph/pas/ar-index.shtml).
2. Oregon voters rejected an effort to repeal the law in November of 1997. Legislation was filed in the United States Congress to override Oregon's statute, possibly by prohibiting the use of federally-regulated medications for assisting death. The use of federal funds had already been prohibited for assisting death. Is this appropriate action by the national government?
3. Note the concern in *Lee* with "standing" — the ability of a person to show he or she is adversely affected by challenged legislation. Essentially, the Oregon statute creates or confers a choice or right. How can this "hurt"?
4. The plaintiffs argue they may be imposed upon as vulnerable people. Does this argument find support in the various opinions in *Glucksberg* and *Quill*? Are there sufficient protections?
5. In *Lee,* the plaintiffs advance four theories — due process, equal protection, First Amendment, and Americans with Disabilities Act (which we have encountered in earlier cases, dealing — *inter alia* — with prisoners, AIDS and alcoholism). How do these differ? Which is most persuasive? Which — if any — find support in *Glucksberg* and *Quill*?
6. Experience in other countries is relevant, as the Supreme Court indicated in *Glucksberg,* although sparse. The Northern Territory of Australia is the only jurisdiction other than Oregon to authorize

assisted suicide by explicit legislation, later overridden by the national legislature. For a comparison between Oregon and Australia, *see* LaFrance, *Physician Assisted Death,* 1 Newcastle (Australia) L. Rev. 16 (1996), contrasting two very different approaches.

The Netherlands has long tolerated assistance in dying, but with unclear authority, criteria and consequences. *See* Groenewold *et al., Physician-Assisted Death in Psychiatric Practice in the Netherlands,* 336 New Eng. J. Med. 1795 (1997); Van der Maas *et al., Euthanasia, Physician-Assisted Suicide in the Netherlands,* 335 New Eng. J. Med. 1699 (1996); Keown, *Euthanasia in the Netherlands,* 9 Not. Dame J. of Law, Ethics & Pub. Pol. 407 (1995); Hall, *To Die with Dignity,* 74 Wash. U.L.Q. 803 (1996).

Canada undertook a comprehensive legislative inquiry in 1994-1995, reflected in an extensive report, *Of Life and Death,* by the Special Senate Committee, chaired by Joan B. Neiman, Q.C., and concluding that no changes be made in existing criminal law. Therefore currently in Canada, assisting suicide is illegal, which was upheld by a 5 to 4 majority of the Canadian Supreme Court in the *Sue Rodriguez* case.

7. The general literature on assisted suicide is huge. Among the better articles are Orentlicher, *The Legalization of Physician-Assisted Suicide,* 335 New Eng. J. Med. 663 (1996) and 38 Bost. Coll. L. Rev. 443 (1997); Meier, *et al., A National Survey of Physician-Assisted Suicide,* 338 New Eng. J. Med. 1193 (1998); Quill, *Palliative Options of Last Resort,* 278 New Eng. J. Med. 2099 (1997); Clark, *Autonomy and Death,* 71 Tulane L. Rev. 45 (1996); Dowme and Sherwin, *A Feminist Exploration of Issues Around Assisted Death,* 15 St. Louis U. Pub. L. Rev. 303 (1996); Boozang, *An Intimate Passing: Restoring the Role of Family and Religion in Dying,* 58 P.H. L. Rev. 549 (1997).

   Two excellent symposia should be consulted, one in 1 *University of Richmond Law Review* (1995) and the other in 4 *Minnesota Law Review* (1998). Most of the leading writers and current thought on this subject are represented in these two issues.

   Among books, the first and the latest are the two best — Elizabeth Kubler-Ross, On Death And Dying (196[illegible]), and Sherwin Nuland, How We Die (1993). Both shed light on the process and experience of dying in ways which should inform constitutional analysis, legislative reform, and the ethical concerns underlying them.

8. *See* Giles R. Scofield, *Natural Causes, Unnatural Results, and the Least Restrictive Alternative*, 19 W. New Eng. L. Rev. 317 (1997); *also see* Larry J. Pittman, *Physician-Assisted Suicide in the Dark Ward: The Intersection of the Thirteenth Amendment and Health Care Treatments Having Disproportionate Impacts on Disfavored Groups*, 28 Seton Hall L. Rev. 774 (1998).

9. The literature on the Oregon assisted suicide statute is extensive. Among the more significant pieces are Woolfrey, *What Happens Now?,* 28 Hast. Cent. Rep. 9 (1998); Graham, *Last Rights,* 31 Will. L. Rev. 601 (1995); Grant, *Relief or Reproach?,* 74 Oreg. L. Rev. 449 (1995). Consider

now the statute itself. A number of states are considering adopting it, in light of the Supreme Court decision in *Gonzales v. Oregon*, *infra*. Should they? How would you improve it?

10. The latest stage in the ongoing saga of Oregon's legislation was reached in 2006, when the Supreme Court rejected the Attorney General's effort to end the practice. That decision follows.

GONZALES v. OREGON

126 S. Ct. 904 (2006)

Justice **Kennedy** delivered the opinion of the Court.

In 1994, Oregon became the first State to legalize assisted suicide when voters approved a ballot measure enacting the Oregon Death With Dignity Act (ODWDA). Ore. Rev. Stat. § 127.800 et seq. (2003). ODWDA, which survived a 1997 ballot measure seeking its repeal, exempts from civil or criminal liability state-licensed physicians who, in compliance with the specific safeguards in ODWDA, dispense or prescribe a lethal dose of drugs upon the request of a terminally ill patient.

The drugs Oregon physicians prescribe under ODWDA are regulated under a federal statute, the Controlled Substances Act (CSA or Act). 84 Stat. 1242, as amended, 21 U.S.C. § 801 et seq. The CSA allows these particular drugs to be available only by a written prescription from a registered physician. In the ordinary course the same drugs are prescribed in smaller doses for pain alleviation.

A November 9, 2001 Interpretive Rule issued by the Attorney General addresses the implementation and enforcement of the CSA with respect to ODWDA. It determines that using controlled substances to assist suicide is not a legitimate medical practice and that dispensing or prescribing them for this purpose is unlawful under the CSA. The Interpretive Rule's validity under the CSA is the issue before us.

I

A

We turn first to the text and structure of the CSA. Enacted in 1970 with the main objectives of combating drug abuse and controlling the legitimate and illegitimate traffic in controlled substances, the CSA creates a comprehensive, closed regulatory regime criminalizing the unauthorized manufacture, distribution, dispensing, and possession of substances classified in any of the Act's five schedules. *Gonzales v. Raich.* The Act places substances in one of five schedules based on their potential for abuse or dependence, their accepted medical use, and their accepted safety for use under medical supervision. Schedule I contains the most severe restrictions on access and use, and Schedule V the least.

To issue lawful prescriptions of Schedule II drugs, physicians must "obtain from the Attorney General a registration issued in accordance with the rules and regulations promulgated by him." The Attorney General may deny, suspend, or revoke this registration if, as relevant here, the physician's registration would be "inconsistent with the public interest." When deciding whether a practitioner's registration is in the public interest, the Attorney General "shall" consider:

> "(1) The recommendation of the appropriate State licensing board or professional disciplinary authority.
>
> "(2) The applicant's experience in dispensing, or conducting research with respect to controlled substances.
>
> "(3) The applicant's conviction record under Federal or State laws relating to the manufacture, distribution, or dispensing of controlled substances.
>
> "(4) Compliance with applicable State, Federal, or local laws relating to controlled substances.
>
> "(5) Such other conduct which may threaten the public health and safety." § 823(f).

The CSA explicitly contemplates a role for the States in regulating controlled substances, as evidenced by its pre-emption provision.

> "No provision of this subchapter shall be construed as indicating an intent on the part of the Congress to occupy the field in which that provision operates . . . to the exclusion of any State law on the same subject matter which would otherwise be within the authority of the State, unless there is a positive conflict between that provision . . . and that State law so that the two cannot consistently stand together." § 903.

B

Oregon voters enacted ODWDA in 1994. For Oregon residents to be eligible to request a prescription under ODWDA, they must receive a diagnosis from their attending physician that they have an incurable and irreversible disease that, within reasonable medical judgment, will cause death within six months. Ore. Rev. Stat. §§ 127.815, 127.800(12) (2003). Attending physicians must also determine whether a patient has made a voluntary request, ensure a patient's choice is informed, and refer patients to counseling if they might be suffering from a psychological disorder or depression causing impaired judgment. §§ 127.815, 127.825. A second "consulting" physician must examine the patient and the medical record and confirm the attending physician's conclusions. § 127.800(8). Oregon physicians may dispense or issue a prescription for the requested drug, but may not administer it. §§ 127.815(1)(L), 127.880.

The reviewing physicians must keep detailed medical records of the process leading to the final prescription, § 127.855, records that Oregon's Department of Human Services reviews, § 127.865. Physicians who dispense medication pursuant to ODWDA must also be registered with both the State's Board of Medical Examiners and the federal Drug Enforcement Administration (DEA).

§ 127.815(1)(L). In 2004, 37 patients ended their lives by ingesting a lethal dose of medication prescribed under ODWDA. Oregon Dept. of Human Servs., Seventh Annual Report on Oregon's Death with Dignity Act 20 (Mar. 10, 2005).

C

In 2001, John Ashcroft was appointed Attorney General. Perhaps because Mr. Ashcroft had supported efforts to curtail assisted suicide while serving as a Senator, Oregon Attorney General Hardy Myers wrote him to request a meeting with Department of Justice officials should the Department decide to revisit the application of the CSA to assisted suicide.. Attorney General Myers received a reply letter from one of Attorney General Ashcroft's advisers writing on his behalf, which stated

> "I am aware of no pending legislation in Congress that would prompt a review of the Department's interpretation of the CSA as it relates to physician-assisted suicide. Should such a review be commenced in the future, we would be happy to include your views in that review."

On November 9, 2001, without consulting Oregon or apparently anyone outside his Department, the Attorney General issued an Interpretive Rule announcing his intent to restrict the use of controlled substances for physician-assisted suicide. Incorporating the legal analysis of a memorandum he had solicited from his Office of Legal Counsel, the Attorney General ruled

> "assisting suicide is not a 'legitimate medical purpose' within the meaning of 21 CFR 1306.04 (2001), and that prescribing, dispensing, or administering federally controlled substances to assist suicide violates the Controlled Substances Act. Such conduct by a physician registered to dispense controlled substances may 'render his registration . . . inconsistent with the public interest' and therefore subject to possible suspension or revocation under 21 U.S.C. 824(a)(4). The Attorney General's conclusion applies regardless of whether state law authorizes or permits such conduct by practitioners or others and regardless of the condition of the person whose suicide is assisted."

66 Fed. Reg. 56608 (2001).

There is little dispute that the Interpretive Rule would substantially disrupt the ODWDA regime. Respondents contend, and petitioners do not dispute, that every prescription filled under ODWDA has specified drugs classified under Schedule II. A physician cannot prescribe the substances without DEA registration, and revocation or suspension of the registration would be a severe restriction on medical practice. Dispensing controlled substances without a valid prescription, furthermore, is a federal crime.

II

Executive actors often must interpret the enactments Congress has charged them with enforcing and implementing. The parties before us are in sharp disagreement both as to the degree of deference we must accord the Interpretive Rule's substantive conclusions and whether the Rule is authorized by the statutory text at all. Although balancing the necessary respect for an agency's knowledge, expertise, and constitutional office with the courts' role as interpreter of laws can be a delicate matter, familiar principles guide us. An administrative rule may receive substantial deference if it interprets the issuing agency's own ambiguous regulation. *Auer v. Robbins,* 519 U.S. 452, 461–463 (1997). An interpretation of an ambiguous statute may also receive substantial deference. *Chevron U.S.A. Inc. v. NRDC.* Deference in accordance with *Chevron*, however, is warranted only "when it appears that Congress delegated authority to the agency generally to make rules carrying the force of law, and that the agency interpretation claiming deference was promulgated in the exercise of that authority." Otherwise, the interpretation is "entitled to respect" only to the extent it has the "power to persuade."

A

The Government first argues that the Interpretive Rule is an elaboration of one of the Attorney General's own regulations, 21 CFR § 1306.04 (2005), which requires all prescriptions be issued "for a legitimate medical purpose by an individual practitioner acting in the usual course of his professional practice." As such, the Government says, the Interpretive Rule is entitled to considerable deference in accordance with *Auer*.

In *Auer*, the underlying regulations gave specificity to a statutory scheme the Secretary was charged with enforcing and reflected the considerable experience and expertise the Department of Labor had acquired over time with respect to the complexities of the Fair Labor Standards Act. Here, on the other hand, the underlying regulation does little more than restate the terms of the statute itself. The language the Interpretive Rule addresses comes from Congress, not the Attorney General, and the near-equivalence of the statute and regulation belies the Government's argument for *Auer* deference.

The Government does not suggest that its interpretation turns on any difference between the statutory and regulatory language. The CSA allows prescription of drugs only if they have a "currently accepted medical use," Similarly, physicians are considered to be acting as [illegible] statute if they dispense controlled substances "in the course of professional practice." § 802(21). The regulation uses the terms "legitimate medical purpose" and "the course of professional practice," but this just repeats two statutory phrases and attempts to summarize the others. It gives little or no instruction on a central issue in this case: Who decides whether a particular activity is in "the course of professional practice" or done for a "legitimate medical purpose"?

B

Just as the Interpretive Rule receives no deference under *Auer*, neither does it receive deference under *Chevron*. If a statute is ambiguous, judicial review of administrative rulemaking often demands *Chevron* deference; and the rule is judged accordingly.

The CSA gives the Attorney General limited powers, to be exercised in specific ways. His rulemaking authority under the CSA is described in two provisions: (1) "The Attorney General is authorized to promulgate rules and regulations and to charge reasonable fees relating to the registration and control of the manufacture, distribution, and dispensing of controlled substances and to listed chemicals," and (2) "The Attorney General may promulgate and enforce any rules, regulations, and procedures which he may deem necessary and appropriate for the efficient execution of his functions under this subchapter," 21 U.S.C. § 871(b). As is evident from these sections, Congress did not delegate to the Attorney General authority to carry out or effect all provisions of the CSA. Rather, he can promulgate rules relating only to "registration" and "control," and "for the efficient execution of his functions" under the statute.

Turning first to the Attorney General's authority to make regulations for the "control" of drugs, this delegation cannot sustain the Interpretive Rule's attempt to define standards of medical practice. Control is a term of art in the CSA. "As used in this subchapter," § 802 — the subchapter that includes § 821 —

> "The term 'control' means to add a drug or other substance, or immediate precursor, to a schedule under part B of this subchapter, whether by transfer from another schedule or otherwise." § 802(5).

The Interpretive Rule now under consideration does not concern the scheduling of substances and was not issued after the required procedures for rules regarding scheduling, so it cannot fall under the Attorney General's "control" authority.

We turn, next, to the registration provisions of the CSA. Before 1984, the Attorney General was required to register any physician who was authorized by his State. The Attorney General could only deregister a physician who falsified his application, was convicted of a felony relating to controlled substances, or had his state license or registration revoked. The CSA was amended in 1984 to allow the Attorney General to deny registration to an applicant "if he determines that the issuance of such registration would be inconsistent with the public interest." 21 U.S.C. § 823(f). Registration may also be revoked or suspended by the Attorney General on the same grounds. § 824(a)(4). In determining consistency with the public interest, the Attorney General must, as discussed above, consider five factors, including: the State's recommendation; compliance with state, federal, and local laws regarding controlled substances; and public health and safety. § 823(f).

The Interpretive Rule cannot be justified under this part of the statute. It does not undertake the five-factor analysis and concerns much more than registration. Nor does the Interpretive Rule on its face purport to be an application of the registration provision in § 823(f). It is, instead, an interpretation of the substantive federal law requirements for a valid prescription. It begins by announcing that assisting suicide is not a "legitimate medical purpose" under § 1306.04, and that dispensing controlled substances to assist a suicide violates the CSA. 66 Fed. Reg. 56608 (2001). Violation is a criminal offense, and often a felony, under 21 U.S.C. § 841. The Interpretive Rule thus purports to declare that using controlled substances for physician-assisted suicide is a crime, an authority that goes well beyond the Attorney General's statutory power to register or deregister.

The Attorney General's deregistration power, of course, may carry implications for criminal enforcement because if a physician dispenses a controlled substance after he is deregistered, he violates § 841. The Interpretive Rule works in the opposite direction, however: it declares certain conduct criminal, placing in jeopardy the registration of any physician who engages in that conduct. The explanation the Government seems to advance is that the Attorney General's authority to decide whether a physician's actions are inconsistent with the "public interest" provides the basis for the Interpretive Rule.

By this logic, however, the Attorney General claims extraordinary authority. If the Attorney General's argument were correct, his power to deregister necessarily would include the greater power to criminalize even the actions of registered physicians, whenever they engage in conduct he deems illegitimate. This power to criminalize — unlike his power over registration, which must be exercised only after considering five express statutory factors — would be unrestrained. It would be anomalous for Congress to have so painstakingly described the Attorney General's limited authority to deregister a single physician or schedule a single drug, but to have given him, just by implication, authority to declare an entire class of activity outside "the course of professional practice," and therefore a criminal violation of the CSA.

The same principle controls here. It is not enough that the terms "public interest," "public health and safety," and "Federal law" are used in the part of the statute over which the Attorney General has authority. The statutory terms "public interest" and "public health" do not call on the Attorney General, or any other Executive official, to make an independent assessment of the meaning of federal law. The Attorney General did not base the Interpretive Rule on an application of the five-factor test generally, or the "public health and safety" factor specifically. Even if he had, it is doubtful the Attorney General could cite the "public interest" or "public health" to deregister a physician simply because he deemed a controversial practice permitted by state law to have an illegitimate medical purpose.

The limits on the Attorney General's authority to define medical standards for the care and treatment of patients bear also on the proper interpretation of § 871(b). This section allows the Attorney General to best determine how to execute "his functions." It is quite a different matter, however, to say that the Attorney General can define the substantive standards of medical practice as part of his authority.

The authority desired by the Government is inconsistent with the design of the statute in other fundamental respects. The Attorney General does not have the sole delegated authority under the CSA. He must instead share it with, and in some respects defer to, the Secretary, whose functions are likewise delineated and confined by the statute. The CSA allocates decision-making powers among statutory actors so that medical judgments, if they are to be decided at the federal level and for the limited objects of the statute, are placed in the hands of the Secretary. In the scheduling context, for example, the Secretary's recommendations on scientific and medical matters bind the Attorney General. The Attorney General cannot control a substance if the Secretary disagrees.

In a similar vein the 1970 Act's regulation of medical practice with respect to drug rehabilitation gives the Attorney General a limited role; for it is the Secretary who, after consultation with the Attorney General and national medical groups, "determines the appropriate methods of professional practice in the medical treatment of . . . narcotic addiction."

The Government contends the Attorney General's decision here is a legal, not a medical, one. This generality, however, does not suffice. The Attorney General's Interpretive Rule, and the Office of Legal Counsel memo it incorporates, place extensive reliance on medical judgments and the views of the medical community in concluding that assisted suicide is not a "legitimate medical purpose."

The importance of the issue of physician-assisted suicide, which has been the subject of an "earnest and profound debate" across the country, *[Washington v.] Glucksberg*, 521 U.S. 702, 735, makes the oblique form of the claimed delegation all the more suspect. Under the Government's theory, moreover, the medical judgments the Attorney General could make are not limited to physician-assisted suicide. Were this argument accepted, he could decide whether any particular drug may be used for any particular purpose, or indeed whether a physician who administers any controversial treatment could be deregistered. This would occur, under the Government's view, despite the statute's express limitation of the Attorney General's authority to registration and control, with attendant restrictions on each of those functions, and despite the statutory purposes to combat drug abuse and prevent illicit drug trafficking.

III

In deciding whether the CSA can be read as prohibiting physician-assisted suicide, we look to the statute's text and design. The statute and our case law amply support the conclusion that Congress regulates medical practice insofar as it bars doctors from using their prescription-writing powers as a means to engage in illicit drug dealing and trafficking as conventionally understood. Beyond this, however, the statute manifests no intent to regulate the practice of medicine generally. The silence is understandable given the structure and limitations of federalism, which allow the States " 'great latitude under their police powers to legislate as to the protection of the lives, limbs, health, comfort, and quiet of all persons.' "

The structure and operation of the CSA presume and rely upon a functioning medical profession regulated under the States' police powers. The Attorney General can register a physician to dispense controlled substances "if the applicant is authorized to dispense . . . controlled substances under the laws of the State in which he practices." 21 U.S.C. § 823(f). When considering whether to revoke a physician's registration, the Attorney General looks not just to violations of federal drug laws; but he "shall" also consider "the recommendation of the appropriate state licensing board or professional disciplinary authority" and the registrant's compliance with state and local drug laws. The very definition of a "practitioner" eligible to prescribe includes physicians "licensed, registered, or otherwise permitted, by the United States or the jurisdiction in which he practices" to dispense controlled substances. § 802(21). Further cautioning against the conclusion that the CSA effectively displaces the States' general regulation of medical practice is the Act's pre-emption provision, which indicates that, absent a positive conflict, none of the Act's provisions should be "construed as indicating an intent on the part of the Congress to occupy the field in which that provision operates . . . to the exclusion of any State law on the same subject matter which would otherwise be within the authority of the State."

Oregon's regime is an example of the state regulation of medical practice that the CSA presupposes. Rather than simply decriminalizing assisted suicide, ODWDA limits its exercise to the attending physicians of terminally ill patients, physicians who must be licensed by Oregon's Board of Medical Examiners. Ore. Rev. Stat. §§ 127.815, 127.800(10) (2003). The statute gives attending physicians a central role, requiring them to provide prognoses and prescriptions, give information about palliative alternatives and counseling, and ensure patients are competent and acting voluntarily. § 127.815. Any eligible patient must also get a second opinion from another registered physician, § 127.820, and the statute's safeguards require physicians to keep and submit to inspection detailed records of their actions, §§ 127.855, 127.865.

Even though regulation of health and safety is "primarily, and historically, a matter of local concern," there is no question that the Federal Government can set uniform national standards in these areas. In connection to the CSA, however, we find only one area in which Congress set general, uniform standards of medical practice. Title I of the Comprehensive Drug Abuse Prevention and Control Act of 1970, of which the CSA was Title II, provides that

> "[The Secretary], after consultation with the Attorney General and with national organizations representative of persons with knowledge and experience in the treatment of narcotic addicts, shall determine the appropriate methods of professional practice in the medical treatment of the narcotic addiction of various classes of narcotic addicts, and shall report thereon from time to time to the Congress."

§ 4, 84 Stat. 1241, codified at 42 U.S.C. § 290bb-2a.

This provision strengthens the understanding of the CSA as a statute combating recreational drug abuse, and also indicates that when Congress wants to regulate medical practice in the given scheme, it does so by explicit language in the statute.

In the face of the CSA's silence on the practice of medicine generally and its recognition of state regulation of the medical profession it is difficult to defend the Attorney General's declaration that the statute impliedly criminalizes physician-assisted suicide. This difficulty is compounded by the CSA's consistent delegation of medical judgments to the Secretary and its otherwise careful allocation of powers for enforcing the limited objects of the CSA. The Government's attempt to meet this challenge rests, for the most part, on the

CSA's requirement that every Schedule II drug be dispensed pursuant to a "written prescription of a practitioner." 21 U.S.C. § 829(a). A prescription, the Government argues, necessarily implies that the substance is being made available to a patient for a legitimate medical purpose. The statute, in this view, requires an anterior judgment about the term "medical" or "medicine." The Government contends ordinary usage of these words ineluctably refers to a healing or curative art, which by these terms cannot embrace the intentional hastening of a patient's death.

On its own, this understanding of medicine's boundaries is at least reasonable. The primary problem with the Government's argument, however, is its assumption that the CSA impliedly authorizes an Executive officer to bar a use simply because it may be inconsistent with one reasonable understanding of medical practice. Viewed alone, the prescription requirement may support such an understanding, but statutes "should not be read as a series of unrelated and isolated provisions." The CSA's substantive provisions and their arrangement undermine this assertion of an expansive federal authority to regulate medicine.

The statutory criteria for deciding what substances are controlled, determinations which are central to the Act, consistently connect the undefined term "drug abuse" with addiction or abnormal effects on the nervous system. When the Attorney General schedules drugs, he must consider a substance's psychic or physiological dependence liability. To classify a substance in Schedules II through V, the Attorney General must find abuse of the drug leads to psychological or physical dependence. § 812(b). Indeed, the differentiation of Schedules II through V turns in large part on a substance's habit-forming potential: The more addictive a substance, the stricter the controls. When Congress wanted to extend the CSA's regulation to substances not obviously habit forming or psychotropic, moreover, it relied not on Executive ingenuity, but rather on specific legislation.

Viewed in its context, the prescription requirement is better understood as a provision that ensures patients use controlled substances under the supervision of a doctor so as to prevent addiction and recreational abuse. As a corollary, the provision also bars doctors from peddling to patients who crave the drugs for those prohibited uses. To read prescriptions for assisted suicide as constituting "drug abuse" under the CSA is discordant with the phrase's consistent use throughout the statute, not to mention its ordinary meaning.

The Government's interpretation of the prescription requirement also fails under the objection that the Attorney General is an unlikely recipient of such broad authority, given the Secretary's primacy in shaping medical policy under the CSA, and the statute's otherwise careful allocation of decision-making powers.

IV

The Government, in the end, maintains that the prescription requirement delegates to a single Executive officer the power to effect a radical shift of authority from the States to the Federal Government to define general standards of medical practice in every locality. The text and structure of the

CSA show that Congress did not have this far-reaching intent to alter the federal-state balance and the congressional role in maintaining it.

The judgment of the Court of Appeals is Affirmed.

Justice **Scalia**, with whom Chief Justice **Roberts** and Justice **Thomas** join, dissenting.

Contrary to the Court's analysis, this case involves not one but *three* independently sufficient grounds for reversing the Ninth Circuit's judgment. First, the Attorney General's interpretation of "legitimate medical purpose" in 21 CFR § 1306.04 (2005) (hereinafter Regulation) is clearly valid, given the substantial deference we must accord it under *Auer v. Robbins,* and his two remaining conclusions follow naturally from this interpretation. Second, even if this interpretation of the Regulation is entitled to lesser deference or no deference at all, it is by far the most natural interpretation of the Regulation — whose validity is not challenged here. This interpretation is thus correct even upon *de novo* review. Third, even if that interpretation of the Regulation were incorrect, the Attorney General's independent interpretation of the *statutory* phrase "public interest" in 21 U.S.C. §§ 824(a) and 823(f), and his implicit interpretation of the statutory phrase "public health and safety" in § 823(f)(5), are entitled to deference under *Chevron U.S.A. Inc. v. NRDC.* For these reasons, I respectfully dissent.

I

The Interpretive Rule issued by the Attorney General (hereinafter Directive) provides in relevant part as follows:

> "For the reasons set forth in the OLC Opinion, I hereby determine that assisting suicide is not a 'legitimate medical purpose' within the meaning of 21 CFR § 1306.04 (2001), and that prescribing, dispensing, or administering federally controlled substances to assist suicide violates the CSA. Such conduct by a physician registered to dispense controlled substances may 'render his registration . . . inconsistent with the public interest' and therefore subject to possible suspension or revocation under 21 U.S.C. [§]824(a)(4)."

The Directive thus purports to do three distinct things: (1) to interpret the phrase "legitimate medical purpose" in the Regulation to exclude physician-assisted suicide; (2) to determine that prescribing, dispensing, and administering federally controlled substances to assist suicide violates the CSA; and (3) to determine that participating in physician-assisted suicide may render a practitioner's registration "inconsistent with the public interest" within the meaning of 21 U.S.C. §§ 823(f) and 824(a)(4) (which incorporates § 823(f) by reference). The Court's analysis suffers from an unremitting failure to distinguish among these distinct propositions in the Directive.

As an initial matter, the validity of the Regulation's interpretation of "prescription" in § 829 to require a "legitimate medical purpose" is not at issue. Respondents conceded the validity of this interpretation in the lower court, and they have not challenged it here. By its assertion that the Regulation merely restates the statutory standard of 21 U.S.C. § 830(b)(3)(A)(ii), the

Court likewise accepts that the "legitimate medical purpose" interpretation for prescriptions is proper. It is beyond dispute, then, that a "prescription" under § 829 must issue for a "legitimate medical purpose."

A

Because the Regulation was promulgated by the Attorney General, and because the Directive purported to interpret the language of the Regulation, see 66 Fed. Reg. 56608, this case calls for the straightforward application of our rule that an agency's interpretation of its own regulations is "controlling unless plainly erroneous or inconsistent with the regulation."

The Court's description of 21 CFR § 1306.04 (2005) as a regulation that merely "paraphrases the statutory language," is demonstrably false. In relevant part, the Regulation interprets the word "prescription" which governs the dispensation of controlled substances other than those on Schedule I (which may not be dispensed at all).

As used in this section, "prescription" is susceptible of at least three reasonable interpretations. First, it might mean any oral or written direction of a practitioner for the dispensation of drugs. Second, in light of the requirement of a "medical purpose" for the dispensation of Schedule V substances, see § 829(c), it might mean a practitioner's oral or written direction for the dispensation of drugs that the practitioner believes to be for a legitimate medical purpose. See Webster's New International Dictionary 1954 (2d ed. 1950) (hereinafter Webster's Second) (defining "prescription" as "[a] written direction for the preparation and use of a *medicine*"); *id.*, at 1527 (defining "medicine" as "any substance or preparation used in *treating disease*") (emphases added). Finally, "prescription" might refer to a practitioner's direction for the dispensation of drugs that serves an *objectively* legitimate medical purpose, regardless of the practitioner's *subjective* judgment about the legitimacy of the anticipated use.

The Regulation at issue constricts or clarifies the statute by adopting the last and narrowest of these three possible interpretations of the undefined statutory term: "A prescription for a controlled substance to be effective must be issued for a legitimate medical purpose. . . ."

A regulation that significantly clarifies the meaning of an otherwise ambiguous statutory provision is not a "parroting" regulation, *regardless* of the sources that the agency draws upon for the clarification. Moreover, most of the statutory phrases that the Court cites as appearing in the Regulation, see *ibid.* (citing 21 U.S.C. §§ 812(b) ("'currently accepted medical use'"), 829(c) ("'medical purpose'"), 802(21) ("'in the course of professional practice'")), are inapposite because they do *not* "parrot" the *only* phrase in the Regulation that the Directive purported to construe.

Since the Regulation does not run afowl (so to speak) of the Court's newly invented prohibition of "parroting"; and since the Directive represents the agency's own interpretation of that concededly valid regulation; the only question remaining is whether that interpretation is "plainly erroneous or inconsistent with the regulation"; otherwise, it is "controlling."

B

Even if the Regulation merely parroted the statute, and the Directive therefore had to be treated as though it construed the statute directly, the Directive would still be entitled to deference under *Chevron*. The Court does not take issue with the Solicitor General's contention that no alleged procedural defect, such as the absence of notice-and-comment rulemaking before promulgation of the Directive, renders *Chevron* inapplicable here.

Setting aside the implicit delegation inherent in Congress's use of the undefined term "prescription" in § 829, the Court's reading of "control" in § 821 is manifestly erroneous. The Court urges that "control" is a term defined in part A of the subchapter (entitled "Introductory Provisions") to mean "to add a drug or other substance . . . to a schedule *under part B of this subchapter*," 21 U.S.C. § 802(5) (emphasis added). But § 821 is not included in "part B of this subchapter," which is entitled "Authority to Control; Standards and Schedules," and consists of the sections related to *scheduling*, 21 U.S.C. A. §§ 811–814, where the statutory definition is uniquely appropriate. In § 821, by contrast, the term "control" has as its object, not "a drug or other substance," but rather the *processes* of "manufacture, distribution, and dispensing of controlled substances." It could not be clearer that the artificial definition of "control" in § 802(5) is inapplicable. It makes no sense to speak of "adding the manufacturing, distribution, and dispensing of substances to a schedule." We do not force term-of-art definitions into contexts where they plainly do not fit and produce nonsense. What is obviously intended in § 821 is the ordinary meaning of "control" — namely, "to exercise restraining or directing influence over; to dominate; regulate; hence, to hold from action; to curb."

When the word is given its ordinary meaning, the Attorney General's interpretation of the prescription requirement of § 829 plainly "relates to the . . . *control* of the . . . dispensing of controlled substances."

II

Even if the Directive were entitled to no deference whatever, the most reasonable interpretation of the Regulation and of the statute would produce the same result. Virtually every relevant source of authoritative meaning confirms that the phrase "legitimate medical purpose" does not include intentionally assisting suicide. "Medicine" refers to "the science and art dealing with the prevention, cure, or alleviation of disease." Webster's Second 1527. The use of the word "legitimate" connotes an *objective* standard of "medicine," and our presumption that the CSA creates a uniform federal law regulating the dispensation of controlled substances, means that this objective standard must be a federal one. As recounted in detail in the memorandum for the Attorney General that is attached as an appendix to the Directive (OLC Memo), virtually every medical authority from Hippocrates to the current American Medical Association (AMA) confirms that assisting suicide has seldom or never been viewed as a form of "prevention, cure, or alleviation of disease," and (even more so) that assisting suicide is not a "legitimate" branch of that "science and art." Indeed, the AMA has determined that " 'physician-assisted suicide is fundamentally incompatible with the physician's role as a healer.' " "The overwhelming weight of authority in judicial decisions, the past and present policies of nearly all of the States and of the Federal Government, and the clear, firm and unequivocal views of the leading associations within the American medical and nursing professions, establish that assisting in suicide . . . is not a legitimate medical purpose."

In the face of this "overwhelming weight of authority," the Court's admission that "on its own, this understanding of medicine's boundaries is *at least reasonable*," (emphasis added), tests the limits of understatement. The only explanation for such a distortion is that the Court confuses the *normative* inquiry of what the boundaries of medicine *should be* — which it is laudably hesitant to undertake — with the *objective* inquiry of what the accepted definition of "medicine" *is*. The same confusion is reflected in the Court's remarkable statement that "the primary problem with the Government's argument . . . is its assumption that the CSA impliedly authorizes an Executive officer to bar a use simply because it may be inconsistent with *one reasonable understanding* of medical practice." *Ibid.* (emphasis added). The fact that many in Oregon believe that the boundaries of "legitimate medicine" *should be* extended to include assisted suicide does not change the fact that the overwhelming weight of authority (including the 47 States that condemn physician-assisted suicide) confirms that they have not yet been so extended. Not even those of our Eighth Amendment cases most generous in discerning an "evolution" of national standards would have found, on this record, that the concept of "legitimate medicine" has evolved so far.

The Court contends that the phrase "legitimate medical purpose" *cannot* be read to establish a broad, uniform federal standard for the medically proper use of controlled substances. But it also rejects the most plausible alternative proposition, urged by the State, that any use authorized under state law constitutes a "legitimate medical purpose." (The Court is perhaps leery of embracing this position because the State candidly admitted at oral argument that, on its view, a State could exempt from the CSA's coverage the use of morphine to achieve euphoria.) Instead, the Court reverse-engineers an approach somewhere between a uniform national standard and a state-by-state approach, holding (with no basis in the CSA's text) that "legitimate medical purpose" refers to *all* uses of drugs unrelated to "addiction and recreational abuse." Thus, though the Court pays lipservice to state autonomy, its standard for "legitimate medical purpose" is in fact a hazily defined *federal* standard based on its purposive reading of the CSA, and extracted from obliquely relevant sections of the Act. In particular, relying on its observation that the criteria for scheduling controlled substances are primarily concerned with "addiction or abnormal effects on the nervous system," the Court concludes that the CSA's prescription requirement must be interpreted in light of this narrow view of the statute's purpose.

Although, as I have described, the Court's opinion no more defers to state law than does the Directive, the Court relies on two provisions for the conclusion that "the structure and operation of the CSA presume and rely upon a functioning medical profession regulated under the States' police powers," — namely the registration provisions of § 823(f) and the nonpre-emption provision of § 903. Reliance on the former is particularly unfortunate, because the Court's own analysis recounts how Congress amended § 823(f) in 1984 in order to *liberate* the Attorney General's power over registration from the control of state regulators. And the nonpre-emption clause is embarrassingly inapplicable, since it merely disclaims field pre-emption, and affirmatively *prescribes* federal pre-emption whenever state law creates a conflict. In any event, the Directive does not purport to pre-empt state law in any way, not even by conflict pre-emption — unless the Court is under the misimpression that some States *require* assisted suicide. The Directive merely interprets the CSA to prohibit, like countless other federal criminal provisions, conduct that happens not to be forbidden under state law (or at least the law of the State of Oregon).

Finally, respondents argue that the Attorney General must defer to state-law judgments about what constitutes legitimate medicine, on the ground that Congress must speak clearly to impose such a uniform federal standard upon the States. But no line of our clear-statement cases is applicable here. The canon of avoidance does not apply, since the Directive does not push the outer limits of Congress's commerce power. The clear-statement rule based on the presumption against pre-emption does not apply because the Directive does not pre-empt any state law. And finally, no clear statement is required on the ground that the Directive intrudes upon an area traditionally reserved exclusively to the States, because the Federal Government has pervasively regulated the dispensation of drugs for over 100 years.

III

Even if the Regulation did not exist and "prescription" in § 829 could not be interpreted to require a "legitimate medical purpose," the Directive's conclusion that "prescribing, dispensing, or administering federally controlled substances . . . by a physician . . . may 'render his registration . . . inconsistent with the public interest' and therefore subject to possible suspension or revocation would nevertheless be unassailable in this Court.

Sections 823(f) and 824(a) explicitly grant the Attorney General the authority to register and deregister physicians, and his discretion in exercising that authority is spelled out in very broad terms. He may refuse to register or deregister if he determines that registration is "inconsistent with the public interest," 21 U.S.C. § 823(f), after considering five factors, the fifth of which is "such other conduct which may threaten the public health and safety

The fact that assisted-suicide prescriptions are issued in violation of § 829 is of course sufficient to support the Directive's conclusion that issuing them may be cause for deregistration: such prescriptions would violate the fourth factor of § 823(f), namely "compliance with applicable . . . Federal . . . laws relating to controlled substances," 21 U.S.C. § 823(f)(4). But the Attorney General did not rely solely on subsection (f)(4) in reaching his conclusion that registration would be "inconsistent with the public interest"; nothing in the text of the Directive indicates that. Subsection (f)(5) ("such other conduct which may threaten the public health and safety") provides an independent, alternative basis for the Directive's conclusion regarding deregistration — provided that the Attorney General has authority to interpret "public interest" and "public health and safety" in § 823(f) to exclude assisted suicide.

The Attorney General is thus authorized to promulgate regulations interpreting §§ 823(f) and 824(a), both by implicit delegation in § 823(f) and by two grounds of explicit delegation in § 821. The Court nevertheless holds that this triply unambiguous delegation cannot be given full effect because "the design of the statute," evinces the intent to grant the Secretary of Health and Human Services exclusive authority over scientific and medical determinations. Far from establishing a general principle of Secretary supremacy with regard to all scientific and medical determinations, the fact that Congress granted the Secretary specifically defined authority in the areas of scheduling and addiction treatment, *without otherwise mentioning him* in the registration provisions, suggests, to the contrary, that Congress envisioned *no* role for the Secretary in that area — where, as we have said, interpretive authority was both implicitly and explicitly conferred upon the Attorney General.

Even if we could rewrite statutes to accord with sensible "design," it is far from a certainty that the Secretary, rather than the Attorney General, ought to control the registration of physicians.

The Court also reasons that, even if the CSA grants the Attorney General authority to interpret § 823(f), the Directive does not purport to exercise that authority, because it "does not undertake the five-factor analysis" of § 823(f) and does not "on its face purport to be an *application* of the registration provision in § 823(f)." This reasoning is sophistic. It would be improper — indeed, *impossible* — for the Attorney General to "undertake the five-factor analysis" of § 823(f) and to "apply the registration provision" outside the context of an actual enforcement proceeding. But of course the Attorney General may issue regulations to clarify his interpretation of the five factors, and to signal how he will apply them in future enforcement proceedings.

. . . .

In sum, the Directive's first conclusion — namely that physician-assisted suicide is not a "legitimate medical purpose" — is supported both by the deference we owe to the agency's interpretation of its own regulations and by the deference we owe to its interpretation of the statute. The other two conclusions — (2) that prescribing controlled drugs to assist suicide violates the CSA, and (3) that such conduct is also "inconsistent with the public interest" — are inevitable consequences of that first conclusion. Moreover, the third conclusion, standing alone, is one that the Attorney General is authorized to make.

The Court's decision today is perhaps driven by a feeling that the subject of assisted suicide is none of the Federal Government's business. It is easy to sympathize with that position. The prohibition or deterrence of assisted suicide is certainly not among the enumerated powers conferred on the United States by the Constitution, and it is within the realm of public morality *(bonos mores)* traditionally addressed by the so-called police power of the States. But then, neither is prohibiting the recreational use of drugs or discouraging drug addiction among the enumerated powers. From an early time in our national history, the Federal Government has used its enumerated powers, such as its power to regulate interstate commerce, for the purpose of protecting public morality — for example, by banning the interstate shipment of lottery tickets, or the interstate transport of women for immoral purposes. Unless we are to repudiate a long and well-established principle of our jurisprudence, using the federal commerce power to prevent assisted suicide is unquestionably permissible. The question before us is not whether Congress *can* do this, or even whether Congress *should* do this; but simply whether Congress *has* done this in the CSA. I think there is no doubt that it has. If the term "*legitimate* medical purpose" has any meaning, it surely excludes the prescription of drugs to produce death.

For the above reasons, I respectfully dissent from the judgment of the Court.

Justice **Thomas**, dissenting.

When Angel Raich and Diane Monson challenged the application of the Controlled Substances Act (CSA), 21 U.S.C. § 801 et seq., to their purely intrastate possession of marijuana for medical use as authorized under California law, a majority of this Court (a mere seven months ago) determined that the CSA effectively invalidated California's law because "the CSA is a comprehensive regulatory regime specifically designed to regulate which controlled substances can be utilized for medicinal purposes, *and in what manner*."

Today the majority beats a hasty retreat from these conclusions. In stark contrast to]*Gonzalez v.*] *Raich*'s broad conclusions about the scope of the CSA as it pertains to the medicinal use of controlled substances, today this Court concludes that the CSA is merely concerned with fighting " 'drug abuse' " and only insofar as that abuse leads to "addiction or abnormal effects on the nervous system.

The majority's newfound understanding of the CSA as a statute of limited reach is all the more puzzling because it rests upon constitutional principles that the majority of the Court rejected in *Raich*. Notwithstanding the States' " traditional police powers to define the criminal law and to protect the health, safety, and welfare of their citizens,' " the *Raich* majority concluded that the CSA applied to the intrastate possession of marijuana for medicinal purposes authorized by California law because "Congress could have rationally" concluded that such an application was necessary to the regulation of the "larger interstate marijuana market." Here, by contrast, the majority's restrictive interpretation of the CSA is based in no small part on "the structure and limitations of federalism, which allow the States 'great latitude under their police powers to legislate as to the protection of the lives, limbs, health, comfort, and quiet of all persons.' "

Of course there is nothing "obscure" about the CSA's grant of authority to the Attorney General. The Attorney General's conclusion that the CSA prohibits the States from authorizing physician assisted suicide is admittedly "at least reasonable," (opinion of the Court), and is therefore entitled to deference. While the scope of the CSA and the Attorney General's power thereunder are sweeping, and perhaps troubling, such expansive federal legislation and broad grants of authority to administrative agencies are merely the inevitable and inexorable consequence of this Court's Commerce Clause and separation-of-powers jurisprudence.

The Court's reliance upon the constitutional principles that it rejected in *Raich* — albeit under the guise of statutory interpretation — is perplexing to say the least. Accordingly, I respectfully dissent.

NOTES AND QUESTIONS

1. In light of the *Gonzales* decision, can Congress explicitly authorize the Attorney General to ban assisted suicide? Make it a crime? Revoke physician licenses? Should it do so?
2. Similarly, should death with dignity advocates now press legislative proposals in states other than Oregon? Should they use the Oregon statute?
3. Was this case about whether assisted suicide is the practice of medicine? How would a court address/decide such a question? How would you present evidence?
4. And should the Court have proceeded to address whether there is a constitutional right to healthcare/medical assistance in dying? Is there such a right — after *Cruzan*? *Raich*? And if there is, may Congress restrict it?
5. Is Scalia right — that the majority creates a rule restricting state authority fully as much as the Attorney General, and more poorly defined?
6. *Gonzales*, of course, is decided on administrative law grounds. Who has the better argument — the majority or the dissents?
7. Finally, we close with a problem of finance: should insurance cover the cost of death?

PROBLEM 4–15 — Death with Dignity

The Oregon Death With Dignity Act provides, in part, as follows:

§ 1.01 Definitions

The following words and phrases, whenever used in this Act, shall have the following meanings:

(1) "Adult" means an individual who is 18 years of age or older.

(2) "Attending physician" means the physician who has primary responsibility for the care of the patient and treatment of the patient's terminal disease.

(3) "Consulting physician" means a physician who is qualified by specialty or experience to make a professional diagnosis and prognosis regarding the patient's disease.

(4) "Counseling" means a consultation between a state licensed psychiatrist or psychologist and a patient for the purpose of determining whether the patient is suffering from a psychiatric or psychological disorder, or depression causing impaired judgment.

(6) "Incapable" means that in the opinion of a court or in the opinion of the patient's attending physician or consulting physician, a patient lacks the ability to make and communicate health care decisions to health care providers, including communication through persons familiar with the patient's manner of communicating if those persons are available. Capable means not incapable.

(7) "Informed decision" means a decision by a qualified patient, to request and obtain a prescription to end his or her life in a humane and dignified manner, that is based on an application of the relevant facts and after being fully informed by the attending physician of:

(a) his or her medical diagnosis;

(b) his or her prognosis;

(c) the potential risks associated with taking the medication to be prescribed;

(d) the probable result of taking the medication to be prescribed;

(e) the feasible alternatives, including, but not limited to, comfort care, hospice care and pain control.

(11) "Qualified patient" means a capable adult who is a resident of Oregon and has satisfied the requirements of this Act in order to obtain a prescription for medication to end his or her life in a humane and dignified manner.

(12) "Terminal disease" means an incurable and irreversible disease that has been medically confirmed and will, within reasonable medical judgment, produce death within six (6) months.

§ 2.01 Who May Inititiate a Written Request for Medication

An adult who is capable, is a resident of Oregon, and has been determined by the attending physician and consulting physician to be suffering from a terminal disease, and who has voluntarily expressed his or her wish to die, may make a written request for medication for the purpose of ending his or her life in a humane and dignified manner in accordance with this Act.

§ 2.02 Form of the Written Request

(1) A valid request for medication under this Act shall be in substantially the form described in Section 6 of this Act, signed and dated by the patient and witnessed by at least two individuals who, in the presence of the patient, attest that to the best of their knowledge and belief the patient is capable, acting voluntarily, and is not being coerced to sign the request.

(2) One of the witnesses shall be a person who is not:

(a) A relative of the patient by blood, marriage or adoption;

(b) A person who at the time the request is signed would be entitled to any portion of the estate of the qualified patient upon death under any will or by operation of law; or

(c) An owner, operator or employee of a health care facility where the qualified patient is receiving medical treatment or is a resident.

(3) The patient's attending physician at the time the request is signed shall not be a witness.

§ 3.01 Attending Physician Responsibilities

The attending physician shall:

(1) Make the initial determination of whether a patient has a terminal disease, is capable, and has made the request voluntarily;

(2) Inform the patient of:

(a) his or her medical diagnosis;

(b) his or her prognosis;

(c) the potential risks associated with taking the medication to be prescribed;

(d) the probable result of taking the medication to be prescribed;

(e) the feasible alternatives, including, but not limited to comfort care, hospice care and pain control.

(3) Refer the patient to a consulting physician for medical confirmation of the diagnosis, and for a determination that the patient is capable and acting voluntarily;

(4) Refer the patient for counseling if appropriate pursuant to Section 3.03;

(5) Request that the patient notify next of kin;

(6) Inform the patient that he or she has an opportunity to rescind the request at any time and in any manner and offer the patient an opportunity to rescind at the end of the 15 day waiting period pursuant to Section 3.06;

(7) Verify, immediately prior to writing the prescription for medication under this Act, that the patient is making an informed decision;

(8) Fulfill the medical record documentation requirements of Section 3.09;

(9) Ensure that all appropriate steps are carried out in accordance with this Act prior to writing a prescription for medication to enable a qualified patient to end his or her life in a humane and dignified manner.

§ 3.02 Consulting Physician Confirmation

Before a patient is qualified under this Act, a consulting physician shall examine the patient and his or her relevant medical records and confirm, in writing, the attending physician's diagnosis that the patient is suffering from a terminal disease, and verify that the patient is capable, is acting voluntarily and has made an informed decision.

§ 3.03 Counseling Referral

If in the opinion of the attending physician or the consulting physician a patient may be suffering from a psychiatric or psychological disorder, or depression causing impaired judgment, either physician shall refer the patient for counseling. No medication to end a patient's life in a humane and dignified manner shall be prescribed until the person performing the counseling determines that the patient is not suffering from a psychiatric or psychological disorder, or depression causing impaired judgment.

§ 3.04 Informed Decision

No person shall receive a prescription for medication to end his or her life in a humane and dignified manner unless he or she has made an informed decision as defined in Section 1.01 (7). Immediately prior to writing a prescription for medication under this Act, the attending physician shall verify that the patient is making an informed decision.

§ 3.06 Written and Oral Requests

In order to receive a prescription for medication to end his or her life in a humane and dignified manner, a qualified patient shall have made an oral request and a written request, and reiterate the oral request to his or her attending physician no less than fifteen (15) days after making the initial oral request. At the time the qualified patient makes his or her second oral request, the attending physician shall offer the patient an opportunity to rescind the request.

§ 3.07 Right to Rescind Request

A patient may rescind his or her request at any time and in any manner without regard to his or her mental state. No prescription for medication under this Act may be written without the attending physician offering the qualified patient an opportunity to rescind the request.

§ 3.08 Waiting Periods

No less than fifteen (15) days shall elapse between the patient's initial oral request and the writing of a prescription under this Act. No less than 48 hours shall elapse between the patient's written request and the writing of a prescription under this Act.

§ 3.10 Residency Requirement

Only requests made by Oregon residents, under this Act, shall be granted.

§ 3.12 Effect on Construction of Wills, Contracts and Statutes

(1) No provision in a contract, will or other agreement, whether written or oral, to the extent the provision would affect whether a person may make or rescind a request for medication to end his or her life in a humane and dignified manner, shall be valid.

(2) No obligation owing under any currently existing contract shall be conditioned or affected by the making or rescinding of a request, by a person, for medication to end his or her life in a humane and dignified manner.

§ 3.13 Insurance or Annuity Policies

The sale, procurement, or issuance of any life, health, or accident insurance or annuity policy or the rate charged for any policy shall not be conditioned upon or affected by the making or rescinding of a request by a person for medication to end his or her life in a humane and dignified manner. Neither shall a qualified patient's act of ingesting medication to end his or her life in a humane and dignified manner have an effect upon a life, health, or accident insurance or annuity policy.

§ 3.14 Construction of Act

Nothing in this Act shall be construed to authorize a physician or any other person to end a patient's life by lethal injection, mercy killing or active euthanasia. Actions taken in accordance with this Act shall not, for any purpose, constitute suicide, assisted suicide, mercy killing or homicide, under the law.

§ 4.01 Immunities

Except as provided in Section 4.02:

(1) No person shall be subject to civil or criminal liability or professional disciplinary action for participating in good faith compliance with this Act. This includes being present when a qualified patient takes the prescribed medication to end his or her life in a humane and dignified manner.

(2) No professional organization or association, or health care provider, may subject a person to censure, discipline, suspension, loss of license, loss of privileges, loss of membership or other penalty for participating or refusing to participate in good faith compliance with this Act.

(4) No health care provider shall be under any duty, whether by contract, by statute or by any other legal requirement to participate in the provision to a qualified patient of medication to end his or her life in a humane and dignified manner. If a health care provider is unable or unwilling to carry out a patient's request under this Act, and the patient transfers his or her care to a new health care provider, the prior health care provider shall transfer, upon request, a copy of the patient's relevant medical records to the new health care provider.

§ 4.02 Liabilities

(1) A person who without authorization of the patient willfully alters or forges a request for medication or conceals or destroys a rescission of that request with the intent or effect of causing the patient's death shall be guilty of a Class A felony.

(2) A person who coerces or exerts undue influence on a patient to request medication for the purpose of ending the patient's life, or to destroy a rescission of such a request, shall be guilty of a Class A felony.

(3) Nothing in this Act limits further liability for civil damages resulting from other negligent conduct or intentional misconduct by any person.

Will this legislation withstand constitutional challenge in the light of *Glucksberg* and *Quill*?

Could it be better drafted? For a comparison to another, quite different legislative attempt, from Australia, *see* LaFrance, *Physician Assisted Death,* 1 Newcastle (Australia) L. Rev. 16 (1996).

PROBLEM 4–16 — Managed Care and Death

You are the acting medical director of an HMO in Oregon. One of your utilization review nurses has denied prior authorization for physician and prescription services to a patient, Janet Adkins, who has Alzheimer disease, and wants to terminate her life before the disease progresses to incompetence; to another patient, Elizabeth Bouvia, who seeks hospitalization maintenance while nutrition and hydration are withheld so she may die to avoid the further onslaught of amyotrophic lateral sclerosis; to a third patient, Cruzan Quinlan, who has a terminal illness and wishes to see an "out of network" physician because those available to her — she fears — favor physician-assisted suicide, and are paid on a capitated basis.

Consult the following three articles: Orentlicher, *Pay My Physicians More To Do Less,* 30 U. Rich. L. Rev. 155 (1996); Furrow, *Setting Limits In The Dying Zone,* 72 U. Det. Mercy L. Rev. 901 (1995); Emanuel et al., *Potential Cost Savings from Legalizing Physician-Assisted Suicide,* 339 New Eng. J. Med. 167 (1998) in deciding what to do.

And (for the last time), what would Rawls do?

You may also wish to consult The Oregon Death With Dignity Act: A Guidebook for Health Care Providers by the Task Force to Improve Care of Terminally Ill (Center for Ethics, OHSU 1998) and Ganzini et al., *Attitudes of Patients with Amyotrophic Lateral Sclerosis and Their Care Givers Toward Assisted Suicide,* 339 New Eng. J. Med. 967 (1998).

PROBLEM 4–17 — Capital Punishment: The Big Sleep

The Supreme Court has held a prisoner may challenge the three part "cocktail" used to put a person to death: sequential injections of sodium pentothal, pancuronium bromide, and potassium chloride as being "cruel and unusual punishment." *Hill v. McDonough*, 126 S. Ct. 2096, 165 L. Ed. 2d 44 (2006), because the condemned prisoner may still feel pain. In an earlier case, the Supreme Court had found no claim was presented where the prisoner's veins were compromised and an unauthorized surgical procedure was needed to insert the needle for the fatal injection. *Nelson v. Campbell*, 541 U.S. 637 (2005). But Mr. Hill alleged that after the pentothal, he might remain sufficiently conscious that he would experience severe pain as the pancuronium paralyzed his lungs and the potassium causes cramping of the heart muscle.

What are the ethical implications here for physicians? For assisted suicide? For the death penalty itself?

TABLE OF CASES

[References are to pages. Principal cases are capitalized.]

[References are to pages. Principal cases are capitalized.]

C

[References are to pages. Principal cases are capitalized.]

D

E

F

[References are to pages. Principal cases are capitalized.]

[References are to pages. Principal cases are capitalized.]

K

L

M

[References are to pages. Principal cases are capitalized.]

[References are to pages. Principal cases are capitalized.]

Q

R

S

[References are to pages. Principal cases are capitalized.]

[References are to pages. Principal cases are capitalized.]

Y

Z

INDEX

[References are to pages.]

A

[References are to pages.]

[References are to pages.]

B

C

[References are to pages.]

[References are to pages.]

[References are to pages.]

[References are to pages.]

E

[References are to pages.]

[References are to pages.]

[References are to pages.]

[References are to pages.]

I

[References are to pages.]

J

L

[References are to pages.]

M

[References are to pages.]

N

[References are to pages.]

O

P

[References are to pages.]

[References are to pages.]

[References are to pages.]

[References are to pages.]

[References are to pages.]

R

[References are to pages.]

S

[References are to pages.]

T

[References are to pages.]

U

V

W